The ten wheeler (6-4-0) built in 1923 bought by Norton Coal Co. in the 1950's to move coal from mine to Ilsley Station

The Long Bros. Tin Shop in Earlington-1920-Harry Long at right

Madisonville Graded School-opened 1904

Nebo in 1908-Two women in buggy are Eliza Hoffman and Allie Barron. Man on right with coat is David Barnett

HOPKINS COUNTY KENTUCKY

VOLUME I - 1988

This photo was taken before the courthouse was razed in 1892. The men in this picture were some of Hopkins County's most prominent citizens. Counting from left to right: 1, 2, 3, and 4 unidentified. 5 James M. Nisbet. 6 and 7 unidentified. 8 S.V. Hall. 9 Forrest Langley. 10 unidentified. 11 Clarence C. Givens. 12 Alonzo L. Jagoe. 13 unidentified. 14 James J. Glenn. 15 Zacharia T. Craig. 16 W. Elwood Jagoe. 17 Rev. Nicholas Lacy. 18 Daniel Brown, jailer. 19 George W. Ramsey. 20 Ruby Laffoon. 21 John Bayless Earle. 22 Herschel Potter. 23 unidentified. 24 Carl Woolford. 25 unidentified. 26 Percy Cunningham. 27 S. Roser. 28 Dr. Hugh Dexter Boyle. 29 Rev. W.R. Booth. 30 Amos Kendall Bradley. 31 unidentified. 32 John Gordon Morton. 33 Unidentified. 34 J. Walter Nisbet. 35, 36 and 37 unidentified. 38 James Buckner. 39, 40 and 41 unidentified. 42 Emmet Kemp. 43 unidentified. 44 Clifton Joseph Waddill. 45 Paul McNary Moore. 46 unidentified. 47 Kinchin Dixon Rodgers. 48 Crutchfield Young.

Copyright© 1988 by
Hopkins County
Genealogical Society
And
Historical Society of
Hopkins County

This book or any part thereof may not be reproduced without the written consent of the Publisher

Library of Congress Catalog Card Number 88-51171

ISBN 978-1-63026-947-0

Manufactured in the United States of America

Limited Edition of 1500 copies of which this copy is number _____

Publishers of America's History
P.O. Box 3101
Paducah, Kentucky 42001

Layout and Design By
Todd Iddings, Publishing Consultant

South Diamond Mine at Mortons Gap between 1890-1900. In front row seated second from right is Edward Lee Hart. In the back row on the far left is Reuben Cortez Harris the Coal Weighman and fourth from left is superintendent Fraudius Brown Harris

TABLE OF CONTENTS

Foreword and Acknowledgements .... 4 & 5
Hopkins County Genealogical Society 6
Historical Society of Hopkins County 7
County History 9
Family History 33
School History 315
Church History 357
Special Features 373
Clubs, Organizations and Memorials 381
Business History 383
Centenarians 431
Index 434

FOREWORD

It was in May of 1986 that the Hopkins County Genealogical Society and the Historical Society of Hopkins County began discussions and making plans to co-sponsor this book. The project had its real beginning in March of 1987.

Our main objective was to aid in preserving our heritage and to give future generations a written foundation upon which to build. It is hoped that this book will inspire everyone to the realization that every family is an important part of history.

We have attempted to bring to readers a feeling of the past and present. We hope that when any future generation reads this work, they will be able to picture their ancestors and the way they lived.

Debbie Hammonds-Editor

The Waltrip home built on Broadway in Madisonville by John B. Waltrip in 1890. Inside the fence L. to R.: Mollie (daughter), John B. (father) Lon, Jim and Will. Outside the fence L. to R.: Walter, Bettie (mother) holding John and Worth

ACKNOWLEDGEMENTS

Harold Ledbetter-County Historian

The Hopkins County Heritage Book Committee would like to express appreciation to those who contributed their efforts to make this treasured book possible.

Special thanks are expressed to those individuals who worked long and diligently to bring about this project: Debbie Hammonds and Rella Jenkins who gave numerous hours to every aspect of the project; Jim Ramsey who contacted the businesses; Dorothy Shoulders, Sharon Johnston, Hazel Gladdish and Winola Mimms who wrote family histories and worked on the school section - Dorothy was also responsible for the Centenarian section; Helen Wilcox and Lou Ann Wolford who processed the mail; Harold Ledbetter who wrote much of the general and community histories and furnished pictures from his private collection; Harold Utley for the history of coal mining; and Donna Slaton who worked on book promotion.

We are grateful to the business community for their interest as reflected in the Business History Section.

Also we would like to thank The Messenger, especially Carole Bailey; the Dawson Springs Progress and editor Jed Dillingham; radio station WFMW and WTTL; Madisonville Cablevision; the Chamber of Commerce; and the staff of the Hopkins County-Madisonville Public Library and the Branch Library at Dawson Springs for their help with publicity for the book. And a special thanks to Mrs. Judith Johnston, a teacher at Dawson Springs High School, for encouraging her students to contribute their family histories to the book.

Beulah Cave about 1902-Front L. to R.: Jasper Robards, Logan Dockery, Sam Clark, Maude Wilkey teacher, Pearl Sisk, unknown, Gusta Clark, Flora Wilkey, unknown, Tavie Dockery Coates, Mary Dockery Howton, Unknown, Unknown,Mary Lola Robards Fuller, Myrtie Robards, Jessie Robards, and Erslie Robards. Second row: Ira Dockery, unknown, Theodora Hicks, unknown, Billy Wilkey, unknown, Floyd Wilkey, Leslie Herron, Oscar Dockery, unknown, unknown, Lillian Lamb (baby), Dorothy Lamb, unknown, unknown, Clyde Wilkey, and Pauline Wilkey. Third Row: Harem Hicks, Thomas Dockery, Curtis Franklin, Delia Hicks, unknown, unknown, unknown, Lula Dockery, unknown, unknown, Bonnie Wilkey (baby), Nola Wilkey, and unknown. Fourth row: Unknown, Dixie Dockery Howton, Cora Hicks Howton, unknown, Flora Franklin Workman, ___ Sisk, unknown, unknown, Mary Ann (Sis) McGregor Franklin, David (Coon) Howton, and Ann Eliza Wade Howton

Hopkins County Genealogical Society

The Hopkins County Genealogical Society was organized in January of 1966 by Mrs. Cletious (Edith) Butler of St. Charles and is now in its twenty-second year. Twenty charter members met at the Courthouse in Madisonville for the first meeting and elected Mrs. Butler the first president.

By 1971, the membership was 67. In 1974, the membership had grown to over 100, many of whom were from outside the county and state. The present membership is 115 plus we exchange periodicals with 28 other genealogical groups.

Some of the earliest members were Eunice Brown, Phil Brown, Betsy, Cherry and Thomas Bruce, Edith Butler, Betty Cox, Mrs. Chester Cunningham, D.O. Dunbar, Maude Ferguson, Marian G. Hammers, Wetonia Harrell, Mr. and Mrs. Thomas W. Hawkins, Lila Kington, Arwana Kyle, Ora Locker, Pauline McClearn, Mrs. Chester Morrow, Mrs. James Frank Pugh, Dr. I. D. Oakley (honorary), Mrs. John W. Parker, Frances and Morgan Pepper, Travis Ridley, Jim Rudd, Elder J.D. Shain and Beulah Stills, all of Hopkins County.

The purpose of organizing this group was to research our family history, learning who our ancestors were. Our "tools" were books of genealogical and historical nature, which were purchased from the proceeds of sales of genealogical books printed and published by the Society. Books published were Courthouse records of marriages, wills and court minutes, census records and cemetery records. The Society has also published records of Christian, Muhlenberg and Webster Counties.

When the Society was organized, Pauline McClearn donated the data she had compiled in copying area cemeteries, work that had begun in 1946. It was with the printing and publishing of the cemetery books that the Society got their financial start. Six members donated $25.00 and were to receive these books when finished. With the $150.00, the Society began their work with old records. There are six volumes of cemetery books.

The Society has had a number of presidents starting with Mrs. Edith Butler and the present day president being Debbie Hammonds, her fourth time around.

The meeting places were several over the years. Starting with the first meeting in the Courthouse, next an office room in Dawson Springs, then the former old downtown Doctors building and one-time Hospital, Carpenters Union Hall, Office of Barney Hopkins, Mobile Unit of Madisonville Community College, later moving with the College in 1973 to meet in the new Library and for the last twelve years at the Hopkins County-Madisonville Library.

The Society wanted the out-of-town members to receive some benefit from the organization, so a quarterly titled YESTERDAYS TUCKAWAYS was initiated in January of 1969. Mrs. Juanita Potts was the long-time Editor of the TUCKAWAYS, resigning in the fall of 1984. Mrs. Rella Jenkins took on the position and remains as the current Editor.

The vast collection of genealogical books owned by the Society was housed in the Hopkins County-Madisonville Public Library for public use until June of 1985. Problems arose with books being taken from the building and the books had to be stored. Since that time, the Society has been working with the Library Board to find a means of making the collection available for public use under safe conditions. It is hoped this problem will be resolved soon and the collection will be available again for public research sometime in 1988. Many researchers have complimented the Society on their collection as being one of the best in the area. Researchers from all over the United States have used this collection.

The Society's major undertaking of 1987 was the co-sponsorship of "The Heritage of Hopkins County 1807-1987" book project.

The Society meets the fourth Tuesday of every month, with the exception of December, at 7:00 in the meeting room of the Hopkins County-Madisonville Library. Membership dues are $10.00 per year.

Hopkins County Genealogical Society-Front row, l-r: Jim and Marie Ramsey, Margaret Kington, and Debbie Hammonds. Second row: Katie Casares, Helen Wilcox, and Diane Gill. Third row: Linda Hayes, Anne Morgan, Sandra Donaldson, and Rella Jenkins. Fourth row: Frank Corum, Charles Lowther, Guy Brownfield, and Tom Wortham

Historical Society Of Hopkins County

The formation of a Historical Society in Hopkins County was first discussed at a meeting in Room 211, Madisonville Community College on Tuesday, December 11, 1973. The meeting was called by Vernon Gipson, Bob Adkins, Tim Cantrell and Joe Gooch.

Lewis C. Woods Jr., a representative from the Kentucky Historical Society, spoke to the group of 17 interested persons on what needed to be done to organize a Historical Society. Committees were formed and the next meeting date was set for February 5, 1974, same time and place.

At the second meeting Vernon Gipson as acting chairman and Tim Cantrell as acting secretary, the Historical Society of Hopkins County was organized. Harold Ledbetter was elected president, a post he held for the next five years; D. W. Dockrey was elected vice president; Faye Cardwell, secretary, and Joe Gooch treasurer.

From this beginning the society has grown steadily until at present the membership totals 488.

Ledbetter received some valuable assistance in those early days from two members, David Jones and Lawrence Casner.

Both of these men helped with every phase of the establishment of the society. Mr. Casner assisted by his wife, Arminta Bowmer Casner, put out the society's first year book only nine months after the society was organized. A year book has been published each year since that time, considered to be one of the society's greatest accomplishments.

Tim Cantrell followed Ledbetter as president serving two terms; then Irene Priest served two terms; Randall Teague, one term; Donna Slaton, two ; Charles Lowther, one, and J. Harold Utley is now in his second term.

Due to the cooperation of the city and county governments of Hopkins County, the Historical Society has been given the former Madisonville Library building at 107 Union Street, as a home, where a museum of pioneer artifacts has been set up.

The society's biggest project to date has been the moving of the log cabin in which Ruby Laffoon was born, from a farm east of Madisonville, to the vacant lot adjoining the Museum site. This was done in the summer of 1987. The cabin was dismantled and moved and repaired in the process. Laffoon was the only Kentucky governor to have been born in Hopkins County.

Harold Ledbetter has been the driving force behind the Society from the beginning and still is.

The Historical Society of Hopkins County Museum and Library

The B.C. Mitchell Home and Business. Students from Seminary School (now the Board of Education Building) would eat lunch here

Members of the Hopkins County Bar and Hopkins County Courthouse officials and court authorities are shown in the 1934 picture made in the circuit court room. Seated in the front row, from left: J.T. Gooch, Charles G. Franklin, Keen Brown, H.F.S. Bailey, L. R. Fox, W.E. "Pappy" Ashby, Walter Branson. Standing, second row, from left: Ruby Ligon, Ruth McNeil Pate, Irene Hatcher, Lonnie Lovan, Elizabeth Kosure, Archie Fox, Thomas E. Finley, B.N. Gordon, James W. Powell, Frank Berry, J.C. Finley, T.D. Hewlett, Carroll Morrow, E.M. Nichols, Benjamin Ashby, Albert Larmouth, Charles E. Barnett, Beth Hoffman, Lalla McCulley, Debbie Hibbs, Margaret Casner Fraelich, John Sugg. Back row, from left: Harry Boyd, Clifton J. Waddill, Major M.K. Gordon, Frances E. Hayes, Beverly B. Waddill, Ruby Laffoon, Dick Crafton (over Frank Berry's head), Judge Charles Wilson, Floyd Wilkey, Abner Johnston and Hirst Brown. Photo courtesy Mrs. Charles Utley

County History

Former Governor Laffoons Birthplace

The Bassett Brothers Livery Stable on the N.W. Corner of E. Center and Franklin St. in Madisonville. The new Police Headquarters occupies this spot now

Early History Of Hopkins Co., Ky.

Into this land two thousand years ago, came the Mound Builders, that race without a history. Who and what they were, whence they came, how long they occupied the land and how and whither they went, no one knows. A debatable question on which the learned ethnologists will differ.

We may surmise that a private tribe of these people held this part of the land for sometime. Their forts, mounds, graves, tools, ornaments and weapons remain to tell us that they were industrious, religious and warlike. Their great earthworks, raised apparently by manual labor with stone and wooden tools, show them educated in cooperation and strongly governed. Their polished axes and tools of hard stone are scattered all over Hopkins County, along with rough flints, which may have been theirs or the weapons of the Indians who succeeded them.

The local center of the Mound Builders was Fort Ridge, standing high above Clear Creek, with an elevation of over 6000 feet. Here they built a rough stone fort encircling the edge of the steep hill, enclosing burial and temple mounds.

Fort Ridge is about two miles from Earlington, northwest, beyond Loch Mary Park. The ridge can be seen from the Richland Road. The Earlington Boy Scouts enjoyed camping there in the early days of scouting. This location was chosen by the Indians to command a long line of communication, as smoke was visible for 25 to 30 miles, in every direction.

They possessed no metal, and so far as known, no letter, and the only traces of their art and skill are found in their stone tools and weapons and pottery and ornaments wrought from sea shells. The material of these weapons and ornaments is all foreign to this region.

In the mounds were a few graves of stone slabs, containing the skeletons of the Mound Builders. They lived, worshipped, worked and passed on. Whether their end came by pestilence, famine or war, or by all of these cannot be known.

Their area of occupation was surrounded in historical times by Indian tribes of Iroquoian, Algonquin and Musgogi stock. They never settled there but regarded Kentucky as a common hunting ground to be visited, but claimed by none, a haunted land where tradition said the ancient vile and treacherous race, who built the mounds, had been massacred and exterminated by incoming tribes and their ghosts haunted the land of Ken-tuck-ee, the River of Blood.

There is an Indian mound southeast of White Plains. This earthen mound is part of the remains of an ancient village site. Mounds of this type were used as ceremonial meeting places which contain no artifacts, as a trench was dug into the back part of the mound many years ago, nothing was found, digging was halted.

The outcrops of native flint made this site inviting to the prehistoric man. From the dome top one may observe the Pond River basin for many miles.

In western Kentucky between Pond River and Tradewater, spread the rolling acres of the 555 square miles forming the county of Hopkins. The region slopes to the valley of each of these rivers, from the slight elevation running nearly north through Madisonville, where it has an elevation of 470 feet above the sea.

Except for the small drainage area of Deer Creek, which flows to Green River, the tributaries of Pond River, MacFarland's Fork, Drakes Flat, Bratton's, Elk and Otter Creeks and their branches drain toward the east, and Tradewater and its tributaries Caney Fork and its streams, Lick, Wier's, Rose, Pond, Poage's, or Greasy Creeks, and smaller runs carry waters to the west.

The Peaks of Otter, west of Mortons Gap hold the highest elevation of 750 feet, while heights of 600 feet remain in Shakerag, the northwestern section of the county. The lowest part are on the rivers, 360 feet where Pond River enters Green River, and 346 feet where Tradewater leaves the county on its way to the Ohio.

Vast and inexhaustible wealth of potash and phosphorus salts lie locked in the subsoil, holding promise of perpetual fertility.

Geologically, the region is in the southern end of the Western Coal Basin. When these coal measures were being laid down, the land subsided beneath the seas in more than a score of ages, and each time was raised to take and hold the deposit of mineral which was metamorphosed to coal so that the structure of the rocks may be linked to that of a vast layer cake, whereof coal is the filler between layers of limestone, sandstone and shale. Faults or cracks run chiefly in a direction from northeast to southwest. Various coals come to the surface or "crop-out".

Us-ki-anō-nuk-ki, the land of growing cane, was the Indian name for Kentucky. A land where the evergreen cane growing thickly along the streams by which they entered the country on their long hunts for game. The cane furnished arrow shafts in plenty and was otherwise useful in the simple economy of those hunting and fishing people.

In pre-Columbian times the country was almost treeless. It was a favorite resort for the Aborigine Indian.

A striking and unique monument is the group of very large "hominy holes" where mass production was carried on. There are six of these round holes, 30 to 40 inches in diameter and about 10 to 14 inches in depth, cut in the jutting hard sandstone on the Tradewater high-point in which it is believed that corn was crushed by large spring-poles and counter weights. This section was inhabited by large numbers of early Americans. It was Indian Country.

After the revolution, the lands southwest of Green River were set apart by the Commonwealth of Virginia to be granted to the soldiers of the Continental Line. In 1748 the surveyors began to lay off to the Virginia soldiers tracts of 1000 acres or larger as called for by their warrents, in the territory lying between Tradewater and Pond River, now Hopkins County. Inspector General, Baron Von Steuben, of Washington's Army entered several thousand acres at Steuben's Lick (Manitou). Tradition has it that he was wounded by hostile Indians on his first visit and abandoned his entry. Congress granted his executors other lands elsewhere in exchange. Some of the land of Major Mace Clements and Ensign John Trabue are still in the hands of their descendants collateral.

In 1776, Virginia divided Fincastle County, erecting Kentucky County. It is interesting to note that in the division of this vast land that the main territory of Hopkins County has formed a part of 13 counties. Henderson County was approved by the General Assembly of Kentucky on Dec. 21, 1798. The small village on the banks of the Ohio River was called "Red Banks" from the color of the clay soil. The settlers who came to make their homes along the great river were grantees of Mr. Richard Henderson and his company. The town was later named Henderson.

The Ohio was the chief highway into the country and flatboats or broadhorns and rafts were the means of its navigation. Most of the men who were financially able to regard the comfort or convenience of their families, acquired lands from Mr. Henderson or others as close to the river as they could, leaving the hinterland chiefly to the more daring and adventurous and the restless. Most were men of fair learning in the three "R's" and of mature years.

Virginia was colonized from rural England and Scotland by the land hungry, and by political exiles, and by paupers sold into services. Tobacco culture was the cause of the growth and prosperity of Virginia.

Unsettled war conditions caused the returning soldiers to seek fresh lands for the growing of tobacco on the western waters.

Military grants in Henderson County were laid off in adjoining surveys of one-thousand acre squares. Larger tracts were granted to officers. In 1784, the price for western waters waste land was thirteen shillings and four pence per one hundred acres.

Whether coming by land from Virginia and the Carolinas, by the Wilderness Road, or from the inland settlements of central Kentucky, or from Virginia by river to the Red Bank, the journey took many weeks, even months.

If by land it was made by foot and horseback, as the was hardly practicable for oxcarts or wagons. The women rode or walked, the men hunted and made camp along the way. The boys drove the few cows, sheep and hogs. Only a small amount of food needed to be carried, as game was plentiful and the long pea-rifle was deadly in the hands of those hunters. Little clothing was brought and that of the roughest and simplest because the people were poor in world's goods, though rich in hope and spirit.

The garments were of homespun cloth and linsey-woolsey, or well tanned skins. The typical garment of the male was the fringed hunting shirt or tunic of leather, with moccasins of Indian pattern.

Every settler who possessed a Bible, or books of any kind, brought it with them. Among the books was Noah Webster's " A Grammatical Institute of English Language" (Hartford, 1783-85) in three parts, the first of which was the "Blue Back Speller".

Their other possessions included the cradle, spinning wheel, a few simple tools, pots, kettles, a little tableware, a little powder and lead, some precious salt, seeds to be planted in the new homeland, plough points, axes, hoe and a few poultry.

At the coming of the white man, no tree above three hundred years of age stood in the county. These forests sheltered and fed herds of elk, deer, buffalo, bear, wolves, foxes, beaver, and lesser animals. The streams protected by the forests were filled with fish and there were birds without number. A hunter's paradise.

Daniel Ashby, residing on Otter Creek, was an early settler. As surveyor, he laid off the John Harvey military survey in 1788. He was a prominent and influential citizen, well and favorably known in the whole country west of Green River. He was the Representative of Muhlenberg, Livingston and Henderson Counties in the State Senate. He earnestly desired his neighbors should be given recognition. To carry out his point, he hit upon the excellent expedient of drafting an act for the division of the Henderson County, and making a new county, and naming the new county in honor of his colleague, General Samuel Hopkins, in the lower house. The act passed and was approved by Governor of the State of Kentucky, Christopher Greenup, Dec. 9, 1806. It was approved by the General Assembly on Dec. 27, 1806. Then on Dec. 29, 1806, a commission was produced by the Governor appointing the first Justices of the Peace of Hopkins County, Richard Davis, Russell Weir, Thomas Anderson, Thomas Adams, Stephen Ashby, Isham Browder, James Logan and the eighth being Joseph Berry. Whereupon, Richard Davis, Esquire, the first named in said commission, administered to Russell Weir, the oath to support the Constitution of the United States, the oath of fidelity to the Commonwealth of Kentucky, and the oath of the Justice of the Peace for Hopkins County. Thereupon, the said Russell Weir, administered the said oaths to the said Thomas Anderson, Thomas Adams, Stephen Ashby, James Logan, Isham Browder and Joseph Berry.

And so a new county was formed, named Hopkins county, the 49th county. And the first Hopkins County Court was held on the 25th day of May 1807.

All of the forefathers of many a worthy son of Hopkins County met now to start the government with the blessing of God, and prayer offered by John Bourland, Minister of the Gospel of the Baptist faith.

Sires without aristocracy of wealth or position, none were graduates of any college. They were men of character and type in every line, not one a coward, cheat, sneak, fool or weakling. They were survivals of the hardship they had suffered.

They came dressed in their best clothes for the celebration and to attend the first court of Hopkins County. What a wonderful day this was and what a beautiful country it was to call it their homeland.

From the south end, came Dick Davis with his long beard and pigtail, in ancient swallow tail coat. Russell Weir, arrayed like a peacock, rode in from the west, wearing a plum-colored coat, red waistcoat or brocade, tight fawn-colored trousers, shiny boots and bell-crowned hat. Bewhiskered Tom Anderson, the blacksmith, with an axe handle-and-a-half across the back of his slick buckskins. Thomas Adams, wiry and fiery, clad in blue homespun thick, heavy and stiff, came from the mouth of Deer Creek. Colonel Stephen Ashby from the Green River country, dressed in his faded regimentals and topped with a coonskin cap with a tail. Isham Browder, pious Methodist and lay exhorter from Elk Creek, with a tall beaver hat, which would weigh two pounds. Joseph Berry, with a ruddy face poised in manner, came attired in neat butternut, from the Flat Creek country. James Logan, short, fat, squinting and merry, came dressed in a bright blue coat. Tom Towles, the man of the law, came from the Red Banks.

There was Sam Woodson and E. Earle, in sober black. And there came Daniel Ashby, the bustling handshaker. There stood the six-foot-three gaunt body of John Gordon, attired in new doeskins and leggins, he had a bony face with high red cheek bones, a shock of black hair. He carried a tomahawk in his belt, leaning upon his jacob-staff, which is a surveyor's rod. At his feet were his saddle bags containing his compass, this was brought with an eye to business. His brother, Billy Gordon, with fiery red hair, rough clad in homespun, with his trousers in big rawhide boots, with spurs, rode in on his gray stallion, "King William". There came a new comer from Fishing Creek, South Carolina, positive and argumentative, told of Colonel Samuel Bratton and his exploits at Huck's Defeat and debated the events of the Revolution with Colonel Abraham Landers, who held out for old Virginia. Old Ennis Ashby, with young Ennis, the first pioneer child born in the wilderness between Tradewater and Pond Rivers. There was Charles Bradley and Asa Sisk, with the broadest jokes, held a small but noisy group. And the boys who came were Ambrose Grayson Gordon, Samuel Gordon, Sam Morton, Samuel Bratton Nisbet, Jim Nisbet and Jim's two fox dogs. There was the McGary children, Stillwell, Barsaiai, Obediah and Levi. Also little Solomon Silkwood.

Mrs. McGary was busy overlooking the cooking. The help was tending the smoking pit where savory venison, mutton and wild turkey roasted to crispy browness resting on lengths of green sapling. In the house on the hearth stone were brown hoe-cakes well baked. At the dug-out milk house at the side of the elm, near the spring were two tubs of cider, one of the hardest, the others fermentation checked by mustard seed. A barrel of persimmon beer, with plenty of gourd dippers.

William Davis, son of Dick Davis, demonstrated his marksmanship under the rise down the path to the left. The were welcoming friends old and new.

The Robert McGary home was a two story log house, located on a rise in the wilderness above a sparking spring, at the head of a little valley opening to the north. First court held here.

There were no roads at this time, only that of the bufflo trace, which was often time followed by man.

There were brief hard winters when the temperature fell to ten below zero, but the forests relieved it by holding off the winds. Snows were infrequent, but lasted longer at a later date when the country was cleared. Spring, summer and autumn were long and pleasant with a few hot sunny days of a hundred in the shade, but the few hot nights made the growing corn crack and snap. The rainfall of 48 inches did not run off in torrents and floods, but dripped from the trees, soaked through the leaf mould and fed perennial springs and slow flowing branches with clean channels.

The hardy and weather beaten pioneers seem to heed all kinds of situations. They were survivors strengthened by vigorous active life in the open, and in bracing temperate climate seemed very hale and healthy.

The characteristic and physique of the pioneer male race was an extreme type. Their height, their high cheek bones, thin faces, prominent nose, powerful jaw, large Adams apple, large ears and coarse hair. They were adapted to any task, physical or mental.

Here our respectable seniors met and accepted their trust, took up the task of county government, amid the applauding of fellow citizens of Hopkins County from far and near. Not only came those who had motions to make, or cause to be heard, but all assembled for merry making and a celebration of new found independence and with high hope for the future. This was a beautiful and glorious day, the settlers had their corn planted and they were all here today for the big occasion.

As the court record gives the account, "Be it therefore remembered: that at the house of Robert McGary, in the county of Hopkins, on Monday, the 25th day of May, 1807, in pursuance of an act of the General Assembly, entitled, An Act Altering the Times of Holding Certain Courts in this Commonwealth, approved the 27th of December, 1806."

Also at that first court meeting, Daniel McGary and Solomon Silkwood produced a writing as follows:

"We do hereby present, promise and agree that should the County of Hopkins think proper to fix the place for erecting the public buildings on our land, we will give forty acres jointly to lie along our line that divides with Daniel McGary's plantation, except as to the water, which the said McGary agrees to allow every privilege to the County of the Hopkins Court aforesaid, the Court allowing us to lay off lots on the opposite side of the street, that given by us to the County, after a town is laid off on said land. This the 25th day of May, 1807."

    Solomon Silkwood (seal)
    Daniel McGary (seal)

The above order appears in Hopkins County Order Book No. 1.

On July 27, 1807, another court was held, this time at the home of Daniel McGary, where invitation for the court to meet at his home was accepted. Sam Woodson's bond as Clerk was presented and approved, and on his motion, Samuel H. Earle was sworn in as his deputy clerk.

Henry F. Delany was sworn in and permitted to practice law in the court. Thomas Towles, Esquire, produced a license to practice as an Attorney-at-Law, was approved.

John Gordon, produced his commission from Christopher Greenup, Governor of Kentucky, dated June 4, 1807, appointing him Surveyor for the county, his official bond was executed by Abner Martin and Lindsay Martin, as sureties. On motion of John Gordon, the following were sworn in as deputies: Thomas Anderson, James Hughes and Thomas Davis.

Daniel McGary was appointed Jailer of the County. Henry Ashby produced his commission as Coroner and took the oath and qualified with Vincent Fugate as his surety.

Thomas Stokes, David Wright, Daniel Ashby, Thomas Anderson, Thomas Adams and Henry Ashby registered their stockmarks.

Roads were in demand, so several men were appointed at this court as viewers, to view a road from and to different directions. The only trails thus far were the traces beaten out by wild animals which were followed by the Indians and the race of men who preceeded them. The main trail in general was beaten out by bison, bear, deer and the Indians, seeking the salt afforded by mineral sprigs, a necessity to their way of life. However, it was found by the early surveyors who were locating the first roads, it was desirable to follow these traces as heavy animals avoided steep hills, ascending and descending.

The plans for the Courthouse were adopted as follows:

"The Courthouse to be of good hewn logs, seven inches thick, twenty feet square, eighteen feet high, with a jointed shingle roof nailed on, a partition of plank above, two below, a plank floor above and below, one pair of stairs, two outside doors below and a door in the partition above, a Judge's bench, a Clerk's table, an Attorney's bar and a Juror's bench above and one below, the whole to be done in good and workmanlike manner."

The plans for the Jail were adopted as follows:

"The Jail to be of hewn timber nine inches square, sixteen feet by twelve feet, seven feet high, the floors laid with timber nine inches thick and squared, a window in the debtors room eight by ten inches and one in the dungeon room of the same size, two doors, one in the debtors room and one from the debtors room into the dungeon with good locks and hinges, the whole to be done in good and workmanlike manner."

Daniel Ashby, John Davis and Robert McGary were appointed commissioners to let the erection of the Courthouse and Jail to the lowest bidder. It was ordered that the next term of Court be "holden" at the house of Daniel McGary.

It was ordered that one moiety (portion) of money be paid to the person undertaking the erection of the Courthouse and Jail, to be paid Aug. 1, 1808, and the other moeity a year later. The buildings to be completely finished and ready for use by the fourth Monday in June, 1808. (This was Aug. 24, 1807, Court)

On this day also Solomon Silkwood being the lowest bidder, undertook the building of the Courthouse for $329.00 and gave bond with Vincent Fugate and Elias Smith as sureties in the sum of $2,000.00. In like manner, he secured the contract of building the Jail at $229.00 and gave like bond. Charles Bradley was allowed two dollars for laying off the public buildings of this county.

No better man could have been chosen for the post of Clerk of the Hopkins County and Circuit Courts, which Samuel Woodson filled for 44 years to the satisfaction of all. The neat, plain signature of Sam Woodson is on every page. He had a genius for detail, a facile pen, good command of plain english. A fine gentleman of the old school, who was well poised and with an active mind. The duties of the clerk in the early years were not onerous, and Mr. Woodson found in them merely an avocation. The few books and scanty papers were kept at his home, but were easily transported and produced at court in due time. When a deed was to be acknowledged or a writ issued, Sam Woodson was to be found on his plantation. If he was ploughing, the attorney or grantor was expected to turn over the papers to the clerk and do the ploughing for the clerk while the clerk went to the house for pen, ink and paper to do his office work.

Our early court was not wholly engrossed with its criminal docket but dealt with many civil matters. Many were suits of debts, ejection, and litigation concerning lands and land lines. Suits for damages for assault and battery were common. Other matters occupying the attention of the court were probate matters, guardianships, administrators, appointments and settlements.

Those who were produced in evidence on the trial of a slave were charged as follows:

"You are brought hither as a witness, and by the direction of the law, I am to tell you before you give you evidence that you must tell the truth, the whole truth and nothing but the truth, and that if it be found hereafter that you tell a lie and give false testimony in this matter, you must for so doing, receive 39 lashes on your bare back, well laid on at he common whipping post."

Harboring a slave without leave of the owner was punished by fine. If more than five were harbored, the offender should forfeit five shillings to the informer for every slave above that number so harbored, provided that slaves of the same owner might meet with his leave upon his plantation or upon the owner's business at any public mill, or on any other lawful occasion by license in writing from their owner, and might go to church to attend divine worship on the Lord's day, or any other day of public worship. No slave was allowed to leave the premises of his master without, a pass, letter or token from his owner or overseer. In 1807, there were 242 blacks in the entire area of Hopkins County. Many large land owners, who had the means of owning slaves, held none at all. And it must be remembered that the churches had from the very first censured slave-holding and dealing. The 242 slaves who were brought to Hopkins County, where in the ownership of 54 persons, 24 of them belonged to one taxpayer. However, in three years the number had increased to 412.

No negro, mulatto or Indian was allowed to keep or carry any gun, powder, shot or any kind of so called weapon and these might be seized by any person when so carried. It was a misdemeanor to hire or induce a slave to ride in a horse race without the master's consent.

The grant to John Fowler is as follows:

"ALL TO WHOM THESE PREMISES SHALL COME - GREETINGS: KNOW YE, that by virtue and in consideration of part a land office Military Warrant W345, there is granted by the said Commonwealth unto John Fowler, Representative of Arthur Lind, deceased, a certain tract or parcel of land containing 1000 acres by survey, bearing the date January, 1785, lying and being in the District set apart for the Officers of the Virginia Line, on the water of Poague's Creek and bounded as followeth, to wit:

Beginning at two small dogwoods and a maple on a ridge S. E. corner to Javin Miller's survey No. 316 and running east 400 poles crossing a branch twice to a dogwood, white oak and hickory, thence north 400 poles crossing two branches to two dogwoods and white oak, thence west to said Miller, thence with his line south 400 poles to crossing a branch to the beginning. WITH ITS APPURTENANCES: TO HAVE AND TO HOLD the said tract or parcel of land with its appurtenances, to the said John Fowler and his heirs forever. IN WITNESS WHEREOF: The said Isaac Shelby, Esquire, Governor of the Commonwealth of Kentucky, hath hereunto set his hand and caused the lesser Seal of the said Commonwealth to be affixed at Lexington on the fifth day of September in the year of our Lord, one thousand seven hundred and ninety-three and of the Commonwealth the second."

(SIGNED) ISAAC SHELBY

The western half of Madisonville is built upon the eastern half of the John Fowler 1000 acre military survey, the north half of which passed through Goldsmith Chandler, Ben Berry and William Allen to Solomon Silkwood, and the south half to Alexander Ashby, the dividing line between them crossing South Main Street near the intersection of Hall Street.

August 24, 1807, term of Court continued-

It was:

"Ordered, that John Gordon, Surveyor of this County, do, on the last day of this month, lay off the Town to be established in this county and that Daniel McGary, Abner Martin, William Davis and Daniel Ashby or any three of them, do superintend and direct the same."

The next term of Court was held at the house of Daniel McGary, Oct. 26, 1807, when the following order was entered.

"On the application of Daniel McGary and Solomon Silkwood for a town to be established on their lands in this county at Flat Creek at the place where the seat of Justice of said county is fixed, and it appearing to the court that it would be advantageous to the good citizens of said county in general that a town should be established at said place and to include 40 acres of land to be called by the name of Madisonville."

"Wherefore, the said McGary, Solomon Silkwood with William R. McGary and Horatio Pidcock as their securities executed bond in the amount of 1,000 pounds conditioned as the law directs, and it is further ordered that the Town be, and the same is hereby vested in Isaac Whyte, James Nisbet, Barnabas Sisk, Horatio Pidcock and William Davis, who are hereby appointed Trustees of the Same."

Madisonville was named for James Madison, Secretary of the State, who helped frame the Constitution in the Convention of 1787. He was a prospective candidate for the Presidency of the United States in the next election. A tradition has it that Samuel Woodson, the young court clerk, proposed it. The Justices adopted the name, and in turn directed the County Surveyor to lay off the streets of the town and the lots, and the appointed Trustees to sell the lots in 1807. The markets for the lots was very limited and but few were bought at first. The Trustees were allowed $24.00 for their services in laying off the town, selling lots and all other services.

The trees were of oak, poplar, gum, elm, hickory, hackberry and sycamore, which covered the site. Enough of the trees had to be cut out and the area cleared for the Courthouse and Jail to be built. The two streets, Main Street and Main Cross, were mere paths, running along among the trees and stumps. Around the north and west sides of the Courthouse were hitching racks built of peeled saplings. A public whipping post was established also.

By 1810, Madisonville was a straggling hamlet which sheltered 37 inhabitants in their log cabins. Frame houses were unknown until 1850. The first brick house in Madisonville was built by Daniel McGary in 1817, on what is now Cardwell Avenue.

In 1810, the Federal Census reported the population for the entire area of Hopkins County as being 2964.

There being few churches and none closer, the villagers worshipped at Browder's Chapel, or the Flat Creek Meeting House, the Courthouse or in the open.

When a preacher came on his usual stated rounds, it was one of his duties to preach the funeral sermon of any member who had passed away since his last visit. A notice would be given as to when the preacher was expected so that the whole countryside might assemble for the occasion. In some instances the deceased had been buried for three or four months longer, then when the preacher came he read a scripture and had prayer at the graveside.

When death came, the body of the deceased was laid out on a plank and a measuring stick was cut and on it was marked with a knife the length and width of the body, and the depth of the coffin was considered also. A rough box was made, pinned together with dowels, as nails were scarce.

And while the preacher was in the countryside, there were weddings to be performed. The traveling preacher also helped the pioneers by writing lines and having them to copy the lines.

Tradition has it that William McLanathan taught reading, writing, and arithmatic in his cabin, just west of the town line. Then in 1816, he received a conveyance of the four acres adjoining the town site for the school from William McGary. The early school masters of the pioneer period were: William H. Moore, James Porter, A. Smith, Claiborn Rice, Samuel Brown and Charles Bradley. Charles Bradley wrote a particularly clear and beautiful hand and doubtless set many a copy. So did Claiborn Rice, but with many more flourishes. When a child finished one book each of the reader, speller (blue back speller) and writing, his education was sufficient for his needs. Much of the training was taught by their parents as had been handed down to them. A child helped with the family chores by the time he or she was three years old, either by helping with the cooking on the open fire, chopping firewood, tending the sheep, hogs, chickens, helping in the fields at planting time and at harvest time, helping with the milking and churning and preparing the butter, using the spinning wheel and the loom and helping their mother with the family sewing, either from cloth or animal skins.

Food was plentiful, easily and bountifully obtained by those who worked in producing food. All of them farmed and hunted, and there was no person who depended upon wages for his sustenance.

The first election of Trustees of the town of Madisonville, the county seat, was held in May 1815. Baxter Townes, Thomas Davis, William McGary, William Wilson and William Noel were elected. William Russell Weir represented Hopkins and Union Counties in the lower house of the General Assembly.

The Circuit Court, presided over by Judge Henry Broadnax, met regularly in its stated session in March, June, and September, the months when the roads permitted access to Madisonville. He was a resident of Lebanon. He was the first Judge of a very large district, appointed when the Circuit Court was first established. Judge Broadnax, wealthy bachelor and a gentleman of the old Virginia School, dressed in the style of his youth, in white cassimere short breeches, sliver knee buckles, white cotton stockings, long white ribbed dimity coat, powdered hair tied behind. He was dignified but brave, and dispensed courageously fair and even. He was a firm believer in the sound principles of government and of the Constitution. He served over 20 years, regardless of political changes, and always with credit and distinction.

The personnel of the Justices composing the County Court was continually changing during this period. Thomas Adams and Isham Browder were longer in office than any other. Among those brought in by change and filling vacancies were Eleazar Givens, James Edmiston, Thomas Davis, Alexander Ashby, George Ashby, Andrew Bell, William McGary, Herbert Browder, James Baker, Wright Willis, Eli Bishop and Charles Bradley.

Israel Davis, son of Joseph Davis, succeeded to the office of Sheriff, but military zeal took this young man to the Battle of the Thames as Ensign in Captain William McGary's Company. His health was so shattered by the hardships and exposure that he died soon after his return. Squire Thomas Adams succeeded him as Sheriff with Henry Ashby, Daniel Ashby, and Daniel Ashby, Jr. as deputies. William Noel, the shoemaker and tavern keeper, still held the office as Jailer. William McGary was also a tavern keeper, and each year the tavern rates were fixed by the court. Benjamin Davis was licensed to keep an ordinary tavern. Below is listed a few rates in force in 1813:

Wine 1/2 pint   25¢
Rum 1/2 pint   25¢
Brandy 1/2 pint   25¢
Whiskey 1/2 pint 12 1/2¢
Lodging 1 night   8 1/2 ¢
Breakfast, dinner
or supper, without
tea or coffee   25¢
1 horse at hay for
12 hrs.   25¢
For corn or oats
(per gal.)   12 1/2¢

****

The Jail which was not occupied by a dozen prisoners for the past few years, was several times repaired. Prison rules were established as follows:

Beginning at each peach tree marked B, standing at the N.E. corner of William McGary's lot and running south 40 poles to a stake S.E. corner of Daniel McGary's lot, thence west 40 poles to S.W. corner to the Benjamin Wickliffe's lots a stake, thence north 40 poles to the beginning, which prison rules were ordered to be made of record. This meant that:

Every prisoner not committed for treason or felony, giving good security to keep within said rules, should have the liberty to walk around. He could go in and out of the prison for the preservation of his health, and by keeping continually within said bounds, should be judged by law as a true prisoner.

Local office holding was not the popular profession. The Jailer was paid $12.00 per year. The County Court Clerk received $15.00 per year. The Sheriff got his commission off of collections.

Jesse Woodson's inspection for tobacco, flour and hemp was established on his land on Tradewater, between Ansel Weir's storehouse and the county line, with Richard Bailey, Samuel Compton and Johnson Gully as inspectors.

The corn was carried to the mill in sacks, on horseback, by the boy of the family who waited his turn. The assembled youths waiting, amused themselves as they could during the long wait. When the miller took his pay or toll for the service, measured by his "toll dish", balanced the sack on the old mare and started the boy home. The corn was hand ground.

Another enterprise of the early days was the making gunpowder. There was according to tradition, such a mill at what is now the northwest corner of South Main and Jagoe Streets. And another where the old Hopkinsville Road in intersected by the Free Henry Ford Road, opposite the Hezekiah Sisk old dwelling.

The Post Office was established in Madisonville, June 18, 1813, in the Caleb Hall Cabin. Baxter Townes was appointed the first postmaster. Later the Post Office was moved to Hogeye Block where a new merchandising establishment was located in a large log building which had been erected. The hogs ran wild in Madisonville among the trees. In the summer time they would wallow in the dust of the town square and in the winter time it was deep mud.

The swine fed principally on roots, nuts and acorns but at times feasted and fattened upon passenger pigeons. Hogs were sometimes driven in herds to places where thousands of pigeons were roosting and where men and boys were armed with sticks and clubs. Plumage was taken to make feather beds.

The last two bears in Madisonville were shot while foraging on the Court House Square in 1810. The bear skins, bear meat and bear grease were in demand and their number lessened.

Our first law against carrying concealed arms, provided that any person in this Commonwealth who wore or carried a pocket pistol, dirk, large knife or sword in a cane, concealed a weapon, be fined the sum of $100.00. This law was passed Feb. 3, 1813. However, no prosecution under this act is recorded.

While Hopkins County was giving of her manhood to the war, its thunders rolled far way and little affected the mode of life and development at home. The tide of immigration continued to flow in, bringing desirable citizenry chiefly from Virginia and North Carolina. These were mostly American born, very few were Europeans.

Every able-bodied Kentuckian between the ages of 18 and 45 is soldier, at least in theory. This legal theory has prevailed since the earliest times. The military training was a small value as preparation for war. Many had served in the Revolutionary War and some of them were the leading citizens holding commissions as officers. Some had followed Mad Anthony Wayne or fought in the Indian War. All were self reliant, bold and daring patriots. Yet there was in the nature of things little discipline and training. As far as equipment, there was none.

A majority of the officers of each regiment might adopt the color of the regimental plume. The privates and non-commissioned officers wore no uniforms, but came in hunting shirts of homespun or buckskin, with hats or caps according to individual means or taste.

Such was the law of Kentucky in pioneer days. Every pioneer was supposed to possess his own equipment, with which he attended the stated musters upon notice duly received. These musters first were held in various neighborhood centers of Henderson County, convenient to the various units, and then after 1807, at Madisonville and later at other places. Sometimes the family attended, bringing baskets of food with them. Whiskey was always plentiful and some drank to excess, which made them hilarious or quarrelsome, according to their nature. Entertainment was afforded in the form of shooting matches, foot races and wrestling. Political oratory was another entertainment. It was nice to see old friends and make new ones, and get the news of the latest happenings of other places.

Eight years since the local government had been set up in the wilderness, but little progress had been made in the direction of easier or more gracious living. Transportation and communication had improved slightly with the beginning of steam navigation on the Ohio. The Island Ford Road was established as well as the Peyton's Ford Road and timber cleared for other roads.

The early pioneers who came into this part of the country, experienced many hardship. Many died of smallpox and other diseases. And many were terrified with outlaws and racketeers, Big Harpe and Little Harpe, whose dreadful violence and outrage before the dawn of the century, alarmed the whole country. This was before Hopkins County was formed.

We are deeply indebted to the hardy pioneers who settled in Hopkins County, cleared its land, built roads and established towns.

Life was hard, the winter often severe, the crop season at times plagued by weather unfavorable for growing crops, causing a scarcity of winter food for man and animal. Their bedrooms without any heat in the winter time and lighted only when necessary by a crude grease lamp. Most cabins were of one room, which served as bedroom, setting room and kitchen. The open log fireplace was their night light as well as their way of cooking.

Even with all of their hardships, they had their days of enjoyment, in hunting, fishing, log-rolling, corn-husking and religious revivals and on occasions a family trip to the county seat.

These pioneers discovered and developed timber and mineral resources. They have passed to us an inheritance worthy of our efforts to preserve and develop.

HISTORY OF HOPKINS COUNTY

The colony of Virginia had many divisions before it was finally named the Commonwealth of Virginia. From it was created the state or Commonwealth of Kentucky, June 1, 1782. From its beginning in a period of 120 years the remaining 111 counties of Kentucky were created and none of them have ever become extinct.

Counties in Kentucky have been named for judges, lawyers, statesmen, senators, congressmen, pioneers and so on. More counties in Kentucky have been named for natives of Virginia than any other state in the Union. Kentucky is truly a daughter of Virginia.

George Washington, surveyor, and afterward, general and president, made the first authorized surveys in the northeast corner of Kentucky. He was assisted by other surveyors.

In July 1790 the eighth Kentucky Convention, looking forward to statehood, petitioned President George Washington and Congress, seeking admission into the Federal Union as a state.

In December 1790, President Washington strongly recommended to Congress that they admit Kentucky into the Union. On Feb. 4, 1791, an act for the purpose of admitting Kentucky passed both houses of the first Congress in its third session, and received the signature of the president.

George Washington (1732-1799) was the President of the United States when Kentucky was admitted as the fifteenth state of the Union, June 1, 1792. He signed the Act. Had there not been some unavoidable delays, Kentucky would have been the first state admitted to the original thirteen colonies instead of Vermont. However, it did not enter the Union until June 1, 1792.

We become confused as to whether Kentucky is a State or Commonwealth. The two designations "Commonwealth" and "State" were synonymous back in the late seventeen hundreds. The term "Commonwealth" dates back to the time of Oliver Cromwell when he created the Commonwealth of States or Colonies. Commonwealth - for the good of all, was the meaning implied. He was ruling England at the time.

A Commonwealth in America is a state having its immediate out growth from one of the original colonies. In seeking its independence from Virginia, Kentucky chose to keep the term "Commonwealth".

Prior to the creating of Kentucky, Virginia had created nine counties. These were in existence when Kentucky came into independence. None of them have ever become extinct.

The area of Kentucky which had not been made into counties prior to its independence, became known as Lincoln County, and from it, as time passed, other counties were formed.

Logan County was created in 1792 with Russellville being the county seat. It was first called Logan Courthouse until it was named Russellville. The southwestern part of the Commonwealth was still owned by the Chickasaw Indians and was their hunting ground. It remained theirs until 1818 when Andrew Jackson and Isaac Shelby negotiated a treaty with the Cherokee Indians in which they ceded their lands along the Mississippi, thus eliminating any Indian Land in Kentucky. Even today this area is called the Jackson Purchase.

Logan County contained a tremendous amount of land and the people in some parts of it desired to establish their own county.

In 1797 Christian County was formed out of the southern part of it and included all the land from the Tennessee border to the Ohio River on the north. Hopkinsville was the county seat of this new county.

Many of the settlers disliked having to travel so many long hard miles to make their court records and agitation began for the establishing of another county so in 1799, Henderson County was formed from the northern part of Christian County beginning at the Ohio River at the north and on to the Christian County line at the south. This still left a large part of the area, especially in the southern part of Henderson County, without a nearby court of law.

In 1806 there was a movement to create a new county out of the southern part of Henderson County. General Samuel Hopkins was representative for Henderson County and Daniel Ashby was the state senator from the same area. Ashby got with General Hopkins and together they brought about the separation of the southern part of Henderson County into a new county. They named it Hopkins County after General Hopkins.

December 9, 1806 the Kentucky legislature passed a bill creating Hopkins County. On Dec. 29, 1806, the Governor signed the act and forwarded it on to Hopkins County, naming justices to set it up and naming a county seat. The Governor's Commission was engrossed in the leisurely manner of the times so the news of the act was brought back by Senator Ashby and this information made known around. When the settlers got their corn planted they decided May 25, 1807 would be a good date for them to meet at the home of Robert McGary. In 1987 the area now is called Eastview Acres. Thus, with the gathering of the duly appointed justices, the plans for the new county and location of the county seat began.

According to the Act of the law, Hopkins County was the 49th county created in the Commonwealth, and it has so remained through the years, with only four minor changes made in its boundary.

In 1819 a part of Christian County was put into Hopkins. This included all land north of a line beginning where the road leading from Highland Lick to Russellville crosses Drakes Creek, near Samuel Williams, then to the mouth of McFarland's Fork, then to the West Fork of Pond River to the mouth thereof, then down the river to the Hopkins County line.

In January 1847 an exchange of lands with Caldwell County made the Tradewater River the boundary line between the two counties.

Feb. 29, 1860 the legislature passed an act creating Webster County, with an effective date of July 1, 1860 and along with Henderson and Union counties, part of Hopkins was included in this new county.

In 1884 the legislature passed an act to settle the county line between Hopkins and Webster Counties. This Act changed the line to include Slaughtersville and its corporate boundary, in Webster. This Act was approved Feb. 20, 1884. Since that time, the boundary of Hopkins County has not been changed.

Joseph Berry, one of the Justices of Peace appointed by Governor Christopher Greenup to administer the beginning of Hopkins County was born near Madison's birthplace in Virginia and having considerable knowledge of Madison, might have suggested the name of Madison for the name of the county seat.

A tradition has it that Samuel Woodson, who came to Hopkins County from Goochland County, Virginia, might have suggested the name.

It was customary to add a suffix to the name of a community to designate what it was, so "ville" was added to Madison's name, making the county seat Madisonville.

In the years from 1780-1820, there was a sympathy in the United States for the objectives of the French Revolution and the French people in particular. The French had helped the Colonies in the war against Great Britain for their liberty, so it is reasonable to assume that this led to the popular adoption of the French suffix "ville" indicating a town or city, (the equivalent of the English, wich or wick - ham - town or ton, or Celtic - don, the English (Danish) - by, the Scottish (or A.S. - burg, with its corruptions boro - bury or burg, the Teutionic - berg, & c, & c.)

As Madisonville was laid out in 1807, as the seat of justice of Hopkins County, James Madison, soon to be president, was a popular man, so that his name naturally suggested itself to our County Court justices, for the combination of Madisonville for this new settlement. Madison was also one who had a large part in the writing of the Constitution of the United States.

There are several small towns in the county, each with a good post office. Manitou, while not incorporated, has had a post office since July 31, 1879 and today it has a post office with a rural route from it.

Earlington, Mortons Gap, Nortonville, White Plains, St. Charles, Dawson Springs and Madisonville all have post offices and have had almost from their beginning. They are nice communities and any one of them would be a good place to live.

At one time there were several small communities in the county, not incorporated, but usually with a store where the post office was located. Later the post offices were combined with those in larger towns and rural delivery was instituted. These communities were Ansonia, Anton, Ashbyburg (first spelled Ashbysburg), Bakersport, Burnett, Beard, Carbondale, Charleston, Chelsea, Clyde, Chalk Level, Clarks, Dalton, Daniel Boone (first called Underwood), Day's Store, Dempstertown, Ella, Ellwood, Gilliland, Hall, Hamby Station, Hazel, Dale, Ilsley, Kingston, Kirkwood Springs, McFareys, McNarys, Mulberry Grove, Olney (first called Iron Bridge), Realus, Richland, Saint Joe, Silent Run, Tweddleville, Vanderburg, Vandetta, Veazey and Yarbro.

However, with the advent of good roads and rural free mail delivery by the Post Office Department, these places soon became just names of an area in which people lived and built their houses. With the passing of time, many moved to other towns, until today, these small places are just names in the books of historians.

Hopkins County is the ninth largest county in Kentucky with good farmland for agriculture, park sites for industry, coal reserves ready to be used, and is a good county in which to live. It has good hard surfaced county roads, is on the Pennyrile Parkway, U.S. 41 and U.S 41A, KY 70, KY 85 and KY 1069. It is also served by the Seaboard System Railroad, which has a large freight yard at Atkinson Junction, at the north limits of Madisonville and the Paducah and Louisville Railway at Nortonville.

It is close to Kentucky Lake and Lake Barkley giving plenty of places for the pleasure of boating or fishing.

The towns in Hopkins County are in good financial condition and the county's finances are also in good shape.

The county schools are consolidated with schools in the following areas: Anton School, Browning Springs Middle School, Charleston School, Dalton School, Earlington School, Grapevine Elementary School, Hall Street Elementary, Hanson School, Madisonville-North Hopkins High School, Mortons Gap School, Nebo School, Nortonville School, Pride Elementary School, St. Charles School, South Hopkins High School, Waddill Elementary School, West Hopkins High School, West Broadway Elementary and White Plains School.

Dawson Springs has its own Independent School System and is not consolidated with the county.

The first dragline in the county dredging Richland Creek in 1900

COMMUNITIES

ANTON

Six miles northeast of Madisonville, on KY 85, is the community of Anton. By name it is thought of as a town, but it is really a community, having never been incorporated. It is populated by many fine people, some who can trace their roots back decades before it was named, when it was a virgin forest inhabited only by many wild animals of various breeds.

It is not possible to state that such and such an area is Anton, in referring today, or when the early settlers came to make this area their homes, unless we know how the community got its name.

In the late 1800's the Federal Government decided that no person should be too far from a post office so it established post offices in many places. Some in homes, others in stores.

Getting a name for its post office was a chore for these people, and after several names were turned down, they named it "Anton" after a good natured Dutchman named Anton Burcken who operated a hoop and saw mill there. The Post office was closed after six years, but the name Anton remained the name of the area and is still so known today.

Many of the early Anton settlers came from Central Kentucky, and the trip was a long hard one over the trails and buffalo traces. Among the early settlers in the Anton area were the Murpheys, Ashbys, Hicklins, Nalls, Slatons, Todds, Batsels and Cardwells. Most of these lived and farmed in the Anton section for several years, or generations, however the Cardwells have been farming their land for five generations. The Cardwells came around 1800, while the Hicklins (from whom all Hopkins County Hicklins come) came about 1814 or 1815. Another large farmer is R.T. Smith, who for several years had a dairy and cattle farm. When the Smiths came in 1920 there was no school in Anton.

Anton had no public school in its area for the first forty years of its existence. What education the children received they got from their parents.

In May 1896 Dr. Boyd T. Arnett arrived, set up a store and did general medical practice.

In 1907 the Madisonville-Hartford and Eastern Railroad Company finished their railroad through Anton, and for a station they set a box car by the railroad. It did not run through where most of the people lived, so they figured out a new name for the station area. It was called New Anton and people gradually began building and moving toward it.

They have four nice churches in the area: Pond River Missionary Baptist in Anton, Bethlehem Christian Church, Browder Methodist Church and the Elm Grove United Methodist.

Anton Elementary School built in 1949

There are several businesses in the area: Basil Preston Garage, Dunnings Garage, Crop Production Company known as the C.P.S. Farm Center, Rite Creek Concrete Company and Short's Grocery.

Short's Grocery at Anton

They also have a nice elementary school in the center of the area. At the north edge, just off KY 85, is the Madisonville Airport which is used by all those flying into and out of the county on business or for pleasure. There is no permanent airline service for passengers. The airport area consists of 216.29 acres, and while entirely owned by Madisonville the city has delegated its authority to an Airport Board. It has a 5,000 foot runway and 26 planes are normally based there.

The Madisonville Airport at Anton

Yes, good pioneer people saw the future of this place and what it held for them, and they made it their place to live.

It also had the honor of having the first woman mail carrier in the United States, Miss Virginia Staples the first rural mail carrier in the United States. She carried mail for seven years and only missed four days work during that time due to illness. Sept. 23, 1911, she married W.A. Smith from Garland, Arkansas and they moved there.

Yes, Anton is a fine community, while no set boundary, its well known reputation makes people proud to say they are from "Anton".

ASHBYSBURG

Ashbysburg, KY (the name was changed to Ashbyburg May 27, 1892) is located on the lofty banks of the beautiful Green River in the northwest part of Hopkins County. It is in some of the most fertile land in the county.

It was established Jan. 3, 1829 and is one of the oldest incorporated towns in the county. It was named for General Stephen

Ashby, son of Captain S.A. Ashby, a Revolutionary War hero. Stephen was born Oct. 14, 1776 and died Oct. 1, 1841 and is buried in Old Salem Cemetery near Slaughters. It was not established as just a place for settlers or passersby, but was set up by well drawn out plans in the 1898 map of Hopkins County by William Shanklin and F.E. Morrow.

The Civil War also touched Ashbyburg. There was a fort built on the only hill near the river, but a few traces now remain of the Confederate fort.

From the very beginning, Ashbyburg was an important river port and in its early days merchandise was shipped there and was carried by wagons all over the county, even as far south as Hopkinsville. Mail was also delivered there. It was an important stop for all steam boats on the river in those days.

Besides the many stores, the town also had a hat shop where the women could go to get hats. There was a hotel where people could wait for a boat or someone to come after them in a wagon. It has been said that after the robbery of the Nimrod Long Banking Company at Russellville that Jesse James spent one night at this hotel, operated by I.G. Gilmore.

First they had a one room school house, then they added another room to it and the children walked two to three miles on dirt roads and through fields and climbing fences until their parents could move to Ashbyburg.

It got its first post office Feb. 14, 1848 and for years mail came there for other towns. They also had a rural route out of the post office.

J.E. Capps was the last rural mail carrier and Mrs. Nancy Carlisle Martin relates making the last mail delivery with him and how sad it was for them. The post office was closed June 30, 1969 and the flag was lowered for the last time.

Lowering the flag for the last time at the Post Office L. to R.: Nancy Carlisle Martin, A.C. Weldon, G.C. Carlisle; Postmistress Mrs. Clarine Fridy Rhodes, E.L. Tomblinson, H.A. Cobb and Jesse Capps

Now as we drive along through the country, we wonder where was this place called Ashbysburg (Ashbyburg). It is just a nice quiet place where there are just modest homes, simply built. Honesty had been handed down from generation to generation, and so it remains today.

Mrs. Nancy Carlisle Martin wrote the history of Ashbyburg for the 1977 Year Book of the Historical Society of Hopkins County. She says she has great pride in saying her home is Ashbyburg where some of the pioneer families were Walter and Will Thompson, Walter being the father of Walter Thompson also of Madisonville. The Carlisles and Timmons (her own family) one of whom was Dr. J.D. Timmons of Hanson, grandfather of Mrs. Hanson Slaton. The Lucks and Will Brown, father of the late Dr. Benson's wife, Mae, and Professor McCulley, The Tomblinsons, Coffmans, Daniels, Ingrams, Hanners, Blue, Arnetts, Nelsons, Wiley, Scotts, Kerrs, Eplys, and Gilmores.

Iley B. Timmons, grandfather of Mrs. Martin, fought in the Union Army and was awarded the Bronze Star for outstanding bravery.

Yes, Ashbysburg is a modest place to live.

BARNSLEY

The Community Center at Barnsley near Mortons Gap about 1919-1920. Front row, second from left-Lener Cates Vincent; Eighth-Oscar Cates. Second Row, fifth-Bud Cates

COILTOWN

Coiltown came into being in the late 1890s when the Coil family of Madisonville leased ground for a camp to a house workers for their coal mines. Coiltown is located at the crossroads of Rosecreek Road and Highway 502, about three miles south of Nebo.

Coil Camp settled on the left side of Highway 502 and the right side was called Circle City Camp. The Coils built and operated a

Bethany Methodist Church at Coiltown in 1942
Front Row L. to R.: Unknown, Mary Jo Lyons, Ronald Bruce, and Unknown; Second Row: Oscar Bannon, Choate Wilson & Wilma Bruce; Top Row: Ella Bannon, Mrs. Mary Bruce and son Roy Douglas

saw mill and lumber yard. Rollin Jenkins operated a livery stable and of course, there was the Coil Company Store. Circle City had their Company Store operated by a Mr. Lynn.

Circle City campers held the Sabbath Day meetings in the bathhouse. About 1900 the town was going strong and two churches were established, Betheny Methodist and Coiltown Baptist. (See church histories in the church section) The Coiltown Holiness Church came later.

The two camps became known as Coiltown. In 1904 butcher shop, ran by James Walter Noel the father of Michael Noel of Manitou, was added to Coiltown. There were two barber shops, one that stayed open all day and one that stayed open all night. This was done to insure that no barbering business was missed as the miners came and went to work. Kennel Clark had a store in the middle of town which was sold in the early 1940s to Champ Winstead, father of Tanner Winstead of Nebo.

As sink holes from the old worked out mines became worse, people sold out and left. By the 1960s, Coiltown was a ghost town. All businesses were gone except for Peyton's Grocery and Gas station on the north side of Rosecreek Road. The churches and school were closed. All that was left was a few of the better homes and Coiltown Lake. Then the strip mines began moving in. In 1963, Sidney Kirkwood and Jimmy Renfro began draining the beautiful lake.

Today, people are once again building and settling in Coiltown.
-Submitted by Dorothy Miller Shoulders

Cox's Store (Pull-Tight)

The Blacksmith Shop at Cox's Store community (also known as Pull-Tight) L. to R.: Carlos Pulley and Washington Jones

Daniel Boone

As with most settlements in Hopkins County, Daniel Boone came into existence due to coal mining.

The Daniel Boone mine was opened in 1904 by the Buffalo Creek Coal Mining Company and was sold to the Daniel Boone Company the same year. On Jan. 1, 1907, Stirling Coal and Coke Company bought the mine. In 1913, the owner became Stirling Coal Company with Paul Gannon becoming Superintendent in 1920.

The Stirling Coal & Coke Co. Store at Daniel Boone

The community had a company store, a post office, a dentist and doctor office, and a depot. Dr. Marvin S. Veal was the community doctor. Thomas H. Rhodes was the bookkeeper for Stirling Coal and also postmaster for close to 50 years. The train would stop in Daniel Boone for passengers. Later, when passengers were no longer picked up, the outgoing mail would be hung on a crane for pickup and the incoming mail bag was thrown off the train.

Lorene Pryor Alexander, now of Hopkinsville, was born in a house that was located directly across the railroad tracks from the Stirling Coal Company Store. Mrs. Alexander's father, Gus Pryor, worked at the Daniel Boone Mine and was one of fifteen men who lost their lives in an explosion at the mine.

On Oct. 27, 1941, around 7:15 in the morning, the mine was rocked by an explosion. An hour after the explosion, 51 men were still trapped in the mine. By noon, 36 men had been rescued and were uninjured except for shock. Fifteen men remained 2400 feet from the mouth of the shaft. A canary that was lowered into the shaft, lived for only a few minutes. Fire departments from Madisonville and Nortonville sent crews of men with rescue equipment. Area mines responded with their first-aid teams. It was not until 4 o'clock the next day that the bodies of 15 victims were recovered.

Other victims besides Mr. Pryor were: Mine foreman Will Compton, Elbertrice Key, Robert Josey, Bert Cunningham, Edgar Adams, Neely Todd, brothers Junior Gamblin and Goldie Gamblin and brother-in-law Obie Wells, Otho Sisk, Benny Martin, Robert Dunning, Dan Pearson and Ike Whitfield. State mine inspectors later said the explosion was caused by a carbide lamp that ignited a gas accumulation. The mine closed in 1944.

Inside the Daniel Boone Mine. The two men in front are L. to R.: Edgar Vandiver and Beecher Goodaker

Mrs. Vergie Spickard Franklin, now a resident of the Dawson Health Center, lived at Daniel Boone. Dr. Veal delivered both of her sons. Mr. Franklin worked for several years at the Company Store and was clerking there when the complex burned, never to be rebuilt.

Daniel Boone School was established to meet the educational needs of the children. (For information on the school, see the school section of this book).

People later bought property in another location from the Stirling Coal Company and built homes. Today, this community is called Cedar Hill.

Lorene Pryor Alexander describes Daniel Boone today as follows: "To drive through the area that was where the little booming coal mine town of Daniel Boone once stood, it is now almost impossible to picture anything ever being there. The area is all covered in a heavy growth of trees, grass, and weeds. Yet many people who are still living have fond memories of Daniel Boone."
- *Written by Debbie Knight Hammonds*

DAWSON SPRINGS

Dawson Springs is about 18 miles southwest of Madisonville on US 62. It has had several different names before the name of Dawson Springs was given and began to be the beginning of the nice, quite town it is in 1987.

Indians were the first inhabitants of this area but after the government sent all the Indians to the Cherokee Strip in Oklahoma, it was soon occupied only by the white settlers that came to the area.

Settlers began to move into the area about 1867 and then when the Elizabethtown-Paducah railroad went through this section, around 1870, more people began moving to this place.

It was formerly called Tradewater but the railroad disregarded the name Tradewater and honored Bryant Dawson, a big land owner, by listing the name of the station as Dawson. The railroad served as a dividing line between the Patten Alexander and Bryant Dawson farms.

On July 14, 1872, before the first train had passed through the town, Dawson donated the tract of land, which is now the American Legion Park, to the railroad for use as a depot.

At the time this took place, the town was made up of the railroad depot, the Galloway brothers commissary and saloon, a blacksmith shop, a small hotel and a mule-powered pump and water tank.

Washington I. Hamby, a captain in the Confederate Army during the Civil War, came to Dawson in 1877 and established a restaurant. Prior to enlisting in the Army, Hamby had farmed in the area.

The railroad influenced the arrival of settlers and though there was not a great number of people in the town, there soon developed the need for a school and in the late 1870's Bush Alexander, Patten Alexander's son, proposed to donate the ground if the county school authorities would erect a school building on his farm.

Hamby's restaurant burned in 1877, so he went into the business of supplying ties for the railroad.

Soon after his restaurant burned, Hamby built one to replace it and added a small hotel to the restaurant. Upon completion of the hotel, it is said that Mrs. Hamby told her husband, "We must have water for this hotel and I think you had better dig a well."

At that time, the hotel stood in what later became Arcadia Park and is now the site of the Commercial Bank of Dawson and the Kentucky Utilities Company Offices. The summer of 1881 was a very dry one, forcing Hamby to have water hauled from the Tradewater River for his business.

Hamby put men to work and on July 2, 1881, water was reached by the workmen. But when the water was tasted, it was found to have a curious taste and not good for use in cooking. He was seriously thinking of filling up the well, however the section of hands of the railroad asked him to leave the well as they found it because the water was apparently good for them and they offered to dig another well free of charge if he would leave the first well. He agreed, and the Dawson Springs mineral water was born.

In 1881, the E&P railroad was purchased by another company and merged with it. At this time, Dawson had a population of about 50 persons.

By 1882, Dawson had a population growth to 150. Its school District No. 82 now had more pupils and the town began growing. Dawson's population by 1885 was about 1,000 people and they thought of themselves as a growing community. This population explosion subsided for a few years until June 1893. During this month while drilling for water again for the Hamby Hotel, W.I. Hamby struck at a shallow depth, a vein of highly mineralized water. This became "Hamby Well" and made Dawson famous throughout the south.

With the building of the Hamby Hotel, to compliment the Southern and Arcadia Hotels, the reputation of Dawson spread throughout the south.

This was the beginning of the "spa era" here. In Europe, "spas" had been the vogue for sometime. Because of the "spa era" in Europe, Baron von Steuben traveled to Manitou to see the mineral springs there, which were part of 2,000 acres of land he had been given by the government, but did not keep. Tradition says he had a skirmish with the Indians there in 1787 and did not stay in Kentucky after this.

Visitors who had traveled from all parts of the country and from abroad claimed the Dawson mineral waters were wonderful for curing diseases. The waters were believed to cure such diseases as stomach troubles, inactive liver, constigout, diseases of kidneys and bladder, female irregularities, rheumatism, gout, nerve trouble, dropsy and Bright's disease.

Seeing the opportunity to make the most of it, the citizens made the area a beautiful spot not only for taking the water cure, but for other visitors. As the town exploded as a health resort, the United States also grew and in 1898, the name "Springs" was added to the name of the town.

Many people think the "Springs" was added because of the mineral springs there, but this is wrong. The mineral water did not come from springs but from shallow wells.

Many fine hotels were built to accommodate the throngs of visitors but unfortunately, fires over a period of time burned them or they were razed and no longer are there any of them for us to admire.

Dawson Springs, in 1910, was definitely a resort town. Stave mills had passed away and mining was on a local scale but not considered much of a business because of the low wages they paid.

The Arcadia Hotel about 1911

Main Street in Dawson Springs in 1910

The establishment of Outwood Hospital by the Veterans Administration in the early 1920's gave Dawson a tremendous boost at a time when her tourist business was declining. It was dedicated Feb. 22, 1922. It closed as a veterans hospital July 1962.

The mining of coal began to increase and two mines were located close to the city, Dawson Daylight Mine, northeast of the town, and the Dawson Colleries Mine. Dawson Daylight began stripping coal in 1923 and closed this operation in 1928 and opened several small underground mines. It ceased operation in 1930.

Dawson Colleries, a subsidiary of Dawson Daylight, started a slope mine on the eastern edge of town on May 27, 1936 and operated until Feb. 21, 1961. There were also several small mines near the town.

The inhabitants were truly glad when the gob pile at the eastern edge of the town was removed in the 1960's and a new bridge was built near the intersection of US 62 and KY 109. This gob pile was created by residue from the Dawson Colleries mine.

With the mines closing, the citizens began to make plans for bringing industry to Dawson. With the good roads (the Western Kentucky Parkway forms the northern limits of the city), the fine school and the other things they had to offer, Dawson Springs residents were certain they would attract new industry to their city.

Dawson had played host to many large meetings of various organizations, local and national. The 1960's and 1970's saw the greatest expansion Dawson had ever experienced. Outwood Hospital was replaced by the state as a school for the retarded; the construction of a new school and gymnasium; construction of Lake Beshear; a housing project; a new post office and building of two industrial parks, one of 41 acres and the other of 120 acres; and expansion of their water works system and secured natural gas.

Dawson Springs is governed by a mayor, elected for a 4-year term, and 6 councilmen elected for two-year terms.

Dawson Springs is not affiliated with the Hopkins County school system but prefers to have its own independent school district.

Although the town has grown much since its early beginning, it still remains the same close knit community it was in early times.

EARLINGTON

Much of the land on which Earlington, KY is located was once farm land owned by John Bayless Earle. Another land owner in the area was Caleb Hall.

Earlington was first called Caleb Hall's Post Office but when John Bayless Earle struck the first pick in the hillside just south of the Madisonville County Club in 1869, it was the beginning of the first commercial mine in Hopkins County. This became the Number 11 Mine of the St. Bernard Coal Company in 1896. In Mr. Earle's honor, the town was called Earlington and was chartered as such by the Kentucky Legislature Jan. 3, 1871.

The St. Bernard Coal Company, later named the St. Bernard Mining Company, was incorporated as the first commercial coal mine in Western Kentucky and in the early days of its existence its chief concern was to develop a new industry - mining coal - in a new field against great odds.

When the railroad was completed through Earlington in 1870, it opened a new operation for St. Bernard. The first railroad engines burned wood and and it was through the efforts of John B. Atkinson,

Skating on the Tradewater River near Dawson Springs ca 1915. Charles F. Cato, Sr., is second from right

superintendent and later president of the company, to use his influence to get the railroad to use coal rather than wood to power its engines. In this he was successful and with completion of the railroad from Evansville, IN to Nashville, TN in 1871, the coal industry of Earlington and the surrounding area began to boom. The last rail on the railroad, which had started from Henderson in 1853 but was delayed by the Civil War, was laid near Mannington, KY in 1871.

The Earlington L & N Depot built in 1900 on the southwest corner of Main-Railroad Streets

At one time, St. Bernard operated eight mines with its main office in Earlington. However, it was sold to the West Kentucky Coal Company in May 1924. In 1963, Island Creek Coal Company, with headquarters in West Virginia, purchased the West Kentucky Coal Company.

Prior to the purchase by Island Creek, West Kentucky moved its offices from Earlington to South Main Street in Madisonville, adding a wing to the former home of Inkerman Bailey. Island Creek also had its headquarters there and added another wing to the house until it closed out its main office in Madisonville and sold the building to Donan Engineering Company.

Earlington began to grow after the railroad came through and was soon a booming town. It continued to grow until the mines began to close after World War II.

John Corliss "Bill" Bassett was Postmaster at Earlington from 1940-1961 - pictured here about 1950

The Earl Theatre-opened Nov. 22, 1949

The L&N Railroad had its yards there and in 1900 erected a very beautiful railroad station which was used until the railroads ceased having passenger trains. It was no longer used after 1963 and was finally razed.

The St. Bernard Coal Company was very generous to the community giving it not only land on which to build schools but also in many instances paying for the building as well.

The Loch Mary Spillway at Earlington

In 1903, the St. Bernard built a power plant which furnished power not only for the mines but for the town as well. Kentucky Utilities purchased this plant from the West Kentucky Coal Company in 1926. The Kentucky Utilities no longer uses the power plant and it is now a work shop.

The city also had two libraries and a hospital during this time.

In the early 1980's the coal business began to slack off and this hurt the progress of the community. The era of company stores ended in January 1983 when the Island Creek Coal Company closed its store. A fire started in the abandoned building and it was destroyed completely in 1987.

Earlington is a good community within four miles of Madisonville and its people are proud of their town and its traditions.

US 41A passes through Earlington and in 1987 their access road to the Pennyrile Parkway should be completed. KY 481 and KY 1337 touch the town and the Seaboard System Railroad serves the community. A four-lane highway, which connects Earlington and Madisonville and KY 112, also are a part of its road system. This gives easy access to all who live and go there.

HANSON

Hanson, KY, five miles north of Madisonville on US 41, has maintained its population of between 500 and 600 people for the past several years. Now in its second century, this little town is inhabited by a number of descendants of the original settlers.

Founded in 1869, Hanson was named for Harry Hanson, a civil engineer who planned the town. History records no connection with the settlement of Hanson for Mr. Hanson. He just appears to have been the right man at the right place at the right time. His picture hangs in the Hanson post office through the courtesy of the family of the late O.A. Ashby.

Hanson was founded on 50 acres of land given for the purpose by Judge Robert Eastwood and the Rev. Roland Gooch.

Construction on the Henderson and Nashville Railroad Company was started about June 3, 1853 and was completed from its southern terminal, Nashville, TN to Hopkinsville, KY. It was completed from its northern terminal, Henderson, KY to Hanson and Hanson remained as its southern terminal until in 1867, when the road was completed from Hanson to Madisonville, where its southern terminal remained until January 1871.

The L & N Depot at Hanson

The railroad was built by Mr. Rankin, a contractor, and the railway was known as a branch of the "Old Southeastern". The first railroad agent was John Anderson.

A few people lived in this area as most of it was virgin forest. Mr. Rankin built a house and set up a saw mill where the town now stands. The town then began to grow as others moved in and other business houses were erected. Had it not been for several disastrous fires, there is no telling how large Hanson would be today.

In its early years, there were several churches in Hanson. At the present, there are only two: The Hanson Methodist Church and the Hanson Baptist Church.

Their first school was very primitive, being located on the Willis Gooch farm in an old tobacco barn. Today, they have a modern school building. At one time Prof. E. McCulley had a college in Hanson in the late 1880's.

When the Hanson community was first settled, mail was brought to Ashbyburg by boat and then transported by stage coach or horseback to Hanson and then distributed to its final point of destination.

Main Street in Hanson about 1890-1900

Perhaps the best known of Hanson's businessmen was E.L. Parish, who operated a store there for more than seventy years.

It is believed that fire changed the history of Hanson. There were four disastrous fires. The four were in April 1889; September 1894; March 1905 and September 1906.

Hanson got its first post office Dec. 7, 1869 with William Anderson as their first postmaster. He served until May 27, 1872 when William H. Weir was appointed. Weir served as postmaster until May 6, 1891.

The town was incorporated Mar. 31, 1873.

In 1987, Hanson is a quite, clean community settled mostly by retired persons and farmers. There is no roughness among its people. Among its attractions is the fine collection of old cars by County Judge-Executive Hanson Slaton.

It is on US 41 and close to the Pennyrile Parkway.

ILSLEY (CRABTREE)

In 1852, a man by the name of Thomas Crabtree began buying large parcels of land near Caney Creek and Caney Fork. He built a log house (larger than a cabin) and settled in the area that became known as Crabtree.

Mr. Crabtree organized a coal mining operation in 1882 that spanned nearly a hundred years (see Crabtree Coal Mining Company).

As a result of the jobs offered by the mine, Crabtree began to grow. The mining company built four-room houses, stables, two churches (one white and one black), two schools (one white and one black), and in 1893 a new Company Store (the other store, built several years before and operated by John and R.M. (Dick) Salmon, had burned earlier that year) and by 1903, Crabtree had a population of 500.

Crabtree proper was about two miles north of the Illinois Central Railroad line. In order to ship coal, a spur track was laid from the mine tipple to the main track. At the main track switch, a depot was built and named Ilsley Station after Edward Ilsley, vice-president of Crabtree Mining Co. (see Ilsley Station).

Era Berryman Adcock and daughter Orene Adcock Russell on the yard engine that carried coal from the mine tipple at Crabtree to Ilsley Station in 1938

In 1923, Crabtree Coal Mining Co. became a part of Norton Coal Co., owned by the Monroe-Warrior Co. of Birmingham, AL.

In the 1920's and '30s, Mrs. Eula Brackett Majors, who ran a boarding house in town, met the train at the station in a spring wagon, at the same time every day, except Sunday, to pick up the mailbag. Her husband, Rufus (Rufe) Majors, drove a large wagon pulled by a team of horses. He hauled water from the Molly Dixon pond for twenty-five cents a load and delivered coal to customers throughout Crabtree, which was by this time called Ilsley to eliminate the confusion of having the train station and the Post Office with different names.

One Halloween, some boys took Rufe Majors big wagon apart, lifted the pieces up and reassembled it on the roof of the company store.

Inside the Crabtree Company Store-Opal Alexander, Mr. Linear, and George McKnight

The Crabtree Company Store was a two-story structure in the center of town. It was a general gathering place, perhaps because the Post Office was there and folks could share news. The barber shop was across the road and run by Earl Alexander and Cal Duncan. Beside the barber shop was a little store called the Hot Cat, owned and operated by Roland Franklin. It had a special attraction for the children in town, as Mr. Franklin sold popcorn, candy, Cracker Jack, and chewing gum, as well as cigarettes and gasoline.

Behind and below the Hot Cat, O.B. Franklin had an auto repair shop, and Walkers Grocery was down the road toward Earlington, near the Salmon house.

The second Crabtree-Ilsley School (see schools) was also built by the mining company, but located beside the Madisonville Road several hundred feet south of the Company Store.

The Presbyterian Church was built just south of the school, with the cemetery between them, in 1926 (see Ilsley Presbyterian Church), and the Holiness Church was built on the north side of the school in 1927.

The Crabtree Company Store burned in 1936 and was rebuilt on the same site but was much smaller and with only one level. The Post Office and temporarily the Company Store were relocated across the road with the barber shop and the Hot Cat which became a grocery store.

Norton Coal Co. closed in the late 1950s and the Post Office and school were closed in the early 1960s. The old businesses are all gone, and few have taken their place. The churches are still here and there is a beauty shop, a welding shop, Martin-Holt Pillow Manufacturing Co., and the "Y" Grocery at the intersection of Highways 112 and 62.-*Submitted by Sharon Riggs Johnston*

ILSLEY STATION

Named for Edward Ilsley, Vice-President of the Crabtree Coal Mining Company, this small community began as a stop on the Illinois Central Railroad's main east-west line.

A depot was built at the main track beside the Crabtree spur track switch. The spur was built so the Crabtree Mine locomotive could pull loaded coal cars to the main track from the mine tipple. The Ilsley Station depot was large enough to accomodate passengers, as well as freight and mail shipments.

The children liked to watch the express train as it sped past. Their interest was not so much with the train itself, as with the way it snatched the mailbag from the extended arm on the pole at the depot.

There were only about eight houses at Ilsley Station, three built on the hill across from the depot and three or four others nearer the track. The only store was run by Monk Menser.

A new depot was built across the main track in the early 1900's and the old depot was turned into a house. Austin Ladd and his family were living there the night that a passenger coach jumped track and rammed into the wall of the house, the family, badly frightened, ran to see what happened. There standing upright in the living room, was the railroad car. The car was removed and the house repaired.

When the mine at Crabtree shut down, the depot was closed and also turned into a house. Ben and Rosia Hoard, whose son Albert gave much of the information for this article, raised their children at Ilsley Station and lived for a time in each of the former depots.

After the closing of the mine and depot, the community became rather isolated and one by one, the families moved away. Finally about 1960, the last man, Ben Hoard, also left Ilsley Station and the road was closed off.- *Compiled by Sharon Riggs Johnston*

LUTONTOWN

The Lutontown Mine

MADISONVILLE

Madisonville early attracted its share of settlers moving west and many of the earlier settlers were German and Scotch. It had an abundance of springs and as water was a much needed item, this caused many to make it their permanent home.

Three years after it was founded, there was still only 37 permanent residents. A census of the time lists eleven men, three women, ten boys, one freedman and eight slaves. These early settlers could not have known that rich mineral deposits underlay nearly all the soil in Hopkins County. Vast deposits of phosphate, potash were matched by coal, oil, gas underground and rich timber above ground.

The early years from 1810 to 1830 show that the town had grown from 37 persons to 112. However, by 1840 the city dropped to 51 persons. The reason for this is hard to determine. In any case, the city started to grow gradually and vigorously and in 1860 its population was 602. By 1870 this had increased to 1022.

The population was not the only indication of prosperity. Madisonville began to assume a more prominent economic role in Hopkins County's progress by the mid 1870s.

By 1889, Madisonville was in a thriving condition. On the sides of the city were fine farming lands. The population had grown as had the number of stores and the population was now 2500.

There were now three flour mills, eight tobacco factories, eight dry good stores, two livery stables, two barber shops and one bank. All of these were established by 1890.

The West Side of Main from Court Street, looking North

Transportation during the first century was basically horse and buggy and travel from town was by stagecoach.

With the coming of the Evansville-Henderson-Nashville railroad in 1869 and its completion on the south to Nashville, the town really began to grow. It was especially a boon to the coal mines for now they could ship coal anywhere. The mines really began to open in various places in the county, giving employment to hundreds of men.

The Masonic Temple and YMCA in Madisonville

Beginning in the early 1900s, the growth was fairly consistent until the depression years came. During this period, the mines almost entirely ceased operation and its growth almost stopped.

Madisonville is the county seat of Hopkins County and is very near the center of the county. It is served by the Seaboard System Railroad. The Pennyrile Parkway is at its eastern boundary and Highways 41 and 41A cross it giving excellent means of travel.

It is a fourth class city with a mayor elected for four years and six councilmen elected for two year terms. Madisonville owns its

Grace Winsteads Restaurant on Dempsey St.

water plant and electric distribution, purchasing electricity from the Kentucky Utilities Company and reselling it to the citizens of the town. This has always been a profitable income for the city.

The city has an excellent Municipal Park, several fine fishing lakes and is assured of a permanent water supply by having Lake Pee Wee as a large reservoir. On Sept. 17, 1978, the 24 inch pipe line to Green River at Ashbyburg was completed and water could now be pumped from the river when the lakes got too low to furnish the town with water. This stopped a water problem which had been with the town since it was founded.

Thompsons Popcorn Factory on the East side of the L & N Railroad. On left is Roy Haley with J.D. Thompson on the right. In the background is the Grand Central Hotel

During the 1920s the city asphalted the streets and began to put electric lights at the intersections.

In 1940, Madisonville was a small town of 8209, with a population that depended largely on agriculture and coal mining. At the beginning of each decade after that, U.S. Census figures show substantial growth. In fact, the 1980 census figures indicate that

The North Side of West Center Street in 1948

Madisonville's population is more than double the 1940 figure, being 16,945 and in 1987 it has no doubt made more progress in its population growth.

With its growth, the city expanded its police and fire departments, water and sanitation departments.

The city has worked hard to attract new industry to the town but was not on the Kentucky Department of Commerce's list of favored cities until it got its permanent water supply.

Madisonville has a fine Hopkins County-Madisonville Library and a YMCA. It also has excellent medical facilities, the Regional Medical Center an excellent hospital and Trover Clinic which has many fine doctors with various skills to take care of the need of Hopkins and nearby counties. Several good nursing homes, three good banks and an excellent city park and golf course are among Madisonville's attractions. It has five grade schools in its limits and Madisonville-North Hopkins High School just north of town. It is also the home of the Historical Society of Hopkins County. Here the museum is stocked with items used by our pioneers and later years and much history of the county.

It has also restored the log cabin in which Governor Ruby Laffoon was born June 15, 1869. It was moved to a vacant lot on Union Street and rebuilt from as much of the original lumber as possible. Laffoon is the only Hopkins Countian to be governor of our Commonwealth. He served from 1931 to 1935.

Madisonville has two nice industrial parks, one on U.S. 41A of 250 acres and one on KY 85 with 75 acres. It has plenty to offer any firm seeking a place to locate a business.

Today there are fourteen manufacturers in and around Madisonville. They are American Mine Tool Inc., Birmingham Bolt Inc., KY Division, Ensign Bickford Co., Filtration Sciences, General Electric Co., Goodyear Tire and Rubber Co., Kentucky Carbide, Kris-Shan Plastics Inc., Ottenheimer & Co. Inc., Polyweave Bag Co., Speed Queen Co., Versnick Manufacturing Co., York International and the Carhartt Co.

It has five shopping centers and other businesses to take care of the shopping needs of anyone. It also has nice business houses in the downtown area.

A wonderful Senior Citizens Center with something for all the senior citizens is located near downtown. The Center has a wide program of services as well as Meals-On-Wheels for the homebound.

The Chamber of Commerce is very aggressive and has done a tremendous job in assisting businessmen and in the search for new industries.

With the close of World War II, the mines in Hopkins County were quite busy and new industry was moving in. Later the mines began a gradual decline and mining eventually ceased to be a major force in employment. The chief sources of employment now are industry, agriculture, mining and service work.

Manitou

Four miles west of Madisonville on US 41A is the community of Manitou. While never incorporated, it has a very interesting history and is, no doubt, the oldest settlement in the county.

Centuries before Kentucky was to become a Commonwealth and Hopkins County was formed, the Indians found Manitou to be a hunters paradise because of the 16 springs there and a great salt lick around it and one about three miles north of it on what is now KY 630.

During the hunting season, the Delawares, Wyandots, Shawnees and other tribes from beyond the Ohio River, and the Catabas, Cherokees and Creeks from the southern country came here to hunt buffalo, elk and deer which roamed this watering place and salt lick in great numbers.

From ancient days, the Indians called Manitou "Tywhopity" after one of their Indian king-gods whose presence the Indians believed to be everywhere. It retained this name until after the Revolutionary War and its name change came about in a peculiar way on two occasions.

Because of the 16 springs and the large salt lick three miles north of Manitou on KY 630, this was a favorite hunting and camping place for the Indians. The original springs dwindled down to 13 then 10 and in 1987 all are gone because motorists kept running into the pumps and knocking them down.

Baron Friedrick Wilhelm Ludolf Gerhard Augiestin von Steuben was a German Army captain but for some reason he left Germany and went into the service of Prince Hohenzollern-Heckigen, who it is believed gave him the title of Baron. After leaving the service of the prince, he went to France where his reputation as an excellent soldier and administrator had preceded him. It was in France he was introduced to Benjamin Franklin and Silas Deade, representatives of the American Colonies who were engaged in war with Great Britian for their independence. They persuaded him that his military skills would be of tremendous assistance to the struggling army of General George Washington. He agreed to help.

It was Baron von Steuben who made the drill manual and drilled Washington's troops to help the nation win its independence. For his services, after the war, he was given grants of land among which were 2,000 acres in Hopkins County around Manitou.

In coming to Kentucky to investigate the land given him at Tywhopity, tradition has it that he was wounded in a battle with the Indians there but there is no record of this among his papers.

In Von Steuben's native Prussia, chalybeate waters were thought to be healthful. It was believed they contained iron in sufficient quantities to warrent their use for anemia. Von Steuben evidently believed he had such waters in Tywhopity but for some reason he did not make use of the land given him in this area. His heirs later surrendered all rights to it.

After his visit, the name of the community was changed to Steuben's Lick and remained that until Nov. 7, 1882. There was a post office at Steuben's Lick from July 31, 1879 until Nov. 7, 1882 when the name changed to Manitou.

C.J. Pratt was responsible for the name change. When he became interested in land speculation around Steuben's Lick is not known but he did become a large landowner prior to 1878.

Mr. Pratt visited Colorado Springs, CO originally called Fountain Colony because of its location on Fountain Creek. Later the name was changed to Colorado Springs because of the springs nearby. Colorado Springs was founded in 1870 while Manitou, CO received its name in 1872.

Pratt was deeply impressed by the fact that the water at Manitou Springs was similar to that at Steuben's Lick. He also found that Manitou, a name given among American Indians to any spirit or supernatural being - good or evil - also applied to any object of religious awe or reverance.

Certainly Mr. Pratt had good reason to want to change the name of Tywhopity to Manitou because of the similarity in the water of the two places and because both had their beginnings as Indian encampments. It took him three years to get the name changed from Steuben's Lick to Manitou.

Manitou has had its name for 105 years. As a settlement, it is the oldest in Hopkins County.

In 1955, the Madisonville Kiwanis Club built a roadside park in Manitou and placed markers designating it von Steubens' Lick Park. The park is at the east limits of Manitou on US 41A. It is a nice place to eat or loaf.

Who the actual first white settlers were in this area is unknown. However, among the early settlers was John W. Oliver who came to the area in 1878. He opened a store there and was the first postmaster.

Cosby and Stella Crow in front of their store about 1947

Manitou has had a post office ever since it became a settlement and that is quite a record for a small unincorporated community.

A three-story tobacco factory was erected in Manitou around 1884 where tobacco was prepared for shipping. In 1929, the factory caught fire, was destroyed and never rebuilt.

There was once a small mine opened near Manitou for wagon trade in coal. The people found they could store potatoes in it during the winter, saving the trouble of fixing another place for them. Everyone stored their potatoes there. Unfortunately, the mine caved in one winter and everyone lost their potatoes.

Today it is a small, quiet place with a store, post office and nice homes of quiet, friendly people and the Manitou Missionary Baptist Church which was organized May 17, 1925.

MORTONS GAP

In 1801, the president of the United States authorized the army to clear out a road from Nashville, TN to Natchez, MS. The route selected from the road generally followed that of a well-known trail which had been used for generations. Frontiersmen taking their products on flatboats down the rivers to New Orleans or Natchez found it difficult to row upstream so they sold their boats. They preferred to walk over the Trace to Nashville and from there on to their homes.

At Nashville, a trace went northward to Russellville, KY to Hopkinsville, continuing north generally along US 41 between the Peaks of Otter along what is now Main Street in Mortons Gap and on northward to the Ohio River.

It is easy to see the Peaks of Otter, or the Gap between them, which resulted in the word "Gap" being added to Mortons, thereby giving the town its name.

Thomas Morton was born in Richmond, VA, later moving to Clark County, KY where he met and married Elizabeth Davis of Fayette County. Apparently they lived in Clark County until sometime in 1797 when, with their three children, they moved westward to what was then Christian County, settling in the central part of it. They evidently reached their destination shortly after Christian County was created out of Logan County Mar. 2, 1797. Here they built their cabin. Its location gave them a way to Hopkinsville and a road north to Henderson on the Ohio River.

They set about clearing the land and improving their living conditions. When the legislature divided Christian County May 15, 1799, creating Henderson County, their home was in the southern part of Henderson County. In 1804 Thomas built a fine brick home which stood for 132 years. The present Mortons Gap school now occupies the site of the Morton home.

Slow in being settled, Henderson County in the 1800s had a population of 1,468 and included all of what is now Hopkins, Union and Webster Counties. By 1810 it only had 2,964 inhabitants so from this it is apparent that there were not too many settlers. In 1810, the nearest towns were Greenville with a population of 75, Henderson with a population of 159 and Madisonville with 37 inhabitants. Madisonville did not have its first post office until October 1809 and as a result, postal service was bad. It was a long travel to Henderson to transact court business, so began agitation for a new county.

Daniel Ashby, who lived on Otter Creek, was state senator representing Muhlenberg, Livingston and Henderson Counties. With the able assistance of General Samuel Hopkins, state representative of Henderson County, Henderson County was divided and a new county named Hopkins was created by the legislature established in May 1807.

As time passed, others began to settle in the Mortons home area and it became known as Mortons Settlement.

There was no church in the settlement until the Christian Church was organized May 25, 1873 and then other denominations began to erect houses of worship.

There has been a post office at Mortons Gap since 1871 and it still has one. From corner groceries, it has grown to have its own nice grocery building. As the town grew, it was decided to incorporate and it was incorporated Mar. 15, 1868 to be known as Mortons Gap.

All of the Evansville, Henderson and Nashville railroad from the Ohio River south to Madisonville and from the Tennessee line north to Hopkinsville had been completed prior to 1868 leaving a gap between Madisonville and Hopkinsville. This missing link was completed in January of 1871 by Henry B. Hanson. This opened up the Mortons area of large scale mining. Two of the best known and largest mines were the Kington Coal Company operated by W.W. Kington and the South Diamond owned by the St. Bernard Coal Company.

On Apr. 10, 1906 the city council passed a motion to erect a jail and courtroom. The jail was 20 X 30 feet and cost $300.

The Planters Bank of Mortons Gap was opened Apr. 1, 1907 for business and continued until it was purchased in January of 1972 by the Kentucky Bank and Trust Company, Madisonville.

The town boomed as long as the Kington Mine, known as White City, and the St. Bernard were operating but after they closed many had to seek other employment.

Mortons Gap has had an interesting and varied history, which included the 1811 earthquake that damaged the home of Mr. Morton and created Reel Foot Lake.

Roy Forrest Robinson and his team of mules in 1904

Ben T. Robinson in his drug store in Mortons Gap

The Nebo Post Office in 1974

Today it is a quiet, industrious town with comfortable homes and peaceful citizens enjoying the heritage carved out of the wilderness for them and proud of the monument of the World War II battle of Iwo Jima. It was erected in 1984 through the efforts of Benny Rash and Charles "Louie" Owens. In 1985, they erected a statue out of coal to the memory of those who died in mine accidents.

Mortons Gap has sent its sons and daughters out into the world and many have covered themselves with honors, reflecting upon the virtues instilled in them by their parents, their excellent school leadership and the people of this proud community.

NEBO

Nebo, located on US 41A about eleven miles west of Madisonville, received its name, we are told, from Alfred Townes a prominent man of affairs, the inventor of the tobacco screw press, and an old time promoter. His picture is on the wall of the Historical Society and Museum in Madisonville.

A history of the State by Battle-Perrin (2nd edition) 1885, page 60, says, "The Nebo District ranks third in the tobacco stemming districts of the United States." It probably increased its tobacco output when the railroad from Madisonville to Providence, which passed through Nebo in 1882, gave them wider distribution.

Actually, Nebo was started as a settlement by Alfred Townes and his family who settled there in 1800. Townes bought 1,000 acres of land for $3.00 per acre and built his home on some of it. He also built the first store near the crossroads of what is now the center of town.

In 1871, the town was incorporated with the state legislature appointing the town officers. Coincidental as it may seem, the year Nebo was officially incorporated, 1871, marked the year of the founder's death. He is buried in Odd Fellows Cemetery in Madisonville.

On Nov. 18, 1840, Alfred Townes was appointed postmaster of Nebo. He probably had the post office in his store.

The town had many business houses as well as saloons. They also, like other smaller communities, had a severe fire in the business district which destroyed a large part of it.

A poultry business was started and it became a booming business for quite a while. However, a fire Aug. 20, 1932 destroyed all businesses on the south side of Main Street. Only the bank, badly damaged, was left. The bank building was repaired and banking continued until 1936 when the bank closed.

The first telephone service for Nebo was established by the Home Telephone Company promoted by J.T. Alexander, Sr. The Southern Bell Telephone Company bought the old system in 1906 and installed the dial system in 1938.

Rural mail delivery was started in 1904 with route #1 and route #2 was started in 1912. The two routes have now been consolidated into one.

Agriculture is now the industry of Nebo. No longer is tobacco the leading crop. Corn and soy beans rank first with wheat and tobacco.

Miss Sarah Barron lives in perhaps one of the oldest homes in Nebo, it being about 127 years old. It was built in 1860 by Ruben Rogers of Logan County, who moved to Hopkins County in 1857. He married Martha Porter and built the house in Nebo. He was in the tobacco business. Soon after the Civil War, Rogers gave up the hotel business and moved to Kansas.

The Sarah Barron home in Nebo in 1988

H.R. Cox, grandfather to Miss Barron, bought the house in 1883 and it has been the family home ever since. Mr. Cox and his wife, the former Jane Chandler of Webster County, had ten children raising five of them to maturity. One of these was Mattie Barron, Miss Sarah's mother, who was born and died in the house in Nebo. Today, Miss Barron lives in the nice old home.

Nebo has made lots of progress over the years in spite of the fires and today, while it is a small community, it has a fire department, nice school, excellent churches and is a warm friendly community.

NORTONVILLE

Nortonville is about 14 miles south of Madisonville, located at the junction of US 62 and US 41, a mile from the Pennyrile Highway.

Nortonville was incorporated as the town of Norton during the 1872 General Assembly, being named after Mr. W.E. Norton, a wealthy gentleman who settled there in 1866.

In 1870, Mr. Norton, seeing the growth possibilities of the community with the location of the then St. Louis and Southeastern Railroad construction, now the Seaboard Coast Line, running north and south, and the Elizabethtown and Paducah Railroad, running east to west, purchased 2,000 acres of land around the junction of what is now the P & L and Seaboard railroad. Later, Mr. Norton sold several lots but kept the remaining land.

Norton was later called "Norton Village" and the name was officially changed to Nortonville in the early 1900's.

Growth of the town was slow, however, in its early history. Soon after the turn of the century it consisted of a post office, one general store, a tobacco warehouse for storing tobacco awaiting shipment, a railroad station and freight depot, one church and a few houses. Most of the original buildings have been razed. The first church building was later moved to Barnsley, where it is still standing.

About 1902, W.S. Elgin, a tobacconist from Hopkinsville, W.B. Kennedy and Frank Fisher of Paducah and others purchased the 2,000 acres from the Norton heirs and opened a shaft coal mine naming it the Nortonville Coal Company.

With the opening of the coal mine, the town began to expand and soon a 20 to 25 room hotel was built opposite the railroad station. For several years, the offices of the Nortonville Coal Company were housed in this building until it was destroyed by fire about 1925 while being operated by O. N. Beshear and family. At one time, Nortonville boasted of 53 business houses and two doctors, but after reaching its peak the shops and stores declined. However, Nortonville's facilities continued later to improve and to multiply.

It got its first water system in 1936, which was a big asset to the community as well water was all that was obtainable prior to this.

Inside one of the stores in Nortonville in 1930's

The Nortonville Post Office in the 1930's. Man in middle is Postmaster Jasper Oates

The streets were blacktopped in 1956, thus eliminating the dirt, cinder and coal gob streets.

In 1960, natural gas was piped into the town and the chimneys for heating with coal gradually disappeared making the air cleaner and healthier.

About this time, they purchased a pumper fire truck. All they had before this was a hose that hooked to the fire hydrants. Later, they bought another fire truck and in 1977 they built a new city hall and completed an $80,000 recreational facility. They also began a $3.5 million sewage system. The lack of a sewage system had kept the city from attracting some industries.

Nortonville is a nice community. The people are friendly and as Eugene "Poss" Rogers, past two-time mayor says, " Our people are our greatest asset".

It now has a nice grade school with a high school at its north limits, a short distance north of the town.

The power plant built in 1925 by the Laniers, coal operators, was purchased by the Kentucky Utilities Coal Company and it continued to operate the plant until 1950 when it was dismantled.

Nortonville is on the site of a prehistoric Indian village from which many artifacts have been recovered. While widely scattered, some good specimens are preserved in the Museum of the University of Kentucky.

The buffalo trace from Nashville, TN on northward to Russellville, KY also passed through Nortonville and many Indian artifacts have been discovered there as it is believed they had a summer camp there.

It is on US 41, US 62 is at its north edge and the Pennyrile Parkway is but a short distance east of it, making it easily accessable. It is served by the Seaboard System and the Paducah and Louisville railroads.

Richland

Located on the banks of Richland Creek, about six miles west of Madisonville, Richland was well named.

This area of our county had much to offer, the first settlers saw an abundance of wildlife in the hills and large stands of virgin timber. The bottom lands of Richland and Clear Creeks would be good for growing crops and the gently rolling upland areas could be cleared, making pasture for cattle and horses. Added blessings of this rich land were underground mineral springs, as well as coal and oil deposits.

Richland became a boomtown in the late 1800's, farms were established, coal was mined, and as the age of the machine dawned, the oil deposits were tapped and pumps dotted the countryside.

A church was built (see Richland Missionary Baptist Church), and a school (see Richland School), as well as several stores. A doctor started a practice here, the Illinois Central Railroad laid an east-west track through Richland, and the government recognized Richland, as the town gained a Post Office in 1893.

Mr. Wm. Cox, who operated a store on what is now Hwy. 70, was Postmaster. This store was torn down about 1925. Frank and Bethel Nourse bought the property and built their own store, which they operated for about fifty years. Another store in Richland was owned by Mr. Hopgood which he sold to E.L. and Martha Trent (see Barton family), still another store on Hwy. 70, facing the Earlington Road, was owned by the Ratliff family.

The railroad depot was just a covered shelter which stood off of the Earlington Rd., across the track from the schoolhouse.

The railroad tracks, then as now, were maintained by a section crew, Frank Teague was the foreman here for many years.

The doctor was Dr. Wm. (Bill) Setzer, a kind, well thought of man, who visited patients and delivered babies as far away as Ilsley.

One morning in the mid 1930's, Dr. Setzer had finished breakfast at the Averitts, as was his custom, and was walking home about

Rad Bowles and his two sons Marvin and Tommy near Richland

7 a.m. He lived on the Earlington Rd. and therefore had to cross the railroad tracks near the depot. He had crossed the tracks many times, but this particular morning, he didn't see or hear the train, no one knows why, and was struck and killed.

Although Richland had a generous supply of mineral water, it never became a resort as did Dawson Springs and Kirkwood Springs, though many folks did come here for the water, as it's healing properties were well known.

Today, Richland is a quiet farming community, without the activity of it's early years. There is no longer a post office, school, depot, or stores, but the Pittsburg and Midway Mining Company's Colonial Strip Mine is digging coal that the older mines could not. Oil pumps still dot the landscape and mineral water can be drawn from the wells.

Richland is a close, family-type community, if a need arises, the people band together to achieve a common goal. In 1986, the need arose for a fire department. There is now a dedicated group of volunteer fireman and E.M.T.'s, and the new fully-equipped fire station stands ready.- *Compiled by Sharon Riggs Johnston*

ST. CHARLES

It is difficult for us, in this modern age, to realize how Hopkins County appeared in the early 1800's. However, our county heritage is full of small communities that grew, with the passing of time, to larger communities and had considerable influence on the development of our growth. Many of them faded away into oblivion, but St. Charles did not.

The second geological map of Hopkins County graphically shows how sparsely settled the county was and the few roads, or trails which connected one part of the county with another and then extended on to other counties. The roads were made mostly by the buffalo whose immense size made the buffalo trails into good roads, with some improvement by the early explorers and travelers.

Going through where Dawson Springs is now located was a trail or road which ran in a north easterly direction across the county and on into Muhlenberg County. The area, where Woodruff, (now St. Charles), became known as the Greenville Road. Travelers and cattle drivers used this road quite extensively.

West of what is now St. Charles was Cane Run Creek and evidently it was of some depth. There was no bridge over the creek but there was a fording place near Woodruff, so it was used by all travelers.

There was a store at this crossing. The name of its operator is not known, but as William Smith had a home near it, it is believed he operated the store but this is not certain.

Just south of Smith's home was the farm of C.B. Woodruff and northwest of his home was the Christian Privilege Meeting House.

It is believed this church was built prior to 1833 and until it burned in March 1980 was the oldest church in the county.

Because of the creek ford, the store and the travel through this area, there grew up a small settlement. Just when it became a settlement of size is not known, but when the railroad was built through there many of the railroad workers settled in the area and in time the village became known as Woodruff, named no doubt because of C.B. Woodruff and the land he owned. The railroad came through about 1869.

Evidently in the early years, around Civil War times, there was a small coal mine in the area for there is mention made of hauling many loads of coal to Hopkinsville from the David Coal Bank (location unknown). It took three days to make the trip and they had certain spots which they tried to reach each day so they could camp at them.

There have been a large number of well known and influential Woodruff's in the area. J.I.D. Woodruff asks a simple question in his booklet letter, "What do you suppose Nathaniel Woodruff, born in Scotland in 1743, would think of his ancestor's today."

The railroad from Elizabethtown to Paducah was eventually completed. However, it went bankrupt and changed hands a number of times. After being the Elizabethtown-Paducah Railroad, it became the Chesapeake, Ohio and Southwestern and later the Newport News and Mississippi Valley. In 1897, it was purchased by the Illinois Central which in 1983 became Illinois Central Gulf. In 1987 it is the Paducah-Louisville Railroad and still serving the same area.

It was in 1872 that the St. Bernard Mining Company purchased the land from J.I.D. Woodruff and laid off their town lots in orderly fashion, as compared to the older settlement.

The Fox Run Mine of the St. Bernard Coal Co. in 1906

Also, the coal company surveyed a railroad spur up by the old Buck Run mine. This was the beginning of the railroad which went up the middle of what is now called St. Charles Street. For a long time it was called Railroad Street and in 1987 it is KY 484.

With the construction of the railroad and the building of the mine just north of town, the community grew but it was still called Woodruff. With the increase of population, a post office was opened Jan. 15, 1873 and is still a post office.

At first, St. Bernard shipped its coal to Henderson to load on barges. But due to damage by flooding, they decided to ship their coal to the Tennessee River.

It is difficult to exactly pinpoint the reason the name of the town was changed from Woodruff to St. Charles, but there are several stories about the reason for the change.

The St. Bernard busy with its mining, was also busy setting up schools for both black and whites, as well as churches. They gave

Greenville Street in St. Charles in 1912

them money to operate schools on a nine month basis. It was in front of the white school that the only source of drinking water was available for a long time.

The town in 1987 is one square mile in limit.

Prior to World War II there was little demand for slack coal. This slack coal was piled at the northwest part of the town and remained there until in 1985 it was finally all moved away and the area made into a trailer park.

With the passing of time the demand for coal ceased to be in great use and the town suffered from this. Many people moved to other areas to make a living. But until the St. Charles mine and the Fox Run mines shut down, St. Charles was a busy place.

Today, St. Charles is a small town without too much activity in it. It contains a county grade school, post office, two grocery stores, several churches and many very fine people.

The first post office was called Woodruff, with William H. Teague being the first postmaster. The name was changed to St. Charles on Mar. 19, 1874

TWEEDLEVILLE-BEARD

When the government decided that people should not have to go so many miles for their mail, they established post offices in many places.

Alford Stevens ran a store and post office on this road, near the Tradewater River, and the government appointed him as postmaster of the post office they established in his store.

Mr. Stevens was nicknamed "Tweedle" and from this nickname they chose "Tweedleville" as the name of the post office. The post office was established May 13, 1903 with Alford Stevens as postmaster. On Oct. 10, 1910, the name of the post office was changed to Beard, with Joseph H. Beard as postmaster. He evidently bought out Stevens. The post office was discontinued May 31, 1911 and the mail delivered to Dalton.

All that remains today is a nice home built where Stevens had his store and the post office was established, the old time well from which he got his water and the old coal house that he used for his coal.

VEAZEY

This community was six miles north of Manitou on the Henderson Road now KY 630, and came into existence long before the Civil War when four Veazey brothers, John Louis, John Comer, Andrew Jackson and Mark M. and their two sisters, Martha and Mary, came to Kentucky from Granville County, NC and settled in northwest Hopkins County.

It became a farming community with several stores in it and in 1888 a post office was established in the store of Louis N. Veazey and he was appointed the first postmaster. He would go by horse back to Manitou and pick up the mail two or three times a week. The post office was discontinued Jan. 15, 1909 when rural routes began operating out of Manitou.

A quarter of a mile east of where the village of Veazey once stood is the Veazey Cemetery where the four brothers are buried. Martha is buried in Odd Fellows Cemetery at Madisonville, while Mary is buried in the Mangum Cemetery a mile east of the Veazey Cemetery.

Veazey lies in what is called part of the "Shakerag" area of Hopkins County, which includes a large part of the northwestern part of the county. However, it has no definite beginning or ending place that can be said with certainity is where "Shakerag" begins or ends.

The name Shakerag goes back to the Revolutionary War, according to Leroy Veazey, a genuine Shakerag citizen. The soldiers training to fight in the war in North Carolina had almost no clothing and many of them were in tatters. Stoker Bill watched his ragged soldiers as they drilled in marching formation with their tattered clothing flapping in the breeze. He is reported to have shaken his head and said, "My poor shakerag boys". The name stuck.

After the war, when they migrated to Kentucky, fond memories of their Shakerag Community in North Carolina caused them to use the same name for their new community in Hopkins County.

Because of the concentration of Veazey's in western Shakerag, the community went by that name. In Veazey were grist mills, stores, a sawmill, a stage route and the Veazey Cemetery first used in 1850.

An old Buffalo Trace in the Veazey area near the home of James Gomer Veazey

With the passing of time, Veazey inhabitants moved away and today there is nothing to mark the spot where this once thriving village stood except the ruins of cellars, cisterns, farm ponds and age old maple trees can still be found on numerous hill tops to make home sites long ago.

WHITE PLAINS

The earliest knowledge of White Plains is of a small nearly treeless plain whose natural prairie like tendency was enhanced by the Indians who burned the area over every year to increase the growth of grass for their buffalo. The earliest eye witness account says, "it was a level, barren plain of several thousand acres that grew nothing but grass. Not even a bush grew upon it."

It has been told that the lower part of the present site of White

Plains was covered with a heavy growth of hazelnut bushes and people came from miles around to harvest the nuts.

There was a buffalo trace which went from east to west and through the middle of what is now White Plains.

It is believed that the first mail to come to this section was brought at intervals by horseback courier riding a route from Greenville. It may have been from Madisonville since the White Plains section was "curtailed" off from Muhlenberg County when Hopkins County was formed.

This small town in the southeast part of Hopkins County on US 62 had four names before it finally got a permanent one: Pond River Mills, Little Prairie, White Plains Station and New White Plains. Its name was changed from Little Prairie to White Plains by the United States Postal Department on Oct. 16, 1874 according to Kermit Lovelace, White Plains historian.

In 1868, Elizabethtown-Paducah railroad began building a railroad between these two towns, which formed its name. We do not have an exact date when it went through White Plains, but it was evidently around 1869. A camp was built in White Plains for the 150 railroad workers. The railroad is still being used but in 1873, the railroad company went bankrupt and has had several different owners since its original laying.

By 1898, the town began to grow and created quite a lumber business. Many rafts of logs and flatboats loaded with white oak barrel staves went down Pond River to points from Evansville, IN to New Orleans.

In 1906 there occurred an event, while not causing a lot of attention at the time, that was to have a tremendous effect on White Plains for many years. This was the establishing of the White Plains Canning Company with Dr. W. N. Bailey, Dr. W.B. Bailey, B.F. Dukes, George W. Putman and W.W. Duncan among the stockholders.

In 1911, the Canning Company stock was sold to W.W. Putman and H.M. Carty and in 1912, Carty became the sole owner. Under his ownership the name was changed to the Carty Canning Company and was known far and wide. He operated the plant until 1944 when it was closed down and only a well marks the spot where it formerly stood.

The town hall was used as a school from 1900-1909. From 1910-1935, school was held in a wooden building. This building burned in 1946. The site of the present school is where this burned structure stood.

On November 26, 1892, the town suffered a disastrous fire which in all destroyed the railroad station and eight other buildings. The town had barely recovered from this shock when, on Mar. 4, 1893, there was another fire which destroyed more buildings.

As the town grew, so did the erection of houses of worship. On August 28, 1903, the Farmers Bank was incorporated and erected a building for it. The bank was in business until May 9, 1925, when it was closed.

Many prominent people in local and state affairs have come from White Plains.

There have been several saw mills in the area with two there today. During the 1930's Morgan Coal Company operated a strip mine at the east edge of the town.

The White Plains business section along the I.C. Railroad in 1950

Today, White Plains is a small but friendly community. For some time the city government was dormant, but in 1976 the people of the town revived its official governing body and they are doing all they can to upgrade the town with buildings and equipment to maintain the streets.

Employees of the Carty Canning Company in White Plains around 1920

Family History

Effie Mae, George W. and John Henry Nichols. Back: Ola Logan-Graham, Pete Nichols and Verda Logan in the Anton Bottoms in the 1930's

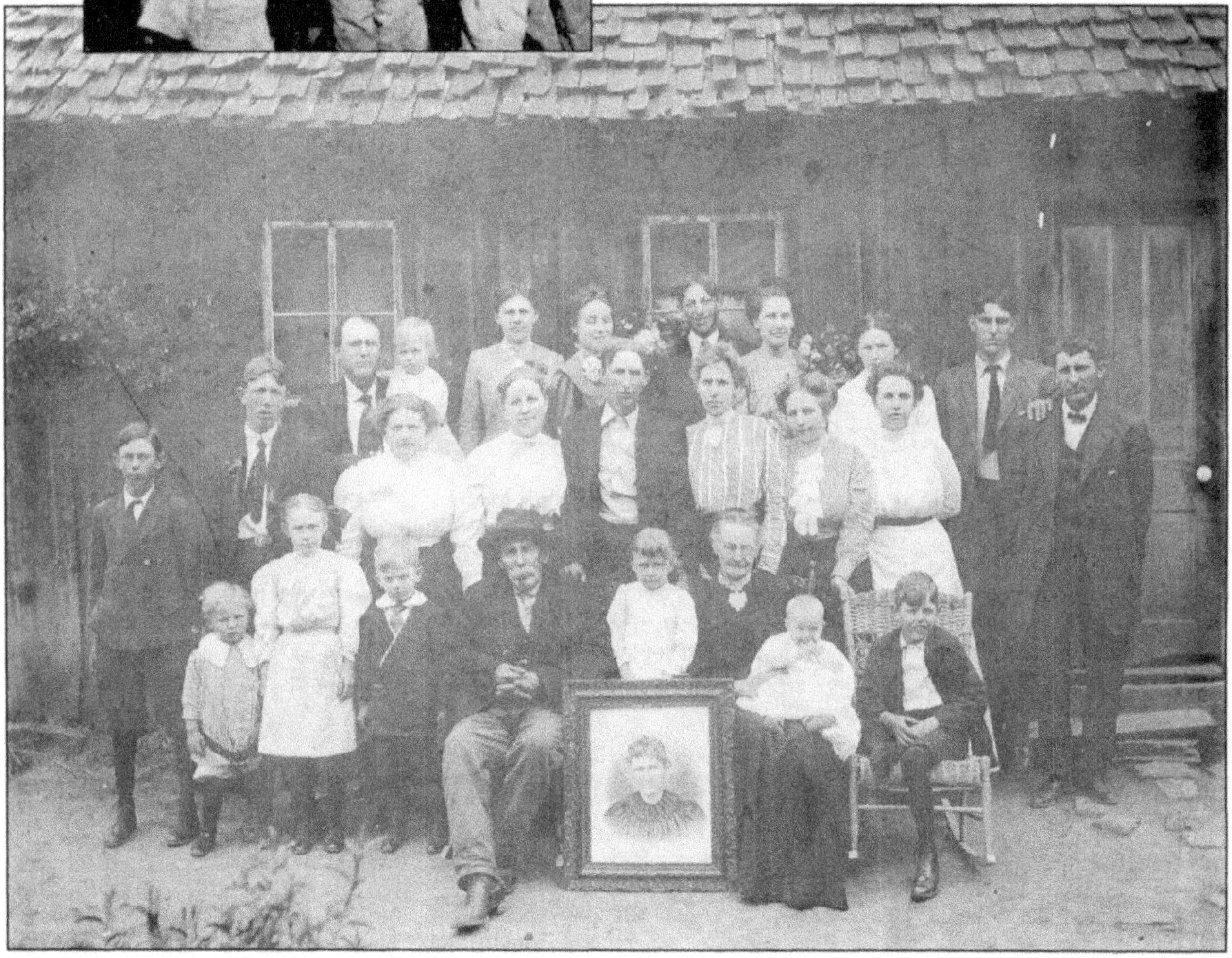

James Robinson (Robertson) Family. Front Row L. to R.: Oscar Summers, Carl Smith, Goldie Summers Lyons, Lucien Baker, James (Jim) Robinson, Marie Summers, Sarah Virginia Robinson holding Gladys Summers Clayton, and Tom Summers. Lady in portrait, Alice Robinson Summers. 2nd row, l-r: James Summers, Lizzie Summers, Agnes Robinson Robinson, William Columbus (Lum) Robinson, Lou Robinson Summers, Cora Robinson Smith, Eugenia Robinson Griffin and Lige Robinson. Top row, l;-r: Neal Summers holding Luther, Berthie Robinson, Minnie Lee Ratliff Robinson, Garland Robinson, Clara Robinson Hawkins, Myrtle Robinson Smith, and Ed Z. Smith

ADAMS

John Adams married Mollie Walker on Apr. 20, 1866, in Hopkins County. They had a son, Rufus, who married Martha Buchanan on Jan. 26, 1876. Their children were: Will, Alice Virginia, Lon, Lula Cammie and Dollie.

Will, born 1878 and died 1959, married Eunice Brown. Eunice was born in 1881 and died in 1963. Both are buried at Olive Branch Cemetery. Eunice's father, Sonny Brown, was opposed to the marriage so they ran away to marry. Moses Harris held the gate open for them to go through. Sonny Brown was very upset and mad at Moses for helping Will and Eunice. Their children were: Homer (married Alma Clayton), John R. (married Beatrice Norwood), Pauline (died at an early age), Robert (married Anna Lou Dement) and Charlie (married Ollie Sandifer).

Alice Virginia was born Nov. 3, 1876, and died Mar. 3, 1954. She married Moses Harris on Oct. 22, 1899. Moses was born Nov. 17, 1872, and died Mar. 1, 1954. Both are buried at Olive Branch Cemetery. (see Harris family)

Lon was born Mar. 25, 1883. He married Minnie Spencer on May 24, 1905. Their children: Arthur (married Ruth Craig), Verna Marie (married first Cosby Arnold, second Rev. John Robinson), Herman (married Alene Neal) and Marvine (married James Monts).

Lula Cammie (named for Cammie Jane Browder who boarded with the Adams family) was born Dec. 10, 1880. She married Ervie L. Adcock who was born Oct. 9, 1879, and died Mar. 24, 1957. They also ran off to get married. They were married in a buggy when the preacher came down the road from the church. Lula's mother was very upset at the marriage and told them that they would have a hard time. That they did, but they lived together for fifty years.

Dollie was born July 5, 1885, and died July 23, 1945. She married Andrew James who was born Jan. 31, 1883, and died Dec. 15, 1959. Both are buried at Olive Branch Cemetery. Their daughter, Hollie Ray, married Robert Ashby Thursby. A grandson, Richard Allen Thursby, died in Vietnam. -*Submitted by Mary Edna Harris*

JOHN RUFUS ADAMS

John Rufus Adams was born Mar. 25, 1905 in Hopkins Co. He was the second child of Willie Henly and Eunice Bell Brown Adams.

He married Johnnie Beatrice Norwood in Springfield, TN, in November 1929. She was the daughter of John Thomas (1885-1961) and Ruby Coffman Norwood (1891-1976).

John was a graduate of Western State Teachers College and was the Assistant Superintendent of the Hopkins Co. School system for 17 years. He retired in 1967 after being an elementary teacher as well as principal of the Hanson and Dalton schools. He was a member, deacon and training unit leader of the Madisonville First Baptist Church. He had served in the Hopkins Co. School system for 42 years. After retirement, John pursued his hobby of farming.

Beatrice was born Apr. 12, 1908, in Hopkins Co. Beatrice attended Bethel College, Murray State University and was a graduate of Western State Teachers College. A school teacher,

John Rufus and Johnnie Beatrice (Norwood) Adams

John was a graduate of Western State Teach- she retired after 29 years of service with the Hopkins Co. School system. She taught at the Dalton, Hanson and Madisonville schools.

John died June 13, 1980, and Beatrice died July 8, 1984. Both are buried in Oddfellows Cemetery.

John and Beatrice were the parents of Martha (1932-1933), Reba Helen, Joe Brown and Mary Doris.

Reba Helen was born Sept. 12, 1934, in Hopkins Co. In December 1960, she married Clarence Dunville, Jr. (born June 11, 1933), the son of Clarence and Nancy Ellen Leech Dunville. Their children: Donna Jane and Dennis Wayne born Sept. 3, 1965, and Susan Lee born Nov. 28, 1967, died Apr. 29, 1982.

Joe Brown, born in Hopkins Co. Jan. 24, 1937, married Diann Weldon the daughter of Freeman and Hilda Long Weldon, on June 26, 1958. They are the parents of: Janet Lynn born July 16, 1959; John Thomas born Oct. 27, 1960; and Douglas Weldon born July 26, 1962. The children were born in Hopkins Co. Janet Lynn married Donald Anderson (born May 15, 1956), the son of Grover and Lorena Greer Anderson, in August 1980 in Nashville, TN. They have two children, Nathan Adams born Feb. 19, 1984 and Lauren Elizabeth born Feb. 9, 1987.

John Thomas married Sherry Mayfield in Owensboro, KY, in October 1983. She was born May 15, 1961, the daughter of Larry Mayfield and Pat Pitchford Aldridge.

Mary Doris was born May 12, 1939 in Hopkins Co. Doris married Frank Daniel on Jan. 25, 1959, in Hopkins Co. Frank was born Apr. 28, 1939, the son of Robert Alvis and Susie Tippett Daniel. Doris and Frank are the parents of Kelly Ann born May 28, 1963, and David Robin born Jan. 15, 1965. Both children were born in Evansville, IN. Kelly married Brian Hood in Monroe, LA, on Dec. 18, 1985. He is the son of John and Faye Vercher Hood. -*Submitted by Linda Hayes*

STELLA ADAMS

Stella Adams was born in Hopkins County on May 17, 1912. Her mother was Lucy Smily Ladd and her father was William Ladd. Stella had ten brothers and three sisters. Her father and most of her brothers worked in the coal mines, but one of the boys was an auto mechanic. The girls helped to take care of the house. Most of Stella's brothers and sisters are deceased.

Stella married Alba Adams on Feb. 2, 1933. Stella and Alba had eight children and 27 grandchildren. Jean was born Aug. 25, 1933, married J.D. Gray, and they have six children; Earl was born June 26, 1936, and he married Maxine Summers. They have three children; James, born Feb. 15, 1938, who married June Suttles. They have five children; Lucille, born on Dec. 28, 1940, married Richard Kimberland. They have three children; Betty, born Jan. 21, 1942, married Donald Martin, and they have three children; Jimmy was born Sept. 10, 1945, and married Nadean Wallace. They have two children; Joe was born Aug. 28, 1948 and was killed in a car wreck; Larry was born Sept. 10, 1951 and married Mary Trotter. They have five children.

Stella used to work for some of the hotels in Dawson Springs, cleaning the rooms and doing the laundry for the hotels. Stella did not get to spend much time in school, but when she was there she tried to keep her grades up high. The times when Stella did not go to school, she spent at home helping to take care of the other kids or working in the fields. Stella had to help do the work in the fields until the others were big enough to help to do the field work.-*Submitted by Mike Adams, grandson*

THOMAS ADAMS

Thomas Adams, the third of eleven children, was born in 1772 in VA. His parents were Samuel and Anne Adams, daughter of William and Mary Walker Adams, Sr.

Thomas and Elizabeth Ann Ashby were married in Bedford Co., VA, in January 1799. They came to this area from Mercer Co. at the turn of the century and settled on 200 acres of land near where Deer Creek flows into the Green River below Onton, KY. This land is now in Webster Co.

Thomas was sworn in as a Justice of the Peace in Hopkins Co. on May 25, 1807 and he was the Hopkins Co. sheriff in 1815. He died about 1829 and his place of burial is unknown.

Elizabeth Ann was born in North Carolina in 1782 and died in Hopkins Co. in 1842.

The children of Thomas and Elizabeth Ann are: James (1806-1840); Samuel (1807-1893); Ann (1809-); William A. (1811-1854); John C. (Aug. 17, 1813-Mar. 21, 1875); Martha A. (1814-1896); Nancy E. (1816-1908); Thomas J. (1818-1875); David Joe (1820-); Mary Susan (1822-).

John C. married America Miller in Hopkins Co. on Dec. 17, 1835. They had: Mary A. born 1838; James V. born 1840; John T. born 1842; and Queentina born 1845. John C. then married Virginia Orten (Dec. 12, 1820-Nov. 14, 1860). Their children were: Rufus R. (Oct. 4, 1848-Jan. 25, 1891); Emily born 1850; and Lorenza born 1852. Virginia was the daughter of Thomas and Mary Polly Ashby Orten. On Apr. 20, 1866, John C. married Mary A. (Mollie) Walker. They had two children, Everett born in 1868 and Laura (Nov. 3, 1869-Aug 30, 1911).

Rufus Radford Adams married Martha Ann Buchanan on Jan. 26, 1876, in Hopkins Co. She was the daughter of Andrew Crawford and

Annie Elizabeth Friday. Martha Ann was born Aug. 2, 1853. Rufus died Jan. 25, 1871, and Martha Ann died Sept. 17, 1906. Both are buried in the Mt. Zion Cemetery near Hanson. Rufus and Martha were the parents of: Alice F. born in 1877; Willie H. born in 1878; Lula C. born Dec. 10, 1880; Lonnie Dow born in 1883; and Dollie C. (July 5, 1885-July 23, 1945).

Willie Henly Adams married Eunice Bell Brown, daughter of John William and Mary Emmaline Bidwell Brown, on Dec. 27, 1902, in Hopkins Co. Willie was a farmer and Eunice was a school teacher. Willie was born Aug. 22, 1878 and died Mar. 1, 1959. Eunice was born Nov. 21, 1881, and died Mar. 7, 1963. They are buried at the Olive Branch Cemetery. They were the parents of nine children:

Homer Luther (Dec. 1, 1903-Apr. 10, 1984) married Alma Clayton on Dec. 20, 1924. Children: Edmund, Jimmy and Dell. Homer is buried at Oddfellows Cemetery.

John Rufus (see his story) born Mar. 26, 1905, married Johnnie Beatrice Norwood.

Ossie W. (Oct. 26, 1907-Nov. 11, 1908).

Chesley Mae (Feb. 21, 1909-Jan 22, 1911).

Mary Pauline (April 1911-Feb. 1937), a school teacher, died of pneumonia after wading a creek to get to the school house.

Paul Brown (Aug. 1917-Apr. 1921) died of diphtheria.

Sarah Elizabeth (June 13, 1920-Nov. 13, 1920)

Robert Eugene born May 21, 1913, married Anna Lou Dement on Dec. 21, 1939. Their children: Julie Ann born May 27, 1944, and Larry (Apr. 6, 1941-Apr. 18, 1961). Larry is buried at Sunnyside Cem. at Beaver Dam, KY.

Charles Henly, born Mar. 7, 1915, married Mary Olive Sandefur in Webster Co. in 1938. Their children: Linda born May 17, 1939; Charlotte born Apr. 3, 1947; Scottie born Feb. 9, 1967; Kandi born Aug. 5, 1968; Melissa born Aug. 23, 1969; and Teresa Renae born May 24, 1972. Mary Olive died May 3, 1987, and is buried at Oddfellows Cemetery. -*Submitted by Robert E. Adams*

ADCOCK-MINTON

Mandrell Lee Adcock was born on Apr. 5, 1941 in a small town in Hopkins County called Ilsley. He was the first of two children born to James Owen and Ruby Pearline Adcock. The second child they had was a son also, David Adcock, born in Hopkins County on Jan. 15, 1943. David is still living in Hopkins County.

James Owen Adcock was born in Hopkins County on Dec. 1, 1919. He was tragically killed in a car accident on Oct. 31, 1956. Ruby Pearline Adcock was born in Rockwood, AL on Mar. 22, 1922. She died in the hospital on Apr. 31, 1985.

Mandrell Lee graduated from South Hopkins High School in 1959. He was class president at South Hopkins during his junior and senior year. At the senior prom, he was voted Prom King. After graduation, he joined the Air Force and served for eight years. He was stationed in Germany for five years and also served in Vietnam. After returning from overseas, he went to college for one year at Louisiana Tech in Louisiana.

Mandrell Lee married Betty Jane Minton on Apr. 20, 1969. She was born in Hopkins county on Oct. 16, 1948. Their first child, a son, was born in Caldwell County War Memorial Hospital on Sept. 22, 1970. He was named Edward Jerome Adcock.

About two and a half years after Edward's birth, the family moved to Elkville, IL. They lived there for about six months. Edward had his second birthday there. Just after his second birthday, they moved back to Dawson Springs, KY.

About three years passed and Lee and Betty had their second child, a daughter, Latasha Lee Adcock born on Feb. 18, 1975.

Edward is now seventeen years of age and Latasha is twelve years of age. All four of them still live in Dawson Springs.- *Submitted by Edward Adcock*

ALCOTT-McGREGOR

Stephen Louis Alcott and Paula Sue McGregor were married May 27, 1972 at First Church of God, Madisonville, KY.

The Alcotts - Steve, Paula and children l to r: Autumn Lynn, Katherine Ann and Mary Paige

Steve is the youngest son of Frederick O. Alcott and Chester Marie Paige Alcott. Fred Alcott is retired from the U.S.D.A.—Soil Conservation Service and Marie Alcott is a retired Todd County teacher. They presently live on their farm at Route 1, Allensville, KY, and still manage the farm.

Steve graduated from Murray State, receiving a B.S. Degree in Agriculture in 1971, after completing high school in Todd Co. Since graduation, he has been employed by the U.S.D.A.—Soil Conservation Service.

Paula Sue, born Jan. 28, 1950, in Hopkins County, is the only daughter of Paul Clark McGregor and Mary Iretta Teague McGregor. (See McGregor-Teague). After finishing Nortonville Elementary School and South Hopkins High School, she graduate Cum Laude from Murray State, receiving a B.S. Degree in Library Science in 1972. She was a member of Kappa Delta Pi, Honorary Educational Fraternity, and president of Alpha Beta Alpha, undergraduate Library Science Fraternity, while there. She received her Masters degree in Secondary Education from Morehead State, Morehead, KY, in 1977.

Paula and Steve met while in school at Murray State. After their marriage in 1972, they lived in Louisville two years. Then they moved to Mt. Sterling, KY, where their first daughter, Mary Paige Alcott, was born Apr. 21, 1975.

Since Sept. 1978, Steve, Paula, and Paige have lived at 805 Guthrie Drive, Murray, KY. Two more daughters were born into the family after the move to Murray: Autumn Lynn Alcott born Aug. 30, 1980, and Katherine Ann Alcott, born July 31, 1982.

Steve is presently District Conservationist, assisting the Calloway County Conservation District in carrying out a Soil and Water Conservation program for Calloway County. Paula is employed by the Murray Independent School System as a librarian for the Murray Middle School (grades 5-8). She has been teaching there since the fall of 1985.

Paige attends Murray Middle School, plays the clarinet in the band and is taking piano lessons. Autumn attends Robertson Elementary School and is active in G.A.'s and Brownies. Katie attends pre-school at Murray Preschool Corporation, Murray State University.

They are active members of the First Baptist Church in Murray, KY. -*Submitted by Iretta McGregor.*

ALEXANDER-SISK

Rufus Alexander and Tressa Sisk of rural Hopkins Co. were married in Springfield, TN. Rufus was killed in a Sturgis mine accident in 1925 at 29 years of age. Tressa bought a small farm at Ilsley and raised the family with the help of her mother, Necie (Mammy) Sisk. Mammy was a good student of her time. She influenced our growth and development and helped with all our studies. She was a loving and knowledgeable grandmother. Rufus and Tressa had five children:

From l to r: Ralph, Faynell, Rex, Virginia (Johnny's wife), Alberta, Johnny and Dot (Rufus's wife)

Ralph Alexander (known to many as Alex) born 8-14-1917 and died Dec. 25, 1983, married Dorothy Coke. Their children: Ruth married Bob Clum and Billy married Tammy Michaels. Ralph taught Agriculture at Union Co. High School until retirement, and Dorothy taught vocal music at Union Co. until her retirement. Dorothy and their children and families reside in Sturgis.

Alberta Alexander born 7-26-1919 lives in Murray, KY. She married John C. Korb who taught math and science in secondary schools in Western KY. He died in May, 1965, a veteran of WW II. Alberta taught Home Ec. in secondary level, and retired from Calloway County

High School in 1981 as Guidance Counselor. They had one son, Danny Korb, living in Dawson Springs. He married Brenda Driver and their two sons are Bryan and Alan.

Faynell Alexander born 5-2-1921 lives in Dawson Springs. She held many jobs in her work years, retiring from Drs. Freeman and Chaney's office in Dawson Springs in 1980. She married Carl Harris in 1939, who was killed in the Battle of the Bulge in WW II. They had one daughter, Glenda Faye Harris, who lives in Tallahassee, FL with her husband, Art Trunkfield. They have two daughters, Paige and Courtney. Two sons, Tim and Kit, were killed in 1976 in a car wreck. Faynell later married Ernest Carroll who had one daughter, Wanda Carroll Fork, who lives in St. Charles with her husband, Wm. E. Fork. Their children: Brenda (Mrs. Joe Gamblin) and Billy, in the Air Force, and they have 2 grandchildren. Faynell and Ernest Carroll had one son, Robert Carroll of Dawson Springs. Ernest died Dec. 19, 1970.

Johnny Alexander born 3-9-1924 lives on Route 1, Nortonville, with his wife, Virginia Plank Alexander. They spent most of their working years in Memphis, TN, where Johnny was Administrator of YMCA and Virginia taught Art. Their 3 children are: John married to Diane Ober, one son, Guthrie, living in VA. James lives in Utah with wife, Susan Thompson, and three children, twins Nathan and Stephanie, and Sydney. Mary Ann married Mike Milligan, two children Margot and Nicole, living in Louisville.

Dr. Rex E. Alexander born 6-1-1935 died in a car accident 3-28-82. He was a professor in the Dept. of Recreation and Physical Education at Murray State, and a member of the faculty since 1952. He was a former basketball, baseball and tennis coach for th MSU Racers. He was married to Doris Snyder of Owensboro. They had two children: Cindy, who married John Wilham and lives in Tennessee with children Tyler, Dane, and Tressa; and David who married Sandy Wilson, with children Rexford and Bret, and lives in Nashville. Rex was in Airforce maintenance in WW II.

At this date (8-22-1987) Tressa and Rufus have 3 living children, 10 grandchildren, and 19 living great grandchildren, ranging from 6 months to 20 years. Our thanks and love to our dear parents and Mammy Sisk who we all loved. -Submitted by Faynell Carroll

EBENEZER ALEXANDER

Ebenezer Alexander and his wife Hannah first settled in Logan County in 1796. It is believed that they came from North Carolina with a relative Matthew Alexander, bought land and set up a salt mine. It is not believed that Matthew and Ebenezer were brothers but were otherwise related. Matthew later moved to Tennessee and Ebenezer sold his holdings and moved to Hopkins Co. sometime between 1801 and 1806. A written history was recently found in South Carolina that indicates there were two Ebenezer Alexanders in Logan County at the same time. No proof has ever been found to substantiate this claim. This Alexander family appears to be of the same family of Alexanders that signed the Mecklenburg Declaration of Independence of May 20, 1775. Because of this declaration, Mecklenburg Co., NC, is often called the birthplace of liberty. Six of the twenty-seven signers were Alexanders.

Ebenezer Alexander gave half the land on which Dawson Springs was founded. The other half of the land was given by the Menser family. Years later a grandson of the Alexanders, Patton Alexander, married Christney Menser. Patton died first and was buried on the Alexander side of town. When Christney died she was not buried beside her husband but was taken to the Menser side of town for burial.

Ebenezer and Hannah Alexander had ten children. Seven of these children have been positively identified. They were: John who married Betsy T. Lavis, Joseph who married Cassandia Brown, William P. who married Agnes Sims, Nancy A. who married William McKenny, Polly who married Andrew Bone and Peggy.

Ebenezer lived the remainder of his life in Hopkins Co., dying in 1825. His wife was still alive in 1825 and it is not known when she died.

Of the seven children little is known. Ebenezer Jr. made several moves and died in Coles Co., IL. He was buried under the title Rev. Ebenezer Alexander. Joseph Alexander lived out his life in Hopkins Co. William P. Alexander is written up elsewhere in this book. -Submitted by Margaret Ladd Sinn

JOE CYRUS ALEXANDER

Joe Cyrus (possibly Josiah) Houston Alexander was born July 27, 1871, in Hopkins Co. He was the seventh of nine children of Moses H. Alexander and Priscilla A. Parsons. On Oct. 23, 1890, he married Mary Ellen Laffoon born June 20, 1877. She was the second of six children of Wiley Elbert Laffoon and Malissa Paralee Sisk.

They were married 59 years and had ten children. Their first born was a girl who died at birth. They had two sons, Bennie Lee and Dennis Edwin, who both died at an early age. Their remaining seven children are as follows:

Elmer Josephine Alexander born Oct. 10, 1894. She married James Porter Hudson in 1914. She had four children. They were Lois Euvena born Apr. 29, 1915, and married Carl Stanford; Edna Irene born Apr. 6, 1917, and married Charles Lewis Davis; Victor Eugene born June 1, 1918, and married Gladys Yandell; Retta Mae born Apr. 20, 1922, and married Vernon Smith.

William Rufus Alexander born in November 1896. He married Tressa Sisk on Nov. 30, 1916. He had five children. They were: William Ralph born Aug. 14, 1917, and married Dorthy Coke; Naomi Alberta born July 26, 1919, and married John C. Korb; Anna Faynell born May 2, 1921, and married first Carl Harris then Ernest Carroll; Johnny Carlisle born Mar. 19, 1923, and married Virginia Plank; and Rexford Eugene born June 1, 1924, and married Doris Snyder.

Ressie Jeanon Alexander was born Apr. 28, 1899. She married George Lee Eades on Aug. 21, 1916. She had three children. They were Joseph Monroe born May 1, 1920, and married Geneva McDonald; James Cleatus born July 27, 1922, and married Catherine Keith; and Mary Elizabeth born Nov. 25, 1931, and married Cecil McDonald.

Luther Laymon Alexander was born June 16, 1904, and married first at age 16 to Anna Ruth Lyell. They had one son, Kendall Lyell, born May 20, 1925. In 1931 Luther married Blanche O'Daniel. They had two children, Witzel Douglas was born July 8, 1932, and died in 1936, and LaNell June, born Nov. 4, 1934, is presently married to Owen Stanley Schriener.

Lelia Opal Alexander was born May 3, 1906, and married first Wilson Lafayette Wright in 1931. She had one son Phillip Eugene Wright born Feb. 6, 1937, and is presently married to Joe Anne Kumlin. In the early 1940's Opal married her second husband Myrtle Clark.

Ruby Agnes Alexander was born Oct. 20, 1910, and married Benjamin Wallace Wade on Apr. 4, 1931. She had five children. They were: Howard Keith, born Nov. 20, 1932, and married Alice Carpenter; Wilma Coleen, born July 3, 1934, and married Gene Lovall; Exie Bonez, born Oct. 11, 1936, and married Robert W. McKnight; Benjamin Alexander, born Mar. 31, 1938, and married first Phyllis Dorr and second wife was Lois Willis; and Katie Lou, born Feb. 2, 1940, and married Lazaro Casares, Jr.

Joseph Cecil Alexander was born Sept. 21, 1915, and on Dec. 1, 1945, he married Rubye Eli Hight, who had one daughter Roberta Gene Hight born June 24, 1941. They had two children. They were: Bettie Joe, born Sept. 15, 1946, and married Michael Singleton; and Joseph Cecil (Joe Jr.) born May 2, 1948, and married Janice Foster Bangs.

Joe Cyrus Houston Alexander, better known as Cy, Uncle Cy or Pa Alec, lived most of his life in Hopkins Co. He was a farmer and was respected as an honest church-going member of the community. He lived the last years of his life on a small farm he owned near Ilsley.

He died July 9, 1949, and is buried in Union Temple Cemetery. His wife, Mary Ellen, continued to live on the farm until she became ill just before her death on Mar. 7, 1956. She is buried beside her husband and several of their children in Union Temple Cemetery. -Submitted by Katie W. Casares

WILLIAM P. ALEXANDER

William Patton Alexander was born June 3, 1787, to Ebenezer and Hannah Alexander. On May 13, 1811, he married Agnes Sims who was born in Spartanburgh Co., SC, on Feb. 10, 1793, to John and Anne Sims of Hopkins Co. John Sims was the son of Nathan and Agnes Bullock Sims. The Sims ancestry has been traced back to 1687 when George Symes emigrated to Surry Co., VA, from the West Indies. John and Anne came to Hopkins Co. in 1800 and John died soon after. Anne died in Hopkins Co. on Apr. 11, 1826.

William Patton and Agnes Sims Alexander had three children: Patton, who was born Feb. 18, 1812, and married Christney Menser; Millie Sims Alexander, who was born Aug. 13, 1813, and married Isaac Beshear; and William A. Alexander. Agnes was pregnant with the third child, William A., when William Patton went to New Orleans to fight in the War of 1812. He fought with the rank of Lt. under Capt. Olney McClean's Company of infantry, 14th Regt. Ky detached Militia. His paymaster sheet states that he was born in Muhlenberg Co., NC. William Patton died on Feb. 3, 1815, in New Orleans from wounds he had previously received. His death came within days of the official notification of the end of the war.

Agnes Alexander then married Larkin Beshear on May 9, 1825. It appears she had three more children: Anderson, Daniel and Presley. She divorced Larkin and never remarried. Agnes died sometime after 1870.

William Patton and Agnes Sims Alexander's only daughter, Millie S. Alexander, married Issac Beshear, son of Issac Beshear on Apr. 4, 1832, in Hopkins Co. They had eight children: Mary Ann, born Feb. 15, 1833, married Sampson Davis; Angeline, born Aug. 11, 1835, married James T. Croft; Mildred, born Aug. 13, 1836, married John Henry Nixon; Stacy, born Oct. 14, 1843, married James W. McKnight; Scothia, born Jan. 24, 1847, married Jo Ann McKnight; Isaac, born Aug. 25, 1850, married Lenora Howell; William Patton, born Nov. 1, 1853, died young; and Manual, born Oct. 10, 1858, married Martha McKnight Nichols.

Mildred Beshear married John Henry Nixon son of Frederick and Jemiah Chandler Nixon on Jan. 31, 1857. They were the parents of three children: William Riley, Veronica and John Henry Campbell Nixon. John Nixon fought in the Civil War and was wounded at Fort Donnelson, TN. He was taken on the steamship "Chancellor" to Mound City, IL, where he died in 1862. There are two recorded death dates for him as the losses were heavy in this battle. It is assumed that he is one of the unknown soldiers buried at the National Cemetery in Mound City. Mildred died in 1863 leaving her three children to be raised by their grandparents, Issac and Millie Alexander Beshear. -*Submitted by Margaret Ladd Sinn*

ALLEN

John Allen born 1715, not known where, possibly immigrant. Married Ann Rhodes, Baltimore, MD. Lived there and at Philadelphia. Built fine buildings at the latter which are said to still stand.

Richard Allen, Sr. 1741-1832. Married Nancy Lindsey, lived in North Carolina. Revolutionary War Service at Kings Mountain. Acquired much land. Public officer and church leader. Put out of church for "anger and land speculation."

James Allen - 1771-1838 - Married Hannah Loving. Lived North Carolina.

John Crittenden Allen 1791-1852. Married 2/14/1811 to Margaret "Peggy" Goad. Lived in North Carolina, Alabama and moved to Hopkins County, KY-date unknown.

James A. Allen - born 1821- married 11/1/1842 to Nancy Caroline Cunningham. (She died 1904). Lived in Hopkins Co., KY. No other dates available. I can confirm this by family tradition.

Richard Carroll Allen - 1847-1936- married Amanda Ellen Barnett, formerly of Todd Co., KY 3/19/1884 at her brother's-John A Barnett. Witnesses J.T. Reddick and W.N. Bailey (both doctors) Minister C.M. Pendley; ordained Missionary Baptist preacher and pastor. Twice moderator Little Bethel Association of Baptist Churches.

Ethel M. Allen Lovelace- 1888-1981, married Oscar L. Lovelace.

Kermit A. Lovelace-born 1915-Baptist minister.

Amanda Ellen Barnett's parents died and were buried in Barnett Cemtery near site of Liberty Church (Baptist), now extinct but location still known in Todd Co. KY. The family came to Hopkins Co. in a sort of wagon train arrangement possibly about 1879, led by her brother John. Her mother was a Porter from Virginia. R.C. and Amanda Allen are buried in Concord Cemetery, White Plains, in the old part. The daughter Ethel as well as a brother of hers is buried in the new part by the church. -*Submitted by Kermit A. Lovelace*

ALLEN

The Allen family in Hopkins County dates back to the early 1800's.

Knowledge of the Allen family postdates John Allen, born in 1715, and Ann Rhoades Allen who married in Baltimore County, MD, on Nov. 24, 1740. They lived in Baltimore for a number of years before moving to Philadelphia, PA, where John Allen established himself as a master builder. He also became a member of The Carpenters Club in 1771, but died before participating in any recorded activities of the club. John and Ann Allen are recorded as the parents of nine sons, but only Richard, likely the oldest, born in Baltimore in 1741, has been identified.

Richard Allen, Sr., achieved status as Col. in the Revolutionary War. He participated in the Carolinas and adjacent areas until 1781. He owned many acres of land in Tennessee and Alabama which were divided among his children at the time of his death.

Evidence suggests that James Allen, Richard's son, lived in Kentucky for a time around 1800 before locating in Franklin Co. AL c. 1819.

John Crittendon Allen, first son of James Allen and Hannah Loving, born in Surry Co., NC, May 4, 1791, settled in Hopkins Co., KY. He married Margaret "Peggy" Goad in Christian Co., KY, on Feb. 14, 1811.

John and Peggy Allen's third son Ezias Earle "Zy" born May 16, 1827, in Hopkins Co., was a farmer in White Plains, KY. He married Rachel G. Allen Apr. 16, 1849. Ezias and Rachel's children were Wm. Frank, born May 22, 1851, and James "Crit" Crittendon, born in 1854, in Hopkins County. Ezias and "Crit" were blinded when they washed their faced in a new wash pan.

Wm. Frank married Amanda Jane Josey on Aug. 25, 1873 in Hopkins Co., KY. Their seven children were all born in Hopkins Co.

Of the seven, only one, Charlie, lived his entire life in Hopkins Co. He worked in the coal mines, farmed, and was in business as a grocer at 654 Hall Street in Madisonville from 1921 until his death in 1967. The store continued in operation under the hands of this wife, Norma Hampton Allen and his daughter, Margie Allen for several years afterward. Son Arnon "Red" Allen operated a filling station in Madisonville for many years until his untimely death in an automobile accident in 1964.

This branch of the Allen family in Hopkins Co. ended with the death of Margie Allen on Apr. 1, 1983. The family is buried in Grapevine Cemetery. -*Submitted by Lorraine Walker*

ALLEN-BAKER

Franklin Pierce Baker b. 10-20-1852 d. 10-17-1929, was the son of James Baker, who is buried somewhere between Richland and Beulah in an area which has since been stripped by Colonial Mines, supposedly leaving the grave site intact. Franklin P. married Cornelia Osburne b. 12-20-1855 d. 7-1-1936. They had 8 children: Falcon O. Baker married Myrtle Goliday; Eula Baker married Joe Majors; Charlie Owen Baker married Claude Ford; Ethel Baker married Oliver L. Weir; Modra Baker married Frank Roark; Calborn Baker married Olga Powell of Cadiz; Susie Baker married John Alexander Powell of Sebree; and Robbie Baker married Claude Bailey Allen.

Claude Bailey Allen b. 2-28-1885 d. 2-15-1957, was the oldest child of Richard Carroll Allen, b. 9-27-1847 d. 5-25-1937, and Amanda Ellen Barnett, b. 1-1-1864 d. 2-8-1953. He married Robbie Baker, b. 2-5-1894 d. 11-26-1965.

Charlie, Norma, Arnon and Margie Allen in Allen's Grocery

Robbie (Baker) and Claude B. Allen

Other children of Richard C. and Amanda Allen were: Clarence, d. as small boy; Ethel Allen married Oscar Lovelace (Kermit Lovelace's parents); Kenneth Allen married Tish Allen; Opal Allen married Wood Lacy; C. Hall Allen married Elnora (Buntin) Battalia. He was Advertising and Sports Editor for THE MESSENGER and first introduced Elmer Kelley to sports on THE MESSENGER.

Claude B. and Robbie Allen had one child, Sue Frances Allen who married Crawford Jent. (see JENT-ALLEN)

As a young man, Claude B. Allen worked in the grocery dept. of the St. Bernard Coal Company Store. In about 1904-5, Mr. Ed McLeod gave Claude a job in the men's dept. of the McLeod Store—dubbed "the Marshall Field of Western Kentucky"—a large store with everthing to feed, clothe, and furnish the home for the family. It had a centralized office with pneumatic tubes that ran from the office to each dept. to carry the money back and forth. In a short time, Mr. Allen organized and became manager of the furniture dept. where he remained until the store was closed in 1929.

Claude B. then worked at the Utley Furniture Store until 1931. In August, 1931, he opened his own store, Allen Furniture Company, in the building presently occupied by McGary Furniture Company. Sue F. Allen worked intermittently in the store, and was assistant buyer with her father. On Feb. 7, 1957, Mr. Allen sold his store to McGary Brothers, just 8 days before his death. On June 16, 1952, Claude B. Allen was elected a member of the American Marketing Congress, this date also being Mr. and Mrs. Allen's 37th wedding anniversary.

Robbie Baker Allen attended the Univ. of Chicago and graduated from Western Kentucky College in 1936, attending through summers and with courses by correspondence and extension classes—without ever having lived on the Western campus during a regular semester. She is believed to have been the first married woman in Hopkins County to have taught continuously in the schools. She taught from January 1919 through 1949, thus breaking the tradition of hiring only single women as teachers. She was the second prinicipal of Hall Street School.

Both Claude and Robbie Allen were devoted members of the First Baptist Church. Claude served as deacon in the Baptist Church, and for 25 years served as secretary of the Sunday School there. They are buried at Odd Fellows Cemetery, Madisonville. -*Submitted by Sue Allen Jent*

ALLEN-DOOM

Donnie and Dorinda Allen reside at Route 1, Dawson Springs, KY. They have one son, James Carrol Locke (Jamey), who resides at the same address. Donnie and Dorinda are employed by the Dawson Springs Board of Education. Donnie teaches High School Special Education and Dorinda teaches Elementary Special Education.

Donnie was born in Madisonville, KY on Dec. 16, 1952. He moved to Dawson Springs in 1958. Donnie Attended Dawson Springs schools until he graduated from Dawson High School in 1970. He attended Murray State University and received a degree in Special Education. He is a member of the First Baptist Church of Dawson Springs. Donnie loves being outdoors and spends his spare time hunting, camping and canoeing.

Dorinda was born in Evansville, IN on Oct. 14, 1952. In 1956, Dorinda moved with her family to Marshall County, KY. She graduated from South Marshall High School in 1970. In 1976, Dorinda began attending Murray State University and graduated in the fall of 1979 with a degree in Special Education. She is a member of the First Baptist Church of Dawson Springs. She enjoys traveling, gardening and helping other people.

Donnie is the son of Joe Ray Allen Sr. and Lovolua Allen. Joe was born May 10, 1924 in Camden, TN. Lovolua was born Dec. 20, 1920 in Pulaski, TN. Donnie has an older brother, Joe Ray Allen Jr. who resides in Dawson Springs.

Dorinda is the daughter of James K. Doom and Ernestine Copeland. James was born Feb. 10, 1923 in Graves County, KY. Ernestine was born Mar. 23, 1927 in Marshall County, KY. Dorinda has an older brother, Gary K. Doom who resides in Calvert City, KY.

Jamey is 15 years old and attends Dawson Springs High School. He was born Feb. 2, 1972 at Fort Campbell, KY. Jamey is Dorinda's son from a previous marriage. -*Submitted by Jamey Locke*

THELMA WOODRUFF ALLEN

Thelma Mae Woodruff Allen was born in St. Charles, KY, Sept. 13, 1925. She is the fourth of five children born to Ernest Boyd Woodruff and Mary Susan Swinney Woodruff. Her siblings are William Thomas (W.T.), Mary Susan, Mildred Coleen, and Ernest Ray (deceased). W.T. married Louise Gamble and still lives in St. Charles. Mary Susan married Lester Devault and lives in Gallatin, TN. Mildred Coleen married Rev. Jack Daniell and lives in Asheville, NC. Ernest Ray married Elizabeth Barnes who lives in Madisonville.

Thelma's father, Ernest Boyd Woodruff, was born Oct. 21, 1889, near St. Charles. He was one of five children born to William R. Woodruff and Annie Nisbet Woodruff. The other children of this union were Mamie, Dixie, Clarence and William (died as a baby).William R. Woodruff later married Ida O'Roark. Their children were Noble, Nick and Jeanette.

The town of St. Charles was named for Charles David Woodruff and Cynthia Davis Woodruff, Thelma's great-grandparents.

Thelma and Cap standing on a shovel used for stripping coal in St. Charles in 1944

John Woodruff, Charles' father, was killed in the Civil War.

The land where the Christian Privilege Church stood near St. Charles was given by Samuel Nathaniel Woodruff, John's father. It was organized in 1832. It burned in 1980.

Annie Nisbet Woodruff's father, James M. Nisbet, was sheriff of Hopkins County from 1881 to 1885.

James M. Nisbet's father, James Nisbet, Jr., was a member of the first town board of Madisonville, organized in 1807. He also donated land for a Christian Church at Grapevine, near Madisonville.

James Nisbet, Sr., served in the American Revolutionary War. His father, Alexander Nisbet, was born at sea as his family fled religious persecution in Scotland. They settled in South Carolina before moving to Hopkins County about 2 1/2 miles southeast of Madisonville.

Mary Susan Swinney Woodruff was born May 19, 1895, in St. Charles, one of four daughters (Lillian, Lara & Carrie) of Royal Ruffus Swinney and Merte Shaw Swinney. Royal's parents were Charles William Swinney and Susan Washington Winfrey. Susan was born in Richmond, VA, in 1832 and died in 1934 in St. Charles. Thelma remembers getting bored as a child listening to Granny Swinney tell stories about President Lincoln. Merte Shaw's parents were Nedham Hamet Shaw, who came to Kentucky from Duplin County, NC, and Mary Francis Putman Shaw of Nortonville.

The daughter of a coal miner, Thelma grew up on a 21 acre farm north of St. Charles. The old home place is now owned by her niece, Marilyn Woodruff Huddleston, the eldest daughter of W.T.

In early 1944 she met her husband, Kenneth Paul (Cap) Allen, superintendent for Miller-Clarkson Construction Company of Dodge City, KS. He strip-mined coal in the St. Charles, Dawson Springs and Carbondale areas. They married Dec. 23, 1944, in Washington, KS, Cap's hometown. They have one daughter, Kona Paulette and live in Independence, MO. *Sources: Cousin Dinsmore Nisbet, Madisonville, KY, R.L. (Bob) Davis, St. Charles, KY.- *Submitted by Thelma Woodruff Allen*

JOSEPH E. ALLINDER

Joseph Edmond Allinder, born Feb. 21, 1868, in Hopkins County, KY, was the second of six children born to Edmond Thomas Allinder and Sarah Ann Steen Allinder, daughter of Wilkerson Steen and Syntha Ann Palmer Steen.

Melissa Agnes (Dame) and Joseph Edmond Allinder

L to r: Mervin Allsbrook, V. LaVerne (Presnell) Allsbrook, Shelley K. Presnell, Elmer W. Presnell and Virginia N. Allsbrook

Edmond Thomas Allinder (born Apr. 17, 1832) first came to Hopkins County from Todd Co., KY in the early 1850's and settled in the Manitou, KY area. He is buried (died Dec. 2, 1906) in the old Steen Cemetery.

The brothers and sisters of Joseph Edmond were: Drucilla Ann, born Aug. 11, 1856; Lucian Lalisca, born 1871; Delora Amzi, born 1874; Sallie Genoah, born 1877; Ambia D., born 1879.

Joseph Edmond married Melissa Agnes Dame (born Sept. 23, 1870-died Nov. 22, 1905). The date of their marriage is unknown. Joseph and Melissa eloped because Melissa's father, James H. Dame, would not give permission for the couple to marry. Joseph and Melissa's children were: Bessie Leona, born Dec. 21, 1887; Lucy Keller, born Sept. 21, 1889; Grover Cleveland, born May 4, 1891 (died young); Emma Genoah, born Oct. 6, 1892; James Edmond, born Aug. 20, 1894 (died young); Clyde, born Apr. 28, 1896; Roy Nunn, born Nov. 8, 1897; David Enoch, born Nov. 26, 1903.

Joseph Edmond was a member of the Madisonville First Methodist Church. He is buried (died Feb. 19, 1935) in Oddfellows Cemetery in Madisonville, KY. -Submitted by Anne Keene Morgan

ALLSBROOK-PRESNELL

In 1810 Gilbert W. Presnell and two brothers, James and Theodore, of English-French descent, migrated from North Carolina westward through Tennessee and Indian country, and settled on a large area of land near Smithland, Livingston County, KY. Gilbert married Nancy Ann Watlington and their children were William Byron and Annie. Annie married a Conners. William Byron married Melvina Ann Robertson and their children were William, Samuel Anderson, Minnie, Belle, Annie, Emma, Gilbert, Frank and Josie.

Samuel Anderson Presnell born 1860 in Livingston County, KY married Elnora McNeeley, born 1861. Their children were: Shelley King, Elmer R., Alpha, and Cleveland.

Shelley King Presnell, b. Aug. 7, 1887, in Princeton, Caldwell County, KY married Nellie K. McCoy, born May 13, 1887, in Eddyville, Lyon County, daughter of Alex Wilson McCoy, b. 1852 in Columbus, MS, and Sinah Emmaline Smith McCoy, b. 1848 in Rockport, KY. Shelley and Nellie were married Dec. 7, 1907. Their children are: Coy R. (8-25-1908) who married Geneva Overton, children Sharon and DeWayne; Virginia LaVerne; Orman A. (3-20-1912) who married Leon, no children; Nell R. (3-12-1915) married Curtis F. Oglesby Sr., their children are Curtis Jr. and Linda; Elmer W. (10-1-1921) married Elaine Wallace, no children; W. Harry (1-3-1924) who married Barbara, one daughter, Anne. Harry died Nov. 18, 1987 at Westbranch, MI.

In 1915 when V. LaVerne Presnell was 5 years old, her family moved to White Plains, Hopkins County. Her father was employed with the Illinois Central Railroad. A few weeks later, the maternal grandparents, (McCoy) moved from Grand Rivers, KY to White Plains where Grandfather McCoy went into the ice delivery business with a wagon and team. The ice was made in the Earlington Icehouse, and delivered along the route to White Plains where Mr. McCoy became very popular and earned the beloved name of Daddy McCoy.

V. LaVerne attended White Plains elementary school and Nortonville School through the last few weeks of the freshman year, when she eloped and married. She has been a member of the United Methodist Church since age 8, and is currently active in the church and community activities.

V. LaVerne Presnell was born Feb. 12, 1910, in Smithland, KY. She married Mervin Allsbrook, born Jan. 1, 1909, in Hopkins County, on Feb. 16, 1927, in the Montgomery County Courthouse, Clarksville, TN, by W.B. Curlew, Justice of the Peace. Mervin was the son of Joseph L. Allsbrook (b. 8-6-1873) and Cleoda French Allsbrook (b. 4-4-1881), of Caldwell County, near Dawson Springs, KY. Other children were: Lenard, Lynn, Bobby and Elmer Francis, twins, Mary F. Pogue, Elmer L., and Maudie Mae Putman. Mervin attended Nortonville and Earlington schools in Hopkins County, was a member of the Nortonville Methodist Church South. He was employed by Norton Coal Company and was with Williams Coal Company at the time of his death, Oct. 19, 1949.

Mervin and V. LaVerne had one daughter, Virginia Nell, born Feb. 25, 1937 at Nortonville. She graduated from Nortonville H.S. and in the fall of 1955 enrolled at Murray State College. In June 1956, Virginia married James B. Gamble, pre-med graduate of Murray State, born 7-3-1934, the son of Eugene and Hazel Harris Gamble of Earlington, KY. In 1960 James graduated from the Univ. of Louisville Medical School and Virginia graduated from the Univ. of Louisville. After residency in Otolaryngology in Miami, FL, a stint in the U.S. Army in Utah near Salt Lake City, two years at Trover Clinic, Providence, KY Dr. Gamble practiced in Broward County, FL, for some years. For the last several years, he has been with the Tri-State Otolaryngology Clinic in Evansville, IN, where the family resides.

Virginia and Dr. Jim have two children: Beth born 6-1-1962 in Utah, a graduate of University of Evansville in nursing, now working in Jackson, WI. Their son, Bart, born 4-13-1964 in Hopkins County, also a graduate of Univ. of Evansville, is now doing graduate work in business at Indiana Univ. -Submitted by L. LaVerne Allsbrook

AMAR

Panfilo Amar, the only son of Severa Ibera and Benito Amar of Tibiao, Antique, Philippines, was born June 9, 1929. When he was seven years old his mother died of pneumonia.

In December of 1942, at the age of 13, he joined the guerilla forced during the Japanese occupation of the Philippines. When Douglas McArthur liberated the Philippines in 1944, he pursued his studies at San Jose Antique High School. In 1946, after the school closed, he went to Manila with a dream to go to America. Three months later he signed a year's contract with the American Graves Registration Service for Marianas Bonin Command. He left for Okinawa, going on to Guam, Saipan, Tinian, Marshall, Kawajalin Islands and Iwo Jima. With the one year contract about to expire, he went back to Guam where he got a job managing the Coney Island Restaurant in Piti Village.

The Korean War broke out and Panfilo was drafted into the United States Army. His basic training was at Scholfield Barracks, Oahu, HI. He was sent to Fort Benning, GA, to be a paratrooper, glider and ranger. After graduation, he was assigned to the 508th Regimental Combat Team at Fort Benning, GA. Four months later he took Parachute Packing Maintenance and Aerial Delivery Training to be qualified Parachute Rigger at Fort Lee, VA. His unit was transferred to Fort Campbell, KY, in early 1953. While stationed there, he met a girl in Madisonville by the name of June King and she became his wife.

In July 1955, Panfilo's unit relieved the 187th Airborne Infantry in Kysuhu, Japan. While he was in Japan his first son, Panfilo Mendoza, was born on Sept. 27, 1955. In the spring of 1956, his unit was mobilized to Fort Campbell to combine forces with the 197th Airborne Infantry reactivated the 101st Airborne Division.

On Mar. 31, 1959, Panfilo was honorably discharged and went to Chicago Heights, IL, and got a job at Ford Stamping Plant. The Lord called him to preach in 1960. He quit his job in 1966 to evangelize in America, Canada and Mexico. In January 1971, he went to the Philippines as a missionary. For the first time in twenty-five years he was reunited with his father and relatives.

While in the Philippines, a son Edward Shane was born Feb. 21, 1971. Three months later, Panfilo started a Bible School in Cebu City to train Filipino evangelists. The first two years God blessed 13 churches and by 1979 there were 32 established churches in Visayas, Mindanao and Metro-Manila.

Panfilo spent 28 months in the Philippines before Shane got sick. He came home and went to work at Huebsch Originators in Madisonville. In 1975 he joined the Livermore National Guard and went to work at River Queen Surface Mine (Peabody Coal Co.). He was transferred to Camp 11 Underground Mine in Morganfield, KY, in 1979. The same year, he left the Guard and joined the 100th Division (TNG) Army Reserve in Madisonville.

In June of 1980, Panfilo and June were divorced. He is now married to Nellie Miller, the daughter of Alford Miller of White Plains, KY.

Nellie M. and Panfilo Amar

Panfilo has two grandchildren: Bonita Angelina born Aug. 18, 1979 and Andres born November 1983.

Panfilo earned service medals during the Japanese occupation of the Philippines. He is also an Honorable Kentucky Colonel awarded by Governor Collins. -*Submitted by Panfilo Amar*

ANDERSON-BALLINGER

Hopkins County and Madisonville have played an important part in the lives of Mildred Ballinger and Bailey Anderson. Mildred was born in Calhoun, KY and moved to Madisonville at the age of five. Bailey was born in Providence and came to Madisonville after World War II, during which he served as a fighter pilot with the 8th Air Force. He was a prisoner of war for a short time in Germany, being liberated in May 1945. Mildred and Bailey were married at First Baptist Church, Sept. 2, 1946.

Mildred and Bailey Anderson, December 1976

Bailey and a partner bought Pate Printing Co., then American Printing Co., and later Messenger Job shop in Owensboro, as well as a shop in Illinois and Florida. In 1964 he became managing editor of the Madisonville Messenger. Six years later he was named publisher of the Sun-News in Las Cruces, NM. After only two years in the Southwest, the Andersons moved to Florence, AL, where Bailey was publisher of the Times-Daily until his death Nov. 18, 1981. Bailey was active in civic affairs and in many organizations such as Rotary, VFW, Chamber of Commerce, United Way, Masons, Downtown Florence, and his Church. He loved to fly and always had his plane to travel for business or pleasure.

Meanwhile, Mildred taught at Madisonville Junior High and Madisonville-North Hopkins. In Florence her cookbook, Shoals Southern Heritage Cookbook was published. As a hobby, she enjoys oil painting. However, most of her time was used to raise their three children:

Patricia Ann (b. May 8, 1948) now living in Greeneville, TN, is married to Attorney Ronald Chestnut. They have two children: Amy Rebecca (b. 7-13-1973) and Alex Anderson (b. 9-11-1976). Trisha is Social Service Director of Tacoma Hospital.

Ruby Elizabeth, known as Wibby, (b. 11-22-1949), presently living in Norfolk, VA, is married to Major Jere Medaris. Four children: Sophia Margaret (b. 5-7-1981), Matthew Anderson (b. 1-28-1983), Jeremy Steele (b. 8-13-1984) and Joshua Ballinger (b. 4-13-1986).

Edwin Bailey, Jr. (b. 3-4-1955) is married to Snow Savich, and lives in the suburbs of Chicago. They have one son, Bailey Lee (b. 6-23-1986) born on his grandfather's birthday.

Mildred, Patricia, Elizabeth and their husbands all graduated from Western KY Univ., Edwin from the Univ. of Arizona, and Snow from Northwestern.

Mildred, still has close ties to Madisonville, for her mother, Mrs. John Ballinger, lives there on Scott Street. Her father died in March 1984. When Mildred is not busy working at the Kennedy Douglas Art Center, Tennessee Valley Art Association, concert series Guild, Salvation Army Women's Auxiliary, Turtle Point Yacht and Country Club or her church, she is busy renewing old acquaintances or visiting family and friends. -*Submitted by Mildred B. Anderson*

ARMSTRONG-GOODAKER

Benjamin Armstrong, born 1797, a native of South Carolina, was of Irish and German descent and settled in Hopkins County. Benjamin married Zelotus E. (Sugg) Armstrong. Benjamin was a captain in the State Militia for many years. He was a soldier in the War of 1812 and participated in the Battle of New Orleans. Benjamin, an elder in the Cumberland Presbyterian Church, died on Jan. 8, 1873, and his wife, Zelotus, died on Sept. 20, 1877.

One son, Newton Jasper Armstrong, born Aug. 11, 1850, married Missouri Bell Wilson, born Oct. 19, 1856. They had seven children. One son, Clyde Clifton Armstrong, born Feb. 14, 1887, married Verdie Cansler Dec. 20, 1908. Clyde and Verdie had two children: Mary Louise and Norris Elwood Armstrong. After Verdie's death in 1918, Clyde married Nettie Riordan. They had two daughters, Billye Joyce and Lynda Lee Armstrong. A daughter of Nettie Riordan, Ethel Mae Harvey, from a previous marriage was also part of the family.

Verdie Cansler's family, Phillip Gantzler (Cansler) emigrated from Germany and settled in Pennsylvania in about 1755. He later moved to Lincoln Co., NC, where he died, leaving four sons and six daughters. One son, James Cansler, born in Tennessee, emigrated to Christian Co., KY, in about 1800. One son of James, Golden Cansler married Betsy McCord and to this union four children were born. One son, Thomas Benton Cansler, married Molly Lyle. They had three children: Calvin, Verdie, and Alger.

Norris E. and Anna Mae Armstrong

Norris Elwood Armstrong and Anna Mae Goodaker were married in Princeton, KY, Dec. 23, 1938. He was born in Dawson Springs, KY, on Apr. 1, 1912. Anna Mae was born in Caldwell Co., KY, on Sept. 8, 1914, the daughter of Dora Goodaker and Ethel Alexander. Norris and Anna Mae were members of the First Christian Church (Disciples of Christ) in Dawson Springs. Norris spent all his working life as a dry cleaner and tailor, retiring in 1976 at age 64. Norris and Anna Mae had one daughter Patricia Ann Armstrong, born in Dawson Springs, Jan. 4, 1941. Patricia married Paul K. Turner, also of Dawson Springs, on Apr. 15, 1961. They have two daughters, Anna Kathleen and Margaret Armstrong Turner.

Anna Mae Goodaker Armstrong was the granddaughter of David W. Goodaker and Mary Ann Egbert, who were married in Caldwell Co., on Mar. 8, 1866. David and Mary Ann had four sons and one daughter. One son, Dora Goodaker, born Feb. 22, 1876, and Ethel Alexander, born Oct. 16, 1889, were married in Caldwell Co. on Feb. 9, 1908. To this union, seven children were born, three sons and four daughters. A son and a daughter died in infancy. The oldest daughter, Anna Mae, was also the granddaughter of David A. Alexander and Casandra Hunsaker, parents of nine children. One daughter, Ethel (Alexander) Goodaker was the mother of Anna Mae. -*Submitted by Norris E. Armstrong*

ARMSTRONG-RAMSEY

Helen Elizabeth Ramsey (7-23-1870 to 9-4-

1940) was a dark-eyed beauty who stuck to her guns. Helen was in love with Sam Armstrong. Her father, John G. Ramsey, said she was not getting married, yet. She and Sam ran off 2 or 3 times and Grandpa always brought her home. The old family story relates that her sister, Minnie, went to bat for her the last time. She told their father to "let her go, Pa," so—he did (Samuel Armstrong, 1866-1942).

She and Sam lived within rock-throwing distance to the family home, as did some of her brothers and sisters. That was a truly family-oriented neighborhood.

They had three daughters, all of them lovely.

Rhea married Clebie Elbert Myers and they had two sons, Marlin and Gene. Marlin married Anna Katherine Hunt and they had one daughter, Myrna Gail. Rev. Gene Myers married Sue Cates and they had a son, Paul Steven and a daughter, Jeanie Suzette.

Coatney married Rufus Yarbrough and they had 2 sons and 2 daughters. Rufus II married Katherine Blalock. Their only child, Jimmy, died early. Helen Elizabeth married Marvin Menser and had one son and one daughter. Their names are unknown. William married a lady named Jeanette (last name unknown). They had 2 children. Corrine married Cleat Braden and they had 4 children. (Again, all facts unknown).

Hurl Armstrong, daughter of Helen Elizabeth Ramsey and Sam Armstrong. Married George Tabor and had two sons, Val and Ira. Grandchildren and great grandchildren still live in Hopkins Co.

Hurl Armstrong married George Tabor and had 2 sons, Val and Ira. Val married Ella Mae Harkins and they were blessed with twins sons, Val Dwayne and Dennis Wayne. Val passed away and left Ella Mae fairly early. She is a retired school teacher. Val Dwayne also married a teacher, Sheila Kay LeGrand and they are the parents of 2 sons and one daughter, Michael Dwayne, Robert Adam and Christie Leigh' Ann Tabor. Dennis Wayne's wife was Kathy Jean Scott. They have 1 son, Russell Wayne and 1 daughter, Shannon Renee.'

Hurl and George's other son and wife have passed away. These are listed, but records are incomplete and not totally reliable. Ira Tabor married Anita Franklin and they had 3 children, probably 2 boys and 1 girl. Stephen Douglas Tabor married and divorced (wife's name unknown). I believe their son's name is Derrick. Ira Tabor died young (very little information). Patricia married a Spanish-American and they lived in Arizona. He may have died or they may have divorced. At any rate, she later married his brother. It is thought that Patty and her first husband had one son. She still resides in Arizona. Stephen Douglas also lives in Arizona. He remains single.

Aunt Helen and Uncle Sam have passed on, long ago. Their little family did pretty well, after so many tries at getting hitched. If they could but see—they'd certainly be proud of their heritage, and deservedly so. (See Robert Winfield Ramsey) -Submitted by Peggy Sullivan Waide

ARNOLD-NISWONGER

William Everett (Bill) Arnold and Lanna Sue Niswonger were married Aug. 11, 1946 in the Methodist Church at Elkton, KY, by Rev. Owen Hoskinson.

Lanna was born Aug. 21, 1928, at Nebo. She is the daughter of Thomas Louis Niswonger and Hortense Lutz. Tommy Louis was born on the old Niswonger farm outside of Nebo (next to the Union Cemetery) Nov. 19, 1895. He is the son of Thomas Jefferson Niswonger and Valeria Elizabeth (Lizzie) Springfield. He was the youngest of three children; John Spencer and Maud Emma. Hortense Lutz was born at Liberty in Webster Co., Nov. 26, 1898. She is the daughter of Jacob Lann Lutz (Dec. 31, 1868) and Vera Gradie Fike (Oct. 20, 1880). She was the oldest of three children, Raymond Price and Lanna Lee Lutz. They were married June, 1914.

Lanna and Bill Arnold

Lanna graduated from Nebo High School and the Univ. of Evansville. She is currently employed as a Chapter I Reading Teacher at Grapevine School. She has taught at Nortonville, Hanson and Seminary Junior High, Reading Clinician at the Reading Clinic, Broadway, and private kindergarten.

Bill was born Nov. 17, 1925 in Madisonville (Grapevine Road) to James Lawson Arnold and Eldee Wilkey. Other children, James Ernest (twin to Bill) and Betty Ruth Roberts Martin. Jimmy (July 7, 1908) was the youngest son of Ernest Newton Arnold and Lena Ann Rock. William Henry (Bub) and Charles Lawrence were his brothers. Ernest was born Oct. 30, 1871, the oldest child of John Lawson (1847) and Mary Ann Ball (1849), other children were Jim, John, Sam, Bessie, Earl, Addie and Martin. Lena (June 4, 1877) one of seven children, Elizabeth (Lizzie), John, Henry, Augustus (Gussie) and Charlie born to Charles Henry Rock and Elizabeth (Eliza) Hahn. Charlie came to Hopkins County and bought property located at the corner of Grapevine Road and Highway 41. He was a shoemaker. Eldee (June 26, 1908) is the daughter of William Everett Wilkey (Oct. 23, 1878) and Mrs. Cora Bell Ligon Logan (Aug. 14, 1876). Other children; Gladys Townzen, Carmen Beshear, Maurice Wilkey, half-brothers Thomas and Joy Logan.

Bill attended Broadway, Waddill and Madisonville H.S. He went into the Army in Feb. 1944 after completing school. His basic training was at Camp Kohler near Sacramento, CA. He was sent to Camp Edison, NJ, for two months and the European Theater with the 3187th Signal Service Battalion, teletype and message center team for the Ninth Army. After being discharged he graduated from Lockyear's College, worked for Hocker Power Brake Company, West Kentucky Coal Company, manager and salesman for Central Mine Supply for thirty years, and last three years as a salesman for Madisonville Recapping Co.

Bill and Lanna have sons, Robert Wayne (Oct. 22, 1951) married Deborah Kay (Debbie) Howser (Feb. 18, 1952), and Steven James (May 16, 1954) married Robin Lynn McCoy (Oct. 10, 1954). They have three grandchildren, Tara Lynn (Nov. 11, 1976), Kelli Ann (Oct. 3, 1981), Curtis Allen (Nov. 2, 1981)-Submitted by Lanna Arnold

FRANK BOWEN ARNOLD

Frank Bowen Arnold (1867-1935) was born in Sacramento in McLean County and came to Earlington as an adult. His parents were Elisha Wesley Arnold and Caroline Virginia (Bowen) Arnold. His grandfather, Benjamin Franklin Arnold is listed in the 1850 census of Muhlenberg County, having come from Virginia with his wife the former Cassandra Marshall—a niece of Chief Justice John Marshall. Earlier ancestors are believed to have come from South Wales as early as the mid-1600's.

Frank B. married Eleanor Josephine Robinson, whose ancestors came to America from the Isle of Man. He and his wife dabbled in real estate and he was for many years cashier for St. Bernard Coal Co. in Earlington, where all their children were born in a house that still stands at the southwest corner of West Main and McEuen Ave. They later moved to Madisonville where he was Trust Officer for Kentucky Bank. Their children, all now deceased, were (1) George B., an aeronautical engineer who managed an aircraft plant for the Chinese government in Hangchow, China, (owned by Curtiss-Wright) in the 1930's and ended his years in South Florida where his widow and sons now reside; (2) Edgar F., long time editor of The Madisonville Messenger, who married Caroline Long of Madisonville; (3) Howard P., a commercial artist who worked in California for Walt Disney in Disney's early years; and (4) Eleanor. Howard and Eleanor never married.

Descendants living in Hopkins County are children of Edgar and Caroline: (1) Edgar F. Jr., who was with The Messenger 24 years and served a term in the Kentucky House of Representatives and is now Chief Right of Way Agent for Dist. 2 of the Ky. Highway Dept.; (2) Mary Ann Crary; and (3) Howard L., a real estate developer. The eldest son, Kenneth L., died in 1966.

Children of Edgar Jr. are Frank E., who lives in Corbin, KY, and Gillis M. who lives in Cary, NC. Children of Kenneth are: Caroline Virginia (Mrs. M.R. Mills) of Madisonville, and Kenneth B., who lives in Virginia. Howard, who married Madisonville native Ann Wright has a son, Bruce, who lives in Madisonville. Gillis has two sons, Robert Edgar and Matthew Walker, to carry on the Arnold name.

War Records: Edgar F. Sr. served in the Army in World War I, while his brother Howard served in the Army Air Corps in both World Wars. Kenneth served in an Army anti-aircraft unit in the South Pacific and was wounded twice. Edgar Jr. was a B-17 Navigator in the Army Air Corps in World War II.

Edgar Arnold Sr., the best-known member of the family to long-time residents of Hopkins County, was with Madisonville's daily newspaper from 1919 until his death in 1963. The Arnold connection with the paper ended in 1970 when it was sold to Worrell Newspapers, a Virginia "chain."-*Submitted by Edgar F. Arnold (Jr.)*

ASHBY-BRANSON

Lorenzo Laton Ashby was the son of Thomas Enoch Ashby (1832-1870). They were descendants of the pioneer Ashby family. Lorenzo married Cora Branson who was born Jan. 19, 1860, and died Jan. 31, 1917. Lorenzo died in August of 1941.

Cora was the daughter of James Murphy Branson and Emily Cardwell. They married in Hopkins County on Mar. 1, 1849. James was born Aug. 23, 1823, and died Mar. 17, 1881. Emily was born Nov. 10, 1829, and died Jan. 14, 1889. Both are buried in New Salem Methodist Cemetery near Jewell City. The other children of James and Emily were: Anna Z., Alice, Indiana, Corella, Howard C., Leota, Emma and Maggie L.

Cora and Lorenzo Ashby had a daughter, Jessie Louise. She was born Mar. 12, 1896, and died Mar. 1, 1919. She is buried at Oddfellows Cemetery in Madisonville. Jessie married James Herschel Hickman (see Harris and Hickman families). -*Submitted by Mary Edna Harris*

ASHBY-DAME

Sarah Ann Dame, (1866-1949) and James Baxter Ashby (1863-1956) were married Apr. 26, 1885.

Sarah Ann (Sally) was born Oct. 10, 1866, to Amanda Blue and Harvey Dame near Hanson, KY. Losing her father at an early age, she lived with an uncle and aunt, Mr. and Mrs. Jack Blue, until her marriage. She attended the local school. Her sisters were Lou Ella, Ida and Betty. Her brothers were John and Ben Dame.

James Baxter (Jim) was born Mar. 13, 1863, to John Pettus Ashby and Eliza K. Robinson in the Shakerag community. Jim attended county school, near Shakerag, where he became close friends with Governor Ruby Laffoon, as they both attended the same fourth grade class. Jim's father died in 1864 during service in the Civil War. (John Pettus was a Confederate soldier.) He left behind five children: John Henry, Laura B., George, James Baxter and Celia.

James B., better known as Jim, after marrying Sally, began farming near Anton. Also, he was active in Baptist church circles, holding a deacon's position first at Liberty Church and later at Nortonville Baptist Church.

Although Jim was a farmer, this was not his sole trade. From 1924 until 1932, he worked as night watchman for Norton Coal Company. From 1943 until 1947, he was employed by the State Highway Dept., also as night watchman.

Jim and Sally were married 64 years and had seven children: Edna, Ona, Homer, Laura, Georgia, James and Anna Mae. Of these seven children, only James and Anna Mae are still living. Sally was 84 years of age at the time of her death; Jim was 93. Both are buried at Oddfellows. *Source: Church records and THE ASHBY BOOK - Compiled by Pansy Wagoner Ashby*

ASHBY-ROSS

Josiah Jackson Ashby and Sarah Wheaton Ross Ashby wre the parents of eleven children. Their children and their number of descendants through six generations are: Charles Willoughby born Nov. 4, 1850, died Jan. 23, 1898 with no issue; Sanford Lee born Apr. 14, 1852, died as an infant; Medor born Nov. 7, 1853, died about 1932 leaving 16 descendants; Lillian Parthena born Aug. 10, 1855, died Nov. 20, 1857; Millard Filmore born Mar. 18, 1858, died Mar. 7, 1936 leaving 133 descendants; Josiah Jackson Jr. born Nov. 7, 1859, died Nov. 14, 1924 leaving 167 descendants; James Shackleford born Sept. 5, 1861, died in 1920 leaving 14 descendants; Wheaton Ross born May 31, 1863, died Aug. 10, 1916, leaving 42 descendants; Perneta Ross "Rose" born May 24, 1865, died Oct. 11, 1941, leaving 24 descendants; Alice Bell, born in 1867, died in 1950 leaving three descendants; and Benjamin J., born Sept. 9, 1869, died Dec. 31, 1891 with no issue.

James B. Ashby's certificate for attending every Sunday at Olive Branch Church Sunday School in 1871

The Josiah Jackson Ashby family in 1880. Sarah and Josiah are seated with Nellie May and Ross (Josiah Jrs. children). Behind are Charles Willoughby, Millard Filmore, Josiah Jackson, Jr., James Shackleford, Wheaton Ross, Benjamin J.., Perneta "Rose", and Alice.

The descendants of all the children total 410. Of the foregoing, there are at least five still living of the second generation and many are still living of the third generation and most are still living of subsequent generations. Through marriages, the above issue carry a total of at least sixty-six (66) surnames as follows: Ashby, Abbas, Ainsworth, Annenson, Bailey, Baker, Beck, Boyd, Braun, Brown, Cates, Coble, Compton, Craig, Crawford, Crutcher, Davis, Dawson, DeWitt, Doan, Doty, Dowling, Drysdale, Duff, Elam, Ellis, Faulkner, Fello, Fowler, Gangle, Gibble, Grimand, Hamby, Hasenmueller, Hewlett, Kondzekowski, Larabee, Long, Lovelace, Luck, Maiami, McBee, McLain, Mayers, Merrick, Morgan, Orton, Parker, Perez, Prow, Qualls, Ramsey, Ranes, Salmon, Schwan, Stewart, Story, Thomas, Townsend, Truitt, Tucker, Waller, Webb, Welby, Weverstad, White, Whitley, Williams, Wilson, and Witteg. We have a lot of cousins, don't we? If I over-

James Baxter Ashby and Sarah Ann (Dame) Ashby

looked you, please let me know. The foregoing does not include the maiden names of females that married into the Clan.

Josiah Jackson Ashby traces his lineage through Willoughby (1793-1835), Enoch (1744-c. 1800), Robert (1710 - 1792) to Thomas (c. 1680 - 1752) who emigrated from Leicestershire, England and settled in Farquier County, VA early in the 18th Century. Ashby is an Anglo-Saxon derivative and is first known as Asebi in the time of Edward The Confessor (1002-1066)

I feel privileged to have known Rose (my grandmother), Medora, Alice Bell, Josiah Jr., Millard, my mother's first cousins and many of their issue. I have fond memories of the annual gatherings of this great Clan at Uncle Millard's. Ginger Brown Parker tells a tale about me driving my father's car through Uncle Millard's picket fence on one of these occasions.

I wish to acknowledge with gratitude, my debt to Sarah Joe Ashby Brown, for much of the information herein.-*Submitted by James K. Ramsey, III*

ASHBY-SOUTHWORTH

William Emsley "Dick" Ashby (b. 11-18-1841 d. 1-18-1918) Hopkins Co. was the son of Lewis Ashby (b. 4-16-1807) and Rosa Ashby (b. 4-13-1811 d. 2-17-1860), grandson of Absalom Ashby, Sr., and Jane Shumate (paternal) and Capt. Stephen Ashby and Elizabeth Robertson (maternal). He married Vitula "Tula" Hopkins Wilson (b. 12-18-1852 d. 4-24-1943) both buried at Oakwood Cemetery, Earlington.

These are the parents of Annie (Ashby) Southworth who lived in Earlington for 90 years, and her sibling as follows:

Mildred Weir Ashby (b. 5-19-1875 d. 3-19-1947) who married Nicholas "Nick" Iradell Toombs (b. 8-31-1857 d. 12-15-1948) on Oct. 20, 1897. Both are buried at Oddfellows. These are parents of Miss Elizabeth Toombs, long-time Elementary school teacher in Hopkins County.

Elizabeth Rolls Ashby (b. 9-10-1876 d. 9-18-1939) married Sept. 8, 1892 to William Burgess Wise (b. 1872 d. 1949), both buried at Oakwood Cemetery.

Nancy "Nannie" Ashby (b. 1-15-1881 d. 11-21-1946) married Dec. 31, 1902 to Amplias O. Sisk (M.D.) (b. 9-8-1874 d. 1-28-1951), both buried at Oddfellows Cemetery.

Henry Ann or Annie Henry Ashby (b. 5-12-1878 d. 9-12-1977) married Feb. 14, 1923, to Brick Southworth (b. 7-1-1879 d. 8-8-1862), both buried in Oddfellows Cemetery. Mr. Southworth was a 1st Lt. in the KY State Guard and an influential civic leader in Earlington. It was through the efforts of "Miss Annie" that the Captain Stephen Ashby Chapter of the DAR was established in Hopkins Co., named for her maternal grandfather.

William Emsley "Dick" Ashby was a younger brother to Lockey (Ashby) Warren in Hopkins Co. (See ASHBY-WARREN family)

Other children of Lewis and Rosa Ashby were: Warren W. Ashby (b. 11-15-1831), married Emily O. Pritchett Tapp; Farris B. Ashby (b. 11-1-1833), married Louisa C. Brown; "Massy" Louisa Ashby (b. 10-27-1835) mar-

Tom (son of Lockey Ashby Warren) and Dovie Warren

ried Orman Sellars; Finley W. Ashby (b. 1-1-1837) died young; Nancy C. Ashby (b.10-29-1839) married Lewis Fugate; Sarah "Sallie" Jane Ashby b. 12-18-1843 first married Charles Joseph Hicklin, and then James H. Hickman; Amanda Ashby (b. 10-6-1845 d. 10-15-1915) married William D. Stodgill (b.1839 d. 1909); Mildred Weir Ashby (b. 4-1-1848) died young; Remus Smith Ashby (b. 2-13-1850 d. 11-10-1919) first married Elizabeth Roberts, then Mrs. Sallie E. Jenkins; Napolean "Pole" Ashby (b. 1-16-1852) married Queen Eliz. Ashby (b. 12-25-1860,) daughter of Daniel B. Ashby and Mary Ann Stodgill, sister to William D. Stodgill, Amanda's husband; Charlotte Ashby (b. 4-10-1855) married John B. "Bee" Washington.

Records show that Rosa died Feb. 17, 1860 and Lewis married Fanny Thomson Bailey on Aug. 8, 1860. They had one son, Virgil "Bud" Ashby (b. 7-?-1861,) who married Martha Jane Jones. Their son, Reuben Ashby, died in 1916 when he was 10 years old.

Birthdates and many of who married supplied to Keith H. Ashby by "Miss Annie" Southworth. -*Submitted by Rella G. Jenkins*

ASHBY-WAGONER

Pansy Elizabeth Wagoner and James Ross Ashby were married Dec. 18, 1937, in Hopkinsville, KY.

Pansy was born Nov. 7, 1915, near Anton in Hopkins Co. She is the daughter of John Wagoner and Ida May Wiar.

The James Ross Ashby family

Pansy attended first and second grades at Wilson School, her teachers being Cattie Stodgill and Delta Merrel, and completed grade school at Browders School. In 1933, while Merril Speck was principal, Pansy, known as "that girl that rides the mule", graduated from Anton High School. She was for many years employed by Western Kentucky Hospital Services, from which she retired in 1976.

She is currently a member of New Salem Baptist Church in Nortonville, an active officer, as well as Past Matron of Nortonville Chapter #243, Order of the Eastern Star of Kentucky, a member of the Daughters of the Nile, Neith Temple #80, a member of the Historical Society of Hopkins County, and a member of the American Association of Retired Persons, Chapter #3391, also of Hopkins County, KY.

James was born Feb. 27, 1905, near Anton. He is the son of James B. Ashby and Sarah Dame.

James attended Medlock School until 1918, then attended New Salem School for two years. Later, he was trained in telegraphy at Romney under the supervision of Bert Scisney, followed by training for main line wires at Nortonville Depot under Bob Ray.

In July of 1922, James began working for the L and N Railroad as a telegraph operator, working at various stations in Indiana, Kentucky and Tennessee. In 1929, he went to Arizona, where he worked for Southern Pacific Railroad for a few months. Due to the Depression, for the next few years, James held a variety of positions with various companies.

James returned to Hopkins County in 1933. He went into mining, working for Trio Coal Company and, later, Norton Coal Company.

In 1942, he returned to the railroad, going with Illinois Central. He worked various stations in the system, including three years at Grand Rivers, KY during the period when Kentucky Dam was being built.

In August of 1949, James became the joint agent for L&N and Illinois Central at Nortonville. While he was working there, the depot burned (Jan. 16, 1959). On emergency basis, the clerk, Alfred Grace, and he moved into a small structure a few yards west of the old depot site. However, this situation lasted until Nortonville Railroad Station was closed on Apr. 1, 1961.

From there, James was transferred to Princeton, KY as the traveling freight agent for Illinois Central Railroad, serving White Plains, Nortonville, Dawson Springs and Princeton, driving an over-sized van to deliver freight daily. He retired in September of 1969 with 40 years of railroad service.

James is currently a member of New Salem Baptist Church, a member of the Historical Society of Hopkins County, a member of the American Association of Retired Persons, Chapter #3391, of Hopkins County, KY, a member and Past Patron of Nortonville Chapter No. 243, Order of the Eastern Star of Kentucky, Ambassador of the Rizpah Temple and a Kentucky Colonel. In the past, he has served as District Deputy Grand Master, District No. 5, F. & A.M. (1965 - 1966) and District Deputy Grand Patron, District No. 16, Order of the Eastern Star of Kentucky (1967 - 1968)

James and Pansy have three children: Patricia Ann Elkins and twin boys, Johnny and Jimmy. They also have six grandchildren and one great granddaughter. -*Submitted by Pansy Wagoner Ashby*

ASHBY-WARREN

Valentine Cook Ashby, b. 8-30-1824 in Hopkins Co., was the son of Robert Ashby (b. ca. 1776 d. ca. 1840) and Margaret "Peggy" Ross, who married Mar. 15, 1818. He married Lockey Ashby, b. 1-9-1829, daughter of Lewis

Ashby b. 4-16-1807 and Rosa (Ashby) Ashby b. 4-13-1811, of Hopkins Co. Lewis' parents were Absalom Ashby Sr. and Jane "Jennie" Shumate, and Rosa's parents were Capt. Stephen Ashby and Elizabeth Robertson.

Valentine and Lockey's children: Rosaline Ashby, b. 1849, married A.B. Galloway Mar. 12, 1869; Orlando Ashby, b. 1851 never married; Margaret (b. 7-11-1853 d. 10-27-1919) married Walter Haynes (b. 8-27-1853 d. 11-10-1884). Margaret is buried at Odd Fellows, Walter at Eastlawn, Hanson; Mary Eliz. Ashby (b. 11-28-1855 d. 5-21-1930); Queen Victoria Ashby b. 1857 married S.J. McDonald, Jan. 21, 1877; John Rollins Ashby, b. 1860; Valentine Cook Ashby Jr. b. 9-15-1863 called "Uncle Tine," married Mrs. Bettie Tucker b. 5-11-1869, on Dec. 25, 1889. Valentine Cook Ashby died 1-29-1863, is buried at Providence Eastlawn, Hanson.

Lockey Ashby, age 36, married Thomas K. Warren, Dec. 4, 1866, at her home in Hopkins Co. Thomas K. Warren b. 1821 in Marion Co., KY, was a mechanic/farmer. Lockey died 2-15-1897, buried at Old Mortons Gap Cem. Thomas K. and Lockey had three children:

Frances "Fannie" Warren, b. 9-28-1869, married William Courtney (4-16-1846) on Dec. 7, 1897. Two daughters: Goldie M. (b. 9-2-1898 d. 1986) and Amber K. (b. 8-27-1900 d. 2-1-1966). Neither married, lived in Nashville.

Rose Annie Warren, b. 1873, married Kenner Jordan, b. 1881 Fairview, Todd Co. KY. Rose died 8-11-1958 in Nashville. Kenner married Trilby Sawyer who died in 1985 in Nashville. Kenner died 6-1963, bur. Nashville.

Thomas Marion "Tom" Warren b. 11-11-1872, Mortons Gap, married Dovie Emma Jordan b. 6-13-1874 at Fairview, Todd Co., daughter of Robert Jordan, b. 1848 d. 1909, and Elizabeth "Bettie" Kenner, b. 1853 d. 1926. Dovie and Kenner were siblings. Thomas K. Warren deserted Lockey and children when Thomas M. was about 14 years old and he had to quit school to work in the mines to support his mother and sisters. He later worked for Inland Steele in Chicago many years before retirement. Dovie Emma died 12-28-1937 and Tom d. 12-7-1942, both buried at Odd Fellows Cemetery, Madisonville.

Dovie and Tom Warren's children were: May Elizabeth Warren, b. 10-10-1898, married Clarence Davis Woodruff, b. 2-15-1895, son of William Roger Woodruff and Annie Nisbet. Clarence died 2-25-1985, and May died Dec. 10, 1987, and they are buried at Grapevine Cemetery. Their son, Marvin Davis Woodruff, b. 6-9-1922, married Wanda R. Outlaw b. 6-16-1928, daughter of Arthur Rhea Outlaw and Ora Hazel Cunningham of White Plains. Marvin retired from Charolais Coal Corp. Their son, Kevin Davis Woodruff b. 10-9-1946, single, works at Charolais. All live near St. Charles.

Opal Fern Warren, b. 8-7-1900, married Charles R. Jenkins b. 4-12-1896. (See Jenkins-Warren, Jenkins-King families).

Farleigh Edward Warren, b. 8-3-1902, married Lois Virginia Peyton, b. 6-18-1906, daughter of William Thomas Peyton and Ruby Foster of Earlington. Edward is retired from Metropolitan Insurance Co.; they live in Louisville.

From l to r: Charlie and Opal Jenkins (celebrating their 50th Wedding Anniversary), Lois and Edward Warren, and May and Clarence Woodruff

Their son, William Edward Warren, b. 1-31-1925, married Margaret Frances Brownell, b 1-23-1925 in Louisville, daughter of Norman Wetherby Brownell and Margaret Frances Denson. William Edward "Eddie" is retired executive with Union Carbide Corp., Victoria, TX. Their son, Douglas Edward Warren b. 8-3-1959, in Charleston, W. VA, married Laurilyn Forsythe on Apr. 4-25-1987. He works for Vistron Corp, Victoria. -*Submitted by Rella G. Jenkins*

CAPTAIN THOMAS ASHBY

Captain Thomas Ashby settled in Virginia in the 1700's. He died in 1752 and was survived by six sons and four daughters. His sons were John (1707-1797), Robert (1710-1792), Thomas Jr., Benjamin, Stephen and Henry. John Ashby fought with Washington and General Braddock in the French and Indian War. He was chosen by Washington to take the news of General Braddock's defeat to the Governor of Virginia at Williamsburg which was a distance of 180 miles. It was said that he made the trip alone on horseback in thirteen hours. John was grandfather of General Turner Ashby and Richard Ashby who lost their lives in the Civil War under the command of Stonewall Jackson.

Stephen died in 1797. He is buried in the Old Ashby Cemetery in Hopkins County. One daughter married James Leeper, son of John Leeper, who shot Big Harp. Another daughter, Rose, married Captain George Timmons. They were buried on the old Timmons Farm but were later moved to West Lawn Cemetery at Providence Church.

Henry Ashby died in 1798 and was buried at Harrodsburg, KY. He and his brother Benjamin helped Washington survey land in Virginia and Kentucky for Lord Fairfax. He married Ellender Nelly Bounds. After his death, Henry's widow and children came to the Madisonville area. She died in 1811 in Hopkins Co. Their children were Elizabeth, Argle, Robert, Bounds, Stephen, Mary, Nancy, George, Sinah, and Sarah.

Elizabeth married Daniel Campbell who was born in 1779 in Virginia. She died in 1846. Argle never married and died 1823. Robert was born 1776 and married Peggy Ross who died before her husband's death in 1844. Bounds Ashby was born in 1779. He married Elizabeth Cardwell (1774-1858) and he died in 1832. They are buried north of Madisonville in High Glory Cemetery.

The descendants of Robert Ashby are Wilson Ross, Crawford B., Valentine, John H. (California Jack), Silas M. and Martha Ann Ashby. Wilson Ross (1818-1855) married Mariah Ann Blue (1827-1905). Crawford B. (1819-1842) never married. Valentine (1824-1863) married Locky Ashby. John H. (1828-1901) married Elizabeth Pritchett (1830-1920), and Martha Ann married Wiley Ross.

The descendants of Wilson Ross Ashby are Frances, John Valentine, Franklin D., Americus Lafayette, Martha and Eliza. Frances (1844-1878) married John S. Bassett. John Valentine (1847-1905) married Elizabeth Tomlinson. Franklin D. (1849-1877) married Adeline Clements. Americus Lafayette (1851-1918) married Mariah Crabtree (1854-1920). Martha (1854-?) married Henry Rickard (1844-1917) and Eliza (1856-?) married Elbert L. Clements (1853-1877).

Home of A.L. Ashby circa 1870

The descendants of Americus Lafayette Ashby are Auzie (1878-1951), Hez (1881-1949), Wilson (1883-1959), Vera (1885-1916), Pearl (1888-1984), Headley (1890-1982), Bertha (1890-1947), and Thomas W. (1894-1972). Auzie married Bessie Brooks in 1904. His second wife was Lillian Carlisle. Hez married Nell Orton in 1900. Wilson married Ruth Orton (1884-1905), Arite Bratcher, Pearl Cates, and Essie McCormick. Vera married Rufe Jordon and Pearl married A.B. Nance (1884-1973). Headley married Lillie Cobb (1895-1934) and his twin sister, Bertha, married Clyde Fox (1888-1975).

Thomas W. married Bertha Hall on Mar. 18, 1916. He was a farmer and their farm is north of Hanson. They lived on the farm until his death. She now resides in Madisonville. They have two children, James Nokomis, Hanson, and Devona Ashby Riley, Madisonville. *Sources: Info. from James N. Ashby and The Ashby Book by Reese, -Submitted by Devona Riley*

AUSENBAUGH-DILLINGHAM

John Ausenbaugh was born in 1945 in Hopkinsville, KY. His father, Johnny Ausenbaugh, was born in 1924 in Dawson Springs, KY. His mother was born in 1926 in Dawson Springs. John has no brothers or sisters. After graduating from high school in 1963, John went to College at Samford University in Birmingham, AL to be a pharmacist.

While in college, John married Margaret Dillingham who was born in 1946 in Dawson Springs. The house she was born in is still in the family; her uncle is currently living there. Margaret has only one brother, Kent Dillingham, born in 1952. He is married and has two children who attend Dawson Springs Grade School.

Amy Ausenbaugh

The parents of Margaret are Kent Norris and Ruth Roam Dillingham. Norris was born in 1927 in Dawson Springs. Ruth was born in 1928 in Pembroke, KY. Ruth had three older bothers who were killed before graduating from high school.

Margaret and Kent attended Dawson Springs High School. Margaret was a cheerleader and Kent played basketball. Margaret graduated in 1964 and went to Western Kentucky U.

In 1969, John and Margaret became parents of their first child, a daughter, Laura Lynn Ausenbaugh, who was born in Birmingham, AL. In 1972, their second daughter, Amy, was born. In 1976, Margaret gave birth to a set of twins, John and Joan.

The family attends the First Christian Church in Dawson Springs. - *Submitted by Amy Ausenbaugh*

BACON

***A thorough search of marriage, deed and cemetery records indicates that Captain James Collins Bacon (June 13, 1839-Nov. 10, 1931) was the first Bacon to settle and live his entire life in Hopkins County. Moving to Madisonville from Frankfort, KY, prior to the outbreak of the Civil War, he married Sarah Frances Davis (May 24, 1844-June 7, 1934).

*Soon after his marriage in Nov. 1863, he recruited one hundred volunteers into a troop destined to become Company A, 17th Regiment Kentucky Cavalry, Union Forces. **As company commander he led this unit in many engagements in the Green River area, Bunker Hill, Hopkinsville and Lyon County. At war's end he worked in Department of Veterans Affairs. *Captain Bacon was to outlive all members of his Company with the exception of R.R. Graham who resided on South Seminary. Captain James and Sarah settled on Hanson Pike and had three children, Virgil Lawrence (June 27, 1866-Sept. 19, 1946), Molly Jane, and Kassey.

In 1888 Virgil married Dixie Brasher (Nov. 3, 1868-Mar. 10, 1931) daughter of Dr. Alonzo W. Brasher (July 1831-Jan. 1919) and Emily Cansler Brasher (July 1831-Nov. 1922) and built a home at 165 N. Seminary (now owned by Mrs. B.C. Bacon, Sr.). Serving as Madisonville Postmaster for fourteen years, Virgil, a staunch Republican and Presbyterian, later owned a general store in Mortons Gap, commuting daily via interurban train known as The Little Dinky. Dixie and Virgil had three children, Brasher Collins Bacon, Sr. (Jan 28, 1892-Feb. 7, 1959), Sarah and Bessie Mae.

In 1916 Brasher, Sr., married Frances Lorene Majors (Oct. 9, 1896/—) daughter of Joseph Alexander Majors (Nov. 22, 1870-Dec. 22, 1930) and Eula Lee Baker Majors (Apr. 23, 1877-June 28, 1953).

Brasher, Sr., a foremost ornithologist in Kentucky, along with Dr. L.O. Pindar and Dr. Gordon Wilson, founded the Kentucky Ornithological Society in April 1923. In the early 1920's he also organized the Spring Lake Fishing Club and Wildlife Sanctuary, a unique private club subscribed to by nature lovers and fishermen of the county.

An employee of Madisonville Post Office for over forty-four years, Bird Egg (nickname by close friends) and Fan Bacon had two sons, Brasher Collins Bacon, Jr. (Oct. 6, 1921/—) and Frank Majors Bacon (Oct. 2, 1927/—). (When B.C. was born he had ten living grand and great-grandparents and vivid memories of nine of them.)

B.C. Jr. graduated from Madisonville High in 1940, and attended Western State College, Bowling Green, KY, prior to Army service in 1943. Two years were spent in France and Germany with 90th Infantry Division, General George Patton's 3rd Army.

On Apr. 30, 1948, he married Nadine Lambert (Oct. 4, 1924/—) daughter of Eulis Grant Lambert (Feb. 19, 1896-Nov. 6, 1956) and Rubie Lois West Lambert (Aug. 23, 1900/—) of Providence, KY. B.C. and Nadine moved to East Lansing, MI where he studied Forestry at Michigan State Univ. Moving to New Albany, IN after graduation in 1950, he followed a career in hardwood lumber production and sales and presently owns and operates with Nadine and son, Mark, B.C. Bacon Hardwood Company.

B.C. and Nadine have three children, Deborah Ann (Jan. 5, 1952), Mark Lambert (Oct. 1, 1953) and Emily Marie (Sept. 7, 1958). Deborah and husband Robert Alexander Minnich, Jr. (Aug. 6, 1950) have two children, Amanda Suzanne (Oct. 13, 1979) and Robert Alexander III (Mar. 30, 1981) *Sources *Family Bible Mollie Bacon Ashby, **History of Kentucky, ***Filson Club, Louisville, Kentucky, * History of Madisonville, J.T. Gooch. - Submitted by Brasher C. Bacon , Jr.*

Four Bacon Generations, 1927. J.C. age 89 , V.L. age 62, B.C. Sr. age 35 and B.C. Jr. age 6

BADGETT

Benton and Lavinia Badgett were the parents of Jesse B., Noah, William B., Tennessee and Mary. All died, leaving no descendants except Noah. Jessie B. was at the Alamo and was elected by the soldiers to represent them at the signing of the Texas Republic. He left several days before the massacre. Jesse B. signed the Declaration of Independence of Texas.

Noah was born in Roy, N.C., (b. 7/7/1809, d. 8/22/1879) and moved to Tennessee around 1816. Records show Noah arrived in Little Rock, AR, in 1825. Thus starting the Badgett roots in Arkansas (Pulaski County). There is a Badgett township and school on the east side of Little Rock. Noah married Lucetta McLain on June 23, 1831, when she was 14 years old. Noah had 12 children, one of which was Dr. Ocus Killian (b. 12/25/1854, d. 6/16/1915).

Ocus married Julia Thomas (b. 7/28/1866, d. 8/24/1901) in 1885, having 6 children. Julia died in 1901, and the remaining 4 children all under 11 years of age (Russell Sr., Owen, Dorothy and Bentley) were raised by Julia's father (Dr. Abner D. Thomas) and her sister (Myra Bell). Dr. Abner was a surgeon during the Civil War and in 1883 opened and operated a cotton mill in Little Rock. As boys Russell, Sr. and Owen worked in the cotton mill for 29¢ per 10 hour day.

Russell Sr. (b. 12/25/1890, d. 8/23/1973) married Mary Rheaetta Rogers (b. 7/30/1893) on 8/12/1915. To this union 4 children were born, James Rogers, Russell Jr., Julia Elizabeth and Thomas Brown.

Russell and Mary Rheaetta (Rogers) Badgett on their 50th wedding anniversary

Russell Badgett, Sr., and his brother Bentley, operated Badgett Construction Company for many years (1920 to 1941). In 1941, his 4 children formed Badgett Mine Stripping Company and strip-mined bauxite in Arkansas and Georgia. In 1943, the company started strip mining coal east of Madisonville, KY, thus starting Badgett roots in Hopkins County. Through the years to date the Badgett's have continued in coal mining under various corporate names. In 1951 Russell Sr. opened Badgett Terminal, a rail to barge coal loading facility at Grand Rivers, KY. Russell Sr. operated the terminal until his death. He is survived today by his wife Mary Rheaetta (94), sister Dorothy (92), brother Bentley (90), his four children, 14 grandchildren, and 20 great-grand-children.

Russell Sr.'s three sons have played a major role in the coal industry in Western KY for the past 40 years. The last active corporation in coal mining is Sextet Mining Corporation formed by Russell Badgett, Jr., in 1962. Sextet was so named for the 6 children of Russell Jr. and Juanita Wadlington Badgett. The latest mine operated by Sextet is the West Hopkins mine near Coiltown in Hopkins County. Three of Russell Jr.'s sons (Russell III, Bentley II, and Joseph) are still active in coal mining in Hopkins County. Genealogy data gathered by Russell Sr. and Bentley I. -*Submitted by grandson Bentley Badgett II*

REV. LEWIS W. BAILEY

Lewis W. Bailey, b. Nov. 8, 1814, Hopkins County, KY, was a son of John Bailey and Martha Patsey Sisk, both from NC, who married Dec. 24, 1809, in Hopkins Co. His paternal grandparents were James Bailey and Parthenia (Bailey) Bailey, both born in VA.

The father died prior to Apr. 13, 1835, the date Martha (Sisk) Bailey was appointed guardian for: Lewis W., Ann, Emily, Matilda, William D., Sally C., and John G. Bailey, orphans of John Bailey, deceased. On Sept. 25, 1836, Martha Patsey Bailey married Hugh Kirkwood, Sr., b. about 1770, Ireland, a farmer in Richland area of Hopkins Co.

Lewis W. Bailey married Margaret Jane Christian on Oct. 12, 1837. They lived in Providence, then in Hopkins Co., now in Webster Co., where Lewis was a farmer. By 1845 he was a Baptist minister in Sharon Church (now First Baptist Church, Providence). About 1851, the family moved to MS for a while. Upon returning to Hopkins Co. they lived in the Silent Run area. After Hugh Kirkwood, Sr., died (1855), Martha (Sisk) Kirkwood lived with her son Lewis W. Bailey. She d. Aug. 8, 1872.

Lewis was a pastor of two other churches, Richland and Silent Run Baptist Churches, and active in Little Bethel Association of Baptists. He was moderator of the Association in 1861 and 1862 and preached the opening sermon for the 1862 annual meeting. After his death, Aug. 18, 1870, Little Bethel messengers passed a resolution as a tribute to his twenty-five years as a minister which was included in the 1870 minutes. Historian John H. Spencer wrote in 1885 that his preaching gifts were not great, but he used them diligently, and made them useful in the Master's cause and that he was a good man much esteemed by his brethren.

Children of Lewis W. Bailey and Margaret Jane Christian which can be accounted for were: Elizabeth K., Martha Jane, Eusibia Ann, John H. (or A), William J. and Lewis, J. (b. 1858, d. 1862).

Elizabeth "Betty" K. (b. Nov. 5, 1840; d. Jan. 15, 1867) a teacher, married (1) May 16, 1861, Rutherford L. Laffoon (b. 1836; d. Feb. 8, 1864) and (2) Dec. 17, 1865, Sidney T. Morrow.

Martha Jane (b. 1843, d. May 7, 1932) married May 20, 1878, James S. Veazey, farmer in Johnson Island neighborhood and attended Johnson Island Baptist Church. They raised Casper Riggins, whose mother died when he was an infant. Years later Casper, his wife, and two children drowned when a hurricane hit Florida, where they lived.

Eusibia Ann (b. about 1848, d. Nov. 19, 1899) married Rufus Owen Kirkwood. (See Rufus Owen Kirkwood) Relatives say Margaret (Christian) Bailey was buried on the Kirkwood lot at OddFellows Cemetery, Madisonville.

John H. (or A) (b. Sept. 19, 1851, Hopkins Co.) was known as "Uncle Doc." In 1871 he was given up for dead and miraculously revived. This experience influenced him to become a physician. He moved to Sturgis in 1870 and began practicing medicine in Union Co. He married Mattie Christian and had one son, Lewis Christian Bailey, called "Lute." After Mattie died John married "Sis" Cooksey.

William J. (b. about 1854 in MS) married Mollie W. Slaton in Hopkins Co. on May 23, 1876. They had Claude, Myrtis, and Lewis Rupert Bailey, who were going to school in Madisonville in 1898. Source: Family Bible, Family history, minutes of Little Bethel Association, A HISTORY OF KENTUCKY BAPTISTS, VOL. I & II, Spencer, 1885 and other documents. - *Submitted by Mary Nell Whitsell Oates*

DR. E. SAMUEL BAKER

Dr. Ephraim Samuel Baker, grandfather of the late S. James Baker, 262 Sugg Street, Madisonville, was an ear, eye, nose, and throat specialist who built a home at 333 S. Scott Street and lived there during his lifetime. The street was called Baker Street until 1921, when it was changed to Scott Street.

James's father, Dr. Samuel James Baker Sr. only child of Dr. E. S. Baker and wife Sallie Douglas both formerly of Muhlenberg Co., raised his family of two sons, S. James Baker Jr. and Ephraim Bernerd (Buddy) Baker and a daughter Gladys Douglas in the Scott Street home.

The family name was Studebaker. Five brothers settled in South Bend, IN, where they had a wagon manufacturing business which later became the Studebaker Automobile Business.

A big museum and National Studebaker Association had been formed. S. James Baker is a member. A family reunion is held each year.

During the Civil War, two of the brothers were Southern sympathizers. They fought for the Confederacy and went to court and had their name changed to Baker.

Dr. Ephraim Samuel Baker was born in Muhlenberg Co. in 1840. The family moved to Hopkins Co. when he was very young.

His life as a doctor was very interesting. At a church service east of town (Liberty Church) a fight took a place on the church lot. He got a kerosene lamp from the church and sewed up a number of knife wounds by the light of the lamp.

After the death of his wife, he turned to the hobby of violin-making and produced several very fine copies of the famous Stradivarius violins of the 1700's. He got some of the wood from England. Some of the wood was 100 years old.

Professor J.J. Glenn's Madisonville newspaper reported Dr. Baker completed his first violin Apr. 30, 1903. It was called a gem. He completed seven violins. Several were on display at Sory and Offutt Drug Store downtown Madisonville. He had his name in all of them. One was played in Carnegie Hall and the tone quality was excellent. He, his son, and grandson S. James Baker were great hunters and fisherman also. -*Submitted by Josephine Baker*

JAMES BAKER

James Baker (1761-1833) was born in England around 1761. He was of English and Welsh decent. He came to this country before the Revolutionary War and settled in Virginia. His brothers were Caleb, Dixon and Elijah.

James entered the war at the age of 15 as a private in the Second Virginia State Regiment and rose to the rank of Sergeant. He suffered greatly at Valley Forge from the cold and hunger.

He received, from the state of Virginia, a land grant of 1000 acres just west of what is now Richland. In 1972 he married Sarah Davis, a double first cousin of Jefferson Davis. From this marriage there were six boys, Richard, the oldest - born about 1798, Dixon, William, Caleb, Elijah and John, and five girls, Mahala, Harriett, Thurza, Elizabeth and Mary.

James served in the War of 1812 in the First Kentucky Volunteer Regiment and he also served in the Company of Kentucky Mounted Rifleman. Although he lived to a ripe old age, he suffered all of his life from the effects of privation and exposure incident to the Revolutionary War. During his closing years his mind became clouded and he lived over and over again the scenes of the War. He died in 1833 and the Daughters of The American Revolution placed a monument at the grave site on the family farm.

His son, William, great grandfather of James G. Baker, married Mary Whitfield in 1836. William remained in this area while most of the other descendants migrated west. William had eleven children. In 1863 he was elected Sheriff of Hopkins Co., serving during the Civil War. He was Sheriff when the courthouse burned. He died in 1869 and is buried just south of Richland.

Franklin Pearce (Pearl), son of William, was born in 1852. In 1875 he married Cornelia Osburn, daughter of Randal Talbot Osburn. They had eight children. Falcon, the oldest, married Myrtle Golladay in 1909. Eula married Joe Majors, Charlie married Claude Ford, Ethel married Oliver Weir, Modra married Frank Roark, Talborne married Olga Powell, Robbie married Claude Allen, Susie married John Powell. Cornelia, grandmother of James G., had the first appendectomy in Hopkins Co. The surgery was performed on her kitchen table.

Falcon Olero Baker, was a founder of Baker and Hickman Department Store. His career began when he bought an interest in E.J. Ashby in 1901. There were two previous locations of the store prior to their move in 1918 to the present building. Falcon was also president of Farmers National Bank from 1912 to 1918. He and Myrtle Golladay had two sons, James and Falcon Jr.

James married Anne Priest in 1944 and they have James G. Baker, Jr., (Jay), William Randolph (Randy) and Mary Holland. Jay married Suzanne Purdy and they have James G. Baker III, Elizabeth Holland, and William Peery. Randy married Jacqueline Neibert and they have twin daughters, Jennifer Anne and Janice

Alicia. Mary first married Miller McPherson and after divorce married David Benin. They have one daughter, Cynthia Faye.

Falcon, Jr., the other son, married Ernestine Magagna in 1938 and they have Charles Edwin and Nancy, neither of whom are married. - *Submitted by James G. Baker (1914-)*

BALDWIN-EADS

Stanley Baldwin, DMD, son of Roland and Stella Walker Baldwin of Campbellsville, KY, was born in Speck (Taylor Co.), KY Nov. 9, 1930. A graduate of Campbellsville H.S. in 1949, he attended Campbellsville Junior College until the activation of his National Guard Unit in the Korean Conflict in which he served from 1951 to 1952. He entered the Univ. of Louisville (KY) in 1953 and graduated from its School of Dentistry in 1957.

Stanley and Charlotte Eads Baldwin

He began his current dental practice in Madisonville (Hopkins Co.), KY in 1957. President of his class and president of Delta Sigma Delta professional fraternity while in dental school, he is a past chairman of the Official Board and past Lay Leader of the United Methodist Church of Madisonville. In 1984, he was selected as Outstanding Alumnus of the Univ. of Louisville's School of Dentistry.

He married Charlotte Ann Eads on Jan. 5, 1951, the daughter of Edward Rouse and Maxine Cook Eads of Campbellsville (Taylor Co.), KY. Charlotte was born Jan. 21, 1932, and is a 1949 graduate of Campbellsville H.S., a 1951 graduate of Campbellsville Junior College (KY), and a 1974 graduate of the Univ. of Evansville, with a bachelor of science degree in Urban Affairs. They are the parents of two sons: Stuart Roland Baldwin, DMD, born Apr. 16, 1952, Ben Eads Baldwin, DMD, born Sept. 12, 1959. They have one grandson, Adrian Eads Baldwin, born Sept. 8, 1979, son of Stuart Baldwin.

Charlotte is former Secretary of the Natural Resources and Environmental Protection Cabinet of Kentucky (1983-87) in the administration of Governor Martha Layne Collins; former mayor of the City of Madisonville (1978-83); former Co-Chairman of Governor John Y. Brown Jr.'s Commission for Full Equality (1982-83); former president of the Kentucky Municipal League (1981); former president of The Garden Club of Kentucky, Inc. (1975-77); and is currently a vice-president of First Kentucky Trust Company of Louisville, KY.

She is a member of the Board of Overseers of the Univ. of Louisville, the Advisory Board of Madisonville Community College, the Board of Directors of the Governor's Scholars Program, and a member of the Selection Committee for Kentucky's Distinguished Student Recognition and Scholarship Award Program.

A recipient of the 1984 Outstanding Alumnus Award of the Univ. of Evansville and the 1984 Outstanding Alumnus Award of Campbellsville College (KY), she also received the 1982 Woman of Achievement Award of the Kentucky Federation of Business and Professional Women, the 1981 Tri-State Mayor of the Year Award of the Evansville Freedom Festival, a 1980 Fellowship for Public Administrators of the National Endowment for the Humanities, and the 1974 Woman of the Year Award of the Madisonville Lions Club.

The Baldwins are members of First United Methodist Church in Madisonville. *Submitted by Charlotte Baldwin*

BANDY-ALLEN

Georgia Mary Allen and Harold Bennett Bandy were married Dec. 16, 1948 in Greenville, KY.

Georgia was born Feb. 24, 1930, near Greenville, in Muhlenberg Co. She was the oldest daughter of James Floyd and Virginia Park Allen. Floyd (Nov. 7, 1895-Mar. 25, 1979) was born in DuBois, PA, to Samuel and Emma Hanna Fye Allen. Virginia Park was born July 18, 1906, near Greenville, KY, to Charles K. and Laura Jane Holland Park. Virginia has one surviving brother, Rev. George D. Park and two deceased brothers: Walter and Otho. Another daughter was born to Floyd and Virginia Allen, Margaret Jane Allen Pearson.

Harold and Georgia Bandy

Harold was born Apr. 27, 1928, in the Weir Community of Muhlenberg Co. to Shelby Eugene (Sept. 16, 1903-Sept. 9, 1967) and Bessie Pamela Heltsley Bandy (Mar. 26, 1903-Sept. 3, 1975). Harold's surviving brothers are James Gerald, Adrian, Morris, and one sister, Shirley Nell Gardner.

Georgia attended Greenville Elementary and High School, graduating in 1948.

Harold attended Hardison Grade School and Graham High School. He joined the U.S. Navy at the age of seventeen, serving two years sea duty in the South Pacific. He graduated from Kentucky School of Mortuary Science in Louisville, KY, and became a licensed Funeral Director and Embalmer in 1951.

Harold and Georgia purchased the Gunn Funeral Home in Nortonville, KY. At the time Harold was the youngest funeral director and embalmer in the state of Kentucky to own an uninherited funeral business. (The Bandy family were farmers.) Georgia became a licensed Funeral Director in 1955.

Harold and Georgia have four children: Michael Bennett (July 11, 1950) married (Sept. 9, 1978) Myrl Elaine Wilkerson (July 24, 1952-May 1, 1985) only daughter of Daril and Virginia Wilkerson, Mortons Gap, KY. They have two children: Michael Scott and Laura Leigh. Michael is a licensed funeral director, embalmer, and partner in the Bandy Funeral.

Linda Jane (Jan. 21, 1953) married (Oct. 15, 1971) Roger Davis Faulk (Mar. 31, 1951) son of Omer and Margaret Faulk, Mortons Gap, KY. They have one daughter: Shelly Lynn.

Robert Allen (July 12, 1954) married (Apr. 6, 1973) Sheila Faye Young (Aug. 13, 1954) daughter of Cleo Young, St. Charles, KY, and Nell Johnson, Hopkinsville, KY. They have two children: Ryan Allen and Amy Michele.

Mary Beth (July 17, 1955) married (Dec 4, 1976) Robert Jerome Hand (Sept. 25, 1952) son of Jerome Hand, Clarksville, TN and Ann Martin, Madisonville, KY. They have two children: Robert Jerome II and Kendal Marie. - *Submitted by Georgia Bandy*

BANKS-HAYES

Helen Elizabeth Hayes, the fifth child, born to Mayme Pritchett Hayes and Charles Richard Hayes of Anton, Hopkins County, KY. Attended public schools of Madisonville, KY, graduated valedictorian from Rosenwald High School in 1938. Bachelor of Arts from Kentucky State Univ., Frankfort, KY. Received the Master of Education degree from Wayne State Univ., Detroit, MI. Further studies at the Univ. of Kentucky, Lexington, KY; Murray State Univ., Murray, KY; Western Kentucky Univ., Bowling Green, KY. Former high school teacher and counselor. Taught in the Madisonville, KY, public schools; Earlington, KY, school system, retired Hopkinsville High School counselor, Hopkinsville, KY. Named Outstanding Secondary Educator of America, 1974. Former member Examination Advisory Team for the Commonwealth of Kentucky. Member of the Wesley Chapel Christian Methodist Episcopal Church, Madisonville. Member of Delta Sigma Theta Sorority. Married Robert Banks, Hopkinsville, KY. A graduate of Kentucky State Univ. Frankfort, KY. Graduate work at the Univ. of Kentucky, and Univ. of Louisville. Former Attucks High School teacher, Hopkinsville, KY. World War II Veteran. Retired from the U.S. Postal Service. Member of Alpha Phi Alpha Fraternity.

Helen and Robert Banks have one child, a son, Robert Darryl Banks, born Madisonville, KY. Darryl, as commonly called, attended early elementary school in Madisonville, KY. Graduated from Hopkinsville High School, in 1968. Magna Cum Laude graduate of Coe College, Cedar Rapids, Iowa. Further studied at Argonne National Laboratory, near Chicago, IL. Darryl is Hopkinsville, Kentucky's first Rhodes Scholar and Kentucky's first Black, 1972. Attended Oxford University,

Darryl Banks and Helen Hayes Banks

Oxford, England. Read for Doctorate Degree in Molecular Biophysics. Has publications in several international scientific journals. Named Outstanding Young Kentuckian, 1968. To date, Darryl is Hopkinsville's only Presidential Scholar, named by President Lyndon Johnson, 1968. Received Governor's Merit Award, 1968. A Phi Beta Kappa, Phi Kappa Phi, member of Lambda Chi Alpha Fraternity, Who's Who Among American Colleges and Universities. A Kentucky Colonel.

Darryl was named Congressional Science Fellow in 1976, by the American Association for the Advancement of Science. Worked with Senate Subcommittee on Health under Senator Edward Kennedy. Represented the United States at the World Health Organization, Geneva, Switzerland, 1980. Worked as Special Assistant to the Administrator of Research and Development with Environmental Protection Agency during President Carter's administration. Panel member on Environment Protection in Tokyo, Japan. Worked as a science researcher for Rand Corporation, Washington, D.C. Presently, Deputy Commissioner of New York State Department of Environmental Conservation. A member of the Board of Trustees for Coe College, Cedar Rapids, Iowa. Committee member for selecting future Rhodes Scholars.

Darryl's wife is the former Margery Baker of Baltimore, MD. A Phi Beta Kappa graduate of the Univ. of Michigan, Ann Arbor, MI. Has a Woodrow Wilson designate Law Degree from Yale University School of Law, New Haven, CT. Served on the legal staff of former United States Senator Dick Clark of Iowa. Former Minority Chief Counsel to Subcommittee on Patents and Trademarks for Senator Howard Metzenbaum of Ohio. Presently, Staff Counsel Chief for New York Department of Public Service. A Kentucky Colonel.

Darryl and Margery have two sons, Adam and David; one daughter, Lauren. -*Submitted by Helen Banks*

BARNES-LAM

B.B. Barnes and Robbie Lam were married Jan. 18, 1919, in the old Hopkins County Court House. B.B's parents were Holly Barnes and Candis Villines Barnes of the Dalton community. Robbie's parents were Dixon Lam and Cora Hancock Lam of the Fiddle Bow neighborhood.

B.B. and Robbie operated a mom and pop grocery for over 50 years in Madisonville, KY. They retired in 1974. B.B died Aug. 31, 1981 and Robbie died Dec. 7, 1987. Both are buried

B.B. and Robbie Barnes

at Oddfellows Cemetery in Madisonville. They had two daughters, Pauline and Ruth Helen.

Pauline was born Mar. 26 1920. She married Cecil Prowse of Nortonville on Apr. 6, 1942. They are both retired and live in Madisonville. Cecil's parents were Roscoe and Opal Prowse of Nortonville.

Cecil and Pauline have one daughter, Modia Ann. She was born Aug. 29, 1946, and is married to Jerry Adams. They live in Princeton, KY. Jerry is a state detective. Modia is cashier and secretary of the board at the Farmers Bank in Princeton. They have two children, Kristy Lynne and Clint Bradley. Kristy is married to Michael Petus of Princeton, KY. He is a graduate of U.K. in Lexington and is manager at the Farm Agriculture in Lexington. Kris is a student at U.K. Clint is a sophmore at Murray State Univ.

Ruth Helen was born Oct. 3, 1923. She and Robert Graham Tucker were married Sept. 12, 1943. They live at 134 Waddill Avenue, Madisonville. Bob's parents were James Tucker and Hortense Graham Tucker. Bob and Ruth have two sons (twins) born Oct. 17, 1946, James Ray and Roy Gilbert.

Ray is married to Sandra Bryant of Greenville, KY. They were married Aug. 27, 1967. They have two sons, John Robert and Bryan Edwards. John was born Aug. 28, 1969. He is a freshman at U.K. in Lexington. Bryan was born July 3, 1972. He is a student at Madisonville North H.S. Ray is area manager for Ladshaw Explosives Co. Sandra is Registrar at Madisonville Community College.

Roy married Jamie Mitchell of Frankfort, KY, on June 1, 1968. They have three sons, Graham, Steven and Nathan. Graham was born in England on May 17, 1971, while Ray was with the Air Force in England. He is a junior at Madisonville North High School. Steven was born Feb. 18, 1975. He is a student at Browning Springs School. Nathan was born Apr. 6, 1979. He goes to school at Anton. Roy is sales manager for Dr. Pepper Bottling Co. and Jamie is a school teacher at Browning Springs School.

Bob retired from Kentucky Bank in 1984. He was vice-president and cashier. Ruth Helen retired in 1981 after 30 years teaching in the Hopkins County School System. -*Submitted by Harold Ledbetter*

BARNHILL

The tradition of the Barnhills coming to America is that the original emigrant was banished from Ireland for publishing a rebel paper, came to Baltimore, MD, and was followed a few months later by his wife who brought with her the printing press and the children.

James Byrd Barnhill was born on Dec. 24, 1804, in Martin County, NC. He was one of five children born to John Barnhill (1781-1845) and Disey Barnhill (- 1852). James Byrd Barnhill (1804-1879) married Levinia Emaline Wynns (1890-1884) on Apr. 2, 1826. Born to this union were the following children: Mary E. (1827-1862), John Daniel (1829-1915), Sarah M. (1831-1852), Artemissa (1834-1913), William D. H. (1836-1837), Josephine (1838-1881), Luticia (1841-1873), Levina E. (1843-1916), Lucy Ann (1846-1847), James W. (1848-), and Susan B. (1852-).

James Byrd Barnhill was married in his native state where he farmed until 1836 when he removed with his wife and family to Henry Co., TN, where he remained for one year. He then came to what is now Webster County, KY, then part of Hopkins Co., bought wild land near Providence and improved a farm upon which he resided until his death on Oct. 30, 1879, in his 75th year. He was buried in the Barnhill Cemetery which was located near the home site. He and his wife were married for 53 years and were members of the United Baptist Church.

John Daniel Barnhill, the first son of James Byrd Barnhill, was employed on his father's farm until he attained his majority when his father gave him a partially improved farm, which he afterward sold. He then bought another farm adjoining, but in Nebo District. He was married on May 12, 1853, to Nancy Frances James in Hopkins County, KY. She was born in Davidson County, TN, on Apr. 23, 1832, and died Aug. 27, 1895, in Madisonville, KY. He was a member of the United Baptist Church and his wife of the Methodist Episcopal Church South. He was an earnest advocate of the temperance cause. To the union of John Daniel Barnhill and Nancy Frances James was born the following children: Willie James (1854-1916), Emma (1856-1938), John Henry (1858-1928), Charley Wright (1861-1898), Sallie Agness (1862-1942), David Lee (1866-1946), Edward Byrd (1868-1913), and Nannie (1870-1944).

David Lee Barnhill

David Lee Barnhill, the fourth son of John Daniel Barnhill, was farmer and horse breeder on the Oak Ridge Farm in Hopkins Co. on the Old Dalton Road. He was married on Mar. 25, 1894, to Emmaline Ramsey who was born on Mar.. 18, 1873, in Webster Co. in the Liberty area near Providence and died Dec. 19, 1956, in Providence. They were members of the First Baptist Church in Providence. The church building was located on land that had been donated by his father. To the union of David Lee Barnhill and Emmaline Ramsey were born seven children: (1) George Daniel (1895-1979) who married Anna Marie Bidwell on Feb. 12, 1923. Their children are Willa Mae, Margaret Lou, Richard Lee, James Edward, and Gary Dean. (2) Addie Rebecca (1896-present) who married Benjamin Ford Barker on Dec. 23, 1922. Their children are Martha Lee, David Barnhill, and Mary Ford. (3) Charley Edward (1898-1971) married Pearl Snow on Aug. 5, 1926. Their child is Emma Belle. (4) Mary Lillian (1900-1978) married Bryan Ford on Dec. 23, 1924. They had no children. (5) Sue Jernigan (1903-1985) married Paul Marcus Hill on Nov. 6, 1930. Their children are Suzanne and Nancy Alice. (6) David Ramsey (1907-1979) married Vera Louise Rich on July 25, 1931. Their child is David Martin. (7) Emma Lou Barnhill (1910-present) is unmarried.

The seventh generation of the Barnhill family is presently living in Hopkins Co. -*Submitted by David Barnhill Barker*

WILLIAM EDWARD BARRON

William Edward Barron (10-10-1844)-(7-2-1887), the son of William A. Barron and Mary A. Puryear, whose grandfathers were John Barron and Hezekiah Puryear, was the father of Wallace Henry Barron I. He and his brothers and sisters were orphans before April 1854, as the will of Hezekiah Puryear revealed. The children: 1. Thomas (who died in Civil War of measles) was not married. 2. William Edward, a Confederate soldier, fought in battle of Missionary Ridge, Chattanooga, TN. 3. Mary Eliza, wife of Tom Forkner. 4. Charlotte Ann, wife of Mr. Ferguson (lived in IL). 5. Laura married Simm Hobgood. 6. Isadora or Dora married Dock Hill Jones.

Wallace Henry Barron I in 1899 at the age of 21

William Edward was discharged from the army with $5, with which he bought a mule to ride home. Dec. 4, 1868, he married Althea Jane Winstead (3-1-1849)-(4-11-1909), daughter of Manley Taylor Winstead (4-12-1820)-(4-15-1907) and Sarah Jane Winstead (7-10-1822)-(12-30-1891) and great granddaughter of Mandley Winstead, Revolutionary soldier. Their children were: 1. William Taylor (12-31-1869)-(1-10-1958), married Agnes Hoffman. 2. Bernice (3-11-1873) - (3-4-1905) m. William Vincent Cox. 3. Wallace Henry I (4-30-1878)-(1-19-1919) m. Mattie Lee Cox. 4. Allie Winstead (6-15-1887)-(1973) m. Gifford Hamilton. William Edward owned 135 acres 3 miles north of Nebo, KY, on which was a comfortable home and a nice orchard. At age 52 he drowned in a pond at home rescuing his wife.

Wallace continued managing the family farm. At age 24, he married (10-19-1902). He and Mattie built their home on the family farm. Around 1908, he moved his family to Madisonville, KY, to manage the dry goods store opened on West Center by father-in-law H.R. Cox. During this time, Mattie was busy with her painting. She majored in art while attending Hamilton College for Girls at Lexington, KY, in 1900.

In 1912, the store was sold and they returned to Nebo. That same year, route #2 mail delivery was established and Wallace was appointed carrier. The family moved back to the farm. Mattie and a hired hand managed the farm while Wallace began his new duties. In good weather, he used a horse and cart, but in winter he delivered on horseback. The winter of 1917-1918 was a real hardship: "the big snow." Drifts were higher than his head, when he was seated on his horse. This was also the year the influenza epidemic raged. In Jan. of 1919, Wallace died of influenza and pneumonia.

These are the children of Wallace and Mattie Barron; Nannie Ruth m. Paul I. Morrow, with issue Anne Mae and Paul Chesterfield, who m. Elaine Dunn. Nannie Ruth m. 2nd Chester Schultz, with issue Patricia Mitchell and Marilyn Faul.

William Chander m. 1st Gladys Baker, with issue, Mary Ellen Low and Barbara Jean Detwiler. William Chandler, m. 2nd Nancy Porter Schmetzer.

Sarah Wallace, teacher 43 years, in Hopkins County.

Herbert Edward m. Mildred Meighan, with issue, Estelle Leigh Huechteman and Jacqueline Freeman.

James Sory m. Jonell Vaughn, with issue, LaLena Utley, James Michael, Stephen Lee, and Terry Joe.

Wallace Henry II m. Rebecca James, with issue, Wallace Henry III and William Edward.

Jane Rice m. Gerald Peyton, with issue, Gerald Richard and Sarah Ann Oxford.

Mary Elizabeth m. Paul D. Wildman, issue, Jane Ellen Watson, Elizabeth Ann Lamb, and Paula Lee Linville.

Anna Grace d. 1-20-1919.

James Sory Barron, a veteran of U.S. Army, W.W. II, South Pacific. W.H. Barron II (H'e) a veteran of U.S. Navy, W.W. II, South Pacific. *Source: Family Bible and DAR Record. -Submitted by Sarah Barron*

BARTON-MARTIN

Trent Barton was born July 15, 1926, in the home his parents bought two years before, at Richland, KY. He was the only son of Wesley and Essie Trent Barton. (See Barton-Trent)

Growing up in the 1920s and 30s, Trent helped his dad run the farm, raising corn and hay, and caring for the cattle and horses. He remembers riding the train to Dawson Springs as quite a treat, and one of the tragedies of the community was the morning Dr. Setzer was hit by a train at the crossing near the Richland School.

Modell and Trent Barton

Trent rode his pony back and forth to Cavanah School and remembers one day in particular. He and Edith Richards, who was teaching at Cavanah and boarding with the Bartons at the time, were riding home after school. A snowstorm had struck during the day, and as evening approached, the temperature was dropping, the wind and blowing snow were bitter cold. What was usually a pleasant ride, became a very long, uncomfortable test of endurance. They rode, crouched in the saddles, dismounting at times to walk in the shelter of the horses and bury their hands in the manes to warm their stiff fingers, finally reaching the Barton home and a warm fire. Besides Cavanah, Trent attended Richland School and graduated from Dalton High School in 1945.

On May 2, 1953, Trent Barton and Modell Martin were married in Springfield, TN by the pastor of the First Baptist Church.

Modell, the daughter of Talburn and Ova Lee Maddox Martin of the Silent Run area, attended Silent Run School and graduated from Dalton High School in 1945. She worked for the Bell Telephone Company (later became South Central Bell) until she retired.

Trent farmed with his father and contracted school buses (owned and furnished buses) and furnished drivers for the county schools, as well as driving the Richland School bus from 1949-52.

Trent and Modell lived in the rock house at the corner of Suthard Drive and Princeton Pike in Madisonville for 18 years. Then after his parents went into a nursing home, they moved out to the family farm at Richland.

Trent and Modell have no children, but spend time looking to the needs of several shut-in friends, as well as Trent's mother in the nursing home.

In pleasant weather, Modell spends time caring for their lawn and working a garden, both of which she greatly enjoys. They are members of Richland Missionary Baptist Church, where Trent serves as a Deacon.

Trent is now serving his 6th year as Magistrate of District 7 and owns an interest in a herd of registered Angus cattle. *Submitted by Trent Barton*

BARTON-TRENT

Philmore and Jane Walker Barton, residing in the western-most part of Hopkins County, were the parents of ten children, one of whom was Wesley Barton, born July 28, 1890 near Dalton, KY. On Sept. 5, 1913, Wesley married Essie Trent, the only daughter of Edward Lambert and Martha Pendgraph Trent.

Edward Trent was a carpenter and worked on a number of buildings in our county, one of which was the first Dalton Baptist Church. In later years, Edward and Martha moved to the Richland community where they owned and operated Trent's General Store and their farm on Highway 70 until Edward's death Oct. 8, 1936.

Wesley and Essie Barton at the Dawson Springs Cliffs about 1912

The Trent's daughter, Essie, became a teacher and taught at several area schools, Dockery, Elam, Jennings, Leach, Richland, Cavanah, and Henson. She was teaching at Richland in 1913 when she married Wesley Barton. While Essie taught, Wesley farmed, spending many happy hours caring for their horses, cattle and crops. The couple spent as much of their spare time together as they could, occasionally managing an excursion to the Dawson Springs Cliffs.

In 1924, Wesley and Essie bought the Charlie Osburn farm, where their only child, a son, Trent was born July 15, 1926. (See Barton-Martin)

When Wesley's health failed and his care became too much for Essie alone, he moved to a local nursing home. Essie loved Wesley dearly and would not stay on the farm without him, so she packed her things and moved to the nursing home too.

Wesley went to be with our Lord Dec. 5, 1986 and Essie still resides in the room she and Wesley shared for so long. - *Submitted by Trent Barton*

THOMAS H. BARTON SR.

Thomas H. Barton Sr. born 1838 in possibly Hopkins County, KY. His parents are unknown but both were born in North Carolina.

Thomas H. Sr. married Judia A. Wicks (born 1840, Kentucky, her parents are unknown as well) on May 15, 1856, in Hopkins County, KY. Their children were all born in Hopkins County, KY, they were: Lennie C. born 1859; William A. born 1860; Peyton L. born 1862; Thomas H. Jr. born 1864; Joseph T. born 1866; Martha Jane born 1868; John Edward born 1870; Harrison F. born 1872 and Wilburn F. born 1876.

Thomas H. Sr., was possibly living in the household of Moses W. Southerd in the 1850's before his marriage. Thomas H. Sr. a farm laborer, possibly rented or worked on different farms, for he was in Charleston in 1860, and Madisonville, Fisher Springs District, in the 1870's and 1880's.

Their son John Edward was in Bonham, Fannin County, TX, in 1894. Here John Edward married Louella D. Brantley (born Apr. 23, 1880, Princeton, Caldwell County, KY, her parents were Marion M. Brantley and Armintast (Minty) Gregston) and on May 6, 1924.

John Edward and Louella Barton children were: Nethan Monroe born 1894; Eula Burchie born 1900; Rosie Lee born 1902; infant boy born and died date unknown; Alice Lee born 1906; Luther Larded born 1908; Harrison Fillmore born 1911; and Edith Snchnetha born 1914.

John Edward was like many people in his time going from one place to another looking for better land and a place where they could raise their children. John Edward lived in the following counties in Texas and Oklahoma. In Texas, Fannin County. In Oklahoma, Greer, Jackson (later became the same county), Cleveland, Johnson and Stephens Counties.

I do not know if Thomas H. Barton Sr. moved to Texas with his son John Edward, for 1880 is the last time I found him.

John Edward died Sept. 15, 1942, in Marlow, OK, and Louella (Brantley) Barton died May 22, 1954, also in Marlow, OK. - *Submitted by Helen Douglas*

HILIOUS E. BASHAM

Hilious E. Basham, one of 17 children, was born Nov. 12, 1884, in Hancock County, KY.

In 1910, he married Anna Kennedy and they were the parents of three children: a son, James, was killed in an auto accident in 1941; daughter Thelma Mahoney lives in IL; and daughter Mary Sanchez lives in Madisonville.

A lover of sports, Hilious and his 11 brothers banded together to comprise the Basham baseball team. He once played shortstop on a semi-pro baseball team. His greatest joy was watching his granchildren play softball.

As a young man he lived and worked in Arkansas, Florida, Iowa, Nebraska and Wisconsin. In Kentucky, he worked at Owensboro Ken-Rad plant and then for General Electric, retiring in 1949. He and Anna then operated a trailer park.

After Anna's death in 1973, Hilious lived with his daughters. He later was a resident at Senior Citizens Nursing Home in Madisonville.

Hilious was a member of the Blessed Mother Catholic Church. He died Aug. 9, 1985, in Hopkins County and was buried at Materdolorsa Cemetery in Owensboro. He is survived by one sister, his two daughters, 10 grandchildren and 12 great grandchildren. *For a photo of Hilious, see "Hopkins County Centenarians." Submitted by Dorothy Miller Shoulders.*

BASSETT

The Bassett family was a prominent family in Kentucky having lived here for many years, since the great grandparents of Amos Bassett came in the early 1800's.

Amos (1815-1899), the second son of Captain John Stout Bassett, served as Deputy Sheriff of Bracken County before coming to Hopkins County in 1841. He married Lucy Waller Nesbit on Sept. 20, 1842. They had eleven children: Lucien, George, William (Bud), Mark K., Elijah, Laura, Samuel, Jenny, Fannie, John and Jessie.

Jimmy and Josephine Baker at retirement party Dec. 30, 1975. Margaret Tapp Noe and H.D. Noe

(I) Lucien married Agnes Pritchett and his children were: James, Alvin Gordon and Mary Lee Bassett.

(II) George (1846-1914) was unmarried. George, William and Elijah owned a livery stable and saw mill in Hopkins Co. George had a contract to do the first paving of Madisonville streets.

(III) William (Bud), farmer and sawmill owner, married Josie Fugate. Their children were: Hirom, Lucy, Lizzie, Sammie, Cordie and Nina (1) Hirom married Ella Wilson and they had three children: (1a) Mary Ruth who married B.L. Hobgood, parents of Byron Lee Hobgood, Attorney, and Carolyn Williams (deceased). (1b) Hiram Jr., who married Mary Etta Beeny, parents of Michael and Beverly Bassett. (2) Lucy, unmarried, reared the family of her sister, Sammie Bassett Tapp (deceased). (3) Lizzie (1894-1910). (4) Sammie married Willis J. Tapp and their children were: (4a) W.R. (Bob) Tapp (deceased) married Mary Eleanor Huston. (4b) Josephine Tapp married Samuel James Baker (deceased). They had one daughter (deceased). (4c) Margaret Tapp married Hugh Davis Noe and had two children, Sarah Noe Davis and Sam Noe. (5) Cordie married James Rich. (6) Nina married Hal Jackson Tapp and their children were: (6a) Lucy Bassett Tapp married Walter C. Hopkins - children Thomas W. Hopkins, Louisville, KY, and Peggy Hopkins Landini, Washington, D.C. (6b) Betsy Tapp of Louisville, KY.

(IV) Mary K. married Dr. Mandley Winstead and their children were: Kate and Amos.

(V) Elijah married Mrs. Cordie Rover and at her death married Margaret Bull.

(VI) Laura (1855-1858)

(VII) Samuel married Mary Jones and had one child, Elizabeth, who married Fred

Earhart whose children were: Ann Earhart and Charles Earhart.

(VIII) Jenny married Yateman Johnson and had two childen: (1) Lucien married Myrtle Tucker and had four children - Sarah Alice, Ray, Frank and Roy. (2) Lucy married R.L. Ferguson.

(IX) Fannie married Ed Kirkwood and had three children: (1) George Bassett Kirkwood (married). (2) Willis Kirkwood. (3) Nan Kirkwood married Mr. Beard and at his death Mr. Shaw. One daughter, Frances, now deceased.

(X) John married Sally Morgan and their children were: (1) Fannie Waller married Lana Graham. (2) Mildred married Strother Branson. (3) Mary Ellen married Robert Nixon. (4) Elijah married Ruth Crick. (5) Sarah married Mr. Wilkerson.

(XI) Jessie married Alvin Sisk and had six children: (1) Samuel Bassett Sisk, (2) Bart Sisk, (3) Hanson Sisk, (4) Alvin Sisk, Jr., married Grace Jones, (5) Jessie Sisk married Ferguson Brown and (6) Louise Sisk married Mr. Newkirk. -*Submitted by Margaret Tapp Noe and Lucy Tapp Hopkins*

ELIJAH BASSETT

Elijah Bassett, who was born in Bracken County, KY, in 1813 was the son of Captain John Stout Bassett and Jane Rogerson. Elijah served as clerk for General Payne and later as deputy sheriff of Bracken County. He came to Hopkins County in 1841, but after five or six years returned to Bracken County where he served as sheriff and later operated a tavern in Brookville. In 1855 he returned to Hopkins County where he farmed near Anton. He married Mary O'Rear Pearl, daughter of John Margness Pearl and Sarah Ann Blackerby in Bracken County and they had five children who lived to be adults: Thomas Karr, John Amos, Sarah Jane, James F. and Gustavus Adolphus. Six children died young. Elijah was shot and killed near the end of the Civil War and his wife, who had been in poor health, died four months later in February, 1865. They are buried in the Bassett Cemetery near Anton.

Their oldest son, Thomas Karr Bassett, was in the Confederate Army and was taken prisoner while visiting his sick mother in October 1864. Despite being captured in uniform, he was executed in Hopkinsville after a drumhead court in reprisal for Confederate raids by Gen. Nathan Bedford Forrest. He was 25 years old and is buried in the family cemetery near Anton.

John Amos Bassett studied medicine under his uncle, Dr. James Bassett, and graduated from the medical department of the University of Louisville. He practiced medicine for many years in Providence. He married Virginia Wetzel and had a daughter, Frances. After the death of his first wife, he married Martha Frances Givens, also of Hopkins County, and they had four sons: John Thomas, James Gustavus, Maurice Kirby and Edgar Barbour Bassett. Dr. John Bassett died in 1912 at age 71.

Sarah Jane "Sallie" Bassett was born in 1853 and married Sylvester Haywood Williams. Their children were Sylvester, Mollie, Melissa, Atriss O'Rear, Martha and Amos. The Williams family lived near Providence and Sallie died in 1925.

James F. Bassett, who was born in 1852, died soon after his marriage to Helen Head Gist in 1891.

A separate article tells of Gustavus Adolphus Bassett, the youngest child of Elijah and Mary O'Rear Pearl Bassett. Submitted by Wm. Kerr Bassett

GUSTAVUS ADOLPHUS BASSETT

Gustavus Adolphus "Gus" Bassett, youngest child of Elijah Bassett and his wife, Mary O'Rear Pearl, was born 11 Aug. 1855 in Bracken County, KY. He came to Hopkins County when he was four months old. When he was nine, his father, who had served as sheriff in Bracken County, was shot and killed. Four months later his mother died and Gus then lived with his sister, Sallie Bassett Williams.

On 25 Feb. 1879, Gus married Misher Izora "Odie" Cunningham, daughter of Joseph Misher Cunningham and Mary Louisa Payne. Both of her parents died when she was very young and she was reared by uncle, Thomas Buford "Uncle Bufe" Payne. For the first years of their marriage, Gus and Odie lived on the Williams farm northeast of Providence but then bought their own farm on Clear Creek in Hopkins County. It was here they reared their children and lived for the next 48 years until his death on 10 Mar. 1929. Later Odie moved to Benton, IL, and lived with her daughter. She died there 7 Jan. 1961 at the age of 102.

Their children were James Payne, Edgar Karr, Jeff, John Corliss, Karr Pearl, Beryl O'Rear and Lawrence Rogers Bassett. James Payne Bassett was born 12 Dec. 1879 and married Nancy Macy Baker on 25 Sept. 1906. They had three children: James Baker, William Kerr and Marjorie. James Payne Bassett owned a livery stable in Providence and later had coal mines in Webster and Hopkins Counties. He was killed in a mine accident on 4 Nov. 1929. The next two little boys of Gus and Odie, "Little Eddie" and Jeff, died young.

They then had twin boys: John Corliss "Bill" and Karr Pearl Bassett, born 20 Sept. 1891. After World War I army service in the A.E.F., Bill worked for many years for St. Bernard and West Kentucky Coal Companies. Thereafter, he served as Postmaster in Earlington for over twenty years. He was commander of the Earlington American Legion Post and also served as District Commander of the Legion. He was one of the founders and served as president of the Brown Meadow Lake Fishing Club. He married Elizabeth Zona Hearin on 7 July 1925. She began teaching school when she was a teenager and received her degree many years later from West Kentucky University after attending summer school almost every year. She was a devoted and talented teacher and served in the Earlington schools for most of her 50 year teaching career. Bill died on 20 Aug. 1965 and Zona on 17 Feb. 1985. They had no children. Karr married Mina Marie Van Metre on 8 July 1917 and they spent most of their married life in Washington state. He was Tax Assessor in Spokane for many years. They had four children: Winston Adolphus, Eleanor Izora, Karlene Marie and Bette June. Karr died 24 Nov. 1863.

Beryl O'Rear Bassett, the only daughter of Gus and Odie, was born 28 Dec. 1893. She married on 5 Sept. 1914 Curtis E. Smith, who visited Providence as a member of the Benton, IL, Silver Cornet Band that played at the county fair. He became a lawyer and she worked in his abstract office for many years. They had two daughters, Berylene Bassett and Sue Carol. Beryl now lives with her daughter, Sue Smith Hawkins in Mobile, AL.

Lawrence Rogers Bassett was born on 23 Aug. 1896 and married Pauline Bullock on 3 Apr. 1923. They lived near Henderson, KY, where he had a large farm a few miles east of town. Lawrence died on 9 Feb. 1967. They had two children: Emma Jean and Robert Lawrence.

The G.A. "Gus" Bassett family. Front l to r: Bill, Gus, Beryl with Lawrence in front, Odie and Karr. Back l to r: Jim, Jeff Cunningham (Odie's brother) and his wife, Daisy.

Gus Bassett was a hard worker and a good farmer; however, he managed to utilize his love of hunting and fishing and his gregarious nature to supplement the income from the usual corn and tobacco crops. His fish nets on Weirs and Clear Creeks provided fish to "peddle" in town along with hams, vegetables and his famous watermelons and cantaloupes. He enjoyed socializing with his adult customers but he delighted even more having some "penny" melons for poor eager children who followed his wagon.

The Gus Bassett place on the Dalton Road was known for its hospitality. The annual family reunion brought Cunningham, Payne, Rogers, Smith, Tapp and other kin from Madisonville, Manitou and Nebo, but the Bassett farm was known best as a year- round gathering place for young people. The boys came to hunt and fish with the Bassett boys, and Beryl's friends came to see the boys. Gus Bassett was a tall strong man and his wife, Odie, was a tiny but energetic woman. She stayed busy cooking and feeding the company that was always there to enjoy the good food of the family dinner table. When she died at 102, people said that she was proof that "hard work never killed anyone." Gus was known not only to his children and grandchildren as "Pap" but also to the many young folk who made the Bassett farm their second home. He always said he had the best neighbors in the world: these included two land-owning Negro families, the Bishops and Rices.

Gus Bassett, a Democrat, a Mason and a

Baptist, was an honest, honorable, generous and hospitable man who, like his wife, Odie, enjoyed living and sharing. -*Submitted by Wm. Kerr Bassett*

JOHN STOUT BASSETT

Captain John Stout Bassett was born 22 June 1791 near Washington (formerly Bassett), PA, as his family migrated from Hunterdon County, New Jersey, to Kentucky. His parents were Amos and Susan Stout Bassett who were with General Symmes' party that came down the Ohio River to found Cincinnati. The Bassetts stopped at Limestone, now Maysville, and lived in Mason and Bracken Counties, KY. John served for 28 years as sheriff of Bracken County. In 1841 he and his family moved to Hopkins County where he bought a farm near Anton.

On 24 Mar. 1811 John Bassett married Jane Rogerson, daughter of William Rogerson, and they had eight children. They were Elijah, Amos, James, William P., Elizabeth, Susan, Emily and Jane Rogerson Bassett. Elijah is discussed in another article. William P. never married; Elizabeth married John Margness Pearl, Jr.; Susan married Lonny Niblick and Emily married William H. Hewlett. All four of these children died as young adults and are buried in the Bassett cemetery near Anton.

Amos Bassett was born 15 Sept. 1815 and married Lucy Waller Nesbit on 20 Sept. 1842. He had farms near Madisonville and members of this family have been prominent in Hopkins County since 1841. The children of Amos and Lucy were Lucien who married Agnes Pritchett, George never married, William "Bud" married Josie Fugate, Mary K. married Dr. Mandley B. Winstead, Elijah married Margaret Elizabeth Bull and then Mrs. Cordie Rover, Laura A. died young, Samuel married Mary Jones, Jenny married Yateman Johnson, Fannie Waller married Ed Kirkwood, John married Sally Morgan and Jessie married Alvin D. Sisk. The Amos Bassett family owned a large tract of land in Madisonville called "Bassett Hill." It ran from Price Street east across what is now Highway 41 and contained two family-owned livery stables, a sawmill and a slaughter house. George Bassett had the first contract to pave streets in Madisonville. The residence of Byron Hobgood on Price Street is on the site of the home of his great-grandfather, William "Bud" Bassett. Byron is President and his uncle, Hiram Bassett, is Secretary-Treasurer of the Bassett-Anton Community Cemetery Association.

James Bassett was the first of the family to come to West Kentucky. Soon after receiving his certificate to practice medicine in 1840, he rode westward to seek a location. He settled in Providence, then in Hopkins County. He married Frances America S. Given, daughter of Eleazer and Mary Eveline Savage Sittler Given. They had no children.

Jane Rogerson Bassett was born 23 May 1828 and married Joe Smith Thomas on 7 Feb. 1848. Their only daughter, Emma, married Henry Burle Williams and they had nine children. Jane and Joe Thomas lived in Hopkins County and are buried in the Bassett Cemetery near Anton. -*Submitted by Wm. Kerr Bassett*

BATES-LUTZ

Vicky Yvonne Lutz and William Stum Bates were united in marriage in 1979 in Sacramento, KY.

Vicky was born Apr. 5, 1955. She is the daughter of Mary Lou Duncan and Rev. Lona Ray Lutz. (See Lutz-Duncan)

Vicky graduated from North Hopkins High School in 1973. She received an Associate Degree in Nursing from Madisonville Community College in May 1987 and is presently employed at Regional Medical Center. Her hobbies include softball, swimming, and bicycle riding.

Vicky was formerly married to Kerry Bruce McCormick. They had one child, Christa Nichole, born Sept. 17, 1975.

William (Bill) was born Dec. 18, 1943. His parents are Mary Elizabeth Moore and Charles Stum Bates. Bill has one brother: Charles Floyd Bates, Sacramento, KY, and one sister: Lavinia (Cathy) Filiatreau of Bloomfield Hills, MI.

Bill attended Anton School and graduated from Madisonville High School in 1961. He also studied agriculture at Western College and Owensboro Wesleyn College.

Bill served two years in the U.S. Army, 1969-1971. He was in the Military Police stationed at Bangkok, Vietnam, during the Vietnam War. He was an expert marksman and won several awards for "Outstanding Trainer."

Bill is a self-employed farmer who enjoys the outdoors. He enjoys working on motors, riding motorcycles and deer hunting.

Vicky and Bill have two sons: William Chad Stum Bates (Jan. 1, 1980) and Adam Wade Bates (Feb. 10, 1981). They are members of Christ the King Church. -*Submitted by Retha Tarter*

BAYER-DAVIS

Anga Lou Davis and David Harold Bayer grew up as childhood sweethearts. On Aug. 30, 1970, they were married in the Apostolic church on Trim Street in Dawson Springs, KY.

Anga was born on Sept. 15, 1952. She is the daughter of Alga Mae Jackson and the late Louis Hershel Davis. Alga was born in Dec. 17, 1919. Hershel was born on Nov. 13, 1914 and died in 1983. Anga has one sister, Linda Kaye Lanham (born Dec. 9, 1942) and one brother, Hildon Maloey Davis (born Dec. 1, 1935).

Anga attended Dawson Springs High School and graduated in 1970. After graduation, she and David were married.

David was born on Mar. 9, 1950. He is the son of Shirley Genieve Buford and the late Edwin Joseph Bayer. Shirley was born on Oct. 4, 1919. Edwin was born Sept. 16, 1916 and died Dec. 9, 1971. David has six brothers and sisters: James Dewayne Bayer (Sept. 16, 1940-1972); Shirley Marie Ramsey (born Apr. 19, 1942); Eugene Allen Beyer (Born Dec. 11, 1946); Loretta Kay Maroney (born Aug. 12, 1948); Kathy Jo Moore (born Sept. 24, 1955); and Mickey Lee Bayer (born May 5, 1965). In 1947, the Bayer family moved from Birdseye, IN to Hopkins County.

David graduated from Dawson Springs High School in 1968. During 1968, he took a radiology class at the University of Kentucky. Then, in 1975, he took a teaching course at Murray State University. Because of his training, he was able to work for two years at the Hopkins County Hospital in the field of radiology and special procedures. He also taught a one-and-a-half year term at the Health Occupations Center in Madisonville, in Radiology Technology. But, perhaps the most rewarding job came in 1972.

In May of 1972, David stepped into his father's shoes and became the pastor of the Apostolic Holiness Church located in Dawson Springs, KY. Within the past 16 years, Rev. Bayer and his family have lived in several locations: Madisonville for two years, Hamby Avenue in Dawson Springs for five years, and since 1977, his residence has been the parsonage located beside the present church on Highway 109.

David and Anga have three children: Chera Diane Bayer (born Oct. 20, 1972); Chad David Bayer (born May 19, 1975); and Mark Daniel Bayer (born Sept. 27, 1977). All the children attend Dawson Springs Independent School System.

During his 16 years of pastoring, Rev. Bayer and his wife have made trips to Mexico (1976 & 1982), The Holy Land (1980), and Canada (1981). In 1986, Rev. Bayer was chosen to go to the White House for a briefing on world and religious affairs.

Rev. Bayer has held many positions during his pastoral tenure. He has been the president of the Ministerial Association for ten years. He is presently the Presbyter of the United Pentecostal Church Section I and also the Bible Quizmaster for the state of Kentucky.

Anga is the vice-president of the Apostolic Ladies Auxiliary. She is also the church organist. She visits various churches to speak on numerous topics, and in 1965 released an album entitled "In the Beginning", which featured her sister, Linda, playing the piano, and Kathy (Davis) Dutton and Jeanetta (Davis) Orange as co-singers. But, first and foremost, she is the pastor's wife, a job that should never be underrated.-*Submitted by Sherry Dismang*

DAVID BAYER

David Bayer grew up to be an excellent individual. He was born on Mar. 9, 1950. He grew up in Dawson Springs, KY in his early years of childhood. He and his family now resides on Hwy. 109 in Dawson Springs, KY. His wife, Anga Lou Davis Bayer, and his children live with him. He has three children: Chera Diane, 15; Chad David, 12; and Mark Daniel, 10.

David's parents are the late Edwin Joseph Bayer and Shirley Genieve Buford Bayer. Edwin Joseph was born Sept. 16, 1916. Shirley Geneive was born Oct. 4, 1919. Both of David's parents were born and raised in Dubois County, IN. David has three brothers and three sisters. They are the late James Dewayne Bayer; Shirley Marie Ramsey; Eugene Allen Bayer; Loretta Kay Maroney; Kathy Jo Moore; and Mickey Lee Bayer.

David is a very well-educated person. He graduated from high school in 1968. After high school, he went to the School of Radiologic Technology at the Hopkins County Hospital for a two-year course. He also took classes at the University of Kentucky extension. He graduated in 1970 at the top of his class and received the Mallingckrodt Award. This was a very special honor due to his outstanding ability. He was the assistant instructor in radiology in 1975-76. While being the assistant instructor, he took instructor classes at Murray State University, in Murray, KY.

On May 10, 1972, David became the pastor of the Apostolic Holiness Church of Dawson Springs, KY.

In 1973, he became an ordained minister. Since 1976, he has been in charge of the Radiology Department at the Outwood Rescare ICF/MR.

During his ministry, David has traveled a number of places including Mexico (twice), Canada, and The Holy Land. His hobbies include playing golf, hunting, and boating. - *Submitted by Chera Bayer*

BEARDEN-LUTZ

Randa Doris Lutz and Calvin Martin Bearden were married Aug. 31, 1960, in the First Baptist Church of Corinth, MS.

Randa was born May 24, 1944, near Manitou, in Hopkins County. She is the daughter of A.W. Lutz and Louise Owen. A.W. Lutz was born Sept. 28, 1916, also near Manitou in what is known as Wolfhollow. He married Louise Owen, the only child of Lonnie Owen and Elizabeth Burton, Sept. 11, 1937 in Rockport, IN. Louise was born Dec. 19, 1917, also near Manitou. A.W. was the son of Pearl Clement Lutz and Bertha Lee Dame. His surviving

Calvin and Randa (Lutz) Bearden

brothers and sisters are as follows: Marie Reid, Elsie Sullivan, and Lonnie Lutz. Those deceased are: Raymond, Douglas Ilene Webster and Rev. Lona Lutz (twin to Lonnie). Seven children were born to A.W. and Louise Lutz: Carroll, Randa, Marshall, Glenn, Joan Howard, Ernie and Delane McKnight.

Randa attended Ashley School for the first grade, her teacher being Eloise Duncan. She attended second and subsequent years at Nebo, graduating in 1961 in the eleventh grade and then attended two years at Oakland City College in Oakland City, IN. She is presently employed by the Hopkins County Board of Education as a Special Education Aide. She has been a member of Concord General Baptist Church since age 12 and is currently the organist at the church.

Other ancestral names are Duke, Buchanan, Winstead, Madison, and Walker from North Carolina to Kentucky and also Hibbs, Osburn, Mathis and Weller from Pennsylvania to Kentucky.

Calvin was born Oct. 14, 1942 in Hopkins County to Davis Bearden and Sarah Ruth Hunter, she being from Tennessee the daughter of John Hunter and Clemmie Hadley. Sarah Ruth was born Oct. 2, 1909. Davis was born Sept. 16, 1910, the son of Herbert and Francis Clayton.

Calvin attended Anton Junior High and graduated from Madisonville High School in 1960. He immediately joined the Navy and received his basic training at the Great Lakes Navel Training Station. After completion of basic training, he was sent to Imperial Beach, CA, for nine months, then to Kamiseya, Japan for three years. He was a Communication Technician while with the Navy. After being discharged from the Navy, he worked for East Side Market for two years, Pryo Mining, Island Creek Coal Company, Star Mines and for the last eleven years South Hopkins Coal Company.

Other ancestral family names are: Little, Pace, West, Asbrooks from Tennessee to Kentucky and Winstead, Yarbrough and Tapp from North Carolina to Kentucky.

Calvin and Randa have two daughters: Krista Marie who married Ricky Eagle and Melissa G. Bearden. They also have a grandson, Eric Eagle, age one. - *Submitted by Randa Bearden*

The construction of Madisonville City Lake off Davis Well Road and South of the L & N crossing in 1932

Taylor Hawkins and J.C. Crockett at Trents store in Richland in 1947

WALTER "BUD" BEASLEY

Walter "Bud" Beasley of Hopkins County, KY was the third child of John Otho Franklin Beasley of Granville County, NC and Sarah Ashby, daughter of Stephen J. Ashby and Melinda Crabtree of Hopkins County, KY. Bud married Annie Mable Robertson while he was working in Kansas City, MO. She was the daughter of William "Bill" Robertson and Elizabeth Ashby of the Old Salem community near Slaughters, KY.

The Beasleys soon returned to Hopkins County where they had two daughters, Annie Mae and Sarah Elizabeth. Bud's mother died one day and his wife the following day. He was determine to keep the two and three year olds together. His older sister, Attie, and husband Theo G. Jones of Hanson volunteered to rear them. Their only child, Ada Lee, married to Whit Haywood, lived with them and they were very helpful in caring for them.

After the children became accustomed to their new home, Bud returned to Missouri to work near the home of his other sister, Ada. She had married Addison Adams and lived in Monett with their children Lorayne, Hubert, and Sara. Bud later went to Detroit, MI to work, but continued to come to Hanson every Christmas to see his girls. He also came for a week each summer, or they went to visit him. When he retired he returned to his home in Hanson where he spent his last days.

Annie Mae married Wayne Finch and lives in Madisonville. Their only child, Robert Walter, lives in Lexington. Sarah married Carl Polley and they live at 108 James Drive, Hopkinsville, KY. Their two sons, Edwin Beasley and Dale Whitcomb, born in Madisonville, live in Brentwood, TN with their families.

The J.O.F. Beasley family lived on Grapevine Road when their fourth and last child, Daniel Otho, was born. J.O.F. practiced law while in Madisonville, but removed to Missouri where he went into business. He died there in 1917.

J.O.F.'s parents, John Franklin Beasley and Alice C. Jones, daughter of Henry W. Jones of Granville County, NC, came to Hopkins County in 1854 and bought a farm, but sold it the next year and went to Texas where he soon died. His wife took their children back to her parents in Granville County.

John Franklin's parents were Robert and Stella Royster Beasley. His grandparents were Robert and Rebecca Wilkins Beasley of Chowan County, N.C. His great grandparents were Robert and Betty Willingham Beasley of Lunenberg County, VA. His great, great grandparents were William and Frances Beasley of Chesterfield County, VA.

Other ancestral family names are: Adcock, Bacon, Bounds, Conway, Davis, Emperour, Fielding, George, Goldsmith, Harding, Hoffman, Hunt, Johnson, McCullough, Nutall, Parker, Prather, Royster, Shepherd, Shumate, Snap, Sprigg, Stepney, Turner, Woodruff, and Wyatt. -*Submitted by Sarah Beasley Polley*

PAULA LUELL MORROW BENTLEY

Paula Luell Morrow was born in Hopkins County, KY, on Aug. 21, 1954, to George Irving III and Wanda Lee Benton Morrow. Her mother was born and raised in Hopkins County; her father was a soldier from California stationed at Fort Campbell.

Roger and Paula Bentley, 1985

Before Paula's birth her father was discharged and returned to California to find employment. Paula was six weeks old when she and her mother went by train to California. It was just the first of 21 moves covering four states the family would make over the next 14 years. Paula and her siblings (Jerry, Angela and Shane) always seemed to be changing schools and friends. In 1968, the family settled down in Santa Ana, CA, where they stayed until the children were grown. But throughout all the traveling and moving they returned to Hopkins County as frequently as possible to visit Paula's grandparents, Will and Pauline Benton.

To this city girl, visits to Hopkins County were a step back in time. Water drawn from wells, pot bellied stoves, homemade biscuits, outhouses, bath in tin tubs and vegetables growing just outside the back door. These county ways are cradled in her memory and now linked to her abundant maternal Hopkins County ancestry.

In 1972, Paula graduated from Santa Ana High School and attended Santa Ana Community College for one year before transferring to Chapman College in neighboring Orange. She graduated magna cum laude from Chapman in 1976, with a bachelors of science in biology. In 1977, she married Roger Boyd Bentley and they are the parents of Rachel, Rebekah, Roger Jr., and Celeste. They have lived in Salt Lake City, UT, since 1982.

Paula's hobbies and interests are varied but at the top of the list are raising her family and researching her family history. By squeezing in a day here and there over the last ten years she has pieced together her Hopkins family ancestry. Her research has etched a picture of what life was like for each of them and more importantly, given her the opportunity to know what each was like themselves. Most were poor and formally uneducated but not necessarily ignorant or unhappy. Some worked hard and reaped satisfaction in knowing they did their best. Some roamed the "backroads" of life and reaped disappointment. But no where did the life of any one individual, good or bad, have no effect on the other family members. Learning about her ancestors has truly taught her that to know them...is to know ourselves. -*Written by Paula L. Morrow Bentley*

BENTON-DAVENPORT

William Richard Benton was born in Hopkins County, KY, to Sylvester and Sarah C. Sisk Benton on Sept. 23, 1885. Since his parents separated when he was 5, Will grew up in the home of his grandfather, Barten Sisk. Those were the years of hard work for the Benton family and Will quit school during the third grade to help make ends meet. In 1912, he married Carrie Wells. Twelve years later the childless couple divorced. In 1924, he married Johnnie Pauline Davenport, the daughter of John W. and Nolie Etta Smith Davenport. Pauline was born in Hopkins Co. on Nov. 5, 1903. Her mother died when she was twelve years old, making it necessary for her to quit school and help her father raise her younger siblings.

William R. Benton and Johnnie Pauline Davenport

Will and Pauline were poor and uneducated but the work habits they developed in youth were the elements that carried throughout the long, hard years of raising their twelve children, all born in Hopkins Co.

Lillie Lucile (Lil) was born in 1924, married Robert Nichols and had eight children: Peggy, Denny, Melvin, Ricky, Gary, Joan, Shelia, and

Pam. She lives in Providence, Webster Co., KY.

John Richard was born in 1926, married and divorced Betty Rumsey. He served bravely in World War II and is the father of six children: Wayne, Linda, Dickey, Johnny, Brian and Michael. He lives in Madisonville.

Thomas Edward was born in 1928. He never married and earned a college degree while serving time in prison. He died in Chicago, IL, in 1976.

Vernon Veon was born in 1929, and married Johnnie Ruth Hall in 1957. He has five children: Libby, Gale, Judy, Tommy and Jimmy. He lives in Madisonville.

Jeraldine was born in 1931, married Herbert Clay in 1949. They have one son, Melvin, and live in Lincoln Park, MI.

Eunice Helon was born in 1933 and married Ralph Rowley in 1953. She has one son, Russell, and lives in Nortonville with her husband, Warren Barnes.

Wanda Lee was born in 1936, married George Morrow in 1954 (later divorced). She has four children: Paula, Jerry, Angela and Shane, and lives in Salt Lake City, UT.

Cecil Ray was born in 1938, married Ruby Jean Keown and they have one son, Jamie. They live in Melvindale, MI.

Norman Victor was born in 1941 and lives with his sister, Jerry, in Lincoln Park, MI where he attends school.

Donnie (Donna) Faye was born in 1946, married Thomas Ball in 1962. They have two daughters, Tina and Brenda, and live in Lincoln Park, MI.

Larry Dale was born in 1947, married Priscilla Camton and died in 1978 in an accident at his home in Nortonville. He had four children: Veon, Bubba, Kathy and Joey.

Janice Marie was born in 1948, married Scott Bearden in 1967. They live in Nortonville and have four children: Brian, Michael, Wendy and Amy.

Will worked as a miner for the Grapevine Mines. He supplemented his income with whatever he could raise, farm, hunt, or fish. Pauline could cook or preserve whatever he could provide. Her days were filled with children and household chores. There wasn't a lot of extra time to play with the children or show each that they were loved but somehow they knew they were.

As the years wore on, the children married and left home one by one, except Victor. Victor was born retarded. In 1975, Will died at the age of 89. After that time Victor was the one thing Pauline had to live for. Then in 1984, Pauline became so ill she and Victor were moved to Michigan to live with her daughter, Jerry. Jerry, her husband Herbert and sister Wanda, took loving care of her with the assistance of other family members until her death on Apr. 14, 1986.

Will and Pauline worked side by side all their lives to raise their twelve children. They are buried side by side in the Grapevine Cemetery in Hopkins Co. -*Submitted by Paula L. Morrow Bentley*

BENTON-SISK

The Civil War was a tumultuous period for many Kentucky families. The deaths of husbands, fathers, sons and brothers not only left grief but often severed the remaining family members from one another in their efforts to survive. This is perhaps the reason a lone 17-year-old young man named Sylvester Benton came to be in Hopkins County, KY, in 1870. Records indicate that Sylvester was born in August of 1853 in Kentucky (or possibly Tennessee). His beginnings in Hopkins Co. were as a farm laborer for James P. Roach. He was a taxpayer, a member of the local militia and appeared to be a rather ordinary person.

In January 1876, he married a local girl named Sarah (or Sallie) Catherine Sisk. Sallie was the daughter of Barten N. and Dicey Vannoy Sisk born in Hopkins Co. on Nov. 9, 1854. The Sisks were a well-established family in Hopkins Co. At first Sylvester and Sallie began their married lives sharing households with others, but later managed to have one of their own.

Sylvester farmed while Sallie was busy with their growing family: Alonzo (or Lonnie) was born Oct. 19, 1876 in Hopkins Co., married Mary Belle Felker in 1902 in Hopkins Co. and died in 1947 in Hopkins Co. They had three sons: George, Virgel and Cuelin.

Nunar Lee was born Dec. 25, 1878, in Hopkins Co., married James M. Jones in 1908 in Mississippi County, MO, and died in 1940 in Mississippi Co., MO. They were the parents of 4 daughters.

Thomas Henry was born in November 1881 in Hopkins Co., married Annie Vincent in 1906 in Mississippi Co., MO, and died in Hopkins Co. in 1936. They are the parents of: Katherine, Chester and Viola.

Ella was born in September 1883 in Hopkins Co., married James A. Todd in 1901 in Hopkins Co. and moved to Union Co. She had several children of whom were: Herman, Vernie, Bennie and Lillian.

William Richard was born Sept. 23, 1885 in Hopkins Co., married Carrie Wells in 1912, divorced in 1924. He married J. Pauline Davenport in 1924, and they had 12 children: Lil, Richard, Thomas, Vernon, Jeraldine, Eunice, Wanda, Cecil, N. Victor, Donna, Larry and Janice. He died in Hopkins Co. in 1975.

Clarence was born in Hopkins Co. in July of 1888.

Charles Vester was born in Hopkins Co. in June of 1891. He moved to Missouri.

Soon after their seventh child was born, there were problems in the Benton household. Sylvester and Sallie separated.

Sallie continued to raise her children the best she could but now under the roof of her father, Barten. Her children would grow up without association with their father or knowledge of their father's family. Sallie and Sylvester never divorced nor remarried. They each designated themselves as "widow" and "widower" on their public documents. Sallie died in 1913, at the home of her daughter, Ella Benton Todd, in Union County, KY.

Sylvester, like many others, had changed his occupation from farmer to miner by the turn of the century. He no longer lived in a home of his own but boarded at the home of others. He went blind sometime after 1900, and became dependent on county resources for his daily needs. It is believed that he died sometime before World War I (1917) at the home of his son Lonnie in Webster County, KY and was buried in the neighborhood Doris-Mays Cemetery. To date no death record or gravestone has been found for Sylvester.

Sylvester was a man who seemingly came from the unknown and left to the unknown. What he left behind were a wife and seven children who tried to do their best in living their lives and raising their own families in spite of the circumstances surrounding their upbringing. As of today, Sylvester and Sallie have hundreds of descendants spread throughout the United Sates. -*Submitted by Paula L. Morrow Bentley*

BERRY-HALE

E. Corean Hale and Gifford W. Berry were married Feb. 7, 1935 by Rev. George Parks at Earlington.

Corean was born Apr. 9, 1913, at Crofton, KY. She is the 7th child of Levi H. Hale and Sarah Melvina Hopper from Caldwell Co. Other brothers and sisters were: Woodrow, Cleatus, Pearl, Earnest, Neal, Lucille, Ruth, Gearaldean and Charles. Corean moved to Nortonville in 1931 from Christian Co. Mr. Hale operated a road grader for the state.

G.W. and Corean Berry with daughters and sons-in-law at their 50th wedding anniversary

Gifford was born Feb. 5, 1914, in the southeast corner of Hopkins Co. His parents were Louis Berry and Laura A. Bilbro. They were born in the same area where Gifford was born. The family moved to Nortonville in 1921. Gifford and Louis operated grocery stores until 1963.

Gifford and Corean attended the Nortonville schools. They were members of the Baptist Church. In 1946, Gifford was ordained to the gospel ministry by the Nortonville Baptist Church. He served as pastor in the following churches in Hopkins Co.: Concord, White Plains, Suthards, Nortonville as interim pastor at New Salem and held pastorates in six churches in adjoining counties. Louis was a deacon and served the Nortonville Church for 35 years as church clerk.

Bro. and Mrs. Berry had two daughters: Jacqueline Jean born Jan. 14, 1937; and Linda Faye born Nov. 13, 1940. Jackie married Dale Webb Jan. 16, 1954. He was from Bardwell, KY. They had four sons: Gregory, Max, Stuart, and

Mark. Linda married Macon A. Ray from White Plains, KY, on Apr. 6, 1957. They had two sons, Wyman A. and Warren B.

Louis' parents were Dick Berry and Louro Dukes. Dick was a son of Gilbert Berry and Jenny Putman. Gilbert was a son of Rev. David Berry, a Presbyterian minister, and Lenora Earle, his second wife. Rev. D. Berry was a son of John Berry. Ancestors back to Rockingham, VA, 1776. John, David, Gilbert and Dick served the Mt. Carmel Presbyterian Church, near White Plains, as elders, deacons, pastor and laymen from 1871 to 1936. Burial plots for the families of John, Bro. David, and Gilbert are in the Fox Cemetery on the Red Hill Road southeast of Nortonville. Louis' brothers were: Walter, Clem, Edwin, and Gilbert and a sister, Alma.

Laura's parents were Rev. John W. Bilbro and Dora Pendly. They had 13 children. The youngest was Murphy. He drowned in the Nortonville lake July 1928. Dora's parents were Ben Pendly and Emily Balcum. Emily was half Cherokee Indian. Ben had come from Butler County in 1845 and settled on a farm near Nortonville in the Pleasant Hill Church area. They came from S.C. and had twelve children.

Rev. Bilbro was a Baptist minister. He organized the White Plains Missionary Baptist Church in 1898. He was ordained by this church and served as its first pastor. He was a farmer and a brick mason. He made brick and fired the kiln on the farm where his family was born. Herbert and Glenn, sons, were excellent brick masons. Burial plots for Ben and Emily, John and Dora and ten of their children are in the New Salem Cemetery at Nortonville. Louis and Laura are buried in the New Salem Cemetery. -Submitted by G.W. Berry

BENJAMIN BERRY

Benjamin Berry, born ca. 1760 King George Co., VA(?), died 1834 Hopkins Co., KY, came to western Kentucky around 1800. The compiler wishes to note that there are no family records of the ancestry of the Benjamin Berry who married Winifred Berry, only court records. A Benjamin Berry married Winney Berry in Frederick Co., VA, Dec. 21, 1789. At that time there were at least four and possibly five Benjamin Berrys living in Frederick County, VA. An additional complication is the fact that there seem to be two Benjamin Berrys who removed to Hopkins Co. at approximately the same time. They were probably the father and husband of Winney Berry. The Berrys were large land holders in Hopkins and Union Counties. The five Benjamin Berrys in Frederick County, VA were:

1) Benjamin, the son of Henry and Sarah. See c. under 1. in section titled "Winifred Berry",.

2) Capt. Joseph's son, Joseph and wife Mary Powers' son, Benjamin. His wife is unknown. See 2. under III.

3) Capt. Joseph's own son, Benjamin who married, Elizabeth Thornley. See 3 under III.

4) Benjamin the son of Benjamin and Elizabeth Thornley Berry. He was born in 1765 and m. Jane Bell. See 3 under IV.

5) Benjamin, the son of Reuben who died in King George County, VA, in 1774. See 9 under III.

(IV). Rueben Berry, (- 1774 King George Co., VA) m. Margaret Martin. 1. Benjamin Berry (ca 1760 VA - 1834 Hopkins Co.)

(V) Benjamin Berry (ca 1760 VA - 1834 Hopkins Co.) m Winney Berry (ca 1770- before 1815 KY) in Frederick Co., VA, 21 Dec. 1789. At a court in Hopkins County, KY, on May 24, 1809, he appointed John Perry of Charles Co., MD, to obtain for him lands which his father, Rueben Berry*, held under lease in King George County, VA Their children were: 1. Henry, a resident of Hopkins Co.; 2. Clarissa Margaret (1796 VA-1885 Henderson Co, KY); 3 Elizabeth, m 1. Franklin Owen, 2. Mr. Baker (children were: John W., James E. and Leander Baker); 4. Lysander, m Mary Rankin in 1827, residents of Henderson Co., KY; 5. Franklin B. resided in Union Co., KY, and m. (1) Roxana, (2) Lucy; 6. Lucy resided in Union Co., m Thomas Berry; 7. Edward.

Benjamin Berry m (2) Sarah Williams Clay of Henderson, KY, 14 Sept. 1815. Sarah was the widow of Marston Clay and the mother of James Williams Clay, who married her stepdaughter, Clarissa Margaret Berry.

VI. Clarissa Margaret Berry, m James Williams Clay on 23 Nov. 1815, Hopkins Co., KY. Their first child:

VII. Benjamin Marston Clay (1816 KY-1900 Henderson, KY), m Abigail Frances McDowell (1823 IN-1909 Henderson, KY), the daughter of Joseph M. McDowell and Abigail Lock (widow of David Lock) of Union Twp., Vanderburgh Co., IN. Their daughter:

VIII. Sarah Elizabeth Clay, m Nathaniel Karr Givens of Hopkins Co., KY. (See Givens.)

*King George Co., VA Deed book 5, #584-588, Reuben Berry leased from George Turberville and his wife Martha on 29 May 1771 for the "longest live" of Reuben, wife Margaret and son Benjamin 318 1/2 acres of land for 2000 weight of tobacco yearly rent.

Bibliography:
Will Book I, King George Co. VA VA State Library, Richmond, VA. "VA. Gen. " Vol 1-2, pp. 5-17, 1957-58. VA. State Lib., Richmond, VA.

Berry and Allied Families compiled and edited by Roberta V. Wiley, 1974. DAR Lib., Washington, D.C. Union Co., KY Ct. File #378. -Submitted by Patricia Randle Gillespie

REUBEN BERRY

Reuben Berry, Sr. was born about 1735-1740 in Virginia and lived most of his life among the Ashbys, as revealed by records in Frederick, Co, VA, Hampshire and Hardy Counties (now W.VA.), Mercer Co., KY, and then Hopkins Co., where his residence predates the organization of the county. He was present at the first court held in Hopkins Co.

Hampshire Co. (W)VA deed records prove that Reuben had a wife named Sarah, probably the mother of most of his children. In 1794 in Mercer Co., KY he married Sinah (Ashby) Featheringille, daughter of Henry Ashby (1714-1798) and Eleanor Bounds. Sinah was born 1760 and died after 1842.

Children of Sinah and Reuben were: Hannah, wife of John Blue (see John Blue story for their descendants), Lucinda, and Parthene, who married Archibald Slaton.

Reuben died in 1829. In 1831 a suit among his heirs, venued to Ohio Co. Circuit Court, contains depositions of 56 persons. Most were early Hopkins Co. residents. The suit, along with Reuben's will, identifies Reuben's older children as Polly (wife of Noah Williams), Anne Hardin, Rebecca (wife of John Williams), Elizabeth (wife of David Brown), Sarah (wife of George Williams), Enoch, William, Joseph, Thomas, Reuben Jr., and Benjamin whose heirs were Granville, Alvin, Thomas, Julia, Margaret, and Malinda. Benjamin's widow, Harriet, married Capt. George Timmons in 1819. In 1828 a Malinda Timmons married John Stubblefield, and compiler suspects that this may be the same Malinda. -Submitted by Mary Louise Parrish Bevers

WINFRED BERRY

WINIFRED BERRY, born ca 1770, died before 1815 , Hopkins Co., KY was the daughter of Benjamin Berry who married Elizabeth Thornley in King George Co, VA. Her lineage follows:

I. HENRY BERRY, the immigrant, died testate in 1677 in Old Rappahannock Co., VA. His wife was Ann. He received a land patent for 140 acres in 1656 and appears prominently in the records of Old Rappahannock Co. He owned land on both sides of the Rappahannock River and resided on the south side of the river on Occupacia Creek. Their children:

1. Henry Berry, d testate in Richmond Co., 1696, m Sarah Harper, only sister of William Harper of Essex Co. Their children: a. Rebecca, m Robert Moody, d. 1776; b. Thomas, m d/o John Gordon; c. Henry, m Sarah, his children mentioned in will, King George Co., VA, 1750: Joel, Henry, Benjamin (a piece of land adjoining Benjamin Stribling), William, George, Enoch, Ann (and her daughter, Eliz. Bronough), Mary, Elizabeth and Sarah. If wife Sarah remarries, cousins Joseph and Enoch to replace her as executors; d. Sarah, m a Mr. McClowd; e. Jane, m first John McKay, second, John Gladen/Golden/Gladwell.; Margaret, m. a Mr. Smith; g. John, m Margaret Smith; h. Elizabeth, m Joseph McClure; i. George Pley (-1720, Essex Co., VA.) Sarah Harper Berry married second John Spiller.

2. William, 3. John , 4., Richard, 5. Martha(Richmond Co., VA Deed Book 7, p. 494 1720. William Berry refers to himself as the son of Henry Berry deceased, to Uncle William, Brother John and sister Martha.)

II WILLIAM BERRY, planter (-1721 King George Co., VA), m MARGARET DOUGHTY, one of the daughters of Enoch Doughty, Gentleman, 1639-1677, Old Rappahannock Co., inherited with her husband, WILLIAM BERRY, a part of Enoch Doughty's land fortune on the north and south side of the Rappahannock River in Stafford, now King Geor. Co., —one patent on the southside containing 4,763 acres. Enoch's father, the Rev. Francis Doughty, clerk, arrived in Massachusetts ca 1639 with his wife, Bridgett and removed to Old Rappahannock Co., VA. Children of William and Margaret Doughty Berry:

1. Capt. Joseph Berry

2. Enoch, (ca 1700-1763, King Geo. Co.) m Dulcibella Bunberry. Enoch's will mentions son Thomas and shares divided into four parts for the children of dec'd dau. Winifred Berry and her husband, Benjamin Berry. It is highly likely that this Winifred Berry's husband was the son of c) Henry Berry and Sarah and that he removed to Fred. Co., VA where he founded Berryville and died in 1810. It is a fact that this Benjamin received land adjoining Benjamin Stribling in King Geo. Co. by his father Henry's will. It is a fact that he named one daughter Sarah (after his mother?) and that she m a Stribling. He named his other daughter, Dulla (after Winifred's mother, Dulcibella Benson Bunberry. Dulla m. James Benson in King George Co., 1771 and Berry Benson approved his grandfather's will in Fred Co., VA in 1810. Benjamin is a son of Henry Berry, late of King George Co., according to a deed recorded in Fred. Co., Bk 16, p 642-648, 1774.

3. Margaret, m Christopher Rogers.

4. Elizabeth, m 1. Robert Strother and 2. William Wheeler of Westmoreland Co., VA.

III CAPT. JOSEPH BERRY, (1691-1749, King Geo. Co.) m CATHERINE SIM COCK.

Children:

1. Frances, born 1721, m 1. Thomas Golding, 2. Thomas Dobyns, 3. James Davis.

2. Joseph (1723-1807, Frederick Co., VA), m 1. Mary Powers and 2. Hulda Hewett, d. 1823, Frederick Co.

3. BENJAMIN BERRY, born 1724, St. Paul's Parish, King Geo. Co.

4. Margaret, died 1725, King George Co., VA.

5. Margaret, (1726-), m Edward Hoyle (-1750, King George Co.)

6. Withers, (-1755, King George Co., VA)

7. Thomas (1733, King Geo. Co. -1819, Frederick Co., VA), m Frances Kendall

8. Baldwin (- -)

9. Reuben, (-1774, King George Co.), m Margaret Martin, who was bequeathed by her father, Francis Martin, by his will filed in King George Co. in 1770, 1/4 of his estate.

IV BENJAMIN BERRY, (1724, King George Co. -ca 1815 Hopkins Co., KY*) m ELIZABETH THORNLEY, d/o John Thornley and Ann Woffendale**and they removed to Frederick Co., VA.

* Only known document referring to his death is in Deed Book D, Henderson Co., KY, 1820. "We the undersigned heirs of Benjamin Berry deceased, in the division of our Father's property agreed among ourselves that Negroe Juber as he had been a faithful servant.....be free." Signed Joseph, Thornley, Reuben, John and Peter Berry.

**King George Co., VA Deed Book 5, p. 1257.

Children of Benjamin and Elizabeth Thornley Berry: (File 378, Union Co., KY):

1. Joseph (ca 1760 VA-before 1849 KY) no heirs.

2. Thornley (1763 King Geo. Co. -1850 Union Co., KY), m Elizabeth "Betsy" Kendall, 1800 in Frederick Co., VA.

3. Benjamin (1765 in VA - 1849, Fayette Co., KY), m Jane Bell.

4. WINNEY, (ca 1770, died before 1815 in KY), m BENJAMIN BERRY (ca 1760, died in Hopkins Co., KY in 1834). They married 21 Dec. 1789, Frederick Co., Va, See heading "Benjamin Berry."

5. Reuben (177? in VA - 1844) Will Bk B, Union Co., KY, no heirs.

6. John, (1776 VA - 1832 KY), m Maria Bell.

7. Peter, (1777 VA - after 1849), wife unknown.

8. Epaphroditus, born 177? in VA, probably died in early manhood in Frederick Co., VA.

9. Mary (178? in VA - 1845 Union Co., KY) , Will Book B, no heirs.

10. Lucy (1785 in VA - 1841 KY), m William Berry (1782 VA-1836 KY) -*Submitted by Patricia Randle Gillespie*

BESHEAR-NICHOLS

Fred Beshear was born in the western portion of Hopkins County on Feb. 6, 1879. Telia Ridley was born in the same locality on Feb. 17, 1884. They married in 1902 and their only child, Opal, was born near Dawson Springs just north of Rosedale Cemetery on July 11, 1904.

Luther Elsworth Nichols was born at Bethany in Caldwell County on Mar. 21, 1874. His given names are the surnames of the first Confederate soldier and the first Union soldier who fell at the battle of First Manassas on July 21, 1861. His cousin Edna Fair Davis was born in Caldwell County on Jan. 25 1880 and they were married in Metropolis, IL on her eighteenth birthday, Jan. 25, 1898. Their first child George Dewey was stillborn on Mar. 11, 1899. Their second child Earle Moren was born in the same house as his father on July 19, 1900, and their third child John Buford was born on Aug. 27, 1905, on the lot in Dawson Springs where the parsonage of the First Baptist Church is now situated.

Edna Fair died in Dawson Springs on Sept. 15, 1920 and is buried in the Davis-Nichols area in Cedar Hill Cemetery in Princeton.

Earle graduated from Dawson Springs H.S. in 1919 and attended the Univ. of Kentucky from which he acquired a law degree in 1926. Opal graduated from Dawson Springs H.S. in 1921 and studied music for one year at Oxford College in Oxford, OH.

Earl and Opal were married on Aug. 25, 1925, by Rev. Oscar Nichols (no relation) in an automobile on the lane in Ilsley on which is situated the Ilsley Christian Church. The marriage license therefore was issued in Scott County, KY.

Luther taught in the Caldwell Co., school system before and during the period that he attended the Louisville College of Medicine from which he graduated in 1903. He practiced medicine (among other places) in Princeton, Crider, Coiltown, St. Charles and Dawson Springs. He ended his career on the staff at Outwood Hospital at his retirement in 1944. Dr. Nichols married Ada Crumbaker of Muhlenberg Co. in 1922 and she survives at This writing in their home on South Jefferson Street in Princeton. Dr. Nichols died on Mar. 28, 1963 and is buried with Edna Fair in Cedar Hill.

Fred Beshear in partnership with Theodore Clark opened Clark, Beshear & Clark, "Furniture, Funeral Directors," in Dawson Springs in 1909. Fred was first elected to the Kentucky House of Representatives in 1931 when Ruby Laffoon was elected Governor, and Fred lost his race for re-election in 1933 due in large part to the 1932 sales tax issue in which he supported Gov. Laffoon. Fred ran twice for the State Senate in 1945 and in 1953 and lost each race to Clarence Maloney. He was elected to the House in 1947 and relected in 1949 but lost in his race for re-election in 1951. His last race was for the House in 1955 which he won and served in the next Regular Session before his death on July 12, 1956.

Telia Ridley Beshear died Jan. 28, 1955, and she and Fred are buried together in Rosedale Cemetery.

Opal Beshear Nichols died of tuberculosis on Sept. 1, 1934.

On Jan. 20, 1937 in Princeton, Earle married Frances Ogilvie who was the daughter of Jimmie Harriss and Dr. Richard W. Ogilvie. Frances died on Nov. 14, 1942, and she is buried with her parents in Cedar Hill.

Earle practiced law in Madisonville from December 1926 until Friday, Jan. 28, 1977, before he died with a heart seizure at home on the following Sunday, Jan. 30.

Opal and Earle are buried with her parents in Rosedale Cemetery.

The younger child of Opal and Earle is Elaine Gordon who was born in Dawson Springs on Feb. 4, 1930, and who married Charles Edward Beshear on Oct. 6, 1963. They live in Russellville, KY.

The elder child is Frederick Elsworth who was born in Dawson Springs on Aug. 4, 1927. He aquired two degrees from the Univ. of Kentucky, the latter of which was a law degree in 1951 and he has practiced law in Madisonville since December 1953. On Jan. 16, 1954, he married Mary Evelyn Pollitte in Harlan. Their three children are Gordon Earle who was born Jan.10, 1955, Christopher Raymond who was born Apr. 2, 1957 and Leigh who was born on Mar. 1, 1967. - *Submitted by Frederick E. Nichols*

STEVEN L. BESHEAR

Although born in Hopkins Co., KY, on Sept. 21, 1944, Steven L. Beshear's roots are also in Christian, Trigg, and Caldwell Counties.

The Joyners (Joiners) and the Westers settled near Canton and the Dry Creek area in 1798 and the early 1800's. Richard and Hannah Boyd Hudson lived in Trigg Co., formerly Christian Co., as well as Gilliam and Nancy Slaughter Ezell, Steve's great, great, greatgrandparents.

Steve's great, great, great grandfather, Issac Beshear, Sr., came from North Carolina with his family and others through Cumberland Gap and finally down Tradewater River to the area now known as Dawson Springs. This settlement was made around the year 1800. Issac Beshear Sr's family consisted of several children, one being Thomas Beshear, born in Hopkins Co. about 1807 and died just after 1860.

Thomas Beshear married Sally Killebrew, born in North Carolina, daughter of James and granddaughter of Kinchen Killebrew, who built the first cabins at the Cerulean Springs resort in Christian Co.

Jane and Steve Beshear and sons Jeffrey and Andrew in front of the Old Governor's Mansion, former home of 33 governors of Kentucky between 1798 and 1914. The house was designated the official residence of the Lieutenant Governor in 1946 after restoration by the Kentucky Historical Society.

The youngest child of Thomas and Sally Killebrew Beshear was James Russell, born in Hopkins Co. June 27, 1847; died July 6, 1927; married Mrs. Nancy Emaline English (Inglis) Eison, born Mar. 12, 1857; died May 12, 1857. They were married Mar. 21, 1878.

Eddie Monroe Beshear, son of the above, was born Jan. 7, 1886; died Feb. 24, 1947. Eddie Monroe married Charlena Ridley Mar. 16, 1905. She was a twin to Melcina Ridley Pool and was born Feb. 28, 1882; died Dec. 11, 1964; to Orlando Petty and Cynthia Catherine Menser. She was born June 1, 1862, and died Mar. 25, 1930.

Orlando Petty Ridley's grandfather was Edward Ridley, born Sept. 9, 1794, in Virginia, and died Feb. 11, 1871, in Hopkins Co., KY.

Edward married Sariah Pendly, Sept. 21, 1815, in Hopkins Co., KY. Sariah was born Apr. 25, 1792, and died Aug. 13, 1869. Edward's father was Thomas Ridley born in Virginia and died in Hopkins Co.

Orlando Petty Ridley's father was Andrew Jackson Ridley, born Jan. 25, 1822; died Apr. 23, 1905; married Rebecca Jane Terry, daughter of Dabney P. and Nancy Terry, Jan. 23, 1848, in Hopkins Co. Rebecca Jane Terry was born Apr. 23, 1824, and died Dec. 12, 1902.

Russell Beshear, son of Eddie Monroe and Charlena Ridley Beshear, was born Aug. 16, 1909, at Dawson Springs and married Mary Elizabeth Joiner of Christian and Caldwell Counties, on Sept. 18, 1937.

Mary Elizabeth Joiner was born Sept. 19, 1914 at Lafayette, Christian Co., KY. She was the daughter of Maxey G. and Nettie Spickard Joiner of Christian and Caldwell Counties.

Steven L. Beshear, the middle son of Mary Elizabeth Joiner and Russell Beshear of Dawson Springs, grew up there. He graduated from Dawson Springs schools as Valedictorian of the 1962 Class.

He also graduated from the University of Kentucky with high honors in 1966 and during his undergraduate years was Phi Beta Kappa and was elected President of the University of Kentucky Student Council.

Steve received his Juris Doctor Degree in 1968 from the University of Kentucky College of Law. While a student in the College of Law, he was a member of the Editorial Board of the Kentucky Law Journal in 1967-68.

Steve practiced law in New York for two years before returning to Kentucky to further his professional career.

He began his career in public service in 1973 when he was elected to the Kentucky House of Representatives, a seat he held for three terms (1973-79) from Fayette County, KY. As a state legislator, Beshear established a reputation for independence, as well as one whose priorities included education, welfare reform, consumer protection and government efficiency.

Named "Outstanding Freshman Representative" by the Capital Press Corps, Beshear pursued a variety of tasks throughout his tenure in the General Assembly. He was House Floor Manager for Bail Bond Reform, a member of the Board of Ethics of the Kentucky General Assembly, vice chairman of the Courts Committee, and member of the Cities Committee and the Judiciary Statutes Committee.

Perhaps his greatest achievement during that period was when he won approval, after more than two years work, for the $10 million expansion and improvement of a much needed neo-natal unit at the Univ. of Kentucky Medical Center, an act to save critically ill infants.

As Kentucky's Attorney General (1979-1983) the Beshear mark was found in many areas, including investigations and prosecutions of welfare fraud, medicaid provider fraud and food stamp trafficking cases, all ultimately saving taxpayers hundreds of thousand of dollars. Beshear was involved in utility rate intervention, in assistance to senior citizens, in drug enforcement for the detection, investigation, and prosecution of illegal diversions of narcotics and in breaking up the largest food stamp criminal ring in history.

As Lieutenant Governor (1983-87) Beshear demonstrated the same aggressiveness, innovation and standards that he had set in the past. He created and chaired a two-year, privately funded, non partisan, citizen statewide planning effort called "Kentucky Tomorrow: The Commission on Kentucky's Future." The project was developed to promote the social and economic revitalization of the State. Beshear also chaired the Governor's Protection Services Advisory Committee which investigated the needs of Kentucky's children. The Committee's findings were endorsed by both the Governor and the General Assembly and resulted in major improvements in children's services. During the 1984 session of the General Assembly, Beshear proposed ten consumer-oriented bills dealing with utilities of which four were approved by the Legislature.

As Lieutenant Governor, Beshear served as President of the Kentucky Senate, the Chairman of the Senate Committee on Committees, and a member of the Senate Rules Committee.

Kentucky Statutes directed that Beshear, as Lieutenant Governor, serve as a member of the Governor's Executive Cabinet and other different committees and commissions.

Steve married Jane Klingner of Lexington, KY on May 19, 1969. She was born Dec. 13, 1946, daughter of Carolyn Graham, Ballard Co. and Fred M. Klinger. Jane is chairwoman of the Kentucky Literacy Commission and active in the affairs pertaining to the operation of the home of the Lieutenant Governor of Kentucky, as well as other committees and commissions.

Their children are Jeffrey Scott, born Apr. 20, 1974, and Andrew Graham Beshear, born Nov. 29, 1977.

Steven was a Democratic candidate for Governor of Kentucky, in the May 26, 1987, Primary election.

Sources: " Seven Generations in and from Flat Lick" by Erleen Joiner Rogers, 1984; "Joiner-Joyner, a History of Our Ancestors" by Pansy Joiner, Jr.; "Census and Tax Records and Marriage Records of Christian, Trigg, Hopkins, Ballard and Caldwell Counties; Bible Records and Vital Statistics of Kentucky. -Submitted by Mrs. Russell Beshear

DONALD LEE BLACK

Donald Lee Black was born in 1938. He has been employed as a coal miner most of his life. He is married to Barbara Ann Black. Her maiden name was Johnson. Barbara moved often often, but grew up in the Dawson/Charleston area. They have three children. Mitch, the oldest son, is serving in the United States Army in Germany. Greg, the middle son, works at Donaldson Creek Coal Mine. The youngest son, George, is now a senior in high school.

Donald's parents are George and Mildred Black. He was born in Pennsylvania where he grew up and spent most of life. Don has four brothers and four sisters. Sam, Jim, Dan, and Roy are his brothers. Marie, Veronica, Bernice and Lana are his sisters. Don's sister, Marie, has had a kidney disorder for the past 11 years. She has since been using a dialysis machine. About six years ago, Don went to Philadelphia to give his sister a kidney. The kidney worked for a few days but her body rejected it.

Donald Black is known as an outstanding miner by many people. He is the "face" boss at Donaldson Creek Mine. He is also a great father, whom I admire very much. *-Submitted by George Black*

BLADES

Ettie Jane Blades was born Jan. 14, 1892, the daughter of Faland Richard Blades and Ellen Carol Dillingham. On July 29, 1909, she married Arthur Pendley, b. Apr. 23, 1889, the son of Roland and Leal Pendley. They were the parents of five children: Gratsie, Delbert and Ray who all died in infancy, Bonnie Rachel Pendley m. Jewell Long, and Corbett Pendley m. Ester Russ. Arthur Pendley died Oct. 16, 1922.

Front row l to r: Hattie Davis, Haywood Davis and Gratsie Pendley. Back row: James Blades, Willie Davis, Fannie Davis, Ellen Dillingham Blades and Etta Blades Pendley Murrah.

On Nov. 16, 1926 Ettie married Arthur Murrah the son of Joshua and Lou Ella (Fox) Murrah. They were the parents of two children: Hazel Ludeama Murrah b./d. 1927 and Jesse Willard Murrah m. Corinne Carlton. Ettie Jane Blades passed away on Jan. 20, 1971, and was buried near her first husband at New Salem Cem.

Faland Richard Blades was the son of William J. (Dee) Blades and Mahala Frances Wilcox. He was born in 1860 in Christian Co. He was married to Ellen Carol Dillingham the daughter of Thurm P. (Printer) Dillingham and Margeret H. Berry. Richard and Ellen were the parents of six other children besides Ettie Jane. They were: Tilman Issac Blades, Rillar Williams Ford, Fannie Davis, James, Bailey and Ralphy. Richard and Ellen Blades were buried at Pleasant Hill Cem. after their deaths.

William (Dee) Blades was the son of Issac Blades b. 1787 in Maryland and Mary b. 1795 in North Carolina. He came to Hopkins Co. with his parents in the 1840's. On Sept. 19, 1858 he married Mahala Frances Wilcox the daughter of James and Nancy Wilcox. They were the parents of seven children. After Mahala's death on May 20, 1878, Dee married Lydia Ann Carlton the daughter of Jeptha and Clicia (Wilkes) Carlton. To their union were born six more children. William (Dee) Blades died Jan. 25, 1895 and was buried at New Salem near Mahala.

Thurm Prentice (Printer) Dillingham was the son of Vachel L. Dillingham and Elizabeth Earle of North Carolina. He was married to Margeret H. Berry the daughter of David and Elizabeth Berry of VA. David Berry was a preacher and one of the original founders of Mt. Carmel Church near White Plains, KY in 1839.

Printer Dillingham b. 1838 and Margeret Berry b. 1841 were the parents of eight children including Ellen: Holland m. Belle Gatlin, Elizabeth, David m. Dickie Dunlap, Lafayette m. Louella Gatlin, Nora m. Dick Berry, Maggie m. Tom Blades and Charles m. Eular.

Vachel L. Dillingham was the son of Jesse Michael Dillingham of South Carolina. He came to Hopkins Co. in the 1840's with his family and settled near White Plains, KY, which was then known as Little Prairie. -Submitted by Willard, Corinne, Lou Ann and Mike Murrah

ETHEL BLANKENSHIP

Ethel was born 5-15-1918 in the Cumberland Mountains of Kentucky. She was the middle child of 7 children of coal miner Balford Struck and wife Nancy. The family moved to the Tennessee state line to live when Ethel was 7. Nancy took in washing to help support the family and died at age 33, when Ethel was barely 10. Balford left the little family to care for themselves. One married and two others were taken in by relatives, leaving Ethel to care for herself, younger twin sisters and a baby barely 2. Many times they begged for food and slept wherever they could. Often Ethel went to neighbors fields to gather corn to parch on the old coal burning stove for herself and sisters. At 12, she lived in the Pine Knott community and attended an evangelistic service and was converted. Neighbors bought her first white dress for her baptismal. When she was 13, she was washing, cleaning and cooking for food and shelter for herself and sisters. They were placed in a children's home in Louisville. Ethel had a furious love for her little sisters and the home complied with her wish to place them in homes before her. It was many years later before she saw them again.

Evangelist Ethel Blankenship

Guy and Sallie Cates, of the Cox's Store community, needed a girl to clean and care for the ailing Sallie. Plaqued with bronchial asthma since she was 5 and very small for her 14 years, Ethel was at first a disappointment for the Cates. She soon proved her worth in housework, gardening and in helping with the farm. That fall, not even knowing her ABC's, she was put in the 3rd grade at Cox's Store School. Learning quickly, she soon caught up with the 4th grade and was promoted to the 5th the next spring. At 15, she was promoted to the 9th grade. At 16, she had to quit, but her thirst for knowledge never stopped. She read every book she could find time for and her Bible every day. She learned music quickly from her foster parents. At 17, she was playing for the choir at Oakley Home General Baptist Church. Her natural ability was used to accompany music groups. Her flaming red hair and sunny disposition won the heart of the church's young deacon, Sidney Blankenship, and they were married when she was 19. Their son, Ferrell, is a musician and owner of Ferrell's Electric Service and daughter Jane, also a musician, is a ward clerk at R.M.C.

Soon after Ethel accepted the call in the ministry, the family left Kentucky. Sidney, a carpenter, joined his wife in what became their life's work. They ministered in Florida, Arkansas, Texas and other southern states. Sister Blankenship became well known for her evangelistic work of 32 years and was on 15 radio stations from Madisonville to Texas for 20 years. She worked in missions, street preaching, tent revivals, visited the sick and dying and ministered wherever her Lord led her. Together they founded the Pentecostal Prayer Chapel at Providence, where Brother Sidney is still active in preaching.

In later years, Sister Ethel suffered from diabetes complications including blindness and kidney damage. Her strong Christian spirit never gave up. She did many of her radio sermons by tape recorder from her sickbed. She died in 1981 and is buried at Oakley Home Church Cemetery. The legacy she left her children and granddaughter, Mrs. Schyrel Osborn and great granddaughter, Sherry, is summed up in her book "From Despair to Glory." - Submitted by Dorothy Miller Shoulders

JOHN BLUE

John Blue was born 1802 to John Blue and Elizabeth McNary who were married in Bourbon Co., KY, and came to Hopkins Co. before 1820. John and Elizabeth and their younger children moved to Green Co., OH, by 1822, and then on to Sangamon Co., IL, where they died in the 1840's.

John (1802) remained in Hopkins Co. and in 1823 married Hannah Berry, daughter of Reuben Berry and Sinah Ashby, early settlers of Hopkins Co. John and Hannah's children were Ann Maria, 1827, who married (1) Wilson Ross Ashby, and (2) Will Rickard; Martha who married (1) Thomas Logan and (2) Hiram Kirkwood; Lucinda J, 1833; Willis, ca 1836; Orleans, ca 1838; Enoch, ca 1841; and 1843 twins Amanda who married Nathan Dame, and Lourana who married William Tomblinson; and John Logan (Jack), 1849.

Hannah evidently died between 1850 and 1864 when John married N. J. Ashby. Their children were Charles F., 1867, and Troy Nathaniel, 1869. In 1873, John married Mrs. Lucretia (Williams) Corbett. Their son Henry J. was born 1880.

Lucinda Blue married William Green Logan in Hopkins Co. in 1853. In 1854 they received a 360 acre headright grant in Tarrant Co., TX, and were living there southeast of Forth Worth. They had gone there with the William Lynn family also from Hopkins Co. Mrs. Lynn was Louisa Logan. By 1860 Lucinda and William G. Logan had returned to Ashbysburgh, Hopkins Co. By 1866 they had moved to Warrick Co., IN.

Children of William G. and Lucinda were: David, 1854; John, 1858; Elnora, 1860 (married James F. Davis and lived in Mt. Vernon, Posey Co., IN); Mary Ellen (Molly), 1866 (married Johnson Rickard and lived in Hanson and Evansville); 1867 twins Theodore (died in infancy) and Theodora (Dora), who married James Clark and lived in Hopkins Co.; Manson, 1869 (lived in Hopkins Co.) and Filson Matthew, b. 1872.

Four months after Filson Matthew was born, tragedy struck the family. Eighteen year old David became ill and died on 30 December 1872. Six days later the mother, Lucinda, died, and the following day, the father, William G. Logan died. The children were returned to the Hopkins Co. area where they lived with various relatives.

Filson Matthew farmed for a short while and married Laura Lee Prather in 1893. Their children: Lucinda Pearl, 1896; Goldie May, 1898; Brodie Franklin, 1901; and Elby Matthew, 1904. In 1894 Filson began working for the L&N Railroad and waved to the children all along the tracks through the Hopkins Co. area. He had a handlebar mustache which delighted the children. He died in 1952. Laura died in 1959.

Laura Lee (Prather) and Filson Matthew Logan in 1943

Lucinda Pearl married Harold R. (Doc) Cobb. Their children: Margaret, Emma, Harold, and Mary Ruth. Goldie May married Norman Parrish and had one child, Mary Louise (b. Hopkins Co.) who married James Bevers and lives in Evansville. (See Wm. Parrish Family) -*Submitted by Mary Louise Parrish Bevers*

BOLES-DAVIS

Anna Doris Davis and Jack C. H. Boles were married May 9, 1941, in Clarksville, TN. Doris was born Dec. 11, 1921, in St. Charles, KY, (Hopkins County) to Robert L. Davis and Eunice Gribble Davis and has two brothers, Jess C. and Charles L. Davis. Robert L. Davis was born July 21, 1892 to Lewis H. Davis (1856-1935) and Minnie Woodruff Davis (1873-1900) in Hopkins Co., KY. Lewis (Lew) Davis was the son of Thomas C. (Red) Davis (1833-1918) and Jane Barnett (1831-1914). Thomas C. (Red) Davis was the son of Thomas (Hopping Tom) Davis (1803-1894) and Elvira Fox. Thomas (Hopping Tom) Davis was the son of John Davis who came to North Carolina from Ireland.

Anna Doris and Jack C.H. Boles

Eunice Gribble Davis was born Sept. 30, 1892, to Charles Gribble (1861-1909) and Mary (Molly) Johnson Gribble (1866-1963). Charles Gribble was the son of John D. Gribble (1818-1890) who came to this country from England at a young age. Charles Gribble's mother was Jane (1820-1898) and was of Welsh ancestry. Mary (Molly) Johnson Gribble was the daughter of Nathaniel P. Johnson (1833-1888) of Galveston, TN and Amanda Beshear of Bullitt Co., KY (1843-1899).

Doris attended first through third grade in Carbondale, KY, grade school and fourth through eighth grade in St. Charles, KY. She boarded in Madisonville with Mr. and Mrs. Pat Collins and attended Madisonville H.S. and graduated in January 1939. After the birth of her children, she worked in various office jobs and retired in July 1986. She has been a life long member of the Christian Church.

Jack was born Dec. 16, 1919, in Terre Haute, IN, to Rex V. Boles (1896-1939) and Agnes Young Boles (1898-1963) and had two sisters, Maribelle and Barbara. Rex V. Boles was born in Farmersburg, IN, to Charles A. Boles (1866-1951) and Alice J. Turner (1872-1938). Agnes Young Boles was born to Herbert Young (1875-1936) and Ora Ann Becktell Young (1878-1950). Ora was the daughter of Samuel Becktell (1852-1909) and Artimissa Preston Becktell (1855-1957). Artimissa was the daughter of Phiness Preston (1819-1899) and Mary Keisling Preston (1819-1907).

Jack attended first and second grade in Terre Haute, IN and elementary school in Madisonville. He graduated from Madisonville H.S. in May 1938 and was employed by Sinclair Coal Company until owning his electrical business for thirteen years. Jack recently retired as plant electrician with the City of Madisonville and has been an active member of First Christian Church for 45 years.

Doris and Jack have four children: Joyce born May 1942 married to Charles L.G. Johnston II and lives in Lancaster, CA, and they have six children and three grandchildren; Robert (Bob) born January 1946, married to Jan Brower lives in Carmel, IN, and has one daughter; Gordon born September 1947 is a pilot with the Alaskan Air National Guard, North Pole, AK; and Martha born December 1956 married Robert Casher, Jr. and lives in Paris, KY. -*Submitted by Doris and Jack Boles*

BOSTICK

The Bostick family was founded in England by Omer DeBostock and was one of the early families entitled to bear arms. The name is recorded in the ancient Domesday Book, compiled by William The Conqueror. The Bostock family being of noble descent, has been traced back to the days of the conquest, for the Baronetcy is one of the finest. Descendants are entitled to be enrolled in the "Americans of Noble Descent. "They are also eligible for membership in exclusive society, "The Colonial Order of the Crown," and other patriotic societies.

Charles Bostick arrived in Virginia before Apr. 7, 1670. Charles and wife Mary, of New Kent Co., VA, were the parents of William b. 1680 d. 6-16-1740; Venecia, John, Mary, Valentine and maybe others. Charles d. 1-4-1700/1701, and Mary d. 12-7-1709.

William Bostick and Elizabeth (2nd generation in America) of Goochland Co., VA were the parents of Charles d. 5-16-1782 Halifax Co.; William; John b. 1710 New Kent Co. d. 11-1767 in St. Paul Parish, GA; Mary Francis and maybe others. John Bostick and Elizabeth Chesley (3rd generation) were married 6-20-1783 in Goochland Co. VA, they were the parents of William b. 1739 d. 1794 Green Co., wife was Agatha; Absalom b. 1740 d. 6-1803 and married to Bethenia Perkins; Chesley b. 1742, d. 1-2-1808 in Louisville, GA. and was married to Jane Jarvis;Jemima b. 1742, married to Valentine Hatcher; Nathan b. 1-26-1746 d. 2-14-1818 Jefferson Co., GA; and was married to Martha Guinn; Littleberry b. 7-10-1751 d. 9-10-1823 Louisville ,GA, and was married to Rebekah Beal, #2 Mary Phillips Richmond Co., GA. Lucy b. 1748, married Marble Stone; Elizabeth married William Garvis. Another daughter married a Corbett.

Absalom Bostick (4th generation) was married to Bethenia Perkins 6-22-1762. She was the daughter of Nicholas Perkins and Bethenia Harding. Bethenia Perkins was born 8-30-1739 and d. after 1809. Colonel Absalom Bostick was a versatile man and a great advocate for Independence, giving both his time and fortune to rid the South of the British. He was a member of the Staff of Colonel Joseph Winston during the Revolutionary War, and was assigned the task of drilling the soldiers, for he was skilled in military tactics. He was a well educated man, and was a member of the Convention that met at Hillsboro in 1778, also a member of the Fayettsville Convention of 1789. He served as a magistrate, sheriff, and coroner, and was elected many times to the General Assembly at Raleigh where he served in both houses. Colonel Bostick's home, "Shoebuckle Plantation" was one of the largest and most historic plantations on the Dan River.

The children of Absalom and Bethenia were John b. 6-18-1765 d. 9-20-1850 married to Mary Jarvis 7-20-1787; Bethenia b. 3-18-1767 d. 1832, married Samuel Hampton; Absalom b. 1769 Pittsylvania Co., VA, d. 1855 Christian Co., KY; Don Ferdinand b. 3-9-1772 Pittsylvania Co., VA d, 3-1825 Stokes Co. NC, married Elizabeth Rand b. 5-28-1779; Susannah b. 1774 Pittsylvania Co., VA, d. 1813 married William Blackburn; Anne b. 1778 married Thornton Preston Guinn. Manoah b. 8-20-1780 d. 7-4-1840, married Jane Scales 12-14-1803, #2 Frances Taliaferro Harvie 6-23-1823; Christiana b. 1785 Stokes Co., NC. Absalom b. 1769 d. 1855 married Nancy Dalton and his children were Dr. Jonathan, Bethenia, Elizabeth, Nancy, Absalom David Dalton, Charles, Thornton T., Susannah Davis. Absalom David Dalton, Charles, Thornton T., Susannah Davis. Nancy Dalton died 1822 in Stokes Co., NC. Absalom Bostick 1769 and #2 Dolly White were married 11-15-1822 (fifth generation.) Dolly was the daughter of Zachariah White and she died in Christian Co., KY, 1865. The children to this marriage were James Z. b. 1824 d. 4-15-1905 Christian Co., KY unmarried; Sarah A. b. 10-10-1825 Stokes Co., NC, married Robert Turner 5-23-1853; Sophia E. 8-1-1828 d. 4-12-1896, married Eli Hiram Sivley 7-11-1850; Catherine b. 1830 Stokes Co., NC died 1905 Christian Co., KY, married Ben F. Simmons Jr., 1863; Edward McNeal b. 5-22-1832 in Stokes Co., NC and died 3-31-1907; Beverly C. b. Stokes Co., NC, 1833, d. Christian Co., KY, 1866, unmarried; Joseph L. b. Stokes Co., NC 1835 d. 9-23-1896 Christian Co., KY, unmarried; Martha C. b. 1838 Stokes Co. and was married to George S. Sivley 4-12-1866. Absolam and Dolly moved from Stokes Co., NC in 1845 with their eight children, to Christian Co., KY. Absolom died at the age of 85, in 1855. Dolly married 2nd to Benjamin F. Simmons Sr. 9-20-1860, witnessed by Edward M. Bostick and George S. Sivley. Dolly d. 1865 in Christian Co. KY.

Barbour Owen and Edward M. Bostick

Edward M. Bostick (6th generation) and Barbour Owen, daughter of Peter T. Owen and Martha Torain, were married 2-25-1863. To this union was born Josephine 1-8-1864 d. 12-6-1953 and married to George Hesselbein, both are buried near Morrilton AR; Mattie B. b. 1866 d. 1945 and buried in Earlington, KY.;Sarah Elizabeth b. 10-1-1868, d. 4-17-1952, was married to Ben Duckworth; Beverly C. b. 1-8-1872 d. 1-4-1949 married 1st Luttie Hill and to this marriage was born Lucian Killebrew b. 1892 d. 1892 6 mo.; Perry Morton b. 1893 d. 1893 6 wks. These two boys were buried at Morrilton, AR. Theodore Arnold b. 10-13-1894, d. 9-30-1957, Mortimer (Red) b. 11-17-1897 d. 9-12-1975, David Beverly 1st b. 12-30-1898, d. 8-2-1984. The youngest child of Edward M. and Barbour, Georgia was b. 9-15-1882 d. 33-20-1969. She was married to James G. Vinson 3-6-1907 in Hopkins Co., KY. Edward M. moved to Hopkins Co. 1900, where he worked for Hecla Coal Co. until his death 3-31-1907. Edward M. and Barbour are both buried in the Earlington Cemetery.

Beverly C. b. 1-8-1872 (7th generation) married #2 Mattie Pearl Hale b. 8-24-1894, d. 3-16-1975 married in Clarksville, TN, 9-20-1918. During the 1890s Beverly C. lived around Little Rock and Morrilton, AR, and in the late 90s, he moved to Hopkins Co. and worked on the hoisting engine for Hecla Coal Co. He returned to Hopkinsville, KY, where he was chief engineer for Ky Utilities. After retiring from the engine room, he spent the remainder of his life farming and building.

There were two children born to this union, Lon Arnold b. 1-31-1920, married to Lena Nell Jordan b. 4-13-1920, daughter of William Revie and Myrtle Pruitt Jordan; and W. Alline b. 2-20-1925 married to Cecil Ray Cornelius b. 1919. - *Submitted by Lon Bostick*

BOSTICK-JORDAN

Lon Arneld Bostick was born (8th generation) 1-31-1920 at 315 W. 15th. St. Hopkinsville, KY. He attended grade school in the Christian Co. School system and was graduated from Sinking Fork H.S. He moved to Bowling Green, KY, where he served his apprenticeship in construction. He was taught by a stern and most capable teacher, a brother Mortimer (Red) Bostick. During this time he was married to Lena Nell Jordan b. 4-13-1920 in Scottsville, KY. She is the GGG granddaughter of William Jordan, I, b. 1771-75, d. 1865 in Barren Co., KY. He was married to Margaret Pinckley b. 1773, d. 9-18-1856 in Monroe Co., KY. She is the GG granddaughter of William II b. 2-10-1812, d. 1-10-1895 at Fountain Run, KY. He was married to Lydia Goodman b. 4-4-1816, d. 1909. Lydia was the daughter of Peggy Hagan and Jacob Goodman of Monroe Co., KY. William and Lydia are buried in the Jordan-Landrum Cemetery near Fountain Run, KY. Lena Nell is the great granddaughter of Jerry M. Jordan b. 12-18-1848, d. 10-29-1914. Jerry was married to Lettie Jane Fults b. 9-15-1846, d. 3-17-1933. Lettie Jane was the daughter of Amanda Silvey and Smith Fults of Monroe Co., KY. They are buried at Rocky Hill Cemetery in Edmonson County, KY. She is the granddaughter of Purnie Britt and William Duncan Jordan b. 10-21-1871 d. 3-18-1947. Purnie b. 3-21-1877 d. 6-5-1954 was the daughter of Eliza Jane Katherine Kelley and Thomas Stephens Britt. Lena Nell is the daughter of Clay Myrtle Pruitt and William Revvie Jordan. Revvie was born 5-16-1896 in Barren Co., KY, d. 10-15-1950. He was accidentally shot while groundhog hunting. He and his parents are buried in Bethlehem Cemetery at Scottsville, KY. Myrtle was born 9-17-1897 in Allen Co., KY and died Mar. 25, 1985, Bowling Green, KY. She is buried in Mt. Union Cemetery, Allen Co, KY. She was the daughter of Amanda Belle Rigsby and Phillip Moses Pruitt.

Lena Nell and Lon started a partnership 6-26-1939 with a sense of direction in life and they have been blessed and fortunate to have been able to maintain this direction and stay on course these many years. To this union was born Carol Yvonne b. 3-29-1940. She is married to Herman Louis Hargrove and they have five daughters, Frankie Jane Brown, Tammy Kay Lamb, Robbie Dean Vaughn, Jackey Lynn Spain and Jerri Ann. Carol has five grandchil-

Lena Nell and Lon Bostick

dren, Stacie Renee and Preston Howard Brown, William Shane Vaughn, Amanda Danielle Huffman and Thomas Heath Huffman Spain. Lon Arneld II and Lonna Sharon (twins) b. 12-16-1941. Lon II was married to Judy Oliver. They had one son Lon Arnled III. They were divorced. His second marriage was to Dixie Lee Oglesby and they have two sons, Christopher Lee and Timothy Blake. Sharon has remained single. Steven Jordan b. 12-10-1956 was married to Sandra Lynn Stevenson. Jeffrey Alan b. 12-8-1958 is engaged to Lillie Sue Hughes of Cadiz, KY.

During World War II, Lon I, served with the 90th 4.2 Chemical Mortar Battalion as a Support Unit in the European Theatre. He was in the battle of the Rhineland and of Central Europe. After the war he returned to Bowling Green and studied Blue Print and Estimating under the GI Bill and is a graduate of ICC. He has been a building contractor most of his life. After the war, Lon joined the Independent Order of Odd Fellows in Bowling Green and served the highest offices there. Shortly after joining the Odd Fellows, he joined the Masonic Lodge and has been a life-long member. He returned to Hopkinsville in 1950 with his family, and they have remained since. In 1955 he was elected Grand Warden of the Grand Lodge of the Independent Order of Odd Fellows and served as Grand Master in 1957-58. Ten years later Lena Nell served as President of the Rebekah Assembly of KY. They are both members of the Eastern Star and the Rebekahs. They are members of the Second Baptist Church. Lon served as President of the Christian Co. Genealogical Society in 1981 and again in 1985. He is a charter member of the John Manire Chapter of the Sons of the American Revolution and served as President of the Chapter in 1985-86. He is a registered Democrat and is semi-retired. He co-chaired the compiling of the Biographical History of Christian Co. along with James T. Killebrew. - *Submitted by Lon Bostick*

BOURLAND-SLATON

John Slaton was born 22 Feb. 1730 in St. Peters Parish, New Kent Co., VA, the son of Arthur and Rachel Slaton. He served as 1st Lt. in the Revolutionary War. On Dec. 20, 1756, he married Susannah Hodges, daughter of Edmund and Nephana (Walker) Hodges. Susannah was born 1734 in Goochland Co.,

VA, where her marriage to John Slaton is recorded. Their children, also born in Goochland Co., were: Sarah (b. 8 Jan. 1758) who married David Walker; James (b. 22 Mar 1760) married Martha Pigg; Rachel (b. Aug 1764) married Isham Browder; Martha (b 13 Aug. 1768) married William Bourland; John Jr. (b. 12 Sept. 1773) married Edith Hibbs; Edmund (b. 13 Feb. 1777) married Nancy Rossner Allen; Arthur Porter (b. 20 Apr. 1780) married Catherine Fugate. Susannah Hodges Slaton died after the birth of Arthur. John Slaton then remarried another Susannah. Children by his second wife, Susannah Groom, were born in Hopkins Co. and are Daniel Slaton (b 22 June 1782) and Mary (Polly) (b. 19 May 1788) who married John Grant.

Martha Slaton, fourth child of John and Susannah, married William Bourland 1786 in VA. They eimigrated to North Carolina where several of their children were born, later settled in the northern area of Christian Co. which eventually became Hopkins Co. William (b. 1765 VA), son of John Bourland, was a Baptist minister and a founder of the first Baptist church established in Henderson Co. He settled and improved 400 acres of land on Flat Creek in Hopkins Co. He died on July 6, 1806 and his will was one of the earliest entered in the records of the newly formed Hopkins County Court. He is buried at Flat Creek Cemetery, Morton Gap, KY. After William's death, Martha married John Snelling Sept. 7, 1814, in Hopkins Co.

Children of William and Martha (Slaton) Bourland were: Susannah (b. ca 1788) who married Joseph Loving Nov. 1806; Mary married Rev. Henry Garrard 12 Oct 1809; Samuel married Martha Snelling; Rachel married John Garrard 26 June 1813; Rebecca married Jesse Herrin 7 Feb. 1814; Martha born 12 Mar. 1798 married Buckner Williams; John M. (born 1800) married Winnifred; Baylis Earl (b 7 Dec. 1804) and James Bourland born Jan. 25, 1807. Their daughter, Martha Bourland (b 1798), was married first to James Newcomb Phillips, on 4 Dec. 1817 in Christian Co. They had a son, William Newcomb Phillips born 23 Sept. 1818 in Hopkins Co. Her second marriage was to Buckner Williams on 25 Feb 1821 and fourteen children were born to this marriage. The youngest, James Harris Williams, was born 27 Dec. 1840. She lived to age 79. - *Submitted by Beatrice Martin*

BOWMAN-TEAGUE

Ishmael Leo Bowman and Evelyn Maria Teague were married in Hopkins Co. on Nov. 17, 1934. Married during the great depression, the family struggled during the first few years. Ishmael worked at several jobs early on, including the Nortonville Power Plant and the W.P.A. He finally went to work for the West Kentucky Coal Company where he eventually retired disabled from mining related injuries. This retirment came in 1960 while working at the East Diamond Mine.

Ishamael, the son of Charles Lesley and Mae Vincent Bowman, had only one sister, named Hattie, who died soon after she was married. Ishmael was born in Muhlenberg Co. on Jan. 13, 1914. He was a star baseball pitcher at the

Ishmael and Evelyn Bowman

Nortonville H.S. in 1931-32. Charles (Charlie), his father, was the son of Martin Gilbert and Almeda Richard Bowman. Martin Gilbert Bowman (called Mark) was born Mar. 27, 1840, and worked as a farm laborer for Lewis Ashby at the age of 15. Mark enlisted in the Union Army in late 1861 or early 1862 and served in the 11th Regiment of the Kentucky Infantry. Mark was wounded in combat at Shilo and Seminary Ridge. He was inducted in the Army at Fort Donaldson.

Mark's father, also named Martin Gilbert Bowman, was born in 1817 and married Nancy, born in 1819. They lived in Muhlenberg Co. He was a tailor by trade. They lived next door to Bennet Bailey who married Martin's sister, Spicy. Martin's mother, Milly, lived with her daughter in 1850 at the age of 67. She had moved to Kentucky prior to 1810 from North Carolina.

Evelyn Maria Teague was born Feb. 3, 1919, in Marissa, IL, the daughter of the Rev. Luther Lovan and Hildia Daugherty Teague. Luther was a Penecostal minister and was instrumental in establishing the Holiness churches at Nortonville and White Plains, KY. Luther was the son of Millard Filmore (1877-1938) and Emilia Pendley Teague (1879-1928) of Bean Bottom (near Nortonville). Millard was the son of John Filmore (1855-1921) and Luna Dillingham Teague (1858-?). John was the son of Moses Teague (1832-?) and Lucy Sneed (1834-?). Moses Teague settled near Pleasant Hill in the mid 1800's.

Ishmael and Evelyn had three children: Glenda (1938), Larry (1940) and Terry (1950). All live in the Nortonville area near their mother. Ishmael died on Good Friday, Apr. 17, 1981. - *Submitted by Terry and Phyllis Bowman.*

BOWMAN-WINDERS

Terry Lane Bowman and Phyllis Ann Winders were married July 4, 1970, in Hopkins Co.

Phyllis was born July 29, 1951 in Madisonville, KY. She is the daughter of Oscar A. Winders and Dorthy E. Faulk. Oscar Winders was born Feb. 10, 1910, in Todd Co., KY, the son of Maynard and Joni Bell Winders. Joni died when Oscar was 18 months old. Oscar married Dorthy E. Faulk on Jan. 13, 1930. Dorthy was the oldest of 10 children of Omer R. Faulk and Dovie E. Mason Faulk.

Phyllis has three brothers: Wallace, Jackie and Bobby; and two sisters: Linda Knowles and Vickie Fox. Phyllis attended Mortons Gap

Terry and Phyllis Bowman with daughters, Misty, Amy, Sarah and Emily

Elementary, South Hopkins High, and Murray State, earning a Masters Degree in Education with a major in history. She has taught in the Hopkins County school system. She is a member of the Mortons Gap Independent Methodist Church. She currently holds the following positions at the church: Secretary-Treasurer, Song Leader, Youth Director in charge of Junior church and choir. Phyllis is currently the 1987-88 Nortonville PTA president.

Other ancestral names are: White, Bell, Mason, from NC, TN to KY.

Terry was born July 12, 1950, in Madisonville, KY to Ishmael L. Bowman and Evelyn Maria Teague. Ishmael was born Jan. 13, 1914, the son of Charley and May Bowman of Hopkins County. Evelyn was the daughter of Rev. Luther Lovan Teague and Hilda Daughtery. She was born Feb. 3, 1919, in Marissa, IL. Terry has a sister, Glenda Wells and a brother, Larry.

Terry attended Nortonville Elementary, South Hopkins, and Murray State, where he received a Masters Degree in Business. Also while at MSU, he was enrolled in R.O.T.C. Upon graduation Terry accepted a position in the purchasing department at the York plant in Madisonville. Currently he is the Purchasing Manager for York International in Madisonville. Terry is a member of the Mortons Gap Independent Methodist Church. He serves as a deacon and is a member of the Board of Trustees.

Other ancestral names: Daughtery, Teague, Williams and Pendley from NC, SC to KY.

Terry and Phyllis have four daughters: Misty Michelle (age 10), Amy Lane (age 7) and the twins Sarah Elizabeth and Emily Maria (age 3). Terry and Phyllis reside in their home on Highway 41, north of Nortonville, KY.- *Submitted by Terry and Phyllis Bowman*

BRACKETT-DUNCAN

Brenda Sue Duncan and Bobby Gene Brackett were united in marriage Mar. 4, 1963, in Shawneetown, IL.

Brenda was born Dec. 4, 1944 in Manitou, KY. Her parents are Edward Lee Duncan and the late Lavena Mae Rhew. (See Duncan-Rhew).

Brenda attended school at Nebo and Madisonville. She is employed by the Hopkins County Board of Education as a school bus driver. Her hobbies include bowling, playing cards, and traveling.

Brenda is known by her friends and family

Brenda Sue (Duncan) and Bobby Gene Brackett with daughters

as a good samaritan. She is truly a caring person and is constantly helping others.

Bobby was born Jan. 11, 1944 in St. Charles, KY. His parents are Edna Franklin and the late Leamon Brackett. Maternal grandparents were Nora Mae Long and Bradley Newton Franklin. Paternal grandparents were Della Melissa Hamby and David Eli Brackett. Other family names are: Calloway, McKnight, Thompson, O'Rourke, McMullin, McLeer, Bailey, Anderson, Soloman, Sisk, Davis, Clark, and Mims.

Bobby has seven brothers and sisters: Ray, Betty Wray, Faye Bumpus, Billy (deceased), Norris, Linda Pendley, and Freida Goodman.

Bobby attended school in St. Charles and Madisonville. He is employed by the CSX Railroad as a carman. His hobbies are fishing, playing cards, coin collecting, and traveling.

Brenda and Bobby have four children. Sherry Lynne (Aug. 23, 1963) (married to Randy Hale), Janice Sue (Oct. 24, 1967), Donna Jean (Nov. 24, 1968) and Kimberly Lynne (Sept. 29, 1976). They also have one grandson, Brandon Lee Hale (Nov. 2, 1983). They live in Madisonville. (See Hale-Brackett.) - *Submitted by Retha Tarter and Lesia Pendley*

BRANSON-KINNEY

Jack Lynn Branson (1948-) and Mary Elizabeth Kinney (1949-) were married Aug. 13, 1967, at First Baptist Church in Madisonville, KY. They have two children, Penny Lee, born Feb. 27, 1969, and David Adams, born Sept. 17, 1970.

Mary Kinney Branson is the daughter of the late Lowell Earl Kinney (1919-1987) and Catherine May Friedel Kinney (1922-). Lowell Earl Kinney was born in Calhoun, KY, and Catherine Friedel Kinney was born in Baltimore, MD.

Jack Lynn and Mary (Kinney) Branson and their children David and Penny, 1986

Jack Lynn Branson's parents are the late Charles Jackson Branson (1918-1976) and Iva Ray Winstead Branson (1924-). Both Charles Jackson and Iva Winstead Branson are descendents of early Hopkins County settlers.

Thomas Jefferson Branson (Jack Lynn Branson's great-great-grandfather) was born in Hopkins County, circa 1815. Thomas Jefferson Branson's father was a veteran of the American Revolution. Thomas Jefferson Branson married Sarah A.J. (Sally) Branson in 1834. One of the five children born to this union was William Washington Branson (1842-1905). William Washington Branson married Cordelia A. Byrom in 1863 and they had six children. Cordelia Byrom Branson died in 1882. In 1883, William Washington Branson married Barbara Ann Joyner. To this union seven children were born, one of which was David Washington Branson (1884-1966). On Apr. 23, 1912, David Washinton Branson married Zala Hollan Gooch (1895 - 1970), daughter of Dudley Barton Gooch (1860-1935) and Charlotte Susan Grant Gooch (1865-1935). To this union, three sons were born: Carroll Gooch Branson (1914-), Charles Jackson Branson (1918-1976), and David Thomas Branson (1928-).

Iva Ray Winstead Branson's parents are the late Ivy Ernest Winstead (1884-1972) and Jessie Manora Adams Winstead (1898-). The grandfather of Jessie Manora Adams Winstead was John Posey McCoy, who was a Union soldier during the Civil War, and died as a Confederate prisoner of war in Florence, SC. During a portion of his incarceration, John Posey McCoy was imprisoned at the infamous Confederate prison camp at Andersonville, GA. John Posey McCoy married Mary Jane Buntin in 186—. One of the children born to this couple was Sarah Frances McCoy (1864-1920). Sarah Frances McCoy married Jessie Yokum Adams (1857-1916) on Feb. 21, 1883. Jessie Manora Adams was born on Aug. 16, 1898.

Jessie Manora Adams married Ivy Ernest Winstead on Feb. 16, 1917. Six children were born to this couple, five of whom are still living.

Jack Lynn Branson is a federal law enforcement agent and Mary Kinney Branson is an Education Specialist at Indiana University-Purdue University at Indianapolis, as well as a professional writer. She has written 13 books, numerous church curriculum units, and television scripts. - *Submitted by Jack Lynn Branson*

BROWDER

John Browder, the son of Edmund, married a Welsh lady named Elizabeth. They had eight children: Arthur, John, Richard, William, Edmund, Ann, George, and Joseph. Son Arthur was born about 1715 in Prince George Co., VA, and died in 1739, leaving an infant heir whose name was Isham. Isham was reared by Arthur's brother and sister-in-law, Richard and Mary Thompson Browder.

Isham married his cousin Martha Browder, daughter of Richard and Mary. Isham and Martha had son, Isham II, born June 12, 1762, in Dinwiddie Co., VA.

Isham II married Rachel Slaton, the daughter of John and Susannah Slaton. Rachel was born about 1764 and died in 1808. She is buried at Browder's Chapel Church Cem. Isham was sworn as one of the first Justices of the Peace on May 25, 1807, in Hopkins Co. Isham died Feb. 19, 1830, in Fulton Co., KY. He was buried in the first grave in Fulton Co. His crude coffin was scooped out from a log and bolted together at each end.

Isham III was born May 3, 1799, in Henderson Co. (what is now Hopkins Co.) Browder Chapel, a meeting house, had long stood on the land of Isham Browder and it had become in need of repair. On Aug. 23, 1821, Isham along with Arthur Slaton, Elias Smith and others built a house of worship. Isham III married Lucretia Langley on Dec. 21, 1820. Lucretia was born Mar. 2, 1799 and died May 11, 1868. Isham III died June 8, 1864. Both are buried at Browder Cemetery. Their children were: John W., Thomas C., William F., Isham IV, Ann J., James E., Lafayette McKendree Harrison and Elizabeth W.

Lafayette McKendree was born Nov. 22, 1838, and died Jan. 31, 1851. He is buried in Browder Cemetery.

Harrison Key was born Oct. 29, 1841, and died Apr. 25, 1911. On Feb. 7, 1861, he married Betty Wilson who was born June 4, 1842, and died Jan. 29, 1901. Their children: Thomas, Cammie Jane (see Hickman family), Evie Elizabeth (married Herbert Slaton) and Arie Belle. - *Submitted by: Mary Edna Harris*

ISHAM BROWDER

Isham Browder was born June 12, 1762, in Virginia. He married Rachel Slaton, probably in Virginia in 1784 (or 1788—date not verified). She was the daughter of John and Susannah (Hodges) Slaydon of Goochland County, VA. She was born 1764, died 1808. In the Revolutionary War, Isham served in the Second Virginia Regiment, Continental Line, was wounded at Monmouth and discharged in 1779. By 1795 he was in Kentucky and in 1799 bought land in Henderson Co.—in the area which was in Hopkins Co. when it was formed in 1806. Here he was a leader in religious, civic and business affairs. He was a devout Methodist, a pioneer in the area in the Methodist Church. He was a lay-exhorter and quarterly conferences were often held in his home. Two of his sons, Josiah and James, became Methodist ministers and his daughter, Mary, married a Methodist minister. He gave land near Madisonville for Browder Chapel (Church) and Cemetery in 1821. Both of his wives and his daughter, Kitty, are buried in this cemetery. Isham was one of the first Justices of the Peace in the county, a member of the County Court, and later a sheriff. He was a farmer and on the 1807 tax roll is listed as owning 2100 acres of land. He was the first in area to be in the tobacco business and owned a tobacco warehouse on Pond River. In 1827, Isham and his second wife, Elizabeth Scearce (married Dec. 20, 1810), moved to Hickman Co. KY, where his two youngest sons, Augustine and David lived. They lived on the farm of Augustine until his death on Feb. 19, 1830. He is buried on the Browder farm near Fulton, KY, the site marked nearby by Kentucky Historical Highway Marker NO. 973. His coffin was made of hollowed out log, bound together with bark strips. His children were: Thomas (ca 1786-1812/3) married Rebecca Harvey 1806; Herbert (Claiborne?) (1788-1815) married Henrietta Sladen; John 1790-1875) married Nancy Allin 1815; Josiah (ca 1792-1854) married Lucinda Brigham 1827, married 2. Rachel Barwick 1834; Pleasant (1794-1830) married Lucy Jane Monroe 1819; Martha (1795-1877) married Joseph Gill 1816; Mary (1797-) married the Reverend Thomas Atterbury 1823; Isham Jr. (1799-1864) married Lucretia Langley 1820; James (1802-1874) married Harriet Smith 1825; married 2. Minerva Turpin 1832; Augustine (1803-1873) married Arena Jackson 1831; David (1806-1894) married Mary (Polly) Smith 1827, married 2. Mrs. Bettie West 1885; Kitty (1811-1813). The first two children may have been from a marriage previous to his marriage to Rachel Slaton. *Sources: Records of Ruth Lewis; Fulton County, Kentucky History; A History of Four Jackson Purchase Families by Mary M. Beadles, - Submitted by Martha M. Thomas - A great-great-great granddaughter*

BROWNING -FISCHER

Henry Lloyd Browning (b. 12-4-1878 d. 9-9-1969) of Hopkins Co., son of Charles Browning and Emma (Bourland) Browning, and Agnes Belle Wyatt (b 1878 d Dec. 8, 1958) daughter of George Wyatt and Sarah (Oldham) Wyatt, were married in 1901 in Evansville, IN. Emma Bourland Browning was the daughter of William Bourland and Margaret (Spann) Bourland. William Bourland was in CSA in the Civil War. He and Margaret had seven children, two remembered as Henry Bourland and William Bourland.

Henry Lloyd Browning was Supervisor of Stores of the West Kentucky Coal Company, was a 32 degree Mason, and the first President of the Earlington Civic Club. He and Agnes Belle Browning were faithful members of the Christian Church of Earlington. They are buried at Grapevine Cemetery at Madisonville. They had one daughter:

Helen Lloyd Browning born Oct. 28, 1907, at Earlington. She married Robert A. "Bob" Fischer in 1936. They had no children. Bob was a pharmacist. They lived in Hammond, IN, and Louisville, KY, before returning to Earlington after retirement. Bob died May 19, 1975, and is buried at Grapevine Cemetery. Helen now resides at Kentucky Rest Haven in Madisonville.

George Wyatt (b 9-15-1853 d. Oct. 1945) and Sarah Oldham Wyatt (b. 2-16-1853, d. 1942) had two daughters: Agnes Bell (Wyatt) Browning, and Georgie Lee Wyatt (b. 1888 d. Jan. 31, 1983), who married John Louis Long (b. Oct. 7, 1887 d. 1941) of Earlington. No children. Both "Miss Georgie" as she was fondly known, and John Louis Long were civic leaders and influential citizens of Earlington for many years. John L. Long was a baker, operating Long's Bakery of Earlington for many years. Miss Georgie was selected one year as "Woman of the Year" by the Earlington Civic Club in recognition of her leadership and good deeds in the community. In their latter years, "Miss Georgie" Long and "Miss Annie" Southworth were good friends and could be depended upon to befriend those in sorrow or in need in Earlington. Mrs. Long was a devoted member of the Christian Church for most of her life. Mr. and Mrs. Long are buried in Oakwood Cemetery in Earlington.

Gabriel Bourland is remembered as a great uncle to Helen Fischer. His tomb rock at Grapevine Cemetery states that he fought in the War of 1812.- *Submitted by Helen L. Fischer*

BRUCE

John Richard "Uncle Dick" Bruce was born in Webster County, KY on Sept. 13, 1869. He was the second son of Abner Joseph Bruce and Mary Elizabeth Armstrong Bruce. At the age of eight, in 1877, he was moved to Missouri, settling near Naylor in Ripley County.

On Aug. 29, 1888, Dick, as he was best known, married his cousin, Laura Jane Bruce. Between 1888 and 1896 they had four children. Sometime in 1897, he moved his family back to Kentucky settling in Hopkins Co. After coming back to Kentucky, he had two more children.

In 1903, his wife died and in 1904, he married Margaret Larmouth and they lived together until her death on June 9, 1957.

When "Uncle Dick" died on Jan. 11, 1970, he had 153 living descendants. These were six children, 29 grandchildren, 74 great-grandchildren and 44 great-great-great-grandchildren. John Richard "Uncle Dick" Bruce lived 100 years, 3 months 28 days. Photo of "Uncle Dick" is included in the Hopkins County Centenarians section of this book.-*Submitted by J. Harold Utley*

BUCHANAN-DAME

Virginia Kay Dame and David Charles Buchanan were married in Hopkinsville on Jan. 15, 1949. Virginia was born June 29, 1928, in Grapevine, to the late Charles William Dame (1902-1972) and Hazel Burns. 'Charlie' (as he was known) was born in Barnsley Oct. 26, 1902. Hazel was born in Benton County, TN, on Mar. 30, 1907, and moved to Kentucky in 1910.

Virginia Kay (Dame) and David Charles Buchanan

Virginia attended the old Grapevine School with Eunice Offutt Brown being her teacher. She later attended Madisonville High School (now Browning Springs). She is a member of Grapevine Christian Church where she teaches The Toddler Sunday School Class. She is also a member of the Auxiliaries of Maurice K. Gordon Post #6, American Legion, Bailey Pride Post 5480 Veterans of Foreign Wars and Lodge 738 B.P.O. E. Other ancestral names are McElvain and Burns, Dobson, Devault, and Pafford from Tennessee to Kentucky.

Charles was born Oct. 23, 1926, across the road from Hicklin Cemetery near Anton. His parents were the late David Ernest Buchanan (1886-1966) and Carrie Bell Stokes (1889-1978).

Charles attended Liberty, Medlock and Nortonville Elementary Schools and is a graduate of Anton High School. Immediately after graduation, he volunteered for military service and was inducted in the Army on Nov. 22, 1944, at Camp Atterbury, IN. He was assigned to Infantry Basic Training at Camp Robinson, AR, just outside Little Rock. Upon completion of basic training, he was shipped overseas as an Infantry Replacement serving with Co. F. 422nd Inf. 106th Inf. Div. in Europe. Upon completion of military duty, he returned to the states and was discharged at Fort Sheridan just outside of Chicago, IL. He is a member of Maurice K. Gordon Post #6, the American Legion serving as Commander in 1964-1965, Life Member of Bailey Pride Post 5480 Veterans of Foreign Wars, Voiture 1381, 40/8 and B.P.O.E. Lodge 738. Other ancestral names are Hibbs and Graham, Yarbrough and Clayton from Pennsylvania to North Carolina and coming to Hopkins County sometime around the 1830's.

Charles and Virginia have two sons: Ronnie

Back row from l to r: Sarah (Oldham) Wyatt, George Wyatt, Henry Browning, little Helen Browning and Agnes Browning. Front l to r: John L. Long and Georgie Lee Long.

(Buck) who is married to Terri Buffington and has one son David Lee who is eight, and Kenny (Bo) who is married to Cindy Lakin and has one daughter Lindsey Nichole who is two. *Submitted by: Charles Buchanan*

BUCHANAN-GENTRY

William Buchanan and his wife Mary Ann Gentry arrived in Hopkins Co., KY, on Christmas Day 1846. Some seem to know the very spot where they camped. They traveled by covered wagon over the Cumberland Pass from Person County, NC. They chartered the Olive Branch Baptist church; the same name of the one they left in Person County, NC. William Buchanan was the youngest of five children all born in Cumberland County, PA. (1). Alexander born 1747 - died 1832; (2). James B. born 1749 - died 1829. Married Amy Burchett; (3). Rebecca born 1756 and married a Graves, Groves, or Grover. Lived in California 1816. (4). Arthur born 1759 - died 1855 Hopkins Co., KY. Married Agnes Graham 5 Mar. 1799, Cumberland Co, PA by Rev. Robert Davidson. A second marriage to Lucy Guthries. (5) William born 1761 - died 1861 Webster Co., KY. Married Mary Ann Gentry 7 Nov. 1799 Person County, NC.

William and Mary Ann Buchanan had five children, all born Person County, NC (1). John Patrick married to Mary Ann Overby 18 Mar. 1850; Hopkins Co., KY. (2). Susan married to Amos B. Pidcock 20 Jan. 1850, Hopkins Co., KY, and John Wicks 18 Mar. 1861. (3). Winnie married William White; (4). Mary Elizabeth married William Springfield; (5) Francis Elizabeth born 1 May 1809 - died 1 Jan. 1887, Person Co., NC. Married William Washington Ramsey about 1832.

John Patrick and Mary Ann Overby had a son John and a daughter Sarah who married Joe Littlepage 17 Nov. 1864, Hopkins Co., KY. They had five children all born Hopkins Co. John T., Sarah A., Mattie, Lizzie, Bertha. John T. married Bertha Hardin 20 Aug. 1905 and they had five children: Walter, Herman, J.R., Everette and Eileen Littlepage.

It appears that all the children of William and Mary Ann Buchanan migrated to Hopkins or Webster Co., KY, except Francis Elizabeth married to William Washington Ramsey stayed in Person Co., NC. They had seven children all born there. Mary Ann married Dit Thaxton; Susan married William Rhenn; Virginia Caroline married Samuel Parham; William Henry wounded and died in Civil War; James Henry died with flu in Civil War; John Dorris born 12 Aug 1843 - died 26 Aug. 1926, Wightman, VA. Married Susan Ann Humphries 7 Dec. 1868, Person Co., NC. France P. married his cousin Geneva Springfield 17 Jan. 1887. He and John Dorris served in Civil War. France in the Navy. He died of consumption as did all the members of his family and are buried in an old neglected cemetery near Vandersberg, KY.

Arthur Buchanan, brother of William Buchanan also moved to Webster or Hopkins County, KY. It appears that many of the families migrated to Kentucky before William and Mary Ann Buchanan.

Ora W. Robinson is descended from William and Mary Ann Buchanan through their daughter Francis Elizabeth, who married William Washington Ramsey. They had a son John Dorris married to Susan A. Humphries, who had a daughter Anna L. who married Charles Harrison Clayton. Then they had eight children. William Joseph Clayton, their fourth child is the father of three, Ora, Norma and William Jr. Clayton.- *Submitted by Ora W. Robinson*

BUNTIN

It is believed that the Buntin family came to Hopkins Co. from Person Co., NC, in about 1839.

It is known that John W. Buntin, Samuel Faucett Buntin and Sarah Buntin were siblings. Evidence also indicates that William Henderson Buntin, Nancy Greenwood Buntin and the following: James Buntin, b. ca 1812/13 who moved to Indiana and may have been in the Alamo (no other information), Matthew b. ca. 1820 who possibly enlisted in Lopez Expedition (no other information), Patsy b. ca. 1815 who 1/ m____Bowers/Boughers and 2/m Jesse Shipman and possibly lived in Central KY and Lucy (1825-1908) who married John Fry and lived in Indiana, were also siblings.

John W. Buntin (1811-1883) was married in Person County, NC, on Dec. 24, 1830, to Jane/Gincy Buchanan (1805-1879). They had no children, but family tradition says that they finished raising Samuel F. and Sarah after the death of their parents in Person County, NC.

Sarah (1827-1861) married Thomas Matthew Hamilton (1822-1877) in Hopkins Co. on Jan. 20, 1846, and removed to Fayette Co., IL, where she died in 1861. Her children were: Winfield Scott (1847-1907) who married Mary Ann Green, John W. (1850-) who married Ida A. ? Claxton, Nancy E. (1853-), David Howard (1854-1933) who married Alyse King and Malissa J. (1859-). After the death of Sarah and remarriage of Thomas Matthew, the family moved to northern Arkansas.

Samuel F. Buntin (1830-1892) married Nancy Jane Coppage (1845-1911) in Phelps County, MO, on Nov. 20, 1860. They returned to Hopkins Co. where their first child was born in May of 1862. During 1864 the family moved to Franklin Co, IL. Their children: Mary (1862-1920) married James P. Crain (1857-1919), Martha Ellen (1864-1949) married Alexander Summers (1850-1921), John Allen (1867-1958), married Loa Davis, William Samuel (1869-1945) married Rosha Manion (1867-1942), James Madison (my grandfather) (1872-1950) married Minnie Crain (1879-1955), Anna Laura (1875-1906) married James H. Whetstone (1866-1904), Charles Washington (1877-1958) married Margaret Clapp (1887-1983), Frank Clarence (1880-1964) married Liva Crain (1883-1966), Guy Ezra (1883-1970) married Ollie Tanner (1885-1970) and Grover Cleveland (1884-1963) married Fern VanNess (1888-1966).

Nancy Greenwood Buntin (1822-1900) married John Gimmeson Hamilton (1820-1897) in Floyd Co. IN, on May 20, 1839. Family tradition says they met "on the Ohio River" as they were migrating to Hopkins Co. They lived in Hopkins Co. until 1854/55 and then removed to Fayette Co., IL. Their children: Sarah Elizabeth (1839 -) married Mike Giles, William Thomas (1841-1868) married ____, John Buntin Hamilton (1845-1867) married Martha E. Pippin, Alexander (1848-1879) married Mary Christman, Nancy Catherine Duval Hamilton (1852-1873) married William F. Cates, Andrew Gimmeson Hamilton (1855-) married Emma Bettie Naue, Martha Jane "Patsy" (1850-) married 1- J.D. Mahon and 2/m Henry Smohl, Mary Frances "Mollie" (1857-1918) married Arthur Henry Wilson (1852-1918) and George Wm. (1857-1861).

William Henderson Buntin (1817-1901) married Betsy Groves (1825-1890) on June 6, 1842, in Hopkins Co. This family remained in Hopkins Co. Their children: John H. (1843 -), Mary Jane (1845-) 1/m John P. McCoy 2/m Ike Stodghall, Julia Ann (1846 -) married Abselem W. Siria, Catherine F. (1848-) married 1- Fleming R. Curual and 2/m Manley V. Winstead, Sarah Frances (1849-)1/m James K.G. Snodgrass and 2/m Poke Walker, Martha E. "Puss" (1851 -) Tom Day and Vonley Parrish, James S. (1854-1866), Thomas Emanuel (father of Charles Givens Buntin 1902-1985) (1856-1935) married Lucille Augustus Hoggart (1866-1938), Lucy F. (1858-) married James R. Teague, America "Jennie" (1861-) married 1-____Mulligan, 2/m ____Franklin and 3/m Manley V. Winstead, William Bradley (1865-1900) married Mary Elizabeth Hodge (1872-1936), and Manley Parrish (1867-1922) married Ella Frances Joiner (1871-1929). *Note: information furnished on William Henderson supplied by chart prepared by Charles Givens Buntin.*

The father and mother of these Buntin children were William Buntin and Sarah Jones who married in Person County, NC, on Sept. 1, 1808. They are listed in the 1830 census there and are thought to have both died there before the migration of the children. It is thought they came with others who later organized the Olive Branch Baptist Church. *Source: Information obtained from family members as well as marriage, census and cemetery records. - Submitted by Jean Buntin Chamness*

BURDEN-BRADEN

Faye Larue Braden and Lennie Eugene Burden were united in marriage Sept. 19, 1959, in Shawneetown, IL.

Faye was born Sept. 9, 1941, in Mortons Gap, KY. She is the daughter of Katie Marie Rodgers

Lennie Eugene and Faye Larue (Braden) Burden

and the late Rosco Authen Braden. Maternal grandparents were Molly Brown and James Rodgers. Paternal grandparents were Nellie Skinner and John C. Braden. John's parents were Jack and Elizabeth Braden. Jack came here from Ireland. Faye has five brothers and five sisters.

Lennie (Eugene) was born Aug. 15, 1941, in Hopkins Co. His parents are Mamie Lucille Felty and the late Lennie Lee Burden. His maternal grandparents were Susan Duke and John Will Felty. His paternal grandparents were Merica Hall and Walter Ennis Burden. Eugene has three brothers: Edward Earl, John Ennis and Richard Norman. He also has two sisters: Rebecca Evelyn Green and the late Betty Lou Braden. (Betty was married to Faye's brother, Ralph). Eugene attended school at Anton and South Hopkins H.S. He has been employed byvarious coal company's in Hopkins and Union County. Eugene's hobbies include woodworking and restoring older homes.

Faye attended school at Mortons Gap and graduated from South Hopkins H.S., in 1959. Faye is a home-maker. Her hobbies include all types of sewing and needlework, crafts and painting.

Eugene and Faye have two sons, David Anthony (Feb. 18, 1961) and Darren Eugene (Mar. 19, 1968). They also have one granddaughter Stephanie Faye (July 24, 1984). - *Submitted by: Retha Tarter*

BURDEN-FORBES

James E. Burden and Luella Forbes were the first to be married under the new blood test law on Jan. 7, 1941, by Rev. W.T. Anderson at Madisonville, KY. James is the son of the late Isiah and Della Daughtery Burden. Luella is the daughter of the late Tom and Florence Durbin Forbes.

Luella and James E. Burden

Mr. and Mrs. Burden have four children:
Sharon Rose born Apr. 23, 1944, is married to Gary A. Wells. They live in Madisonville and have two children, Gwendolyn Hope McCoy, born Apr. 6, 1969, and Taylor Mack Wells, born Aug. 12, 1977.

Brenda Faye, born Oct. 10, 1947, is married to Capt. Bruce A. Messinger. They live in Fort Knox, KY, and have two children, Shari Renee Hawes, who was born Jan. 3, 1966, and is married to Jeffery Taylor and lives in Madisonville, and Joshua David Messinger, born Oct. 3, 1981.

Alisa Diane born Mar. 22, 1958, and is married to David W. Betts. They have two children, Andrew Keith Dawney, born Dec. 6, 1978, and John David Betts, born Nov. 21, 1984. They live in Madisonville.

James Allen Burden, born Dec. 29, 1961, is single and lives in Madisonville also.

James E. has been a farmer, a ship-builder during the war, worked at Vogue strip mine for over 34 years, pastored several small churches, the longest being 25 years at Pond River Baptist Church where he is now a deacon. He still fills in at churches needing a pastor and enjoys fishing.

Luella is a homemaker, she enjoys babysitting for her grandchildren, making quilts, raising flowers and entertaining her children and grandchildren on Sunday afternoons.

They have lived in Madisonville 30 years and enjoy traveling. They are both active members of Pond River Baptist Church. - *Submitted by Rev. James E. Burden*

ISAAC BURDEN

There lived a man of gentle nature in Hopkins Co., KY. He came from a long line of ministers. His father, his father's father and his great grandfather, James Burden, a soldier in the Revolutionary War, were all ministers. This man, Isaac Burden, was born in Butler Co., May 31, 1867. Yet, he spent his young productive life here in this county, moving to Anton as a young lad of seventeen. He received much from the people of this county, and those who knew him were greatly enriched as well.

I know I was! I remember as a child of four, my dear Grandfather. The awe and warmth of emotion his presence brought, when he came to visit us. My father, William Burden, who married Verta Forbes, was his only son.

For, families are what Hopkins County is made up of, isn't it? It is the deepest, dearest root and core that makes up any county, any city, any state in this union.

My fond memory conjures up a picture of my grandfather. His visits brought laughter, sweet, sweet laughter, and a closeness that was and should be with any child.

He had a boom in his voice that was edged with kindness. A broad smile on his tanned face, and eyes that were crinkled at the edges, from his own merriment of life. There was a commanding authority to his voice that suited him to a tee.

What I remember most about my grandfather, was a warm feeling of being loved. He would gather my two older brothers, Gus and Charles, and my younger sister Vickie and me around him. And the feeling of family surrounded me. For, in that tiny room by the fireplace, he would take me on his knee, and sing in his deep bass voice, "COME TO THE CHURCH IN THE WILD WOOD." I still recall that song, as it vibrates through my mind and pulls at my heart strings ———————
————"OH, COME TO THE CHURCH IN THE DELL."

He is a legend, for around Anton and Madisonville people remember him still, although it has been forty years since his death. He is remembered as a big, broad-shouldered man. Not so tall a man, but strong enough to carry two railroad cross-ties on one shoulder, with what seemed like little effort at all. He died May 23, 1945. His remains can be found in the Hicklin Cemetery in Anton, KY, but his spirit lives on———————and his spirit spurs me onward, as I live in Hopkins County, the town, the state, and the Country that I love. May I carry on my heritage and tradition. Dedicated to my two wonderful sons, Stuart and David. For, they are the future generation! - *Written by Alice Burden Monhollon History Teacher/Writer*

BURTON-MADISON

My great grandmother, Frances Ann Walker Burton, always claimed that she was "kin to President James Madison." Below is her line of descent from the Madison's. To date, the direct link to President Madison is unknown, but in their daily hum-drum lives this probably was something that they talked about and were proud that a President was in their family lines, however remote it might be.

There were at least four Madison sisters who married in Granville Co., NC, and came to Hopkins Co. around the mid 1850's. They are as follows: Margaret (Peggy) (Jan. 6, 1825-June 1, 1866) buried at Veasy Cemetery, m. Oct. 18, 1845 to John Richard Burton; Martha (Patsy) (Jan. 13, 1823-Aug. 9, 1875) buried Silent Run Cemetery, m Apr. 23, 1939, to Larry Talbot Burton; Mariah b. ca. 1830, death date unknown, m. June 13, 1849, to Jesse J. Burton, they may have moved to Agness, AR; Eliza (1827-1917) m. June 17, 1852, to Hiram Satterfield (1813-1893), both buried Veasy Cem. James Madison, who married Phoebe Forsythe, was thought to be a brother. (See Madison-Hibbs). Their father is thought to be Peyton Madison, although it remains unproven at this time.

John Richard Burton with his second wife Louisa (Luda) Roberts and their children Ben and Naomi.

The children of Peggy Madison and John Burton are: John Y. (May 23, 1846-1865) died fighting in the Civil War, buried at Camp Chase; Jesse J. (Oct. 15, 1847-Dec. 1861) died near Burkesville, KY, during the Civil War; Paul b. Sept. 28, 1849, m. Etta Fauquar; Missouri A. (Aunt Dude) (July 15, 1851-Feb. 28, 1890) buried Cox Cemetery, m. John Cox; Ellis Sabrina (Jan. 29, 1853-Apr. 16, 1931) buried Olive Branch Cemetery, m. first Addison Walker, m. second William Presley Jackson; Martha R. (Mar. 6, 1854-Oct. 17, 1931) buried

Martha Bowles, daughter of John Richard Burton and Margaret Madison.

Odd Fellows (Madisonville), m. W.T. (Bob) Bowles;Richard (Sept. 25, 1856-1931) buried Pleasant Grove, m. Susan W. Massey (Aunt Polly Dick); William (Apr. 22, 1861-Dec. 29, 1942) buried Odd Fellows (Madisonville) m. Mrs. Mary F. Ashby; Louisa (Mar. 12, 1859-Oct. 21, 1866) buried Veasey Cem.; Mary L. (Feb. 22, 1863-Mar. 23, 1865) buried Veasy Cem.

Ellis Sabrina Burton and Addison Walker's children were: Mary P. (Molly) (1870-Nov 4, 1943) buried Burton Cem., m. Joe Parish; Francis Ann (Jan. 6, 1873-Jan. 26, 1955) buried Burton Cem., m. Dec. 19, 1894, in Jasper, Spencer Co., IN to Joseph Norman Burton (Oct. 29, 1874-Apr. 10, 1953) also buried Burton Cem.; John Henry Walker b. Aug. 29, 1874, buried Burton Cem. m. Laura Cates; Willis T. Walker b. Aug. 31, 1882, buried Burton Cem. , m. Minnie Adams (he supposedly weighed 17 pounds when born); Ellis Walker (Jan. 1, 1878-Sept 11, 1931) m. Emma Riley, buried Burton Cem.; Alberta (Babe) (Feb. 5, 1884-May 6, 1976) m. Virgil David Cates, buried Union Cem., Nebo.

Sabrina and William Presley Jackson (Oct. 19, 1850-Aug 12, 1917) buried Olive Branch Cem., children were: Chester Jackson, Naomi Jackson Day and William Thomas (Will Tom).

France and Joseph Burton had the following children: Thenie and Cecil who died young; Flora Elizabeth Burton b. Sept. 25, 1897, still living in 1987, m. Lonnie Owen (Oct. 18, 1892-Feb. 9, 1966), he's buried at Concord Church at Manitou, where they were both members; Virgia Burton b. Aug. 6, 1903, residing in Brown's Rest Home in 1987.

Flora and Lonnie Owen had one daughter, Louise b. Dec. 19, 1917, who married Sept. 11, 1937, in Rockport, IN, to Arthur Walton (A.W.) Lutz b. Sept. 28, 1916.

The children of Louise and A.W. Lutz are: Carroll Lutz, Randa Lutz Bearden, Marshall Lutz, Glenn Lutz, Joan Lutz Howard, Ernie Lutz, Delane Lutz McKnight.- *Submitted by Randa Bearden*

BYRUM

Grover Cleveland Byrum, born Feb. 24, 1889, in Hopkins Co., KY, was the youngest of 12 children born to Erastus "Polk" Byrum and Martha Frances "Fannie" Boyd Byrum. They were married Oct. 24, 1866.

Erastus "Polk" Byrum, born in NC in 1844 to John R. Byrum (1807-1867) and Altha Ann Ross (1815-1880), married in Granville, NC, on Dec. 14, 1835. Polk Byrum died in 1888 and is buried in Olive Branch Cemetery in Hopkins Co. Martha Francis "Fannie" Boyd Byrum, born Apr, 3, 1850, to John C. Boyd (1822-1858) and Martha J. Boyd (1823-1868), died Jan. 19, 1915 and is buried in Nebo Union Cemetery.

On Jan. 20, 1915, Grover Cleveland Byrum married Irene B. Brinkley, daughter of John W. Brinkley (1874-1945) and Mamie A. Lynn Brinkely (1874-1962). Grover and Irene lived in the Coiltown and Nebo areas and had 5 children, 11 grandchildren, and presently 9 great-grandchildren.

George Mass Byrum was born in Coiltown to Grover and Irene, who then moved to a farm house belonging to Alfred and Eula Corbin, Grover's brother-in-law and sister, on the Nebo-Coiltown road, where Margaret Linda Byrum was born Dec. 28, 1917. An adjoining farm of John Ramsey is the birthplace of the last three children: Mildred Sue (Jan. 6, 1920), Maymie Lee (Mar. 26, 1922), and Grover Cleveland Jr. (Aug. 20, 1925). All five children still live in Madisonville.

George Mass Byrum has never married. Margaret Linda Byrum married John Priest "J.P" Edwards on Nov. 24, 1937. A son, Richard Daniel "Dickie" Edwards was born July 29, 1939, and married Joyce Ann Head, Philpot, KY, Aug. 17, 1962. Their two children are Ross Daniel Edwards (Oct. 28, 1964) and Mary Kelly Edwards (Apr. 23, 1967), both born in Madisonville. The second child of Margaret and J.P., Mayrene, born Aug. 17, 1948, died Nov. 14, 1949. In Nov. 1952, Margaret and J.P., adopted Julia Ann Edwards. She was born Feb. 29, 1947, in Murray, KY and married Charles E. Beal Sr. (b. Aug. 18, 1931).

Mildred Sue Byrum married Orville Bradford Johnston, Oct. 25, 1952. Orville was born Apr. 14, 1919. Their children: Alfred Allen "Fred" Johnston, born Jan. 15, 1955, married Valerie Lynn Lovan (b. June 22, 1959) in Springfield, TN, on Dec. 11, 1981. Valerie had one daughter, Allison Salmon (b. Aug. 11, 1979); Phyllis Lynn Johnston (b Oct. 27, 1957) married David Hill (b. Sept. 11, 1957) on June 11, 1983. Their son, Tyler Bradford Hill was born Jan. 21, 1986.

Maymie Lee Byrum married James Howton Dorris on Apr. 1, 1948 in Henderson, KY. (See Dorris-Byrum family.)

Grover C. Byrum Jr., born Aug. 20, 1925, married Jo Nell Thompkins (born Jan. 4, 1934) but have since divorced. Their children are: Linda Sue Byrum (b. Jan. 6, 1954) and Timothy Lynn Byrum (b. Sept. 19, 1958). Linda married Henry Bruneau of Paris, France, and they have twin daughters, Danielle and Michelle, born Feb. 1, 1981. - *Submitted by Maymie Dorris*

SALLIE CAIN

Sallie Brown was born Dec. 5, 1882, near the Dalt 900, Sallie married Ernest (Guy) Cain. Guy was born Nov. 5, 1873, and was the son of Ruthedge Cain Sr. and Mattie Hill. Guy's brother's were Orvell and Ruthedge Jr. and he had a sister, Erma.

The Cains were the parents of: Louis who married Bonnie Hart (see Pernecia Hart); Robert; and Naomi. There are seven grandchildren and three great grandchildren.

Guy died Apr. 23, 1957. In later years, Sallie was a resident of Brown's Rest Home. She died Feb. 19, 1985, at the age of 102. Sallie and Guy are buried at Beulah Cemetery.

A photo of Sallie is included in the Hopkins Co. Centenarians. -*Submitted by Dorothy Miller Shoulders*

Irene and Grover Cleveland Byrum

The interior of Morton's Theatre in Madisonville in early 1900's

ALLIE MAE CAMPBELL

Miss Allie Mae Campbell was born Sept. 9, 1883, in Christian Co., KY, near Castleberry Church. She was the daughter of Allen M. Campbell (Apr. 11, 1848-Dec. 30, 1924) and Cordelia A. Campbell (July 17, 1848-Aug. 1908).

Miss Allie Campbell

In the 1890's, the family moved from Christian Co. to the Nebo area of Hopkins Co. where Allie's father owned a large farm.

Allie taught school at Crofton Independent School for about 12 years. She then taught school in Nortonville until she retired in 1955, completing a 52 year teaching career. After her retirement, she began teaching again as a kindergarten teacher at Nortonville until she became ill and underwent surgery in Dec. of 1957.

Allie was a 32 year member of the Hopkins Co. 4-H, a member of the Nortonville Christian Church where she taught Sunday School for years and sponsored the Christian Endeavor, and she promoted and helped organize the Nortonville Alumni Association in 1955 which is still active today. She was involved in civic affairs and gave to a lot of benevolent causes. Allie was always considered a good neighbor and was very devoted to her family.

Allie died May 7, 1958, in Hopkins Co. Hospital. She is buried in Union Cemetery in Nebo next to her parents. - *Submitted by Mrs. Herman Gladdish and Debbie Knight Hammonds*

JAMES SAMUEL CAMPBELL JR.

James Samuel Campbell Jr., born September 1910 in Caldwell Co., KY, was the first of five children born to James Samuel Campbell and Jewell Grace Christ.

James married Pearl Grace Carner, born April 1917, of Caldwell Co., KY. Her parents were Job Carner and Eliza Jane Oates.

In 1950, James and Pearl Grace moved to Hopkins Co. James worked for the Illinois Central Railroad and later as a security guard at the old Hopkins Co. Hospital. James died in February of 1977.

Pearl Grace worked at several nursing homes in Madisonville, the last one being Trover Convalescent Home.

Six children were born to James and Pearl Grace. They are: Janice C. Franklin, Jewell A. Wint, Linda F. Franklin, Larry W. Campbell, Judith Karen Adams (died Sept. 1980) and James W. Campbell (died May 1982).

The four oldest children attended the old Munns School, Seminary Street School, and the old Madisonville High School.

James and Pearl Grace have eight grandchildren. They are: Daniel Bryan Buie (died June 1987), Scott Buie, Troy Wint, James Lowell Wint, Genia Franklin, Lynn Adams, Chris Campbell, and Christy Campbell. - *Submitted by Janice Franklin*

SHARON KAYE CANSLER

Sharon Kaye Cansler was born on Oct. 27, 1968 in Hopkins County Hospital, Madisonville, KY. Her mother, Gladys Blanton, 43 years old, was born on Feb. 1, 1944 at Madisonville Hospital and her father, Calvin Cansler, was also born at Madisonville Hospital.

Sharon has two brothers and two sisters who are in order of age as follows: David Glenn Alsbrooks, age 25; John Carl Alsbrooks, age 23; Mary Louise Alsbrooks Tyler, age 21; and the writer, Sarah Lou Cansler, age 17. We were all born and reared in Hopkins County.

Sharon lives at 114 Water Street, Dawson Springs, KY. She and her family have occupied the same premises for over twenty years. Sharon and Sarah are the only two children at home.

Sharon is currently employed at the Hickory Pit and Gift Shop where she has worked for over two years. She describes the Hickory Pit as her "home away from home" - her closest friends are found there. She calls her fellow workers and her employers her "second family".

Sharon is a private and secluded person. She spends many hours alone in her room drawing. Everyday after school (that is when she is not going straight to work) she goes to the Public Library and sits for hours pouring over various art books. When she finally reaches home, her arms are loaded with art books.

Sharon loves to work with her hands. She has won various awards for her skillful handywork. Someday, she hopes to be an accomplished artist. Her work is sometimes shown at the local art exhibit show. Sharon will draw almost anything and she does many different types of woodcrafts. She loves to woodburn various designs into different forms that she has carved from wood. Someday, I believe that Sharon will be a great asset to Dawson Springs.

Sharon is a senior at Dawson Springs High School. She often draws and creates pictures and slogans for school plays and different activities that are happening in our school. She has taken art classes at every opportunity but she still wants more.

Her family life, her work, and her drawing are the three most important aspects of Sharon's life. Sharon is a very special and a very unique person and I hope that she will someday get the world-wide recognition that she deserves. I am very fortunate to have Sharon as a sister. Although sometimes we do not get along, I still love her. - *Submitted by Sarah Cansler*

CAPPS -THOMAS

Jesse Everett Capps and Laura Pearl Thomas were married Mar. 26, 1921, in Caldwell Co. Four days later they traveled by train from Princeton, KY, to Evansville, IN. In Evansville they met Mr. J.L. Allen, an Ashbyburg resident, who assisted them in the purchase of their furniture. The furniture was loaded on a boat, THE EVANSVILLE. They traveled with their furniture on the Ohio and Green Rivers to Ashbyburg, where Everett had accepted a position as a rural mail carrier, a job he held for the next 41 years. Mr. Capps began his all-day job on muddy, unpaved roads traveling in a buggy pulled by horses or on horseback.

In 1937 when the Green River flooded the small community of Ashbyburg, Mr. Capps was unable to deliver his mail. He spent his time keeping one jump ahead of the rising water. As the water flooded homes, families would move in with others whose homes were on higher ground. Three families moved in with the Capps family: The Bennie Love family, the Hailey Tomblinson family, and a family from McLean Co. The water continued to rise and could be heard hitting the sides of the house. Furniture was placed on scaffolds and everyone moved to higher ground. The Capps family moved into the Oliver Tomblinson home with four other families: J.L. Allen, Billy Ashby, Hailey Tomblinson, and Cleve Carlisle, where they waited for the waters to crest. When the water receded, the Capps family returned to their home, finding an 18" water line.

Everett was the son of James David Capps and Sarah Magdelen Cantrell. He was born Oct. 20, 1894, in Christian Co., and died Dec. 16, 1974, in Hopkins Co. His surviving sisters are: Elza Massamore, and Amanell Grisham. Those deceased brothers and sisters are: Edgar Capps, Hershel Capps, Omer Capps, Lelia Capps, Erba Capps, and Lura Lature.

Pearl is the daughter of Ephriam Newton Thomas and Nancy Elizabeth Hopper. She was born Dec. 16, 1901, in Caldwell Co. She was the youngest of six children. Her deceased brothers and sisters are: Beecher Thomas, Milton Thomas, Bertha Eli, Minnie Haile, and Reuben Thomas.

Pearl and Everett Capps with daughter Bonnell

Everett and Pearl have two daughters, Bonnell Crabtree and Rebecca Jane Clayton. Bonnell and Rebecca chose teaching as their profession. Bonnell taught in Hopkins Co. until her retirement. Rebecca is currently a teacher in Hopkins Co.

Bonnell was born Aug. 29, 1922, in Ashbyburg. She married Calvin Douglas Crabtree Jan. 30, 1946. They have three sons. Douglas Everett was born June 30, 1947. Thomas Warren was born Mar. 19, 1954. John Wesley was born Aug. 27, 1962. Doug married Delores Ruth Polley June 29, 1968. They have one son, Marc Douglas born Oct. 6, 1977. Tommy married Sherry Darlene Nance June 14, 1975. They have one son, Eric Thomas born Sept. 14, 1981. John married Trisha Gaye Sheets May 31, 1986.

Rebecca was born Aug. 8, 1941, in Hopkins Co. She married Max Alan Clayton Nov. 19, 1966. They have one daughter, Anna Laura Clayton, born Apr. 5. 1971. - *Submitted by Rebecca Clayton*

CARD-JONES
James Lee Card and Beverly Jane Jones were married Dec. 6, 1969, in Memphis, TN. They moved to Madisonville in January, 1970. They have one child.

The Card family - Jimmy, Beverly and Jonathan

Jonathan was born June 19, 1972, in Madisonville. He is attending Irmo High School in Columbia, SC, and has returned to Madisonville every summer for a visit.

Jimmy now works for The Pantry Convenience Stores. He was transferred to Columbia as Regional Director of S.C. in January 1986.

Beverly worked for Peoples Bank and Trust Company for 10 years and is now enjoying early "retirement". - *Submitted by Beverly Card*

CARDWELL-MURPHEY
William Ray Cardwell (b. 3-21-1913) and Carrie Lucille Murphey (b.9-6-1915) were married Dec. 16, 1936 in Princeton, KY.

Ray is the son of William Everett Cardwell (b. Hopkins Co. 3-25-1886, d. 6-29-1970) and Bessie Ray Stodghill (b. 3-22-1887, d. 5-20-1962). William E. and Bessie Ray marrried on Oct. 10, 1906. William E. was the son of William Evermont (b. 11-11-1825, d. January ? 1900) and Emma Gibson Mauzy (b. 1864, d. 1-28-1903). William Evermont emigrated to Hopkins Co. from Mercer Co. where his parents, James and Nancy Cardwell, lived. Bessie Ray was the daughter of Jeff and Prince Stodghill.

Lucille is the daughter of Finis Ewing Murphey (b. 11-5-1894, d. 5-18-1975) and Mattie Mae Hanner (b. 9-19-1900, d. 7-25-1952) who were married in 1914. Finis was the son of Charles N. (Dick) Murphey (b. 1857 d. 1924) and Hattie E. Crumbaker (b. 1863, d. 1920) . Mattie Mae was the daughter of James R. Hanner (b. 4-26-1864, d. 11-26-1935) and Ethel M. Fowler (b. 2-6-1869, d. 5-11-1948).

Ray and Lucille's children are: Betsy Ann Cardwell Sellers (b. 8-20-1938); William Ray Cardwell Jr. (b. 9-19-1940); and twin sons Everett Holman and Finis Coleman Cardwell (b. 3-24-1946). The Cardwell's have eight grandchildren.

The Cardwells live east of Madisonville in the Anton community and have lived on the family farm since marriage. Ray and his father farmed the land inherited from his grandfather, William Evermont Cardwell, until later on when Ray and his three sons and grandson Everett Holeman (Buddy) Cardwell Jr. continue to farm on the land that has been in the family five generations.

Ray and Lucille have been active since marriage in community affairs including but not limited to: Farm Bureau, PTA, 4-H, Hopkins Co. Saddle Club, Homemakers and Hopkins Co. Fair. Ray enjoys hunting, fishing, and horseback riding. Lucille enjoys cooking, needlework and a variety of handicrafts. Lucille has been named Lions Club Woman of the Year, Master Farm Homemaker for Hopkins Co. and the Pennyrile Area, and a Kentucky Colonel.

In December of 1986, Ray and Lucille were honored by family and friends with a 50th Wedding Anniversary celebration. - *Submitted by Lucille Cardwell*

CARLTON
Ruby Whitson Carlton was born on Dec. 31, 1905, in Christian Co., KY, the son of Jeptha Dickerson Carlton and Annie Elizabeth Keith. On Nov. 22, 1922, he married Eunice Bailey Winsett, b. Dec. 4, 1904, the daughter of Charlie W. Winsett and Sallie Jane McCracken. To their union were born seven children: James C. "Duck" Carlton m. Willa Dean Choates, Geneva m. Howard "Bill" Wilson, Arbie Carlton m. Janice Butler, Edward Lynn and William Whitson who died in infancy, Corrine m. Jesse Willard Murrah, Rodney Wayne m. Ruth Ann Smith.

Ruby and Eunice (Winsett) Carlton on their wedding day, Nov. 22, 1922

Ruby was employed by Norton Coal Company and Island Creek Coal Co. He is retired and lives in Christian Co. at the present time. Eunice Winsett Carlton passed away Jan. 25, 1965. She was laid to rest at New Salem Cemetery. She was a kind woman mourned by all who had known her.

Jeptha Dickerson Carlton was born Jan. 12, 1871, in Hopkins Co. the son of Daniel Wade Hamilton Carlton and Martha Tennessee Putman. On Jan. 11, 1893, he married Annie Elizabeth Keith, b. Mar. 16, 1874, the daughter of Joseph Johnston Keith and Susan E. Dukes. Jeppie and Annie Carlton were the parents of seven children including Ruby. They were: Eron Crick Pyles, Lawrence Carlton, Florence Crick, Charlie Carlton, Jewell Carlton, and Eural Carlton. Deptha Dickerson Carlton died on Mar. 26, 1928. He was buried at Coles Chapel Cem. as was Annie E. Carlton who died on Apr. 28, 1953.

Daniel Wade Hamilton Carlton was born Sept. 13, 1844, the son Jeptha B. Carlton and Clicia Ann Wilkes. On Apr. 5, 1867, he married Martha Tennessee Putman, b. Mar. 5, 1847, the daughter of Noah Putman and Elizabeth J. Carlton. Wade and Martha were the parents of two other children besides Jeppie: Louis Benjamin, Arra V. Keith. Martha Carlton died on July 14, 1873, and was buried at Rock Bridge Cem. After her death Wade married Amanda Keith Hunter, b. July 17, 1841, the daughter of Alexander Keith and Ellen Wadley. After her death he married Mary Keith Knight, b. July 1, 1830, Amanda's sister. Wade Carlton was a member of the Masonic Lodge and a great fiddle player. He died Mar. 2, 1930. He was laid to rest beside his first wife Martha.

Jeptha B. Carlton was born Nov. 1, 1823, in Williamson Co., TN, the tenth child of fourteen belonging to Thomas Carlton and Nancy Anna Wade. He was married Clicia Ann Wilkes on May 25, 1840. They came to Kentucky in the 1850's where they lived when Jeptha fought in the Civil War. He was a school teacher, a millwright, and a farmer by trade. He died Jan. 30, 1869, and was buried in the Fox Cem. near Nortonville. Clicia did not die until Feb. 6, 1910. She was laid to rest by his side.

From Thomas and Nancy Carlton back through North Carolina, Pennsylvania and Massachusettes to England. The Carlton family is documented to Baldwin de Carleton who fought alongside William the Conqueror in the Battle of Hastings in 1066. - *Submitted by Willard, Corrine, Mike and Lou Ann Murrah*

CARSON-CLARK
Steven Eugene Carson and Charlene Marie Clark were married June 26, 1970, in the Second Baptist Church of Madisonville.

Steve was born Nov. 10, 1951, in Bowling Green, KY, in Warren Co. He is the middle son of Johnny Henry Carson and Ivy Lou Sears. The Carsons moved to Madisonville in 1959. Steve graduated from Madisonville North Hopkins High School in 1969. He started to work for Mr. and Mrs. Fred Strother at Barnett-Strother Funeral Home in October 1968. He served 2 years with U.S. Army as a prison guard at Ft. Leavenworth, KS, from 1973 to 1975. He attended Kentucky School of Mortuary Science from 1975 to 1976. Steve is a licensed funeral director and embalmer as well as the manager of the funeral home. He and his wife are part owners of the funeral home with Mrs. W.F. Strother.

Steve has two brothers: Johnny Dale Carson, who lives with his wife, the former Suzann Allen; and Dennis Alan Carson of Madisonville. Steve and Charlene are members of 2nd Baptist Church and have two children;:Steven Eric Carson, born in 1971; and Samantha Leigh Carson, born in 1976.

The Carson family-Steve, Charlene, Steven Eric, and Samantha Leigh

Charlene was born May 24, 1951, in Uniontown, KY, in Union Co. She is the oldest child of Wilbur Lee Clark and Patricia Ann Clements. The Clarks moved to Madisonville in 1964. She attended grade school at St. Agnes Parochial School in Uniontown until moving to Madisonville. She graduated from Madisonville North Hopkis High School in 1969. She was employed by the Hopkins Co. Hospital as a E.K.G. Technician. She continued her cardiology training at Norton's Childrens Hospital in Louisville and worked as a cardiology technician until moving back to Madisonville in 1976.

She is now a licensed funeral director and is working as a partner with her husband at Barnett-Strother Funeral Home.

Charlene's sisters and brother are Greg Clark, Anita Patterson, Patty Cotton, Joann Fritz, and Natalie Clark. Other ancestral names are Pike, Whitlock, Rathman, and Bratton. *Submitted by Steve and Charlene Carson*

CARTER

According to John Carter's Revolutionary War record, he was born in Chester Co., PA, and moved to Chester District, SC ca 1763. His gravestone in present Fulton Co., KY, records his birth as December 1747 and death as September 1839. The John Carter family arrived in Henderson - now Hopkins - Co., ca 1800 according to the early land grants he received. Shortly after arriving in Henderson Co., John and his children began obtaining grants of land, and by 1816, they had acquired 3645 acres in Clear Creek/Tradewater River area. John's wife's exact name is not known, but all indications are that it was Dorcas, nick-named Patsy. There was a Dorcas Carter 'birid Aug. 4, 1824' in the old Carter Cemetery near Beulah, and Dorcas was a family name. John and wife had the following children: Hannah - ca 1780, Henry - 15 June, 1781, Jane - ca 1782, Martha D. - 1784, Ezekiel - ca 1786, John Jr. - ca 1788, Dorcas - 1790, William F. - ca 1792 and Polly - ca 1800. There is no proof nor disproof that William was one of John's sons. William signed a document indicating that he might be a family member in 1817 and so far as can be determined, there were no other Carters in the area at that time. Hannah became Stephen Rash's second wife on 9 Sept. 1823, but was soon his widow. She followed her family to Hickman, later Fulton Co., where Henry had moved ca 1826-27. Henry had married Ebenezer and Mary Given's daughter-Mary (Polly) on 18 May 1815. They had 8 children who helped settle Hickman Co. and Obion Co., TN. Jane married into another early Hopkins Co. family-George Gill. After serving in the War of 1812, George and Jane migrated to northeastern Arkansas where he became a pioneering Baptist minister. Martha D. and John Chappell were married in 1808 but she was widowed in 1824, being left with 8 children. She married Abraham Ellis of Caldwell Co. and they migrated with her family to Obion Co. in late 1820's. Polly was living with Hannah in Hickman Co. in 1840 but disappeared after Hannah died. Ezekiel married Sally (Sarah) Parrish, daughter of Jesse Parish of Hopkins Co. Ezekiel and Sally also moved to Obion Co. at about the same time as the rest of the family. According to her will, they had 5 children before he died ca 1844. However, there were unaccounted for children in his household during 1830 and 1840 censuses. John Jr. married an Elizabeth in Hopkins Co. and they had 2 children. John and family also went to Obion Co. ca 1827-28 and no spouse nor children were listed for him in 1830 census. However, he was living next door to Ezekiel and there was a sudden increase of children in Ezekiel's family. Were the 2 extra children John Jr's? William F. married Elizabeth Ann Conn in Union Co. in 1823. In 1830 census there were two children but nothing more is known about William. Dorcas married into another Hopkins Co. family - Ebenezer Alexander, Jr. They, too went to Obion and Hickman Co. but in 1832 they migrated to Coles Co., IL, where they raised a large family. Ebenezer became a minister in a pioneer church which later became Methodist. MANY descendants of this couple still live in that area.

Source: *John Carter and His Descendants* by Virginia Carter Graham. A copy of this book is in the Hopkins Co. Library. - *Contributed by Virginia C. Graham*

CARTWRIGHT

Robert Cartwright, native of Princess Anne Co., VA, after serving his country in various civil and military capacities, both in Virginia and South Carolina, joined the Col. John Donaldson expedition. They left Fort Patrick Henry on the Holsten River, Dec. 22, 1779, and arrived at Big Salt Lick, Apr. 24, 1780. Robert Cartwright (b. 2-22-1722 d. 12-24-1809) married Anne Huggins, daughter of Robert Huggins, had one son, William b 7-14-1746. She died 3-17-1747. He then married on 4-20-1749 to Mary Hunter, dau. of John Hunter and Jacamine. Their issue: Martha 5-14-1750, Mary 8-11-1753, Anne 6-2-1755, Susannah 9-4-1757, Robert (b. 12-17-1759 d. 3-23-1776), John Hunter 2-26-62, Thomas 11-20-1763. She died ?-22-1764. He then married Pembroke Hunter in 1764. Issue: Pemmy 2-28-1765, Jacob 2-21-1767, James 2-14-1770, William Hunter 10-4-1772, Elizabeth 9-2-1776, Jesse Hunter 1778, Robert 1780, and David 1782.

Thomas Cartwright (b. 11-20-1763 d. 1822) wife Martha. Issue: Samuel (1786-1822), Thomas, Hezekiah, Sally, Patsy, Susannah.

Samuel Cartwright (b. 1786 d. 6-14-1856) married Letty Moore Mar. 20, 1810. In 1830 census they had 3 boys and 3 girls. He married Minerva Ellis on Oct. 17, 1841, their issue: James 1842, Elizabeth 1844, William 1849.

Thomas Cartwright (b. 7-18-1813 d. 10-19-1876) married Mary Fisher on Jan. 4, 1838. She was the dau. of Jacob Fisher, and was born June 21, 1820, died 5-8-1906. Thomas and father Samuel came to Butler Co. 1850. Issue: John Monroe 1839, Phillip 1840, Louisa J. 1842, Samuel Wilson 4-15-1843, James Henry 1845, William 1847, Hezekiah 1850, Martha 1852, Mary Caroline 1855, Thompson 1855, Silas, Erastus.

Samuel Wilson Cartwright (b. 4-15-1843 d. 9-29-1924) married Amanda Alice McCoy (b 1-6-1846 d. 3-20-1900), daughter of Rueben McCoy and Helen Daughtery. Issue: Joney, Henry, Lydia, Finas, Susan, Denny, Thomas, Elizabeth, Archer and Lizetta. (See Cartwright-McCoy) - *Submitted by Dorothy Abbott*

CARTWRIGHT-HOWTON

Uria and Ozelia Cartwright were married on Sept 4, 1926, in Madisonville and have lived in Hopkins Co. for the majority of their lives.

Ozelia was the former Ozelia Howton who was born Jan. 31, 1908, near Lafayette Church in southwestern Hopkins Co. She was one of six children born to Riley Arthur Howton and Aremently Purdy Howton, both of Kirkwood Springs. Riley Howton was a former magistrate from the Sixth District, a farmer, auctioneer, and music teacher. Ozelia's maternal grandparents were Bassett Purdy and Sara Jane Harris Purdy, and her paternal grandparents were Alfred Howton and Polly Anna Harris Howton. The Howton family members were long-time residents of HopkinsCo. as Alfred's father, Henry Howton, was the original landowner of the property near the current Lafayette Church.

Uria and Ozelia Cartwright on their 60th wedding anniversary, Sept. 4, 1986

Uria Lewis Cartwright was born on May 11, 1903, in Rochester, Butler Co., KY, to his parents, Dennie B. Cartwright and Bertha Mae Arnold Cartwright, who had two other sons and one daughter. The Cartwright family moved to Hopkins Co. in 1921; the family traveled from Butler Co. to Madisonville in a wagon with the trip starting at 4 a.m. and arriving at Hopkins Co. at 11 p.m. Uria's paternal grandparents were Samuel Cartwright and McCoy Cartwright, who originally moved to Kentucky from the Tennessee area. Uria's maternal grandparents were Bill and Amanda Arnold.

After moving to Hopkins Co., Uria worked on the construction of Illinois Central Railroad near Madisonville and married Ozelia on Sept. 4, 1926, in Madisonville. The couple lived in their residence (which Uria built in 1923) on Grapevine Road from the date of the marriage until the present, except during the Depression when they lived in Dawson Springs and briefly in Indianapolis, IN. Uria was a farmer and a coal miner, having been a U.M.W.A. member who worked at the Pleasant View, Sunset, Curtis, Grapevine, New Coal and North Diamond mines.

Ozelia spent a great amount of her time raising their five children, Bremen, Billy, Jo Ann, Peggy and Bobby. The Cartwrights have ten grandchildren and currently have seven great-grandchildren.

A history of the family would not be complete without a reference to the Grapevine Baptist Church. Uria and Ozelia were charter members of the church and raised all of their children and many of their grandchildren in the church. Ozelia has also taught the Mary Helen Sunday School Class for approximately 30 years. -*Submitted by Uria and Ozelia Cartwright*

CARTWRIGHT-McCOY

The children of Samuel Wilson Cartwright (b. 4-15-1843, d. 9-29-1924) and Alice McCoy (b. 1-6-1846, d. 3-20-1900) (See Cartwright story) are:

Joaney married 5-29-1879 to George Wester. Issue: Dolph married Lona Huggins; Harve; Finley married Essie Hill; Floyd married Lydia Brown; Marvin married Etta Shimmer; Arvin married Blanche Summers; Clarence; Adorum; Carlie married Fannie Howton; Elsie married Joe Hill; Alice Ann married Vert Adkins; Aula married Bill Kirby; Novella married Jack Jenkins; and Della married Harry Abbott.

Henry (b. 3-27-1865, d. 8-27-1935) married Lum. Issue: Nancy married Calvin Stearsman; Homer H. married Pansy Irene Pendley; Harvey married Leora Baker; Effie married Sandy Hammer; and Seva married Claude E. Andrews.

Lydia married Charlie Jenkins, Delmer Cook married Gusta Wester, Lou married Perry Hartis.

Finas Ashley (b. 10-13-1869, d 1-20-1952) married Stella Ann Arnold (b. 3-23-1873, d. 9-7-1958) Issue: Fred married Rosa Davis; Marion married Lula Bell Lee; Erdine died as a baby; Lossie married Sammie H. Ferrell; Vernie married Leera Thomason; Tommy married Pauline Egbert; and Johnnie married Gladys Wilson.

Susan married Thomas Hammers. Issue: Joseph died a baby; Luzettie married Johnny Arnold; Virgil married Kester Conley; Erdie; Minnie married Jesse A. Pendley; Festus married Elsie Moore Kirby; and Ustus married Leona Fortner.

Denny (b. 3-10-1874, d. 6-1936) married Cora Bertha Arnold (b. 5-20-1883, d. 1-10-1975). Issue: Latney married Pauline Shoate; Uria L. married Ozelia Howton; Edna married Henry Rice; and Estel married Lucille Mullins.

Tommie (b. 10-20-1876, d. 8-25-1936) married Effie Arnold (b. 12-23-1889, d. 2-2-1981). Issue: Martin married Jessie Howton; Edith married Malcolm Noffsinger; Henry Hamilton married Lawcerner Pyle; Exie married Joe Downey; Recie married Mitt Barker; and Ray remained single.

Lizzie/Elizabeth married Billy White. Issue: Arvillie married Nettie A. Arnold; Leslie married Goldie Belamy, 2nd Laura —.

Archer (b. 1-18-1884, d. 5-27-1963) married Sybil Hardesty (b. 5-26-1900). Issue: Keever, Hugh, Warren, J.D., Lois Marie, Marion Wayne, and Sylvia.

Lizetta Harriet (b. 2-14-1888, d. 11-3-1966) married Sam Abbott (b. 11-10-1884, d. 9-7-1967). Issue: Luther, Kester, Rufus, Rupert, Henry, Flora, Parlon, Charles, Norman, Wilbur, Nancy, Mildred and Bonnie. *Submitted by Dorothy Abbott*

CARTWRIGHT-UTLEY

Keith and Rene Cartwright and their son, John Thomas Cartwright, 1042 Parkwood Drive, Madisonville, KY, are a family with a long history in Hopkins Co. and Western KY.

Rene is the former Debbie Rene Utley, who was raised in nearby Providence and who was born on Dec. 14, 1960, in Madisonville, with her parents being Thomas Earl Utley and Thelma Marie Utley. Rene has one brother, Harold Utley, and one sister, Marie Utley Brown. Her father, Thomas Utley, was a native of the Stoney Point/Dalton area in Hopkins Co. as were his parents, John Utley and Eva Johnston Utley. Rene's maternal grandparents were Clay Villines and Fannie Sigler Villines of Dixon, Webster Co., KY. Rene's father died on Oct 21, 1973, and her mother remarried Floyd Coffman of Dalton in 1983.

Keith was born on Nov. 2, 1958, in Madisonville, KY, with his parents being Billy Rudolph Cartwright and Nell Katherine Wiley Cartwright. He has one brother, Kevin Marion Cartwright. Keight father was the son of Uria Lewis Cartwright and Ozelia Howton Cartwright of Dawson Springs and Grapevine.

Nell's parents were Milford Otis Wiley and Jewell Almaranda Timmons Wiley of the Ashbyburg Community in Northern Hopkins Co.

Keith lived in Madisonville until age nine when his family moved to Providence. He graduated from Providence High School in 1976. Rene lived all of her childhood in Providence and graduated from Providence High School in 1978. Keith graduated from Madisonville Community College in 1978 and Murray State University in 1980 and then entered the University of Louisville School of Law. Rene graduated from Murray State University in 1982, and Keith and Rene were married on July 31, 1982, at Rene's home church, Victory Baptist Church, in Providence. After their marriage they moved to Louisville, where they lived until Keith finished law school. After his graduation from law school, they moved to Madisonville in July 1983.

Keith is currently an attorney with the law firm of Moore, Morrow & Frymire. Rene is a registered nurse with the Hopkins Co. Health Department, and she has formerly worked with the Regional Medical Center, and Jewish Hospital of Louisville. They are both members of the First United Methodist Church of Madisonville; Keith is active in the Madisonville Lions Club and Rene is a member of the Greater Madisonville Lions Club and Rene is a member of the Greater Madisonville Lioness Club.

Another generation of Cartwrights in Hopkins Co. was established in 1985 when John Thomas Cartwright was born on Dec. 3, 1985. He was named for his father, whose first name is John, and for his maternal grandfather, Thomas Utley, and maternal great-grandfather, John Utley. *Submitted by Keith Cartwright*

CASTLE-GREEN

Eugene Allen Castle and Lula Margaret Green were married Apr. 12, 1958, in the First Baptist Church in Middlesboro, KY. They moved to Hopkins Co. July 1958.

The Cartwrights. Front row l to r: Archer, Samuel Wilson Cartwright, Amanda Alice, Joanie, Lizetta. Back row l to r: Henry, Finas, Dennie, Thomas, Lydia, Susan and Lizzie.

Eugene (Gene) was born Sept. 2, 1918, in McAlester, OK, the only child of the marriage of Elmer Burl Castle (1900-1982) and Mabel Grace Pascoe (1901-1976). Elmer was the only son of William Henry Castle and Eleanor (Nora) Connally. William and Nora also had a daughter, Vivian Castle Overand (1903) who lives in Oklahoma City, OK. Mabel Pascoe was the only daughter of William Pasco (died 1918) and Sophia Bernhardt (died 1961). Mabel had two brothers, Earnest William (1910-1974) and Augustus (Gus) (1905) who still lives in McAlester, OK.

Lula (Lu) was born Oct. 23, 1923, at Insull, KY, in Harlan Co. She is the daughter of the late Robert Clinton Green (1903-1979) and Rose Hensley Green, who now lives in Knoxville, TN. Rose and Clint were both born in Bell Co. and were married Dec. 22, 1922, at Cubage, KY. Clint Green was the only son of James Lee Green (1866-1946) and Betty Head Green (1872-1931). He had five half-sisters: Nancy Green Boatright, Ida Green Thompson, Margaret Green Daniels, Elizabeth Green Taylor and Mary Green Wilson. Clint Green was a descendent of Lewis Green (1750-1836) who served in the Revolutionary War from 1776 to 1783. Lewis, whose father was a vestryman in the church at Kilgore Station in Scott Co., VA, married Esther Kilgore and moved to Kentucky about 1800. Lewis and Esther had ten children and Clint Green descended from their oldest, James, who was born in 1784 and married Nancy Arnett, born 1788. Rose Hensley was born Mar. 4, 1906, the second of eleven children of David Crockett Hensley (1886-1927) and Dora Bell Hensley (1889-1970). The other children were: Lillie H. Pace, Cecil Hensley, Grace H. Green, Elsie H. Scott, Milford Hensley, Verna H. Carroll, Flossie H. Daniels, Hazel H. Campbell, Arlus Hensley and Ruby H. Walters. Rose was a descendent of Lewis Hensley (1782) who was the first Hensley to come from North Carolina to Kentucky. He settled in what is now Bell Co. and married Nancy Hoard (later changed to Howard) daughter of Samuel Hoard (1762-1840). Samuel Hoard served in the Virginia Continental Line during the Revolutionary War and was with Washinton at Valley Forge and at the surrender of Cornwallis at Yorktown.

Lula Green Castle graduated as a registered nurse in 1945 from the Knoxville General Hospital School of Nursing in Knoxville, TN. Eugene Castle served six years in the U.S. Infantry during World War II, attaining the rank of Captain. He was a prisoner of war and received the Purple Heart and the Presidential Citation. He gradeuted from the University of Oklahoma School of Medicine in 1953 and after specializing he moved to Middlesboro, KY, in 1957. He joined the Trover Clinic in Madisonville, KY, in 1958 and was head of the OB-GYN department until his death Apr. 6, 1985. Lu and Gene had two children: Margaret Rose Castle (1959) and E. Allen Castle, Jr. (1961). - *Submitted by Lula G. Castle*

CATES-HILLYARD

Mary Elizabeth Hillyard and Aubrey Lee Cates were married Jan. 5, 1928 in Springfield, TN. Mary was born July 9, 1909, in Crittenden Co. near Marion. She is the daughter of Henry Guy Hillyard and Elnor Celeste Waide Hillyard. She has five brothers and five sisters. They are Wilbur, Budie Agatha, Minnie Frances Cates, Mary Elizabeth Cates, Robert Winderd, Glades Syvesta Cunningham, Louvinia Waide Larimore, Lawrence Henry, Georgia Franklin Hennebut Mitchem, Virginia Lee Peyton and David Guy.

Aubrey Lee and Mary Elizabeth Cates

Mary moved to Nebo in the early 1920's. She attended school at Nebo completeing the sixth grade. She played basketball on the girl's team. She quit school to help at home on the farm. She became a member of the Nebo Methodist Church as a teenager in the 1920's

Aubrey Lee Cates was born July 1, 1906, in Hopkins, north of Manitou. He is the son of Lonnie Ruby Cates and Effie Mae Cates. He has two brothers and three sisters. They are Lonnie, Aubrey, Hazel, Cora Hardy, Josephine Marks, and Lilian Peyton.

Aubrey went to the Greenwood School north of Nebo. At thirteen he quit school to help work the family farm because of his father's death. He is a member of the Nebo Methodist Church. They have lived in the Nebo community most of their lives. He is a retired farmer and employee of Chrysler Corporation.

Mary and Aubrey have seven children. They are Naomi Love Knox, Douglas Wayne, Rosetta LaVonne Crask, Ruby Henry, Celeste Lou Krietzer, William David, and Sharon Gail Harris.- *Submitted by Sharon Harris*

LANNA MARS CATES

Lanna Mars Cates, born Mar. 26, 1903, in Hopkins Co., KY, was the fourth child of Robert Franklin Cates and Roslin Deborah Jones. Robert and Roslin's other children were: Velma Francis, Alva Vernon, and Verlia Nancy Isadora. On Sept. 17, 1926, Lanna married Sam E. Peterson in Charleston, MO. Their children were: Marie (Thiesern) born 5/7/27; twins Velma Corrine (Roberts) and Thelma Nadine (Schroller) born 10/28/29; Mary Ann (Lewis) born 6/22/34 and Dixie Lee (Briegel) born 4/13/42.

Robert Franklin Cates, born Jan. 2, 1869, died Jan. 10, 1944, was the eighth of thirteen children born to Thomas Jefferson Cates, 1831-1899, and Nancy Caroline Benton, 1835-1905, of Hopkins and Webster Counties. Robert's siblings were: Mary, 1855-1870; William L. 1856-1925; John Newton 1857-1940; Richard E. 1859-1936; Thomas J. 1863-1865; Samuel 1864-1940; James W. 1866-1950; George W. 1861-?; Theodore Guston 1873-1942; Tinna 1875-1950; and Minnie L. 1879-1958.

Thomas Jefferson Cates was the son of John Cates, 1793-1869. John Cates first shows up in Hopkins Co. between 1810 and 1820. Abner Cates, who we believe was a brother of John Cates, was a constable of Hopkins Co. in 1815. John Cates' wife was Frances, maiden name unknown. John Cates came to Hopkins Co. from North Carolina. The county minute books show that John settled in the Knob Lick area of Hopkins Co. with another possible brother, Alexander.

Roslin Deborah Jones, 1875-1954, our subject's mother, was the fourth of eight children of Doc Hill Jones, 1846-1932, and Isadora W. Barron, 1845-1909. Doc Hill Jones' parents were Moses Jones, 1808-1863, and Meleana Harriet Clay, 1818-1885. Moses Jones arrived in Hopkins Co. about 1855. His first eight children were born in Granville Co., NC., the last four in Hopkins Co. Isadora Barron's parents were William Jacob Barron and Mary Ann Puryear. It is not known when William Barron arrived in Hopkins Co., but he married Mary Ann Puryear in 1839 in Hopkins Co. William and Mary Ann both died young and their seven children were split up into various relative's homes. Isadora grew up in the home of W.T. Overby. Mary Ann Puryear's parents were Hezekiah Puryear, 1790-1855, and Mary Hudson ?-1821. She was born in Mecklenberg

Front row: Robert and Roslin (Jones) Cates. Back row: Velma, Alva, Verlia and Lanna

Co., VA, and came to Hopkins Co. with her father about 1835.

Lanna Mars Cates Peterson died Jan. 29, 1982, in Sylvania, OH. She is survived by five daughters, 16 grandchildren and 21 great-grandchildren. This article was written by her granddaughter. - *Submitted by Kathy Thiessen Risher*

CHARLES F. CATO

In July of 1635 John Cato and wife Joan embarqued from Geavesend England, on the ship Assurance de Lo for the American Plantation Colony. On arrival he was awarded a patent of 300 acres of land on the East Branch of the Elizabeth River in the newly formed county of Norfolk. That patent lies in what is today the city of Norfolk, VA. He was awarded this acreage for furnishing transportation to America for six persons. This included food, clothing and supplies for one year. The people's names were listed on the patent and only one was Cato. John Cato. He was allowed 50 acres for transporting himself. Nothing for the rest of his family. He received 250 acres for the other five people.

Skipping along for four generation we come to another John Cato. He married Jane Cooke and settled in Brunswick Co., VA. In the mid-seventeen hundreds he sold this land and moved to Lancaster Co., SC. Most of his family went with him, including a son Henry Cooke Cato. Henry was named after his maternal grandfather. In 1806, after John died, Henry Cato and wife Tabitha moved to Christian Co., KY.

For three generation the Catos farmed, built wagons, made harnesses, fiddled at square dances and dabbled in a jack-leg law practice. They sold, swapped and bartered farms. "I'll give you this wagon, that team of mules and my land across the creek for your fifteen acres above my place." This was usually done with a handshake. No deed. This occurred in the areas around Pennyrile Park and Northeast Trigg Co.

William Wiley Cato, born 1850, married Mary Jane Glover and moved to Dawson Springs. There he was known as 'W.W.' He went into the hotel business. When a son Charles F. Cato, born 1875, came home from being a drummer (salesman) in the 'wild west,' he purchased a part interest in W.W.'s holdings and they started Cato's Busy Store. W.W. died in 1928. The Crash of '29 wiped out all of the family's holdings.

Charles F. Cato Sr. about 1900

In 1933 Charles F. Cato, Sr., with wife Rosa Lou Gleaves Cato and family, moved to Madisonville. 'Charlie' was again a traveling salesman. Rosa Lou died with cancer in 1941. Charles F., Sr. died in 1962. Their children were:

Baker G. Cato, born 1912, married Etta Geneva Clayton. They later moved to Tennessee. He died at Rockwood, TN, in 1970.

Mary Rose Cato, born 1915, married Maurice Caruthers. She retired from Hopkins Co. Hospital. Maurice retired from Kentucky Bank and Trust Co. Mary Rose died 1980. Maurice later married Eva Lloyd Trathen, a life-long friend of Mary Rose.

Charles F. Cato, Jr., born 1929, moved to CA when he worked for the Division of Forestry. He married Berniece K. Sitz Pate. After his medical retirement they moved to Utah. Berniece died in 1987. He plans to finish his days in Pleasant Grove, UT, with visits to Madisonville. *Submitted by Charles F. Cato*

WILLIAM McVEY CHANDLER

William McVey Chandler born Jan. 16, 1829, in North Carolina to Washington and Letha Morrow Chandler. He married Eliza Jane Parker, daughter of Jonas Parker and Ruth Tapp, 4th child of William Tapp, Revolutionary soldier, and Rebecca Fowler. Through this William Tapp, the Chandler line was dated back through three other generations of William Tapps to Thomas Tapp of London, Middlesex Co., England, circa 1628-May 18, 1689. Thomas Tapp migrated from England to Charles River Co., VA.

William McVey Chandler

William McVey's grandparents, John Chandler 1780-1860 and Rebecca McVey Chandler, 1783-1860, were married in North Carolina, Nov. 22, 1800. Great grandfathers were Joel Chandler, Ensign Revolutionary War and John McVey, Revolutionary soldier. Sons of American Revolutionary Chapter in Henderson, KY, called John McVey S.A.R. Chapter in honor of this Revolutionary soldier.

Children of William McVey and Eliza Jane Chandler were: Martha Jane, married H.R. Cox, Mary A. married B.F. James, Sarah, married Dr. L.J. Couch, Lurticia married Thomas Powell. By second marriage to Bettie Isbell were William and Betty.

Mr. Chandler farmed until 1882, then engaged in milling business in Sebree, KY, until his death Nov. 21, 1885.

Martha Jane Chandler (May 18, 1850-Mar. 24, 1935) married Hezekial Rice Cox (Sept. 27, 1845-Sept. 21, 1918), son of Alexander Bailey and Martha Ann Puryear Cox, Nov. 22, 1866. Mr. Cox sold his farm in Webster Co. in 1878 and bought land near Nebo, KY. He moved to Nebo and bought a store on site of present business, Lantrip's gas station. In 1883, he bought a home and store across the street from first business. At one time, Mr. Cox owned five stores, and at his death four; one each at Sebree and Richland and two in Nebo. He was a large stockholder in Nebo Citizens Bank, organized Apr. 29, 1902. At his death, he was the president of the bank. He planned to retire, but he met with an accident which took his life. He drove a high-spirited horse, which was frightened by noise from a threshing machine. He was thrown from the buggy and dragged. He died of multiple injuries, six days prior to his 73rd birthday.

The home Mr. Cox bought in 1883 was built in 1860. It has been home for three family generations. Presently, it is home to his granddaughter, Miss Sarah Barron, a retired teacher. Her mother was born shortly after it was purchased and died there 88 years later.

Mr. and Mrs. Cox had nine children, but only five reached maturity. They were: Anna Eliza (3-24-1866, who lived 102 years and eight months). W.B. (Aug. 9, 1869-Feb. 16, 1951), Laura Vaden (Feb. 18, 1872-Feb. 16, 1916), Mattie Lee (Dec. 10, 1883-Dec. 21, 1971), and Nannie Rebecca (Apr. 15, 1885-May 30, 1978).
Source: History of the Tapp Family, Family Bible - Submitted by Sarah Barron

CHILDERS-ARBUCKLE

Elsie Trusty Arbuckle and James Madison Childers were married Dec. 1, 1943, in Morganfield, KY. They moved to Hopkins Co. in 1950 from Webster Co.

Elsie was born Sept. 26, 1924, in Henderson, KY, the only daughter of Enoch Bradshaw Arbuckle and Lola Pearl Trusty. She attended grade school in Fredonia, KY, and 8th grade through high school and two years business college at Midway College, Midway, KY. Some of the positions she has held in Hopkins Co. are: first Hospital Secretary for Trover Clinic; bookkeeper for Coca Cola Plant; office assistant at Woolworth; 25 years as loan, feed grain and conservation reserve clerk at the Agricultural Stabilization and Conservation Service (ASCS) Office in Madisonville. Since retirement in 1980, she has operated a commercial recording studio, Trusty Tuneshop, and music publishing company, Trusty Publication BMI, with office and studio located 11 miles west of Madisonville on Hwy. 1034 (Rose Creek Road) where she resides on their 125 acre farm.

Due to work as Executive Director of Bill Monroe Day, Merle Travis Day, Pee Wee King Day and Duke of Paducah Day held in Madisonville, yearly from 1969-1972, Gov. Wendell Ford made her a Kentucky Colonel. She has written over 450 songs, many of them being recorded and featured on TV and radio shows and concerts. She is a member of Johnson Island Baptist Church where she has been pianist and soloist for 35 years.

Elsie and J. M. Childers in the Bahamas in 1986

James, "Bud" to his friends, was born Mar. 13, 1918, in Webster Co., near Providence to William Shirl Childers and Anna Ora Villines. He has one living sister, Frances Rachel Hobgood of Robards, KY, and one deceased sister, Geraldine Lynn. Bud attended McGaw School and graduated from Providence High School in 1935. He was assigned to the 448th Bomber Div., 8th Air Force, after volunteering for service during WWII. He was stationed near London, England, and flew 28 missions as a tail gunner on a B-24 bomber before enemy fire over Keil, Germany, destroyed their plane and all crew members bailed out into enemy territory. He and all his crew spent the rest of the war in German prisoner of war camps or being marched back and forth across Germany or riding in cattle cars as the German Army moved them away from the Russians closing in on one side and our own forces (Allied) closing in on the other side. On V-E Day, they were all set free.

Bud farmed, worked at Stoney Point coal mines and Servel, Inc., in Evansville, IN. He then worked for ASCS & Soil Conservation Service for 18 years, retiring in 1980.

Elsie and Bud have two sons: Terry of Tanner, AL, and Jimmy of Frankfort, KY. They have two granddaughters, Christine, 18, and Amy, 7. - *Submitted by Mr. & Mrs. James Childers*

CHRISTIAN

I. CAPTAIN GILBERT CHRISTIAN born ca. 1677 in Ireland, m MARGARET RICHARDSON. They came to New Castle, PA, in 1726 and to Augusta Co., VA, in 1732 with three sons, John, Robert and William, and daughter, Mary. With Gilbert when he came to Virginia were his nephew, Israel Christian, and his wife, Elizabeth Starke. Their only son, William, married Anne Henry, sister of Patrick Henry, and was an officer in the Rev. War. They had five daughters. Christian Co., KY, was named for Israel's son, William Christian. Christian's Creek which drains into Middle River in Augusta Co., VA, was named for Gilbert's sons. They received a 1,600-acre grant along its headwaters in the Beverley Patent in 1739. It was a part of the Walnut Hills Campground, approximately six miles south of Staunton in 1985. Gilbert's son, William was famous as a Captain in the French and Indian War and was in the Augusta Co, VA, Militia in 1776. For more information, see Chalkey and Draper's Preston and VA Papers.

1. Robert Christian m. Isabella Tiffins
2. John Christian m. Wilson
3. Mary Christian m. 1st 1724 John Moffet (- 1746) 7 ch and m. 2nd 1755 John Trimble, 1 son.
4. WILLIAM CHRISTIAN (1725 Ireland - before AUG 1779 Augusta Co., VA).

II. WILLIAM CHRISTIAN m MARY CAMPBELL, d/o Patrick Campbell and (?) Thompson. Issue:

1. Margaret Campbell Christian (1745-1790) m. Capt. Andrew Russell.
2. Gilbert Christian (1747-1796) m.
3. Elizabeth Christian
4. Mary Christian
5. PATRICK CHRISTIAN (ca 1745 Augusta Co., VA - before March 1811).

III. PATRICK CHRISTIAN m. 1st 20 June 1766 ELIZABETH ROBERTSON (-after 1776), d/o Matthew Robertson and Martha. He served in the Rev. War and was Sergeant at Yorktown in 1781. His will probated 25 March 1811 Augusta Co., VA. FRANCES GIVENS RANDLE (1868 KY - 1948 KS) joined the Henderson, KY, DAR Chapter through Patrick Christian. Her national number is 273938.

1. William Christian
2. Martha Christian (ca 1770 - before 1829 Hopkins Co., KY) m. 21 March 1793 Augusta Co., VA, Philemon Richards, Jr. (ca 1770-before March 1793 KY), 4 children.
3. MATTHEW CAMPBELL CHRISTIAN (ca 1772 Augusta Co., VA - 1853 Union Co., KY)
4. John Christian
5. Mary Christian m. 18 Feb. 1796 David Bell

PATRICK CHRISTIAN m. 2nd Mrs Elizabeth Bradford Hayes.

6. James Christian
7. Elizabeth Christian
8. Nancy Christian

IV. MATTHEW CAMPBELL CHRISTIAN m Augusta Co., VA, JANE BLACK. Their daughter:

V. ELIZABETH R. CHRISTIAN (5 AUG 1803 KY - 21 APR 1871 KY) m. JAMES KERR GIVENS, son of Thomas Givens and Elizabeth "Betsey" Kerr. Their son, NATHANIEL KARR GIVENS m. SARAH ELIZABETH CLAY.

See GIVENS family for later generations of ELIZABETH R. CHRISTIAN and JAMES KERR GIVENS. - *Submitted by PATRICIA RANDLE GILLESPIE*

CHRISTOPHER

Oscar C. Christopher was born Jan. 8, 1888, in Maury Co., TN. He was the second of ten children born to Milton and Mattie (Pugh) Christopher. He got very little education but he could figure out most anything in his own way. During his lifetime he was a farmer, a blacksmith, a construction worker, a carpenter, a coal miner and a merchant.

The Christophers and the Morgans lived on adjoining farms in the early 1900's. In 1911 Oscar helped Mrs. Morgan and her daughter, Annie, with their crop after Mr. John Morgan died . On Sept. 10, 1911, Oscar C. Christopher and Annie Morgan (b. Aug. 14, 1894) were married, and they lived on the Morgan farm. Mrs Laura (McGrady) Morgan (b. 4-17-1872) and Annie operated a store and Oscar and brother started a freight delivery service in Mt. Pleasant.

In 1912, their first child, Jonnie , was born. Later in St. Charles she married Oscar Knight on Apr. 8, 1935. They had four children: Joyce, Phillip, Frances and David. Both Jonnie and Oscar are deceased.

On 9-5-1914 a son, Harold, was born. Their third child, born Dec. 15, 1918, was named C.D. for his Uncle Culess, killed in France during WWI. C.D. married Dorothy Carroll (b. 10-30-1923) of Earlington. They have one daughter, Martha Lynn Riddle (b. 7-22-1952).

In 1923 the Christopher family moved from Mt. Pleasant, TN, to St. Charles, KY, then a booming coal town. Mrs. Morgan also moved and lived with the Christophers until her death in 1958. After several years of carpentry, farming, working in the mines, Oscar Christopher bought a grocery-general merchandise store in St. Charles, which he and Annie operated until 1959. He died a few years later. C.D. bought and still operates Christophers Store.

Harold, fondly known as "Chris," grew up in St. Charles and worked at many odd jobs like shoe shining, cleaning the barber shop, clerking and delivery in a grocery store, working in the mines, and hauling coal. He finished the 8th grade at St. Charles and went to Dawson Springs to high school. In 1937 he got a job in the West Kentucky Company Store in Earlington in the credit department, was store manager at Wheatcroft for a while, then became credit office manager in Earlington, a job he held for 36 years until early retirement because of ill health. Chris died Mar. 24, 1987.

Harold "Chris" and Gertha (Oakley) Christopher

Harold Christopher and Gertha Oakley (b. 11-5-1916) were married Nov. 23, 1936. Gertha was the daughter of Woodson Oakley of Earlington and Sophie Gropengeiser of the Vandetta community. Her grandfather was a German who was a merchant on a tugboat that plied the Green River. Mr. and Mrs. Oakley had 5 children. In 1919 Mr. Oakley was killed in a St. Bernard Coal mine accident. Mrs. Oakley then married Edward Wiles and they had 9 children. She later married Joe Morris when she was 75 and he was 80. Sophie died in March 1981.

Harold and Gertha had one daughter, Ann, born 2-1-1939 in Earlington. She married Donald Egbert (b-7-8-1937) son of Buck and Earline (Fike) Egbert. Donald works for Peabody Coal Company and Ann works at the Water Company in City Hall at Earlington. They have two children: Chris (b. 4-17-1958) graduate of Georgetown University and Southern Baptist Seminary, Louisville, where he is now a Baptist minister. He married Patricia Powell (b. 5-9-1961) on Nov. 20, 1981. Shana (b. 9-1-1972) is a student at University Heights, Hopkinsville, KY.

Annie Christopher, died Dec. 5, 1987, at 93, and is buried in Oakwood Cemetery in Earlington. *Source - "Autobiography of Harold Christopher, 1914-1987". Submitted by Mrs. Ann Egbert*

CLARK-ADAMS-HOLLIE

On the Eighteenth day of May in the year Eighteen Hundred Ninety-Six the matriarch of our family was born, Verdie Lee Clark, in Hanson, KY. The daughter of Lewis and Clara Rendie (Lunsford) Clark. Earlier, Lewis Clark had migrated from Rome, GA, to Kentucky, where he and his wife Clara settled and began their home. There were five children born to this union who were as follows; Corrine Clark-Cross (her daughter was Viola Watkins); Goldie Clark-Browder (her daughter was Onieda B. Robinson); Ida Clark-Warfield-Akins (her daughters were Roberta and Catherine Warfield and son was Henry Akins Junior); Frederick Clark; and V.L. Clark-Hollie. The Clarks nurtured their children with a warm sense of family pride, high morals, and deep admiration for the Lord. Mr. L. Clark was a devout Sunday School instructor and was also known as a great singer. He attended A.M.E. Zion Methodist Church in Hanson, KY. He expired in Nineteen Hundred-Nineteen.

Lewis Clark (father of Verdie Lee) and Verdie Lee Clark Adams Hollie

During the early Twentieth Century Ms. Clark met Edward Cornelious Adams (born Apr. 2, 1890-died Dec. 5, 1975) and they were married in Nineteen Hundred-Nine. He was the son of John and Doane Adams. Their other children were: John Adams Jr.; Will Adams; Annie Bell Adams-Bell (her children were Agnes L. (Bell) Robinson; Calantha (Bell) Woodson; Curtis Bell; Catherine Bell; Ruby Bell); and with Mary Lizzie Adams-their daughter was Lelia Adams. John Adams Sr.'s brothers and sisters as well as their children are as follows: Abe (Molly) Adams, parented Lula (her children were Jim, Molly, Grace); Harry; and Addie Adams who married Jesse White; Henry (Ms. Eastwood) Adams, parented Lelia, Charles, with (Ms. Grady) Jesse, Harry Lee; and Rosie (Adams) Slaughter, her children were Belle, John, Rob, his daughter was Aileen Webb.

Children born to Edward and Verdie were: Ophelia Adams, born 1913 died at 5 years old; General Lee Adams, Aug. 10, 1915; Clara Geneva (Adams) Scisney, Dec. 19, 1917; Anna Frances (Adams) Taylor, Aug. 8, 1919; John Edward Adams, Sept. 11, 1922; Frederick Lewis Adams, July 17, 1924 (died Dec. 20, 1947); and Frankie Louise (Adams) Nichols, July 14, 1927. Edward's son Garth Riggins (Adams).

Later in Nineteen Hundred Thirty-Six, Ms. Verdie was united in Holy Matrimony with James Franklin Hollie (born July 3, 1886-died Oct. 27, 1945). James Raymond Hollie was born to this union.

Early in childhood, Mrs. Hollie professed faith in Christ, having been directed to Christ by her father in the A.M.E. Zion Church in Hanson, KY. In Nineteen Hundred Thirty-Two, she allied herself with East View Baptist where she served faithfully for a period of over thirty-seven years. She was an active member of the Missionary Society, Mothers Board, and the Senior Choir of which she served as president. Mrs. Hollie was also an active member of the Ladies Auxiliary of Post 161.

Mrs. Verdie Lee C. Hollie pictured with the Eastview Baptist Jubilee Choir in 1957. She is the fourth from the left in the second row.

Although her formal education was limited, after attending Akinson College on West Broadway, she had a vast knowledge of the Lord's purpose and support in her life. Sister Verdie Lee Hollie departed this life on Apr. 23, 1970. She left the memory of her courageous, undaunting spirit which will continue to inspire each generation of the family and those who encountered her virtuous character. Proverbs Thirty-One and Ten!- *Compiled by Elder John H. Nichols Jr., 1987. Mother, Aunt Anna, and Cousin Ellen Franklin*

CLAYTON

When William the Conqueror invaded England in 1066, one of his loyal retainers was Robert De Caudebee. Caudebee is a town in Normandy, which is shown in the 1970 census as having a population of 9270.

For his services in the invasion, King William gave him the Manor of Clayton in Lancashire, he then anglicized his name to Robert of Clayton, later dropping the "of" to become Robert Clayton - the first "Clayton".

In the succeeding centuries the Claytons spread over England and eventually to America. Probably the first Claytons in America were two brothers, Richard and Barnabas, who came from London to Salem, MA, in 1629.

Most of the Claytons in western Kentucky are descended from settlers who came from the area around Roxboro, Person Co., NC, where Claytons are as plentiful today as they are in Hopkins Co., KY.

The Clayton coat of arms carries the motto "Probitatem Quam Devitias" which freely translated means "truth and honor are better than riches."

In 1833, Robert and Lucretia (Tapp) Clayton came to Hopkins Co. They and their neighbors named their new community "Shakerag" as they had come from the "Shakerag" area of Person Co., NC.

In 1840, the Warham and Richard Clayton families had followed them to "Shakerag." Many other families by other names had also immigrated to this area.

Robert and Lucretia had four sons and four daughters. My grandfather, the youngest son was named Richard Dallas Clayton, the "Dallas" in honor of George M. Dallas, vice-president under President James K. Polk. Since then many descendents have had Dallas as part of their names.

Due to bad weather and roads at the time of her death, Lucretia was buried in their orchard, the beginning of "Clayton Graveyard," where anyone regardless of name could be buried, with no charge for burial plot. In earlier days all met annually to clean off the graveyard.

Two Claytons from Shakerag are listed in Adam R. Johnson's "The Partisan Rangers of the Confederate States Army," my grandfather Richard Dallas and his cousin William J. Clayton, later known as "Uncle Dick" and "Uncle Bill Solly" Clayton. They enlisted when the rangers were encamped at Olive Branch Church. I believe there is a historical marker at Browning Spring in honor of General Johnson and the rangers. They were a detachment from John Hunt Morgan's cavalry.

Most Claytons in Hopkins Co. have been respected, respectable, hard-working farmers, teachers, preachers, businessmen, etc. and even some politicians.

Richard Dallas Clayton married Dianah Teague. They had three girls and five boys. Their third son, Willie Eli (1872-1956), was my father. He married Nila Josephine Cunningham (1877-1958) on June 18, 1893. To them were born two girls, seven boys:

Bernis, school principal and superintendent; Pratt, farmer; Jesse, teacher at Georgia Tech and Annapolis; Emma, housewife; Cecil, teacher and Inspector Dept. of Agriculture; Raymond, Naval Officer; Lonnie, Army and Post Office; Marvin, Naval Academy Graduate, Lt. Commander, N.A.S.A. Missile Program; Macil, housewife.- *Submitted by Cecil D. Clayton*

CLAYTON-BROWN

Audrey Mae Brown and Ruby E. Clayton

were married in 1922 in Madisonville, KY. Audrey, born Aug. 4, 1903, and died Oct. 29, 1984, was the daughter of William Berry Brown and Rhoda Dixie Edmiston of Dalton community, where she attended her early years of school. The family moved to Providence where Audrey went to Browns Academy and a middle school on Broadway Street. In her early teens, the family returned to rural Dalton where her formal education stopped, but Audrey's quick mind never stopped learning. She took her homemaking serious, enjoying sewing and caring for others. This trait served her well and endeared her to many in years to come. One could never go into the Clayton home without seeing the dining room table that doubled as a sewing table, covered in a new project or covered with an abundance of food she had prepared for a threshing crew or summer guests. The Clayton home always smelled of good food. Audrey's warm heart and helping hands were wherever needed, whether in illness or death, or support in a birth of new babies of the community. Audrey had only one full sister, a widow, Verble McCoy lives in Madisonville. By previous marriages, she had many half sisters, Ruby, Emma, Fannie, Ann, Mildred, Ella and Carrie and her half brothers were Anderson, Ambrose, and Green.

Audrey Mae and Ruby Clayton

After their marriage, the Claytons lived in Chicago, where Audrey worked at the famous Massey's Restaurant. The widowed Mrs. Brown lived with the Claytons for 23 years before her death in 1958.

Ruby (Rube), born May 18, 1882, and died Jan. 26, 1964, was the son of William A. Clayton and Clarkie Jane McCoy of Webster Co. His brothers were Forrest, David Paul (Potter), William Cosby (Doc), Herbert (Chub) and Kermit. His sisters were Ora and Nancy Elizabethann, who died as a small child from a fall, and Gertrude, who never married and is living in Madisonville. Rube left school at an early age to work. He worked at many types of jobs. Barbering for the patients at Hopkinsville State Hospital gave him a hobby for later years. Most of his neighbors could boast they had had at least one "Rube hair cut." His other hobby was reading. His favorite subjects were history and geography. Later years his reading and studying turned to the Bible's Old Testament. Rube served in WWI in France, as Corporal, and was later a co-owner of a merchandise store in Chicago. He was with the I.C. Railroad about 10 years. In 1932, he bought a farm on Highway 502, north of Nebo. The Claytons moved from Chicago in 1933 to their new home in time for the birth of their first daughter, Deloit Jean on Feb. 26, 1933. The second daughter, Beverly Laine, was a Valentine girl born Feb. 14, 1939. Jean graduated from Nebo High School and married Eugene B. Dame, another Nebo alumni. The Dames own a farm north of Nebo and have one son, Clayton "Clay" Eugene, who graduated from West Hopkins High School and is now attending Evansville ITT College. Beverly also graduated at Nebo and married Paul J. Buntin from Dawson Springs and he graduated from Charleston High School. They have a daughter Cynthia Ann now in Nebo Jr. High. The Buntins also live on a farm near Nebo. Beverly's step-daughter, Amanda, has one child.

After Ruby's death, Audrey regretfully closed her large house and moved into a trailer home near the Dame's. She continued to be a gracious hostess until illness forced her to accept the daughters' invitation to live with each part time. The Claytons attended Tirzah Primitive Baptist Church in the Liberty community of Webster Co. and were buried in the Tirzah Cemetery.- *Submitted by Dorothy Miller Shoulders*

CLAYTON-CLAYTON

The Clayton family has been prominent in Hopkins Co. since about 1834 when Robert Clayton and his wife Lucretia (Tapp) migrated from Person Co., NC, to Hopkins Co.

They came from a community in Person Co. called Shakerag. It is believed that the name "Shakerag" followed them to Kentucky.

When Solomon Thomas Clayton, only child of Richard Jefferson and Rowan Slaughter Clayton, was eight or nine years old, he came across the mountains with his parents and other Clayton families including his uncle, Alexander, in 1858. The trip took about seven weeks in covered wagons. They settled on a farm near Olive Branch Church.

Jesse and Sally Buchanan lived near Friday School with their five sons and only daughter, Elizabeth Ann.

When Solomon Thomas was 24 years old and Elizabeth Ann was 15, they married and lived with her parents for several years. They had 15 children, among them James Lewis Clayton born Sept. 3, 1885.

Alexander Clayton, born about 1819, also settled in Hopkins Co. His second wife was Mary Ann Clayton, the oldest daughter of Robert Clayton. They had four girls and one son, William Alexander, July 19, 1863. Sometime later they moved to Webster Co. where William Alexander met and married Clarky Jane McCoy. They had nine children including Ora Ethel Clayton, Feb. 10, 1886.

James Lewis' second marriage was to Ora Ethel Clayton performed by Elder J.D. Shain Dec. 16, 1914. They settled in Hopkins Co. in or near what was known as Shakerag. James Lewis was a hard working farmer all his life, and during depression days, provided the necessities for his family while paying for his farm. He didn't depend upon any one farming operation but carried on a variety of activities to earn his living. In all his endeavors, Ora Ethel was by his side.

Their first child, Waurika, was born June 12, 1916. She was one of many grandchildren in James Lewis' family but was the only grandchild in Ora Ethel's family until Jan. 6, 1919, when her brother, Arden Jewell, was born. They remained the only grandchildren for four or five years when other grandchildren began to arrive.

Waurika married William Dame Dec. 27, 1934, and had one child, Geraldine, born May 28, 1936. Later she married Guy Leon Nix July 12, 1953. Arden married Eva Grace Grable and had four children: Fayetta Oct. 12, 1944; Nancy Lou Mar. 2, 1946; Donna Gail May 16, 1953; Louis Earl July 25, 1958. Arden and Eva have three grandchildren.

James Lewis and Ora Ethel remained on the farm until 1959 when their farm home burned. They then moved to Madisonville where they lived the rest of their lives. Ora Ethel died June 25, 1974, six months before they had been married sixty years. James Lewis grieved for Ora Ethel until his death from a stroke Mar. 28, 1981. They were both interred in Olive Branch Cemetery about 1-1/2 miles from where they had spent most of their married life.- *Submitted by Waurika Clayton Nix*

CLAYTON-TIPPETT

Anna Mae Tippett and Leslie Roland Clayton were married Apr. 16, 1938 at the home of Rev. W.E. Siria near Madisonville, in Hopkins Co.

Anna Mae was born Jan. 22, 1919, near Madisonville in Hopkins Co. She is the daughter of Robert Lee (R.L.) Tippett and Ada Frances Day. Two other children born to them were, Otho Tippett and Susie Tippett Daniel. Ada Day was born to Susan Jane Buchanan and William Joseph Day, Aug. 26, 1880. R.L. Tippett was born July 3, 1875, to Jonah Tippett and Ann Rebecca Bailey, north of Hanson near Oakland School in the Deer Creek Section of Hopkins Co. Kendral Jonah Tippett was one of the fifteen children born to William T. Tippett and Arena Adcock who came to Hopkins Co. from Jones Co., NC, in 1857. They traveled in two covered wagons pulled by oxen. Kendral Jonah served in the Civil War for the Confederate Army and is said to have helped remove

James Lewis and Ora Ethel Clayton with Elder J.D. Shain on their 50th wedding anniversary

the records from the Hopkins Co. Courthouse before it was burned.

Anna Mae and Leslie Clayton with their great granddaughter, Amie Katherine Cartwright

Other ancestral names are: Cox, Yeager, Groves, Overby, Brown, Haskins, Pettus, Jordon, Giles, Cocke, and Sugg.

Anna Mae attended Pleasant Grove School from the first grade through the eighth and graduated from Madisonville High School Jan. 24, 1936. She became a member of Pleasant Grove Baptist Church at age 10. She was employed in Hopkins Circuit and Quarterly Courts and State Public Assistance and Social Services for 25 years.

Leslie was born Jan. 9, 1914, near Manitou in Hopkins Co. in what is known as Wolfhollow, to Myrtle Harris and John Aaron Clayton. They moved a little later near Madisonville. Other sons are Raymond Vance and Ollie Wallace (O.W.). O.W. lost his life in WW II in France in November 1944. Myrtle Harris was born to Lelia Bourland and Roland Gooch Harris. John Aaron was born to J. William Clayton and Sara Agnes Daniel.

Other ancestral names are: Yarbrough, Winstead, Tapp.

Leslie attended Columbia and Pleasant Grove Schools. He helped out with farming at home at an early age. He has been engaged in farming most of the time; however, he has worked in several other occupations.

In 1945, they moved from west to east of Madisonville. Church memberships were transferred to Liberty Baptist Church soon after that. Leslie was Hopkins Co. Magistrate for the 3rd District for eight years, and also served on the Hopkins Co. Hospital Board for that time.

At the present time he is farm supervisor for Goldenrod Farms.

Leslie and Anna Mae have one son and one daughter: Max Alan married Rebecca Capps; Rita Lisa married Otis Cartwright. One grandson, Ray Alan Cartwright, married Kimberly Montgomery; granddaughter, Malisa Ann Cartwright, married Troy Killough; granddaughter, Anna Laura Clayton, age 16; great-granddaughter, Amie Katherine Cartwright, age 6; Kahra Beth Cartwright, age 2; great grandson, Phillip Van Killough, age 2.- Submitted by Mrs. Leslie R. Clayton

CLAYTON-WOOTON

Bernice Coleman Clayton, son of Alexander Coleman Clayton and Nancy Jane Villines Clayton, and Ora Elizabeth Wooton, daughter of Benjamin Terry Wooton and Mary Ellen Villines Wooton, were married Dec. 25, 1917, in Hopkins Co., KY.

Bernice and Ora Clayton

Bernice and Ora had four daughters: Margaret, Bonnie, Bee and Nell. Along with Coleman Lee, a son born to Bernice's first wife Nellie Sutton who died at Coleman's birth, they lived on a farm in Shakerag Hills and raised cattle, corn, tobacco, watermelons, and a great vegetable garden. After twenty years of married life on the farm, they moved to Madisonville and opened Wooton and Claytons Grocery on the corner of Nisbet and Hanson Streets with Ora's parents, Ben and Ellen Wooton, as partners.

COLEMAN, who worked for Peabody Coal Co., was married to Minnie Rae Taylor. They had four children: Nellie Belle (died at 2 yrs.); Lee Roy (died at birth); Dorothy, who works for McCoy Oil Co. and is married to Edward Wilson of Harris Funeral Home, has two sons, Allen and Tim, and one grandchild, Alle Marie; and Jerry who works as a fireman for the Madisonville Fire Dept. and is married to the former Nancy Duvall, they have two daughters, Amy and Alicia.

BONNIE, married Eugene F. Smith who works for Semo Security. The Smith's live in Evansville, IN. They had two children: Sharon (died at birth) and Michael who died in an accident in 1979, just six weeks after his marriage to Cheryl Jones.

BEE married Hughston Cunningham, Sr., in 1948 and they had four children: Larry, Marlene, Lola and Ruth. Hughston had three children from a previous marriage to Tempie Nance. They are David, Dean and Hughston, Jr. Hughston, Sr., worked for Peabody Coal Co. for 35 years and was killed in an accident while on his way to work on the morning of Aug. 28, 1978.

Larry is married to the former Diane Bruce and they have three children: Shawna, Tracy and Brandon. Larry drives a truck for Mine and Mill Supply Co. in Dawson Springs, and Diane works for Kentucky Rest Haven.

Marlene was first married to Roger Dale Wells. They had two children, Marla and Kimberly (Kim died at 2-1/2 months). Marlene is employed by American Mine Tool and is now married to Jack Simms who is employed by Kentucky Forge. The Simm's have a grandson, Chad Allen.

Lola is married to Roger Dale Ball, who is employed by Cimarron Coal Co. Lola is a former Radiologist at R.M.C. The Balls live in Dalton and have one daughter, Jennifer Charity.

Ruth was married to Kenneth Norris and they had three children: Reggie, Anitra and Rhiona. Ruth then married Roger Dale McCarty and they have two children, Roger Dale and Steven.

David was married to the former Sandra Buchanan and they had three children: Alan, Lisa and Nathan. They have nine grandchildren. David also has a son, David, Jr. David is an over-the-road trucker out of Jeffersonville, IN, and Sandra works for Clinic Convalescent.

Dean is married to Aubrey Gene Baggett, they have three children: Brentley, Vicki and Jason. They also have two grandchildren, Bradley and Julie. Dean works for Edwards IGA and Gene is employed by Industrial Mill Supply Co.

Hughston, Jr., (Mac) is married to the former Linda Yell and they have two children, Christy and Sonya. Linda had a son from a previous marriage, Timmy. Mac works for MAPCO Coal Co. at Dotiki Mine.

NELL was married to Marvin W. (Jack) Cunningham, who was employed by Peabody Coal Co., and was killed on the job in September 1957. They had four children: Rita, Terry, Anthony and Mary. Nell also has five grandchildren and one great grandchild, and works at Senior Citizen.

Rita was married to James McCarty and had two children, Keith and Angie. She then married Bobby McKinsey and had two sons, Jason and Jeremy. Rita is employed by Country Meadows Nursing Home and Bob was employed by the Speed Queen Company until his death in 1987.

Terry (Dr. Terry A. Cunningham, DMD) is married to the former Vicki Dillingham, who is Terry's part-time assistant in his office at 1340 S. Main St., Madisonville.

Anthony (Tony) was married to the former Patricia Harley. Tony is an avid photographer and while not on the job at Speed Queen, he operates Cunningham Photography. Patricia is employed by Senior Citizens Nursing Home.

Mary is married to Mike Barnett, they have one son, Michael. Mary is an Avon Lady and Mike is employed by Pyramid Mining.

MARGARET Clayton never married but stayed home to help with the operation of Wooton-Claytons Grocery (later named Clayton Sisters Grocery until the rest of the girls married and moved out). The store was then named Clayton's Grocery, and with her parents' deaths, Margaret remained as owner and operator until the store closed for the final time on Jan. 1, 1974. Margaret is very active in church work at the First Baptist Church, where she teaches a Sunday School Class for five year olds.- *Submitted by Mrs. Hughston Cunningham*

GABE CLAYTON

Gabriel Lee Clayton was born May 24, 1895. He was the son of Soloman Thomas Clayton and Elizabeth Buchannan. His grandparents Richard Jefferson and Rowan Clayton came to Hopkins Co., KY, in 1858, moving from Person Co., NC.

Gabriel was one of fifteen children born to

the Soloman Clayton family. The family lived on the Dr. Waller farm in Shakerag. Gabe attended Buntin's School and Fridy School.

On Jan. 26, 1916, Gabriel Clayton and Ruby Brown were married at the home of the bride's parents, John W. Brown and Mary Emily Bidwell Brown. The Reverend D.S. Edwards presided over the ceremony. Witnesses were Nettie Brown Edwards, sister of the bride, and Rowland Gooch.

Ruby Brown Clayton was the youngest of nine children. The Brown home was on the old Henderson Road one and one-fourth miles west of Hanson.

The Clayton home on 1069, torn down in 1984

Gabe and Ruby lived for a few years in a small house on the Soloman Clayton farm or Dr. Waller farm as it was called. Three of their five children were born there. On May 6, 1931, they purchased the John Wallace Brown farm.

Frieda Mae Clayton was born Aug. 3, 1917, and died May 25, 1942. Frieda married James Curneal and there were three children. Mona Sharon born May 13, 1938, died Oct. 13, 1938, Sandra born Jan. 28, 1941, died May 25, 1942. Frieda and daughter Sandra died in a house fire. Frieda and James' oldest daughter Jerry Sue was born July 21, 1935.

Anna Lois Clayton was born Feb. 15, 1921. She was married to William Thomas Rudd June 8, 1941. They have a daughter Kathy.

Mason Lowell Clayton was born Mar. 2, 1924. He and Betty Jo Harris were married Nov. 2, 1946. They had a daughter Sherry Clayton Tomes married Kenneth Tomes. They have four daughters, Dawna Tomes Smith, Holly, Rachel and Brooke. Mason and Joy Clayton are parents of a daughter Stacy Clayton Harrelston.

Norma Zane Clayton was born June 10, 1932. She married Thomas Edward Roach. They are parents of Michael David, Robin Edward and Debra Bates.

Larry Dahl Clayton was born Dec. 12, 1937, he married Helen Warren. There are five children Chris, Lori, Suzie, Kathlene, and Nicholas.

Ruby Brown Clayton died March 10, 1959, and is buried in Olive Branch Cemetery.

Mr. Clayton farmed for many years. He raised black Angus cattle and grew tobacco and other crops.

Gabe and Delcia Arnold Agee Clayton were married May 1, 1960. They lived on Seminary Street in Madisonville until 1985. Delcia Clayton now resides in a Louisville nursing home and Mr. Clayton resides at Kentucky Rest Haven in Madisonville. -Submitted by Sherry Clayton Tomes

SIM CLAYTON

The Claytons from Person Co., NC, came to the Western Coal Field Region of Kentucky in the early to mid-eighteen hundreds. Among these cousins of Simeon Thomas "Sim" Clayton were his brothers and sisters who came to Hopkins Co.

Sim Clayton, whom this little sketch is about, never came to Hopkins Co., or if he did he didn't stay. Sim and his brother John D. "Forty Dollar" Clayton were the only sons of Solomon Clayton, Sr. (ca 1775-1849), and Frances Carver Clayton, (1775-ca 1860), who didn't migrate to Kentucky.

The brothers of Sim Clayton, (1813-1890), who came to Kentucky were Solomon, Jr., Alex, William and Richard Clayton. His sisters were Nancy Owens, Betsy Villines, and Malinda Poole.

In Hopkins Co. they lived in the area of Hanson, Madisonville, Manitou, and Slaughters, KY, near the L & N Railroad.

Seated l to r: Simeon Thomas Clayton and Simeon Albert Clayton. Standing: Madison Thomas Clayton

The children of Sim and Mary Painter Clayton (1811-1871) were Betsey Clayton (1833-after 1880), Logan Green Clayton (1835-1876), Solomon C. Clayton (1838-1905), William Rufus Clayton (1839-1914), Frances S. Clayton (1842-ca 1922), Mary I. Clayton (1844- ?), Madison Thomas Clayton (1848-1916), Simeon Albert Clayton (1850-1928). All these are North Carolina cousins of the Hopkins Co., Kentuckians; nearly all of them are buried at Wheeley/Wheeler's Primitive Baptist Church near Hurdle Mills, Person Co., NC.

Solomon C. and William Rufus Clayton fought with the 50th Regt. North Carolina State Troops, C.S.A. during the Civil War, lived through it signing their Oaths of Allegiance in 1865.

The children of Sim and Mary Clayton called them "Muh" and "Fah," pet terms for mother and father. They were all tobacco farmers with the exception of William Rufus Clayton, a miller by trade in later years. They loved laughter and playing practical jokes on one another. All of them leaned toward the Primitive Baptist faith. The churches they attended were Ebenezer and Wheeler's P.B. Church near Hester's Store and Hurdle Mills respectively. Didn't think preachers should stand while praying.

They loved the winding, white, dusty roads of Person Co. and walked miles to visit family and friends, especially on Sunday. They loved the "sosations" or "meetuns" (Associations), held periodically by Primitive Baptists. These Associations would last several days with preaching under brush arbor and singing without the accompaniment of musical instruments. Someone would set the musical pitch of the song by beginning to hum.

Many of these Clayton men were of hearty, robust stock with hardened, red, leather-like hands and faces. They were men of the soil in its truest meanings. John Thomas Clayton, grandson of Sim and Mary, was one of the last of these men in this Clayton line to be given back to this soil. The occurance was on a sultry-hot humid day in late August 1974. It was his kind of day; he always liked this kind of weather for reasons unknown to most of us. Family and friends stood in every shady spot available, women fanned themselves with hats and handkerchiefs beneath the great oaks of the church-yard. Myriads of sweat-bees adorned the handles of pick and shovel. Across the field trees seemed to dance slowly in the waves of rising heat. How long must a man stay away from his Lord?, the preacher asked. Papa was eighty-nine.

Jim Clayton who resides at 610 Cameron St., Burlington, NC, researches Person Co., NC, Claytons and their colonial North Carolina and Virginia origins. -Submitted by Jim Clayton

Sources: Family Bible, John T. Clayton, Thomas A. Clayton, Wheeleys P.B. Church Records at NC State Archives.

CLEMENTS

The Clements family, of Scotch-English ancestry emigrated to Essex Co., VA, about 1680. John Clements was sent to England for his education as a physician. After returning to Essex Co. he was married and fathered several children, Mace, Ewen, Pittman, Smith and others. John Clements died in 1767. Mace Clements also became a doctor and enlisted in the Virginia Continental Line in 1776, serving as Regimental Surgeon until 1783. For his seven years service, at the rank of Colonel, he received a 7,000 acre land grant, 4,000 acres in Limestone, Northwest Territory, an early name for Maysville, KY, and 3,000 acres in Hopkins Co., KY, near what is now the intersection of U.S. Highway 62 and the Pennyrile Parkway near Nortonville, KY.

In 1795 William Clements moved from Richmond, VA, to Wilkes Co., GA, where his son Meriwether was born in 1804.

In 1818 William Clements traveled to Hopkins Co., KY, to survey a 1,000-acre tract from his Uncle Mace's 3,000 acre land grant.

In 1858 Meriwether Clements moved from Franklin Co., GA, to Hopkins Co., KY, and settled on his father's 1,000 acre tract.

Meriwether Clements had four sons, William, Mace, Walter and George as well as several daughters.

Walter, a First Lieutenant in the Confederate States Army, was killed at Fort Donelson, TN, on Feb. 16, 1862, at the age of twenty-two.

George Clements married Manerva Harrison of White Plains, KY, and had three sons, George, Charles and Harrison.

Several descendents of these men still live in Hopkins Co., KY. -*Submitted by John B. Clements*

CLEMENTS-CLARK

On June 7, 1940, J. Pat Clements and Thelma Cecelia Clark were married at Immaculate Conception Church in Earlington, KY. Pat was from Union Co. and was the son of Lewis and Anna Cambron Clements. He was one of eight children. Thelma was the daughter of Joseph E. and Nellie Newcom Clark of Jewel City and later on Earlington. She was one of fourteen children.

Pat had opened up Clements Jewelers and Thelma was working at the credit bureau when they met. To this union three children were born. All three went to school at Immaculate Conception School kindergarten through eighth grade with Carmel also attending her freshman year there.

Carmel Jeanne was born Nov. 28, 1943. After grade school, she attended and graduated from Madisonville High School in 1961. She was a member of the Beta Club. She attended college at Nazareth in Louisville and Murray State in Murray. After two years she started to work with her father in the family business. On Sept. 4, 1980, she and Don Abbott of Madisonville were married. Don was born May 23, 1951. Don had been an electrician for many years and in November 1983 he started working for himself. In June 1986 he hired his first employee and named his company Abbott Contractors. They bought a lot on the edge of Shake Rag near Wicks Well and built most of their own home.

Steve was born on Mar. 30, 1950. After grade school, he went to and graduated from Madisonville North Hopkins High School in 1969. On Apr. 27, 1974, he and Meryl Adams of Empire, KY, were married at Christ the King in Madisonville. They have two children. Sara Ashley was born July 29, 1975, and is in the seventh grade at Browning Springs Middle School. She has taken dancing for about seven years and is learning to play the french horn and the cello. Matt was born Dec. 14, 1976, and is a fifth grader at West Broadway. He takes tap and plays the violin. He and Sara both take gymnastics. Steve started working at Clements Jewelers while he was in high school and trained under his father. Meryl is a Nuclear Medicine Technologist at Regional Medical Center. They have bought the family home in Homewood after the death of his mother.

Rebecca Ann was born Mar. 27, 1954. After attending and graduating from Madisonville North Hopkins she attended and graduated from Western Kentucky University with a degree in clothing and marketing. She worked in Atlanta for a couple of years and then came back to Madisonville and worked in the family jewelry store for about a year before marrying Bernard Leroy Williams from Glasgow, KY, on June 21, 1980, at Christ the King. Bernard worked for his father in the family oil business before going to work for the Chamber of Commerce in Glasgow. Becky works for a bank in Glasgow and they have a daughter named Lauren born Feb. 27, 1984. They have bought Bernard's grandfather's home and completely rebuilt it.

Steve and Carmel still operate the family business after the death of Pat on Mar. 23, 1973, and the death of Thelma on Mar. 5, 1981. - *Submitted by Carmel Jeanne Clements Abbott*

CLENDENING

A name, not common, made fun of, called a lot of things. Hard to spell (10 letters). I am happy to have the opportunity to tell you where our name originated.

In 1737, the spirit of emigration was high among Presbyterians in the northern parts of Ireland, in Scotland and the adjacent parts of England. The Irish Presbyterians were Scotch-Irish because of their Scotch extraction. Among these were the Clendenings who came to America and were residing on Burdens Grant as early as 1753.

John, Archibald, and Charles Clendening were the three brothers who migrated. Archibald and his children were massacred.

On Oct. 10, 1774, at Point Pleasant, VA, riflemen defeated the federation Indian tribes led by Shawnee Chief Cornstalk. It is the most important battle between the Indians and the whites. The roster inscribed on the Point Pleasant Battle Monument lists six Clendenings in that battle: Adam, Alexander, Charles Clendening, Captain George and Robert Clendenin, and Captain William Clendening.

The Battle of Point Pleasant was recognized as the first battle of the American Revolution by the Congress of the United States, Senate Bill No. 160, on Feb. 12, 1908.

Kanawha Co. was formed Nov. 14, 1788, and organized Oct. 6, 1789. Among gentlemen justices qualified as members of the County Court were Robert Clendenin and William Clendenin.

The military organization of Kanawha Co. lists: George Clendenin, County Lieutenant; William Clendenin, Major; Alexander Clendenin, Ensign; Daniel Boone, Lt. Colonel. These have been honored with others on a memorial stone in Charleston, WV, erected by the County Court of Kanawha Co., 1930, at the request of the John Young Chapter, National Society of Daughters of the American Revolution.

George Clendenin furnished the books for the county for which the court allowed him 1,900 lbs. of tobacco.

Fort Lee, locally called Clendenins Fort, was built in 1788 for the protection of the early settlers against the Indians. A memorial marker has been erected in Charleston, WV, on the site.

Oct. 10, 1774, Clendenin Fort was used as a courthouse when Kanawha Co. was formed. Thirteen votes were cast. George Clendenin was sent to the Virginia Legislature, and at the end of the second election in 1791, George Clendenin and Daniel Boone were sent.

While in Richmond, George Clendenin bought from his commanding officer, Colonel Thomas Bullett, 4,000 acres. He gave 104 acres, tract 40 in 1794, to found Charleston, WV. He named the town for his father, Charles Clendenin.- *Submitted by: Brenda Tapp*

CLENDENING-LYNCH

William H. Clendening and Wilma Hazel Lynch were married Feb. 22, 1943. They have six children: Brenda Faye Tapp, Betty Kathryn Thompson, Sharon Sue Oldham, Jeannie Ann Samples, Sandra Gail Wallace, and Donnie Ray Clendening.

Brenda lives in Madisonville, is married to Eugene Tapp. They have three children, Steven Eugene Sept. 10, 1965-Dec. 8, 1965, Jeffrey Owen, and Eugenia Faye July 6, 1968-May 13, 1972.

Betty lives in Morganfield, KY, married to Gary Thompson and they have one son, Derick Dwayne born Aug. 17, 1980. Betty has one son by a previous marriage, Curtis Ray Todd born Dec. 22, 1966.

Sharon lives in Shakerag Hills, is married to Ralph Oldham and they have two children, Sue Lynn born Aug. 31, 1969, and Anthony born June 26, 1970.

Jeannie lives in Kuttawa, KY; is married to Johnny Samples. They have four children: Lisa Ann born Nov. 22, 1969, John Wayne, Tricia Jean, and James Ira born May 12, 1973.

Sandra lives in Indian Mound, TN, is married to Ted Wallace. She has three children by a previous marriage: Steven Michael, Cathy Michelle, and David Wayne born May 9, 1973.

Donnie Ray lives in Madisonville, has one daughter, Brandy who lives in California.- *Submitted by Brenda Tapp*

CLOUSE-WOOD

Nellie Sue Wood is the middle child of Olus Vance and Mary Thelma Nixon Wood. She was born June 21, 1945, in Caldwell Co. She married Allen Benjamin Clouse, the only son of Benjamin Martin and Alice Blossom Clouse, Nov. 2, 1963, in Montgomery Co., TN. They have two sons, Jeffery Allen Clouse born Aug. 22, 1964, in Caldwell Co. and Kevin Michael Clouse born Sept. 26, 1968, in Asmara, Ethiopia.

Allen and Sue Clouse

Jeffery graduated Valedictorian from Wakefield High School, Arlington, VA, Class of 1982. Jeff was in Who's Who Among American High School Students his junior and senior years. Jeff was a Magna Cum Laude 1985 graduate of Virginia Tech in Blacksburg, VA. Jeff is a member of Phi Beta Kappa, Phi Kappa Phi, and Upsilom Pi Epsilon honor societies. Jeff presently lives in Falls Church, VA.

Kevin is a senior at Central High School in

Maryland. Kevin was in Who's Who Among American High School Students and the National Honor Roll his junior year. He is employed by the Army Air Force Exchange Service.

Sergeant Major Clouse has 25 years in the United States Army. He has had two overseas assignments, Korea and Ethiopia. The family has also lived in Tennessee, Massachusetts, Texas and 14 years in the Washington, DC, area.

Allen was born July 18, 1944, in Valparaiso, IN. When he was four, his parents moved to Arizona. His maternal grandparents were Russell D. and Ettie Maud Stradler Coleman. His paternal grandparents were Lafayette and Mary Edwards Clouse.- *Submitted by Sue Wood Clouse*

COATS-WOMACK

John Coats was born in Tennessee about 1817, the son of Thomas Coats. The Coats family was from Bell Buckle, Bedford Co., TN. Thomas Coats was from North Carolina, and had three sons, Thomas, James, and John, and one daughter, name not remembered, who married Riley Howard and went to Missouri.

Mary Jane (Coats) Phelps, daughter of John and Mary (Womack) Coats

John Coats, the subject of this sketch, married Mary Womack, daughter of Hawkins and Mary Jane (Cooper) Womack. A romantic story has been handed down about John and Mary. John was working as overseer on the Womack plantation, and Mary fell in love with him. Her parents opposed her wish to marry this "lowly overseer," but their love prevailed and they eloped and were married. She was no longer welcome at her parents' house, and when Mary's younger sister married, the sister didn't even speak to Mary at the wedding party.

Their children, born in Tennessee, were Talitha, m. William Edens; Mary Jane, m. Absalom Phelps; Wilson B., m. Matilda Howton; Sarah, m. John R. Davis after her sister Nancy's death; Hawkins; and Nancy, m. John R. Davis. Mary (Womack) Coats died when Nancy was an infant, and John fed the baby with a bamboo-cane nipple, keeping the bottle in his bosom at night where it would be warm for the night's feeding. Sometime during the 1850's he moved with his children to Hopkins Co. and married a widow, Mrs. Mary Webb, who had a son, Robert. This Robert took the name Coats from his step-father. From this second marriage John also had a son George. His second wife died, however, and again he remarried, this time Mary Levina (Chappell) Young. Two children were born to this union, Mary and Lewis.

John Coats died in 1865. He has numerous descendants in Hopkins Co. today, though most of the descendents of his son Wilson B. live in the west. They hold an annual reunion in Colorado.- *Submitted by Sanford G. Etheridge*

COOPER-OLDHAM

Patricia R. Oldham Cooper married Hugh Cooper on June 4, 1960. They have six children and reside in Rosemont, IL. She is the sixth and youngest child of Claude Lee and Cyntha Lam Oldham, former residents of Dawson Springs, KY, until the early 1940's when they moved to Chicago, IL.

Pat's grandparents were Lewis B. and Malissa Ann Mary Barnes Oldham of Caldwell Co. Her search goes on for information about George T. and Mary E. Tomasson Oldham, her great grandparents, Hopkins Co.

A romance with family ancestry and subsequent genealogical endeavors inspired by a good friend, Pauline McClearn, bring the Coopers "home" to Dawson Springs three to four times per year.- *Submitted by Patricia Cooper*

COPELAND

Donnie Copeland, a welder for P&M Coal Company, is my father. He is about 5'8" in height and was born on Aug. 23, 1948 - that makes him 39 years old. Ann Paul, now Ann Copeland, is my mother. She is about 5'7' tall and was born on Nov. 24, 1949. She works for a sewing factory in Dawson Springs. Donnie and Ann married at an early age. They have been married for 20 years.

Their children are Greg Copeland and Cynthia Copeland. Greg, who is currently in high school, is 16 years old. He was born Jan. 10, 1972. Cynthia, a high school graduate, is now attending college at Western Kentucky University. She was born Sept. 6, 1967. These children are good students on the average. Cynthia holds a 4.0 grade average and Greg holds a 3.5.

Donnie and "Sissy", a nickname for Ann, have very respectable parents. Donnie's parents are Ellis and Jewel Copeland. They live in Caldwell County, just outside of Dawson Springs. Ann's parents live on Oak Heights, a residential street in Dawson Springs. Their names are Bill and Pat Kinsolving. Both sets of parents are well respected around the Dawson Springs area. Bill and Ellis are both retired coal workers.

The only great-grandparents that were still living when Greg was born were William and Thelma Moore. William was a busy person. He seemed to stay working all of the time. He was one of those men who had a minute for anyone and loved to be around children. He was a very handyman when it came to fixing things. Thelma, better known as "Gemmy", is still living. She lives with Donnie, Ann, Greg and Cynthia. These two people were the nicest a person would probably ever meet.

Donnie has a brother named David. He lives in Dawson Springs and has a daughter, Shannon. He mines coal for a living, just as the rest of the family does. Ann has a brother, Bill Paul. He is an anesthesiologist at Marianna, FL. He has a son, Devin Paul, and a daughter, Wendy Paul.-*Submitted by Greg Copeland*

CORUM

Otto Franklin Corum, Jr. (Frank), was born in Hopkins Co., KY, May 11, 1943. He is the second of two children born to Otto Franklin Corum, Sr., and Kathryn Herod Beasley. Ann Kathryn Corum Gibson being the first born. Otto Franklin Corum, Sr., was born Sept. 17, 1910, in Hopkins Co., KY, and died in Hopkins Co., KY, July 15, 1982. He was the third of four children born to John Robert Corum, M.D. and Mallie Lee Major, Cordelia Corelli Corum Henderson, Nancy Brown Corum, and Lyle Waller Corum Casner being the other children. Kathryn Herod Beasley was born in Smith Co., TN, Mar. 7, 1915. She was the first of two children born to Rufus Cleveland Beasley and Emma Burford Herod. Ann Ellen Beasley Deavours being the other child. John Robert Corum was born in McLean Co., KY, Jan. 20, 1879, and died Feb. 11, 1968, in Hopkins Co., KY. He was the second of eight children born to Samuel Chesley Corum of Grainger Co., TN, and Lucy Suvilla Dodson of Ohio Co., KY. Mallie Lee Major was born in Hopkins Co., KY, May 24, 1879, and died in Davidson Co., TN, Aug. 28, 1961. She was the last of four children born to Richard Franklin Major of Hopkins Co., KY, and Martha Warran Timmons of Hopkins Co., KY. Rufus Cleveland Beasley was born in Smith Co., TN, May 12, 1893, and died in Warren Co., KY, Nov. 10, 1963. He was one of eight children born to Jerome Beasley of Smith Co., TN, and Ellen Taylor, probably of Macon Co., TN. Emma Burford Herod was born in Smith Co., TN, Nov. 28, 1894, and is still living in Hopkinsville, KY. She was the first of two children born to Peter Clay Herod of Smith Co., TN, and Clara Jones of Monroe Co., KY.

Frank Corum first married Carole Jane Dupay Good of Lawrence Co., PA, Feb. 8, 1974. There was no issue of this marriage.

Frank Corum was next married to Janet Howard Woodall Reichmuth of McCracken Co., KY. She was born Feb. 10, 1948, the third of three daughters born to William Howard Woodall and Alma Holt. The other two daughters being Judith Holt Woodall, wife of Robert Hauman of Toledo, OH, and Linda Elizabeth Woodall, wife of George Burgess Carey of Lexington, KY. From this marriage, Frank and Janet have been blessed with the birth of one son, Otto Franklin Corum III, born Feb. 8, 1979, in Hopkins Co., KY.

Frank Corum was blessed with the benefits of two caring parents and good educational opportunity. He was a June 1962 graduate of Culver Military Academy and a June 1966 graduate of Vanderbilt University with a Bachelor of Science degree in Civil Engineering.

He served in the United States Army Reserves from June 1966 to June 1972. He has used his opportunities to obtain some degree of success in construction, land surveying, asphalt paving, coal mining, banking, investing, and stock raising. He is a United Methodist.- *Submitted by: Frank Corum*

CORUM-BAKER

Bill Corum and Glenna Reece Baker were married in Lexington, KY on June 28, 1941.

Bill Corum was born Oct. 6, 1918, in the Ashbyburg community of northeast Hopkins Co., KY. He was originally "Billy" or "Billy Sunday" on his birth certificate, but later legally changed this to "Bill." He is the youngest child of Marshall Ashby and Lesbia Cobb Corum.

About 1919, Bill Corum moved with his family to Madisonville. His brothers were W.B. (Apr. 9, 1908) and Kenneth (Apr. 4, 1910) and his sisters were Emma Louise (Apr. 24, 1914) and Frances Marie (Sept. 27, 1915). He attended public schools in Madisonville and graduated from Madisonville High School in 1938. He played guard on the first basketball team from Madisonville to play in the state tournament. He played center and was captain of the football team and was named Outstanding Athlete his senior year.

He entered the University of Kentucky in the fall of 1938 and was a member of Lances, a junior men's honorary fraternity and a member of Sigma Nu social fraternity, where he served as president. It was there he met his future bride, Glenna Baker. The war interrupted his college work and Corum entered business with his father and family in the construction of a large ammunition plant near Charlestown, IN. Also, Corum became involved in the family farming operations during the war time period.

About 1947, Bill Corum entered U.C. Milk Co., Inc., a dairy processing and packaging company his father and uncle had started in 1927. He became president in 1954 and currently serves as Board Chairman (1987).

Bill Corum served three years as president of the Madisonville Chamber of Commerce during the middle 1960s, a period which saw the first of several major industries move to Madisonville. He was instrumental in securing the Goodyear Plant for the community.

He served as president of the Kentucky Dairy Products Association, The Southern Association of Ice Cream Manufacturers (1957), and the Madisonville Kiwanis Cub (1966).

He served as president of the Junior Chamber of Commerce and Chairman of the Hopkins County Hospital Fund Drive. He is a member of the First Methodist Church and he is a Kentucky Colonel. He was awarded the Lions Club Outstanding Citizen of Madisonville in 1965.

Bill Corum is a director of Kentucky Bank and Trust Co., served on the advisory board of the Madisonville Community College and is a director of the Hopkins County Development Corp.

Glenna R. Baker was born Mar. 14, 1921, in Greenville, TN, the daughter of Henry Reece Baker and Rena J. Brown Baker. She attended local schools and graduated from Vassifern School for Girls in Hendersonville, NC, in 1939. She attended Transylvania College and the University of Kentucky for one semester each and was a member of Chi Omega Sorority.

Glenna and Bill Corum have two children, William Montgomery (July 14, 1942) and Elizabeth Josephine (Aug. 16, 1949). Bill and Glenna Corum currently live at 2209 S. Main St., Madisonville. See photo with M. Ashby Corum.- *Submitted by William M. Corum, son*

CORUM-FERGUSON

William "Billy" Corum and Frances "Fee" Corum were married June 19, 1965, at the First Methodist Church in Madisonville, KY. To their union two children were born; Caroline Ferguson (Mar. 3, 1967) and Ashby Toland (Aug. 28, 1969).

William M. and Frances Ferguson Corum

William Corum was born at 48 Lake Street, Madisonville, Hopkins Co., on July 14, 1942. He attended Seminary Elementary School and graduated from Madisonville High School in 1960. As a youth he was active in 4-H, with prize dairy cattle. He was State Showmanship Champion in 1957 and his animal won the Kentucky Grand Championship Female in 1956. He was ninth at the National Gurensey Dairy Show.

Corum entered the University of Kentucky in the fall of 1960 and was a member of Kappa Sigma social fraternity where he served as Grand Master of Ceremonies. He graduated in 1964 with a B.S. in Business Administration. He attended the University of Kentucky Law School for one year.

William Corum became associated with U.C. Milk Co., Inc. (Goldenrod Dairy) in May of 1965, where he served as purchasing agent, vice-president, and is currently serving as president. The company had been started by his grandfather in 1927.

William Corum has served as President of Madisonville Kiwanis Club (1973-74), President of Hopkins Co., UK Alumni Club, President of Dixie Dairy Products Association and as Vice-president of the Madisonville Chamber of Commerce.

He has served as director of the University of Kentucky National Alumni Association, Madisonville Country Club, Hopkins Co. Fair, Hopkins Co. YMCA, and Kentucky Dairy Products Association. He is a Kentucky Colonel.

Corum traces his ancestry to a William Coram, transported from England about 1727 as an indentured servant and to Peter Francisco, a Revolutionary War hero.

Frances Ferguson was born Sept. 30, 1942, in Little Rock, AR, the daughter of Dr. Frederick Fielding Ferguson and Janis Caroleen Toland Ferguson. She attended schools in Memphis, TN, and Nashville, AK, before moving to Madisonville in 1953. Her father was one of the first seven doctors to be associated with Trover Clinic.

She graduated from Madisonville High School in 1960 and entered the University of Kentucky where she was a member of Alpha Delta Pi social sorority. She was rush chairman in 1963.

Frances Corum has been active in the education of her children having served as officer of several PTAs. She has been active in summer and high school swimming activities, having served as conference chairman and booster club chairman.

Frances Ferguson traces her ancestry through Betty Washington Lewis, sister of George Washington, and to Edward I, II, III and to Henry III, Kings of England.

William M. and Frances Corum live at 1029 Princeton Pike in Madisonville.- *Submitted by William M. Corum*

ASHBY TOLAND CORUM

Ashby T. Corum was born in Hopkins Co., KY, Aug. 28, 1969, the son of William M. and Frances Ferguson Corum. He entered Grapevine School in the fall of 1975 and moved to West Broadway School in 1977 when his family moved from Parkwood Drive to Princeton Pike. He attended Browning Springs Middle School and was named Outstanding Math Student in the eighth grade.

Ashby Toland Corum

As a young man, Corum received numerous awards. He was a four year letterman on the Madisonville-North Hopkins High School soccer and swim teams. He became an Eagle Scout in 1986 and was named Kentucky's Most Outstanding Eagle Scout in 1987. Ashby won the Second Region of Kentucky Math Competition in 1986 and 1987 and competed at the state level. He was a member of the high school academic team and the Beta Club. He was a Class Marshal his junior year and Vice-president of the Student Council his senior year. He is a Kentucky Colonel.

Upon graduation from high school in 1987, Corum received a Presidential Scholarship to attend the University of Kentucky and the Downey Scholarship for Civil Engineering. He was also invited to apply for the award of Scholastic All-American.

Ashby T. Corum will enter the University of Kentucky College of Engineering in the fall of 1987, majoring in civil engineering. - *Submitted by William M. Corum-father*

CAROLINE FERGUSON CORUM

Caroline Corum was born Mar. 3, 1967, in Hopkins Co., KY, the daughter of William M. and Frances Ferguson Corum.

She attended Grapevine Elementary School where she was a cheerleader, Seminary School and Browning Springs Middle School. She graduated from Madisonville-North Hopkins High School in 1984 after three years. During that time she was class treasurer. She was active in summer and high school swimming. She was high point swimmer in her age group in the Southcentral Swimming Championship in 1983. She earned six letters in high school swimming and was selected All-Conference in 1982. She was one of the youngest persons to earn a high school "M," having lettered in the sixth grade. Caroline was Most Valuable Swimmer in high school in 1981, 1982, and 1983.

Caroline Ferguson Corum

After graduation, Caroline entered Sweet Briar College, then attended the University of Kentucky. She was a member of Kappa Alpha Theta sorority, where she was secretary. She is a senior at American University in Washington, DC.- *Submitted by: William M. Corum-father*

M. ASHBY CORUM

Marshall Ashby Corum was born July 23, 1887 in McLean Co., KY, the fourth son and one of eight children born to Samuel Chesley Corum and Lucy Suvilla Dodson Corum. About 1900 the family moved to the Ashbyburg community in Hopkins Co.

He attended school in Bowling Green, KY, and later graduated from the Louisville College of Pharmacy, class of 1908, where he was president of his senior class. After graduating, he opened a small drug store in South Carrollton on the Green River in Muhlenburg Co. His brother, Dr. J.R. Corum was a graduate of the Louisville Medical College and together they planned to practice as a team, physician and pharmacist. However, river traffic brought much business to Mr. Corum's drug store and after one year he sold the store for a sizable profit and decided on a more flexible lifestyle, becoming a businessman. The 1910 census shows that he was a sales clerk in his father-in-law's store at Ashbyburg.

He married Miss Lesbia Cobb on Aug. 7, 1907. She was the daughter of C.C. Cobb and Nannie Ashby Cobb of Hopkins Co. To that union five children were born; W.B. (Apr. 9, 1908), Kenneth (Apr. 4, 1910), Emma Louise (Apr. 24, 1914), Frances Marie (Sept. 27, 1915), and Bill (Oct. 6, 1918).

Ashby Corum began trading in livestock and during World War I he would purchase mules and resell them to the U.S. Army. At the conclusion of the war he had several mules, but the Army was no longer purchasing mules. When the men began to return to civilian life after the war, many could not find jobs. Mr. Corum combined this available labor and his stock of mules and started a construction business with his brothers, William Burnice, Dr. J.R., and Arthur, already operating as CORUM BROS. They built many two lane roads and highways in western Kentucky in the 1920's and 1930's. One of the more popular projects was the contract to build Dade Park, now called James C. Ellis Park in Henderson Co., a horse racing track near the Ohio River.

In the 1920's, as the construction business flourished, Mr. Corum organized and established, with his brother-in-law, John Utterback, the U.C. Milk Co. (GOLDENROD DAIRY). The new pasteurization company was established to process, package, and distribute the milk from the Corum-Utterback dairy herds. This endeavor helped other farmers in the area, because they could sell their milk at "Grade A" and command a higher price for their cream and milk.

Mr. Corum was able to survive the depression because the government was building roads and the construction business remained busy. The dairy processing company progressed as pasteurized milk became a necessity as well as a convenience.

About 1940, Corum Bros. was awarded a contract to partially build the large ammunition plant at Clarksville, IN. After the job was complete, the government refused to pay for a major portion of the work, citing a breach of contract by Corum Bros. After a lengthy trial, the Corums were awarded their rightful pay for work performed.

Bill Corum and his father M. Ashby Corum about 1941 at Corum Bros. office, 758 S. Main, Madisonville. The building was just north of the Cates Motor Co. showroom.

During the 1930's and 1940's Ashby Corum purchased land in the Ashbyburg area and a farm between Madisonville and Earlington, upon which he made his home. During the late 1940's, Corum Bros. Contractors disbanded and Ashby Corum formed a separate construction business as a partner with Nick Edwards. The company was called Corum & Edwards, Inc. This company did much road and blacktop work until about 1964 when Ashby Corum sold his interest to Otto Corum, his nephew.

During the 1940's, with his son-in-law, Charles Ben Ashby, Mr. Corum formed an automobile business called Corum Motor Co. This business was a Dodge-Plymouth dealership.

Also during the 1940's, Mr. Corum started an appliance business with another son-in-law, Rayburn Whitledge. The MID-STATE Co. was located at about 56 South Main St. in Madisonville.

Ashby Corum was the first President of the Hopkins Co. Agricultural and Industrial Fair. He served on the Kentucky State Fair Board during the planning and early construction stages of the Kentucky Fair and Exposition Center in the mid 1950's. It was his idea to build ramps instead of steps in Freedom Hall. He served as president of the Kentucky Association of Highway Contractors in 1929. He was a charter member of the Madisonville Kiwanis Club, and a Kentucky Colonel.

Ashby Corum made his home in Ashbyburg, then moved to Madisonville about 1919. In the 1920's he moved to a home at the corner of Center and Scott Streets, directly in front of the Methodist Church. He then moved to the location of the Goldenrod Farm on South Main St. in the 1930's. About 1949 he moved to 48 Lake St. Then, in the 1960's to a small house at 150 Waddle Ave.

M. Ashby Corum died Aug. 21, 1968. He and his wife are buried at Odd Fellows Cemetery in Madisonville, KY.- *Submitted by: William M. Corum, grandson.*

SAMUEL CHESLEY CORUM

Samuel C. Corum was born Aug. 15, 1857, in Grainger Co., TN. He was the son of Robert N. Corum and Sarah E. Morgan Corum of the Little Valley community near Blaine. His mother died when he was about six years old and his father married a Mary Jarnagin. He had one full brother, R.L. Corum, of Morgan Co., TN. Also, a half-brother, William A. "Billy" Corum. Most of William A. Corum's family settled in McLean Co, KY, about 1880 or later.

At the age of 14, Samuel Corum climbed from the second story of his family's log home in the mountains of Eastern Tennessee and ran away. His father had died about 1872 and he was left to be raised by his step-mother.

He settled in McLean Co., KY, near Beech Grove and the Green River. He met Lucy Suvilla Dodson and they were married Aug. 1, 1875. She was only 15 years old at the time.

To that union eight children were born: William Burnice, (June 27, 1876); John Robert, M.D., (Jan. 20, 1879); Arthur D., (July, 7, 1883); Ethel, (July 12, 1885); Marshall Ashby, (July 23,

Samuel C. Corum and Lucy Suvilla Dodson on or about the date of their marriage

1887); Emma Sarah, (Oct. 4, 1890); Samuel Pascal, (Jan.10, 1894); and Mary Veatrice, (Sept. 6, 1896).

Samuel Corum was a prominent farmer and businessman and his business kept him away from home much of the time. Most of the farming chores were left to his wife and the children. He was a trader in livestock and would purchase animals in and around McLean Co. and sell them at Evansville. He lived about three miles from the Green River landing at Wrightsburg, near Onton, KY, and it was quite a chore to move the animals the three miles to and from the steamboat landing and his farm.

About 1899, Samuel Corum built a fine home in the Ashbyburg community of Hopkins Co. and moved his family to be closer to a river landing. He owned numerous farms in McLean, Hopkins, and Butler Counties.

In his later years he "spotted ties." Much of the Green River bottomland was being cleared and leveled for farming. Trees were cut into railroad ties and laid on the banks at the river landings. He would check and purchase ties for the railroads and would mark the end of each tie with a colored marker. Thus, when the ties were loaded on boats to travel the river, the rightful owner could claim his ties at their river landing destination.

Samuel C. Corum died a young man on Nov. 21, 1904, just 47 years of age. His wife did an excellent job of raising a large family, many of whom became very prominent people in Hopkins Co.'s history and progress.

Lucy Suvilla Corum died Aug. 25, 1937, in Madisonville. Both Samuel and Lucy are buried in the Little Bethel Baptist Church Cemetery at Beech Grove, KY.- *Submitted by William M. Corum, great-grandson*

WILLIAM BURNICE CORUM

William Burnice Corum was born June 27, 1876, in McLean Co., KY, the oldest child of Samuel Chesley Corum and Lucy Suvilla Dodson Corum.

He married Hallie Bell Thomas July 17, 1899, in Vanderburg, Co., IN. To this union six children were born: William Chesley (Apr. 5, 1900); Thomas Worthington (July 10, 1903); Girtie Lee (June 28, 1906); Lucy Virginia (Nov. 2, 1909); James Coleman (Dec. 29, 1913); and Bernice Mae (July 9, 1916).

Burnice Corum, as he was known to his family and friends, was said to be one of the most energetic businessmen of the area during his time. Being the oldest of eight children, he received much counsel and guidance from his father concerning business matters and his father always encouraged his children to "stick together" in their business lives. He followed this advice throughout his lifetime.

In his early life, he worked on his father's farm, attending county schools. As a young man he studied at Bowling Green and secured a certificate to teach. He taught in Muhlenburg and McLean counties for a few years, then followed his family to Ashbyburg in Hopkins Co. and began farming. There he formed with his three younger brothers, Dr. J.R., Ashby and Arthur, a firm known as Corum Brothers. They set up a general merchandising store at Ashbyburg. The store became a clearing house for a vast river territory along the Green River. It was said that anything from a hay rake to a steam shovel could be purchased from the store.

With William Burnice Corum as the "ramrod" of the firm, Corum Brothers began operating on a large scale. The brothers began farming several thousand acres and after World War I entered the contracting business.

About 1920 the Corum families began moving to Madisonville, as the river ceased to be the primary mode of transportation. William Burnice lived in Madisonville until about 1930 when he was forced by ill health to retire from active business.

He was one of the first appraisers for the Federal Land Bank, and his duties took him to the states of Tennessee, Indiana and Kentucky. He was a Republican and ran for the county offices of Jailer and Sheriff.

The following is quoted from an obituary appearing at the time of Mr. Corum's death:

"He recognized no schedule of work hours. He took no vacations. He worked and worked, many a time through day and night without stopping, because he loved work for its own sake. He was a big man, weighing considerably more than two hundred pounds, but he handled his bulk with as much ease as a jockey gets about. He was strong physically. As strong as any man could want to be. But he died at 58 because his tremendous energy had burned up the power house. He died with a telephone at his bed, through which only a few moments before he had issued orders to some of his associates, with him to the last."

William Burnice died Sept. 26, 1934, in Hanson, and he and his wife are buried in Bethel Cemetery at Beach Grove. -*Submitted by: William M. Corum, great-nephew*

COTTON-HOOK

Freda Mae Hook and James Wallace Cotton were married Aug. 18, 1956 in Shawneetown, IL.

Freda was born on June 12, 1938, in Hopkins Co. She is the daughter of William Herman Hook and the late Anna Mae (Dexter) Hook.

James was born in Hopkins Co. on Feb. 24, 1936. He is the only son of William Cotton and Nora (DeArmond) Cotton.

Freda attended first grade at Munn's School. Both attended the old Anton School and remember moving into the new school which was built there. Freda attended Madisonville High School while James dropped out to work.

Freda was previously married and had a son. J.W. and Freda have five children born and raised in Hopkins Co. The children are: Darrel Wayne Watson born May 2, 1956; James Dale Cotton born July 18, 1957; Judith Ann Cotton born Jan. 19, 1961; Keith Earl Cotton born June 5, 1964; Nora Mae Cotton born Apr. 3, 1968; and Amanda Jane Cotton born Oct. 8, 1978. Five of their six children are married and have families of their own.

Darrel W. Watson married Brenda Vickery. They have three children and reside and work in Madisonville. Their children: Jimmy Wayne Abbott born June 26, 1973 (Darrel's stepson); Chassity Gale Watson born June 14, 1977; and LaDonna Kaye Watson born May 28, 1982.

James Dale Cotton married Sandra Lee. They reside and work in Madisonville with their two children: William Dale Cotton born July 2, 1979 and Lisa Marie Cotton born Jan. 25, 1982.

Judith Ann Cotton married Ronnie Carl Vickery. They reside near Anton with their three children. Ronnie is an employee of Coca-Cola and Judith Ann is employed at Regional Medical Center. Their children: Shawn Steven Vickery born June 17, 1979; Brandy Nichole Vickery born Apr. 27, 1983; and Christopher Scott Vickery born Oct. 31, 1986.

Keith Earl Cotton married Carolyn Davis. He graduated from M.N.H.H. School in 1982, and Carolyn graduated from Dawson Springs High School in 1982. They have no children. Keith is an employee of Western Kentucky Distributors and Carolyn is an employee of Wal-Mart. They reside in Dawson Springs.

Nora Mae Cotton married Allan Anthony Jones. They reside in Anton and Anthony is an employee of Western Kentucky Distributors. They have two sons: Matthew Earl Jones born July 9, 1985, and Douglas Wayne Jones born Oct. 31, 1986.

Amanda (Mandy) Cotton is eight years old and lives with her parents in Anton. She will be a 3rd grader when school starts this fall. She has been in Brownies for two years, and an active member of Lantrip's Karate Studio.

James Wallace Cotton supported his family by working in the underground coal mines. He started out working for Nashville Coal Company and presently works for Island Creek Coal Company at the Providence #1 Mine. He has worked in underground coal mines for 32 years. Earning his 20 and 30 year pins from Island Creek.

We feel our contribution to Hopkins Co. is our children and grandchildren! Some of the children carry on the traditions and thoughts that were taught to us by our parents and grandparents. Sometimes when we are all together, I look at each one and wish only the best for all of them. Later we hope they can remember and look back to us with love as we love them all!- *Submitted by Freda Mae (Hook) Cotton*

JAMES DANIEL COUCH

James Daniel Couch, son of Daniel, grandson of James Couch, was born in Albermarle Co., VA, Feb. 16, 1803. His grandfather, (Capt.) James Couch, of Buckingham Co., VA, was said to have been born 1750 in England. James D.'s mother's name is unknown, but his father, Daniel, died in Bedford Co., VA, 1811, ca. age 37, leaving five young children: Thomas Jefferson Couch b. ca. 1797, Elizabeth b. ca. 1800, James D., Dolly b. ca. 1801, and a son John. One source states that James D. was reared in Buckingham Co. This is likely as there were many relatives living there — the Couch's, Low's, Anderson's and Howard's.

James D. Couch's uncle John (Jr.) of Buckingham Co. was the first born of Capt. James Couch, and seems to have been a dominant one in the family — he lost his first wife, and administered the estates of his father, and three brothers before leaving Virginia for Kentucky. In 1833 John Couch and his wife Mary Anderson, daughter of (Capt.) Thomas Anderson and Sarah Howard, settled on a plantation of 1000 acres in Hopkins Co., KY, and John took the Citizenship Oath. John had thirteen or fourteen children, one of them was named Mary Ann.

In July 1835 in Hopkins Co., James D. Couch and Mary Ann were married by Rev. C. Campbell. At about this period in time, there was a big land rush going on in Mississippi after the Treaty of Pontotoc Creek was signed with the Chickasaws in 1832. James D.'s brother-in-law Aaron Root (Elizabeth's husband) was the first Sheriff in this area and owned an extensive stage and mail line. James D. and several of Aaron's brothers were in Mississippi around this same time. James D. bought land in De Soto and Monroe counties, MS. He evidently decided he would rather live in Kentucky because around 1836 James D. Couch gave power-of-attorney to Aaron Root to sell property for him in Mississippi. James D. and Mary Ann lived out their lives in Hopkins/Webster (1860) counties. He died Apr. 11, 1866 and is buried in Mt. Carmel Cemetery. She died 1904 and is buried at Slaughter, KY, Cemetery. They had ten children.

James D. Couch's sister Dolly and brother John have not been traced. His brother Thomas Jefferson is found on the 1850 Hopkins County Census living with James D. and Mary Ann. Thomas Jefferson Couch's will, 1856, names James D., four of his nephews, two of his cousins, and parents D. and J.

All my ancestors migrated to Hopkins Co. from Virginia or North Carolina from the late 1790's to the mid 1840's. I was born 1920 in Webster Co., and moved to Evansville ca. 1922. My father was Roy A. Couch, son of Joe Daniel Couch, son of James Powhatan, son of James Daniel and Mary Ann Couch. -Submitted by Mrs. Catharine (Couch) Kello

COULTER

James Garfield Coulter was born Apr. 19, about 1877 (he was unsure of the year of his birth because he was an orphan) and died May 9, 1963. He was raised in Jamestown, TN, by an Indian woman named Mary Woods.

James Garfield (Mr. Jim) Coulter, Mary Elizabeth Harris-Workman, and Mary Easter Howton-Miller-Coulter

Jim (referred by all who knew him as "Mr. Jim") was a faith-healer. People would come from all over Dawson to have him "blow in" their children's mouth to cure thrash. His specialties were taking off warts, curing shingles, and stopping bleeding. Mr. Jim came by this "gift of healing" when at one point in his life he went into a "trance" and people thought he was dead. When he came out of the trance he later discovered he had the "gift." He met Mary Easter Howton-Miller in Dawson Springs when he came through Dawson while working on the railroad. They married Mar. 9, 1921, in Caldwell Co., KY, and made their home on what is now known as Walnut Street in Dawson Springs.

This was both Mary and Jim's second marriage. Mary was married previously to Burl W. Miller by whom she bore all six of her children. They are Minnie Bell Miller-Brown, Louella Miller-Powell, Mary Frances "Fanny" Miller-Messamore-Adams, Nancy Catherine Miller (died at age 16 months), James Louis Miller, and Rosa Lee Miller-Brown-Harris.

Mary Easter Howton-Miller-Coulter was born Feb. 18, 1873, and died Oct. 16, 1962. She was the third child and only daughter out of four children. Her parents were Charles Louis Howton (born July 27, 1847; died July 11, 1884) and Easter Catherine Steel-Howton (born Apr. 23, 1842, in North Carolina; died Jan. 25, 1907). Paternal grandparents were Harvey Howton and Mary W. Galloway-Howton. Paternal great-grandparents were Lewis Howton (born Dec. 16, 1793; died July 1, 1874 in Hopkins Co.) and Sarah Ridge-Howton (born Jan. 14, 1802 and died Sept. 19, 1851 in Hopkins Co.). Paternal great-great-grandparents were Jonathan Howton and Ann E. Trover of Hopkins Co.

Mary and Jim Coulter never had any children of their own but after raising Mary's children they also took a grandchild of Mary's to raise when she was a few months old after believing the child was not being raised in the proper atmosphere and was being neglected. This child was Mary Elizabeth Harris-Workman. (See Harris-Workman story).

Mary and Jim Coulter are buried in Walnut Grove Cemetery in Dawson Springs. - Submitted by Kathy Annette Workman

COX

Tradition relates that members of a Cox family left Virginia with the intention of settling in the west, possibly Missouri; this seems to have been in the early years of the 19th century. The story continues saying that serious illness struck one family member and the group stopped in the area now known as Hopkins Co., and waited for the patient to recover enough to travel. However, the patient was enduring a lengthy illness, and a part of the family decided to travel on to Missouri, while the others remained in Kentucky, planning to join the Missouri group when the crisis ended. Perhaps the Kentucky group found life in Hopkins Co. more appealing, because they decided to remain and become residents. The Missouri Coxes and the Coxes of Hopkins Co. were still in touch as late as the 1950's; Bowling Green, MO, and neighboring Lincoln Co. seem to be the area which the Coxes settled in.

Horace W. Cox with son John Henry Cox about 1932

Back in Virginia, the last generation which did not join the trip west was headed by John Cox (1710-1793) who resided with his wife Lucretia Wynne in Mecklenburg Co. John was descended from Richard Cocke, the immigrant and founder of his family in Virginia, born in England, and in Virginia by 1636.

The first member of the Cox family to settle in this area of Kentucky appears to have been a son of John Cox of Virginia; he was Samuel Cox, born 1753, died 1820. Samuel and his wife, Temperance Bailey (1761-1824) both died in Hopkins Co., and there is no indication as to their place of burial. Some of their eleven children were born in Person Co., NC, which is not very far from their Virginia home. Records suggest that they arrived sometime between the marriage of one of their children, Elizabeth, in May 1809, in Person Co., NC, and the marriage of another of their children, Wyatt, in May 1815, in Hopkins Co. To follow the lineage of this large family would require volumes, so only an account of their son's line will follow; he was the eldest child, Meredith Cox, born in Virginia in the year 1778. His wife was Margaret Harris McFarland (1768-c. 1830). Meredith eventually traveled on to Missouri and died there in Lincoln Co. after 1818. Meredith and Margaret became parents of twin sons, Apr. 5, 1804, but it is unclear where they were born. One of the twins was John Bailey Cox (1804-1850). John's wife was Bathsheba (1801-1881). They were living in Hopkins Co. when John died in 1850, and his will bears the date of May 13 of that year. They seem to have been farming on the land where they are buried, about one mile east of Brown

Road, that farm being the one owned by Walton H. Cox at the time of his death in 1960. (Walton was a great-grandson of John Bailey Cox.)

The eldest of the ten children of John Bailey and Bathsheba Cox was Meredith Franklin Cox (1832-1910). He was a farmer in this same area east of Brown Road, and married Caroline Pritchett, who soon died. He then married Caroline's cousin, Agnes Jane, a daughter of Horace and Lucy Goodloe Pritchett. Meredith and Agnes Jane, who are buried at Grapevine, had three children, only one of whom has descendants in 1987. The one who has descendants was Horace William Cox (1862-1936), their eldest. Horace William was a farmer and road contractor, and married first Irene Vernleigh Hayes who died young, leaving Horace with two daughters, Anna Mabel and Agnes Annie.

Ed and Iley Cates with son Claud, about 1911

John Henry Cox and David H. Pritchett (with cap). Both lived to be grandfathers to the same children, the ones born to Bill (William M.) and Edith Ann Pritchett Cox

Later, in 1905, Horace married Ola Logan, who became the mother of his only son, John Henry Cox, born 1909, died 1980. Horace and his family lived a part of their lives on his farm, but settled finally in Madisonville on Harrig Street in 1920. Horace lived to see two grandchildren, Ola Hayes Gill (Mrs. Jasper Clayton), daughter of Annie and Jesse Gill, and Mary Whitfield Cox, daughter of John Henry and Mary Elizabeth "Betty" Whitfield. John Henry Cox, a farmer and political figure, married Betty on Dec. 7, 1930, and in addition to Mary, had two sons, John Horace Cox in 1938, and William Meredith Cox in 1942. - *Submitted by John Horace Cox*

ILEY CATES COX

Iley Polley, born July 13, 1883, died May 22, 1985, was the daughter of Peter Polley and Katherine (Katie) Cobb of Webster Co. (see Polley-Jones).

Iley married Ed Cates when she was 16. Ed Cates, born 1874 died 1951, was the son of Sam Cates (1845-1916) and Mary Catherine (Molly) Averitt. Ed's brothers were Guy (see Ethel Blankenship), Hugh and Watt. His sisters were Cora and Victoria (Vick).

Iley and Ed built their home on a farm on Highway 120 in Webster Co. Their only child, Claud (1901-1959), married Valera Hidgen of Hopkins Co. Claud and Valera's only child, Inez, married Lloyd Whitmore. Inez has lived in California for 34 years. She and her husband are retiring and returning to the Nebo community in the fall of 1987, where they have bought a home. Inez has two children and three grandchildren.

Iley's hobbies were needlework and wood crafting. She enjoyed landscaping and gardening. Her neat well-groomed yard was a community show place with its rock garden and miniature well stocked with gold fish. During the late 30's and 40's, she bred and raised beautiful singing canaries.

A member of Oakley Home General Baptist Church since she was a teenager, where Ed was a deacon, Iley loved music. She played piano and the French harp and sang for school and church specials. She was an excellent cook and enjoyed entertaining. Sharing her husband's love of the farm, she was a good horsewoman. She kept a saddle mare for riding until just before selling the farm. After the death of Ed, she stayed on the farm for a few years renting out her ground. Finally selling her farm she lived in Nebo for awhile before buying a house in Manitou.

At this time, she married Herman Cox. She was heartbroken when the marriage ended in divorce after a few years. Again she sold her home and moved into a trailer on the farm of a niece near Nebo. Even in her 80's and 90's, she had a yard of lovely flowers. At 90, she attended the wedding of a great great niece and was the life of the reception that followed.

Iley's last move was to a local health care center in Madisonville where she continued to attend Sunday morning church services and community singings. After she was confined to a wheelchair, she still attended the church services held by different local churches in the home. Her clear soprano voice could be well heard. She had memorized all the old hymns, as her sight was now dim.

The home's staff helped her celebrate her 100th year. Not so alert she had to be told who some of her relatives were. She always apologized for her poor memory, but no one minded.

Iley never tired of talking over old times with her last friend her age, Charley Oakley (see his story). She loved recalling the good times at church revivals and homecomings. Her pride was her only granddaughter, Inez, and great grandchildren in California she so missed and that some day she just might get on a plane and visit.....

See "Hopkins County Centenarians" for a picture of Iley Cates Cox. - *Submitted by Dorothy Miller Shoulders*

SALLY COX

Sarah Temperance Cox was born Mar. 20, 1831, in Ashbyburg, KY. She was the daughter of Peyton Cox and Sally Sugg.

Sarah, better known as Sally, married Samuel Champion Cox (a distant cousin) on May 13, 1850, in Hopkins Co. He was born May 11, 1827.

The children of Sally and Samuel Champion were: Mary (Molly) Susan, Sarah Louisa, Francis Marion, Nannie J., Annie Elizabeth, Ella Temperance, Samuel Peyton and Eva Vaden.

Sally and Samuel lived in Nebo, the corner of what is now Highway 41-A and South Hoffman Street.

Samuel Champion Cox died Feb. 3, 1907, and Sally died Aug. 22, 1931, at the age of 100. Both are buried in the Barron-Cox Cemetery at Nebo. - *Submitted by Dorothy Miller Shoulders*

JOSEPH CRABTREE

The Crabtree ancestors were Irish descendants. The exact year of their departure from Ireland is not known, but they first settled on the coast of North Carolina. From there the family of Joseph Crabtree moved into Washington Co., TN. After a few years, they made their journey into Kentucky in 1811. They settled in Hopkins Co. near what is known as the New Salem area.

Joseph Crabtree was born July 7, 1792, and died Aug. 22, 1863, at Prathersville. He married Ellender Prather who was the daughter of Thomas Prather. Their children were: Rosa A. (1820-1894), Phillip P. (1823-1853), Thomas W. (1825-1899), Willis Y. (1829-1893) who married Louisa E. Jackson from Tennessee, Orlean B. (1833-?) who married Priscilla Ashby in 1870 and Barbara A. (1835-?).

Thomas W. Crabtree (1825-1899) was first married to Pernetta Prather, daughter of Phillip Prather. They had one child, Sarah Elenor Crabtree who married Austin P. Ashby. To this union two children were born, Addie L. Ashby, 1872, and Conrad Ashby 1873-1964.

After the death of his first wife, Thomas W. married her sister Zella Ann Prather in 1853. Their children were: Mariah Louise (1854-1923) who married A.L. Ashby, Phillip D. (1856-1922) who married Mattie Hughes, Barbara L. (1858-1859), Willie L. (1865-1942) who married Birdie Lutz, William M. "Bill" (1865-?) who married Docia Brown, Joanah who died in 1868 and Thomas, Jr. (1874-?).

After his marriage into the Prather family, Thomas W. was engaged in the tobacco buying business. His father-in-law was owner of a general store and tobacco factory at Prathersville, a settlement named after him.

A railroad was started through Prathersville a few years before the Civil War. Construction halted during the War, and it was not until 1869 that he first train rolled through the area. Several contractors had the job of putting the railroad through, but many went broke. Finally, Mr. Hanson was successful in getting it completed. Since Prathersville was so close to Slaughters, which made it inconvenient for the trains to stop that close together, they moved Prathersville up. Prathersville became Hanson, named for the successful railroad contractor, Henry Hanson.

The Prathers and the Crabtrees were church-going people. They attended Salem Chapel which was located near the Roland Gooch farm west of Hanson. While the Civil War was brewing the church split over the ownership and rights of the slaves. The southern wing pulled away and built a new church about two and one half miles south of Slaughters. During the Civil War the Salem Chapel was burned.

Thomas Crabtree took great pride in raising fine horses. During the Civil War the northern soldiers raided him and took his horses. They were often compelled to cook for the Yankee soldiers.

Thomas W. died at the age of seventy-four years and he was survived by one daughter, Mariah, and four sons, Phillip, Willis, William and Thomas Crabtree, Jr.

Information from James N. Ashby and the late Richard Brown. - Compiled and written by James N. Ashby and Devona Riley

CROFT-FERGUSON

Margaret Florence Ferguson and Thomas Dale Croft were married Oct. 22, 1945, at the Hopkinsville, KY, court house.

Margaret was born Nov. 13, 1928, in Ferguson Town, KY, Hopkins Co. She is the daughter of Ural and Goldie Ferguson. Ural was born Feb. 11, 1906, in Ferguson Town, KY. He married Goldie Hatfield in Old Shawnee Town, IL, in 1924. Goldie was born July 24, 1908, in Leweshearn, KY, Muhlenberg Co. Ural was the son of Johnnie Ferguson born February 1884 and Fannie Mitchell born 1884. Two children were born to Johnnie and Fannie Ferguson: Ural and Gertrude. Goldie was the daughter of Jim Hatfield born Oct. 6, 1864, and Margaret Alice Whelchels (Wilkie) born 1865. They were married Jan. 9, 1885, and she was of Indian descent. Goldie was a descendant of the Hatfields of the Hatfield and McCoy Feud. There were eleven children born to Jim and Margaret Hatfield. There were three children born to Ural and Goldie Ferguson: James Harold, Margaret Florence, and Eva Nell.

Margaret went to school at the Old Charleston School in Charleston, KY. Upon marrying Thomas, they moved to Chicago where they presently live. She worked in factories until retiring to raise their two children. She is presently helping her son raise his three daughters.

Thomas was born Mar. 3, 1929, in Cambria, IL, Williamson Co. to Cordie Dempsey Croft and Maude Francis Thomas, the daughter of Luther Thomas born Oct. 21, 1879, and Nancy Lindsey born Aug. 4, 1883. Cordie Croft was born March 14, 1902, and Maude Thomas Croft was born Mar. 2, 1902. Cordie was born on the old Doc Earl Place in Kentucky. Cordie's grandmother was of Indian descent. Thomas has a sister named Wanda.

Upon arriving in Chicago, Thomas went to work for Northwestern Railroad, and then onto Advance Transformer where he has been employed for 34 years. He was a race car driver for 15 years until he retired from racing in 1968.

Thomas and Margaret have two children: Veronica Gale born Oct. 17, 1954 who married Larry Bruce Latimer and Thomas Dale Jr. born Apr. 9, 1958. They have three granddaughters: Margaret Lynn born May 30, 1977, Alyssa Gayle born Oct. 1, 1979, and Eileen Michelle born Jan. 27, 1982. - *Submitted by Veronica Gale Latimer*

CROW-HUTCHISON

It is said the Crow name originated in Scotland, which country they left because of persecution and went to Northern Ireland, before coming to Virginia.

Many of the name can be found in early records of Augusta, Botetourt, and Essex counties of Virginia. References to the early-day Crows living as neighbors to families with whom the Crow family are known to have intermarried lends credulity to the belief that these Crows are the family from whom the Crows of Hopkins Co. descend.

By the 1790's, some families of the Crow name had left Virginia. Many appear to have emigrated to Kentucky.

One of the early Crow emigrants to Hopkins Co. was John S. Crow (born ca. 1789/90-died 1877), son of John Crow who died 1802.

John S. Crow was living in Mecklenburg Co., VA, where his marriage to Nancy Hutchison (born 1796-died 1874) took place. Consent for the marriage was given by Nancy's mother, Amy Hutchison, according to the marriage bond, dated June 23, 1814. William Hutchison, the father of Nancy, and the husband of Amy, had died in Virginia previous to 1814.

Family tradition is that four Crow brothers left their Virginia home, in the Mecklenburg area, traveled over the Wilderness Road as far as the Cumberland Gap, where two of the brothers turned south into Alabama and became founders of the southern branch of the Crow/Crowe family and two, John S. and William, traveled westward into Kentucky, settling in the Nebo and Corinth neighborhoods of Hopkins Co.

A wagon caravan of family members came on that journey. John S. Crow brought with him his young wife, Nancy, and their infant daughter, Elizabeth (Betsy). Other members of the group included: William Crow, brother of John S., Amy (Brown) Hutchison, the mother of Nancy, Amy's daughter, Elizabeth, and sons Thomas and John Wesley. A third daughter of Amy (Brown) Hutchison, Martha (Patsy) with her husband, Thomas A. Compton, were also in the caravan.

There were other related families, from Virginia, who made their way in that wagon train of fifteen wagons, with accompanying riders, along the Wilderness Road into the fertile lands of Western Kentucky. Each family had with them a second wagon loaded with supplies.

The time of this journey was after the 22nd of May, 1815, which was the birth date of Elizabeth, the first child of Nancy and John S. Crow.

John S. Crow was both a carpenter and farmer. John S. Crow served his country in the War of 1812. He was allowed a military pension on Nov. 4, 1872.

The land holding of John S. Crow were about 1000 acres in Hopkins Co. Tradition is that he homesteaded some of the land and added to his holdings by purchase of tracts to accumulate this acreage.

The children of Nancy and John S. Crow included Elizabeth, born in Virginia, and the following ten children, all of whom were born in Hopkins Co., KY: William H. born 1817; Alzada born 1819; Elvira born 1821; Nancy born 1823; Mary Virginia born 1824; Louisa born 1826; Clementine born 1829; Orpha born 1831; Caroline born 1835 and John Wesley born 1836.

Descendants of this family still reside in the Hopkins Co. area. - *Submitted by Catherine D. Austin (Mrs. Clarence C.)*

SAMUEL D. CROWE

Samuel Delaney Crow(e) was born in Hopkins Co., son of John Wesley Crow and Nancy M. Compton.

John Wesley Crow, (born Dec. 11, 1836, died Jan. 22, 1916) on his father's farm two miles north of Nebo, was the tenth child and second son of John S. Crow. He married Nancy M. Compton Sept. 20, 1860 (born Sept. 14, 1839, died May 16, 1876). Their children: John, Will, Sam, Allie and Mattie. He then married Mary Francis Hobgood, and two children (one child, Jim, survived) were born before her death in childbirth in 1884. The third marriage was to Sara A. Daniels, and a son Green Daniels was born before her death in 1910. John Wesley was engaged in farming on his father's farm until his marriage, when he purchased land adjoining the homestead, where he made the culture of tobacco a specialty.

Margaret and Tom Croft dancing after renewing their wedding vows in 1983

John S. Crow 1789/90-1877 and Nancy Crow 1796-1874

John Wesley Crowe family about 1908 at the homeplace. John Wesley is in the front row with the white beard.

John S. Crow, (born Apr. 30, 1790, died Jan. 28, 1877) and his wife Nancy W. Hutchinson, (born Apr. 30, 1796, died Apr. 28, 1874), the parents of John Wesley, were natives of Virginia, and of English and Irish descent respectively. He served in the War of 1812 at Norfolk, VA. In 1814 he and his wife homesteaded land two miles north of what is now Nebo in Hopkins Co. He cleared and improved the farm upon which he resided until his death. The Crow graveyard is on this farm, and many of his descendents are buried there.

Samuel Delaney Crowe (the "e" was added to the name in his generation), our subject, managed his father's farm until his marriage to Mary Alice Hart (born Aug. 17, 1879, died July 10, 1967). Molly, as she was called, was a descendent of Richard Parker, Chirurgeon (1629-1680), the son of James Parker of Trangoe, Cornwall, descendant from the ancient family of Parker of Browsholme, England. The first land grant for Richard Parker was recorded in his name in Nansemond Co., VA, in 1654. Descendants moved to South and North Carolina, Kentucky and Hopkins Co. There Molly Hart was educated and taught school before she met and married Samuel Delaney on Jan. 31, 1903, at the end of a school term. Samuel purchased property next to land his father had given him. He continued to farm this land until his death Nov. 16, 1941, (birth May 15, 1872). This land is still owned by the children and grandchildren of Samuel Delaney.

The oldest son of Samuel and Molly was Compton Cardwell (Jan. 29, 1904-March 1981). He served as teacher, principal and superintendent in Hopkins Co. school system for fifty years. The oldest daughter, Auvergne Blythe Carneal (born Sept. 23, 1905) was a teacher and principal for forty-five years. Other children: Marion Victor (born Aug. 15, 1908, died Feb. 9, 1976); Vera Marjorie Collier (born Sept. 15, 1911, died Feb. 16, 1987); Gwen Hart Crowe (born Aug. 16, 1916, died Dec. 17, 1944 while serving in the Army in the Battle of the Bulge in WWII) and Lilly Dale Boyd (born Sept. 8, 1918). Of the fourteen grandchildren of Samuel Delaney and Mary Alice, six now live in Hopkins Co. in the Madisonville area. There are twenty great great grandchildren and six great great great grandchildren. *Sources: Some Ancestors and Descendants of Richard Parker, Chirurgeon 1629-1680 by Eleanor Davis McSwain, Kentucky Genealogy and Biography Vol. IV and personal research. - Submitted by Dale Crowe Boyd and Mrs. Walter Carneal*

CULLEN-TOWE

On Nov. 3, 1939, Thomas Ray Cullen was born in Hopkins County, KY, the son of Herschel and Nova Cullen.

Hershel and Nova are also the parents of: David who married Jean and they have three children, Elaine, Beverly, and Regina; Billy who married Geraldine and they have two children, Barry and Randy; Dale who married Eva and they have five children, Timmy, Brian, Angela, Brenda, and Joseph; and Jimmy who married Marsha and they have four children, Holly, Jane, Robby and Cindy.

On Jan. 6, 1940, Norma Jean Towe was born in Bowling Green, KY, the daughter of Bruce and Flo Towe. Norma's brothers and sisters are: Billy who married Sharon and they have three children, Keith, Mark and Krystal; Larry who is not married; Wandra Lantrip who has two children, Candy and Lisa; Carolyn who married Rodney Hail and they have one child, Malissa; and Sandy who is not married.

Norma Jean and Tommy were married on Mar. 21, 1959. They are the parents of two children. Steven Ray Cullen was born Nov. 19, 1959. He and his wife, Cheryl have two children, Rhianna and Justin. Sherry Jean Cullen was born Jan. 29, 1961 and married Jerry Cain.

Norma Jean and Tommy graduated from Dalton School. Both are Baptists. Tommy is self-employed. They live on Fergusontown Road.-*Submitted by Lisa Lantrip*

CUNNINGHAM-DAME

Hugh Cunningham, an early pioneer of Hopkins Co., was born in 1854 and died in 1932. He married Jennie Dame, born 1856 and died 1942. Hugh was a farmer, and the couple lived a great deal of their life in the Shakerag community near Fridy schoolhouse. They had 14 children. Those who are remembered are: Macy, Ebb, Ernest, Jess, Johnny, Noah Dexter and Ezra B. They are buried at Olive Branch Cemetery.

Noah Dexter Cunningham, thought to be the oldest of the children, was born 1873 and died 1959. He married Mary Jane Daniel, born 1876 and died 1958. They operated a grocery store in their home on North Seminary for many years. They are buried at Olive Branch Cemetery. Their children were: Elmer, Selby Lee, Allie, Welby, Elby, Laura, William, Verdie and Strother.

Elmer Cunningham married Flora Cates; Allie Cunningham married Lanerline Taylor; Welby married Bennie Daniel; Elby Cunningham married Goldie Taylor, sister to Lanerline; Laura Cunningham married John Clayton; William married Mary Poole; Verdie Cunningham married Ruby Clayton; Strother Cunningham married Betty Todd.

Selby Lee Cunningham first married Nevaline Baker. They had three children: Morris Cunningham who married Geneva Roberts; Amos Lee Sr. who married Clarice Brawner; and Dorothy who married Jack Waggoner. Selby Lee Cunningham and Almer Milum, daughter of Ed and Rosie (Furr) Milam, were married on Nov. 5, 1930, at Dixon, KY. Selby Lee was born Dec. 6, 1897, and died Oct. 31, 1971. Almer was born at Gordonsburg, TN, on July 29, 1914, and died Mar. 30, 1967. They are buried at Odd Fellows Cemetery. Their children are:

Rosie Jane Cunningham born Jan. 10, 1932, d —, married Ruby R. Davis; Thelma Jean Cunningham born Dec. 31, 1933, married George Albert Moore (see MOORE-CUNNINGHAM), Ruby Juanita Cunningham born July 2, 1935 married Donald Powless; Martha Helen Cunningham born Mar. 16, 1938, married Harold Wayne Babb; Talmadge Townes Cunningham born Mar. 9, 1942, married Patricia Morgan; Ford Lee Cunningham born Aug. 19, 1943, married Mary Bestine Scott.

Selby Lee later married Mary Frances King who survives. - *Submitted by Thelma Jean Moore*

CUNNINGHAM-TEAGUE

Chester Lee Cunningham b. Nov. 19, 1913, the son of Jasper and Gabie Lou Ella Murrah Cunningham of Hopkins Co., KY. Chester attended grammar school at Oak Hill and Mortons Gap. He graduated from Nortonville High School. Chester served several months in the CCC.

Agnes and Chester Cunningham

Chester married Agnes Teague b. Jan. 15, 1919, the daughter of George Anderson and

Effie Rachel Lyell Teague. They moved to Detroit, MI, where Chester was employed approximately 10 years at Difco Laboratory, Inc. They came back to Kentucky in 1947 and Chester was employed by the Chesley Franklin Coal Co. and Decola Coal Co. for approximately 18 years until the mine closed in 1968. Chester and his son, Joe, operated the Standard Oil Station and Garage for a number of years. He retired in the late 70's.

Agnes was employed at the Chesley Franklin Coal Co. and Decola Coal Co. to weigh coal and keep the books for approximately 20 years.

Chester and Agnes reside in Nortonville and are members of the First Christian Church there.

They are the parents of one son, Joe Murrah Cunningham, b. Oct. 29, 1938. Joe attended grammar school in Detroit, MI, and in Nortonville, KY. He graduated from South Hopkins High School, entered the Army and served time in Korea. He married Priscilla Lane Crick b. Sept. 24, 1941, the daughter of Jewell Floyd and Sarah Lile Crick of Hopkins Co., KY. They lived in Detroit, MI, for a few years where Joe was employed as a welder. They moved back and he went into business with his father. He operated an auto store for a few years and then sold the business. At the present time, he operates a used car lot in Nortonville. Joe, his dad and his uncle A.D. Cunningham have operated a service station and garage in Nortonville for several years. Priscilla is a housewife and mother. She is a member of the First Christian Church in Nortonville. They reside in Nortonville and are the parents of four children:

Sandra Leigh b. Feb. 15, 1960, married Calvin Gamblin who works at Dotiki Mines owned by Mapco Coal Co. Sandra is a housewife and mother. They live in the New Salem area near Nortonville, KY, and are members of the Mannington Baptist Church. They have one son, Joshua Carl, and a daughter, Sarah Marie.

Shelia Carol b. Feb. 3, 1963, married Timothy Joseph Martin who is employed at First Federal Savings & Loan in Madisonville, KY. Shelia is employed at Blue Grass Carpet. Tim attends Christ the King Church and Shelia is a member of the First Christian Church in Nortonville. They live on McLaughlin Street, Madisonville, and are the parents of a daughter, Whitney Lane.

Susan Myreah b. Dec. 4, 1965, is employed at Ormonds in the mall at Madisonville. She is single, living at home and a member of the Mannington Baptist Church.

Chester (Chet) Murrah b. Oct. 10, 1970, is a senior at South Hopkins High School. He lives at home and attends Mannington Baptist Church. - *Submitted by Agnes Teague Cunningham*

KIMBERLY JANE SHOULDERS (CUNNINGHAM)

Born Marcello Kay Sullivan on Aug. 1, 1957, in Whitley Co., KY, at 11 months was placed in the foster home of Ernest and Edith Prewitt of Corbin, with other welfare children. Suffering from some malnutrition, but not as severe as her older half-sister, Karen, the girls were placed for adoption in April of 1959. They gained another sister, Lola, when James and Dorothy Shoulders of Manitou became their legal parents. Marcello was by then Kimberly Jane, the namesake of Grandmother Betty Jane Shoulders of Webster County (see Miller and Shoulders).

Kimberly Jane Shoulders (Cunningham) 1957-1983

Kim's first memories were at her home in Manitou. Adoring family, lots of cousins, a big Collie dog, birthday parties, chickenpox and a much-desired bride-doll for Christmas. Her first three grades were in Hobbs, NM, where she excelled in reading, receiving a certificate for finishing 4th grade reading by the end of the 3rd year. She had a pet horntoad lizard, was a Brownie Scout, learning to do the hula and sang in a trio with her two older sisters. "The Bible Song Birds" sang throughout the South West. Back in Kentucky for 4th grade, she began private music lessons, voice, rhythm and piano. At Nebo School she was a drummer for Jr. High band, later drummer and majorette at West Hopkins. She was in Chorus, All District Chorus and Quad-State, also Quad-State Singers of Mixed Ensemble and Senior Girls Ensemble, graduating as "Female Most Talented" in 1975. She turned down an offer to tour and travel with the musical group of "Up With People" and married classmate Gary Cunningham on September, 1975. In October 1976, her daughter Kimberly Kayôna was born. Kim was a member of the Concord General Baptist Church on Highway 630, a member of the Church Guild Girls and Youth Choir. She played organ as well as piano, accompanied solos, duets and weddings, also church V.B.S. She returned to Madisonville's Health Occupation School where she now lived. She won at state level a 2nd place silver trophy for her school, Spelling Medical Terminology, graduating in 1982. Kim worked at R.M.C. and then Trover Clinic. She was a medical secretary at Trover Clinic at the time of her illness, entering R.M.C. on June 23, 1983, due to a kidney failure and other complications and in spite of the care of the R.M.C. staff, Kim went back into a coma July 10. She died July 18 and was buried in Concord Cemetery on Highway 630 near Manitou.

This quote by older sister, Lola: "Time, you thief, tell why! You took the brightest star in the sky? She was my baby sister, I loved her so much. We had so many good times, laughing, talking and such". - *Submitted by Dorothy Shoulders*

CURB-WAIDE

Suzanne Camille Waide is the daughter of Peggy Sullivan Waide and Harry Doyle Waide of Earlington, KY. She was born in Hopkins Co. Hospital in Madisonville, KY, on June 15, 1960, at a time when the Waides lived in Providence, KY.

She attended Madisonville city schools and, in 1978, graduated from Madisonville North Hopkins High School.

The Harry Waide family, Christmas 1986. In front l to r: Wei Qiang Dong, a Christmas visitor from Shanghi, China, Clay N. Curb, Mary Mae Curb in front of Kent Waide, Uncle Spaulding "Sugie" Ringo, Hannah Jo Curb and Harry D. Waide. Back row l to r: Peggy S. Waide holds Muppy J. Puppy, Suzanne Waide Curb and Forrest L. "Ben" Waide.

Suzanne migrated to Houston, TX, in 1981 and worked at Avis-Rent-A-Car Systems at Hobby Airport. She met Clay Neal Curb, of Houston, who worked at the same facility.

Clay and Suzanne were married in St. Mary's Episcopal Church, Madisonville, by Rector Robert A. King and First United Methodist Minister, Dr. Wallace Thomas.

Clay is the son of Jo Nell Swanzy Curb and Wayne Gray Curb of Fort Worth, TX. Clay had two brothers: Grayling Wayne Curb and Patrick Ruel Curb of Houston. He has a half brother, Paul Bell, of Ft. Worth. Paul is his mother's son by her first marriage.

Suzanne has two brothers: Forrest Lynn "Ben" Waide and Kent Waide of Earlington.

The Curbs have two daughters: Hannah Jo (Sept. 7, 1982) born in Houston, TX, S.E. Memorial Hospital and Mary Mae (Apr. 23, 1984) born in the same facility. Both girls were christened at St. Mary's Episcopal Church on Christmas Eve following their respective birth dates.

Suzanne is a member of the First United Methodist Church in Madisonville and Clay is a confirmed member of St. Mary's.

Suzanne is a housewife and Clay is employed by Ruby Concrete Company.

At present, Hannah Jo is attending Kindergarten at Waddill Avenue elementary school, the fourth female in a successive line starting with her great-grandmother to attend Waddill School.

(See Waide-Sullivan; F.L. Waide; Kent Waide; Ramsey-Ringo and Sullivan-Ramsey). - *Submitted by: Peggy Sullivan Waide*

DANIEL

The known progenitors of the Daniel family in Hopkins Co., KY, were Mathew Daniel (b. before 1755 (1), d. 1825) and his wife Rachel Satterfield, daughter of John I. Satterfield and his wife Lucy.

According to family tradition, Mathew was the son of John Daniel of Virginia who was granted land in St. James District, Caswell Co., the area that became Persons Co., NC. Mathew owned land on both sides of the Dan River in Pittsylvania Co., VA, Rockingham Co., NC, where he operated a ferry.

On Oct. 9, 1809, in Rockingham Co., NC, a marriage agreement was filed for Mathew Daniel and Agatha Paine. (The widow of Robert Payne, Agatha was also widowed by her first husband Constantine Perkins.) They moved to Pittsylvania Co., VA, by 1810, living there until his death. (2)

Mathew's will (3) in Pittsylvania, VA, dated January 1825, proved Mar. 25, 1825, listed five children, making sons John and Green his executors.

1. Lucy married William A. Griffith Feb. 19, 1822, lived in Rockingham Co., NC.
2. Mathew b. May 23, 1786, in Orange Co., NC, d. April 1869, in Persons Co., NC.
3. Jane "Jeney" married Robert Wallis in Person Co., NC.
4. Green born 1788 married Elizabeth Day Mar. 2, 1814. They lived in Pittsylvania Co., VA. He bought land from the heirs of his brother John before they moved to Kentucky.
5. John and wife Elizabeth lived in Persons and Rockingham Cos., NC, died about 1827/1829. Brother Green was his executor. His daughter Agatha married Joseph D. Griffith and remained in Leaksville, Rockingham Co., NC. In later years taking care of her mother Elizabeth who had been widowed by the death of her second husband Bartlett Estis.

John Daniel's son William and his wife Katy, with their three daughters, migrated from Rockingham Co., NC, to Hopkins Co., KY, in 1835, settling on Pond Creek. The families of his brothers and sisters came here a short time later. They included James and wife Mary, Rachel and her husband John Cahall, (5) Sarah and husband Johnathan Harrelson, (6) Mathew who married Mary Yarlbrough, and Green who married Hester Sisk, all buying farms in Hopkins Co.

William and Katy's son John was born Apr. 9, 1836, in Hopkins Co., living there until his marriage in 1860 to Sarah Jane Tapp (1843-1876), the daughter of William Isham Tapp and Phobe Ann Harrelson. He then moved to Vandersburg, Webster Co., KY. After the death of Katy, William married Jane Winstead Feb. 5, 1839. They lived in the Nebo area until his death Sept. 27, 1869. Jane had died three weeks earlier. (7)

Of William and Katy's three daughters: Elizabeth married 1st James S. Mitchell, Oct. 22, 1850, 2nd Thomas Clayton Dec. 6, 1863, 3rd John Harwick 1870; Catherine married Irwin B. Bauldwin May 3, 1852; and Sarah married Elijah G. Mitchell Oct. 26, 1852.

Sources: (1) 1800 Persons Co., NC, Census, (2) #1798 Contract, Deed Book O, Rockingham Co., NC, (3) Pittsylvania Co., VA, Will Bk. 1-2, (4) Rockingham Co., NC Deed Bk. 2DE, 2DF and 2DV, (5) Pittsylvania Co., VA deed bk. 35, (6) Hopkins Co., KY, Deed Bk. 8, (7) Hopkins Co., KY, Civil Case #10025.-*Submitted by: Barbara S. Bishop*

JOHN DANIEL

John Daniel (Apr. 9, 1836-Dec. 1, 1913) was born in Hopkins Co., KY, the only son of William and Katy "Ann" Cahall Daniel. (1&2) He married Sarah "Sally" Jane Tapp (1843-1876), the daughter of William Isham Tapp and Phebe Ann Harrelson within the census year of 1860. (3) They made their home with John's sister Catherine Bauldwin at Nebo, KY, where they attended Pleasant Grove Baptist Church. (4) In April 1861 they moved to Vandersburgh, Webster Co., KY, where John was a farmer. Their children were:

1. Phebe born c. 1863, married Elijah Harris Oct. 23, 1878. They had two children John and Laura.
2. Virginia born September 1865, married George Garst (Oct. 16, 1854-Apr. 16, 1907) on May 25, 1887. Their children were Guy M. (March 1889-1953), Edgar L. (Jan. 1, 1895-Sept. 15, 1895), and Girty F. born January 1898.
3. John Green "Bob" (July 12, 1868-May 25, 1950) who married Rosa L. Bassett (June 6, 1867-Apr. 12, 1918) on Sept. 20, 1918, at Rumsey, McLean Co., KY. (5) Rosa was the daughter of John Synette Bassett and Francis C. Ashby, the daughter of Wilson Ross Ashby and Mariah Ann Blue.

Rosa had come to Hopkins Co. to visit her aunt. John saw her crossing a field between the two farms, and decided this was the girl for him. So the courtship began, and a date set for the wedding. Then Rosa discovered John had a previous date to take her cousin to a dance. Rosa postponed the wedding a day, insisting John honor his obligation to her cousin. (6)

Rosa's father, John Synette Bassett (Nov. 13, 1843-May 28, 1912), was the son of William Henry Bassett, whose parents were Abner Bassett Jr. and Nancy Galloway, (7) and his wife Nancy Lynne, the daughter of James Lynne Jr. of Beech Grove, Daviess Co., KY. They were members of Cumberland Presbyterian Church in McLean Co. John was married at least seven times (5): 1. Francis C. Ashby July 27, 1863, 2. Mary Francis Ashby July 22, 1879, 3. Mrs. Amanda Mattingly Oct. 22, 1885, 4. Mrs. Ellen Clark Branson Feb. 5, 1890, 5. Elizabeth Whaling Sept. 28, 1899, 6. Francis listed as wife in 1900 census in McLean Co., KY. 7. Mrs. Rosa Corum Apr. 25, 1903.

4. Charles "Pete" born c. 1871, married Birdie M. Barnett Apr. 20, 1890. He was a bartender at the Soaper Hotel in Henderson, KY.
5. Martha W. born c. 1874. After her mother's death in 1876 (4), she lived with her maternal grandmother Phebe Harrelson Tapp Humphrey at Vandersburgh, Webster Co., KY.

John Daniel married second Alpha Elizabeth Bumpass (December 1854-Jan. 20, 1945) on Dec. 8, 1876. Alpha was the daughter of Edward and Nancy Childers Bumpass from South Carolina. She was a school teacher and poetess. At that time they moved to Hopkins Co., KY, again, first living in the Kitchen District. By 1900 they were living at Hanson, later moving to Ashbysburgh. John and Alpha had five children.

1. Edward born c. 1878.
2. Robert Hamilton "Ham" (June 29, 1881-Nov. 24, 1959) married Florence Beal (Dec. 26, 1884-Feb. 17, 1972).
3. Sarah J. born February 1882, married H.T. Hopgood Apr. 9, 1895.
4. Washington Raymond born 1889, married Susie Branson Nov. 16, 1904, 2nd. —Goad.
5. George born May 2, 1891.

Source: (1) Rockingham Co., NC, marriage records. (2) Hopkins Co., KY, death certificate, (3) Hopkins Co., KY, 1860 census, (4) Pleasant Grove Baptist Church records, Hopkins Co., KY, (5) McLean Co., KY, Vital records, (6) John Green Daniel, (7) Daviess Co., KY, deed recorded Nov. 17, 1838. Grantor John Galloway, Grantee William H. Bassett, (8) Cumberland Presbyterian Church records, McLean Co., KY, (10) Personal knowledge.-*Submitted by: Barbara Curren Bishop*

JOHN GREEN DANIEL

John Green Daniel born July 12, 1868, in Vandersburgh, Webster Co., KY, was the son of John Daniel and Sarah Jane Tapp. They lived in Vandersburgh until his mother's death in 1876. His father married again to Alpha Ann Elizabeth Bumpass and moved to Ashbysburgh, Hopkins Co., KY, taking John and Virginia with them. The three remaining children, Phebe, Charles and Martha lived with their maternal grandmother Phebe Harrelson Tapp Humphry in Webster Co.

John Green married Rosa Lee Bassett (June 6, 1867-Apr. 12, 1918), who was the daughter of John Synette Bassett and Francis C. Ashby. Rosa was born at Ashbysburgh, KY, where her family lived until the death of her mother, Feb. 17, 1878, at which time they moved to Rumsey, McLean Co., KY.

The Daniel family about 1905. Front row l to r: Geneva, Laura Hazel, and Ruth Belle. 2nd row: Nettie, John Green Daniel and Rosa Lee. 3rd row: Grace, Nolia and Willia Mae.

John Green and Rosa had 11 daughters:
(1) Grace born August 1889 married Clarence Smith Nov. 25, 1906 and died in childbirth in 1907.

(2) Willia Mae "Dids" (May 31, 1892-1965) married (1) William Woods Mar. 8, 1911; (2) Charles Henry and (3) Jack Tomblinson of Ashbysburg, KY. They lived in Madisonville until their deaths, at which time the "Daniel Family Bible" disappeared.

(3) Nolia Francis (Apr. 14, 1894-Jan. 9, 1965) married Charles Francis McNeely Nov. 30, 1912. They had five children: 1. unnamed child, Aug. 23, 1913; 2. Charles Daniel born July 27, 1914; 3. Marion "Bud"; 4. Ruth Elaine born Aug. 9, 1920 and 5. Bobby Joe.

(4) Nettie (Feb. 17, 1895-Dec. 25, 1978) married (1) Louis Sharer, Mar. 30, 1915, by whom she had two children: Arthur Kirth (Sept. 28, 1915-1918) and Grace Elizabeth (May 3, 1917-June 12, 1943). She married again to Rudy Sandefur (Aug. 21, 1900-Jan. 29, 1979). They were the parents of two children: Jack R. Sandefur born Jan. 16, 1927 who married Dorothy Prince and Shirley Diane born Feb. 6, 1937 who married Jerry Kiesel.

(5) Geneva (Mar. 16, 1898-Jan. 30, 1986) married first to Vernie Edmundson Mar. 30, 1915. Then to Bee Washington Ellis (January 1885-Feb. 20, 1945). Bee Ellis was an undercover agent with the Army working in the Hawaiian Islands during WWI. After WWI, he went to work for the Evansville, IN Fire Department and remained there for 25 years, becoming their Fire Chief. Their daughter Marion Hazel was born Apr. 27, 1918. She married Omar Godfrey "Toby" Wegrich. They lived in Elkhart, IN where they raised three children, Toby Dale, John and Karen Sue. O.G. Wegrich was an executive of Miles Laboratories until his retirement when they moved to Berrien Springs, MI.

(6) Ethel born September 1898. The only known information on her is the 1900 census where she is listed as a daughter.

(7) Laura Hazel (Sept. 9, 1900-Apr. 30, 1932) married Fredrick Henry Reis Apr. 22, 1916. Their only son Welburn Lee married Isabelle Clark.

(8) Ruth Belle born May 31, 1902 married William Reed Blick (Sept. 2, 1900-June 1, 1980) July 23, 1924. They moved to Detroit, MI where Reed worked for Briggs Mfg. Co. They had two sons William Robert and Paul Reed.

(9) Hallie Clay (Mar. 28, 1905-Oct. 3, 1971) married Caldwell Curren in 1926. Married the second time to James C. Smith, Jr. Apr. 26, 1930 and the third to Charles Clark. Her only child is Barbara Voncille Curren born Mar. 17, 1927. Hallie continued using the name of Smith thru her lifetime. Moving to Santa Monica, CA she became a Christian Science nurse working at that occupation thru her adult life.

(10) Tinia born 1907 died 1909.

(11) Nora Hettie Mar. 25, 1909 - married Oscar Byers Apr. 20, 1926 and had three daughters, Constance Maxine, Lois Ann and Janet Fay.

John Green worked as a logger and tobacco farmer in Kentucky. Around 1910, he moved his family by train to Evansville, IN. There he worked at Heranles Wagon Works, later opening a restaurant on Morton Street.

He was a tall, thin man with hazel eyes and a warm, easygoing nature. He was greatly respected by all that knew him. His greatest delight was to line his grandchildren up, each having a turn across his knees, while he sang "Old Miss Morgan Played the Organ". Father beat the drum, sister played the tamborine and father beat the Boom! Boom! Boom! Each boom ending with a spank. Thus, he left his grandchildren with a lifetime of joyful memories.

Sources: McLean Co., KY tax record, Hopkins Co., KY tax record, census and court records, Vanderburgh Co., IN vital records, city directories and personal knowledge.-Compiled by Barbara Voncille Curren (Mrs. Amos Alton) Bishop

DAUGHERTY-BAIZE

Moncy Phillip Daugherty was born in Daviess Co. on Aug. 12, 1878. Via Tula Baize was born in Ohio Co. on May 18, 1880. They were married in Tula's home in Renfrow on the 17th day of December 1900. They had three children: Hilda (Dec. 20, 1901), Raymond (Mar. 20, 1903) and LeEtta (Mar. 1, 1906). Raymond died at the age of 12 from a ruptured appendix. This left a lasting impression on Tula till her dying day in 1976. The effects of Raymond's death are expressed in a poem entitled "My Child" that Tula wrote in 1916.

Tula and Moncy Daugherty in 1950 at home north of Nortonville (Bean Bottom)

Terry Bowman writes this in loving memory because of Tula's (Grandma's) perseverance and determination. She was an intelligent woman, but due to the lack of quality education in the 1890's she went through the 8th grade twice.

When she married Moncy (Old Dad) he was a salesman, selling to retail stores.

On Jan. 21, 1901, she was sworn in as Postmaster of the Post Office in Renfrow, KY. Her certificate is signed by the then Postmaster General of the USA, Charles Emory Smith.

Hilda married Luther Teague at Nortonville on May 20, 1918. Sometime after that, they all moved to Marissa, IL where Terry's mother was born, Evelyn Maria Teague Bowman. While there, LeEtta met and married Doice McGough. They lived their life out in Illinois. The Daugherty's and Teagues moved back to Kentucky in the mid 20's.

Moncy was the son of Preston and Louisa Cook Daugherty, they were of Irish descent. Tula was the daughter of Mathias and Sarah E. Ashley Baize. Tula was an only child. Later Mathias married again and had four children: Thomas, Jesse, LeEtta and Buna.

As a great grandchild, Terry remembers many stories Grandma told. The most lasting story was of seeing Halley's Comet in 1910. She recalled that it was so bright you could see it in the late afternoon while the sun was still out. It was reported that the tail of the comet would pass through the earth on May 18 (Tula's 30th birthday). She said that the people were so afraid that one of her aunts went to hide under the bed.

She took the time to smell the roses of life. A good Christian, she must have written over two hundred poems many of which the family still has. Moncy, Tula, Hilda and Raymond are buried at New Salem in Nortonville.-Submitted by Terry Bowman

DAVENPORT-HIBBS

Issac Barber Davenport was born in either Christian or Hopkins Co., KY, in October of 1849. He was the son of John W. and Cynthia Ann Walker Devenport. His nickname was JB or Bud. JB married Miss Mamona Nora Hibbs in Hopkins Co., on July 5, 1870. Mamona was just 13 when they married. Family tradition tells she was a very beautiful red-head who at one time modeled. Mamona was the daughter of James R. and Mary J. Todd Hibbs, born in September 1856.

JB did some farming and some ranching and was also what was called a "street preacher". He died in a tragic accident in Earlington in the early 1900's when he was run over by a wagonette. Mamona remarried to James Boyce who had come to Hopkins Co. from Nebraska from England. As time went on, two of Mamona's sons would marry two of James' daughters. By 1910, Mamona was a widow again. She may have married a third time before her death; whom is not known.

JB and Mamona had six children. They are:
James E., born circa 1872, and died as a boy.
John W., born in Earlington on Oct. 23, 1874. He married Nola E. Smith in Hopkins Co. in 1896 and they had nine children: Carl, Cil, Archie, J. Pauline, Lawrence, Nellie, Frank, John and Mabel. He died in Detroit, MI, on July 19, 1938.

Minnie G., born in Hopkins Co. on Apr. 20, 1876, married John Fagan in Hopkins Co. in 1900. They had two daughters and maybe a son. Minnie died Oct. 9, 1908, two days after the birth of their second daughter and is buried in the Oakwood Cemetery.

Walter N. was born in March 1885, in either Kentucky or Tennessee. He was married briefly to Miss Annie Fox in 1906. He married his second wife, also his step sister, Nellie Boyce, in 1907. They had at least one child: Ruthie. There is evidence to suggest he married a third time in 1922 to Annie Dockery.

Cecil H. was born in June 1887. He married his stepsister, Mary Boyce, on July 18, 1908, in Hopkins Co. They had three children: Marvin, Ethel and a stillborn son. Cecil died on May 23, 1919, and Mary on Jan. 10, 1919, both in Hopkins Co.

Burnice was born in Earlington, Hopkins Co., KY, on Sept. 5, 1892. She married Charlie Ray in Hopkins Co., on Nov. 24, 1907, and had two children: Robert and Charlie E. She died on May 22, 1914, and is buried in the Oakwood

Cemetery.-*Researched and submitted by Paula L. Morrow-Bentley*

DAVENPORT-SMITH

John Washington Davenport was born on Oct. 23, 1874, in Manitou, Hopkins Co., KY, to Issac Barber (J.B. or Bud) and Mamona Nora Hibbs Davenport. Nolie Etta Smith was born on Jan. 23, 1878, in Earlington, Hopkins Co., KY, to Robert Alexander and Amanda Oldham Smith. John and Nola were married in Hopkins Co. on Apr. 8, 1896.

John W. Davenport in Detroit, MI, in 1935

John worked as coal miner while Nolie kept busy bearing and raising their nine children. In 1915, Nolie died of tuberculosis. She was only 37 and John was left with their seven surviving children aged 1 to 18 to raise.

John remarried in 1916 to Nona Holmes Sisk. They all moved to Herrin, IL, but weren't there long before John and Nona separated and John took his family back to Hopkins Co. He had sold everything to finance the trip and thus he and his children had to live in a tent until more permanent housing could be had.

All during this time the older children helped raise the younger and worked to support them all. There was little time for school, so the Davenport children didn't get much schooling. The lessons they learned were the practical, common-sense lessons of life.

As the years passed the children (all born in Earlington) grew up and left home:

Carl Westley, born July 11, 1897, joined the armed forces and most likely fought in WWI. It is not believed he ever married. He died in the 1960's or 1970's in a VA hospital.

Mabel was born in February of 1898, and died a few years later.

Amanda Lucille (Cil), born Apr. 9, 1902, moved to Chicago, IL, married and later divorced Bob Williams. She then moved to Detroit, MI, and married Victor Porter. She died there in 1978.

Johnnie Pauline, born Nov. 5, 1903, was the only one of the children to stay in Hopkins Co. She married William Benton and raised 12 children: Lil, Richard, Thomas, Vernon, Jeraldine, Eunice, Wanda, Cecil, Victor, Donna, Larry and Janice. She moved in 1985, to Detroit, to live with her daughter because of her declining health. She died there in April 1986, and is buried in the Grapevine Cemetery of Hopkins Co.

Lawrence Edward, born Aug. 31, 1907, married Ethel Hurt. They are the parents of Wilma, Mary Jo, Lorrie and Barbara and currently live in Fowlerville, MI.

Nellie Marie, born Sept. 30, 1910, married George Travis after moving to Detroit. They were parents to Patricia and Joyce. Nellie is currently living in a nursing home in Riverview, MI.

Frank Alexander, born Mar. 7, 1912, moved to Detroit and married Annie Paddock. They are the parents of Frank Jr., Sherry, Sharon, Virginia and Richard. Frank died in 1986, in Taylor, MI.

In 1926, John W. Davenport married a third time to Mattie Smith Morgan. Whether they divorced or Mattie died is unknown. John finally moved to the Detroit area himself and died there on July 19, 1938, he was 63.-*Submitted b: Paula L. Morrow-Bentley*

NELLIE DAVENPORT

Nellie Marie Davenport was born to John W. and Nolie Etta Smith Davenport on Sept. 30, 1910, in Earlington. Weighing only 3-1/2 pounds at birth, her parents had to pin her to the bedsheets so she wouldn't "get lost."

Nell Davenport Travis

When Nellie was five years old, her mother died. The coming years were a bit unsettled for the Davenport family. Nellie was raised by her siblings. She attended school in Earlington until the 5th grade and had to quit because of poor eyesight.

At the age of 12, Nellie left Hopkins Co. and moved to Chicago, IL, with her brother Frank and sister Lucille. Lucille kept house for them. Later, they all moved to Kinoshia, WI, and when Nellie was 17, they all moved to Detroit, MI.

In Detroit, Nellie found employment with the Mills Bakery on the bread line. She rented a room and shared it with a girlfriend, Lola Nichols (from Webster Co.). Her father had moved to the Detroit area by this time and rented a room across the hall. Not long after, Nellie fell in love with George Travis and on Apr. 6, 1930, they were married.

George and Nellie had two daughters: Patricia Mae Travis (Dec. 8, 1937) and Joyce Marie Travis Miller (July 4, 1941). They raised a foster daughter, Betty Lou, the niece of her former roommate Lola Nichols.

They lived in Detroit until 1945, when they bought a house in the suburb of Melvindale. George died in 1976 and Nellie still owns her Melvindale home. She lived there until failing health made it necessary for her to move to a nursing home in Riverview, MI, where she is now. She has two grandchildren: Michael Miller, 21, attending Michigan State University and Tricia Miller, 15, in high school. Also two foster grandsons: Joseph Savino, 34, works at Ford Motor Co. in Dearborn and Philip Savino, 22, who lives in Florida.-*Submitted by Patricia M. Travis*

DAVIS

William Davis was born June 8, 1761, in the eastern part of Virginia.

He served as a private in the North Carolina Militia during the Revolutionary War and took part in the battle of Kings Mountain in October 1780.

In Wilkes Co., NC, on Nov. 15, 1780, William Davis married Anna Loving, daughter of Gabriel Loving, Sr. Anna Loving Davis was born Apr. 28, 1766, in Virginia and died after 1856, probably in Hopkins Co., KY.

William and Anna Loving Davis migrated to Hopkins Co., KY, in the early 1800's, joining others of their family. William and Anna were the parents of twelve children: John Davis born June 23, 1782; James Davis born Feb. 3, 1784, married Nancy Moore Morton; Elizabeth (Betsy) Davis born Oct. 29, 1786, married Daniel Fox; Loving Davis born Feb. 13, 1789; Vincent Fugate Davis born Mar. 3, 1791 married (1) Susanna Sisk and (2) Delina Sisk; William P. Davis born May 23, 1793, married Darcus Baker; Polley Davis born Sept. 7, 1795; Rebekah Davis born Oct. 9, 1797; Katharine (Kate) Davis born June 11, 1800, married Caleb D. Franklin; Hannah Davis born May 1, 1801; Thena Davis born Feb. 17, 1804, married Amos P. Lacy and Jacob Bonapart Davis born July 21, 1807, married Nancy Sisk.

William Davis died in Hopkins Co., KY, on Feb. 6, 1838, and is buried in Flat Creek Cemetery near Mortons Gap. On the stone marking his place of burial is the following inscription: William Davis, Revolutionary Soldier, "Erected to the memory of...Hero of King's Mountain...He was deacon of the Baptist Church, his life was devoted to religion and the good of mankind."

Sources: Revolutionary War Record W-8657 and Family Bible- *Compiled by Daniel W. Dockrey*

DAVIS-JENNINGS

Carl Nevin Davis, of St. Charles, KY, and Mayme Denton Jennings, of Sacramento, KY, were married on Feb. 9, 1924 in Madisonville, KY. Mr. Davis's parents were John Dixon Davis and Edmona Lynch Davis and Mrs. Davis's parents were Orville Francis Jennings and Maggie Denton Jennings. They have three daughters, Elaine, Louise and Maxine.

Elaine is married to Ruby W. Poe, of Dawson Springs, who works for the Paducah and Louisville Railroad. Elaine is a retired teacher. The Poes have four children: Charisse, who married Jesse Taylor Richardson; Randall, who married Sandra Russell; Margaret, who married James R. Purdy; and Kimberly Poe. They have five grandchildren: Jessica and Taylor Richardson, Chris and Angel Poe, and Chele Purdy.

Mayme and Carl Davis

Louise married Forrest R. Foe of St. Charles who works for Sextet Mining Co. Louise is a teacher in the Hopkins Co. School System. They are the parents of three children: Carol, who married Clifton Drennan; Neil, who married Rosemary Cummins; and Karen Foe who died in infancy. They also have three grandsons; Jerry Pollard, Aaron Huddleston, and Neil Foe, Jr.

Maxine married Troy D. Smith of St. Charles, who works for the Colonial Mine of P & M Coal Co. Maxine is a former teacher. They also own and operate the S & S Coin Laundry in Madisonville. They are the parents of one daughter, Christiane, who married George E. Brooks. The Smiths have two granddaughters, Allyson Lea and Ann Kristen Brooks.

Mr. Davis was a rural mail carrier for nearly fifty years, carrying mail at Nortonville for one year, and the remainder of the time at St. Charles. Mrs. Davis was his substitute carrier for 25 years.

They formed lasting friendships over those years and had many rewarding experiences. Some of their experiences were also exciting, as on the day that an irate bull lifted Mr. Davis's A-Model Ford mail car off the ground by hooking his horns under the back bumper. Then there was the day that Mrs. Davis pulled her car up to a mailbox and saw that the family's house was burning. She ran inside and helped the lady of the house to safety.

Mr. and Mrs. Davis's first home in St. Charles was on what is now the Lake Grove Road, overlooking what was then called Cat Hill Lake. Their second home was in St. Charles near the old St. Charles School and next door to the EMBA Hall. In 1937, they purchased a farm west of St. Charles on Highway 62, where Mrs. Davis still lives.

The Davis family attended Christian Privilege Church for a number of years. Elaine and Ruby Poe are members of Adriel Missionary Baptist Church at Dawson Springs. Louise Foe is a member of the Lake Grove General Baptist Church at St. Charles. Maxine and Troy Smith are members of the Grapevine Christian Church at Madisonville.

At the time of Mr. Davis's death in 1978, the couple had been married for fifty-four years. Those years had seen St. Charles change from a thriving coal-mining town to a much less active economic community. The quiet roads had become thoroughfares for fast-moving traffic of all kinds.

The scene has changed but the memories linger on, and the lives of Mr. and Mrs. Davis's children, grandchildren and great grandchildren will always be enriched by the warm and loving legacy of their home and their Christian example.-Submitted by Ruby Poe

DAVIS-LOVING

William Davis, born June 8, 1761, in Wilkes Co., NC, a volunteer at King's Mountain, married Anne Loving, daughter of Gabriel Loving, Sr., Nov. 10, 1780. Children named by William were: William P., Vincent F., Betsy, Polly, Rebecca, Katherine, and Hannah. Jacob Benton Davis is named a son of William and Anne in some sources, but William's will made him a special legatee. Was Jacob an orphan nephew or cousin? Family connection among William Davis of Flat Creek, Richard Davis of Madisonville, and Clement Davis of Christian Co. seems nearly certain, for they were of similar ages and may have been brothers or cousins originating in North Carolina.

Colonel William Davis received Kentucky Land Grants and moved his family to Christian Co. about 1805. When Hopkins Co. was organized in 1806, he moved near Madisonville and later moved near Flat Creek Chapel in present Morton's Gap community where he served as trustee for sometime and lived there until he died in 1838. His grave in Flat Creek Cemetery has a Revolutionary War Soldier marker.

Vincent F. Davis married Susanna Sisk, Apr. 30, 1826, and married Delina Sisk, Aug. 12, 1867, but bride(s) of William P. Davis and the daughters' husbands are not known precisely, though the will gave some clues. Nor do we know a name for Jacob's first wife, but he had two daughters before he married Nancy Perimon Sisk, daughter of Robert and Mourna Sisk and sister of Susanna, Feb. 11, 1834. One of Jacob's daughters married a Brown. The other, Mary Ann, married William Woodruff in Hopkins Co., 1857, and they later moved to Parker Co., TX, where they lived in old Cougar Community and were buried in nearby Hill Cemetery, about twenty miles southwest of Weatherford. Children of Jacob and Nancy were: Robert Earle, 1835, William, 1838, Charles H., 1841, and Hezekiah Butler, 1844. After Jacob died in 1845, Nancy Sisk Davis lived near Madisonville until 1850, when she married Elijah Wristen and later moved to New Madrid, MO, then to Parker Co., TX, where she died in 1856. Her grave is among the oldest in Spring Creek Cemetery, seven miles southeast of Weatherford, TX, and her sons became pioneers of West Texas and Oklahoma.

References: Hopkins Co., KY, Records, Sisk Family History, History of Parker Co., TX, 1980-Submitted by Sam & Wilhelmina Andrew

HEZEKIAH BUTLER DAVIS

Hezekiah Butler Davis, fourth son of Jacob Benton and Nancy Perimon Sisk Davis, was born in or near Madisonville, KY, May 10, 1844, only about a year before his father died. With brothers: Robert Earle, William, and Charles H., he moved with his mother, Elijah Wristen, his stepfather, and the Wristen children to New Madrid Co., MO, in 1851. In the fall of 1855, the Wristens moved to new land in Parker Co., then being organized on the Texas Frontier, and settled in Irby Community on Spring Creek.

When his mother died in 1856, H. Butler Davis soon moved out of his stepfather's household and worked for neighbors until he, at 17, and Charles enlisted in Company E, 6th Texas Cavalry, CSA, and fought at Pea Ridge, AR. He was ordered back to Texas with the horses, but the orders were changed and he was discharged as underage. Charles came home sick a few months later and when he recovered, both joined Captain Wills' Company, 31st Texas Cavalry, in which they served until the war ended. William Davis had also entered Confederate Service and he died and was buried on Galveston Island in 1863. While furloughed home, Butler married Sarah Elizabeth (Lizzie) Battern on Dec. 22, 1864, and they raised six children in Parker Co. Charles H. Davis married Mary Jones of Parker Co., raised several children, and was a farmer the rest of his days near Dennis and Brock on Brazos River.

Wild Indian days were drawing to a close about 1875, and Uncle Butler Davis and Aunt Lizzie believed it safe to build a large house in isolated country south of Brazos River, near the Weatherford to Stephenville stagecoach trail, which began old Cougar Community. An ordained Predestinarian (some say Hardshell) Baptist Preacher, Uncle Butler served as Road Commissioner several years, and conducted church services in Cougar and many nearby camp meetings until they moved into Weatherford about 1914. Aunt Lizzie died about 1920, but he lived until 1925, when he died at age 81 and was buried beside his wife in Hill Cemetery near Cougar. Anecdotes of his life in the Parker Co. History (Published in 1980) almost read like "Tall Tales", but enough verified truth survives to prove H. Butler Davis was a true pioneer and Father of Parker County.

References: U.S. Census, 1860, 1870, 1880, 1900, 1910; Parker County, TX, Records; Parker Co. Genealogical Society Newsletter ("Trails West") all volumes, located in Weatherford Public Library and the Texas Archives, Austin, TX.-Submitted by Sam & Wilhelmina Andrew

JUDY MASON DAVIS

Judy Mason Davis is the oldest daughter of Ernest Sr. and Mayme L. (Starks) Mason (see Ernest Mason Sr. story).

She graduated from Rosenwald High School with honors and now resides in Champaign, IL. She attended the University of Indiana in Bloomington, IN before enrolling in and graduating from the Kentucky School of Mortuary Science and is presently a licensed Funeral Director and Embalmer.

She is employed by the State of Illinois Postal Service and has been employed for fifteen years with this agency.

Judy has one son, Andra, 15, and they are members of the Wesley Chapel C.M.E. Church in Madisonville.-Submitted by Mayme L. Mason

MARTHA CHILDRESS DAVIS

Martha Childress Davis was one of eight children born to Mattie Elizabeth and George Childress. She was born Jan. 26, 1948. Martha graduated from Caldwell County High School in May of 1966 and went to work at Arvin Incorporated on June 6, 1966. She married Edward Wilson and had two children: Elizabeth Jewel born Feb. 6, 1967 and Shelley DeAnn born Sept. 15, 1970. Martha then married Donald Wayne Davis and had two more children: Cory Don born Feb. 27, 1976 and Brett Durand born Sept. 9, 1986.

Martha has six living siblings: Jessie Childress, George Childress, Rudell Childress, Roy Cecil Childress, Loray Childress Cotton, and Lou Ella Childress Cotton. Martha has one deceased sibling, Rosa Mae Childress Cook.

Martha now lives in Caldwell County and has a full life. She is an avid reader, likes walking, gardening, and leathercraft. Martha enjoys taking care of her youngest son and just spending time with her family. She is an active parent in the Cub Scouts and Boy Scouts of America. She and her husband have been leaders as their son Cory has gone through the many steps of becoming a Boy Scout. Martha's daughters, Lisa and Shelley are both active in the city and school sports and have played softball together for several years. They also enjoy swimming, walking, jogging, and spending time with the family.

Martha is a housewife who enjoys working on the farm with her husband. She has previously worked for Buckhorn Incorporated in Dawson Springs and for the Hosiery Mill in Princeton. - *Submitted by Shelley Wilson*

ROBERT EARLE DAVIS

Robert Earle, first son of Jacob Benton and Nancy Perimon Sisk Davis, was born in or near Madisonville, KY, July 14, 1835. After his father died in 1845, and his mother married Elijah Wristen in 1850, Robert accompanied the Wristens to New Madrid Co., MO, 1851, where he married Margaret Ellen Wristen, Apr. 17, 1853, when he was 18, and Margaret was 17. Robert and Margaret moved to Lamar Co., TX, 1854, then on to Weatherford, Parker Co., 1855, then being laid out by surveyors, where Robert filed pre-emption on 160 acres located near the town's northwest corner.

Their first son, William Riley, was born in 1855, and in 1858 gold was discovered in Arapaho Co., Kansas Territory (now Colorado). Robert moved his family to Golden, where he mined a little, kept store, and preached in the Primitive Baptist Church, and he preached in every place they lived thereafter. Mary Emma was born in Golden, 1859, but in spite of difficult travel in Indian and Civil war times, family tradition places them back in Parker Co. when David was born in 1864. Their other children were: Robert Harvey, 1866, Noah Benton, 1869, Ira Elijah, 1871, Eva Ellen, 1873, Charles Elbert, 1876, Minnie Alice, 1878, Alfred Claude, 1879, and Elizabeth, birthdate unknown, died at age 3. They lived in Irby and Balch where Robert had a mill, cotton gin, and general store, a few years as partners with Margaret's brothers, Daniel and Frank Wristen. Riley Davis opened a store on a crossroads which became Brock in 1880. Robert and Riley continued storekeeping until they moved to Floyd Co., TX, in 1889, where they opened at least two more general stores.

Robert Davis and his sons were among founders of Lockney and Floydada in Floyd Co., where Robert was active in real estate, after which they moved to the Cimarron Strip of Indian Territory, and Robert built one of the first brick buildings in Woodward, OK, 1893, for the Davis Drug Store which carried that business name until sold about 1970. Great Grandmother Margaret Ellen died in Woodward, Mar. 19, 1907. Great Granpa Robert then lived in Uncle Alfred Claude Davis' home and worked in real estate until shortly before he died in 1922, leaving a considerable Estate to descendents in Texas, Oklahoma, and California. Robert and Margaret had long been known as "Granpa and Grandma Davis" to old Woodward residents.

References: U.S. Census, 1880, 1900, 1910; History of Parker Co., TX, 1980; History of Floyd Co, TX; Woodward Co., OK, Records.- *Submitted by Sam & Wilhelmina Andrew*

WILLIAM DAVIS

William and Anna Loving Davis (1766-186?), came to Hopkins Co. from Wilkes Co., NC around 1805. They were married in 1780. Anna was the daughter of Gabriel Loving, Sr. Their children were: John, James, Elizabeth, Loving, Pleasant, William, Mary, Rebecca, Catherine, Hannah, Thena, Vincent and Jacob.

William served over two years in the Revolutionary War, was captured by the British but managed to escape. He is buried in Flat Creek Cemetery at Morton's Gap, KY. On his tombstone are these words, "To the memory of William Davis, Revolutionary soldier, hero of King's Mountain. Born June 8, 1761, died Feb. 6, 1838. He was a deacon in the Baptist Church, his life devoted to religion and the Good of Mankind."

In 1807, William and Anna owned 200 acres on Pond River, Vincent and Jacob were born there.

Vincent Fugate Davis (1807-1892) married, 1826, Susanna Sisk (1807-1866) daughter of Robert and Mourning Sisk. Robert served in the Kentucky Militia during the War of 1812. His father, Daniel Sisk, was killed in the Battle of King's Mountain. Vincent, a farmer, married in 1867 Delina Sisk. Vincent, Susanna and Delina are buried in Flat Creek Cemetery. Vincent and Susanna's children were: Louisa, William Jackson, Martha, America, Thomas, Benjamin and Susan.

William Jackson Davis (1833-1901) married, in 1857 McLean Co., KY, Mary Malinda Vance (1838-1882), daughter of Joseph and Elizabeth Green Vance. Joseph and Elizabeth are buried in Old Buck Creek Cem. William Jackson, a farmer, served in the Civil War. He and Malinda are buried at Bethel Baptist Church Cemetery, Beech Grove, KY. Their children were: Malissa, Susan, Margarite, Tilda, Leona, Thomas, Sarah, Rena and Alice.

Sarah Davis (1873-1968) married 1893 William Eugene Alvey (1870-1945), son of Henry, Jr. and Theresa Isabelle Thompson Alvey.

Will and Sarah Davis Alvey on their wedding day, Jan. 3, 1893

Henry and Theresa are buried at St. Alphonsos Cemetery, St. Joseph, KY. Sarah and Will, with their children, Mary, Verna, Aubrey and Alice, migrated to Marshall Co., KY in 1899. They settled in the Calvert City area. Guy, Lillian, Lessie, Margaret, Michael and William Chester were born there. Sarah and Will were members of the Catholic Church. They are buried at Calvert City Cemetery. Mary Mable Alvey (1893) married, 1912 Paris, TN, Artie Owen Petway (1895-1978), son of James Willis and Eliza Jane May Petway. Willis's great grandfather, Micajah Petway, was a bodyguard of George Washington at Valley Forge.

Owen worked many years for the NC and St. L Railroad. Their children were: Velvin, Ruby, Evelyn, Verna, James, Guy, Artie, Sarah, Robert, Randall and Doris.

Sarah Allene Petway, married 1944 Daytona Beach, FL, Forest Richard Edwards, son of Coral Mitchell and Tennessee Belle Hughes Edwards. Forest served three years in the US Navy during WWII. He graduated from the University of Kentucky and received a Master's degree in Electrical Engineering from Purdue University. He retired from Union Carbide, Paducah, in 1983. They are members of Immanuel Baptist Church and enjoy golf, fishing, gardening and antiques. They have four daughters: Patricia, Vicki, Cynthia and Susan Michal.-*Submitted by Sarah Petway Edwards*

WILLIAM JACKSON DAVIS

William Jackson Davis was born in Hopkins Co., on Oct. 20, 1833 to Vincent Fugate and Susanna Sisk Davis. His grandparents, William and Anna Loving Davis and Robert and Mourning Sisk, migrated to Hopkins Co. from Wilkes Co., NC. On Sept. 17, 1857 in McLean Co., he married Mary Malinda Vance, daughter of Joseph and Elizabeth Green Vance, who had come to McLean Co. from Knox Co., TN. William was a farmer and fought in the Civil War. He died Jan. 2, 1901. Mary died July 10, 1882. Their children were: Malissa m. John Dant; Susan (1861-1865); Margarite (1863-1886); Tilda (1866-1870); Leona m. William Elliot; Thomas m. Mary Anna Alvey; Sarah; Rena m. Jesse Eubanks; and Alice m. Nance Coomes.

Sarah Davis born in McLean Co. on Jan. 24, 1874, married Jan. 3, 1893 William Eugene Alvey. The Alveys, from Maryland, were early

William Jackson Davis

settlers of Washington Co., KY and neighbors of Abraham Lincoln, grandfather of the 16th president.

Sarah and Will moved to Marshall Co., KY in 1899. They separated about 1926 and never lived together again. They are buried side by side in the Calvert City Cemetery. Their children were: Mary; Verna m. George Chambers; Aubrey m., at age 50, Winfred Peck Key; Alice (was so pretty she was called Dolly) m. Harry Redmond; Guy m. Bertie Noles; Lillian m. Nesby English; Lessie died 1937 in freak train accident; Lois m. Raymond English; Royce, twin to Lois, m. Nina Barnes; James m. Frances LaFountaine, (he survived a plane crash in 1948. After a three week search, he was found 50 miles south of Casper, WY, high in the Haystack Mountains. His friend, the pilot, was killed.) and William Chester m. Virgina Kimmett.

Mary Mable Alvey born McLean Co. Nov. 17, 1893, married May 12, 1912 Artie Owen Petway, whose great, grandfather John Petway came in a wagon train, pulled by oxen, from Edgecombe, NC to Livingston Co., KY in 1835. Mary and Owen lived in Marshall, Calloway, Graves and McCracken Counties. Their children were: Velvin m. Rhoda Jane Jones, 2nd Mable Hyatte; Ruby m. Charles Howard; Evelyn m. Eugene Vasseur; Verna Louise (1918-1919); James m. Eulalah Myre (he served three years in US Army during WWII); Guy (1922-1936); Artie; Sarah m. Forest Edwards; Robert m. Leona Kinsey (he served 20 years in US Air Force); Randall died Thanksgiving Day 1941 in a car-train accident which killed six members of another family; and Doris m. Gene Arnold.

Artie Alvey Petway born Mar. 29, 1924 married 1942 in Charleston, MO. Melva Irine Korner, daughter of Gottloeb and Sophronia Herzog Koerner. Artie served three years in the Air Force in WWII. He is a retired Pipefitter. His hobbies are gardening and fishing. Melva's are sewing and genealogy. They enjoy camping in their Air Stream trailer. Their children are: Arlene, Ronald and Randle.-*Submitted by Melva Koerner Petway*

RILEY P. DAWSON

Riley P. Dawson was born in 1833, the second of eight children, in Caldwell Co. He was the son of John W. Dawson, who came from Virginia, and Drucella Mason, daughter of Elisha Mason from Illinois.

On Oct. 2, 1855 he married Rebecca Hooper, daughter of Enoch Hooper, in Caldwell Co. They lived there until 1869, when with his brother Bryant N. bought 250 acres from David Menser. This tract of land lying in Hopkins and Caldwell Cos. on Tradewater River and was purchased for one thousand dollars.

Riley is listed in the 1870 census, starting the move of Dawsons to Hopkins Co. The Paducah-Elizabethtown Railroad was constructing a 183 mile stretch of track when Bryant and Riley proposed to the company that if they gave the right of way and the land for a depot, would they establish it on their land. The company accepted and the town, which was to become Dawson Springs, was laid out.

The railroad was completed in 1872 and on Sept. 6, 1872 the first train to make the trip between Elizabethtown and Paducah stopped at the station known then as Tradewater Station.

Riley died that year leaving a widow and eight children, the third of which was John Enoch who was born Feb. 2, 1859. On Feb. 8, 1880 he married Rebecca Huddleston born July 6, 1869. To this union, three children were born: Eddie William, Claude, and Ella, who married Ira Peyton. John and Rebecca are buried at Rosedale Cemetery in Dawson Springs.

John Enoch and Rebecca Huddleston Dawson

Eddie William was born Mar. 10, 1887 and married Gurthie Vandiver on Feb. 22, 1911. She was born Feb. 5, 1894, the daughter of Hollie Vandiver and Melinda Bryant. They were the parents of eight children: Artie Eulies born Aug. 24, 1912, Lula Eloise (Mrs. Clarence Dame) born Feb. 16, 1914: Edna Mae (Mrs. Wayne Phillips) born Jan. 24, 1916, Stella Rosetta (Mrs. Ray Utley), born Oct. 16,1916, Lee Estil born Mar. 15, 1920, Justin Paul born Mar. 13, 1922, Albert Elvis born Aug. 17, 1925 and Audrey Pauline (Mrs. John Selby) born Mar. 31, 1929. Eddie died Mar. 20, 1970 at the age of 83 leaving 85 descendents. Gurthie died Feb. 22, 1979.

Albert Elvis married Pauline Frances Tanner (born Mar. 16, 1923) on Mar. 24, 1943. She was the daughter of Willie West Tanner and Ruth Elma Fugate. They are the parents of five children: Sandra Kay (Mrs. Terry Miller) born Dec. 17, 1943; Trudy Ann (Mrs. Kenneth Ezell) born Oct. 14, 1947, Rodger Dale born July 20, 1950,Hank Garland born Mar. 8, 1953 and Steve Allen born Oct. 2, 1956.

Sandra Kay married Terry Wayne Miller on Feb. 24, 1962 in Gallatin Co., IL. Terry was born Jan. 16, 1941 the son of Marshall Truman Miller and Margaret Whelan. They have one child Troy Scott Miller born Nov. 20, 1966 in Hopkins Co., KY.-*Submitted by Sandra K. (Dawson) Miller*

DEBOW-ADCOCK

James William DeBow came to Hopkins Co., KY., ca 1909 from Christian Co., KY. (see Archibald James DeBow) and on July 30, 1910, he married for the second time to Almeda Dessie Adcock (b. May 2, 1894 to Roland and Mary Frances (Fanny) (Masoncup) Adcock in Hanson, Ky.) She died Oct. 26, 1966 and is buried by her husband at Odd Fellows Cemetery.

Children:

I. Ethel LuVera DeBow- b. May 13, 1911 in Muhlenberg Co., KY. -m. James A. (Buster) Brown - June 12, 1935 in Madisonville, KY. Vera died June 19, 1986; buried along side of her parents. No issue.

II. Roy Bryant De Bow - b. Sept. 2, 1912; d. Aug. 12, 1957. (see sketch).

III. Vivian May DeBow - b. Nov. 26, 1914 - Hopkinsville, KY.; m. June 16, 1914 to Cecil Ray Jones; (b. Jan. 15, 1913, Howell, IN; parents: Caphal Mylin and Florence Alice (Baldwin) Jones); m. Evansville, IN. No issue.

IV. James J. DeBow -b. Apr. 26, 1916; died Mar. 17, 1920; buried beside of grandmother, Mrs. Fanny Adcock in Odd Fellows Cemetery in Madisonville, KY.

V. Herschel Franklin DeBow- b. July 4, 1918 in Madisonville; died Apr. 14, 1945 during W.W. II near Kothen, Germany. Burial at Breuna, Germany but now rests beside of his parents. Never married.

VI. William Issac DeBow - b. Feb. 8, 1921 in Madisonville; m. Elsie M. Nance (b. Mar. 21, 1916, Hanson, KY) in Hopkinsville, KY. Billy died Jan. 23, 1983; buried at East Lawn Cemet., at Hanson, Ky. No issue.

VII. Mary Elizabeth DeBow - b. May 13, 1922, Madisonville; m. Morris Frank Harris (b. Aug. 24, 1920, Madisonville to Willy Elzy and Nancy (Durham) Harris) on Dec. 7, 1940, Madisonville, KY.

Children: (1) James Ray Harris - b. Sept 16, 1941; m. Feb. 26, 1960 in Shawneetown, Il to Sharon G. Cates (b Nov. 20. 1943, Providence, KY to Aubrey Lee and Mary Elizabeth (Hillyard) Cates). (a) James Christopher (Chris) b. Apr. 17, 1961, Tampa, FL, (b) Andria Charlene - b. June 20, 1964, Madisonville; graduated from Oral Roberts Univ. May, 1987.

VIII. Margaret Louise DeBow -b. July 19, 1924 in Madisonville; m. (1) Paul (Jack) Ligon, Jan. 30, 1949 in Hopkinsville Ky. Jack b. Oct. 15, 1910; d. Apr. 8, 1981; buried Odd Fellows Cemet. in Madisonville, m. (2) John Ed McGregor (b. June 14, 1917, Madisonville) m. in Springfield, TN on Sept. 27, 1983.

Children: (1) Larry Jay Ligon - b. Nov. 19, 1949; Dawson Springs, KY.; m. (1) Dec. 20, 1969 at Glynco Base, GA to Dayle Burcher (b. Feb. 13, 1948 to Earl and Betty Lou (Weinburgh) Burcher; divorced; (2nd) m. Dolores (Wallace) Hoffman, Apr. 24, 1982 at Dawson Springs, KY; (2) Teresa Kaye Ligon -b. Jan 21, 1952, Dawson Springs, KY.; m. Mickey A. Grant (b. Dec. 26, 1956, Madisonville to Clivie Lee and

Maxine (Callahan) Grant Nov. 18, 1976. (a) Robert Lee Grant - b. May 5, 1977, (b) Amanda Lynn Grant - b. Dec. 20, 1979. - *Submitted by Emily Grace Owen DeBow*

DEBOW-OWEN

Roy Bryant DeBow was born Sept. 2, 1912 at Nortonville, KY; son of James William and Almeda Dessie (Adcock) DeBow. He married Emily Grace Owen on Dec. 24, 1936, daughter of Robert Dale and Daisy Elizabeth (Friend/Smith) Owen, and I was born Apr. 16, 1918, Madisonville, Ky (see OWEN).Roy Bryant died Aug. 12, 1957 and was buried at Odd Fellows Cemet. at Madisonville. Two children:

(1) Sherry Ann DeBow - b. Nov. 5, 1938 in Madisonville. Married Apr. 12, 1957 to Melvin Ross Carlisle b. Apr. 4, 1937, son of Edwin Carlisle, Sr. and his wife, Carrie (Hicklin) Carlisle. Sherry works as a bookkeeper for a tool and die company; Melvin R. is a mine superintendent for Peabody Coal Company in Muhlenberg County. Two children: (a) Melvin Craig Carlisle - b. Aug. 25, 1958 at Madisonville - m. Apr. 25, 1981 to Debra (Debbi) Lois Littlepage b. Apr. 2, 1963 in Madisonville to Henry Jefferson and Mary Kathyrn (Duvall) Littlepage. (b) Mark Ross Carlisle - b. Apr. 27, 1966 in Madisonville; received scholarship from the U.S. Navy, Apr. 18, 1986; entered the service - August 1986; attends school at the University of Florida.

(2) Royce Kingsley (King) DeBow - b. Oct. 20, 1943 in Madisonville; m. May 2, 1964 in Chicago, IL to Donna Kay Shafer b. Feb. 6, 1943 in Benton Harbor, MI; dau. of Lester Newton Shafer and Doris Elaine (Peterson) Shafer. King works for Rudig Trophy Co., Milwaukee, WI and Donna works for Board of Education, West Bend, WI They are residing in Cedarburg, WI. Three children: (a) Royce Kingsley DeBow, Jr. - b. Oct. 6, 1964, Evanston, IL. Entered U.S. Navy on Apr. 2, 1985; trained in telecommunications and now he is stationed in Iceland working in television as newscaster; (b) James Bryant DeBow - b. June 20, 1967; St. Joseph, MO; attending Univ. of WI; (c) Pamela (Pam) Lynn DeBow - b. Mar. 25, 1969 in Port Washington, WI; will graduate from West Bend, Wisconsin High School, June, 1987. - *Submitted by Mrs. Emily Grace Owen DeBow*

DEBOW-WOOSLEY

James William DeBow was born in Christian Co. KY, on July 25, 1876 to Archibald James and Elizabeth Jane (Bryant) DeBow (see Archibald James DeBow). Jim, as he was called, was killed by a train on June 12, 1925, while walking to work at Madisonville, KY. He is buried in Odd Fellows Cemetery, Madisonville, KY.

He was twice married - 1st to Iona Mildred Woosley of Christian Co., KY, on Sept. 3, 1897 and in that county. She was born Mar. 21, 1880 to Wilson Henry and Eliza Mildred (Renshaw) Woosley. She died Oct. 7, 1940 and is buried in Woosley Cemetery in Christian Co., KY.

Three children:

I. Gaspard Noel DeBow (Apr. 22, 1899-Oct. 19, 1969). Married Nov. 16, 1936 to Hallie Mae Harper (b. May 7, 1917 in Christian Co., KY to Richard and Cora Estelle (Turner) Harper), in Hopkinsville, KY. Gaspard N. is buried at Bainbridge Cemetery in his native county.

Issue: 2 sons

1. Gilbert Curtis DeBow (June 27, 1937-Oct. 18, 1958) in Christian Co., KY. Buried at Bainbridge Cemet. of same county. Never married.

2. Richard Noel DeBow b. Sept. 27, 1939 Cerulean, Trigg Co., KY; died May 20, 1965 in Christian Co., KY. Buried at Bainbridge Cemetery.

Richard Noel married Martha Ann Sneed (b. Dec. 9, 1944 in Christian Co., KY) on Feb. 16, 1961 in Hopkinsville, KY. Her parents: Benjamin and Cleo (Lancaster) Sneed.

Two children:

(a) Linda Ann DeBow - b. July 24, 1962 married Bradley Don Minton - b. Nov. 14, 1961 - son of Don Gary and Phyllis Ann (Wallace) Minton.

(b) Richard Noel DeBow - born Dec. 27, 1965.

Gilbert C. and his brother, Richard Noel DeBow lost their lives in motorcycle accidents some six years apart and almost at the same place on the same highway in Christian Co., KY, a short distance from their home.

II. Lee Roy, b. Dec. 29, 1901 - Caldwell Co., KY - d. Mar. 24, 1970 in Veterans Hospital, Memphis, TN. Burial in Veterans Cemet. Shelby Co. TN. Married Angilee Logsdon in Montgomery Co., TN. Her parents: Goldman D. and Cora (Mitchell) Logsdon. No issue.

III. Houston DeBow - born 1904 and died 1925. Burial in Woosley Cemetery in Christian Co., KY. Never married. - *Submitted by Emily G. (Owen) DeBow*

ARCHIBALD J. DEBOW

Archibald James DeBow was born 1848 in Wilson Co., TN, the older of two sons born to James Ballow DeBow (1827-1855) and Evalina N. Harris (1829-1871). His brother was Richard Winn DeBow. After her husband's death, Evalina married William H. Stone in 1856 and he died 1862; then she married Richard H. Cartwright in 1866.

Ca. 1866, Archibald came to the Bainbridge area of Christian Co., KY to live with his mother's sister, Harriett Frances who had married Stephen Allen Wade III. In 1869, Archibald married Elizabeth Jane Bryant (b. 1851, Campbell Co., GA) daughter of John William Bryant, Jr. (1832-1908) and Mary Daniel Wood (1827-1917). Archibald died 1906 and Elizabeth in 1931; both are buried at Riverside Cemetery, Hopkinsville, KY. Their children, all of which were born in Christian Co., KY were:

Mary Susan Evalina (1870-1899) married W.B. Dunning 1894 in Caldwell Co., KY. She is buried in Dunning Cemetery, Caldwell County.

Chestina Josephine (1873-1944) married George Wylie Mitchell (1868-1925) in 1892 in Caldwell Co., KY. Both are buried at Riverside Cemetery, Hopkinsville, KY.

James William (1876-1925) married Iona Mildred Woosley (1880-1940) in 1897 in Christian Co., KY. In 1910, he married Almeda Dessie Adcock (1894-1966) at Madisonville, KY. Iona is buried in Woosley Cemetery, Christian Co., KY. James William and Dessie are buried in Odd Fellows Cemetery of Madisonville, KY. (see sketch on James William DeBow)

Sonora Pauline (1882-1932) married Harry Frank Smoth, 1903 in Hopkinsville, KY. She is buried at Riverside Cemetery, Hopkinsville, KY.

Griffie (1885-1953) married Mattie Jewell Freeman born 1896. They were married 1910 in Clarksville, TN. He is buried in Riverside Cemetery, Hopkinsville, KY. She resides on Blane Drive.

Ethel LuVera "Vera" (1889-1975) married Guy Wolfe (1883-1935) in 1915 in Clarksville, TN. Both are buried at Riverside Cemetery, Hopkinsville, KY.

Henrick de Borg (d'Boogh) of Amsterdam, Holland, had four children who emigrated to America in the 1640's. Archibald's line descends from a son, Capt. Frederick, a trader who sailed a vessel in the Hudson River. Frederick's son, Solomon born 1660, had a son Frederick (1686) who settled in Monmouth Co., NJ. His son, Solomon born 1714, began spelling the name DeBow and he moved to Orange Co., NC.

This second Solomon had a son Frederick born ca. 1759 the third of this name in the lineage. Frederick married Rachel Rogers, niece of Anne Rogers Clark, the mother of Gen. George Rogers Clark. Frederick was a Captain in the Militia of North Carolina, Virginia and South Carolina during the Revolutionary War. Among Frederick's children was Archibald born ca 1797 who married Susanah Ballow, daughter of Capt. James Ballow. One of their children was James Ballow DeBow. This family settled in Smith Co., TN as early as 1798, some moved on to Wilson Co., TN prior to 1830.

The name of this family appears in at least thirty forms in records. - *Submitted by Mrs. Gladys Wolfe*

DENTON-EARLE

Una Rosaline Earle and Thomas Jefferson Denton were married Oct. 5, 1876.

Una Rosaline Earle, eighth child of John Orville Earle (b. 1818-d. 1895) and Mary Melvina Dillingham Earle (b. 1827-d. 1912) was born Nov. 1, 1860 and died Oct. 2, 1940. See EARLE's OF VIRGINIA.

Thomas Jefferson Denton and Una Rosaline Earle Denton

Thomas Jefferson Denton, son of Daniel G. Denton and Orlena Agnes Almon Denton, was born Oct. 5, 1845 and died Mar. 14, 1918.

Children born to this union: Uva Matilda

Denton, born Aug. 8, 1878, died 1943; Lilly Vitulla Denton, born Jan. 1, 1881, died Sept. 21, 1963; Ida Charlie Denton, born Mar. 31, 1883, died Feb. 23, 1962; Willie Everett Denton, born Dec. 18, 1885, died May 19, 1953; Jessie Edward Denton, born Apr. 20, 1888, died Mar. 28, 1966; Mary Izetta Denton, born Jan. 18, 1891, died July 11, 1956; Sue Grace Denton, born Mar. 3, 1893, death unknown; Cora Lee Denton, born Feb. 3, 1896, died Aug. 7, 1977.

Una Rosaline Earle Denton and Thomas Jefferson Denton lived on their farm just north of the farm of John Orville and Mary Melvina Earle, Una's parents.

Una Rosaline and Thomas Jefferson Denton are buried at Good Hope Cemetery. - *Submitted by Iretta McGregor*

DEVENPORT-WALKER

John W. Devenport and Cynthia Ann Walker were married in Todd Co., KY, on Dec. 17, 1836. Both were born in Kentucky circa 1816.

In their early married life they lived in Todd and Christian Counties. Sometime after 1850, they settled in Hopkins County in the Elk Creek area where they raised their family.

John was a farmer and carpenter. He owned a great deal of land in Christian and Hopkins County. He grew tobacco, corn, wheat and hay. He raised hogs and other farm animals. He owned slaves. In 1863, he added more responsibility by becoming the guardian to his widowed sister-in-law's (Mary J. Walker Dukes) ten children. Cynthia bore him eight children:

Furby (Phoebe) Ann was born circa 1839. She married Henry Reynolds in Hopkins County in 1858. They had seven children: Mack, William, Emma, George, Mary, Susan and Lydia.

Parthenia was born circa 1840 in Christian Co., KY, and married William McDaniels in Hopkins County in 1859.

James Alexander was born May 16, 1844, in Christian Co. He married Sarah E. Henderson in Hopkins County in 1867. They had eleven children: James D., John, William W., Robert P., Herman Issac, Claude, Walter T., George, Lula, Annie and Bessie. James died in 1936, his wife died in 1917. Both are buried in the Grapevine Cemetery.

Eliza was born circa 1846, in Christian County and married Jacob Shanks in Hopkins County in 1868.

Issac Barber (JB or Bud) was born in October of 1849, most likely in Christian County. He married Mamona Nora Hibbs in 1870, in Hopkins County. They had six children: John W., Minnie, James E., Walter N., Cecil and Burniece. He died in Earlington in the early 1900's.

H.R. was their sixth child, a son, born circa 1851.

Thomas O. was born June 17, 1854, in Hopkins County and died three months later.

George W. was born May 6, 1857, in Hopkins County and married Mary Phelps in 1876, also in Hopkins County.

During the period of 1870 - 1877, Cynthia died. In 1877, John married a much younger Mattie Parker in Hopkins County. He fathered a daughter, Mary, in 1878. John died sometime between 1880-1900. Burial places for John and Cynthia are unknown. - *Submitted by and researched by Paul L. Morrow-Bentley*

DEXTER

Charles P. Dexter was born in 1852, the son of Charles and Martha James Dexter.

On Feb. 4, 1874 in Muhlenberg Co., KY, he married Luetta Roberts. She was born in 1855, the daughter of Wiley Roberts and Rowan Washington who were married July 11, 1848 in Granville Co., NC.

The children of Charles and Luetta were:

Ulyless Grant born ca. 1875, married Minnie Sisk May 13, 1894 in Hopkins Co., their children: Bertha Mae, Retha Bell, Charlie Mason, Rosa Lee and Chester Noble.

William Wiley born 1877 married Serena Mae Hook (1877-1947) on Dec. 27, 1894 in Hopkins Co., their children: Charlie born and died in 1887; Rufus (1895-1897); Cammie (1898-1899); Mayme Marie born Oct. 27, 1899, married James Hershel Hickman (Jan. 25, 1897-Nov. 8, 1952) on Dec. 21, 1919, their children: Eva Imogene (Gossett), William Harrison Hickman (d. November 1982), and Edna Mae (Harris). James Hershel and William Harrison are buried at Odd Fellows Cemetery; Elison Lee married Ella Pearcy of Henderson Co., KY on Jan. 30, 1924, their children: Isabelle (Browning), Mae Mallory (Babb), Agnes Lee (Lynch), and Carl Ray Dexter; Rosa Bell married Ross Marks. Their children: William Lee, Mildred (Faust), Lorene (Holeman) and Dorothy (Hobgood); Paul married Margie Wood, children: Carmezelle (dec'd) buried Hicklin Cemetery, William (Pete) and Violet Carolyn; Estes Everett married Evelyn Jones, their children, Carroll and Harold. Elison Lee and Paul are buried at Hicklin Cemetery as are William Wiley and Serenna Mae.

Knol K. married Essie Duree. Their children: Waunita married Clarence Madison, children: Lawrence Dexter Madison and Nevaline Madison Rodgers; Pauline and Willie.

Lorenzo (Nov. 15, 1886-Dec. 10, 1961) married Annie Babb on Oct. 2, 1915. Their children: Annie Mae (Hook), Vicie (Proctor) and Dorothy (Thomas). Lorenzo and Annie are buried in Hicklin Cemetery.

Sarah Elizabeth married Franklin Hook on Dec. 23, 1896 in Hopkins County. Their children: Louette, Jeanette, Leffie, Martha, Elizie and Theador.

Martha born Feb. 10, 1890 married Shelby Farris. They are buried in Hicklin Cemetery. Their children: Marvin, Cicel, Roy James, Ruby Winbadger, Medies Gibson and maybe more.

Walter married Rodie Farris. Their children: Nora Mae (Richardson) and John Dexter of California. Walter died July 4, 1924 in the copper mines at Bisbee, AZ.

The Charlie Dexter family lived in the Shakerag area on what is now the J.D. Buchanan Road. The family is mentioned in "Hillbilly Heritage" by Rea Walker. They attended Mt. Zion Methodist Church, which has been torn down.

(See Hook story) - *Submitted by Mary Edna Harris*

WILLIAM C. DEXTER

William Charles "Bill" Dexter was born in Hopkins Co., KY on Oct. 13, 1905 to Knol K. and Elsie (Duree) Dexter. He had two sisters, Wanedta and Pauline.

After his parents divorced, he lived with his grandparents, Mr. and Mrs. Charles P. Dexter until 1919 when he joined his mother in Denver, CO. She had remarried some years before to C.L. Wainwright from San Bernardino, CA.

Late in 1919 Bill, his mother and half brother, Lawrence Wainwright, joined his stepfather at Moorcroft, WY. Wainwright was drilling exploratory wells for oil in the area. They spent the rest of 1919 and part of 1920 at drilling sites about forty miles north of Moorcroft. In 1920 Bill's mother was seriously injured in an automobile accident near Hulett, WY. The Wainwrights returned to California for her medical treatment where they remained. Bill stayed in Wyoming and worked on ranches. In 1923, he went to work for the U.S. Biological Survey (later renamed U.S. Fish and Wildlife Service) as a government trapper.

In 1927, Bill and Edna M. Pollock were married in Gillette, WY and made their home in and around Moorcroft. Edna, born on a homestead near Hulett, WY was one of seven children born to Edward K. and Dell (Grenier) Pollock.

After Ed Pollocks death in 1930, Bill and Edna purchased her parents ranch near Oshoto, WY. They operated it until 1936, while Bill continued to trap. In 1936, they leased the land and moved back to the Moorcroft area to be nearer schools. In 1940, Bill was transferred to Clearmont, WY where he continued to work for the Fish and Wildlife Service until 1950 when he resigned to devote full time to his livestock business.

Bill and Edna had four children. They are: William Donald, Elsie Louise, Paul King and Charles Edward.

Don and his wife, the former Sadie Todd, have two children: Kevin and Kerri. They have lived in Cheyenne, WY since 1965.

Louise is married to Guy Hopes and lives in Bakersfield, CA. They have three children: Glenda, Guy Dee, and Gary.

Paul married Glenda Fowler and had three sons: Bruce, Timothy and Scott. Paul died following a traffic accident in Oregon in 1965.

Charles married Thelma McCue and had two sons: Russel and Jerry. Charles and Thelma purchased a farm in Minnesota in 1960, which Charles continues to operate.

Bill and Edna sold their livestock in 1978 and retired. Bill continued to trap during the winter months. He had a fatal heart attack while he and Edna were checking one of his trap lines in a remote area near the Powder River on Nov. 13, 1981. Edna managed to move him from behind the steering wheel of their pickup and drive to a ranch house for assistance. Edna moved to Sheridan, WY in 1982, where she now resides. - *Submitted by W. Donald Dexter*

DICKINSON-WALDROP

Thomas Hagan Dickinson and Sandra Faye Waldrop were married June 14, 1969 in Rome, GA. They are adopted Hopkins Countians, coming to this county from Todd County.

Tommy is the son of Mimms Hagan Dickinson, born June 30, 1915 in Todd County, and Hazel Ruth (Gray) Dickinson, born Feb. 14, 1923, in Christian County. Tommy has two sisters Mayme Ruth Wilson, Cunningham, TN and Jo Ann Holder, Trenton, KY. Mimms (Mickey) Dickinson died of a heart attack while at work at the Division of Forestry in Madisonville, Aug. 21, 1973. Hazel died at home of an unexpected death Dec. 3, 1966, while she was employed at the Western Kentucky State Hospital.

Tommy was a newspaper pressman with the Leaf-Chronicle Newspaper, Clarksville, TN before coming to the Madisonville Messenger in 1972. He presently is a professional cross-country truck driver for TMI, a California based company leased to Ligon Nationwide. Tommy is a former Nortonville City Councilman and has been active in the Vol. Fire Department since he was a teenager in Todd County.

Sandy is the daughter of James Lewis Waldrop, born Feb. 13, 1928, Christian County, and Mary Leona (Hyams) Waldrop born Aug. 14, 1933, Todd County. Sandy's oldest sister and brother are twins, Wanda Lois Perry, Trigg Co. and Wayne Douglas Waldrop, Christian Co., her youngest brother, Stephen Dale Waldrop is in the United States Navy stationed in Lemmore, CA. Sandy's father James Lewis Waldrop is an independent cross-country truck driver, and her mother Mary Leona Waldrop is retired from the dry cleaning profession. Sandy has been employed with the Hopkins County-Madisonville Library System since 1980, and she presently is the head librarian at Dawson Springs Branch Library. Sandy is a member of the Kentucky Library Assoc.

Tommy and Sandy have one child, Sherry Lynn Dickinson, born Nov. 14, 1970. She graduated from South Hopkins High School where she was active in several clubs. She was president of the French Club, treasurer of the FBLA and parliamentarian of Beta Club. Sherry won first place in business computer applications in state competition of Future Business Leaders of America. This made her eligible to compete nationally on July 4, 1987 in Anaheim, CA at the Future Business Leaders of America/Phi Beta Lamda National Conference. Sherry placed 10th in the nation in this event. She plans to attend Western Kentucky University and major in computer science.

Tommy and Sandy bought their home in Nortonville in 1978 when they decided to make Hopkins County their permanent home. They thank God for their family, friends and the many blessings that He has brought them. - *Submitted by Sandra Dickinson*

DILLINGHAM

James Bethel Dillingham was born Dec. 24, 1918 in Dawson Springs, KY. His parents are Nannie Eison Dilligham born Dec. 23, 1892 and Berlin F. Dillingham born Dec. 29, 1894, both in Hopkins County.

James Bethel was an only child and grew up in Dawson Springs. He and Berlin jointly owned a Buick garage in Princeton and the family attended the Apostolic Holiness Church of Dawson Springs. James Bethel served in the United States Navy during World War II.

James Bethel Dillingham married Audry Mae Orange when he was 16 years old. They had three children, who are Martha Jane born Dec. 26, 1935, Linda Nell born Feb. 9, 1944, and Marcia Kaye born Mar. 10, 1947. Audry Mae Dillingham died on Aug. 13, 1964. Bethel later married Margaret Bushnell from Denver, CO.

Martha Jane, Bethel's first child, married Billy McNamer and had two children, Jan and Larry Dale. The middle child, Linda Nell, married Philip Mejia and had three children, Stephen, Rebekah and Melissa. The youngest of Bethel's children, Marcia Kaye, died at age twenty on July 6, 1968. She was never married

Martha McNamer now lives in Corpus Christi, TX. Linda Mejia resides in Dawson Springs, KY. James Bethel Dillingham is living with his wife, Margaret, in Louisiana. -*Submitted by Melissa Mejia*

JOHN DOCKERY, SR.

John Dockery, Sr. was born between 1755 and 1765. He lived in Wake and Orange Cos., NC and in Hopkins Co., KY.

John Dockery married Sary Perry in Wake Co., NC on the 30th of May, probably 1789 or 1790. (During the time that Alexander Martin was governor of North Carolina.) Sary Perry was born between 1755 and 1765 and died in North Carolina between 1820 and 1826.

Census records indicate that John and Sary Perry Dockery were the parents of at least nine children; however, only four have been identified. Their known children were: Polly Dockery who was born circa 1790 and married Vincent Wilkey in 1808 in Orange Co., NC; Richard Perry Dockery who was born circa 1792 and married Margaret "Peggy" Lam in 1815 in Orange Co., NC; John Dockery Jr. who was born between 1794 and 1797 and married Huldah Ann Watson (believed to be the daughter of Robert Watson) in 1816 in Orange Co., NC and Robert Dockery who was born between 1794 and 1800 and married Catherine "Caty" Jessup in 1820.

Richard Perry Dockery and his wife, Margaret Lam Dockery were the first of this family to migrate to Kentucky. They arrived in Hopkins Co., KY and purchased 67 acres of land in 1818.

Vincent Wilkey, husband of Polly Dockery, died in North Carolina sometime before 1826; Sary Perry Dockery, wife of John Dockery, Sr., had also died by this time. In 1826 John Dockery, Sr., his widowed daughter, Polly Dockery Wilkey and her young children made the trip from Orange Co., NC to Hopkins Co., KY to join the Richard Perry Dockery family.

After the death of John Dockery, Jr. in 1836 or early 1837, Huldah Watson Dockery, with her children, migrated to Hopkins Co., KY. They came to be with Huldah's father-in-law, John Dockery, Sr. and other relatives, arriving in Hopkins County circa 1837.

Hulda Ann Watson Dockery

The known children of John Dockery, Jr. and Huldah Ann Watson Dockery were: Peyton Dockery born circa 1818; Absalom Dockery born in 1820; Watson Dockery born circa 1824; Sarah Ellen Dockery born circa 1825; Nancy Dockery born circa 1827; Julia Dockery born in 1833 and Cornelia Dockery born circa 1836. All of these children of John and Huldah Dockery migrated to Hopkins Co., KY. Most of them married and reared families in Hopkins County. Huldah Watson Dockery died in Hopkins County circa 1883 and is buried in Beulah Cemetery in Beulah, Hopkins Co., KY. - *Submitted by Daniel W. Dockrey*

DANIEL DOCKREY, SR.

Daniel William Dockrey was born Jan. 16, 1881 in Beulah, KY. He was the son of William Harrison Dockrey and Martha Lamson Dockrey. Daniel William grew up in the Beulah community.

Daniel William Dockrey Sr., about 1900. Carrie Lee Bobbitt Dockrey, May 20, 1902.

Daniel William Dockrey married Carrie Lee Bobbitt in Christian Co., KY Oct. 15, 1902. She was the daughter of Emsley William Bobbitt and Nancy Deborah McCord Bobbitt and was born near Kelly, Christian Co., KY June 18, 1884.

After their marriage Dan and Carrie Dockrey lived for a time in Kelly, KY, moving to Providence, KY around 1905. In 1906 the Dan Dockrey family moved to Madisonville, KY.

Dan and Carrie Bobbitt Dockrey were the parents of six children: Roy Lee Dockrey born Oct. 30, 1903; Pearl Dockrey born Oct. 5, 1905; Ola Jeanne Dockrey born June 26, 1908; Kathryn Dockrey born May 4, 1914; Ruby Dockrey born June 10, 1922 and Daniel William Dockrey, Jr. born Aug. 4, 1928.

Dan Dockrey worked as a carpenter and cabinet maker. He was for many years Mill Foreman for Ruby Lumber Company in Madisonville. He was in charge of razing the Hopkins County Court House in 1935.

Daniel William Dockrey was a member of Madisonville First Baptist Church. He died Sept. 19, 1974. Carrie Bobbitt Dockrey was a member of the Seventh Day Adventist Church. She died Nov. 4, 1975. They are buried in Odd Fellows Cemetery on West Center Street in Madisonville, KY. - *Submitted by Daniel William Dockrey, Jr.*

WATSON DOCKREY

Watson Dockrey was born circa 1824 in Orange Co., NC, the son of John and Huldah Watson Dockery. He migrated to Hopkins Co., KY in 1836 or 1837 with his mother, brothers and sisters.

Watson Dockrey married first Martha Burton on Jan. 31, 1850 in Montgomery Co., TN. They were the parents of one child, Virginia F. Dockrey. Martha Burton Dockrey died shortly after the birth of her daughter and is buried in Lick Creek Cemetery in Hopkins Co., KY.

Watson Dockrey married second, Serena Carver Franklin on Oct. 14, 1851 in Hopkins Co., KY. Serena was born circa 1834 in Hopkins County, the daughter of Jeremiah and Elizabeth Jackson Franklin. Serena Dockrey died Nov. 30, 1913 and is buried in Beulah Cemetery in Hopkins Co., KY.

Watson and Serena Dockrey lived on a 280 acre farm on the south east side of Beulah, KY. They lived in a log house; two large rooms separated by a "dog trot". Each room was heated by a fire place. One fire place had a chimney made of sand stone; the other had a "stick and dirt" chimney. Fire wood for the winter was stored in the dog trot. Their house was built on a hill and at the foot of the hill was a spring called Cold Springs. This was where they got their drinking water.

Watson had a large brown stud, his prized horse, which he hid in the "thickets" during the Civil War whenever word was received in the area of approaching Union or Confederate forces.

Watson was a member of the Universalist Church at Beulah and later a member of the General Baptist Church.

Watson and Serena Franklin Dockrey were parents of seven children: William Harrison Dockrey born Sept. 21, 1852; John R. Dockrey born Aug. 13, 1854; Mary C. Dockrey born Feb. 20, 1856; Pernesia J. Dockrey born circa 1859; I. Elizabeth Dockrey born circa 1862; Rebecca A. Dockrey born circa 1863; Willis W. Dockrey born circa 1868 and Valentine Dockrey born circa 1871.

Watson Dockrey died Sept. 6, 1893 in Beulah, KY and is buried in Beulah Cemetery. - *Compiled by Daniel W. Dockrey*

WILLIAM DOCKREY

William Harrison Dockrey was born on Sept. 21, 1852 near Beulah, Hopkins Co., KY. He was the son of Watson and Serene Carver Franklin Dockrey.

On Nov. 27, 1872 William Harrison Dockrey and Martha Lamson were married at the home of Martha's parents, William and Elizabeth Wyatt Lamson. Martha Lamson Dockrey was born in 1857 in Hopkins Co., KY and died on Nov. 30, 1886 in Hopkins County. She is buried in the Lamson Cemetery between Dalton and Providence, KY.

William Harrison Dockrey 1852-1938

William H. and Martha Lamson Dockrey were the parents of five children: Amy Virginia Dockrey born Aug. 12, 1873, married William Albert Franklin; Edward Ashmore Dockrey born Aug. 16, 1877, married (1) Jennie Howard and (2) Lou Lam; Daniel William Dockrey born Jan. 16, 1881 married Carrie Lee Bobbitt; Henry Wesley Dockrey born Feb. 24, 1884 married (1) Mammie Simmons and (2) Louise Young; Mary Louanna Dockrey born May 4, 1886.

William Harrison Dockrey was a farmer. After the death of his first wife, Martha Lamson Dockrey, he married Mrs. Jennie Biggs on Sept. 25, 1895. William Harrison Dockrey died on July 11, 1938 and is buried in Beulah Cemetery in Hopkins Co., KY. - *Compiled by Daniel W. Dockrey*

DONALDSON-FURGERSON

Roy Eugene Donaldson and Sandra Grace Furgerson met at Iowa State U. They were married on Feb. 24, 1962, the same day that Roy graduated from Iowa State U. with a degree in chemical engineering. The first year Roy worked for Goodrich Gulf Chemical Company which was located in Nitro, WV. The following year Roy started working for Silas-Mason, Mason-Hanger Co., which was located in Burlington, IA. Roy was in process engineering which was the trouble shooting department in charge of the different bombs and ammunitions that were being made for the army. As the Vietnam War increased, he was transferred to the ammunition plant in Grand Island, NE. He and his family stayed in Grand Island until 1969. He moved his family in February, 1969 to Nebo, KY, where he began a new career in farming.

Gene and Sandra Donaldson, 1962

Roy Eugene was born in Burlington, IA, on Feb. 27, 1939, to Roy Oscar Donaldson and Macey Viola Good. Roy O. has a farm at Carman, IL. Roy E. has one sister, Donna Kay who, married Gary Campbell. Sandra was born on Feb. 28, 1941, in Hopkinsville, KY, to Charles Emmett Furgerson and Thelma Geraldine Townsend. Roy and Sandra have four children. Therese Anne was born in Burlington, IA, on Feb. 11, 1963. She graduated from West Hopkins High School, where she played basketball and tennis. She and her husband (James Edward Logan) graduated from the U. of Kentucky in 1985. They presently live in Elizabethtown, KY. Roy Eugene II (Butch) was born in Madisonville, KY, on April 1, 1965. He graduated from West Hopkins High School where he played basketball and baseball. He is currently attending East Tennessee State U. where he has a basketball scholarship. Michael Townsend (Mike) was born in Grand Island, NE on July 27, 1966. He also graduated from West Hopkins High School, where he played basketball, tennis, baseball and track. He is attending college at the U. of Kentucky. David Gerald was born in Madisonville on May 9, 1972, and will be attending Webster County High School in 1987-1988. David's interests lie in hunting, fishing, basketball, football, track and softball.

Other ancestral family names are: Furgerson, Whitfield, Fox, Graddy, Bruce, Coleman, Outlaw, Davis, Robertson, Kornegay, Moreman, Williams, Barefield, Bryan, Goodman, Rombeau, Needham, Coghill, Grayson, Donaldson, Goode, Jones, Kirkham, Self, Tyson, Byers, South, Gay, Low, Bellamy, Delong, Campbell, Lockridge, Warwick and Dunlap. - *Submitted by Sandra Donaldson*

DORRIS-BYRUM

Maymie Lee Byrum Dorris was born in Nebo, KY on Mar. 26, 1922, dau. of Grover Cleveland Byrum Sr. and Irene Brinkley Byrum, natives of Hopkins County. Grover Sr. was born Feb. 24, 1889, and died Apr. 20, 1968. Irene was born Sept. 5, 1897, and died Feb. 28, 1965. Grover and Irene had four other children: George Mass Byrum (Dec. 7, 1915), Mrs. J.P. (Margaret) Edwards (Dec. 28, 1917), Mrs. Orville (Mildred) Johnston (Jan. 6, 1920) and Grover C. Byrum Jr. (Aug. 20, 1925). All were born and reside in Hopkins County. (See Byrum family.)

Maymie Byrum Dorris

Maymie graduated from Nebo School in 1940. In 1942, she moved to Evansville, IN, where she worked four years at the Chrysler Defense Plant as instructor over the inspectors.

On Apr. 1, 1948, Maymie married James Howton Dorris in Henderson, KY with Orville Johnston and Mildred Byrum as witnesses. Howton was the son of the late Jim Dorris and

Georgia Howton Dorris Clark, born near Rabbit Ridge in Hopkins Co., Aug. 31, 1920. He entered the Army in 1942, serving in Hawaii, the Philippines, and Okinawa during WWII; he was discharged in 1945 and returned to Hopkins Co. and worked in the coal mines before taking a job with Kentucky Utilities in Earlington, where he worked as a line foreman for 19 years until his death Nov. 14, 1965. He is buried at Odd Fellows Cemetery, Madisonville.

Maymie and Howton had four children: Susan Jo Dorris (b.Dec. 28, 1952), Janice Jai (b. July 1, 1955) married Anthony Taylor (b. Oct. 13, 1954) on June 18, 1977. They have two sons, Harrison Andrew Taylor (Nov. 21, 1981) and Christopher Thomas Taylor (Sept. 8, 1985); Joni Lee (b. Nov. 9, 1958), on Apr. 24, 1981 married Gary Offutt (b. Dec. 11, 1953). They have one son, Nathan Embry Offutt (Oct. 5, 1983); and James Allan (Jim) Dorris (b. Aug. 17, 1961), married Mary Kay Reimer (b. Apr. 7, 1961) on May 25, 1985. All of the children live in Madisonville.

Maymie has resided on Lake Street in Madisonville since July 1957. She is an active member of the First Baptist Church in Madisonville, was a choir mother and Sunday School teacher for several years. She belongs to the Starlite Homemakers Club, is a past Worthy Matron of the C.S. Hoffman Chapter of Eastern Star, and is a credentials committee member for the Kentucky Grand Chapter of Eastern Star. She was active in PTA while her children were in the Madisonville school system, receiving three life memberships in the PTA from three different schools, and was a Girl Scout leader for seventeen consecutive years. She retired from the Hopkins Co. Extension Office on Mar. 26, 1987, after working as an assistant Home Extension Agent for sixteen years. - *Submitted by Susan Dorris*

RUSH W. DOZIER, SR.

Rush Watkins Dozier, Sr., dean of the Realtors in Madisonville, was born in Louisville on Oct. 29, 1917. His mother had gone to her hometown of Louisville for the birth because Madisonville at that time did not have a hospital.

He is the son of E.W. Dozier (1888-1963), a real estate professional in Madisonville from 1919 until his death, and Cornelia Watkins Dozier (1895-1958). Both his parents attended college — E.W. at the Greenville, TX, business college and Cornelia at the Southern Seminary in Virginia. As a young man, E.W. Dozier taught school in Arkansas. He was a prominent civic leader in Madisonville, who served on the city council and ran for mayor. He was an Elk and a Shriner as well as a charter member of the Madisonville Country Club and the Madisonville Kiwanis Club.

Besides Rush Dozier, Sr., who was named after his maternal grandfather, Rush C. Watkins, a Louisville businessman and civic leader, the couple's children were E.W. (Buddy) Dozier, Jr., of Louisville; Mrs. Cornelia Dozier Cooper of Somerset; and William L. Dozier. There were eight grandchildren.

Rush Dozier was graduated from Madisonville High School in 1936 and from Van-

Rush W. Dozier Sr.

derbilt University with a B.A. degree in 1940. He volunteered for army service in 1941 and was graduated from Signal Corps officers training school in 1942 as a second lieutenant. In early 1943 he was sent to England attached to the 65th fighter wing of the 8th Air Force. He served as a communications officer in England and Europe during World War II and retired from military service in September 1945 with the rank of captain. He entered the real estate business with his father in 1946 and has been a Realtor ever since.

In 1949 he married Patricia Sisk of Nogales, AZ. Her father, Hanson Ray Sisk, was a native of Madisonville who became a renowned Arizona newspaper editor and publisher.

Rush Dozier was one of the founders and an early president of the Madisonville-Hopkins County Board of Realtors. He holds the advanced professional designations of CRB, CRS, and GRI. He served on the Kentucky Association of Realtors (KAR) board of directors and was a founding member of the KAR Legal Affairs Committee.

He has had a lifelong interest in real estate education. His work with the Legal Affairs Committee helped earn the Kentucky Real Estate Commission the 1986 award for having the best real estate education program in the nation. He was a charter member of the 200 Club of the KAR Honor Society and received an honors teaching award for his work in the Kentucky Community College system's associate degree program in real estate. His local board of Realtors recognized him with its lifetime achievement award and in 1984 he was named Realtor of the Year for Hopkins County. In 1981 he was named Madisonville Man of the Year.

His wife, Patricia Dozier, attended the University of Arizona. While working at the Madisonville Community College, she was one of the founders of its learning laboratory. She also helped start a learning laboratory at the Madisonville Vocational and Technical School. She received an outstanding achievement award for chairing a four-county area, including Hopkins County, for the Kentucky Educational Television outreach program.

The couple have two sons, Rush W. Dozier, Jr., and Raymond Lee Dozier. Rush Dozier, Jr., received his undergraduate degree with honors in government from Harvard University and his law degree from Vanderbilt University. After serving as city editor of the Lexington Herald newspaper, he joined the administration of Governor John Y. Brown, Jr. He rose to the position of executive assistant and general counsel to Governor Brown. He now serves as the vice chairman of the Public Service Commission of Kentucky. He is a founder and chairman of the board of the Governor's Scholars Program, a statewide summer program for outstanding high school students.

After graduating from the University of Kentucky, Raymond Lee Dozier became a fourth-generation real estate professional. He has his own commercial real estate office in Lexington. He and his wife, Judy, have two daughters.

Rush Dozier, Sr., is co-broker of Century 21 Dozier-Fazenbaker, Inc., Realtors. - *Submitted by Rush W. Dozier, Sr.*

W. BERTRUM DOZIER

William Bertrum "Bert" Dozier was born in Arkansas, the second of ten children of Robert G. and Martha H. Dozier. For more than 50 years, Bert Dozier was a prominent businessman in Madisonville. He came to Madisonville from Texas in 1919, after service in the First World War, to enter the real estate business with his brother, E.W. Dozier, who had preceded him to Madisonville. The two men organized and operated two businesses: Dozier Brothers Real Estate, whose offices were in the old Hotel Madison building on Union Street, and Dozier Brothers Auto Sales, a Hudson and Essex automobile dealership on North Main Street next to the present Post Office.

W.B. Dozier

Bert Dozier was associated with the late Walter Ruby, Sr. in the buying and selling of coal properties. At one time he operated a small mine, but soon gave up mining itself for a career as a promoter. He was one of the outstanding promoters of the coal industry in Hopkins and surrounding counties. In the early 1920's, he and E.W. Dozier were instrumental in the bringing the B.F. Weber mining firm of Chicago into Hopkins County, resulting in the opening of coal mines east of Madisonville.

Bert Dozier married Hellen Morton Hickman. He and his father-in-law, L.K. Hickman, were partners in many coal and oil ventures. After Mr. Hickman's death, Mr. and Mrs. Dozier owned an interest in the Baker & Hickman department store in Madisonville. He was a founding member of the Madisonville Country Club, and was both an Elk and a Shriner. He was a member of the First Methodist Church.

His wife, Hellen, died in 1985. Besides E.W. Dozier, his brothers who lived in Madisonville were Frank, Hugh, and Jack Dozier. All are deceased. His other brothers and sisters, all deceased, were William Dozier, Ila Dozier, and Ruth Harris. He has one living sister, Rosa Roberts of Clovis, NM. He has many nieces and nephews, including Rush W. Dozier, Sr., of Madisonville, E.W. "Buddy" Dozier, Jr., of Louisville, and Cornelia Dozier Cooper of Somerset, KY. Bert Dozier died in Madisonville on Apr. 3, 1979. - *Submitted by Rush Dozier, Sr.*

DRENNAN-SLATON

Ice patches lingered only in the shadows; the remains of the snow that had fallen just days before were almost gone. The date was Dec. 22, 1973. James "J.D." Drennan and Marilyn Slaton were married. Rev. Jim Thornton performed the double-ring ceremony in his home with Charlie and Ann Walker as witnesses.

After a brief honeymoon trip to Paducah, the couple resided for a short time with Marie and Rufus Ausenbaugh, J.D.'s mother and step-father, in Dawson Springs. They then moved into their own home at 207 South Parker, Dawson Springs. In June 1975, they moved to 751 Choctaw in Madisonville. Thirteen months later came an additional move to their present address, Beagle Park Circle.

In October, before their marriage, J.D. had purchased a business and opened it as J.D.'s Standard, a full-service gasoline station at 102 E. Center. Some years later when Standard Oil changed to Chevron USA, the business name was changed to J.D.'s Chevron. In May 1983, Chevron USA closed this leased location and the business was moved to 1115 E. Center, where it still operates. A second business was purchased in July 1978; the gasoline station at North Main and North Streets became North Main Chevron. It presently operates at this location.

J.D. and Marilyn have two children, Jared Davin (b. Feb. 12, 1975) and Jana Diane (b. Dec. 27, 1977). Jared attends Browning Springs Middle School where he served as vice-president for the sixth grade Beta Club. Jared plays Alto saxophone in band. He also completed in May his fourth year of Children's Choir at First Baptist Church. Jana is a student at West Broadway School. She enjoys music and also has attended four years of Children's Choir at First Baptist Church. She likes to collect baby dolls and stuffed animals but her favorite and largest collection is jewelry pins. Her stepgrandfather has helped her add to her collection with finds at local yard sales, and the collection has increased to 70+ pins.

The entire family attends Liberty Baptist Church, Hwy. 85 East, where they are members. Jared and Jana are part of various children's classes and activities. J.D. serves as a trustee and Marilyn is involved in numerous volunteer works within the church.

J.D. (b. Oct. 23, 1945) is the son of Geneva Marie Jones Ausenbaugh and Harvey B. Drennan (1916-1980). Marilyn (b. Sept. 17, 1950) is the daughter of Alma Nellie Breedlove Slaton and John Marion Slaton. - *Submitted by Marilyn Drennan*

DULIN

Robert Smith Dulin, son of Rice and Catharine Myers Dulin, was born in Christian Co., KY in 1837. He moved to Hopkins County in 1853 and engaged in farming for many years. In 1877 he and Chesley Williams opened a sawmill in Mortons Gap. They also had farming and real estate interests. In the 1880's they with John G. Morton opened the Victoria Coal Mine at Monarch which was productive through World War II. Mr. Dulin sold his interest in the mine, retaining mineral rights, in 1904 and moved to Springfield, TN, where he died in 1911.

In 1860 Mr. Dulin married Mary Jane Clements, daughter of Meriwether and Elizabeth Kidd Clements of Wilkes Co., GA. In 1858 she and her two brothers moved to Hopkins County to live with their uncle, Dr. Mace Clements, on his farm located between Nortonville and White Plains. They moved to Mortons Gap, after their wedding. They had five children, Kate C., 1861; Walter J., 1863; Hanson L., 1866; Mollie E., 1868; and R. Smith, 1878.

In 1884 Walter Dulin with his brother-in-law, Edward G. McLeod, husband of his sister Kate, opened Dulin-McLeod Department Store in Earlington. Hanson Dulin and Neel Glenn, husband of Mollie Dulin, became partners in the store in the late 1880's. In 1895 Walter Dulin and Edward McLeod moved Dulin-McLeod Department Store to Madisonville and located on court house square. Hanson Dulin and Neel Glenn moved to Springfield, TN, and opened Dulin-Glenn Department Store.

In 1905 Walter Dulin sold his interest in Dulin-McLeod Department Store to Edward McLeod who changed the name of the store to McLeod's. Walter Dulin opened Dulin's Department Store on South Main Street in Madisonville in 1906. His brother, R. Smith Dulin, became a partner in the store at that time. Dulin's Store went out of business in 1937, Walter Dulin having died in 1922. R. Smith Dulin moved to New York City in 1928 and on to Boyle Co., KY, near Danville in 1932 and lived there until his death in 1954.

Lucy Beaumont and Walter Dulin

Walter Dulin married Lucy H. Beaumont, daughter of William Henry and Penelope Hibbetts Beaumont of Nebo, KY, in 1896. They had three daughters, Nell B., 1897; Mary E., 1899; and Louise B., 1902. All three are living today, Nell and Mary in Madisonville and Louise in Columbia, SC.

In 1923, Nell Dulin married Eldon Guy Brownfield of Warren Co., KY, who moved to Madisonville in 1916. They had two sons, Eldon Guy, 1924 and Walter D., 1931. Eldon Guy Brownfield resides in Madisonville, and Walter Brownfield resides in Ridgefield, NJ.

In 1927, Louise Dulin married Laurence S. Barringer of Florence Co., SC, and they moved to Columbia, SC. They had three children, L. Beaumont, 1929; Mary S., 1936; and Laurence S., 1937. Beaumont B. Palmer, wife of Paul T. Palmer, Jr., and Laurence S. Barringer, Jr. reside in Columbia, SC. Mary B. Rooker, wife of William A. Rooker, Jr., resides in Atlanta, GA.

Kate Dulin married Edward G. McLeod of Hopkins County in 1882. They had two daughters, Lanna, 1883, who married J. Clarence Nisbet of Madisonville and Jane, 1900, who married Hoyt H. Coil of Madisonville. The Nisbets had no children to survive, and the Coils had one daughter, Kate. All are deceased. The Nisbets and Coils, except for Kate, resided in Hopkins County all of their lives. Kate Coil Holeman Ballard moved to Pinellas Co., FL, in 1952 and lived there until her death in 1974.

R. Smith Dulin married Jean W. Cecil of Boyle Co., KY, in 1899. They had one daughter, Lily Cecil Dulin, 1911, wife of Joe Wallace of Shelby Co., KY. They reside in Boyle County and Louisville, KY. - *Submitted by Guy Brownfield*

CLINT DUNBAR

Clint Dunbar has been a resident of Dawson Springs all of his life except for three years in which he lived in Caldwell County. He was born in Hopkins County Nov. 6, 1908. He is married to Glenna Dunbar and they have one son, Donnie, who is married to Carla Bowles. Donnie and Carla have a son, Auston, who was born Oct. 1, 1979.

Clint Dunbar has been a coal miner, sawmill worker, farmer, and he also worked at Outwood Mental Health Care Center. His hobbies include gardening. Mr. Dunbar attends Prospect Church near Dalton. His wife attends Dunn Church.

Mr. Dunbar went to Howton School where he graduated from the eighth grade. The teacher he remembers the most is Flossie Calvert, his eighth grade teacher. Mrs. Dunbar went to Kirkwood Springs School. She is retired after working thirty years at Ottenhiemers Sewing Factory.

Mr. Dunbar said the thing he remembers about his grandfather is that he came from Ireland on a boat when he was six years old and that he fought in the Civil War on the Union Side.

Mr. Dunbar's mother, Viney Dillingham, was born in Tennessee on June 1, 1870. His father, Johnson Dunbar, was born in Caldwell County on Dec. 1, 1853.

Mr. Dunbar has contributed old mining tools and other things to the Dawson Springs Library. He really loves nature. He has a garden to which he is very dedicated. He loves children and enjoys being around them. His step-grandson, Josh, stays with him and

Glenna whenever he can. All of the neighborhood children like him alot and he lets the children play ball and camp out on his land.

Clint Dunbar is a very peaceful man who never harms anyone or anything - *Submitted by Christy Abbott*

HAROLD RAY DUNBAR SR.

Harold Ray Dunbar Sr. grew up most all of his life in Hopkins County. He was born on July 8, 1942 in Hopkins County. The parents of Harold are Garland Dunbar and the late Elizabeth Dunbar. They were the parents of two other children: Sue Riley of Acworth, GA and James O. (Jim) Dunbar of Edmonton, KY. Sue had three children and four grandchildren. Jim has three children and two grandchildren.

Harold Sr. has two children: Tonya Suzanne Dunbar and Harold Ray Dunbar II. Harold Ray II was born in Owensboro, KY on Oct. 11, 1969. Tonya was born in Owensboro, KY on Oct. 11, 1969. Tonya was born in Owensboro on the Mar. 26, 1972. Harold Sr. and his wife, Adeline, moved back to Princeton from Owensboro with their two children.

Harold Sr. is a graduate of Dawson Springs High School. After he graduated, he entered the Air Force where he stayed for four years.

Harold Sr. is now employed at General Electric in Madisonville, KY as a tool maker. He and his family are members of Northside Baptist Church in Princeton, KY. They all enjoy showing cars.

Harold Ray II is now 18 years old and a graduate of Dawson Springs High School. He currently works at the Dairy Queen in Princeton, is a freshman at Hopkinsville Community College and plans to attend Murray State University majoring in History.

Tony Suzanne Dunbar is 15 years old and is a sophomore at Dawson Springs High School. She is a member of the band and plays the flute.

Adeline, Harold Sr.'s wife, is a third grade teacher at Dawson Springs Elementary School. She graduated from Caldwell County High School and attended Murray State University.

- *Submitted by Tonya Dunbar*

JAMES RUFUS DUNBAR

James Rufus Dunbar was born July 14, 1927 in a small rural community called Ilsley. His parents are Lelia Gertrude Ashmore, born Apr. 19, 1905 in Caldwell County, and the late Volney Johnson Dunbar, born Sept. 9, 1898 in Hopkins County. James was the first born son of Volney and Lelia, and he was followed by a brother, Floyd Wayne Dunbar, and a sister, Willa Dean. Wayne and his wife, Beverly, live in Lockport, NY. They have four children. Willa Dean married Allen Burries and they live in Dawson Springs along with their son, David.

When James was young man he traveled quite often, until he married Dorothy Marie Davis in October of 1948. They lived in Dawson Springs and James went to to work in an underground mine. That was the beginning of a thirty-five year career in the mines. It ended in 1953 when he suffered his third serious injury and had to retire.

James and Dorothy have three daughters. Their eldest, Phyllis Ann, was born Aug. 15, 1949. She has two children, Shelia Marie Carroll, 18, and Kimberly Lynn Carroll, 15. James and Dorothy's second daughter Patricia Lynn, born May 19, 1955, lives in Hopkinsville, KY with her husband, Jed Simons, and their daughter, Shawna Nicole, who is nine years old. The third and youngest daughter, Twylia Michelle, was born July 15, 1966. She is unmarried and lives at home.

Two years ago, James had open heart surgery. He has recovered well and stays busy restoring and repairing all types of guns. He loves to trade guns and he tries to do target practice once a week with friends. His family always has something for him to repair and he is a whiz at repairing small appliances.

James is a very family oriented person and likes to have his children and grandchildren close. He is the mainstay of the Dunbar family and respected and loved by all.-*Submitted by Kim Carroll*

DUNCAN-BARNES

Randy Joe Duncan and Dana Lucille Barnes were united in marriage June 1, 1966 in Elizabethtown, IL.

Randy was born May 1, 1947. He is the son of Edna Louise Rhew and Joseph B. Duncan (See Duncan-Rhew). Randy has one brother, Anthony Keith Duncan.

Randy, Dana and Ethan Anthony Duncan

Randy has lived and worked in Hopkins County his entire life. He attended Nebo School and graduated from West Hopkins High School in 1967. He has been employed by Goodyear twenty years. He received the "Goodyear Good Spirit Award" in 1978. He is a member of the C.S. Hoffman Masonic Lodge #252 at Nebo, KY. Randy joined the lodge in 1979, has held several offices and was Master of the lodge in 1983.

Randy is an outdoorsman. He enjoys hunting (deer, quail, duck, geese and turkeys), archery and fishing. He belongs to the Goodyear Bass Club and has participated in Redman and Professional Bass Fisherman Tournaments. Randy has won numerous trophies and awards.

Dana was born Apr. 14, 1949, in Washington, DC. Her parents were Opal Marie Harris and Ralph Thaddeus Barnes. Her maternal grandparents were Jessie B. Tucker and William Lee Harris of Madisonville, KY. Her paternal grandparents were Annie Julia Alsop and Elmer O. Barnes of Washington, DC. Dana has a twin sister, Dona Louise Barnes. She also has another sister: Anna Marie Costin and one brother, Ralph Lee Barnes.

Dana attended school in Washington, DC, Maryland, and in Hopkins Co., KY.

Dana enjoys sewing, quilting, cross stitch, crocheting, and knitting. She has been a volunteer teacher of adult reading. She is now a volunteer craft teacher at Nebo Elementary School. She likes the outdoors and enjoys growing flowers.

Randy and Dana have one son: Ethan Anthony Duncan (Mar. 26, 1979). Ethan, a Cub Scout of Pack 129 at Nebo, is following in his Dad's footsteps of enjoying the great outdoors. - *Submitted by:Dana Duncan*

DUNCAN-FRENCH

Georgia Geneva French was born Aug. 20, 1908, in Caldwell County. Both her mother, Edna Florence Egbert, and her father, William David French, were from Caldwell County. She had three sisters, Lovie, Jewell, and Zada, and one brother, Archella. The family attended Lewistown Christian Church when they could. Georgia and her brother and sisters went to the White Schoolhouse. Georgia was on the basketball team and enjoyed an active youth. She completed her eighth grade year. After completing her eighth grade education, Georgia returned to the school in the afternoons to play basketball with her friends. Her social life consisted of play parties and square dances. The dances were at people's homes around the community. Georgia probably met Clarence at one of these dances.

Georgia Geneva Duncan

Clarence Canel Duncan was born Apr. 10, 1908, in Hopkins County. He was the son of William Duncan and Jimmie Lou McNeely Duncan. Georgia and Clarence often went to the square dances together under the supervision of Georgia's father. Sometime Georgia and Clarence went to prayer meetings in order to see one another. Clarence came to see Georgia every Sunday evening. They sat in the parlor with the rest of the family until night when Clarence had to leave.

On Feb. 3, 1934, Georgia and Clarence were married. The couple lived in Caldwell County at first but later moved to Hopkins County. They had six children, one boy and five girls. Georgia and Clarence had high hopes for their children. They wanted all of their children to graduate from high school. Not only did all the children graduate, but two of the daughters also attended Murray State University; Jane, who is a teacher at Dawson Springs High School, and Thressa, who is an assistant-principal at Webster County High School.

Georgia and Clarence later moved into

Dawson Springs. Clarence died in September of 1973. Georgia, however, still lives in Dawson Springs with her daughter, Brenda Duncan.-*Submitted by Nikole Williamson*

DUNCAN-PARISH

Oscar Lee Duncan and Luetta Parish were united in marriage in 1918.

Oscar (born June 17, 1898) the son of the late Betty Brinkley and George Duncan.

As a small child, Betty traveled with her family from North Carolina to Kentucky in a covered wagon. She was married first to a Moody. They had two children: John and Joe Moody.

Oscar Lee and Luetta (Parish) Duncan

George Washington Duncan was married first to Mary Elizabeth Villians. They had six children: Jeff, Jim, Wash, Elsie, Edd, and Nora.

Betty and George had six children: Doc, Bunt, Arthur, Fannie Harris, Dessie Clark, and Oscar.

Luetta (Dec. 7, 1897-July 31, 1955) was the daughter of the late Mollie Walker and Joe Parish. She had two brothers: Lee and Jim and one sister, Myrtle Oakley. She also had a half brother, Bart Parish (son of Joe Parish and his first wife, Pip Cox).

Luetta, with her American Indian heritage, had high cheek bones, long black hair, and dark complexion. She was of a loving but stern nature, an immaculate housekeeper, and excellent cook. She enjoyed playing the guitar.

Oscar and Luetta had three children: Edward Lee (Feb. 27, 1920) (See Duncan-Rhew), Mary Lou Lutz (July 16, 1923) (See Lutz-Duncan), and Joseph B. (Feb. 28, 1926) (See Duncan-Rhew).

Oscar was converted in 1917. He has been a member of Concord General Baptist Church near Manitou since the age of twenty-one. He was ordained as a General Baptist preacher Mar. 29, 1930. His pastorate was: Concord, Star Hope, Oakley Home, Cumberland Valley, Freedom, Pleasant Union, Cedar Grove, Gum Grove, Tilden, Mt. Olivet, Beulah, Madisonville, Union Temple, Union Cross Roads, Sebree, Greens Chapel, New Hope, Union Grove, Carters Chapel, Midway, and Pleasant Grove.

Reverend Duncan always put God's work first. In his early ministry, Reverend Duncan walked or rode a horse to his churches. He often stayed overnight in the homes of the congregation. His pay was chickens, vegetables, apples, and a few coins. Luetta took care of the children and literally kept the home fires burning.

Fond memories are of drawing a pail of cool water from the well to drink from a dipper, lying on a feather bed, watching the fire flicker in the grate, and a white fluffy cat named Snowball.

After Luetta's death, Reverend Duncan married widow Eunice Crittenden Latham in 1956. She has stood by his side in the Lord's work. Reverend Duncan now resides in Senior Citizens Rest Home, Madisonville, KY. - *Submitted by: Granddaughters, Retha Tarter and Lesia Pendley*

DUNCAN-RHEW

Lavena Mae Rhew and Edward Lee Duncan were married June 1, 1940 in Dixon, KY.

Lavena was born Oct. 7, 1920, the daughter of the late Mamie Mae Arnold and Benjamin Rashley Rhew (See Rhew-Arnold). Lavena was a home-maker, devoted to her family and church. She was a faithful and active member of Concord General Baptist Church near Manitou, KY. She enjoyed working with the young children of the church and singing alto in the choir. Her hobbies included sewing, quilting, and embroidering. She was a 4-H volunteer and active in the Hopkins County Republican Party.

Lavena Mae (Rhew) and Edward Lee Duncan

Edward (Edd) was born Feb. 27, 1920, the son of Luetta Parish (deceased) and Rev. Oscar Lee Duncan (See Duncan-Parish). He served thirty years as a United States Postal employee. His hobbies include growing flowers, carpentry work, coin collecting and going to auctions.

Edd and Lavena had six children: Jerry Edward (Mar. 17, 1941) (See Duncan-Simmons), Larry Benny (Oct. 3, 1942), Brenda Sue Brackett (Dec. 4, 1944) (See Brackett-Duncan), Retha Carol Tarter (Aug. 13, 1948) (See Tarter-Duncan), Lesia Arlene Pendley (June 4, 1959) (See Pendley-Duncan), and Neal Casey (Oct. 3, 1962). There are thirteen grandchildren and one great-grandchild.

Fond memories are of Christmas with all the family home, packages piled high under and around the tree, home-made candy, and Rudolph with his shining nose on the front porch.

Lavena died Oct. 9, 1969 at home and was buried at Concord Cemetery on Hwy. 630 near Manitou. Edd was left with Lesia (age 10) and Casey (age 7) to raise. It was difficult at times, but was a job well done.

After Lesia and Casey were grown, Edward married Francis Sue Baldwin Gish, May 30, 1986. They reside in Madisonville, KY. - *Submitted by: Retha Tarter and Lesia Pendley*

J. DUNCAN-RHEW

Edna Louise Rhew and Joseph B. Duncan were united in Holy matrimony Apr. 30, 1944, in Greenville, KY, by Reverend Lona Lutz.

Louise was born May 12, 1927, to Mamie Mae Arnold and Benjamin Rashley Rhew. (See Rhew-Arnold) She has been a life-long resident of Hopkins Co. She is employed as a data entry operator by the Department of Transportation, Bureau of Highways, District Two.

Edna Louise (Rhew) and Joseph B. Duncan

Louise is a high-spirited individual, who loves working, sewing, and being with her grandchildren. No job ever seems too hard for Louise to tackle.

Joseph (Joe) was born Feb. 28, 1926, to Luetta Parish and Reverend Oscar Lee Duncan. (See Duncan-Parish) Joe has lived and worked in Hopkins County his entire life, except for twenty months served in World War II.

Joe served in the U.S. Navy Amphibious Corps May 27, 1944-Jan. 31, 1946. He traveled overseas on the USS Transport "General U L Scott." After a stay on the New-Hebrides Island, Joe was stationed with a landing craft repair unit in the Soloman Islands, Guadal Canal, Tulagi, and later the Philippines.

Joe is a member of Concord General Baptist Church near Manitou, KY. He is a fun-loving person with a great sense of humor and is a terrific Pappaw!

Joe and Louise have two sons: Randy Joe (May 1, 1947) (See Duncan-Barnes) and Anthony Keith (Nov. 16, 1953). They also have two grandsons: Ethan Anthony (Mar. 26, 1979) (See Duncan-Barnes) and Joseph Andrew (May 18, 1986). - *Submitted by: Dana Duncan*

DUNCAN-SIMMONS

Jerry Edward Duncan and Brenda Jane Simmons were united in marriage Oct. 5, 1966.

Jerry was born Mar. 17, 1941, in Manitou, KY. He is the son of Edward Lee Duncan and the late Lavena Mae Rhew Duncan (See Duncan-Rhew).

Jerry graduated from Nebo High School in 1959. He attended Bethel College and Western College. He also attended the "Andrew School of Music" in Lowell, IN.

Jerry was employed nineteen years by United States Steel in Gary, IN. He worked as a steel charger. His hobbies include: quilting, repairing string musical instruments and playing the violin.

Jerry is a member of Concord General Bap-

Brenda Jane (Simmons) and Jerry Edward Duncan

tist Church near Manitou, KY. He is an accomplished violinist, a humble man, who has dedicated his musical ability to the Lord's work. He enjoys playing his violin in church and for weddings. He visits Hopkins County rest homes regularly and plays his violin for the elderly. He has received numerous awards and trophies by playing his Mittenwald German violin.

Brenda was born Apr. 25, 1948, in Tuckerman, AR. Her parents are Ella Williams and Thurman Lonzo Simmons. Maternal grandparents are Pearl Jane and the late Arthur Williams. Paternal grandparents are the late Maggie Jane and Lonzo Simmons.

Brenda's hobbies include quilting and crocheting.

Jerry and Brenda have three children: Michelle Darlene (Feb. 18, 1968), Timothy Edward (Sept. 6, 1969), and Mark Lee (Oct. 12, 1973). They reside in Madisonville, KY. - *Submitted by Retha Tarter*

DUNN

Peggy Jean Dunn was born on Sept. 11, 1950 in the Madisonville Hospital. She lived in Madisonville most of her school life. Peggy went to five different schools which were Waddill Elementary, Hall Street Elementary, Seminary Jr. High School, Madisonville North Hopkins High School and Dawson Springs High School. Peggy's parents are Louise Rhew and Joseph Thomas Rhew. Louise Rhew is a nurse aid and Peggy's father was a carpenter before he retired. Peggy has three sisters, their names are Brenda Rhew, Jennifer Rhew and LaDonna Rhew.

Peggy went to work when she was very young. She started to work when she was fifteen at a restaurant in Dawson Springs called the Hickory Pit. Peggy worked at the Hickory Pit until she graduated from high school.

A few months after Peggy graduated from high school, she married Bobby Joe Dunn, who had just gotten out of the Navy. After she married my father, she started work at Ottenheimer's when she was eighteen, and worked there for six months. Then she began work at the Ramada Inn and she was nineteen when she worked there. While she was working at the Ramada Inn she became pregnant with her daughter, Wendy Leigh Dunn.

Two years after she worked at the Ramada Inn, she began work at General Electric in Madisonville. Peggy has been working at General Electric for fifteen years. While she was working there, she became pregnant with her son Jonathan Logan Dunn.

Peggy is now living in Dawson Springs, KY. She has two lovely children and is very pleased with the way everything has turned out in her life. -*Submitted by Wendy Dunn*

DURHAM

Virginia Ann Ford was the first of eight children born to John Laban Ford of Caswell Co., NC and Lucy Ann Elizabeth Staples of Virginia.

John Laban Ford was the son of Levi Ford of Caswell Co., NC and Arritta Davis. Lucy Ann Elizabeth Staples was the daughter of John Burton Staples and Nancy A. Turner both of Virginia but moved to Muhlenberg Co., KY when Lucy was a baby.

David Monroe Durham and Virginia Ann Ford Durham with great grandson Richard Monroe Burton, about 1920

Virginia Ann Ford was born Dec. 28, 1842, in Muhlenberg Co., KY. Brothers and sisters are: Aritta, John Levi, Samuel Henry, George William, James Riley, Napoleon Monroe and Laborn Gaines Ford.

On Aug. 19, 1857, Virginia Ann Ford married David Monroe Durham who was born in Virginia but lived most of his life in Caswell Co., NC. He came to Kentucky in 1853 to visit family and friends. Virginia and David's family were friends so he stopped to visit with them and met Virginia Ann, and never returned to North Carolina. After their marriage they lived for awhile in Muhlenberg Co., KY, but moved to Hopkins Co., KY, with their children.

Virginia and David Durham were the parents of eight children: 1. America Ellen, born Aug. 25, 1858, and married James Connelly. 2. Nancy Jane was born Apr. 8, 1860, and married William Harris. 3. Mary Isabelle was born March 1863 and married James T. Hibbs. 4. Patrick Monroe was born Jan. 26, 1866, and married Fannie Lea Hall. 5. David Milton was born June 17, 1868, and married Ella Temperance Cox. 6. Louisa Elizabeth was born June 26, 1871, and married Charles E. Hibbs. 7. Nellie was born Nov. 16, 1873, and married Charles Henry Durham. 8. Lillian May was born Mar. 22, 1876, and married William Thomas Hibbs.

David Monroe Durham served with the Kentucky Calvary of the Union Army during the Civil War. He died on Aug. 24, 1897, in Nebo, KY. Virginia Ann Ford Durham died on May 16, 1931, in Nebo, KY. Both are buried in the Durham Cemetery on Ray Duncan's mother's farm. I believe the cemetery is gone now. - *Submitted by Pat Brock*

DURHAM-SMITH

Margie Ann Smith is the sixth child of Whit and Janie Smith. She was born Mar. 8, 1926, at Earlington, KY. While attending Mortons Gap School in the 5th grade, her friend Bessie pointed through the schoolroom window and said, "See the boy with the black cap over there shooting marbles, that's my new boyfriend, Dorris Durham." The next year when Bessie missed the schoolbus, Dorris saved Margie a seat by him and the romance began.

Dorris Durham and Margie Smith

Dorris Elijah was born in Christian County on December 22, 1923. He is the fourth son of Amy Lee Lacy Durham, born May 15, 1897, and Walter Sherman (Tom) Durham, born Oct. 4, 1891, died Apr. 3, 1935. His parents married on July 1, 1915, at Kelly, KY, in a double wedding with her sister. Tom and Amy sat in a horse drawn buggy and Elise with her groom in the other buggy, side by side, while the preacher read the vows from his porch.

In 1945, Margie graduated with honors as salutatorian of her class. Her grades had tied for the valedictorian honor, but because she had no means of transportation, she could not attend the extracurricular activities and the honor was given to her best friend. She also won the Beauty Queen title her senior year. After graduation she attended Lois and Glen Beauty College in Bowling Green, KY. She was voted Miss Lois and Glen Queen and earned her beautician license.

Dorris's schooling ended in the 8th grade because of his father's death. He began working in the share-croppers' fields to help feed a family of seven. He graduated from a mechanic school in 1949. On Aug. 28, 1959, he graduated from the School of Industrial Electricity.

In Hopkinsville, KY, at a Baptist minister's home which was beautifully decorated for the Christmas holidays, Margie and Dorris were married on Dec. 21, 1946. The tiny raven-haired, green-eyed bride wore a light blue dress, black velvet sandal heels and a winter white coat. The newlyweds then moved into an apartment on Clay Street.

Dorris has always been an excellent provider for his family and relatives by working a variety of jobs, taxi driver, bellhop at the Sun-tag Hotel in Evansville, IN, L & N Railroad and mechanic, to name just a few. Dorris has a big, soft heart and has sacrificed many times for his family, relatives and friends.

In 1947, the young couple remodeled a small, yellow schoolbus tailored just for two in Crofton, KY. In the fall of 1948, on September 21, Karol Kaye was born in Christian County. In the fall of 1955, Linda Faye was born in Hopkins County Hospital.

In 1965, Whit Smith, Margie's father, sold the homeplace farm on the Barnsley Loop, just outside of Mortons Gap, KY, to Dorris and Margie. They remodeled the house and moved in where they still reside.

Karol married William Augustus Welch, born June 10, 1947. They have one son, Nathan Travis, born Feb. 26, 1973.

Linda married Richard Lee Lam, born July 16, 1955, and they have two children: Joshua Lee, born July 15, 1974, and Katie Scarlett, born Mar. 27, 1985.

As gifts, Margie and Dorris gave each daughter property so their families could build new homes and hopefully continue the tradition of passing the farm to the children. - *Submitted by Linda Lam and Karol Welch*

DAVID MILTON DURHAM

The Reverend David Milton Durham, son of David Monroe and Virginia Ann Ford Durham, was born near Greenville, KY, in a one-room, round-log cabin, on June 17, 1868. At the age of six he moved to Hopkins Co., KY, where he grew to manhood, working on his father's farm and attending the public schools. When about twenty years old, he commenced teaching but also attended the Academy of Morganfield under Professor Lemon. He also studied Scriptures under his uncle, the Rev. G.W. Ford, who was minister of the First Christian Church of Morganfield. He later studied under the Rev. W.Y. Allen and Thomas H. Smith.

Front l to r: Ella Temperance Cox Durham, David Giles Durham, David Milton Durham. Back: Carl Milton Durham and Morris David Durham

On June 13, 1894, David married Ella Temperance Cox, of Nebo, KY. It is interesting to note that Ella's mother, Mrs. Sallie Temperance Cox, celebrated her 100th birthday anniversary in 1931 in Madisonville. She was living at the home of another daughter, Mrs. Vaden Cox of Madisonville.

David and Ella both continued teaching and conducting Bible schools in Nebo. They had three sons, Morris David, Carl Milton, and David Giles. In 1900, David Milton was the census taker of Hopkins Co., and much of the records is written by his hand. The family lived in Nebo until moving to Illinois, where David gave himself wholly to the ministry. He continued in this for thirty years—by choice mostly in weaker churches where he felt the need greater.

David Milton was one of eight children. His brother, Patrick Monroe, also devoted his life to Christian ministry. His six sisters were America Ellen Connelly, Nancy Ann Herron, Mary Isabell Hibbs, Louisa Elizabeth Hibbs, of Nebo section, Lillian Hibbs, of Madisonville, and Nellie Durham.

David Milton died in Albion, IL, on Sunday, Sept. 11, 1932. His beloved wife had passed away on July 22nd of the same year. - *Submitted by Dorothy D. Pierce*

JOHN YOUNG DURHAM

John Durham was born Nov. 22, 1889, in Hopkins County. His parents were Patrick Monroe and Fannie Hall Durham. Patrick Durham was a native of Muhlenberg Co., KY, and Fannie Hall was born in Nebo (Hopkins Co.). John was the third of nine children born to Patrick and Fannie Durham. John's sisters and brothers are Iva Elizabeth, Clara Ann, Clayton and Clinton (twins), Tina Pearl, Mertyl Mae, Virginia Lee and Marvin Monroe Durham.

John Young Durham

As a young man John moved to Edwards Co., IL, where his father was a pastor in a Christian Church. John attended College in Albion, IL, and taught school for several years. In March 1911, he married Alma Alice Bond the daughter of George Henry and Emily Ida Crawford, both natives of Edwards Co., IL.

John and Alma were the parents of two daughters: Janelle Bond and Marjorie Lee.

Janelle Bond Durham was born Apr. 1, 1916. On Dec. 25, 1935, she married Frank Porterfield of Wayne Co., IL. Their daughter, Patricia Lee Porterfield, was born July 22, 1939, in Madisonville, KY. Patricia married Alvin Brock of Edwards Co., IL, on July 16, 1956. They have three sons: Andrew David, James Frank and John Patrick.

Marjorie Lee was born July 4, 1922, and she married Marion E. Fisher of Wabash Co., IL, on Apr. 20, 1941. They have two sons: John Charles Fisher born Nov. 8, 1943, married Suzanne Alanson, parents of Lisa Anne and Nathan Scott; and James Durham Fisher born Feb. 15, 1953, married Sherree Jones, parents of Adam Christopher.

John Young Durham died on Mar. 12, 1937, in Evansville, IN. His wife Alma died on July 4, 1952. Both are buried at Graceland Cemetery in Albion, IL. - *Submitted by Patricia Brock*

PATRICK MONROE DURHAM

Patrick Monroe Durham was born Jan. 22, 1866, in Muhlenberg Co., KY. He was the fourth of eight children born to David Monroe Durham of Caswell Co., NC, and Virginia Ann Ford of Muhlenberg Co., KY. Brothers and sisters of Patrick were: America Ellen, Nancy Jane, Mary Isabelle, David Milton, Louisa Elizabeth, Nellie and Lillian May Durham.

Patrick Monroe Durham and Fannie Lea Hall Durham

As a young man Patrick moved to Hopkins Co. with his parents. Here he met and married Fannie Lea Hall on Jan. 6, 1884. Fannie was born Jan. 7, 1869 in Nebo. She was the daughter of John E. Hall of Virginia and Sarah Elizabeth Lawson of Kentucky. John Hall served with the Confederate Army during the Civil War.

Patrick started his married life as a farmer in Hopkins Co., but after a few years he was called to preach. After attending school to be a minister he pastored at many Christian churches in Kentucky, Mississippi and Illinois.

Patrick and Fannie were the parents of nine children (all born in Hopkins Co.): Iva Elizabeth born May 23, 1885 (married O.W. Taylor); Clara Ann born Dec. 3, 1887 (married Jess Burton); John Young born Nov. 22, 1889 (married Alma Bond); Clayton born July 3, 1892, (married Olive Lovelette); Clinton (twin of Clayton) born July 3, 1892 and died Sept. 28, 1893; Tina Pearl born Jan. 31, 1895 and died Feb. 2, 1895; Mertyl Mae born Aug. 13, 1896 (married Lyman Gill); Virginia Lee born Sept. 12, 1899 (married O.C. Shurtleff); and Marvin Monroe born Mar. 1, 1905 (married Grace ?).

Patrick Monroe Durham died Nov. 10, 1946, in St. Louis, MO. Fannie Mae Lea Hall Durham died Aug. 15, 1953, in Wabash Co., IL. Both are buried at Graceland Cemetery in Albion, IL. - *Submitted by Patricia Brock*

VIRGINIA LEE DURHAM

Virginia Lee Durham was born Sept. 12, 1899, in Hopkins Co., KY. She was the eighth of nine children born to Patrick Monroe Durham and Fannie Lea Hall Durham. Both were born in Kentucky.

Brothers and sisters of Virginia Durham were: Iva Elizabeth, Clara Ann, John Young, Clayton and Clinton, Tina Pearl, Mertyl Mae, and Marvin Monroe.

Virginia Lee Durham, 1919

While still in school, Virginia moved with her parents to Edwards Co., IL, where her father accepted to pastor a church. On Jan. 25, 1928, Virginia married Orris Clark Shurtleff on Wabash Co., IL. He owned and operated a Tin Shop in Mt. Carmel, IL. They had one son: John Orris Shurtleff. John attended four years of college with a major in music prior to joining the Air Force. He retired a Major and during his career was a jet pilot and pilot instructor. He married the former Shirley Hurst of Alabama and they have two children: John Clark Shurtleff and Jennifer Lee. They make their home in Ana Heim, CA, where he is involved with the real estate business.

Orris Clark Shurtleff died about 1954 in Mt. Carmel, IL, and is buried at Highland Memorial Cemetery.

Virginia Lee Durham Shurtleff later married Cecil Howey and made their home in Anaheim, CA. She died Oct. 6, 1974, and is buried in Anaheim. - *Submitted by Pat Brock*

EARLES OF VIRGINIA

1st Gen. The founder of this branch of Earles in America was John Earle, born in England about 1614, who emigrated to America in 1649, with his wife, Mary, and their children, Samuel, John, and Mary, settling first in St. Mary's Co,, MD, and in 1652 in what was then Northumberland Co., afterwards Westmoreland Co., VA. He was awarded a grant of 1700 acres of land, lying on the Potomac and Yeocomico Rivers and Earle's Creek. His will was proved in 1660, and an inventory of his estate was recorded at the Clerk's office at Heathsville, Northumberland Co., VA.

2nd Gen. Samuel Earle, born in England 1638; died in VA 1696; married 1st. Bridget Hale; second, Matilda (Allerton?).

3rd Gen. Samuel Earle, Jr., born in Westmorland Co., VA; died there in 1746; married Phillis....

4th Gen. Samuel Earle, 3rd; born in Westmoreland Co., VA. 1692, died in 1771; married first, Anna Sorrell; 2nd. Elizabeth Holbrook.

5th Gen. Judge Baylis Earle, born 1734; died Jan. 6, 1825; married Apr. 16, 1757, Mary Prince, and about 1773 removed from VA and settled in Spartanburg County, SC.

6th Gen. Edward Hampton Earle, sixth son of Judge Baylis and Mary Prince Earle, was born in South Carolina Oct. 15, 1780, and was twenty years old at the time of his migration to Kentucky. He married Susan Davis in Kentucky and had issue: Thomas, Richard, Aspasia, William, John, Anne, Josephine, and Burkley (or Berkley). His wife was the dau. of Richard Davis, one of the first magistrates of Hopkins Co., and a sister of Dr. Thomas Chiles (or Childs) Davis, who was on Col. Allen's staff and was killed at the River Raisin. Edward Hampton, being younger, lived to a good old age and as "Uncle Ned" was a connecting link with the old South Carolina days. He was a man of prominence and, according to the records patented, owned more land than any of the others except his nephew Samuel H. Earle. He was sheriff of the county about 1827, and his name appears on many documents after that as a witness, etc. His descendants are numerous, two being Claiborne Baker and Mrs. Edna Martin Robinson living in Madisonville.

Susanna Davis was born Dec. 12, 1782; died Jan. 20, 1851, married Sept. 18, 1803.

John Orville Earle homeplace in Hopkins County

7th Gen. John Orville Earle, born Nov. 1818; died May 14, 1895; married Mary Melvina Dillingham Oct. 4, 1841 (born Jan. 1, 1827; died Feb, 1, 1912). Children born to this union:

1. Manilus Valerius Earle, b. Dec. 23, 1842; d. Jan. 12, 1873
2. Florence Vitula Earle, b. Sept. 15, 1844; d. Mar. 19, 1918
3. Norman Robert Earle, b. July 15, 1846; d. May 6, 1864 (Killed in Civil War at Slaughterville, KY)
4. Edward Eprahim Earle, b. Nov. 27, 1848 (Was in Civil War)
5. Mary Susan Earle, b. May 1, 1851; d. Dec. 28, 1940
6. Richard Franklin Earle, b. Aug. 17, 1853
7. John Orville Madison Dillingham Earle, b. Mar. 17, 1856; d. Nov. 12, 1873
8. Una Rosaline Earle, b. Nov. 1, 1860; d. Oct. 2, 1940 (See DENTON-EARLE)
9. Margaret Melvina Earle, b. Dec. 24, 1863; d as an infant
10. Ida R. Sophia Earle, b. Oct. 14, 1867

It was related to me by William Bunyan McGregor, that the large tree seen to the right in the picture, was a small sapling when John Orville Earle settled here. John drove the wagon over the tree and Mary said, "Don't kill that tree; I want it in the yard."

The J. O. Earle house was torn down about 1954 and Paul and Iretta McGregor (great-granddaughter of John Orville Earle) used the stone chimneys to build a fireplace in their home across the road from the site of the old house. - *Submitted by Iretta McGregor*

MARK E. EASTIN, JR.

Mark E. Eastin, Jr. was born Sept. 1, 1904 in Sturgis, KY, the son of a small town banker. Mr. Eastin was reared a Methodist. He graduated from Sturgis High School and attended Bowling Green Business University, Ogden College, Western Kentucky University in Bowling Green, KY and graduated in 1929 from Vanderbilt University, Nashville, TN, majoring in Commerce and Business Administration.

Mr. Eastin married Alma Davis of Bowling Green, KY on June 17, 1929 and entered the employment of West Kentucky Coal Company in its General Sales Department in Paducah, KY in the fall of 1929. He was transferred to Louisville, KY in 1932 as Manager of Wholesale and Retail Departments there and returned to Paducah General Sales Department in 1934 as Assistant to the Vice President of Sales. He then transferred to Earlington, KY as Sales Manager of the St. Bernard Division of the West Kentucky Coal Company in the fall of 1936, and when the General Sales Offices of the parent company (West Kentucky Coal Company) were consolidated with the Sales Offices of the St. Bernard Coal Company, became Assistant Sales Manager and later Sales Manger of the combined companies, progressing to Assistant to the President, Vice-President, and following the consolidation of the Operating, Engineering, Sales and General Offices of the company in Madisonville in August 1948, became Executive Vice President and a Director of the West Kentucky Coal Company.

Mr. Eastin was elected President and Chief Executive Officer of the company and its subsidiaries on Mar. 16, 1956. The subsidiaries were: St. Bernard Coal Company; Nashville Coal, Inc.; River and Gulf Transfer Company; Baltimore Insular Lines, Inc.; and Allied Supply Company.

Mark E. Eastin, Jr.

Eastin also served for a number of years as: Member and Director of the "Executive Coal

Conference", Washington, D.C.; Director and Regional Vice President of the National Coal Association, Washington, D.C.; Vice President and Director of Rail to Water Transfer Corporation, Chicago, IL; Vice President and Director of Mid-West Coal Producers Institute, Chicago, IL; Member of Solid Fuels Unit of the Interior Department Executive Reserve, Washington, D.C.; Regional Vice President and a Director of Kentucky Chamber of Commerce, Louisville, KY; Director of Spindletop Research Center, Lexington, KY; Member of Economic Development Commission, Frankfort, KY; Member of Madisonville Junior College Advisory Board; Director and President (1965-1983) of Trover Clinic Foundation, Madisonville, KY; Member of the Commonwealth of Kentucky "Advisory Council for Health Facilities", Frankfort, KY; Member of the Pennyrile Comprehensive Health Planning Council; Member of Madisonville Municipal Airport Board; Kentucky Colonel on staffs of Governor Bert Combs and Governor Ned Brethett; and Member of Elks Lodge.

Island Creek Coal Company acquired control of the West Kentucky Coal Company in the fall of 1963, and Eastin, while continuing as President of West Kentucky Coal Company, was elected a Vice President and Director of Island Creek Coal Company on Nov. 5, 1964, and when the West Kentucky Coal Company and it's Subsidiaries were merged into Island Creek on Dec. 15, 1964, he became President of the West Kentucky Division of Island Creek, continuing in this position until his retirement on June 30, 1965.

Eastin continued as Director of Island Creek Coal Company until it was merged into Occidental Petroleum Corporation on Jan. 26, 1968.

Eastin is a member of the Sigma Chi Fraternity, a past president of the Paducah Junior Chamber of Commerce, past President of the Madisonville Country Club and past President of the Madisonville Kiwanas Club. He has two children, a son, Mark E. Eastin III of Madisonville, KY and a daughter, Mrs. Gerald Poynter of Owensboro, KY, and four grandsons, Mark E. Eastin IV, Stephen Hancock Eastin, Parker Davis Eastin and Brady Gerald Poynter, and two granddaughters, Alyson Dean Poynter and Leigh Ann Poynter.

Eastin is presently a Director and Vice President of Hopkins County First Federal Savings and Loan Association, Madisonville, KY.-*Submitted by Mark E. Eastin, Jr.*

BASIL EDMISTON

Basil Edmiston, born about 1826, in Hopkins Co., KY, was the 6th child of James and Mary Matthews of South Carolina. Other children of James and Mary Edmiston, included Logan, Samuel, John, Isaac, and Dickerson. Basil Edmiston married Rhoda C. Bishop. To this union were born Mary Jane Edmiston Harris, Martha Isabel Edmiston Rogers, Julia A. Edmiston Graham, James Irwin Edmiston, Larentine Edmiston Wyatt, William Logan Edmiston, Basil Everett (Eb) Edmiston, Francis H. Edmiston Dockery, twin sons named Melton (Met) and Whitnell (Whit) Edmiston, and Rhodia D. Edmiston Parrish.

William Logan Edmiston, the sixth child of Basil and Rhoda Edmiston, was born Aug. 15, 1854, in Hopkins Co., KY. Around 1880, he married Mary Elizabeth Coffman, daughter of Isaac Shelby Coffman and Elizabeth Lynn. To this union were born Clyde Wallace Edmiston, Zera Edmiston Brinkley, and "Little Tibe" (only known name). William Logan Edmiston died in 1937, and Mary Elizabeth Edmiston died in 1946. They are both buried in the Coffman Cemetery in the Dalton area in Hopkins Co., KY.

Clyde Wallace Edmiston was born Dec. 14, 1892, in Hopkins Co., KY. On Dec. 24, 1914, in Springfield, TN, he married Dolan Flossie Fox, daughter of Robert Tyson Fox and Cora Idella Sisk. To this union were born Robert Logan Edmiston, Clyda Mae Edmiston Winstead Jordan, and identical twin daughters, Amma Nell Edmiston Edwards, and Blon Dell Edmiston Burgess. Clyde Wallace Edmiston was a farmer, miner and blacksmith. He always enjoyed a good laugh at his neighbors' expense and enjoyed many a good one, liking all his neighbors and they liking him. Dolan was the person in the neighborhood who was depended on by all to help with their sick and coming. Clyde Wallace Edmiston died Apr. 18, 1968, of heart failure at his home. He is buried in the family cemetery, Homesite, in Hopkins Co., KY.

Log cabin on Edmiston Farm

Robert Logan Edmiston, the first born of Clyde and Dolan Edmiston, was born May 23, 1916, in Hopkins Co., KY. On Nov. 8, 1941, in Christian Co., KY, he married Anna Lilith Franklin, daughter of Benjamin Louis and Lora Virginia Downing Martin Franklin. To this union were born Virginia Renee' Edmiston Harned and Lillith O'Shann Edmiston Triplett Edmiston. Robert Logan Edmiston was elected to the Hopkins Co. Board of Education in 1962 and has served 4 consecutive terms as of this writing in 1987. He served 52 months in the 28th Infantry during World War II and was decorated for heroic achievement during the Battle of the Bulge with a Bronze Star.

The Edmistons first settled in Hopkins Co., KY, in the Dalton area in 1810. The picture is of the log cabin which was built around this time. The cabin was built with two big rooms separated by a hallway called a "dog trot." Big fireplaces were built in the ends of the two large rooms. The upper rooms could be reached by ladder from the dog trot. There was a kitchen at the back connected to the rest of the house, but this was torn down in the 1950's. A front porch runs the entire length of the house. The property is still in the Edmiston family, currently occupied by Mrs. Clyde Edmiston, whose late husband was a grandson of Basil Edmiston.- *Submitted by Lillith O'Shann Edmiston*

EGBERT-BARNES

Brady Crockett Egbert and Laura Mae Barnes were married in 1899. Born to them were nine children; two died in infancy.

This bit of history is a tribute to my mother, Laura Mae, her father John Quincy Barnes, his father Asha Barnes and mother Julia. Asha Barnes was lost at sea - Great Grandmother Julia came from North Carolina with her children and nieces and nephew, all children. They came by ox-cart. My grandfather, John Quincy, was 9 years of age and walked all the way.

My father, Brady, was killed in 1923 in construction of the Illinois Railroad. My mother was a brave woman. Back in those days it was rough, but she could always make do and get more food out of a little. I can see the beautiful vegetable gardens and always flowers too, tables of apples drying in summer, and

Brady Crockett and Laura Mae Barnes Egbert in 1916 with children. Standing in back l to r: Reta Pauline, Artie Owen, Edna Beatrice and Everett Marion. In front: Juston Edward, Hustler Bedford, and Marie Carmon in chair.

rows and rows of canned fruit and vegetables, sorghum cookies and beautiful quilts. Her fingers were always busy. She lived to be 92 years of age; she died in 1972.

Reta Pauline married Tommie Cartwright. Born to them were: Tommie Alfred, Ansley Earl, Omba Ruth (deceased) and Uldine, eight grandchildren and three great-grandchildren.

Artie Owen (deceased) married Fairy Lovan.

Edna Beatrice married Kirah Hancock (deceased). Born to them were: Herman Ray, Anna Louise, Mary Beth, Kirah Jr. (deceased), twins Nannie Mable and Cora Mae, Ruby Harold, James Rodney, twenty grandchildren, thirty-five great-grandchildren and two great-great grandchildren.

Everett Marion (deceased) marred Artie Louise Stearsman. Born to them were: Billie Louise, Marion Earl (deceased), Danny Clifton (deceased), Jane Sharon, James Edward, eleven grandchildren, six great grandchildren and eight great-great- grandchildren.

Juston Edward married Effie Mae Cartwright. Born to them were: Joanna Marie, Wanda Lamerrel, Thelma Laverne, Barbara Maxine, ten grandchildren, seven great-grandchildren.

Hustler Bedford married Mary Earline Fike (deceased). To them three children: Donald Lane, Marilyn Sue, Judy Ann, six grandchildren and one great grandchild. Hustler is now married to Betty Capps.

Marie Carmon married William Lawrence Fugate and has one daughter, Norma Jean. - *Submitted by Carmon Fugate*

JOSEPH VERNON ELI

Joseph Vernon Eli was born Mar. 12, 1911, the fourth son of Levi David Eli and Nancerine Parker Eli. He was born in a log cabin out from Dawson Springs just a few miles from Hwy. 109, near the Christian Co. line. His mother (Nancerine) died when he was six months old; Levi David kept his older sons, Herman age 10, Eurie age 8, and Jim age 5, with him but arranged for Joseph Vernon Eli to be raised by a family in St. Charles, KY, Jim and Estella Samples.

Dixie (Burton) and Joseph Vernon Eli

Vernon's first memories are with the Samples on Niles farm (in the Union Temple area) when he was around three years old. Then they went to an area called Deleany (6 miles from Princeton, KY) where Jim Samples worked at a sawmill. Samples bought a 60-acre farm on the outskirts of St. Charles and had a new home built under the construction of Luther Childress. This home was built when Vernon was 9 years old; Vernon stayed until his marriage at age 23.

Vernon's first years of school were at Piney Grove, where he went for 3 years. He went to Hamby Station School for awhile, and then at age of 15 he went to a testing for several schools in the area and got his eighth grade diploma. This testing was held at St. Charles. He went to Dawson Spring High School for 1 1/2 years. At the age of 19, he went to Crabtree School (located in Ilsley) until he was 20 1/2 years old; he got an eleventh grade education. After this, Vernon worked for a while on the construction of Highway 62 from the Y at Ilsley to Nortonville, KY.

At the age of 23, Vernon Eli married Dixie Berton Ashmore, age 21, the daughter of George Virgil Ashmore and Ollie Anna O'Roark (or Ro'Ark). Rev. J. P. Clevenger of Earlington performed the ceremony on Mar. 31, 1934. They lived several years in the St. Charles and Daniel Boone Road area; they had 5 children during this time. In the spring of 1947, they bought a farm between Nortonville and White Plains, KY. Four more of their children were born while they lived on the farm. Vernon farmed on this until he sold it in the spring of 1963.

Vernon worked for Norton Coal Co., from 1941 for approximately 18 months under the supervision of Pokey Saint and Orten Dillingham. He worked the L&N Railroad between Mar. 21, 1950, through the Sixties as a laborer. During layoff periods, Vernon worked as a laborer on the construction of South Hopkins High School and also the Pennyrile Parkway. In 1963, he became assistant foreman for L & N Railroad, then 3 years later he became foreman and retained that position until his retirement in 1976. During the years of 1963 through 1976, he traveled with the railroad in the areas between Goodlettsville, TN, to Evansville, IN, and the area between East St. Louis to Louisville to Henderson, KY; owning property in Nortonville and Madisonville, KY, during these years. Then in 1980, he bought property on the outskirts of White Plains and had a home built. Dixie died Dec. 7, 1986. Vernon sold the home in the fall of 1987.

Vernon was ordained a General Baptist Minister in 1942; Ministering to number of churches in Caldwell, Hopkins, Muhlenberg, Christian and Ohio Counties. He pastored churches in Hopkins and Muhlenberg Counties. He is in the Long Creek Association.

The Joseph Vernon Eli children, November 1987

Vernon and Dixie had a total of nine children; Katherine Kari born in 1935, James Vernon born in 1937, Jurild Thurman born in 1939, Estella Anna born in 1942, Mamie Georgia born in 1945, Mary Frances born in 1947, Joseph Herman born in 1949, Carolyn Sue born in 1951, and Charlotte Joan born in 1956.

In 1950, Vernon checked into some documents and found that possibly his name was spelled Vernice at birth; he also found at this point that he was also called Joseph, thus his name Joseph Vernon. From the time Jim and Estella Samples took care of him up to 1950 he thought his name to be Vernon, only.

Levi (Vernon's father), after raising his other sons to adults, remarried. Levi married Mabel Mitchell of St. Charles and to this union 5 children were born: Betty Lou, Ester May, Mary Ann, Billy Gene and Alice Faye.

Joseph Vernon's parents, Levi and Nancerine, were buried in Shyflat Cemetery off Highway 109 between Dawson Springs and Hopkinsville, KY. Levi Eli's lifespan was 1878-1962, Nancerine Parker Eli's lifespan was 1877-1911. Levi's father was Elisha (one of the twins of Michael Eli and his third wife Elizabeth).

Vernon's ancestors can be traced and documented back to England, when his ancestor Robert Eli I came over from England at the age of 14 on the "Primrose" in 1635 bound for Virginia. From Robert Eli I to Vernon were 10 generations. - *Submitted by Georgia Eli Miller*

ELLIOTT-LEWIS

Sanders Elliott and Mary Bell Lewis (b. 5-9-1883 d. 1970). dau. of Will Lewis and Amy Frances Samuels Lewis, were married and moved to Madisonville from Cadiz, Trigg Co., KY, where both were born. The coal mining town of Madisonville afforded few jobs other than in the coal mines, or the tobacco factories, for men to support their families.

Three Elliott children in 1981 with their niece, Gloria (Van Leer) Williams and husband, Harold Williams. L to r. Otis, Willie Mae, Gloria, Harold and Edward Elliott

Sanders Elliott was blessed with an inventive mind and at one time he invented a balancing scale, but there was not much opportunity for blacks, or Negroes, so these things were never recognized by the public. He made a partial living by fixing clocks. He passed away at the age of 70.

Mary Bell Elliott was one of the best cooks in Hopkins Co. In her later years, when she was about 65, she received her diploma as LPN from the Chicago School of Nursing. She was a Sunday School teacher in the East View Baptist Church for 38 years, and matron for the church Flower Girl's Club for 50 years. She was 86 years old when she passed away.

Sanders and Mary Bell Elliott had four sons and two daughters: Durwood Elliott received his education from Ross-Delmont Elem. and H.S. on KY Ave., where Rosenwald was later built. He inherited an inventive mind from his father, and at present he has a new invention which is almost completed. He is a successful realtor in South Bend, IN, having left home in Madisonville at the age of 16.

Edward Elliott also received his education from Ross-Delmont Elem. and H.S. in Madisonville. He is a licensed funeral director for Kentucky who is on the staff of Elliott Mortuary, Madisonville.

Willia Mae Elliott graduated from Rosenwald High School and from Gupton-Jones College of Mortuary Science—the youngest to have graduated from the college at that time. She is a licensed funeral director for KY and TN, and is owner/manager of Elliott Mortuary and Ambulance Service, being in business for more than 40 years. She was the first black candidate for Coroner in Hopkins Co.

Elizabeth Elliott Van Leer married Robert G. Van Leer and lives in Madisonville. (See VAN LEER-ELLIOTT)

Two sons, Otis Elliott and James B. Elliott are deceased.

Sanders and Mary Bell spent some wonderful years together, and the six children born to this family felt blessed that they were our parents. They contributed a good life to us in Hopkins Co., and left pleasant memories to all.

Sanders Elliott's niece, Lula Vinson, taught school in Trigg Co. for many years at McUton, Rocky Point, Linton, Cerulian Springs, and Trigg Co. High School. She took early retirement. When the all-black school, Free State, closed from busing problems, Lula bought the school building. Sanders Elliott's nephew, Elliott Vinson, drove a school bus for many years, driving for all schools after the black school closed. - *Submitted by Elizabeth Elliott Van Leer*

ETHERIDGE-CREEKMUR

William Henry Etheridge, son of Miles Bartlett and Charlotte (Howton) Etheridge, was born in 1847 in Hopkins Co. and married Sarah Elizabeth Creekmur, daughter of John and Nancy Jane (Howton) Creekmur, on Dec. 5, 1872. They had two children who lived to maturity, George Bartlett (1875-1940), unmarried, and Ida A. (1876-1959), who married Len Beshear. Two other children who died young were Joseph N. (1873-1873) and Willie E. (girl, 1884-1888). All except Ida are buried in the Etheridge Cemetery near Dawson Springs; Ida is buried in Rosedale Cemetery.

The Will Etheridge place was located one mile west of Charleston. Little is related of him except the manner of his death: he was killed in April 1884 by a neighbor while bending over a log at a "log-rolling" (communal construction of a new house). He received a blow on the head with a "hand-spike" (a pole or lever for rolling logs). It happened "about dinner time," according to one report, "and Will was able to

William Henry and Sarah Elizabeth (Creekmur) Etheridge with children George and Ida. In the back is Mrs. Etheridge's sister, Alice.

eat some custard for lunch, and then he was taken home, and died that night." According to another report, he lived a few days. It is fair to add that while both the nature of the quarrel (children running across a field) and the name of the assailant are known, it is not known who started the quarrel or whether such an unfortunate result was intended.

"Bett" Etheridge later married an elderly man, Miles Hanner, whom she survived. She died in 1928. - *Submitted by Sanford G. Etheridge*

ETHERIDGE-HOWTON

Miles Bartlett Etheridge was born ca. 1819 in Trigg Co., the son of Cornelius and Frances (Creekmur) Etheridge, who had emigrated to Kentucky from Norfolk Co., VA, ca. 1818. Cornelius was descended from Thomas Etheridge, who came to Norfolk, Co., VA from England ca. 1640, as follows: Thomas the immigrant; William; Thomas; Samuel; Thomas William; Joshua; Cornelius. Miles had several brothers and sisters, as well as a half-brother and two half-sisters from a previous marriage of Cornelius. One half-sister, Amelia Ann, was the second wife of Lewis Howton of Hopkins Co. and is buried beside him at Old Beulah Cemetery. One of his brothers, William E., was in the Confederate Army and was killed in action. Another brother, David D., was the great-grandfather of Mrs. Eva Grace (Etheridge) Martin of Princeton. His youngest sister, Mary Ann, married James J. Bush on Jan. 22, 1849, and they have numerous descendants in Trigg Co. today. His father Cornelius ("Neely") died in 1834, and his mother Frances in 1843.

Miles Bartlett Etheridge

Miles himself married Charlotte Howton on Feb. 24, 1840, in Hopkins Co. Charlotte, born ca. 1822, was a daughter of Lewis Howton and granddaughter of Jonathan Howton. Her mother, Sarah (Ridge) Howton, the first wife of Lewis Howton, is also buried beside him at Old Beulah. The couple settled down in the Charleston district (near Dawson Springs) to engage in farming, and raised a large family. The Etheridge place was near the present Walnut Grove Church, the house being situated on a rise to the west of the church, on the north side of the road. No trace of it remains. Their family cemetery, the Etheridge Cemetery, is on the south side of the road. The first grave in the cemetery was that of their son, Cornelius Lewis ("Neely") who died in the Army of measles in Princeton shortly after enlisting in 1863.

Their children, all born in Hopkins Co. from 1841 to 1863, were Sarah Frances, m. James H. Hicks; Amelia Ann, m. John Wyatt; Cornelius Lewis, unmarried; William Henry, m. Sarah Elizabeth Creekmur; Charlotte Susan, m. John Wyatt after the death of her sister Ann; Miles Stanford, m. Martha Malinda Miller; James Harvey, unmarried; Martha Elizabeth, m. D. S. ("Sant") Young; George Whitson, m. Rebecca Jane Phelps; David Grant, unmarried.

As late as 1958, oldtimers still remembered the good times and hospitality they had enjoyed as young people at the Etheridge home. But for the family itself, the post-civil-war times were increasingly hard times. Miles suffered from declining health, and in addition to that had to declare bankruptcy after he had co-signed a note for a neighbor. Miles died in 1888, Charlotte in 1897. Of their 10 children, only 5 had children, and only 4 (Susan, Sanford, Martha, and Whitson) had grandchildren. - *Submitted by Sanford G. Etheridge*

ETHERIDGE-MILLER

Miles Sanford Etheridge, son of Miles Bartlett and Charlotte (Howton) Etheridge, was born on Mar. 21, 1853, near Dawson Springs. He married Martha Malinda ("Sissy") Miller on Dec. 2, 1875. Their children were Stella, who married Clarence McElroy; Kelly, who married Cora Alpha Traylor; and Evelyn May ("Eva"), who married John N. Knight. Sanford's first wife Martha died about 1887 and is buried in the Etheridge Cemetery, together with an infant who died at about the same time. Sanford then married Nancy Froman, but the marriage did not last, and his children were later brought up by Sarah and Jim Hicks, Sarah being Sanford's oldest sister, herself childless. About 1892, when he had a drugstore in either Benton or Hardin, because of some difficulty (real or imagined) with the law, he left Kentucky with a third wife, Della Parson, and was never after heard from by the family. He kept in touch with his close friends in the Masonic Lodge, however, and they affirmed he had gone to Arkansas, but they would never divulge his exact whereabouts. They also said he had raised children by his third wife. His brother George Whitson claimed to have seen him through the window of a saloon in East St. Louis in 1896 while watering his horses outside. He didn't go in,

Miles Sanford Etheridge

however, because, as he said, he "didn't want to start any trouble."

Each of the three children named above had families, and "San" and "Sissy" now have grandchildren and great-grandchildren in Kentucky, Ohio, Florida, West Virginia, and throughout the west. - *Submitted by Sanford G. Etheridge*

ETHERIDGE-PHELPS

George Whitson Etheridge, son of Miles Bartlett and Charlotte (Howton) Etheridge, was born in Hopkins Co. on Nov. 10, 1860, and died on his ranch at Guernsey, WY on Nov. 12, 1923. He married Rebecca Jane Phelps (1865-1955) on Dec. 24, 1885. Rebecca was the daughter of Absalom ("Tap") and Mary Jane (Coats) Phelps. In 1887, "Whit" and "Becky", together with the Absalom Phelps family and the Wilson B. Coats family (he was Becky's uncle) and one or two other families, formed a wagon train and emigrated to northeastern Colorado, near the now extinct towns of Bryant and Leslie.

George Whitson and Rebecca Jane (Phelps) Etheridge with their son Obie

In 1894 after 2 years of panic and drought, they followed the other settlers from that section to the irrigated sections of Colorado, as hundreds of farms were abandoned. In 1895, they bundled up their 5 children and made the trip back to Kentucky by covered wagon, and after a few months' stay in and around Dawson Springs, struck out again to repeat the wagon trip west they had made nine years before. This time they settle in Wyoming.

"Whit" visited Dawson Springs again in 1919. He wrote home that he was particulary depressed by the run-down condition of his boyhood home. At his death in 1923 he was survived by his wife and eight children: Ivan, b. 1886; Obie, 1889; Stella, 1890; Ellis, 1892; Charlotte, 1894; Absalom, 1897; Beulah, 1899; and Ferne, 1901. Of these, Beulah—who was named for the community Beulah in Hopkins Co.—is the sole survivor in 1987. - *Submitted by Sanford G. Etheridge*

EVANS-TEAGUE

Thomas Meade Evans (6/27/1902-10/14/1984) was the son of Wm. and Agnes Stubb Evans of Livingston Co., KY. He worked with the Signal Corp for ICRR for a number of years. He married Thelma Pearl Teague (1/31/1909-1/23/1982), the daughter of George Anderson and Effie Rachel Lyell Teague.

Thomas Meade and Thelma Pearl (Teague) Evans

Thomas worked for West Kentucky Coal Co. as Tipple Foreman and other coal companies until his retirement. Pearl was a housewife and mother. They were members of Grand River Baptist Church and resided in Madisonville at their deaths. They are buried in New Salem Cemetery in Nortonville. Their children:

George William b. 7/8/1926 married Doris Wyatt b. 9/4/1927. G. W. is an electrician for P & M Coal Co. Doris is a housewife and mother. They reside on Eastview Dr. in Madisonville and are members of Grapevine Christian Church. Their children: Cheryl Jean who is single, works as a medical transcriber at Holmes RMC in Melbourne, FL; and Jaynet Gail who married Dunham Pascal Box who works at Sextet Coal Co. Jaynet Gail is an RN at RMC in Madisonville. They reside in Madisonville with their two children, Wm. Pascal and Carrie Renae.

Earl Thomas b. 7/8/1931 married Faye McGregor b. 7/9/1937. E.T. is employed at American Mine and Tool. Faye is employed at Harvey's Department Store. They reside on Sugg St. in Madisonville and are members of Grapevine Christian Church. Their children: Debra who married Rick Starr. Rick is the Pastor of the Christian Church in Oblong, IL. They are the parents of Sarah, Bethany and twin sons Joshua and Jacob.; Carolyn and Brian who are still at home.

Jane Ann b. 6/23/1934 married Charles Edward Robinson. Charles was employed at Penwalt Corp., Inc., in Calvert City, KY. He died of a heart attack in 1969 and is buried in Dixon Cemetery at Grand Rivers, KY. Jane and the children moved to Madisonville. Their children: Barry Mark who married Kim Smith, and works at Cimmaron Mines. Kim teaches Lamaze classes at RMC. They are members of the First Baptist Church and reside on Montrose Dr., Madisonville. Their children are Rebecca, Andrew and Adam.; Sharon Dawn married Randy Hassler. Randy works for Peabody Coal Co. They are members of the Baptist Church and reside in Owensboro, KY. Their children are Matthew and Elizabeth; and Alan Mark married Kathy Drake. They reside in Paducah, KY, where he is employed at the Triangle Insulation Co. Alan has three children by former marriages, Emily, Bradley and Seth.

Charles Meade b. 11/11/1937 married Sue Watts b. 4/17/1940. They reside in Paducah, KY, where he is a boilermaker at V.M.V Enterprises. They are members of the Baptist Church. Their children: Charles Meade, Jr., Tracy Karan and Nathan Andrew.

James Larry b. 12/29/1940 married Wanda Keeling b. 1/1/1942. Larry is a welder at Walker's Boat Dock in Paducah, KY, and Wanda is a housewife and mother. They belong to the Baptist Church and reside in Grand Rivers, KY. Their children: Lisa Kay married Jefferey Timmons. Jeff is self-employed. Children: Mandy Brook and Jill Beth; James Larry, single, works at Heating and Air in Westland MI; Lonnie Dean married Scarlet Johnson. Lonnie is self-employed and their children are twins Rhea and Andrea and a son, Kristin; Lori Mae married Rick Hensley, a mechanic who is self employed. They are the parents of Kayce and Kayla; and Lesle Earl who is single and lives with his parents. He works for Gardner. - *Submitted by Agnes Teague Cunningham*

GEORGE FAULL

George H. Faull, born in Cornwall, England, in December, 1850, came to the United States at the age of 18 and located at Ducktown, TN, where he secured employment in the copper mines. Later he moved to Coal Creek, TN, where he became a coal miner and in 1878 to Kentucky and for one year worked in the coal mine at Empire. His next location was at St. Charles, where for a quarter of a century he was mine foremen of the St. Bernard Mining Company, at the end of which he retired on a pension and moved to Earlington in 1904. He died at Herrin, IL, in January 1914 while visiting a son, Henry Faull, and was buried in Christian Privilege Cemetery at St. Charles. He served effectively as a member of the school board of St. Charles, for a number of years as a member of the city coucil, and always possessed in full degree the respect and confidence of his associates and fellow citizens. He was a devout Christian and a faithful member of the Methodist Church, South, and his fraternal affiliation was with the Masons.

In Ducktown, TN, he married Elizabeth Ann Roberts or Robards, who was also born in Cornwall, England, in February 1851. Her father, Johnathan Roberts, born in England migrated to the United States in 1855, settling near Pittsburgh, PA, where he lived a number of years moving then to Ducktown, TN, where he died. He was life-long miner and a devout Methodist Circuit Rider in Pennsylvania, Knoxville, TN, and Coalcreek, TN.

George H. Faull

The children born to George and Elizabeth Faull were William J. in 1872 at Ducktown, Mary Ann in 1873 at Coalcreek, Ena between 1873 and 1883, Ella born in the 1870's, (died at the age of three), Barton in 1886 at St. Charles, and Nora in 1883 at St. Charles.

William J. married Joan McAllister in 1896 and Mary Anne, Joseph Basil Hibbs Oct. 2, 1889. Henry married Sally Todd of St. Charles and Ena, Horace Harrison. Barton died at the age of forty-four, unmarried, a World War I veteran. Nora, unmarried, died at the age of twenty-nine of tuberculosis.

George and Elizabeth Faull, Barton and Nora are buried in the family plot at St. Charles, in the Christian Privilege Church Cemetery. Mary Ann and Joseph Basil Hibbs, Ena and Horace Harrison are buried in the same cemetery. William J. and Joan McAllister are buried at Dawson Springs where they lived for many years and Henry's family in Herrin, IL, where they lived and reared their family.

The men all worked for St. Bernard Coal Company at St. Charles in the early years. William J. became the office manager of the St. Bernard Coal Company at St. Charles, later moving his family to Dawson Springs where he owned and operated a drug store. They had five children: Mona Meade born in 1897, Marjorie who died at the age of 17 months, Perry Kemp born in 1900, Margaret Elizabeth born in 1903, and Mary Sue born in 1911. -*Submitted by Kathleen Trover Davis*

FERGURSON-MITCHELL

John Henry Fergurson and Fannie Florence Mitchell were married in 1902. John Henry was born Feb. 24, 1884, in Fergurson Town, KY, Hopkins Co. His ancestors founded the town.

John Henry and Fannie, born March 1884, had two children: Gertrude born 1904 in Hopkins Co. and died 1976, and Paul Ural born Feb. 11, 1906 in Hopkins Co. and died Mar. 1, 1935. John Henry died in 1965 and Fannie died July 6, 1937.

John Henry ran the only grocery store for miles around in the 1900's. He was also a blacksmith and a farmer. He was married four times. John Henry was the son of William Buck Fergurson and Martha Ellen Franklin. William Buck was born Sept. 27, 1856, and died Apr. 15, 1936. Martha Ellen was born June 15, 1860, and died Feb. 18, 1934. She was the daughter of Dal Mitchell.

John Henry had three sisters: Mamie, Meadie, and Maude, and one brother James William. William Buck had a twin sister named Sarah Emily. She died June 17, 1936. John Henry's grandparents were James William Fergurson and Nancy E. Wicks. James

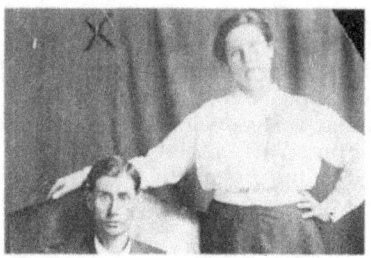

Johnnie and Fannie Mitchell Fergurson

William was born Oct. 26, 1821, and died Feb. 28, 1862. James and Nancy were married May 28, 1855. Nancy was born in 1837. -*Submitted by Margaret Fergurson Croft*

FINLEY

One foggy night late in the 18th century, a crowd was dancing on a boat docked at Liverpool. It was a farewell party for emigrants who were to sail to America at dawn. A lad of 17 years - of Scotch-Irish parentage - slipped aboard during the confusion and hid in the hold. He took roots in the soil of the Carolinas.

In 1810, one of his three sons, Howard Finley, came to Hopkins County and settled in the Suthard Community.

Six years later a son was born, Thomas Helm Finley, who in young manhood married Miss Mariah Malin of the same county. He died in 1899, his wife a few years earlier. Five sons and one daughter were born to this union.

The oldest child was Richard Newport. He was wounded while fighting with Union Forces in the battle of Shiloh and died shortly after in Paducah.

The second son was James William who was also a soldier in the Union Army.

The sister was Mary Elizabeth and she married James H. Laffoon.

Dr. and Mrs. Finley

John Howard was born on Dec. 9, 1845. He was a prominent farmer and was known as "Doctor" Finley because he possessed a divine gift for healing. He was known in his day as a "Faith Doctor." He would take no pay for his services, saying that it was a Gift of God.

George Finley lived in Madisonville and with his sons operated a hardware store for many years.

Dr. Thomas Randolph Finley was a physician and practiced medicine in St. Charles for many years.

They were a pioneer family that became extensive landowners from Carbondale to Richland. They were all very hearty, living to be 90 + years old. There were lawyers, doctors, merchants, teachers, and farmer born to these pioneers. - *Submitted by Ruth F. Osburn*

CHESTER ARTHUR FINLEY

Chester Arthur Finley, born July 12, 1883, in Hopkins Co., KY, was the fourth of six children born to James William Finley and Helen Mary Castleberry Finley, daughter of George Washington Castleberry and Nancy Jane Malin Castleberry.

James William Finley (born Nov. 27, 1840) served in the Civil War in the Union Army. He and his four brothers and one sister owned land in the Carbondale-Suthards area of Hopkins Co., KY. James William died Feb. 2, 1935. He and his wife are buried in Oddfellows Cemetery in Madisonville, KY.

The brothers and sisters of Chester Arthur were: James Lemuel, born 1876, (died young), George Randolph, born June 30 1878, Nancy May, born Sept. 29, 1879, Pearl born Feb. 15, 1885, Martha Elizabeth (Bessie), born Jan. 31, 1891.

As a young man, Chester Arthur traveled to Canada and worked as paymaster for a railroad company. He returned to Hopkins Co., KY, and went into business with his half-brother Thomas Finley, son of James William Finley and his first wife, Cassandra R. Leach Finley. Chester and Thomas purchased the New Providence Merchantile Company in Providence, KY. Chester Arthur sold his interest in the business to Thomas in 1912.

Chester Arthur was hired by the Bureau of Census to be Enumerator of the Carbondale-Suthards area for the 1910 Census.

On Dec. 17, 1913, Chester Arthur married Ora Judia Cowan (born July 17, 1892-died Oct. 22, 1917). They had one son, James Arthur, born May 25, 1917.

Chester Arthur Finley and Emma Genoah(Allinder) Finley

Chester Arthur married Emma Genoah Allinder (born Oct. 6, 1892) on Dec. 20, 1920, in Springfield, TN. They had two daughters: Melissa Agnes, born July 28, 1921, Thelma Jean, born Jan. 20, 1930.

Chester Arthur and family lived on his father's farm at Suthards, several miles south of Earlington, KY. He worked as a barber in Earlington in the first years of his and Emma's marriage. After his father's death, he became a full-time farmer at Suthards.

Chester Arthur (died July 5, 1957) is buried at Oddfellows Cemetery in Madisonville, KY. - *Submitted by Anne Keene Morgan*

HOWARD FINLEY

Howard Finley was born in North Carolina in 1767 and died in Hopkins Co. in 1840. He came to this area in the early nineteenth century and settled in what is now known as the Carbondale and Southards area. At one time, the Finley acreage extended from there to Richland. To this day a section of Highway 112 is known as the Finley Levee. Howard Finley's wife was Betsy Ann Helm.

The settlement of Howard Finley's estate as recorded in 1840 included cash on hand $102.12; many tools and necessities for everyday living; guns; watches; nine slaves. The inventory also included one colt; a horse; one lot of flax; one loom; a cotton patch; a lot of tobacco; a barrow; leather; potatoes; and hogs. The total value was $1300. However, the land later proved to have valuable coal deposits.

Thomas Helm Finley, the son of Howard and Betsey Helm Finley, was born in 1815 and died in 1899. He married Maria Malin a neighbor, on Jan. 3, 1838. Maria was the daughter of John Malin of the Carbondale area. Malin was a soldier in the Hopkins Expedition against the Indians in 1812. He was also a large land owner.

Both Howard and Thomas Helm Finley are buried in Cane Run Cemetery, which is located near the Malin property. No trace of the Finley or Malin houses remains.

Five children were born to Thomas Helm and Maria Malin Finley. The oldest, Richard Newport Finley, born in 1838, was killed in the Civil War Battle of Shiloh.

James William Finley, another son, was married twice and had seven children: Thomas E.; James Lemuel; Chester; George; May; Pearl; and Bessie. Thomas E. Finley's children are Thomas E. Jr., James Campbell, and Gordon Bennett. George's children are Garland, Ardath, and Louis. May's children are Helen Ruth, Dorothy, and Vemont. Pearl's children are Finley Davis, Virginia, and Dicie Helen. Bessie's two children are Bessie and Wanda.

Thomas Helm Finley's only daughter, Betty, was married to James Laffoon. Their only son was Sidney.

John Howard Finley's children were Ruby, Rosa, Ruth, and Sophia. George Alleny Finley's children were Lonnie, Floyd, Everett, Ernest, and Lena. Lonnie's daughter is Lillian Bassett. Everett's daughter was Margaret Lena's daughters are Bethel, Karleen, Emily Sue, Georgia Mae, and Mary Ruth.

Dr. Thomas Randolph Finley was the youngest son and his children were Maud Finley Ashmore, Kimmel Hart Finley, and Dr. Austin Flint Finley.

The fifth generation, the descendants of Howard Finley, are listed in the accompanying article, Thomas Randolph Finley and Austin Flint Finley. - *Submitted by: Mary Hart Finley*

THOMAS R. FINLEY AND AUSTIN FLINT FINLEY

Thomas Randolph Finley, the youngest of Thomas Helm and Maria Malin Finley, was born at the Carbondale home on Aug. 2, 1850. He died on Dec. 26, 1947, in Madisonville and is buried at Oddfellows Cemetery. He married Mariah Isabel Hart, who had come to Kentucky as a child from Louisa County, VA, after the War Between the States.

He received his medical education at Missouri Medical Academy, now Washington University, in St. Louis and practiced in St. Charles, which at that time was a prosperous mining community of the St. Bernard Coal Company. His office was across the street from the company store. The Finleys were members of Christian Privilege Church and lived near the church. Dr. Finley often sang there and continued to sing at First Christian Church after he retired and moved to Madisonville. "Amazing Grace" and "When The Roll Is Called Up Yonder" were among his favorite hymns.

In Madisonville his loafing places were Ligon's Harness Shop, Senator Rash's shuffleboard court, and the Hotel Madison.

His children were Kimmel Hart Finley, now deceased, with one son Thomas Randolph Finley, and Maude Finley Ashmore, also deceased with two sons, John Randolph Ashmore, now deceased, and Thomas Austin Ashmore.

Dr. Austin Flint Finley, the oldest son of Dr. Thomas Randolph Finley are Mariah Hart Finley, was born in St. Charles on Oct. 24, 1881, and died in Madisonville in August 1962, and is buried at Oddfellows Cemetery. Dr. Finley was named for Dr. Austin Flint, a famous doctor of that time.

Dr. Finley graduated from the University of Kentucky Medical School which was in Louisville then. He also graduated from Male High School there, as his parents had a home in Louisville in order for the children to attend school in the city.

Dr. Finley married Mary Agnes Salmon, who at the time of their marriage lived in Ilsley. Mary Agnes Finley was born on June 12, 1890, and died May 20, 1984. She was educated at South Kentucky and Ward Belmont Colleges.

Dr. Finley began his practice in Ilsley and there he was in the influenza epidemic of 1917. He made his rounds on horseback, and he was always interested in Kentucky saddle-bred horses. In 1920 he moved to Madisonville where his offices were in the McLeod Building and in the old Madisonville Hospital. He performed the first blood transfusion in Hopkins County and continued to keep informed of the latest medical findings. He was Director of the Hopkins County Health Department at the time of his death.

Dr. Finley enjoyed hunting and had several famous bird dogs-Whit and Frank. He was also an avid sports fan and reader. Cooper and Kipling were among his favorite writers.

Mary Hart Finley, Agnes Isabel Finley, and Jane Rash Finley Bone are the three daughters of Dr. and Mrs. Finley. Jane Finley Bone is married to James Glenn Bone. Their three children are Flint Finley Bone, James Rash Bone, and Mary Agnes Bone.

Flint Finley Bone is married to Martha Cochran Bone, and their two sons are Aaron Flint Bone and Benjamin Cochran Bone.

James Rash Bone is married to Jane Vaughan Bone and his children are Rebekah Elizabeth Bone and Matthew Jacob Bone. - *Submitted by Mary Hart Finley*

FLEMING

1st Generation - Robert Fleming of Virginia; 2nd Generation - William Fleming of Virginia; 3rd Generation - William Buck Fleming of North Carolina and Florida; 4th Generation - Edward Fleming of Hopkins Co., KY; 5th Generation - Edward Henry Fleming of Webster Co., KY; 6th Generation - William Edward Fleming, Tip Calvin Fleming and Steve Alvin Fleming.

Edward and Louisa Fleming with daughter Anna and son Henry (baby)

Edward Thomas Fleming, born 1862 in Lake City, FL, was one of four children born of the marriage of William Buck Fleming, born Dec. 15, 1788, died May 7, 1872, and Mary Eliza Thomasson, born 1834, died July 24, 1919. Buck's and Mary Eliza's other children were Suzannah, born in North Carolina but married Wade F. Bailey of Dixon, KY; Molly, born in North Carolina but married Walton Wamock of Webster Co.; and William, born in Florida but married Frances Ashby of Webster County.

Edward Thomas Fleming married Dec. 7, 1887, Miss Louisa Prather, born 12 Mar. 1860, daughter of John and Louisa Branson Prather of the Slaughters area. Ed and Louisa settled on a farm in the Vandetta Community near Hanson and there they raised their five children, who attended the common schools of the area and grew to adulthood, married neighborhood boys and girls and established homes of their own. Their issue were: 1. Anna, married (1) Arch Parker and had issue Marvin Ray and Charlie J. Anna married (2) Joe Brown, no issue; 2. Edward Henry, married 21 Dec. 1913 Dona Alice Hancock, daughter of the prominent family of Lewis and Sally Bradshaw of the Onton area. Their issue are: William Edward, who married Edna Bryant of Mishawaka, IN; Tip Calvin, who married Jane Warren of Evansville, IN; and Steve Alvin, who married Louise Page, daughter of James Blanton and Virgie Springfield Page of Madisonville, KY. Steve and Louise's issue are Anna Lisa who married Jim Lee Kennedy of the Kirkwod Springs community, Hopkins Co., and Julie Page who married Marty Ray Walters of Louisville, KY; 3. Johnny, married William Orten and had issue Maxine and Willadeane; 4. Ina, married Albert Ashby and had issue LaRue, Oneal, R.H., and Georgie Lou; 5. Iva (twin to Ina) married Richard Parker and adopted son, Eugene.

Edward Thomas Fleming died 4 Sept. 1931. Louisa Prather Fleming died 19 Apr. 1923. Both are buried in Slaughters Cemetery. - *Submitted by Steve Fleming*

FOX-DAVIS

Daniel Fox was born circa 1785 in North Carolina the son Titus and Elizabeth Wright Fox.

In the Pendleton District of South Carolina on Aug. 29, 1803, Daniel Fox married Elizabeth (Betsy) Davis daughter of William and Anna Loving Davis. Elizabeth Davis Fox was born on Oct. 29, 1786, in North or South Carolina and died July 24, 1865, in Hopkins Co., KY.

Record has been found of four children of Daniel and Elizabeth Davis Fox, but probably there were others: Azel T. Fox born circa 1821 married Nancy Bruce; Daniel Crittenden Fox born May 12, 1826, married Margaret Ann Russell; Louanna Fox born in 1810 married George Wyatt, Jr.; Zalmon L. Fox born in 1820 married Rebecca Brown.

Daniel Fox was a farmer and a Baptist minister. He died in Hopkins Co., KY on Dec. 13, 1848. - *Compiled by Daniel W. Dockrey*

FOX-GALBRAITH

Nathan FOX and wife Rebecca GALBRAITH (b. ca 1797, VA) of Hopkins Co. were relatively newly married in 1820 with only a son and daughter: George W. who married Altha JOYNER in 1839, Livingston Co, KY, and Elizabeth Ann born 13 Apr. 1820. They soon added Susan who married John RAY, Esther Clarissa (b. 14 June 1824), Irena (b. Christmas Day 1826), and Nathan D. (b. 26 Mar. 1828). Johnathan TODD sold Nathan 50 acres for $1 in 1823 and John & Ellen WILSON (went MO) sold him 100 acres in 1825 for $100.

Yet by 1830, the family had moved to Pope Co., IL, along with early Hopkins Co. settlers Daniel and Elizabeth FOX who, upon arriving, applied for a revolutionary war pension. Daniel's son Pleasant had come to Pope Co. ten years earlier. The winter after old Daniel and Pleasant moved across the Ohio River to Livingston Co., KY, Nathan FOX died. His widow Rebecca acted as executor of his will (24 Jan. 1838, Pope Co. Probate Bk D. pgs. 94-95).

Their eldest daughter Elizabeth Ann married James McCARVER about the same year. By 1840 Sarah Fine was born; she married George W. WEEKS. John and Martha "Julia"

Francis Marion Moseley, grandson of Nathan and Rebecca Fox

were born next. "Julia" (1845-1928) married 1st Sidney BELL and had Josie Bell GARRETT, David BELL and Lura Bell; she m. 2nd Mr. ATHEY and had Earl, Raymond, Maggie SHARP wife of Wm. SHARP.

When William McCarver died, "Betsy" married widower William MOSELEY (1802-1869), son of Clement Mosely, newly arrived in Massac Co., IL, from Caldwell/Christian Co., KY. William had 5 children and served Jackson Precinct as justice of the peace. He and Betsy FOX had 5 more children: William Smith (1849-1914), Francis Marion (1852-1888), Louisa Elmina (16 Feb. 1853-18 Sept. 1932) married Samuel JOHNSTON (son Stuart was mayor of Paducah), David (1856-1883), and Clement Nathan (b. 1859, named after both parents fathers!). Betsy's widowed mother, Rebecca FOX, was often in the household when not in Livingston Co., KY, with daughter Susan RAY and grandchildren: Nathan A., Mary, Alley, and John W. On 29 Sept. 1861 Betsy MOSELEY died leaving eight children and five step-children.

Rebecca Galbraith FOX seems to have moved around among her children, helping out and enjoying the affection of her many grandchildren. In 1860, she lived with son Nathan DeKalb and wife Emeline (b. ca 1832, TN) in Pope Co. and enjoyed grandsons Pleasant, Francis, and Thomas. Nathan served Nathan served as worshipful Master of Farmers Masonic Lodge No. 232 in 1867, farmed, served as a Baptist minister, and gave the first Republican speech in Metropolis at the Massac Co. Courthouse. - *Submitted by Karen Kerr Jensen*

FOX-JULIAN

It began with James Fox who moved to Kentucky between the years of 1801-1805. James brought a daughter and two sons with him. One son was named Titus. James and his wife Elizabeth sold their land in Wilkes Co., NC and moved to Burke Co., NC. In the 1800 census, they were in Pendleton Dist., SC. The family then moved to Kentucky near White Plains. Titus was born about 1760 and married Elizabeth Wright in 1780. He served in the Revolutionary Army around this time. He and Elizabeth had nine children: Amelie, Daniel (married Elizabeth Davis, who is buried at Browns Cemetery), Rachel Hankins, Sarah Matthews, James (who died in 1845), Mary (Polly) Sisk, Allen, Jess (born in 1805 in Ky, lived in Christian Co.) and Malinda (married Greenberry Mathew). Allen, Mary, James and Sarah stayed in Hopkins County. Titus died Sept. 24, 1845.

Allen, son of Titus, was born in 1801 in SC. He married Temperance Julian, the daughter of John Julian from SC. They were the parents of: Isiah, Lucinda, John Julian, Virginia, Isaral H. (Edd), Avarilla F. and Flora.

John Julian, son of Allen, was born July 4, 1835, and married Frances Elizabeth Oldham the daughter of Cadel Oldham. They were married Oct. 18, 1866. Their children were: Eniss Wesley, Emmit Edman (who died very young) and John Medley (born 1876, died 1908 of typhoid fever, married Holland Webster).

Emmit E. was born Feb. 4, 1870. On Apr. 12, 1892, he married Addie Hardwick who was born on July 9, 1876, and died July 19, 1951. Both are buried at Ilsley Cemetery. Emmit farmed and worked in the coal mines. Their children were: Mary married Orbey Sisk and had one son who lives in Hopkinsville; Ivy Frances married (1) Gordan Ashby on Apr. 12, 1914, in Hopkins Co., (2) K.K. Kennedy on Sept. 15, 1934 in Christian Co.; Jess F. who was born Sept. 23, 1901, married (1) Jewel Eli in 1920, (2) Berdie Steadman; Grace who died at age 2; William Julian born Feb. 18, 1905, died June 27, 1975 (married Verna McKnight in January 1928); and Johnnie Mae born July 8, 1911 and died July 4, 1977 (married Charles Johnson).

Berdie (Steadman) and Jess F. Fox

Jess F. had two children from his first marriage to Jewel Eli: Louise (married Douglas Jackson from Maury Co., TN, and had a son Kenneth) and Harold who died Oct. 4, 1986 (married Dorthy Nell Workman who died Dec. 5, 1986, they had no children).

Jess F. maried Berdie Steadman on Mar. 23, 1929. Berdie was born in Alabama. Their children are: Gwyn and John E.

Gwyn was born Apr. 22, 1931, and married John R. McDonald who was born in Tennessee and moved to Dawson Springs in the early 1920s. Gwyn and John now live in Illinois. They have three children: Johnny (living in Wyoming), Barbara (married Monty Johnson of Illinois) and James (not married, lives and works out of Chicago).

John E. was born July 2, 1932, and married Billie Sue Bean in 1950 while he was in the Navy. They now live in California. Their children: William F. (married Mary and has two children) and Diberia (married David Bittler and lives in Pennsylvania).

Many descendents of this family still live in Hopkins County. Joseph J. Fox returned to Hopkins County in the past few years. He is descended from John Medley and Holland Webster Fox, both deceased. Joseph has a large family, none living in Kentucky. - *Submitted by Berdie S. Fox and Joseph J. Fox*

FOX-RUSSELL

Titus Fox came with his wife, Elizabeth Wright, and their family to Hopkins County by 1802. They were both born in Wilkes Co., NC. Titus, born ca 1760, died in Hopkins County on June 22, 1825. Elizabeth, born ca

Gravestones at Prospect Cemetery of John, Daniel Crittenden, Margaret Ann and Nancy Fox

William Preston Fox (1807-1878)

1766, died in Hopkins County on Sept. 24, 1849.

Their oldest son, Daniel, remained in North Carolina. He married Betsy Davis, daughter of William and Anna Davis, in Pendleton District, SC, on Aug. 29, 1803. They soon followed his parents to Hopkins County. Daniel died on Dec. 13, 1848. Betsy died on July 24, 1865. She is buried in the Brown Cemetery in Hopkins County. Near her stone is that of a small grandchild.

Daniel and Betsy had, at least, seven children. The youngest son, Daniel Crittenden, was born in Hopkins County on May 12, 1826, and died in July 1884. He was married to Margaret Ann Russell, the daughter of James Russell. Margaret Ann was born May 24, 1824, and died Dec. 30, 1894. They are buried in Prospect Cemetery at Dalton. Their graves, along with the graves of two of their children, are enclosed inside a private fence.

Daniel Crittenden Fox and Margaret Ann Russell were the parents of nine children. Daniel Francis, born at Dalton on Jan. 14, 1853, was the third child. He was married on Jan. 7, 1875, to Victoria Davis, daughter of a John Wigginton Davis and Melissa Jones of Caldwell County. Daniel Francis and Victoria made their home in the Dalton area for a few years and then settled in Caldwell County. Daniel Francis died in 1936 and Victoria in 1930. Both are buried in the cemetery at Shady Grove, KY.

Information was obtained from deed books, will books, Titus Fox's Revolutionary War pension application, censuses, cemetery records, and family records. - *Submitted by Evelyn Arduese, and Virgina D. Smith*

FOX-WILSON

William P. Fox was born in 1841 and died in 1919. He was the son of William Preston Fox (1807-1878) and Mary (Polly) McGregor (1809-1865). He married Maranda Wilson (1842-1936), daughter of Mitchel Wilson and Matilda Wyatt Wilson. William Preston and Mary McGregor Fox are buried at Lick Creek. Mitchel and Matilda Wilson are buried at Lick Creek. William P. and Maranda Fox are buried at Mencer. William P. and Maranda were the parents of five children: Mary (born 1863 and died 1866), Wilson, Dury, Charlie and Hardy.

Wilson (1864-1950) was a farmer. He married Leanda Densmore Jackson (1862-1904), the daughter of Densmore and Nan Franklin Jackson, in 1885. They were the parents of five sons: Clell, Clyde, "Joe" Charles B., Clifton and Archie. Clell was born in 1886 and died in 1934. Clyde was born in 1888 and died in 1975. "Joe" was born in 1890 and died in 1936. Clifton was born in 1894 and died in 1971. Archie was born in 1899 and died in 1985. Wilson, Clell "Joe" and Clifton are buried at Dunn. Leanda is buried at Lick Creek. Clyde is buried at Rose Dale. Archie is buried at Herrin, IL.

Dury, who was a farmer, was born in 1867 and died in 1922. He married Marcella Franklin. They were the parens of one daughter, Vivian, who was born in 1897 and died 1977. Dury, Marcella and Vivian are buried at Rose Dale.

Charlie, who was a barber and a farmer, was born in 1873 and died 1955. He married Virginia Dockery. They were the parents of two sons, Loral and George. Loral was born in 1897 and died 1967. George was born in 1903 and died 1973. Charlie, Virginia, Loral and George are buried at Rose Dale.

Hardy, who was a photographer, working with Isaac Willingham, was born in 1878 and died in 1961. He married Bertha Boitnett. They were the parents of a daughter, Nell and a son, William. Nell now lives at Madisonville and William lives at Paducah. Hardy and Bertha are buried at Rose Dale.

William P. and Maranda lived on the Fox family farm, which was located on Hurricane Creek. This location is between Dawson Springs and Charleston, on what is now known as Fox Road. The house they lived in and part of the farm is now owned by the Joe Walker family. Later William P. and Maranda lived in Dawson Springs at a location that is now 207 E. Hall St.

Some of the decendants of William P. and Maranda living in Hopkins County today are: Charles Dixon, son of Vivian; Niles Fox, son of Clyde; Virginia Fox Chappell, daughter of "Joe"; Larry Chappell, son of Virginia; Brett, Shane and Mance Chappell, sons of Larry; and Brandon Chappell, son of Brett.

Some of the other decendants who are deceased are: Ashby Fox, son of Clyde; Richard and William L. "Bill" Fox, sons of "Joe" and Bobby Fox, son of Archie.

Virginia Fox Chappell, with her husband, Lawrence, is the only decendant now owning and living on a part of the Fox family farm. - *Submitted by Virginia Fox Chappell*

DANIEL FOX

Daniel FOX was born in Virginia's Shenandoah Valley on 1 Jan. 1766. In 1780 he enlisted at N.C.'s Wilkes Co. Courthouse under Captain Joel LEWIS and Col. GREEN and marched to Guilford Courthouse where he joined the 7th N.C. Regiment as a private and fought the British under Lord Cornwallace. He served with Titus Fox, son of James FOX of Burke Co., NC, who died in Hopkins Co. in 1812, another early Hopkins Co., KY, settler. In 1787, Daniel married Elizabeth in Burke Co. and in 1809 he entered land by certificate from Henderson Co. and became an official Hopkins Co. settler.

Hendley WADE knew Daniel, 1807, had 15 yr. old child and one older child and John B. CUNNINGHAM, 1813, knew Daniel's fourth child, a grown man. Daniel's revolutionary pension papers (W9443) only list his surviving children of 1845: Pleasant FOX who moved to Pope Co., IL, by 1820 and Nancy (born 16 June 1793, NC) who married Rueben REEVES (born 13 Aug. 1795); their children: John (24 Jan. 1815), Mary Ann (1 Mar. 1817), Elijah (18 Apr. 1819), Manurvy (8 Aug. 1821), William (17 Aug. 1823) who acts as executor of his grandmother FOX'S estate in 1851, and Absolom (14 Aug. 1825). Perhaps if the other Daniel FOX children can be identified, someone will be able to submit DAR papers on the patriot Daniel.

In 1830, Daniel and Nathan FOX (1794-1838)

William P. Fox and Maranda Wilson Fox Family. Seated l to r: Leanda holding Clifton, Hardy, Maranda, William P., Charlie and Virginia. Standing l to r: Wilson, Clyde, Clell, Dury, "Joe" and Marcella.

moved to Pope County. The only other FOXs living the area were Pleasant, who served as 2nd Lt. in IL Militia in 1828, and James N. FOX (1770/80 - 9 Mar. 1835). This James N. served as Captain in 3rd Reg. IL Militia in War of 1812, was J.P. , and ran for legislature in 1822; by 1830 he'd moved across the Ohio River to Livingston Co., KY where he died; his issue: William, Henry, David, Daniel C., Sarah who married James R. RAMAGE, James J., Jasper, Nancy Elizabeth who married Maston POE, and a daugher who married Benjamin CLOUD and had child Sarah.

Daniel FOX, age 67, applied for a pension (1833) and in 1836-7, he moved to Livingston Co, KY with son Pleasant. The next winter, Nathan FOX, in Pope Co. died. Daniel and wife Elizabeth moved away to Marshall Co., KY, where Daniel died 22 Apr. 1845 (no will). Widowed Elizabeth then went to live with her surviving daughter Nancy REEVES in Graves Co., KY, where she died 27 Sept. 1851 (no will).
- Submitted by Karen Jensen

TITUS FOX

Titus Fox was born in Wilkes Co., NC, the son of James Fox. On Aug. 25, 1780 in Wilkes County, Titus married Elizabeth Wright. Elizabeth was born in 1766 in Wilkes Co., NC and died Sept. 24, 1845 in Hopkins Co. KY.

Titus and Elizabeth Wright Fox migrated to Hopkins Co., KY, in the early 1800's. They were the parents of eight known children: Amelia Fox born Jan. 2, 1782; Daniel Fox born circa 1785 married Elizabeth Davis; Sarah Fox born circa 1793 married _____ Matthews; James Fox born circa 1795; Mary Fox born July 14, 1799, married E.B. Sisk; Allen Fox born circa 1802, married Temperance Julian; Jesse Fox born circa 1805, married Elizabeth Knight; and Malinda Fox born circa 1808 married _____ Matthews.

Titus Fox died in Hopkins Co., KY on June 22, 1825. - Compiled by Daniel W. Dockrey

FRANKLIN-TEAGUE

Chesley M. Franklin b. 5/28/1898, was the son of Thomas Randell and Salley Ezell Franklin. Chesley's dad was superintendent of coal mines. Chesley went to work in the mine as a small child, starting the pump in the morning or any other task a small lad could do. When he received his wages he gave it to his parents and received pocket change in return. He married Orva L. Teague b. 9/17/1898, the daughter of George Anderson and Effie Rachel Lyell Teague of Christian Co., KY.

Chesley M. Franklin and Orva L. Teague Franklin

Chesley operated a grocery store in Mannington, later moving to Nortonville while still employed at Williams Coal Co. They moved to Dawson Springs in the mid-thirties and opened a small truck mine at Beulah, KY. He only employed a few men. They hand dug the coal, hauled it outside, where Chesley hand loaded it on a truck and hauled it between the rivers to sell. He unloaded it by hand and returned home. On a short haul he could get two loads sold in one day. He operated Chesley Franklin Mine, The Chesley Franklin Coal Co., with his son-in-law E. D. Harrell as partner and the Franklin & Franklin where his son Decola was a partner. The Decola Coal Co., where his son Decola and daughter Wetona were his partners. He was successful in business and continued until his death July 30, 1967.

Orva was a housewife and mother. They were members of the First Christian Church. They had 50 years together. Orva died Dec. 22, 1975 and is buried at Petersburg Cem., Christian Co., KY Their children were:

Leamon Madison b. 11/17/1917, d. 5/2/1918.

Decola Wayne b. 12/17/ 1920, d. 6/17/1978. Decola attended Nortonville and Dawson grammar school, graduating from Dawson Springs High School and Lindsey Wilson College. He taught one year at Nortonville and served in the Navy during WW II. He went in the coal business with his father and sold it after his father's death. Decola married Burnett Russell. Decola drown in Lake Beshear and is buried at Rosedale Cem., Dawson Springs. Decola and Burnett had two daughters: Patricia Joyce married Wm. Schoefield who is a corporate lawyer and diplomat in the State Dept. in Washington, D. C., Patricia is Vice Adm. of the Kennedy Institute in Washington; and Orva DeNell married Edward Storms who is employed at Buckhorn Inc. in Dawson Springs. DeNell is a teacher's aide at Dawson City School. They reside in Dawson Springs and have two children, Shannon and Jonathon.

Wetona Joyce b. 12/31/1928 married Kenneth Cotton. Wetona and Kenneth attended grammar school and graduated from Dawson City School. Kenneth served in the Navy and is employed by Peabody Coal Co. in Indiana. Wetona was employed by her dad and later became a partner in the coal business. They reside in Booneville, IN, and are members of the Christian Church. Wetona had three sons by a former marriage: Dale Franklin Harrell who married Barbara Mills from Georgetown, KY. Dale is employed by The Bradenton <u>Herald</u> in Info. System and Barbara is with Tropicana. They live in Bradenton, FL. Dale has two sons by a former marriage, Steve and Mike; Lynn Avery Harrell married Joyce Beshear and had one daugher, Christy. Lynn died in a car accident on Hwy. 62 near St. Charles, KY in 1973 and is buried in Rosedale Cem. in Dawson Springs.; and Dennis Reed Harrell who is single and serving in the Air Force Combatic Logistic Support Squadron, stationed at Ogden, UT. - Submitted by Agnes Teague Cunninham

BENJAMIN FRANKLIN

Benjamin Louis Franklin, born Oct. 7, 1860, in Hopkins Co. was the first child born to Finis E. Franklin and Sarah Wilson, daughter of Louis Wilson and Sallie Sisk. Other children born to the union were Frank Lee and David G. Finis Franklin was born ca 1841 and was the third child of Stephen Franklin and Temperance Mason. Stephen and Temperance (Tempie) were married Dec. 29, 1836, in Caldwell Co. To this union were born Rebecca Jane (Lynch), Newton, Finis E., Nancy (Jackson), Stephen Addison, John Riley, Foster M., Thomas J., James Winchester and Bryant D. Stephen Franklin, was born Nov. 19, 1810, in KY and died Feb. 9, 1856, is buried in Lick Creek Cemetery in Charleston, Hopkins Co. Temperance Mason Franklin was born ca 1816 in Tennessee and her date of death is unknown at the time of this writing.

Benjamin Louis, the first born of Finis E. and Sarah Franklin, married Jefferson (Jeffie) Davis Mason from Tennessee, on Sept. 11, 1879, in Hopkins Co. To this union were born Ila Birch (Finley), Charles Greenleaf, Nellie L., Flora Mae, Ruby, Della Mabel (Wilkey), Vaden (Fitzsimmons), Bryant Leslie, Mary Ruth (Ridley) and twin boys not named. After the death of Jeffie on Jan. 24, 1904, Benjamin Louis married Lora Virginia Downing Martin, daughter of John Bryant Downing and Anna Eliza Nichols, on Nov. 27, 1907, in Caldwell Co. To this union were born Thelma Ray (Monroe) and Anna Lilith (Edmiston).

Anna Lilith, born Mar. 23, 1918 in Hopkins Co. married Robert Logan Edmiston, son of Clyde Wallace and Dolan Flossie Fox Edmiston, on Nov. 8, 1941 in Christian Co. To this union were born Virginia Renee' (Harned) and Lillith O'Shann (Triplett) (Edmiston).

Benjamin Louis Franklin and Anna Lilith Franklin Edmiston, October 17, 1940

Benjamin Louis lived most of his life in Charleston, Hopkins Co. He conducted a successful mercantile establishment in Charleston for 53 years. He was a democrat, member of the Universalist Church and affiliated with Beulah Lodge No. 609, A.F. and A.M. for over 50 years. He also was a member of the Hopkins Co. Board of Education. This must have taken a great deal of dedication, considering he had to travel 5 hours by horse and buggy to attend the meetings.

Franklin's original store consisted of three floors. He sold everything you could want and ask for, from food to clothes to coffins. The original store was torn away to make a more compact store as many articles were obsolete that were previously carried. The new store was constructed in 1937. The area residents would come to Franklin's store, purchase large quantities of meal, flour, potatoes, seed, etc. to last till harvest. Once the crops were harvested, these same people would come back, settle their account and purchase said items again for the next winter.

In 1922, strange faces started to appear when the I.C.R.R. was put through Charleston. At night the railroad workers would bring music intruments to the store which stayed open until 11 and 12 p.m. They would sing sad songs of love and home as most of them were from other states which were far away in those days.

There was always an on-going checker game. The store was equipped with one of the few radios and people would gather at the store to listen to the sounds coming from this strange box. Franklin would also read the newspaper aloud each night, as most people in the area could not read.

Franklin was always impeccably dressed and always had a smile and a kind word for his fellow man. He had a dry sense of humor which made his personal jokes very humorous as well as original. He was an avid reader of the Bible and quoted it often. He would apply the passages to everyday happenings and predictions which he often told his family would come to pass, which at the time seemed ridiculous to them, but which some of them have lived to see come to pass.

Benjamin Louis died June 1, 1944, in Hopkins Co. and is buried in Rosedale Cemetery at Dawson Springs in Hopkins Co. - *Submitted by Lillith O'Shann Edmiston*

JEREMIAH FRANKLIN

Jeremiah Franklin was born in 1805 in Kentucky, the son of James and Rachel Franklin.

On Jan. 10, 1826, in Hopkins Co., KY, Jeremiah Franklin married Elizabeth Jackson, daughter of Christopher and Rebecca Croft Jackson. Elizabeth Jackson Franklin was born in 1807 in South Carolina. She died in 1856 in Hopkins Co., KY, and is buried in Lick Creek Cemetery near Beulah, KY.

Jeremiah and Elizabeth Jackson Franklin were the parents of ten known children: Christopher James (Kit) Franklin born in 1827 married Nancy Dockery; James A. Franklin born Aug. 16, 1827 married Nancy H. Southard; Logan Ashmore Franklin born in 1829 married Martha E. Jackson; David N. Franklin born Nov. 3, 1832, married Elizabeth Clark; Serene Carver Franklin born in 1834 married Watson Dockrey; Rebecca A. Franklin born in 1836; Jeremiah H. Franklin born in 1839 married Mary E. Brown; Thursey Franklin born Nov. 17, 1839, or 1842, married William J. Franklin; Lafayette Franklin born in 1844 married Rachel Harriet Webb; and Orlando Franklin born in 1853 married Florissa Sisk.

After the death of Elizabeth, Jeremiah Franklin married Nancy Brown Mar. 13, 1858, in Hopkins County, KY. The date of his death is not known. He is buried in Lick Creek Cemetery in Hopkins County, KY. - *Compiled by Daniel W. Dockrey*

MINNIE SUGG FRANKLIN

Minnie, above all else, loved her family and home. She had three children and enjoyed spending a quiet time reading to each of them. She also loved working in the yard. It must have provided some much needed time to herself. Whenever possible, she would work in her rose garden and tend to the jonquils, mock orange, japonicas and all the other beautiful growing things she loved.

Minnie and Charlie Franklin

Because she was somewhat shy, she found public attention very unpleasant. Her husband, Charles G. Franklin, was a lawyer (probably Hopkins County's first law school graduate) and politician. Because he was so adept at both, the two created a certain amount of limelight, which Minnie deftly sidestepped as much as possible. To her horror, one night at a campaign rally, Charlie called on Minnie to speak when a scheduled speaker failed to show. Anger overcame her fear, and she delivered a fine speech, but it was nothing compared to the one she gave Charlie when they returned home.

Even Mr. Alexander, who sold home grown vegetables from his wagon, bestowed unwanted attention. Invariably as he rounded the corner of Seminary to Broadway, he would bellow "Okay, Miz 'Charles', get your veg-a-gables....tomatoes, beans, squash. "Miz 'Charles' would frantically hunt for her purse while sending anyone she could grab out to stop Mr. Alexander from shouting her name to the neighborhood.

Although she was reserved with those not close to her, family and friends saw the capriciousness she occasionally displayed. For instance, they vividly remember one certain Christmas back in the Thirties when one of the children was given a BB pistol by a sibling. Obviously anticipating with pleasure a little target practice, Minnie suggested innocently that the pistol be tried out right there in the house... and at all things, the Christmas tree ornaments. Stunned for a second or two, the children were simply ecstatic. Her husband was somewhat less enthusiastic. The better part of that Christmas day was spent sweeping up the pieces of colored glass and excitedly talking about a Christmas no one would ever forget.

Minnie had a keen sense of humor and loved to laugh and entertain her family with stories of growing up in a large family. Her father, John Will Sugg, first married the eldest daughter of the Johnston family (Anna). After her death, he married the youngest Johnston, Frances Arminta. Minnie was born in Madisonville in 1888. Her brothers and sisters were Emma Carroll, Neva Ernestine, Charlotte Frances, Lora Margaret, John, Berry and Mary (who died in infancy). Minnie died in Dec. 1980, twenty-one years after Charlie's death.

She, unlike Charlie, did not have an extensive education but was a lover of books. She was a member of the Blue Stocking Club, a literary group which met once a month. A glance at the program showed quite a variety of interest. In the 1916-1917 year, Minnie gave a paper on Verdi; in the 1928-29 year, her topic was Jean Ribaut and the Hugnenots. These women were smart, active and capable.

Minnie and Charlie married in 1914 and had three children; Frieda Wells, Carroll Franklin (lawyer and city Judge), Mimi Gordon and seven grandchildren. They are Michael Sugg Franklin, Peter Crowe Franklin, Charles G. Franklin II, John Lee Franklin, Alice Blackwell Franklin, David Laurence Gordon an Carroll Halliday Gordon. -*Submitted by Frieda Wells and Mimi Gordon*

CARMEN DELLA FREY

Carmen Della Frey, born July 25, 1955 in Hopkins Co., KY, was the third of three children born to Edgar Mitchell Frey and Helen Canepa Frey.

Edgar Mitchell Frey, born July 8, 1910 in Henderson Co., KY, was the only child of John Madison Frey and Della Billings Frey.

Helen Canepa Frey, born Apr. 22, 1915, in Yuma, AZ, was the first of two children born to Edward Joseph Canepa and Carmen Canepa.

Edgar and Helen Frey first came to Madisonville, KY, in March 1943. Edgar was working for Mauger Construction Co. when he moved his family to Madisonville. He retired in 1975, after 32 years of service with Peabody Coal. Co.

Carmen has one sister and one brother. Her sister, Linda Frey Hall, married William Earl Hall and they currently reside in Louisville, KY. They have three sons; Robert Mitchell Hall, Randall William Hall, and John Frey Hall.

Carmen's brother is John Edward Frey. He is currently living in Madisonville, KY.

Carmen Della Frey has received her B.S. Degree from Belmont College, Nashville, TN, and her M.A.E. Degree from Western Kentucky University, Bowling Green, KY. She is working for the Simpson County Board of Educaiton in Franklin, KY. She has been teaching in Franklin for the past ten years.- *Submitted by Carmen Della Frey*

GEORGE FUGATE

George Fugate was born circa 1765. It is known that he lived in Virginia and in Bourbon, Muhlenberg and Hopkins Co., KY. He was living in Hopkins Co., KY by 1807, as his name appears on the Hopkins County tax list of 1807. George Fugate owned two hundred acres of land on Pond River in Hopkins County and had joint ownership with Arthur Slaton of another one hundred acres on Pond River.

George Fugate was married to Martha Howell, daughter of William Howell (who served in the Virginia Continental Line during the Revolutionary War) and Letitia Lewis Howell.

George and Martha Fugate were the parents

of seven known children: Sally Fugate born 1784 (or before) married William Berry; Katherine Fugate born Apr. 20, 1790, married Arthur Slaton; Letty Fugate born in 1791, married William Clift; Zachariah Fugate born circa 1794 married Elizabeth Wilson; Lewis Fugate born July 5, 1797 married Nancy Ashby; Martin L. Fugate born in 1804 married Nancy Wilson; and Polly Fugate.

George Fugate died circa 1830 in Hopkins Co., KY. - *Compiled by Beverly H. Dockrey*

ZACHARIAH FUGATE

Zachariah Fugate was born in Kentucky circa 1794, the son of George and Martha Howell Fugate.

In Hopkins Co., KY on Sept. 4, 1820, Zachariah was married to Elizabeth (Betsy) Wilson, daughter of James Wilson, Sr. Elizabeth Wilson was born in Virginia circa 1804 and died in Hopkins Co., KY between 1870 and 1880.

Zachariah and Betsy Wilson Fugate were the parents of eight known children: Thomas Fugate born circa 1821, married (1) Nancy Raines and (2) Martha S. Foley; George Washington Fugate born circa 1822, married (1) Miranda E. F. Lovan (2) Emmeline H. Coleman and (3) Mary C. Wise; Nancy Ann Fugate born Aug. 23, 1828, married John Wesley Lovan; James Clark Fugate born Mar. 25, 1831, married Ruth Ann Stride; Mary Jane Fugate born circa 1832, married Hilliard Littlepage; Sarah Elizabeth Fugate born circa 1837, married William Richard Morgan; William L. Fugate born July 8, 1838, married Alice M. Lovan; Henry H. Fugate born circa 1841.

Zachariah Fugate was a farmer. He died May 31, 1871 in Hopkins Co., KY and is buried in Flat Creek Cemetery near Mortons Gap, KY. - *Complied by Beverly H. Dockrey*

HERSHELL FULMER

Born 2/20/1906 in Tennessee, Hershell was one of 10 children, one dying in infancy. He was the son of Mary Ellen and George Fulmer. He attended school in Centerville, TN, where his father was a policeman. Fellow students gave him the nickname of "Flea", because of his short stature and quickness on the football field. One of his schoolmates was the now-famous "Minnie Pearl" of Grand Ole Opery fame. Hershell worked for the Borden Milk Company, married Louise Banks and had no children.

Hershell Fulmer

He served in the Merchant Marines in W.W. II and was stationed in Liverpool, England. He went to work for the Greyhound Bus Lines as a traveling auditor. After his divorce he came to Madisonville and bought the bus depot in 1945, where he later met his 2nd wife. Hershell built the present station as it stands now. He was married in 1948 to Isabelle Lloyd Mitchell. Isabelle had a son, William Lee, by a former marriage (see Cates and Lloyd). William Lee was the only child in Hershell's life and so became his pride and joy, as were the 4 grandchildren in later years. Hershell sold the bus station in 1950 and went to work for Western Ky. Gas Co. After 17 1/2 years, he retired in 1967. The picture above was made at his retirement dinner.

In the 50's, the Fulmers bought a few acres of land north of Nebo on Liberty Road. The Webster Co. line ran just behind the new home they built, putting a part of their acreage in both counties. Hershell's hobby was growing things, mainly vine fruits. His strawberries, blackberries, raspberries, gooseberries and vegetable gardens were his pride. Many of the neighbors reaped the benefits. His profit was more enjoyment that the revenue he received. Hershell was a member of the Eagles and Elks Lodges, also the Lion's Club. He attended the Nebo Baptist Church. His mother-in-law, Mrs. Ila Lloyd, made her home with the Fulmers for 19 years. Hershell's first heart attack came in the late 1970's. Surgery soon followed, a plastic tube was inserted in the lower artery of the heart. The tough little "flea" had to slow down, no longer jump through or run the "passes"; but his eternal youth and quick wit still made him a good host and entertainer. Hershell's warm smile and "Howda Neighbor!" will ever be remembered. - *By Dorothy Miller Shoulders*

FURGERSON-TOWNSEND

Thelma Geraldine Townsend was born in Webster Co., KY on Apr. 28, 1910. Her father was Aaron Hubert Townsend who was born in Webster Co., KY on Sept. 25, 1890, to Roland Gooch Townsend and Sallie Evelyn Clayton. He died in Webster Co., KY, on Aug. 12, 1979. He married Grace Curtright on Apr. 8, 1909 and to this union Geraldine was the only child. Grace Curtright was born in Hopkins Co., KY on Jan. 26, 1892 to Wilbur Forest Curtright and Florence Marshall Springfield. She had one sister Hattie Curtright and a half sister Vaden Killough. Grace was a well-known successful farmer and was also very active in politics. Grace died in Madisonville, KY on Jan. 27, 1970. Geraldine lived on the farm with her mother and maternal grandmother. At age 12, she was sent to Providence, KY to attend high school and then to Bethel Womans College at Hopkinsville, KY. She attended the University of Kentucky from which she received a B.A. Degree. She did graduate work at the Western Reserve University, Cleveland, OH.

She married Charles Emmett Furgerson of Nortonville, KY, on June 15, 1938. They had one child, Sandra Grace Furgerson (Donaldson). She taught school for eight years during her life and finally found her niche in life when she was employed by the state of Kentucky as a child welfare worker for fifteen

Thelma Geraldine (Townsend) Furgerson and daughter Sandra Grace

years. Her education in psychology was continued while working. She retired at age 62 from the state, but was sent to Little Rock, AR, by her mother to help administer the estate of M.D. Springfield, her great uncle. She attempted to retire again but was called to Kentucky by the illness of her mother in 1968. She was administrator to her mothers' estate.

When you receive and leave legacies there is no complete retirement until death. The following are legacies left to her by her ancestors:

"Your word is your bond," "Bankruptcy is a disgrace," "When you spend a nickel you can never get it back," "A stitch in time saves nine," "Do it right or don't do it at all," "Take good care of your chattels," "Everything has a place," "Never condemn a man until you have walked in his moccasins for three moons," "You reap what you sow," and finally the greatest saying of all: "Get an education because no one can take that away from you."

In 1976, Geraldine built a two story home, of Classical Greek Revival architecture, in memory of her ancestors. She named the home "Grace Lands" in honor of her mother, Grace Curtright Townsend.

Other ancestral family names are: Townsend, Curtright, Clayton, Springfield, Humphrey, Miller, Kirkwood, Steen, Ramsey, Cain, Yarbrough, Willis, Henson, Davey, Palmer, Green, Norman, McGriff, Dugan, Carver, Winstead, Tapp, Bourne, Barrick, Johnson, Wroth, Weir, Bumpass, Ashburne, Coffman, Lusk, Herber, Cates, Turner, Cahusac, Gendron, Maham, Mazyak, and Cooper. - *Submitted by Sandra Donaldson*

LINDA RATLIFF GANTT

Linda is a Madisonville native, born Dec. 16, 1947, to Jimmy and Nora Howton Ratliff. She had one brother, Darell Kent Ratliff (May 11, 1954).

She stayed with her grandparents, A.W. and Winnie Gamblin Ratliff, while her parents worked. At five years old, Linda started school with Miss Anna Lou Hatcher at Seminary Street School. Her third grade was in the newly completed West Broadway Elementary, then back to Seminary for 7th and 8th grades. Then she went to Madisonville High School. Western Ky. University was where she did her

Linda Lou Ratliff Gantt

undergraduate studies in Health and Physical Education and minors in Sociology and Mass Media.

Earning a B.S. in education, she started an 8-year teaching career at North Hardin High School in Radcliff. She taught P.E., Anatomy and Physiology, Health and Journalism. She also coached girls' track, helped the J.V. cheerleading and sponsored the school newspaper, "The Trojan."

During this time, Linda met her future husband, Mike Gantt. They married on her 25th birthday and after the brief 1972 Christmas break, went back to work. While teaching, Linda went to night classes, then summer courses at Western to complete her M.A. in Guidance Counseling.

The next year, she and Mike moved to Ft. Sill, OK, for his Advanced Training courses for the Ky. Army National Guard. While there, Linda became the class newsletter editor/publisher and editor of the cookbook they presented as the final issue. She also became a volunteer at the Western Hills Christian Church.

Since the Gantts had hoped to have a family by this time, they finally believed they would not be blessed with children.

Change comes with time, and after settling in Madisonville and getting a home of their own, they were surprised to discover that the flu that prevented them from a Christmas family reunion in Ohio was in fact their first of three children in his beginnings.

Believing she had the flu, she made an appointment to see Dr. C.W. VanHooser, an Internal Medicine specialist, to help her get better. It was he who informed her that she was indeed expecting a child. Being a person of short patience, Linda called her husband at work and told him. He turned pale, got wobbly and said he wouldn't believe it until Dr. Eugene Castle confirmed it, which he did.

Gabriel was born July 25, 1979, and Dr. Manojukmar Shah helped deliver him as well as their other two babies, Rebecca Lynn (Nov. 21, 1982) and Christopher Michael (July 13, 1985).

Christianity has been very important in the Gantts' lives and continues to give guidance, direction and comfort to them. Mike began in Church of God and Pentecostal Church while Linda went to Richland Missionary Baptist, then First Christian Disciples of Christ in Madisonville and Bowling Green, then both served in Elizabethtown Independent First Christian Church where Mike was baptized. In Oklahoma, they were members of Western Hills Christian and now they are members of Grapevine Christian Church where they strive to serve Jesus Christ.-*Submitted by Linda Ratliff Gantt*

MICHAEL FRANK GANTT

Michael Frank Gantt was born in Bellevue, OH, on Jan. 20, 1948, to James Marion and Maxine Weeston Gantt. Mike's father, Jim Gantt (June 1, 1924) was from near Concord, NC, where his parents, Frank Alexander Gantt (May 5, 1896-June 9, 1961) and Lillian Mathitas Crisco (May 23, 1903-Mar. 2, 1984), were born.

Michael Frank Gantt

Maxine Weeston Gantt (Aug. 21, 1923-Feb. 27, 1969) was an Ohio native whose grandparents all had emigrated from Germany in the late 1800's. Her parents were Frank Henry Weeston (1893-1961) and Helen Gertrude Baumann (1895-Aug. 26, 1973).

Mike's siblings are John Allen (Aug. 27, 1951), James Robert (June 18, 1950), Judith Kay (Sept. 18, 1955), and half-siblings are Peggy Jean (Dec. 11, 1972), Paul Andrew (July 13, 1974) and Jennifer Sue (Nov. 23, 1976).

As the oldest child, Mike learned to work hard and share his income to help the family. He began as a newspaper boy and has been working, going to school or both ever since.

At school he showed his athletic abilities particularly in high school football, winning the "most fumbles caused" trophy for his senior year. After his 1966 graduation from Bowling Green Senior High School, he went to Bowling Green University for a short time.

Only two months after his mother was killed in a car accident, Mike was drafted into the Army as many were during the Viet Nam War. Basic training was at Ft. Gordon, GA, were he also took M.P. school. Officers' Training school was at Ft. Sill, OK.

Mike came to Ft. Knox as a training officer, fully expecting to be sent into combat at any time, but was spared that experience. It was during his last year of active duty that he met Linda Lou Ratliff, a native of Madisonville, KY. It was nearly two years later (Dec. 16, 1972) that they wed.

After they married, Linda continued to teach in Radcliff while Mike worked in the Kentucky Army National Guard and had a job in internal operations at Radcliff's Ft. Knox Bank. He went to the Elizabethtown Community College, then completed his accounting degree at Western Ky. University in 1977.

Mike's NG position called for an Advanced Officers Training, so Linda quit teaching and they both went to Ft. Sill, OK, to be "regular Army" for an eight month's stay.

Returning to Kentucky, the Gantts searched for a permanent home and a steady job for Mike. The middle of 1978 he started with York in Madisonville and August 29, they moved into their new home.

Their children are Gabriel Baxter (July, 25, 1979), Rebecca Lynn (Nov. 21, 1982) and Christopher Michael (July 13, 1985).

As of 1987 Mike is Battalion Commander of the 1/623 Field Artillery Post in Glasgow and is Senior Accountant Analyst at York International Corp.'s Madisonville plant. *Submitted by Linda Lou Ratliff Gantt*

REV. ROBERT GARDINER

Reverend Gardiner was one of the pioneers of Methodism in Madisonville. His granddaughter, the late Isabel Gardiner, was active in the Madisonville Methodist Church for over fifty years, and the present Isabel Gardiner Sunday School class is named for her.

Jacobena E. Wright Gardiner and Rev. Robert George Gardiner

Robert George Gardiner was born May 22, 1806, in Aldington, County Kent, England. A graduate of Oxford, he spoke three languages and led a studious life, keeping up well with the current thought of the times in theology, science, literature, and the humanities until a few days before his death on April 23, 1888.

Confirmed in the Church of England, Robert Gardiner joined the Wesleyan Methodists in August, 1922. On Mar. 17, 1830, he set sail for America and landed in New York on May 17. In 1836 Reverend Gardiner was received on trial by the Kentucky Conference and preached over a great part of Kentucky for the rest of his life, including the Shelby, Madisonville, Princeton, Hodgenville, Greensburg, and Bowling Green circuits. Redford's "Western Cavaliers," Nashville, 1878, states: "He was a most industrious and useful preacher." When Reverend Gardiner rode the Madisonville Circuit on horseback, he had forty-one different appointments to fill. It is said he carried with him a claw hammer so that he could bark the trees as he went on his rounds to thus enable him to retrace his steps.

He married Jacobena Eleanor Wright of Graves Co. in 1840. Together they established and conducted the Hardinsburg Female High

School from 1852 until the Civil War.

A chaplain in the 27th Regiment, Kentucky Infantry during the Civil War, his sympathies and careful nursing help were active with the blue and grey alike, when sick in hospital or wounded on the field of battle. He was a strong man physically, and although he died lacking one month of being eighty-two years of age, it is probable his life was cut shorter by exposure on the tented field. Active as a preacher, mason, lecturer, and faithful worker in the Chautauqua Circle, he died Master of his Lodge and Chaplain of the Grand Lodge of Kentucky.- *Submitted by Margaret Berry*

DR. THOMAS GARDINER

Thomas Wright Gardiner was born Oct. 9, 1848, in Daviess Co., KY, near Owensboro. He was the son of the Reverend Robert G. Gardiner and Mrs. Jacobena Eleanor (Wright) Gardiner. Reverend Gardiner, a Methodist Episcopal Church minister, served as a chaplain during the Civil War and often was accompanied by his son. (See Rev. Robert George Gardiner article.)

Dr. Thomas W. Gardiner and Mollie Weatherly Gardiner

Thomas W. Gardiner graduated from Louisville Medical College in 1872. Dr. Gardiner moved to Madisonville in 1876 and was a practicing physician until 1886 when he entered the drug business, although he continued to aid those who sought his advice. He was senior member of the Gardiner & Bowmer drug firm of South Main Street until his death, Aug. 7, 1929.

In 1886 he married Mollie Weatherly, daughter of Henrietta and George L. Weatherly of Madisonville. (See George Lawson Weatherly article.) Miss Weatherly had received the first School Teacher's Certificate of record in Hopkins Co. on Aug. 9, 1879. It was a First Class Certificate good for four years and the general average given to her on the examination was the unbeaten figure of 100.

In 1888 Dr. Gardiner built the brick house on the Northeast corner of Sugg and Seminary Streets. The house remains in the Gardiner family today, soon to celebrate its 100th birthday.

Recognized throughout Kentucky as a mental disease specialist, Dr. Gardiner was appointed superintendent of the Western Kentucky State Hospital, Hopkinsville, in March 1897 by Governor W.O. Bradley, Republican. As superintendent, he recommended and fought for reform in the treatment of the mentally ill. In his report to Governor Bradley in 1898 he stated: "There was an unusual number of old, harmless, incurable, idiotic and imbecile patients admitted who should have been kept at their homes or maintained by their respective counties." He criticized the lunacy laws saying: "Trial of a case of lunacy by a jury, usually composed of farmers or others equally ignorant of mental diseases, is a travesty, if not a serio-comic farce. Before such a tribunal, an accusation of insanity by a friend or relative is usually sufficient to cause a verdict of guilty and the accused becomes a charge upon the state. Mental disease is not considered a crime, and a person so afflicted should not be tried by criminal procedure." Governor J.C.W. Beckham, Democrat, appointed Dr. Gardiner Chairman of the State Board of Control, which became the Charities and Corrections Board, and had jurisdiction over the State's Penal Institutions and Hospitals. He served as a City Councilman in Madisonville and as a member of the Board of Education. He was a member of the County Election Board at the time of his death.

Dr. Gardiner was a very perceptive man, and the years he spent as a state official saw the institutions over which he had control flourish under the modern, wholesome methods he inaugurated.- *Submitted by Margaret Berry*

JOYCE GARRETT

Joyce Miller Garrett was born in McLean County at the residence of her parents, approximately five miles from Island, KY on May 16, 1943. She has one older sister, Darlene B. Bowman. She also has three older brothers and one younger brother: Kenneth D. Miller, Billy R. Miller, Duard A. Miller who is her twin, and Rufus M. Miller.

Joyce's mother was Mildred Davis. She was born at Rumsey in McLean County on Mar. 6, 1908, the youngest of twelve children.

Joyce's father was Marvin Augustus Miller. He was born in McLean County at Livermore on Sept. 14, 1908, the youngest of three children.

On Dec. 21, 1963, Joyce married Donald R. Garrett. They are the parents of three children: Robin Dawn was born on Sept. 5, 1964 and is married to Jimmy D. Suttle and they reside in Dawson Springs; David Paul was born on Aug. 27, 1969; and Jonathan Troy was born on May 7, 1972. Both sons still reside at home. David, Jonathan and their father are avid golfers and enjoy other sports also.

Joyce has been employed for the late Dr. James Salmon and also at Outwood. She presently is employed for Dr. James F. Britt at Britt Chiropractic Life Center. She enjoys gardening, growing roses and reading. - *Submitted by Johnny Garrett*

GATLIN-BERRY

Charles M. Stodghill (b Jan. 17, 1880 d Nov. 25, 1951) and Leona Sisk (b. Sept. 26, 1879 d. Mar. 4, 1954) were married in Hopkins County. They were the parents of Bonnie (b July 27, 1900 d Dec. 21 198-) who married Clinton William Gatlin (b Jan. 22, 1898 d. Oct. 7, 1985); Paul Stodghill who married Idell Newman; and Raymond M. Stodghill (b May 29, 1906 d Mar. 3, 1937). Charley, Leona and

W.C. (Dub) and Beth Owen Gatlin on their 50th Wedding Anniversary April 3, 1987

Raymond are buried in Grapevine Cemetery, also Bonnie and Clinton Gatlin.

Bonnie (Stodghill) Gatlin and Clinton Wm. Gatlin were parents of W.C. (Dub) Gatlin, born May 5, 1918. He is married to Beth Owen Berry b. Oct. 14, 1919, dau. of Andrew D. (Andy) Berry (b. Mar. 24, 1892 d Apr. 17, 1942), and Jessie (Owen) Berry (b Dec. 21, 1891 d Dec. 8, 1983), dau. of the late Emily Jane Webster and Robert Nathanial Owen of Manitou.

Andy Berry was the son of John Wm. Berry (b June 21, 1860 d Sept. 24, 1923) and Virginia (Winders) Berry (b Nov. 11, 1859 d Apr. 17, 1947). They moved from Todd Co. to Hopkins County and lived near St. Charles. They are buried in the St. Charles Christian Privilege Cemetery, and Grapevine Cemetery, respectively.

W.C. and Beth Gatlin reside in Madisonville. W.C. is semi-retired from farming-mining, and Beth is a retired Beautician. They observed their 50th Wedding Anniversary on Apr. 3, 1987. They have four children:

Charles Wayne Gatlin b Feb. 13, 1938, married Carolyn Nance b Nov. 16, 1943, daughter of Raymond Nance and the late Dorothy Nance of Slaughters. Charles is employed at Charolais Strip Mining Co., and they live in Madisonville. Children are Lori Ann Gatlin born Oct. 11, 1961 who married Joey Dickerson, b Apr. 27, 1959. They have one son, Kyle Joseph Dickerson b Dec. 9, 1985. Tara Denise Gatlin born Dec. 27, 1971 is a sophomore at Madisonville-North Hopkins.

Betty Jean Gatlin b Nov. 25, 1940 married Lewis Stanley b Oct. 14, 1938, son of Lewis and Lucille (Fletcher) Stanley of near Mortons Gap. Lewis is a Federal mine inspector and teaches classes at Madisonville Community College. Their children are Kimberly Jo Stanley b Oct. 16, 1959, who is an LPN at Donaldson Hospital, Donaldson, TN; Ginger Gail Stanley b Mar. 12, 1964, employed at the Log House Pre-School, Madisonville; Amanda Elizabeth b Apr. 6, 1977, is in 5th grade at Hanson School. The Lewis family lives in Madisonville.

Judith Gail Gatlin b May 10, 1943 (twin) is married to Herman Edward Adkins Jr. b Mar. 20, 1942, son of Herman and Marie (Babb) Adkins. He is employed at U.C. Milk Co. Their children are: Robert E. Adkins b Feb. 21-1963 who married Tammy Burden b May 3, 1962. Robert works for the City of Madisonville;

Patricia Gail Adkins b Apr. 27, 1966 is married to Roy Hibbs b Oct, 5, 1960, who is employed by Madisonville Cablevision. They have one son, Jeremy Ryan Hibbs b. Feb. 19, 1987. They live in Madisonville.

Robert (Bob) Dale Gatlin b May 10, 1943 (twin) is single, lives in Jacksonville, FL and is an employee of Cain and Bultman, Inc. distributors.

Andy and Jessie Berry also had a son, W.D. (Dub) Berry b Feb. 11, 1921 who married Jo Ann Bojak of Chicago. They have three children: Barbara Jo married Mike Bold, resides in Chicago; Susan Berry married Donald Marzonia, and they reside in Cape Coral, FL; Michael David Berry is married and lives in Chicago.

Andy Berry at age 11 became delivery boy with wagon and team in St. Charles for St. Bernard Coal Co., and later he worked in the Company Store. He served as St. Charles Police Judge for five terms, with appointments coming from Gov. Ruby Laffoon and Gov. A.B. Chandler.

Beth's grandfather Berry was bedfast the last few years of his life, and she remembers that he would hook his walking cane handle around the necks of the children to pull them close to his bed to talk to them. Se was afraid of him so she tried to avoid getting "hooked". Beth remembers that she and brother Dub Berrry would slide down the hug slack pile in St. Charles, and then get whippings for getting their clothes black with slack dust. -*Submitted by Beth Owen (Berry) Gatlin Written by Rella G. Jenkins*

R. HARPER GATTON

R. Harper Gatton was born Feb. 1, 1891, in Madison, IN, the son of a Baptist minister, J.S. Gatton, and Amy Smallwood Gatton. At his age 2, the family moved to Eminence, KY.

In 1912, Mr. Gatton graduated from Georgetown College, earned an M.A. from Univ. of Chicago, did graduate work at Columbia University and returned to Georgetown College for his Doctorate in 1936.

In 1912, Mr. Gatton came to Madisonville to become high school principal, at the age of 21. Because of his excellent leadership, in 1914 he became superintendent of the Madisonville Public Schools, a job he held for 38 years (1914-1952). Through his influence and guidance, great improvements in the school system were made, with more schools being built, the curriculum improved, accreditation achieved for the schools, and Madisonville High School accepted as a member of the Southern Assoc., which enabled MHS graduates to enter college without having to take an entrance exam. He went beyond the call of duty to achieve what he believed to be the best.

Other educational achievements were active member and president of KEA; for 47 years a trustee of Georgetown College, and 23 years as trustee of Univ. of KY; he served as chairman of the KY Textbook Commission; and was president of the National Beta Club.

In his zeal for civic improvements, Mr. Gatton served as president of the local Kiwanis International in 1927, and later as governor of the KY-Tenn. Kiwanis District. He was on the International Board, was Vice-Pres., and then became International president in 1935-36.

Other organizations benefitting from Harper Gatton's outstanding abilities were Rizpah Shrine Temple as potentate; Federal Emergency Relief Administration as state director; and his membership in KY Crippled Children's Commission. For years he was a local leader in the Chamber of Commerce, and in 1951 he left Madisonville to become executive Vice-Pres. of the Kentucky Chamber of Commerce in Louisville, where he remained until 1961. He then returned to Madisonville where he remained faithful in the local Chamber of Commerce until his fatal illness.

Harper Gatton was first married to Miss Margaret Frances Lackey, who died Dec. 20, 1920. Their two daughters are Winona (Gatton) McCandless McCall, and Margaret (Gatton) Findt. In the summer of 1927, while Mr. Gatton was teaching at Western KY State College in Bowling Green, he met Miss Alice Linkenberg of Louisville, who was then teaching music at Western. They were married Feb. 16, 1928, and lived in Madisonville, with Mr. Gatton as Supt. of Schools and Mrs. Gatton teaching music at Madisonville H.S.

The talented Mrs. Gatton developed a program of vocal music in the school system, which brought honors and inspired many young people to pursue music careers. For many years she served as organist and choir director at the First United Methodist Church.

Mr. Gatton was active in First Baptist Church, being a deacon and an outstanding Bible class teacher for many years.

He was much in demand for speeches to civic and educational meetings. He was admired and respected by all who had the privilege to benefit from his teachings and acquaintance. He had countless friends everywhere, throughout Kentucky and across the nation, being one of Madisonville's most outstanding and long-remembered citizens.

Harper Gatton died Oct. 27, 1965, at the age of 74, after giving 53 years of service to education, civic affairs, church, business and industry—a man who excelled in everything he did.- *Submitted by Rella G. Jenkins for Winona (Gatton) McCandless McCall*

THE GILL BROTHERS

Accompanying their mother Mary Gill, two brothers arrived in Hopkins Co. by 1805 after traveling from Chester Co., SC, over the arduous Wilderness Road. They had turned south through the middle of Tennessee, then north into Kentucky just before reaching Nashville. These two brothers, George and William Gill, left Hopkins Co. in its early history, but another brother, Isaac, who had stayed back in South Carolina, later moved to Hopkins Co. and left descendents in the area.

George Gill Jr. (1775-1848) married Jane Carter, daughter of John and Patsy Carter, and paid taxes in 1807 on over 1,200 acres in Hopkins Co. The next year he and three other men were authorized by the Hopkins Co. Court to "view a way for a road to be made from Madisonville to the county line toward Shawneetown."

In November, 1811, George fought under the command of General Harrison in the Battle of Tippecanoe. During the winter of 1815 he and his family left Kentucky, making their home on the White River near Batesville, AR. He was an early Justice of the Peace and surveyor there, and was the earliest circuit riding Baptist preacher in northern Arkansas. A prolific writer of articles and sermons, he was known as "George the Scribe." The children of George Jr. and Jane Gill were: Tabitha, born 1806; Isaac, 1807; Addison, 1809; Mary, 1812; William, 1814; John C., 1816; George III, 1818; Silas Redmon, 1821.

William Gill left Hopkins Co. by 1811, and may have been the one who showed up in Union Co., KY, that same year. He was a farmer, who with his wife Mary had at least two sons, one named William, and several daughters. He served on the first grand jury of that county, and at his death in 1848 his estate inventory showed he owned many books.

Isaac Gill (-d. 1834) was a watchmaker like his father, and while living in South Carolina he patented a timepiece in 1810. In 1820 he and his wife Ann Caroline moved to Hopkins Co. He bought Madisonville town lots 60, 61, and 62 (across the street from the northeast corner of the public square, running north). Two of those lots were later sold to his nephew, Orlean Bishop of "Bishop and Woodson and Co." By 1830 he had moved to Henderson Co., and died there four years later. Ann Caroline died in 1839, leaving children: Mary E. Barnard, Eliza G., Maria Louisa, William Y., and Joseph L. Gill.

Joseph Gill (1789-1855) married Martha Browder, daughter of Ishram, in 1816, and lived on a farm near his mother in Hopkins Co. However, by 1820 they left for Missouri, where he bought farm land and several town lots in Fayette. He was also a watchmaker, and served as one of the first trustees for the town. He later moved to Benton Co., MO, where he died. Joseph and Martha's children were: Zereldah (moved back to Henderson Co., KY), Edwin R., Elbert J., Thomas, Ira, William T., and Mary.- *Submitted by Twyla Gill Wright*

GILL-DURHAM

Mertyl Mae Durham and Lyman L. Gill were married Aug. 21, 1915 in Edwards Co., IL, by her father, Rev. Patrick M. Durham.

Mertyl (Durham) and Lyman L. Gill on their 50th wedding anniversary, 1965

Mertyl was born in Nebo, KY, in Hopkins Co., Apr. 13, 1896, the 7th of nine children born to Patrick Monroe (1866-1946) and Fannie Lea (Hall) Durham (1869-1953), she being the daughter of John E. Hall (1841-1910) and Sarah Elizabeth (Lawson) Hall (1846-1895). Patrick M. and Fannie Lea Durham's children were: Iva Elizabeth Taylor (1885-1972); Clara Ann Burton (1887-1959); John (1889-1937); Clayton (1892-1964); Clinton (1892-1893); Tinia Pearl (1895-1895); Mertyl Mae Gill (1896-1965); Virginia Shurtleff (1899-1974); and Marvin (1905-1974).

Mertyl's paternal grandparents were David Monroe Durham (1832-1897) and Virginia Ann Ford Durham (1842-1931). The David Durhams were parents of eight children: America Ellen Connelly (1858-1947); Nancy Ann Harris (1860-1936); Mary Isabel Hibbs (1863-1954); Patrick Monroe (1866-1946); David Milton (1868-1932); Louisa Elizabeth Hibbs (1871-1952); Nellie Durham (1873-1918); and Lillian May Hibbs (1876-1954).

The maternal grandparents of Mertyl (Durham) Gill were: John E. and Elizabeth (Lawson) Hall. They were the parents of Robert (1866-1926); Fannie Lea Durham (1869-1953); John F. (1874-1934); Edmund (1877-?); Annie Morgan (1879-1960); and Grace Keller (1888-1942).

Patrick M. Durham and his family moved to Edwards Co., IL, in the early 1900's, where he was engaged in the ministry until his death. This is where Mertyl met Lyman L. Gill and they were married with the following children being born to them: Robert (1917-1976); Kenneth Monroe (1922) and Virginia Elizabeth (1925).

Robert was minister of Christian Church of Jacksonville, FL, at the time of his death. He was ordained into the ministry by his grandfather, Rev. Patrick M. Durham. His widow is Nelle Irene (Dunn) Gill, and his two daughters are Kathy Marsh (1951) and Cheryl (1954), all of Jacksonville, FL.

Kenneth Gill married Anna Louise Hogue (1923-1963) in 1941. They had two daughters, Charlotte McKechnie (1944), of Albion, IL, and Karin Gray (1948), of Ada, MI. After the death of his first wife, Kenneth married Patricia (Henderson) Hedrick and her children are: Cindy Hocking (1950) of Albion, IL, Scott (1953) of Noble, IL; and Gil (1956) of Ada, MI. Kenneth and Pat have nine grandchildren.

Virginia Gill married John Tice (1923) and they reside in Olney, IL. They have two sons, John Jr. (1943), of Olney, IL, and Steven Ray (1947), of Springfield, IL. Virginia and John have three grandchildren, Amy Elizabeth (1970), of Olney, IL, Anthony Christopher (1971) of Springfield, IL, and Jennifer Ann (1975) also of Springfield, IL.- *Submitted by Virginia Tice*

GILL-WALLACE

Wilma Jean Wallace was born in Fairfield, IL on Nov. 10, 1930. On May 28, 1949 in Evansville, IN, Jean married H. Ralph Gill. Ralph was born Apr. 6, 1924.

Ralph and Jean have three children. Debi Layne, the oldest, was born Dec. 9, 1950. Mark Duane was born Dec. 20, 1955, and Joy Lynn was born June 10, 1958. Debi Layne is married to Bill Vance who is the pastor at a Baptist Church in Ridgetop, TN. They are the parents of two daughters, Casey Lynn who is 12 years old, and Cathy Jean who is nine years old.

Mark Duane is married to Debbie and they have no children. Mark works as a Youth Minister in the Dawson Springs First Baptist Church. They lived in Madisonville from March 1986 to December 1986, when Mark was a Youth Minister in the Second Baptist Church. Joy Lynn has a son, Evan Tate Faulk, who is five years old and attends kindergarten.

Ralph and Jean moved to Paducah, KY in 1969. After four years, they moved to Madisonville, Hopkins County, KY. Ralph started out at Grapevine Baptist Church, but is now the pastor of Park Avenue Baptist Church in Madisonville.

Jean is a very talented lady and her favorite hobby is tole painting. She paints for the joy, but some of her work is just as good as professional paintings. The Oliver's Restaurant in Dawson Springs, KY has some of her paintings exhibited. When the Gill's lived in Cadiz, KY, some of her work was on exhibit at the Trigg County Welcome Center. Jean does not only like to paint, but she also likes to sew. Most of the presents the Gill's give away are made by Jean and most of the decorations in their home are her work.

Since Ralph is a pastor, church is an important factor in their life. The church has helped them to rear their children in a peaceful home and with God's help, the Gill's have a happy life. - *Submitted by Linda Mathisen*

HILDA KIRKWOOD GILL

Hilda Baird Kirkwood was born Aug. 4, 1921. She was one of four children. Elizabeth (1920) married Alfred Grace (1920) and they have two children. Mac Grace (1948) married to Patricia Adams, and George Grace (1949) married to Elizabeth Smith. They reside in Henderson. James Gamblin Kirkwood was a twin to Elizabeth. He was killed in World War II. He has one son, James Utley. Mary Ray Kirkwood (1918-1973) married Rodman Clark (1916-1979). Two children: Serena Kay Clark (1955) married Kenneth Thomas Williams (1953), they have two children; and David Michael Clark (1960) has two children. They all reside in Providence.

Hilda Baird Kirkwood Gill

Hilda was born in Hopkins Co. She moved only shortly during the war while her husband worked in the shipyards in Evansville, IN. She worked as a beautician in Dawson before her marriage to Kenneth Marlow Gill of Earlington on Dec. 29, 1941. She is retired from the Enro Shirt Factory. They reside in Earlington. They have three children. Kenneth Kirk Gill born Nov. 27, 1943, married Dianne Hauprich born Aug. 7, 1945. They have two children: John Kirk born Aug. 16, 1971, and Katrina Lynn born June 25, 1975. They reside in Sebree.

Joseph Lee Gill born Nov. 16, 1945, married Lee Mills born Sept. 11, 1947. They have two children: Joseph Scott Gill born Aug. 19, 1969, and Michelle Lea born May 27, 1972. They reside in Madisonville. Martha Ann Gill Downing born Feb. 4, 1946, has one daughter Melissa Ann born Oct. 19, 1980. They reside in Earlington.

Hilda's great great great grandfather, Hugh Kirkwood, came here as a small boy from Ireland. He is mentioned in "Major Gordon's History of Hopkins County" as being a pioneer of Hopkins Co. He fought with General Jackson at the Battle of New Orleans. Kirkwood Springs is named for Jim Kirkwood. It was once a thriving spa of hotels, a stagecoach line, post office, and mineral springs.

The Kirkwoods were for the most part farmers in Hopkins Co. However, they were also druggists, grist mill and saw mill owners, and soldiers.

Hilda's father, George Rudy Kirkwood (1894-1965), married Clara Edith Gamblin (1891-1961). Hilda's paternal ancestry is: grandparents - George Dallas Kirkwood (1849-1924) married Mary L. Curtwright (1865-1922). Great grandparents - Isaac Newton Kirkwood (1825-1917) married Lucinda Utley (1825-1908). Great great grandparents - James Kirkwood (1803-1858) married Mary Polly Sisk (circa 1806). Great great great grandparents - Hugh Kirkwood from Ireland (1767-1855) married Catherine (circa 1768) and the second Martha (circa 1771). Her maternal ancestry is: grandparents - Charles Madison Gamblin (1854-1936) married Mary Ray Browning (1856-1876). Great grandparents - Madison Gamblin (circa 1821) married Lou Anna Franklyn (circa 1828). William Browning (1828-1882) married Mary Doll Lovan (1831-1863). - *Submitted by Dianne Hauprich Gill*

JAMES GILL

James Gill came to Hopkins Co. in the 1850's. He and his son William and William's family moved from Olive Hill, Wayne Co., TN. Part of their land was also in neighboring Hardin Co. They resided in the Rose Creek area of Hopkins Co.

James' first wife was Nancy per the 1850 Tennessee census. However, when James appeared in the 1860 Hopkins Co. census, Malissa Peyton is listed as his wife. After James' death Malissa married James Givens.

The children of James and Nancy were Hamilton (B Circa 1831), E. Green (B Circa 1833), James (B Circa 1838), Frances (B Circa 1840), Harrison (B Circa 1841), E.E. (B Circa 1843), John Taylor (B Circa 1846). William was born circa 1821. William's trade was blacksmith. James and E. Green remained in Tennessee to oversee their father's land and business there.

Hopkins Co. courthouse records show that on Apr. 17, 1889, William Bird Gill donated 7/

8 acre to Rose Creek Church and the Rose Creek neighborhood for a cemetery. On Nov. 20, 1894, William donated one acre of his Rose Creek farmland for the construction of the Bethany Methodist Episcopal Church. However, I cannot find whether or not the church was ever actually built.

While it cannot be connected at this time, it should be noted that in 1798 to 1800 widow Mary Gill and her children settled in the same Rose Creek area. Mary and her children, George, Isaac, Joseph, William, Mary Bishop, and Hannah Graham came from Fishing Creek, Chester Co., SC. Mary is buried in Rose Creek Cemetery. With a twenty year Gill absence, James and William moved to the same area of Rose Creek.

James Gill is the great grandfather of Dudley Gill of Madisonville and Kenneth Marlow Gill of Earlington. William Bird Gill is the grandfather of Dudley, and John T. is the grandfather of Kenneth.- *Submitted by Dianne Hauprich Gill*

KENNETH MARLOW GILL

Kenneth Marlow Gill was born Jan. 17, 1914. He is the oldest of three children. Emma Nelda Gill was born Mar. 31, 1919, and resides in Indianapolis with her husband Thomas Bryant, born June 12, 1914. They have two children, Kenny Wayne and Kay Elaine. They and their children also live in Indianapolis. Harold Dudley Gill was born Apr. 2, 1917, and died Aug. 20, 1917.

Kenneth Marlow Gill

Kenneth was born in Earlington where he has lived most of his life, only leaving to work in the shipyards in Evansville, IN, during the war. He worked at North Diamond Mine and retired from Pleasant View Mine.

On Dec. 29, 1941, Kenneth married Hilda Baird Kirkwood, born Aug. 4, 1921, from Suthards. They have three children, Kenny Kirk Gill, born Nov. 27, 1943. He is married to Dianne Hauprich, born Aug. 7, 1945, from New York. They have two children, Katrina Lynn Gill, born June 25, 1975, and John Kirk Gill, born Aug. 16, 1971. They reside in Sebree, KY. Joseph Lee Gill, born Nov. 16, 1945, married Lee Mills, born Sept. 11, 1947, from Mortons Gap. They have two children, Michelle Lea Gill, born May 27, 1972, and Joseph Scott Gill, born Aug. 19, 1969. They reside in Madisonville. Martha Ann Downing, born Feb. 4, 1947, has one daughter, Melissa Ann, born Oct. 19, 1980. They reside in Earlington.

The Gills have been in Hopkins Co. since early 1800's. George Gill surveyed the road from Madisonville to Shawneetown, IL. Mary Gill, a widow, migrated from Chester Co., SC, with her children. They settled in Rose Creek area. Kenneth's great grandfather came to Hopkins Co. from Tennessee also settling in the Rose Creek area.

Kenneth's father Green Gill (1885-1928) married Lavona Belle Oldham (B 1889). His paternal ancestry is: grandparents - John Taylor Gill (1846-1918) married Laura Scott (1844-1891), great grandparents - James Gill (1801-1863) married first Nancy (B 1804) and second Malissa Peyton (B 1814). Laura Scott's parents were Adam D. Scott (1811-1889) and Jamima Howard (1821-1889). Kenneth's maternal ancestry is: grandparents - Hiram Oldham (1860-1918) married Lucy M. Lamb (1861-1924), great grandparents William Jackson Lamb (B 1834) married Amanda Roark (1838). Frances Marion Oldham married Martha Boyd.- *Submitted by Dianne Hauprich Gill*

MARY GILL FAMILY

Into the Kentucky hills, shortly after 1800, rode the fifty year old widow Mary Gill, her two young daughters and three sons. Just a few years before, in 1795, they had buried her husband, George Gill, Sr., in Chester Co., SC. She and George had migrated there from Lancaster Co., PA, in 1767. Not only had her husband been a yeoman farmer, but also an established clockmaker, reader of books, and a staunch Presbyterian. As a militiaman under General Sumter in the American Revolution, he had been imprisoned by the British in 1780.

Rose Creek Cemetery, shown in circle

After arriving in present Hopkins Co., KY, Mary Gill claimed 200 acres north of Clear Creek in 1805. The family built a log house on her acreage and cleared fields for planting. Two of her sons, George Jr. and William, soon claimed or bought land around her. Two other sons, Isaac and Abraham, had stayed behind in South Carolina. Abraham and his wife Agnes died there in 1815, and Isaac lived in Charleston, SC. All of Mary's sons eventually left Hopkins Co., but her two daughters, Mary and Hannah, established families whose descendents continued to make their homes in the county.

Young Mary Gill, born in Chester Co., SC, about 1783, married Eli Bishop in Hopkins Co. on Mar. 9, 1809. Eli was a farmer and deputy surveyor in the early decades of the county. To them were born two children. Orlean Bishop, born 1811, married Sarah J.G. Woodson on Nov. 26, 1840. He later became long-time Hopkins Co. Clerk of the Court. His sister, Elvira Bishop, born 1813, married Berry Nichols on Aug. 10, 1836. After Mary's death, sometime between the birth of Elvira and 1818, Eli remarried and had two more daughters: Rosaline, born 1831, and Celeste, 1835.

The widow Mary Gill was perhaps closest to her younger daughter, for Hannah and her husband bought land next to Mary and were there to help care for her in her old age. In 1818 Mary turned her farm and legal affairs over to her daughter's husband.

Hannah Gill was born in Chester Co., SC, in 1785. She married Richard S. Graham, who was a Hopkins Co. yeoman farmer, owner of a tannery, and the "legal eagle" for the family. Their acreage lay next to her mother's on Rose Creek in Nebo district. When Richard died in 1838 he owned considerable property and 10 slaves. He specified that his daughters were to receive as much inheritance as his sons: Harvey, born 1808; Paulina, 1810, m. John Peyton; Alzada, 1811; Elmina, 1815, m. Wiley Parker; Miranda; Olivia, 1823, m. Elijah Baker; Zereldah, 1823, m. Moses Clift; Elvira, 1830, m. R.A. Harris; Leroy; and Cyrus. When Hannah died in 1862 her estate was valued at $17,000.

The Grahams and Mary Gill attended Rose Creek Cumberland Presbyterian Church, which was established near their homes. The widow Mary Gill died in the 80th year of her life on Dec. 15, 1825. She is buried in Rose Creek cemetery, south of Nebo, where her gravestone still stands.- *Submitted by Twyla Gill Wright*

CLARENCE E. GILLESPIE

Clarence Edward Gillespie was born on June 27, 1943 in his grandfather's house in Dawson Springs, KY.

Clarence graduated from Dawson Springs High School in 1961. He enlisted in the Marines in May of 1961. Clarence left the Marines after four years as a corporal.

On Nov. 6, 1965, Clarence married Anna Ruth Laffoon. Their first child, Julie Ann Gillespie, was born on July 10, 1967. Their second child, Laura Lee Gillespie, was born on Mar. 6, 1970.

In April, 1977, Mr. Gillespie became a member of the Star Mine First Aid and Mine Rescue team and the captain of the first aid team.

To keep the teams ready for any emergency, the Mine Heath and Safety Association of the U.S. Government and the Kentucky Department of Mines and Minerals hold contests on the local, state and national levels every year. The Star team has won local contest in Alabama, Illinois and West Virginia. They have won the national titles for first aid in 1983 and 1987 and for combination in 1987.

In December 1979, the team was called into action when a fire broke out on a beltline of Peabody's Mine 10 near Springfield, IL. The fire was fought for several days until the mine had to be sealed off to smother the fire. Tests were run to see if the fire had been smothered. The fire was out, but the percentage of methane was at explosive levels. Six teams, including the Star team, worked for six days using self-contained breathing apparatuses before they reached the area of the fire and assessed the damage.

On another occasion, Mr. Gillespie was called from a dinner engagement in Paducah due to a fire at Peabody's Camp 2 mine in Union County, KY. A fire on the track had gotten out of control. The fire was in an area that had very bad roof conditions, many falls and poor ventilation. The smoke was so thick that they literally could not see their hands in front of their faces.

Mr. Gillespie has never been involved in a mine rescue operation that involved looking for trapped miners. However, when Emory Mine Company's Winberg Mine caught fire in December of 1986, 28 men were trapped and the Star team was making plans to go there. About this time, the fire got totally out of control, and the mine had to be sealed off. Before the mine was sealed, all 28 bodies were found but could not be recovered.

Mr. Gillespie said, "We train hard at something that I hope we never have to use."*Submitted by Laura Gillespie*

GIVENS

The prominent Givens family migrated in numbers to Hopkins Co., KY, from Virginia.

SAMUEL GIVENS*, the immigrant, in 1739 obtained a 1,000 acre grant in Orange Co., VA, soon after entering the colonies via New Castle and Lancaster Co., PA. Four hundred acres were recorded for him in Frederick Co., VA, *Survey Book 1734-58,* land lying on the north side of the James River above Craig's Creek in present day Botetourt Co., VA. SAMUEL (ca 1693 County Antrim, Ireland-1740 Orange Co., VA) m SARAH CATHEY (ca 1700 County Antrim, Ireland-1766/69 VA). SARAH m (2) Rev. Robert Allen of Frederick Co., VA. SAMUEL was one of the founders of the Old Stone Church in Augusta Co., VA, a Justice of the Peace and captain in the militia. Their son:

JOHN (1719 Ireland - 1790 Augusta Co., VA) m MARGARET CRAWFORD (?). JOHN was the father of THOMAS GIVENS who bought 920 acres of land on the Clear Creek branch of the Tradewater River recorded in 1812 in Hopkins Co., Deed Book 1, p. 149. JOHN's sister, Elizabeth Givens, m General Andrew Lewis, a personal friend and favorite officer of George Washington.

THOMAS GIVENS (1767 Virginia-1848 Hopkins Co., KY) m. 1. ELIZABETH "BETSEY" KERR (1769 Virginia-1826 Hopkins Co., KY), d/o James and Jean/Jane Kerr. The Kerr ancestral home, built ca 1740, is still standing in Augusta Co., VA, at the confluence of Christian's Creek, Long Meadow Run and Middle River. It was built by James Kerr's father, James Kerr, the immigrant.

JAMES KERR GIVENS (1794 Virginia-1855 Hopkins Co., KY) m 1. Margaret Poage Given. Issue: Thomas Karr Givens and Eleazer Robertson Givens. m 2. ELIZABETH R. CHRISTIAN* (1803 Kentucky-1871 Kentucky). See CHRISTIAN family. Children of James Kerr and Elizabeth R. Christian Givens: Margaret P.; Mathew, died young; John Christian; Elizabeth Jane; Mathew Campbell; Helen Mar; NATHANIEL KARR (1837 Kentucky-1871 Hopkins Co., KY); James M.; and Martha Jane. NATHANIEL KARR GIVENS and his brother, James M., both served in the Kentucky Confederate Cavalry.

These families, with one known exception—the omission of Margaret-one of John Givens' (1719-1790) eleven children-who married James Agnew in 1788—are all enumerated in *Some Webster County Kentucky Families* by Minerva Bone Bassett, published by Gateway Press, Inc. 1983.

At Home

Dear Children:

It is a source of inexpressible gratitude to me to think that I am once more permitted to write to you and the more to, when I thank that in all probability this may be the last that I shall ever be permitted to write, though I hope that it may be otherwise. I say that it may be the last for you well know my feeble condition and in addition to that I am becoming advanced in age. I have already lived my three score and one years. Consequently I could not expect to live much longer, even were I in the enjoyment of health. Considering my age and many infirmities and seeing that we are so far separated it is hardly reasonable to suppose that we will ever again be permitted to meet this side of Eternity. But then I shall ever hope and expect to meet you. You are both doubtless well apprised of the great importance of being prepared to meet death knowing that He is no respector of persons, falling not only upon the old, but upon the middle aged and even young. Knowing this fact you will not only be prepared for death yourselves, but will impress its importance upon your children also. You should be very careful to instruct your children in the principles of morality and Religion so that they may be our amounts to your family, to society and useful in the hands of the Lord.

You are living in a country where more than ordinary care should be taken of the morals of children. And you may be assured of being doubly compensated in after life for this attention which you bestow upon your children in infancy.

We would be exceeding glad to see you all again, but entertain little hopes of ever so doing. Notwithstanding we are so far separated and have almost — of ever seeing you again. You must think not that our affections for you are by any means weakened or obliterated. We ever expect to cherish those affections for you which parents alone can cherish for their children.

My general health is as good as usual for this season, though I am poorer than I have ever been in my life. Your Mother's health is good. The health of the family is good also.

Matthew is at home for the present. Helen is still going to school at Princeton. We heard from Eleazer and Martha a few days since. All were well. Judith and Artimissa, each have a fine daughter.

We received your minature from Mrs. Hodge. We prize it very highly. We will try and get ours taken and send them to you this summer. We make you a present of this Medical work. Times are very hard. Many poor people are bound to suffer. Corn is worth one dollar here and many places it is light. But as the Lord would have it we made a better crop last year than usual.

Write to us when you receive this.
As ever your affectionate
father and mother
J.K. and Elizabeth Givens

T.B. & Margaret Parker

T.B. Tell Son, Billy and Daughter that we want to see them very much. Tell them to write to us. Douglas more especially for we want to see some of his handi-work. Mr. Hodge says that Billy is the smartest boy that he has ever seen.

(Letter written by James Karr Givens (who died Apr. 7, 1855, just 17 days later) to his daughter, Margaret, and her husband, Thomas B. Parker.)

V. NATHANIEL KARR GIVENS, m SARAH ELIZABETH CLAY (1848 Indiana-1925 Coats, Pratt Co., KS) on Dec. 20, 1865, at her parents' home in Henderson, KY. NAT and SALLIE first met while she was attending a tobacco auction with her father, B.M. Clay.

Nathaniel K. Givens home built in 1866 located on old Lutontown Rd. Burned. In picture are Frances Givens Randle and Fan Bassett Price.

Nat was selling tobacco and Mr. Clay was buying it. SALLIE was very beautiful, with dark hair and eyes, and NAT fell in love with her at first sight. After their marriage they lived on his farm near Providence on the Webster-Hopkins Co. line where he had chosen a lovely site for their home on high ground overlooking the gently rolling farm land inherited from his parents. Their daughter, FRANCES/FANNIE ABIAH GIVENS was born at the home of SALLIE's parents, now Madisonville, on Dec. 29, 1868. NATHANIEL GIVENS died tragically of a heart attack at the age of thirty-four and SALLIE remarried in 1874 to Sherwood Hicks Woolfolk. They lived in Madisonville where he practiced law, but the financial panic of 1873 was to change their lives in ways never imagined. By 1880 they had moved onto Nat Givens' land in Hopkins Co. to try and restore their flagging finances. The children loved living on the farm near Providence and for them life was idyllic with a cook, maid and laundress to look after them and the beauties of nature all around them. They looked upon it as a paradise—with long visits to and from friends and relatives and the almost unceasing activities connected with a large farm and a large family. But times were still hard and Woolfolk was determined to move on, so after a brief stay in Madisonville and with a very sad and reluctant family, he moved to Pratt Co., KS, in 1886. Their life was one of a typical pioneer family on the prairie—a great struggle to reach a comfortable old age. FANNIE GIVENS made several trips back to Kentucky, staying with family and friends and no doubt consulting with her guardian, Mathew C. Givens, about the farm in Hopkins Co. She married in 1893, GEORGE SIMMONS RANDLE (1867 Illinois-1957 Wichita, KS). See RANDLE family.- *Submitted by Patricia Randle Gillespie*

GLADDISH-PARKER

Herman Manual Gladdish (1902-1974) and Hazel Toy Parker (1900-) were married in Springfield, TN, May 25, 1929. They lived the first nine years at Crofton, KY, in Christian Co. In 1938, they moved to Nortonville on New Salem Circle Road about one-fourth mile from Highway 41. In 1943, a disaster befell them. Their house burned. They moved west on the same road and lived there until 1963. They moved to Nortonville on Highway 41A.

Herman and Hazel T. Gladdish

Both of them were born in Christian Co., west of Crofton — he in Castleberry and she in Adams (West Grove) school district. He lived in the same place during her entire single life.

Her parents moved to Hopkins Co. when she was fifteen months old and lived there until her seventh birthday. She attended her first school in Nortonville. Her teacher was Miss Mary Quinn. Her parents moved back to their home in Christian Co. in 1907. In 1917, they moved to Crofton in Christian Co.

Hazel graduated from Crofton High School. She attended Western Kentucky University, Bowling Green, KY, and two summer terms to Washington University, St. Louis, MO. She became a teacher and taught thirty-one years. She taught in Christian, Muhlenberg, Leslie and Hopkins Cos.; also, in Crofton Independent system. Her longest period of service was in Hopkins Co. She retired on service from South Hopkins High School in 1963, being the first teacher to retire from South Hopkins.

Herman was a farmer, equipment operator and U.M.W.A. miner. He retired from Island Creek Coal Company in 1963.

Both of them were members of New Salem Baptist Church, Nortonville, KY.

Herman Manual was the son of William Felix (1871-1950) and May Woodruff Gladdish (1880-1940). William F. and May's children were: Nicy Gladdish Cansler (1897-1974); William Columbus (1899-); Herman Manual (1902-1974); Verlis Clay (1909-).

Herman's paternal grandparents were Columbus (1844-1922) and Mary Ann Brown Gladdish (1842-1904). Columbus was a Civil War Union soldier. Both generations were born at Castleberry.

Herman's paternal great grandparents were William and Louisa (Step-mother) Gladdish who were born in Warren Co., KY, and Pascal (1814-1883) and Jolina Brown (1814-1883). Both born in North Christian Co. Pascal donated land for Castleberry Church and Cemetery in October 1877. He is buried in this cemetery and has a memorial purchased and erected by his great grandson, W.C. Gladdish.

Herman's paternal great, great grandparents were Nathaniel Brown and Ann Croft Brown, married in 1813. They had one son, Pascal. His great, great, great grandfather was James Wright Gladdish.

Herman's maternal grandparents were James Benjamin (1852-1887) and Fanny Wheeler Woodruff (1850-1906). His great grandparents were Hiram and Lounicey Crabtree Woodruff. Herman and Hazel have two nephews: Horace E. Cansler, Dawson Springs Route 2 and David Cansler, Wichita, KS; one niece, Terry Sue Wells.

Hazel's father was O.S. Parker (1845-1928), a man of many talents and contributions to his community. He was farmer, teacher, Civil War veteran, held several elected and appointed offices in Christian Co. He was Republican Representative from Christian Co. in the Kentucky Legislature (1873-1875). In later years he maintained his own office.

Hazel's mother Mary Ann was married to J.J. Dunning in 1872. He died in 1876. They had no children. In 1880, Mary Ann Downey married Obadiah S. Parker in Nashville, TN. They

O.S. Parker (1845-1928) State Representative in Ky. Legislature 1873 to 1875. Mary Ann Parker (1857-1928)

had three children: Edith Blanche (1882-1962); Elbridge E. (1884-1965) and Hazel Toy (1900-).

Blanche was a teacher in Christian Co. for many years. She died in Memphis, TN, in 1962. She had lived there 25 years. She is buried in Riverside Cemetery, Hopkinsville, KY.

Elbridge E. was a World War I veteran, and prior had served three years in the army, two of which were in Jolo Island, Philippines; he retired from the Frisco Railroad, at Memphis, TN. He was buried in Riverside Cemetery.

Her paternal grandfather was Obediah Parker, born in South Carolina. He came to Kentucky in 1818. He married Mary (Polly) Thornberry in Christian Co. They had 13 children. Her paternal great great grandfather, John Parker, born in South Carolina, a Revolutionary War veteran came to Kentucky (1818). All of Mary Ann Downey Parker's relatives were born in Carey Co., Ireland. She alone was born in the United States. Her parents were naturalized citizens.

Her mother, Hazel's grandmother, was Mary Murphey Downey. She married C.C. Downey (1855). They came to America and helped build the railroad from Louisville to Nashville. Mary Ann was born near Clarksville, but her parents moved to Nashville when she was an infant. Her mother died in 1867 and was buried in the Catholic cemetery in Nashville. Her father died at Crofton, KY, and is buried at Old Liberty Cemetery in Christian Co. Her grandmother (Hazel's great grandmother) was Mary Murphy. She died and was buried in Ireland.

Herman and Hazel had four children. A son, Herman Gladdish, Jr. graduated from Nortonville High School in 1947. He served in the Korean Conflict and later in Japan. He was a farmer and had also worked for IC Railroad; after moving to Louisville, KY, he worked for International Harvester until his death. His widow still lives in Louisville, KY. He married Peggy Martin and they had three children: Gary, a brick mason in Louisville, has one son, Steven Gladdish; Mark, who is in the Coast Guard is stationed at Saute St. Marie, MI, and has one daughter, Jessica May; Jeffrey, a printer, lives in Louisville with his wife and daughter, Lauren, born September 1987.

Their eldest daughter, May Downey Gladdish, married Herbert Barnard, Jr., from Alexander City, AL. She is a teacher. He moved to Florence in 1957 and is employed as Budget Officer with TVA, Division of Research, National Fertilizer Development Center, Muscle Shoals, AL. May and Herbert have lived in Florence, AL, their entire married life.

Jacqueline and Jean, their other two daughters are twins.

Jackie married Charles E. Markham from Western Kentucky. She is a teacher and taught in Ohio, Hopkins, McLean and Fayette Co. schools. Her longest period of service was in Fayette Co. She is retired on a 31-year service period. Her husband, Charles E. Markham, is a musician. He taught band, served as a music director, church organist, and plays for various occasions. He, also, gives concerts. He retired on service. They live in Lexington, KY, during the summer and Arizona in the winter.

Jean married Rev. Richard D. Hagen from Arizona. He has pastored churches in Louisiana, Mississippi and Tennessee. Since 1977, he has been the pastor of the Kentwood Independent Baptist Church in Kentwood, LA. He also owns and operates the Hagen School of Kentwood, a Christian elementary and high school. Jean is the supervisor for the school. Richard is also interested in scientific research.

Jean and Richard have two sons: Sidney D. and Timothy H. Hagen. Sidney received both a Bachelor of Arts and Master of Arts in Bible from Bob Jones University, Greenville, SC. He married Dianne Helen Kliewer of Hollister, CA. Sidney will be a supply pastor for Tom Walker, who is a missionary serving in Erickson, Manitoba; Timothy H. is a computer operator for Tensor Geophysical Service Corporation. He is also working on a degree from University of New Orleans. Timothy and his wife, Carol, have one son, Richard Colin Hagen.

The 1970's were a time of stress and sorrow in our family. Herman died Sept. 5, 1974, after a period of long illness. On Dec. 12, 1976, also after a period of long illness, Herman Gladdish, Jr. died.

Hazel still lives in their home 148 South 41 in Nortonville, but she spends the winters with her two daughters in the south and her daughter in Arizona.- *Submitted by Jean Hagen*

GLASS-DUNNING

George Davis Glass and Shelia Ray Dunning were married July 8, 1950 at Bowling Green, OH.

George was born July 19, 1927 at Lewistown near Princeton, KY. George is the son of Walter Glass and Alta Egbert. Walter married Alta on Apr. 13, 1917. During their 54 years of marriage, Alta gave birth to ten children. George's surviving brothers and sisters are as follows: Owen Glass, Frank Glass, Donnie Glass, O'Leta Fletcher, Willmia Hart, Dean Chambers, Mary Asby and Charlotte Thomason. George's oldest brother, Reathel Glass, was killed on a battle ship during World War II.

George was reared at Lewiston and attended school at White School House. At the age of 22, George joined the Navy. After serving five years in World War II, he and his wife moved to Marion, KY. George worked at the Kentucky Utilities Co. and was transferred to Princeton, KY for three years and was again transferred to Dawson Springs. George has lived in Dawson Springs for 21 years and has worked for the Kentucky Utilities Co. for 32 years.

Shelia was born Dec. 18, 1930 in Dawson Springs, KY. Shelia is the only daughter of Robert Roy Dunning and Elizabeth Griffith. Shelia's father was born in Livingston County and her mother was born in Hopkins County.

Shelia graduated from Dawson Springs High School in 1948 and started working at Dr. Jones Jr. D.M.D. office. After working at the doctor's office, she moved to Marion and worked for the Kentucky State Department of Security for five years. When she moved to Caldwell County, she worked at the Caldwell County Attorney's Office and then for the Caldwell County Board of Education. When Shelia and George moved to Dawson Springs, Shelia worked on the Dawson Springs Board of Education for three years and then she was the City Clerk of Dawson Springs for nine years. Shelia is presently working at the State of Department in Madisonville, KY.

George and Shelia have two children: Reathel David and Anna Lea. David married Teresa Ennis and Anna Lea married Ron Claxton. George and Shelia have three grandchildren: Tonia Glass, 17; Brian Glass, 13; and Dustin Glass, 6.

George and Shelia were divorced in 1975. Both are still living in Dawson Springs, KY. - *Submitted by Tonia Glass*

GOOCH

The history of this pioneer family is given beginning in Granville Co., NC, up until the present.

Thomas Gooch was born on Apr. 10, 1784, in Granville Co., NC, at age 18, married to Miss Jermima Hester, immigrated to Hopkins Co., KY, in 1840, and died Nov. 22, 1859.

Thomas Gooch had six children: 1-Eliz born 1804, died 1860 and married James J. Rust, 2-Willis L. born 1807, died 1842 and married Rachel Cozart Mangrum, 3-Haywood born 1811, and married Linny, 4-Joseph Hester born 1815, died 1878 and married Emily Louise Philpot, 5-Mary was married to Soloman Jones, 6-Roland (Reverend) born 1822 North Carolina, died 1873 (Gooch Cemetery) and married Louisa Francis Coffman.

Roland Gooch, son of Thomas, had six children: 1-twin infant daughters born 1845, died 1845, 2-Jemima Florence born 1846, died 1916, 3-Genoa Fletcher born 1848, died 1881, 4-Willis Haywood born 1851, died 1924, 5-Joseph Withers born 1860, died 1925.

Jemima Florence Gooch married Reverend James C. Hopewell and had four children: 1-Nora born 1870, 2-Willis born 1872, 3-Mamie born 1874, 4-Elsie M. born 1876.

Genoa Fletcher Gooch married John S. Whittinghill and had five children: 1-Eva born 1872, died 1872, 2-Helen born 1874, 3-Nina P. born 1876, 4-Eunice born 1877, 5-Genoa.

Willis Haywood Gooch married Elizabeth Childs Brown and had two children: 1-Roland Brown born 1898, 2-Delia Nora born 1900.

Roland Brown Gooch and Delia Nora Gooch

Joseph Withers Gooch married Emma Wells and had five children: 1-Aubrey Lytton born 1884, died 1954, 2-Wilby T. born 1885-Professor at Baylor University, 3-Joseph Harold born 1889, died 1925, 4-Elizabeth Lucile born 1895, died 1919, 5-Joe Wells born 1900, died 1966.

Dr. Wilby T. Gooch married Artie Burton Muse. They had two children: 1-Wilby T., Jr., born 1909, 2-Lucy Frances born 1911.

The part of Hanson west of the railroad, was donated by the Gooch family to start the town of Hanson. The road west of Hanson has a steep hill. This hill at winter's first snow provides the children of Hanson a place to test their new sled. This hill caught the eye of a famous educator, Dr. Henry Hardin Cherry,

Seated l to r: Willis H. Gooch, Roland B. Gooch, Lizzie Gooch, Delia Gooch and Tiny Brown. Standing l to r: Crawford Strum (brother of Tiny Brown) and Tyler H. Brown, (son of Tiny Brown, brother of Lizzie Gooch).

who was looking for a location to build Western Ky. State Teachers College.

The log house, that housed several generations of the Gooch family still stands. The stable across the road housed some fine work mules and one special mule to Mr. Roland named Tom. Behind the stable is the Gooch Cemetery.

This spring after the death of Mr. Roland Gooch, it was necessary for the administrator, Mrs. Iola Brown, to hold a public auction. People came from several states to buy. The Hopkins Co. Historical Society, purchased a corded bed to place in the former Governor Ruby Laffoon cabin. The Gooch family is a credit to the history of Hopkins Co.- *Submitted by Franklin W. Livingston, a life-long friend of the Gooch family.*

JOE THOMAS GOOCH

A collateral descendant of Sir William Gooch, Baronet, colonial Governor of Virginia 1727 to 1729, Joe Thomas Gooch, born 1941, is from a Hopkins Co. family that migrated to Kentucky from Granville Co., NC, and before that from Goochland Co. that Governor Gooch created in 1727 from the shire of Henrico, one of the original eight "shires" of Jamestown colony. His immediate family includes his father, Alonzo Joseph (Jody), an uncle, John Thomas, a former Madisonville attorney, four aunts, Claudia, Zala, Claire, and Tina Sue, a brother, Wendell, and two nephews, David and Jeremy. Jessica Terri is his daughter. Clexton Beatrice Hobgood, his mother, was the daughter of Lewis P. Hobgood of Slaughters; there are four uncles from the mother's family: Verble, Wallace, J.D., and Raybal. Related are the Hobgood, Townsend, Pool, Grant, Madison, Waller, and Branson families.

Joe Thomas Gooch

Gooch's grandfather, Dudley Burton Gooch, migrated to Hopkins Co. in 1867 and in 1909 purchased on Highway 1069 the Hal Jackson farm, the site of the stagecoach stop. This area known as the Irv Adcock Store neighborhood and sometimes called "ribbon city" was home to the Gooch family. They attended the Olive Branch Missionary Baptist Church just a short distance away, and many family ancestors and relatives are buried in this church cemetery. There is also a family burial plot behind the house on the farm.

A graduate of the University of Evansville and Indiana University, Gooch has been teaching U.S. History and Sociology at Madisonville Community College since 1970. He is a charter and life member of the Historical Society of Hopkins Co. and holds membership in the Kentucky Association of Community College Professors, Phi Theta Kappa, Pi Gamma Mu, Anthropologists and Sociologists of Kentucky, and the Grant-Lee Association.

He has coordinated the Hopkins Co. PTA Scholastic Bowl contest since 1980; he has been president of the Pennyrile Performing Arts Association 1982-1985, president of the Kiwanis Club of Greater Madisonville 1986-87, and president of the Grant-Lee Association since 1981.

His publications include: *Just the Other Day: A History of Madisonville, Kentucky,* 1981; a book review of George Snyder, *A History of Georgetown College, The Filson Club History Quarterly,* January, 1981; *The Pennyrile: History, Stories, Legends,* 1982; "The Case of Asbury Harpending, Jr.," *The Journal of Kentucky Studies,* Northern Kentucky University, July, 1984; *The Story of Shakerag,* 1984; and articles in the *Yearbook* of the Historical Society of Hopkins Co.

A few of the collateral relatives of Gooch in Hopkins Co. include Bartlett Louis Gooch of Civil War fame who was with John Hunt Morgan on the raid into Ohio in 1863; another was Tom Gooch of the "Army of Six" that defended Madisonville at a site near where Browning Springs Middle School is located today; yet another is Roland Gooch whose family donated land to start the town of Hanson.- *Submitted by J.T. Gooch*

GOODAKER-JENNINGS

Efra Vincent Jennings and Arnold Rufus Goodaker were married June 6, 1935, in Dawson Springs by Rev. H. Corbin Adcock of the First Christian Church at his residence.

Efra and Arnold Goodaker

Efra was born Feb. 20, 1910, in Hopkins Co. near Dawson Springs. She is the daughter of Ruthie A. Jennings and Lula Belle Fox who married in 1906 and had another daughter who died in infancy. Ruthie was the son of Allen V. Jennings and Paralee Franklin. Lula was the daughter of Nelson Fox and Mattie Floenda McGregor.

Efra graduated from Dawson Springs High School. She was cashier for Purdy Brothers Groc. and later bookkeeper for City Water and Sewer System until retirement in 1973. Other ancestral names: Bishop, Dockery, Dunn and Simms.

Arnold was born Nov. 21, 1908, in Caldwell Co. to Dora Goodaker and Ethel Alexander (m. Feb. 9, 1908). Other surviving children: Anna Mae, Lois and Paul. Deceased: Earl, Alyene and Oleta.

Ethel was the daughter of Emily Hunsaker and David Alexander. David's grandfather, Lt. Wm. P. Alexander, died in the Battle of New Orleans on Feb. 3, 1815.

The Alexanders came from Logan Co. in the early 1800's and settled in what is now a part of Dawson Springs. David (b. Mar. 7, 1845) plowed where Main Street is now. Other ancestral names: Menser and Shull.

Dora was the son of David Whitt Goodaker and Mary Ann Egbert. Whitt was a Union Soldier in the Civil War. An ancestor, Thomas Goodaker from North Carolina, took a 200-acre land grant in Caldwell Co. Mar. 19, 1805. Other ancestral names: Carter, Townsend and Franklin.

Arnold attended school in Caldwell Co.; graduated from Dawson Springs High School. He was a postal employee at Dawson Springs for 42 years and retired in 1971. He did public service work with the Community Benevolent Service, Public Housing and Rosedale Cemetery, Inc.

Efra and Arnold enjoy fishing, gardening and golf. They are members of the First Christian Church where he is an Elder, Emeritus.

Arnold and Efra have one son, Arnold Wayne (b. Feb. 21, 1939 in Dawson). He graduated from Dawson Springs High School, attended WKSU and graduated from UK with a civil engineering degree. After college he served two years in the Army and became a 1st Lt. At present he is a civilian employee of the Louisville District Army Corps. of Engineers and is the Area Engineer at Ft. Campbell. He married Gloria Lynn Eldridge, Sept. 9, 1961, in First Baptist Chapel in Princeton.

Gloria (b. Sept. 16, 1941, in Madisonville, daughter of Wm. H. Eldridge and Henrietta Hogan) has a brother, Carney. She graduated from Caldwell Co. School, attended MSU, graduated from UK and has an MA from WKSU.

Wayne and Gloria's son, Andrew Wayne (b. Apr. 17, 1965 in Louisville) is a chemical engineering senior at U of L. Their daughter, Amanda Ruth (b. May 14, 1970, in Owensboro) attends Christian Co. High in Hopkinsville where the family resides.- *Submitted by Arnold R. Goodaker*

BLANCHE GOODRIDGE

Blanche Dora Lewis was born in Todd Co., KY, on Jan. 15, 1882, to Will Lewis and Frances Samuels. She was the second of twelve children. Born into a farm family, she learned early to work. She worked in the tobacco patch and barn and plowed the fields with the horses and mules.

Her mother, Frances, was one of the daughters of the renowned Mrs. Mary Thornhill (her master's name) Samuels (see Samuels-Thornhill-Lewis) who was born a slave. Mary's husband to be, Mr. Samuels, bought her and freed her before marrying her. Their marriage took place in a church instead of "jumping the broom stick" as most slave ceremonies were held. Thus began a legacy that will forever live as the family increases. The elder Mrs. Samuels lived to be over 110. Frances died at 75.

Blanche married Buck Goodridge (1880-1962) about 1900. A coal miner, he moved his family (of three at that time) to Madisonville in 1909. Their children: Iloa, Margaret, Nathan, William, Ethel, Lester, and Theodor (Ted). One child died in infancy. Sons Will, Lester and Ted served in World War II.

Blanche is a member of Flower Grove Baptist Church in Madisonville. Age has slowed down her attendance, but she still holds the title of "Church Mother."

She always enjoyed her gardens and insists hard work never hurt anyone. She will ask her guests if they raised a garden and if it produced good. In years gone by she raised a lot of pretty flowers, a son reports. What did Blanche do in her spare time? She made many quilts for her growing family. She still has several in use even today.

The Goodridge's have 16 grandchildren, 39 great grandchildren and six great great grandchildren.

In spite of a weakening surgery when she was about 100, Blanche still lives at home. Her son Lester stays with her and cares for her needs that she can not do alone. Still very alert, she enjoys company in the late afternoon. One of Madisonville's great little ladies. For proof go visit with her.

Photo of Blanche Goodridge is included in the section "Hopkins County Centenarians." - *Submitted by Dorothy Miller Shoulders*

BENJAMIN GORDON

Benjamin Norris Gordon, son of John Breathet Gordon, was born in Todd Co., KY, near the small settlement of Gordonsville in the late 1880's. He was educated in Elkton, KY, and taught school for a short time. He then became a court reporter, and moved to Madisonville, KY, in 1908. He studied law while he was reporting court cases, and was soon approved as an attorney, obtained his law license, and began the practice of law in Madisonville.

Benjamin Norris Gordon and Judge Laurence T. Gordon

In 1910 Mr. Gordon married Mary Watson, who was a music teacher, and a native of Cadiz, KY. Mary Watson's grandfather was Thomas Tennessee Watson, who was a doctor of chemistry, and collaborated with William Kelley of Peaches Mills, TN, to invent a process of making steel from pig iron which was the forerunner of what is now known as the Bessemer Process. He also established the first iron foundry in Kentucky in the 1930's. This foundry was known as the Empire Iron Works, and was located on the Cumberland River in what is now Kentucky Woodlands National Wildlife Refuge.

Mr. Gordon became a law partner with Letcher Fox, and they practiced law for many years in Hopkins Co. with their offices located at the north west corner of Main and Sugg Streets in Madisonville.

Mr. Gordon was mayor of Madisonville from 1930 to 1937, during which time he continued his law practice. He died in 1957. Mr. and Mrs. Gordon had three children: Norris W. Gordon, Laurence T. Gordon, and Virginia Gordon. Norris W. Gordon, who was a civil engineer, and worked with Jones and Donan, Engineers in Madisonville for several years. He died as a result of an automobile accident in the year 1938.

Virginia Gordon, the only daughter, graduated from high school in Madisonville, went to Christian College in Columbia, MO, and studied art in Cincinnati, OH. She married Albert Rau from Cleveland, OH, and they now live in Phoenix, AZ. They have one child, Susan Rau, who now teaches school in Ocean Beach, CA.

The second son is Laurence T. Gordon, who was raised in Madisonville, and who also became a lawyer. He practiced with his father and Letcher Fox for a few years, and was County Attorney of Hopkins Co., KY, from 1950 to 1962. Laurence T. Gordon married Mimi Franklin, daughter of Charles G. Franklin and Minnie Franklin; and in 1962 became a law partner with Carroll S. Franklin, son of Charles G. Franklin. Later Byron L. Hobgood joined this law firm, and the partnership continued until Laurence T. Gordon was elected as the first District Judge of Hopkins Co. under the new Court system of Kentucky which was established in 1978 under the Constitution of Kentucky. He served as District Judge until 1986 when he returned to the practice of law with his old firm, now composed of Charles G. Franklin II, (son of Carroll S. Franklin), Laurence T. Gordon, Byron L. Hobgood, and W. Michael Troop.

Laurence T. Gordon and Mimi F. Gordon have two children: David L. Gordon and Carroll H. Gordon, both of whom graduated from High School in Madisonville, and from the University of Kentucky in Lexington. David worked in the Kentucky Bank & Trust Company in Madisonville for a few years, and in the year 1985 began work in the Property Valuation Office in Madisonville.

Carroll worked with the accounting firm of Wilson, Bruce and Ramsey in Madisonville and then moved to Lexington in 1986 where he obtained his license as a Certified Public Accountant, and became associated with the accounting firm of Woollard & Company, Certified Public Accountants, of Lexington, KY. SOURCES: *Family History and Bible Records- Submitted by Laurence T. Gordon*

GORDON LAWYERS IN HOPKINS COUNTY

Following the death of John Gordon II, a Captain of the Kentucky Militia in the Battle of Blue Licks in 1782, the last battle of the American Revolution, his son John Gordon III (1774-1824), a surveyor by occupation, was dispatched to the Hopkins Co. area by the Governor of Kentucky in 1806 for the purpose of surveying the boundaries of Hopkins Co. which was then being created from part of Henderson Co. John Gordon III was elected County Surveyor at the first organizational meeting of Hopkins Co. government on May 25, 1807. He likewise by survey laid out the town of Madisonville by court order in 1807 and for the remainder of his life accomplished most of the military land grant surveys in payment for military service in the Revolution to veterans living in Hopkins Co.

John Gordon III and his wife, Elizabeth Wright, married Aug. 23, 1802, and were survived by one son, Ambrose Grayson Gordon (1803-1860), and two daughters. Until his death in 1860, A.G. Gordon practiced law in Madisonville with his uncle, William Gordon, brother of John Gordon III. He was a man of wide business interests which included contracting with the Federal Government for mail route deliveries throughout western Kentucky, dealing in land markets and mineral rights and, served as President of the first railroad constructed from Henderson to Nashville which became a part of the Louisville & Nashville Railroad system in 1880. At the time of his death, he was a partner in the law firm of Gordon and Gordon with his son, William L. Gordon (1837-1930).

William L. Gordon was admitted to the bar in 1859. He was married to Cordelia A. Arnold (1840-1897) and they had six children, three daughters and three sons, namely W.L. Gordon, Jr. (1863-1933), John Fleming Sale Gordon (1866-1930), and Maurice Kirby Gordon (1878-1974), all three of whom became practicing attorneys in Madisonville in their father's firm known as W.L. Gordon and Sons.

William L. Gordon, Sr., served in the Union Army, was a confirmed Republican once making the race for Lt. Governor of Kentucky. He was General Counsel of the St. Bernard Coal Company and later of the West Kentucky Coal Company. Always active in political and governmental affairs, he served as Federal Referee in Bankruptcy for the Western District of Kentucky for more than twenty years retiring therefrom at the age of 85 years.

His eldest son, W.L. Gordon, Jr., left the legal profession and became the General Superintendent of the St. Bernard Coal Company.

Maurice Kirby Gordon actively practiced law in Madisonville for more than 65 years. While serving as Inspector General of the 36th Division AEF, World War I, he proposed the name "American Legion" for our largest veterans organization at its first caucas in Paris, France, in 1919. The local American Legion Post in Madisonville is named in his honor and memory.

John Fleming Sale Gordon served many years as Judge of the Hopkins Circuit Court and was a founder and first president of both the Kentucky Bank and Trust Company in Madisonville, and Peoples Bank in Earlington.

Judge Flem Gordon, as he became known, was the founder and first Exalted Ruler of the Madisonville Elks Lodge. In 1913 he married Ruby James (1876-1978), sister of the then Kentucky United States Senator Ollie M. James. Their only child, James Fleming Gordon, practiced law in Madisonville twenty-five years prior to his appointment as United States District Judge for the Western District of Kentucky by President Lyndon Johnson in 1965. Judge James F. Gordon married Iola Young of Providence, KY, in 1942, and have three children: Maurice Kirby Gordon II, James Fleming Gordon, Jr., and Marianna Gordon Dyson, all three of whom are attorneys. The sons are now jointly practicing in Owensboro, KY.

When Judge James F. Gordon, upon appointment to the Federal bench, closed the Gordon law office in Madisonville, it was the oldest continuous business in Hopkins Co. — five direct generations in business since 1806.- Submitted by\ James F. Gordon. Collins Kentucky History, History of Hopkins County - M.K. Gordon, Gordon Family Bible, Vol. IV of Hopkins County Minute Book, page 123, Livingston Law Register, 1851, Kentucky History Illustrated, 1885, Vol. 15, No. 104 - Madisonville Messenger, Congressional Record, 89th Congress, July 22, 1965

GRACE

Roscoe Louis Grace was born Apr. 24, 1908, in the Orange Grove Community of Christian Co. He moved to Nortonville in the late 40's where he operated several businesses until his death on July 3, 1983. His philosophy of life was "Better to laugh than cry" and indeed his smile and whistling as he went through his daily activities were testimony to this.

He married on Mar. 10, 1930, in Hopkins Co., KY. His bride was Eunice Wynn, born Oct. 2, 1909. Their early years together were financially difficult due to the depression. Eunice always worked alongside her husband in farming and business. They had two children: Laurel Ruth, born May 25, 1933, and Carroll Douglas, born Jan. 29, 1941.

Laurel married July 12, 1952, in Springfield, TN, to Joseph Carroll Whitfield. He was born Feb. 12, 1934, the son of Ruby and Naomi Ashby Whitfield. Their daughters are: Belinda, born Apr. 7, 1953, and Tina, born Mar. 7, 1956. Belinda married Paul Cox, born Mar. 26, 1952, on Oct. 10, 1977. His is the son of David and Wandalea Grayson Cox. Tina married Steve Nichols, born Oct. 11, 1953, on Aug. 1, 1975. He is the son of R.C. and Honey Lou Burden Nichols. Steve and Tina have two daughters: Sarah, born Oct. 14, 1983, and Emily, born May 6, 1986.

Carroll Douglas married July 20, 1961, in Hopkins Co., KY. He married Pearl Elizabeth Grace, born Apr. 13, 1943, daughter of Hobart and Myrtle Agee Lyell. They have a daughter, Diana, born Apr. 9, 1964.

Roscoe's family goes back to Nathaniel, born about 1648 in England. Roscoe's parents were Noah, born Mar. 10, 1878 (died June 12, 1959), and Nancy Keith Grace, born June 17, 1883 (died Feb. 26, 1970). Their children were: Willie (1901-1980), who married Lucille McIntosh; Ella (1905-1956), married Albert Skimehorn; Garland born 1912, first married Verna Crick, second marriage to Mary Beshears; Vivian, born 1913, married Louise Hight; and Alene, born 1919, married W.H. Chadwick.

Eunice is the daughter of James W. Wynn (May 24, 1873-June 17, 1963) and Francis E. Hendrix (Sept. 3, 1880-June 4, 1960). Their other children were: Mable (1897-1972), married William Barnett; Mollie (1898-1899); Jewel (1904-1986), married Paul Whitfield; and Newel, born 1907, married Berchie Young.- *Submitted by Laurel Whitfield*

GRACE-ROBINSON

John Lawson Grace and Ethel Robinson of Madisonville, Hopkins Co., KY, were married in the year 1928. Ethel Robinson Grace a housewife. Husband, John, was an industrial arts teacher at Rosenwald High School. Well-known in the community for his woodwork and architectural abilities. Drew the blue print for the East View Baptist Church that stands today. Both are deceased.

The parents of four children, namely: John David Grace, graduate of Kentucky State University, Frankfort, KY. Retired brick layer. Married Bernice Daly of Pittsburgh, PA. John and Bernice have three children - John David Grace, Jr., Philadelphia, PA. Pamela Grace, Wharton, NJ; Jonathan Charles Grace, Secane, PA. Resides in Madisonville, KY.

Charles Edward Grace (deceased). Retired inspector of Republic Steel, Cleveland, OH. Married Helen Crawford of Cleveland, OH. Charles and Helen have three children - Charles Jr., Gregory and Carmen of Cleveland, OH.

Dorothy Jean Grace Henry, graduate of Kentucky State University, Frankfort, KY. Retired teacher, having taught at the Branch Street and the Waddill Avenue Schools. Member of Alpha Kappa Alpha sorority. Married James Henry, assistant principal of Madisonville North Hopkins High School. Graduate of Arkansas A & M College, Pine Bluff, AR. Member of Omega Psi Phi Fraternity.

Loretta Robinson Grace Striplin, graduate of Kentucky State University, Frankfort, KY, and Murray State University. Retired school teacher. Named Outstanding Elementary Teacher of America, 1974. Married the Reverend Cephas A. Striplin (deceased). Graduate of Western Kentucky University, Bowling Green, KY. A Christian Methodist Episcopal minister, presiding elder and Equal Opportunity officer for the Pennyrile Allied Community Services.

All four of the Grace children attended the public schools of Madisonville, KY.- *Submitted by Loretta Grace Striplin*

RICHARD RUMSEY GRAHAM

A history of Richard Rumsey Graham and an account of one direct line of his descendants. He was a retired agriculturist and life-long resident of Madisonville, Hopkins Co., KY, born Dec. 6, 1845, to Harvey (born 1808) and Mary Ann Baker Graham (Aug. 5, 1822), both born in Hopkins Co. His grandfather Richard S. Graham was born in Ireland about 1775 and emigrated to South Carolina as

L to R: Richard R., Rupert K., Rupert Earl and Rufus Edgar Graham

a young man; married Hannah Gill (born 1784 in South Carolina) and moved to Kentucky in the early 1800's.

On Dec. 12, 1870, Richard R. Graham married Mary Ellen Utley (Oct. 1, 1847-Dec. 3, 1929, Hopkins Co.). They had ten children all born in Hopkins Co.: Kirk (Apr. 26, 1872-Oct. 1, 1890); Rufus Edgar (Nov. 6, 1873-May 22, 1955); George Wilbur (July 6, 1875); John Will (Jan. 26, 1877-Nov. 16, 1878); Frank Hill (Nov. 25, 1878-Nov. 6, 1879); Mary Harp (Oct. 23, 1880-Dec. 27, 1951); Walter G. (Aug. 9, 1882-Jan. 16, 1885); Shannon (Aug. 8, 1884-1973); Richard W. (Mar. 15, 1886-1958) and Scott Homer (Oct. 3, 1888-Sept. 2, 1967). Rufus E. was first to marry on Dec. 13, 1896, to Elizabeth "Lizzie" Helen Osburn (May 13, 1877-Jan. 2, 1965). They had two sons born in Madisonville, KY: Rupert Kirk (May 24, 1898) and Homer Montgomery (Dec. 13, 1901).

During World War I, Rupert served in the U.S. Navy. When he returned to Madisonville in 1918, he married Edith Crow (Dec. 19, 1894-Oct. 15, 1978) of Manitou on Aug. 1, 1918, and moved to Detroit, MI, where Rupert Earl was born Oct. 20, 1919. Because of ill-health, they moved to Portales, NM, where James Wollard was born Aug. 11, 1922. From 1923 to 1943 they resided in Evansville, IN, and in 1943 moved to Long Beach and later to San Diego, CA. Rupert K. died Mar. 23, 1956, and is buried in the National Military Cemetery at Fort Rosecrans, CA.

From 1942 to 1974 Rupert Earl served in the U.S. Navy and retired as a Captain in the Supply Corps. In 1947 he married Agnes Koli of Los Angeles, CA, and they reside near Sisters, OR. (No children)

During World War II, James W. served as an officer in the U.S. Marine Corps. In 1942 he married Barbara E. Kay of Charleston, WV. From 1946 to 1986 he was affiliated with Evansville, IN, school system and retired to Naples, FL. They have two children, daughter Bonnie married to Tad Randolph of Indianapolis, IN, and living in Battle Creek, MI, with their children, Jay, Ross and Erin. Son, James Kirk married to Jennie Vagnoni of Pittsburgh, PA, and living in Las Vegas, NV. (No children)

Concluding the history of Richard Rumsey it should be noted he not only farmed during his lifetime, but was active in politics and served as a member of the Kentucky Legislature about 1896-1900 (?). During the Civil War he served with Company E, 27th Kentucky of the Union Army. He died at age 98 (Apr. 8, 1943) and is buried in the Oddfellow's Cemetery at Madisonville, KY. He was the last survivor of the Grand Old Army of the Republic of Kentucky.

Other ancestral names are: Cox, Slaton, Slack, Fowler, Carmack, Wilkey, Wilson, Montgomery, Parker, Clift, Mangrum, Peyton and Brooks.

Sources: Who's Who in Western Kentucky (F-450, W56 page 163) Library of Congress, Family Bible and Hopkins Co. Courthouse Will Book. -*Submitted by Mr. and Mrs. R. Earl Graham*

GUGE-FRANKLIN

Mary Florence Franklin and George Linsey Guge were married Sept. 5, 1936, in Madisonville, KY.

Florence was born Mar. 5, 1909, in Hopkins Co. She is the daughter of Samuel Turner Franklin and Elsie Ellen Laffoon. Samuel was born Jan. 1, 1878, in Hopkins Co., near St. Charles. He is the son of Bartley Winchester Franklin and Lucy Jane Clark. Sam's brothers and sisters are: Sarah Florence Sizemore, Ida Belle Hamby, Charles David and Eugene (died in infancy). Samuel married Elsie Laffoon Dec. 24, 1901, near St. Charles in Hopkins Co. Elsie is the daughter of Alexander Boston Laffoon and Martha Elizabeth Southard. Elsie's brothers and sisters are: Cordie Phillips, Thomas, William Herbert, and Verna Brown. Eleven children were born to Samuel and Elsie: Almon, Ruby Parks, Florence, Naomi Trathen, Mattie Rodgers, Woodrow, Thelma Brandt, Foch, Ellyn Ward, Josephine Phaup and June Lavell (died in infancy). Sam and Elsie lived and raised their family in the Daniel Boone community. Sam was a school teacher, miner and farmer. Elsie was a housewife but also pedaled the vegetables and products they raised on the farm in the mining camps. Florence quit school at an early age to help at home. At the time of her marriage to George, she operated a small grocery store in Madisonville. Soon after their marriage she became a housewife and reared her family. In her later years Florence was a sitter with the sick, retiring in 1985.

George L. and Florence Guge

George, a native of Graves Co., was born July 20, 1910, at Fancy Farm, KY. He is the son of Charles Henry Guge and Gracie Catherine Toon. He came to Hopkins Co. in 1930 to work in the coal mines starting at the Workman's Coal Co. near Charleston. He was working at Flat Creek Mine during the 1937 flood. There were four men drowned in the mines and George helped to get three of them out. The fourth one was blown out by an air explosion. They found the last man after 62 days. This was an experience that will never be forgotten. He later worked at Dawson Colleries, Redbud Coal Co., Cardinal Coal and Bell & Zoller Coal Co. retiring after 42 years in July 1972. While employed in the mines George also built several houses and operated a peach orchard for two years.

George and Florence are members of First Church of God, 617 South Kentucky Ave., Madisonville, KY.

George and Florence have three daughters: Mary Elizabeth married Phil Slygh. She had two children by a previous marriage: Deborah Lynn Eisenhauer and Robert Glenn Gibson. Elizabeth has one grandson: Scotty Lynn Eisenhauer. Rita Juanita married Ellis O. Potts. They have two daughters: Tijuana Leigh Rickard and Tonia Renee Gibson. Ellis and Juanita have four grandchildren: Micah Kern, Kalen Ryan, and Bryce Linsey Gibson and April Nicole Rickard. Fredia Faye married Wesley Owen Bowles and they have three children: Lisa Lynn Hunt, Starla Denise, and Wesley O. Bowles, Jr. Faye and Wesley have seven grandchildren: Brandon and Jeremey Chappell, Tiffany and Starla Hunt, Wesley III, Brittany and Linsey Bowles.- *Submitted by Juanita Potts*

HALE-BRACKETT

Sherry Lynne Brackett and Randy Lynn Hale were united in marriage Apr. 30, 1983, at Concord General Baptist Church by Reverend Oscar L. Duncan (Sherry's great-grandfather).

Sherry was born Aug. 23, 1963, in Madisonville, KY. Her parents are Brenda Sue Duncan and Bobby Gene Brackett. (See Brackett-Duncan).

Sherry graduated from Madisonville North Hopkins High School in 1981. She attended Madisonville Community College 1981-82. She presently works for Home Medical Equipment Sales & Rental. Her hobbies include tole painting, bowling, swimming and camping.

Randy and Sherry Hale

Randy was born Apr. 29, 1963, in Orange, CA. His parents are Greta Kittinger Padgett and the late Gerald Hale. Maternal grandparents are Lavinia Ellis and the late Robert Kittinger (see Kittinger-Ellis). Paternal grandparents are Agnes Purdy Smith and the late Clarence Hale. Randy has a twin sister: Sandy Lynne. He has two brothers: Barry Durand and Terry Wayne. He also has a half brother, Steve Hale.

Randy graduated from Madisonville North Hopkins H.S. in 1981. He attended Madisonville Community College 1981-82. He is presently employed by Hardin-Graybill Printers, Inc., Owensboro, KY, as a pressman. Randy enjoys outdoor activities such as swimming, camping, etc.

Randy and Sherry have one son: Brandon Lee Hale (Nov. 2, 1983). They live in Madisonville and attend the First Baptist Church. -*Submitted by Sherry Hale*

HALE-PEPPER

William Cordell "Cordie" Hale was born Feb. 22, 1865, in Christian Co., KY, the son of Silas Hale (1820-1873) and Nancy Ann Johnson (1823-??).

In 1888, he married Margaret "Maggie" Mildred Pepper. She was born in Todd Co., KY, on Apr. 1, 1870, the daughter of Noel Pepper (1832-1913) and Bell Jane Faughender (1844-1930).

Soon after their marriage, Cordie and Maggie moved to Earlington in Hopkins County, where their three daughters were born: Buena, Mayona Bell, and Hazel Lee.

Seated, Margaret Mildred Hale with her daughters; standing from l to r: Hazel Hale Smith, May Hale Hammonds and Buena Hale Wyatt and William Cordell "Cordie" Hale

Buena was born Mar. 8, 1889. She married John Wyatt on Dec. 23, 1906, in Hopkins County. They were the parents of two sons, John and Bill, and a daughter, Lola Bell. Buena died in 1964 and is buried in Grapevine Cemetery in Madisonville.

Mayona Bell "May" was born Oct. 14, 1890. She married Monroe Asberry Hammonds (see Hammonds-Hale) on Nov. 17, 1913, in Hopkins County. They were the parents of a son, Garrett Monroe (see Hammonds-Vance), and a daughter, Hazel Imogene (see McGar-Hammonds). May died Sept. 13, 1965, and is buried in Oakwood Cemetery in Earlington.

Hazel Lee was born July 25, 1893. She married James R. Smith on Jan. 21, 1912, in Hopkins County. They had no children. Hazel died Feb. 8, 1986 and is buried in Grapevine Cemetery in Madisonville.

Buena, May and Hazel attended Munns School.

Cordie worked at the Hecla Mine running the water shaft.

Cordie died Aug. 3, 1936, and Maggie died Jan. 15, 1944. Both are buried in Grapevine Cemetery in Madisonville. - *Submitted by Debbie Knight Hammonds*

HALL

The Hall family in Hopkins County begins June 23, 1951, when Donald, Nell and their two children moved to Madisonville from Hopkinsville. Their roots were in Christian County. Nell's fifth great-grandfather, Jesse Cornelius, had settled in Christian by 1798. Don's third great-grandfather, Peter Hall, had bought land in Christian in 1817. In the Revolutionary War, Nell's fifth great-grandfather, Aaron Quisenberry Sr., supplied beef to the Continental Army, and Don's third great-grandfather, James Purvis, was a North Carolina private.

Nell is the daughter of Ennis (1902-1984) and Lorene Sizemore (1903-1974). She also was reared by her grandparents, James and Penina Smith, and her stepfather, Garnett Burt. Don is the son of William (1900-1981) and Eudora Shadoin Hall (1897-1953). He was reared by his mother and his grandmother, Katherine Roake Shadoin, a native of Staines, England, who died Sept. 26, 1955, in Madisonville.

Nell was born Aug. 28, 1925, near Hopkinsville and graduated from Sinking Fork High School. Don was born June 17, 1923, and began selling newspapers at age 6 in Hopkinsville. In 1934 he became a fan of the Detroit Tigers; he still follows the Tigers. At Hopkinsville High, he was starting halfback on the undefeated 1940 state football champions, and graduated in 1941 as athlete with the highest academic standing. In 1942 he and his father took a 3-month course at radio school in Madisonville. During World War II, Don served with the Army in the Philippines and New Guinea.

Don and Nell married Mar. 26, 1947, at Hopkinsville. He graduated from Southern School of Printing and became a linotype operator at Kentucky New Era in Hopkinsville. In 1951 he was hired at Hopkins County Times. He joined Madisonville Messenger in 1953. In 1957 Don and Nell formed Small Fry Baseball League for children age 8 to 10. For 15 years they operated the league, which eventually grew to 12 clubs; in 1963 the Lions Club selected the Halls "Team of the Year" in Madisonville. In 1964 Don and Nell launched Hall Printing Co., a job printing business, on a part-time basis. Don left The Messenger in 1966 and began operating his business full-time at 686 Cherry.

Nell began substitute teaching in 1957. The following year, she started her full-time career at Pride Avenue School, where she eventually taught fourth, fifth and sixth grades. She earned degrees at Bethel College and Kentucky Wesleyan. In 1986 she retired after teaching at Pride for 28 years, the longest term for any Pride teacher.

Nell and Don have a son, Robert, and a daughter, Donna.

Bob, who was born Feb. 22, 1948, is a copy editor for The Evansville Press and part-time journalism instructor at University of Southern Indiana. He holds a master's degree from University of Evansville. On Aug. 22, 1971, he married the former Ruth Jahn, who was born June 18, 1950, in Huntingburg, IN. She is a former beautician and office worker. Their daughter, Renee, who was born Jan. 20, 1981, attends Vogel School.

Donna, who was born Nov. 28, 1950, is in her 16th year as health, physical education and geography teacher at Hopkinsville High. A graduate of Austin Peay State U., she holds a master's and a Rank I certification from Murray State. On Apr. 25, 1987, she married Dale Baggett, a teacher and swim coach at HHS. Dale was born Feb. 14, 1950, at Tennessee Ridge, TN. A graduate of Western High in Detroit, he holds a master's from APSU. While attending APSU he was an Olympics-class swimmer. Dale also is a commercial fisherman. Donna and Dale have a home in Hopkinsville and a trailer at Tennessee Ridge. - *Submitted by Nell S. Hall*

CALEB HALL

Caleb Hall, Jr., was born Apr. 3, 1775, in Bedford Co., VA. He was the son of Caleb Hall, Sr., and the grandson of Leonard and Joanna Letton Hall.

The Hall family took part in the westward migration of the late 1700's. Records show that Leonard Hall married in Maryland, lived in Virginia and Kentucky and was living in Barren Co., KY, when he died in 1809. Caleb Hall, Jr., migrated with his parents to Bourbon Co., KY, in the early 1790's.

Caleb was married to Martha (Patsy) Ligon Davis, daughter of Thomas and Ann Ligon and widow of James Davis, Jr., by December, 1802, when he was listed in Henderson Co., KY, records as guardian of Patsy's two young children, James and Nancy Davis. Martha (Patsy) Ligon was born July 11, 1780, in Virginia. She was a charter member of the Grapevine Christian Church in Hopkins Co., KY, on Apr. 28, 1834. She died Sept. 6, 1854, and is buried in Grapevine Cemetery on McLeod Lane in Madisonville, KY.

Before December 1802, Caleb Hall, Jr., had settled in Henderson Co., KY, in the area from which Hopkins County was created in 1807. Caleb Hall appeared on the Hopkins County tax list of 1807 with property on Pond and Tradewater Rivers. His holdings totaled more than one thousand acres. His farm included a large portion of the present site of Earlington, KY. In the early 1800's this area was called Caleb Hall's Post Office.

The first two recorded cases in the Hopkins County Circuit Court involved Caleb Hall, who was brought before the Grand Jury for profane swearing. Apparently he uttered an oath "at Daniel McGary's" on Sept. 28, 1807.

In 1807 Caleb Hall purchased three lots in the town of Madisonville. Two of his lots (Lots No. 17 and No. 24) were on what was later to become famous as the Hog Eye Block (present day Court Street). A third lot (No. 61) was located on what is now Federal Street. These lots cost Caleb Hall $27.50. By 1810 Caleb had purchased six additional lots in Madisonville.

Caleb and Patsy Hall were the parents of eight known children: Eveline Belmont Hall who married Charles C. Young; Elizabeth Hall who married Turner O'Bryan; Rachel Hall who married Hardin H. Thomasson; Dixon Hall who married Sarah Henson; Samuel H. Hall who married Eliza Ann Goodloe; Julia Ann Hall who married (1) Dixon H. Thomasson and (2) James S. Rose; Caleb Mastin Hall who married Elizabeth Oldham and Martha Hall who married Thomas Goodloe.

During his later years, Caleb Hall had a brick home located on the west side of what is now Main Street of Earlington, KY, near the present Loch Mary. This house burned one night in 1860 or 1861. After his house burned Caleb divided his time between his children until his death. He died at the home of his son, Samuel Hall, Apr. 22, 1861. Caleb Hall is buried in Grapevine Cemetery on McLeod Lane in Madisonville, KY. - *Compiled by Beverly H. Dockrey*

DIXON HALL

Dixon Hall was born in Hopkins Co., KY, Apr. 29, 1811. He was the son of Caleb and Martha Ligon Hall.

Dixon Hall was married in Hopkins County

Donald Hall family, 1987

on Dec. 17, 1832, to Sarah (Sallie) Henson, daughter of Bartlett and Ann Henson. Sarah Henson was born July 4, 1815, in North Carolina and died Sept. 6, 1873, in Hopkins Co., KY. She is buried in Flat Creek Cemetery in Hopkins Co., KY.

Dixon and Sarah Hall were the parents of ten children: Bartlett Henson Hall, William Henry Hall, Caleb Mastin Hall, Martha Ann Hall, Susan Asburreen Hall, Thomas Freeland Hall, Mary Elizabeth Hall, Robert Mahlon Hall, Sarah Ann Dixon Hall and John Gordon Burnett Hall.

Dixon Hall 1811-1894

Dixon and Sarah Hall began housekeeping in a two room log house to which they added rooms as their family grew. This log house was built on their farm which was given to them by Dixon's father, Caleb Hall. The farm was located on the north east border of the present town of Earlington, KY.

Dixon and Sarah Hall were members of the Primitive Baptist Church. Dixon served as Moderator of the Flat Creek Association for many years.

In 1861, Dixon Hall served as Deputy Sheriff of Hopkins County under Sheriff John Cargile. He also served as Justice of the Peace for eleven years. Dixon served as Judge of Hopkins County from 1878 until 1882.

In 1866 the Hall family moved to Madisonville into a house on Sugg Street. Dixon and his sons had cut and prepared the lumber from trees on the family farm, hauled the lumber to town in a horse drawn wagon and built the house.

Sarah Hall died in 1873 and in 1883, Dixon Hall moved from Hopkins Co., KY, to Windom, McPherson Co., KS, a western station in the pioneering days of that state. Dixon Hall was accompanied on this move by his two daughters, Mary Elizabeth and Sarah Ann Dixon Hall, and his son, Robert Mahlon Hall. At this time, Dixon's daughters were unmarried and his son, Robert Mahlon was married to Mahala Pritchett. Dixon and his family were joined in 1885 by another son, John Gordon Burnett Hall, who was later elected as the first County Attorney of Stevens Co., KS. John G.B. Hall was elected for two terms during the turbulent pioneering years of that county. Later he returned to Madisonville, KY.

At some time prior to October 1886, Sarah Ann Dixon Hall returned to Madisonville and on Oct. 28, 1886, was married to Marcellus W. Bishop, owner of a dry goods store in Madisonville.

In 1888, Dixon Hall and his daughter Mary Elizabeth (Betty) moved to McPherson, McPherson Co., KS, to join Dixon's, son, William Henry Hall.

Dixon Hall returned with his daughter Betty to Madisonville in 1892. After returning to Madisonville, Dixon lived first with his son, John G.B. Hall, and then with his daughter and son-in-law, Dixie and Marcellus W. Bishop. It was at the home of Marcellus W. Bishop that Dixon Hall died July 29, 1894. Dixon Hall is buried in Flat Creek Cemetery in Hopkins Co., KY. - *Compiled by Beverly H. Dockrey*

JOHN G. B. HALL

John Gordon Burnett Hall was born on his father's farm near Earlington, KY, Sept. 23, 1857. He was the son of Dixon and Sarah Henson Hall.

John G.B. Hall was educated in the schools of Madisonville and attended the Lincoln University at Lincoln, IL, in 1877 and 1878. After leaving school he read law with Polk Laffoon and William L. Gordon and was admitted to the bar in October 1879. He was a partner with Polk Laffoon in the practice of law for one year.

Judge John G.B. Hall and Helon Ada Morton Hall in 1948 on their 50th wedding anniversary

On Oct. 12, 1883, John G.B. Hall and C.C. Givens established the Hopkins County Gleaner, a weekly newspaper which reached a circulation of four thousand copies in fifteen months. This was said to be the largest circulation of any newspaper in the state, outside of Louisville. In 1885 Mr. Hall sold his interest to Mr. Givens and went to Hugoton, KS, where he assisted in the organization of Stevens Co., KS. He was elected first county attorney of the new county in 1886 and was re-elected in 1888. In July 1889 Mr. Hall resigned his office as county attorney, returned to Madisonville, KY, and resumed the practice of law. In November 1894 he was elected County Judge of Hopkins County, serving two terms.

On Nov. 7, 1898, after an engagement of 20 years, Judge Hall married Helon Ada Morton in the parlor of Morton House. Helon Ada Morton, born July 28, 1859, in a log cabin on the South Main site of Morton House, was the daughter of John Gordon Morton and Nancy Elizabeth Young Morton.

Judge John G.B. and Helon Ada Morton Hall were the parents of one child, a daughter, Helon Morton Hall, born Oct. 27, 1900, and died Nov. 29, 1936.

Prominent in church, civic and political activities, John G.B. Hall served as Representative in the Kentucky Legislature. Judge Hall was a member of Madisonville First Christian Church, holding numerous offices in the church, and was elder emeritus at the time of his death.

Helon Ada Morton Hall was significantly involved in the establishment of the Madisonville Public Library. She and Judge Hall gave the lot on Union Street where the library was constructed and she served as the first president of the Library Board. Mrs. Hall was an active member of the Madisonville First Christian Church.

Judge Hall died Dec. 18, 1953; Helon Ada Morton Hall died Feb. 12, 1955. They are buried in Grapevine Cemetery on McLeod Lane in Madisonville, KY. - *Submitted by: Beverly Harris Dockrey*

THOMAS FREELAND HALL

Thomas Freeland Hall was born in Hopkins Co., KY, on his father's farm near Earlington Dec. 26, 1845. He was the son of Dixon and Sarah Henson Hall. He lived on the farm with his family, helping with the farm and logging operations until the date of his marriage.

On Dec. 24, 1872, in Hopkins Co., KY, Thomas Freeland Hall was married to Talitha Elizabeth Lovan, daughter of John Wesley and Nancy Ann Fugate Lovan of Mortons Gap, KY.

Thomas Freeland Hall 1845-1886 and Talitha Elizabeth Lovan Hall 1853-1947.

Talitha Elizabeth Lovan was born in Hopkins Co., KY, Dec. 30, 1853. She was a member of the Salem Baptist Church near Mortons Gap and later of the First Baptist Church in Madisonville.

Thomas and Talitha Hall lived in Mortons Gap, KY, for several years after their marriage. Thomas worked as a carpenter and in the logging and saw mill business.

Thomas Freeland and Talitha Hall were the parents of seven children: Annie Dixon Hall born Apr. 3, 1874, married Reuben Cortez Harris; George Wesley Hall born 1875; Rose Elizabeth Hall born Feb. 19, 1877, married Lee Lucas Kosure; Lonnie Williams Hall born 1878, married Charlotte F. Sugg; Lenora Hall born 1880; Loyette Hall born 1882, married Thomas Henry Browning; and Robert Freeland Hall born Jan. 26, 1885, married (1) Pearl Ilene Pool (2) Lana Gatlin.

On July 28, 1885, Thomas Freeland Hall purchased a lot at 124 South Seminary Street in Madisonville and began construction on a home for his family.

In the summer of 1886, Thomas Freeland was injured in an accident at the Coil Saw Mill where he was employed. This injury resulted in his death on Aug. 16, 1886. Thomas Freeland Hall is buried in Flat Creek Cemetery near Mortons Gap.

Relatives helped Talitha Hall to complete construction of her house in Madisonville and she lived there until her death at the age of ninety four. Talitha Elizabeth Hall died at her home in Madisonville, KY in the summer of 1947 and is buried in Flat Creek Cemetery in Hopkins Co., KY. - *Compiled by Beverly H. Dockrey*

HAMMONDS-HALE

Monroe Asberry Hammonds was born Apr. 25, 1893, in Christian Co., KY. He was the son of Isaac Sherman (Oct. 20, 1866-May 2, 1920) and Tennessee Alice (Craig) (Feb. 3, 1873-May 10, 1925) Hammonds.

Alice Craig Hammonds, mother of Monroe

His brothers and sister, all born in Christian County, were: Vaden H. (January 1891-1948) married Jethro Armstrong; Duden Edgar born March 1898, date and place of death unknown; Eura Houston born Jan. 24, 1902, married Ethel Mae Greer, lives in Michigan; John Malburn (June 18, 1905-May 7, 1977); and William K. born Jan. 28, 1908, believed to have died in Missouri.

On Nov. 17, 1913, Monroe married Mayona Bell Hale. She was born Oct. 14, 1890, in Hopkins County, the daughter of William Cordell and Margaret Mildred (Pepper) Hale (see Hale-Pepper).

Monroe Asberry and Mayona Bell Hale Hammonds

Monroe and May were the parents of two children: Garrett Monroe (see Hammonds-Vance) and Hazel Imogene (see McGar-Hammonds).

Monroe worked for Kentucky Utilities, North Diamond mine and retired from L & N Railroad.

May died in Earlington on Sept. 23, 1965. Monroe died in Earlington on Feb. 14, 1967. Both are buried in Oakwood Cemetery in Earlington. - *Submitted by Debbie Knight Hammonds*

HAMMONDS-KNIGHT

Timothy (Tim) Wayne Hammonds was born Jan. 27, 1952, in Lafayette, IN, the son of Garrett Monroe and Iva Mae (Vance) Hammonds (see Hammonds-Vance). Tim has two brothers, Michael Shepherd and Gary Hammonds, and a sister, Glenda Shepherd Lutz, all residing in Madisonville.

When Tim was five years old, the family moved to Earlington as this was his father's birthplace. Tim attended school in Earlington, graduating from Earlington High School in 1970. He then attended Lockyear Business College in Evansville, IN, graduating in 1972. In June of 1972, he began working at Cates Olds-Cadillac, Inc. in Madisonville. He continues to work there in the position of Business Manager.

In September of 1972, Tim enlisted in the Army Reserves and left for basic training at Fort Jackson, SC, in February of 1973. He served six years in the Army Reserve.

On Nov. 3, 1972, Tim married Debra (Debbie) Kay Knight at St. Mary's Episcopal Church in Madisonville.

Debbie was born Aug. 19, 1953, in Hopkins County, the daughter of the late Wayne A. Knight and Doris (Hatcher) Knight (see Knight-Hatcher). Debbie has a sister, Cheryl Lynn, who married Gregory Bennett and resides in Alexandria, VA.

Debbie attended grade school in Madisonville and graduated from Madisonville North Hopkins High School in 1971. While in high school, she was a member of Tri-Hi-Y, Pep Club, and president of Teens Who Care. She also held a part-time job as a Pharmacy Technician at the Hopkins County Hospital. Debbie attended Madisonville Community College.

Jason, Debbie, Leslie and Tim Hammonds

After her marriage, Debbie began working at Speed Queen holding various positions, the last being Production Supervisor. In 1980, she decided to become a full-time homemaker.

Tim and Debbie are the parents of a daughter, Leslie Marie born Mar. 21, 1980, who is a second grader at West Broadway School and a son, Jason Wayne born Nov. 21, 1983.

Tim is an avid golfer. He is a member of Earlington First Christian Church. Debbie is a member of St. Mary's Episcopal Church and her hobby is genealogy. She is serving for the fourth time as president of the Hopkins County Genealogical Society. A great deal of her time this past year has been spent working on "The Heritage of Hopkins County" book project. - *Submitted by: Debbie Knight Hammonds*

HAMMONDS-VANCE

Garrett Monroe Hammonds was born Mar. 26, 1915, in Earlington, Hopkins, Co., KY. He was the son of Monroe Asberry (Apr. 25, 1893-Feb. 14, 1967) and Mayona Bell (Hale) (Oct. 14, 1890-Sept. 23, 1965) Hammonds (see Hammonds-Hale). Garrett has one sister, Hazel Imogene (see McGar-Hammonds). He attended school in Earlington, graduating from Earlington High School in 1934.

Garrett and Iva Mae Hammonds

On Oct. 3, 1936, Garrett entered the Army taking his training at Fort Knox, KY. On May 10, 1942, serving with the 1st Armored Division, he left New York on the "Queen Mary." He was in Scotland, Ireland and England while training for battle. He left England and participated in the invasion of North Africa on Nov. 8, 1942, remaining there throughout the North African Campaign (Algeria, Morocco, and Tunisia). In the Italian Campaign, he participated in the invasion of Salerno on Sept. 9, 1943, almost reaching Rome. At Anzio, he was wounded when he was blown out of a tank. He was hospitalized in Naples, then going to Casablanca, Morocco, and Oran, Algeria. He was shipped back to Norfolk, VA, and later assigned to Fort Campbell, KY. His next assignment was to Lafayette, IN, where for the next seven years he was ROTC Instructor at Purdue University, later assigned to Nike Guided Missile Unit, 71st Nike Missile Battalion stationed at El Paso, TX, for training. His final station was at Fort Meade, MD, receiving his discharge on Jan. 31, 1957.

In June 1949, Garrett married Iva Mae (Vance) Shepherd. She was born Aug. 5, 1918, the daughter of Leo Harry and Neola Fern (Praim) Vance. Iva Mae had two children from a previous marriage: Glenda Mae Shepherd who married Robert Lutz and Michael Alan Shepherd who married Jo Salmon. Glenda and Mike reside in Madisonville with their families.

Garrett and Iva Mae had two sons, Garrett Monroe, Jr., and Timothy Wayne (see Hammonds-Knight). Both were born in Lafayette, IN.

In 1957, Garrett brought his family to Earlington. On Apr. 1, 1957, he went to work for West Kentucky Coal Company, later Island Creek Coal Company, as a time clerk and payroll manager. He retired in July 1977.

Iva Mae worked for several years at Clinic Convalescent Center.

Garrett is a member of the V.F.W., American Legion, Elks Lodge and Masonic Lodge #548.

Garrett and Iva Mae are members of the Earlington First Christian Church where Garrett is past chairman of the board, past treasurer, past elder and deacon emeritus and teacher of the mens' Sunday School class.

Garrett and Iva Mae still reside in Earlington. - *Submitted by: Debbie Knight Hammonds*

JOHN PRICE HANKS

John Price Hanks was born on Apr. 12, 1862. He was the youngest child of Hopkins County pioneers Robert Mansfield and Phoebe Lewis Hanks.

In 1882, in Johnson Co., IL, he married Isabelle Jones. To this union eight children were born: Ellen Loretta, Sept. 13, 1883; Addie Roselle, Nov. 6, 1885; Brydie, Dec. 17, 1887; Gracie May, Feb. 11, 1890; Nick M., Mar. 25, 1892; Zelma C., Feb. 4, 1895; Willie Wilford, Sept. 16, 1897; and Charles Vernice, Mar. 3, 1900.

J.P. and Isabelle (Jones) Hanks

As a younger boy, John Hanks worked to build the Illinois Central Railroad that travels through White Plains in Hopkins County. Later he farmed in Hopkins County. He was at one time a Sheriff's Deputy in Hopkins County and wore his gun wherever he went.

He was always proud of his heritage and ancestors. John Hanks made the claim that he was a second cousin to President Abraham Lincoln, as Lincoln's mother was Nancy Hanks.

John Hanks was a prominent and active Democratic worker in both local and county campaigns of his party for many years. And for his contributions, John P. Hanks Road was named after him in Hopkins County.

John Hanks died six weeks after his wife on Oct. 28, 1949. He had 36 grandchildren, 43 great-grandchildren and 3 great-great-grandchildren. He and his wife are buried in Concord Cemetery in White Plains, KY. - *Submitted by Craig A. Whitfield*

HARMON-HOWTON-ASBRIDGE

Gladys Mae Asbridge (July 9, 1907-Jan. 24, 1981) was born to Althus Zacharire Asbridge, a railroad man, and Nora Franklin (Feb. 14, 1883-Oct. 8, 1907) who died three months later. Gladys was raised by her grandmother (Mammy) Parthenia Elizabeth Franklin Franklin. She married Steven Newton Franklin and had eight children including Gladys' mother, Nora. The other children were: twin sons Dee and Lee; Martha Jane (Janie) wed Rufus Chandler; Charlie wed Cle Price; Cynthia (Seenie); Danny; and Lemuel. Mammy was a widow without a home, so she and Gladys stayed with each child one month at a time. They continued to move each month until Gladys wed Baxter William Howton in 1924 and Mammy lived with them.

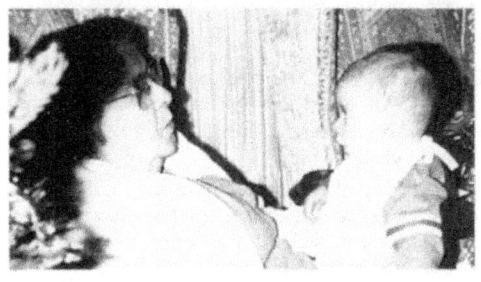

Gladys Mae Howton Harmon and great grandson Gabriel Baxter Gantt, age 5 months, Christmas 1979

Baxter was fun-loving and hard-working, not afraid of very much, while Gladys was superstitious and more cautious, but just as hard-working as her husband. On Sept. 5, 1925, James Baxter (J.B.) was born and died. A year later John Harold was born (Sept. 6, 1926-Feb. 24, 1948); he wed Dorothy Riggs on Dec. 7, 1946, and was killed in Dawson Daylight mines. Nora Lou wed James Darrell Ratliff on the same day Johnny was wed, neither knew the other was getting married. Laura Elizabeth (Lib) (Jan. 5, 1930) wed Billie Wayne Prince the same year Gladys married Walter Harmon (Sept. 4, 1905-May 25, 1975) in 1950. George William (July 23, 1932) was found to have polio at eight months and the doctor wanted to put him in a body cast when George started having convulsions, but his parents refused. They were guided to Dr. Earl Frye, a chiropractor in Providence, who worked with George until he improved and later was able to walk. George later wed Fay Nell Terry. Jerry Earl (named for Dr. Frye) (Feb. 22, 1945) wed Lorita Kingrey.

Baxter died soon after Jerry was four months old, then exactly one month later Janie Chandler's husband Rufus died. Janie talked Gladys into coming to Beulah to live with her, bringing the children along. Janie helped care for the baby while Gladys worked. At first Gladys used the insurance money to buy a coal truck for Johnny to haul coal and support the family. Nora was in business college at the time and able to send some money to help out and Lib worked at Woolworths when not in school. Then after graduation Johnny was gone, so Lib was the sole support as she worked at Ottenhiemer factory.

As time passed, Gladys worked many places, owned two restaurants in Beulah as well as ran the Madisonville Bus Station. She also sold many things house-to-house and really enjoyed her customers.

Her family remained the focal point of her life and she was extremely proud of her grandchildren. They were: Linda Lou Ratliff (Dec. 16, 1947) wed Michael Frank Gantt an Ohio native, and had Gabriel Baxter (July 25, 1979), Rebecca Lynn (Nov. 21, 1982) and Christopher Michael (July 13, 1985); Darrell Kent Ratliff (May 11, 1954); Bradley Lewis Howton (George's son) (Apr. 19, 1956); Jeffery Wayne Prince (Aug. 26, 1957-Sept. 16, 1959), struck by a car; Deborah Fay Howton (George's daughter) (Feb. 4, 1960) wed Kenneth Ray Groves and had Haley Danielle (Nov. 20, 1984); Paula Ann Prince (Jan. 5, 1961) wed Roy Ower McGregor and had Brandon Shayne McGregor (Dec. 21, 1981); William David Howton (Jerry's son) (Nov. 15, 1971). Jerry and Rita were divorced and David stayed with his mother who remarried. - *Submitted by Linda Gantt*

GILES BAKER HARRALSON

Anderson Bailey Harralson, b. 1776 in South Carolina, married Phoebe Cox, b. 1781. They went to Tennessee and later in 1816 came to Hopkins County. He went before the court, stating his desire to be a Kentucky citizen, coming only for farming and not to buy or trade slaves. He purchased land approximately 3-1/2 miles north of Nebo; built a family house and cabins for his slaves. Across the road is the Old Harralson Cemetery, where the older generations are buried. Part of the old house still stands on a farm presently owned by Kenneth Roberts.

Anderson died several years before Phoebe in 1861. After her death, their slaves were appraised at $19,000.00. They were the parents of eight children, one of which was Anderson Bailey Harralson II b. Nov. 23, 1812, d. Jan. 24, 1884. He married Elizabeth Bailey b. May 18, 1816, d. Feb. 22, 1896. They were the parents of eight children: Anderson Bailey III, married Mary Wynn; Peter married Sallie Gray; William d. 1876, never married; Mary married Roger Hewlett; Elizabeth married Charlie Cox; Phoebe married Hugh Kirkwood; Jane married Robert Austin; and Giles Baker b. Aug. 20, 1847, d. Feb. 7, 1932.

Giles Baker Harralson married Lilly Ashby on May 29, 1888. They were married by Bro. Story. Lilly b. Jan. 18, 1860, d. Dec. 20, 1946. They were the parents of five sons: John (Jack) Henry, William, Hayden, Sammie Giles and Ruby.

Lilly and Giles Harralson with grandchildren Sue and Gwendolen

Dr. John (Jack) Henry Harralson died in 1951. He married Agnes Simpson who died in 1983. One son, John Henry Jr. married Sarann Salsburg and they had four sons: John Henry III, James and twins Thomas Giles and Benjamin.

William Harralson died 1977. He married Alisa Cox who died 1980. One son, D.B. Harralson, died 1978, married Lillian Mills, died 1982, and they had one son Dr. David Harralson, whose daughter is Ellen Harralson.

Hayden Harralson, died 1967, married Helen Hoket, died 1981. Their son Hayden Jr., died in 1954. Hayden Jr. had one daughter, Sharon Sue, who married Elwood West.

Sammie Giles Harralson, died Sept. 23, 1983, married Gwendolene Clayton. They had one daughter Sue who married Davis Howard Crowe. Their children are Carol who married Doug Watkins and Howard who married LaRhue Ange. Howard and LaRhue are the parents of Andrea and Justin.

Ruby Harralson married Nellie Morrow, she died in 1934. He married 2nd Helen Campbell in 1963. Ruby died in 1971.

Giles and Lilly's first home was just below Greenwood School. Sons Jack and Will were born there. In 1892, Giles bought a farm and larger house from Robert and Sallie Craig. It was located across the road from Old Republican Christian Church before it was moved to Nebo. The church is now called Nebo Christian Church, with the 5th generation of Harralsons still attending today.

In 1924, the farm and house were sold to son Sammie. The old house burned December 1949. A smaller modern house was then built on-site. Giles and Lilly lived in Nebo from 1924 till their deaths. They are buried in Nebo Cemetery. The farm now belongs to Mrs. Sam Harralson and daughter Sue H. Crowe.

Many descendants of Anderson B. Harralson live in Hopkins County. Among them are Mary Lu Sharp, Linda Sue Crowe Franklin, Marie Hill, Ila Lee Ashby, the Hewletts, Sue and Davis Howard Crowe and family. - *Submitted by Mrs. Sammie Harralson*

HARRIS

George Washington Harris was a blacksmith in Cannon Co., TN. He lived near a town by the name of Readyville. In 1879, he and his family moved to Webster Co., KY, arriving by wagon and team. Later they moved to Hopkins County.

George Washington Harris was born Aug. 2, 1831, and died July 8, 1902. He married Ruthie Sauls. Ruthie was born Sept. 18, 1831. Her date of death is unknown. Their children were: Robert, Emmon, Jessie, Emily S., Janie (married a Givins), Jerucie (married Grover Puckett), Clistie (married Grover Bryant), Maggie E. and Moses.

Elmer and Mary Edna Harris

Robert was born Nov. 13, 1856, and died May 28, 1911. He married Tinnie Harris who was born Mar. 4, 1861, and died Mar. 14, 1930. Both are buried at Olive Branch.

Emily S. was born in 1869 and died in 1933. She married James I. Moore who was born in 1860 and died in 1937. Both are buried at Olive Branch.

Maggie E. was born in 1876 and died Sept. 11, 1897.

Moses was born Nov. 17, 1872, and died Mar. 1, 1954. He married Alice Virginia Adams (see Adams family) on Oct. 22, 1899. Both are buried at Olive Branch. Their children were: Roseanna, Carroll Everest and Elmer Clifton.

Roseanna was born Sept. 15, 1909, and married Lawrence Pool who was born on May 5, 1898 and died Dec. 1, 1985.

Carroll Everest was born Mar. 15, 1912, and married Louise Villines.

Elmer Clifton was born Jan. 29, 1908. On Apr. 9, 1949, he married Mary Edna Hickman (see Hickman family). Their children are: Elmer Ray, Alice Jean and Carroll Daniel.

Elmer Ray was born Jan. 27, 1952. He married Chyrel Orange Lovell on May 5, 1984. They have a daughter Crystal Curry.

Alice Jean was born Dec. 15, 1949. She married Mike Rittenhouse on May 21, 1981. They have a son Jason James born May 1, 1982.

Carroll Daniel was born Feb. 5, 1955. He married Judith Lynn Oglesby on May 28, 1977. Judith Lynn, daughter of William C. and Naomi Rodgers Oglesby was born June 23, 1951. Carroll and Judith had two sons, Jeremy Daniel born Feb. 10, 1979, and William Ray born Jan. 24, 1985, and died Mar. 4, 1985. - *Submitted by Mary Edna Harris*

HARRIS-AUSENBAUGH

James Newman Harris was born May 12, 1932. His parents were Harvey U. and Ruby A. Harris. Harvey was born 9-27-1904 in Hopkins County. Ruby Alene was born 1-7-1911 in Evansville, IN. James Newman was born on a small farm, in Hopkins County, near Beulah, KY. Being born at home, his first visit to a doctor was at age eight. James had one older sister, Betty Alene Harris.

Chores were learned at an early age, milking cows, feeding livestock and harvesting crops. The first three years of school were at Elam School. One teacher taught the first grade through the eighth grade. There was no running water or electricity in the school building. In early fall, the boys would gather wood. One large wood stove heated the one room school. The only way to keep warm was to sit close to the stove. Students walked to school, some a short distance, others walked two miles. The fourth year of school was at Dalton, KY. Fourth and fifth grades were taught by one teacher. Students were picked up by buses. Junior high school was taught by three teachers. A large coal stove was in each classroom. The boys carried in the coal for heating the rooms. Every winter, students were absent from school with measles, mumps, chicken pox, whooping cough and scarlet fever. The principal of the school taught algebra and math. James's favorite subjects were health and biology. Senior year, the new building at Dalton was completed and twelve students graduated in 1951.

After graduation, James left the farm. First employment was a Prow Brothers Plumbing Company, at Madisonville, KY. His wages were seventy-five cents per hour. To receive higher wages, he left Madisonville and went to work at a factory in Evansville, IN.

In 1952, James began to date Datha Lorene Ausenbaugh. She was from Dawson Springs and had graduated from Dawson Springs High School in 1952. She was employed by the Illinois Central Railroad. They were married in 1955 and lived for two years in Henderson, KY. In 1957, James and his wife returned to Dawson Springs. They bought a house and farm on the Olney Road. James worked at Dawson Daylight and Dawson Colleries Mines and farmed part time. Datha continued working for the railroad thirty one years, before retiring.

On Feb. 3, 1970, their only child was born. Born in the Hopkins County Hospital, he was named James Harvey Harris.

In 1957, the farm consisted of 185 acres. In 1988, the farm is over 700 acres. Beef cattle are raised. Hay, corn and tobacco are grown. James Newman's hobby is his horses. Traveling to horse shows and showing his Missouri Fox Trotting horses is what he enjoys. He is a hard working farmer and my Dad, whom I love and respect. -*Written by James Harvey Harris*

HARRIS-CATES

Sharon Gail Cates married James Ray Harris in Shawneetown, IL, on Feb. 26, 1960. She is the daughter of Aubrey Lee Cates and Mary Elizabeth Hillyard Cates. Sharon was born Nov. 20, 1943, at the Cardwell Hospital in Providence, KY.

Sharon attended Nebo School graduating in eleven years in 1960. She is presently employed as a certified dental assistant with expanded functions for John A. Roy, DMD. Sharon was Dental Assistant of the year for the state of Kentucky in 1986. She is a member of the Sixty Six Homemakers Club, serving as Vice President. She has been a volunteer in many organizations - Hospital, Girl Scouts, Boy Scouts, 4-H, Hanson School, and church. She has three brothers and three sisters. They are Naomi Love Knox, Douglas Wayne, Rosetta LaVonne Crask, Ruby Henry, Celeste Lou Krietzer, and William David.

Sharon Cates and James Ray Harris

James Ray Harris was born Sept. 16, 1941, in Madisonville, KY. He is the son of Morris Frank Harris and Mary Elizabeth DeBow

Harris. Jimmy attended school at Seminary and Madisonville High School graduating in 1959. He entered the Air Force for four years that fall studying electronics. He was stationed in Texas, Colorado, Florida and Okinawa. He worked for Kentucky Finance, National Life Insurance, Zeigler Coal Company and Peabody Sinclar as an electrician. He is now employed at Graham Hill #3, Peabody Coal Corporation.

He has one sister Lisa Lou Harris Berry. Lisa married Dan Berry from Morganfield, KY.

Sharon and Jimmy have two children. They are James Christopher and Andrea Charlene. Chris graduated from Madisonville North Hopkins High School and is employed as a technician in the pharmacy at Regional Medical Center. Charlene graduated from Madisonville North Hopkins High School and Oral Roberts University with a degree in business administration with a minor in computers.

The family attends Christian Assembly in Madisonville, KY. - *Submitted by Sharon Harris*

HARRIS-POOLE

Lemuel Washington Harris (b. Apr. 29, 1889, d. Dec. 25, 1971) and Novella Poole (b. Mar. 10, 1889, d. Dec. 29, 1980) were married Dec. 24, 1911, in the Hanson/Shakerag area and raised their family in the East Broadway/Caroline St. section of Madisonville. For many years, "Lem" Harris worked for the Hopkins County Road Department as foreman who regularly checked out road conditions throughout the county. This tall, lanky, pipe-smoking driver in the Ford pick-up truck was well-known by people from Olney in the west to Vandetta in the north and by those on the Frostburg Road in the east to Daniel Boone in the south. While serving as road foreman, Lem and Novella lived at 537 W. Arch across from Browning Springs School (then MHS) with the county truck department housed in the nearby warehouses (now the Youth Center). At retirement, their first purchased home was at 305 Lawrence Street.

Lem was the only son of Thomas Harris and Genoah Fridy Harris from the Shakerag area near Hanson and had three sisters: Nannie Nichols, Alice Lutz and Alma Brinkley. Other ancestral names are Buchanan and Fridy. Novella was the second child of Andrew J. Poole, who came to the Olive Branch community from North Carolina, and Magnolia Alice Bowles Poole (Hanson area) and had six brothers: John Will, Elmer, Wallace Beckum, Aubrey, Robert (Bob), Lester and three sisters: Naomi Daniels, Lula Skaggs and Mada Uzzle. Other ancestral names of Novella are: Bowles, Wooten and Buchanan.

Of the seven children born to Lem and Novella Harris, the five that lived to be grown (with their families) are: (1) Clifton "Slim" (Maymie), who worked at the Grand Central Shoe Shop until his death at age 67, (2) Modest Smith (Roy) has daughters Eloyse Jean Groves Merrell (grandchildren: Terri Bundy and Jacki Holland), Wilma Sue Phillips (grandchildren: Steve, Jeff, Karen, Shelley) and Carolyn Uplinger (grandchildren: Mark & Travis) (3) Cora Lee Moore (Lawrence) lived in Evansville (now Madisonville) has son, James (grandchildren: Joan, David, Sherry, Julie and James L.), (4) Nora Kathryn Stokely lived in Texas and New Orleans until her death at age 54, (5) L.W. (Dub), Jr. (Dorothy, Virginia) lives in Henderson and has children Claudia, Janice, Paula, Dennis, Peggy and their grandchildren.

Lem and Novella Harris lived a long and eventful life. Novella was a devout Primitive Baptist Church member, always read her Bible daily and regularly attended services until her health prevented it. Lem was of the Missionary Baptist faith and enjoyed listening to the services and gospel singing programs on the radio. Much of his spare time (before the television age) was spent in a rocking chair with his ear bent toward the radio. Lem at the age of 82 survived through grandchildren and great-grandchildren of four generations. Novella, at 91, saw five of the fifth generation offspring. The first two were: daughter Modest Smith, granddaughter Eloyse Jean Groves, great-granddaughter Terri Bundy, and great-great-grandsons Paul and Alan Bundy. Her daughter Modest's second child, Sue Phillips and son Jeff's son, Brian were another. Cora Lee's son James's daughter Joanie had Pete and Richard who were also 5th generation great-great-grandchildren for Novella Harris. - *Submitted by Jean Groves Merrell, granddaughter*

HARRIS-WILSON

Raymond R. Harris was born Aug. 1, 1904, in Hopkins Co., KY. He was the son of Roland (1867-1907) and Lela (Bowling) Harris (1875-1963). Roland and Lela were married Dec. 20, 1893, in Hopkins County. They were also the parents of a daughter, Myrtle, who married Erin Clayton. After Roland's death, Lela married Jim Clayton and they had a son David Clayton.

Raymond and Ora Harris

On Sept. 15, 1945, in Christian Co., KY, Raymond married Ora Bell Wilson. Ora was born May 8, 1907, in Christian County, the daughter of Nathaniel Henry (1867-1951) and Iva Lee (Reynolds) Wilson (1876-1914) of Christian County.

Raymond was in the Army during World War II, serving in England. He worked at Ruby Lumber Company in Madisonville and was a member of the Pleasant Grove Baptist Church.

Before her marriage, Ora worked at the cigar factories in Madisonville, Louisville, and Evansville. She then went to work in Madisonville at the S.J. Campbell Parachute Factory and, later, worked in a restaurant.

Ora and Raymond lived on Broadway, Scott Street and on a farm on Rose Creek Road. It was while living on the farm that Raymond died on Jan. 5, 1963. He is buried at Odd Fellows Cemetery in Madisonville.

In 1968, Ora moved back into Madisonville where she still resides. She is a member of Salem Primitive Baptist Church. - *Submitted by Debbie Knight Hammonds*

FRANCIS BROWN HARRIS HART

Frances Brown Harris (Hart) was born Nov. 9, 1868 in Rockcastle, Trigg County, KY. She was the daughter of F.B. and Cornelia Frances Harris (See Fraudius Brown Harris story.) She died on Nov. 13, 1968, in Charleston, WV, just a few days after her one-hundredth birthday. She is buried in Grapevine Cemetery in Madisonville, KY.

The Harris family moved to Hopkins County, KY when Fanny was quite young and she attended school in Morton's Gap.

Fanny Harris was married May 9, 1888 in the Christian Church in Morton's Gap to Edward Lee Hart. They were married by Rev. J. W. Hardy. Edward Lee Hart was born in 1861 in Virginia, died May 15, 1940 in Madisonville, Hopkins County, KY and is buried in Grapevine Cemetery in Madisonville. Lee Hart was working as a carpenter at the time of his marriage and later worked as a coal miner.

Fanny and Lee Hart were the parents of four children. Lillie Louise Hart died as an infant. Brent Hart was born Feb. 5, 1889 and was prominent for many years in Hopkins County coal mining circles. He died July 13, 1959. Sibyl Stuart Hart was born Sept. 13, 1892 and died Feb. 7, 1987. Winnie Davis Hart was born Nov. 20, 1898 and is presently living in Lillian, AL.

"Aunt Fanny", as Mrs. Hart was best known, lived most of her adult life in Madisonville and was an active member of the Madisonville First Christian Church. When she was 88 years old her children asked her to give up her ancient Dodge car, which was famous in her neighborhood as the "Church Chariot". Her car was a four door sedan and she used it to drive her friends to church.

After living alone in Madisonville for 26 years, Aunt Fanny moved, at the age of 97, to Charleston, WV to live with her daughters, Mrs. George Merryman and Mrs. Winifred Calfee.

On her 97th birthday Aunt Fanny was the subject of an article in the Daily Mail, a Charleston, WV newspaper. During that year she had pieced two Cathedral quilts and was busy knitting bandages for lepers, a project of her church.

"I still do everything I ever did", she said. "Figures don't mean much to me. I never think about being old. As long as they make hand lotion and rouge I will invest in it. I think one ought to have pride and look decent as long as they can. Women get to be old by wearing long skirts and stockings with crooked seams."

A picture of Fanny Hart is in the Hopkins

Co. Centenerians Section. -Compiled by Beverly H. Dockrey Great niece of Mrs. Hart

FRAUDIUS BROWN HARRIS

Fraudius Brown Harris was born Mar. 21, 1845, in Trigg Co., KY. He was the son of Reuben and Malinda Thomas Harris. His maternal grandmother was Sally Rucker, daughter of Kentucky pioneer Baptist preacher, James Rucker, who migrated from Virginia to Woodford Co., KY, in 1785 and died in Caldwell Co., KY, in 1800.

Fraudius Brown Harris and Cornelia Francis Harris

Mr. Harris had four brothers and one sister: Joseph T. Harris, Martha Ann Harris, John T. Harris, William F. (or Frances M.) Harris and Achilles Calloway Harris.

When Fraud Harris was about sixteen years of age, he along with a group of other boys damaged a Union boat on the Cumberland River. It was then that his mother, Malinda allowed him to join the the Confederate forces and serve during the Civil War. He enlisted as a Private under the command of Colonel T.G. Woodard in Company B, 2nd Regiment, Kentucky Cavalry. He served variously as a courier, a wagon master and assistant paymaster under Brigadier General J.H. Kelly, Major C.S. Severson and Major General Bennett H. Young, respectively. After the war ended, Fraud returned to Trigg Co., KY, and was married in 1866.

F.B. and his wife, Cornelia Frances Harris (born in 1847) were the parents of four children: Lillie Ann Harris born Jan. 6, 1867; Frances Brown Harris born Nov. 9, 1868, married Edward Lee Hart; Alice Sanders Harris born Nov. 16, 1870, married Walter H. Morton; and Reuben Cortez Harris born May 13, 1874, married Annie Dixon Hall.

In 1879 the Harris family moved to St. Charles, Hopkins Co., KY, and later to Mortons Gap, KY, where F.B. was employed by St. Bernard Coal Company as Superintendent of South Diamond Mine. F.B. Harris was the first mayor of Mortons Gap, serving until 1904.

F.B. and Cornelia Frances Harris were for many years members of the Christian Church. F.B. Harris was made an Elder of the Mortons Gap Christian Church in 1889.

In 1910 the Harris family moved to Madisonville, Hopkins Co., KY, where they resided on East Broadway.

After the Civil War, F.B. Harris became a charter member of the Madisonville Camp No. 528 of the Confederate Veteran's Association and was commander of this camp, holding the rank of Major on the staff of General W.J. Stone. In 1916, when General Stone was elected Commander of the Kentucky Division of Confederate Veterans Association, F.B. was unanimously elected by the Confederate Veterans of the Second Kentucky Brigade as Commanding General.

F.B. Harris died Jan. 19, 1918, and Cornelia Frances Harris died Nov. 17, 1920. They are both buried in Grapevine Cemetery in Madisonville, KY. *Sources: An article about Mortons Gap written by Richard Henry Mar. 23, 1925, and published 1974 by Historical Society of Hopkins Co., Inc. <u>Original Atlas and Historical Data of Hopkins County, Kentucky</u>. Family records. Compiled by Beverly H. Dockrey.*

FREELAND FRAUD HARRIS

Freeland Fraud Harris was born May 27, 1898, in Mortons Gap, KY. He was the son of Reuben Cortez Harris and Annie Dixon Hall Harris.

The Harris family lived in Mortons Gap until around 1911 when they moved to Providence, KY, living there until 1912. They moved to Madisonville in 1913 when Freeland was in the ninth grade.

Freeland F. and Georgie (Myers) Harris

While Freeland was attending high school, he began working at <u>The Hustler,</u> the local newspaper. He also worked at the Willard Hotel and later <u>The Messenger</u>.

Freeland was working for the L & N Railroad in 1917 when the United States entered World War I. On June 5, 1918, he enlisted in the United States Navy. Most of his time in the navy was spent aboard the battleship Texas. Freeland was aboard the Texas in the North Sea when it was part of the fleet that received the surrender of the German Navy on Nov. 21, 1918. The Allied fleet escorted the German fleet to Scappa Flow. He was also on the Texas when the battleship, along with the other ships of the Sixth Battle Squadron, met the convoy escorting President Wilson (who was on the George Washington) on Dec. 13, 1918, and accompanied him to Brest, France, where the President attended the Paris Peace Conference. Freeland was released from active duty and returned to Madisonville July 1, 1919.

Freeland Harris married Georgie Elizabeth Myers July 4, 1928. She was the daughter of John William Myers and Ida J. Lyons Myers and was born in Madisonville, KY, July 11, 1904. At the time of their marriage Freeland was working as a supervisor for the Tradewater Grocery Company and Georgie was working in the office of the Cumberland Telephone Company.

Freeland and Georgie Myers Harris were the parents of three children: Beverly Ann Harris born June 14, 1929; Freeland Harris, Jr. born Nov. 24, 1930, and Jeanette Harris born Jan. 16, 1936.

In 1939 Freeland and Georgie Harris bought a neighborhood grocery at 55 Spring Street. Specializing in personal service to their customers all over the community, they continued to operate this grocery until 1969.

Freeland and Georgie bought the Standard Motel on South Main Street in Madisonville in 1953. This business was operated until Mar. 20, 1971.

Freeland and Georgie were both members of Madisonville First Baptist Church. Georgie M. Harris died on Feb. 27, 1954. Freeland Harris died Oct. 6, 1979. They are buried in Odd Fellows Cemetery in Madisonville, KY. - *Submitted by Beverly Harris Dockrey*

HUBERT HARRIS

Hubert Y. Harris was born in Sumner Co., TN, Sept. 12, 1907. He and his wife, the late Myrtle Jenkins Harris, came to Hopkins County in 1944. They came to Kentucky shortly after Mr. Harris's sister Eunice Francis Harris Perry and her husband Ezra had arrived.

The Harris' purchased the Brown farm located one mile west of Hanson, KY. The farm adjoined the Rowland Gooch farm and Gabe Clayton farm.

The Harris family includes six children, Betty Jo, Charles Allen, Dorothy, Robert Young, Clara and Brenda.

Betty Jo born Oct. 6, 1928, was married to Mason Clayton and has one daughter Sherry Clayton Tomes. Betty Jo resides in Madisonville.

Charles Allen was born Sept. 23, 1930, and married Margie Proctor. They have two children, Steven and Melissa. Charles resides in Madisonville.

Dorothy Jean was born May 8, 1936, and married Boise Pillow. The Pillows reside in Evansville, IN, and are the parents of four children, Constance Jo Wedding, Boise Glenn, Tamara Young and Timothy.

Robert Young was born Jan. 26, 1938, and married Mary Helen Thompkins. They have two children, Sonya Davis, and Micheal Robert.

Clara Mae was born May 21, 1941, was married 1st to Charles Taylor and 2nd to Thomas Parker. Her children are Vicky Taylor, Kevin Taylor and Teresa Parker. Clara lives in Owensboro, KY.

Brenda was born Dec. 31, 1948, and married Bailey Joe Skaggs. They are the parents of two daughters, Lori Jolene Strader and Jessica Erin. They live on Route 2, Hanson.

Myrtle Jenkins Harris died on Nov. 23, 1976.

Mr. Harris is a retired carpenter, he is a farmer and is employed as custodian at Hanson Elementary School.

Hubert Harris and the former Edith Wilcox were united in marriage on July 6, 1981.

Mr. Harris has resided at his Route 2, Hanson home forty two years. - *Submitted by Sherry Clayton Tomes*

REUBEN CORTEZ HARRIS

Reuben Cortez Harris was born May 13, 1874, in Scottsburg, Caldwell Co., KY. He was the son of Fraudius Brown and Cornelia Frances Harris. In 1879, when Reuben Cortez was five years old, the F.B. Harris family moved to Hopkins Co., KY. They lived first in St. Charles and then in Mortons Gap.

R.C. Harris married Annie Dixon Hall Dec. 25, 1895. Annie was the daughter of Thomas Freeland and Talitha Elizabeth Lovan Hall and was born Apr. 3, 1874, in Mortons Gap. Reuben Cortez and Annie were married at the home of the bride's mother, 124 South Seminary Street in Madisonville. Following the wedding ceremony the groom's parents held a wedding reception in their home in Mortons Gap.

Annie Dixon Hall Harris and R.C. Harris

At the time of their marriage R.C. Harris was employed as a weighman for St. Bernard Coal Company at South Diamond Mine. Annie Hall began teaching in 1890 when she was sixteen years old and taught for five years in the Hopkins County school system at Moss Hill near Mortons Gap.

R.C. and Annie Hall Harris were the parents of five children: a stillborn son in 1896; Freeland Fraud Harris born May 27, 1898, who married Georgie Elizabeth Myers; Carl Whitson Harris born Jan. 17, 1903, who married Bonnie Hewlett; Mabel Dixon Harris born June 27, 1907, who married Robert Lee Harned and Paul Turner Harris born Jan. 2, 1914, who married Martha Katherine Whitfield.

The R.C. Harris family lived in Mortons Gap and Providence, KY, before moving to Madisonville in 1912. Shortly after moving to Madisonville Mr. Harris went to work as an insurance agent, first for Kentucky Central Insurance Company and later for Metropolitan Insurance Company.

R.C. Harris was a member of the First Christian Church and Annie Hall Harris was a member of the Old Salem Baptist Church, moving her membership to the Madisonville First Baptist Church in 1894. Mrs. Harris was active in her church and in the PTA. She was a charter member of the Madisonville American Legion Auxiliary and active in its child welfare work.

R.C. Harris died Jan. 22, 1960, in Madisonville. Annie Hall Harris died in Madisonville May 17, 1961. They are both buried in Odd Fellows Cemetery in Madisonville, KY. - *Compiled by Beverly Harris Dockrey*

PERNECIA HART

Pernecia was born June 11, 1881, in the Silent Run area of Hopkins County. She was the daughter of Orlando Franklin and Florica Sisk. Her brothers were Theodora and Silas.

On Dec. 26, 1900, in Hopkins County, she married William Benjamin (Ben) Hart. Ben was the son of Rufus Hart and Rebecca Cardwell. Their other children were: Dudley, Thomas, Garland, Walter, Ruby, twins Lloyd and Floyd who died as children, Ema, Mary (Molly), Sarah, Vera and Versa.

The children of Pernecia and Ben were: Bonnie married Louis Cain (see Sallie Cain story); Florisa (Davis); Thelma (Maddox); Sybil (Schaut); Helen; Franklin; Durwood; Claybourn; Amplias and Buford. There are 35 grandchildren, 65 great grandchildren and more than 23 great great grandchildren.

Ben died in 1931. Pernecia was a member of the Pentecostal faith. At the time of her death, Aug. 24, 1981, she was a resident of Brown's Rest Home in Madisonville. She and Ben are buried in Silent Run Cemetery.

For a picture of Pernecia, see "Hopkins County Centenarians." - *Submitted by: Dorothy Miller Shoulders*

SOLOMON W. HART

Solomon W. Hart was born Dec. 22, 1808, in Hopkins Co. His parents were John Solomon and Esther Parker Hart. Born 1780 in Onslow Co., NC, John came to Kentucky about 1800. He and Esther (dau. of Peter and Sarah Barnes Barnes Parker, migrated from Gates Co., NC) were married 1805. Esther was born 1788, and her first child, William was born 1806, so Solomon was the second child.

John Hart died 1821 in Union Co., leaving seven children. Esther remained a widow until 1835 when she married Thomas Ashby. (Her 3rd marriage was to Andrew Phillips 1840.) Solomon married Jan. 18, 1835, moving to Hopkins Co. where his bride, Sarah Hibbs' parents lived. (Nathan and Mary Bourland Hibbs.) In December, he purchased his first farm of 130 acres.

Solomon and Sarah Hibbs Hart's children were Tolbert born Dec. 7, 1835, teacher and store keeper, died 1866 of Civil War causes; Martha Ann born July 12, 1837, married Eli Mangum, died Dec. 15, 1899; Mary E. born Nov. 23, 1840, died age 8; Benjamin N. Hart born 1844, married Jennie L. Hibbs, died Jan. 3, 1876; Anastasia Denola "Nolie" born Sept. 6, 1846, married George W. Buchanan, died Apr. 2, 1911, buried Olive Branch and Rufus Owen (my grandfather) born June 22, 1849, married Marion Rebecca Cardwell Nov. 24, 1870. The 5th daughter of William Hamilton and Sarah Catherine Parker Cardwell, she was born Aug. 21, 1850 (died Nov. 16, 1908, Providence). Rufus Hart died at Nebo Nov. 26, 1918. Both buried Odd Fellows Cemetery.

Sarah Hart died June 23, 1849, day after Rufus Owen was born, buried Old Parker Cemetery, Providence. After his wife died, Solomon asked his brother, Benjamin, if he and his wife, Sarah, would keep baby Rufus for awhile. Sarah placed the baby on a pillow in front of her, and rode horseback home to Union Co. Her own baby was born the following March, not long after little Rufus had gone home. This baby was also named Rufus Owen after his cousin.

Solomon married Nov. 19, 1853, Sarah Jane Cardwell, born Sept. 18, 1831, daughter of John and Mary Ann Carnahan Cardwell. Their children were Frances born Feb. 22, 1855, married James Buchanan Lutz; Joseph S. born Nov. 27, 1856, married Mollie Utterback; Julie Maranda born Sept. 26, 1858, married R.W. Buchanan; Henry Clay born June 25, 1860, married Elizabeth F. Marshall; J. Ebenezer born Aug. 18, 1862, left Kentucky 1883, TEX?; Dr. George Emmit born Jan. 31, 1865, married Alice Nichols; Annie born Jan. 26, 1867, married John O. Jenkins; Ella Margaret born Nov. 7, 1868, married Edward Cosby Rice and Janey P. born Mar. 15, 1870, married Jefferson D. Price. Sarah C. Hart died Jan. 7, 1877. Both she and Solomon are buried at Olive Branch.

In Spring of 1878, Solomon married a distant cousin, Mary Headley. She died June 1878, a month before he died July 21, 1878. Solomon was a good farmer, owned several farms, prospered, loved and cared for his large family. - *Submitted by Betty Waltrip Irwin (a great-granddaughter)*

HARVEY-WEATHERLY

Isabel R. Weatherly (1862-1933), second daughter of G.L. Weatherly (see GEORGE

House built by John B. Harvey on Seminary Street in Madisonville

LAWSON WEATHERLY article), married John B. Harvey (1847-1923) of Hopkins County. J.B. Harvey was Madisonville Postmaster from July 1912 to 1916 and a dealer for the Cincinnati wholesale house of F. Strauss and Company. In 1878 Mr. Harvey purchased the lot at 175 North Seminary Street, Madisonville, from Polk Laffoon. He obtained the services of the firm of George F. Barber and Company, Architects, Knoxville, TN, to design his Victorian house. The present owners, Mr. and Mrs. John William Bassett, have the original set of drawings, which are in India ink on line paper.

Mr. and Mrs. Harvey entertained many prominent persons in their home, probably the most notable being President William Howard Taft. The property remained in the Harvey family until Dec. 31, 1949. - *Submitted by Margaret Berry*

HATCHER-SMITH

John (Jesse Lorne) Hatcher was born at No. 9, Arkansas on June 6, 1904, the son of William Loring and Lula Carraway Hatcher. At birth John was named Jesse Lorne by his mother but his father disliked the name saying it reminded him of Jesse James. So John is what he began calling his son and the name stuck.

Ada and John Hatcher on their 40th wedding anniversary

John's siblings were: Ronnie, Jane Elizabeth and Drayton. William Loring died May 24, 1911, and Lulu married Hicks Lewis and they were the parents of a daughter, Edna. Lulu and sons Ronnie and Drayton died during the flu epidemic in 1918. Jane Elizabeth and Edna were taken in by relatives. John was on his own at the age of 14. He traveled freely about the country.

On Mar. 12, 1932, in Blytheville, AR, he married Ada Mae Smith. Ada was the daughter of William Henry Harrison and Effie Elsie Taylor Smith who were the parents of fourteen children. Ada was born Aug. 2, 1913, in Tyler, MO.

John and Ada were the parents of: Doris Jean (see Knight-Hatcher), Joann, Drayton, Patty Jane (all born in Arkansas), and John Micheal (born in Hopkins County).

John farmed in Arkansas. In 1943, the family moved to Hopkins County and John went to work for Badgett Mining Company. Around 1956/57, John, Ada and John Micheal moved to Gibson Co., TN, for two years and then returned to Hopkins County. John went to work for L & N Railroad. He retired in 1975.

The grandchildren of John and Ada are: Debra Knight Hammonds (see Hammonds-Knight), Cheryl Knight Bennett, Michael Dean Ashby, Christopher Leigh Ashby, Teresa Lynn Hatcher Medeiros and Sundie Ann Hatcher. There are seven great grandchildren.

Due to his being on his own at such a young age, family was always very important to John. He always wanted his children and grandchildren near. During the later years of his life, family Sunday dinners became a tradition and birthdays were always and still continue to be occasions for a get-together. John died Nov. 27, 1977, and is buried at Odd Fellows Cemetery in Madisonville.

Ada has always put her family first. She continues to reside in Madisonville where you can always find a child, grandchild or a great grandchild in her home at most any hour of the day. - *Submitted by Debbie Knight Hammonds*

HAYES

Charlie R. and Mayme R. Hayes had six daughters (see Hayes-Pritchett).

Viola Hayes Drake attended WJIC in Paducah and had two children: Charles Wyatt (Aug. 26, 1940), attended In. State U. in Bloomington, has three children, Timothy, John (Mar. 9, 1962) and Monique (Mar. 16, 1966) and lives in Pasadena, CA; Lois Carolyn has a BA degree from Murray State U. and lives in Louisville with husband Robert King and two children, Nichole Hayes (June 5, 1980) and Robert Hayes (Oct. 18, 1981).

The Hayes daughters

Willie Hayes Williams, lives in Louisville, employed by Jefferson Co. Schools, has one son, James Andrew (Mar. 18, 1951), who attended Eastern KY U. and is Program Director at WJYL in Louisville and has two children, Christina Marie (Feb. 4, 1986) and Christopher Ray (Oct. 22, 1986).

Anna Hayes South retired from the Army Finance Ctr. in Indianapolis, has two daughters: Patricia Ann (Nov. 17, 1941) who has a BA from Murray State U. and an MA from IL State U., is a Documentation Representative to the Defense & Civils Programs Office at the Jet Propulsion Lab in Pasadena, CA, has two children, Jennifer LeAnn Ransaw (Oct. 10, 1969) and Randy Ransaw (Oct. 11, 1973), lives in Los Angeles; Phyllis Marie (Oct. 5, 1944) has a Bachelors in Pre-Law from Ball State U., is a Systems Consultant Executive with AT&T in Indianapolis, has two children, Karen Marie Campbell (Sept. 6, 1969) and Christina South Campbell (Sept. 4, 1974).

Myrtis Hayes Evans, has a BA from KSU in Frankfort, an ME from Wayne State U. in Detroit, a retired educator from Detroit schools, Los Angeles & Hopkins Co., living in Madisonville. Formerly married to Robert Elliott, they had two sons: Robert Hayes Elliott (May 29, 1946) has a major in Psychology and a minor in Physics at Mich. State U., lives in Tempe, AZ, is the Chief Housing Loan Officer & SBA Specialist with the Kleinbeck Financial Group and a Housing Consultant for the Washington, DC, Center for Community Change and ACORN of New Orleans; Ronald Spencer Elliott (Aug. 14, 1948) enlisted in USAF from 1967-1971 spending part of his tour in England and the Continent, rec'd degree in Auto Mechanics at Henry Ford Comm. College in Dearborn, MI, an Associate Degree in Chemistry and Physics, cont'd studying Physics at Ga. Tech. U., lives in Knoxville, TN, as a professional photographer.

Helen Hayes Banks, BA from Ky. State U. in Frankfort, ME from Wayne State U. in Detroit, retired educator from Earlington and Christian Co. Schools, lives in Hopkinsville. Son Robert Darryl (July 1, 1950) a Rhodes Scholar (see Banks-Hayes) lives in Niskayuna, NY, with wife Margery Baker and their three children, Adam Baker (Feb. 28, 1981), David Baker (Aug. 30, 1983) and Lauren Baker (Aug. 10, 1985).

Ernestyne Hayes Shelton lives in Indianapolis, IN. She and her husband have six children: Richard Leon (Feb. 11, 1956) attended In. State U. in Terre Haute & Clackmus Jr. College in Oregon City, OR, is now a Distributor for <u>Indianapolis News</u> & a Dist. Sales Leader for A.L. Williams Investments, lives with wife, Lisa, and child, Rishanan (July 13, 1979); Kevin James (Apr. 4, 1957) attended Ky. State U. in Frankfort & Clackamus Jr. College in Oregon City, OR, is presently a typist for Center Township Trustees; Kimmery Ann (Jan. 25, 1960) graduated from In. State U. with a degree in Political Science and one in Forensic Studies, and a degree in Law from the U. of Mi. in Lansing, is now a Deputy City Attorney in the District Attorney's Office in Santa Monica, CA, lives in Los Angeles; Kent Hayes (Dec. 30, 1964) is a senior at Purdue U. at W. Lafayette; Michael (Aug. 17, 1967) is a sophomore at Butler U. in Indianapolis; Michelle (Aug. 17, 1967) is a freshman at IUPUI in Indianapolis. - *Submitted by Myrtis Hayes Evans*

HAYES-PRITCHETT

Charlie Richard Hayes, b. Nov. 7, 1887 d. June 8, 1968, and Mayme Roberta Pritchett, b. Oct. 19, 1890 d. Apr. 22, 1974, were married in Evansville, IN. Both began their public education in Anton at the Hayes School.

Charlie R. Hayes' parents were James M. Hayes Jr. and Hattie Belle McNary who were married Jan. 13, 1876. His paternal grandmother, Mary, came to Kentucky from Virginia. Charlie's siblings were Lonnie, Mack, William, Fletcher, Roy, Mollie, Lena, Ludie, Lizzie, Willie and Bessie. His maternal grandmother was Mary McNary.

Charlie Richard and Mayme Roberta (Pritchett) Hayes

Mayme Roberta's parents were Vicie Louise Scott, died Nov. 6, 1911, and Walter Pritchett both born in Hopkins County. Her maternal grandmother, Ann Scott, lived on the William Cardwell farm in Hopkins County as a house-servant. Mayme's siblings were William, Mabel, Annie, Fannie, Georgia, Bertha and Lovie.

Charlie and Mayme had six daughters (see Hayes story). Viola Bell (Nov. 28, 1919 to May 31, 1978) married Lavonia B. Drake from Slaughters, KY; Willie Lee b. Sept. 9, 1913, married James Williams (dec. Sept. 23, 1985) of Louisville; Anna Ruth b. Nov. 17, 1915, married Willmott South from Mt. Sterling, KY; Myrtis Marie b. Sept. 25, 1917, is now married to Thomas Evans from Kansas City, KS; Helen Elizabeth b. Dec. 5, 1919, married Robert Banks from Hopkinsville, KY; and Ernestine b. July 29, 1929, married Robert Leon Shelton from Sebree, KY.

Charlie, Mayme and family lived in Anton until late 1920 when they moved to Madisonville and he became employed by Coil Mines Coal Co. The residence at 427 Branch St., which is still maintained, became known as their homeplace. Their very loving, supportive and courageous spirits were instilled in their children. These traits and attitudes continue to be exemplified through three generations of their immediate family.

The Hayes grandchildren have so many pleasant memories and so much appreciation for the warm reception, guidance, and love shown them by their grandparents over the years, that they and their children returned to the homeplace in August 1980. In commemoration, this four day gathering was called the "1st Grandchildren's Re-Union." They returned from Los Angeles, CA; Phoenix, AZ; Washington, DC; Atlanta, GA; Indianapolis, IN; and Detroit. There were eight grandchildren with four spouses, six great grandchildren, and one former son-in-law. It resulted in four days of happy memories and an update on accomplishments, announcements and expectations. - *Submitted by Myrtis Hayes Evans*

ALONZO GARFIELD HAYWOOD

Alonzo Garfield Haywood was born Feb. 5, 1881, near Hanson in Hopkins County, the son of Willis Bird Haywood and Martha Denola Webb.

He spent his entire life in Hopkins County with the exception of a brief time when he mined copper in Arizona and Mexico. The early part of his life, he farmed in the northern section of Hopkins County. The latter part he worked as a coal miner for the old Sunset and Coil Mines around Madisonville and the Hart Coal Company of White City.

Wedding picture of Alonzo G. and Sally Price Haywood, 1902

On Feb. 2, 1902, he married Sallie Ann Price born June 29, 1883, the daughter of Simon Peter Price (1843-1914) and Sarah L. Tomlinson (1850-1898). Their children were: Franklin Emerson born Nov. 21, 1904, Fred born Apr. 12, 1906, Mary Elizabeth born Oct. 22, 1907, Fairy Jeanette born Aug. 3, 1909, William Robert born Feb. 25, 1910, John Paul born Oct. 29, 1912, Charley Edward born Sept. 2, 1914, Major Garfield born Dec. 14, 1916, Jonell born Jan. 1, 1919, Kenneth Price born Aug. 2, 1923, and Jack Densmore born June 11, 1929.

Alonzo died 1951, Sallie died 1937. They are buried in East Lawn Providence Church Cemetery, east of Hanson. - *Submitted by Kenneth Price Haywood*

JAMES HAYWOOD

James Haywood, born May 4, 1815, in Montgomery Co., NC, was the son of Partin Haywood (Hagood) and the grandson of Bird Haygood (the writer is unable to explain the change in spelling of the family name).

The Partin Haywood family moved to Carroll Co., TN, in 1826. On May 26, 1842, James married Lucretia Ann Rust (born Oct. 13, 1821 in Greenville Co., NC) the daughter of James J. Rust and Elizabeth Gooch Rust.

James Haywood with son Willis Bird about 1849

In 1850 the family moved to Hopkins Co. near Vandetta where James taught school for one year for $150.00. The next year they raised a crop and moved back to Carroll Co., TN, in

Lucretia Rust Haywood with son Benjamin Franklin about 1849

1852 where he taught school and farmed until 1864.

As in many cases, the Haywood family had divided loyalties during the Civil War. James was a Union sympathizer and was outspoken in his beliefs. His brother, Hillbird Haywood, had two sons James R. and Jefferson Green in I Co. 7th Tennessee Cavalry (Union) who were captured and imprisoned in the infamous confederate stockade at Andersonville, GA. They both died and were buried there.

One cold night in November 1863, guerrillas or nightriders came to the James Haywood home and demanded money or his life. They knew that he had sold some land and was paid in gold. He was hanged three times but was released each time before death but he did not reveal where the gold was hidden. He decided to return to Hopkins Co. after that episode. They were searched several times during the journey but his gold coins were concealed in the bottom of a wooden keg and covered with lye soap.

James and Lucretia's children, all born in Carroll Co. were: Willis Bird born Feb. 9, 1846, Benjamin Francis born Mar. 12, 1848, Joseph Dow born May 3, 1850, John Rust born Dec. 21, 1852, James Jr. born August 26 and died Sept. 9, 1855 and Alonzo born Jan. 25, 1860.

James in his old age was nearly blind. One day while walking in the horse lot he stumbled into a mule that kicked him over a log. Shortly after this, he died on June 26, 1898. Lucretia died July 5, 1900. They are buried in East Lawn Providence Church Cemetery, east of Hanson. - *Submitted by Kenneth Price Haywood*

WILLIS BIRD HAYWOOD

Willis Bird Haywood was born Feb. 9, 1846, in Carroll Co., TN, the son of James Haywood and Lucretia Ann Rust. He was named after his great grandfathers Bird Haygood and Willis Gooch. He moved with his parents to Hopkins County in 1864.

On Jan. 15, 1868, Willis married Martha Denola (Nolie) Webb (born 1852), the daughter of Walker T. Webb (1803-1884) and Harriett Malin (1810-1897). Their children were: William Benjamin born 1868, James Walker born 1870, Ulysses born 1872, Rowena born 1873, Henry H. born 1875, Emerson Ethridge born 1878, Alonzo Garfield born Feb. 5, 1881, and Willis Bird born Mar. 15, 1883.

Willis was a farmer and a strong Republican, as was his father. He named two sons after Republican presidents Ulysses S. Grant and James Garfield. He took typhoid fever in

Willis Bird Haywood with son William Benjamin ca. 1875

1883 and died September 25 at the age of 37. Martha married two more times, to R.B. Utterback in 1898 and J.C. Russell in 1901. She died in 1927. They are buried in East Lawn Providence Church Cemetery east of Hanson. - *Submitted by Kenneth Price Haywood*

HEDGES-HALEY

Shirley Ann Haley and Clifford O'Neal Hedges were married on Mar. 4, 1966, in Louisville, KY.

Shirley was born Apr. 2, 1946, near Graham, in Muhlenberg Co. She is the daughter of Millie Colburn and William Wallace Haley. Wallace Haley was born Jan. 5, 1897, near Graham, in Muhlenberg County. He married Millie Colburn, the child of George Miligan Colburn and Theodocia Woosley, Feb. 15, 1927. Millie was born Aug. 14, 1909, in Butler Co., KY.

Clifford and Shirley Hedges with daughters Freda and Rita

William Wallace was the son of Gus Haley and Elsie Mae Milton. His brothers and sisters were: Lee Haley, Rufus Haley, Charlie Haley, Damer Haley, Maymie Lewis, David Haley, Lucy Uzzle, George Haley, and Jack Haley.

Shirley attended Graham High School, graduating in 1964, and then attended Ky. Wesleyan College in Owensboro for several semesters. Shirley and Clifford became foster parents for the state of Kentucky July 1975 and from then to the present have kept 129 foster children in their home. Shirley was elected to the Hopkins Co. Board of Education in 1984 and is presently serving. Shirley and Clifford attend the Grapevine Baptist Church where Shirley has been in charge of the nursery for the past 12 years.

Shirley has five sisters and one brother: Doshie Mae, Mirdie Dean, Joan Drucilla, Norma Jean (deceased), and William Robert.

Clifford was born May 26, 1943, in Jefferson Co., KY, to Eirsie Callie Hedges and Nora Loraine Wisehart.

Nora Loraine was born July 27, 1923, the daughter of Jordon B. Wisehart and Anna Lee Hardin in Jefferson Co., KY.

Eirsie Callie was born Aug. 11, 1920, the son of Callie Hedges and Eirsie Belle Wiley in Shelbyville, KY.

Clifford has two brothers: LeRoy Calvin (deceased) and Ralph Earl.

Clifford graduated Ahrens Trade High School Louisville, KY, in 1961. He was drafted into the Armed Forces in May 1966. He took his basic training at Fort Knox, KY.

Clifford and Shirley went to Germany in September and October of 1966 and their oldest daughter, Freda Cheryl, was born in Augsburg, Germany, on Aug. 4, 1967.

Clifford is now employed as a machinist with LEBCO Co.

Clifford and Shirley have two daughters: Freda Cheryl, a junior at Brescia College in Owensboro, KY and Rita Gale, a senior at Madisonville North Hopkins High School. - *Submitted by C.O. Hedges*

CHARLES I. HENRY

Charles I. Henry was born June 5, 1892, in the Cherry Hill community of Muhlenberg Co., the son of the late James Rudolph Henry and Mary Easter Isbell.

He served in the U.S. Army in France and Belgium in WWI.

He graduated from University of Kentucky, and received his M.A. degree from Univ. of Chicago in August 1927. He was associated with the Shelby Co. schools, Bagdad, KY, before coming to Madisonville in 1922.

C.I. Henry on his 94th birthday

In 1922 he married Mildred Bennett born July 23, 1893, in Greenville, KY, and brought his bride with him to Madisonville. She was a teacher in the Hopkins Co. schools for several years. They had no children. Mrs. Henry died July 9, 1979, and is buried at Evergreen Cemetery in Greenville.

Mr. Henry was hired by Harper Gatton, Supt. of Hopkins Co. Schools, on the recommendation of Delmont Utley, Chairman of the Board. He was principal of Madisonville High School on So. Seminary, built in 1923, where grades 7-12 were taught there from 1923 to 1937. They then moved to the new MHS at Browning Springs, where Mr. Henry remained as principal until 1940.

The Henrys left Madisonville in July 1940, for him to become Supt. of the Mayfield school system, but returned to Madisonville on Jan. 1, 1946, when he became cashier and later a Vice President of the KY Bank and Trust Co., remaining there until his retirement June 30, 1966. He had been a member of the Board of Directors of the bank for 40 years, having missed only 5 of 175 director's meetings.

Mr. Henry was a very active member of the First Baptist Church, where for 25 years he taught the men's Baraca Sunday School class, which was broadcast on radio each Sunday.

Mr. Henry was a Kiwanian for 65 years, and was presented a plaque by the Kiwanis Club in acknowledgement of his 65 years of service. He was fondly known as "Mr. Kiwanis." He served as president of the local club, Lt. Gov. of the division, Gov. of the KY-Tenn district, and was Chairman of the International, extensively active throughout Kentucky in Kiwanis and education for over 70 years. His last public appearance, other than church, was his presentation of the "History of the Kiwanis Club" in February 1987, before his death in March.

He was an ardent member of the Hopkins Co. Retired Teachers Assoc. and attended meetings through the June 1986 meeting, at which time the group sang "Happy Birthday" to him for his 94th birthday. Other activities in which he participated were member of the Madisonville Community College Advisory Board, and a member of the Advisory Board of the Hopkins Co. Senior Citizens Center.

Mr. C.I. was a familiar figure in the community, with a cheerful word and warm handshake for all. He enjoyed visiting with students, educators, and friends as he met them. His marvelous mind enabled him to quote poetry phenomenally and he was a teller of subtle jokes, according to his closest friends.

During their last several years Mr. and Mrs. Henry were fortunate to have tender loving care from their dear friends they called "family": Mr. and Mrs. Thurman Clark, Mr. and Mrs. Crawford Jent, Mr. and Mrs. J.P. Edwards, Mr. and Mrs. Bill Page, Dr. and Mrs. Wm. Jernigan, Mr. and Mrs. Charles Schmitz of Greenville, and Joyce Jackson, his personal secretary. For his last annual Christmas Breakfast in 1986, all 35 invited guests attended. His last large function was to attend the 44th Wedding Anniversary of Sue and Crawford Jent in February 1987.

C.I. Henry died Mar. 21, 1987. Two nephews survive. Funeral services were conducted by Dr. Harold Purdy and Rev. Archie Oliver. Burial was in Evergreen Cemetery, Greenville. - *Submitted by Rella G. Jenkins*

JOSEPH HENRY

The record of this family begins with Joseph Henry, born Nov. 13, 1772, who left his birthplace, Dublin, Ireland, going first to the southwest coast of Scotland, before coming to America. He was in Augusta Co., VA, at about the age of 30 years, where he married Lucy Shumate (born ca. 1783/85), the daughter of Bailey and Mary (Dodson) Shumate of Albermarle Co., VA. Permission for that marriage was given by Bailey Shumate, dated Sept. 7, 1802.

In Augusta and Albermarle Counties of Virginia are found records of Henrys living in the area as early as 1759. It would seem that Joseph came to relatives living in Virginia, when he left his homeland.

Many of the early families used the same names for their children as did Joseph, which is another reason to believe a relationship existed. Many of the same Henry families emigrated to Kentucky from Virginia at about the same time as did Joseph and his wife, Lucy (Shumate) Henry.

In the First Tax List of Hopkins Co., KY, of 1807 is found Joseph Henry, owning 100 acres of land on the Tradewater. In 1818, records show Joseph Henry bought 30 acres of land "lying in the county of Hopkins on the waters of Wier Creek, a branch of the Tradewater," for which he paid $40. Joseph Henry was appointed surveyor of the road from "Stubin's Lick to Given's Horse Mill" in July 1815.

The Henry family home in Hopkins County was a large two story house built of logs - (as were others in this area). There were two large rooms in front connected by a wide hallway with stairs, with a large room attached at the rear. The upper floor was a duplicate of the lower floor. Every room had a fireplace. The rooms were sealed with cedar and had hand-hewn cedar beams.

A burial plot was set aside on the family farm, as was the custom in Virginia. Later, the family stones were removed, by an owner of the land, and used to fill in "a wash." It is very likely that the emigrant, Joseph, and his wife, Lucy's, gravestones were among those used to fill "the wash," so that their burial place is now lost.

The Henrys were active in organizing the Star Hope General Baptist Church in Webster County.

The following is a list of the children of Joseph and Lucy (Shumate) Henry with their approximate birthdates: Sarah born 1804; James born 1805; Thomas born 1806; Polly born 1807; Nancy born 1810; Racheal born 1813; Lucy born 1816; Bailey born 1817, and Joseph born 1819.

Descendants of these Henrys are still living in the Western Kentucky area. - *Submitted by Catherine D. Austin (Mrs. Clarence C.)*

BARTLETT HENSON, JR.

Bartlett Henson, Jr. was born circa 1775, the son of Bartlett Henson, Sr. of Burke Co., NC.

Bartlett Henson, Jr. and his wife Ann migrated from Burke Co., NC, to Hopkins Co., KY, in the fall of 1815. They made their journey to Kentucky in wagons when their youngest child, Sarah was "a babe in arms."

Bartlett and Ann Henson had seven known children, who were all born in North Carolina: Abner F. Henson, who was born circa 1796 and married Mahalia Davis in Hopkins Co., KY, in 1817; Elizabeth (Betsy) Henson, who was born circa 1799 and married (1) Thomas Herrin (2) John Clark and (3) John Kirkwood; Polly Henson who was born circa 1801 and married Hugh Kirkwood, Jr. in 1820 in Hopkins Co., KY; Ann Henson who married George W. Utley in 1827 in Hopkins County; William Henson who was born in 1810 and married (1) Elizabeth Dixon and (2) Sallie Sisk; Susanna E. Henson who was born in 1811 and married John B. Laffoon in 1832 in Hopkins County. (They were the grandparents of Ruby Laffoon, Governor of Kentucky.) and Sarah Henson who was born in 1815 and married Dixon Hall in 1832 in Hopkins Co., KY.

Bartlett Henson, Jr. died between 1820 and 1821 in Hopkins County and Ann Henson died July 3, 1835, in Hopkins Co., KY. - *Compiled by Beverly H. Dockrey*

HEWLETT

Our authentic record of the Hewlett family began in the year 1786, when Martin and Jane Hewlett and family left Henry Co., VA. After stopping in North Carolina and Eastern Kentucky, the family settled in Hopkins Co., KY, about the year 1800.

The Hewlett family originated in France, then went to England, then to America to settle on Long Island, NY about 1660, and then migrated South to Virginia.

Our family first settled on Pond River near Anton, then moved to the area between Madisonville and Hanson, and were prosperous farmers and business people in the area, also doctors and lawyers.

Members of our family have served in every war our country has fought. Martin Hewlett fought in the Revolution; his son, Lemuel Green Hewlett, was one of the few injured in the Battle of New Orleans. We had members of our family serve in the Confederate Army in the Civil War. In World War I, Dr. Lan Hewlett of Hanson, KY, was gassed while in France caring for the wounded and died soon afterward. In World War II one Hewlett was in the Bataan Death March and died in a Japanese Prison Camp in the Philippines.

Thomas and Lena Hewlett about 1925

Thomas Dewitt Hewlett, a brother of Dr. Lan Hewlett, was an attorney in Madisonville from 1922 until his death in 1954. He was elected twice as County Attorney and served in the State Legislature in 1952-1953.

The Hewletts have gone to other states from here. One branch went to California and have established the large computer company of Hewlett-Packard. - *Submitted by: Gladys Hewlett Kelley*

HEWLETT-KIRKWOOD

On a December day in 1900, a 26 year-old man pulled up to the home of his bride-to-be with a buggy pulled by two rented, white horses. The snow was gently falling, which made the scene like something out of a storybook. It would be an event which the young girl would remember for the rest of her life. They drove to the train station and proceeded to Robertson Co., TN, where they were married on Christmas Eve 1900.

Lola Dempsey Kirkwood, the bride, was born in Madisonville Jan. 16, 1882, daughter of Thomas Jefferson Kirkwood (1853-1921) and Louisa Elizabeth Sisk (1858-1909), both born in Hopkins County. Her grandparents were Jef-

Lola Kirkwood and Giles B. Hewlett on their 50th wedding anniversary, 1950

ferson W. Kirkwood and Florella O'Bryan, and William Henson Sisk and Pernecia O'Bryan.

Giles Baker Hewlett, the groom, is believed to be born in Webster County, on the border of Hopkins near Nebo, May 4, 1874. His parents were Emery Roger Qualls Hewlett (1835-1898) and Mary Temperance Harrelson (1841-1920), both of Kentucky. His grandparents were Lemuel Green Hewlett and Rebecca Harvey Browder, and Anderson Bailey Harrelson and Elizabeth Mary Ann Bailey. All left their native states to settle in Hopkins County. Lemuel fought in the Battle of New Orleans in 1815, and was wounded, losing several fingers.

Their eight children are:

Robert Pratt (1901-1987) married Hilda Juntunen in Detroit, MI. Their children are Helen Fay, Robert Allen, Donald Ray, Roger Giles and Carol Janis. After Hilda died, he married Theresa Radziejewski.

Owen Manley (1902-1944) died serving his country in a Japanese prison camp, near Manila in the Philippines. He succumbed to starvation days before MacArthur began his invasion of the Philippines.

Raymond Earl (1904-) married Pauline Hibbs and had Raymond Terry. Later he married Elizabeth (Betty) Jugas and had Ronald Jugas, David Earl and Susan Ann. He now resides in the Detroit area.

Ila Lee (1908-) married Bradley Ashby of Hanson, KY. Their four children are Marjorie Lee, Bradley Carroll, Wayne Gerald and Lola Belle.

Aubrey Dempsey (1910-) married Frances Hobgood in 1930. They have resided in Nashville most of their lives; they're still there today. They have Barbara Ann, Stephen Owen, Pamala Ruth and Lola Faye.

Clara Giles (1913-1965) married Elmer Daniels in Detroit, and had Marlene Elaine and Gloria Jean. After Elmer's death, she married Bernard Suino.

Sammie Ray (1922-) and Lola Faye (1922-1924) were twins. Sadly, Lola choked to death on a bean at the age of 23 months. Sammie married Lorene Brown; Richmond, VA, is their home. Their children are Garland, Kevin and Lynette.

Although they spent most of their lives farming near Hanson, circumstances took Giles and Lola to Arizona one year and to Detroit during the depression. They were members of the Hanson Baptist Church. Both died of heart attacks; Giles on Feb. 6, 1960, Lola on Apr. 1, 1972. They were buried in the East Lawn section of the Providence cemetery near Hanson. Their 50th wedding anniversary picture is shown above. They were married a total of 59 years. - *Submitted by James E. Gunnis - a great-grandson*

LEMUEL GREEN HEWLETT

Lemuel Green Hewlett (1790-1877) came to Hopkins County with his parents, Martin and Jane Hewlett, in the year 1800. As a young man, he helped build houses in the new town of Madisonville, and gave some land for the building of the First Methodist Church in Madisonville.

When Andrew Jackson recruited men from this area, he volunteered and fought in the Battle of New Orleans. He lost two fingers in the battle. Andrew Jackson passed on his horse and threw Hewlett a kerchief from around his neck to wrap his hand. After the battle, the soldiers were discharged in New Orleans and they had to walk home. They came up the Mississippi River to the Ohio River and then home. On the way, they ate with Indians who had camps on the rivers.

At the battlesite in New Orleans there is a museum that has the records of Lemuel Hewlett's activity. Also, there is a similar record in the Archives Building in Frankfort, KY. - *Submitted by Gladys Hewlett Kelley*

JAMES RUSSELL HIBBS

James Russell Hibbs, was born in 1833 in Hopkins County on a plantation of some thousand acres belonging to John S. Hibbs, born in 1817. John's father was probably Nathan A. Hibbs, born in 1782 in Virginia and married in Hopkins County in 1808 to Polly Bourland, one of the first marriages in the county.

John Hibbs died in 1834; his will at the Hopkins County Courthouse provides: "I give unto my brother Nathan Hibbs, my sorrell filly three years old next spring and request that my said father in law to give and to possess the plantation and to keep it until my son James comes of age." The settlement lists James R. Hibbs, orphan of decedent, his only heir with Tolbert Hibbs guardian. His wife was Eliza Dorriss, the daughter of John Dorriss.

James Russell Hibbs was living with the Tolbert Hibbs family in the 1840 census and the 1850 census. He was married twice, first to Mary J. Todd, Aug. 3, 1853, in Madisonville; they had two children, Daniel and H.R. (a girl). December 15, 1863, he married Melissa Jane Hibbs, born in 1840, the daughter of Joseph and Mary Hibbs and either his third or fourth cousin. Joseph Hibbs is buried in the Flat Creek Cemetery. He was born 1801 and said both his parents were born in Kentucky. He was listed as a farmer in both 1860 and 1870 census.

The children of James Russell and Melissa Jane Hibbs were: James Ernest, born in 1865; John Edward, born in 1866; Joseph Basil, in 1867; Oscar C. in 1869; Amyrillas Evelyn and Carrie Ivo.

James Russell Hibbs probably inherited the land his father left him. Several transactions are listed in the Hopkins County Courthouse in Madisonville in his name; 1852, 200 acres on Tradewater River to Ira Dorris; 1861, 85 acres on Clear Creek to Ben F. Nixon; 1862, two tracts on Lick Creek to Elisha Williams; 1863, acreage to Isaac Lynn; 1863, 100 acres on Pogner Creek to B.D. Robertson; 1863, 100 acres on Clear Creek to Ben Nixon; 1865, 100 acres on Clear Creek to Tolbert Hibbs; 1866, 1-1/3 acres to Mary H. Frost; 1866, 150 acres on Pogner Creek to Lloyd Browning; 1867 with Melissa J. two lots in Madisonville to P.N. Bradley.

He and his wife owned and operated a grocery in Madisonville, located directly across from the Courthouse on the site where the Bank is now located. The grocery was burned by the Union soldiers when they burned the Courthouse.

The Hibbs families in Kentucky were originally from Hardin and Nelson counties, farmers and Quakers, so James Russell returned to Hardin County during the Civil War and later to Louisville where he operated a dry goods store. Later the family moved to Springfield, TN, and operated a tomb stone business. Melissa died before 1892 and is buried in the Flat Creek Cemetery. James Russell returned to Hopkins County, traveled on horseback as a peddler selling a medicine, a balm of some sort he had perfected, and was known as Dr. Hibbs. He died at the home of his son, Joseph Basil, in St. Charles and is buried in the Christian Privilege Cemetery on their burial plot.

Ernest Hibbs owned and operated a music store in Madisonville for many years until his death. Ernest had one daughter, Ernestine. Oscar owned and operated a grocery store in Cairo, IL, until his death. Oscar and his wife had no children. Carrie married Mr. Lynn, who worked for the railroad. They lived in a bungalow on West Main Street in Madisonville and raised a family there. - *Submitted by Kathleen Trover Davis*

JOSEPH BASIL HIBBS

Joseph Basil Hibbs was born Oct. 2, 1867, in Louisville, KY, on the corner where the Brown Hotel now sits, the son of James Russell and Melissa Hibbs. Joseph Basil Hibbs married Mary Anne Faull on Oct. 2, 1889. They lived in St. Charles where he worked as a mine superintendent in a St. Bernard Coal Company mine. Their first child, Ethel, born 1890, died in 1892. Ruth was born Nov. 27, 1892, Lonnie Clyde in 1898, Raymond in 1905, Thelma in 1912, all at St. Charles.

For a short period around 1900, Joseph Basil (known as "Bass") Hibbs was a salesman for the Singer Sewing Machine Company. He had fought for safety measures in the mines and for the union and was finally blacklisted by the coal company. He owned several small farms in the Suthards and Carbondale section, buying back part of the original family farm, but the house burned and the family lived in a log cabin on the place for two or three years, then moved to Earlington so their daughter, Thelma, could attend high school.

Mary Anne died Feb. 27, 1941, at Earlington and was buried in the Christian Privilege Cemetery at St. Charles, as was Joseph Basil, who died in 1949.

While the family was living on a 50-acre farm in the Suthards section, purchased from Z.F. Trover, Ruth married Barton Crutchfield Trover, Feb. 20, 1910. Clyde, at 19 years of age, was a private and ambulance drive in France during World War II. Returning home after the Armistice, he soon married Edna Harper from Carbondale and they had one son, Hamill, who died at the age of seven. Raymond married Mary Moore Randolph, a teacher, of Earlington in 1944. Two children were born to them, Barbara and Joseph Randolph. Thelma married Aubin Higgins in 1940 and bore two sons, Michael and Lexis.

The earliest Hibbs settlers came into New Jersey in 1625 and were practicing Quakers. They were said to have been two brothers who were ship builders. Joseph Basil did build houses, the Suthards Christian Church and other carpentry at various periods in his life. He died at the home of his son, Raymond, in Earlington. - *Submitted by Kathleen Trover Davis*

MARY MAY HIBBS

Mary May Tucker was born in McLean Co., KY, on May 1, 1883. In 1902, she married Ben Hibbs (born Nov. 8, 1872 in Hopkins County), a farmer.

For two years they lived in Old Mexico, where Ben was a foreman in a copper mine. In the 1930's, they were with Springfield-Hibbs Funeral Home in downtown Madisonville.

May and Ben were the parents of five children. There are now 11 grandchildren, 16 great grandchildren and two great great grandchildren. Ben died on Mar. 28, 1961, and he is buried in Olive Branch Cemetery.

May was very active in Hanson's rural Homemakers much of her life. She has been a member of Olive Branch Baptist Church for more than 80 years.

Until 1981, she lived in her home in Hanson. She then moved to her daughter's in Madisonville. In 1986, May became a resident of Senior Citizen Nursing Home in Madisonville.

Photo of Mary May Hibbs is included in the section "Hopkins County Centenarians". - *Submitted by Dorothy Miller Shoulders*

HICKERSON

Carol Elaine Hickerson was born in Hopkins County Hospital in 1972. Carol was 15 on Nov. 24, 1987 and she attends Dawson Springs High School. She has a younger sister and brother. Her sister's name is Emily Jo Hickerson. She was also born in Hopkins County Hospital, in 1977 and was 11 years old on Jan. 6, 1988. Emily attends Dawson Springs Elementary and is in the 5th grade. Carol's brother is Jason Steven Hickerson. He is 6 years old and will be 7 on Nov. 14, 1988. He also attends Dawson Springs Elementary; he is in the 1st grade.

Carol's mother is Kathy Jo (Bivins) Hickerson. She is a housewife who is 36 years old. In her spare time, she likes to go to homemakers and likes to work with arts and crafts. Carol's dad, Andy Steven Hickerson, is 36 years old. He was born Feb. 16, 1950. He works at Sextet Mining Corporation. Andy is a boss of one section of the many sections of miners.

Carol wants to be a Psychiatrist. Her sister, Emily, wants to be a Pediatrician. Her brother, Jason, wants to play for the Boston Celtics. The family attends First Baptist Church in Dawson Springs. They live in Dawson Springs by the Western KY 4-H Camp.

In Carol's spare time, she enjoys swimming, talking to her friends, playing softball and Junior Varsity basketball. She plays Junior Varsity Basketball for Dawson Springs as a forward and also plays softball, of which she plays second base. She also enjoys riding her 4-wheeler, and loves to play with animals. She is very outgoing. Carol's sister, Emily, plays a clarinet in the Elementary band.- *Submitted by Trish Matheny*

HICKLIN

This family is of Scotch origin. On account of persecution received in Scotland, Arthur Hicklin left his native land and settled in County Tyrone, Ireland, probably about 1730. After a residence here of more than twenty years, the times were again stormy, so much that he concluded to go to America where he might serve his God in his own way and under his own vine and fig tree.

Sometime in the decade 1750-1760, Arthur brought his family over and settled in Lancaster Co., VA, taking up a large body of land along the eastern bank of the Catawba at Browns Ferry. The name of Arthur Hicklin's wife was Jane. It is likely he was married before he left Scotland. His children were George, William, Arthur, Hugh, John and Elizabeth.

Some years of peace were spent in the forest, but "the dogs of War" were turned loose and the Revolution was on hand. Having some experience in the treatment of the Royal Government the sons of Arthur Hicklin, one and all soon decided on which side they would serve.

Hugh Hicklin's wife was named Elizabeth, their son was Thomas Hicklin and his wife was Elizabeth Carlisle, their son was James Hicklin born Nov. 15, 1785. - *Researched by: Darrell Hicklin*

Around 1814 James Hicklin (b. Nov. 15, 1785) and wife Catherine Scearce Hicklin (b. Aug. 30, 1789) settled in Hopkins County. James, Catherine and small daughter Permelia rode down horseback from the Bluegrass area of Kentucky. Their children were Permelia Hicklin, born Dec. 25, 1812, David Hicklin born June 13, 1815, Thomas Hicklin born Nov. 9, 1818, William G. Hicklin born Nov. 20, 1820, James Hicklin Jr. born Nov. 23, 1822, Catherine Mary Hicklin born Jan. 19, 1824, Linsey Hicklin born Dec. 27, 1825, Wesley Hicklin born Jan. 19, 1828, Sarah Margaret Hicklin born July 22, 1832, Louisa Hicklin born Nov. 27, 1830. James Hicklin died in 1854. He and Catherine are buried in Browders Cemetery.

Missaniah Murphy (b. Jan. 5, 1837) and Wesley Hicklin (b. Jan. 19, 1828) were married Aug. 25, 1853. Their children were: Charles T. Hicklin born Aug. 25, 1854, Lutetia C. Hicklin born Oct. 7, 1856, Corrilla C. Hicklin born Nov. 16, 1858, Ada Hicklin born Oct. 25, 1862, Annie M. Hicklin born Mar. 4, 1865, America M. Hicklin born Sept. 25, 1866, James E. Hicklin born Jan. 26, 1869, Washington Noel Hicklin born Nov. 18, 1871, John Wesley Hicklin born Aug. 12, 1874, and Permelia Myrtle Hicklin born Aug. 28, 1877. Missaniah and Wesley donated one acre of ground for a cemetery that is now known as Hicklin Cemetery, Anton, KY. Both are buried there.

Willie Lee Livingston (b. Feb. 20, 1893) and John Wesley Hicklin (b. Aug. 12, 1874) were married Dec. 25, 1907. Their children were John Wesley Jr. (died in infancy) Katharine Hicklin (b. Aug. 23, 1913) and Willie Ruth Hicklin (born Aug. 30, 1919). Willie Lee and John W. are buried in Hicklin Cemetery. (See Malcolm Jackson Family) (See David Jackson Family) - *Source: Hicklin Family Bibles. Compiled by Katharine and Ruth Jackson*

HICKMAN

James Hickman married Martha Roberts and their children were James and Henry Harrison. Henry Harrison was born in 1856 and died in 1939. He married Cammie Jane Browder (see Browder family) on Jan. 18, 1882, in Hopkins County. Cammie was born in 1862 and died in 1928. They are both buried in Oddfellows Cemetery in Madisonville. Their children were: Leslie Key and James Herschel.

Leslie Key was born Dec. 9, 1883, and died Feb. 4, 1960. He married Lula Edwards who was born July 14, 1888, and died Nov. 30, 1973. Both are buried at Oddfellows. They were the parents of Helen Morton who married Bert Dozier and second Phillip Hubbert. She was born Aug. 27, 1910, and died Dec. 5, 1985. Leslie Key was a senior member of Baker & Hickman Department Store. He purchased an interest in the business in 1910.

James Herschel was born Jan. 25, 1897, and died Nov. 8, 1952. He is buried at Oddfellows. He worked for the State Highway Department. He married first Jessie Louise Ashby (see Branson-Ashby family). Their children were Mary Edna and J.A.

J.A. was born and died in 1919.

Mary Edna was born Jan. 3, 1918, and married first John Taylor Clark Jr. Their daughter Serena Ann was born Dec. 19, 1941, and died Jan. 14, 1982. Serena married Robert Andrew Thursby. Serena and Robert's daughter Mary Ann was born Oct. 3, 1961.

Mary Edna married second Elmer Clifton Harris (see Harris family).

After the death of Jessie Louise in 1919, James Herschel married Mayme Marie Dexter. Their children were Eva Imogene and William Harrison.

William Harrison married Doris Catherine South.

Eva Imogene married Dewey Gossett and their children are Leslie Wright (married Robbie Jewell Blanchard), Anna Marie (married Tommy Kelley), Patricia Lee, Herschel Dewey, Wayne Harrison and Violet Dawn. - *Submitted by Mary Edna Harris*

HICKS-SISK

Patricia Sisk and Trumon Earl Hicks were married June 26, 1955 in a double wedding ceremony. The ceremony took place at the home of the bride.

Patricia was born June 14, 1939 to Edna A. Menser and D. Garnett Sisk. She was active in the 4-H club during her shcool years and graduated from Charleston in 1956. Over the years, Patricia has been in Homemakers and the Parent-Teacher Association. She has been a member of the Friends of the Library since the organization started in 1978 and recently joined the garden club. Currently, she is in her twentieth year as a Dawson Springs High School band booster mom. One of Patricia's favorite hobbies is skillfully baking and decorating delicious cakes. Others are decorating her home and growing plants.

Truman and Patricia Hicks

Trumon was born Sept. 15, 1935 to Dollie R. Roberts and T. Arnold Hicks. Trumon was also involved in the 4-H Club as well as being a member of Charleston's basketball team. He graduated Valedictorian of his class in 1953. Trumon has worked for Island Creek for twenty years and is presently a shop mechanic at Providence No. One coal mine. His favorite pastimes include fishing, hunting, gardening, and reading. He also likes to collect stickers and has a collection of more than thirty-five.

Trumon and Patricia have lived in Hopkins County all their lives. They have lived in Dawson Springs on Oak Heights since Dec. 7, 1963. Trumon cut all of the lumber for their house on his father's farm in Beulah. They enjoy traveling and have been in thirty-five states. Their favorite trips include one to Yellowstone National Park and one to view the historical sites in Washington, D.C. During nice weather, they often barbecue outdoors on their backyard patio.

On Aug. 3, 1956, Patricia and Trumon had a son who is now Dr. Steven E. Hicks. Their next child, Randal J. Hicks, was born on Jan. 19, 1959. Their only daughter, Joan Hicks, was born May 15, 1970. Randal married Tana V. Russell of Dawson Springs on Apr. 7, 1978 and they have a daughter, Korrie D. Hicks, who was born May 10, 1987 in Pusan, Korea. Steven married Sally A. Fisher of Moscow, OH on Dec. 15, 1984. Joan is a high school senior and will be attending college next fall.

Other ancestral family names are Wilkey, Fitzsimmons, LaMar and Laffoon.-*Submitted by Joan Hicks*

HILL

Robert T. Hill migrated to Hopkins County from Tennessee when he was twelve years old. Upon attaining manhood he married Luaretta Meelin (who had moved to Hopkins County from South Carolina) and became a Cumberland Presbyterian minister. In the 1840's, he ministered at the Rose Creek Presbyterian Church near Nebo.

The pioneer minister expired in 1846. He was survived by his widow and three daughters. A son, Robert Porter Hill (1846-1938) was born after his death.

In 1854 his oldest daughter Mary traveled by oxcart in a wagon train across the plains and mountains, being the first settlers to pass through the Natches Pass in Montana, to the Washington Territory. The purpose of her perilous journey was to marry her fiance, Rev. David F. Byles.

Following the Civil War her brother, Robert P. Hill, went to join her. He worked as a surveyor for several years before returning to Hopkins County. He purchased land on the Rose Creek Road seven miles west of the small city of Madisonville. Here he built a home and lived with his widowed mother until her death.

During this time the former surveyor acquired the name Robert Porter "Oregon" Hill to distinguish himself from two other 'Bob Hills' served by the Nebo post office. He entered into a tobacco business that was ill-timed and suffered a financial loss, selling much of his real estate to fulfill financial obligations. What was left of this former prosperous and well-plotted family farm was sold twenty years ago by his two sons and now awaits ravaging by a coal company.

Following the death of "Oregon Bob's" mother, he married Mary Langley Hoffman, a school teacher and daughter of a prominent Nebo family. C.S. Hoffman Masonic Lodge #252 is named for her father who was a charter member of the fraternal group.

To this marriage two sons were born. David Byles Hill was born in 1891, married Alverdia Oldham and was the father of four children. He expired in 1977 at the age of 86 in Cincinnati, OH. None of the children reside in Hopkins County. Robert lives in Cincinnati, OH; Donald F. lives in Evansville, IN; Mary Lou Hill Whitledge lives in Evansville; and Gerald W. Hill lives in Lexington, KY. There were five grandchildren, four survive, one in Indiana; one in Tennessee; and two in Kentucky. There are now four great-grandchildren.

The younger son Frank Hoffman Hill was born in 1902 and when he passed away in 1981, he was survived by his second wife, Marie Craig Hill and two sons, and seven grandchildren.

Frank's two sons, Kenneth and Charles Hill now reside in Madisonville. - *Submitted by Robert Hill*

HILL, BONE, PEYTON, FIKE, KNOX DESCENDANTS

The Bones, Lansdens, Knoxes, Polks, and Hills left York and Lancaster counties in a large caravan to travel down to Mecklenburg and Rowan counties, NC. They later moved on to Tennessee and settled in Wilson Co., TN. They moved on to Hopkins Co., KY. The Triggs, Grahams, Teagues, Fikes, Kings and Peytons also moved down to North Carolina but came across the mountains and across Kentucky to Hopkins County. Little Granny Peyton told that they came by mule with all their belongings in small trunks strapped to a mule. They were all associated with the Cumberland Presbyterian Church and several of the sons became ministers in the Church. They settled in the NW part of Hopkins Co. The Rose Creek Cumberland Presbyterian Church was built by them. The families intermarried.

Jane Bone married James Hill Sept. 4, 1790. They had eleven children; Thomas Logan, William N., John Bone, Elizabeth Witherspoon, James M., Hugh Bone, Jane Givens, Robert Potts, Altezera Loving, Patsy Ann, and Suzannah.

Col. Thomas Logan (war of 1812 and Indian Wars) married Anne Lansden, daughter of Robert Thomas Lansden and Suzannah Bone. They had three children: Abner Emerson Hill, Caroline A. Stone and Susan J.

Abner Emerson Hill (Nov. 7, 1823) married Ann C. Peyton (Nov. 4, 1831) married Nov. 7, 1854. Ann died June 2, 1856. He married Hannah Peyton in 1858. They had three children: Annie, Abner Emerson and Martha (Mattie). The 1860 census shows him as a retired merchant and he had died before the next census.

Mattie (July 25, 1861) married J.W. Fike. They had two daughters: Vera Gradie Lutz and Jimmie Lee (Tott) Lutz. Her second marriage was to J.W. Jackson. They had a son, Boone Jackson.

Annie (Mar. 6, 1860) married Thomas Bone Knox. They had three children: Jimmie (died very young), Retta (never married) and Tommie Hill.

Abner Emerson married Mattie Weir in October 1886. They had seven sons and four daughters: Hannah E., Leon L., Hugh Davis, Eugenea Hannah, Alice Ameila, Annie Weir, Amzee Hooker, Emerson Clifford, Paul Marcus, Carol Bone and Elmer Austin.

A.E. Hill as he was known was a merchant and tobacco man. He was associated with tobacco factories in Nebo, Manitou and Madisonville. - *Submitted by Lanna Arnold*

HILL-HANCOCK

Ruben Hill was born in Hopkins County Sept. 5, 1875, died Nov. 16, 1978, and is buried in Union Cemetery at Nebo. He was the son of Edd Hill and Susan Yarbrough. Edd and twin brother Abney, at age 17, lied about their age and joined the Union Army during the Civil War. Ruben's brothers were: Eddie, John and William. His sisters were Mary and and Odie.

Mr. and Mrs. Ruben Hill

Ruben married Stacy Jane Hancock in 1905. Stacy was born May 10, 1878, in Hopkins County and died May 7, 1975. She was the daughter of Fletcher Hancock and Nancy Cates.

Stacy enjoyed working in her flower garden, raising chickens and quilting. Her brothers were: Doc, Louis, Dick and Smith. She had a sister, Betty.

The Hills were active members of the Methodist church, first in Coiltown and then at Nebo for 75 years.

Ruben, a farmer, bought a farm on Happy Lane in 1920. The Hills lived there until Stacy's death. Ruben was over 100 before his health forced him to move from his farm home. He lived part time with his daughter and in the Clinic Convalescent Center. A sportsman all his life, Ruben always owned one or two dogs. He went squirrel hunting with his grandson, James Hibbs of Nebo, when he was 93. The grandson reports, "The best marksman around in spite of his age." Another close relative relates how Ruben would drive his tractor to cross fields to his favorite fishing hole when he was in his late 90's.

Ruben and Stacy were the parents of Maggie Gertrude (Gertie) and Alie Floyd. There were five grandchildren, five great-grandchildren and two great-great-grandchildren.

For a photo of Ruben Hill, see section on "Hopkins County Centenarians". - *Submitted by Dorothy Miller Shoulders*

HILLYARD-WAIDE

Elnor Celeste Waide and Henry Guy Hillyard were married Sept. 14, 1902, in Crittenden County. She was the daughter of Edwin Waide and Minnie Taylor Waide. She was born Nov. 12, 1883, in Crittenden County. She died Jan. 2, 1981. She had nine brothers and four sisters. They are William, Elnor Celeste, Todd, Goldie, Woodford, Florence, Adah McDowell, Ewell Susie East, Alvie, Richard (Dick), Berdie, Minnie Lloyd, and Earl.

The Hillyard family.

Celeste's ancestors came from England in the middle 1500's. Dr. Roland Taylor came to America to escape the wars of England. This is the family line of President Zachary Taylor and President James Madison. President Madison's grandmother and President Taylor's grandfather were brother and sister, their younger brother George is our descendent.

Henry Guy Hillyard was born Mar. 27, 1882, in Crittenden County. He is the son of George Washington Hillyard and Rachel Frances Lowery Hillyard. He has six brothers and seven sisters. They are Nancy, John Irwin, Laurah Ellen Sheridan, Ulysses Ewell Grant, Fines Albert, Ida Mae Tudor Andrews, Aldora Jane Northern, Irene Jean, Algie Ninn, Henry Guy, Victor Elmer, Ollie and Effie (twins), and Fred Harrison.

Eleven children were born to Henry and Celeste. They are Wilbur, Budie Agatha, Minnie Frances Cates, Mary Elizabeth Cates, Robert Windred, Glades Syvesta Cunningham, Louvinia Waide Larimore, Lawrence Henry, Georgia Franklin Hennebut Mitchem, Virginia Lee Peyton, and David Guy.

Henry was a farmer. They moved to Providence then to Nebo in the early 1920's. They were members of the Nebo Methodist Church. Henry died Sept. 10, 1961. - *Submitted by Sharon Harris*

HOBGOOD

Before the American Revolution in 1776 Hobgoods had settled in Halifax Co., NC, near the Roanoke River in an area where the small town of Hobgood is now located. After fighting in the Revolutionary War the Hobgoods returned to their homes and some families moved from Halifax County to Ebgecombe Co., NC.

The Hobgood families were lawabiding. A search of court records revealed only one Hobgood indicted 1790-1830 and he was pardoned by the state legislature.

A review of the 1790 to 1850 United States Census for the area of North Carolina revealed that during the 1830's several Hobgood families migrated from North Carolina to the new land west of the Allegheny Mountains. The 1830 census for Halifax County prior to the migration revealed the following Hobgood families: 1. John Hobgood; 2. John B. Hobgood; 3. Sterling Hobgood; 4. Thomas Hobgood.

It was on the long journey from North Carolina to Kentucky that the writer's great great grandfather, "Ell" Hobgood, met his wife to be Sally Parker.

The descendants of the several Hobgood families that moved west settled in Webster County near Vanderburg, KY, and in Union Co., KY. In Webster County the Hobgoods were and still are successfully engaged in farming. During the civil war Thomas G. Hobgood was a southern sympathizer and his farm was accordingly raided and burned by the union forces and his livestock and crops were confiscated. He never forgot this. He was even buried facing north, so that he could rise up to fight the union.

From the marriage of "Ell" Hobgood and Sally Parker was born George Thomas Hobgood, the great grandfather of the writer. George Thomas Hobgood married Polley Ann Winstead. From that marriage Charles Green Hobgood was born in 1887 in Webster County. He moved his family to Hopkins County in the early 1900's where he farmed, mined coal, worked at the Lime Cola Bottling Plant, operated a filling station and the "Wagon Wheel," and during World War II he did defense plant work. Later in life he operated a garage with his son, B.L. Grandfather of Byron Hobgood, Charles Green Hobgood, lived to be 92 years of age. He married Bessie Prow. They were married 71 years. Bessie Prow was the daughter of Beauregard Lee Prow and Nettie Ann Neisz. Bessie Prow had twelve other brothers and sisters. There were 13 children in her family and for a large family all of the brothers and sisters were uncommonly close to each other.

Of the marriage of Charles Green Hobgood and Bessie Prow three children were born, Mabel Hobgood, Beauregard Lee Hobgood and Lucille Hobgood Cox. Beauregard Lee

Bessie and Charles Green Hobgood, Christmas Day 1945

Hobgood known as B.L. married Mary Ruth Bassett. A history of the Bassett family is found elsewhere in this edition of the Hopkins County Heritage Book. From the marriage of B.L. Hobgood and Mary Ruth Bassett two children were born, Byron Lee Hobgood and Carolyn Sue Hobgood Williams. Carolyn Sue Hobgood Williams married Edward Williams and of that marriage two children were born, Brenda Williams Huddleston and Susan Williams Winstead. Carolyn Sue Hobgood Williams passed away at age 30 and her daughters were raised by Edward Williams and his second wife, Wanda Wagner. Brenda Williams Huddleston married Billy Huddleston and one child was born, Andrea Huddleston. Susan Williams Winstead married Ricky Winstead and one child was born, Jonathan Winstead. Byron Lee Hobgood and Joan Hobgood have two children, Laura Ashlee Hobgood and Erin Jane Hobgood.

Mabel Hobgood passed away without children. Lucille Hobgood Cox married Palmer Cox and was mother of four children, Linda Cox, Chipper Cox, Robert Cox, and Beverly Cox. Chipper Cox passed away while a child, Linda, Robert and Beverly Cox have each married and have children living in the states of California and Washington. - *Submitted by Byron L. Hobgood*

HOBGOOD-PERKINS

Marlin Hobgood was born Apr. 10, 1905, in Hopkins Co., KY. He was the son of Bert (1881-1923) and Sallie (1883-1957) Hobgood.

Upon the death of his father, Marlin had to quit Madisonville High School at the age of 18. He assumed the route of mail carrier that his father had held for 10-1/2 years, earning the job by scoring the highest grade on a postal exam. Marlin carried the Nebo route for the next 42 years.

Marlin Hobgood at age 18 as he delivered the mail with Old Hunter

When he began the route, it was 22 miles long and before his retirement on July 27, 1965, it was just over 40 miles long. In the early years, he used horseback, wagon and buggies to deliver the mail. Sometimes it took all day and a part of the night to make his rounds. In later years, using a car, it would take 3 to 3-1/2 hours. In the 1937 flood, Marlin hired three men to help him and they used four boats to deliver the mail.

Marlin always enjoyed the people on his route, considering them to be friends. Before the time of the telephone, the mailman was called on to deliver all sorts of messages from one farm to another. Because of this, the mailman pretty much knew everything about the folks on his route.

Marlin met Margaret Perkins while delivering mail to the home of her parents, George C. (1866-1924) and Johnnie (1870-1952) Perkins. He watched her grow from a little girl with long curls to a pretty young lady. Margaret was born Nov. 18, 1911, in Hopkins County. In November 1941, they were married in Charleston, MO.

Marlin and Margaret had one son, Marlin (Eddie) II. Eddie lives in Centersburg, OH, and has two daughters and one son.

Marlin Hobgood at retirement, after 42 years of delivering the mail

Marlin and Margaret attended the First Christian Church in Madisonville, KY, in which he was an elder. He was also a member of the Masonic Lodge and a Kentucky Colonel.

Marlin died on June 29, 1985, and is buried at Union Cemetery in Nebo, KY. Margaret continues to reside in Nebo. - *Submitted by Margaret Perkins Hobgood*

ELIZA HOFFMAN

Annah Eliza Cox was born Mar. 24, 1868, the daughter of Hezekiah Rice (H.R.) Cox and Martha Jane Chandler.

On Dec. 17, 1885, in Christian Co., KY, Eliza married Christian Stover Hoffman II born Feb. 7, 1858, died January 1930. He was the son of C.S. Hoffman I and Elisheba Temperance Harralson.

Eliza and C.S. were the parents of: Joseph McNary, a World War I veteran; Edward Lee who was in the mercantile business with his father in the heart of Nebo; and John Henry who was also a World War I veteran.

Eliza and her family were members of the Nebo Christian Church. The church was next to their home. When the new church was built with its parking lot, the old Hoffman homeplace was sold to make way for the new building.

Eliza died Nov. 14, 1970, at the age of 102. She is buried in Union Cemetery at Nebo.

Information supplied by Sarah Barron of Nebo from the book "Cockes and Cousins Vol. II, the Descendants of Thomas Cocke 1639-1697".

For photo of Eliza Hoffman, see Hopkins County Centenarians. - *Submitted by Dorothy Miller Shoulders*

HOLLAND

Richard Holland died in 1863 at the age of 62 after a fall from a horse. He married Lucy Diggs who died about 1872 at the age of 82. Both were natives of Virginia and migrated to Kentucky.

Their son was Ulysses J. (U.J.) Holland who was born in Fluvanna Co., VA, on Mar. 13, 1816. U.J. had two brothers, Richard and Shannon, and sisters. I have no account of them. When the family moved to Kentucky, they settled in Christian Co. U.J. was reared on his father's farm. He learned the trade of wagon maker.

In 1846, U.J. moved to Tennessee. He married Almyra Gaines Yates (b. ? 15, 1824, possibly Virginia) in 1843, the daughter of Col. James Gaines Yates and Mary Browning Yates. The Yates lived on a farm or plantation in the delta of Red and Cumberland Rivers between Port Royal and Clarksville, TN. This place was the ancestral home of the Yates. Col. Yates and members of the family are buried in a rock-ribbed enclosure in a limestone knob on the old plantation. It seems that many of the Holland children were born on this plantation near Port Royal and came to Madisonville when they were children.

To U.J. and Almyra were born: James Manford Holland, Dec. 16, 1846; Elizabeth M. Holland, Aug. 11, 1848; Ann Lou Holland, Dec. 21, 1849, who died in Madisonville, KY, May 30, 1939 (the last of the family); James R. Holland, Apr. 3, 1852; Mary Florence Holland Moremen (my grandmother) Aug. 20, 1856, died May 3, 1906; Jack Holland Aug. 24, 1858, died Oct. 15, 1859; and Tennessee Holland (a girl) Jan. 10, 1862, died Jan. 14, 1862.

In 1860, U.J. and family moved to Hopkins Co. In this county, he owned a farm or farms that totaled 300-400 acres. He kept all or part of his farms and moved to Madisonville in the county. Here he lived at 419 W. Center St. The family residence was kept in the family until after his daughter, Anna Lou Holland, died May 1939. The house was rented for a while and finally sold to the Myers family. This family sold it and lot to the A & P Company for a store location.

In Madisonville, U.J. Holland operated a flour mill and a planing and saw mill. I, Virginia McCalister, a great-granddaughter, visited in Madisonville several times in my life when my great aunts, Anna Lou and Christina Holland Ross, lived at 419 W. Center. The house was a modest six room frame on the first floor and two rooms on the second. It was located about three squares from the heart of the town. It was on a large lot. The family kept a lovely vegetable garden. The women had hired help, part black and part white. The family had collected some very old pieces of walnut and cherry furniture. When Anna Lou, the last heir, died, the furniture was divided among her three nieces and a nephew. My sister and I inherited about seven pieces from my mother Ernestine R. McCalister, granddaughter of U.J. Holland. We have restored them and enjoy the use of them now. The members of the Holland family are buried in the Old Odd Fellows Cemetery in Madisonville.

The children of Mary Florence Holland Moremen (dau. of U.J.): Wade W. Moremen (August 1878-June 1953); Eula Almyra Moremen Tierney (Jan. 1, 1880-Sept. 6, 1968); Ernestine R. Moremen McCalister (July 23, 1882-Apr. 8, 1973); and Johnnie Beard Moremen (May 19, 1889-Dec. 15, 1976). Eula Moremen Tierney and Johnnie B. Moremen (spinster) had no children. Wade Moremen had four children: Wade W., Walter W. (dec'd 1985), Wm. D., and Mildred Moremen Clark. Ernestine Moremen McCalister's children were Virginia M. McCalister born Nov. 19, 1905, and Henrietta L. McCalister born Sept. 22, 1909.

Two descendants of Richard Holland lived in Hopkinsville, Richard Holland (a bachelor) and Johnnie Beard (a spinster). They were first cousins to my grandmother, Florence Holland Moremen. Other members of this Holland family live now in the Paducah area. We have lost contact with these interesting people. I visited as a 12 year old in the Richard Holland and Johnnie Beard home in Hopkinsville. They lived in a lovely home. They had fine silver, linen sheets, and a butler. They met us at the train in a coach with a black driver. I felt real luxury. Sources: Newspaper clippings, family Bible, History of Ky., 1885 by Battle, Perrin and Kniffin, and my mother, Ernestine Moremen McCalister. - *Submitted by Virginia M. McCalister*

ASHLEY HOLLOMAN

Ashley Holloman (1860-1949) was the only child of the pioneer family of Samuel Harrison Holloman and Sara Jenkins Holloman, both from Dalton, KY. His mother died when Ashley was a young boy and his father remarried a short time later to Julia Bradley and she raised him as a son. Ashley named his only daughter after her.

In 1886, Ashley married Mary Marjorie Williams and she bore him three children: Chesley Williams Holloman (m. Dot Waller); Samuel Harrison Holloman (m. Hallie Ligon); and Missaniah Julia (m. David F. Ramsey).

Ashley made his livelihood as a farmer and tobacco man. Each of his children had one child: Mary Jane Ramsey Mullins of Trigg County, KY, C.W. Holloman, Jr. of Centerville, OH, and Mary Ligon Holloman Whitehead of Birmingham, AL. There are 10 grandchildren and three great grandchildren. Ashley is buried in the family plot in Odd Fellows Cemetery in Madisonville. - *Submitted by Mary J.R. Mullins*

HOOK

A young boy 12 years old, with his parents, came to the U.S. from Germany. The parents' names remain unknown, so far. (They are great, great, grandparents of Freda Hook Cotton on the Hook side.) However, the names of their children are known. There were nine children of this family born in Pennsylvania and Ohio.

They are: Levi, Eli, Charity A., Sarah E., Mathis, Benjamin, John, Elizabeth and Amos Hook (Freda's great grandfather). Five of the brothers of this family were soldiers in the Civil War and all returned from that sanguinary conflict without serious wounds.

Eli Hook enlisted as a private in Co. F, 21st Ohio Volunteer Infantry on Sept. 5, 1861. He was discharged Dec. 31, 1863, and re-enlisted. He was born in Seneca Co., OH, on Feb. 20, 1844, and married Lucy Crocker on Dec. 12, 1865. He participated in several principal battles and was with Sherman when he made his march from Atlanta to the sea.

In October of 1908 the members of this family were to have a family reunion in Dahlgren, IL, at the home of Eli Hook. Three of the family members had already passed away, Benjamin, John and Elizabeth.

Mrs. Charity A. Fesnot of Wichita, KS, Mr. & Mrs. Levi Hook of Broadland, SD, and Amos Hook of Hanson, KY, were re-united with Eli Hook. Sickness kept away Mrs. Sarah E. Ebright of Owosso, MI, and a brother Mathias Hook of Columbus, KS. It had been 58 years since Levi and Amos had last met.

Amos Hook born May 14, 1845, (Freda's great grandfather) and his wife Martha Harriman born June 18, 1847, came to Kentucky with their family in a covered wagon, when their young son was three weeks or three months old. They settled at one time in Shakerag country. There were eight children born in this family: Mary Adline, July 22, 1867; Benjamin Franklin, Jan. 29, 1870; Albert Agustus, Sept. 9, 1872; Anna Lea, Oct. 4, 1874; Serena Mae, Apr. 25, 1877; Ocia Ole, Feb. 27, 1881; Katherine Isabelle, Feb. 4, 1884; and Fredrick Amos Hook, Aug. 5, 1887 (Freda's grandfather).

Fred Hook married Cora Elizabeth Arnold (born Feb. 17, 1885) on Apr. 13, 1911. They had five children: Bonnie Lee, Feb. 23, 1912; Wm. Herman, Apr. 9, 1913; Lula M., Sept. 15, 1914; Ollie Franklin, Apr. 22, 1920; and Nellie Ray, July 27, 1923.

They purchased a farm at Anton, KY, in 1918 and raised their family there. Fred worked his farm mostly, but during the winter time worked at two local coal mines. He worked at Trio and New Coal mines. He was a member of

Herman and Mae Hook with children-Freda, Wm. Franklin and Don Gary in 1946

Elm Grove Church and also registered to serve in W.W. I and probably would have served if the war had not come to an end when it did. His son Ollie served in W.W. II. He entered the Army on Nov. 5, 1942, and was released on Feb. 19, 1944, as ST. SGT. He earned a few ribbons and medals during this time.

Wm. Herman Hook (Freda's father) married on Feb. 13, 1937, Anna Mae Dexter, born July 5, 1916. They raised three children: Freda Mae, June 12, 1938; William Franklin, Nov. 14, 1939; and Don Gary, May 13, 1945.

Freda's father worked at New Coal mines, hauled coal for schools, and later in his life worked for different coal companies, retiring from Peabody Coal Co.

Freda's mother worked for several years at the old hospital in Madisonville, KY. She then went to the new Hopkins Co. hospital, Regional Medical Center, when it was completed. - *Submitted by Freda Cotton (Hook)*

HOWSER-KING

Aug. 31, 1947, at Hillsdale Baptist Church, Franklin, KY, Edith Mary King became the bride of H.B. Howser (both of Franklin, KY).

Edith's parents are Nina-Violet Finn King and John Taylor King, Sr., Franklin. H.B.'s parents are Vercie Cretia Law Howser and John G. Howser. Nina-Violet Finn was raised in Simpson County and married John Taylor King of Kansas City, MO. They decided Franklin, KY, was the spot to raise a family, and run a farm and general merchandise store. The family included three other children: John Taylor King II; Charles Layman King; and Patricia Kaye King (Mays).

H.B. and Edith King Howser at the Opryland Hotel in Nashville, TN, in April 1985

The senior Howsers came from Tennessee. H.B.'s mother, Vercie Cretia Law Howser was from Macon Co., TN, and John B. Sr. was from LaFayette, TN. Their family included three other children: Ewell Homer; Earl Duane and Lillian May Howser (Leath).

H.B. was principal of Middleton school in Franklin until 1952, at which time he was employed by U.C. Milk Company. He has remained with U.C. for 35 years and is Vice President and Sales Manager.

Edith worked for a number of years as the Downtown Retail Merchants Association Executive Secretary. She just recently retired after 16 years in the men's department of Baker & Hickman, Madisonville's oldest department store.

They have two children, Deborah Kaye Howser, born in Carter Moore Hospital in Franklin on Feb. 18, 1952. Debbie is married to Robert Wayne Arnold, son of Lana Niswonger Arnold and Bill Arnold of Madisonville. They have two daughters, Tara Lynn, born Nov. 11, 1976, and Kelli Anne, born Oct. 3, 1981. They live in Bowling Green where they are all engaged in various and many community activities. The Howser's second child was John Charles Howser (Feb. 3, 1962) born in Hopkins County Hospital in Madisonville.

Debbie and John have their college degrees. Debbie is a librarian in the Bowling Green school system and John is Medical Photographer for Vanderbilt Medical Center, Nashville, TN.

John married Betsy Blayne House on Aug. 8, 1987, in Springfield, TN. Blayne's parents are Mr. and Mrs. J.B. Craft of Springfield and Mr. and Mrs. George Pearson House, Hermitage, TN.

The Howsers enjoy traveling, entertaining, church and most of all, each other — after 40 years together.

All family members are Methodist, except Bob Arnold. He is Presbyterian.

God has truly blessed this union. - *Submitted by Peggy Sullivan Waide*

HOWTON

Howton is a family name long in the local books. Hopkins Co. is the original settling place for the Howton family, and Silent Run in particular. Around 1800, a very young Englishman named Johnathan Howton was so anxious to come to America that he actually stole money from the mattress where his mother kept her cash. Then he slipped on board a sailing ship and hid in the crows nest where he stayed until the ship wouldn't be able to send him back to England. After he felt safe, he was allowed to work his passage across. "A Howton always pays his debts" he said and sent the very same money he'd stolen back to his mother in England.

From l to r: unknown, Uriah Howton, unknown, unknown, James William Howton, son Baxter William Howton and wife Louisa Jane DeArmond Howton

Jonathan married Ann Trover, had a son David who wed a girl named Elizabeth (July 27, 1792-? 25, 1878), they had a son David who wed Sarah Chappell Aug. 1, 1845, then wed Mary A. Blue (May 10, 1830-Sept. 15, 1907) on June 28, 1852. David (Oct. 13, 1823-June 23, 1892) and Mary had at least nine children: Mary Jane wed James L. Nickleson who became the 1st Master of the Beulah Masonic Lodge then a year later left the lodge and his wife to join the Jesse James gang; Nathan wed Paralee Kirkwood Aug. 7, 1883; Susan wed James Edward Kirkwood; David M. (Buck) (Mar. 4, 1855-Mar. 12, 1890) wed Lenora R. Wade (?-Dec. 21, 1876); Uriah B. (Uncle RAR) (July 28, 1853-Oct. 1, 1934) wed Susan Purdy (1855-Mar. 25, 1890) on Dec. 10, 1875, they had four children all initials U.H. (stood for child of Uriah Howton) all born dead; Joel W. (Pop) (1858-1913) wed Mollie (1869-1944); Laura (1863-1949) wed J.B. Adkins (1855-1912) on Dec. 13, 1881; Kathryn (1870-19?) wed Joseph Beard (1866-1911); and James William (Feb. 19, 1866-Aug. 21, 1952) wed Louisa Jane DeArmond (Dec. 7, 1876-Feb. 19, 1950) on Nov. 15, 1896.

The parents (David and Mary) lived in a log cabin with an unfinished floor and something happened to cause a rift between them that both were too stubborn to work out. It was so bad that they lived in opposite sides of the house, coming together only for meals and then talking only to the children even to the point they told their children to tell the other to pass the food, etc. He made the living, she cooked and he would eat anything she prepared, but he was afraid to drink the coffee for fear she might poison him. He made his own coffee. Mary kept the grudge to the grave. David died first and she had him buried on his side then when she died she had made a special request that she be buried beside him, but on her side with her back to him. The request was carried out.

Their son James William and his wife had a son, Baxter William (Oct. 7, 1904-July 11, 1945) wed Gladys Mae Asbridge in 1924. Their children: James Baxter (born and died Sept. 5, 1925); John Harold (Sept. 6, 1926-Feb. 24, 1948) wed Dorothy Riggs; Nora Lou (Mar. 25, 1928) wed James Darrel Ratliff (Oct. 12, 1925) had Linda Lou (Dec. 16, 1947) and Darrell Kent (May 11, 1954); Laura Elizabeth (Jan. 5, 1930) wed Billie Wayne Prince, had Jeffery Wayne (Aug. 16, 1957-Sept. 16, 1959) and Paula Ann (Jan. 5, 1961); George William (July 23, 1932) wed Fay Nell Terry (May 15, 1933), had Bradley Lewis (Apr. 19, 1956) and Deborah Fay (Feb. 4, 1960); the baby was Jerry Earl (Feb. 22, 1945) wed Lorita (Rita) Kingrey (daughter of Dorothy Riggs Howton and her second husband Ernie Kingrey) and had William David (Nov. 15, 1971), later divorced and she remarried.

See story on Baxter and Gladys Howton for more information. - *Submitted by Linda Lou Ratliff Gantt*

HOWTON-DAVIS

Elvie Howton (June 20, 1919-Feb. 24, 1983) was the son of Mr. Huey Howton (Apr. 28, 1892-Oct. 16, 1970) and Mrs. Atha Stallins Howton (Jan. 24, 1897-Sept. 21, 1970). Bernice Davis Howton (born June 20, 1919) was the daughter of Mrs. Cynthia Davis (Feb. 16, 1898-Aug. 1, 1937).

Elvie and Bernice were raised as friends

from birth. They lived across the Tradewater River in Caldwell County, were married Sept. 10, 1938, and lived happily together until Elvie died in 1983.

Elvie had two brothers and one sister who have passed away and two sisters, Gertrude Howton Roberts and Marie Howton Hulsey, still living. Gertrude is now living in Wisconsin with some of her children. Marie is living in Dawson with her husband. Bernice has one sister, Dorothy Davis Dunbar, who lives in Dawson with her husband.

Bernice quit school in the eighth grade. She attended a little one-room school in Olney, KY. Bernice and her family tried to attend a Holiness Church but there were only two churches in Olney, and they were both Baptist.

Elvie worked on a farm until 1926; then he was hired by the coal mines. He worked in the mines until he retired 17 years later because of his health, mainly "black lung". Elvie's hobbies were hunting and dancing. He loved these things when he was able to do them.

Bernice worked at home raising the children, cooking, and keeping the house tidy. Her hobbies consist of dancing and playing cards, which she still does.

Bernice and Elvie moved to 706 Union Grove Avenue in 1969. Bernice still lives there with one of her sons.

Bernice and Elvie had ten children, nine sons and one daughter. They are: Donnie, Jerry, Ricky, Larry, Billy, Dale, Sue, Sandy Fay and Randy Kay (twins) and Rocky.

Donnie was born Mar. 18, 1941 and married Linda Mitchell. He is a preacher and runs the Parkway Gulf. Their children are Debbie, Teri, Tammy, Nathan, Joni, and Cindy. Debbie has three children: Mikey, Chassity and Crystal.

Jerry was born Feb. 17, 1943 and married Wanda Oliver. He is employed by South Central Bell. Their children: Michael now deceased, and David. David has just recently married Holly Darnell.

Ricky was born Feb. 9, 1945 and married Mildred (Milly) Latham. Their children are: Missy, Ricky Jr., and Rhonda. Ricky is employed by Webster County Coal Company.

Larry was born Sept. 7, 1947 and married Betty Eli. They have one child, Troy. Larry is employed by Pyro Coal Company.

Billy was born July 3, 1949 and married Mae Eli, a sister to Betty. Their children: Chris, Brad, and Nicholas. Billy is employed by Webster County Coal Company.

Dale was born Oct. 24, 1950 and has never married. His occupation is hunting and dog trading. He lives with his mother.

Sue was born Feb. 19, 1955 and married Bobby Cotton. Their children are Kandi and Bobby Junior (B.J.) Sue does domestic work.

Randy Kay and Sandy Fay (twins) were born Aug. 15, 1956 and died Aug. 21, 1956.

Rocky was born Mar. 9, 1960 and married Shirley (Sissy) Cotton, a sister to Bobby. Their children are Robyn and Christy. He is employed by the Earlington Police Force.

This brings up to the present generation of the very large Howton family. I am the grandson of Bernice and Elvie, and the second eldest son of Billy and Mae. - *Submitted by Brad Howton*

HOWTON-ELI

Betty Lou Eli and Larry Joe Howton were married June 29, 1968 at the Lighthouse Mission Pentecostal Church in Madisonville, KY. Both Betty and Larry have lived in Hopkins County since their births.

Betty was born Mar. 18, 1950 at the Hopkins County Hospital in Madisonville, KY. she is the daughter of Levi Davis Eli (born Mar. 6, 1878 in Kentucky; died Dec. 21, 1962) and Mable Mitchell (born Nov. 21, 1916, in Hopkins County). At age 64, Levi married 27-old Mable on Feb. 14, 1944, in Christian County. Levi and Mable had six children of their own. The children are as follows: Larry Junior Eli (born September 1948; died 6 weeks later), Betty Lou Eli Howton (born Mar. 18, 1950), Eska Mae Eli Howton (born Sept. 26, 1951), Mary Ann Eli Ebert (born Apr. 18, 1953), Billy Gene Eli (born June 17, 1955), and Alice Faye Eli Cotton (born Oct. 8, 1956). Levi is the son of Elisha Eli and Mary Trotter. He has one surviving half-sister, Della Huddleston, who lives in Dawson Springs. Mable is the daughter of James Tinsley Mitchell and Rosa Henderson. Mable has only one brother who is still living; his name is Eugene Mitchell (born Nov. 22, 1921), and he lives in Madisonville.

Betty attended St. Charles School from the first grade through the eighth grade. She then went to South Hopkins High School for the next two and one-half years. She completed her schooling at Dawson Springs High School when she graduated in 1968. Betty went to work for Ottenheimer and Company in May 1968 and worked there until July 1979. She is now a homemaker and part-time employee.

Larry was born Sept. 7, 1947, in Dawson Springs, KY. He is the son of Elvie Huie Howton (born June 20, 1919 in Caldwell County; died Feb. 24, 1983) and Bernice Ovelia Davis (born June 27, 1920, in Caldwell Couuty). Elvie and Bernice were married Sept. 10, 1938. They had ten children of their own. The children are as follows: Donnie Morris Howton (born Mar. 18, 1941), Jerry Wayne Howton (born Feb. 17, 1943), Ricky Dane Howton (born Feb. 11, 1945), Larry Joe Howton (born Sept. 7, 1947), Bill Ray Howton (born July 3, 1949), Gary Dale Howton (born Oct. 24, 1951), Kathy Sue Howton Cotton (born Feb. 19, 1955), Randy Kay Howton (born Aug. 15, 1956), Sandy Fay Howton (born Aug. 15, 1956), and Rocky Lynn Howton (born Mar. 9, 1960). Randy and Sandy were twin boys who died six days after their birth. Elvie Howton is the son of Alfred Huie Howton and Aethia Stallins. He has two surviving sisters—Marie Howton Hulsey of Dawson Springs and Gertude Howton Roberts of Sheboygan, WI. Bernice Davis is the daughter of Cynthia Davis. Bernice has one sister who currently lives in Dawson Springs; her name is Dorothy Davis Dunbar.

Larry attended Dawson Springs High School until his ninth grade year. He attended Charleston School during his ninth grade year and then returned to Dawson Springs High School. He completed his education at Dawson Springs High School when he graduated in 1965. Larry went to work for Ottenheimer and Company not long after his graduation. He worked there until 1979 when he was hired by the Pyro Mining Company in Sturgis, KY. Larry has worked for Pyro ever since.

Larry Joe Howton and Betty Lou Eli have one son, Troy Don Howton. He was born Mar. 21, 1970, at the Hopkins County Hospital in Madisonville. Troy will also become a graduate of Dawson Springs High School in 1988. Submitted by Troy Howton

BAXTER WILLIAM HOWTON

Baxter William Howton (Oct. 7, 1904-July 11, 1945) was the only child of James William Howton (Feb. 19, 1866-Aug. 21, 1952) and Louisa Jane DeArmond (Dec. 7, 1876-Feb. 19, 1950). They had plans for Baxter to become a doctor or lawyer and would have done anything to help him to become a "professional" man, but he had other ideas. He was a coal miner working independently and for larger mines. He was a road-grader driver for the county and had a real desire to be a mechanic. At one time when his dad had a 1919 Model-T Ford, Baxter kept at him until he was allowed to modify the car. He put in a foot control for the accelerator to be used instead of the hand lever control that came with it. James William had said he couldn't understand why Baxter wanted to put that pedal in, but after he got used to it he had to admit it was a lot handier.

Baxter Howton (on left), with friend J.D. Schmetzer, sitting on one of the old cars he worked on

Hopkins Co. had been the home place for the Howtons since James William's great-grandfather Johnathan (see Howton story) had come over from England many years earlier. Silent Run was the main area where the Howtons settled and it was in this area Baxter lived most of his life, including the flood of 1937 that hit the area hard.

In 1924 he married the only child of Althus Zacharire Asbridge and Nora Franklin Asbridge (Feb. 14, 1883-Oct. 8, 1907). Gladys Mae (July 9, 1907-Jan. 24, 1981) was born only three months before her mother died and her father was a railroad man who was travelling most of the time, so her maternal grandmother, Parthenia Elizabeth Franklin Franklin, took care of her. They didn't have a home of their own, but Parthenia had her children to stay with one month at a time. She and Gladys would go to one of the homes then the next month they packed and moved to another of the homes and at the end of that month, they moved to the next. She hadn't known about exchanging gifts or special dinners at Christmas until she married. Their children were J.B. (James Baxter) (Sept. 5, 1925-Sept. 5, 1925); John Harold (Sept. 6, 1926-Feb. 24, 1948); Nora Lou (Mar. 25, 1928); Laura Elizabeth (Jan. 5, 1930); George William (July 23, 1932) and Jerry Earl (Feb. 22, 1945).

Christmas was now a time of celebration for Gladys and Baxter; one of the most memorable traditions was when Baxter would go to the store and buy bushel baskets of oranges, apples and candies and a whole stalk of bananas, then whenever friends and family came over they shared in the treats. Every weekend one of the children would have a friend stay over, they took turns so no one was left out.

Hot weather brought other festivities. Since there wasn't electricity there, the ice wagon came and Baxter would buy two 100 lb. blocks of ice, one to cool the cistern where they kept the milk and butter, the other was to make ice cream. He also got a 25 lb. block to float in a #2 wash tub and filled it with lemonade and sliced lemons. Gladys made cakes (no mixes) to have with the ice cream. Then all the neighbors and kinfolk would come have a great time.

Baxter was well known as a man who loved children and he took time to be with them. Once he took his daughter Nora hunting (he always took her big brother Johnny, but not this time). When he killed a squirrel, she cried and he took her home and never took her hunting again. He was very proud of his children and pleased when Jerry was born (Baxter died just 4-1/2 months later).

(See story on Gladys Mae Asbridge Howton Harmon for update.) - *Submitted by Linda Lou Ratliff Gantt, granddaughter*

PETER HOWTON

Peter Howton, son of Lewis Howton Jr., son of Lewis Howton, son of Jonathan Howton believed to have been born around 1757 in England.

Peter, born 1852, first married Dec. 19, 1874, in Hopkins County, a Sarah Woolard, born 1852. Their children were: William born 1876, George born 1878, Sam born 1881, Ben born 1885, Mary Jane born 1886, Peter Gilbert born 1892 and died 1893, and Allie born 1894. Sarah died 1895 leaving Pete with six living children from 19 years to one year of age. Sarah is buried on the east side of Lafayette Church Cemetery along side Peter Gilbert.

Minerva E. and Peter Howton

Second, Peter married Minerva Ellen Martin Fuller, widowed and left with four children from seven years down to two years of age. They were: Hattie born 1888, Idealia born 1890, Mose born 1892 and Johnny born 1894.

Over the years the story has been told, that seeing the advantages of combining two households, he rode his horse up to the front porch of the widowed Minerva Ellen Martin Fuller's home and without dismounting asked her to marry him. It is unclear at this point if she answered a firm yes right away. But it is a fact that on turning his horse to leave the yard he was thrown.

Peter and Minerva were married Dec. 24, 1896, with 17 years difference in their ages and a combined family of 10 children. They were together for 42 years and produced four children of their own, two of which lived to adulthood. They died two years apart, she in 1938 at age of 69, he in 1940 at the age of 88. Both are buried at Lafayette Church Cemetery. Their children were: Vera born 1898, Ethel born 1901, Icie born 1903 and Lena born 1906.

Vera, born 1898, died 1969, married Nov. 21, 1915, at Beulah, Jasper Simpson Robards born 1893, died 1975. Both are buried at Lafayette Church Cemetery. Their children are: Eugene born 1918, Dorothy born 1921 and Edith born 1926.

Ethel born Dec. 20, 1901, died Nov. 28, 1902, buried at Lafayette Church Cemetery.

Icie, born Sept. 1903, died Feb. 4, 1904, buried at Lafayette Church Cemetery.

Lena, born May 28, 1906, died Mar. 12, 1951, married May 23, 1918, James Earsley Robards, born Dec. 5, 1895, died Feb. 7, 1964. Both are buried at Lafayette Church Cemetery. Their children are: Florella, born 1919, Kate born 1921 and Norman born 1923. (See Robards) - *Submitted by Norma Towe Cullen*

HUDDLESTON-BOSWELL

Haze Huddleston was born in Centerville, MO on Feb. 17, 1924 to the proud parents Thomas Franklin and Loretta Huddleston. Haze's father died when Haze was only two years old. In a few years Loretta, Haze's mother, married Bill Russell. Haze had to quit school and go to work when he was only sixteen because his step-father broke his back and someone had to support the family.

Later Haze met a girl, whom he fell in love with, by the name of Irene Boswell. Irene was born in Tula, KY on Mar. 20, 1920. Her parents were Plez and Bessie Boswell. Haze and Irene were married and lived in Marion, KY for many years. In 1958, they moved to Madisonville, KY where he worked for Scott McGaw Motor Company for sixteen years. Haze worked as foreman of the auto body department.

Haze and Irene had three boys. Tom was the first, born on Dec. 2, 1946. Encil was the second, born on Sept. 27, 1948. Ronny was the third, born on May 10, 1958. They too went into the auto body repair business like their father. Tom and Encil worked for Scott McGaw Motor Company when they were young. When all three of the boys grew up, the four of them started their own business. Haze, Tom, Encil and Ronny became partners of the business

called Huddleston's Body Shop. For fourteen years, it has been a very successful business in Madisonville. It is the largest independent body shop around this area. Huddleston's Body Shop had made a name for itself that people in this area all know and trust.

Tom married Sherry Jefferies from Evansville, IN. Tom and Sherry had one son, Brent Huddleston, born Jan. 12, 1967. Encil married Sharon Todd from Dawson Springs, KY. Sharon and Encil had one son, Robert Dale Huddleston. Robby was born on Jan. 12, 1970, exactly three years after Brent was born. Ronny married Renee Driver from Paducah, KY. Ronny and Renee had two children, a son Ronny Wayne Huddleston and a daughter, Stephanie Huddleston. Ronny Wayne was born on May 25, 1979 and Stephanie was born on Dec. 2, 1981.

The whole Huddleston family lives in the Hopkins County area. Haze and Irene live at 1601 Scott Drive in Madisonville. They have lived in Madisonville for thirty years, and here they will live out their lives with the family that loves them close by. Haze Huddleston has built a strong bonding family and business that will live and go on forever. We will always remember and love Haze and Irene Huddleston. - *Submitted by Robby Huddleston*

HUDDLESTON-WOODRUFF

Joe G. Huddleston and Marilyn J. Huddleston of R. #2, Dawson Springs, KY, were married Apr. 24, 1965, by Rev. Jim Camplin, St. Charles, KY. They have two children.

Anthony (Tony) Joe, born Dec. 30, 1967, graduated from South Hopkins High School in 1986 and is now serving in the United States Marine Corps. At this time, he is stationed at Camp Lajuene, NC.

Marilyn and Joe Huddleston

Amy Darlene, born Sept. 14, 1969 (on her Dad's birthday), graduated from South Hopkins High School in 1987. She won a $200 scholarship from Reader's Digest and while still residing at home, plans to work and save her money and enter Nursing School as soon as possible.

Joe's mother, Mary M. Crook Huddleston, was born Nov. 8, 1919, and now resides at the New Dawson Springs Rest Home. His father, William Claud Huddleston, was born Mar. 25, 1911, and died Feb. 29, 1976. Claud was a retired coal miner and farmer. Joe has two brothers and also two half-sisters from his father's previous marriage, one of whom is now deceased.

Marilyn's father, W.T. Woodruff, was born July 5, 1915, and is a retired coal miner. Her mother, Alma Louise Gamble Woodruff, was born Jan. 31, 1924. They live within walking distance of Marilyn's and Joe's home. Marilyn has two brothers and one sister.

Joe and Marilyn both are graduates of South Hopkins High School. He worked for the State Highway Department until he became disabled in 1975. She once worked for the Enro Shirt Co. until the children were born, then became a full-time housewife and mother.

The Huddlestons own the small farm that once belonged to Marilyn's paternal grandparents, which still holds a lot of fond memories of her childhood. Her brother Darrell owns the home where the Woodruff children were raised. Joe's younger brother, Paul, owns the home where he and his brothers grew up. Who says "You can never go home again"?

The family attends Earlington Assembly of God Church and enjoys the outdoors a great deal, hunting, fishing and camping whenever possible. In fact, their son Tony has proudly displayed on their living room wall a trophy 8 point buck to prove it. - *Submitted by Joe and Marilyn Huddleston*

JAMES E. HUDDLESTON

James E. Huddleston was born Apr. 16, 1886, in Hopkins County. He was the son of George Washington Huddleston (1863-1916) and Mary E. McKnight Huddleston (1867-1957) who are buried in Union Temple Cemetery in Hopkins County.

James married Bertha Robinson, a widow with a three-year-old daughter, Carmie. They became the parents of two daughters, Cloria and Georgia. All three children still live in Hopkins County. Bertha died in 1929.

James was a timberman and carpenter. He played the fiddle, banjo and harmonica. He was a resident of Route 1, St. Charles until he entered the New Dawson Springs Nursing Home.

On Oct. 10, 1987, James passed away. He was buried in Piney Grove Cemetery in Caldwell County.

Besides his three daughters, James was blessed with 12 grandchildren, 21 great-grandchildren and six great-great-grandchildren.

(For photo of James E. Huddleston, see Hopkins County Centenarians section.) Information from Cloria Menser, a daughter. - *Submitted by Dorothy Miller Shoulders*

HURLEY-CANSLER

Glenda Mae Cansler and Joel Grubbs Hurley were married Oct. 9, 1947, by Rev. Edward Coffman in Russellville, KY.

Glenda was born Jan. 18, 1927, in Christian County, youngest daughter of Ezma Poole and Herman Cansler. Her sisters are Catherine Dunning, Crofton and Pauline Coates, Dawson Springs.

Glenda attended grade school at Crofton and Hopkinsville. She attended seventh and subsequent years at Dawson Springs, graduating in 1944. She has more than 38 years Federal

Joel G. and Glenda Mae Hurley

Service and is presently employed with Department of Army, Fort Campbell, as Chief, Manpower and Civilian Personnel and staff member of the Commander, Medical Department Activity. Represents the Commander for union negotiations with AFGE, Local 2022. Served as a member of the supervisory committee Fort Campbell Credit Union. Prior to working for the Army was employed by the Veterans Administration as Finance Officer at Outwood and Columbia, SC.

Joel was born July 9, 1923, in Earlington, youngest son of Dot Bean and William Creed Hurley. His brother, William Creed Hurley II, resides in Long Beach, CA.

Joel attended school in Earlington and graduated from Earlington High School in 1942. He attended Western Kentucky University until he joined the Army. After completion of basic training at Camp Grant, IL, he attended several Medical Technical Schools. He served three years in the Army Medical Corps with 17 months in New Guinea and Philippines. After discharge from the Army he worked in Oregon and Arizona. Returning to Kentucky, worked at VAH, Outwood, in charge of the Medical Laboratory. Joel served as Sheriff 1945-1957 and Judge 1958-1961 of Hopkins County. Served three years on Board of Directors of The Kentucky Sheriff's Association. He has been a Specialty Advertising Consultant for more than 20 years, forming his own company in 1962.

They are the parents of a daughter, Deborah Dianne Hurley, and a son, Joel Kent Hurley. Dianne is employed by the U.S. Army, White Sands, NM. Kent is employed by Peabody Coal Company, Muhlenberg County.

They are members of the First Christian Church, Dawson Springs. Joel serves on the Board of Deacons.

Both Joel and Glenda have held positions of leadership. Joel is Past Potentate of Rizpah Shrine Temple; Past President Cabri Chapter 88; Past Worthy Patron, Order of Eastern Star; Past President of the Parent Teachers Association; Past Cub and Scout Master; and a former 4-H leader; Past Commander of American Legion and Disabled American Veterans; Past All State Commander VFW Post 5359 in 1983-84 and 1984-85; Third District Commander 1984-85. At VFW State level, served as Sergeant-At-Arms; Chief of Staff; Judge Advocate and presently Jr. Vice Commander which is tantamount to the Office of State Commander.

Glenda is Past Secretary, American Society of Military Comptrollers; Past Queen, Daughters of Nile, Rizpah Temple; Past Secretary, Order of Eastern Star; former 4-H leader; Past Commander Unit 163, First District and State Judge Advocate of Disabled American Veterans Auxiliary; Past President VFW Auxiliary Post 5359, District 3 and Color Bearer #1 at the State level. - *Submitted by Joel G. Hurley*

JACKSON-OLIVER

John William Jackson born Feb. 8, 1915, in Lyon Co., KY, the son of Benjamin and Mary Alice Fitts Jackson, married Jan. 31, 1935, in Caldwell Co., KY, to Ella Mae Oliver. Ella Mae was born Apr. 30, 1911, in Lyon County, the daughter of Charles Loyd and Mary Susan Oliver. They have one son, John Morgan Jackson, born Sept. 10, 1939, in Lyon Co., KY.

Ella Mae (Oliver) and John William Jackson

John Morgan married Mary Frances Wood, the daughter of Olus Vance and Thelma Nixon Wood, on May 23, 1959, in Caldwell Co. They have two daughters: Donna Sue and Susan Lynn.

Donna Sue was born Dec. 28, 1960, in Caldwell Co. She married Joseph Victory "Buddy" Radford, on Oct. 7, 1983, at her parents home in Lyon Co. No issue. Joseph "Buddy" is the son of James Dudley and Elizabeth Mae Robertson Radford.

Mary Frances (Wood) and John Morgan Jackson

149

Susan Lynn was born Sept. 6, 1966, in Caldwell Co. She married Ralph Allen Hillyard on Aug. 9, 1983, in Springfield, TN. Ralph Allen is the son of Tommy and Lacey Jayne Keel Hillyard. They have one son, Jason Jeffrey, born Jan. 31, 1984, in Caldwell Co. Ralph is in the U.S. Navy, stationed aboard the USS Oliver Hazard Perry. - *Submitted by John and Mary Jackson*

BECKLEY JACKSON

Beckley Jackson was born in Mecklenburg Co., VA, on Mar. 9, 1788. He was the son of Matthew and Elizabeth Jackson. He went to Hopkins Co., KY in 1815 and died there, Dec. 28, 1859. He is buried behind the Old Jackson Homeplace, which is the Old Jackson Cemetery. He married Martha Brown, daughter of Thomas and Mary (Pettus) Brown on June 12, 1809, in Mecklenburg Co., VA. She was born Jan. 20, 1789, in Mecklenburg Co., VA, and died on June 11, 1856, in Hopkins Co., KY. She is also buried in the Old Jackson Cemetery.

They lived on Old Henderson Road in Hopkins County and their home was known as The Stagecoach Inn in the 1830's. Men stopped here to change horses, when going from Henderson to Hopkinsville, KY. Their children were: Pernetta, born Dec. 11, 1810, married Thomas Browder, Aug. 5, 1830, died Feb. 19, 1886, buried Mt. Carmel Cemetery, west of Slaughters, KY; Arena, born Feb. 11, 1813, married Augustine Browder, June 16, 1831, died Nov. 23, 1887 near Fulton, KY, buried Palestine Cemetery, near Fulton; Sterling Brown, born Feb. 19, 1815, probably died young; Tabatha Ann, born Jan. 16, 1816, married Williamson Reynolds, Dec. 29, 1834; Andrew, born Dec. 24, 1818, married Eliza —, married 2. Sarah Yandell, May 31, 1854; Fertina, born Sept. 10, 1820, married John C. Winstead, Jan. 24, 1833, married 2. Edwin Ruby, Apr. 22, 1845, died Aug. 6, 1866; William Harrison, born Mar. 24, 1823, married Sarah Pritchell, Aug. 20, 1846, died Dec. 6, 1905, buried Old Jackson Cemetery; James, born Mar. 24, 1823, died at birth; John Washington, born Sept. 16, 1824, married Martha Hamton, June 11, 1846, died Sept. 17, 1891, buried Pleasant Grove Cemetery, Hopkins Co., KY; Thomas Jefferson, born Jan. 12, 1826, married Emily Jane Marrow in 1856, in Hopkins County, died July 9, 1894; Matthew James, born May 18, 1829, married America V. Fugate, Nov. 6, 1850, married 2. Martha E. Slaton, Nov. 11, 1857, died Oct. 27, 1864, buried Old Jackson Cemetery; Nancy John, born June 4, 1830, married Issac M. Eison, Mar. 25, 1864.

Beckley Jackson had four brothers: Bins, Burwell, Francis and Nathaniel. Burrell and Nathan Jackson listed in the Hopkins Co., KY, Census in 1850, may have been his brothers. Sources: Records of Mattie Belle Wolfenberg, Weatherford, Texas; Palestine Cemetery, Fulton, Kentucky; Records of Bernice Stroud, Fulton, Kentucky. - *Submitted by Martha M. Thomas, a great-great granddaughter.*

BENJAMIN JACKSON

Benjamin Jackson born Feb. 13, 1870, in Hopkins Co., son of Christopher and Sarah Ann Tirey Jackson, married Mary Alice Fitts Dec. 5, 1901, in Lyon Co. He died June 12, 1952, in Caldwell Co. Mary Alice born Dec. 4, 1873, in Lyon Co., the daughter of John and Mary Eliza Dunning Fitts, died Dec. 2, 1957, in Lyon Co. Both are buried at Cedar Hill Cem. in Caldwell Co. Children: Stella, Ethel, Edd, Jessie, Myrtle Mae, Elwood, Sally Mae, Charley Jacob, John William (see his story), Mary Lee and Virgie.

Benjamin Jackson and Mary Alice Fitts Jackson, wife of Benjamin

Stella, born Oct. 16, 1902, married Clyde Edward Oliver, Dec. 2, 1919, Lyon Co., died May 26, 1937, Caldwell Co. Clyde Edward, born June 3, 1900, son of Charles Loyd and Mary Susan Oliver Oliver, died May 10, 1977, Caldwell Co. Both are buried in Oliver Cem., Lyon Co. Children: Robert Glenn, Jim Wallace, Shellie Woodson and Wylie Calbert.

Ethel, buried in an unmarked grave, Friendship Cem., Lyon Co.

Edd, born Dec. 25, 1905, married Maudie Mae Oliver, Jan. 24, 1923, Lyon Co., died Feb. 16, 1947, Caldwell Co., buried Oliver Cem., Lyon Co. Maudie Mae, born Sept. 7, 1905, daughter of James Fratis and Julia Ann Oliver Oliver. Children: Mary Beatrice, Norman, Charolene, Virginia Nell, Edd Jr., Forrest Elwood, Dorothy and Cecil Edward.

Jessie, married Nov. 8, 1923, Caldwell Co., to Leonard Teague, died Nov. 6, 1933, Caldwell Co., buried in unmarked grave in Friendship Cem., Lyon Co. Children: R.B., Edna, Jennie Kathryn, Louise and Bobby.

Myrtle Mae, born Feb. 8, 1909, married Robert Lee Helton, Jan. 16, 1926, McCracken Co. Robert (Nov. 11, 1875-July 10, 1961) buried Rose Brower Cem., McCracken Co. Myrtle Mae then married Reinus David Holley, Sept. 23, 1965, McCracken Co. He was born Feb. 14, 1909, Mayfield, KY, died Sept. 21, 1981, McCracken Co., buried in Maplelawn Cem. there.

Elwood, born Feb. 7, 1910, married Loraine Orange (b. Feb. 10, 1913) Jan. 3, 1931, Caldwell Co. Elwood died Nov. 18, 1986, Caldwell Co., buried Witherspoon Cem. there. Children: Barbara Jean, Ella Florance, Elwood Jr. and Roger Dale.

Sally Mae, born June 16, 1913, married first Dennie Teague; second, Dec. 14, 1963, Caldwell Co., to Dennie Teague; third, to Woodrow Sloan and fourth, to Elmer White. Sally, died Apr. 12, 1985, Evansville, IN, buried Memorial Park there. Children: David Leroy, Ruby Nell, Prudie, Rose Mary and Peggy Ann.

Charley Jacob (twin to John William), born Feb. 8, 1915, married Cortney Eserine Oliver, Jan. 3, 1936, Caldwell Co., died Nov. 24, 1976, Nashville, TN, buried Oliver Cem., Lyon Co. Cortney Eserine, born Dec. 6, 1919, the daughter of William Gobel and Lucy Frances Gilkey Oliver. Children: Charles Hollis, James Wilburn, Nellie Frances, Ronnie Gale, Richard Dale and Ruthie Irene.

Mary Lee, born Apr. 8, 1917, married Clyde Allen Oliver, Jan. 30, 1933, Caldwell Co. Clyde Allen, born Apr. 8, 1910, Caldwell Co., son of Melrose and Sara Sells Oliver, died Aug. 7, 1976, Caldwell Co., buried Fairview Cem., there. Children: Nellie, Charles Allen, Barbara Sue, Clyde Jr., Jerry Anthony, Kenneth Earl, Shirley Jean and Billy Joe.

Virgie, born Apr. 15, 1919, married Clyde Edward Oliver, Nov. 24, 1939, Caldwell Co. No issue. Clyde Edward, born June 3, 1900, son of Charles Loyd and Mary Susan Oliver Oliver, died May 10, 1977, Caldwell Co., buried Oliver Cem., Lyon Co. Virgie had a son, Kenneth, born Oct. 3, and died Oct. 14, 1937, buried Pleasant Hill Cem., Lyon Co. Virgie raised her sister's children. - *Submitted by Mary Frances Jackson*

CHRISTOPHER JACKSON

Christopher Jackson was the son of Joseph Jackson, who died in Hopkins Co., KY, in 1813 and Elizabeth Jackson.

Christopher Jackson was married first, to Rebecca Croft daughter of Frederick and Catherine Croft. After Rebecca's death, he married Sarah Moore on May 30, 1816, in Hopkins County. His third marriage was to Rebecca Thomas.

Christopher and Rebecca Croft Jackson were the parents of seven known children: Joseph Jackson; Jacob Jackson married Betsy Wyatt; William Jackson, born in 1800, married Elizabeth Butner; Nancy Jackson, born 1802, married Dabney Terry; Elizabeth (Betsy) Jackson, born 1807, married Jeremiah Franklin; Nathan Jackson, born 1808, and Rebecca Jackson, born 1813, married James Franklin, III.

There were three other children of Christopher Jackson, probably of his third marriage to Rebecca Thomas: Seintha Jackson, born 1835, married Hutcheson B. Lamb; Edith (Edy) Jackson, born in 1842, married Thomas G. Chapel and Isaiah Jackson married Matilda S. Menser.

Christopher Jackson died on Oct. 9, 1848, in Hopkins Co., KY. - *Submitted by Daniel W. Dockrey*

CHRISTOPHER JACKSON

Christopher Jackson was born ca. 1848 and married Sarah Ann Tirey on May 21, 1869, in Hopkins Co. Christopher was killed, while working in timber, near Pleasant Hill Community in Lyon Co. about 1890. Sarah Ann was born in Obion Co., TN and died May 22, 1924. She is buried in Liberty Cemetery in Lyon Co. Their children: Rebecca, Jacob, Rufus Marion, Benjamin (see his story), Nancy, Daniel Slayton, Christopher, John and Andrew.

Rebecca was born ca. April 1870 and married John Tirey.

Jacob was born ca. 1871.

Rufus Marion was born Sept. 19, 1873

(Morgan Funeral Home Records say Sept. 19, 1865), and married Necie Wilson on Dec. 15, 1904, in Caldwell Co. He died Jan. 3, 1960, in Caldwell Co. and is buried at Cedar Hill Cemetery. Their children: Alma, J.D., Maude, Nannie Louise, Rufus Mae, Anna Florance and William Garnett.

Nancy (date of birth not known), married James Brisco.

Daniel Slayton was born Feb. 14, 1880, in Hopkins Co. and married Minnie Fitts on Dec. 1, 1901, in Lyon Co. Their children: Willie, Arene (R.E.), Malloy, Mary Ann, Herbert Slayton, Janice Catherine, Glenn and A.B. His second marriage was to Emma Byrd Farless on Dec. 9, 1939, in Lyon Co. He died, Nov. 6, 1941, in Lyon Co. and is buried in Pleasant Hill Cemetery.

Christopher's date of birth is not known.

John was born ca. 1888 in Hopkins Co. and married Virgie Crow on Apr. 11, 1910, in Caldwell Co. He died on Mar. 4, 1957, in Caldwell Co. and is buried at Liberty Cemetery, in Lyon Co. Their children: Birdie Mae, Harold, Raymond and Odie Anna.

Andrew was born May 3, 1891 (Lyon Co. Health Dept. Records), in Hopkins Co. and married Daisy L. Wynn on Nov. 8, 1903, in Lyon Co. He died Aug. 29, 1947, in Lyon Co. and is buried in Pleasant Hill Cemetery there. Their children: Lucy, Coy L., and Minnie M. Andrew married second, Maude Jackson and had: James Andrew, Thelma Ruth, Ella Lee, Nannie Mae, Wanda, Rosie Lee and two infants who did not survive. - *Submitted by Mary Frances Jackson*

D. JACKSON-HICKLIN

Willie Ruth Hicklin, b. Aug. 30, 1919, and David Todd Jackson, b. Apr. 6, 1920, were married in Madisonville, KY, on July 14, 1940. The wedding was performed by Rev. B.F. Cato, in the presence of Jeanette Woodruff (Qualls) and Walter Qualls. Ruth is the daughter of Willie Lee Livingston Hicklin, b. Feb. 20, 1893, and John W. Hicklin, b. Aug. 12, 1874. David is the son of Mary Belle Todd Jackson, b. July 28, 1890 and Herman F. Jackson, b. Nov. 8, 1890. They have two children; Ruth Ann Jackson Street, b. Sept. 4, 1942 and Maurice Edward Jackson, b. Jan. 10, 1947.

David Todd and Willie Ruth Hicklin Jackson

David is retired from the U.S. Post Office as a thirty-five year letter carrier. He is a veteran of World War II, an Elder in the First Christian Church, a member of F & AM Lodge 143, Woodman of the World, V.F.W. and a Kentucky Colonel. Ruth is a housewife, active in Lelia Dempsey Missionary Group and Homebuilders Sunday School Class of First Christian Church. She is a member of the Anton Homemakers and a lifetime member of the Hopkins County Historical Society.

Ruth Ann, b. Sept. 4, 1942, is married to George C. Street, b. Nov. 10, 1941, of Louisville, KY, and they live in Louisville, KY. Both are graduates of the U. of Kentucky. Ruth Ann is an office manager for Primary Devices and George is Project Manager for The Omegas Group, this pertains to computers and software. Their daughter, Sarah Elizabeth Street, b. Oct. 15, 1966, and her horse Poco, are at this time attending Meredith Manor Equestrian School in Waverly, WV. She is specializing in Dressage Riding and plans to ride and teach Dressage. Their son, George C. Street, Jr., b. Mar. 1, 1969, will graduate from Waggoner High School in June 1987 and will take a six week trip to Germany on an exchange program.

Maurice E. Jackson, b. Jan. 10, 1947, is married to Sara Biven Jackson, b. Oct. 1, 1949, of Louisville, KY. They live in Bowling Green, KY, and both are graduates of Western Kentucky U. They have two children, Carrie Ann Jackson, b. Oct. 2, 1974, and Daniel Todd Jackson, b. Feb. 3, 1983. Maurice is a Sales Representative of Conwood Corp., Inc. of Memphis, TN. Sara is an Elementary School Librarian in Warren Co. Their daughter Carrie Ann is an Honor student at St. Joseph Catholic School, Bowling Green, KY. Their son, Daniel Todd is the youngest grandson and they all make life very interesting for David and Ruth. - *Submitted by Ruth H. Jackson*

M. JACKSON-HICKLIN

Katharine Hicklin, b. Aug. 23, 1913, and Malcolm Jackson, b. Mar. 27, 1906, were married Sept. 6, 1929, at the Methodist Parsonage in Nebo, KY, by Rev. Owen Hoskins. They have lived in Madisonville, KY, for most of their married life. They are members of the First Christian Church and have three children; John Paul Jackson, b. Aug. 23, 1931; Marian Rita Jackson, b. Oct. 2, 1934; and George Malcolm Jackson, b. July 8, 1938.

Malcolm is an Elder of the First Christian Church, a member of the Woodmen of the World. He has served as secretary of Lodge 25 for many years and in 1982 he was awarded an Honorary Plaque as Outstanding Citizen by the Woodmen of the World Life Insurance Society. He is a member of the Kiwanis Club and received a pin for thirteen years of perfect attendance. He is a Kentucky Colonel. Malcolm has served as a Deputy Tax Commissioner, a Deputy Sheriff of Hopkins County. He was Madisonville City Treasurer for ten years, Quarterly Clerk for one and a half years for the County Judge. Malcolm retired after serving twenty-two years as County Treasurer.

Katharine is a member of The Lelia Dempsey Missionary Group of First Christian Church, Madisonville B.P.W., the Anton Homemakers and Woodmen of the World. Katharine was employed by Trover Clinic for twenty-seven years. She was first a Receptionist, then an Ophthalmic Dispenser and for twenty-two years served as a Medical assistant for Dr. John W. Pate. Since retirement she and Malcolm have done some traveling to different parts of the country. Katharine enjoys quilting and needlework.

John Paul Jackson, b. Aug. 23, 1931, and Jane Ann Robinson were married on Aug. 31, 1956. They had two children; Paul Wesley, b. Sept. 10, 1957, who was killed in an industrial accident in Texas, in 1982, and daughter, Katharine Ellen, b. Mar. 17, 1961, is married to Daniel Dowdy and they have one son named, Benjamin Dowdy.

In 1978, John Paul Jackson and Brenda Dempsey were married and they have one daughter Kammie Len Jackson, b. Mar. 20, 1979, who is a student at Anton School.

Rita Jackson, b. Oct. 2, 1934, is married to Mark A. Dees, b. Sept. 15, 1935. They live in Wauwatosa, WI, where both are Chemistry teachers. They have two children; Thomas A. Dees, b. Apr. 16, 1970, and Carol Marian Dees, b. June 12, 1972.

George Malcolm Jackson, b. July 8, 1938, who lives in Owensboro, KY was married to Ann Wells and they have three children: Rita Jane Jackson, b. Nov. 26, 1959; James Michael Jackson, b. Feb. 10, 1963; and Leslie Jackson Keller, b. Feb. 20, 1966. George M. Jackson is married to Anna Sue Allen and they have one daughter, Dannett Allen Jackson, b. Jan. 17, 1971. George is also the proud grandfather of two granddaughters, Savannah and Katherine Elizabeth Keller.

When all the family get together occasionally for a picnic at the home of John Paul and Brenda, who have a lovely home at Anton on the land of their Hicklin ancestors, it is indeed a joyful day. - *Submitted by Katharine Jackson*

HERMAN JACKSON

The residence at 526 East Broadway in Madisonville, KY, was the permanent home of Herman Franklin and Mary Belle Todd Jackson for all their nearly 55 years of married life, and before that, was Mary Belle's home, since the age of 14. Herman and Mary Belle were married, Nov. 19, 1913, at the home of the First Christian Church minister, Bro. J.M. Gordon, on Lake St. in Madisonville.

Front l to r: Herman Franklin, Mary Jane, Mary Belle, Margaret Ann, Sarah Ethel, Alexander Franklin Todd, and Daniel Todd Jackson. Back row l to r: John Franklin Jackson and Mary Helen Cox.

Herman Franklin Jackson (a twin) was born on a farm near Onton, KY, on Nov. 8, 1890. His parents were John Sanford and Florence Toombs Jackson. During Herman's early years, his family, who were farmers, moved several times to different farms in both Hopkins and Webster counties, before settling on a farm near Anton in Hopkins County, when Herman was 15 years old. Herman taught school for about four years before entering the grocery business in 1917, and this remained his occupation until his retirement in 1961. His grocery store was named Jackson Brothers Grocery, since part of the time, his brother, Ruby C. Jackson, was his partner, and was located on the corner of East Broadway and Hipple streets. Herman became a Christian at the age of 10 and became a charter member of the Belcourt Christian Church in Webster County. Later he became a member of the Bethlehem Christian Church, finally moving his membership to the Grapevine Christian Church, where he served faithfully, as both a deacon and elder and was an elder emeritus at the time of his death, July 27, 1978. He was also an active member of the Woodmen of the World.

Mary Belle Todd was the daughter of Alexander Franklin Todd (1855-1950) and Margaret Ann Story Todd (1865-1896). She was born, July 28, 1890, on her parents' farm, east of Madisonville, part of which is now Madisonville City Park. At the age of 14, she and her family moved to the home at 526 East Broadway. Mary Belle graduated from Madisonville High School (the Waddill Ave. School today) in May 1910 and in June 1910, after taking an exam was awarded a teacher's certificate, but never took a teaching job. Instead she worked, for awhile, for Williams Cleaning Co. as a bill collector. Mary Belle was an active lifelong member of the Grapevine Christian Church, where her maternal grandfather, J.F. Story, had been a minister from 1885-1893. One of Mary Belle's greatest interests was her flower gardens, where she spent many happy hours. She also was an active member of the Women's Christian Temperance Union. Mary Belle died, May 18, 1968, and she and Herman are buried at Grapevine Cemetery.

All their children were born at home and their names, birthdates and spouses are as follows: John Franklin, Apr. 3, 1918, m. Mary Peveler; David Todd, Apr. 6, 1920 m. Ruth Hicklin; Sarah Ethel, July 16, 1923, unmarried and now owns and lives at homeplace on East Broadway; Mary Jane, Jan. 21, 1925, m. James P. Hulsey; Margaret Ann, Aug. 20, 1927, m. James L. Wooton; Mary Helen Cox, Oct. 11, 1914, m. Harry Bolin (Helen is Mary Belle's niece reared in her home). - *Submitted by Margaret Jackson Wooton*

JOHN SANFORD JACKSON

John Sanford Jackson (1861-1915) and Florence Toombs (1863-1962) were married Mar. 18, 1886, and lived on several different farms mostly in Webster County until, finally settling on a farm near Anton in Hopkins County in 1905. John's father, Julius Augustus "Gus" Jackson (1829-1906), was one of the famous forty-niners, who went West in search of gold, but returned to Kentucky in 1854, to marry a Nebo girl, by the name of Nancy Ruby Cox. Julius became one of Webster County's first sheriffs and the story is told that one day during the Civil War, he had been out collecting taxes and had returned to his home when a group of Confederate soldiers arrived. He thrust the bag of tax money into the hands of one of his house slaves, Aunt Mary Drake, and told her to hide it. As the Rebels were dismounting at the front door, Aunt Mary slipped out the back way and hid the money under the wash kettle. One of the young Jacksons saw her, and tried to tell the Rebels, who were turning the house upside down looking for money and valuables, but fortunately for the Jacksons, the child was too young to talk plain and the soldiers paid no attention to him.

John's grandfather, Charles King Jackson (1806-1894), was born in Sussex Co., DE and was a direct descendant of Elder William Brewster, one of the Plymouth Colony settlers, who arrived in America on the Mayflower, Dec. 21, 1620. John's grandmother was Jane Dunville Jackson (1807-1880), whose father came to this country from Ireland.

Florence Toombs, who grew up on a farm in Webster Co., was a twin daughter of Frank and Lucy Moore Toombs. Frank was of Irish descent and Florence was always proud of her Irish blood. She also had a strong Christian faith, which sustained her through some difficult times of caring for her family, after the death of her husband, at the age of 54. John S. Jackson was also a Christian, having been converted at a meeting, at the High Glory Union Church, near Hanson, sometime after his marriage to Florence. Another interesting fact about Florence is that she was born on Valentine's day, died on Good Friday and was buried on Easter!

John Sanford and Florence Toombs Jackson became the parents of seven children, all of whom, have remained for most of their lives, as residents of Hopkins County, with the exception of Marvin, who moved to Florida. The children and their spouses are as follows:
Russell Emit (1888-1978), m. Lennie Slaton; Henry Augustus (1890-1985), m. Dolly Slaton, Tinnie Thompson, Mary Nisbet; Herman Franklin (twin to Henry), (1890-1978), m. Mary Belle Todd; Lola Ethel (1887-1918), unmarried; Marvin Austin (1894-1979), m. Pauline Paris, Ruth Brown; Ruby Cox (1895-), m. Mary Agnes Cox; John Malcolm (1906-), m. Katherine Hicklin. - *Submitted by Margaret Jackson Wooton*

Front l to r: Lola Ethel, John Sanford, J. Malcolm, Florence Toombs, Russell E., Mildred, and Lennie Slaton. Back row: Ruby Cox, Marvin A., Herman Franklin, Henry A. and Dolly Slaton.

JAGOE

Abraham Jacob Jagoe was born in Cork Co., Ireland in 1769. He came to America as a young man and settled in Virginia, where he pursued his trade as a saddle-maker. In 1800, he married Susanna Short of Botetourt Co., VA. Around 1822, Abraham, wife and seven children came to Kentucky and settled in Muhlenberg County near the Hopkins County line along Pond River. Two sons, Benjamin, b. 1803, in Virginia and William, b. 1818, in Tennessee, joined their father in farming large amounts of land in Hopkins and Muhlenberg Counties.

After Abraham's death in 1833, Benjamin purchased all of his father's properties and continued to farm. In 1846, he married Mary Kittenger Lindley. They had seven children:

(1) Mary E. (1847-1916), married Wm. W. Nisbet and raised eight children, one of whom was Maymie, who married M. Kirby Gordon, the Madisonvillian, who named the American Legion.

(2) Nancy (1851-1933) who married Wm. A. Nisbet owner of an old established livery stable in Madisonville.

(3) Marcellus, who married Courtney Darnell and moved to Cadiz, where they raised six children.

(4) Lucy F. (b. 1861), married Forrest Ellis, owner of an Ice Plant in Hopkinsville.

(5) Ephriam Brank (1853-1914), married Corella Hicklin, from the Anton area. Their only child to reach adulthood was Mary Ada, who later married Benjamin Browder McKinsey of Madisonville. Corella died at age 27 and Ephriam married Miranda A. Harris. They had two children; Lucy C., wife of Charlie Lowe, was a nurse during the great flu epidemic of 1918; and William whose only son, William Ernest, now resides in Whittier, CA.

(6) William Elwood (1850-1920), came to

Hopkins County in 1874 and in 1882 married Jemie Nisbet. They lived on Hanson Road, where their seven children were born and raised. In 1882, W.E. was elected Tax Assessor and in 1897 was elected for the first of two terms as magistrate of the Kitchen Dist. In 1904, he ran, unsuccessfully, for County Judge. His seven children were: Jessie E., married Henry Clay Brogdon of Calhoun, GA; Marietta, who was a "hat-dresser" in Madisonville, and married William Grizzell of Tennessee. They moved to Chattanooga, where Mr. Grizzell owned a Drug Store; Robert Elgin, who married Myrtle Haynes; Elizabeth, who married Eugene Knight; Ola Rhea, also a "hat-dresser", as well as an accomplished artist, who married Wesley A. Miller; James Kemp, an employee for the Southern Pacific RR in Phoenix, AZ; and Laura E. Jagoe born in 1893. She was a secretary to County Attorney, Tom Gooch, as well as a school teacher in Hopkins County for many years. She married the late, Dan Suthard. Mrs. Suthard, now 94, still lives at home in Madisonville.

Ovie and Naomi Cates, and Beulah and Wilbur James in 1958.

Front row adults l to r: W.E. Jagoe and A.L. Jagoe. Back: Cyrena Davis Jagoe

(7) Alonzo Livermore (1858-1936). A.L. married Cyrena Davis in 1879 and they had four children: Earl (1880-1931); Ellis (1882-1962); Davis P. (1889-1966), who was a personal Liason Messenger to Gen. "Black Jack" Pershing, during WWI; and Cyrena Helon Jagoe (1892-1972) who married Robert S. Pride and had two daughters, Fredrica, who married Ruby W. Robinson, Gov. Ruby Laffoon's grandson, and Jane Pride, who married Norvell Moore. Alonzo was the Vice-President of the Farmer's National Bank, from 1908 through 1916. Mr. & Mrs. Jagoe owned a considerable amount of property along both sides of the Old Hopkinsville Road (now South Main). Sometime before 1898, an East-West access road, which for many years was the southernmost city limit of Madisonville, was established which ran through his farmland and in the family's honor it was named, Jagoe Street. - *Submitted by Tom Wortham*

JAMES

Beulah Ashby, daughter of Lillie Crabtree Ashby and Thomas Ashby, and Wilbur E. James, son of Mary Nelson James and Andrew Lee James were united in marriage on Nov. 2, 1918, at Hanson, KY. The ceremony was performed by the Reverend Maddox, a Missionary Baptist minister. Their attendants were Naomi and Onie Cates.

Beulah and Wilbur lived at the James homeplace, west of Hanson. To this union, eight children were born; Kathryn, Evelyn, Raymond, Genenia, Wilbur J., Betty, Carroll and Kenneth.

Wilbur was interested in literature. He studied the Bible daily. He enjoyed reading the works of American authors. His favorite poet was Henry Wadsworth Longfellow.

Beulah's family kept her busy. She enjoyed sewing for her girls, crocheting and gardening.

Both Beulah and Wilbur were members of Olive Branch Baptist Church. Each of their children, at one time, was a member of this church. Wilbur taught the Men's Bible Class for 25 years. Beulah was happy to work with children in the church. Beulah worked in Bible School when she was eighty-two years old.

Beulah and Wilbur traveled over most of the United States. They enjoyed seeing new places and meeting new people.

Wilbur died Aug. 7, 1977, at the age of 80. Beulah lives north of Madisonville. She is still active in church and Sunday School. She still enjoys meeting new people and making new friends.

The walls of Beulah's house are lined with pictures of her eight children, thirty-seven grandchildren, fifty-three great grandchildren and her three great great grandchildren. - *Submitted by Marquerette J. James*

JAMES-DARNELL

My name is Lee James and I am a member of a family of five. I have one brother, Jordan Heath James, who was born Mar. 4, 1987. I also have a sister, Kelly Elizabeth James, who was born Aug. 1, 1977.

My mother is Rebecca James, formerly Darnell, who was born May 26, 1950. She has one brother, Terry Darnell, who was born July 12, 1952 and is married to Conie Darnell. They have a son, Adam Darnell, and a daughter, Joy Beth Darnell. My mother also has a sister, Elizabeth Morris, who was born on June 23, 1954. She is married to William Morris and they have two daughters, Jonie and Jamie Morris. Jonie is blind and is attending the Kentucky School for the Blind in Louisville, KY. My mother's parents are John Darnell and Irene Darnell, later becoming Franklin due to divorce. My great grandmother's name is Frace Gordon.

My father, Eldon James, was born on July 14, 1946, and comes from a family of five. His sister, Faye, was born Feb. 2, 1947, she is married to Frank Orten and they have two children, Cindy and Randy. My father's brother, Jarvis James, was born on Mar. 14, 1948. He is married to Beth James and they have one child, Chera Beth James. My father's parents are Robert and Geneva James.

I was born on Sept. 10, 1971. The James family moved to Hopkins County in the year 1957 from Crittenden County. - *Submitted by Lee James*

JAMESON

In the early 1800's, Andrew Jameson married a widow from Logan Co., KY. Issac Browning had died and left his wife, Henrietta, with three children: Joel, Joshua, and Elizabeth. Andrew and Henrietta made their home in Hopkins Co., KY; they had two children: James Solmon and Mary Catherine. Mary Catherine married Moses Baugh. James Solmon married Rose Ann Branson; they had Daniel Lee, James Preston, Sarah, Selena (who died when she was twelve years old), and Mary Catherine called "Molly".

Daniel Lee Jameson

James Preston married Helen Bartlett; Sarah married Commodore Ashby; "Molly" married Baker Pidcock. On Feb. 11, 1869, Daniel Lee (born Nov. 4, 1842; died May 5, 1907), married Louisa McGrew from Cox Creek, KY, in Nelson County. In November 1887, they purchased 140 acres of land in the Anton community, from Louisa's nephew, Lonnie McGrew. They paid from $.50 to $1.50 per acre for the land. The farm is located on Route #3 in the Anton community. Louisa and Daniel Lee had three sons: Edwin called "Ed" (born Nov. 23, 1869; died Sept. 6, 1950); Baker (born Mar. 22, 1872; died Mar. 20, 1958); and Will (born July 24, 1877; died Mar. 23, 1937).

When Ed and Will were young men, they did carpentry work and built many of the barns in the Anton neighborhood. They rented the top floor of a store on Center Street in Madisonville, KY, and set up a broom factory. They delivered the brooms by horse and wagon, making stops in Sacramento, Bremen, Central City, Greenville, and back to Madisonville.

Baker married Lulla Francis Browning; they had three sons: Clarence (born Sept. 27, 1901; died June 26, 1972); Earnest Lee (born Mar. 22, 1906; died Dec. 22, 1941); and Edwin Haden (born Aug. 28, 1920). Edwin Haden lives in Hopkins Co., KY. Will married Mary Sally Coffman; they had Andrew Jackson called "Jack" (born Oct. 17, 1909; died Mar. 5, 1980).

On Nov. 30, 1902, Ed married Elffie Howard Barr (born July 3, 1871). They lived for one year, at Anton, KY, on the farm with her father, John Alford Barr, and her mother, Summerville Ashby Barr. Summerville had inherited this farm from her father, Colonel John Ashby, Jr.

On Sept. 22, 1903, a daughter, Mary Laura, was born to Ed and Elffie. The family moved to Madisonville, KY, and Robert Clifton was born Apr. 3, 1905 (died Sept. 11, 1985). The story is told that he was really born on April 1, All Fool's Day. The family, thinking this was unlucky, changed his birth date to the third. In October the same year, Elffie died of typhoid fever. Mary Laura was almost two years old, and Robert Clifton was six months old. Ed moved his two children back to Anton, Route #3, to live with his mother, Louisa, and his father, Daniel Lee. Here, Mary Laura and Robert Clifton grew up.

On Sept. 10, 1925, Robert Clifton married Verbe Lillian Floyd (born Nov. 6, 1907). They made their home on the John Alford Barr farm, at Anton, KY. They had Robert Lealand (born Aug. 7, 1926; died June 22, 1984); Rita Aleen (born Jan. 14, 1931); and Norma Alice (born Oct. 14, 1933).

On July 22, 1934, Mary Laura married Aaron David Nall (born Sept. 2, 1900; died Sept. 18, 1960); they had Aaron Howard (born June 30, 1935, died Apr. 23, 1942); Mary Patricia (born Apr. 1, 1940); and Nancy Lillian (born Feb. 17, 1943, died May 29, 1943).

When Ed died Sept. 6, 1950, Robert Clifton inherited the John Alford Barr farm, where his wife, Lillian, still lives. Mary Laura inherited seventy acres of the original Daniel Lee Jameson farm, which she still owns. November 1987 will mark 100 years, that it has been in the Jameson family. - *Submitted by Mary Patricia Nall Underwood*

NANCY MASON JASPER

Nancy Mason Jasper is the daughter of Ernest Sr. and Mayme (Starks) Mason (see Ernest Mason Sr. story).

Nancy attended Branch Elementary and graduated from Rosenwald High School. She is a graduate of Kentucky State U. receiving a degree in Education and taught at Waddill Avenue School and Madisonville Junior High for two years.

Nancy is married and has two children. Her husband, Harvey Jasper, Jr., graduated from Southern Normal, a private school in Brewton, AL. He attended Alabama A&M in Huntsville, AL, and at present owns and operates Jasper's Towing Company, where he has four workers in his employ.

Their son, Tremaine Mason Jasper, 13 years of age, is an honor student and a member of National Junior Honor Society. Tremaine is a recent graduate of Mountain Sky Junior High and plans to attend Thunderbird High next year.

Heather Mechelle Mason Jasper, 10 years of age, attends John Jacobs Elementary where she participates in Project Potential, a program for accelerated students.

Nancy and her family reside in Phoenix, AZ, and she has been an educator with the Phoenix School System for the past thirteen years. She teaches the eighth grade at Valley View School and is the newly appointed Program Coordinator for Project Rising S.T.A.R., a project designed to provide opportunities that will encourage at risk of dropping out of school to achieve their academic potential.

Nancy and her family are active members of Tanner Chapel A.M.E. Church in Phoenix, AZ. - *Submitted by Mayme L. Mason*

JENKINS-KING

This Jenkins family is thought to be of Welch origin, coming from Wales in about 1700, first settling in Chester Co., PA, then in Monongahela Co., WV. William Costello Jenkins, born Mar. 3, 1844, in Monongahela Co., WV, was the son of Bartholomew (ca. 1797-d. 1863) and Nancy Eliza (Baker) Jenkins. He first came to Hopkins Co., KY, in October, 1873, where he became a salesman for St. Bernard Coal Company, in the thriving coal town of St. Charles. W.C. died June 4, 1916.

Annie King was born Oct. 8, 1857, in Spottsville, PA, daughter of Joe and Sarah (Gill) King (b. Dec. 15, 1827), who came from Lancaster, England in 1857, and from Pennsylvania to St. Charles, KY. Annie died Sept. 13, 1927.

William Costello Jenkins, first of the Jenkins to go to St. Charles, 1873

William C. Jenkins and Annie King were married in Hopkins County, Nov. 4, 1888, and were the parents of five children: Willie Mae (b. Nov. 23, 1889; d. Apr. 26, 1964), married John Clay Woodruff (b. Apr. 29, 1887; d. Sept. 15, 1930), a merchant and owner of Slate Ford Mine, in partnership with brother, Jimmy. Their only child, Hilda Mae Woodruff (b. Mar. 26, 1921; d. June 14, 1984), married Orvil E. Smith (Oct. 15, 1917). (See Smith-Woodruff family in this book). The second child, Maud Ella Jenkins (b. July 29, 1891; d. Dec. 20, 1951), married William J. Gribble (b. Apr. 1, 1888; d. Oct. 14, 1948), a druggist in St. Charles and old Eddyville, KY. No children. George Bartholomew Jenkins (b. Sept. 21, 1893; d. Nov. 13, 1918), married Charlie B. Woodruff (b. Jan. 1, 1893; d. Nov. 15, 1918), sister to Clay Woodruff. Their son, Richard Costello Jenkins (b. Mar. 18, 1918; d. Oct. 13, 1972), was eight months old when George and Charlie died, two days apart in the WW I flu epidemic. Richard was reared by grandparents, the Gribbles, and Willie Mae Woodruff. He was a pharmacist, never married. Charles Robert Jenkins (b. Apr. 12, 1896), married Opal F. Warren. (See Jenkins-Warren story in this book.) The youngest, Jettie Isabella Jenkins, (b. July 21, 1898; d. Dec. 28, 1964), married Thomas Ell Blanks of Mortons Gap. He was born Aug. 28, 1897; d. Sept. 26, 1942. Jettie's second husband, George F. Agate, of Michigan, died July 22, 1953. Tom and Jettie had one daughter, Margaret Jenkins Blanks (b. July 27, 1923; d. Dec. 21, 1981), married John E. Kaake, b. Jan. 11, 1918, of Peck, MI. They had four children: Peggy JoAnn (b. Jan. 1, 1944; d. Oct. 24, 1951); Kathleen Margaret (b. Feb. 20, 1945), married Jeffrey Mathew Taylor (b. Aug. 24, 1941) has three children: Wendy Kathleen (b. Jan. 23, 1965), Melissa Leigh (b. July 31, 1968) Mathew John (b. June 29, 1971); Roberta Lynel (b. Mar. 15, 1947), married a Williams and they had Ian Anthony (b. Aug. 21, 1971). Her second husband, Robert E. Brown (b. Dec. 23, 1952), and they have Erin Elizabeth (b. July 10, 1976); next is Suzanne Beth Kaake (b. Oct. 25, 1953) and John Ed Thomas Kaake (b. Aug. 19, 1958), both are unmarried. They all live in Michigan. In 1936 Tom and Jettie adopted a daughter, Loretta Ann Koehler (b. Sept. 10, 1933), at age 3, in Oakland Co., MI. She married Richard Giovannini (b. Dec. 5, 1932), they have three sons, Erick John (b. Apr. 30, 1954), married Denise McGlinch, who have Erick John Jr. (b. Mar. 28, 1978) and Emilie Joy (b. Oct. 9, 1980); Kenneth Alan (b. Aug. 7, 1955) and Thomas Glen (b. June 18, 1966).

Before 1900 Joe King presumably returned to England, leaving Sarah (Gill) King in St. Charles. She later married Joe Mosely (b. Apr. 19, 1831; d. unknown). Joe and Sarah King had a son, George King, born 1855, in England, just about two years before the parents came to the U.S. (See the King family in this book.) Sarah King Mosely died Dec. 25, 1903. - *Submitted by Rella G. Jenkins*

JENKINS-WARREN

Charles Robert Jenkins, born Apr. 12, 1896, in St. Charles, KY, was the fourth child of William Costello and Annie King Jenkins, who married in Hopkins Co., KY, on Nov. 4, 1888. William Costello was the son of Bartholomew and Nancy Eliza (Baker) Jenkins of Monongahela Co., WV, near Morgantown. Annie was the daughter of Joe and Sarah (Gill) King, who came to the U.S. from Lancaster, England in 1857. (See JENKINS-KING)

Charlie Robert Jenkins grew up in St. Charles. He and Opal Fern Warren, born Aug. 7, 1900, in Mortons Gap, were married Sept. 23, 1917, in Clarksville, TN, with attendants Alma and Harlan Kinnett of St. Charles. Opal was the daughter of the late Thomas M. and Dovie Emma (Jordan) Warren of Hopkins Co. Opal has one sister, May Woodruff, age 88, St. Charles, and one brother, F. Edward Warren, age 84, Louisville. Opal is retired as lunchroom supervisor of St. Charles Elementary School, and lives in Madisonville near her son and family.

Charlie served in WW I in the Medical divi-

Standing l to r: Charles W. and Rella Jenkins, Janine and Wesley K. Moore, and Pam and Warren Jenkins. Seated - Opal Jenkins, age 87.

sion. For many years he was a motorman at old Fox Run Mines, and later was maintenance man at St. Charles Elementary School. He was an avid hunter and fisherman. Charlie and Opal observed their 50th Wedding Anniversary on Sept. 23, 1967, and Charlie died Nov. 29, 1967. He is buried at Odd Fellows Cem. in Madisonville.

Charlie and Opal had one child, Charles Warren Jenkins, born Mar. 28, 1919, at Earlington. He graduated from Nortonville H.S. and Murray State College with B.S. and M.A. degrees and has 30 advanced hours in Administration. He served 4-1/2 years in the U.S. Air Force in WW II, where he was assigned to Hq. and Hq. Company of the Air Force at Jefferson Barracks, MO, for three years, on detached service with the Signal Corps in Signal Maintenance and Operations. He was at San Angelo Army Air Field (Bombardier School) San Angelo, TX, as Communications Chief and Cryptographer for 1-1/2 years. He taught at Lynn Grove H.S. in Calloway Co., Steele, MO Elem. School, was principal at Sharpe H.S., Marshall Co., Principal of H.S. at Puryear, TN, and for seven years was the first principal of South Hopkins H.S. For four years he was Director of the Madisonville Cooperative Extension Center in Madisonville before it became affiliated with the UK Community College System as Madisonville Community College in 1968. He was Acting Director of Madisonville Community College for one year, and was with the MCC as Business Office Administrator for 15 years before his retirement in December 1984.

Charles W. Jenkins and Rella A. Gibbs, born June 23, 1917, in Calloway Co., met at Murray State College, and married Apr. 25, 1943, at Jefferson Barracks, St. Louis, MO. During WW II, Rella was Secretary to the Band Leader at Jefferson Barracks, and for a time was Secretary to the Colonel at Hq. and Hq. on the Post. She is the daughter of the late Jesse and Jersye (Roark) Gibbs of Murray, Calloway Co., KY. She has one brother, Virgil N. Gibbs and family who lives in Calloway Co. Rella graduated from Murray Training School and Murray State College (now University) with B.S. and M.A. degrees, and taught Business subjects at Springville, TN H.S., Old Nortonville H.S., South Hopkins H.S. for seven years, and at Madisonville High School, and Madisonville-North, for seven years. She was Counselor/Administrative Assistant in Student Services at Madisonville Community College from 1968 until her retirement in June, 1982. She is active in Genealogical and Historical Societies, Retired Teachers Assoc., Pennyrile Arts and Crafts Guild, and Friends of the Library. Rella has given much of her time to "The Heritage of Hopkins County" book project.

Charles W. and Rella have two children: Pamela Janine (Jenkins) Moore, b. Oct. 4, 1944, in Murray, KY, married to Wesley Kim Moore b. Oct. 13, 1957, son of George A. Moore and Thelma Jean (Cunningham) Moore in Madisonville. Janine is a graduate of Murray State University with B.S. and M.A. degrees, and presently teaches at Madisonville-North Hopkins H.S. being head of the Fine Arts Department and is yearbook sponsor. Wesley graduated from Madisonville - North Hopkins H.S and presently is Home Food Distributor for Schwan's Sales Enterprises. Both are active in Community Theatre. Charles Warren Jenkins II, b. Aug. 6, 1953, in Murray, KY, is a graduate of Murray State University with B.S. degree. He is lead guitarist and song writer for the rock band HARDSTREET, and is employed by the Kentucky Administrative Office of the Courts as Court Designated Worker in Hopkins County. He is married to Pamela Gwendolyn (Ruff) Jenkins, born May 29, 1962, in Orlando, FL, daughter of Robert and Ann (Durham) Ruff of Madisonville. Pam graduated from Madisonville-North H.S. She is singer and keyboard player with HARDSTREET Band, and is Manager of TACO CASA in the Parkway Plaza Mall in Madisonville. - *Submitted by Rella G. Jenkins*

JENT-ALLEN

Crawford Lee Jent, b. Feb. 18, 1913, is the son of Richmond M. Jent, teacher/farmer/carpenter, and Ida Cornett Jent, of the Red Fox community near Hazard, Knott Co., KY. His father died in 1916 when Crawford was only three years old, and his mother died Aug. 24, 1974.

Crawford graduated from Carr Creek H.S. in 1934, and attended Western KY State College for two years. In 1936 he came to Madisonville, employed in Soil Conservation 1936-38. He then went to Berea College in 1938 and graduated in 1941. In 1939 he worked a short while for the WPA at Pennyrile State Park checking soil build-up. He worked for the Dept. of Interior, at Piedmont National Wildlife Refuge, Roundoak, GA.

Mr. & Mrs. Crawford Jent on their 44th wedding anniversary

During WW II, Crawford was in the 1st Marine Div., and was wounded at Guadacanal Oct. 9, 1942. As a young Marine he went to Klamath Falls, OR on New Years 1942-3. In 1944 an article in COSMOPOLITAN Magazine related that a group of housewives were so impressed with his manners and conduct that they decided to sponsor bus loads of the Marines into Klamath Falls for entertainment. Crawford was discharged Nov. 25, 1945.

Crawford Lee Jent and Sue Frances Allen met in Madisonville in 1936, and were married Feb. 14, 1943. She was the dau. of Claude Bailey Allen and Robbie Baker Allen, born Apr. 4, 1916. (See ALLEN-BAKER) From 1946 to June, 1963, they operated a Dairy Farm on Laffoon Trail where they now live. In the fall of 1962, Crawford decided to return to WKU to work on certification. From February 1963 thru 1965 he taught Eng., Math, and KY History at Seminary Jr. H.S. From 1967 to 1978, he taught American History in Jr. High at Browning Springs. For 24 years, Crawford Jent served on the Draft Board #40 of Hopkins County. Since his retirement in 1978, he has served hundreds of hours of volunteer work at Regional Medical Center, which he continues to enjoy.

Both Crawford and Sue are members of the local and state educational organizations, and held offices in the Hopkins Co. Retired Teachers Assoc. and other civic organizations.

Sue Frances Allen Jent graduated in 1933 from Madisonville H.S. and attended Bethel Women's College, Hopkinsville, receiving an Associate Degree (AA) in 1935. Earned an A.B. degree in 1939 from Oberlin College and Conservatory, Ohio, with Eng. and Music majors. In 1959, she received an M.A. degree in Education and Area in Music from WKU, and in 1971 she received an M.A. Plus Degree, equivalent to today's Ed. S.

In 1939-42, she taught at Bethel in the Academy and Jr. College. In 1942-43 she was band director in south Hopkins Co., where she put together the first band from students in three high schools—White Plains, Nortonville, and Mortons Gap, while they were still attending these individual schools. In 1943-44, Sue taught Math at the Claude D. Swanson Jr. H.S. in Arlington, VA.

For the next 30 odd years, Sue held various jobs in the city schools and Hopkins Co. school system, teaching Math at MHS; 1951-52 Band Director at Nebo and Hanson; 1952-59 String Instructor in Madisonville schools; 1959-66 was Elem. Music Supervisor; 1966-78 Instructional Supervisor, when she retired June 30, 1978. In 1971-74 and 1978-86, she also served as a part-time Music Instructor at Madisonville Community College. From 1979 to the present, she has a private string studio using three other teachers working with her.

In addition, Sue started teaching a Sunday School class at the First Baptist Church when she was 16 years old, and has continued to the present time. She has served in a phenomenal number of organizations in various capacities in the educational field, music field, and agricultural field. In education: HCEA, was first Finance Educational and Salary Scheduling Comm. in Hopkins Co.; helped develop Professional Practices Comm. as a part of State

Govt.; President of KY Assoc. for Supv. Curr. Development; Board of Directors for ASCD 2 yrs.; Comm. for KY Assoc. Edu. Supervisors; Pres. of KY Alliance Arts Education; on 1st Comprehensive Arts Planning Commission; Comm. for Rev. of Minimum Foundation Program. Agriculture, locally: Member of Farm Bureau Women; Women's Adv. Council Member; So. States Coop; Organizer and Charter member Beacon Homemakers; was Dist. Judge in FFA, FHA and 4-H Club projects.

In music: National Board Member of National Federation Music Clubs; National Chairman of Jr. Festivals; National Student Advisory Committee; on Ex. Comm. NFMC; State Pres. four yrs. KY Fed. of Music Clubs; Vice-Chmn. of KY Bicentennial Parade of American Music, which sent a program of music by KY Composers/Performers to Kennedy Center in 1976; Organizer of Madisonville Music Society in 1965, been Pres. twice; Among the organizers of the Pennyrile Performing Arts Assn.—she wrote By Laws and drew up the Organizational Chart. She was Chmn. of Co. Mother of the Year; Cancer Drive; Educational Chmn. for 1st Drug Abuse Comm.; on Edu. Sub-Comm. for the All American Competition for Madisonville; Charter and Organizer of Cardinal Garden Club.

Organizations Sue belongs to are: Phi Theta Kappa (Honorary Jr. Colleges); Chi Delta Phi (Honorary Literary Soc.); National Advisory Council of Brevard Music Center (NC) for four years; She is a KY Colonel; Duchess of Paducah; Personalities of the South Yearbook; Outstanding Educator of America 1973-74; Life Fellow of Dict. of International Biography, and various Who's Who. - *Submitted by Sue Allen Jent*

ALEXANDER T. JOHNSON

Alexander T. Johnson, the son of Louis W. and Nancy Graven Johnson, was born May 12, 1822, in Louis Co., VA. He moved with his family to Hopkins Co., KY, in March of 1837, to a farm his father purchased and cleared six miles southwest of Nebo. He worked with his father on the farm until he was eighteen. He then attended school for three years in East Tennessee, after which time he returned to Hopkins Co., KY, and taught school for a few years. He made one trip to New Orleans with a flat boat. In 1847, he purchased uncleared land which adjoined his father's farm, built a home, and continued to acquire adjoining land until he had accumulated 600 acres. This land, located in what is known as the Johnson's Island community, has remained in the Johnson family and is now operated by Alexander's grandson, Clifton Powell Johnson. He also owned some valuable property in the town of Nebo. The farm was used for producing corn, tobacco, wheat, and raising hogs, cattle and horses. On Oct. 14, 1847, he married Mary Lamson, a native of Hopkins County. She was a daughter of John Lamson, a native of Massachusetts, who was among the early pioneers of Hopkins County. To this union six children were born. Mary and Alexander were both members of the Missionary Baptist Church. She died in 1863. He married Elizabeth G. (Betty) Smith on Mar. 21, 1866. Seven children were born to this union. Alexander was a mason and a life-long Democrat. - *Submitted by C.P. Johnson*

CLIFTON PRATT JOHNSON

Clifton Pratt Johnson, son of Alexander T. and Elizabeth G. Smith Johnson, was born Jan. 9, 1879, in Hopkins Co., KY. He resided most of his life on the family farm that was cleared by his grandfather, Louis W. Johnson and his father, Alexander T. Johnson in the Johnson's Island community six miles southwest of Nebo. Upon the death of his father, he purchased the interests of his brothers and sisters in the family farm. He added acreage until the farm totaled 762 acres. The farm was used for the production of corn, tobacco, wheat, pasture, hogs and cattle. He purchased livestock throughout Hopkins County and parts of Caldwell, Webster, and Christian Counties. He married Vada Frances Cates, daughter of William L. and Rolie Victoria Cates of Hopkins Co., KY. To this union two sons were born—Clifton Powell (born Jan. 19, 1918) and James Raymond (born Feb. 5, 1920). C.P. Johnson currently resides in Madisonville, KY, and continues to operate the family farm. J.R. Johnson lives in Ocala, FL, and is a retired aeronautical engineer. Clifton Pratt and Vada were members of the Johnson's Island Missionary Baptist Church. He was a life-long Democrat and precinct election officer for many years. The family moved to Madisonville in 1936. Clifton died on Mar. 20, 1951, and Vada died on Aug. 27, 1964. They are both buried in Oddfellows Cemetery. - *Submitted by C.P. Johnson*

LOUIS W. JOHNSON

Louis W. Johnson, born Jan. 27, 1797, was a native of Virginia and was of Irish descent. He learned the brick mason's and plasterer's trades in early life in his native state and followed his trades for several years. He was a veteran of the War of 1812, and was at the burning of Fredericksburgh, VA. He married Nancy D. Graven (born Oct. 27, 1800) and had seven children before moving to Hopkins Co., KY, in March of 1837. Alexander T. Johnson, born May 12, 1822, accompanied his family to Kentucky and worked with his father on land that was purchased and cleared in an area located six miles southwest of Nebo in a community later named Johnson's Island. Two more children were born to Louis and Nancy in Kentucky. Nancy died Aug. 30, 1844, and is buried beside Louis, in the Rose Creek Cemetery. Louis married Suzannah B. McKinney May 7, 1845, and had one child, Clara A. who was born in 1846. Louis died Nov. 22, 1859. - *Submitted by C.P. Johnson*

JOHNSON-UTLEY

Mildred Katherine Utley, born Dec. 31, 1916 in Hopkins County, KY was the second of two children born to Edna Katherine Castleberry Utley and Oliver Perry Utley. On Oct. 20, 1934, she married Everett Victor Johnson, born Aug. 4, 1912 in Hopkins County. Originally, the name Johnson was spelled with a "t", but over the years it was dropped by the family. Mildred Katherine Utley had one sister, Mary Lorene Utley Weir, who is now married to Ancle Weir, both in Hopkins County. Mildred and Everett Johnson had five children: John Norman, born Aug. 8, 1935; Donald Lynn, born Oct. 7, 1938; Sue Katherine, born Sept. 21, 1940; Everett Micah, born May 10, 1952; and Perry Lee, born May 28, 1954. All were born in Hopkins County, and three presently live in Hopkins County. The others live in Evansville, IN and Morganfield, KY.

Mildred is the proud grandmother of ten children and is a great grandmother to three. Everett was a farmer and a coal miner. His mother, Susan Francis Ausenbaugh, was born Aug. 15, 1881. J.E. Johnson, his father, was born Apr. 12, 1871. Mildred worked at the Clinic Convalescent Center for twelve to fifteen years.

Edna Katherine Castleberry Utley, Mildred K. Johnson's mother, was born on June 23, 1881 and died on Dec. 15, 1970. Mildred Johnson's father, Oliver Perrry Utley, was born on Feb. 10, 1871 and died on Sept. 14, 1927. Mildred and family settled on Grapevine Road in Hopkins County. She is a faithful member of Grapevine Baptist Church in Hopkins County. -*Submitted by Robin Johnson*

ARCHIE D. JOHNSTON

Joaiah Johnson brought his son JACOB from North Carolina to Muhlenberg Co., KY about 1810 and died in 1845.

JACOB is the forefather of almost all of the Johnson's in Muhlenberg Co., some of whom spell their name Johnston.

JACOB m. Elizabeth Wells and were the parents of Alfred, John, Jacob Jr. (Proctor), BURT H. (HARVEY), Hines, and James.

BURT H. JOHNSTON-Jan. 26, 1824-Apr. 24, 1900 was m. Sept. 22, 1845, in Clarksville, TN, to Martha A. McKinney, Feb. 13, 1829-Apr. 4, 1857. Their children were JOHN SMITH, Jacob M., Perina E., Susan, Henry Nicholas, Martha Ann, Bert Harvey Jr. When his first wife died, BURT H. m. Nancy Shelton (Mar. 16, 1837-Sept. 12, 1881), she died, and BURT H. m. Tabatha Word. They had a daughter May, who m. a preacher ? Casey.

JOHN SMITH JOHNSTON-Oct. 12, 1847, Todd Co.-Oct. 31, 1903 buried Heltsley Cem. Kirkmansville, KY, m. Oct. 28, 1869, in Christian Co. to Mary L. Dulin (b. Apr. 30, 1854 in Christian Co. d. Feb. 21, 1933, buried Clark Cem., Christian Co.) Their children were John Evan (Doc), AUSTIN BERT, Amy, Laura Bell.

AUSTIN BERT JOHNSTON-b. Sept. 16, 1875 in Christian Co., d. Feb. 21, 1957, m. Jan. 26, 1989 in Christian Co. to Rosie Renshaw (b. Feb. 22, 1883 d. Feb. 26, 1904), both are buried in Clark Cem. They had four children: Bessie, Nolie Lee, Leo, and an infant that lived only four days.

Rosie died and AUSTIN BERT m. Oct. 25, 1907, in Hopkinsville to Ida Mae Boxley (b. July 26, 1884; d. 1938 buried in Clark Cem.). To this union were born 10 children: Austin Julian, Edna, Claria Angeline, Madaline, Carl Chester, John Ralph, ARCHIE DULIN, Susie Kathleen, Elizabeth May, and Ernest Kenneth.

ARCHIE DULIN (A.D.) JOHNSTON-b.

Hilda Hamby Johnston and Archie D. Johnston with children Ron, Dan, David and Jeanne

July 27, 1918, in Christian Co. m. Aug. 14, 1944, in Hopkinsville to Hilda Elizabeth Hamby (b. Oct. 31, 1924 in Christian Co.) dau. of Byron Leslie & Myrtle Aline Carmack Hamby.

Archie & Hilda moved to Hopkins Co., in February of 1952, and bought a house on Railroad St. in Earlington. They lived there until June of 1969, when they bought a house on Shop St. in Mortons Gap where they now reside.

Archie is a retired L&N engineer and Hilda owns and operates Johnston's Speedy Office Services (tax preparation & Notary Public), from their home. They have four children.

(1) Lawrence Daniel-b. July 17, 1945, m. Aug. 15, 1967, to Patricia Carol Clevenger (b. July 14, 1947), dau. of J.P. & Beulah Mae Crick Clevenger. Danny & Pat are the parents of Sherie Danette (July 31, 1969-July 31, 1985), and James Patrick-b. July 23, 1972.

(2) Rev. Robert David-b. May 15, 1948, m. June 13, 1969, to Barbara Lynn Simons (b. Sept. 13, 1949), dau. of William E. (Bill) & Thelma Nadine Grant Simons. They are the parents of Robert David II (b. June 25, 1972), and Michael Alan (b. Aug. 25, 1975). Bro. Davis is, at this printing, Pastor of Temple Baptist Church in Laurens, SC.

(3) Ronald Wayne-b. Sept. 13, 1952, m. Sept. 1, 1972, to Sharon Kaye Riggs (b. Sept. 22, 1952), dau. of Henry D. (Buck) & Elizabeth Terzah (Terry) Adams Riggs. (see Alfred G. & Duessie Davis Riggs) Ron & Sharon are the parents of Kenneth Austin (b. June 29, 1975), and Sarah Elizabeth (b. Sept. 23, 1977).

(4) Jeanne Elizabeth-b. Jan. 25, 1960, m. May 25, 1979, to Kenneth Richard Spain (b. Dec. 29, 1958) son of Robert Wayne & Judith Ann Putman Spain. They have a son, Casey Daniel (b. Dec. 30, 1979). - *Compiled by Patricia C. Johnston. Submitted by Sharon R. Johnston*

JOHNSTON-SISK

Edgar Franklin Johnston was born on Aug. 1, 1892, to Benjamin Franklin Johnston (1856-1932) and Mary Frances (Eades) Johnston (1855-1930). Cannie Mae Sisk was born on Oct. 25, 1893, to James F. Sisk (1869-1954) and Docia (Kirkwood) Sisk (1870-1958).

Edgar and Cannie married on Feb. 6, 1912, in Hopkins County. They had nine children:

1) Dudley Alzo Johnston was born on Aug. 22, 1912, and died on Dec. 27, 1981. He married Ola Brunette Villines in 1931, and had six children: Ola Mae (Johnston) Peyton, Dudley Edward Johnston, Austin Earl Johnston, Lilith Nadine Johnston, Melba Jo (Johnston) Mashburn and Glendal Leo Johnston. Brunette died in 1985, and is buried in Odd Fellow's Cemetery alongside her husband.

2) Infant daughter, born Nov. 26, 1914 and died Nov. 26, 1914. She is buried at Silent Run Cemetery near Beulah, KY.

3) James Elgin Johnston was born on Aug. 11, 1916. He is married to Irene (Willis) Johnston and resides in Evansville, IN. Elgin has one son from a previous marriage, James Estel Johnston, who resides in Chicago, IL.

4) Orville Bradford Johnston was born on Apr. 14, 1919. He married Mildred Sue Byrum in 1952, and had two children: Alfred Alan Johnston and Phyllis Lynn (Johnston) Hill. They reside in Madisonville.

5) Katherine Virginia Johnston was born on Aug. 25, 1921. She married Robert Herman Gibson in 1946, and had two children: Sandra Kay (Gibson) Cain and Robert R. Gibson. They reside in Evansville, IN.

6) Eve Evelyn Johnston was born on Apr. 16, 1924. She married in 1947 to Lawrence A. Peters. They had three children: Larry Wayne Peters, Janis S. (Peters) Gordon and Sherri Jo (Peters) Allgeier. They reside in Louisville, KY.

7) Edgar Franklin Johnston, Jr. was born on Mar. 1, 1927. He married Gusta Mae Rhodes Stewart in 1966. They reside in Madisonville. Edgar, Jr. had five children from a previous marriage to Martha Lou Qualls: Kathy Lou Johnston, Karen Sue (Johnston) Davis, Debra Jean Johnston, Deanna Elaine (Johnston) Hayes and Edgar Franklin Johnston, III.

8) Ben Algene Johnston was born on Oct. 20, 1932. He married Marie Cunningham in 1949. They had two children: Vickie Lynn (Johnston) Mattingly and Barry Algene Johnston. They reside in Owensboro, KY.

9) Ernest Edwin Johnston was born on May 31, 1934. He is married to Paula (Priest) Johnston and resides in Henderson, KY. Edwin had three children from previous marriages: Teresa (Johnston) Parker, Mark Johnston and Kimberly Ann Johnston.

Edgar Franklin Johnston, Sr. died on Oct. 16, 1950 and is buried at Odd Fellow's Cemetery in Madisonville. Cannie Mae died on Feb. 20, 1969, and is buried alongside her husband. - *Submitted by: Phyllis Hill*

JONES-HOWTON

Benjamine Lee Jones, born in McLeansboro, IL, June 20, 1847, and Nancy Elizabeth Howton Parrish, a widow born in Hopkins Co., KY, Oct. 24, 1871, were married in Hopkins Co., Jan. 1, 1901. A son of Nancy Elizabeth, Jesse Delano Parrish, whose father had died prior to his birth, was nine years old.

Jesse Delano Parrish (deceased) married Addie Brown. They had one daughter, Pansy Marie Parrish, married Carl Terry. To this union two children were born: Phillip D. Terry, who has two sons, Parrish Winn and Phillip Brandon; Carole Ann Terry Staton, who has one daughter, Charity Lane.

The Jones union produced five children, four still living in Hopkins County.

John Paul Jones (deceased) married Lillian Wilson; no children.

Ruth Ellen Jones married Alvin Kirkwood. To this union two sons were born. Dr. James

Nancy Elizabeth Howton and Benjamin Lee Jones

Benjamine Kirkwood married Ola Leticia Hehl; no children. Edward Ray Kirkwood married Naomi Ruth Poe (deceased). They had two daughters: Nancy Ellen Kirkwood Alfonso, who has one son, Derrick Benjamine, and Elizabeth Rae Kirkwood Paris, who has one son, Matthew Glenn.

Nancy Josephine Jones married Elgie Clayton; no children. She married Bailey Hight Maxwell (deceased); no children.

Edna Lee Jones married David Corbit Robards (deceased). They had one daughter, Hilda Jeraldene Robards, married Alfred Nathaniel Creasey (deceased). To this union two sons were born. David Blake Creasey has one son David Scott, and Gregory Alfred Creasey has one son, Jason Corbit.

Mary Magdalene Jones married Dr. Elmo Vane Morse. They have one son, Jerry Vane Morse, married Judith Ann Hicks. To this union three sons were born: Jevan Maxwell-Dare, Jerry Aldon-Cole, and Jerad Christian-Lemar.

The beginning, as related by the daughters. Our father was a bachelor when he came to Hopkins Co., KY. He was a skilled carpenter at the time, although at one time he had been a teacher. He was the one who helped us with our homework and encouraged us to achieve. The "Lee" part of our father's name came from Robert E. Lee. His father had come to Illinois from Virginia and there he and Lee had been friends. Our mother received little education. She was reared by her father along with other young children when their mother died. She married young, and when she was left with a child, she worked in the homes of relatives and friends to support herself and her child. Our parents were life-long Democrats, and although they differed in their religion (he Cumberland Presbyterian; she Primitive Baptist), there was no friction. He was a Mason; she a member of the Eastern Star. They are buried together in the Beulah Cemetery in Hopkins County. - *Submitted by Mary Jones Morse*

BETTIE ANN JONES

Bettie Ann Hobgood was born June 27, 1886. She was the daughter of Buck and Kitty Hobgood.

Bettie was married to Frank Jones. They had no children. Bettie was a widow for 39 years.

For approximately 60 years, Bettie was a resident of Barnsley, Hopkins Co., KY. She was a member of St. James Baptist Church at Barnsley for over 40 years.

Bettie was a resident of Senior Citizens

Nursing Home. She died in the Regional Medical Center at Madisonville on Aug. 24, 1986, and was buried at Elliott Memorial Gardens in Madisonville.

She left four nephews: Rev. Harry D. Radford, Sam T. Hobgood and Elroy Hobgood all of Madisonville and Paul Hobgood of Chicago, IL, and one niece, Vera Swainigan of Indianapolis, IN.

A picture of Bettie is included in the section "Hopkins County Centenerians". - *Submitted by:Dorothy Miller Shoulders*

JAMES HAYES JONES

James Hayes Jones, b. Mar. 8, 1857, Caldwell Co., KY; d. Aug. 19, 1919, Mortons Gap, KY, son of Charles Clay Jones (b. Apr. 18, 1824, Caldwell Co.), and Catherine Mary Lander, (b. Feb. 25, 1832, Christian Co., KY). Charles Clay was son of Charles Jones, who had moved to Caldwell Co. from Campbell Co., VA. When the Civil War broke out, Charles Clay and family (which at that time contained six children), were living in Wallonia, on Fork of Little River, operating an Inn. He was for the North, believing the Union must be kept together, while most of his neighbors were Southern sympathizers. They told him to leave town, but when he didn't, they loaded the whole family in a boat, with only what they could carry, and made them leave. They settled at Dycusburg on the Cumberland River in Lyons Co., where he died Feb. 5, 1869. His wife, Catherine, d. Mar. 29, 1908, Mortons Gap, KY. She was the daughter of Jeremiah Foster Lander (b. 1807, Clark Co., KY; d. 1834, Christian Co., KY), and Mary McAtee (b. 1810 Fayette Co., KY, daughter of John McAtee-b. Maryland; d. 1855 Trigg Co., KY). Jeremiah Foster was son of William Lander, b. 1765, Loudoun Co., VA, and Letitia Strode, b. 1775, daughter of Capt. John Strode, b. 1730, Virginia and Mary Boyle, b. 1739, Virginia. Capt. John Strode built Strode Station, Clark Co., KY, 1779. The fort was located about two and one-half miles from Winchester on the Lexington Road.

James Hayes Jones

Charles Clay and Catherine Jones had the following children who lived to be adults: Alice Cordelia, b. 1848, m. John A. Couch; Lucy Clay, b. 1852, m. John Grasty, lived Mortons Gap; Willie Clay, b. 1844 m. William Pickering, lived Evansville, IN; James Hayes, b. 1857, m. Henrietta Wallace; Annie Maude, b. 1865, m. Herman Kirchoff, lived Dayton, OH. Four children d. young.

James Hayes Jones, in 1880, was living in Trigg County close to his sister Lucy Clay Grasty, and was a flat boatman. A few years later the Grasty family moved to Mortons Gap, and on a visit to them, he got a job with St. Bernard Coal Company, in charge of loading coal on the train cars. He married Feb. 14, 1887 - Henrietta Wallace, b. Feb. 5, 1850, Trigg Co., KY; d. July 29, 1949. Henrietta was daughter of Dudley William Wallace, b. 1830, Stewart Co., TN; d. 1914, Grand Rivers, Lyons Co., KY and Eliza Jane Jordon, b. 1836; d. 1888, Trigg County Furnace. Her grandparents were: Axum Green Wallace (b. Martin Co., NC), Elizabeth Ross, Tillman Jordon, Cassendra Hensley. Axum Green Wallace had moved his family to Trigg County, when in about 1844, he took a raft loaded with produce to New Orleans to sell and on his way home, up the Natchez Trace, in Mississippi, he was robbed and murdered. A family living nearby found his body and enough identification to notify his family. The two oldest sons made the trip to Mississippi and brought his body back and he was buried near Golden Pond, which is now on Rt. 68 in Land Between the Lakes.

James Hayes and Henrietta Jones had the following children, all born and lived in Hopkins Co., KY: Clay McKinley, b. 1889, m. 1910, Elgie Herman Sisk; Lila Jane, b. 1892, m. 1912, Oswald McMinnus Kington; Paul M., b. 1898; d. 1976 m. 1) Faye Moore: m. 2) Margaret Qualls; Wallace D., b. 1898 (twin) d. 1956 m. 1922, Edna O'Bryant, d. 1986. - *Compiled by: Lila Jones Kington. Submitted by Margaret Clark Kington*

MOSES JONES

Moses Jones was born 1808 in the Granville Co./Person Co., NC, area. America Jones and Levina Wheeler were his parents. In 1832, in Granville Co., Moses married Malina Harriet Clay, daughter of Doctor Clay and Betsy Hill.

In about 1851, neighbors and relatives from the Granville/Person Co., NC, area formed a 14 family wagon train and migrated to Hopkins Co. Moses, Malina, and their eight children ranging in age from 17 to one were among them. Other families included: Hobgoods, Vaughns, Oakleys, and Carnals.

The family of Dock and Isadora (Barron) Jones about 1905

(Compiler would welcome additional information about this trip from anyone). The William Parrish family made the same trip about this time, but it is not known if they were together or not. On Oct. 23, 1852, Moses Jones purchased 125 acres on Poplar Creek. Moses died in 1862, and Malina Harriet died in 1885. Both are buried on the Hurtis Cline farm on Hwy. 1030.

Children of Moses and Malina were: James T., born ca 1834; Permelia Taylor, ca 1836, married (1) Jackson Cozart and (2) Allen Groves; Susan Cornelia, born ca 1838, married Jacob Groves; Lucy Ann, ca 1840, wife of Charles A. Cates; Nicholas Y., 1843; Robert H., 1844; Doctor Hill, b. Feb. 23, 1847; William P., 1850; Alexander, 1855; and Averilla (Rilda), born ca 1858, unmarried in 1885.

Doctor (Dock) Hill Jones married Isadora Barron in 1867, daughter of William Barron and Mary Ann Puryear of Hopkins Co. Isadora died in 1909 and Dock died in 1932. They are buried in Browder Cemetery.

Children of Doctor Hill Jones and Isadora were: Cora, born ca 1868, married (1) James R. Dunkerson, and (2) James Madison; Delora, born 1870, married Robert Lacy Parrish (see Wm. PARRISH STORY FOR HER DESCENDANTS); Lindsey, born 1873, married Minnie Cates; Rasaline, born ca 1875, married Rob Cates; Elby Hill, born ca 1879, married Maude Carnal, parents of Fay Todd and grandparents of Florence Etta Tompkins, both of Slaughters; Frank W., father of Frank J. Jones of Newburgh, IN, and twins Finis and Amplis. Amplis died in infancy. - *Submitted by Mary Louise Parrish Bevers*

T.G. JONES

Theodore Gooch Jones of Hanson, was the ninth of twelve children born to Thomas Marshall "Tom Pet" Jones and Lucretia Jane Ashby, daughter of Wilson W. Ashby and Charlotte McEuen. T.M. was born in Stem, NC, Granville County, to Thomas Jones and his second wife, Jane "Jensey". After Thomas died, Jane married Thomas D. Fowler and they came to Hopkins County bringing her two small children; Loton and Thomas M.

T.M. was Hanson's fist postmaster. Mail was brought to Ashbyburg by boat and then transported by stagecoach or horseback to

Jones' Stand. T.M.'s country home was a white two-story house on the left past the Hanson Cemetery. It was later owned by a Mr. Gammon.

T.M. and Lucretia's other children who had issue were: Don, who married Ella Pritchett; Loton Gus, married Mary Emma Masoncup; William, married Molly Hobgood; Lula J., married Robert Calvin Tapp; Annie Ledia, married Thomas Dudley Givens; Florence, married John F. Bailey; and Minnie, married Edward L. Parish.

Charlotte McEuen was the daughter of Felix McEuen and Lucretia Montelle. Lucretia's parents, Augustus and Charlotte Le Chere Montelle, came to Lexington, KY, from Paris, France. In Lexington they established a boarding school on Richmond Pike, across the street from "Ashland". Mary Todd, future wife of Abraham Lincoln, was one of their students.

Theo G. Jones married Attie Beasley, daughter of J.O.F. and Sarah Ashby Beasley, while she was teaching at Old Salem School. She had attended Van Horn Institute, a boarding school, at Slaughters. The account of their wedding is on microfilm in the Hopkins County Historical Library on the front page of THE HUSTLER, Apr. 2, 1891. Her Aunt's home, where the wedding took place, was a two-story on N.W. corner of Noel and Seminary Streets in Madisonville.

The couple moved to Hanson where he went into business and later had the Hanson Hotel. Their home was across the street from the Methodist Church, where he was Sunday School Superintendent for thirty years. He was a charter member of that church and the last to die. He and Attie celebrated their sixty-fifth wedding anniversary. He was President of East Lawn Cemetery at Providence Rural Methodist Church, east of Hanson. He, his parents, and several brothers and sisters are buried there.

Theo and Attie's only child, Ada Lee, married Whit Haywood. Ada Lee and Whit had no children and lived with her parents. She worked at Peoples Bank at Hanson, and Whit was a partner in Finley Hardware Company in Madisonville.

Attie's mother was living with them at the time of her death. Attie's brother, Walter "Bud" Beasley, lost his wife the next day, so they took his two and three year old girls, Annie Mae and Sarah Elizabeth and reared them. - *Submitted by Sarah Beasley Polley*

WASHINGTON F. JONES

From North Carolina they came in covered wagons, the Jones and Newton families. A carpenter by trade, Washington Franklin Jones (1855-1919), better known as "Uncle Wash", and Loucris Newton (1862-1952), better known as "Aunt Kit", were married ca. 1880. To this union eight children were born and reared around N. Hopkins County. Their children:

Queen (1882-1963), married Almont Morrow and had nine children, with five surviving: Audrey, married Mable Nance, live in Oklahoma, parents of two sons with one decd.; twins Lloyd and Floyd. Lloyd married Alice Clark and they have eight living children.

Front row l to r: Gertie holding Othello, Queen holding Floyd, Audrey, Wash Jones, Carrie, Loucris, Annie and Sallie holding Opal. Back row l to r: Frank, Roy Morrow, Almont Morrow holding Lloyd, Sindy, Linnie, Luther and Carlos Polley

Floyd married Mary Lou Dame and they had two sons and one daughter; Rowena, who married Otto Hibbs, and lives in Sturgis; and Clarence. Queen was an excellent cook and had a deep sense of caring for her many grandchildren.

Linnie Merandia (1884-1969), never married, but spent her life caring for her widowed mother. She taught school and was also known for her fine stitchery and quilt making.

Sallie Lee (1887-1968), married Carlos Polley (d. 1957), parents of three daughters: Annie Lue (d. 1975) married Arthur Miller (d. 1951), had three children (see Shoulders-Miller); Opal Mae married Rev. Thomas Wilson (d. 1986), had two sons and one daughter who died in infancy; and Illy Kathleen married Huston Vanvactor and live in rural Hanson. Helping out in her fathers carpenter shop gave Sallie a love for wood carving, a hobby that served her well in later years. She left a legacy of beautiful poems and songs.

Gertie Mae (1890-1981), married Roy Morrow and had: Othello, married Roy Russel, had six children, one died, lives in New Hampshire and Louette who married Robert Cates and lives in Hopkins County. "Aunt Gert" was a member of the choir at Oakley Home Church on Hwy. 630. Also known for her fine stitchery and quilting.

Lousinda (1892-1923) died as the result of childbirth. Married Minis Clark (d. 1974). Their children were Katherine and Bonnie Helen. "Sindy" shared with her brothers and sisters a love of music. She played the guitar.

Luther (1894-1928) married Gusta James, who preceded him in death. Their son, Harold, died in 1986. Little is known of Luther, as he spent most of his married life in Chicago, where he died of TB.

Franklin (1896-1964) married Coralee Cates (now dec'd.), had eight children: Douglas, Virginia, Curtis, Adell, Carroll, L.H., Billy, and Connie. Frank served his country in France during WW I. He followed his father's trade as a carpenter all his life.

Carrie Victoria (1904-1981) married Duane Crawford. Their children were Margret, Jerry and Neal. Carrie was a dedicated worker with the youth in D.V.B.S. in the Nebo Baptist Church, a leader in the local homemakers and loved working in crafts. - *Submitted by: Dorothy Shoulders, a great granddaughter*

JOYCE-RAMSEY

She had the soft, slow voice of a southern lady and the patience only years of difficult times can bring forth. Aunt Annie was still a pretty woman in her 70's. Watching her comb her long white hair was something I looked forward to.

Another was cherry pudding pie. Aunt Annie made it for my dad and me every time she knew we were coming to the farm. He loved it—still does.

Frank Morrison Larkin, infant son of Annie Ramsey and Albert Larkin

Born Annie Victoria Ramsey (Oct. 15, 1879), she was the fifth and last daughter of John G. and Louiza G. Ramsey of the Dalton area of Hopkins County. She was my grandfather's (Ernest D. Ramsey) sister.

Growing up in a Christian family made its mark on this child. God would be her strength through many hard trials.

All the Ramsey children had to have some formal education and there had to be a church. Grandma kept asking Grandpa, but it was put off. I'm not certain the year they were built, but built they were. My great-grandmother took a stand for her children and the neighborhood. Every thriving community was only as progressive as its children's education.

The church was Methodist and built by my great-grandfather, J.G. "Doc" Ramsey. The school was one room and was to house many a student as they started the ladder to success. My grandfather, Ernest Ramsey, and Lex Bell (later President of Kentucky Bank in Madisonville), attended that one room school. They remained life-long friends.

My great-grandmother was said to be filled with the Spirit. I always heard Grandma was quite adept at holding babies on her lap. If she got a bit happy in the service, she knew how to balance little ones and still clap and shout (back when Methodists still did that).

Aunt Annie was a radiant bride when she married Thomas Allen Joyce. They had three children: Ernestine Marion (Nov. 5, 1905); a son, Parl, (1902-1904), died in a freak accident in infancy; and Gilliam (1903-1924), who died in a mine explosion at Victoria Mine in Hopkins County. She also lost Uncle Tom in 1907.

I'm not sure when, but Aunt Annie also lost her home to fire. Nothing was salvaged.

Marion grew up and spent a good bit of time at my grandparents, Ernest and Opal Ramsey's, in Madisonville. She went to school there. They shared a name and a birth date.

In 1916, Aunt Annie married Albert Larkin in Madisonville. They had one son, Frank Morrison (July 25, 1920). He and his son, Dwayne, are the only two descendants still living in the Government Section.

Marion married Hubert Davis (Mar. 10, 1901-Nov. 25, 1971) in my grandparent's living room, Nov. 25, 1928. They lived in Henderson, KY, until 1958 when Chrysler moved to St. Louis, MO. They made their home in Ellisville, MO.

To their parents a daughter, Joyce Ann was born (July 22, 1930 to June 10, 1970). Joyce was a most enthralling, accomplished musician, wife and mother. She passed on at 40. Her husband was Roger Snow. Their three children are David, Susan and Audrey Snow. They live in Chicago.

Frank married Pauline Kirkwood (Oct. 12, 1920), daughter of Minnie and Robert Kirkwood of Dalton. The ceremony was performed at the General Baptist Church in Dawson Springs (Oct. 28, 1939). They had 11 children, all married. In order they are:

Roger Audmond, Jan. 18, 1941; Frank Mitchell, Mar. 30, 1943; Jerry Wayne, Feb. 6, 1925; Myrna Joan, Dec. 10, 1946; Barbara Lynn, Dec. 14, 1948; Patricia Neal, Aug. 3, 1952; Debra Dale, Mar. 26, 1955; Deana Kay, Feb. 7, 1957; Brenda Gail, Apr. 28, 1960; Morris Dwayne, Oct. 3, 1964 and little Carrol Henry, July 5, 1966, who was stillborn.

After Uncle Albert (1873-1936) passed, Aunt Annie lived part time with her children and down home. She passed Aug. 16, 1971, after 35 years of widowhood.

I can still hear your voice, Aunt Annie, it never lost its softness. - *Submitted by Peggy Sullivan Waide*

JOYNER-DAY

The earliest account of Joyner ancestors is William Joyner, born 1799, in North Carolina and his wife Mary, born 1810, in Tennessee. Their children: John C., b. Sept. 4, 1830; David, b. 1838; Sarah, b. 1836.

In the 1860, 70 and 80 Hopkins County Census, John C. and wife Emily Ballard (b. Aug. 25, 1838) are shown. Their children: John; Sallie married Jonah Tippett in 1887; Ella married Coon Buntin in 1888; Dave married Nancy Cunningham in 1886; Barbara Ann married William W. Branson; Mary married Will Frazier in 1894; Dora married O.W. Cates in 1894; Susan married Willis Oakley in 1894; and William Bennett born in 1883 in Hopkins Co. married Callie Lee Day, born 1884.

Home of Henry Day at 418 S. Seminary St. in 1925. William and Callie Joyner with children Jewell, Rea, Geneva and Evelyn.

Callie's ancestors include: America Caroline Buntin (1861-1924) and J. Thomas Day (1856-1925). Betsy and Billy Buntin, Mary Elizabeth Hobgood and Henry Burnett Day. Callie's siblings were: Bobby Hess; Martha Jane married Rufus Stodgill; Leony; Henry married Cora Parrish; Thomas married Maud; Bertha; Roy; Laura married George Mitchell; and Pearl.

William and Callie married in 1903, and lived in the Shakerag area until 1915. Their children were: Bennett, b. 1904; Roy, b. 1906; Bracie, b. 1909, married Versie Ruth Dixon and had children Sue Melton and Joyce Dorris; Jewell, b. 1915 married Burl King and had a son James Carl; Rea, b. 1918, married James Walker and had children June Landrum and Shirley Thomas; Geneva, b. 1920, married James S. Thomas and had children Jim, Ellen, Joan, Jennifer and Fredrick; Evelyn, b. 1923, married first Lee Roy Grant with children Doris Hawkins and Patricia Stokes, married second Wm. B. Brashear with stepchildren: Mark, Alisa, and Tracie.

The Joyner family moved in to the Nebo farm area in 1915, and misfortune took the lives of the first two children. The last three were born in this new location. Bracie, Jewell and Rea had attended school at a one room building named Porter and Payne, taught by Miss Auvergne Crow (she later married Walter Carneal and taught in Nebo School when the children moved to Nebo).

Bracie died in 1964, his wife Ruth lives in Madisonville.

In 1942, William met with a fatal accident from a driver asleep at the wheel and Callie later married Elgin Jagoe of Hopkins County. They lived in the Hanson area for many years before his death in 1964. Callie died in 1968. - *Submitted by Rea Joyner Walker*

WILLIE MITCHELL KEENE

Willie Mitchell (W.M.) was born Nov. 15, 1900, in Macon Co., TN, the first of nine children born to James Elisah Alexander Keene and Camilla Myrtle Barber Keene.

W.M. first came to Hopkins County as a young man looking for work in the coal mines. He returned to Macon Co., TN and married Liza Elender Herald, daughter of Noah Herald and Lydia Katherine Blankenship. W.M. and Liza were married in Macon County on Oct. 31, 1920.

Willie Mitchell and Liza Elender (Herald) Keene

W.M. and Liza's first two children, Kermit Leston, born Aug. 5, 1921 and Wilma Dean, born Mar. 9, 1923, were born in Macon Co., TN. The family moved to Hopkins County in 1923. On May 28, 1926, twin daughters, Elma Ray and Velma Ray, were born. Velma Ray died Dec. 31, 1926 and is buried in Grapevine Cemetery. The family moved back to Macon Co., TN in 1930. The last child, a daughter, Aminell, was born Sept. 18, 1937 in Macon County.

W.M. and family moved back to Hopkins County for the last time in 1938. He was involved in the forming of the Union while he worked for Dawson Daylight Coal Company in Dawson Springs, KY. He worked for West Kentucky Coal Company until Island Creek Coal Company bought them out. He worked for Island Creek Coal Company until his retirement with a mine pension. He owned land and farmed in the Oak Hill Community near Nortonville, KY. He is buried (died Aug. 26, 1986) in Suthards Cemetery, south of Earlington, KY. - *Submitted by Anne Keene Morgan*

KENNEDY-RINGO

She is my grandmother's half-sister. The first child of Benjamin Franklin Ringo (Aug. 17, 1864 to June 20, 1962) and Lena Gertrude Sigler Ringo (Aug. 6, 1888 to Nov. 7, 1974). She is my Aunt Alice.

B.F. Ringo (I will call him Poppa) lost his first wife, Florence Dye Ringo (Mar. 1, 1872 to June 12, 1907) and was left with three of their four children: Leavy Novelist (Dec. 8, 1889 to Aug. 22, 1971), Opal Vivian (May 25, 1895 to May 4, 1967) and Ben Spaulding Ringo (b. Mar.

26, 1898). Opal was my grandmother. Little Leah Pauline only lived from May 11, 1893 to Oct. 20, 1894.

Poppa later met and married Lena Gertrude Sigler (b. Aug. 6, 1888) from across Tradewater River in Caldwell County. Her father owned a large farm on the road to Shady Grove. Poppa owned a large farm on the Hopkins County side.

She was a young girl when she married and Poppa was many years her senior. They worked in the fields side by side.

They had two daughters, Alice Reba (b. Oct. 3, 1910) and Zeola Virginia (b. Nov. 12, 1916). If that name sounds different, its probably because they let little Alice name her baby sister.

Albeit, they are half-great-aunts, I never knew any difference in my feelings for them.

My precious Aunt Alice would be the pianist for my wedding at the "Old Ramsey Homestead" in the Government section of Hopkins Co. She always had a great humor and good wit. Growing up on the Ringo farm meant helping with all the chores. Her humor was a great asset.

I never knew my own great-grandmother, Florence. Mrs. Gertrude (pronounced Ms.) was my great-grandmother and was always good to me. I often think how hard life was for her. I loved her very much.

Aunt Alice married John Givens Kennedy of Providence, KY on Nov. 4, 1933 in Madisonville, Hopkins Co. They were married by Rev. Anderson in the Baptist parsonage.

They made their home in Webster County. Their only child, James Franklin Kennedy, was born July 16, 1938. Uncle John had a son, John Reed, by a previous marriage. He lives in Oregon.

Jimmy and I were special cousins. I felt as close to him as a brother. He married a friend of mine, Lucinda Ruby, daughter of Edwin and Mary Comer Ruby, of Springlake Woods, Madisonville. They later divorced and he married June (NMI) Ferris (b. Mar. 22,?) of Owensboro. They adopted a son, John Charles Kennedy (b. Apr. 22, 1971).

Uncle John (Dec. 26, 1906 to July 23, 1959) passed away early in life. Poppa passed in June of 1962. Aunt Alice and Mrs. Gertrude made their home in Calvert City, Lyon Co. She worked at the Gilbertsville, KY Holiday Inn for some years.

We lost Mrs. Gertrude Nov. 7, 1974. Jim has retired after 20 years in the Air Force. He and June live in Goldsboro, NC as does his mother.

Aunt Alice did marry again. His name was Howard Dorris (July 31, 1910 to Oct. 12, 1979) and she had known him for many years, but she became a widow again in 1979. She enjoys her church and her friends, still plays the piano, attends church regularly and recently attended a big birthday party in her honor.

I miss them all and I love them all.

(See Ringo-Dye, Seymour-Ringo, Ringo-Arnett, Ramsey-Ringo, and Mather-Ringo). - *Submitted by Peggy Sullivan Waide*

GEORGE KING

Joe King and Sarah (Gill) King came to the United States from Lancaster, England in 1857. Their son, George King was born in Lancaster, Eng. in 1855, and their daughter, Annie King was born Oct. 8, 1857 in Spottsville, PA, a short time after they landed in the U.S. From Pennsylvania they migrated to Kentucky and settled in St. Charles, a thriving coal mining town.

Paul King Sr.

George King grew up in St. Charles, attended school studying pharmacy, and is said to be the first pharmacist in St. Charles. For many years he operated King Drug Store in St. Charles and later, King Drug Store in Earlington. On Apr. 20, 1881 he married Mary Ella Robinson, b. Aug. 16, 1863 from Wisconsin, dau. of Thomas Robinson (b. Maine) and Elizabeth Chigudder (b. England) Robinson.

George and Ella had four children: E.O. Gilbert King, b. 1885, who married Maggie Turner. Gilbert designed a prototype of a military Army tank which is on display at Smithsonian Institute in Washington, D.C. He died in 1921, buried at Christian Privilege Cemetery, St. Charles.

Norris King b. 1886, was also a pharmacist for a number of years in Madisonville. He married Nell Blair, and during their last years they resided in St. Petersburgh, FL. No children.

Paul King b. June 21, 1891 first married Lucy Fawcett b. Sept. 20, 1893, dau. of J.E. and Dixie (Jordan) Fawcett. She died Mar. 14, 1942. They had one son, Paul King Jr. On Oct. 19, 1948, Paul married Julia Maddox b. June 26, 1920, who retired in 1985 as Assistant Vice-Pres./ Branch Manager of the Southside Branch of Peoples Bank, after 23 years. She presently lives in Earlington and works part-time in the office at Wal-Mart Department Store. Paul taught school and coached at Nortonville, traveled for Wright Machine Co., worked at King Drug Store in Earlington, during his younger years. He was a prominent civic leader in Earlington and served as Mayor, City Judge and on the City Council for many years. He died June 29, 1973, is buried at Grapevine Cemetery.

Paul King Jr. b. Oct. 21, 1922 at Earlington, married Jean Spicer b. Aug. 26, 1926 dau. of Benjamin Wm. Spicer and Hallie Simpson of Lexington, KY. Paul Jr. is Professor of Psychology at the University of Missouri, Columbia, MO, where he has been for a number of years. Their children: Susan Gail b. Jan. 3, 1953, married to Dean France b. May 3, 1954, son of Cecil Lee and Jane (Kehr) France. He is a policeman, and Susan is a newspaper writer. Karen Lee b. Sept. 9, 1954 married Gerald Robert Silvoso b. Nov. 9, 1948, son of Joseph A. and Wilda L. (Miller) Silvoso. They have one dau. Amy Jordan born Feb. 15, 1982. Dr. Gerald Silvoso is a physician at Little Rock Diagnostic Clinic, Little Rock, AR, and Karen is an RN. - *Submitted by Rella G. Jenkins with approval of Mrs. Julia King*

KINGTON-JONES

Lila Jane Jones and Oswald McMinnus Kington were married Nov. 6, 1912 in Earlington at the home of Elgie and Clay Sisk (Lila's sister and brother-in-law). Elgie was Oswald's first cousin.

Both were born in Mortons, Lila on Jan. 14, 1892 and Oswald on Dec. 23, 1891.

Lila was the daughter of Henrietta Wallace Jones and James Hayes Jones. Hayes Jones ran the power house for St. Bernard Coal Company at South Diamond Mine until his death in 1919. Henrietta Wallace Jones died at Owensboro in 1949. Lila had one sister, Clay McKinley Jones Sisk (1886-1977) and twin brothers, Wallace Dixon Jones (1898-1956) and Paul Moore Jones (1898-1977). Paul was City of Madisonville Engineer during his career. Wallace was a route salesman for Armour Packing Company.

Oswald was the son of William Ward (1861-1944) and Emma Louisa Lovan Kington (1866-1914). He had one living brother, George M. Kington, and the deceased members are: Katherine K. Oates, Willie K. Davis, Goebel K. Trathen, Rena Mae Jones, Alice Marie Kington, and Hammonds Lovan Kington.

Oswald was a mine operator at White City, Uniontown and west of Madisonville until 1936. He served on the rationboard in the World War II period, was appointed County Judge, serving for six months in 1947, declining to seek election. He served as Deacon Chairman of the First Baptist Church from 1945 until 1965 and was a director of the Kentucky Bank & Trust Company for over forty years.

Three children were born to them, William Hayes (1915-1977), Betty Jane Gilford born 1920 and Oswald M., Jr. born 1931. They have eleven grandchildren and sixteen great grandchildren.

William Hayes married Margaret Elizabeth Clark, Sept. 12, 1940 in Lebanon, KY. They had three children, Barry Clark, Sept. 2, 1942, Janet Elizabeth Kington Dickey, Aug. 17, 1944, and William Hayes, Jr., May 2, 1949. There are six grandchildren.

Betty Jane Kington married Floyd Robert Guilfoil, Jr. of Syracuse, NY, in Carmel, CA in 1943, while Robert was in the army. They have three children, Anne Kington Gilfoil Borrusch, July 29, 1946, Betty Jane Gilfoil Briggs, Oct. 20, 1949, and Floyd Robert III, Sept. 16, 1956. There are four gransons.

Oswald M. Jr. married Jane Allen Judge in Carlisle, KY, Feb. 6, 1954. They have five children, James McMinnus, Dec. 19, 1954, John Harlan, Dec. 14, 1955, Sarah Allen Kington Patterson, Jan. 1, 1958, Mary Jane Kington Popham, Apr. 11, 1959, and Charles Allen, Jan.

3, 1962. There are six grandchildren. - *Submitted by O.M. Kington Jr.*

WILLIAM WARD KINGTON

William Ward Kington, b. July 14, 1861, Hopkins Co., KY; d. May 2, 1944, Madisonville, KY, son of George Washington Kington, b. 1839 Morgan Co., TN and Susan O'Bryan, b. 1845 Hopkins Co., KY. His grandparents were: Bernard M. Kington, b. 1804 Sullivan Co., TN; Sarah Ann Snodgrass of Walker Co., GA (they came to Hopkins Co., KY about 1846; Thomas L. O'Bryan, b. 1820 Hopkins Co.; Louisa Loving, b. 1825 Hopkins Co.

William Ward m. Feb. 28, 1883 - Emma Louisa Lovan, b. Feb. 14, 1866; d. May 17, 1914, daughter of James Porterfield Lovan, b. 1840 Hopkins Co. and Angeline Hankins, b. 1839 Hopkins Co. Her grandparents were Russell Gray Lovan, b. 1808 Hopkins Co.; Mary E. Ezell, b. 1809 Virginia; Houston J. and Mary Hankins.

William Ward and Emma Louisa Kington had eight children: Katherine, b. 1884 m. Omer J. Oates; Willie Glenn, b. 1889 m. William E. Davis; Oswald McMinnus, b. 1891 m. Lila Jane Jones; Rena Mae, b. 1893 m. Witson Jones; Goebel, b. 1899 m. J. Ries Trathen; Hammond Lovan, b. 1901 m. Ruby M. Collins; Anna Marie, b. 1904; d. 1914; George M., b. 1909 m. Helen W. Sugg. William Ward m./2 1916-Mrs. Minnie Lee (Mock) Spivey; m./3 Bernie Walker.

William Ward's parents were divorced in 1874. His mother, Susan O'Bryan m./2 J. Millard Frazier and moved to Harrodsburg, KY. She left her three children, William Ward, Martha Katherine and James Miller with her parents, Thomas and Louisa O'Bryan, who lived a few miles east of Mortons Gap. Their father, George Washington, about a year later left for the West, place unknown.

W.W. Kington

William Ward was only twelve years of age when he went to work in a coal mine. His first employment was with the old South Diamond Coal Co., and his first duties consisted of greasing cars. He eventually held practically every position in connection with the operation of a coal mine. His first venture into the coal business was in 1901, when he operated the Kington-Wolfe Mine near the south city limits of Mortons Gap. In 1906 he closed it as a commercial mine, incorporated Kington Coal Company, and the next year opened a mine four miles east of Mortons Gap. He also started a town, with small company houses, a general store, and later a hotel. All the houses were painted white, thus the town was called White City and the mine, White City Mine. He built a railroad from Mortons Gap to the mine. He developed its properties until the mine had a capacity of 1,500 tons per day. At the height of the season's production 350 men were working in or about the mines. In 1920, he sold this mine to Hart Coal Company and opened a mine in Union County, west of Morganfield, with business offices at Mortons Gap. This mine was closed in 1935.

W.W. Kington's home at Mortons Gap

The profits of his business were diverted to other enterprises, chiefly in his home community of Mortons Gap. He was one of the organizers in 1907 of the Planters Bank of Mortons Gap, and was elected president. He was also president of the Mortons Gap Ice and Light Company, built the local plant in 1914, but sold his interest in May 1920. Much of his capital went into a building program in Mortons Gap. He erected a substantial brick business block on Main and Cross Streets in 1904, selling it in 1920. For twenty-three years he was a member of the City Council, a supporter of the Baptist Church, contributing the land and helping build the church edifice. During his life he was accomplished at the following occupations: farmer, coal miner, carpenter, brick maker, brick layer, undertaker, baker (made crackers), merchant, canning factory and banker. Information: "History of Kentucky", Vol. 5. Editor - Judge Charles Kerr, Publ. 1922; "1986 Historical Society of Hopkins County, Kentucky"; Oswald and Lila Kington. - *Submitted by Margaret Kington*

KIRKWOOD

Hugh Kirkwood came to America as a small child from Ireland. In Hopkins County history, he is considered a pioneer. He was in his late thirties; early forties, when he put down roots in the Silent Run area. The Kirkwood family has contributed to the growth and development of Hopkins County.

In Major Gordon's HISTORY OF HOPKINS COUNTY, Hugh Kirkwood was mentioned as being an active volunteer of the War of 1812. He was a first sergeant in Captain William R. McGary's Company of Hopkins County 5th Regiment. In the 76th Regiment of militia commanded by Colonel Ashby, Hugh was a Captain and later a Major. He fought at the Battle of New Orleans under General Jackson.

His first wife was Martha Amanda. His second wife was Patsy Bailey. The children of Hugh and Martha were Hugh Jr. (b. circa 1800), James (b. circa 1803), John (b. circa 1798), Hiram (b. circa 1808), Jefferson (b. circa 1812), and Frances (b. 1813). His children were farmers and businessmen as was Hugh. Hugh Jr. and James were among the first in Hopkins County to construct horse power grist mills. James resided at Silent Run and Hugh Jr. in the Charleston District. Later he moved to the Kitchen Precinct.

Kirkwood Springs named for Jim Kirkwood brought business and tourists to Hopkins County in the late 1850's. In its day, it was a busy, bustling resort spa. Hotels, baths, stagecoaches, railroads, and horses and carriages transported people in and out. While the summers were busy and productive, the winter months brought severe weather and isolation. The surrounding areas grew and prospered.

The Kirkwoods for generations were involved in grist mills, saw mills, farming, and raising livestock (especially hogs). Some of the Kirkwood land is still in the family.

Hugh Kirkwood is the great great grandfather and James the great grandfather of Hilda Kirkwood Gill of Earlington. - *Submitted by Dianne Hauprich Gill*

KIRKWOOD AND SLATEN

The Hugh Kirkwood who died in 1855 was born in Ireland; he was the son of Hugh Kirkwood, Sr. (p. 27, HOPKINS COUNTY, KENTUCKY RECORDS, Volume V). Several descendants of Hugh Kirkwood, Sr., were named Hugh. Those identified by the writer are:

1. His son, whom I had thought of as Hugh Sr. (until I found the above facts), evidently should be called Hugh Jr. Note, however, that he was referred to as Hugh Sr. in all but one of the records found by me. This Hugh Kirkwood fought with Andrew Jackson in the War of 1812. He was married and had small children when he went to war as the first sergeant of Captain William R. McGary's Company, Kentucky Mounted Volunteer Militia—commanded by Colonel Henry Renick (p. 146, SOLDIERS OF THE WAR OF 1812, REPORT OF THE ADJUTANT GENERAL OF THE STATE OF KENTUCKY, Frankfort, KY, 1891). The children of this veteran of the War of 1812 were John, James, Hiram, Jefferson W., Nancy (wife of Thomas J. Alman), and Sophia (wife of Isham B. Slaton) (pp. 539-542, Deed Book 21, Hopkins Co., KY).

2. The next Hugh is referred to as Hugh Kirkwood, Jr. in several sketches (pp. 86-88, "Biographical Sketches," HOPKINS COUNTY, KENTUCKY RECORDS, Volume V) perhaps should be called Hugh Kirkwood III. He was born in Kentucky in 1800 and died in 1868. His wife was Polly (Henson) Kirkwood of North Carolina. Two of their sons were James W., born Jan. 29, 1823 (husband of Misaniah Potts, a native of Green Co., SC).

3. Hugh Jefferson Slaten, Sr. was born in Hopkins Co., KY, in 1830, probably between the end of July and the end of December. His date of birth was estimated from the date of his

first marriage, July 19, 1856, age 25 and the date of his third marriage, Dec. 20, 1880, age 50. Hugh J. was the son of Isham B. and Sophia B. (Kirkwood) Slaton. Hugh, Sr. was the grandson of John an Elizabeth Hibbs Slayden (p. 19, THE SLATON FAMILY AB ANTIQUITAS, 2nd edition) and Hugh Kirkwood, who died of old age (age 88) in Hopkins Co., KY, Nov. 21, 1855 (p. 27, HOPKINS COUNTY, KENTUCKY RECORDS, Volume V). Hugh Jefferson Slaten, Sr. was called Jeff. Jeff had three wives and twelve children. He married Nancy Linn (Lynn?) in McLean Co., KY; Jerusha A. Durham (of South Carolina) in Saline Co., IL; and Martha Ann Lewis in Labette Co., KS.

4. The son of Jeff and Martha Ann (Lewis) was Hugh Jefferson Slaten, Jr., who was born in Labette Co., KS, on Jan. 20, 1882, and died at Erie (Neosho County), Kansas, on Jan. 21, 1965. Hugh Jefferson Slaten, Jr. married Nora Orleapha Guy of Erie, KS. One of their two children was a son named Hugh J (no middle name and no period).

5. Hugh J Slaten, born Jan. 13, 1919, in Erie, KS, has been married two times. The names of his wives are Margaret Katherine Treadway, who was born in Parsons, KS; and Kathleen Burgess of Stillwater, MN. Hugh J is the last person named Hugh in the Slaten family. However, one of Hugh J's grandsons (J.J.) is named Jefferson James Slaten; thus, Jefferson, which was passed down from the Kirkwood family, is a current name of a Slaten child. - *Submitted by Dr. Lenell M. Slaten*

KIRKWOOD-CASTLEBERRY
Wooed But Not Won.

The vows were all forgotten,

The ring asunder broken.

"On last Wednesday morning Mr. E.N. Newbury of Blue Mound, IL, arrived in our town after having procured the necessary papers to make one of Kentucky's blue-eyed belles, Miss Emma Castleberry, his wife. With fond anticipations and bright hopes for the future he came, not thinking that one so fair could be so false, nor dreaming that dark clouds would gather and the chill wind of disappointment blow....They proceeded to make final arrangements, when alas, without knowledge or consent, Mr. W.E. Kirkwood of the vicinity of Silent Run, KY, and the would-be-bride hied away to the nearest county seat and were quietly married."

So reads the newspaper account of the Mar. 14, 1893 marriage of Nancy Emma Castleberry (born Dec. 26, 1870 to John Castleberry and Minerva E. Wilson) and William Edgar Kirkwood (born Aug. 13, 1871 to Jimmy K. Kirkwood and Miriah Wilson). Five daughters were born to this union: George Ruth (born Nov. 23, 1894, called Ruth, but named for Dr. George Brown, the physician who delivered her); Alyne Matilda (May 9, 1897 to Dec. 19, 1933); Elfa Grace (Feb. 18, 1901); Lelia Elizabeth (Oct. 18, 1905); Margaret Elaine (Dec. 22, 1908). Emma and William E. lived with his parents on the Kirkwood Farm outside Dawson Springs for some years after the marriage until he became a Singer Sewing Machine agent. He traveled from farm to farm selling sewing machines from a specially-designed buggy with a trunk in back to carry the ma-

L to r: William Edgar Kirkwood, George Ruth Kirkwood, Nancy Emma Castleberry Kirkwood and Alyne Matilda Kirkwood

chines. He took produce of all kinds in payment, including garden vegetables, chickens, and other items.

In 1904, William E. was promoted to manager and moved his family to Madisonville, where his office was located. Unfortunately, Emma's health was not robust. In 1910 they moved back to Dawson, where Emma could take the waters and where William E. could more easily travel back and forth from Louisville on the train. (William E. was by then working for Baldwin Piano Company, headquartered in Louisville.) Tragically, Emma died Nov. 17, 1910, leaving William E. with daughters ages 15, 13, 9, 5, and 2 years.

After a brief stay with Mr. & Mrs. LaRue of the Owensboro College and Conservatory, William E. moved his daughters back to the Kirkwood farm where his widowed mother, Miriah, and his three younger brothers still lived and worked. William's work required that he travel a great deal and he lived in a number of different states before his death on Mar. 31, 1931 in Philadelphia, PA. - *Submitted by: Mrs. Ruth Logan*

HUGH KIRKWOOD
Hugh Kirkwood came to this country as a small boy and all records indicate from Antrim, North Ireland. His father Hugh, Sr. was granted 250 acres in the Granville Section of South Carolina on the Flagbranch of Little River, waters of the Savanah, by King George III and was witnessed by the Hon. William Bull, Esq. on July 20, 1772.

Hugh, Sr. joined the Revolutionary Army on June 6, 1776 and was a Sgt. in the 2nd Company of the 5th Regiment of South Carolina. He was severely wounded on Oct. 9, 1779 in the battle of Savanah. His last will and testament on record in the Court House at Addeville, SC, District 96, states that he died from these wounds and that he appointed Capt. John Bowie as guardian of his three young sons, Hugh, Jr., Nathan and Robert.

In the revised 1790 Georgia State census, it shows Hugh, Jr. and Nathan members of the Wilkes County Militia in Washington, GA in 1793. Then records indicate Nathan returned to South Carolina and Hugh lived for a period in Tennessee. He shows up next in the 1802 tax list of Muhlenberg Co., KY with 200 acres on Pond River. He received a land grant in 1809 of 200 acres in Hopkins County. On the 30th of January, 1809, the 76th Reg. of the Kentucky Militia was formed, and among the Regimental Captains' was Hugh Kirkwood. In 1812 General Harrison called for volunteers and Hugh was listed as Ensign under William McGary, in Hopkins County Militia. In December 1814 he was serving as Major.

He was appointed Justice of Peace in 1817.

He and his first wife, Catherine, had seven children, (1) John (Johnnie), (2) Hugh, Jr., (3) James W., (4) Jefferson Wm., (5) Hiram, (6) Sophia, (7) Nancy. His wife Catherine died between 1830-1836 and he married his second wife Martha (Patsy) Bailey in 1836. He died in November 1855 in Hopkins Co., KY. In the Hopkins County Vital Statistics at his death in 1855, he was listed at age 88, died from old age.

His five sons were all very successful farmers in the Dalton, Richland and Silent Run areas.

There are now estimated over 1200 descendants from the Hugh and Catherine union. Sources: Kentucky State Historical Society, Frankfort, KY; Kentucky Archive, Frankfort, KY; Tennessee State Archive, Nashville, TN; South Carolina State Archive, Columbia, SC; Williard Library, Evansville, IN; Latter Day Saints Library, Evansville, IN; Washington, D.C. National Archives; Probate Court Records, Addeyville, SC; Greenwood, S.C. Library; Georgia Historical Society, Savanah, GA; Historical Society, Charleston, SC; Court Records, Anderson, SC. - *Submitted by John W. Kirkwood, Jr.*

RUFUS OWEN KIRKWOOD
Rufus Owen Kirkwood was born Aug. 30, 1844, in western Hopkins Co., KY, to Jefferson William Kirkwood, of Irish ancestry, and Florella O'Bryan, both natives of Hopkins Co. His maternal grandparents were: Reddick O'Bryan and Elizabeth Bourland, daughter of Rev. John Bourland, first pastor of Richland Baptist Church which they helped to organize in 1837.

Rufus Owen Kirkwood, early 1900's

When R.O. Kirkwood was about 15 years old his father died leaving him the responsibility of caring for his mother and twin brothers, Hiram T. and Thomas Jefferson Kirkwood, age seven. Sisters already married were: Virginia, wife of Thomas Younger, and Irene H., wife of John A. McGuire (McGuyer).

The family owned a farm near Richland which was ransacked during the Civil War by Union soldiers who stole food and horses. When they stole R.O.'s pony he joined the Confederate army to try to get his pony back. When or where he served is not known, but a granddaughter remembered when he attended Confederate reunions.

Rufus Owen Kirkwood married (Mar. 11, 1869) Eusibia Ann Bailey (b. ca. 1848), daughter of Margaret Jane Christian and Rev. Lewis W. Bailey, an ordained Baptist minister and farmer. The young couple lived on the Bailey farm before moving to Earlington.

They had two daughters: Cora Elizabeth, (b. Nov. 16, 1870; d. June 26, 1916) and Johnnie Mae (b. Mar. 11, 1884; d. Dec. 8, 1965). Cora married William Tolliver McGary and Johnnie Mae married his brother, John Oliver McGary. (See Tolliver Young McGary).

R.O. Kirkwood was a blacksmith at a coal mine before moving to Madisonville. There he opened R.O. Kirkwood's Blacksmith Shop on E. Center St., about where the police station is now. For a while his son-in-law John O. McGary was his partner.

After Eusibia Ann (Bailey) Kirkwood died Nov. 19, 1899, R.O. later married Annie (Veazey) Lynch, a widow, who survived him.

Rufus Owen Kirkwood died Nov. 18, 1916, and was buried in Odd Fellows Cemetery, Madisonville. A stone anvil atop his tombstone is evidence that he was proud to be a blacksmith. He was a Baptist by faith and a member of the Odd Fellows lodge. Sources: Family Bible, oral history and other documents. (See McGary Families) - *Submitted by Mary Nell (Whitsell) Oates*

KITTINGER-ELLIS

Lavinia Ellis and Robert Kittinger were united in marriage Dec. 20, 1924 on a cold snowy night in the home of Brother George Alston in Sacramento, KY.

Lavinia was born Jan. 21, 1910 in Sacramento, KY. She was the daughter of Addie Macky and Silvester Ellis. Her maternal grandparents were Nannie Ray and Scott Macky. Her paternal grandparents were Ellen McLaughlin and Bud Ellis. She has three sisters: Miladene Ray, Moriel Arnold and the late Nannie Ellen Durbin. She also has four brothers: Welborn and the late Robbie, Barnnie and Hobert Kittinger.

Lavinia attended school at the Adam's School House in Sacramento. It was a one room school house. Lavinia had to walk about two miles to and from school daily.

Lavinia is a faithful and active member of the Cumberland Presbyterian Church where she enjoys singing in the choir. She also enjoys sewing, quilting, crocheting and visiting with friends and family.

Robert (b. Dec. 11, 1902, d. Sept. 28, 1952) was the son of Betty Mize and Claude Kittinger. He had one sister: Ruth Greer. He worked for the Madisonville State Highway Department as a mechanic for several years. Robert was a member of the Cumberland Presbyterian Church.

Lavinia and Robert had four children: Greta Ann Hale Padgett (Dec. 14, 1933), Roy Gene (July 16, 1931), James Wallace (May 19, 1926) and Ellis Hugh (b. Apr. 23, 1929, d. Sept. 11, 1968).

After the death of Robert, Lavinia went to work at the Enro Shirt Factory and worked there for 23 years. She is presently living in Madisonville. - *Submitted by Sherry Hale*

KNIGHT-HATCHER

Wayne Augustus Knight was born Sept. 26, 1932 in Christian Co., KY. He was the son of Albert Richard (1903-1953) and Minnie Florence (Wilson) Knight (see Knight-Wilson)

Wayne attended school in Christian County and in Hopkins County. The family moved to Hopkins County in 1942.

In 1950, he enlisted in the Kentucky National Guard progressing to the rank of First Sergeant in 1955. He served on state active duty at Clay, KY the following year. He was called into active federal service with Company C, 3rd Battalion, 123rd Armor in 1961, serving some eleven months as First Sergeant. He spent twenty years in the Kentucky National Guard.

On Feb. 14, 1952 in Shawneetown, IL, Wayne married Doris Jean Hatcher. She was born Dec. 7, 1932 in Blytheville, AR, the daughter of John (1904-1977) and Ada (Smith) Hatcher (see Hatcher-Smith). Doris graduated from Hanson High School in 1951.

Wayne and Doris were the parents of two daughters: Debra Kay born Aug. 19, 1953, married Timothy Wayne Hammonds (see Hammonds-Knight) and Cheryl Lynn born July 6, 1958, married Gregory Bennett. Cheri now resides in Alexandria, VA where she is Administrative Assistant to the Sheriff of Alexandria.

Wayne worked for Servel in Evansville, In, Lincoln-Mercury in Madisonville as a car salesman, Pleasant View mine until it closed (he helped with the sealing of this mine) and at East Diamond mine as Assistant Mine Foreman. He was a member of the Masonic Lodge and the American Legion. He liked to hunt and raised beagles to hunt with and for show.

It was at the East Diamond mine, on July 18, 1970, that Wayne lost his life in a roof fall. He is buried at Odd Fellows Cemetery.

After Wayne's death, Doris continued to remain at home to be a full time mother to the girls. She later went to work for the Kroger Company. She is a member of St. Mary's Episcopal Church and loves to travel. She continues to reside in Madisonville. - *Submitted by Debbie Knight Hammonds*

KNIGHT-WILSON

Albert Richard Knight was born Sept. 20, 1903 in Christian Co., KY. He was the son of James Walter (1874-1914) and Vandora (Sizemore) Knight (1874-1951) of Christian County.

On Jan. 21, 1925, in Montgomery Co., TN, he married Minnie Florence Wilson. Minnie was born Apr. 25, 1909 in Christian County. She was the daughter of Nathaniel Henry (1867-1951) and Iva Lee (Reynolds) Wilson (1876-1914) of Christian County.

Richard and Minnie were the parents of three children, all born in Christian County:

Minnie and Richard Knight

Winfred Earl born June 7, 1926, died Nov. 1, 1927; Wilda Lee born July 25, 1929, married Richard Olp Aug. 11, 1951 in Hopkins County, died Mar. 28, 1985 in Christian County; and Wayne Augustus born Sept. 26, 1932, died July 18, 1970 in Hopkins County (see Knight-Hatcher).

At the time of their marriage, Richard was farming in Christian County, between the towns of Crofton and Kelly. Over the years the family left Christian County twice following better job opportunities. Once Richard worked in a plant at Old Hickory, TN, the other time was a move to Bowling Green, KY to farm. In 1942, the family left Christian County for the last time, settling in Hopkins County.

Richard went to work for the Dr. Pepper Bottling Company in Madisonville and later Servel in Evansville, IN. Minnie went to work for the S.J. Campbell Parachute Factory and later Enro Shirt Factory. Richard and Minnie attended the First Baptist Church in Madisonville.

On June 30, 1953, Richard died in Hopkins County. He was buried in Macedonia Cemetery in Christian County.

Minnie retired from Enro in 1970 and continues to reside in Madisonville.

Richard and Minnie have four grandchildren: Debra Knight Hammonds, Cheryl Knight Bennett, Richard Dwight Olp and Mark Stephen Olp, and three great grandchildren: Leslie Marie and Jason Wayne Hammonds and HilaryLee Olp. - *Submitted by: Debbie Knight Hammonds*

FRANK JOHN KRAUTHEIM

Frank John Krautheim was the third of four children of Mary Angela Delli Venneri and Michael Stephen Krautheim.

Frank had two older brothers, Joseph Krautheim and Michael Raymond Krautheim, and one younger sister, Mary Anne Krautheim.

Mary DelliVenneri was born July 27, 1910 to Candida and Joseph DelliVenneri. She was the first of three daughters. On Aug. 11, 1938, she married Michael Krautheim, who was born Feb. 28, 1908, the son of Michael and Catherine Krautheim. On Apr. 23, 1943, Mary and Michael had their third son, Frank Krautheim.

Frank Krautheim grew up in Parsippani, NJ and his family moved to Point Pleasant Beach, NJ in 1963. After graduating from Parsipanni High School with a letter in baseball and band in 1961, he went on to Patterson State College in Patterson, NJ. After two years at Patterson, he went to Murray State College at Murray, KY. It was at Murray that Frank met his wife-to-be, Lou Nell Morris from Dawson Springs, KY.

Lou Nell Morris was born in Princeton, KY on Feb. 28, 1945. She was raised in Dawson Springs, where she graduated from high school in 1963. Lou Morris went to Murray State College. Lou Morris's parents, Nell Rose Smith and Douglas Holeman Morris, had four other children: Douglas Holeman Morris Jr., Susan Jane, William Lee, and Millie Dee.

Just before Frank Krautheim graduated in 1966, he married Lou Morris on Oct. 9, 1965. After graduating, they moved to Dawson Springs, where he obtained a job at Outwood Hospital as a teacher and later as head of the Foster Grandparent Program. He began teaching at Browning Springs Middle School in 1975. He also worked as a volunteer fireman in the Dawson Springs Fire Department.

On Sept. 25, 1967, Frank and Lou had their first son, Frank John Krautheim, Jr. He graduated from Dawson Springs High School and is presently attending college at the University of Kentucky. On May 9, 1972, their second son was born, Michael Stephen Krautheim. He is presently attending Dawson Springs High School.

Frank Krautheim died on May 14, 1982, when he had a heart attack while fighting a fire. He was 39 years old. He is buried in Rosedale Cemetery. - *Submitted by Stephen Krautheim*

EDD LEE LACY

Barthelmew Lacy was born in 1785, in North Carolina. He moved to Christian Co., KY, and married Charlotte Prince on May 28, 1811. They had two sons; James (born in either 1822 or 1823 and died in May of 1855) and John.

James Lacy married Lucetta Reynolds on Feb. 5, 1846. They had four children: Sara Ellen, Rachel, William Wesley and James II.

William Wesley Lacy (born June 21, 1854 and died Dec. 16, 1919) married Cordelia Elizabeth Lantrip on Nov. 23, 1876, in Hopkinsville, KY. Cordelia was born on June 2, 1854, and died on Mar. 30, 1927, in a rest home in Nashville, TN. She and William Wesley are buried in Christian Privilege Cemetery in St. Charles, KY.

William and Cordelia moved to the Crabtree area of Hopkins Co., KY, where their three sons, William Clinton, Edd Lee and Charles, who all attended school in St. Charles. Oldest son, William Clinton, (born on Oct. 12, 1877, and died Mar. 21, 1932), attended Draughn Business School in Nashville, TN, and married Nancy Marie (Mae) Finley on May 27, 1901. They had one son and two daughters: Edwin Vemont (born on July 23, 1904, and died in Hopkinsville, Apr. 13, 1956, where he is buried), who married Lillian Louise Joiner on Mar. 21, 1931; Helen Ruth (born on June 7, 1902) who married Robert L. Russell; and Dorothy May (born on June 28, 1908), who married Claude F. Nix. William Clinton Lacy divorced Mae Lacy and married Harriet Saunders. They had one child, William Clinton, Jr. William Clinton, Sr., is buried in the Christian Privilege Cemetery in St. Charles.

Helen (Miller) and Edd Lee Lacy on his 75th birthday.

Edd Lee Lacy (born March 27, 1884, and died on May 28, 1960), married Helena Emilia Miller on Apr. 18, 1911. Helen had previously been married to Ed Willis of Evansville, IN. Edd and Helen had three children; Ruby Catherine, Carrie Elizabeth and Charles Edward. A son, Charles Edward, was born to the Edd Lacys on July 4, 1915, and died in infancy on July 11, 1915. He is buried in the Grapevine Cemetery in Madisonville, KY. Ruby Catherine (Katy) (born Jan. 3, 1912, in Glasgow, KY), married William Hammack Tapp on July 9, 1935, in Madisonville, and lived in Winston Salem, NC, where she died Sept. 23, 1974 (her remains are in Oak Hill Cemetery in Evansville, IN). Carrie Elizabeth (born Oct. 13, 1913, in Glasgow, KY) married William Lyalls Stewart, of St. Charles, on Apr. 24, 1937 in Mortons Gap, KY. They have three daughters: Catherine Eulalia, Sandra Lyle and Carrie Elizabeth II. Catherine Eulalia (Layle) (born June 2, 1939, in Madisonville), married Jackson Ralph Luckett on June 23, 1967, in Washington, D.C., and lives in LaJolla, CA. Sandra Lyle (Sandy) (born May 6, 1942, in Madisonville) married Millard John Morgan, Oct. 8, 1966, in Beaufort, SC; they have two children: Millard Lyall (Charlie) and Elizabeth Alice. They currently live in Lompoc, CA. Carrie Elizabeth II (born Sept. 14, 1949, in Hopkinsville) currently lives in Shelby, NC.

Edd Lacy moved to Madisonville and worked at the Lee Jackson Barber Shop as a barber for 33 years before moving to the Hotel Madison Barber Shop until his retirement. He was a member of the Elks Lodge of Madisonville and secretary-treasurer of the Barbers' Union.

Helen Lacy was an accomplished seamstress and worked at home on custom sewing and tailoring. She received a commendation from the Elks Lodge for hand-sewing a silk United States flag containing 35 stars, honoring the soldiers who lost their lives in World War I. The flag adorned the wall of the Elks Club reception room.

Helen and Edd Lacy are both buried in Oak Hill Cemetery, Evansville, IN. Refer to: Emil George Miller; Merritt Omer Stewart; William Lyalls and Carrie Elizabeth Lacy Stewart. *Submitted by Mrs. Lyall Stewart*

VERONICA NIXON MILLER LADD

Veronica Nixon was born July 6, 1860, in Christian Co., KY. She was the daughter of John Henry and Milly S. Beshear Nixon. When she was two years old her father died and when she was three years old her mother died. She was raised by her mother's parents Issac and Millie Sims Alexander Beshear in Hopkins County.

On Mar. 16, 1877, she married Thomas Miller and had three children: Alice Effie, John Riley, and Nora. In 1886 Thomas Miller died leaving Veronica to raise their three children. Veronica married William Austin Ladd in Hopkins County on Aug. 1, 1892. William was the son of Jason and Mary Duncan Ladd and a veteran of the Civil War. He had been first married to Nancy Ladd and had four children: Annie, Lillie, William G., and Della May. These seven children ranged in age from 21 to 7 when William and Veronica combined their families.

Standing: Effie, Margaret, Veronica. Sitting: Jason, Earl, Lona.

Their lives were spent between Dawson Springs and Marion, IN. Three more children were born: Henry Jason, Millie Margaret and Earl, the first two children being born in Hopkins Co. and the third being born in Marion. On Sept. 24, 1902 when Earl was two years old, William was working with a street car crew and was riding on a street car when it was struck by a train at a crossing. He was killed. Veronica followed him in death on Apr. 11, 1911. All of their children had grown to maturity except Henry Jason, Millie Margaret and Earl. To them it was history repeating itself. Their mother and great grandmother had been orphans before them. Jason was 16 years old and was on his own. Margaret and Earl were raised at the Soldiers and Sailors Home in Knightstown, IN.

It is not known what became of the first Ladd children. Of the Miller children's lines Alice Effie had one daughter, Lona, of Ft. Lauderdale, FL, John Riley had five living children: Tom, Georgia Lou, Henry, William, and Norman. Georgia Lou Alexander of Dawson Springs remains in the area. Nora had no children. Henry Jason Ladd left two children: Paul who had no children and James who had children. Millie Margaret Ladd had no children and Earl W. Ladd had two daughters and lived his life in Valentine, NE. - *Submitted by: Margaret Ladd Sinn*

LAFFOON

The original name of this family was Lafon or Lafond, and there are several branches which maintain this spelling I am told. The Lafonds were French Huguenots. John Bledsoe Laffoon, was born 1790 and died Sept. 23, 1873, in Hopkins Co. John married Lydia Knox on Jan. 13, 1817. They had two children. Lydia, his first wife died and on July 8, 1832, he married Susan E. Henson. John was a wealthy farmer and represented the Legislature in the session of 1851 and 1852, being the first representative after the adoption of the new Constitution. John had another seven children by his second marriage. James K. Polk Laffoon was one of the seven and he was born Oct. 24, 1844, in Hopkins County. In 1860 he is listed on the census as a science student.

At the beginning of the Civil War he entered the service as a 2nd Lt., in the Confederate Army. He was taken prisoner at the battle of Ft. Donelson and was imprisoned for seven months before being exchanged. He then served under Morgan's command and was again captured at the Ohio Raid. At the end of the war he returned to Hopkins County and taught school for two years. He was admitted to the bar in 1867. He married Hattie Evelyn Parker on Dec. 15, 1869. In 1872 he was elected County Attorney of Hopkins County. In 1884, he was elected by the Democrats as a member of the 49th Congress and re-elected to the Fiftieth in 1886.

Polk Laffoon and Hattie had four children, namely; Guy Laffoon; Lena, who married Wallace D. Crenshaw; Emma who married Phillip Watt Nisbet; and James K. Polk Laffoon Jr., who married Emily Woodall and lived in Covington, KY. Emma and Phillip W. Nisbet had three children; Guy Laffoon Nisbet, Jessie Parker Nisbet, and Mary Frances Nisbet. Guy moved to Charleston, WV, and married Martha Baldwin, Mary F. married John E. Carr and lived in Auburn, KY, and Jessie P. Nisbet married Charles K. Ashby and lives at 148 E. Broadway, Madisonville, KY. - *Submitted by: Jessie N. Ashby*

LAFFOON

George Washington Laffoon was the son of Rutherford and Sarah Hill Laffoon. The Rutherford Laffoon Family came to Hopkins Co., KY when George Washington (G.W.) was an infant. Rutherford and Sarah are buried in Southards Cemetery in Hopkins County.

G.W. was born on June 30, 1810 in South Carolina. On Jan. 31, 1830 in Hopkins County, he married Lucinda Julian. G.W. and Lucinda were the parents of six children: John Henry, Dr. William R., Mary Elizabeth, Senate N., Sarah R. and Columbus B.

Dr. William R. Laffoon was born Nov. 24, 1832 in Hopkins County. Dr. Laffoon was educated in KY and later attended the Medical Department of the State University of Michigan at Ann Arbor, MI.

Upon the outbreak of the Civil War, he enlisted in the 2nd Arkansas Cavalry. He served through the war as hospital steward and assistant surgeon. He participated in battles at Nashville, Murphfreesboro and Shiloh. After the war he began his practice in Arkansas, later giving it up to farm.

In 1865 Dr. Laffoon married Miss Mary Ann Ragland. She was born Apr. 9, 1832 in Georgia, the daughter of John and Charity (Cress) Ragland.

Dr. Laffoon and Mary were the parents of: Arvilla L., Lulu W. and William Nash. - *Submitted by Herbert Laffoon.*

LAFFOON, FOX, FARMER

William Laffoon, a Hugenot, was born in France ca 1750. He was living in the Pendleton District of South Carolina in the 1800 census, published in 1963. The original spelling of the name was LaFond.

William migrated to Hopkins Co. about 1814, and he appears in the 1820 census. His will was written on Nov. 26, 1821. William's will listed several children, a former son-in-law, Robert Orton, who married his granddaughter Cynthia, daughter of Mark and Sarah Laffoon, and William's wife Susannah. Nine of William's children can be identified: Washington, Alexander, Mark married Sarah (?); Rutherford married Sarah N. Hill; John Bledsoe married first Lydia Knox and secondly Susan Henson, Cynthia married Noah Fox, Sarah married Abner West, Susannah married a Wilson; and Mary married John Malin.

Cynthia, who married Noah Fox, was born ca 1782 in South Carolina. They had at least nine children: George Washington married Mary Wyatt, Jenny married William Martin Castleberry Jr., Altha married Nathan W. Castleberry, Elvira married Thomas Davis, John Crittenden married Mahla Moore, Martha A. married Jousha Todd, Evelina married William Todd, Elizabeth married Hiran Woodruff and a female married David Woodruff. Noah died after 1850 and Cynthia after 1860.

Jenny Fox married William Castleberry in Hopkins Co. on June 14, 1818. His father was William M. Castleberry Sr., a Revolutionary War Soldier, his mother was Elizabeth Smith. There were seven children from this union: William, Flemming, Daniel, Enoch, Nancy Caroline and Mary Ann. The family moved to Marshall Co., KY. A land sale to a Shadrick Gowen in 1845 is the last known record of William Castleberry. On the 1850 census, Jenny was listed in Union Co., IL as a widow. Jenny died after 1870.

Nancy Caroline Castleberry married Newton Anderson on May 22, 1851 in Union Co., IL. Newton served in the Civil War with Co. B, 81st Illinois Inf. They were the parents of eleven children: Thomas R., Jefferson, Sabrina, La Mina Alice, William, Helen Post, Willis, Corah Ann, Victoria, Eliza Jane and Earnest.

La Mina Alice was first married to Benjamin Wood, and secondly, to Jonathan Scaniel Farmer Jr. Jonathan, was born in 1815, in Marshall Co., KY, the son of Jonathan and Susannah Hill Farmer. Susannah was the granddaughter of Thomas Hill, a Revolutionary War Soldier. Four children were born of the union of La Mina and Jonathan Farmer. Two of the children died in infancy. James Tanner and Cyrus Benjamin lived to adulthood. From newspaper accounts, at the time of his death, Jonathan was the last Confederate Soldier in Massac Co., IL. He served in Co. A, 3rd Ky. Inf., Mounted. Jonathan died on Feb. 29, 1928. His wife, La Mina, died July 1, 1935.

Cyrus Farmer married Mellie Trout, the daughter of James and Flora Gilbreath Trout of Johnson Co., IL. There were four children of which two daughters survived. The oldest daughter, Virginia, married Dr. William Gordon and are residing in Hinsdale, IL. They have one daughter, Anne Clare. The other daughter, Elizabeth, married Thomas Crosson and they have six children: Thomas, Stephen, Robert, Danielle, Lora and Kathryn. They reside in Colorado Springs, CO. Cyrus and Millie are deceased and are buried in the Reevesville Cemetery in Johnson Co., IL. - *Submitted by Elizabeth Crosson*

RUBY LAFFOON

Governor of Kentucky 1931-1935. Ruby Laffoon, the only native of Hopkins County to be elected governor of Kentucky, was born Jan. 15, 1869 in Hopkins County. He was the third of three children born to John Bledsoe Laffoon and Martha Henrietta Earle Laffoon.

Ruby Laffoon married Mary Nisbet Jan. 31, 1894. Mary Nisbet was the daughter of John Crittenden Nisbet and Mary Elizabeth Bryant Nisbet (Mary Elizabeth Bryant was from New York. She met and married John C. Nisbet in Clinton, KY) Mary Nisbet Laffoon was born in Texas Feb. 13, 1874, and died June 5, 1972 in Hopkins County. Both she and Ruby Laffoon are buried in Grapevine Cemetery.

Ruby Laffoon and Mary Nisbet Laffoon had three daughters - Laura Isabelle, born Feb. 15, 1895, married Charles Harrod Boyd (no issue) Lelia Holeman, born in 1904, married Edward Lindsey (1 daughter, Lelia) - Martha Lou born Jan. 1, 1900, married William Reese Robinson June 1, 1920.

William Reese Robinson and Martha Lou Laffoon Robinson's children were - R.W. Robinson born Mar. 20, 1921, died Feb. 21, 1975, married Freddie Pride(three daughters, 1 son: Nancy, Barbara, Jane and John) - Roy Thomas Robinson born July 20, 1929, married Betty Brinkley (1 daughter Laura Beth, 1 son Roy Thomas).

Printed in the <u>Madisonville Messenger</u>, Dec. 10, 1935, as follows: "The honor of the governorship of his native state has come to no other Hopkins Countian. His town and his county have won distinction through him no other son could have earned for them.

"Ruby Laffoon made a fearless governor. Assailed on all sides by predatory interest, by wolves of special privilege, by social unrest, by the poor, the hungry and the jobless, he held to his course mapped by an ambition to make "Kentucky the best governor she ever had." He has been responsible for more constructive policies than any other governor since the state's formative years. Historians will accord to him the place he has earned as a statesman.

"He is entitled to rest, to peaceful communion with tested friends. We welcome him and his gracious wife and talented daughter back to their home. They have served their state well and brought honor and distinction to their people." - *Submitted by Martha Lou Laffoon Robinson*

LAMB-HAMBY

The Lamb family was established in the first settlement of Caldwell County, near 1800, by John Lamb, thought to be the son of Longshear Lamb and born in 1793 in South Carolina. He married Aug. 24, 1816, Mary Polly Clayton, daughter of Phebe and Moses Clayton. Their son, Jessie Lamb, was born Mar. 28, 1828, in Caldwell County, married Sarah Melvina Scott, born Sept. 14, 1833, in Caldwell County, on Nov. 7, 1850. Their son, Albert Grigsby Lamb, born in Caldwell County Nov. 21, 1851, married George Ann Smith, born in Caldwell County Oct. 4, 1853, daughter of Rhoda Jane Glass and Simeon Smith. Their daughter, Zorah, born May 11, 1876, was one of twelve children. Zorah married Ezekiel Golden Hamby Dec. 3, 1898. Other ancestral names include Woolf, Jennings, Seaburn and Rogers.

Ezekiel Golden and Zorah Hamby

The Hamby family was established in Christian County by Jeremiah Hamby, born possibly in 1767 in either, North Carolina or Ireland. He was married to Elizabeth Thompson, born in South Carolina. Their son, Isaac Hamby, born ca. 1802, married Katherine McKnight, daughter of William and Charlota Hamby McKnight. Their son, J.T., born Mar. 15, 1827, married Cassie M. Galloway, born Aug. 15, 1837, daughter of Charles and Lettica Smith Galloway, on Feb. 7, 1861. Their son, Ezekiel Golden, was born Feb. 29, 1868, one of eight children.

Ezekiel Golden, known as "Gold", owned a farm in Hopkins County near White Plains for several years. He attended one-room schools and taught at the Oak Grove School for two years. He and his brother, Ike (Isaac) ran Hamby Station, a train depot and general store near St. Charles, for several years.

Gold and Zorah had three children who died in infancy, and are buried at Cranor School House Cemetery. Their fourth child, Eudenah, was born Nov. 12, 1910. In 1916, the Hambys moved to Dawson Springs, where Gold built several houses, and continued farming on a smaller scale. They were members of the Dawson Springs First Christian Church. On June 3, 1934 Eudenah married Laban Littleton Perry (see HAMBY-PERRY), and they have two children; Susan Gayle, who married James Mestan, and Kenneth Littleton, who married Sharon Thomas. The Mestans have two children; Sheri Lynn, Arlington, VA; and Sean, Murray, KY. The Kenneth Perrys have one son, Brian Littleton, and live in Versailles, KY.

Gold preceded Zorah in death in October 1956. Zorah died in 1963, and they are both buried at Rosedale Cemetery in Dawson Springs, KY. Sources: Family records, court records. - *Submitted by Eudenah Hamby Perry*

JOHN LAMSON

John Lamson was born circa 1798 in Massachusetts.

In Hopkins Co., KY on Mar. 11, 1823, John Lamson married Rebecca Carter, daughter of Moses and Mary Carter. Rebecca Carter Lamson was born circa 1805, and died on Oct. 17, 1843, in Hopkins Co., KY. She is buried in Lamson Cemetery, three miles south of Providence, KY.

John Lamson was a farmer. He and Rebecca were the parents of seven known children: Samuel Lamson, born Apr. 6, 1825, married Sarah Elizabeth Stalions; Mary Lamson born July 16, 1827, married Alexander T. Johnson; John Lamson, Jr. born Apr. 10, 1829, married Rebecca Vinecia Wyatt; William Lamson, born Jan. 24, 1831, married Elizabeth I. Wyatt; George Washington Lamson, born Oct. 25, 1832, married (1) N.A. Bruswell (2) Mary C. ?; Betty E. Lamson, born Feb. 19, 1835; Sarah K. Lamson born Sept. 16, 1836, and Francis R. Lamson, born Sept. 29, 1839 married John Lowrey.

John Lamson died on Feb. 28, 1856, in Hopkins Co., KY and is buried in Lamson Cemetery. - *Submitted by Daniel W. Dockrey*

WILLIAM LAMSON

William Lamson was born Jan. 24, 1831, in Hopkins Co., KY the son of John and Rebecca Carter Lamson.

On Feb. 18, 1851, in Hopkins Co., KY William Lamson married Elizabeth I. Wyatt, daughter of George Wyatt, Jr. and Louanna Fox Wyatt. Elizabeth Wyatt Lamson was born circa 1837. Family tradition states that this was Elizabeth Wyatt's second marriage. According to this tradition Elizabeth first married a Mr. Parish (against her parents' wishes) and Mr. Parish was struck by lightning and killed as he and Elizabeth left the minister's house following the wedding ceremony.

Elizabeth Wyatt Lamson 1837-?

William and Elizabeth Wyatt Lamson were parents of six children: Daniel William Lamson born Feb. 9, 1853, married M. Jane Wright; a son, born Dec. 6, 1854 and died Dec. 12, 1855; Vinecia Catherine Lamson, born Nov. 24, 1855, married George W. Parish; Martha Y. Lamson born Mar. 18, 1858, married William Harrison Dockrey; John D. Lamson, born Sept. 4, 1866; and Louanna M. Lamson born June 8, 1869.

William Lamson was a farmer. He died on Apr. 16, 1873 in Hopkins Co., KY and is buried in Lamson Cemetery near Providence, KY. - *Submitted by Daniel W. Dockrey*

LANDRUM-WALKER

Barbara June Walker and Phillip Wayne Landrum were married in 1958 in the Nebo Christian Church. Both had graduated from Nebo High School that year.

June was born in 1940, the first child of Rea Joyner and James Hoard Walker (see Walker-Joyner). She was born in Hopkins County, living in the house her grandparents (Winsteads) had raised their family. June went to Nebo School all twelve years, the same school both her parents graduated from. June was a cheerleader for several years for the Nebo Purple Aces Basketball team of which Phil was a member.

June (Walker) and Phillip Landrum

Phil was born in 1940, the son of Vergie Irene Tidwell and Samuel Luthur Landrum. Phil was born in Hopkins County but lived for a while in Evansville, IN moving then to Dixon, KY, and then to the Nebo area where he attended school.

Phil has a sister, Joyce Ann, born in 1937, who married Quentin Eli Demoss. They are the parents of two children: Joy Quenell, married Doyal Brasher (parents of Gwendolyn Ann) and Dudley Earl Demoss, married Lori Parker (parents of Sara Christanne, Katie Virginia and Samuel Jacob).

Vergie Tidwell Landrum was born in Hayti, MO, the daughter of Abby Dilbeck and John Thomas Tidwell. Abbey's parents were Elizabeth Ann Vaughn and Benjamin Dilbeck. John's parents were Martha Barnes and Robert Tenson Tidwell.

Sam Landrum was born in Rockport, KY, the son of Nancy L. Tinsley and Robert Aaron Landrum. Nancy's parents were Emma Benton and Martin L. Tinsley. Robert's parents were Mahalia F. Sinclair and Samuel Isum Landrum.

Sam died in 1985 and Vergie lives in St. Charles.

When June and Phil married, he was stationed at Ft. Leonardwood, MO in the U.S. Infantry. He was sent to the Panama Canal Area where he was stationed for two years. Their children were born there. Bret David was born in 1959 and Lisa Lyn in 1961. In 1961, the family returned to the U.S. to live in Florida and parts of Texas. In the early 70's, Phil owned and operated a camera store in Austin, TX. During this time, he felt the need for a more active life in Christian work and accepted an offer to serve as associate minister in the Southwest Christian Church of Austin where he has served since 1978. Besides being a housewife and mother, June holds a position with I.R.S. of Austin.

Bret married Gaylynn Deveraux and has a son Bret Ryan born in 1982. Lisa married Karl Parcher and had a daughter Britney Aaron born in 1985. - *Submitted by Rea Joyner Walker*

ELIZABETH LANGZELL

Elizabeth Yates Langzell was born Oct. 22, 1883 near Richland and attended Munns School.

At age twenty, she married Eber Langzell (Feb. 2, 1882-Apr. 9, 1964) who had come from Dyersburg, TN when he was a very young boy. He came on a houseboat, not ever knowing or remembering his parents or any of his people. He was adopted by a Merrill family.

Eber and Elizabeth soon started moving around from place to place. On leaving Richland, they moved to Madisonville and from there to Earlington, Mortons Gap, Nortonville and White Plains.

The Langzells also lived in different areas, Trabue, Concord, and Clements districts. Their two younger children attended school at Clements.

They were the parent of five children: William T., Wallace, Charles (all deceased), Martha Helen Henery who lives in Detroit and Richard who lives in Florida

They later moved to Detroit, MI, where Mr. Langzell died. Later Mrs. Langzell went to Florida, where she died at the age of 101 (June 4, 1984). Both are buried at Grapevine Cemetery in Madisonville.- *See Hopkins County Centenarians. Submitted by Bonnie Slaton Langzell*

LANTAFF-DANIEL

Ormsby Logan (O.L.) Lantaff is the fourth generation of Lantaff's living in Hopkins County, and he is Madisonville's present Mayor. James L. Lantaff (b. 1833 d. 1912) was said to be the first Lantaff to settle in Hopkins Co. He is buried at New Beulah Cemetery. (See James Lantaff story). His son was John Edward Lantaff, whose son was Ernest Logan Lantaff (b. Dec. 26, 1886 d. Mar. 17, 1948), who married Maude E. Ferguson in 1912. Maude (b. Feb. 28, 1892 d. Dec. 11, 1959), was the dau. of Mr. and Mrs. William H. Ferguson of Hopkins Co. They are buried at Odd Fellows Cemetery.

Ernest L. and Maude E. Lantaff were parents of five children: O.L. Lantaff b. Oct. 21, 1912; Arvan Lantaff; Edith Earle Lantaff, b. 1917 and killed by a car in 1924 at age 7; Connie L. Duncan, who lives in Greenville, KY; and Alton Lantaff.

O.L. Lantaff married Clara Edith Daniel b.

Madisonville Mayor O.L. Lantaff

July 20, 1920, dau. of Jess Daniel (b. Sept. 17, 1885 d. June 5, 1966), and Maude Walker (b. Mar. 17, 1890 d. June 15, 1968). The Daniels were married July 17, 1907, and lived in Hopkins Co. They are buried at Odd Fellows Cemetery. O.L. and Clara Lantaff have one dau., Norma Jean (Mrs. Rudy) Stone, who lives in Madisonville. Their children are Teresa Joan Jones, Gary Wayne Tomblingson and Troy Scott Tomblingson.

At a very early age, Ormsby L. Lantaff was a grocery delivery boy for B.B. Barnes Grocery on South Madison St. Years later, in 1960, he bought the grocery store from H.E. Jenkins, and for 20 years he and Mrs. Lantaff operated the Lantaff's Grocery on Madison St.

During WW II, O.L. missed leaving for induction into service by one hour, when he was notified that under the lowering of the upper-age limit, he was too old for service. During wartime, the groceryman had to cope with rationing by the Federal Government, and exchanged ration stamps for merchandise. Gasoline, tires, sugar, coffee, meat, shoes, cigarettes, and soft drinks are a few of the scarce items which were rationed.

For 17 years, from 1966 to 1983, O.L. Lantaff served as city councilman for Ward 2 of Madisonville. In 1983, when Mayor Charlotte Baldwin was appointed to Governor Collins' cabinet, O.L. Lantaff was sworn in as Mayor for the remainder of Baldwin's term, and was elected for four more years in 1985.

There have been many complex problems and some sleepless nights for the Mayor, but there have also been some very satisfying accomplishments for Mayor Lantaff's administration. He feels that the improved relations between the city and county governments has been a great accomplishment, attested to by the joint city-county venture in completing the Senior Citizens Center on North Main.

The Mayor points with pride to other improvements during his administration: the renovation and improvement of the downtown city building for city government offices; a run-way and lighting improvement project for the airport at Anton, with an F.A.A. grant; general up-grading of many streets to include improvements to sidewalks, water and sewer lines and drainage; work on the city park, including sprucing up the restrooms, the stadium, golf course, and No. 1 city lake there; the building of new docks for fishing at Lake Pewee; and major new equipment received by the Madisonville Fire Dept. and other city departments.

The office of Mayor requires full-time attention and great dedication to the welfare of the city, without adequate compensation in salary. And, O.L. Lantaff could not have taken on the responsibility, had he not been retired from his grocery business. Mayor Lantaff agrees that cities the size of Madisonville are always likely to have some limitations on the number and types of people who will run for mayor. - *Submitted by: O.L. Lantaff - Written by Rella G. Jenkins*

JAMES LANTAFF

According to his "Last Wishes" written in 1909, and his tombstone in New Beulah Cemetery, he was born on July 22, 1833, but other records indicate that he may actually have been born a year or two later. According to his ship's passenger list, James sailed from England to New Orleans in 1853, with his parents, William and Mary (Bowles) Lantaff, and a younger brother and sister, William Bowles Lantaff (born Apr. 24, 1837), and Mary Ann Lantaff (born in 1840). The family departed from Liverpool, England on February 21, landed in New Orleans on April 29, and on May 9, 1853 landed in Earl, IN (now considered part of Evansville) where they were engaged in farming.

Mary and James Lantaff

James Lantaff was married (February 1859), to Mary Ann Blanchard, the daughter of Samuel Blanchard and his wife, who were also English immigrants. James and Mary Ann became parents of four children in Indiana: John Edward Lantaff (born Oct. 25, 1863), Hannah P. Lantaff (born in 1866, and married James D. McGregor in 1881), William Sam Lantaff (born Dec. 4, 1866, and married to Tabitha Jane Howton on Oct. 12, 1890), and Emery A. Lantaff (born July 1869, and married to Minnie F. Tapp on Jan. 8, 1890).

James Lantaff served in the Indiana Infantry during the Civil War (November 1864-July 6, 1865), and then returned to farming in Indiana. In 1877 he sold his farm and bought a farm in the Silent Run area of Hopkins Co., KY. He lived on this farm until his death (June 29, 1912). He and his wife are buried in New Beulah Cemetery.

The oldest child of James and Mary Ann Lantaff, John Edward, was married to Sarah Elizabeth "Betty" Dockery on Oct. 15, 1884. Born on Apr. 15, 1866, she was the daughter of

George W. Dockery and Mary Priscilla (Southard) Dockery of the Beulah-Charleston area of Hopkins County. John Edward was engaged in farming in the Beulah area and had three sons: Ernest Logan Lantaff, George James Lantaff and Edward Gothard Lantaff. John Edward Lantaff (died Mar. 3, 1926), and Sarah Elizabeth Lantaff (died Mar. 18, 1951) are buried in New Beulah Cemetery.

Ernest Logan Lantaff was born Dec. 26, 1886. He married Maude E. Furgurson in 1912, and they were the parents of five children: Ormsby L. Lantaff, Arvan Lantaff, Edith Earle Lantaff, Connie (Lantaff) Duncan and Alton Lantaff. All are deceased except Ormsby L. (now mayor of Madisonville) and Connie Duncan, who lives in Greenville, KY.

George James Lantaff was born Sept. 10, 1889. He married Greek Furgerson, daughter of William Anderson Furgerson and Rebecca Jane (Clark) Furgerson, on Dec. 28, 1911, and they were the parents of three children: Ethel Mae (Lantaff) McGuyer, James Fredrick Lantaff and Bobby George Lantaff. Ethel and James now reside in Madisonville, while Bobby lives in Venus, TX.

Edward Gothard Lantaff was born on Sept. 6, 1898. He was married to Clora Cornelia Brown on Mar. 13, 1916. They had one child that survived infancy, Marvin E. Lantaff, now deceased. - *Submitted by Roberta Brinkley*

LORI ANN LANTRIP

When Lori Lantrip, at age five, began practicing judo under her father, Jim, and switched to Karate in the 1970's, she probably never thought that in 20 years she would possess the title of World's Champion in Featherweight Karate, a signal honor so very few people in the world achieve. These 20 years have not been without long hours of hard work at practice, dedication, frustration, pain, and sacrifice. The biggest payoff came with the gold medal when Lori led the United States to victory in the World Karate Kick-Boxing Championship at Munich, Germany, defeating reigning West German and European champion, Gerda Mack, in double overtime sudden death, 11-10. The U.S. team had no corporate sponsorship and designed their own costumes and paid their own expenses to Germany.

Lori Ann Lantrip, Featherweight Karate Champion of the World.

On Saturday, Oct. 10, 1987, Jim Lantrip, her coach, stood in the Olympic Stadium, Munich, Germany, and watched his daughter, Lori, in the center of the competition ring, receive the gold medal as the best lightweight semi-contact karate fighter in the world. It was an indescribable, powerfully emotional moment, representing the U.S. in a competition featuring 30 countries, before a sold-out crowd of 11,000 people of all nations, and this was the world championship! When the national anthem was played and the Stars and Stripes were flown, it was the greatest over-whelming moment of their lives for both Lori and Jim.

Jim Lantrip, present Hopkins County jailer, had a 20-year career in the U.S. Air Force as a policeman. He and family traveled all over the U.S. and were 10 years in Asia—Japan, Philippines, and Korea. From the beginning workout in Roswell, NM, in 1960, Jim is now a veteran judoka and karate instructor. Since returning to Hopkins Co., he opened a karate studio and has been a law enforcement officer, including deputy sheriff, before jailer.

While in Munich, Germany, Jim served as assistant coach for head coach Jeff Smith of Washington, DC, and refereed two crucial final-round bouts between Great Britian and Germany. He attended the World Karate Congress meetings, while in Munich before the world championship competition, and was named President of the World Association of Kick-Boxing Organization in America.

Not only is Lori now world champion in her class, she was featured in the "Fighter International" Magazine, 1987 summer issue, as the beautiful centerfold poster girl (fully clothed) and other pictures showing her beauty as well as talent. The Magazine was a sell-out of thousands, and Lori was much in demand for her autograph. In 1984, Lori was one of the few females in history to be featured on the cover of the national martial arts publication "Karate Illustrated's" 1982 "Rookie of the Year" which she had won.

Lori is a 6-time National title holder, and has placed in almost every major tournament in the U.S. in both fighting and hard/soft forms. Lori got her black belt in 1980, and was nationally ranked by 1982. She fought on National Cable-TV (ESPN) at the Battle of Atlanta in 1983, which was a proud and major achievement for her. Some of her other titles: In 1982: AKA Grand National, Chicago; Ft. Worth Pro-Am at Dallas; and the U.S. Open at St. Petersburg, FL. In 1983: Battle of Atlanta, GA; L.A.M.A. Nationals, Chicago; and AKA Grand National. In 1984: L.A.M.A. Nationals; U.S. Top Ten Nationals, Stockton, CA; U.S. World Championships, Washington state. In 1985: AKA Grand Nationals; California Grand Nationals. In 1986: NAKC Liberty Classic, New York; NAKC Mid-West Championships, Columbus, OH. And among her exciting wins, she was interviewed on NBC's TODAY SHOW.

Lori Ann Lantrip was born Dec. 20, 1961 in Madisonville, daughter of James A. "Jim" Lantrip, b. Aug. 18, 1942, and Elizabeth (Thorpe) Lantrip, b. Mar. 14, 1942, dau.of John C. and Helen (Mathis) Thorpe of Ilsley. Although Lori attended many schools over the world, she graduated from Madisonville-North H.S. and attended Madisonville Community College. Jim is the son of the late James A. "Al" Lantrip and Doris (Darr) Lantrip of Nortonville. Al was a well-known law enforcement officer and died while Sheriff of Hopkins Co. Jim and Liz are both graduates of South Hopkins High School.

They have a son, Michael Jonathan "Mike" Lantrip, b. Nov. 1, 1962 in Newfoundland, and a graduate of Madisonville-North H.S. He is presently serving as Deputy Jailer. He is also a black belt and an accomplished fighter in the martial arts, and teaches in the Lantrip Karate School in Madisonville. He is a two-time National Judo Karate Champion at ages 10 and 11. The mother, Liz Lantrip, is also a black belt in karate, having started her training while living in Japan in 1964.

The Lantrip Karate Studio is a very popular place with the young people especially, perhaps on the road to winning some national crowns, emulating their very talented and popular instructors Lori, Mike and father, Jim.

What a remarkably competitive family to have in Madisonville, KY. We are very proud of your accomplishments. Keep up your winning records! - *Written by Rella G. Jenkins with approval of Lantrip family*

LEDBETTER-PAYNE

Harold George Ledbetter of 450 South Seminary St., Madisonville, retired insurance executive, veteran affairs leader, of Scottish ancestry, was born Mar. 23, 1912 on N. Elm St. in Clay, Webster Co., KY the son of Sidney Harmon and Vera Ethel (Cranor) Ledbetter. He was educated in the schools of Madisonville.

Winter time in the late 1930's or early 1940's in front of Company Store in Earlington

On Dec. 7, 1935, Harold married Thelma Imogene Payne of Madisonville. They are the parents of two daughters; Alice Faye born in 1948 and Patricia Ann born in 1951.

Harold was associated with the Madisonville Police Department, beginning his career as a radio dispatcher in 1940. Upon his return from the army, after three and a half years, he was assigned as a police patrolman.

Left Front: Buddy Cardwell-Grandson, Thelma Ledbetter, Fay (Ledbetter) Walker, Kellie Anne Cardwell-Granddaughter and Patricia Ann (Ledbetter) Atwell. Back Left: Harold Ledbetter, Charles Walker and Harold Atwell.

On Jan. 5, 1948, he was promoted to assistant chief of police, a position he held until Sept. 10, 1950, when he resigned to take a position with the State Auto Mutual Insurance Company.

Long active in the Veterans of Foreign Wars affairs in KY, he was Commander of the 3rd District; Chairman of the State Membership Committee; Chairman of the KY V.F.W. News Control Board, establishing a state paper for the Dept. of KY V.F.W.; and Chaplain of the State V.F.W. for 8 years.

On Sept. 29, 1960, he was appointed Director of the Hopkins County-Madisonville Civil Defense Organization and established Civil Defense groups in all the towns in the county. He held this position until Nov. 3, 1964. Harold has been active in many other organizations and civic affairs: Director of the Hopkins County Safety Council 1958; Director of the Hopkins County Fair Assoc. 1949-50; Chairman of the Hopkins County Chapter of American Red Cross 1956-57; President of the High Twelve Club 1949-50; voted Outstanding Citizen of Madisonville by the Lions Club in 1949; Lay Minister of the Christian (Disciples of Christ) Church, beginning on Dec. 20, 1964 and in 1987 is still an active Lay Minister; Treasurer of the West Area, Christian (Disciples of Christ) Church in Kentucky for 15 years; is an Elder Emeritus of the Madisonville Christian (Disciples of Christ) Church; and on Feb. 14, 1986 was appointed by the Hopkins County Fiscal Court as Official Hopkins County Historian.

Thelma Imogene, his wife, is the daughter of William Lewis Payne and Bertha Qualls Payne (1891-1970) and was born in Christian County, KY on Nov. 30, 1917. She moved to Madisonville when she was 10 years old.

Thelma has been a member of the Anton Homemaker's for many years; Treasurer of the West Broadway P.T.A.; Treasurer of the Christian Women's Fellowship of the Christian Church; President of the Lelia Dempsey Circle of the Christian Church; and active in other community and civic affairs.

Both Harold and Thelma are democrats and members of the Madisonville Christian (Disciples of Christ) Church.

Their youngest daughter, Patricia Ann, married Harold Atwell and they live in Madisonville.

Harold and Thelma have two grandchildren, Kellie Ann (Scott) Miller and Everett "Buddy" Holeman Cardwell Jr., who live in Madisonville. Their mother, Mrs. Alice Faye (Charles) Walker lives in Paris, TN.

Harold's hobby (one he has had for over 40 years) is Hopkins County history and also keeping up with the progress of the small town of Ledbetter, Livingston Co., KY, which his great grandfather, Wiley K. Ledbetter, settled in the late 1800's. The small town has continued to grow and is quite a prosperous little town today.

The Ledbetters's enjoy their work in the church and both keep busy, he with preaching and she in helping him.

Yes-they still live in "The Best Town On Earth", Madisonville, KY.-Submitted by Harold Ledbetter

LEWIS-WILKEY

Arthur Lewis was born Oct. 2, 1914, in Crittenden Co., KY, the son of Gid and Anna Farley Lewis. He married Beulah Leanne Wilkey who was born Feb. 7, 1914, in Hopkins Co. Her parents were James H. and Anna Laura Franklin Wilkey.

Arthur and Beulah are the parents of James Arthur (born Jan. 17, 1939) and Judith Ann (born Aug. 27, 1947).

Arthur was a merchant and service station operator at Beulah, KY. Beulah worked in the store and was an office clerk at Chesley Franklin Coal Co. and Roberts Brothers Coal Company at Beulah. Submitted by Arthur Lewis

MARY T. MASON LIGHTSEY

Mary Threasa Mason Lightsey is the youngest daughter of Ernest Sr. and Mayme (Starks) Mason (see Ernest Mason Sr. story).

Mary attended and graduated from Madisonville North High School and received a B.A. Degree from Western Kentucky University in Bowling Green, KY. Mary is presently employed at Human Resources Unemployment Insurance Agency as a Senior Examiner.

She married Roosevelt Lightsey Jr., who also attended and graduated from Western Kentucky University. Roosevelt is employed at the Corrections Department as a Probation and Parole Officer.

Mary and Roosevelt have two sons Tracy and Byron. They reside in Louisville, KY and attend Community Baptist Church. - Submitted by Mayme L. Mason

LISANBY-MENSER

Bertha Jane (Menser) Lisanby was born Oct. 5, 1894 in Christian County, KY. Her mother was Perniece Arma Relia Ellis (Huddleston) Menser. Perniece married Forest H. Menser. Both Perniece and Forest were born in Christian County.

Bertha's brothers and sisters who died at early ages were: Elsie at age 18 George at birth, Benjamin at age 15, and Relia at age 2 because she chewed on a discharged gun shell. Bertha's other brothers and sister are: Mary, Ada, Henry, Louella, Thomas and Clarence.

Bertha's grandfather built and ran the Lisanby boarding house, which was once in Dawson Springs. It was later torn down. Bertha belonged to the Baptist Church. She constantly sewed quilts for her family. After her parents passed away, she had to run the boarding house, so she stayed in Dawson all the time. Bertha's grandchildren called her Grandmaw Lisanby.

Grandma Lisanby had eight children:

Nina was born June 13, 1914 and married Clyde Poole. Their children are: Arnold Poole; Deloris Dearing; Clyia Sue Monks; Gary Poole; Connie Littlejohn; Madonna P'Pool; Randy Poole; and Brenda Wallace.

Rufus was born July 31, 1916 and married Olan Thomas. They have five children: Nancy Schelleburg; Beth Sanders; R.A. Lisanby; Tara Summers; and Sheila Walker.

Polly was born Dec. 27, 1920 and married Ralph Mason. They had three daughters: Linda Jenkins; Nicole Saturally; and Cindy Scholar.

Cara Lou was born July 28, 1924 and married L.B. Craytor. Their children are Janice Harp and Bert Craytor.

Dean was born Jan. 26, 1927 and married Roscoe Kem. Their children: Stanly Kem; Larry Kem; Michael Kem; and Karen Lacy.

Elaine was born Apr. 1, 1930. Elaine first married Harold Hickerson and had two children, Andy Hickerson, my father, and Rick Hickerson. She divorced Harold and married Junior Davis. Junior died and she then married Hoyt Thomas.

Howard was born May 19, 1932 and married Ellene Pinnegar. Their children: Janice McFarlin; Rhonda Slaton; and Kevin Lisanby.

Wayne was born Sept. 7, 1935 and married Fran Amos. They never had any children although they do have a mentally retarded boy living with them.

Phylis was born Feb. 25, 1938. She married first John Winfree and had three children: John Winfee Jr.; Mark Winfree who died at the age of ten; and Leslie Winfree. Phylis divorced John and married Dr. Carl Caplinger. Carl died a few years ago and Phylis has not remarried.

Grandmaw Lisanby lived in and around Dawson Springs all of her life. She was one of the first people to sell her land so Lake Beshear could be built.

My name is Carol Elaine Hickerson. Grandmaw Lisanby was my great grandmother. I was born Nov. 24, 1972.-Submitted by Carol Hickerson

DANIEL R. LITTLEPAGE

Daniel Rufus Littlepage was born Jan. 21, 1893 in Mortons Gap, KY. He is the third of ten children of Thomas Gooch Littlepage and Rodelia Foster Littlepage.

On Feb. 12, 1911, he married Maggie Delene Marshall, the daughter of John W. Marshall and Suzie Moore, in Hopkins County. The marriage was performed by J.W. Bilbro. To this marriage were born six children: an unnamed female died at birth in 1912; Evelyn was born Jan. 21, 1914; Annie Lucille was born Sept. 5, 1917; Helen Irene was born Nov. 3, 1920; John Thomps was born June 8, 1922; and Nell Ruth was born Mar. 1, 1925.

Ira Belle and Daniel Rufus Littlepage in the late 1960's

On May 1, 1926, his wife Maggie died. She was buried in Concord Cemetery in White Plains, KY.

On Nov. 28, 1928, he married Ira Belle Oldham of Mortons Gap, KY. She is the daughter of William Oldham and Stella Outlaw Whitfield. To this union he had twelve children: William Daniel, Fairy Elaine, Lois Marie, Joy Estell, Millard Loren, Peggy Sue, Windal Carroll, Carolyn June, Bobby Darrell, Glenda Kay and Timothy Craig.

D.R. Littlepage was a life-long farmer in Hopkins County. He was a member of Concord Baptist Church in White Plains. D.R. Littlepage died Dec. 20, 1982. He was buried in Concord Cemetery. He left behind thirty-three grandchildren, twenty-five great-grandchildren and nine great-great-grandchildren. - *Submitted by Craig A. Whitfield*

JOHN LITTLEPAGE

John Littlepage was born prior to 1760, in Virginia. He was the son of Richard Littlepage and Elizabeth Epps.

On May 25, 1785, in Campbell Co., VA, he married Amy Scott. She was the daughter of John and Elizabeth Scott. To this union six children were born: Epps, James, Richard, Ellis, Elizabeth and Polly.

In the late 1700's, John Littlepage and his wife made Hopkins Co., KY their new home. Records show he sold land in Bedford Co., VA, in 1798.

John Littlepage served his country in the American Revolutionary War. He was a private in a Regiment commandeered by Col. Baylor of the Virginia line for a term of three years. For his service, he received a pension and Bounty Land Grant in Kentucky. It is inscribed in the Rolls of Kentucky that he began receiving $8.00 per month on the 8th day of July 1818. The pension was paid till the day of his death.

John Littlepage and his children had a conspicuous part in the settling of Hopkins Co., KY. Records show that his family owned acres of land on the waters of Pond River in Hopkins Co. and were some of the first settlers.

The Kentucky Agency Rolls of American Revolutionary War Pensions show that John Littlepage died in Hopkins County on Mar. 23, 1820. His wife Amy died in Hopkins County in 1834. - *Submitted by Craig A. Whitfield*

LIVINGSTON

Arthur Wilson Livingston, born in Granville Co., NC, in 1826, son of a hatter by trade.

As a young man, he wanted to be with his brother Jim Livingston who was in Kentucky. Leaving North Carolina for Kentucky, he stopped at the Rev. Roland Gooch farm in Hopkins Co. His brother, Jim, had gone on to Texas and he decided not to follow him and settled here in Hopkins Co. He worked on the Gooch farm for sometime.

Margaret Catherine, Annie Elizabeth, and Arthur Wilson Livingston

Arthur Wilson Livingston in 1848 married Mahulda Ashby born in 1830, and died before 1884. Children by Mahulda were: Laura, who married Daniel Demoss; James R., born 1852; Flora, born 1855 married W.H. Mullins; Henry N. born 1857, died 1942 married 1876 to Henrietta Wilson; Lee born 1863, married 1882, to Rhoda Ashby, (Lee was killed working on the Railroad and was the first person buried in East Lawn Cemetery at Providence); John C., born 1867; and Francis M., married first Cintha McEuen and had children Pearl and Alice, 2nd marriage to Laura Brown.

Arthur Wilson Livingston married second, Annie Elizabeth Marks, born 1860, died 1942. Their two children were: Margaret Catherine born 1887, died 1948 married Frank Madison born 1884, died 1949; and Arthur Southall Livingston born 1885, died 1967 married to Lora Lee Todd born 1894, died 1975.

Arthur Southall and Lora Lee Todd Livingston were the parents of: Franklin Wilson Livingston; Margaret Catherine married Jack Newcomb; Charles Arthur Livingston; and Mary Jane married William S. Blue.

Arthur Wilson Livingston purchased the farm from his brother Fredrick Washington Livingston in 1884. This farm has remained in the Livingston family for over 100 years.

The Livingston farm was cut into by the L & N Railroad. This upset Arthur Wilson. His wish was he hoped never to see the first train cross his farm. His wish was granted. At the same time they were leaving the farm house with his body, the first train started across the farm.

Arthur Wilson was one of many who left North Carolina to settle in Hopkins Co. He died July 4, 1911, and was buried in Olive Branch Cemetery west of Hanson, KY. - *Submitted by Franklin Wilson Livingston*

LLOYD-CATES

Ila Lee Cates and Roy Edward Lloyd were married 1917. Ila, born 1897 and died 1982, was the daughter of Will B. Cates and Cordelia Rodgers of Hopkins Co. where she attended school. She was a member of Nebo Methodist Church, where she enjoyed singing and other hobbies. She enjoyed all types of handicraft and loved gardening. Ila furnished flowers from her own yard for most of Nebo High School's functions. As a young adult and later in years she enjoyed going to community socials and old fashion "Pound Parties". Community young people would gather at one home and would bring a pound of homemade candies, a cake or such, and in the evening they would enjoy singing, square dancing and games. The Lloyd children are sure this is the way their parents met. Ila's brothers were Huffman, died at age 9, Johnny, Felix (Jack), and Willie Morton (Doc) and her sisters were Eula, Isabelle, and Mildred.

Ila Lee and Roy Lloyd

Roy, born 1892 and died 1962, was the son of John Edward Lloyd and Sallie Brinkley of Webster County. The Lloyd family can trace their roots to England. Brothers were Strother, Clarence and Johnny and sisters were Jenny and Maggie. Roy loved music and played the French harp and guitar for family fun and community socials. A member of Corinth Baptist Church, just over the Webster Co. line on the Grace Townsend and Corinth Church Road. He farmed most of his life and was custodian for Nebo High School for 22 years. The job became so demanding as the school grew that Ila became his assistant. Roy's hobby was wood carving, the old fashion way, whittling. He delighted Nebo students with his work. A daughter still has some of his best accomplishments, a tiny linked chain carved from a wooden kitchen match, and a pair of scissors that will cut paper and a pocket knife that the blade will close.

The Lloyd children are William Edward, who married Geneva Oldham and has two boys, one girl, seven grandchildren and one great grandchild; Obie Lee, who married Martha Lou Hunt, had a boy and girl, and later married Gaynell Fowler and had two girls and one boy. He has six grandchildren. Martha Isabelle, who married James Mitchell, and had one son. She later married Hershell Fulmer, no other children. Isabelle has four grandchildren. All three of the Lloyd children live in Hopkins Co. The grandchildren live in Hopkins Co. except one who lives in Ohio and one in Arizona. The Lloyds gave the county many professionals: nurse, school teacher, policeman, Korean war vet, musicians, hand crafts, college student and one great grandson has announced his plans for entering into the field of Christian ministry. - *Submitted by Dorothy Miller Shoulders*

LOCKRIDGE-THOMAS

Andrew Lockridge (b. 1770-80) came to Hopkins Co., KY sometime after administering the 1799 estate of his father John Lockridge (widow: Anna Rhea) in Augusta Co., VA. He married Sarah Thomas (possibly the daughter of Edward and Jane Thomas, who came from Muhlenberg Co., in 1814) in 1815, and raised eight children: (1) John who moved to Clayton Co., IA, (2) Jane Hanking, (3) Sarah Ann, who married John F. Wade Sept. 16, 1835, Pope Co., IL, (4) James, who married Nancy Randolph Sept. 30, 1849, Posey Co., IN, (5) Elizabeth, who married Jonathan Forcum Oct. 27, 1848, (6) Martha, who married John Wade's cousin, Thomas Wade Jan. 22, 1846, (7) William R., who inherited his father's lands along with James; and (8) Susannah.

Left to right: Joshua Kimbrell, Eleanor Wade Moseley and John Wesley Wade, about 1919

Andrew, the grandson of Major Andrew Lockridge (1740-1791) of 2nd Battalion during the American Revolution and Jean Graham (1742-1796), died in August of 1833 leaving Sarah with six children at home. Daughter Sarah Ann Wade, migrated to Posey Co., IN and helped found Wadesville. Some siblings followed: Martha and Thomas Wade with toddlers Harriett and Andrew, James and Nancy Randolph Lockridge with Enock (b. ca 1851), and John (b. ca 1857), and Elizabeth and Jonathan Forcum with William (b. 1850).

John F. Wade (1816/17-1882 or earlier) and Sarah Lockridge (1819-1855) had six children: (1) James D. (no issue), (2) Nancy, who married Walter Conoway; issue: Susan, John, (3) Martha, who married Walter Dunn, (4) John Wesley, Apr. 23, 1846-Mar. 12, 1926, who married Lenora Rice in 1864, (5) Susan, who married William E. Webb July 2, 1870 and had daughter Rachel; and (6) Rachel, born 1855, who married Joe Umpries (no issue). Shortly after Rachel's birth, Sarah died. John returned to Hopkins County and married Mary Ann Coleman; they had daughter Elvira about 1860. The family then farmed in Massalon Twp, Wayne Co., IL from 1857 thru 1870's.

John Wesley Wade, grandson of Andrew & Sarah Thomas Lockridge, raised his family in Wayne Co. near his wife's parents, William & Carolina Crow Rice. His eldest daughter Sarah Caroline Wade (Sept. 3, 1865-Sept. 5, 1942) married Joshua Kimbrell (May 20, 1868-July 22, 1941) and is the great grandmother of this biographer. - *Submitted by Karen Kerr Jensen*

LOGAN

Among the very first Justices of the Peace in Hopkins Co., was James Logan, appointed Dec. 29, 1806, by Gov. Christopher Greenup. James Logan was, as the name suggests, of Scottish extraction, and was born in Morris Co., NJ, in 1755. He died in Hopkins Co., KY, Feb. 28, 1835, at some eighty years of age. During the Revolutionary War, Logan served in the United States Army. He served in the New Jersey line, and was receiving the veteran's pension at the time of his death. To whom he was married, and that date, are not known now, but records show that he left New Jersey to live in Hampshire Co. in Virginia, and later moved to both Mercer and Bourbon Counties in Kentucky. His last home was Hopkins County, where he held about four hundred acres. A document from the year 1836 lists Logan's living children as Thomas, Polly, Nancy Logan Lynn (Mrs. John W. Lynn), Ann Logan Ashby (Mrs. William B. Ashby), all of Hopkins Co. No attempt will be made to account for all of Logan's descendants, but one line will be mentioned.

Dixie Lois Logan, a teacher and principal in Hopkins County for 43 years, with her grandfather Samuel McNary Logan on his 90th birthday, July 27, 1947

In the year 1860, records show that Logan's son Thomas had a wife, the former Martha E. Blue; Thomas was then seventy, and his wife was twenty-seven. Tradition tells us that Thomas was a surveyor. In 1860, the couple had two little sons, Thomas Owen Logan (1853-1939), and Samuel McNary Logan (1857-1949). Both of these sons came to have large families of their own. Thomas Owen Logan married Dorothy Colleen Jewell, Mar. 30, 1870. They are buried at Silent Run. Their children were Aletha, Jeff, Mary Belle, Dixie, Jewell, Annie, and Justin. Among their descendants living in 1987 are A.O. Richards, Logan Richards, Blanche Logan Calvert, Jewell Wyatt Logan, and Ben Logan Sisk.

Samuel McNary Logan married Dixie Lynch, Dec. 24, 1879. They are buried at Odd Fellows Cemetery, Madisonville. Their children were Mack, Ola, Clint, Tom, Brad and Ray. An infant daughter, Bonnie Queen, lived only a short while. Among their descendants are Dixie Lois Logan, Helen Lynch Albritton, Virginia Scudder, The Rev. Samuel M. Logan, Sue Logan Brown, Mary Cox Whitfield, John Horace Cox, William M. Cox, Jenny, Tom, Lori, and John Logan. - *Submitted by John Horace Cox*

LOGAN-KIRKWOOD

Clint Morton Logan (Aug. 3, 1886), was the fourth of six children born to Samuel McMary Logan (1856-1949), and Dixie Lynch Logan (1865-1927). Clint worked on the family farm and played fiddle and bass fiddle for dances in Dawson and elsewhere. Another favorite hobby was fox hunting. The object was not to kill the fox, but to release him to run another day. Clint participated when the National Fox Hunters Association met in Hopkins County. The hunters came from a number of states including Virginia and West Virginia and stayed at the New Century Hotel in Dawson.

Clint first saw Ruth (George Ruth Kirkwood, born Nov. 23, 1894, to Edgar Kirkwood and Nancy Emma Castleberry Kirkwood), on a moonlit summer evening in 1912. She was dancing at a "play party"-an outdoor dance at the neighboring Eison farm while he and some friends provided music. Clint pointed Ruth out to his brother and said, "That is the girl I am going to marry." Later, Clint arranged to be introduced to Ruth in Dawson and courted her. They were married Dec. 19, 1915, in the parlor of Ruth's Grandmother Miriah Wilson Kirkwood (1844-1934), near Dawson in Hopkins County.

L to r: Clint Morton Logan, Dixie Lois Logan and Ruth Kirkwood Logan

After marrying, Clint and Ruth moved to the Logan farm about four miles from Charleston, Hopkins Co., KY. There, a daughter, Dixie Lois Logan, was born Nov. 3, 1916. Clint moved his family into Madisonville when Dixie was about a year old. He was associated with the Havoline Oil Company. In 1936, Clint and Ruth sent Dixie to Western Kentucky State

College in Bowling Green. She received her two year certificate in 18 months. Dixie began a teaching career at Charleston School in a six room building with first through tenth grades and a pot-bellied stove to provide heat.

Clint died on the operating table during goiter surgery on June 17, 1940. Ruth went to work for the Sixth Vein Coal Company and later for Cates Motor Company.

In 1941, Dixie accepted a position as a fourth grade teacher at Madisonville Waddill Avenue School. By attending college during the summers and on Saturdays, Dixie earned both a Bachelor's and a Master's degree from Western Kentucky State College. During a 40 year career as a teacher and principal, Dixie has served the people of Hopkins County. Mrs. Ruth Logan celebrated her 90th birthday Nov. 23, 1984 and is the oldest active member of the Madisonville First Christian Church. - *Submitted by Mrs. Clint Logan (George Ruth Kirkwood Logan)*

LOGAN-WYATT

Jewell Logan (1885-1941), and Archie Wyatt Logan (1892-1982) were married Feb. 29, 1912. Jewell was the son of Thomas Owen Logan (1853-1939) and Dorothy Coleen Jewell Logan (1851-1942), of the Kirkwood Springs community. He is also the great-grandson of James Logan, who was one of the first justices of the peace of Hopkins County, when it was formed in 1807.

Archie Wyatt Logan was the daughter of George Green Wyatt (1857-1942) and Amanda Holloman Wyatt (1865-1941), of the Dalton community. Jewell and Archie Logan had two children, Eva Blanche Logan (1913) and Jewell Wyatt Logan (1926).

Blanche Logan married Walton Edward Calvert on Dec. 25, 1932. He is the son of Finis A. Calvert and Rosa McNeely Calvert. Blanche was a school teacher and deputy County Court Clerk in Hopkins County.

Walton Edward Calvert was a school teacher, farmer, served in WW II (1942-1945), and Hopkins County Court Clerk (1962-1974). Blanche and Walton retired in 1974, and live on their farm on Walnut Grove Road, in Dawson Springs, KY. They have one son, Walton Logan Calvert (1946). He married Jacquelyn Beeler of Bardstown, KY, on Aug. 17, 1968. They graduated from the U. of Kentucky at Lexington. He is an attorney and she is a teacher. She received a Masters degree in Library Science from Vanderbilt U. in Nashville, TN. Logan is the Hopkins County Attorney, having been elected in November, 1977. Jackie is employed as Library Director at Madisonville Community College. They have one daughter, Whitney Ross Calvert, born Apr. 13, 1975. They live in Madisonville, KY.

Jewell Wyatt Logan married Joyce Polley on June 4, 1956. She is the daughter of Vernon and Hattie Alice Little Polley of Nebo. Jewell was a basketball coach and teacher in Hopkins County and he served in WW II (1945-1946). He and Joyce own and live on the farm his parents owned on Highway 70 West near Dalton. Joyce was a school teacher in Hopkins County and is now Principal of the Health Occupations School, in Madisonville, KY.

Jewell and Joyce have one son, James Edward Logan (1962). He married Therese Donaldson of Nebo on July 14, 1984. They graduated from the U. of Kentucky at Lexington, he is in business administration and she in education. He is employed as a civilian personnel manager at Fort Knox, KY, and she is a school teacher and girls' basketball coach in Hardin County. They live in Elizabethtown, KY.

This is a short account of only one part of the Logan family of Hopkins County. There are several people living in Hopkins County who are descendents of James Logan, who was here in 1807. - *Submitted by Logan Calvert*

WOODSON NORMAN LONG

One owns something that is precious, memorable and untouchable. That something is one's history. One's history cannot, in any circumstance, be taken away from the owner. In the following paragraphs I will share a portion of the vivacious history of Woodson Norman Long, my father.

Woodson Long was born in a four-room modest building that his family called a home. He was born on a cold snowy morning at 1:00 a.m on Feb. 20, 1927. He was brought into this world by Dr. Caudil from Hopkinsville, KY, who had to drive a car 10 miles to a small village called Herdon and then take a two mile, bumpy, horse and buggy ride, to my grandfather's house where my grandmother was expecting a child.

This seven and a half bouncing baby boy was born to the loving arms of Isaac and Alma Long. Isaac was born on May 5, 1882 in Herdon. Alma was born Apr. 4, 1898 in Churchill (about 10 miles from Herdon).

My grandparents worked hard to see that all six of their children (three boys and three girls) lived a happy and enduring life. They owned approximately 267 acres of fertile land in South Christian County. If not for the land, my father and his family would not have managed the depression as well as they did. Isaac also had a very good job with the L & N Railroad as a section foreman. The job paid well and had very good benefits. Isaac worked for the L & N Railroad for 26 years. My grandmother was basically a housewife, but she did write a local column every week for the Kentucky New Era.

My grandfather's parents were, in a sense, much more exciting than my grandmother's parents. Samuel Long, my great grandfather, at one time rode with Jesse and Frank James who I am kin to. Sam was very tough. My grandfather told my father that Sam could knock the bark off the tree with his fists and he could drink boiling coffee right out of a coffee pot. My other three grandparents were as exciting.

My father has lived a very enthusiastic life. He graduated from South Christian High School, where he was voted as a member of the all-time South Christian basketball team. At the age of 16, he played lead guitar and sung in a family oriented band called The Little River Ramblers, which had a weekly radio show. He played music with Roy Acuff and his band in 1946. He then went to the Army and fought in the Korean War. After the war, he married Nancy Fowler in 1957. Together they went on to have four beautiful children of their own: Lisa, Mike, Mark and Angie.

Although I never got the chance to meet any of my great grandparents, I will always remember what they mean to me. Through my father I have grown to know and love everyone in my past family. - *Submitted by Mike Long*

THOMAS LONGSTAFF

Thomas Longstaff was born Oct. 10, 1847, in Newcastle-upon-Tyme, Northumberland Co., England, the son of Robert Longstaff and Ruth Plett.

He married in England about 1866, to Jane Maie Anderson, born Apr. 16, 1849/50, in Whitehaven, Cumberland Co., England.

Jane Maie Anderson Longstaff about 1924

Thomas worked as a foreman in the coal mines of Newcastle before being sent for by Wm. F. Anderson (possibly a relative of Jane Maie), who was Secretary-Treasurer of the St. Bernard Coal Mine, in Earlington, KY. He brought his pregnant wife and two sons to Kentucky around 1869, or 1870, where he was hired as a company foreman. He lived, reared a family of 11 children and died in Earlington. Thomas died Oct. 18, 1913, and is buried in Oakwood Cemetery as is his wife, Jane Maie, who died Nov. 7, 1927.

Children of this marriage are: (1) Alexander (b. Apr. 8, 1867 Eng.); (2) Robert (b. Apr. 6, 1869 Eng.); (3) James (b. Apr. 26, 1870 Kentucky); (4) Ruth (b. Apr. 25, 1873 Kentucky m. Mr. Mitchell d. 1938); (5) John (b. July 16, 1875 Kentucky m. Cornelia Jennings 1900); (6) Margaret (b. Feb. 13, 1878 Kentucky m. Henry B. Long 1895 d. 1951); (7) Archibald (b. Oct. 27, 1880 Kentucky m. Fanny ?); (8) May (b. Mar. 17, 1882 Kentucky m. Pete Herb 1900); (9) Thomas (b. June 3, 1884 Kentucky m. Maryanna Smiley d. 1938); (10) William (b. Sept. 17, 1886 Kentucky); (11) Elizabeth (b. Mar. 27, 1889 Kentucky m. Earl Allsbrook).

In the 1880 Census Hopkins Co., KY, Thomas and wife are listed with seven children. Alexander, the eldest, was listed as age 13 and working in mines.

Robert, second son, lived for a time in Colorado Springs, CO. He was an electrician. He is buried in Washington Park Cem., Indianapolis, IN with a Masonic emblem on headstone. Beside him is his brother James. Both had worked in the coal mines in Kentucky and Colorado and died in Indianapolis.

John and wife went to San Francisco, CA, sometime after their marriage in 1900.

Archibald (Archie) and wife Fanny owned a railroad hotel in the Howe Area of Evansville, IN.

May married Pete Herb, son of Pete J. Herb 1854-1899, buried in Oakwood Cem. Hopkins Co. Pete was an engineer on the L & N Railroad out of Corbin, KY and reared six children.

Thomas was a conductor for the L & N Railroad and lived in Evansville, IN. One son was born in 1922.

William was a professional gambler. He died in Earlington, KY.

Margaret married three times (1) Henry Bernard Long, Mar. 10, 1895 ,Earlington, Hopkins Co., KY; (2) Richard Harrison; (3) John Yatsko. There were two sons by first marriage and one daughter by second marriage. He was living with his daughter at time of death in 1951 in Athens, AL. - *Submitted by Johanna Pierce Long*

JOHN WESLEY LOVAN

John Wesley Lovan was born in Hopkins Co., KY Nov. 22, 1828, the son of Reuben Parks Lovan and Talitha Foley Lovan.

On Dec. 16, 1847, John Wesley Lovan married Nancy Ann Fugate, daughter of Zachariah and Elizabeth (Betsy) Wilson Fugate. Nancy Ann Fugate was born in Hopkins Co., KY, Aug. 23, 1828. She died in Hopkins Co., KY July 7, 1897, and is buried in Old Salem Cemetery at Mortons Gap, KY.

John Wesley Lovan 1828-1900 and Nancy Ann Fugate Lovan 1828-1897.

John Wesley Lovan first farmed on rented land and then on one hundred ninety acres which he purchased when he was twenty five years of age. In 1871, he moved to Mortons Gap, KY and opened a general merchandise business. On Mar. 15, 1888, when the town of Mortons Gap was incorporated, J.W. Lovan was appointed as one of five men to serve on the Board of Trustees. At one time he also served as Magistrate in Hopkins County.

John Wesley and Nancy Ann Fugate Lovan were the parents of four children: George Yell Lovan who married Melissa Mitchell; Miranda White Lovan, who married James Marion Coil; Reuben R. Lovan, who married (1) Viola H. Lovan and (2) Dora Coomes and Talitha Elizabeth Lovan, who married Thomas Freeland Hall.

John Wesley Lovan died Jan.6, 1900, in Mortons Gap, KY and is buried in Old Salem Cemetery at Mortons Gap, KY. - *Submitted by Beverly H. Dockrey*

REUBEN PARKS LOVAN

Reuben Parks Lovan was born Apr. 30, 1806, in Hopkins Co., KY, the son of John and Fanny Parks Lovan.

On Nov. 15, 1827, in Hopkins Co., KY, Reuben Parks Lovan was married to Talitha Foley. Talitha was born in Hopkins Co., KY, the daughter of James and Susanna Campbell Foley. Talitha Foley Lovan died in Hopkins Co., KY after 1880. Family tradition says she died at about ninety years of age.

In 1841, Reuben and Talitha Foley Lovan were charter members of the Salem Baptist Church near Mortons Gap, Hopkins Co., KY. Reuben Parks Lovan gave the land for the first Salem Baptist Church building. This church was near a place then known as McDowell's Lick and near the site of the present church.

Reuben and Talitha Lovan were the parents of seven children: John Wesley Lovan born Nov. 22, 1828, married Nancy Ann Fugate; Susan Lovan born circa 1831, married Jefferson Davis; James Marion Lovan, born Nov. 2, 1832, married Louisa V. Bone; America F. Lovan born 1838, married Thomas Pritchett; Sylvanus Lovan born 1840, married Elmina J. Coleman; Salina Lovan born 1840 (twin to Sylvanus); and Florella Lovan born July 15, 1847, married William A. Gatlin.

Reuben Parks Lovan died June 27, 1858 in Hopkins Co., KY and is buried in Flat Creek Cemetery near Mortons Gap. - *Submitted by Beverly H. Dockrey*

LOVELACE

Samuel Newton Lovelace lived in Tennessee. Married Angeline Francis Webb (of Dutch Extraction). Served in Civil War but don't know which side. Stationed near home. Old family tradition that he would slip off and go home. When soldiers came looking for him would go through trapdoor in floor into a small cellar. Wife would drop a sheepskin rug over trapdoor, put a chair on and sit there and rock while the house was searched. Story that she was walking one day with washing of clothes on back in a sheet. Walked between two patrols that started firing on each other. Ran to the nearest. Unhurt but a musket bullet went completely through the bundle of clothes on her back. Came to Kentucky by wagon. He died years first and is buried in Rock Bridge Cemetery in Christian Co. Location grave lost. She is buried at Old Burg Cemetery near Mannington. Grave unmarked but location known to some relatives.

John B. Lovelace - 1864-1896. Married a Bailey. Four children of which only Oscar L. lived to be more than three years old. John was killed in a gunfight when he was Marshall at White Plains, trying to arrest a man wanted for murder in McLean County. He and the three small children buried in old part of Concord Cemetery near White Plains. His wife married again and buried by second husband in same cemetery.

Oscar L. Lovelace married first Ethel Allen. One son Kermit A. Lovelace. Married second to Mabel Allen (little relationship if any) and two sons were born. One died while small. The other, James Oscar Lovelace was mortally wounded opening a booby trapped pillbox in the Siegfried Line in World War II. He left a wife and daughter. Oscar and James Oscar buried in Oddfellows Cemetery, Madisonville, KY. - *Submitted by Kermit A. Lovelace*

GABRIEL LOVING, JR.

Gabriel Loving, Jr. was born circa 1760 in Virginia, the son of Gabriel Loving, Sr. The name of Gabriel Loving, Jr.'s first wife is not known, but it is known that he married Mrs. Rachel Sisk, widow of Daniel Sisk in Wilkes Co., NC on Aug. 27, 1781. Daniel Sisk was killed in the battle of King's Mountain during the Revolutionary War, and in 1784, in Wilkes Co., NC, Gabriel Loving, Jr. was appointed guardian of "the orphans of Daniel Sisk": Betty, Gabriel, Robin and Nelly Sisk. Tradition says that Gabriel Loving, Jr. married a third time to Polly Sumpter, after Rachel died, but no proof can be found.

According to DAR records, Gabriel Loving, Jr. served as a Lieutenant in the Continental Army during the Revolutionary War.

In 1803, Gabriel sold his property in North Carolina and by 1805, he was living in Hopkins Co., KY. A Hopkins Co., KY, tax list shows Gabriel Loving, Jr. as the owner of two hundred fifty acres of land on Pond River, adjacent to property owned by Ebenezer and John Bourland. Two of Gabriel's sisters, Mary and Abigail, had married John and Ebenezer Bourland.

It is believed that Gabriel Loving, Jr. had several children, whose names have not been recorded. His children of whom record has been found are: John Loving, born Sept. 7, 1779; Jane Loving, born 1782; William Ransom Loving, born 1784, or 1785; Joseph Loving born Apr. 18, 1786, and Wiseman F. Loving, born Dec. 18, 1803.

Gabriel Loving, Jr. was living in Hopkins Co., KY in 1810, for he appeared in the federal census of that year, but it is not known when or where he died. - *Compiled by:Beverly H. Dockrey*

JOHN LOVING (LOVAN)

John Loving (Lovan) was born Sept. 7, 1779, in Wilkes Co., NC, the son of Gabriel Loving, Jr.

John Loving was married on Jan. 1, 1801, in Wilkes Co., NC to Frances (Fanny) Parks, daughter of Reuben Parks. Fanny Parks was born in North Carolina Apr. 10, 1783. She died in Hopkins Co., KY, July 25, 1841.

John and Fanny Parks Loving migrated to Hopkins Co., KY, between 1803 and 1805, along with John's father, Gabriel Loving, Jr. and other members of the Loving family.

It was with the John Loving family that the spelling of the surname was changed in Hopkins Co., KY, from LOVING to LOVAN. The latter spelling is presently used by Hopkins Co., KY, descendants of John Loving.

Thirteen children were born to John and Fanny Lovan: Gabriel Gilbert Lovan, born Dec. 17, 1801, married Frances Wilson; Nancy Ray Lovan, born Apr. 14, 1804, married James Kennedy; Reuben Parks Lovan, born Apr. 30, 1806, married Talitha Foley; Russell Gray Lovan, born Feb. 11, 1808, married Mary E. Ezell; William Merritt Lovan born, June 13, 1809, married (1) Permelia Adkins and (2)

Maria C. Carnahan; Mary Ransom (called Polly Malin) Lovan born July 12, 1811, married William Ezell; Alice Medora Lovan born Feb. 24, 1813, married John Kennedy; John Gilpin Lovan, born Dec. 3, 1814, married Mary Kennedy; Oscar Fritzlin Lovan, born Apr. 16, 1817, married (1) Sarah A. Littlepage, (2) ? and (3) Elizabeth Pidcock; Amanda Melvina Lovan, born May 16, 1819; Ethelred Thomas Lovan, born Sept. 10, 1821, married Louisa London; Daniel Riley Lovan, born Mar. 7, 1823, married Sarah (Sally) Ezell; James Marion Lovan, born June 25, 1827, married Mahala Jane Martin.

John Lovan died Jan. 30, 1844 in Hopkins Co., KY. - *Compiled by Beverly H. Dockrey*

LOWTHER

The name, Lowther, originated in Westmorland (now Cumbria) Co., England, where a village and river by that name remain. Sir Hugh de Lowther, Attorney General under Edward I in 1292, served with Henry V at the battle of Agincourt. A Crusader's cross is carved on his stone at Lowther Church.

Sir Richard Lowther was Lord Warden of the Western Marches when Mary, Queen of Scots fled from Scotland to England in 1560.

The Lowther family in Hopkins County traces its origin to William Lowther, born at Tober (now Derry County) Ireland in 1694. He and his wife, Martha, and family, who were Quakers, immigrated about 1729, settling near Doylestown, PA. He died in 1750 and she in 1752.

William's son, Robert, (1714-1780), married Aquilla Reese on Feb. 20, 1736. The Reese family had migrated with William Penn. In about 1740, Robert and family moved to western Virginia.

Their son, William (1742-1814) was born in Albermarle Co., VA. In 1763, he married Sudna Hughes, sister of Jesse Hughes, for whom the Hughes river in West Virginia is named. William served in the American Revolution on the western frontier and as an Indian fighter thereafter. He rose to the rank of colonel. He also was the first justice of the peace and sheriff of Harrison County and served in the Virginia Assembly.

William's third son, William (1769-1857), married Margaret Morrison (1768-1850), in 1789. They had 12 children. Their third son, also named William (1793-?) married Melicent Maxwell. The town of Cairo, WV is laid out on their homestead.

Their second child, Alexander (1836-1908), married Amanda Mann (1858-1917), daughter of C.B. Mann and Sarah Roberts Mann. Their son, Ernest, came to Christian Co., KY in the early 20th Century, where he was a telegraph operator. Subsequently, he was a mail carrier until retirement. Amanda also moved to Kentucky and is buried at Crofton. Family legend says that Mannington may have been named for her brother, Charlie Mann, first stationmaster at Mannington.

Ernest (1884-1962) married Greta Eddins (1888-1959), daughter of Benjamin Downer and Margaret Moodie Eddins. They had seven children: Benjamin Eddins; Mildred Ruth; Mary Elizabeth; Edgar Mann; Ernest Raymond; Charles Herbert; and James Edwin.

Edgar and his family moved to Hopkins County in July 1951. - *Submitted by: Charles E. Lowther*

LOWTHER-CARROLL

Charles Ernest Lowther, fourth child of Edgar Mann and Margaret (Evans) Lowther was born at Hopkinsville, KY, Apr. 25, 1951. In July 1951 he and his family removed to Nortonville, where his mother and two sisters and their families still reside.

Charles and Shelia Lowther and daughter, Clara

Charles graduated from South Hopkins High School in 1969. Thereafter, he graduated from Western Kentucky U. in 1973, majoring in history with minors in English and Government. The following year, he completed 24 hours toward a Master's degree in history at Western.

During the period from August 1974 through August 1977, Charles worked at a number of occupations, including insurance agent (National Life and Accident Company), assistant loan manager (Kentucky Finance Company), substitute teacher in the Hopkins County School System, and underground coal miner (Island Creek Coal Company).

Charles attended the College of Law, U. of Kentucky, from 1977 to 1980, graduating in May 1980. In October 1980, he was licensed to practice law. He has been associated with Mills, Mitchell and Turner since May 1980.

Sheila Lee Carroll Lowther, eldest child of Vernon Ray and Audrey (Barnett) Carroll, was born at LaFollette, TN on Mar. 17, 1955. In 1958, her family moved to Bromley, KY. She graduated from Dixie Heights High School in 1973. She attended Transylvania U. as a merit scholar and graduated in 1977 with a degree in Political Science. In the summer of 1977, she received an English-Speaking-Union fellowship to the U. of London. She graduated from the College of Law, U. of Kentucky, in 1980. She has also been licensed to practice law since October 1980, and has been associated with Mills, Mitchell and Turner since May 1980.

Sheila and Charles were married at Lexington on Aug. 19, 1979. They have one daughter, Clara Elizabeth, born at Madisonville on Feb. 13, 1984.

Charles is a past president of the Historical Society of Hopkins and currently is vice president of that organization. He is a member of the Hopkins County Genealogical Society and the Kentucky Historical Society. He serves on the Boards of Directors of Western Kentucky Legal Services and Hopkins County Academic Boosters. Sheila is on the Board of the local Red Cross chapter. Both belong to the local, state and national Bar associations.

Both Charles and Sheila enjoy reading in their spare time. Consequently, they have acquired a library of about 2000 books. Charles also collects metal soldiers and maps. - *Submitted by Charles E. Lowther*

LOWTHER-EVANS

Edgar Mann Lowther, fourth child of Ernest and Greta (Eddins) Lowther was born at Crofton, KY, on June 15, 1916. He attended school in Christian Co., KY.

Edgar worked as an underground miner for in excess of 30 years at the Williams mines near Mannington for Williams Coal Company and its successors. He was last employed by Island Creek Coal Company in June 1969 when he sustained a disabling heart attack. He worked as a belt-mechanic, mechanic and electrician. He was a graduate of the School of Industrial Electricity in Madisonville.

He sustained serious injuries in the mines in 1952 and 1965. In the first accident he injured his back in a rockfall. In the second accident he received a crushing injury to his head and arm. However he was able to return to work within a year after each injury.

He died July 7, 1973, and is buried at New Salem Cemetery near Nortonville.

Margaret Frances Evans, eldest child of James Estle and Hattie Mary (Cayce) Evans, was born at White City, Hopkins Co., KY, on Dec. 31, 1915. At an early age she moved to Christian County and received her formal schooling there. She lived primarily with her grandparents, Samuel Morton Crews Cayce and Margaret (Beard) Cayce, while she grew up.

Edgar and Margaret Lowther

Edgar and Margaret married on Feb. 21, 1935, in Christian County. In July 1951, they moved to Nortonville.

The had five children: (1) Dale Wayne, born Jan. 18, 1936, married Mary Jeannette Scott on June 1953. They have four sons: Anthony Scott; Richard Wayne; Steven Dale; and John Kevin.

(2) Margaret LaVerne, "Peggy", born Oct. 14, 1937, married William Edgar Bond on Feb. 18, 1961. Their children are Damon Russell and Rhonda Lynn.

(3) Shirley Ruth, born Mar. 18, 1943, married Wesley Darrell Creamer, Sr. Their children are Tonda Louise and Wesley Darrell, Jr.

(4) Charles Ernest, born Apr. 26, 1951, mar-

ried Sheila Lee Carroll, on Aug. 19, 1979. They have a daughter, Clara Elizabeth.

(5) Kimberly Faith was born Aug. 6, 1960.

Both Edgar and Margaret were and are members of Nortonville Baptist Church, where Margaret had taught Sunday School for a number of years. - *Submitted by: Charles E. Lowther*

LUCAS-KING

Mayme H. King was born July 11, 1889, the only child of Ira Wright King (Nov. 3, 1864-Dec. 13 1949) and Clementine (Tina) D. Cates (Oct. 10, 1869-Nov. 15, 1965) who were married Oct. 17, 1888 in Hopkins Co.

Mayme grew up on a farm near Nebo, KY and attended a rural one-room school. In December 1909, she married her teenage sweetheart George Jasper Lucas. George (Sept. 12, 1886-Nov. 13, 1966) was the son of Winfield T. Lucas (1859-1934) and Minnie N. Lucas (1870-1943). Mr. W.T. Lucas was a saw miller.

George and Mayme were the parents of one child, Gladys (Nov. 19, 1910-Mar. 20, 1977), who married Ernest G. Lansden (Apr. 3, 1905-May 30, 1960/61). They were the parents of Gail born Aug. 25, 1938. Gail was married July 26, 1958 to Leo King Jr. (born Apr. 6, 1932).

About 1920, George and Mayme moved to Nebo to operate a general store. A few years later, a partnership was formed to with J.E. Wooton under the name of Lucas & Wooton. The business expanded to deal in poultry, which was shipped by rail to Chicago and New York. Mayme would say, "He'd (George) go off a chicken feeder and come back a gentleman." On one trip to New York, George saw the musical "Sonny Boy" performed by Al Jolson. He came home filled with excited descriptions of the event, and later, when the film was shown in Madisonville he was elated to take Mayme and Gladys to see it.

On Aug. 20, 1932, a fire which destroyed a business block at Nebo, consumed Lucas & Wooton Store and Poultry Warehouse. Soon after the Lucases moved to Henderson, KY to establish a new home and business.

In February 1988, Mayme was interviewd by columnist Judy Jenkins for the Henderson Gleaner. She found Mayme at age 98 years and 7 months with an alert mind and interested in "doings" of her only grandchild, Gail, and her three grandchildren, Elizabeth (Beth) King Scherer, Nancy Terry King, and Leo Lansden (Lanny) King. Though George, Gladys, and Ernest have been deceased for many years, Mayme has maintained her own household. Until November 1987, she did much of the housework and cooking. At that date she fell while visiting a relative on the 14th floor of a Florida condominium and broke her hip. The doctors and nurses were amazed that at age 98, she was hospitalized for the first time. In three days after surgery, she was walking and a week later, she was headed for home by regular flight.

During the interview, Mayme pointed out a picture of Gladys as a baby wearing a long flowing dress. The lady who arranged that dress for the photographer was a survivor from the Titanic tragedy. The Providence, KY resident, during the portrait setting, enthrolled Mayme with the personal story of events from that night in 1912 when the doomed ship sank into the icy water of the Atlantic.

Mayme has lived to see many events come to pass: discovery of x-rays; the Wright Bros. flying the first plane; the telephone; women winning the right to vote; the first motion picture with sound; the first atomic bomb; polio vaccine discovery; man walking on the moon; the U.S. Bicentennial celebration; and the first artificial heart implant.

Mayme's love and constant companion is Pete, a blue parakeet who is Lord of the house and enjoys singing duets with Mayme while perched on her shoulder.

Sources: Judy Jenkins interview, Family Bible and cemetery records; and the Madisonville Messenger, Aug. 20, 1932. -Submitted by Sarah Barron

LUCKETT-STEWART

Catherine Eulalia (Layle) Stewart Luckett was born on June 2, 1939, in Madisonville, KY, to Carrie Lacy Stewart and Lyall Stewart.

Layle attended school in Madisonville, graduating from Madisonville High School in May 1957, where she played clarinet in the band, served as stage manager of the senior class play and was a member of the Beta Club. She received her B.A. degree from Randolph-Macon Woman's College in Lynchburg, Va in June 1961 where she was secretary of Alpha Delta Pi sorority, a member of the Young Democrats, the Outing Club, Sock and Buskin Dramatic Club, The Marketing Club and International Business Club, the Potpourri Literary Magazine staff and church relations chairman for the YMCA. Layle graduated from the Harvard-Radcliffe program in business administration in 1962 and earned her masters in business administration from the Harvard Graduate School of Business in 1965, where she was a member of the Harvard Law School Forum. She also studied at the Brazilian American Cultural Institute, Alliance Francaise in Paris, France, where she was an exchange student trainee with the Association International Des Etudiants Scientific Et Commerciale and completed her studies for her PHD in management at UCLA and Golden Gate University in San Francisco.

Layle designed and conducted management development seminars for the U.S. Departments of Labor and Health, Education and Welfare and for state and private employment agencies and enterprises. As she traveled

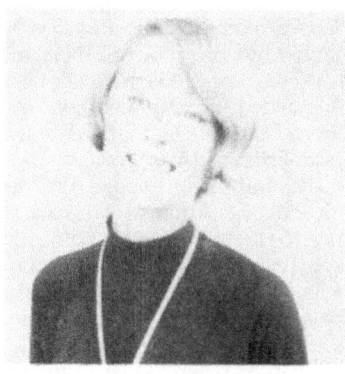

Layle Luckett

with her U.S. Marine Corps husband, she taught management and marketing courses at the U.S. International University in San Diego, the University of Maryland, George Washington University in Washington, D.C., Golden Gate University in San Francisco and the Dominican University in Marin Co., CA.

Other work experience included The Vogue in Madisonville, Filene's and the Red Garter of Boston, Woodward and Lothrop on Washington, D.C., L.S. Ayres in Indianapolis, Clairol, Inc., at the 1965 New York World's Fair, and as consultant for Planning Research Corporation, Arthur D. Little Company and Harbridge House in Washington, D.C.

Layle married Jackson Ralph Luckett (born June 15, 1929), on June 23, 1967. After Jack retired from the Marine Corps as a Lieutenant Colonel, while he was serving as Assistant City Attorney for Los Angeles, Layle attended UCLA, studying for her PHD.

The idea of travel was in their blood so they retired from "normal" life, stored their possessions and on Feb. 1, 1974, started a world tour which lasted until December 1975, when they finally settled in Jack's hometown of San Francisco. During this time, Layle studied six foreign languages.

Layle is listed in the 1970 edition of Outstanding Young Women in America and the 1973 editions of Who's Who in American Women and Two Thousand Women of Achievement.

Layle joined the First Christian Church in Madisonville at seven years of age and on June 11, 1984, was ordained a minister through The Church of Gospel Ministry, Inc. She and Jack now make their home in La Jolla, CA. Refer to: Edd Lee Lacy, M.O. Stewart, Emil George Miller, William Lyall and Carrie Lacy Stewart. - *Submitted by: Mrs. Lyall Stewart*

LUTZ-DAME

Pearl Clinton Lutz was born Feb. 7, 1878 in Hopkins Co., the son of Robert Franklin and Almedia Frances (Winstead) Lutz. On Oct. 31, 1900, in Hopkins Co., he married Bertha Lee Dame, the daughter of James William and Aerie Ella (Boyd) Dame. She was born Oct. 9, 1880, in Hopkins Co. Pearl Clinton died Apr. 21, 1952 in Hopkins County and Bertha Lee died Aug. 4, 1955, in Hopkins County. Both are buried at Olive Branch Cemetery. Their children:

Johnny Raymond, b. 1903, d. 1974, married

Mayme Lucas, age 94 standing beside her cousin Helen Cox, age 92

Pauline Oldham and their children: Paul, Danny and Jo Evelyn, who married 1. Bunton and 2. Bruce.

Verda Marie, b. ca. 1906, still living 1987, married 1. Dixon and 2. John Reid. No issue.

Douglas, b. 1909, d. 1963, while checking oil wells fell from a tank, married Lola B. Harris, children: Rev. Charles Lutz and Dennis Lutz.

Edith Ilene, b. 1912, d. 1962, of cancer, married Leslie Webster, children: Duane, Shelby (female) m. Howard and Gail m. Whitaker.

Arthur Walton, b. Sept. 28, 1916, still living 1987, m. Louise Owen (b. Dec. 19, 1917, married Sept. 11, 1937). Children: Carroll, Randa Bearden, Marshall, Glenn, Joan Howard, Ernie, and Delane McKnight.

Lonnie, b. Dec. 18, 1918, still living in 1987, married Dorothy Clayton. Children: Kenneth, Sharon Beaver, Joyce Hopple and Roger.

Lona, b. Dec. 18, 1918, twin to above, d. Feb. 7, 1986, m. Mary Lou Duncan. Children: Phil, Shelia Sharky, and Vicki, m. 1. McCormack and m. 2. Bates.

Elsie, B. January 1924, living in 1987, m. Henry Sullivan. Children: Dr. Jerry Sullivan, Judy Clark, Jimmy Sullivan, Janice ?.

The children of Arthur Lutz and Louise Owen:

Carroll Lutz, b. Sept. 24, 1938, m. 1. Hilda Galloway, div., m. 2. Rosemary Lamb. Children: Jeff.

Randa Doris Bearden, b. May 24, 1944, m. Calvin Bearden, children: Krista Marie married Ricky Eagle and they have one son, Eric b. Apr. 26, 1985; and Melissa Gay Bearden.

Marshall Lutz, b. Nov. 30, 1947, m. 1. Nancy Helm and had two children: Kathy and Marsha, m. 2. Gayle Mitchell.

Glenn Lutz, b. May 13, 1950, m. 1. Charlotte Lewis, m. 2. Pam Phillips, children: Misty and Amanda.

Joan Lutz, b. July 23, 1951, m. Kenneth Howard, children: Kenny and Micheal.

Ernie Lutz, b. Nov. 20, 1955, m. Diane Carroll, div.

Delane Lutz, b. Sept. 2, 1957, m. Craig McKnight, div., children: Steven Ray McKnight. - *Submitted by Randa Lutz Bearden*

LUTZ-DUNCAN

Mary Lou Duncan and Reverend Lona Ray Lutz were united in marriage Mar. 1, 1941 in Clarksville, TN.

Mary Lou was born July 16, 1923. Her parents are Reverend Oscar Lee Duncan and the late Luetta Parish Duncan. (See Duncan-Parish). She is an excellent home-maker. She has an outgoing personality and a great sense of humor.

Rev. Lona Ray Lutz and wife Mary Lou (Duncan)

Mary Lou is a member of the Madisonville First General Baptist Church. She was deeply devoted to Lona and stood by his side in the Lord's work.

Lona (Dec. 18, 1918-Feb. 7, 1986) was the son of Bertha Dame and Pearley Clinton Lutz. He was the twin brother of Lonnie Clay Lutz. His other brothers and sisters were Raymond, Douglas, A.W., Marie Reid, Eilene Webster, and Elsie Sullivan.

Lona was ordained as a General Baptist minister Apr. 23, 1942 at the Dixon General Baptist Church. He attended Oakland City College in Oakland City, IN, for two years.

Reverend Lutz served as pastor of the following churches: Concord, Tilden, Free Union, Beech Grove, Cumberland Valley, Sebree, Union Hill, Beulah, Lake Side Church, Oakley Home, and Madisonville First General Baptist.

Rev. Lutz was an excellent speaker. His thoughts were well organized and his words were articulated very well. Many people were blessed by his ministry.

Rev. Lutz was of a calm nature. He enjoyed gardening, fishing, and was an excellent carpenter. He possessed a wonderful sense of humor.

God blessed Mary Lou and Lona with three children: Phil Ray (Mar. 23, 1943) (See Lutz-Ramm), Shellia Diana Sharkey (May 24, 1949) (See Sharkey-Lutz), and Vicky Yvonne Bates (Apr. 5, 1955) (See Bates-Lutz).

Lona and Mary Lou were happily married for forty-five years. - *Submitted by Retha Tarter*

LUTZ-KELLY

Jacob Lutz, born Sept. 9, 1810, in Nelson Co., KY, was the tenth child of Jacob and Catherine Mathis.

Jacob (born Apr. 4, 1769, in Pennsylvania; died Sept. 3, 1837 in Nelson Co.) and Catherine (born Aug. 26, 1771; died June 12, 1854 in Nelson Co.) both are buried at St. Lukes Lutheran Cemetery, Nelson County. Their oldest children are recorded at Apple's Church, Thurmont, MD, (Frederick Co.); the others were born in Kentucky. They are Mary Lutz (May 4, 1792), Margaret Lutz (Dec. 7, 1793), Benjamin (Apr. 16, 1795), Phebe (Apr. 25, 1797), Elizabeth (Dec. 21, 1798), John (Dec. 2, 1800), William (Dec. 29, 1802), Charles (Apr. 18, 1805), Sarah (July 29, 1808), and Jacob.

The Chris Lutz Family: Chris, Mollie Kelly, and C.M.

Jacob married Matilda Osborn (June 23, 1816) in Nelson County. Nov. 1, 1832. She was the oldest child of Isaac Osbourn and his first wife Jane Threlkile.

In 1845 they, their children, Isaac Osbourn with his second wife Mary Lutz, most of Isaac's children and their families moved to Hopkins Co. near Madisonville. Jacob and Matilda lived in Wolf Hollow. Their children were Mataline Gregory, Christopher Columbus "Chris", Robert Franklin, Jacob Hefley, James "Polk", Margaret Swope, James Benjamine "Buck", Franklin Pearce "Purd", Rosecran Grant "Ross" and Susan Warenner.

The Griffins-Hugh, Eugenia and Louise at 211 E. Moss St. in Earlington

177

Christopher Columbus (June 4, 1836), married Mary "Mollie" Kelly (Feb. 5, 1837), Nov. 20, 1862 in Hopkins Co. She was the daughter of Quinton Kelly and Lucy Ann Woodson and granddaughter of Frederick Kelly and Mary (Rolly) Havenhill. They had four children; Mollie Farlin (Feb. 15, 1864), Columbus Marion (Nov. 11, 1865); Jacob Lann (Dec. 31, 1868), and Lou Emma McEuen (Jan. 14, 1871). Mollie Farlin lived only a few hours. Chris served with Company A, 17th Regt. of Kentucky. He served mostly in the Hopkinsville, Russelville area during the Civil War. After his return home, he taught school and farmed.

C.M. or "Lum" as he was known by his family, wanted to teach. Getting an education was not an easy task in those days. He attended school in Nashville and taught several years in the Hopkins County schools. He married Jimmie Lee "Tott" Fike, the youngest daughter of Mattie Hill and James Fike. They had no children. They both taught at East Texas State College in Commerce, TX.

Jacob Lann told of cutting timber and clearing land where Lake Pee Wee is to help send his brother to teachers' college. As were most of the Lutz men, he was a well-known carpenter. At the age of thirty, he married Gradie Fike, oldest daughter of Mattie Hill and James Fike. They had three children, Hortense Niswonger Porter, Raymond Price and Lanna Lee.

Emma married George McEuen. He operated a mercantile store in Earlington and at Star Hope in Webster County. Later, they returned to Earlington and operated a jewelry store. After his death, Emma moved to Commerce, TX where her brother lived and opened a jewelry store. - *Submitted by Lanna Arnold*

LUTZ-OSBURN

Jacob Lutz was born Sept. 9, 1810, the son of Jacob and Catherine (Mathis) Lutz. On Nov. 1, 1832, in Nelson Co., KY he married Matilda Osburn the daughter of Isaac and Jane (Threlkile) Osburn. Matilda was born June 23, 1816. Jacob and Matilda came to Hopkins Co., KY, ca. 1847 and lived around the Richland area. They went to Texas ca. 1856, Burleson County, and were back in Hopkins Co., KY by 1860. Jacob died Apr. 5, 1884, and Matilda died Nov. 12, 1894. Both are buried at Odd Fellows Cemetery in Madisonville, KY.

Jacob and Matilda Osburn Lutz

The children of Jacob and Matilda:
Almarinda Matilda born Nov. 25, 1833, in Nelson Co., KY, died Apr. 18, 1881, married Wilson Gregory, buried Pleasant Grove Cemetery in Hopkins Co., KY.

Christopher C., born June 4, 1836 in Nelson Co., KY, died July 13, 1920 in Hopkins Co., KY. and is buried at Oddfellows. He was married Nov. 29, 1862, in Hopkins County. to Mary M. Kelly.

Robert Franklin, born May 4, 1839 in Nelson Co., KY, died June 2, 1919, married 1st Louisa J. Martin, married 2nd Almedia Francis Winstead (born Jan. 13, 1846, died Feb. 27, 1934), married Oct. 10, 1866, in Hopkins Co., KY, by Elder I.H. Henry, General Baptist Minister. Fanny Winstead was the daughter of William H. Winstead and Alafar Hibbs, granddaughter of William Hibbs and Elizabeth Arlige. Robert and Almedia are buried at Olive Branch Cemetery near Hanson, KY.

Jacob Hefley born Sept. 7, 1841, in Nelson Co., KY, died in 1929, in Christian Co., KY, married Lucinda Cordelia Crabtree on Feb. 23, 1870 in Hopkins Co., KY. Buried in Christian County.

James K. Polk born May 30, 1844, died June 2, 1917 in Hopkins Co., married Oct. 17, 1866 to Lovinia Catherine Sisk, buried Silent Run Church Cemetery near Beulah, Hopkins Co., KY.

Margaret Jane, born Apr. 28, 1850 in Hopkins Co., KY, died Aug. 4, 1929 in Hopkins Co., KY, married Feb. 17, 1878 to J.W. Swope. Buried Odd Fellows Cemetery, Madisonville, KY.

James Buchanan, born Apr. 28, 1850 in Hopkins Co., KY, died Sept. 23, 1917, married 1st. Francis Hart on Dec. 3, 1873, married 2nd Genoah Gooch on July 10, 1884. Buried Olive Branch Cemetery near Hanson, KY.

Franklin Purd, born May 19, 1853 in Hopkins Co., KY, died Oct. 29, 1904. Was killed on the Jockey grounds in Madisonville in a fight. Buried in Odd Fellows Cemetery in Madisonville, KY. Married Jan. 2, 1878 to Elizabeth Hughes.

Rosecran (Ross), born Jan. 4, 1857 in Texas, died Aug. 12, 1918 in Hopkins Co., KY, married June 16, 1886 to Rebecca Alice Gooch. Buried Olive Branch Cemetery near Hanson, KY.

Mariah Susan, born Sept. 5, 1860 in Hopkins Co., KY, died Oct. 27, 1925, married George W. Warrinner on Nov. 25, 1878 in Shawneetown, IL. Buried Odd Fellows Cemetery in Madisonville, KY. - *Submitted by Randa Lutz Bearden*

LUTZ-RAMM

Phil Ray Lutz and Virginia Marie Ramm were united in marriage July 2, 1970, in St. Petersburg, FL, by Reverend Lona R. Lutz.

Phil was born Mar. 23, 1943, in Hopkins County. His parents are Mary Lou Duncan and the late Rev. Lona Ray Lutz. (See Lutz-Duncan).

Phil attended school at Nebo and Madisonville. He graduated from Madisonville High School in 1961. Attended UK Extension Center in Henderson, KY, two years and graduated from Western KY University in 1965, with a BA in math. Phil continued his education at Florida State U. and received his MS in statistics in 1967. He has been employed by General Electric for twenty years as a Quality Control Specialist.

Virginia (Ginger) was born Dec. 29, 1945 in Aurora, IL. Her parents are Marie Irene Gerry

Phil and Virginia Lutz with children Brian Ray and Amanda Marie

and Arthur Carl Ramm. Her maternal grandparents were Julia Josephine Ebinger and Frank Joseph Gerry. Her paternal grandparents were Teresa Reimer, (born in Austria) and Charles Carsten Ramm (born in Denmark). Ginger has one sister: Linda Merlyn Nalevanko.

Ginger graduated from West High School, Davenport, IA in 1964. She received her LPN license in 1966 from Eastern Iowa Community College. She is a Girl Scout leader, Past President of her local PTA, and runs the clinic at her local Middle School.

Phil and Ginger have two children: Brian Ray (May 15, 1974), and Amanda Marie (Aug. 2, 1977). As a family, they enjoy camping, gardening, shelling, and swimming. They reside in Largo, FL, and are members of the Calvary Baptist Church in Clearwater, FL. - *Submitted by Retha Tarter*

C.M. LUTZ

C.M. Lutz was born near Madisonville Nov. 11, 1865, the son of Chris and Molly Kelly Lutz. His closest boyhood friend was his younger brother Jacob Lann. He didn't go to school until he was 12 years old. They lived too far from a school. He recalled that a subscription teacher came around to their house when he was eight but he didn't want to attend her class. When he started school he walked five miles each way to Munns school. He started his teaching career in 1884 at Munns School, it was a one room school at that time. From there he went to Johnson Island School. He studied in his spare time and then entered Colman Academy in Nashville. From there he entered Vanderbilt University. He was principal of Madisonville High School for three years. Principal in those days was equivalent to the title of superintendent today.

Professor C.M. Lutz and Mrs. Tott Lutz, 1911

For one term 1889 to 1890, he taught at the old Madisonville Academy. In a newspaper interview while visiting Madisonville in 1937, he said that even though the academy building had been gone many a year he could picture the surrounding territory. He told about a woolen mill near the academy that completely processed the wool, making it into yarn and spinning it into fabric. He also talked about the streets by the academy being lined with trees and that there was a great stir about cutting a lot of them so that telephone and electric wires could be strung.

After receiving his MA from Vanderbilt, he taught in Jacksonville, FL and Mobile, AL.

He married Jimmie Lee "Tott" Fike, daughter of James and Mattie Hill Fike. She was born and raised in the Nebo area. She attended school under Mr. Lutz, later taught in the Hopkins County schools and was principal in the old East Broadway school.

They moved to Commerce, TX, in 1911, where he taught at the Mays Normal School. When the school became a state institution in 1917, he was selected to receive the keys of the school for the State of Texas. He remembered this as one of the great experiences of his life. He was head of the East Texas State Chemistry department. Tott Lutz was dean of women.

The Lutz's had no children, although they financially aided 15 students in acquiring their college education. When he retired in 1941, one of his students gave the following tribute to him, "I think he was the greatest man I have ever known; he was so simple in his wants, so sincere in his purpose, so uncompromising in his standards of excellency, so untiring in helping those who were in need; he gave so much of himself and asked so little in return."

They were members of the Christian Church.

C.M. died July 18, 1951; Tott died Nov. 13, 1951. They are buried at Odd Fellows Cemetery, Madisonville. *Submitted by Lanna Arnold*

JACOB LANN LUTZ

Jacob Lann Lutz, youngest son of Chris and Mollie Kelly Lutz was born Dec. 31, 1868. He was raised on a farm near Madisonville and was taught the family skills of farming and carpentry. Schools were not close to the farm, therefore the children were taught elementary skills by their parents. His father, Chris had taught before serving with the 17th Regt. of Kentucky during the Civil War and his mother Mollie Kelly had attended the Academy near Madisonville. (We were always told that it was located in the area where the Bill Day farm is today. Her grandfather Fredrick Kelly owned a large farm in the same area.) He married Gradie Fike (Sept. 29, 1880), Sept. 29, 1897, at Mother's home. Gradie was the oldest daughter of James Fike and Mattie Hill Fike Jackson. She was born on a farm near Nebo (it was later known as the Will Porter farm). Her father Jimmy Fike was killed while a group of young men were playing a game of leap frog, in a freak accident. Gradie and Tott were very young. Her mother married J.W. Jackson and they moved to his home in Nebo.

Lann and Gradie bought a farm at Liberty in Webster County. Liberty Store was operated by George and Emma Lutz McEuen. Later Lann operated the store. Here their three chil-

The J.L. Lutz family in 1930 at the homeplace in Dixon. Front: Gradie, Lanna Lee, and Hortense. Back: Lann and Raymond.

dren were born, close family ties were built and the foundation of education and the future were laid. The family often gathered around the study table with its bright kerosene lamp. The three children; Hortense, Raymond and Lanna Lee, were inspired to set high values and goals. Education and family togetherness were important values. Hortense lived in Nebo a year so that she could ride the train to Madisonville and attend high school. She went to Commerce, TX the second year of high school. By that time Raymond was old enough for high school and they rode from Liberty to Providence, horse back to school.

The Lutz moved to Dixon when Lanna Lee reached high school age. They lived a short time at a house on the north side of Dixon, then bought a house on the south side of town where they lived for 32 years. Lann worked for Ruby Lumber Company. At that time they were building bridges throughout Kentucky, and Lann was the foreman for many of these. He took great pride in the fact that he was foreman in the building of the present Webster County Court House. He was injured on this job and was in an Evansville, IN hospital during the flood of 1937.

He and Rev. Pearcy built the present brick General Baptist Church in Dixon. The women worked just as hard quilting to pay for new pews and hymnals.

They went hand in hand through joys and sorrows that they encountered in their fifty-four year journey together. (See J.L. Lutz children.) - *Submitted by Lanna Arnold*

J.L. LUTZ CHILDREN

Hortense Lutz, oldest child of Jacob Lann and Gradie Lutz, married Tommy Louis Niswonger, son of Tom Niswonger and Lizzie Springfield. They had two children; William Louis (Bill) and Lanna Sue Arnold. Hortense taught her first school in Webster County at Lick Skillet. She rode horseback to school as there were no cars at that time. She boarded with the Ashers during the week, returning home on the weekend. She taught several years at Greenwood school in Hopkins County. At the beginning of WW II, she went back to teaching, first at Stoney Point, then at Nebo Junior High and later the lower elementary grades. She set up the lunch room program at the Nebo School.

In 1961, she married Ebenezer Porter. She was an active church member from early childhood and raised in the General Baptist Church,

Raymond Lutz and Ebenezer and Hortense Lutz Porter, 1979

but changed to the Methodist Church when she moved to Nebo. She and Ebenezer were active in building the present Methodist Church building in Nebo. At their deaths, they were members of the Madisonville Methodist Church.

Raymond Price Lutz married Sibyl Harralson from New Boston, TX, July 3, 1929. They had three children: Sybil Marion Severance, Raymond Price Jr. and William Lann. Raymond graduated from Purdue with a Masters Degree in electrical engineering in 1926. He taught at Purdue and the Mellon Institute for three years. He joined Western Electric in 1929, in Chicago. In 1951, he was appointed Superintendent at the Burlington and Greensboro, NC, plants. He was transferred to Sandia, NM, as Superintendent in 1954, where he was made Vice President. He died in 1957; at that time he was head of the new Western Electric laboratory in Princeton, NJ.

Lanna Lee Lutz graduated from Texas Northeastern Teachers College in Commerce, TX. (Sibyl Harralson was her roommate.) She taught school and coached girls basketball in Western Texas. She took pneumonia and died at age 25. She never married. See Jacob Lann Lutz. - *Submitted by Lanna Arnold*

ROBERT FRANKLIN LUTZ

Robert (Bobby) Franklin Lutz was born May 4, 1839, in Nelson Co., KY, the son of Jacob and Matilda (Osburn) Lutz.

On Jan. 8, 1862, in Hopkins Co., KY, he married Louisa J. Martin and they were the parents of Jeneva Lutz (1864-1884), who was engaged to or married to a Phil Brewer.

On Oct. 10, 1866, he married second Almedia Frances Winstead, the daughter of William H. Winstead and Alafar Hibbs. Fanny was born Jan. 13, 1846, in Hopkins Co., KY. Robert died June 2, 1919 in Hopkins Co. and Almedia Frances died Feb. 27, 1934, in Hopkins County. They are both buried at Olive Branch Cemetery near Hanson, KY.

Their children:

Naoma, born Aug. 27, 1867, died Mar. 13, 1939, married June 23, 1883, in Hopkins County to Thomas Rhew. Both are buried at Daniel Cemetery located off Wolf Hollow Road out from Manitou, KY.

Claude Emus (Bud) born Nov. 26, 1869, died Nov. 6, 1947, married 1st Alice Bowles on Dec. 16, 1891, in Hopkins Co., married 2nd Mrs. Nanny Tucker Lutz, widow of his brother Lemuel. Buried Olive Branch Cemetery near Hanson, KY.

John Virgil, born Feb. 2, 1872, died Aug. 16, 1959 in a car wreck, married Johannah Buckannan on Jan. 5, 1888 in Hopkins Co., KY. Buried Olive Branch Cemetery near Hanson, KY.

Lemuel F. born Nov. 23, 1874, died Nov. 14, 1903, married Nanny Tucker on Jan. 12, 1892 in Hopkins Co. Buried Olive Branch Cemetery near Hanson, KY.

Elmo Pratt born Feb. 27, 1876, died May 19, 1962 in Hopkins Co., KY, married Ella Daniel on Oct. 3, 1900 in Hopkins Co. Buried Olive Branch Cemetery near Hanson, KY.

Pearl Clinton born Feb. 7, 1878, died Apr. 21, 1952 in Hopkins Co., married Bertha Lee Dame born Oct. 9, 1880, died Aug. 4, 1955, married on Oct. 31, 1900 in Hopkins Co. Buried Olive Branch Cemetery near Hanson, KY.

Ora Ethel (Ode) born May 5, 1880, died Dec. 12, 1962, married Robert Utterback on Dec. 27, 1899 in Hopkins Co. Buried Olive Branch Cemetery near Hanson, KY.

Inace (Ine) born Jan. 15, 1883, died Feb. 14, 1934 of brain tumor, married James Alonzo Dame born July 12, 1882, died Mar. 19, 1919. Buried Oakley Home Church Cemetery between Manitou and Dixon, KY. Lonnie Dame was a brother to Bertha Lee.

Ezra Clyde (Edd) born May 21, 1885, died Oct. 17, 1975 in Hopkins Co., married Macie Cunningham. Buried Olive Branch Cemetery near Hanson, KY.

Ailcy Nimma born Feb. 26, 1890, died Apr. 8, 1980 in Hopkins Co., married George Beeny on June 2, 1907. Both buried Odd Fellows Cemetery at Madisonville, KY.

Mirtle born Sept. 5, 1887, died 1972 in Hopkins Co., married Ebb Anderson. Buried Odd Fellows in Madisonville, KY. - *Submitted by Randa Lutz Bearden*

SOLOMON S. LYONS

Solomon S. Lyons was born Oct. 26, 1841 in Hancock Co., KY. He was the son of Ephraim Lyons, Jr. and Barshaba Phillips Lyons.

Solomon Lyons married Josephine Whittinghill circa 1863 or 1864. Family tradition states that Solomon and Josephine eloped on horseback, Josephine riding behind Solomon on his horse. Josephine was the daughter of David and Margaret Phillips Whittinghill and was born Aug. 24, 1846 in Hancock or Ohio Co., KY.

'Solomon S. Lyons 1841-1877 and Josephine Whittinghill Lyons 1846-1936.

Solomon and Josephine Whittinghill Lyons lived at Trisler, (near Fordsville), Ohio Co., KY, for several years after their marriage.

They were the parents of six children: Ida J. Lyons, born Nov. 23, 1864, married John William Myers; David Ephraim Lyons, born Dec. 20, 1866 married Molly Lucky; Lucy Frances Lyons, born Nov. 30, 1868; Idra Elmo Lyons, born Mar. 9, 1871, married Amma Fox; Birtie Lyons, born Feb. 18, 1873, married James Adcock; Chester Solomon Lyons, born June 26, 1875, married Mattie Barnhill.

Solomon and Josephine Lyons moved from Ohio County to Hopkins Co., KY circa 1876. Solomon died Mar. 30, 1877 in Madisonville, Hopkins Co., KY and is buried in Pleasant Grove Cemetery at Pleasant Grove Baptist Church on Rose Creek Road near Madisonville.

After Solomon Lyon's death, Josephine went with her children to live with her parents, David and Margaret Whittinghill, on their farm near Manitou in Hopkins Co., KY.

After her children were grown, Josephine Whittinghill Lyons married Apr. 25, 1895 in Hopkins Co., KY, I.T. Osburn. I.T. Osburn was born Oct. 10, 1827, died Mar. 18, 1912 and is buried in Odd Fellows Cemetery in Madisonville.

Josephine W. Lyons Osburn died July 31, 1936, in Madisonville, Hopkins Co., KY. She is buried in Odd Fellows Cemetery on West Center Street in Madisonville, Hopkins Co., KY. - *Compiled by Beverly H. Dockrey*

McALISTER-FULCHER

Maria Gail Fulcher was born Nov. 12, 1949 at the Hopkins County Hospital located in downtown Madisonville, KY. The parents of Gail are Ollie Mae Fulcher and Forest Monroe Fulcher. Ollie Mae was born Dec. 11, 1924 in Christian County. Forest Monroe was born Feb. 8, 1929 in Calloway County. Gail has one sister who was born July 23, 1951; her name is Sharon Darlene Kane.

Gail grew up in Dawson Springs, KY and attended Dawson Springs Independant School. The house Gail and Sharon grew up in is located on Oak Heights in Dawson. When Gail went to school, she had Mr. Phillip Back as her algebra teacher. Mr. Back is now the principal of the high school. Gail also had Mr. Carl Buzzard for biology and Mr. Bill Outland for a high school sponsor. Mr. Buzzard is still at Dawson Springs teaching Biology I in the year 1987. Mr. Outland is now the principal of the elementary school. During Gail's senior year of high school, she was voted "Flirtiest" in the entire senior class. Gail graduated in May of 1967 with a class of 25 students.

In June of 1967, Gail married Earl Wayne McAlister of Princeton, KY. When Wayne and Gail married, Wayne was in the Air Force. They moved to California in July of 1967, where Wayne was stationed at Travis Air Force Base. Wayne and Gail moved to Princeton in December of 1968. Wayne was sent to Vietnam in February of 1969 and returned home in July of 1969.

In May of 1970, Wayne and Gail became the proud of parents of a son whom they named Michael Wayne McAlister. Mike was born at the Caldwell County Memorial Hospital in Princeton, KY. When Mike was two, he became a big brother to a sister, Kimberly DeNae McAlister. Kim was born June 15, 1972 at the Hopkins County Hospital. Both Mike and Kim attend Dawson Springs High School., Mike is a senior, and Kim is a sophomore and a varsity cheerleader.

Wayne works at the Kentucky State Penitentiary as a guard. Gail works at Ottenheimer & Co. The McAlisters now reside on Cadiz Hill Road in Dawson Springs. - *Submitted by Kim McAlister*

McCHESNEY- FIGERT

Patrick Kent McChesney and Denise Lynn Figert were married June 9, 1977 in Sylva, NC.

Patrick was born at Jennie Stuart Hospital in Hopkinsville, KY, the son of Mr. and Mrs. James McChesney. Patrick's father, James, was born Dec. 16, 1913 in Princeton, KY. James married Hazel V. Moorefield on July 26, 1936 at the First Baptist Church in Henderson, KY. Hazel was born Dec. 11, 1916 in Hernadon, KY. James' brothers and sisters are: John who died in 1927, Chesley who died in 1969, Mary Eli who died in 1981, and Ursula Cotton who is still living. Hazel has a brother, Robert (Bob) Moorefield, and a sister Josephine.

Denise was born Jan. 10, 1958 in Mercy Hospital in Quincy, IL, the daughter of Daniel W. Figert and Grace Thomas Figert. Grace was born Sept. 14, 1940 in Marblehead, IL. Daniel was born Dec. 18, 1939 in Wabash, IN.

Patrick attended Dawson Springs High School and after graduation, he attended the University of Kentucky, He also attended Management School at Transylvania in Lexington.

Denise attended a number of schools from Colorado to Illinos. One of her grade schools was the Immacualte Conception in Earlington, KY. She attended junior high at Seminary School and high school at Madisonville North Hopkins in Madisonville, KY. Denise's first job was at a Sav-Rite Drug Store where she ran the jewelry department. Patrick's fist job was taking up tickets at the Strand Theatre.

Patrick's main interest is cooking. However, he flies ultralights, shoots black powder guns and runs the Hickory Pit and Gift Shop.

Denise loves to read and write. She keeps a record of her dreams to see if they are of any relevance to daily life. She also enjoys crafts and loves to watch the snow fall. She doesn't like to be out in snow, but to just watch it fall.

Patrick has a sister, Jan, who was born Aug. 3, 1954 in Madisonville. Jan is married to Patrick Lucas and they have two children, a son Kent and a daughter Caroline.

Denise on the other hand, has many brothers and a sister. Denise is the eldest. In order from eldest to youngest: Danny Eric Figert, Derek Thomas Figert, Mark Andrew Figert, and Jessica Ann Figert.

Patrick has a son, Christian Eric McChesney, who was born Oct. 7, 1970. He has always attended the Dawson Springs Schools. Chris is in Beta Club, plays the sax in the band, has a car, is on the annual staff, and is the manager of the girls basketball team. - *Submitted by Sharon Kaye Cansler*

McCLEARN-DAVENPORT

Edith Mae Davenport was born May 11, 1915, in Crofton and Dexter Alison McClearn was born Feb. 12, 1909, in Barnsley. She graduated from Crofton High School and they were married May 11, 1934.

Wedding picture of Dexter Alison and Edith Mae (Davenport) McClearn

Edith's parents were Maggie Helon Grace (June 1874-October 1947) and John Thomas Davenport (January 1872-November 1946). They owned a farm east of Crofton.

Deck's parents were John Randolph McClean (February 1868-1922) and Cynthia Hulda Clark (February 1879-February 1967). His father supplied props for White City Mines and died at age 54. Deck, being the older boy, went into the mines at age 14 driving a bank mule to haul coal outside. He and his mother raised five younger sisters and one brother. He operated a cutting machine from age 18 until he lost a leg at age 32 in a mine fall. He was miner for 32 years.

Later Deck and Edith owned and operated a grocery store at East Center and Park Avenue from 1949 until 1969. Deck died July 18, 1969.

Edith's grandparents were Lucy Butler (1842-1919) and George Davenport (1840-1930). He operated a broom factory in Crofton and delivered brooms in a wagon from store to store. His parents owned a farm in Tennessee and owned slaves. They gave each child a slave or $1000 when they married. George took money and bought a farm east of Crofton where Edith's father was raised.

Edith's maternal grandparents were David Crocket Grace (April 1843-April 1921) and Jennie Palmer (August 1840-1915). She was a bed and chair patient with locked knees for 35 years. Maggie Grace never saw her mother stand or walk. David's father homesteaded 500 acres east of Crofton where Edith's mother was born and raised. David was a horse soldier in the Civil War, as his father was in the American Revolutionary War.

Edith and Deck had two children. Lynn Gail (Apr. 20, 1935) graduated from Draughn's Business College and married C.B. Utley, Jr., (May 22, 1932) Nov. 26, 1954. He spent two years at Western and 2 years in the Army. They own and operate Happy's Inc. of Madisonville. Their daughter, Lisa Gail (Apr. 15, 1960) has two associate degrees from Western and is in the Trust Department of Kentucky Bank. She married John T. Miller, Jr. (10-3-61) a service technician at Happy's and an employee for United Parcel Service.

John Dexter McClearn (Nov. 14, 1937) graduated from Western and also received his commission in the Army Reserve. Now a Colonel he is Assistant Superintendent of Hopkins County Schools. He and Dorothy Jean Rudd (June 16. 1937), who attended Bowling Green Business Univ. married Mar. 28, 1959. They have two sons: John Keith McClearn (Nov. 11, 1961) graduated from Murray and received his Army Commission. He is a Captain at Fort McClellan, AL. Joseph Kevin McClearn (Feb. 3, 1965) is a junior civil engineering student at Tennessee Technological University. - *Submitted by: Edith McClearn*

McCULLEY-CHAPPELL

Audrey Chappell was born in 1904, in Linton, IN, the twin daughter of William Claude (of Charleston, KY) and Bertha Nixon Chappell. The birth was difficult, and as a consequence Bertha died, as did Audrey's twin. Audrey had one sister, Thula, who later moved to St. Louis, MO and worked as nurse in a hospital there. She continues to reside in St. Louis.

According to her son Bill, Audrey was raised by two aunts, Betty and Bell Nixon. She attended Huckleberry School in Hopkins County and high school in Benton, IL. Audrey returned to Kentucky to attend Western Kentucky University for three years. After graduation, she moved back to Hopkins County to teach. Her first teaching position was at Henson School for the 1924-25 term. She then taught at Leech School from 1925-29, while boarding with Owen and Iva McCulley Laffoon.

Graduation picture of Audrey McCulley, 1926

On Jan. 4, 1930, Audrey married Edney Clifton McCulley, the son of George Baxter and Ollie Todd McCulley. Ed was one of six children, he had four brothers, Joseph A., John Ray, William Isaac and Myron Glen, and one sister, Iva, with whom Audrey had been boarding.

When the school term began in July of 1930, Audrey was teaching again, this time at Hucklebery where she attended school as a child, and continued there through 1932. Audrey taught at Munns School from 1933-1940. During this time, she and Ed had a son, William D. (Bill), born in July 1934 at St. Louis where Audrey's sister lived. Bill lives in Madisonville with his second wife, Ruth, and has five children and seven grandchildren.

Audrey taught school at Suthards from 1940-1943, where she and Ed also owned and operated a grocery store in the early 40's. She then taught at Anton from 1943 until she retired in 1957.

While she taught at Anton, Ed was a meat cutter for Fox's Meat Processing and Market on Hwy. 109 in Dawson Springs, as well as Teague's Shoprite Foods on South Main St. in Madisonville. They bought a home on West Center St. in Madisonville.

After she retired, Audrey missed working with children, so she opened a kindergarten in her home in 1959, and taught through the late '60s. Parents and students, as well as neighbors Ruth Finley Osburn, Mrs. Vic (Mary) Crowe, and Minnie Pressley, all had many nice things to say about Audrey as a teacher and as a friend. Kenneth Roberts of Madisonville attended school at Anton and says she was a sweet, considerate teacher and also a good disciplinarian. Mrs. Harold (Shirley Stearman) Sisk attended school at Suthards under Audrey and her daughters went to Audrey's kindergarten. She had great regard for her.

Audrey had parties for the children, was always interested in her students' activities in and out of school, and she had pictures of her students from all of the schools she taught.

Audrey and Ed also bought and sold antiques. They traveled to sales all over and had a great number of antiques in their home.

The McCulleys lived happily together for forty-eight years. Ed passed away Mar. 17, 1978. Audrey took comfort in their grandchildren and the pleasant memories of their years together. She joined Ed on Feb. 20, 1986. They are buried, as they lived, side by side in Old Suthards Cemetery. - *Submitted by Sharon Johnston*

WILLIE A. McDONALD

My great-grandfather, Willie McDonald, was born Sept. 13, 1885 in Trigg County, KY. At a young age, he moved with his family to the Sardis Community of Lyon County, KY in what is now the Land Between the Lakes area across the river from Eddyville, KY.

Willie attended the Sardis Elementary School where he completed the eighth grade. Also attending the Sardis School was a young lady, Lillian Baker, who was one year younger than Willie. These two were married on May 24, 1908. In 1909 their first child, Herbert, was born in Lyon County, KY.

In 1911, hard times hit the Sardis area, so Willie and his family moved to Truman, AR. Here he found employment with a Singer Sewing Machine Factory. While in Arkansas their second child, Kathleen, was born; however, she lived only six months. In 1917 their third child, Marie, was born. By this time, World War I was in progress, and many families left Truman. Transportation in that day was not conducive to moving all one's possessions over long distances, so they sold all of their possessions and returned to Lyon County, KY in 1919.

Willie farmed in Lyon County until 1924. During this time, in 1921, they had their fourth child, Geneva, who is my grandmother. She is now married to Joseph Eads of Dawson Springs, KY. In 1923, Willie and Lillian's fifth

181

and final child, Cecil, was born in Lyon County.

In 1924 economic conditions again forced Wilie to seek employment elsewhere. This time, he relocated to Hopkins Co., KY where he settled in a mining camp at Dempster, KY. The mining camp was two to three miles east of St. Charles. This move was made in horse-drawn wagons and required overnight camping along the way.

In 1925 he moved his family to St. Charles where he would remain until 1942. His mining career took him from the Dempster mine to the Fox Run mine also located near St. Charles, KY.

Later, the automobile and gravel roads made travel possible for men to commute longer distances to work. This enabled several men from St. Charles to seek employment at the Six Vein mine at Charleston, KY. Willie worked at the Six Vein mine until the early 1930's when the depression found him out of work.

Unable to find employment, he turned to the newly formed W.P.A where he worked until 1935. At this time, he purchased a large truck and began to do general hauling.

In 1942 he moved to Ilsley, Ky where he became a night watchman for Norton Coal Company. He ended his mining career here a few years later.

All the while he was working as a night watchman, he continued his trucking business doing well in ice and coal. By 1947 most of the outlaying area around Ilsley had received electric service, and people had bought refrigerators so he closed the ice business.

In 1948 he purchased a small place in the Menser community, three miles east of Dawson Springs on Highway 62. He became a truck farmer which he continued until his death in 1969, at an age of eighty four years. - *Submitted by Bobby Egbert*

McGAR-HAMMONDS

Howard Curtis McGar was born Oct. 30, 1918, in Earlington, Hopkins Co., KY. He was the son of Bradley Curtis McGar (d. 1931) and Esther Mae (Williams) McGar (d. 1976). They were also the parents of another son, Vernon Lee (Nov. 15, 1913-Oct. 4, 1965). Bradley Curtis McGar was the son of Charlie and Molly Brewer McGar. Esther was the daughter of Hampton and Delia Scott Williams.

On Dec. 17, 1941, Curtis married Hazel Imogene Hammonds. They were married in Hopkinsville, KY, by Brother A. R. Casey.

Imogene was born Mar. 17, 1921, in Earlington, Hopkins Co., KY. She was the daughter of Monroe and Mayona Bell (Hale) Hammonds (see Hammonds-Hale). She has one brother, Garrett Monroe Hammonds (see Hammonds-Vance). Imogene graduated from Earlington High School in 1940.

Curtis entered the service in July 1941. He was stationed at Fort Monmouth, NJ, Camp Crowder, MO, and Camp Maxie, TX. He also was stationed in the Aleutian Islands. He was discharged in January of 1946 with the rank of Staff Sargent. Upon returning home, he went to work for West Kentucky Coal Company and Island Creek Coal Company. He retired from the East Diamond mine in 1980 after 34 1/2 years on the job.

Imogene worked as a clerk at the West Kentucky Coal Company Store, later Island Creek, in Earlington for number of years.

Curtis and Imogene are members of the Earlington United Methodist Church, having served on the official board and also as trustee. They live on Farren Avenue in Earlington. - *Submitted by Debbie Knight Hammonds*

DANIEL McGARY

Col. Hugh McGary came into Kentucky in 1774 or 1775, bringing his family from the Yadkin River area of North Carolina, and accompanying the family of Daniel Boone. He had married Mary Buntin Ray, a widow with several children, in 1768. They had three McGary sons at this time, and settled on a farm in Mercer County, KY near the fort of Harrodsburg. When Indians were on the warpath, the family moved inside the fort for protection.

Daniel McGary was born in North Carolina in 1770; Robert McGary was also born in North Carolina in 1772; William Ray McGary was born in North Carolina in 1774 and they were the small children when they arrived in Kentucky.

Sometime around 1798, Daniel, Robert and William Ray McGary came into Henderson County to an area which would eventually become Hopkins County and settled in what would later become the city of Madisonville. Their mother, Mary Buntin Ray McGary died in 1779, and Dad, Col. Hugh, remarried in 1780 to Catherine Yocum. They may have settled on land that Col. Hugh had received for service in the Revolutionary War.

Daniel McGary married Nancy Berry in 1790, and they are both buried in the Flat Creek Cemetery near a now extinct settlement known as McGary's Station. This station had a post office and was located south of the present Grapevine Community. Nancy Berry McGary died in September 1834, and Daniel died in September 1841. They had four children: Mary, who married Isaac Whyte; Thomas; Tolliver; and Samuel Goode Hopkins McGary.

Upon the formation of Hopkins County, Daniel proposed to give 20 acres off the west side of his farm, to form Madisonville as the county seat. This offer was accepted, and the 20 acres was surveyed as a strip of land one acre wide (the distance between Main St. and Union St.) and 20 acres long extending from the present McCoy Avenue on the south to North Street on the north. The Soloman Silkwood family gave a similar 20 acres on the west side of Main Street. - *Submitted by Edwin B. McGary*

THOMAS EDWIN McGARY

Thomas Edwin McGary was born at the McGary farm in Richland, KY on May 14, 1836 and worked as a farmer and teamster until being attacked by a band of Yankees as he was making a delivery of goods from Ashbyburg to Madisonville. This encouraged him and two of his brothers, Charles C. and Tolliver Young McGary, to go to Princeton, KY, to enlist in the Confederate Army. The three brothers apparently served together and fought in several battles including Shiloh and Brices Cross Roads before being stranded in northeast Mississippi at the end of the war. Thomas Edwin married Mary Elizabeth Smith of Monroe Co., MS on Jan. 2, 1868, and they became the parents of four boys, all of whom were born in Mississippi and all came to Richland, KY, in 1887 when the three stranded McGary families returned to Kentucky.

The sons and their families are as follows:
(1) William Loton McGary, born Feb. 3,

Curtis and Imogene McGar

At the McGary Homeplace, May 1910. Front row l to r: Mary Elizabeth and Thomas Edwin McGary. Back row l to r: William Loton, James Monroe, Charles Thomas and Jess Watkins McGary

1869, married Dec. 11, 1889 to Mary Fears and they had four children: Clarence Edwin, born Oct. 29, 1890; Jimmie Fears McGary born Aug. 17, 1893; Curtis Loton, born July 5, 1907; and Agnes Lee, born Nov. 23, 1902. Clarence Edwin never married. Jimmie F. married Jeff Russell and they had 3 children: Jeff Russell Jr., Mary Agnes and George William.

Curtis and Agnes met tragic deaths. Curtis swallowed a nail and choked to death and Agnes Lee, about 20 years old, was sitting in a porch swing in the family home on South Scott St. in Madisonville during a thunderstorm and lightening struck the swing chains and she was electrocuted.

(2) James Monroe McGary, born Dec. 1, 1870, married Mar. 3, 1908 to Letress Alto Osburn and they had two children: Harry Hosea McGary born Sept. 18, 1909, married Emma Clayton Veazey and they had no children; and Margaret Lucile McGary, born Mar. 9, 1915, married to Harlan Haywood and they had no children.

(3) Charles Thomas McGary, born July 23, 1873, married Dec. 23, 1902 to Lizzie Lynch and they had two children: Edwin Logan McGary, born Jan. 27, 1904, who died in infancy; and Era McGary born Jan. 26, 1905, married to Fred McGuyer and they had no children.

(4) Jesse Watkins McGary, born Feb. 20, 1876, married Sept. 2, 1926 to Sarah Lou Basinger. Jesse W. was the youngest of the Thomas Edwin McGary boys and he remained single and lived with his mother at the Richland homeplace until her death in 1925.

The four McGary boys were all musicians and were very much in demand throughout the area to entertain and play for dances and neighborhood "gatherings". It was said that "Aunt Molly" (Mary Elizabeth, their mother) never cooked breakfast until she checked the boys bedrooms to see how many stray young men had spent the night and would be hungry.

In 1925/1926, Jesse W. sold the farm and elected to semi-retire at 50 years of age. First, though, he took a trip to Mississippi and then to Texas to visit family he hadn't seen in years. However, a visit with "Aunt Lou" Eden (Lucy Clarissa Smith, his mother's sister) would change his plans and in effect change his entire remaining life. "Aunt Lou" could not tolerate the idea of a man leading a peaceful existence alone, so she arranged to have Miss Sarah Lou Basinger, a neighboring young lady (age 33) in for dinner to balance out the dining arrangements. Jesse W. innocently (maybe) fell right in line with the plot and in September 1926 he and Sarah Lou were married near Richland, KY and at ages 50 and 33, started a family, producing 4 boys. Now Sarah Lou Basinger was the daughter of Margaret Louella Taylor Basinger, who was the stepdaughter of Charles C. McGary, who was a brother of Thomas Edwin McGary (see Charles C. McGary section of Tolliver McGary story).

The four sons of Jesse W. and Sarah Lou are as follows: Edwin Burwell (Burl) who married Mary Lanna Kington and had three children: Robbie Lou who married Paul Key; Lisa Ann who married David M. Rumph Jr.; and Daniel Edwin McGary who married Paula Jane Holloman and they have a daughter, Lauren Nichole who was born Apr. 20, 1987.

Jesse Jeptha McGary married Rose Ellen Blair and they have no children.

James Loton McGary who married Carma Newmann and they had one son, James Eric, who met a very untimely death in 1982 in a motorcycle accident at age 18.

Bobby Franklin McGary married Sandra Cates and they have 2 children: Jesse Franklin McGary who married Carolyn Ibis, no children; and Patricia Ellen who married James Ray Wyatt and they have a son, Jake Austin Wyatt.

The McGary family is probably one of the few families that has been in Hopkins County continuously since before its inception. - *Submitted by Edwin B. McGary*

TOLLIVER McGARY

Tolliver McGary was born Dec. 15, 1802, before Hopkins became a county, and married Elizabeth Dorinda Young on Aug. 18, 1825. Tolliver was a giant of a man, being 6'4" tall and weighting 350 pounds. However, he was very athletic, and frequently participated in foot races, jumps, and other competitive activities. He died in 1846 from complications of injuries received in being thrown from a horse. His widow, Elizabeth, died in August 1854 and they were buried in a cemetery near the present intersection of West Center and Seminary Streets, in an area known as "Tabernacle Burying Ground." As Madisonville expanded, these graves were moved and it is believed that Tolliver and Elizabeth are buried in Flat Creek Cemetery near the extinct settlement of McGary Station. During the moving of these graves, it was reported that workmen opened a large grave, which they surmised must be that of Tolliver McGary.

While Tolliver was widely known for his athletic ability, he also became very proficient in other activities. He became the father of 12 children. The 12 children of Tolliver and Elizabeth McGary are as follows:

(1) Nancy L. born May 15, 1826, married William Wilson and they had 7 children: Elizabeth, Nannie (probably Nancy), Sallie, Vitulia, William, Jack and Theo.

(2) William H. born Sept. 29, 1827, married Jennie Arnold and they had 8 children: Annie, Elizabeth, Delia, Jennie, William, Charles, Walter and Frank.

(3) Mary born Aug. 6, 1829, died in infancy.

(4) Charles C. born in 1831. With his brother Thomas Edwin and Tolliver Young McGary, he joined the Army of the Confederacy in the early 1860's and all three apparently "soldiered" together and fought in a number of Civil War battles, including Shiloh and Brices Cross Roads in northeastern Mississippi. They were stranded in this area after hostilities subsided (they didn't cease for years) and all three married local girls in Monroe, Clay and Pontotoc counties in Mississippi. Charles C. married Mary Jane Rodgers Taylor, a young widow whose husband, James R. Taylor, had been killed in the war just prior to the birth of Margaret Louella Taylor on July 13, 1862. Charles C. and his two brothers moved back to Kentucky (Hopkins Co.) in 1887, but Charles returned to Mississippi and remained there until his death. He is buried in Lebanon Cemetery in southern Monroe Co., MS. Although Charles C. and "the widow "Taylor" had two children, William and a daughter (name unknown), the McGary clan would hear more from Margaret Louella Taylor in the Thomas Edwin McGary family story.

Margaret Louella Taylor married Burrel (Burl) Basinger and they had 7 children: Willie, Mary Alena, John W., Sarah Lou, Sophronia, Laura Belle and Burrel A. Sarah Lou Basinger will reappear in the Thomas Edwin McGary Story.

(5) Sarah A. born Feb. 29, 1833, married Al Hewlett and they had 6 children: William, Heck, Buddy, Laura, Emma and Julia.

(6) Elizabeth R. born Sept. 15, 1834, married Thomas McEuen and they had no children. Mr McEuen was an officer in St. Bernard Coal Company and the family was pleased that Elizabeth had married so "well." She was highly respected in and around Earlington where she was known as "Aunt Bet."

In 1886, "Aunt Bet" went to Mississippi to visit her three brothers who had been stranded there since "The War." She was appalled at the poverty that her 3 brothers and their families were enduring, so she returned to Kentucky and made arrangements to bring the three families back to Hopkins Co. In early 1887, the three families gathered at Strong Station in northern Clay Co, MS and boarded an IC Railroad Passenger Train for the trip home to Kentucky.

(7) Thomas Edwin born May 14, 1836 (see Thomas Edwin McGary story).

(8) Paulina A. born Feb. 24, 1838, married Dr. Loton Jones and they had four sons: Loton Jr., William, Charles Edwin and Henry Glover Jones.

(9) Judith D. born Dec. 31, 1839, died at a very young age.

(10) Vitulia born Nov. 23, 1841, died in infancy.

(11) Tolliver Young born Dec. 12, 1843. He was the third of the McGary bothers who were stranded in Mississippi after the Civil War, and he married Sarah Rodgers of Pontotoc Co., MS (she may have been related to Mary Jane Rodgers Taylor who married Charles C. McGary). For Tolliver Young McGary story, see article by Mary Nell Oates.

(12) Franklin W. born Feb. 18, 1846. No information available. - *Submitted by Edwin B. McGary*

T. Y. McGARY

Tolliver Young McGary (b. Dec. 12, 1843; d. May 18, 1899) was one of 12 children of Tolliver McGary (b. Dec. 15, 1802; d. Nov. 26, 1846 and Elizabeth Dorinda Young (b. Oct. 12, 1806, N.C.; d. Aug. 6, 1854, KY.) His paternal grandfather was Daniel McGary, Hopkins County pioneer and eldest son of Hugh McGary, Sr., who came from NC to the Kentucky territory in 1775. His maternal grandfather, Thomas Cadet Young, Jr., a Revolutionary War soldier who came to KY from NC was of English ancestry.

Front row l to r: Mary Elizabeth, Tolliver Young, Sarah Ann, John O. Back row: Finis E., William Tolliver and Charles Clifton. About 1886

T.Y. and brothers Charles C. and Thomas Edwin McGary joined the Confederate States Army, went south, fought in the battle at Shiloh, and were in Mississippi when the Civil War ended in 1865. All three married there.

Tolliver Young McGary married Sarah (Sallie) Ann Rodgers (b. Aug. 12, 1839), Ponotoc Co., MS, where their five children were born. The family moved to Earlington, Hopkins Co., KY, in Nov. 1886. Sarah Ann d. Jan. 10, 1898, and Tolliver Young McGary d. May 18, 1899. They were buried in Oakwood Cemetery, Earlington.

Their children were: Charles Clifton (b. d. Oct 12, 1899) who married (June 1, 1892) Della Brasher; William Tolliver (b. Dec. 16, 1871; d. Mar. 19, 1941) m. Mar. 11, 1891, to Cora Elizabeth Kirkwood; Finis Edwin (b. 1872; d. 1960) who m. Issie B. Stanfield (b. 1886; d. 1936), Mary Elizabeth (b.-; d. Nov. 16, 1894) who m. D. B. Hancock on Dec. 9, 1886; and John Oliver (b. 1880, d. Nov. 17, 1965) m. Johnnie Mae Kirkwood (b. Mar. 11, 1884 d. Dec. 8, 1965). They had been married nearly 66 years. *Source: Family Bibles, Family histories, and other records (See R.O. Kirkwood, W.T. McGary Family. - Submitted by Mary Nell (Whitsell) Oates*

WILLIAM TOLLIVER McGARY

William Tolliver McGary, born Dec. 16, 1871, in Ponotoc Co., MS, was a teenager when he moved to Hopkins Co., KY in 1886, with his parents, Tolliver Young McGary, Hopkins Co. native, and Sarah Ann Rodgers, of Mississippi and settled in Earlington. Other children, all born in Mississippi, were Charles Clifton, Finis Edwin, Mary Elizabeth and John Oliver (See T.Y. McGary family)

W.T. "Tollie" was already a coal miner when, on Mar. 11, 1891, he married Cora Elizabeth Kirkwood, daughter of Rufus Owen Kirkwood and Eusibia Ann Bailey, at her home in Earlington. They lived in the Hecla mining community prior to 1895, then moved to Madisonville, where W.T. worked at Reinecke mine.

For six years (1904-1907 and 1912-1913) W.T. was a member of the Madisonville Police Force. At that time patrolmen walked their beats and carried night sticks. Later he was a foreman at Coil Mine.

The children of Cora E. Kirkwood and W. T.

W.T. McGary family. Seated: William Tolliver and Cora with Robert Owen. Standing: Mattie Mae, Lena and Kathleen. About 1906.

McGary were: Lena (b. Feb. 17, 1892; d. May 10, 1976), Mattie Mae : (b. Jan. 30, 1895; d. Sept. 18, 1968), Kathleen (b. Nov. 5, 1896), Jimmie D. (b. Oct. 6, 1899; d. Jan. 31, 1901), and one son, Robert Owen McGary (b. Feb. 16, 1902).

Lena, a 1912 graduate of Madisonville High School, married John Leslie Greer, of Ohio Co. Both were teachers. Lena taught in Owensboro, KY for 40 years. Their only daughter, Kathleen Elizabeth Greer (b. Nov. 5, 1916, Hopkins Co.,), widow of Jacob William Snyder, Jr., lives in Owensboro.

Mattie Mae, 1914 graduate of MHS, married George Herbert Whitsell. (See G. W. Whitsell). She was an accomplished seamstress and an employee at The Vogue Dress Shop, Madisonville, for 30 years. Their two daughters are: Mary Nell Whitsell (b. July 10, 1916), wife of George Louis Oates, Jr., Madisonville, and Mildred Louise Whitsell (b. Aug. 4, 1919, Webster Co.) widow of (1) Luther Conrad Brewer and (2) Frank Mann Curtis. Mildred Curtis lives in FL.

Kathleen McGary, a teacher for 35 years, lives in Owensboro. She married Robert Earl Hale, also a teacher. He was Daviess Co. Representative to the Kentucky Legislature when he died Apr. 6, 1966. Kathleen was elected to finish his unexpired term.

Robert Owen McGary, a retired engineer, graduated from Owensboro High School and University of Kentucky. He was a co-founder of Buensod-Stacey, Inc., New York City, a supplier of air-conditioning for large industries, and became president of the firm before he retired. He and his wife, Mary Jane Lyle McGary, live in Louisville. Their daughter, Doris Elizabeth McGary (b. June 3, 1932, NJ), married James Trabue Taylor of Elizabethtown, KY, where they reside.

William Tolliver McGary (d. Mar. 19, 1941) and Cora (Kirkwood) McGary (d. June 26, 1916) were members of First Baptist Church, Madisonville. They were buried at Odd Fellows Cemetery. - *Submitted by Mary Nell (Whitsell) Oates*

Source: Family Bibles, Family History, Other documents (See R.O. Kirkwood) (See Oates-Whitsell)

McGAW-WILLETT

George Edwin McGaw, the son of William Patten McGaw and Dora Ann James was born on Nov. 9, 1905, near Lisman, Webster Co., KY. At St. Peter's in Waverly, KY, on Apr. 21, 1945 George Edwin McGaw married Miss Mildred Martin Willett, the daughter of Boyd Aubrey Willett and Cala Harrison Martin. Mildred was born Jan. 5, 1906, on Willett-Highland Creek farm three miles northeast of Waverly, KY. They were residing in Madisonville, at the time of Edwin's death on July 19, 1985.

Edwin and Mildred McGaw, January 5, 1978.

Edwin received his formal education in Webster County and held several certificates in coal mining management.

Mildred was a high-school graduate of St. Vincent Academy in Union County, KY and was graduated from Western KY with a Bachelor of Arts Degree.

She was an elementary school teacher for forty-seven years, including nineteen years in Union County; twenty-four years in Hopkins County; four years in other systems (including the government Indian Service in New Mexico) and seven years as substitute teacher in Hopkins County. At the time of her retirement in 1973, she had been a teacher at West Broadway School for fifteen years.

The McGaws moved from Webster County to Madisonville in 1950 when Edwin was employed as superintendent for five years of the new Atkinson Mine of the West Kentucky Coal Company. Mildred was employed by the Hopkins County School System as a sixth-grade teacher at Seminary School. That same year they built the first residence in Country Club Heights Subdivision on Wesco Drive.

Edwin had held several positions with the Company until 1955 when he was promoted to general superintendent of mines of West Kentucky Coal Company and its subsidiary, Nashville Coal Company, Inc. When Island Creek Coal Company got controlling interest of West Kentucky Coal Co., he was made safety director.

At the time of his final retirement in 1970, he had forty-seven years of experience in the coal mining industry, including seven years as mine inspector for the Department of Mines and Minerals for the Commonwealth of Kentucky.

Their two children are Deborah Ann McGaw, born Sept. 17, 1952, married Daniel Wayne Smith at Immaculate Conception

Church in Earlington, KY on July 14, 1972; Judy Ann McGaw born June 3, 1953, married Archie Lewis Coburn June 18, 1972 at Christ the King Church in Madisonville.

Both daughters were high-school graduates of Madisonville North Hopkins High School. Deborah holds and Associate of Arts Degree from Madisonville Community College; Judy has an Associate of Arts Degree from Henderson Community College.

Deborah and Daniel Smith have two children, Brian Edwin Smith born Feb. 28, 1974 and Leslie Camille Smith born Dec. 13, 1977.

Judy and Archie Coburn have two children, Andrew Wayne Coburn born Mar. 14, 1973 and Keri Lynn Coburn born Jan. 28, 1976.

Edwin was affiliated with the Western Kentucky Mining Institute - past president Mine Inspectors Institute of America; National Mine Rescue Association, Post #2 and #4. He received a medal of honor, the highest honor in bituminous coal mining from Joseph A. Holmes Safety Association, Washington, D.C. and an honorary title as Kentucky Colonel from Governor Bert Combs.

Mildred is a member of the Delta Kappa Gamma Society, Business and Professional Womens Club, Hopkins County Retired Teachers Association, Kentucky Retired Teachers Association and the Captain Ashby Chapter of the National Society of the Daughters of the American Revolution.

She was a charter member and past president of Hill 'n' Dale Garden Club and an active member for twenty-nine years.

Mildred and Edwin were members of the Immaculate Conception Church in Earlington, KY.

They owned Mildred's family farm in Union county, northeast of Waverly, KY. However, they were residing at their home on Wesco Drive, Madisonville. - *Submitted by Mildred W. McGaw*

McGREGOR

Between 1807 and 1809 William McGregor Sr., born ca. 1772, who came from Scotland at age nine with his mother Molly to Charleston, SC, came to Hopkins Co. to find land to settle on. He settled around "Old Lick Creek" near Charleston. He and son Samuel gave a section of the land for the church to be built on. About 1811, he returned to Charleston for his family to remove to Hopkins Co. between 1812 and 1818. He joined the church ca. 1826, died 1833. He and a man on the street got into an argument. He went to court and was fined $1.00 for saying a "swear" word. He is probably buried at Old Lick Creek. His wife was believed to be Amelia Clark. Their children were: John (1796-1863); Samuel (1798-1851); William Jr. (1799-1889); James (1804-1865); Moses (1805-1860); Levi (born ca. 1807); Mary (Polly) (1809-1865) and Dison (1812-1888).

John married in 1818 Mary Alice Franklin (1800-1863). Their children: Filander; William; Mary; John; James; Eddy and Martha. John married 2nd Lucinda Creekmur.

Samuel married in 1820 Elizabeth Jordan (1804-1882) daughter of Woodruff Jones. Children: Viana; Millie; Mollie; Paulina; Rebecca; Samuel Jr.; William; Martha and John.

William married 1820 Elizabeth Waid (1802-1881). Children: Rebecca; William C.; James; Levi Bartlett; Serilda; Dyson; Mary; Henly Preston; Ursula and Permelia. William Jr. was moderator of the Primitive Baptist Church. His son, Dyson Addison was SGT. in Co. "A" 15th KY Vol. Cavalry. Dyson married Frances Stallings and died 1861. Henly Preston was Private in Co. "A", same as Dyson Adison. He returned to Benton, KY with wife Vivian and moved to Glenn Allen, MO. Dyson was age 54 when he applied for a pension and Henly received a pension until his death in 1913. They both were grandsons of William McGregor Sr.

James married Elizabeth Chappell (1808-1860). Children: Shadrach; Alfred; Wylie; Elizabeth; James Jr.; Margaret; Rebecca (in 1860 married William Goodaker who joined Co. "C" 48th Mounted Inf., got sick and died 23 Nov.. 1863, leaving one son William Bayless born 1861); John; Ava; Barnett; Bailey and Lydia. James Jr. grandson of William McGregor Sr., was a Private in Co. "C" 48th Ky. Vol. Mounted Inf. He went home to wife, Nancy, where they lived in Dalton.

Moses married in 1826 Sarah Hankins (1806-?) daughter of William Hankins. Children: Sarah; John; William; Moses Jr.; Joel; Nancy and David.

Mary (Polly) married in 1827 William Preston Fox (1807-1878) son of Jeremiah Fox. Children: Adison; Mary; Martha; John; William; Sarah and Rosha.

Dison married 1832 Margaret Goodaker (1816-1878) daughter of Johnny Goodaker and Filander Franklin. Children: Mary; William; Elizabeth; John; Filander; James; Barney; Paten; Serilda; Noah; Martha and Reson Titus. Son John was a Private in Co. "A" 15th Reg. KY Cavalry. He returned home to Princeton, KY where his wife Mary and son Loton lived. Both John and Mary died before the pension act was passed. John was the grandson of William Sr. - *Submitted by Ora B. Locker and Howard McGregor*

McGREGOR-GRAHAM

William Clark McGregor and Nancy Doylene Graham were married Mar. 17, 1984, in Summersville Baptist Church, Summersville, KY.

Doylene and William McGregor

Doylene is the youngest daughter of Doyle Graham and Vivian Lucille Bale Graham of Route 3, Greensburg, KY. Doyle and Lucille Graham are retired dairy farmers having lived in Green County all of their lives.

Doylene completed high school, third in her class, at Green County High in 1976, being active in the band there. While a student at the University of Kentucky, Lexington, she worked as a Research Animal Care Technician, doing cardiovascular research at the Wenner-Gren Research Laboratory. She graduated from the University of Kentucky and Auburn School of Veterinary Medicine, Auburn, AL. She did her preceptorship at the Veterinary Clinic in Pryor, OK.

William Clark McGregor, born Nov. 26, 1958 in Hopkins Co., KY, is the youngest son of Paul Clark McGregor and Mary Iretta Teague McGregor. (See McGREGOR- TEAGUE). He attended Nortonville Elementary School, and South Hopkins High School, being active in the Beta Club. He graduated from the University of Kentucky in 1980, receiving a Civil Engineering Degree with an option in Mining and Hydraulics. He was a member of Chi Epsilon, National Civil Engineering Honor Society, being an officer in the Kentucky Chapter in 1979-1980.

He worked as a Civil-Mining Engineer for Wiley Engineering in Farmington, NM, for a time before moving to Welch, OK, where he worked for Ranchers Coal, Inc., in the same capacity, later becoming Vice President of the company.

William and Doylene presently live in Bernice, OK, where Wm. is employed as a Civil-Mining Engineer for Trans-Western Coal Co., in Claremore, OK.

Doylene is co-owner, operator of Grove Small Animal Hospital, Grove, OK.

They attend church at First Baptist Church in Grove, OK. - *Submitted by Iretta McGregor*

McGREGOR-HOFFMAN

James Rhett McGregor and Roberta Virginia Hoffman were married on Oct. 6, 1973 at Highview Baptist Church, Louisville, KY.

The Rhett McGregor family, Kristen, Jayson, Roberta and Rhett

Roberta is the daughter of the late William Carroll Hoffman of Ansted, WV and Katheran Virginia Ferguson Hoffman of Ansted, WV. William Hoffman was a retired electrician before his death in January 1985. Katheran, "Kat," is a retired elementary school teacher, having taught in the Fayette County School System for a number of years. She is an active member of the Ansted Baptist Church and is an excellent golfer. She has won numerous trophies including the club championship at the Hawksnest Golf Club.

Roberta attended elementary and high school in Ansted, West VA. She graduated from the West Virginia School of Dentistry, Morgantown, West VA. After graduating she taught in the School in Dentistry at West Virginia University and later was in private practice in Beckley and Ansted, W. VA.

James Rhett McGregor born July 1, 1947, in Hopkins Co.. Ky is the oldest son of Paul and Iretta McGregor. (See McGREGOR-TEAGUE). He completed grade school at St. Charles, having attended Nortonville Grade School in grades 1 thru 7. He also graduated from South Hopkins High School in 1965 and entered the University of Kentucky, Lexington, KY and studied Civil Engineering. While at the University of Kentucky, Rhett was an active member of the Phi Kappa Tau Fraternity. He received a scholarship from the American Institute of Mining Engineers as he graduated with a civil engineering degree in 1970. Rhett became a Registered Professional Engineer in 1974 while living in Colorado where he worked for Consolidation Coal Company.

After Rhett and Roberta married they moved to Denver, CO where Rhett worked in the mining industry on projects in Utah, CO and Wyoming. Roberta was on the faculty of the University of Colorado School of Dentistry as an Associate Professor. In 1980 Rhett and Roberta moved to Cumberland, MD where Rhett was a Project Manager for AMCA Resources and Roberta was an Associate Clinical Professor at West Virginia University Dental School. In 1981 they moved to Louisville, KY, and in 1984 they moved to Cincinnati, OH. Presently, Rhett is employed as Senior Product Engineer for Price Brothers Company.

Rhett and Roberta have two children, Kristen Virginia and Jayson Rhett. Kristen is a senior honor student at Princeton High School and Jayson is in the seventh grade at Princeton Junior High. Kristen is a member of the Student Council, the drill team, the Academic Challenge team and she enjoys playing the piano. Jayson participates in basketball, soccer, golf and tennis, and he is also an excellent student.- *Submitted by Iretta McGregor*

McGREGOR-McGREGOR

As far back as 1215 the MacGregor Clan can be found in Glen Orchy of Scotland. In the early 1800's the records show many of them now called McGregor in several Kentucky counties including Hopkins.

William Bunyon McGregor and Mona McGregor with sister, Lou

Mona Florence McGregor was born June 15, 1882 in Dalton Community, the daughter of James McGregor and Nancy Jane Utley. One of 12 children, only 8 reached adulthood.

In December 1908, Mona married William Bunyon McGregor. William was born Apr. 19, 1876 in the St. Charles Community, the son of Dyson Asidon McGregor and Mary Elizabeth Teague. He was the only son and the youngest of 5 children and better known as Bunyon. The family joke Bunyon and Mona always told was that they were 15th cousins. Both could proudly say each father, the two elder McGregors, was Civil War Veteran of the Union Army. Also as far back as either could remember their families were staunch Primitive Baptist (see McGregor Book) and children are still of that faith.

With little formal education Bunyon began as farmer, becoming well-known as a hard worker. He was self-taught and learned quickly. A test driller for a local coal company, a business man an an honest trader, he also became known as a user or loaner for neighbors and friends. A judge of good character, his daughter proudly remembers her father as being able to help others while bettering himself without much loss financially. Bunyon died in August of 1968.

Bunyon and Mona's children: Nell Jean married Julian Teague and died at the age of 27 leaving no children; Paul Clark married Mary Iretta Teague (see their story); Nana Lou married James S. Powell and had two children. Mona and Bunyon had five grandchildren and nine great grandchildren.

Mona enjoyed knitting. Her specialty was socks with a turned heel and toe. Her children often wore them as houseslippers. A petite but strong little lady, she was in her late 50's when she took up horseback riding for the second time and became quite the old-fashioned way, side saddle! In her 90's, she was made a Kentucky Colonel. A day before she was 96, she had major surgery and the family feared for her life. She bounced back dramatically.

At the age of 97, Mona's son took her on a month vacation, touring the western states. At a motel indoor swimming pool, she decided she would like to try it. When asked by her daughter after she returned home what sort of swimsuit she wore, Mona replied "Why my petticoat, of course!" Not to be stopped by age, she visited the World's Fair in Tennessee at the age of 100.

Her daughter visited England and found in London the one gift Mona most desired, a piece of the McGregor Clan Plaid. It was made into a lovely scarf. The colors, the large part being a fire engine red, the smaller strip of double forest green and a tiny bit of white to form the plaid pattern.

Doctors from U.K. Medical Center in Lexington have visited Mona and have financed her trip to U.K. for tests on her longevity. She laughing told her family she was put in a box and banged on.

Since her move from her daughters home in Madisonville to Brookfield Manor in Hopkinsville two years ago, she has become a legend. Nearing her 106th birthday, Mona is still alert. Impaired by failing eyesight and hearing, she still can walk about her room when assisted.

Nana Lou, her daughter, reports "Mother doesn't live in the past as most older do, but lives her life one day at time." (See "Hopkins County Centenarians". - *Submitted by Dorothy Miller Shoulders*

McGREGOR-TEAGUE

Paul Clark McGregor and Mary Iretta Teague were married May 12, 1946 at Earlington Baptist Church.

The Paul McGregor family - 1964

They have lived on the farm near Daniel Boone in Hopkins County since that time. The farm is known as the "Jack Earle" (John Orville Earle) farm and their home is located across the road from the site of the log house of John Orville Earle. Iretta's great grandfather, John Orville Earle was the fourth child of Edward Hampton Earle who came to Kentucky from South Carolina in 1800.

Paul was born Nov. 1, 1912 at St. Charles, KY. He is the son of William Bunyan McGregor (b 1876, d 1968) and Mona Florence (McGregor) McGregor. Mona McGregor is still living and was 105 years old June 15, 1987.

Mr. and Mrs. Bunyan McGregor were both born in Hopkins County and lived in the St. Charles area all of their married life, with the exception of two years when they lived in Greenville, KY.

Paul graduated from Dawson Springs High School and Western Kentucky State University, Bowling Green, KY. He is a veteran of World War II, serving in the VIII Corps in the European Theatre of Operations. He is a retired school teacher and farmer and was elected a member of the Hopkins County Board of Education in 1964.

Iretta was born Aug. 30, 1926, near St. Charles, KY. She is the daughter of William Kenneth Teague (see his story) (b. 1896-d 1970) and Cora Lee Denton Teague (b 1896-d 1977). After attending grade school at Good Hope and St. Charles, she finished high school at Nortonville and attended Western Kentucky University at Bowling Green, KY.

Paul and Iretta have three children: James Rhett, born July 1, 1947; Paula Sue, born Jan. 28, 1950, and William Clark born Nov. 26, 1958.

Paul and Iretta are thankful that God has blessed them to live in America and to have three children and their families. They feel that to love God supremely, home, family and friends are life's greatest blessings. - *Submitted by Iretta McGregor*

McGUYER-LANTAFF

Ethel Mae Lantaff and Fred Clifton McGuyer were married on June 25, 1947, in Hopkinsville, KY. Fred was previously married to Era McGary from July 12, 1932, until her death on Jan. 30, 1946.

Ethel and Fred McGuyer on their 25th wedding anniversary - 1972

Ethel is the oldest child of George James Lantaff of Beulah and Greek (Furgerson) Lantaff of the Richland area. George was the son of John Edward Lantaff and Sarah Elizabeth "Betty" (Dockery) Lantaff. He was a farmer and coal miner most of his life, but also taught school one year and ran a small grocery on Lake St. for a while. Greek was the daughter of William Anderson Furgerson and Rebecca Jane (Clark) Furgerson. George and Greek were married on Jan. 28, 1911 in Richland.

Ethel was born on Jan. 28, 1913. When she was six, her family moved from western Hopkins County to Madisonville. She attended West Broadway and Waddill Ave elementary schools and graduated from Madisonville High School on Seminary St. in 1931. Between 1932 and 1945 she worked as a clerk-typist in the following government offices: Federal Emergency Relief Administration P.W.A., W.P.A. and Post Engineer Office-War Dept. at Camp Breckinridge, KY. Her last employment was for the Solid Fuels Administration from June 16, 1945 until Apr. 30, 1947. After marrying in 1947, she devoted her time to home, family and church work. She and Fred joined St. Mary's Episcopal Church in 1955. Here Ethel sang in the choir for about 25 years, held a number of offices in the Church women, lead a prayer group and was editor of "The Red Doors" newsletter. She also was the first woman at St. Mary's to serve on the vestry.

Fred McGuyer is the oldest son of William Rufus McGuyer and Georgia Geneva (Hibbs) McGuyer. Rufus was farmer born in the Pleasant View area of Hopkins County. He was the son of John A. McGuyer and Irena Hoyt (Kirkwood) McGuyer. Georgia was the daughter of William F. "Billy" Hibbs and Alice Florence (Webb) Hibbs of the Nebo area.

Fred was born on Feb. 16, 1904, in a log house across the road from Circle City Mines. He attended school at Smyrna, a one-room school near Circle City, 2 miles south of Nebo. He began working in the coal mines at 13, during the months when school was not in session. He worked for a number of coal mines in Hopkins County (a total of 36 years altogether). He also operated several small mines. a trucking business and a salvage business with Harlan Haywood on Caroline St. Then in 1954, he went into business with James W. "Jake" Gentry on North 41 between Hanson and Madisonville. It was called M & G Salvage and evolved into an automotive generator and starter business that moved to S. main St. in 1966. The partnership dissolved in 1972 when Fred retired.

Fred and Ethel McGuyer have two daughters: Pamela Joan (McGuyer) Furgerson, born Nov. 27, 1949 and Roberta Gail (McGuyer) Brinkley born June 27, 1951. Pamela married Robert E. Furgerson on Mar. 15, 1969 and they have one child, Jeremy David, born Jan. 14, 1977. Roberta married Joseph Michael Brinkley on Dec. 30, 1972, and they have one child, Cynthia Carole born July 27, 1975. - *Submitted by: Roberta Brinkley*

JOHN A. McGUYER

John A. McGuyer (born Jan. 1, 1837 near Wortrace, TN) was the first McGuyer (McGuire) in Hopkins County. He was the grandson of Revolutionary War veteran William McGuire and the son of John William McGuyer and Mary Fabra (Ditto) McGuer. His family owned a large farm in Beford Co., TN. His father died in 1837, on his way back to Tennessee after service in the Texas Revolution. His mother also died when he was infant, leaving him to be raised by an older sister, Elizabeth "Betsey" (McGuyer) Pruitte. His other brothers and sisters were: Cynthia (McGuyer) Mullins, Ben McGuyer (killed in the Civil War), Fabra (McGuyer) Snellings, Sarah E. (McGuyer) Arnold and William D. McGuyer (desendants in Muhlenberg Co., KY and in Missouri and Illinois).

McGuyer Homeplace on Gentry Lane

John A. McGuyer left Tennessee and traveled around through Kentucky, Illinois and Missouri. He married Geneva Irena Hoyt Kirkwood (July 25, 1861 in Hopkins Co.) who was the daughter of Jefferson W. Kirkwood and Ovella Florella (O'Bryan) Kirkwood, both of whom were members of pioneer families of Hopkins County. John A. was a farmer and the father of eight children. Four children were born in Hopkins Co., Benjamin Wayne McGuyer (born Aug. 2, 1862), who married Laura Moore in Missouri; Jennie McGuyer (born 1867), who married Henry Anderson; William Rufus McGuyer (born 1872), who married William D. Coil. Three children were born in Illinois: Ella Mae McGuyer (born Sept. 18, 1875) who married James W. Hooker; Thomas T. McGuyer (born 1876 who married Eula Whitfield; and Cora McGuyer (born Feb. 16, 1879) who married E. H. Sisk. The eighth child, Mary E. McGuyer, was born Sept. 12, 1880 in Missouri, but died there as a child. John A. and his family moved back to Hopkins Co. from Missouri and lived in the Pleasant View area. He died on Feb. 6, 1887 and his wife on Nov. 6, 1901. Both were buried in Pleasant View Cemetery.

William Rufus McGuyer, the third child of John A. McGuyer, was married (Jan. 11, 1902) to Georgia Geneva Hibbs, daughter of W. F. "Billy" Hibbs and Alice Florence (Webb) Hibbs of Hopkins County. They lived in Circle City near Coiltown and farmed in this area of Hopkins County until 1919 when they moved to a farm near Madisonville with a two-story home at the end of what is now called Gentry Lane. They lived here until the house burned on Dec. 9, 1938. Seven children were born in Cicle City: John William McGuyer (born 1902, died in infancy), Fred Clifton McGuyer (born Feb. 16, 1904), Thomas Cornelious McGuyer (born Feb. 1, 1907), Geneva Alyne (McGuyer) Rogers (born Feb. 4, 1910), Pearl Rudell McGuyer (born Aug. 7, 1912), Fannye Mae (McGuyer) Blakely (born Feb. 7, 1915), and Willie Kathryn (McGuyer) Taylor (born Oct. 26, 1917). Their eighth child, James Sory McGuyer, was born Mar. 31, 1925 in Madisonville. William Rufus McGuyer died on Oct. 4, 1942 and his wife on Apr. 17, 1958. They are buried in Grapevine Cemetery. Five children survive in 1987: Fred, Fannye and James live in Madisonville, Rudell lives in Eldorado, IL and Alyne lives in Muskogee, OK. - *Submitted by Roberta Brinkley*

BENJAMIN C. McKINSEY

Benjamin Cotton McKinsey was born in Christian Co., KY July 22, 1859 son of Wm. C. McKinsey (1818-1906) and Alicy Hunter McKinsey (1830-1901) and grandson of James McKinsey, all of Christian County. Benjamin married Mary Catherine Wilson (1856-1931), of Hopkins Co. in 1877. By 1906 they had sold all of the 300 acres left to them by Wm. C. McKinsey, and in 1907 Benjamin purchased farmland north of Madisonville, near what is now Hwy. 1069. Of the 8 children born to this couple, only five survived to adulthood. They were; (1) William Vego (1879-1959), (2) Alwin Claude (1883-1946), (3) Louis Ivan (1885-1955) (4) Shellie Estill McKinsey (1899 -). In 1922 Shellie, a teacher in Hopkins Co. married Aubrey D. Walker (1893-1955) a farmer in the Vandetta area. Shellie was always active in the Methodist Church in Madisonville and for many years taught the Susannah Wesley class. Shellie and Aubrey had three children; Nell Rose Walker (Tapscott) now living in Princeton, KY, Carroll Walker who was killed in an auto accident in 1955, and A. Calvin Walker who married Evelyn Hoskins of Hopkins Co. in 1958. Mr. and Mrs. Calvin Walker live in Madisonville, while their two daughters, Vicki

R. Eshelman and Suzy D. Walker live in Newark, OH and Indianapolis, IN respectively.

Mary Catherine Wilson McKinsey and Benjamin Cotton McKinsey

The second son of Benjamin C. McKinsey was Benjamin Browder McKinsey (1881-1942) born in Christian Co. In 1907, Browder married Mary Ada Jagoe (1879-1960) daughter of Ephriam B. Jagoe and Corella Hicklin Jagoe. From 1910 to 1931, Browder was a "miller"; working first for the Madisonville Milling Co. then Thompson and Hankins Milling Co. From 1931, until his death in 1942, he was the superintendent of greens at the Madisonville Country Club. Browder and Ada had two children; Benjamin Brank McKinsey (1909-1962) and Mary Carnell McKinsey (1912 -) In 1925, Brank entered service with the Madisonville Fire Dept. Nine years later he married Cleone Clayton (b 1913), In 1936, he was made Assistant Fire Chief under B. K. Toombs. Their only child, C. Brank McKinsey, was born in 1937, and is currently the owner of The House of McKinsey catering in Madisonville. In 1936 Brank, Sr. was promoted Fire Chief. He suffered a fatal heart attack, fighting a fire in 1962. Carnell graduated from Madisonville HS in 1930 and began work as a secretary for E. M. Vaught of the Miller Ice Cream Co. in Madisonville. In 1939 she married Hollis W. Wortham (1904-1965) who had begun working for the Illinois Central RR in 1920. At the time of his death he was a Trainmaster of the Western KY Division. Hollis and Carnell had two children; Tom H. Wortham (b 1943) and Cochran (b.1948 -) from Ashland, KY. They have three sons: Michael David (1970 -). Chad Cochran (1972 -); and Jeffrey Hollis (1978 -). David is presently a teacher in the city school system in Elizabethtown, KY. - Submitted by Tom Wortham

McLEAN

William James McLean was born in Hopkins County on May 15, 1877. He married Addie May Bailey on Nov. 16, 1898. Addie was born on May 9, 1880. Her homestead still stands near Manitou, KY. They were parents of five girls: Anna May, born Nov. 2, 1899; Jessie Pearl, born Mar. 7, 1902; Reesie Lee, born Oct. 27, 1905; Dora Agnes born Aug. 6, 1907; and Elizabeth, born Aug. 23, 1911.

The McLean's were the writer's husband's grandparents and she and her husband are the third generation to reside in the Gordon Ave. home. The original structure burned on Dec. 24, 1925. Mr. McLean was a carpenter and rebuilt the home as it now stands. Mr. McLean was a carpenter and rebuilt the home as it now stands. Mr. McLean's mother was a Yates from Manitou, KY, who came originally from Virginia. His grandfather served in the Revolutionary War and then became an ordained minister. Mr. McLean's brothers were Elvy, Robert, Jessy and Wallace. He had one sister whose name was Lela.

Painting of home on Gordon Ave

Addie McLean, who had the good looks of the Irish, had three sisters, Inez, Pearl and Maude. Addie was a homemaker of the finest kind and departed this earth Feb. 8, 1969 four years after her husband who died Apr. 21, 1965. Their oldest daughter, Anna Mae, married Artie Elmo Lutz on June 2, 1917. They lived in Earlington, Ky and had two children: Nevoline Banks Lutz born Feb. 17, 1918 and Artie Elmo Lutz, Jr. born Oct. 14, 1923.

Nevoline married Jack Bennett on Dec. 25, 1941. Their children are: Jackie born June 24, 1946; and David born June 15, 1956 and died October of that same year. Jackie married David Bossuet and they have tow children, Michelle and Scott.

Artie Elmo Lutz Jr. served his country for thirty years in the United States Navy earning many medals including the Presidential Unit Citation for Bravery during the sinking of the Yorktown by the Japanese during World WW II. He married Joyce Ann South on July 17, 1956.

Their children are: Steve born May 15, 1957; Margaret, born Nov. 4, 1958; Judy, born Dec. 23, 1959; James born Feb. 5, 1962; and Jason, born Feb. 26, 1974. Margaret married James R. Brown and they have two children, Christopher and Lauren. Judy has one daughter, Delia Beth Rivers. James serves his county in the United States Marine Corps, currently stationed in Okinawa, Japan. Steve resides in Cookesville, TN, and works for the state as Community Planner.

The McLean's second daughter, Jessie Pearl, worked for forty years as legal secretary and bookkeeper for the firm of Gordon, Gordon, and Morrow. She did not marry and lived her entire life at the Gordon Ave. address. Miss McLean died in September of 1971.

Reesie Lee McLean died on Apr. 13, 1926 and Dora Agnes McLean died on Feb. 12, 1931, both from complications of respiratory ailments.

Elizabeth McLean married Henry Gatlin of the Grapevine section and they had three children: William Douglas, born Feb. 25, 1938; James Leonard born Apr. 19, 1942; and Richard Henry, born June 7, 1948. William married Alice Mullinix and they had three children; Douglas, Freda and Leigh Ann. William was injured in an accident and died in 1966. James married Nellie Coker and they have two children, James II and Michelle. Richard married Jean Cates and they have two children, Ricky and Jeff.

The painting of the Gordon Avenue home appearing with this article was done by Megan Starke of Madisonville. - Submitted by:Joyce A. Lutz.

McLEMORE

Thomas and Cora McLemore have been residents of Madisonville, KY for many years now. On the clear, cold night of Jan. 30, 1937, Cora Evelyn Kirkwood married Thomas McLemore in the little town of Sebree, KY, in nearby Webster County. To this union, three children were born. The first of the three children to be brought into this world was Jerry McLemore, who is presently a resident of Atlanta, GA. Jerry was born on Feb. 4, 1941 and married Miss Betty Potts, also of Atlanta, GA. The second of the three children is Mrs. Pamela Ann Butler, who presently resides in Dawson Springs, KY. Pamela was born on Apr. 1, 1948. Pamela is not married at this time. The third and last child is Mrs. Cherrie Christian, who resides in Madisonville, KY. Cherrie was born on Sept. 28, 1954 and is married to George Christian, also of Madisonville.

Thomas and Cora are also the proud grandparents of six wonderful grandchildren - Jeff McLemore, John McLemore, William Latham, Kristal Moore, Susan McLemore and David Christian.

Cora McLemore was born on Oct. 31, 1915 in the town of Townley, AL, in Walker County. Thomas McLemore was born on June 24, 1913, in Hopkins County, at 342 West Lake Street, where this couple presently resides.

Thomas was a self-employed painter and carpenter, who also enjoys fishing as a hobby. Cora is presently an employee of Ligon Nationwide for sixteen years. She enjoys working with her flowers in her spare time.

I am very proud to have Thomas and Cora McLemore as grandparents. - Submitted by Willie Latham

McLEOD

John McLeod of Scotland from Lewis Clan was the father of Richard and Edgar McLeod (Dec. 27, 1831-Aug. 9, 1906), of Spotsylvania Co., VA. Richard married Maria S. Day on Nov. 7, 1843. On Jan. 10, 1854, Edgar married Margaret Lewis Morse (July 7, 1834-Apr. 1, 1887) at Jerdone Castle, Louisa Co., VA. The Rev. G.M. Bagby officiated. Jerdone Castle was the home of Gen. William Coleman where he raised his niece who was orphaned at an early age. Margaret was a first cousin of Samuel F. B. Morse, inventor of the telegraph.

The children of Margaret and Edgar McLeod, born in Spotsylvania Co., VA were: Ida Lewis (Sept. 8, 1855-Apr. 4, 1895), Edward

Glanville (Nov. 2, 1856-Dec. 6, 1937); and Mary Field (Sept. 16, 1861-Oct. 18, 1861)

During the Civil War, Edgar sold shoes to the Confederate Army. After the conclusion of the Civil War, he moved his family to Christian Co., KY where he bought land to farm. It was here Margaret gave birth to their fourth child, William Coleman McLeod on July 29, 1869. He died in Hopkins Co. Jan. 29, 1938.

After retiring from farming, Edgar moved his family to Earlington, KY. It was here in 1877 that Edward Glanville founded The McLeod Store beginning his life-long career in retailing. He married Kate Dulin and they had two daughter, Lana Dulin McLeod, who married Clarence Nisbet and Jane McLeod who married Hoty H. Coil. Their child, Kate Coil Ballard was the only grandchild of Edward Glanville McLeod. When Edward joined his in-laws in the retailing business in Madisonville they formed the Dulin-McLeod Store on South Main St. When they split their business interest, Edward formed a partnership with his brother William Coleman McLeod and they moved the new McLeod Store to West Center St. at the northwest corner of Seminary St. In The early years of the twentieth century, Edward purchased more property on South Main St. across from the courthouse and Madisonville's largest general retail store moved to South Main. The McLeod Store was the first to introduce a self-service grocery store to Hopkins Co. with its Piggly Wiggly self-service system.

William Coleman McLeod continued to pursue his interest in real estate which would lead him to become one of the largest individual land owners in Hopkins Co. He married, on Mar. 8, 1916, Pearl Carmack (Apr. 11, 1884-Apr. 3, 1970). They had two children, Margaret Marie born, Mar. 18, 1917 and William Edward (Jan. 22, 1919- Feb. 4, 1961)

William Edward married Dorothy Laffoon and they were the parents of: Margaret Ann born Oct. 9, 1949 and Elisabeth Kay, born Jan. 20, 1953.

Margaret McLeod married William Strauther Winstead (Sept. 16, 1902-Aug. 10, 1976) of Madisonville, KY, on Nov. 4, 1935. For many years Strauther owned and operated the Acme Packaging Company, located on McLeod Lane. The children of Margaret and Strauther:

Charles William born Sept. 16, 1936, married Betty Burnett on Oct. 5, 1956. Children: Charles Michael, born Sept. 20, 1957; Robert Lynn, born Apr. 27, 1959, Katherine Ann, born Apr. 3, 1964 and Carolyn Elisabeth born May 16, 1966.

Elisabeth Ann born Oct. 18, 1937, married Willis N. Dever on Dec. 23, 1956. Children: Rhea Elisabeth born Sept. 24, 1958, and Mark Edward born Aug. 28, 1960.

Robert Edward born Feb. 23, 1943, married Marlyne Hogue on Sept. 15, 1963. Children: Mariann Marie born Dec. 30, 1965, Susan Elisabeth born Nov. 11, 1967, Robert Edward II born Apr. 18, 1973 and John Michael born Sept. 7, 1978.

Richard McLeod Winstead born Dec. 9, 1946, married Beverly Gayle Easterly on July 24, 1976. Children: Rachel Elizabeth born Jan. 18, 1979 and Richard Andrew McLeod Winstead born July 19, 1983. - *Submitted by Margaret M. Mcleod Winstead.*

McNARY-WARDERS

Rufus Edward McNary Sr., and Florence Warders McNary lived on the southwest corner of Arch and Lunsford Streets in a house built by her father, Rober Warders, who was a carpenter in Hopkins County. He built A.M.E. Zion Temple Church on Church Street. He died in Danville, IL, in 1925. Florence, a native of Christian County, had two sisters: Julia Warders and Nellie Brooks Lowery; three brothers: Leslie and Robert Warders, Henry Brooks. She was an elementary teacher and seamstress. Member of AME Zion Church. Died Feb. 5, 1918.

From l to r: Cheryl Lynn Ashe, Theresa Mae Harrison Ashe and Linda Sue Ashe-Ford

Rufus, born in Hopkins county, had three brothers: Robert ("Mitch"), Virgil, Sugg; two sisters: Rose, Ealie M. Walls. He operated a three-chair barbershop, and was an insurance agent for Domestic Insurance Company in Louisville. Active in Odd Fellows, Masonic, and Knights of Phythias Lodges, Republican Party, trustee in A.M. E. Zion Church. Four children: Guy Clinton, Reginald, Rufus, Jr., Rose Elizabeth (See McNary-Warders Children). In 1921, he married Elsie Harrison from Greenville, KY. He regarded her granddaughter, Theresa Mae Harrison (Ashe), who became a permanent member of his family when she was nine months old, as his own child. He died Oct. 10, 1932.

After high school in Madisonville, Theresa entered Kentucky State University. After three years in college, she moved to South Bend, IN to live with her father, Harold Harrison and wife, Velzora. Her mother, Leora Rouse, lived in Chicago. Returned to Kentucky State, joined Delta Sigma Theta Sorority, graduated 1945, B.A. Degree, sociology-economics. Caseworker, St. Joseph County Department of Welfare, South Bend; finance counselor and caseworker, Mishawaka; retired 1979 from Children's Center, South Bend. Married Charles S. Ashe, Jr., 1948. Two daughters, Cheryl and Linda Sue Ashe-Ford. Her grandmother, who moved to South Bend with her husband, Vergil Lynch in the early 60's, was an active choir member of A.M.E. Zion Church. She died in 1965.

Husband Charles graduated from Talledega College, AL, 1941, B.A. degree, Sociology-Psychology, Omega Psi Phi Fraternity. Retired after 38 years of service at St. Joseph County Department of Public Welfare. Was Administrative Supervisor of Adult Services.

Cheryl Lynn - B.A. in Theatre-Art History, Earlham College, Richmond, IN. Master's degree in Library Science, Indiana University, Librarian/Specialist for handicapped in Savannah, GA Public Library System.

Linda Sue Ashe-Ford, B.A. in Theatre-Communications, University of Hartford, CT. Master's degree in Education-Administration, Antioch University, Keene N.H. Director, Trinity Episcopal Day Care Center, Portland, ME. Husband James Ford, graduate of University of North Carolina, Chapel Hill; Master's degree in Business Administration, Hobart College, Geneva, NY. Underwriter for Union Mutual Insurance Company, Portland. *Submitted by Rose McNary Banks*

Rufus E. McNary Sr.

McNARY-WARDERS CHILDREN

Guy C. McNary moved to Columbus, OH after finishing high school in 1921 at Atkinson College, a private A.M.E. Zion church school in Madisonville. Became a licensed embalmer and funeral director in Ohio. Married Helen Lash of Middletown, OH, who had one daughter, Virginia. Most of his adult years were in the hotel business in Columbus. He died in Ohio in 1962. Reginald died in infancy.

 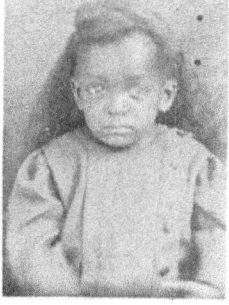

Guy C. McNary and Rufus "Mack" McNary, Jr.

"Mack" (Rufus, Jr.) was a product of Madisonville Public Schools. He died in 1933 at the age of 25.

Rose, who resides in Louisville, was valedictorian of Atkinson College's 1928 graduating class. Attended Wilberforce University (Ohio) and Ohio State University. Married John A. Banks (Hopkinsville) 1933. Finished former Louisville Municipal College (University of Louisville), English-Library Science, 1941 "with distinction." Teacher-librarian,

Lincoln Institute (Shelby County), 1941-43. Graduate of Atlanta University Library School, BLS degree, 1944. Librarian, Louisville Municipal College (U of L), 1944-1951; Assistant Reference Librarian, Fisk University (Nashville). Summer term, Columbia University Library School. Master's in library Science, University of Michigan Library School, 1952. Member of library staff and instructor, Department of Education for four summers at Tennessee State University (Nashville). Junior high and middle school librarian, Jefferson County Public School System, 1952-1981. Retired, June 1981. Member of Kentucky Retired Teachers Association, Jefferson County Retired Teachers Association, Kentucky Library Association, Louisville Friends of the Library Club, American Association of University Women, University of Michigan Alumni Association plus the Louisville Chapter, University of Louisville Alumni Association, Louisville Urban League NAACP, National Council of Negro Women, Louisville Urban League Guild, Zeta Phi Beta Sorority, and an ordained deacon of Plymouth Congregation United Church of Christ.

Rose McNary Banks

Husband John is a graduate of Lane College, Jackson, TN, B.S. degree in physics. A former high school coach in Tennessee and Kentucky. Was basketball coach at the former Rosewald High School (Madisonville). His team was Kentucky State champion in 1936 and National Champion at Tuskeegee (AL), 1936. Life member, NAACP, Alpha Phi Alpha Fraternity, Epicurean Club (men's social club), and Immaculate Heart of Mary Catholic Church. Retired from U.S. Post Office, 1972. - *Submitted by Rose McNary Banks*

SAMUEL McNEELY

Samuel McNeely (1765/70?) followed the trail of many others as he made his way to Hopkins County. He was born in Ireland, as indicated by the marriage certificate of his son, Mathew (second marriage). Samuel had a daughter 16-18 according to the 1810 census of Hopkins County, so had to be married by at least 1794. Since no marrige record for him can be found in the Carolinas, Pennsylvania or Virginia he was probably married in Ireland. Although family tradition locates him at one time in North Carolina, the first real evidence of his life in the U.S. is in South Carolina where his son, Joseph, is born in 1796. He was probably the Samuel McNeely who witnessed a will in Abbeville District, SC, Dec. 31, 1795 (Abstracts of Old Ninety-six and Abbeville District Wills and Bonds, by Young, page 218). Abbeville came out of District 97 which touched York, a part of Camden District, and was very close to East Tennessee. So it is not surprising to find Samuel in 1800 tax list in Blount County, TN (Early Tennessee Tax Lists by Sistler), as he makes his way West, pausing in East Tennessee. He is on the same tax list in 1801, although he owns no property, and is listed under Captain Alexander's Company. He is involved in a legal case in Apri, 1802, but is not on the tax list that year so it is assumed that he moved on at that time to Kentucky.

Samuel appears in Hopkins County in the censuses of 1810 and 1820.

He does not have a wife in the 1820 census and married Elizabeth Brown on Dec. 3, 1821 in Hopkins County. Samuel is listed as one of several witnesses R/E for James Keykendall (page 12, Kentucky Records, Hopkins County, KY Deed Book, No. 1, 1808-1816, Order Book 1-A, 1807-1818). Also, in Minute Book, 1818, Samuel is listed as inspector of tobacco for Hopkins County. Gordon's **History of Hopkins County** records Samuel as "granter or grantee" or "witness" to deeds and is on the Hopkins County Tax List 1811-1821.

While in Hopkins County at least two of Samuel's children were born: John W. in 1813 and Mathew in 1814. It appears that three daughters married in Hopkins County: Isabella, Marian and Elizabeth. A fourth daughter, Nancy, married in Caldwell County. Marian was born in South Carolina and it appears that all four daughters were born before Samuel arrived in Hopkins County.

Samuel McNeely next appeared in Caldwell County in the 1830 census, together with sons Joseph, Mathew and John W. Here Samuel signed the marriage bond for Mathew and Louisa M. Walker, Mar. 26, 1833. John W. married Nancy V. Hobby Nov. 11, 1833.

The author of this study is a descendant of Mathew; his son, John N.; grandson, Albert; and great grandson, Clifton. Clifton was born in Hopkins County as some of the family once again crossed the Tradewater River. - *Submitted by Gerald A. McNeely*

THE MABREY FAMILY

Will Mabrey (William or Willis) (1829-1862) brought his family from North Carolina, probably through Tennessee, to Muhlenberg County, KY before the Civil War and settled near Graham. Will and his wife raised three children, Mary, William and Thomas Pinkney. Like many border state families they were bitterly divided by the war and the slavery and states rights issues. Will and his son, Thomas P. opted for the Confederacy, while young William left Kentucky, served in the Union Army and changed the spelling of his name to Mabry. Will, the Mabrey patriarch was killed in the defense of Fort Donaldson in 1862.

Thomas Pinkney Mabrey (1851-1948), (grandfather to James T.) grew up on the family farm, which he worked for several years before becoming a merchant in Central City. He married Florence Wilson (c. 1857-1951) and they raised nine children; Luella (1883-1903), Robert Samuel (1885-1947), Thoms Cleveland (1887-1962), Mary Dora (1889-unknown), Willis (1890-1959), Ivy (1892-unknown), Pauline (1894-unknown), Raymond (1895-1917) and Roy (1900-1966).

Robert Samuel Mabrey, father to James T., married Leila Woodward (1888-1982) at Cedar Hill, TN in 1904. They had had seven children, Otis (1906-1929), Mabel (1908-1929), Macy (1910-1970), James T. "AL" (b. 1912), Mary Edith (b. 1914), Mildred (b. 1916) and Robert Richard (1919-1980). Robert Samuel was a coal miner in Muhlenberg County for many years before moving to Madisonville in 1925 to work at Grapevine mine. Many of his and Leila's children have strong roots here.

Macy married Cecil Preston and their son Lowell graduated from the United States Naval Academy. He is now a college professor in San Diego, after retiring from the Navy as a Rear Admiral.

Mary Edith married Glenver Brown who was a school teacher here until his death in 1971. They had three children; Mark who married Linda Snelling, and they have one daughter, Wendy; Cherry who married Joe Clemson and they have one child, Sean Clemson; and Jud who married Barbara Kiss and they have one child, Amber.

James T. "Al" married Marjorie Wilkins in 1947. They had two children: Jennifer Lee (b. 1950) who has one child, Polly Radebaugh; and Jill (b. 1953) who has three children, Robert, James and Rachel Hinchcliffe. Al and Marjorie were divorced in 1960.

In 1963 Al married Marie Robinson Brown, widow of James Brown, by whom she had two sons, William and Robin. Robin married Margaret Lutz and they have two children, Christopher and Lauren.

Marie and Al Mabrey

Mildred and her son Samuel Rich reside in Bradenton, FL. Richard (1919-1980) married Mary Tierney and had two children; R.R., Jr., "Dick" and Gail. Dick married Elease Arnold and they have two children, Rick, III and Laura. Gail married Robey Crowe and they have two children, Kelly Sarah and Robbie.

James T.'s first cousin, Raymond Brenton Mabrey (b. 1919) (eldest son of Thomas Cleveland and Audrey Todd Mabrey) married Esther Bergman (b. 1917) and they have four children and eight grandchildren. Raymond is a retired doctor who lives in Apalachicola, FL. - *Submitted by James T. "AL" Mabrey.*

MADISON-HIBBS

James Madison was born Jan. 28, 1809 in North Carolina, thought to have been Granville County, died Nov. 20, 1910, in Hopkins Co., KY, buried at Olive Branch Cemetery near Hanson. He married Phoebe Forsythe, Oct. 25, 1837 in Granville, Co., NC, she being born Mar. 16, 1822 in North Carolina, probably Granville Co.; died Aug. 18, 1905 in Hopkins Co., KY and is buried in Olive Branch Cemetery near Hanson.

In Hopkins Co., James Madison purchased 100 acres of land on Deer Creek in 1853 from Thomas Hamilton. In 1857, he purchased another 100 acres on Deer Creek from George Bailey.

The children born to this union are: William M., b. Oct. 30, 1838; Julia Ann, b. Feb. 12, 1844; Saludia Margaret b. 1846; John W. b. 1849; Nancy J., b. 1850; George Thomas b. Oct. 24, 1852; Mary E b. Apr. 1. 1855; Henry b. July 15, 1858; Lucy b. 1860; Ziba b. Jan. 13, 1862 and Dixie b. July 10, 1864.

James and John Madison, John and Martha Madison

John W. Madison married Martha E. Hibbs in Hopkins Co., KY, Sept. 19, 1866, she being born in 1852 in KY, d. in 1933. Both are buried in Olive Branch Cemetery, near Hanson. Martha is the daughter of Nathan A. Hibbs and Nancy D. Utley. Nathan A. Hibbs is the son of Nathan H. Hibbs and Mary Rachel Bourland, born Jan. 1, 1825, KY and d. Sept. 19, 1909. He was married (1) Nancy Utley, (2) Isabella H. Herrin (were divorced), (3) Sarah Mitchell, married 4th at age 74 to Polly Satterfield, daughter of Hiram Satterfield and Eliza Madison. They were married June 29, 1899 in Concord General Baptist Church near Manitou. Nathan A. is buried beside his 3rd wife Sarah in Odd Fellows Cemetery in Madisonville.

Nathan A. Hibbs has been listed among some of the first teachers of the first school built in Providence, Webster Co., KY. The school was said to have been built around 1819. It was a rude cabin with a dirt floor. Its furnishings were simple and primitive, possibly consisting of benches made from split logs, a fire place possibly built across one end of the building, and a narrow opening for windows covered with heavy shutters, as were the sort of educational buildings typical of the times.

The children of John W. Madison and Martha Hibbs are: Mary b. ca 1868; James N. b. ca 1871; Sarah E. b. ca 1876; Lucy P. b. ca 1878; and Lovelace b. 1879 d. 1956 buried Olive Branch Cemtery who married Etta Belle

Lovelace and Etta Belle Madison on their 50th wedding anniversary

Oakley, daughter of John Oakley and Misha Fawcett. Their children now living are; Virginia Ruthy Mae Beshear, Veneda Martha Belle Corum, Lena Bracie Buchanan, Vera Elizabeth Drake, Those deceased are Clarence W. and David E. Madison. *Source: The Clayton Book by Pat Brown Harris . Some Early Pioneers of Western Kentucky, Their Descendants and Ancestors by: Helen E. Hart Peyton Vaneda Madison Corum personal records . - Submitted by Vaneda Madison Corum*

JAMES T. MADISON

William (Buck) Madison was born on Oct. 30, 1838 to James and Phoebe Forsythe Madison. Buck Madison fought in the Civil War. He married Indiana Mangum on Mar. 22, 1866. The children born to this union were James T. Madison, born on Jan. 31, 1867; Jasper N., born Oct. 25, 1868; Nanera M., born Sept. 21, 1870 who married Joe Tippett; George Smith, born Oct. 7, 1874 who married Julia Tippett; Izora M., born 1876 who married John Trice. After the death of Indiana Mangum, Buck Madison married Loretta Parrish. To this union was born Watt M. (1881), Frank M. and Basil Madison.

Front row l to r: James T. Madison, Hallie, and Temesia. Back row: Bennie and Cam Madison.

James (Jim) T. Madison married Temesia Parrish in Hopkins County, KY. They were both members of the Olive Branch Baptist Church and were buried in the Olive Branch Cemetery near Hanson, KY. James and Teme-

Vera and Bennie Madison

sia Madison had three children. They were: Joseph Cam Madison who married Claudie Gooch; Hallie Madison who married Vernon Smith; and Bennie Madison born Apr. 14, 1891. On Nov. 17, 1917, Bennie Madison married Vera Mullenix, daughter of Ed and Florence Buchanan Mullenix. Vera was then teaching at a one room schoolhouse at Cox's Store. After this union, they lived on a one hundred eight acre farm on the Old Hanson Road that they bought from Ed Mullenix. Bennie had a dairy farm. He sold milk and farm products retail to residents in Madisonville and Earlington for 62 years.

On Nov. 27, 1918, their daughter Florence Geneva Madison was born in their home. She is the only descendant from James T. Madison. In 1938 Florence Geneva married Melvin Rudd, son of Ulus and Flossie Rudd. After their marriage, they lived on the farm with Bennie and Vara Madison where they continued to milk cows and do general farming. In 1984, Bennie Madison died at the age of 93.

The children of Florence and Melvin Rudd are: Mildred Ann Rudd, born Aug. 13, 1951 and Pamela Sue Rudd, born Dec. 17, 1953. On Dec. 30, 1971 Mildred, a local school teacher, was married to Randal Louis Littlepage, D.M.D. They have one child, Benjamin Rudd Louis Littlepage. Pamela Sue, a music teacher, was married on June 7, 1975 to Harold Neil Helton, Ph.D. They have one son, Johathon Rudd Helton. - *Submitted by Mildred Rudd Littlepage*

WILLIAM MAJOR II

William (Bill) Morris Major II, was born 7-7-1915 in Kansas City, MO, to Morris S. and Emily J. Gross Major b. MO. Grandparents are: Wm. M. and Mary G. Hern Major and Wm. S. and Antoinette Geobel Gross b. Mo. A sister Jane Major Dana, CA.

Bill graduated from high school in MO, attended college in CA. In 1940 he enlisted in U.S. Army Air Corps, was stationed in Hawaii and was present at the attack on Pearl Harbor 7-7-1941. He served through-out the war in the Pacific theater; his last duty was the Iwo Jima engagement. Bill was a Tech/Sgt. in charge of mess halls for the 45th Fighter Squad throughout World War II.

William Morris and Florence Ruby Bennett Major

William Morris Major II and Florence Ruby Bennett married 3-15-1946 in the First Christian Church, Miami, FL. At that time Bill was employed with J.P. Riddle Co. and was sent to Brazil for one year. On their return to the U.S. Bill, owned and operated a Western Auto store in Madisonville for 31 years. He was active in civic affairs, charter member of VFW Post 5480, Retail Merchants, Rotary Club.

Florence Ruby Bennett b. 10-5-1923, Texas Co., MO, daughter of E.L. Bennett and Melissa Ann Carder Bennett, b. MO: other children are Hadley and Ervin Bennett and Audra Bennett Bowers, OK and MO.

Bill and Ruby's three children are graduates of MNH High School. Ruby Ann Major b. 4-21-1954 Nashville, TN, attended George Peabody College and graduated fro SMU Dallas, TX, with a BS degree in Phy. William Morris Major III, b. 7-15-1957 Madisonville, attended University of KY, M.C.C., Western KY University. He enlisted in U.S. Army Corps of Engineers, 1984 and served a two year tour of duty in Germany. bill III was awarded numerous merits of awards for outstanding performances during his term of enlistment. Robert Bennett Major, b. 8-20-1960, Madisonville, graduated from Western KY University with an A B Degree in Bldg. Constr. Bob is currently self-employed.

Bill and Ruby have two grandchildren: Emily Nicole Hartwig, b. 9-11-1978. Emily's parents are R. Ann Major-Hartwig Click and Fenton W. Hartwig. Christian Major Click b. 8-12-1984, is a son of R. Ann Major Click and Grady H. Click, Austin, TX.

The Majors are members of the First Christian Church, Madisonville. Bill retired in 1978. He and his wife Ruby currently reside at their home in Madisonville.

The young Majors are direct descendants of 13 Major family generations beginning with Richard and Jane Ere Monger Major who came form England, settled in VA mid 1630;s. The Major ancestors came from VA to KY with Daniel Boone and settled at Boonesboro. Woodford Co. pioneer John Major, Sr. (1740-1808) American Revolutionary Soldier, received a land grant for his services in the war. His son Col. James Major, his grandson Joseph M. (son of James) were soldiers who served in various Colonial Wars. Some of the early ancestors moved Westward to Missouri mid-1800's. William Boone Major (1825-1909), son of Joseph M. and Bill's great-grandfather, m. Prudence Warder, MO. He served in the Mexican War and was Captain in the Confederate Army. Capt. Major was kinsman to Daniel Boone. During the Pony Express era, Capt. Major was Station Master at Salt Lake City, UT, and a kinsman of Alexander Major, partner in the Pony Express.

Other Kentucky ancestral family names: Redd, Minter, Trabue, Dupuy, Flournoy, LaVillion. *Submitted by Mr. and Mrs. Wm. M. Major II*

MARTIN-ADAMS

Streve Alvie Adams was born May 24, 1916, and Mrs. Stella Ladd Adams was born to Mr. and Mrs. William and Lucy Ladd on May 17, 1914.

Betty Lou Adams Martin was born to Alvie and Stella Ladd Adams on Jan. 21, 1943 in Dawson Springs, KY. Betty went to school until she was in the 11th grade of high school, when she married Donald Morris Martin on Oct. 28, 1960 and began her own family.

In addition to Betty Lou, Mr. and mrs. Alvie Adams had these other children: Jean Gray, Earl Adams, Lucille Kimberland, James Adams, Joe David Adams, and Larry Wayne Adams.

Betty Lou and Donald Martin have three children: Barbara Lou, Timothy Moris, and Julie Estella. Barbara Lou graduated from high school in 1978 and is married to Neal Shipp. They are the parents of two children, Keith and David. Timmy is a carpenter and he graduated in 1973. Julie is an honor roll student in the 10th grade.

Betty had done many different things and has many hobbies. She has worked at Ottenheimers as a colloar setter. She also farms, sews, is a homemaker, cake decorator, plumber, carpenter, electrician, water truck driver, veterinarian, a mother and grandmother. (See the Stella Adams story) *-Submitted by Glen Adams*

MARTIN-BAKER

Nancy Iona Baker was born Feb. 14, 1886, in Caldwell Co., KY. she married Clark E. Martin in 1905. Clark (Feb. 2, 1886-July 17, 1964) was a carpenter and built several homes in Hopkins County. He became an ordained Baptist minister and pastored Oak Grove in Madisonville, Mt. Zion in Earlington, and Shipps Chapel in Ilsley. Still building houses and churches, they pastored in Murray, KY. Upon retiring, they returned to Madisonville in 1960 when Rev. Martin was 74.

Nannie (as her husband called her) was devoted to her husband's pastorate and work. She taught Sunday School, was in the Mission Circle and was a church usher until she was 85.

As a young housewife, Nannie cared for her growing family, raised turkeys to sell in the fall to help provide Christmas for her family and others. "No job too small or large," a granddaughter relates. "Grandma-ma could hammer nails and climb a ladder as much a Pappa and never wore a pair of pants to do it,"

Nannie would rise early to cook, then be on the building job with her menfolk, by 7 a.m. Her granddaughter relates how she as a child would go along to "help." At noon, Nannie would serve her meal from a large blue and white granite oval shaped dishpan. With a large table cloth to spread under a shade tree, it was like a picnic. Work would end by 4 or 5 p.m. so that Nannie could prepare the evening meal and have time to visit the sick, help a neighbor or piece on one of over 100 quilts she quilted in her lifetime.

"No distance was too far: remembers her granddaughter, "for Grand-ma-ma to walk to help her church mission work." After her children were adults, Nannie worked in private homes and to help her daughter graduate from nursing school.

At age 75, Nancy retired from work outside the home, but stayed very active in church and community work until past the age of 85. A daily Bible reader, Nancy attributes her long life to hard work and her deep faith in God.

The Martin did well in raising their two children. Their son followed in Dad's footsteps. Rev. Carlton D. Martin died July 30, 1985. A daughter, Viorah (Martin) Shane still resides in Madisonville. There are three grandchildren: Rev. Clark E. Martin II, another minister; James H. Martin and Mari Ola (Martin) Madison. There are 9 great-grandchildren and three great-great-grandchildren.

Always a pillar of encouragement to her growing family, nancy would admonish them "to be somebody" and "do well in school." She has lived to see her dream come true: a doctor, a lawyer, two in real estate, a journalist, a poet, one in security and two yet in college. (See "Hopkins County Centenarians"). *- Submitted by Dorothy Miller Shoulders*

MASON-WHITE

Robert Wesley Mason and Hester Elizabeth White were married on Dec. 1, 1892 in Hopkinsville, Christian Co., KY, by Judge Landers. Their witnesses were Elias White and Sarah Frances White. Robert and Hester were born in Christian County. Hester grew up in the community of Kelly in Christian County. She was the daughter of Elias White, who was born Apr. 7, 1831 and Ivy Cavannaugh White who was born on June 18, 1833. They were married Mar. 9, 1854. The following were the children of Elias and Ivy White: Nancy Jane (Jan. 28, 1851), William Henry (Mar. 3, 1857),

Wedding day 1905, of Nancy Iona Baker and Clark E. Martin. Photo Courtesy of granddaughter Mari Ola Madison

Martha Calrisy (Oct. 27, 1859), Sarah Francis (Jan. 17, 1862), Charles Allen (Dec. 15, 1865), Mary Alice (Aug. 2, 1866), Hester Elizabeth (June 2, 1869) Georgia Ann (June 16, 1870), John Lindsy (Apr. 21, 1872), David Elias (July 16, 1874), Joseph Alford (Apr. 15, 1877) and Elia Thomas (Jan. 8, 1899). The Whites came from Virginia to Kentucky.

Robert Wesley Mason and Hester Elizabeth White Mason, 1905

Robert W. Mason was born on May 24, 1868. He had a brother, John, and a sister, Maude.

Robert and Hester Mason had the following children: Dovie Udella (Dec. 20, 1893), Bluford B. (Sept. 25, 1895), Jewell L. (Mar. 30, 1897), William W. (Oct. 27, 1903) and Jessie Alice (Apr. 12, 1908).

Dovie Udella married Omer Ray Faulk of Mortons Gap, on June 20, 1912 in Springfield, TN. Their witnesses were Garland Kennett and Grace Lovan of Mortons Gap. Their children were: Dorthy Elizabeth (July 8, 1914), Otis R. (Jan. 19, 1916), Erma M. (Mar. 21, 1918), James (Mar. 4, 1920), Omer J. (July 10, 1921), Robert W. (Apr. 5, 1923), William (Aug. 23, 1925), Anna M. (Dec. 4, 1927), Wilma (Apr. 1, 1930), Eugene (Sept. 20, 1932), Dempsey (July 20, 1934) and Carl (Aug. 31, 1937).

Dovie Udella and Bluford Mason with Carlo, 1905

Jessie Alice married Dave Webster and to this union one daughter was born, Wanda. After the death of Dave, Alice married Andrew Oglesby of Mortons Gap.

Bluford B. Mason fought in Europe in WW I. He never returned home alive; he died in Europe after developing pnuemonia.

Robert and Hester were life members of the Mortons Gap Methodist Church. After the original church, which was located on Cross St., was completely destroyed by fire in 1930's, Robert and Hester were responsible for the church to be rebuilt in a new location on Crooked Street in Mortons Gap. This structure, after many years of renovation, still stands today; and houses the present Independent Methodist Church. There is a memorial in memory of the Masons located in the lobby of the church. -*Submitted by Terry and Phyllis Bowman*

ERNEST MASON SR.

Ernest Mason Sr. was born May 7, 1914 in Webster Co., KY to the parents, William and Mary Fuqua mason. Ernest was the fourth son born in a family of ten children.

Ernest Mason Sr.

Being a large family, where the father was a sharecropper, an offer of assistance from a white family was well received. The family of Fred Tapp, owners of Tapp Funeral Home in Dixon, KY, offered to raise Ernest if his parents would allow him to stay with them and care for the Tapp's elderly mother.

Hence, the beginning of a future started. Ernest was fascinated by the mortician's profession at an early age and Mr. Tapp realized that Ernest's interest was genuine and encouraged him. He would allow Ernest to stand on a wooden box to be able to watch the procedures of preparation. Mr. Tapp continued to educate Ernest and kept him in school in Dixon, KY, and later Ernest attended Rosenwald High School in Providence, KY.

In 1932, Ernest attended the Kentucky School of Mortuary Science in Louisville, KY and became a licensed Funeral Director and Embalmer in 1936. He became the first black licensed mortician to reside in Providence, KY.

After residing in Providence for a few years, Ernest decided to make his move. And with the assistance of the Earle Montgomery Funeral Home of Providence, Ernest Mason Sr. moved to Madisonville and located his business, Mason Funeral Home, on East Noel Avenue. Upon on moving to Madisonville, Mason wasn't the only black mortician and was not being contacted by any families to provide his services.

But, he remained cheerful and befriended a special person, Mary Bennett. Mary Bennett was a terminally-ill neighbor that encouraged him to continue and not be discouraged. A special bond was formed and Mason would check daily on Mrs. Bennett. He would even go fishing and invite her to eat fish that night. Mary Bennett died two days before Mason Funeral Home's first year anniversary. A letter was read and in the latter a name had been scratched and a new name added, Ernest Mason Sr........his first funeral.

Mayme L. Starks, the daughter of Mayme S. and Clarence Starks, and Ernest were married June 11, 1936. A graduate of Rosenwald High School of Madisonville, she served as Lady Attendant for the funeral home. Ernest and Mayme united with Wesley Chapel C.M.E. Church in Madisonville and Mayme is still a faithful member.

Ernest progressed in his business but owned not one piece of equipment. Everything he used belong to Mr. Montgomery. When Mr. Montgomery died, Mason was allowed to purchase the equipment for $500.00, $100.00 and down and the rest to be paid in six months. Mason's mother-in-law- Mayme Starks, gave him the $100.00 for the downpayment and in six months the Madisons were debt free.

In 1965, Mason Funeral Home moved to a new location, which is the present location and the name was changed to Mason and Sons.

On Nov. 25, 1971, Ernest Mason Sr. departed this life, leaving behind his wife and a family of three boys and four girls. They were the children that had been raised with strict discipline and a firm emphasis on religion and education. They are: Ernest Mason Jr., Judy Mason Davis, Helen Keith Mason Tinsley, Mary Threasa Mason Lightsey, and Roth Starks Mason. (See their stories) - *Submitted by: Mayme L. Mason*

ERNEST MASON JR.

Ernest Mason Jr. is the oldest son of Ernest SR. and Mayme L. (Starks) Mason, (see Ernest Mason Sr. story)

Ernest Mason Jr.

He graduated from Rosenwald High School in 1956, and attended the University of Louisville before enrolling in and graduating from the Kentucky School of Mortuary Science with distinction. He immediately joined his father and in 1965, the name changed to Mason and Sons Funeral Home to reflect the partnership, and they worked together until his father's death.

In 1962, Ernest married the former Cynthia Palmer who presently holds a B.S. Degree in Business Education from Kentucky State University, a Master of Arts Degree and an Education Specialist Degree from Western Kentucky University in Counselor Education. She is a counselor at Madisonville North Hopkins High School where she is the College Board

Representative and also the Advanced Placement Coordinator.

Ernest and Cynthia have two children: Lori Ann, who is a senior at the University of Kentucky in Lexington (received an academic scholarship) and Scott Palmer who is a sophomore at Madisonville North Hopkins High School and an active member of Beta Club (National Honor Society).

Ernest served in the U.S. Army (1963) and was honorably discharged after a short time because of his father's health. He was an active member of the Army Reserve for six years, City Councilman for two full terms (the first Black elected official in the city of Madisonville) and is a Deacon and Trustee at East View Baptist Church in Madisonville where his wife and children are also members.

Presently, Ernest is operating the family business, Mason and Sons Funeral Home in Madisonville, and he is also in partnership with his brother William at Masons Funeral Home in Evansville, IN, which William owns and operates. -*Submitted by Mayme L. Mason*

ROTH STARKS MASON

Roth Starks Mason is the youngest child of Ernest Sr. and Mayme (Starks) Mason (see Ernest Mason Sr. story)

Roth Mason

Roth is a graduate of Madisonville North High School. He attended the University of Louisville preceding his enrollment and graduation from Mid-America College of Mortuary Science in Jeffersonville, IN. He has been associated with Mason Funeral Home of Evansville, IN, and Mason and Sons Funeral Home of Madisonville.

Roth just recently became owner-operator of Rutledge-Mason Funeral Home in Murray, KY. Roth is also the owner-operator of Roth's Limousine Service.

Roth resides in Murray, KY and attends Cleaves Memorial Church in Evansville, IN. - *Submitted by Mayme L. Mason*

WILLIAM C. MASON

William (Billy) C. Mason is the son of Ernest Sr. and Mayme (Starks) Mason (see Ernest Mason Sr. story).

William graduated from Madisonville North High School and attended Western Kentucky University in Bowling Green, KY, before enrolling in and graduating from the Kentucky School of Mortuary Science. He is a licensed Funeral Director and Embalmer in the states of Kentucky and Indiana. William is the owner-operator of Mason Funeral Home in Evansville, IN.

William Mason

William is married to the former Gwendolyn Brown, a native of Sturgis, KY, and the daughter of Mrs. Loretta Brown. She is a graduate of Union County High School in Morganfield, KY, and recieved a B.S. degree in Elementary Education from Indiana State Univeristy, and a M.A. degree from Murray State University. She is presently employed as a fourth grade teacher in the Henderson County School System in Henderson, KY.

William and Gwendolyn have three children: Jabbar, Christopher, and Tiffany. They are active members of the Cleaves Memorial Church in Evansville, IN. - *Submitted by Mayme L. Mason*

RICHARD L. MASSAMORE

Richard (Dick) Massamore is the son of James Ruffey Massamore and Elza Lorena Capps-Masamore. James Ruffey was born on Dec. 8, 1899 in Hopkins Co. His ancestors came to Hopkins County between 1795-1805. On June 3, 1923 he married Elza Capps who was born Aug. 8, 1904. When they were married, he had his name changed to Massamore. They had one son, Dick, on Mar. 27, 1924. James Ruffey died on Aug. 25, 1971. Elza now lives in Dawson Springs.

Dick married Dora Jean Simons on Oct. 5, 1946. Jean is the daughter of John Alvin Simons born Feb. 8, 1903 and Manda Belle Tirey-Simons born Feb. 3, 1906. John Simons married Manda Tirey on Oct. 11, 1924 and had Jean on Oct. 12, 1925. John died on Dec. 27, 1963 and now Manda lives in Dawson Springs.

Jean and Richard Massamore

Dick and Jean had three children. David G. Massamore born on July 1, 1948 is the oldest child. David married Sharon Byrant in July 1971. She was born on Sept. 14, 1953. They now have two children, Sarah Elizabeth born Dec. 20, 1977 and Scott Alan born June 1, 1982, and live at 1000 Ballard Lane in Madisonville. David is an attorney. He has offices in Madisonville and Dawson Springs.

Jean Ann is their second child. She was born on Apr. 18, 1951. She married Raymond Ivan Farmer on June 21, 1969. He was born in Christian County on Dec. 27, 1950. They had two children, Lee Ann born Feb. 11, 1970 and James Raymond born June 16, 1971. Ann and Raymond divorced in February 1972. Raymond now lives in Durgin and owns Farmer's Market. On May 5, 1972, Ann married Larry Edmund Hyde. He was born on June 28, 1948. My sister, Lori Alyson Hyude, was born Aug. 9, 1973. Larry now lives in Caldwell County, and Ann lives on Huckleberry Road in Charleston

Jane Ellen born, born Apr. 15, 1954, is Dick and Jena's youngest child. Jane married Rev. Stephen Graham Stout on Dec. 30, 1977. Jane and Steve had a son, Benjamin Graham, on May 13, 1982. They live in Lancaster, KY.

Dick and Jean have six granchildren two of which, Lee Ann and Jim, live at 402 South Main Street in Dawson Springs. Both Dick and Jean graduated from Southern Law University and Jean from Memphis Academy of Arts, both in Memphis, TN.

Dick is a retired mailman. Dick and Jean are self-employed at Massamore Tax Service, Inc. They are members of the Dawson Springs First Christian Church, and both are very active in the community.- *Submitted by Lee Ann Farmer*

WALTER R. MATHENY

Walter Robison Matheny, born May 28, 1883 in Muhlenberg Co., KY was the oldest of six children born to William Eli Matheny and Mariah Loney. Walter's brothers and sisters were: William Wesley, bonr Dec. 16, 1886; Everett Austin, born Mar. 9, 1888; Edgar Harrison, born Feb. 21, 1889; Gala Leora, born Aug. 15, 1891; Julie, born June 16, 1895. His half-brother and sisters were: Miriam, born Oct. 15, 1899; Leslie Elizabeth, born Oct. 30, 1902; Ancil, born Aug. 29, 1905.

Walter R. and Lizzie Matheny with son Rollie about 1908

Walter came to Hopkins County at the age of 47 in 1936 and resided here until his death Feb. 28, 1979. He married Elizabeth Jane Stewart, daughter of Green Crawford Stewart and Sarah Ellen Spinks, Nov. 5, 1903. Unto this union were born two sons: Rollie William Green Matheny and Everett Eli Matheny.

The Mathenys, of which Walter is descendants, are of French descent and were among the Hugenots driven from France in 1685 and emigrating to America in 1730. When the Shenandoah Valley was opened they settled in four of the valley counties.

Walter lived in several locations around Hopkins County including the old Ed and Rufas Short place, in one of the oldest log houses in that area then. He also lived and farmed for several years on a farm belonging to Fletcher Slaton. During my childhood he lived in th old Lonnie Stum place another of the old log homes, which at one time was a small country grocery store. It was later torn down and made way for what is now Rice Supply on Highway 85.

Walter enjoyed hunting as a past-time, especially coon and fox hunting. He, in part, made a living for a while selling coon hides and also serving as the community's only barber for quite some time. Some of his hunting partners were other Hopkins countians such as: Rex Slaton, Will and Grover Cardwell, and Fletcher Slaton.

Walter's oldest son, my grandfather, Rollie Matheny, was born Aug. 18, 1904. He married Grace Tyson, daughter of Elzie Tyson and Anna Stewart, Mar. 2, 1926. They owned and operated the 85 Drive Inn Restaurant on Highway 85 for 29 years. After Rollie's death, Oct. 25, 1969, Grace continued to operate the restaurant until her retirement in 1977. Unto their union were born two sons: Carl Donald Matheny and Earl Ruby Matheny. Carl, my father, continues to earn his living on the same grounds where his parents started their business 39 years ago. He is the owner and operator of the Lawnmower Center on Highway 85.

Carl married Geneva Stewart, daughter of Albert Stewart and Hattie Noffsinger, Sept. 14, 1946. Unto their union were born six children: Don, Dannie, Pam, Carla, Valisa and Mark.

Carla was born Oct. 30, 1955, in Hopkins Co. and has lived her all her life. Se married Hank Dawson, son of Albert Dawson and Pauline Tanner, Dec. 14, 1973. They have two children: Stefanie Danielle and Matthew Shane. - *Submitted by Carla Kay Matheny Dawson*

MATHER-RINGO

My Aunt Virginia always remembered me on Christmas when I was a little girl, packages with new pajamas among other things.

She had left the farm of her father, Benjamin Franklin Ringo (8-17-1864 to 6-20-1962) and made her way to the big-city working world of Indianapolis.

Born Zeola Virginia Ringo, 11-12-1916 in Hopkins County, she is the daughter of the late B.F. and Lean Gertrude Sigler Ringo (8-6-1888 to 11-7-1974). Their farm fronted the Tradewater River in Hopkins County. At some point they moved to the Blackford area of Webster County and later bought a large farm between Providence and Clay.

Aunt Gin was my grandmother Opal's (Big Mama) half-sister. They shared a father, whom we called Poppa. He and Ms. Gertrude were special to me. I had a four generation picture made at my wedding, Poppa, "Big Mama," Mother and me. I wish I had taken time to have a five generation picture after my oldest child Suzanne, was born.

Time and distance prohibited my seeing her as much as Aunt Alice.

While working in Indianapolis, she met Robert Lee Mather (11-20-1915). They were later married there on 10-12-1942 and made their home there.

Their only son, Ben, was born Aug. 12, 1947. He married Janet Imus, also of Indianapolis, at the Christian Church there and had two sons. Eric Ian was born Oct. 11, 1977, and Brett Justin Mather on Dec. 15, 1978. Ben and Janet later divorced. She has not remarried and still lives in the Indianapolis suburb of Carnel with the boys.

Ben married Kate Gerencer (9-19-1956) on Aug. 16, 1986. They are the parents of a son, Logan Holmes, born July 27, 1987. They live in Indianapolis.

Aunt Gin lost Uncle Bob Sept. 6, 1966. She continued living in the same home for many years and kept her job at L. Strauss until retirement, June 6, 1980. She now lives in an apartment very close to all her grandchildren and family. We stay in contact and get to see each other rarely.

Poppa and Ms. Gertrude passed away long ago; Aunt Alice is a widow and lives in Goldsboro, NC. Their two half-sister, Opal and Leavy, have passed on leaving only my precious "Sugie" (Uncle Spaulding Ringo) in this vicinity. He lives on Hall St. in Madisonville and is 89.

I am very thankful for the sweet relationships and am very blessed. - *Submitted by Peggy Sullivan Waide*

MAUK-SLATON

James Lewis Mauk was born near Glasgow, KY, and was married to Effie Prowse of Nortonville. They settled in Central City, KY, where he operated a grocery store for many years. They are buried at Unity Cemetery in Muhlenberg County. Their children were James Lewis Mauk Jr., who lives in Scottsdale, AZ, and Edward Mauk of Madisonville.

Edward Mauk born 2-23-1927 of Muhlenberg County is a retired coal miner married to Ada Slaton born 12-17-1932, daughter of Clyde Slaton (b. 2-27-1892 d. 10-8-1969) and Addie Woodson (Walker) Slaton (b. 1-7-1898 d. 12-3-1962) of rural White Plains.. Ada's grandparents were Conn Slaton and Beatrice (Lacey) Slaton, and Jonah Walker and Ollie (Allen) Walker. both men were farmer in the White Plains community. (See SLATON-CALLIS)

Edward and Ada Mauk have three son: Edward Alan Mauk born 9-19-1954 who married Barbara Jo Nance born 9-21-1957, daughter of Charles Edward Nance (b. 4-2-1922 d. Aug. 1958) and Mary Helen (Brooks) Nance born 10-10-1921 who lives in Earlington. Eddie attended Earlington High School and is now employed at Goodyear in Madisonville. Barbara graduated from Earlington High School and attended Madisonville Community College. They have one son, Joseph Edward Mauk born 8-2-1981. They live in Earlington. (See NANCE-BROOKS).

Clyde Marshall Mauk born 8-27-1958, graduated from South Hopkins H.S. He is married to Sunni Lee Stokes born -15-1958, daughter of Carmon L. "Poochie" Stokes Jr. and Billie (Bernard) Stokes of Earlington.

Clyde works at Badgett's KY. Lake Dock at Grand Rivers, KY, and Sunni Lee is a pharmacits at Regional Medical Center, Madisonville. Sunni Lee graduated from Madisonville-North Hopkins H.S. and received her doctorate in Pharmacy from University of Kentucky. They reside in Madisonville.

Mark Lewis Mauk born 3-14-1961 is married to Amy Blades born 11-8-1964, daughter of Tommy Blades and Brenda (Lewis) Blades of Nortonville, Mark is employed at General Electric in Madisonville, and Amy is employed at the Regional Vocational Office in Madisonville Community College. They have a son, Brandon Lewis Mauk born 11-8-1986. they reside in Madisonville. - *Written by Rella Jenkins*

SALLY MAXWELL

Sarah Elizabeth Knight was born Nov. 16, 1880, the daughter of D.H. Knight and Nancy Hight of Rock Bridge in Christian County, KY. Her father, D.H., was a Civil War Veteran.

Sarah, more affectionately known to her family and friends as "Sally," was raised on a farm near White Plains. She married Charlie Tyson and had three children. All preceded her in death.

In 1921, she married Albert Maxwell, a lay minister of the Church of Christ. To this union a son, Wallace Earl was born. Wallace Earl, also a Church of Christ minister, now pastors in Florida.

Sally was a resident of Clinic Convalescent Center in Madisonville at the time of her death Sept. 27, 1981. She was buried in Hight Cemetery near White Plains.

Taylor Ezell of Mortons Gap was the responsible person and supplied this information. For a picture of Sally Maxwell, see "Hopkins County Centenarians." -*Submitted by Dorothy Miller Shoulders*

MELTON

My name is Joan Melton. I was born in Caldwell County, on Feb. 20, 1969, the youngest of four children. I have two sisters, Beverly, born Jan. 6, 1954, and Sharon, born Dec. 31, 1962, and one brother Russell, born Apr. 24, 1959. Our parents are James Melton, born Oct. 14, 1930, and Shirley Beshear Melton, born May 21, 1936. James and Shirley married June 8, 1957.

Among some of our interest are riding our horses and just being out in the country.

I attend Dawson Springs High School and have attended Dawson Schools since kindergarten, and I am a senior now. I have been involved in the computer club since 8th grade, on the honor roll several times and recieved a certificate in Business Math on Awards Day.

I live with my mom and dad in Dawson Springs. My brother and his wife, Dorene, also live in Dawson Springs as does my sister Beverly and her two children. My sister Sharon and her husband John and her two children live in Oak Grove, KY, near Ft. Campbell.

When my dad was a teenager, he and some friends had a group called The Pine Vally Pals. The group played music and sang for a local radio station in Hopkinsville, KY. One of the guys in the group used to be Dolly Parton's road manager. My dad was in a singing contest and came in first place against Pat Boone. My family attended a Holiness Church for many years. My dad has played the guitar in all the churches we have attended, and I have been involved in youth services which included Bible Drill, singing, Bible Baseball and much more. -Submitted by Joan Melton

MELTON-WEBB

Mary E. Webb was born May 16, 1850, the daughter of Francis Jackson Webb (1827-1907) and Rebecca Carithers Webb (1829-1907). Mary married Jack J. Melton, born May 15, 1851, and they were the parents of a son, name unknown, and two daughters, Rebecca born Nov. 6, 1875 and Delia born Feb. 28, 1878.

The family took a sudden notion to go to Texas in a covered wagon, driving two little mules named Donk and Donkey. They stayed in Texas for a few years and then started home. On their way back, the son became very ill and died. The family stopped by the wayside and buried him, then sadly returned to their Kentucky home.

The family spent the remainder of their lives on their farm in the Clements School District in Hopkins County.

Jack died Feb. 21, 1923 and Mary died Jan. 27, 1941. Both are buried at Ridge Top Cemetery, near Crofton, in Christian County, KY.

MENSER

Jonas Mentzer came to Kentucky from Pennsylvania circa 1794, as a surveyor. He was born in 1760 and died Dec. 24, 1830. Having served in the Revolutionary War under Captain Finley, Lancaster Co., PA, he surveyed and claimed large parcels of land and built a double log house in Dawson Springs, KY.

Jonas had been engaged to marry Sallie Smith, daughter of Henry and Sarah Smith in PA. After he had built their home, he traveled back there to claim his bride. They came as far as Eddyville by waterway, possibly the Ohio River. There they were met by someone driving an oxcart and traveled overland on to Dawson Springs. Sallie was born Mar. 8, 1784 and died Apr. 3, 1860.

Eight children were born to this union: Christene, who m. Patton Alexander; Jim Daniel m. Melinda Ashmore; Henry Solomon m. Mary Jemima June Beshears; Drucella m. James Cook; Jonas, Jr. never married; David m. Gracie Cranor; Mary Sarah m. Anderson White; and Elizabeth m. C.H. Coleman.

The children of Henry Solomon and Jemima were: Henry David m. Frances Beshear; Charlie m. Martha Beshear; Harper Forest m. Pernecia Huddleston; James Daniel m. Annie White; Necie m. Dr. G.W. Beshears; Benjamin m. Fannie Vickery; Patton m. Bertie Linville; and Will m. Zela Alexander.

Harp and Necie (daughter of Ellis and Carolyn Parsons Huddleston) were the parents of eleven children. Six reached adulthood. Harp died in 1911, after a beating by the Night Riders, and was buried in Parson's Cemetery. Necie then married John Orten. She died in 1948 and was buried in Piney Grove Cemetery beside daughter Elsie.

From the union of Harp and Necie, five children raised families. Mary m. Eaph Hopper, farmer, Caldwell Co. After the birth of their first two daughters, they moved to Carbondale, IL. Daughter Esta m. Casey Jones. Aline m. first Dean Crews, second Geddes Riggins. Margarite m. _____.

Bertha and Albert farmed most of their lives in the Piney Grove Community. Their children were: Nina Mae m. Clyde Poole, Dawson Springs; Rufus m. Olan Thomas (he was a Nazarene minister), raised a family in Peoria, IL; Pauline m. Ralph Mason, now lives in Hopkinsville, KY; Cara Lou m. L.B. Craytor, Eugene, OR; Elaine m. Harold Dickerson, now m. to Hoyt Thomas; Wayne m. Frances Amos, Dawson Springs; and Phyllis m. John Winfree, m. second Dr. Bruce Caplinger, deceased.

Nola m. Herbert Hopper, Sr. He worked as a mechanic in Dawson Springs. Their children: Marie m. Joe Parker, deceased, lives in Chicago, IL; Imogene m. James Lile, Detroit, MI; Herbert, Jr. m. Sue Johnson, they live in Madisonville; and Harvey m. Louise Clark, Dawson Springs.

Ada and Lewis Thomas, a truck farmer and coal miner, lived on the Dawson-Princeton Rd. Their children: Glenn m. Josephine Gardner, deceased, Caldwell Co.; Lillian m. Guy Taylor, Valley Station, KY; Don Owen m. Doris Blackburn, Princeton, KY; Carolyn m. Richard Jackson, Liviona, MI; Bill m. Lydia Hodiac, Chicago, IL; and James E. m.Vera Hutchinson, Eldon, OK.

Henry m. Edith White, daughter of George and Sudie Cline White. He worked as a plumber and steamfitter in Hopkins, Caldwell and Christian Cos. He was also a Pentecostal minister. Their issue included seven children. Three died in infancy, Kaye was killed by an automobile in 1952, at age eight. Three daughters reached adulthood:

Deane m. J.B. Renshaw, Crofton, KY. They are the parents of Gayle m. Bob Rogers, Murray, KY;Johnny m. Debbe Foster, Crofton, KY; and Brenda m. Bates Payne, Jr., Pembroke, KY. They have seven grandchildren.

Donna m. Don Matheny. They reside in Dawson Springs and have two sons: Kevin is in the U.S. Coast Guard stationed in TX; and Darrin m. Melissa Parker and lives in Dawson Springs.

Suzanne Epley Barnett resides in Hollywood, FL. She has two children: Micheal Epley and Melody Epley, both reside in Miami, FL.

The Mensers are buried in Macedonia Cem. Pennyrile Park. The Lisanbys, Thomases and Hoppers are buried in Piney Grove and Tabernacles Cemeteries. Twenty-four of the twenty-six cousins from the Harper Menser family are still living. They meet regularly for a reunion at Pennyrile State Park, Dawson Springs, KY.- Submitted by Deane Menser Renshaw

MERIDETH-ALFRED

Gerald Glendon Merideth Jr. and Penny Elaine Alfred were married Feb. 7, 1987.

Gerald was born Apr. 29, 1965 in Tacoma, WA. He is the son of Gerald G. Merideth Sr. and Wilhelmina Heid. Gerald G. Merideth Sr. was born May 10, 1938 in Chicago. He married Wilhelmina Heid, born Jan. 24, 1936 the daughter of George and Louise Heid (both deceased), on Jan. 18 1963 in Germany. Gerald Sr. was the son of George Meredith and Leona Giffin (both deceased).

Gerald Jr. attended Charleston school his first four years. He attended fifth grade and subsequent years at Dawson, graduating in 1986. He is presently employed with the United States Army Reserve as a Sergeant. He was recently employed with Delta Express in Madisonville. He was a member of the First Baptist Church for four years. His surviving brothers and sisters are as follows: Karl Heid, Andrew Heid, Usula Nolan, Leana Merideth, Larry Merideth and John Merideth.

Penny was born Feb. 3, 1969 in Hopkins County to William Earl Alfred and Janie Lee Duncan, she being from Grayson County, KY the daughter of Otha P. Duncan (born May 29, 19192, died Feb. 6, 1976) and Sarah Jane Webster field (born July 12, 1960). Janie was born Jan. 1, 1946. William was born Apr. 18, 1933, the son of Lennie Alfred and maudie Farris.

Penny attended Dalton school for eight years, West Hopkins for 1 1/2 years. She attended 10th grade and subsequent years at Dawson and is finishing thre rest of schooling at Dawson. She will graduate in 1988.

Some of Gerald Jr.'s hobbies are hunting, fishing and basketball. Some of Penny's hobbies are reading and taking care of her family. Penny's surviving brothers and sister are as follows: Beverly Ezell, Thomas Alfred, James Alfred and Randall Alfred. Gerald and his family are and recently settled in Dawson.

Gerald and Penny have one daughter, Holly Michelle Merideth, born Dec. 29, 1985. -Submitted by Penny Merideth

LEWIS DANIEL MERRELL

Lewis Daniel Merrell, born 14 Oct. 1892 in Hopkins Co., KY was the third child of seven born to Chapman N. and Susan Samantha Gunn Merrell, daughter of Vinson D. and Mary Ann Sisk Gunn.

Chapman N. Merrell (b. February 1843 in AL; d. 2 Nov. 1903 in Hopkins Co.) first came to Hopkins co. in 1856. Chapman N. was found in 1860 on the Census Schedules, living with his mother, Lucretia McGregor Merrell, as head of household, and a younger brother James K, Polk Merrell. Also a known married sister, Mary Jane Merrell Butler (b. 6 Dec. 1838 in AL; d. 7 Apr. 1916 in Hopkins Co.) also listed in the 1860 census in a separate household with her husband Daniel and family.

Chapman N. was married twice. His first wife, LouVina Ann Welch b. 1844 and d. ca. 1885. They married on 8 Jan. 1862 in Hopkins Co. and to this union there were seven children born. Chapman N. and his second wife Susan Samantha (b. 12 Apr. 1870, d. 22 Dec. 1943) also had seven children. They married on 16, Jan. 1887. Chapman worked as a farm laborer and a shingle maker. Chapman and Susan Samantha are both buried at Old Salem Cemetery in Hopkins Co.

Chapman N. and Susan Samantha's children were: Jimmie Polk female, b. (July 1888; Lottie M., female, b. 3 Nov. 1890; Lewis Daniel b. 14 Oct. 1892; Cy Thaniel, male b. 16 Nov. 1894; William b. Jan. 1896, d. 12 July 1906;

Lewis and Mossie Merrell's children at family reunion in July 1980 at Madisonville City Park. Back row l to r: Raymond, Carl, Edward, Paul, Lewis, Ray, Marlin and Chapman. Front l to r: Lorine, Lola May, Waffrieda and Pauline

Della, female, b. 18 May 1900; and Chapman E., male, b. 3 Sept. 1902.

Lewis Daniel Merrell married Mossie Lee Barber (b. 16 Jan. 1896, d. 5 May 1961) on 31 Dec. 1911 in Hopkins Co. Their children were: Raymond Lee b. 3 Mar. 1914; Carle Cemen b. 12 Apr. 1916; Edward Lewis b. 26 Jan. 1918; Lorine b. 23 Nov. 1921; Paul Daniel b. 13 Sept. 1923; Lewis Dewy b. 12 Apr. 1925; Monroe Lee b. 18 Feb. 1927, d. 14 Nov. 1974; Junior Ray b. 2 Mar. 1929; Marvin Speed b. 18 Oct. 1930, d. 25 Sept. 1931; Lola May b. 4 Mar. 19322; Marlin Dee b. 27 May 1934; Chapman Donald b. 10 Jan. 1936; Waffrieda b. 10 June 1937; Pauline b. 9 Dec. 1938.

Lewis Daniel Merrell and Mossie Barber Merrell about 1911

Lewis attended a few years of schooling at the Munn School House for his education. When his father died, at the age of eleven he helped run the farm at his home in Mortons Gap. He was the eldest son. Lewis married when he was nineteen years old, and Mossie just lacked being 16 by a few days. They lived in the country outside St. Charles. Their first son, Raymond, was born here. They moved to White City and Carl was born. Their third son was born in their third home on Lewis's mother's property on White Plains Road in Mortons Gap. The house burned down and they moved to a three room house and porch out on Oak Hill where the remaining eleven children were born. The home on Oak Hill had no electricity or running water for years. The eldest son Raymond did run electricity into the home later on, but the water was always drawn up out of a well and carried to the home by buckets.

Lewis worked for Moss Hill Mine in Muhlenberg Co. and Norton Coal Mining as a coal miner. Lewis worked for Sterling Coal Co. from 1920 until the strke in 1929. He was out of a coal mining job in 1929 and could only find employment through the WPA as a civilian painter at Fort Knox. He did this for 13 years and lived away from home during the week, coming back home on weekends by train. He then retired in 1957. Due to a dispute about his pension, he was short just one year to qualify to receive it.

Lewis enjoyed playing cards and nipping at the whiskey bottle when he couldn't be seen by his wife, Mossie. I remember watching him watch the wrestling matches on T.V., how he loved to watch them. He was a hardworking man and a loving father and grandfather. - *Submitted by Sandra Reynolds Goolsby*

MESSAMORE-PHELPS

Brenda Phelps married Wayne Messamore on July 28, 1966. They were married for three years when on Aug. 28, 1969 their first child, Anthony Wayne was born. They also had two more children, Ricky Lynn on June 4, 1972 and Lori Kaye on May 1, 1978. Lori is a very talented girl. She sings in the church choir. She is a beautiful girl even though she did not win the Little Miss Dawson Pageant. Ricky won an academic award for achievement. Ricky and Lori presently go to West Hopkins School. Andy works for Wayne Howton.

Brenda Kay Phelps was born Sept. 6, 1947 to Nancy and Churchill Phelps. Brenda is in charge of the youth group at the Missionary Baptist Church, and has taught Sunday School for the last seven years. Brenda enjoys sewing and makes most of her own clothes. She has worked at Ottenheimer's for the last eighteen years. She belongs to Don Howton's Church.

Brenda's mother, Nancy was married to Churchhill R. Phelps. He was killed in a factory accident a day after his birthday. He was born on June 9, 1910. Nancy was left to rear Brenda and her nine brothers and sisters. Her sisters are as follows: Glenda Dearing, Linda Phelps, Pauline Allen, Gevada Phelps. Her brothers are Glen David, Freddie, Rodger and Robert Phelps.

On Apr. 27, 1943 Wayne Messamore was born Ressie and Walter Messamore. Ressie and Walter were married on Oct. 12, 1924. Messamore died. Wayne was reared in Hopkins County. He attended grade. He is a member of Don Howton's Missionary Baptist Church in Dawson Springs. Wayne is one of eleven children. Clair, Doris Gibson, Wanda Peak, Connie Jackson, Ola Maye Clark and Marie Bershears. Wayne works at Sullivan Plumbing in Madisonville. He enjoys sleeping after coming home from work. If one were to ask what Wayne's favorite hobby is, he would say, "aggravating people". - *Submitted by Vickie Dearing*

JACOB MESSAMORE

Jacob Messamore was born in South Carolina. After moving to Kentucky, he married Charlotte Parker on Oct. 23, 1826. Their son, George, resided in Hopkins County and then moved to Christian County where he married Margaret C. Lantrip on Jan. 5, 1848. She was the daughter of Shadarack Lantrip, born September 1777, and Catherine Croft, born 1789. George and Margaret had a son, Malbert Lincoln Messamore, born Sept. 5, 1865. Malbert married Viola Jane Parker on Jan. 15, 1880. They had a son, James Rufey Messamore, born Dec. 8, 1899. He married Elza Lorena Capps, born Aug. 8, 1904, on June 3, 1923. Her parents were James David Capps, born Feb. 14, 1870, and Ida Elizabeth Cline, born Nov. 26, 1882.

James David Capps' parents were Miles Robinson Capps, born Dec. 8, 1837, and Emily Frances Glover, born Mar. 24, 1837. Ida E. Cline's parents were Charles Douglas Cline, born 1860, and Frances Delilah Miller, born 1861. Miles Robinson Capps parents were David Capps and Berthera Hunter. Frances Miller's parents were James Miller and Nancy C. Blaylock.

James Rufey Massamore and Elza L. Capps had a son, Richard L. Massamore, born Mar. 27, 1924. He married Dora Jean Simons, born Oct. 12, 1925 on Oct. 5, 1946. They now reside in Dawson Springs. Dora Jean's parents were John A. Simons, born Feb. 8, 1903, and Manda Belle Tirey, born Feb. 3, 1906. They were married on Oct. 11, 1924. John Simon's parents were George (Vought) Simons, whose parents were from Germany, born 1864, and Dora Viola Wever, born Apr. 12, 1863. George (Vaught) Simon's parents were (unknown) Vaught and (Eva) Wyman born May 14, 1834. Dora Viola Wever's parents are unknown.

Manda B. Tirey's parents were George Washington Tirey, born July 29, 1872, and Iva Pearl Armstrong, born May 9, 1878. They resided in Hopkins County. George W. Tirey's parents were Joseph Tirey, born Mar. 11, 1838, and Manda Jane Sisk, born Aug. 2, 1850. Iva P Armstrong's parents were Newton Jasper Armstrong, born 1850, and Missouri Belle Wilson, born 1856. The Tireys and the Armstrongs resided in Hopkins County.

Joseph Tirey's parents were Andrew Tirey, born Mar. 23, 1808 and Sallie Wilkey, born 1820. Manda Jane Sisk was a daughter of Robert B. Sisk, born 1822, and Mary McCully, born May 25, 1824.

Newton Armstrong's parents were Benjamine Armstrong and Selotus Sugg. Missouri Belle Wilson's parents were John T. Wilson and Elizabeth Utley.

This information was submitted by Jim Farmer, a great, great, great, great grandson of Jacob Messamore. Jim lives with his grandfather, Richard L. Massamore in Dawson Springs, KY.

THOMAS L. METCALFE, JR.

Thomas Lee Metcalfe was born in Hopkinsville, KY, Sept. 23, 1898. He was the son of Thomas L. Metcalfe, Sr., and Clara Virginia Orr.

Thomas Lee Metcalfe Jr.

The Metcalf family first came to Kentucky from Virginia and settled near Paris in 1783. In 1824 they moved to East Tennessee and established the first cotton factory in that part of the state. In 1859 they settled in Hopkinsville, KY. Thomas Metcalfe, Sr., was active in many businesses, owning at one time a printing plant, a confectionary business, and chain of laundries before getting into the floral business. He built several greenhouses in Hopkinsville and bought stores in Jackson, Clarksville, Chattanooga and Murfreesboro, TN, and Madisonville, KY.

Thomas Jr. spent his childhood playing in his father's greenhouses, and as soon as he was old enough to do chores around the greenhouses, he was put to work. He often accompanied is father on train trips to Madisonville to check on the business. Flowers grown in Madisonville were shipped to Hopkinsville, and then to larger markets throughout the south.

In 1918, Thomas was sent to Madisonville to repair damage to the greenhouses done by the winter of 1917. He never returned to Hopkinsville. He began working toward buying the business from his father and after a few years became the owner of Pleasant View Greenhouses, which is still in operation today.

In 1923 he married Nina Elizabeth Myers, daughter of John and Annie Denton Myers. They were parents of four children, Robert McCarley, Virginia Ann, Mary Elizabeth and William Orr.

They lived for many years in a small house across from the greenhouse office, which Mr. Metcalfe built soon after he came to Madisonville. After World War II, they bought and remodeled a large brick home on Princeton Road, where they moved in 1952.

Thomas's hobyy was working with wood, which he collected for many years. He supplied hardwood for paneling for his children's homes, and used it extensively in his home, the summer cottage in Michigan and the houses he built around greenhouses.

Thomas died January 1983

He had built Pleasant View Greenhouses up from one greenhouse, 250 feet long, to a successful floral business, both wholesale and retail with eighteen greenhouses. His sons, Buddy and Bill, operate the business today and three of his grandsons, Thomas L, Mark L. and Robert are associated with the greenhouse. Pleasant View Greenhouses is one of the oldest businesses in Madisonville. *Submitted by Robert M. Metcalfe*

MIDKIFF

In 1943, Herman Midkiff, the son of Mary and Arnold Midkiff, married Wanda Russell, the daughter of Everett and Mae Russell. Herman was born on Nov. 19, 1922. Wanda was born Jan. 20, 1929. At the time of their marriage, Herman was twenty and Wanda was fourteen.

Mary and Arnold Midkiff had one other child, Marvey Midkiff. Other children of Everett and Mae Russell are: Ray Russell, Floy Russell, and Audrey Russell, all married.

Wanda and Herman live in Hartford, KY. They had four children, all boys. Mike Ray Midkiff was born May 6, 1945. Steve Jay Midkiff was born Sept. 1, 1952. Brent Midkiff was born Sept. 8, 1957. Timothy Scott Midkiff was born Dec. 27, 1964.

In the summer of 1961, Herman had major surgery. Eighty-five percent of his stomach was removed due to ulcers. Herman's job was as a contractor for Jet Coal Company in Charleston, Hopkins County, KY.

Since Herman was in the hospital, his oldest son Mike took over his job at the age of sixteen. Mike drove every morning at five o'clock from Hartford to Charleston. He supervised the loading and delivery of coal. Mike worked for twenty-one days without a day off. Usually, his only means of transportation to and from work was a dump truck. Herman took over again after recovering from his operation.

Herman and Wanda Midkiff

Both Mike and Steve graduated from the University of Kentucky. Mike graduated with a major in business and Steve graduated with a major in Psychology. Steve went on to Harvard University and earned his master's degree in Psychology. Brent attended Western Kentucky University for two years. Tim attended Madisonville Community College for two years.

Mike married Glenda Green, the daugher of Robert and Opal Stanley. While living in Georgetown, KY, Mike and Glenda adopted a son, Michael Ray Midkiff, Jr. Michael was born on Nov. 4, 1971. Soon Mike and Glenda moved to Central City where they had a son, Matthew Shane Midkiff. Matthew was born on Oct. 2, 1973.

Mike bought a grocery store three years later in Dawson Springs, Hopkins County, KY. The store was bought on the first day of August in 1976. When Mike and his family moved to Dawson Springs, a daughter, Amanda Kathleen Midkiff, was born. Amanda was born on Oct. 27, 1979. Mike is still the owner of Mike's IGA and his children attended Dawson Springs School.

Steve and Brent went their own ways, and both married. Tim, however, stayed in Dawson Springs and married Stephanie Russell of Dawson Springs. Tim also works at Mike's IGA. -*Submitted by Mike Midkiff*

EMIL GEORGE MILLER

Emil George Miller was born Oct. 3, 1853, and died Sept 6, 1911, of Bright's Disease. He attended public school in Evansville, IN, on Apr. 15, 1869, received a diploma from Evansville Business College with honorable examination in business application double entry bookkeeping, including steamboat bookkeeping, commercial calculations and penmanship.

Catherine and Emil George Miller

He was the son of John George Miller who was born in Delkenheim, in the duchy of Nassau, Germany, and who came to Evansville, IN on June 28, 1848. On Oct. 31, 1866, in Vandenburge, Co., IN, John George Miller became a naturalized citizen of the United States. John George was initiated into the Scheiller Lodge, IOOF, on May 29, 1857, and was elected secretary in 1867, Noble Grand in 1866 and Treasurer in 1870. John George Miller married Catherine Cristina Bastein, who was born in Germany in 1816 and died July 21, 1873.

Starting in 1870 and continuing until the confinement and continuing until the confinement caused his health to fail, Emil George and his father John George Miller, owned and operated the first shoe store in Evansville, Miller Shoe Store, 501 Main Street. Then they purchased a dairy farm on West Franklin Street in Evansville, IN, which was later moved to Kentucky Avenue.

Emil, George Miller married Catherine Roehrig on Jan. 21, 1875, in the Evangelic Church in Evansville, IN. Catherine, the daughter of John Jacob Roehrig (born on Mar. 21, 1825 and died on Apr. 2, 1879) and Magdalena Schneider (born on July 29, 1828 and died on May 25, 1887), was born on May 27, 1854 and died on Apr. 16, 1936. John Jacob and Magdalena, who was of French descent from Alsace Lorraine, met in Dusseldorf, Germany, where they married and came to the United States, traveling by covered wagon from Schenectady, NY to Booneville, IN, where they settled.

They had five daughters and one son, all born in Evansville:

1) Their son, John George Jacob, was born on Sept. 27, 1876, and died on Sept. 15, 1927. He was married to Maria Catherine (May) Dickman. They had three children, Harry Hobert, Lillian Catherine and Cecelia Maria. John came to Madisonville around 1900 and liked it so well he persuaded his parents move there in May of 1903, where they purchased and operated the Lucille Hotel and Restaurant at 122 Sugg Street, across from the Railroad Depot. The family then moved to Texas where John owned and operated The Traveling Miller Circus. John buried in San Antonio, TX.

2) The oldest daughter, Ida Emma, was born on Sept. 26, 1878 and died Mar. 30, 1903.

3) Catherine Lena was born on Aug. 8, 1881, and died on May 26, 1965. She married Hugh Beresford on Apr. 22, 1911, and moved to Seattle, WA, then later Honolulu, HI, where he was plant manager for Armour Meat Packing Company. They had one, son Robert Miller, who was born on Aug. 6, 1912, and died in January 1980, in Millbrae, CA. Catherine died while visiting in Madisonville; her remains are in Tacoma, WA. She was an active member of the Christian Science Church.

4) Helena Emilia was born on Jan. 2, 1884. She graduated from Central High School in Evansville, IN, on June 14, 1901. On May 18, 1904, she married Ed Willis in Evansville; however, they were divorced in 1911. She moved to Madisonville and married Edd Lee Lacy on Apr. 16, 1911, in Hopkinsville. Helena Emilia died in Madisonville on Feb. 13, 1928 as a result of a car/train accident a"Dead Man's Curve," west of Madisonville. Helen and Edd are buried in Oak Hill Cemetery in Evansville, IN. They had two daughters, Ruby Catherine and Carrie Elizabeth and one son, Charles Edward, who died in infancy.

Ruby Catherine (Katy) was born on Dec. 3, 1911, in Glasgow, KY, and died on Sept. 24, 1974, in Winston-Salem, NC; her remains are in Oak Hill Cemetery in Evansville, IN. She graduated from Madisonville High School in 1929 and married William Hammack Tapp, July 8, 1935, son of Hugh Tapp and Wesley Murphey of Madisonville.

Carrie Elizabeth was born on Oct 13, 1913, in Glasgow, KY. Her family then moved back to Madisonville. Carrie graduated from Madisonville High School on May 22, 1931. She was married to William Lyalls Stewart of St. Charles, KY, on Apr. 24, 1937. They had three daughters, Catharine Eulilia, Sandra Lyle and Carrie Elizabeth II.

Charles Edward Lacy was born on July 4, 1915, and died the following week on July 11, 1915. He is buried in Grapevine Cemetery in Madisonville area.

5) Adeline Nettie was born on Apr. 13, 1886, and died in Madisonville on Sept. 4, 1976. She married Pearl Chester Williams on May 14, 1911. They had four children, all born in Madisonville: Catherine Elvira was born Aug. 6, 1912; Thelma Louise was born on Jan. 1, 1915; Emil Johnson was born on Nov. 23, 1916; and John Edmond was born on July 5, 1919, died Nov. 25, 1965, and is buried at Odd Fellows Cemetery in Madisonville, KY.

6) Carolina Elizabeth was born on June 11, 1889, and died on June 15, 1915, in Evansville, IN, following surgery for appendicitis. She had graduated from Central High School and Lockyear's Business College in Evansville, IN. She worked in Madisonville as cashier for Dulin's Department Store and was a member of the First Presbyterian Church.

Refer to: William Lyalls and Carrie Elizabeth Lacy Stewart. Submitted by Mrs. Lyall Stewart

FERN WOOLFOLK MILLER

Mary Fern Woolfolk was born Mar. 7, 1877, at Madisonville, KY. She was the daughter of Sarah Elizabeth Clay Givens Woolfolk and Sherwood Hicks Woolfolk. Her mother, Sara (Sallie), had been married to Nathaniel Givens, and after his death, married Sherwood H. Woolfolk at Madisonville on Jan. 23, 1874. Sherwood Woolfolk had been married earlier to Mary Magruder until her death in 1867. From these marriages Mary Fern had a half sister, Frances Givens (Fannie), and a half brother, Lillburn Woolfolk. May Fern was the second of five children from her parent's marriage: Maggie Mae, Mary Fern, Agnes, Clay, and Samuel Snowden Woolfolk.

Fern Woolfolk Miller

Mary Fern was called Fern and attended school in Madisonville. Her father, Sherwood Woolfolk, was a lawyer at Madisonville in partnership with his brother-in-law, John Bayless Earle. Sherwood Woolfolk also served in the Kentucky State Legislature from 1871 to 1873. While in Kentucky, the family lived at Madisonville, except for a few years (probably 1880 to 1884) when they lived on a tobacco estate near Providence, KY. Mr. Woolfolk had served in the Civil War as a Captain for the Confederacy in Co. I, 8th Co. of Confederate Volunteers. He was captured at Chester, OH, and imprisoned along with 67 other officers at Columbus, OH. His health was impaired due to this, so he moved to the drier climate of Kansas, and to the call of cheaper lands in the West.

Fern lived in Kentucky until she was nine years of age. The family moved to Kansas, arriving in Pratt County on Apr. 1, 1886. Life was hard at first on the Kansas prairie with prairie fires and the wind sweeping across level fields, but the Woolfolks preserved and had a good life. Fern had such fond memories of her childhood in Kentucky that she wrote a book at the age of 85 about those recollections. These interesting insights led her descendants to return several time to Hopkins County for visits with relatives and viewing the beautiful Kentucky countryside. Other Kentucky ancestral names are Berry McDowell, Williams and Clay.

Fern married George David Miller on Mar. 16, 1897, in Pratt, KS. George Miller was the son of Marion Co., KY, parents who had also moved to Kansas. George and Fern lived during their marriage on farms in Pratt and Barber Counties of Kansas until they moved in November 1912 to Sawyer, KS, to gain a better education for their four sons: Marion John (b. Jan. 5, 1898; m. Sybil McReynolds), Percival Sherward (b.. Nov. 28, 1902; m. Dorothy Davis), George Junior (b. June 2, 1907), Loyce Veryl (b. July 24, 1909; m. June Eberle). George Miller was a farmer and rancher until his death Oct. 28, 1954. Fern had a true pioneer spirit that enabled her to endure hardships and make a good home for her husband and sons. She remained remarkably active until her early 90's when failing energies slowed her pace.

She passed away Jan. 39, 1971, at Pratt, KS, in her 93rd year. Fern and George Miller are buried beside her parent's graves at the Coats, Kansas Cemetery.

Their grandchildren are: Mac Wendell Miller (m. Harriet Johnson), Wayne Eugene Miller (m. Shirley Allen), Margaret Corinne Miller Davis (m. Ronald Davis), Twyla Fern Miller Dubois (m. Martin Dubois); great grandchildren: Marcia Dawn Miller, Mercer Wayne Miller, Lesa Renee Miller Sailor (m. John Sailor), Lori Gail Miller Buchholz (m. Glenn Buchholz), Mark Ronald Davis (m. Susan peters), Alan Sherwood Davis (m. Beth Herzet), Steven Christopher Davis, Leslie Renne Dubois, Jacqueline Ann Dubois; and one great-great-granddaughter, Kelli Lynn Davis. *Submitted by M. Corinne Miller Davis.*

LESTER MIMMS

Had circumstances been different or society a bit more advanced in the early years after the turn of the century, Lester Mimms might have been a professional athlete or president of a major company or even a member of Congress. He had both the talent and drive to excel in any profession. But he was far ahead of his time....so he had to settle for one of the most successful careers in education that any teacher has ever had. For forty years, Hopkins County prospered from the dynamic, intelligent leadership that Lester provided.

Lester Mimms

The early 1900's were tough times for most people in Earlington. the St. Bernard Coal Company was the city's only employer, and miner's wages were too low to support a family. Most men subsidized their incomes by working long hours in their fields after they had completed shifts in the mines. Women did domestic work, raised the children, took care of the homes and worked with the men in the fields. It was a constant struggle for most families to keep enough food on the table and maintain an adequate place to live.

Emma Mimms, Lester's mother, was determined that her son would have a better life. He was going to get an education. For most people, such a goal was unrealistic. When children were old enough, it was expected that they would lend their efforts to help support the family, but this tradition was not in Emma's plan for Lester. She wasn't discouraged that her idea required money, an item that Jesse, Lester's father, had little of. No detail of such minor importance would ruin her dream; she had faith. So with pockets full of little more than his mother's faith and a bag bursting wither her expectations. Lester enrolled at the Simmons Academy in Louisville when he was only fourteen.

The Simmons Academy was both a high school and a college. All students were housed together in two dormitories—one for men, one for women. Any 14 year old kid was lucky to survive the first semester. Lester compressed his growing up into a few short months. Not only did he adapt to the new environment at Simmons, he soon became a campus leader, starring on the school's basketball and football teams.

After graduation, Lester returned to Hopkins County — not by choice, but the great depression forced it. Already, he had missed more meals than he cared to recall and to try to survive this national crisis in Louisville would have been suicide.

His first job was in St. Charles where he ran their one-room school program. He was hired to teach at Earlington's Million High School the following year.

Over the next thirty-two years, Lester transformed a typical "school for colored" to one of the most exciting and successful secondary institutions for learning in the south. Million High School put Earlington on the map. The school's reputation for producing superior students and good basketball teams spread from Evansville to Nashville and from Harlan to Paducah. Million instilled a fierce competitive spirit and a sense of pride in its students that other schools could not match. It was Lester's philosophy of education that made the difference.

In his role as school bus driver, counselor, basketball coach, math and science teacher, and principal, Lester was able to inject his positive, all-encompassing approach to education in every fiver of the school system. He believed that a good school had to provide and atmosphere conducive to learning — so he managed Million with the efficiency of a well-run business. He believed that school buildings and grounds should be clean — so he joined teachers and students in details to pick up trash. He believed that motivation was essential in the teaching process —so he spent a lot of time complimenting other teachers, students, and parents for anything positive that he could identify. Most of all, Lester believed that the total individual had to be involved in the learning process — so he insisted that teacher show legitimate concern about each student as a person - whether they were eating properly and had warm clothes to wear in winter. When students had needs that the school could not deal with, Lester contacted the churches and social service agencies to solicit help.

Million's students went forward to excel in professions ranging from education to business and from coal mining to auto mechanics. Lester had often said that his school never produced a failure; some students were simply more successful than others.

In 1966, Earlington consolidated the "colored" and "white" high schools. Lester joined the faculty of the newly integrated Earlington High School as a social science teacher. But in the second year of its operation, Lester was appointed principal becoming the first black person to hold the position in an integrated school in the south.

Soon the entire city of Earlington knew that Lester's approach to education that succeeded at Million was not "black" magic. It worked equally as well for white students.

As incredible as it was, Lester found time to do other things during his teaching career:

He was superintendent of the Cherokee State Park (The South's Finest Park for Negroes) on Kentucky Lake for two summers in the early 1950's. He was the first black person to hold such a position of employment in the State Department of Parks.

He earned his Masters Degree with honors from the University of Indiana.

He served on the Board of Regents for Kentucky State University.

Lester retired in 1970. Any person with a lesser sense of duty would have assessed his long list of accomplishments as an overpayment of his debt to society and looked forward to the serene days at the fishing ponds and golf courses. But Lester could not resist the challenge that the Pennyrile Area Community Action Program offered to direct the Head Start project for pre-school age children in Muhlenberg and Hopkins Counties. So after only a few months, he came out of retirement. Again, he implemented the policies that supported his teaching philosophy, and they worked as well with the little children as they had with older students. In a short time, Lester's Head Start Program achieved a high level of success than similar programs had attained in other communities after years of operation.

Later, Lester was asked to develop and implement a program for senior citizens. He led the efforts to remodel the recreational facility and he worked with people in the community to establish projects that matched the needs of the elderly.

He retired again in 1973.

Lester Mimms was one of the most talented and intelligent leaders of his time. He knew a better way to teach. And he made Earlington a better place in which to learn. *Submitted by Corria Mimms and written by Ronald Mimms*

MITCHELL

In approximately 1850, Ambrose Mitchell moved his family from North Carolina to Hopkins County, KY, settling north of Madisonville. They settled on a 900-acre farm, much of which is presently in the Madisonville city limits. He had four daughters; Frank Mitchell Strum, Cornelia Mitchell Denny, Sue Mitchell Slaton, and Sally Mitchell; and four sons, Sam Mitchell, Wiley Mitchell, Bud Mitchell and the youngest Jesse Nathaniel Mitchell.

The Mitchell sisters - Jessie Lee Mitchell Mangum, Pella Othella Mitchell Powers and Earnestyne Mitchell Buchanan

Jesse Nathaniel Mitchell married Cordelia Hopgood and they had six children; William Ambrose Mitchell, Pella Othella Mitchell Powers, Jessie Lee Mitchell Mangum, Oather Harland Mitchell, Gracie May Mitchell (who died at birth), and Earnestyne Mitchell Buchanan, who is the only one still living.

In 1917, Earnestyne married Eros Thomas Buchanan, son of Johnnie Franklin Buchanan and Nola Pinkston Buchanan. His brothers were Myrlah F. and Vernon. Earnestyne and Eros Buchanan had one child , a daughter, Sarah Ruth Buchanan Mock, who was born on the site which now accommodates the Madisonville Community College. They had one granddaughter, Judy Gaddis, and one great-grandson, Mitchell Fielding Gaddis, who was named for his great-grandmother.

Part of this aforementioned farmland is now owned by the Madisonville Community College, Lakeshore County Club and the Madisonville Industrial Park. Approximately one-ninth of this original farm still remains in the Mitchell Family, on which the family of Earnestyne Mitchell Buchanan's granddaughter now resides. -*Submitted by Judy Gaddis*

MOORE-CUNNINGHAM

Scott Milton Moore was born May 11, 1876, the son fo Charlie Moore, born 1837 died 1917, and Miss Matt Chamles, b. —died Feb.. 13, 1882, from Robertson Co., TN. Scott M. was first married to Fannie Smith, and they had one daughter, Beulah Moore, born 1-11-1908, who resides in Louisville. IN Hopkins County on Oct. 30, 1920, Scott M. Moore married Leona Belle Parker, born Apr. 30, 1893, daughter of John Parker, born 1842 died 1913, and Martha Jane Dunning. They are all buried at Union Temple Cemetery near St. Charles, KY. Scott and Leona's children were:

The Moore family. From l-r: Back row: Wesley and George II. 2nd row: Janine, Cindy and George Steele. 3rd row: Thelma and George Sr. Front - Justin Jennings

1. John Robert Moore, born June 19, 1925, died 1929, age four years.

2. George Albert Moore, born Apr. 29, 1927 in Hopkins County.

3. Leona had one daughter, Martha Elizabeth "Betty" Terry born 1-8-1919, who lives in Florida. Se is married to Louis Jerome "Red" Vogt.

George Albert Moore and Thelma Jean Cunningham married July 16, 1949, at Hopkinsville, KY. George is a truck operator at Cimmaron Mines. They have four children:

Cynthia Diane 'Cindy' Moore, born Nov. 17, 1953. She graduated from Madisonville High School, and is retired from the office at Krogers. She is married to George Ivy Steele, who works at Steele's Car Wash/Station.

George A. Moore II, born Oct. 20, 1956. He is single, graduated from Madisonville High School, and attended Madisonville Community College. He has been a City Councilman, Ward 5, in Madisonville for 12 years, since he was 18 years old.

Wesley Kim Moore, born Oct. 13, 1957, is married to Pamela Janine Jenkins Moore, daugher of Charles W. and Rella G. Jenkins. (See JENKINS-WARREN).

Scott Jerome Moore, born May 1, 1963, is a graduate of Madisonville-North Hopkins High School. He was employed in produce at Krogers before enlisting in the service. He is married to Lori Brink of New York whom he met while they were in service in Texas.They have one daughter, Kaitlyn Diane Moore, born Aug. 20, 1987. They reside at Hastings on the Hudson, NY. Scott is employed by a Produce Company Warehouse. - *Submitted by Thelma Cunningham Moore*

MOORE-HOPPER

Zelma Hopper, born May 6, 1912, is the daughter of Fulton Hopper and Virdie Ann grace. Her grandparents were Franklin and Mary Hopper, and Houston and Alydia Lauderdale Grace who was a Cherokee Indian.

Leslie Moore, born June 13, 1910, is the son of Callie Matheny and James Jackson Moore, who died in January of 1917. His grandparents were Thomas Ray and Mary Moore and Al Matheny.

Leslie was six years old when his father died and was forced to work the fields of the family farm. He was a descendant of Irish immigrants, who were o strangers to hard work. At the age of fifteen, he took a job in the coal mines with Hart Mining Company of White City. there, he met the beautiful dark-haired, blue-eyed Zelma Hopper. Her father was employed by the same mining company, so they lived in the same mining camp community. Leslie and Zelma soon fell in love and wanted very much to marry. She was fifteen, he was seventeen, and their parents would not allow it. Leslie arranged to "steal" Zelma away, with the help of Ulas Uzzle, who has a Model-T Ford. On July 16, 1926, Zelma met Leslie at his house and Ulas Uzzle planned to drive them to Clarksville, TN to marry. They began their journey but soon had to turn around because they couldn't push the Model-T up Moss Hill. The rain had made the dirt road too muddy and slick. Leslie was determined to make Zelma his bride, so they detoured through Mortons Gap where the roads were flat. They made it to Clarksville, and were married that day.

Leslie and Zelma lived in the mining camp in White City and began their lives as man and wife. They would sit in a small park in the evenings and listen to another resident of the camp sing "Bonnie Blue Eyes" for Zelma, because her eyes were such a beautiful blue. Leslie continued his work in the mines.

To this union seven children were born. Hallie Lee, who died in infancy, Edith Gordon, Jo Merit, Kenneth Ray, Jewel Lester, Gloria Mae, and Michael Glen. They have fifteen grandchildren and sixteen great grandchildren. - *Submitted by Sharon Lam*

DONALD WAYNE MOORE

Donald Wayne Moore was born on Aug. 17, 1944 in his home in Hopkins County.

Don's mother was Mary Carter who wasborn in Muhlenberg County in 1909 and died in 1947. His father was Lucian Moore who was born in Christian County in 1900 and died in 1967. Mary and Lucian where the parents of eleven children, six daughters and five sons. The daughters were Janie, Loretta, Teen, Mari and Hilda. Hilda is now deceased. The five sons, were Ezra, Leon, Eual, Don and Earnest. Earnest is now deceased.

Don's father, Lucian, was also married to Pauline Gresby and they had two children, a daughter Lela and a son Johnnie.

Don married Barbara Bourland and they had two daughters, Teresa and Donna. Teresa was born on Mar. 7, 1962 in El Paso, TX on an army base. Donna was born Aug. 29, 1964 in Madisonville, Hopkins County, KY. Teresa is married to John Alexander and has two daughters, Tara and Misty. Donna is married to Mark Martin and has two daughters, Lindsay and Sandra.

Don was also married to Pamela McLemore. They had a daughter, Kristal, who was born in Madisonville, Hopkins County, KY on Dec. 21, 1972. She is a sophomore at Dawson Springs High School in Dawson Springs, KY.

Don is presently married to Judy Parrish. From this marriage, he has three stepchildren. Kevin, the oldest, is 24 and single. Karen is 23 and has two children, Michael and Tabetha. Keith the youngest, is 21 and single. Don and Judy live on Carter Drive in Madisonville. They have been married eleven years.

Don is currently employed with P&M Coal Company at Colonial Mines. He has been with the company for 22 years. He has worked as a shovel operator, dragline operator, welder, temple man and now is the supply clerk. He has also owned and operated his own wrecker and sanitation company. He operated both for seven years and recently sold his sanitation business but kept his wrecker service.

Don was a Boy Scout for six years. He served 5 1/2 years in the Army, stationed in Germany for 2 1/2 years. While in the Army, he guided missile maintenance. He received a good conduct medal and was "Soldier of the Month" in 1960 in West Germany. Don received his G.E.D. in the Army and attended vocational school in 1962.

Some of the clubs and organizations Don had been involved with are the Dixie Flyers, which began in 1971, and he was Past Master of the Masonic Lodge 143 in Madisonville in 1970 and Beulah Masonic Lodge 609 in 1980. -*Submitted by Kristal Moore*

EDWARD WELDON MOORE

Ed Weldon was born in Madisonville, KY, July 6, 1930. He was the only child of William Edward "Bill Ed" Moore and Aurelia Weldon. He was raised at 336 Hall Street and attended Hall Street Elementary School. He graduated from Madisonville High School in 1948 as valedictorian. He played the trumpet in both his high school and college bands. Ed Weldon received a B.A. Degree in Chemistry from Vanderbilt University in 1952, and his M.D. in 1955. He performed his internship and residency at Harvard (Boston City Hospital). Additional graduate work was completed at Harvard, MIT and Tuft Universities.

Doctor Moore performed cancer research at the National Insitutes of Health for two years. He returned to Boston in 1959 to spend a year with Harvard Medical Services, Boston City Hospital. In 1960 he resumed research at the Lemuel Shattack Hospital for several years.

Presently Dr. Moore is a Professor of Medicine, Physiology and Pathology at the Medical College of Virginia, Richmond, VA. He has had many visiting lectureships and has published many articles in the medical field.

He married Carolyn Rice, daughter of Nathanial "Than" Rice and Leota Rice of Madisonville on Sept. 11, 1954. They had four children: Emilie and Valerie, twins born on July 14, 1955, Edward Nathaniel "Ned", born on Aug. 26, 1958, and Angela Patricia, born on Mar. 17, 1960. They divorced in 1961. He then married Inge K. Rasmusen in Denmark on Sept. 5, 1963. They have two children: Niels Edward, born on July 22, 1968, and Karen Lisa, born on Jan. 29, 1975. - *Submitted by Robert P. Moore*

JAMES A. MOORE

Jim Al Moore was born in Madisonville, KY on Oct. 20, 1915. He moved to Washington with his father and mother in April of 1924. He graduated from Western High School in 1931, with many honors. He was a finalist, National High School Oratorical contest, 1931; class treasurer 1931; Student Council 1931; Debating Team 1930-31; and Cadet Captain 1931. He attended prep school at Lavilla, Lausanne and Grindelwald, Switzerland, in 1931 and 1931. He graduated from the University of Kentucky with an AB degree, cum laude in 1936. College found Jim Al on the tennis team in 1934 through 1936 and as co-captain in 1936.

He was an Omicorn Delta Kappa in 1936, on the debating team in 1935-36; and the winner of the Oratorical Contest in 1935. He was also an ROTC Cadet Captain in 1936 and served on the student council in 1936.

Jim Al graduated from Harvard University with an LLB in 1939 and was a member of the Harvard Law School Legal Aid Bureau in 1937-39.

He married Dorothy Marie Kelly in 1941. They were divorced in 1968. They had three children: Marjorie M. Eickel, James Kelly Moore, and Kathleen M. Marozzi.

He became an associate in Pepper, Bodine, Stokes, and Schoch (now Pepper Hamilton and Scheetz) in 1931 and became a partner in 1951. He later headed the tax department and was a member of the Executive Committee. He opened the Washington office of the firm in 1969. Jim Al retired in 1977 to devote more time to the Camelback Ski Area.

Jim Al served in the United States Naval Reserve as an Ensign Lieutenant from July 4, 1942, to Dec. 7, 1945. He later retired as a Lieutenant Commander.

He was a member of the American Law Institute, formerly on Tax Advisory Committee, member of the tax section, American Bar Association, formerly chairman of and Special Advisor to Exempt Organizations Committee.

He was one of the founders of Camelback Ski Area and the president of Camelback Ski Corporation from its incorporation in 1962 until 1986. Jim Al is listed in Who's Who in the South and Southwest from 1975 to 1980, listed in Who's Who in America since 1980 and is the author of various published articles pertaining primarily to the tax law and the ski industry. - *Submitted by Robert P. Moore*

JOHN TAYLOR MOORE

John Taylor Moore is my paternal grandfather. When John was eighteen, he went into World War II as a cook. When he was twenty-one, he met my grandmother, Nell Catherine Farar. At the age of twenty-three, they got married and had their first of three sons, Johnny Wayne Moore, husband of Janet Johnson and father of John Moore, Jr., and Sherry Moore.

After Johnny Wayne, Tommy Jackson Moore was born, the husband of Roxann McGregor and the father of Tommy Alan Moore and Brian Daniel Moore.

Next Jimmy Moore was born, the husband of Kathy Jo Bayer and the father of James Jeremy Moore and Joshua David Moore.

Tommy Moore is my father and he is currently working at Green River Coal Company. Jimmy and Johnny Moore are currently unemployed, but were also former coal miners.

When John Taylor was twelve years old, he dropped out of school to help out with the family chores. Since he lived on a farm, there was much to be done. He had two brothers, Dewey Wayne Moore and Verlan Moore. Dewey, the oldest of the three, is a coal miner and has never been married.

Verlan, the youngest of the three, is married to Roena Kay Johnson and is the father of Kenny Moore. Kenny Moore is the husband of Carole Davis and the father of Ryan Moore.

John Taylor never got more than an eighth grade education but he has worked all his life. He lived in Hopkins County when he was twenty-seven and is currently living in Christian County at Hopkinsville.

Since John Taylor has retired, he can't do much, so now he works at an automatic car wash in Hopkinsville. John is a very religious man and wherever he goes, if it is on Sunday, he will find some church to go to. His original church is the Apostolic Holiness Church in Dawson Springs. He has known Rev. David Bayer all of his life. -*Submitted by Brian Moore*

JAMES HOMER MOORE

Jim Moore graduated from Marion High School and later Kentucky State College (now the University of Kentucky) at Lexington, with a degree in Agriculture.

At age 22, he enlisted in the United States Army on Sept. 19, 1917, at Marion, KY. He was honorably discharged at Camp Zachary Taylor, KY on Oct. 25, 1918, as a Regimental Sergeant Major. The reason stated on the discharge was to accept a commission as a Second Lieutenant, AG-DUSA.

While a Corporal at Camp Zachary Taylor, he married Ina Darnell, the daughter of James Allen and Elzora Darnell. She was a high school English teacher at Danville, KY. They were married in Louisville, KY on Nov. 28, 1917. Ina Darnell graduated valedictorian from Paducah High School in 1912, and later moved to Nashville, TN, with her parents.

After the war, they moved to Tennessee where Jim taught and was the high school principal at Murfreesboro and Shelbyville. At one of these high schools he was also a baseball coach. He claims to have coached Tommy Bridges, who later became a truly great pitcher for the Detroit Tigers—better than a twenty-game winner several times and pitched for the 1934 and 1935 pennant winners.

In 1935 or 1936, Jim and his two brothers, Virgil and Abe, formed a partnership to buy a farm at Vandetta near Hanson, KY. Jim lived there on what was called the "bluff" and was the managing partner of the farm until it was sold in 1957.

Ina was a 1916 graduate of the University of Kentucky. She taught in schools in Monticello, Danville and Marion, KY, before returning to Hanson school in 1936. She taught at Hanson until retiring in 1963. She was also principal during the last eight years of that time.

Jim and Ina are buried at West Lawn Cemetery near Hanson. -*Submitted by Robert P. Moore*

JAMES L. "MONK" MOORE

James Lawrence (Monk), the second oldest of four children born to Richard Edward Moore and Lorena "Lora" Mae Hall, was born at home—416 East Broadway, Madisonville, KY, on Feb. 6, 1905. He graduated from Madisonville High School and attended the University of Kentucky.

Monk went to work at the post office June 27, 1923, as a substitute carrier. He advanced to regular carrier on Nov. 6, 1923, and was promoted to post office clerk Dec. 17, 1923. In June of 1929, he was promoted to Assistant Postmaster of the Madisonville Post Office, a position he held until his retirement on Jan. 1, 1963.

Monk served in the United States Army during World War II in the Pacific Theater. He entered active duty on Feb. 1, 1943, and served as postal officer with the 15th Base Post Office, Army Post Office #59. He was relieved from active duty on Aug. 21, 1946, with the rank of Captain. Among his decorations and citations were the American Theater Service Medal, Asiatic Pacific Service Medal and Victory Medal. Prior to his active service, he completed approximately twenty years with the Kentucky National Guard. He was the "ranking" second lieutenant prior to activation.

He married Katherine Eades Overall, the daughter of James Dreyfus Overall and Goldie Katherine Eades, on Oct. 3, 1927. They had one daugher, Martha Eades Moore, born on Aug. 14, 1932.

Katherine received her B.A. Degree from Kentucky Wesleyan College, 'having completed three years at Georgetown College. She taught several years before going back to college to complete her degree. After graduation, Katherine taught math and reading in junior high school for seventeen years before retiring.

Monk died of cancer at age 58, and is buried at Oddfellows Cemetery, Madisonville, KY. Katherine presently lives at 47 West Noel Avenue, Madisonville, KY. - *Submitted by Robert P. Moore*

LEVI M. MOORE

Levi M. Moore owned land in Hopkins Co., KY in 1838, a lot in Providence, that he bought from William Jenkins and wife. In 1842, Levi M. along with his brother Simpson M. Moore and his brother-in-law John Smith bought land on Tradewater River, from Samuel Montgomery and wife. By 1848, Levi M. and family were in Desha County, AR, where Levi M. and his wife died of cholera.

Levi M. Moore was born about 1808 in Kentucky, the son of Levi Moore, Sr., who died 1820 in Muhlenberg Co., KY. He had the following brothers and sisters and possible more: Edith who married Kinyard Hay; Absale Ann who married John Smith Jr.; Susannah who married Oliver Harper; Amariah who married Elenor Bogus; William M. who married Delila McPherson; Joseph W. who married Ann H. Boyd; Simpson M. who married first Fannie W. Rice, second Martha Barnhill; Alney M.; Ira; and Silas.

Levi M. was found in the 1830 census of Morgan Co., IL. He married Margret Vertress in 1830 Morgan Co., IL. She was the daughter of John and Nancy Haycraft Vertress. They were the parents of three children: Apsala Ann married first H.H. Marsh and second Thomas Quartron in Morgan Co., IL, Josephus and Nancy.

I am the great-great-granddaughter of Levi M. and wife Margret Moore. - *Submitted by Mrs. LaVerl Quarton Hilyard.*

MARTHA EADES MOORE

Martha was the only child born to James Lawrence Moore and Katherine Eades Overall in Madisonville, KY, on Aug. 14, 1932. She attended grade school at Waddill Avenue (except for the 6th and 7th grades when she moved to Washington, DC, while "Monk", her father, was in the Army). She returned to Madisonville in 1945 and graduated from Madisonville High School in 1950 as Valedictorian.

She received her B.S. Degree in Chemistry from Georgetown College in 1954, graduating summa cum laude. She also served as president of the chemistry fraternity. Her first job was as a chemist with Meade Johnson in Evansville, IN. her roommate in Evansville was a friend of the Alldredge family and she was introduced and eventually married Gordon Alldredge, son of Floyd and Amy Redenour Alldredge, on Dec. 8, 1956. They had two children: Larry, born May 15, 1960, and Kathy, born Mar. 1, 1963.

Gordon Alldredge, who studied agriculture at Purdue University, was a fourth generation farmer from Mt. Vernon, where they lived after their marriage. They raised grain and livestock on approximately 200 acres. Martha left Meade Johnson when Larry was born. Gordon died Sept. 17, 1983. He was an elder of the Mt. Vernon First Presbyterian Church. Martha became an elder in 1983. She is very active in church affairs and is the choir director.

Martha has always been a Girl Scout and is still active the Raintree Council. Martha is also active with Red Cross and teaches classes in first aid and CPR. Her first-aid class was taught by her aunt, Jane Pride Moore, in 1947 or 1948, when Martha was a Girl Scout. - *Submitted by Robert P. Moore*

NEVILLE "ABE" MOORE

Neville "Abe" Moore was a prominent Madisonville attorney for fifty years. He retired from practice on Jan. 1, 1970 ending an active career that began in 1920 when he started his legal career with his late father, Allie C. Moore, an association that lasted until 1923.

Abe graduated from Marion High School in 1916, and received his LLB degree from the University of Kentucky in 1920. In 1923, he joined the well-known law firm of Gordon, Gordon & Moore, an association that lasted until 1951. In 1951, he became associated with Carroll Morrow under the firm name of Moore & Morrow, which later became Moore, Morrow & Frymire.

Abe was married May 28, 1936, to Floriene Ellis. He was a member of the Republican State Central Committee from 1932 to 1940; supervisor of the Census of the Second Congressional District in 1930; was a director of Madisonville Building and Loan Association; and a director of the Kentucky Bank and Trust Company for years until he relinquished that office in 1967. He was a member of the Madisonville Elks Lodge and a member of the Madisonville Chamber of Commerce.

Abe was inducted into the United States Army at age 42 on Aug. 25, 1942, in Evansville, IN. He was discharged a Master Sargeant on July 17, 1943. He was stationed at Fort Campbell, KY, where he applied his legal training in the staff Judge Advocate Office. He was believed to have also served in the United States Army during a portion of World War I. - *Submitted by Robert P. Moore*

NORVELL HALL MOORE

Norvell Hall Moore was the third of four children of Richard Edward Moore (10 Apr. 1876 - 4 mar. 1959) and Lorena "Lora" Mae Hall (25 July 1881 -11 Dec. 1938), the others being William Edward "Bill Ed" Moore (b. 26 Jan. 1903), James Lawrence "Monk" Moore (6 Feb. 1905 - 25 Mar. 1963), and Anita Belle Moore Poole (b. 8 Nov. 1916). He was the grandchild of Judge James Alexander Moore (29 Oct. 1836 - 24 Nov. 1924) and Martha Bourland (14 Feb. 1845 - 18 Sept. 1930) of Marion, Crittenden Co., KY.

Norvell was born in his parents' home at 416 East Broadway, Madisonville, Hopkins Co., KY, on 29 Dec. 1912. This was his residence at death, having acquired the home from his father in 1946. He attended Madisonville High School, Western Kentucky State College and the University of Kentucky where he studied toward an electrical and mechanical engineering degree. He joined the Kentucky National Guard at the age of 16 and at the outbreak of World War II was activated with the 149th Inf., 38th Div.

He was a much noted sharpshooter with the rifle and pistol and qualified as one of the top 100 marksmen in the nation during the 1936-39 National Rifle Matches at Camp Perry, OH.

On June 4, 1943, in New Orleans, LA, Norvell married Jane Lillian Pride (21 Aug. 1917 - 3 Mar. 1986), the daughter of Robert Silas Pride (1 Dec. 1880 - 6 May 1942) and Cyrena Helon Jagoe (26 Apr. 1882 - 5 June 1972).

The day his unit was called to active duty (6 Jan. 1941), Norvell was commissioned a Second Lieutenant. During WWII he served in four campaigns: Marianna, New Guinea, Phillipines and Rynkyu. During his service in the Pacific, Norvell served on the staff of General John R. Hodge, Commander of the 24th Corps. He also served for a brief time on the staff of General Douglas MacArthur. After V-J Day, he served in Korea as its first Provost Marshall. He was also the protocol officer for the surrender of the Japanese forces in Korea on 9 Sept. 1945.

While in Hawaii with the 38th Division, Norvell was transferred to the newly-formed 24th Corps and was selected as a project officer for a highly specialized school to train specially selected men to perform reconnaissance from rubber boats launched from submarines. Due to his outstanding performance as a commandant of this school, he was selected to be the assistant operations officer (G-3) for the V Marine Amphibious Corps which was being formed for General MacArthur. He was one of two Amry personnel serving with the Marines. It was while serving with his famous unit that he participated in the amphibious assaults on the Marianna Island, the Phillipines, New Guinea, Ryukya and several other less publicized landings. He became known throughout the Pacific Theater as an expert in assault landings.

Among the decorations he received were the Amry Team Badge, Combat Infantry Badge, Bronze Star with device for second award, Asiatic-Pacific Ribbon, tow Bronze Service Stars from the Marianna Island Campaign, the Army Liberation Ribbon with two Bronze Service Stars, a Battle Star for the Ryukya Campaign, the Bronze Arrowhead for the Assault Landing on Saipan, and the Navy-Marine Citation for Amphibious Operations with the V Amphibious Corps.

Following deactivation, he organized the National Guard in Western Kentucky. He was commander of the 3rd Battallion, 149th Infantry. In 1950, he resigned from the National Guard to form an Army Reserve Battalion, which was part of the 100th Division. He was succeeded by his good friend, Wilbur Meredith of Bowling Green. A graduate of the Army Command and General Staff College, he also taught in that school's branch at Ft. Meade, MD, for several years.

In 1952, General Hodge, his Pacific commander, took over as commander of the Continental Army Command at Fort Monroe, MD, and requested that the then Colonel Moore to be assigned to his headquarters in a reserve capacity working in the G-3 operations section.

Norvell and Jane Moore had three sons: Norvell Hall Moore, Jr. (b. 13 Apr. 1944), who married H. Marlene Fusting of Louisville, KY; Robert Pride Moore (b. 12, Aug. 1946), who married Judith Ann King of Upton, KY; and Richard Edward Moore II (b. 26 Dec. 1950) who married Cynthia Lynn Coburn of Madisonville, KY.

Novell Moore was a longtime businessman in Madisonville. He was a painting contractor for approximately 40 years; a partner of R.E. Moore & Son Hardware Store for 10 years; and the preparation plant manager for Caney Creek Coal Mines for three years. He was a member of the St. Mary's Episcopal Church where he served on the vestry and as senior warden. He was a member of the Benevolent and Protective Order of the Elks, Lodge No. 738, and was the first commander of the Bailey Pride V.F.W. Post.

Norvell is buried in Grapevine Cemetery, Grapeview Road, Madisonville, KY. He died of cancer on 3 May 1986 at the age of 73, exactly two months after the death of his wife, Jane. - *Submitted by Robert P. Moore*

NORVELL H. MOORE, JR.

Norvell Moore, the oldest son of Norvell Hall Moore, Sr. and Jane Lillian Pride was born in Nashville, TN, on Apr. 13, 1944. He attended Hall Street Elementary School, Seminary Junior High School and graduated from Madisonville High School in June of 1962. Norvell attended Western Kentucky State College for two years before enlisting in the Kentucky National Guard on June 3, 1964. Norvell returned from active duty on Dec. 12, and enrolled for another semester at Western. In May of 1965, he was selected as one of two Kentucky National Guardsmen to attend the Officers Candidate School at Fort Benning, GA. Norvell graduated from O.C.S. as a Second Lieutenant, Infantry, on Aug. 23, 1965. Again he enrolled for another semester at Western Kentucky University.

Sometime in December of 1965, Norvell was asked if he would go to work for the Pittsburgh and Midway Coal Mining Company. On Jan. 31, 1966, he started to work for P&M in Waycross, GA, as a Drilling Coordinator and worked all over southern Georgia and northern Florida prospecting for phosphate. In April, he was transferred to DeCovan, KY to work on a drill rig, coring coal for the DeCovan Mine. During a National Guard summer camp in 1965, he met Marlene Fusting, daughter of Thomas Fusting and Beatrice Barrett of Louisville, KY, whom he married on May 13, 1967. On Nov. 1, 1967, Norvell and Marlene were transferred to Columbus, KS. As a prospect driller for P&M, his work took him to Illinois, Kansas, Colorado, New Mexico, Missour and occasionally back in Kentucky. Some time during 1968, he moved to Fort Scott, KS, and on Dec. 14, 1969, his first son Michael Hall was born. In June of 1970, Norvell, Marlene and Michael moved back to Kentucky. Norvell went to work at the P&M Paradise Mine as a Mine Foreman. While living in Greenville, KY, a second son, Stephen Thomas, was born on May 11, 1971. In March of 1974, Norvell was transferred to the P&M Colonial Mine as the Master Mechanic responsible for all mine maintenance. In September of 1981, he was promoted to Superintendent. He was transferred to the Pleasant Hill Mine as Superintendent on Jan. 15, 1984. In Mach of 1985, Norvell was assigned Special Projects Maintenance Manager for P&M, and he went to Kansas and Colorado to rebuild two draglines. On Sept. 1, 1985, he was transferred to the Midway Mine as the Superintendent of Maintenance and he and his family presently live in Butler, MO. On Jan. 5, 1987, he was reassigned as the Production Superintendent for the Midway Mine.

As a young man, Norvell was active in Boy Scouts. He earned the rank of Eagle while a member of the First Christian Church, Troop No. 1, Ben Ashmore was is scoutmaster. He was a member of th Order of the Arrow. He is a member of St. Patricks Catholic Church, Butler Missouri. He also served on the board of Christ the King School while in Madisonville. - *Submitted by Robert P. Moore*

RICHARD EDWARD MOORE

Richard Edward Moore was one of ten children (eight of whom lived to be adults) born to Judge James Alexander Moore(29 Oct. 1836 - 24 Nov. 1924) and Martha Bourland (14 Feb. 1805, Almance Co., NC, - 9 Apr. 1870 Crittenden Co., KY) and Margarete Carrick (20 June 1806, Charleston, SC - 15 Mar. 1876, Crittenden Co., KY). Martha was the daughter of David Bourland (11 Mar. 1819 - 1877) and Elizabeth Vickers (1825- 29 Nov. 1861) of Hopkins Co.

R.E. as he was called, was born in Marion, Crittenden Co., KY on 10 Apr. 1876. In 1899, R.E. moved to Madisonville, Hopkins Co., KY where he met and married Lorena "Lora" Mae Hall (b. 25 July 1881), the daughter of William Lorenzo Hall (22 June 1858 - 4 May 1939) and Jennie Belle Crawford (6 Dec. 1860 - 23 Aug. 1924), on 12 Oct. 1900.

His father-in-law, W.L. Hall, was a prominent masonary contractor and owned a brickyard located on the property now known as McCoy Avenue. He built homes for his three children, Roy, John and Lora, on Hall Street and Broadway. R.E. and Lora's home was built at 416 East Broadway.

R.E.'s Uncle, Harry Bourland, was then working for Belknap Hardware Company and agreed to set R.E. up in a bicycle shop located on Center Street where Parrish Drug Store was later located. He shortly moved into a full line of hardware and in 1905 moved the hardware store down East Center Street to where Fox Hardware Store was later located. The store was known as "Bourland and Moore." In 1926, he sold the sheet metal portion of the business to Phil B. Simmon, father of Cotton Simmon, and grandfather of Reggie Simon.

Along came the great depression and R.E's bankruptcy in 1930 which found him working for Whit Haywood and Lonnie Finley at the City Hardware Store . In 1933, he again opened his own store at 48 South Main Street, and was joined by his oldest son, William E. "Bill Ed" Moore. He retired in 1956 when his son, Norvell Hall Moore, joined the partnership of R.E. Moore & Son Hardware.

R.E. and Lora had four children: William Edward "Bill Ed" Moore (b. 26 Jan. 1902) who married Aurelia Weldon (b. 4, Sept. 1903), James Lawrence "Monk" Moore (6 Feb. 1905-25 Mar. 1963) who married Katherine Eades Overall (b. 2 Sept. 1906), Norvell Hall Moore (29 Dec. 1912 - 3 May 1986) who married Jane Lillian Pride (21 Aug. 1917 - 3 Mar. 1986), and Anita Belle Moore (b. 8 Nov. 1916) who married David Gray Poole (19 Aug. 1910 - 19 Jan. 1984)

Lora died 11 Dec. 1938 and on 11 Dec. 1940, R.E. remarried Agnes Curtis, the widow of Frank Curtis Sr. R.E. died 4 Mar. 1959 and Agnes died 16 Apr. 1969. R.E. and Lora are buried at Oddfellows Cemetery in Madisonville. Agnes is buried in Calhoun, KY.

R.E. served on the Madisonville City Council, representing the Sixth Ward for eight years in the 1920's. He was a Republican and active in politics for many years. He was a member of the First United Methodist Church. - *Submitted by Robert P. Moore*

RICHARD E. MOORE II

Richard Edward Moore II, the youngest son of Norvell Hall Moore, Sr., and Jane Lillian Pride, was born in Nashville, TN, on Dec. 26, 1950. He attended Hall Street Elementary School, Seminary Junior High School, and graduated from Madisonville North Hopkins High School in 1970. Ed lettered in track two years and football all four years at North Hopkins under Coach Bill Welburn and Coach Dennis Sexton. His senior football awards included Outstanding Offensive Lineman, the "Thin 27" Award and the award for the Most Yards gained in Penalties. He received a football scholarship at Western Kentucky University where he was "red shirted" the first year and lettered the second.

He was offered a full scholarship by and transferred to Georgetown College where he lettered three years. He also lettered in wrestling one year at Georgetown. He was awarded the NAIA all Conference Offensive Lineman and elected Team Captain. He was president and treasurer of the Lambda Chi Alpha Fraternity. He received his B.S. degree in Business and Accounting and a minor in Physical Education in 1975.

Having worked some 15 years part time in the painting business for his father during summers and after school, his first job after college was as controller of McCoy Management Services in Madisonville, KY. After four years, he took a controller and general manager position with Big Truck Sales and Service. In May of 1981, he resurrected his father's painting contracting business and grandfather's hardware store and greatly expanded the service and geographic area under the name of R.E. Moore Paint Company, Inc. In 1982, the company split into two: one for retail sales and one for contracting.

On Jan. 23, 1976, he married Cynthia Lynn Coburn, daughter of Charles "Red" Coburn and Sadie Putman Coburn. They have two children: Richard Edward III, born Jan. 19, 1982, and Jonathan Hall, born Dec. 14, 1985.

Ed was and is an active scout and scouter. He earned the Eagle Rank in 1968, and has been active in the Green River District of the Audubon Council in several different roles including Scoutmaster of Troop 103, SME chairman, and Advancement Chairman. He and Cindy are active in the Presbyterian Church where he serves as deacon. Ed was a trustee of the local Elks Lodge and is an active Kiwanian. He received the Ed Calloway Award for the most outstanding Kiwanian in 1987.

In 1986, he purchased the "homeplace" at 416 East Broadway as well as the Roy Hall home at 424 East Broadway where he runs part of his businesses. Ed's wife, Cindy, is a graduate of Madisonville North Hopkins High

School and has an Associate in Applied Science Degree from the University of Keentucky in x-ray technology. She worked at Trover Clinic for five years until the birth of her second son. - *Submitted by Robert P. Moore*

ROBERT PRIDE MOORE

Robert Pride Moore, the second son of Norvell Hall Moore, Sr., and Jane Lillian Pride, was born in Nashville, TN, On Aug. 12, 1946. He attended Hall Street Elementary School, Seminary Junior High School and graduated from Madisonville High School in June of 1964. Bob received a B.S. Degree from Western Kentucky University in February of 1970; an M.S. Degree from the University of Kentucky College of Education in May of 1974; and a J. D. Degree from the University of Kentucky College of Law in May of 1977. Bob clerked for Honorable James F. Gordon, United States District Court Judge for the Western District of Kentucky in Owensboro, upon graduation. He returned to Madisonville and entered the partnership of Adams, Massamore & Moore until Apr. of 1981, at which time he formed the new partnership of Massamore & Moore. In October of 1982, he then entered the partnership of Calvert & Moore. He served as Assistant Hopkins County Attorney from November of 1980, until the present time.

To date, Bob has 23 years service in the Army Reserve, having enlisted while in high school in December 1963. He served with various units of the 100th Division (Training) and obtained the rank of Master Sergeant before receiving a direct commission to First Lieutenant in July of 1976. He is a graduate of the Armor Officer Basic and Advanced Courses as well as the Command and General Staff College. His latest assignment was that of Detailed Inspector General for the 100th Division Headquarters in Louisville, KY.

Bob has served as a member and Chairman of the Hopkins County, Madisonville Joint Planning Commission and is active in the First United Methodist Church serving on the Administrative Board and as Scout Master of Troop 528.

On June 27, 1970, he married Judith Ann King of Upton, KY, daughter of Raymond Amos and Wilma Gertrude Vance King. They first resided in Georgetown, KY, until 1977. They spent a year in Owensboro and have resided the remaining time in his hometown of Madisonville, KY. Bob and Judy have two sons: James King Moore, born July 19, 1976, and Matthew Pride Moore, born Oct. 5, 1981.

Bob's wife, Judy, received her A.A.S. Degree from Elizabethtown Community College; her B.S. degree from Western Kentucky University; and her M.A. degree from the University of Kentucky in Business Education. She taught at Georgetown College from 1971 to 1973, was a sales representative and later product planner for Internation Business Machines (IBM) in Lexington, KY, from 1973 to 1979, and presently is an Associate Professor for the Madisonville Community College in Madisonville, KY. - *Submitted by Robert P. Moore*

VIRGIL YANDELL MOORE

Virgil's father, Alfred Clay Moore, was a great friend and admirer of William Yandell, co-owner of the leading dry goods store in Marion, Yandell and Guggenheim. He asked Mr. Yandell to be the godfather and to name his first son. Mr. Yandell was flattered and said that he would be proud if the boy bore his middle name. Additionally, as a keen latin scholar, Mr. Yandell gave the parents a choice of Rex or Virgil as a first name. Virgil's mother is said to have picked the lesser of the alternative evils and named him Virgil. The initials V.Y. have been distinctive and have served him well through life.

Virgil received his AB degree from the University of Kentucky in 1909 and his L.L.B. degree in 1911. He then practiced law with his father and married Dorthy Ina Price, daughter of a Presbyterian Minister and a high school classmate. She had attended music school in Nashville.

Virgil's trial work attracted the attention of Judge Flem Gordon, who offered him a job in Madisonville with Gordon, Gordon and Cox. It is believed that he moved to Madisonville in 1913 or 1914. His wife, Dorthy taught piano.

After the war came the federal income tax and Gordon, Gordon and Cox represented many coal companies. Virgil, being the youngest of the firm was given the task to learn about the new income tax. Mr. Cox later left the firm or died and Virgil was made a partner. This was during the time when Virgil was trying some tax cases in Washington in an era when there were lots of Washington tax lawyers with lots of clients and little or no trial experience. He received an offer of partnership from Andrew Smith and Tom Johnson who had offices in the Transportation Building (17 and H.N.W.). He accepted, the firm became Smith, Johnson & Moore, and he moved to Washington in the spring of 1924.

Mr. Johnson died and the firm became Smith and Moore. Later, Robert Lucas, a noted Kentucky politician who had been chairman of the National Republican Party under Hoover, and later commissioner of the Internal Revenue Service, joined the firm which then became Smith, Moore & Lucas. They then moved to the National Press Building at 14th and F.N.W. Sometime in the mid-30's the partnership ceased. Virgil had been handling cases for various accounting and legal firms all over the country — some for the Philadelphia firm of Pepper, Bodine, Stokes and Schoch. Sometime in the mid-30's he entered in association with this firm and was the "Washington Office".

When his wife became terminally ill, he retired completely. In 1933 or 1934, they had bought a farm on the Patuent River in California, MD which they named Crittenden after the county of their birth. They sold this in 1942 and moved to Fort Lauderdale, FL where they already owned a small house. His wife died in January of 1942 and Virgil remarried in 1945 to the former Emma Brown, who had been his secretary in the National Press Building. They bought a home in Miami Shores. Emma died there in June, six months after Virgil's death.

Virgil was very active in Kentucky Republican Politics even after he moved to Washington. In those days there was very little radio and a candidate had to have a "stable" of speakers. Virgil traveled all over the state. He was well enough known to be given a lead speech at the Republican State Convention in 1919. He also spent some time in Kentucky campaigning for Senator Ernest (1925-1926) and for Hoover in 1928. - *Submitted by Robert P. Moore*

WILLIAM EDWARD MOORE

"Bill Ed" was the oldest of four children born to Richard Edward Moore and Lorena "Lora" Mae Hall. He was born at home — 416 East Broadway, Madisonville, KY, on January 26, 1902. His first schooling started at age 5 with Granny Davis, a private teacher living at the corner of Caldwell and Franklin Streets. The next four grades were taken at the Broadway School at the corner of Scott Street and Broadway. West Broadway had the sixth through eighth grades. High school was completed in 1920. The high school was located on the corner of Waddill Avenue and Scott Streets.

In 1920, he went to work in his father's hardware and sheetmetal store. It failed in 1930, during the great depression. He then worked for Denton Hardware until October 1931. His father, Richard Edward "R.E." had gone to work at City Hardware where Bill Ed joined him for two years. Pay was $15.00 per week. On Apr. 15, 1933, he joined his father as a partner in R. E. Moore & Son Hardware located at 46 South Main Street (the Hog Eye block). His father, R.E., retired in 1956, and shortly thereafter, his brother, Norvell, purchased a one-half interest. Bill Ed retired from the store in 1974, at the age of 72.

He married Aurelia Weldon, the daughter of Jessie and Maud Weldon. They have made their home at 336 Hall Street since June 1, 1928. Bill Ed was active in Farm Bureau, the Chamber of Commerce, Retail Merchants (president, twice), Lions Club and Rotary.

Bill Ed was on the Board of Stewards of the First United Methodist Church for 30 years. He also served on the house committee.

Bill Ed and Aurelia have one son, Doctor Edward Weldon Moore, born July 6, 1930. *Submitted by Robert P. Moore*

The Grand Central Hotel in Madisonville-About 1936

MORGAN

Hubert Eugene "Gene" Morgan and Joyce Ann Roskosky were married July 3, 1958, in the First Christian Church of New Albany, IN. Joyce was born Sept. 16, 1939, the only child of George Curtis Roskosky (1919-1972) and Wilma Elsie Phillips (1922-1983) of Louisville, KY. The Phillips family have lived for several generations in Louisville but Joyce's paternal grandfather was an immigrant.

Gene and Joyce Morgan on their 25th wedding anniversary

Born about 1893, near Kiev, Russia, Michael Roskosky was a subject of Tsar Nicholas II in a turbulent era when Russia was destined for a devastating war and, ultimately, a brutal revolution. Michael fled his country, eventually arriving in U.S.A. and by 1912, had made his way to Louisville. There he married Emma Heina of that city and before his death in 1955, they produced five children.

Gene was born Apr. 24, 1936, in Hopkins County, the first of three children to Cecil Audie Morgan of Hopkins County and Velma Arrietta Jennings of Providence. Gene, his brother Kenneth Ray and sister, Ammie Katherine (Kitty) grew up in western Hopkins County and attended school at Dalton under the able administration of principals A.O. Richards and Thornton Devers. After graduation in 1954, Gene worked at farming and coal mining until 1955, when he secured employment in Evansville, IN. In 1956 he entered the consumer credit industry as a trainee and by 1958 had been transferred to Louisville, where he and Joyce met. In 1962 he was promoted to branch manager and transferred to head his company's office in Caldwell, ID.

In the years following, there were numerous career relocations within the western states taking the Morgans to Colorado, Montana, Washington and back to Idaho.

In 1969 Gene accepted a position in the retail automobile business and since 1975 the Morgans have made their home in Caldwell, ID. He has remained in that business working in retail and fleet sales, fleet and lease manager and presently is business manager for a multi-franchised G.M. dealership in the nearby city of Nampa. Joyce has worked for several years as a specialized cost accountant for Selkirk Metalbestos also in Nampa.

They have three children, Theresa Lynn, Steven Douglas and Todd Mitchell and two grandchildren, Nichole Annette and Sarah Elizabeth by their daughter, Theresa.

The first of Gene's fathers family to settle in Hopkins County was Nathanial Morgan born about 1844, the son of Webber Morgan (ca 1825) and Nancy Walker (ca 1827) of Todd County. Nathaniel came to Hopkins County about 1865. His mothers family descends from Louis A. Jennings Sr. (ca 1755) of Virginia, a Continental Soldier of the 6th S.C. line who patented a military land grant in Christian (now Caldwell) County in 1803. The predominant family in Gene's ancestry is Fox. Both his father and mother descend from James Fox, Sr., whose family was among the early settlers from North Carolina about 1805. Other ancestral names are (from NC) Brown, Bird, Davis and Loving. (From VA.) Curneal (or Carneal). (from TN) Ayres. - *Submitted by H. E. "Gene" Morgan*

SANDRA STEWART MORGAN

Sandra Lyle Stewart was born on May 6, 1942, in Madisonville, KY, to Carrie and Lyall Stewart, their second daughter. She has been a life-long member of the First Christian Church in Madisonville. Sandy attended Seminary Street Elementary School where she was active in Girl Scouts and began taking music lessons, seventh grade at the the Old Madisonville High School and then returned to Seminary Street School for her last year of junior high school where she was a cheerleader. While a freshman and sophomore at Madisonville High School, she sang in the Glee Club, played clarinet and saxaphone in the high school marching band and violin and viola in the orchestra. During these years she was also active in CYF (Christian Youth Fellowship), through which she did her first community volunteer work, trick or treating for UNICEF.

The Millard Morgan Family, 1985

She graduated from Stuart Hall in Stuanton, VA, in June 1960, and from Transylvania College in Lexington, KY, where she became a member and secretary of Delta Delta Delta Sorority and the Young Republican Club and served on the Dean's Advisory Committee and the Panhellenic Scholarship Committee. She also attended Evansville College one summer. Sandy continued to work summer and Christmas jobs at the Vogue, Seibert's Music Mart, as a hostess at the Holiday Inn, the County Court Clerk's office and Pennyrile State Park.

Upon graduation from Transylvania in 1964 with a Bachelor's Degree in History and Psychology, Sandy was commissioned a Second Lieutenant in the United States Marine Corps. She was stationed at Quantico, VA, served as an administrative officer at Parris Island, SC, and as an educational officer at Headquarters Marine Corps in Washington, DC, during which time she married Millard John Morgan (born in Camp Forrest, TN, on Apr. 28, 1943), son of an Army colonel, whose mother's family (Schwankert) was from Newark, NJ, and whose father's family was from Perry Co., MS. They have two children, Millard Lyall (nicknamed Charlie or Chuck) and Elizabeth Alice.

Upon discharge from the U.S. Marine Corps, Sandy and Millard moved to Albuquerque, NM, where Sandy worked in Public Relations for Presbyterian Hospital Center and Millard attended the University of New Mexico.

They moved to Santa Monica, CA, in 1968 and Sandy became active in the Santa Monica First Christian Church, singing in the choir, organizing the Young Women's Circle, and organizing and serving as secretary of the Young Adults.

In 1971, she obtained her lifetime California elementary teaching credential from California Lutheran College in Thousand Oaks, CA, and taught elementary school in Simi Valley and Goleta, CA. In 1973, she earned her Master's Degree in Elementary Reading and Linguistics with emphasis on Diagnosis and Remediation of Learning Disabilities from the University of California at Santa Barbara and was selected for membership in Delta Gamma Rho, an educational honorary, for her outstanding academic achievement.

After moving to Lompoc in 1979, she served as a member of the Lompoc Valley General Plan Advisory Committee, an advisory group to the County Board of Supervisors. She was selected to serve in 1981-83 as a member of the Santa Barbara County Grand Jury, one year as Parliamentarian and Secretary and the second year was appointed Foreman.

She is a member of four General Federation of Women's Clubs: GFWC Alpha Literary and Improvement Club of Lompoc where she has held most offices and major chairmanships, is past president of GFWC Town and Country Women's Club of Santa Barbara, and was named their "Outstanding Volunteer" in 1986, GFWC Las Unidas and GFWC Primeras Damas. She is currently serving as President of Tierra Adorada District of the California Federation of Women's Clubs and has been selected to serve 1988-90 as the Citizenship Chairman for the California Federation of Women's Clubs. She served as Processional Chairman at the 1987 International Convention of the General Federation of Women's Clubs in San Diego. Sandy was honored in 1986 as "Outstanding Volunteer for Tierra Adorado District." In 1987, she organized a new GFWC Lompoc Junior Woman's Club.

Sandy has also been a member of the Santa Barbara County Republican Central Committee, the Lompoc Valley Republican Club, the Lompoc Valley Federated Republican Women's Club, the America Association of University Women, and PTA. *Refer to William Lyalls and Carrie Elizabeth Lacy Stewart, -Submitted by Mrs. Lyall Stewart*

VENSON PAUL MORGAN

Venson Paul Morgan, born July 19, 1885, in Hopkins Co., KY, was the seventh of ten children born to Watson Calhoun Morgan and Margaret Marie Hilburn Morgan.

Watson Calhoun (Cal) was born April 1843, in Dade Co., GA. He died Nov. 13, 1913 in

Muhlenberg Co., KY. Cal came to Hopkins County before 1880 with his family to work in the coal mines. He lived most of his adult life in Earlington, KY. He and his wife are buried in Oakwood Cemetery in Earlington, KY.

The brothers and sisters of Venson Paul were: Alice, born 1872, Amanda, born Nov. 1874, Joseph, born 1878, Alfhansus Leo, born Aug. 6, 1879, Francis C., born Mar. 3, 1881, Bernard, born Aug. 20, 1883, Pat Henry, born Mar. 19, 1888, Herman, born Mar. 23, 1890, Aloyisus and Ignatius, born Oct. 14, 1891 in Arkansas.

Venson Paul married Fanny Burns (born 1890, died 1909), on Apr. 24, 1907 in Hopkins Co., KY. Fanny was the daughter of William Tandy Burns and Sarah Agnes Ayers Burns. Venson Paul and Fanny had one son, Venson Paul, born June 16, 1909.

Venson Paul married second to Orie Mae McCoy and had one son Orvil. Venson Paul is buried (died Apr. 2, 1916) in Oakwood Cemetery in Earlington, KY.

His son, Venson Paul (2) married Stella Mae Jones June 7, 1926. Their children were: Manual Ray, born May 12, 1927 (died young), Audrey Pauline, born Dec. 11, 1928, James Clidy, born Aug. 1930 (died young), Lois Ann, born Jan. 2, 1934, Mary Faith, born Aug. 28, 1938, Paul Keith, born Dec. 4, 1940, Sarah Ellen, born Sept. 19, 1943, Carlos Omar, born July 15, 1945, Niles Robin, born July 8, 1946.

Venson Paul (2) worked for West Kentucky Coal Company and Island Creek Coal Company until his retirement. He is buried (died Dec. 9, 1968) in Forest Lawn Cemetery, in Madisonville, KY. - *Submitted by Anne Keene Morgan*

MORROW-DENNIS

Henry Hilliard Morrow, a Hopkins County native, born in Madisonville, Feb. 22, 1902, and Willie Dennis, born in Wheatcroft, KY, in Webster County, Aug. 25, 1906, were married in Shawneetown, IL, Jan. 30, 1931.

Hilliard and Willie Morrow

Willie resigned her school teaching position in Wheatcroft after they married and began her life as a farmer's wife on the Morrow farm just south of Nebo, KY, where they lived happily and raised their children.

Hilliard's death, September 1971, and Willie's approaching retirement from teaching school, a job she had enjoyed during many years with the Hopkins County School System, caused her to leave the farm physically and move to Clarksville, TN, near her daughter. The rural life of Hopkins Co. and the two generations in some families of children she taught are a large part of the many memories she holds dear today, and loves to talk about to her Tennessee friends. Willie is a member of Rose Creek Cumberland Presbyterian Church near Nebo. She has a sister, Carrie O'Bryant, who lives in Madisonville.

Hilliard and Willie have two children, four grandchildren and two great grandchildren. A son, Alton Boyd, was born Mar. 30, 1933 and is married to Ruth Galbreath. Alton has worked many years in the coal mines, mine inspector and construction. He has a son, Dana, that lives in Madisonville.

A daughter, Sue, was born Jan. 22, 1935, and is married to Harold Bell. They live in Clarksville, TN, and Sue is employed at Ft. Campbell, KY, and Harold is Navy-retired and employed part-time. They have three children, Merri, Rebecca and Paul. Merri is married to David Six and they live in Germany with their son Shawn. Rebecca is married to Steven McLeskey and they live in Clarksville, TN, with their son, Joshua. Paul is still at home with his family, attending college and working. - *Submitted by Alton B. Morrow*

MORROW- WINSTEAD

William Morrow b. ca. 1772, d. after April 1815 (will date), married in Person Co., N.C., on Oct. 8, 1793, to Mary Ann (Polly) Underdown. She was the daughter of Stephen Underdown born in Caroline Co., VA, on June 9, 1755, and married Mary Elizabeth Edwards in 1776.

Their children *Ann Morrow married David Chandler; Archibald m. Patsy Parker; *John b. ca. 1793 d. Nov. 14, 1877, age 84 years old, m. Mary Winstead, daughter of William Winstead who died ca. 1828 in Person Co., NC, and Sarah who died ca. 1831 in Person Co.; *Sarah died ca. 1845 m. William Winstead (see Winstead-Morrow); Winifred m. James Fowler; Benjamin m. Margaret Love; *Leatha M. Washington Chandler; *Mary Ann b. ca. 1811 m. George T. Winstead (bro. to the above); *Stephen b. ca. 1812 or 1815 m. Mary Ann Chandler; *William b. Feb. 7, 1813, m. first to Nancy Newton in KY, Jan. 28, 1839, m. second Amanda J. Swearingen in Clinton Co., MO, in 1855. (Asterick denotes those who came to KY.)

The children of John Morrow and Mary Winstead are: Robert b. Oct. 10, 1821, d. Mar. 14, 1898 m. Mar. 5, 1849, in Hopkins Co. to Francis J. Davis (dau. of John), both buried at Odd Fellows; John Jr. b. ca 1827 d. after 1882, m. Mary Susan Davis (sister to Francis) she died after 1890; William B. ca. 1834, m. Sarah T. Cox Feb. 12, 1854; Emily J. b. ca. 1833, m. Thomas J. Jackson on Sept. 27, 1856; Sidney T. b. July 16, 1830, d. Sept 5, 1889, m. 1st Drucilla Chandler d. Jan. 15, 1865, two children David C. and Mary R. (Molly), wife of E.D. Cox, m. 2nd Mrs. Bettie L. Bailey Laffoon d. January 1867, m. 3rd Alcy Ann Mitchell Morrow, widow of William (M. or W.) Morrow; M.A. m. a Yarbrough.

Children of Robert Morrow and Francis: Robert P. b. ca. 1853; John C. b. ca. 1854; Sidney A. b. ca. 1855; Charles B. b. ca. 1857; and James T. b. ca. 1859.

Children of John Morrow Jr. and Mary Susan Davis: Sarah O. b. ca. 1855, probably married R.P. Nichols; Francis R. b. ca. 1856 (female); John T. b. ca. 1858, m. on Dec. 2, 1879 in Webster Co. to Maggie Booth (according to his grandson, Floyd Morrow, he came in and ate a big dinner, got up from his chair and fell over dead at the age of 23); W.B. b. 1860 d. 1946 m. Ada Bone, both buried in Union Cemetery; Lelia I. b. ca. 1863 probably m. I.O. Crabtree; Minnie b. ca. 1868 may have m. E. L. Herren; Charlie b. 1868 d. 1946 m. 1st Viola Kirkwood, m. 2nd Willie Hughes, Edgar D. b. ca. 1870 m. Nora Simmons; Boyd b. ca. 1872 m. Emma Ligion; Walter C. b. 1874 d. 1940 m. Ella N. Byrum.

Children of John T. and Maggie Booth are: Roy McNary Morrow b. Mar. 4, 1888, d. June 21, 1943 m. Gertie Jones, both are buried at Oakley Home; John Almont Morrow b. Aug. 5, 1881, d. Nov. 1, 1938, m. Queen Jones (sister to Gertie), both buried Oakley Home; and Myrtle b. Jan. 20, 1883, d. July 28, 1966 m. Cap Cates.

Children of John Almont and Queen are: John Floyd b. June 10, 1909 m. Mary Lucinda Dame; Lloyd Washington (twin to Floyd) m. Alice Clark; Clarence b. Oct. 1920, m. 1st Lucille Sizemore, m. 2nd Mary Ipock; Rowena Morrow b. Feb. 4, 1914, m. Otto Hibbs and lives in Sturgis; and Audry Morrow m. Mabel Nance and they live in Oklahoma. - *Submitted by Randa Bearden*

WANDA BENTON MORROW

Wanda Lee Benton was born May 2, 1936, on a farm in the Grapevine area of Madisonville, Hopkins Co., KY, the seventh child of William Richard and Johnnie Pauline Davenport Benton.

Wanda Lee Benton Morrow, 1986

Wanda grew up in one of the poorest families imaginable. Looking back she says, "I was happy as a child, I didn't realize just how poor we were. There was always something to eat on the table and we had clothes, never mind that they were hand-me-downs. My playmates were my 11 brothers and sisters and the neighboring Fugate children. Our play-

207

grounds were the railroad cars and woods. We made our own toys from anything we could find. A lump of coal wrapped with string and other stuff made a ball. We made sleds from wood, rolled down hills in barrels, climbed trees, chewed "gum" from gumwax trees, made mud pies and built playhouses in the woods. We had a lot of fun."

Wanda attended school at the old Grapevine school until she was 15. It was then she took her first job as a nanny in Paducah, KY. At age 17 she moved to Detroit, MI, and worked as a nanny there. She returned to Madisonville, KY, when she was 17 and married a soldier named George Iriving Morrow III on New Year's Day, 1954.

Her parents had prophetically named her Wanda, which means "wanderer. Wanda has wandered from state to state since she married and left home. She and George have lived in Kentucky, Indiana, Michigan and California while raising their four children: Paula, Jerry, Angela and Shane. By the time they divorced in 1985, they had moved 24 times.

Since 1985, Wanda has lived in Kentucky, Michigan, California and Utah. She has seven grandchilden: Joseph, Rachel, Rommel, Rebekah, Shawn, Roger and Celeste.

Wanda currently lives and attends school in Salt Lake City, UT. - *Written by Paula L. Morrow Bentley*

MORTON

William Chenault Morton, son of John Gordon Morton II and Margaret Kuykendall Brooks Morton, was born Aug. 21, 1935. He was admitted to the practice of Law in 1965 and is presently practicing law in the firm of Logan & Morton. On Apr. 20, 1957, he married Beverly Ann Gipson. They were married in the Morton House. They have one son, William Chenault Morton II, a student at the University of Kentucky.

William Chenault Morton is one of three sons born of the union of John Gordon Morton II and Margaret Kuykendall Brooks. John Gordon Morton III, a journalist, graduated from Western Kentucky University. He worked for several newspapers including the Jacksonville Times and Miami Herald. John died in 1964. Brooks Browning Morton graduated from Northwestern University after which he moved to New York City, seeking and finding a career in the theatre. An accomplished musician, Brooks had several Broadway shows to his credit, the last being "42nd Street." Brooks died in 1984.

John Gordon Morton II, was one of three children born to the union of William Caleb Morton and Maude Ruby Morton. The other children being Mary Ruby Morton Browning, wife of Woodson Browning, a long-time co-owner and publisher of The Madisonville Messenger and William Clint Morton, who served for many years as secretary of the Madisonville Building & Loan Association. His wife of 50 years, Alice Whayne Hickman Morton, resides at 114 E. Broadway.

William Caleb Morton was one of six children born to the union of John Gordon Morton and Nancy Elizabeth Young Morton. John Gordon Morton was a prominent business man and was thought to have been the first banker in Hopkins County owning and operating Morton Bank. William Caleb Morton was an Architect. Among the buildings he designed in Madisonville was the old Hopkins County jail and the building located on South Main Street which once housed the Farmers Bank & Trust Company.

Also born to the marriage of John Gordon Morton and Nancy Elizabeth Young was: Elizabeth Morton McPherson who is survived by Robert L. Schlotman, Jr., Julian Schlotman and Elizabeth Schlotman Stone, of Madisonville; David Ambrose Morton; Mollie Morton Hendricks, who is survived by Elizabeth Essington Carson of Chicago, IL; Helen Morton Hall wife of Judge John G.B. Hall; and Charles Everett Morton who is survived by Clyde Ruby of Madisonville.

The Mortons also owned and operated The Mortons Theatre which was located on the site of the former Capitol Theatre building on which is now located the offices of Brown and Holloway Insurance, Union Street.

Morton House located at 140 South Main Street was the home of John Gordon Morton which became the home of Helon Morton Hall and John G. B. Hall until their death and then was occupied by Mary Ruby Morton Browning until her death. Morton House is now the location of the Greater Madisonville Chamber of Commerce.

Margaret K. Brooks was the only daughter of Basil Murphey Brooks and Margaret Ogden Brooks.

Willis Chenault Brooks, Margaret's brother is retired from the Grain, Fertilizer and Tobacco business and is married to Mary Utley Brooks and presently resides in Madisonville.

Basil Murphey Brooks for many years operated the Brooks Loose Leaf Floor and was well well known as a sheep farmer working hard to promote the wool industry. He served as Mayor of Madisonville in the 1920's and was president of the Slaughters Bank from 1912-1914.

The Brooks family has long been prominent in agriculture and business in Hopkins and Webster counties. - *Submitted by William C. Morton*

MUNNS

John Munns was born Apr. 26, 1834, in England. He married Eleanor Robinson and they were blessed with eight children.

In 1865, this family came to America. When Munns was 43 years old, he moved to Madisonville and bought some land known as the Thomas Yates farm. It is part of this land that was donated for a school house which was called Munns School. In recent years, the school has been restored.

A few years later, the Munns family moved to Dawson Springs and built a hotel. They were very active in the town and well-liked. On digging a well for his hotel, Munns accidentally discovered the first salts well, known as Old Munns Well. Munns was the first person to manufacture liquid and dry salts in Dawson Springs. His property, which he bought from Mrs. Alexander, was close to the Heckley Mines and was underlaid with coal. Munns was a shrewd businessman and bought his three and one-eighth acres of land cheaply. Later, Munns' hotel burned.

Eleanor Munns died on June 28, 1883, at the age of 51. She is buried in the Arcadia Hill Cemetery in Dawson Springs.

Munns remarried. His new wife, Matilda, and his youngest daugher, Nora, opened a millinery. As the leading millinery in Dawson Springs, the ladies shop carried all of the latest styles at reasonable prices. Matilda was also a minister at the General Baptist Church.

John Munns died on July 27, 1905, at the age of 71. He was buried in Arcadia Hill Cemetery.

Before he died, Munns was quoted as saying "Dawson Springs will some day be famous for the wonderful medicinal qualities of her waters."

Appropriately, this active family has Munn Street in Dawson Springs named after them. The Munnses were present at the birth of the town and had much more than just an idle curiosity in its future. - *Submitted by Joan Hicks, a Senior at Dawson Springs High School*

MURRAH

Chester Arthur Alan Murrah was born Nov. 4, 1889, in Hopkins Co., KY. the son of Joshua Murrah Jr. and Lou Ella Ann Fox. On July 26, 1910 he married Willie Reeder b. Aug. 18, 1895. To their union were born Howard Earl Murrah m. Eunice Addison and Marvin Murrah who died in infancy. Willie Murrah died of pneumonia on Nov 25, 1913. After her death Arthur joined the Army where he fought in World War War I. Upon being honorably discharged he married Zena Smith b. May 9, 1986. Their only child was William G. Murrah m. Mary Springfield. Zena died of pneumonia on Nov. 30, 1925, in Nortonville and was laid to rest at Concord. Arthur's third marriage was to Etta Jane Blades on Nov. 16, 1926. They were the parents of two children: Hazel Ludeama Murrah b/d. 1927, Jesse Willard Murrah m. Corinne Carlton.

Arthur Murrah

Arthur worked in several coal mines around the Nortonville area, but his last job was as a cook in the Outwood Veterans Clinic near Dawson Springs. He died on Jan. 31, 1945, and was buried with military honors at New Salem Cem. Etta Jane Murrah was a member of Pleasant Hill Baptist Church in the 1930's. In later years she attended services at the Trinity

Gospel Tabernacle in Nortonville. She passed away Jan. 20, 1971, at the home of her son Willard Murrah, near Cross Roads at the age of 79.

Joshua "Pig" Murrah was born in August 1863 the son of Joshua Murrah Sr. and Emily E. Givens of Logan Co., KY. He was married to Lou Ella Ann Fox b. Feb. 19, 1863, the daughter of Matt Fox and Nancy Furgeson. They were the parents of seven other children besides Arthur. They are as follows: Hazel b. 1887, Fannie b. Apr. 4, 1891, Lucy Dillingham b. Aug. 15, 1893, Gaby Cunningham b. Apr. 5, 1895, Dalton b. Aug. 5, 1896, Mattie Kirkman Cobb b. Apr. 16, 1902, and an unnamed infant b/d Aug. 13, 1905. Joshua worked for the railroad as well as farming the land he owned south of Flat Creek in Mortons Gap. Joshua died around 1906. Lou Ella died in 1943. Both are buried at New Salem Cem.

Joshua Murrah Sr. was born in March 1819 in Logan Co., KY. On July 15, 1853 he married Emily E. Givens. Emily was born in 1838 to Jonathon and Maria Givens of Logan Co., KY. In 1860 they lived in Adairsville, KY where both Joshua Murrah and Johnathon Givens were in the carpentry business. Joshua and Emily Murrah were the parents of seven children including Joshua Jr. They were: Viola J. Bean, John Murrah, Joe Murrah, Annie, Gabriella, and Amelia J. Murrah.

Joshua Murrah Sr. was a descendant of Joshua and Lucy Murrah of Wilkes Co., NC; who fought against the British in the Rev. War. They came to Kentucky in 1805. They settled on a 640 acre land grant in southern Logan Co. - *Submitted by Willard, Corinne, Mike and Lou Ann Murrah*

MUSIC

William Music was born Mar. 24, 1915 in Auxier, KY. His parents were Laura Honeycutt and William Jefferson Music. His mother was born June 11, 1881 in Bayes Branch, KY. His father was born Oct. 8, 1876 in East Point, KY.

William has six brothers and two sisters: Calloway C. Music, Irvin M. Music, James Paris Music, Frank Music, Okra Music, Ted (Theodore) Music, Edna Music and Carrie Music.

William graduated from high school and then attended two years at Alice Lloyd College in Knott County, KY. He moved to Dawson Springs in 1960 because of a job promotion. He worked as a supervisor for the Division of Forestry. He is now retired. William has attended the First Christian Church for twelve years. He resides at 210 Park Avenue in Dawson. His honors and awards are poetry award, Rotary basketball award and president of the Rotary. He likes fishing, hunting and collecting Indian artifacts. He is a good typist.

Bill's first wife died in 1967 of a ruptured pancreas. He is now married to Freida Evelyn Huddleston (Music). They met at a grocery store. Freida would follow Bill around the store and and look to see what he had in his shopping cart. They finally got together for dinner. Bill and Freida like to play cards and every week they play with other couples. They will be married sixteen years in July.

Freida has two children: Polly Hardegree and Steve Gray. Polly has a son and a daughter. Steve has two sons and one daughter. Freida has attended the First Christian Church since 1934.

Bill has five children: Douglas Irvin Music born June 4, 1942; Darvin Music born June 2, 1948; Wayne Music born Jan. 12, 1948; David Music born June 6, 1953; and Jan almon born July 3, 1950.

Doug has been divorced from his first wife, Sherry Jean Hawkins, for almost three years. She is now married to Jeff Jennings. Doug is married to Barbara Jean Wilguess (Wilson). Doug has one daughter, a step-daughter and a step-son.

Darvin is married to Mary Cartwright and has one daughter.

Wayne is married to Mary Brock and has a son and a daughter, and three step-daughters.

David was married to Brenda Scott and is now divorced. He has one son and a step-daughter.

Jan is married to Vernon Lee Almon. She has one daughter. -*Submitted by Alexia Music*

MYERS-SIGLER

Lou Gore Sigler was the daughter of Sarah (Sally) Isabel Ramsey Sigler and Robert Lee Sigler. Her grandmother was Louiza Elvina Gore from Elizabethtown, IL. Louiza married John Gilliam Ramsey of Dalton, KY.

Taken at the "Old Ramsey Homestead", John Gilliam "Doc" Ramsey with his trusty Kentucky long rifle and his wife Louiza Elvina (Gore). Circa 1890's.

The Ramseys had 12 children. "Sally" was their eighth child, born 3-24-1874. It was a time when people visited, "for a spell." It was not unusual for one to visit for 1-2 years. Traveling was very difficult.

During "Sally's" first three years, her grandmother, Rejoina Gore, from Illinois visited Louiza and her family, from about November 1876 to Aug. 8, 1877, at which time she died unexpectedly.

This was a very formative time in little "Sally's" childhood. It is entirely plausible that she would name her only daughter after her mother and possibly, remembering the grandmother she was able to enjoy for so short a period.

Sally married Robert Lee Sigler on Sept. 24, 1913—just 16 days before her mother died of Pneumonia. She was to be in poor health most of her life. Lou Gore Sigler was born 5-9-1915. They also had one son, stillborn.

They lived on a farm close to Duvin mine in Webster County. Lou Gore remembers the tragedy of Duvin Mine. Thirty-eight men died in an explosion. This tragedy touched nearly every family in Webster and Hopkins counties. Lou Gore would never have guessed that her future husband was one of the rescue squad brought in from Dawson Springs, KY.

The Sigler's later moved into Providence, where Lou Gore graduated from Providence High School in 1932. She became an experienced seamstress and made her way for a time when seamstresses were in great demand.

In research for this history, it has come to my attention, that my husband's (Harry Doyle Waide) grandmother, Belle Riley Price, was first cousin to Robert Sigler, my great uncle by marriage. Belle was one of 13 children. They lived in Webster County.

After Robert passed away (2-17-1952), Lou Gore cared for "Sally" until her death, Nov. 24, 1958, and she worked at Cooper's Department Store.

After the death of his wife, Rhea (who was Lou Gore's first cousin), Clebie Elbert Myers continued to fellowship in the family circle. Eventually, he and Lou Gore started courting and decided life should be shared. They married July 27th, 1962, in Shawneetown, IL, and moved to Madisonville.

Clebie worked throught the years at Dawson Daylight and West Kentucky #7 mines, as a state Mine Inspector and retired from mining at Pyro. He later worked for Munday Homes in Madisonville.

Clebie was the son of Jim and Mary Mabry Myers of Fredonia area.

Lou Gore's knowledge of materials and her pleasantness, gave her an open door to work for J. C. Penneys, Johnston, Big B and Kwik Kleen Cleaners.

Lou Gore and Clebie had no children but his and Rhea's children remained close. There were two sons, Marlin married Anna Catherine Hunt and had Myrna Gail; Rev. Gene Myers married Sue Cates and had Paul Steven and Jeanie Suzette.

Lou Gore lost Clebie, June 12th, 1976. Albeit they had but a few years—they were good loving years. She makes her home in Madisonville, loves to travel, still sews, and enjoys life as the Lord unfolds it before her. (See Ramsey-Stevens-Gore) - *Submitted by Peggy Sullivan Waide*

BENJAMIN JACOB MYERS

Benjamin Jacob Myers was born Feb. 19, 1823. in Christian Co., KY, the son of George and Nancy Boisseau Myers.

Benjamin Jacob Myers married Elizabeth Shelton Quisenberry, widow of Garland Quisenberry and daughter of James and Elizabeth Shelton, on July 5, 1853, in Christian County. Elizabeth Shelton Quisenberry had one son at the time of her marriage to Mr. Myers, James Edward Quisenberry, born June 4, 1847, probably in Christian County.

Benjamin Jacob and Elizabeth Shelton Myers were the parents of four sons: Richard

Benjamin Jacob Myers 1823-1895

Mansfield Myers, born July 21, 1856, in Christian Co., KY; George Myers, born Sept. 2, 1859, in Muhlenberg County, KY; Benjamin E. Myers, born Mar. 4, 1862, in McLean Co., KY; John William Myers born Mar. 9, 1864, in McLean Co., KY and Daniel Ellison Myers born May 7, 1866, in McLean Co., KY.

Elizabeth Shelton Myers died Dec. 23, 1871 and Benjamin Jacob married Elizabeth Jane Coffman on July 25, 1872. They were the parents of two daughters: Sallie Myers born June 23, 1875 and Fairy Elizabeth Myers born Apr. 25, 1877.

Elizabeth Coffman Myers died Dec. 1, 1878 and Benjamin Jacob married a third time to V.K. Plain on Sept. 4, 1879. There were no children of this marriage. At the time of her marriage to Benjamin Jacob Myers, V. K. Plain was the mother of a daughter by a previous marriage, Sue Jan Plain born Aug. 5, 1858.

Benjamin Jacob Myers moved with his family to a farm in Hopkins County, KY between 1880 and 1890. He died Dec. 4, 1895, in Madisonville, KY, at the home of his son, John William Myers, and is buried in Odd Fellows Cemetery in Madisonville, Hopkins Co., KY. - Compiled by Beverly H. Dockrey

JOHN WILLIAM MYERS

John William Myers was born Mar. 9, 1864 in McLean Co., KY. He was the son of Benjamin Jacob and Elizabeth Shelton Myers. John William moved with his family to Hopkins Co., KY, sometime during the 1880's.

On Jan. 8, 1891, in Hopkins County, KY, John Williams Myers was married to Ida J. Lyons. They were married by the bride's grandfather, David Whittinghill, a Baptist minister. Ida J. Lyons was born Nov. 23, 1864 at Trisler (near Fordsville), Ohio County, KY. She was the daughter of Solomon and Josephine Whittinghill Lyons.

John Williams and Ida Lyons Myers were the parents of five children: Herbert Hopewell Myers born Feb. 10, 1892, who married Annie Moore; Gladys Josephine Myers born June 4, 1895, who married Darrell K. Veller; Benjamin Jacob Myers born Nov. 16, 1897, who married (1) Mary Wilson and (2) Agatha Shanks; Dexter Marie Myers born Dec. 15, 1900, who married William Goebel Wilson; and Georgie Elizabeth Myers born July 11, 1903, who married Freeland Fraud Harris.

John William Myers worked as a farmer until 1902 when he and his family moved to Madisonville and he went to work at Victoria Mine No. 11 as an electrician.

On Christmas Eve (Dec. 24), 1906, John William Myers died in Madisonville, KY, of typhoid fever. Ida J. Lyons Myers died Jan 27, 1953 in Madisonville. They are both buried in Odd Fellows Cemetery in Madisonville, KY. - Compiled by Beverly Dockrey.

NANCE-BRADEN

Dolores Fay Braden and Eugene Willis Nance were married Oct. 26, 1952 by Rev. O.L. Duncan in his home at Manitou, KY.

Dolores was born July 16, 1933, in Clay, Webster Co., KY, the daughter of the late Wallace Braden Sr. and Martha Elizabeth Potts. Wallace and Elizabeth were married July 9, 1932. They were also the parents of a son, Wallace Jr. Wallace Jr. has four children: Gail Baunhofer, Martha Burton, Cindy and Rodney Carroll. Sarah Lynn and Christopher are the grandchildren.

Eugene and Dolores Nance

Wallace Sr. was the son of the late Elder George T. Braden and Vertie Lee Perkins. Elder Braden was a long-time minister of the Primitive Baptist of Webster and Hopkins Counties. Thirteen children were born to this union, with four surviving.

Elizabeth was the daughter of Jacob Ray Potts and Monta Ardell Alley of Union County. Four children were born to this union, with one now surviving.

Other ancestral names are Cates, Dail, Coffman, Kirkwood and Meazles.

Eugene was born Nov. 27, 1925, the only child of the late Willis C. Nance and Ina May Carnal of Hopkins Co. Ina was the daughter of the late Jimmie Carnal and Phoebie Ann Hawkins. Phoebie's father died while serving in active duty in the Union Army during the Civil War. Three children were born to this union, none survive.

Willis was the son of the late Henry Nance and Ruthie Trice of Hopkins County. Henry was born in North Carolina in 1870. Five children were born to this union, one now survives.

Other ancestral names are Wright, Suit and Strum.

Eugene attended Cox's Store, graduating in 1942. At this writing, Eugene has just received his G.E.D. He is presently employed at Federal Crop Insurance.

Dolores attended school at Red Oak in Webster County, graduating from the 8th grade in 1946 and high school in 1950, at Dixon.

Dolores and Eugene have one son, Michael David, who resides in Speedway, IN. He is married to Roberta Ann Turner, daughter of Mrs. Margaret Turner and the late Robert F. Turner, Jr. Mike and Roberta have one daughter, Rebekah Elizabeth. She was born Nov. 16, 1983.

The Nances are members of the Oakley Home General Baptist Church in which Eugene is a deacon, songleader and Sunday School teacher. Both joined this church in 1953 and were baptized in Jack Wilson's pond. - Submitted by Dolores F. Nance

NAPIER-CARTWRIGHT

Judith Kay Cartwright and Paul Frances Napier were married May 28, 1965 in Joplin, MO.

Judith was born Nov. 27, 1940 in Webb City, MO, the daughter of Roy and Virginia Cartwright. Virginia Cartwright was born June 15, 1920 in Webb City. Roy Cartwright was born Dec. 26, 1919. Judith has one sister, Jean Anne Moore, and one brother, Ronald Cartwright.

Judith attended school at West Side Elementary School and Webb City High School in Webb City, MO. After her high school graduation, she attended Pittsburgh State University in Pittsburgh, Kansas. Judith was very interested in music and was a concert violinist for several years. She finished her education at Southwest Missouri University in Springfiedl, MO where she decided to major in elementary education. Later she moved to Kentucky with her husband and daughter, Jeannie Marie Napier. She received her Masters Degree at Murray State Univ.

Judith began teaching in 1962. Her first teaching job was at Eugene Fields Elementary School in Webb City, MO and in 1978 she began teaching at Dawson Springs Elementary School where she is still employed.

Paul Frances Napier was born June 23, 1934, the son of Jess and Hazel Napier. Jess was born Apr. 2, 1912 and Hazel was born May 4, 1914. Paul has one brother Joseph Napier.

Ida Lyons Myers

Paul attended Fairbank Elementary School and Pipkin Jr. High School in Springfield, MO. Later, he attended Monett High School in Monett, MO. After his high school graduation, Paul attended Southwest Missouri State University in Sprinfield, MO. He received his masters degree in psychology at Kansas State College of Pittsburgh in Pittsburgh, KS. Paul later moved to Detroit, MI where he received his specialist degree in psychology.

Paul and Judith live in Princeton, KY where they enjoy gardening not only as a hobby but as a business.- *Submitted by Jeannie Napier.*

PRESSLEY ELLIS NICHOLS

Pressley Ellis Nichols was born Sept. 20, 1918 in Hopkins County at Anton. He was the fourth of five children born to James A. Nichols and Josephine Ellis.

James A. Nichols was born in Webster Co., KY at Lisman on Nov. 29, 1878. He was the seventh of eight children born to Press Nichols and Sarah Skinner.

Pressley Ellis Nichols

Press Nichols was born July 18, 1837, in North Carolina and came from there to Webster County. He died Nov. 30, 1897. Sarah Skinner was born December 30, 1844, and died Feb. 8, 1885.

Josephine Ellis was born in McClean Co., KY, July 13, 1887, the fifth child of William Azro Ellis and Ailcy Roberts.

William Azro Ellis was born Nov. 17, 1857, and died Dec. 14, 1937. He came to Hopkins Co. from McClean Co.

Ailcy Roberts was born Oct. 31, 1853 in Hopkins Co. and died June 12, 1914.

James A. Nichols and Josephine Ellis were married Aug. 10, 1910. James A. died Jan. 28, 1965, and Josephine died Mar. 2, 1956.

Pressley Ellis Nichols began work with the Chrysler Corp. in Evansville, IN, on Dec. 29, 1942. He was laid off on Jan. 7, 1944. He then worked for Republic Aviation Corp., also in Evansville making P47 thunderbolts (a fighter plane for the Army Air Force). He was again laid off on Aug. 14, 1945.

On Mar. 8, 1948, he went back to work for Chrysler and worked there until Aug. 8, 1959. He was transferred to St. Louis, MO, where he worked until May 31, 1977. On this day he retired with over thirty years with the Chrysler Corp. - *Submitted by Pressley E. Nichols*

WILLIAM "PETE" NICHOLS

William Colonias "Pete" Nichols born in Anton, KY, Hopkins Co., was one of four children born to John Nichols and Cordie Scott-Nichols (1874-1900), daughter of William Scott and Annie Scott (1849-1901). The brothers and sisters of William C. were: Henry Nichols (1899-1967); Birdie Nichols-Hall (1891-1985); Ruby Nichols Baker-Foster (1893-1973).

Mother Nichols and family on Dec. 25, 1958. Front l to r: George William, Mother Marie, Carlene Claybon and Pete Jr. Middle row: Effie Mae Buell and Annie Nell. Back row: John Henry, James Columbus and Lee Roy Nichols.

During the great war, World War I, William C. served as a foot soldier from 1916-1918. Shortly after returning from serving his country he united in matrimony with Ethel Marie Logan, born Dec. 25, 1900, daughter of John Logan (1871-1915) and Ludah Pritchett-Logan (1869-1910). Her brother and sisters were: Sammie Jack Logan; Amanda Logan-Hayes (1896-1986); Melissa Logan-Johnson; Verda "Polly" Logan; Pearline Logan.

Pete and Marie located in the Anton bottoms. As they worked and built their home, eight children were added to them as follows: George William (1922); Effie Mae Nichols-Buell (1924); John Henry (May 18, 1926); James Columbus (Nov. 22, 1928); Lee Roy (1930); Annie Nell (Apr. 30, 1932); Carlene Claybon (1934); and Pete Jr. (February 1936).

William Colonias "Pete" Nichols and Ethel Marie Logan Nichols.

When it looked as if the near future would yield the bountiful fruits of labor for Pete and Marie, tragedy struck! One afternoon in November, after waking at his sister's home in Madisonville, Pete went to pick up his children from Rosenwald school. While attempting to cross the railroad tracks at Main and Noel, he was struck by a train. His family was shattered.

In the midst of pain and sorrow, relatives offered to take individual children to ease the load. But Marie remembered the unity she and her husband once had and conquered the minds of division and took on the task of nurturing and maintaining her family. As a result of her sacrifices and devotion during the formative years for blacks in Hopkins County, the Nichols Family continues to blossom and grow. - *Compiled by Elder John H. Nichols, Jr.*

NISBET

The surname, Nisbet, was a family name before 1139 A.D., and one of the oldest families in Scotland. The Castle of Nisbet is on a fine estate of more than 200 acres of Scotland, near Duns, Berwickshire, a former border stronghold. "There is an intense fascination about the old house of mystery and romance with spiral staircases, secret chambers and underground passages."

Nisbet Coat of Arms

The progenitor of most Nisbets in America, Canada, and England, and most prominent in the religious life of early Protestantism in Scotland and America, was Murdoch Nisbet, b. 1470 A.D. in Ayshire, Scotland. He was a very learned scholar and completed the translation of the New Testament from Wycliff's version into the Gaelic (of Scots) in 1510. He was severely persecuted and fled to Belfast, Ireland, because of his preaching and teaching his doctrine to the people. In about 1500, he returned to his homeland and died in 1558. He left his son, Alexander Neisbet, heir to the New Testament, who in turn left it to his son, James Neisbet, born 1602. This James had two sons, James Nisbet (b. 1625 d. 1684), and John Nisbet (the martyr) (b. 1627 d. 1685).

James married Janet Gibson in the Parish of Loudon, where he settled and became an earnest and active upholder of the "Covenants." Although he did not take as prominent a part as his brother, John, in battling for the conceived rights of the Covenanters, he did and said enough to be executed at the Howgate Head, Glasgow, on June 5, 1684. He and Janet had two children, James Nisbet III, a merchant, came to America on Dec. 20, 1685, the same month that his Uncle John Nisbet (martyr) came to a martyr's end on the scaffold in Edinburgh.

James III went to Perth Amboy, NJ, to Woodbridge, then on to Newark, NJ. He married Abigail Harrison in 1695, and died there in 1720. Had sons Samuel, b. 1723; James 1718-1792; John 1725-1812; dau. Abigail b. 1720.

James Nisbet Jr. and Janet's second son, John, b. 1657, known as, "The Younger", to distinguish him from John, "the martyr". He was arrested as a Covenanter, tried, condemned and hanged on Apr. 14, 1683.

John (martyr), married Margaret Law in 1651; three sons survived: Hugh b. 1664, James, b. 1667; and Alexander, b. 1671. Scottish historians acclaimed him as "British soldier, Covenanter, and Martyr". In 1664 he united with the Presbyterian form of church government, and was active in the uprising of the oppressed Scots against the Catholic Church and King in 1666. He fought, was captured, severely wounded, escaped, denounced as a rebel with 5,000 marks on his head for capture. His property was confiscated, he and family suffered untold hardships, until he was captured, cast in prison, sentenced, and hanged, Dec. 4, 1685. He died courageously with nine of his near relatives; never lost faith in God.

Alexander's son, Will Nisbet b. 1695; Elizabeth (1730-1813) married Charles Weir, granddaughter, Agnes Weir Robertson (1789-1866).

James (1667-1728) married Agnes Woodburn, had two known children: Alexander b. 1701 and John 1705. See JOHN NISBET (American Ancestor). Source: <u>Nisbet Narrations</u> as collected by Newton Alexander Nisbet Crayton Printing Co., Charlotte, NC 1961. - *Submitted by Mrs. Laura Suthard. Compiled and typed by Rella Jenkins*

NISBET

The Castle of Nisbet is located on an estate in Scotland and covers more than 200 acres. It is situated about two miles southeast of Duns Berwickshire, originally a border stronghold.

Samuel Bratton Nisbet, second child of James Nisbet Sr., was born Apr. 21, 1794 in Lancaster Co., SC, died Aug. 17, 1876, buried in Grapevine Cemetery, Madisonville, KY. Samuel came with his parents from South Carolina to Kentucky in 1800.

He married Agnes Pritchett on Apr. 11, 1922 and to this union were born nine children. The sixth child of this union was Francis Marion Nisbet, born Sept. 3, 1830, in Hopkins Co. He married Mary Woodson Morgan June 30, 1863 and to this union were born seven children, the fifth child was Phillip Watt Nisbet who was born Sept. 27, 1872; died Apr. 27, 1945. Phillip W. Nisbet was a painter. He married Emma Laffoon on June 6, 1901. They had three children, namely Guy Laffoon Nisbet, Jessie Parker Nisbet and Mary Frances Nisbet. Guy moved to Charleston, WV, and married Martha Baldwin of Logan, WV, Mary Frances married John E. Carr and lives in Auburn, KY; Jessie P. married Charles K. Ashby and lives in Madisonville, KY. - *Submitted by Jessie N. Ashby*

NISBET-JAGOE-SUTHARD

James Nisbet Jr., b. Feb. 23, 1796, 3rd child of James Nisbet Sr. married Mary Ann Butler Pritchett, on Mar. 12, 1821 in Hopkins Co., and were most prominent and influential citizens of Hopkins Co. and Kentucky. In October 1840, he was appointed magistrate where he served over 20 years. He was a Lt. and later Captain in the Militia, and was a land processor for over 25 years. Most of the family were charter members of the Old Grapevine Church. They raised 11 children as follows:

Samuel Rhea, Lucy Waller, Agnes Jane, Mary Elizabeth, James Moore, John Crittenden, William Alexander, Benjamin Franklin, America Washington, Laura Ann, and Virginia Franklin Nisbet.

Laura Jagoe Suthard and great grandfather, James Nisbet Jr. (1796-1881)

James Jr. died Apr. 19, 1881, and Mary died Sept. 18, 1856; both are buried in Grapevine Cemetery, Madisonville. (See Wm. Kemp Nisbet)

Samuel Rhea Nisbet b. Feb. 12, 1822, oldest child, was educated in the medical profession and practiced in Hopkins Co. He first married a Miss Prunty, and they had Nonna Nisbet and Joseph Nisbet. Joseph married a widow Oldham, and their children were: Emma Nisbet, married a Perkins ;and Sarah (Sallie) Nisbet married a Franklin.

Dr. Samuel Rhea Nisbet married second, Elizabeth Winstead, and they had four children: Charlie (girl), Jemie (Jennie), William Kemp and Etta. Dr. Nisbet died Aug. 6, 1884, is buried in Grapevine Cemetery.

Charlie Nisbet, b. Oct. 29, 1867, married Hollie E. Turner (b. Sept. 2, 1852 d. July 27, 1888), on Dec. 10, 1878. Their one daughter, Aetna Turner, b. Oct. 30, 1883, married James T. Williams—one son, James Nisbet Williams, b. Jan. 1, 1903. Charlie died Apr. 30, 1930.

Jemie/Jennie Nisbet, b. Dec. 8, 1859, married Elwood Jagoe, b. Mar. 20, 1850. Their seven children were: Jessie Jagoe b. Feb 26, 1883; Etta Jagoe, b. Jan. 11, 1850, married W.L. Grissell; Elgin Jagoe, b. Aug. 30, 1891; Elizabeth (Betty) Jagoe, b. Apr. 4, 1889; Ola Rhea Jagoe b. Aug. 30, 1891; James Kemp Jagoe, b. Jan. 26, 1900; and Laura E. Jagoe, married J. Daniel Suthard. Jemi died Dec. 18, 1958, and Elwood died Sept. 29, 1920.

Laura Emerine Jagoe, born Sept. 12, 1893, sixth child of Jemi Nisbet and William Elwood Jagoe, is a direct descendant of Col. William Bratton who fought in the Rev. War and was present at Yorktown when Cornwalis surrendered to Gen. Washington. Laura was born at home in the country now Hanson St. She graduated from Madisonville H.S. in 1913 and lived with a sister in Calhoun, GA, where she attended teachers college, Univ. of GA in Athens. She returned to Hopkins Co. where she successfully passed the "Teachers Test" and received a First Class Teaching Certificate. She taught in the elementary schools in Hopkins Co. until WW I when she was made principal of Ilsley School at age 22. She says that some of her students were almost as old and some boys larger than she.

In 1926, she became secretary to Attorney Tom Gooch and she wrote the last warrant for the last hanging in Hopkins Co. ("Bunion Fleming and Nathan Barnes").

In 1930, Laura E. Jagoe, married J. Daniel Suthard (b. Mar. 26, 1884 d. Nov. 27, 1963), a successful farmer in Mortons Gap area, later a coal miner. One daughter Sara Suthard Ellison, now lives in Detroit, MI. In 1950, while Sara attended Murray College, Laura returned to teaching at Mortons Gap for seven more years before retiring.

Sara and Robert Ellison, had a son, Rodney Ellison, b. May 20, 1952 who married Carol Larmouth, b. Mar. 22, 1958, on Aug. 16, 1975. Their two children: Jennifer Ellison b. Feb. 27, 1976, and Matthew, b. Dec. 7, 1977. Rod and Carol live in Madisonville. He is Technician/Service Advisor for Madison Square Nissan. (See Wm. K. Nisbet for other children of Dr. S.R. Nisbet). - *Submitted by Laura E. Suthard. Compiled by Rella G. Jenkins. Source: Nisbet Narrations as collected by Newton A. Nisbet, 1961*

JAMES FRANKLIN NISBET

James Franklin Nisbet, fifth child of James Moore Nisbet (1829-1915), was born Mar. 12, 1859. He married Francis Patilla Woodruff of St. Charles. They lived on Davis Well Road, where he was a very fine veterinarian, who helped people far and near as neighbor and friend, and was a public road overseer, trustee of his school district, farmer. Their children:

Charles Alexander Nisbet, b. Nov. 1, 1886, married Martha (Mattie) Wilkey; James Wm. Nisbet, b. Nov. 5, 1888, married Elizabeth Sisk, b. Dec. 20, 1892. Their children: James Nisbet Jr., born Dec. 30, 1915, married Virginia Rawlins Carter; Lounicy York Nisbet, b. Jan. 30, 1918, served in WW II, married Kathryn James Oct. 13, 1945—one dau. Linda Kay Nisbet, b. Sept. 6, 1947; Howard Brazzleton Nisbet b. Apr. 12, 1920, served in WW II, married Jan Ann Nichelson, their children: Sharon Louise, Diane Eliz., and James Wm.; Robert Cantrill Nisbet b. Sept. 17, 1922, graduate of GA Tech, Civil Engineering, married Sara Mac Lewis, b. June 6, 1926, RN. Their four children: Barbara Gail, Edward Lewis, David Wayne and Susan Beth.

Lounicy York Nisbet, third child of James Franklin Nisbet, b. Feb. 3, 1890, d. Oct. 5, 1914, of typhoid fever.

Benjamin Dinsmore Nisbet, b. Apr. 17, 1893, married Mabel Bell Pillow, a school teacher, graduate of Transylvania College, on Dec. 23, 1926. He was graduate of Bowling Green Western KY Normal College. Taught school for over 25 years, was County Supt. of Hopkins Co. schools for eight years, school supervisor of music for three years. He served in WW I in the Navy and witnessed the surrender of the German Fleet at Scapa Flow. Their children:

Emma Mildred Nisbet, b. Mar. 5, 1930,

married Glen Gould and they have two sons. They live in Pennsylvania; Benjamin Dinsmore Nisbet Jr., b. Feb. 25, 1933, a graduate of Transylvania College in 1955, studied in Bible College to be a Christian Minister. Was Assistant Minister of the Christian Church in Cynthiana, KY, for many years. He married Joann Pearce June 3, 1956.

Other children of James Franklin Nisbet were Elijah Bassett Nisbet, b. July 11, 1895, grad. of medicine, married Sadie Wilgus Pollion, settled in Odessa, MO; Mary Louise Nisbet, b. Jan. 28, 1898, married 1st a Menter, 2nd to Henry A. Jackson, no children; Emma Lucille Nisbet b. Aug. 14, 1900, married Roy H. Whalen, both school teachers in Louisville. Two children: Charles Roy Whalen b. Mar. 15, 1933, UK grad; Martha Louise Whalen b. Nov. 25, 1934, UK grad.; Dixon Franklin Nisbet, b. Oct. 3, 1903, married Eva Brooks Dec. 24, 1931. Is grad. of Western KY College, Bowling Green, is a school teacher. One dau. Susan Brooks Nisbet b. Sept. 19, 1932, married Herman E. Spivey Jr. One dau. Eva Kathryn, b. June 3, 1954. - *Submitted by Laura Suthard. Compiled by Rella G. Jenkins. Source:* Nisbet Narrations *as collected by Newton A. Nisbet, 1961*

JOHN NISBET

It is thought that John Nisbet (b. 1705), and his wife, Sarah, and two young sons, Alexander and James, first settled in the southern part of Anson Co., where North and South Carolina are divided, now known as Lancaster Co., SC.

John received his first land grant in April, 1753, for 350 acres. This community was growing very fast by families from Pennsylvania and Charleston, SC. Among the families was Col. Alexander Osborne, Hugh McWhorter, whose son, Rev. Dr. Alexander McWhorter, was a close friend and advisor of George Washington, and was President of Queens College in Charlotte, NC, James Hall; Andrew, and Isreal Pickens, James and Robert Davis, whose descendents intermarried into the family of John Nisbet's descendents.

Of John Nisbet's children: Alexander, b. 1731 (at sea); James b. 1733, Lancaster Co., PA; William b. 1735; John b. 1737, Rowan Co., NC; David, b. ca 1736, North Carolina; Thomas B., North Carolina, and Elizabeth.

John later moved south out of Pennsylvania into Carolinas, Rowan Co., where he died Nov. 19, 1755, at the early age of 50. He was buried in Old Thyatira Presbyterian Churchyard—his the oldest marked grave in this cemetery. Sarah, wife, died October 1764, and their 2nd son, James, who died 1763, are buried by his side.

Alexander Nisbet married at about age 20 to Agness Ramsey b. 1727. They moved further south into the Carolinas following an old Indian Path, settling in "the Garden of the Waxhaws," Jacksonham District in Craven Co., SC. He also received a land grant of 390 acres. Some of their neighbors were the families of John McDow, Thomas Gamble, James Huey, and John Walker.

Alexander and Agness had nine children, Martha, b. 1752; William, b. 1753; Margaret, b. 1756; John, b. 1759; Alexander, b. 1762; James, b. 1765; Benjamin, b. 1768; Joseph, b. ?; and Isabell, b. 1773.

Alexander died at age 42, leaving Agness with the small children to raise. They are buried in Old Waxhaw Presbyterian Church Cemetery.

The sixth child of Alexander Nisbet and Agness Ramsey was James, who was in the Revolutionary War. "James Nisbet served in his brother, Col. William Nisbet's Company, from May 1778 to Aug. 1779."

James married Jane Bratton, daughter of Col. William Bratton of York District, in 1791. They had four children: Alexander (1792), Samuel Bratton (1794); James Jr. (1796); and Andrew M. (1799) all born in Lancaster Co., SC.

James Nisbet and family, along with brother, Alexander and family, joined wagon trains that were moving further "West". Alexander and his family moved to eastern Tennessee and settled in Rutherford County. James and family moved on further "West" into Kentucky, and settled in Madisonville, KY, arriving on Christmas Eve 1800. This was a recently formed county of Henderson, formed from Christian County in 1798. (See Nisbet-Jagoe-Suthard) - *Submitted by Rella G. Jenkins with approval from Mrs. Laura Suthard. Source:* Nisbet Narrations

WILLIAM KEMP NISBET

William Kemp Nisbet, fifth child of Dr. Samuel Rhea Nisbet (1822-1884), and Elizabeth Winstead Nisbet, b. Apr. 28, 1863, married Jan. 25, 1894, to Eva McGregor in St. Charles, KY, daughter of Alec and Amelia McGregor (both died young). Amelia's maiden name was Cheguidden, whose parents were from Wales, England, and Alex's parents were from Scotland. Dr. William Kemp Nisbet practiced medicine in Earlington for about 50 years. He served in the U.S. Army during the Mexican border trouble (1915-1916), also as Col. in the Army Medical Corps in WW I. They had one son, Kenneth Rhea Nisbet, b. 1896 in St. Charles, who married Gladys Whitford of Earlington. He was Chief of Engineers U.S. Army for many years and a 2nd Lt. in Infantry in WW I, a Lt. Col. in the U.S. Air Force in WW II. In 1961 he lived in Arlington, VA. Had one son, William Kenneth Nisbet, b. 1934.

William Kemp Nisbet and Elizabeth Winstead Nisbet, mother of William Kemp Nisbet.

Etta Nisbet, sixth child of Dr. S.R. Nisbet, b. Aug. 28, 1865, married Charles B. Kingham, had several children, including: Albert, Kate, and Charles Jr. She died in 1945, buried in Grapevine Cemetery. *Submitted by Laura Suthard. Compiled by Rella J. Jenkins. Source:* Nisbet Narrations

NISBET-BASSETT

The second child of James Nisbet Jr. (1796-1881), was Lucy Waller Nisbet b. Aug. 1, 1823, in Hopkins County, married Amos Bassett, b. Sept. 16, 1815. They had 10 children: Lucian, married a Pritchett; George, b. Jan. 13, 1846; William, b. June 29, 1848; Mary married Dr. Winstead; Elijah b. Dec. 14, 1851 married first Cordie Johnson, second to Margaret Buhl of Evansville; Samuel b. Oct. 5, 1857, d. 1902, married Mary ?, one child, Elizabeth; Jennie, b. June 18, 1861, married Yateman Johnson, two children: Lucian Johnson married Myrtle Tucker, Lucy Johnson married Robert Furgeson; John A. b. June 29, 1865 married a Miss Morgan, children, Sarah, Mary, Ellen, Eligh, and Francis; Jessie (girl) b. Aug. 25, 1868 married A.D. Sisk, children, Bassett Sisk, Bart, Hanson, A.D. Jr.; William Nisbet youngest of 10, married Miss Finley, two children, Elizabeth and Martha. *Submitted by Laura Suthard. Compiled by Rella J. Jenkins. Source:* Nisbet Narrations

NISBET-RASH

Agnes Jane Nisbet, third child of James Jr., b. June 6, 1825 was married Dec. 16, 1846 to Benjamin Lewis Rash b. July 31, 1820. Their son Adolphus Franklin Rash b. Sept. 6, 1847, on Oct. 25, 1882 was married to Fannie C. Jones b. Aug. 20, 1835.

Adolphus Franklin Rash was a medical doctor in Hopkins Co. for many years. He died Feb. 21, 1889. Fannie died Nov. 30, 1898.

Adolphus and Fannie had a daughter Mary Nisbet Rash b. Nov. 6, 1885. She married Feb. 15, 1906 to Ernest Claytor b. May 16, 1871. They had two sons, James Rash Claytor b. Jan. 2, 1907 and Ernest Claytor Jr., called "Son". James Rash married Frances Sheffer b. Nov. 18, 1914, and he died Aug. 1, 1973. She was married Roy Allen Apr. 7, 1978 and they live in Madisonville. Ernest Jr. "Son" married Roberto Clements born Dec. 9, 1901, d. in 1975 or 1976. He was born Jan. 7, 1910 and d. Jan. 2, 1974.

Other children of Benjamin L. and Agnes J. Rash were: Otway Watkins b. Jan. 30, 1850 d. June 18, 1928, married Sarah Elizabeth Robertson b. 1851 d. 1933. Their children: James Robert Rash b. Oct. 9, 1872, served in Spanish American War, served as Postmaster in Henderson. Married Jane Browlee, had sons Dr. Jack O.W. Rash and James R. Rash Jr. (See James Rhea Rash family.) - *Compiled by Rella G. Jenkins approved by Frances Clayton Allen. Source: Nisbet Narrations, 1961 and Frances Clatyor Allen*

JOHN H. NISWONGER

John H. Niswonger, native of Ohio Co., WV was born Feb. 28, 1828. He married Luttitia Coffman, Oct. 19, 1853, the youngest child of Isaac Coffman and Mary A. Harbor, both natives of Kentucky, (he of Hopkins County and she of Woodford County.) Their other children were Hiram, Isaac S., Huldak, Annie, Elisha J., Joel H., W.C., Mary L., James R., and Mildred.

The paternal grandparents were Isaac Coffman, a native of Maryland and Annie French, of Scotland. They were pioneers of Hopkins County. The maternal grandfather, Amos Harbor married a Miss Husted. He died in Tennessee and she in Woodford County.

John H. taught school in Webster and Henderson Counties for several years. He bought a farm adjoining Luttitia's parents in what is now Webster County where he farmed and taught school. After this he taught in Henderson County for several years, moving to Hopkins County in 1872. He bought a farm next to Union Cemetery south of Nebo. They had eight children, four lived to adulthood: Elisha J., Sept. 21, 1854-Aug. 1868; triplets were born Apr. 10, 1856. John H. Jr. died August 22; William B. died August 17; Mildred (Jenny) married E.B. Rodgers and died Sept. 21, 1938. Alexander (Alex) Nov. 16, 1857, he moved to Providence, KY, in 1882 where he operated a drug and general merchandising store. Twins were born Mar. 31, 1862; Josey married Elmer Edger II. She moved to Florida and died there. Thomas (Tom) Jefferson married Valerie Elizabeth (Lizzie) Springfield (Dec. 16, 1870), the daughter of John H. Springfield and Cynthia Townsend Ramsey. She was the only child of this marriage. (John H. had three daughters by his first marriage to Mary L. Coffman, Genova A. Ramsey, Mary Banks Pemberton and Mildred Overby (Cynthia's first marriage was to William H. Ramsey.) They were also early pioneers of Hopkins County.

Tom and Lizzie Niswonger with children Maud, Tommy Louis and John

Tom Niswonger remained on the family farm operating it even after unsuccessful cataract surgery left him blind in 1905. They had three children; John Spencer (Sept. 2, 1888), Maud Emma (Oct. 19, 1891), Thomas "Tommy" Lewis (Nov. 19, 1895).

John Spencer married Helen Hill Winstead (Oct. 10, 1890). Their children are Mary Elizabeth Wright, Lillie Pearl Hoffman, Nell Grace Clayton, Lois, John Thomas; Emma Jean Hibbs, Helen Josephine Stewart Sexton, and Charles. John farmed the home place with his father and was also the iceman for the Nebo area.

Maude never married.

Tommy Louis married Hortense Lutz (Nov. 26, 1898) daughter of Jacob Lann and Gradie Fike. Their children are William Louis and Lanna Sue Arnold. He worked for the State Highway and Sentry Mines as a dragline oiler. They were divorced after sixteen years. Tommy's second marriage was to Opal Rich. Hortense was a school teacher for many years in Hopkins County Schools. She married Ebenezer Porter in 1961. - *Submitted by Lanna Arnold*

JOHN HENRY NIXON

John Henry Nixon, son of Frederick and Jemimah Chandler Nixon, grandson of Absolom and Edith Farmer Nixon, was born in 1828.

His grandfather, Absolom Nixon was born in 1759, Prince Co., VA, married May 27, 1783 in Surry Co., NC to Edith Farmer of Stokes Co., NC. Absolom served in the Revolutionary War as a foot soldier for the state of South Carolina. After the war, his family moved to Laurens Co., SC; to East Tennessee near Knoxville; to Rutherford Co., TN; then to Christian Co., KY.

Absolom and Edith had a large family of nineteen children, raising fourteen. A partial list follows: Uriah, Phoeby married Jan. 1, 1823 in Christian Co.; William Duncan; Adaline married William B. McCullock; Needham T. married Mary S. Hopson; Edith; Hester; Temperance; Absolom Jr. and Frederick. Absolom Sr. died July 27, 1836 in Christian Co.

Frederick Nixon married Jemimah Chandler Apr. 9, 1817 in Christian Co. Children: William; Samuel T.; Benjamin T.; Elizabeth L.; Narcissa Adaline; Henerette; John Henry and Zekiah Nixon.

John Henry, farmer, married Mildred Sims Beshears (born Aug. 13, 1836) on Sept. 18, 1857 in Hopkins Co. He enrolled in the Civil War at Ashbyberg, Nov. 3, 1861, in the 17th KY Volunteer Infantry (later the 25th Infantry). He was wounded in the battle at Fort Donelson, TN, taken aboard the steamboat "Chancellor" where he died on or about Mar. 2, 1862 upstream at Mound City, IL. There are two records of his death, as loss of life was heavy in this battle. He is believed to be one of the unknown soldiers buried at the National Cemetery in Mound City.

His wife Milly died June 20, 1863 leaving three small children: William Riley (born Sept. 23, 1858 Cedar Co., MO); Vironica (born July 6, 1860) and John Henry Campbell Nixon (born July 31, 1862). These children were raised by their mother's parents, Issac C. and Mildred Sims Alexander Beshears Jr. of Hopkins Co. - *Submitted by: John and Mary Jackson*

JOHN HENRY C. NIXON

John Henry Campbell Nixon born July 31, 1862 married first Rachel Marcella Howell Apr. 9, 1883 in Hopkins Co. No issue. His second marriage was to Martha E. (Mattie) Keller Apr. 12, 1888 in Christian Co. Mattie is buried in an unmarked grave at Newson Cem. in Caldwell Co. Their daughter, Georgiana, born July 17, 1889, married Oscar Starling Dew on May 23, 1906 in Christian Co. Children: Verlie Jane Branson Casteel and Verna Lee Stokes. His third marriage was to Mary Etta (Mollie) Blackburn Oct. 6, 1890 in Caldwell Co. Mollie was born June 5, 1868, daughter of James and Mary Maddox Blackburn who came from Robertson Co., TN. Their children: Barney (no dates, buried in family plot near Outwood Hospital where they lived); Mildred

Mary Etta Blackburn Nixon, Mildred Mae Nixon Taylor, Jennie Lee Nixon Menser, Georgiana Nixon Dew, John Henry Campbell Nixon and John Robert Nixon.

Mae; Jennie Lee; John Robert; Charles Anderson; Lona Frances; Nettie Niles and Mary Thelma.

Mildred Mae (Mollie) born Dec. 16, 1892, died Mar. 29, 1979, buried Crabtree Cem. at Ilsley. Married first-Charles Frank Collins May 16, 1909, Caldwell Co. Married second-Thomas Pickering Taylor Aug. 20, 1945, Christian Co. Married third-Thomas Gresham Sept. 6, 1965, Hopkins Co. No. issue.

Jennie Lee born July 6, 1895, died Feb. 22, 1985, buried Crabtree Cem. at Ilsley, married William Lester Menser Apr. 7, 1910, Hopkins Co. Children: William Harvey; Arvil Hershal; Geneva Loreanne Inglis; Leo; Elvis Vinson; Earnest and Morris Charley.

John Robert born July 20, 1897. Married first: Ester May Messamore Mar. 28, 1918, Hopkins Co., died in childbirth, buried in unmarked grave at Shyflat Cem.; second marriage, Rachael Pearl McIntosh Apr. 14, 1922, Caldwell Co., children: Rachel Pauline Johnson, Fleda Jean Boswell, Mack Aubrey , Mary Sue, Johnnie Bolden and Claybourne; third marriage, Manthas Parker Martin Jan. 12, 1946, Christian Co. was brief, no issue; fourth marriage, Esmer Messamore Carroll Nov. 19, 1946, Christian Co., no issue.

Charles Anderson born Dec. 10, 1900 married Flora Moore Dec. 21, 1920, Caldwell Co. and had a daughter Lucille Ambrose. Second marriage, Beatrice Cansler Feb. 14, 1935, Hopkins Co. Children: Charlena Utley and Bobby Gene. Charley was killed in the coal mines June 7, 1954, buried Crabtree Cem., Ilsley.

Lona Frances born Feb. 14, 1903 married first William Hanson Andrews Oct. 4, 1919, Hopkins Co. Children: Margaret Kaiser Winters and Lorena Jeanette Ayotte. Second marriage, Robert "Jack" Andrews. Third marriage, Henry Lowe. No issue. Lona died July 9, 1975, buried Glen Eden Mem. Gardens, MI.

Nettie Niles born Apr. 8, 1908; married first Michael Dropp Oct. 31, 1925. Children: Michael Jr. and Marcella Simko. Second marriage, Jerome Anderson Jan. 29, 1942, had a daughter, Geraldine Bostic. Nettie died Mar. 4, 1974, buried Crabtree Cem., Ilsley.

Mary Thelma born June 24, 1912 married Olus Vance Wood Nov. 21, 1927, Caldwell Co. Children: Mitchell Olus; Lewis Alton; Mary Frances (see Jackson); Jo Ann; Nellis Sue; Barbara Fae, Mildred Marie and Ralph Douglas. - *Submitted by Mary Frances Jackson*

CHARLEY F. OAKLEY

Charles Frank Oakley (1885-1987) married Roxie Overtine Neal on Oct. 31, 1906 in Shawneetown, IL. Born in Webster County and reared in Hopkins County, he was the son of Jessie Robert Oakley, born 1856 and died 1935, and Mary Jane (Jennie) Wilkerson, born 1852 and died 1943. Charley's brother was Reverend W.W. (Willie Woodson) Oakley, a well-known General Baptist minister. His sisters were Sallie, Bessie and Doanie. His wife Roxie, born 1889 and died 1967, was the daughter of William M. Neal, born 1855 and died 1936, and Cordie A. Dame, born 1866 and died 1928. Roxie's brothers were Claud, George and James Henry (Jim). Her sisters were Jonnie, Sallie (see Ethel Blankenship) and Mary Effie.

Charles Frank Oakley with wife Roxie Neal on their wedding day.

Charley, a farmer in his youth, was always full of dreams for the future. A distant relative, Greenville Louis Oakley, gave ground for a church and burial ground in 1898 on Highway 630 in the Cox's Store Community known as Pultight. The church was and still is known as Oakley Home General Baptist Church. As a lad in his early teens, Charley helped in building the first white-framed building in September 1899. His job, as he proudly told his children in years to come, was pulling and hammering straight the used or bent nails. At 17, he was baptized and joined the newly-built church with its large steeple and huge bell that could be heard for miles calling worshipers to services. His brother Reverend W.W. became his pastor in later years. About age 40 Brother Charley, as he was now known, was ordained Deacon of Oakley Home, an office he served in for over 60 years.

Charley's children were born on a farm he owned on the Yarbough Hill and Cox Store Road. He lived in Indianapolis, IN off and on for more than 20 years. He worked as a sander for General Motors. One week he worked two shifts straight but was only paid for one. He complained and his boss told him he couldn't find another job that paid $70 a week. Charley informed his boss he had land in Kentucky and he hadn't forgot how to farm and left. He later returned to Indiana and worked making airplane parts during WW II until the war was over.

His little family always came home for Oakley Home Church's Homecoming and Revivals. Always a pusher of his dreams, Brother Charley saw his beloved church remodeled in the late 30's. In the early 50's it went to electric. The Oakley's had made the move twice back to the farm before Brother Charley sold it. Now retired, he and Roxie lived in Madisonville. His church soon to go full time, so was Brother Charley. A new building was needed and from his personal savings Charley loaned a large sum of money, interest free, on the heating system of the buildings.

Not to be put aside, at 65 Brother Charley began a new career house painting. Many home and businesses around Hopkins County were painted including Harris Funeral Home. At 80, at the insistence of family and friends, he hung up his paint brush for hire. Giving generously again, his dream of Oakley Home's parsonage came true in 1984. At 101, he was still attending his place of worship and dreaming again for the future.

The Oakley's had a son, Ralph Debartis, who died in 1975. He had three children: 1st Betty Lou who had Wayne and Victor before her own early death, 2nd Ralph who died as a child, and 3rd Jerry who had Ruth Ann and Jeari Lynn. The Oakley's daughter, Blanche, married Durwood Veazey and lives in Madisonville. Her son, Dwight Charles Veazey is also of Madisonville. There were six great great grandchildren.

Charley became known as "Pappy" Oakley in his last years and lived in a local nursing home. He was well loved by staff and other residents. It is said he lived so long because he loved life and enjoyed it so much and gave so much love to others. - *See "Hopkins County Centenerians." Submitted by Dorothy Miller Shoulders*

OATES

The Oates family is one of the pioneer families of the White Plains community. Like most families, historians disagree on their origin and lineage. They are believed to be of English decent. Originally, they may have been Danes and invaded England with the Vikings, or Normans and come in with William the Conqueror in 1066. The name was then spelled "Otes". It is disputed whether the first Oates to come to America has been found. One source lists him as John Oates who married in Ireland "before 1732" and settled in Chester Co., PA in 1734; later moving to North Carolina.

Historians do agree that the first Kentucky Oates was Major Jesse Oates, who fled Perquimans Co., NC about 1800, accompanied by a negro slave, after killing his brother-in-law a Mr. Coghill, in a duel. Tradition says Oates served in the Revolutionary War under Colonel Francis Marion, known as "the Swamp Fox". Records show him reaching Captain rank. Records say Coghill's friends pursued him to near the present site of Hopkinsville where they lost his horse tracks in a sea of buffalo tracks. He settled near the present town of Graham, in Muhlenberg County, where tradition says he and slave lived awhile in a huge, hollow Poplar tree. Later he obtained much land, built a home and sent to North Carolina for his family.

His second son, Jethro (pronounced Jeether then) forded Pond River and bought 500 acres of land in Hopkins Co., southeast of White Plains. The river crossing is still known as "Jeethers Ford". His oldest, William (who brought the family to Kentucky about 1807) also bought land in both Muhlenberg and Hopkins and married in Hopkins. One of William's sons, James Wilson Oates, married Elizabeth Caroline Herring and may have settled on land originally owned by the Herrings. James Wilson had a son, Alney Filander "Fie" Oates, who in turn had a daughter Virginia Oates Neathery who still lives on what is believed the property. She has a tax receipt on it dated 1827 and made to her great grandfather, Pete Herring. It is in same general area as the Jethro land. It is known the last two rooms of the dwelling house were added in 1872. The rest is much older. Union soldiers raided there and took some horses, and the outlaw Jesse James once spent the night there with James Wilson Oates. The house is described in the 1979 Yearbook of Hopkins Co. Historical Society as "in excellent condition, cheerful, cozy and comfortable".

Mrs. Neathery's son, James Tilford Neathery July 27, 1942, lives in a new house on the same farm. He is married to Suzanne Fitch Apr. 1, 1951, owns and operates Neathery Dance Studios on McLeod Lane in Madisonville. Both he and his mother have followed a career in teaching and education. He has one son, James Leif Neathery, born Dec. 21, 1983.

OATES GENEALOGY IN KENTUCKY

Major Jesse Oates—1756-1831—Married (1) Laruhama Stevens 1782, (2) Zilpha Mason 1789.

William Oates—1783-1833—Married Elizabeth Earle 1807 (Died on Miss. River - buried either Island 100 or West bank at Stackland reach.)

James Wilson Oates—1825-1884—Married Elizabeth Caroline Herring 1845

Alney Filander "Fie" Oates—1867-1941—Married Annie Hight 1896 born 1875, died 1977.

Virginia Oates Neathery—1911—Married Harlan Neathery 1931 born 1910, died 1983.

James Tilford Neathery—1942—Married Suzanne Fitch 1976 born 1951.

James Leif Neathery—Dec. 21, 1983.

- *Submitted by James T. Neathery*

OATES-WHITSELL

George Louis Oates, Jr., and Mary Nell Whitsell were married Nov. 5, 1937, at First Baptist Church, Leitchfield, KY and her cousin John Hardy Morton, Jr. (b. Oct. 2, 1916) married Nell Katherine Addison (b. July 16, 1917; d. Apr. 1, 1986) in the double ceremony performed by Rev. Hollis S. Summers, Madisonville FBC pastor. Only witnesses were Rev. T. Emerson Wortham, host pastor, and Mrs. T.E. Wortham.

George Louis and Mary Nell Oates

George L., Jr. was born Jan. 21, 1906, in Vine Grove, Hardin Co., KY, where his father, George Louis Oates, Sr. (b. Sept. 17, 1864, Hopkins Co.; d. Dec. 30, 1951, Warren Co., KY) was a merchant. His mother, Ida Blanche Stader (b. 1874; d. Jan., 1921, Hardin Co.) died before his fifteenth birthday. The younger children were: Mary Elizabeth and Robert Stader Oates, both deceased, and William Mason Oates, Salinas, CA.

Mary Nell was born July 10, 1916, Hopkins Co., to George Herbert Whitsell and Mattie Mae McGary. Her only sister, Mildred Louise, widow of (1) Luther Conrad Brewer and (2) Frank Mann Curtis, lives in Florida. Her two sons: Conrad Allen Brewer and Timothy David Brewer, both born in Hopkins Co., live in Colorado.

George L. graduated from Vine Grove High School and attended the former Bowling Green Business U., Bowling Green, KY. He came to Madisonville in 1935 with the Area Office of Works Progress Administration (WPA). Later he was payroll clerk for Trio Mine and Pine Hill Mine until they closed. For many years he worked for Cedar Bluff Stone Co. as weighman and was manager of the local rock yard for ten years.

Mary Nell, 1934 graduate of Madisonville H.S., attended Murray State Teachers College one term and studied with Professor E. McCulley in his Madisonville Business College.

For more than 50 years George L. and Mary Nell have been active members of First Baptist Church, Madisonville. He was ordained as deacon in 1955, and is now a deacon emeritus. He served as clerk of Little Bethel Association of Baptists for seven years (1966-1972). Mary Nell was clerk of the Association for ten years (1973-1982). Also, she was employed as office secretary of Little Bethel Association for 12 years before retiring in 1981.

FAMILY OF GEORGE L. AND MARY NELL W. OATES

1. George Louis Oates, III (b. May 5, 1939, Hopkins Co.) married Sept. 13, 1959 to Jo Anne Brizendine (b. Feb. 21, 1938, Sumner Co., TN). They have one dau.: Mary Louise Oates (b. June 5, 1962, Sumner Co., TN) m. Dec. 28, 1985 to David Michael Driver (b. Dec. 6, 1961, Trousdale Co., TN).

2. William Robert Oates, PhD (b. Aug. 24, 1943, Hopkins Co.), m. May 9, 1981 to Rita Elizabeth Haugh (b. June 28, 1950, Minnesota). They have one dau.: Elizabeth Haugh Oates (b. Sept. 2, 1984, Miami Beach, FL).

See G.W. Whitsell and W.T. McGary Family. - *Submitted by Mary Nell Whitsell Oates*

OFFUTT

John Sanford Offutt was a confederate soldier of the Civil War. When the war ended he was in Mississippi. His officer gave him a mule to ride to his home in Madisonville, KY.

When he arrived at the Mississippi River near Paducah, the Captain of the boat would not let him bring the mule aboard the boat. So he got on the boat and forded the mule across the river.

After crossing the river Offutt got on the mule again and rode to Hopkins Co., KY. When he arrived home about six o'clock p.m., at this time the negro housekeeper had just finished washing dishes and was about to throw the dishwater out the back door, when she saw John S. Offutt ride in on the mule. She became so excited she threw the dishwater, pan and all into the air. She yelled out - "Master John is home, Praise the Lord, Master John is home."

The twelve children of John Sanford Offutt are all deceased, however many descendants are living in Hopkins Co., KY and other states.

HEADS OF THE OFFUTT FAMILY IN U.S. ARE AS FOLLOWS:

Generation I: William Offutt I, d. 1734, m. Mary Brock about 1697 Montgomery Co., MD, daughter of Capt. Edward Brock.

II: James Offutt (b. ca. 1703, d. 1750) m. 1. Rachel Beall (d. 1740) and m. 2. Sarah Beall.

III: William Offutt, III (b. ca. 1700-1737) m. Jane Joyce, will probated Aug. 23, 1810.

IV: Thomas Offutt, Jr. (b. ca. 1760, d. Scott Co., KY 1816) m. Marcia Minor, daughter of John and Ann Westmam Minor.

V: John Minor Offutt, (b. Oct. 12, 1778, d. 1862) m. Ann S. Wright, Sept. 24, 1829.

VI: John Sanford Offutt (b. Aug. 24, 1835, d. Feb. 23, 1920) m. 1. Mary Goodloe 1848, 2. Clara Laffoon 1859.

VII: Elijah Benjamin Offutt (b. Jan. 21, 1880, d. June 5, 1957) m. Lena B. Hewlett (b. June 14, 1884, d. Dec. 2, 1967) in 1905.

Children: VIII: Essie, Eunice, John William, Everett Benjamin, Clifton Ray, James Hammack, Betty Lou, and Robert Strother Offutt.- *Submitted by Eunice O. Brown*

OLDHAM

Gardner Oldham (b. 1886 d. 1928) was the son of Jim Oldham of the Pleasant View community in Hopkins County. He married Dixie Bowles (b. 1886 d. 1949), and they were parents of James Bowles Oldham (b. 1912 d. 1929); Kinchloe Oldham who resides in Richland Community; Mrs. Redmon Utley who lives at the old Gardner Oldham homeplace; and William Marion "Bill" Oldham who lives on part of the old Jim Oldham farm in the Pleasant View community.

Gardner Oldham was a merchant and an inventor, and was prominent and well thought of in the county. He was loved by the neighborhood children because he slipped some candy in the sacks of groceries that the parents bought. He had one of the first telephones of the community about 65 years ago, and the people came from all around to the grocery to use the phone to call the Dr. Before telephones the neighbors would shoot guns to let a distant neighbor know that something was wrong.

Gardner Oldham also bought the first radio in the Pleasant View neighborhood, and people would come from miles around to see and hear the radio. At that time, Bill Oldham was just a small boy, but he remembers they would have to adjust the knobs and then the "squeaking" and "sqwaking" would come on and he would get a quaint feeling to hear someone talking in the radio. He remembers a Mr. Clayton, a violinist from Hopkinsville ("We called them fiddle players") who played one night and everybody came around to listen. That was a great thing and the Oldhams felt that they could not be more "modernized" than they were right then. People would come on Saturday night to listen to the Old Barn Dance and other programs until they went off the air at 12 o'clock.

Gardner Oldham invented the electric brooder and incubator for hatching white leghorn chickens. He substituted light bulbs for warmth, with alternating On and Off switches, instead of the little kerosene heater formerly used outside the brooder. He received a card of the patent pending, but never got a patent on it. He sold the white leghorn chickens for 50¢ each.

Although Mr. Oldham died when Bill was 7 years old, he has many fond memories of his father, and many people have told him what a "fine fellow" his father was.

The family had an orchard and an apple house, where they stored apples in the fall to be used all winter. They had popcorn to pop and eat during the winter. They would make popcorn balls with sorghum molasses, and boy! they were good Bill remembers.

When Bill was growing up, for entertainment they had play parties and played games, such as "Skip to my Lou"; pound parties where each person brought one pound of candy or other foods. They went to Munns School house for community soup suppers, where individuals brought in chicken, tomatoes, corn, whatever to go into the soup. Bill's Uncle Frank Wright used to be the soup maker for the neighborhood and Bill though he made the best soup he ever tasted! The men usually chipped in a dime each to buy the crackers. A soup supper was quite an occasion.

For ice cream suppers, the women would bake cakes and pies and sell them with the homemade ice cream. Money was often donated to the school, and that is how lots of school projects were paid for.

Munns school was also used for Sunday School, called Union Sunday School at that time. All denominations in the neighborhood enjoyed the spirit of fellowship. A Mr. Wilson was the first Sunday School Supt. that Bill remembers. The people "stopped to smell the roses" and were thankful for what they had.

One dollar a day pay was considered a good job. A dollar twenty five per day was an extra good job. In the Pleasant View neighborhood, people swapped work. If it was wheat threshing time—hay baling-or harvesting of crops—and there were not enough people in the family to do the work, the men would trade work and were not out any money. If someone got sick, all the neighbors would put the crop out so he would have a crop coming on, and if it was in the fall, the men would harvest the crop so the family could have something to live on during the winter. Bill said, "We didn't figure we owed one another, that was just our way of life and we enjoyed it. We felt like we had done something to help our fellow man, which was a great feeling—we had given something".

William Marion Oldham was named for his uncle Marion Oldham who was killed in France in World War I. He is married to the former Ethel Katherine Swain of Muhlenberg County, KY. He is retired and enjoys his woodworking shop and grows vegetables in a hot house that he designed. He is an avid supporter of the Pennyrile Arts and Crafts Guild (of which he is a member) in the restoration and preservation of Munns School as a museum of memorabilia of the times when he was a student there. He lectures to student groups who visit Munns about the "days of yore" when he attended Munns School. - *Written by Rella G. Jenkins. Submitted by William "Bill" Oldham*

OSBORN-SHOULDERS

Betty Ruth Shoulders and Curtis Casmer Osborn were married in the chambers of Judge Hattley in Dixon, KY on Oct. 16, 1953.

Betty Ruth was born Nov. 4, 1939 in Webster County, the youngest daughter of Ott Shoulders and Betty Jane Hopper (see Shoulders-Miller). Daddy Ott's brothers were George and Tom, better known as Bud. Sisters were: Zenner, Neicee, Ora and Mable. Mother Betty's brothers were: Tommy, Harrison and Leonard. Sisters were: Cordelia and Sibie.

Betty and Curt Osborn

Betty Ruth attended schools in Webster County and at Nebo and Adult Education in Madisonville for a G.E.D. She worked at the plastic factory in Providence for 13 years. Betty has turned her craft hobby into a profitable work. She makes floral arrangements, dolls and many other beautiful things. She and her husband have been members of the Pentecostal Prayer Chapel for 25 years, where she has served as a Sunday School teacher, church clerk and treasurer.

Curtis was born May 8, 1936 in Hopkins County, the oldest son of Curtis Hershel Osborn and Artie Mae Simms. Daddy Curt was born in 1903 in Webster County, youngest son of Luther Osborn and Maggie Loyd. Artie Mae was born in 1907 in Hopkins County, the daughter of Joe Simms and Lula Jones. The other children of Curtis Hershel and Artie Mae: Eula Mae Landtrip, Paul Barton and Bobby Joe.

Curtis C. attended school at Nebo. He has worked at Providence plastic factory for 33 years as head mechanic. A musician, he plays guitar and has written several gospel songs. He is lay-pastor for the Pentecostal Prayer Chapel. Other family names: Brinkley.

Betty and Curtis have two sons. Richard Wayne married Teresa Schyrel Blankenship of Madisonville, their children Sherry Lee age 10 and Richard Wayne Jr. who died in infancy. The other son is Jeffery Alan. Both sons are West Hopkins High School Alumnis. - *Submitted by Betty Osborn*

ISAAC OSBURN

Isaac Osburn, born 1792 Coxes Creek area of Nelson Co., KY, the son of Nicholas and Rachel (Hibbs) Osburn, natives of Virginia. Isaac grew up and married his first two wives while living in the area around Coxes Creek. That whole area was swarming with his relatives. He bought several tracts of land. Then in 1844, he started thinking about going elsewhere and journeyed to Hopkins Co., KY where he bought a tract of land. Then he returned to Nelson Co. sold off his land there and took his family, except for his daughter Lavina who was married and she and her husband did not want to leave, together with a number of other relatives, and they went by wagon train to Hopkins Co. They all settled in and around Madisonville, KY.

Isaac married 1st in Nelson Co., Sept. 12, 1815 Jane Threlkile, orphan of Thomas Threlkile and niece of James A. Brashear, her guardian; 2nd in Nelson Co., Jan. 1, 1836 Mrs. Mary Lutz, widow of William Lutz and also the previous widow of Elias Hefley, the daughter of John Wiseheart; 3rd in Hopkins Co., Dec. 24, 1846 Mrs. Eliza Rehling, widow of Henry H. Rehling, Eliza was a Hibbs prior to marrying Henry.

Isaac amassed considerable wealth before he died just prior to Apr. 18, 1881. The exact date of death and place of burial are not yet known.

Isaac's children were:

Matilda b. June 23, 1816, d. Nov. 12, 1894, m. Nov. 1, 1832 Jacob Lutz, bur. Odd Fellows Cem. Madisonville, KY. Both born Nelson Co., KY.

Talbot b. Apr. 15, 1818 in Nelson Co., d. Dec. 10, 1872 in Hopkins Co., bur. Old Richland Cem., m. 1st in Nelson Co. Jan. 9, 1840 Susan Taylor the daughter of Isaac Taylor, m. 2nd in Hopkins Co. Oct. 21, 1849 Mrs. Nancy (O'Bryan) Hefley, m. 3rd in Hopkins Co. Luvina (Franklin) Ayers. He had eight children.

Elizabeth b. 1819 in Nelson Co., KY, d. ?, m. in Nelson Co. Dec. 30, 1837 to Tolbert Hibbs.

Lavina b. 1823 in Nelson Co., m. in Nelson Co. Jan. 2, 1845 to Taylor W. Samuels. They were founders of a whiskey called T.W. Samuels.

Isaac T. b. Oct. 10, 1827 in Nelson Co., d. Mar. 18, 1912, m. 1st in Hopkins Co. to Mary in 1852, m. 2nd in April 1895 to Josephine.

William Thomas b. Mar. 15, 1831 in Nelson Co., d. July 29, 1896 in Hopkins Co., m. Nov. 15, 1860 to Ann E. Waetzel.

Laura C. b. Apr. 14, 1833 in Nelson Co., d. June 22, 1916, unmarried.

John V. b. Feb. 14, 1837 in Nelson Co., d. Nov. 5, 1920, m. June 9, 1867 to Susan E. Slaton (a descendant of Elizabeth Hibbs b. ca. 1772, m. 1791 to John Slaton in Virginia).

Roseanna b. 1839 in Nelson Co., d. 1915 in Hopkins Co., m. Apr. 5, 1859 in Hopkins Co. to John A. Osburn, widower and cousin.

Margaret E., b. ca. 1843 in Nelson Co., m. Mar. 3, 1857 in Hopkins Co. to Joseph Hibbs. - *Submitted by Randa Bearden*

OWEN-DUKE

Pleasant Prell Owen b. June 5, 1824 in North Carolina to Joshua Owen and Henrietta Buchanan. He died July 24, 1898 and is buried in Owen Cemetery, located across the road from Concord General Baptist Church. He married Jan. 7, 1847 in Hopkins Co., Mary Ann Springfield who was born Dec. 6, 1829 in North Carolina and died Oct. 17, 1897. She was the daughter of William Springfield and Elizabeth Buchanan. She was at first buried beside her parents, but due to a family disagreement was later moved to Owen Cem. and is buried beside her husband. Their children are: Emily F. (Puss) married William L. Gaston; John Washington married Indiana Duke; Elizabeth called Sis married Lyhue Coffman; Margaret A. married 1. Denney, married 2. Vanover; Joshua E. married Rossie Mitchell; William E. married Martha Buchanan; Nancy (Nanny) R. married John W. Springfield; Yancy W. (stillborn twin to Nancy); Mary E. married William Duff Webster; Robert Nelson (Tawsey) married Emily Webster; and Thomas T.

John Washington Owen was born Sept. 14, 1850 in Hopkins Co., KY and died Jan. 21, 1930. He married Indiana (Ann) Duke on Dec. 25, 1870, she being born Aug. 10, 1856 in North Carolina and died June 29, 1936. Both are buried in Owen Cemetery. She was the daughter of Nelson Duke and Margaret (Peggy) Wilkerson. Ann along with her parents and sisters came to Hopkins Co. with several families in 1869, they being the Brinkley, Wilkerson, Mangrum, Hampton, Obryan and Duncan. Ann loved to dance and always claimed that she danced all the way from North Carolina with Nick Wilkerson who was an infant at that time.

Their children: William Owen b. Sept. 20, 1872, d. July 4, 1874, buried Olive Branch Cem.; John C. b. Apr. 30, 1874, d. Nov. 12, 1951 married Maggie Friday, buried Oakley Home Cem.; James Preston b. Mar. 27, 1876, died as an infant (William and James were both burned to death in the open fireplace at different times), buried at Olive Branch Cem.; Martha Della b. June 1, 1878, d. July 8, 1940 married 1. Walter Satterfield (see Satterfield-Madison) married 2. James Oliver, buried Owen Cem.; Edd Romulus b. Mar. 13, 1880, d.

Feb. 3, 1960, buried in Concord General Baptist Church Cem. where he was the custodian for over 50 years, married Elizabeth Higdon; Cora Ann b. Nov. 21, 1881, d. July 11, 1960, buried Concord Gen. Bapt. Church Cem., married James Bard; Mary Ida b. Aug. 31, 1883, d. July 26, 1959 married Ellis Hawkins, buried Carbondale, IL; Lottie Victoria b. Mar. 20, 1885, died as an infant, buried Olive Branch Cem.; Charlie Arthur b. Jan. 2, 1887, d. Mar. 18, 1935, never married, buried Owen Cem.; Bennie Irvin b. Apr. 6, 1889, d. Feb. 20, 1963, buried Concord Gen. Bapt. Cem., married May Vanvactor; Lonnie Clemont b. Oct. 18, 1892, d. Feb. 9, 1966, buried Concord Church Cem., married Nov. 14, 1916 to Flora Elizabeth Burton still living in 1987 (see Burton-Madison); Mirdle died as an infant; and Ernest Cecil b. Feb. 20, 1898, d. Dec. 10, 1981, buried Concord Gen. Bapt. Church Cem., married 1. Annie Veasey, married 2. Virginia Haley. - *Submitted by: Randa Bearden*

OWEN-WEBSTER

Robert Nathaniel Owen (Mar. 20, 1865-May 21, 1949) was the youngest son of Pleasant Prell (June 5, 1824-July 24, 1898) and Mary Ann (Springfield) Owen (Dec. 6, 1829-Oct. 17, 1897). Robert N. married Emily Jane Webster (Dec. 5, 1866-Sept. 18, 1945) in Hopkins Co., KY on Oct. 13, 1886. He was a farmer, carpenter before coming to Madisonville to work for C.E. Owen in his hardware store and then later had his own grocery on E. Center Street.

Robert Nathaniel Owen and Emily Jane Webster on their wedding day, Oct. 13, 1886

To this union were born: (1) Inah Leonia Owen; born Oct. 23, 1887; d. June 19, 1889; buried in Owen Cemetery, Hopkins Co., KY. (2) Pleasant Pratt Owen; born Oct. 6, 1889; m. Aug. 12, 1912 to Mary Schimmel; died ca. 1962 in Algonquin, IL and both are buried there; three children: Helen; Robt. Charles and Louise. (3) Jessie Anna Frances Owen; born Dec. 21, 1891; m. (1) Robt. Green - Mar. 23, 1913, Henderson, KY; (2) Andrew David Berry on July 6, 1918, Hopkinsville, KY; two children Elizabeth (Beth) Owen and Walter David Berry. (4) Dollie Emily Owen; born Feb. 12, 1894; m. W. Grover Allen, May 4, 1914; died Dec. 8, 1983 in Chicago Hgts., IL and is buried there; two children: Frances and Elise. (5) Robert Dale Owen; born Feb. 23, 1896; m. Daisy Elizabeth Friend/Smith in Evansville, IN on Jan. 15, 1917; died Mar. 26, 1959 at his home in Webster Co., KY and is buried in Odd Fellows Cemet., Madisonville, KY. Seven children: Emily Grace; Robbie Elizabeth; Robert Bradford; Walter Pratt; Franklin Dale; Rudolph David and Donald Wayne Owen. (6) Dewey Lamb Owen; born Nov. 12, 1897; died Nov. 15, 1898. Buried in Owen Cemetery. (7) Goldie Pearl Owen; born Apr. 30, 1901; m. Oct. 22, 1921 to Al Burton; died in Chicago, IL on May 6, 1948 with burial at Owen Cemet. but later at Odd Fellows Cemet. Four children: Emily Frances; Richard Owen; Beatrice and Shirley Burton. (8) Walter Harvey (Brother) Owen; born Aug. 25, 1903; he never married; served in the Air Force during World War II in the European Theater; died Sept. 15, 1957 and is buried at Owen Cemetery. (9) Elsie Lucile Owen; born Apr. 8, 1907; died Mar. 1, 1908 with burial in Owen Cemetery.

Emily Jane Webster Owen and Robert Nathaniel Owen on their 50th wedding anniversary

This poem was written by Pleasant Pratt Owen, the oldest son of Robert Nathaniel and Emily Jane (Webster) Owen. Pratt lived in Chicago, IL at the time of his parent's fifty-fifth wedding anniversary on Oct. 13, 1941.

PA AND MA OWEN
Of course we'll have our biscuits
And honey for them too
To be without hot biscuits
In Kentucky - wouldn't do.

Folks will come for miles around
And youngsters by the score
To a dear and kind old couple
Whom we love more and more.

Pa and Ma, just get along
The way God meant them to
And tried to tell their youngsters
That's the proper thing to do.

May God Bless and keep them
As now they're growing old
And let us all remember
The things that we were told.

A Son
- *Submitted by Emily Grace Owen DeBow*

PADGETT-RATZLAFF

Wesley Padgett, Jr. and Deloris Jane Ratzlaff were married Aug. 26, 1966, in the First Church of God, in Marion, SD.

Wesley was born in Linton, IN, on Aug. 1, 1944, to Wesley S. and Dorothy Padgett. Deloris was born on Sept. 4, 1945, in Sioux Falls, SD, to Lloyd and Bertha Boese Ratzlaff.

Deloris and Wesley Padgett Jr.

Wesley moved with his family to Madisonville when he was a small boy. He graduated from Hopkins County High School in 1965 and attended Gulf Coast Bible College in Houston, TX. Deloris graduated from Marion High School in Marion, SD, in 1963, and attended Anderson College in Anderson, IN. In 1965, she transferred to Gulf Coast Bible College in Houston, TX. Wesley and Deloris met in college and were married. Their first child Ruthann Joy was born Nov. 10, 1967, and their son Russell Lloyd was born Mar. 26, 1969, in Houston, TX. In July of 1969, the family moved to Madisonville. The Padgett's bought a home at 104 Buckner Street in Madisonville and lived there until 1975, when they bought their current home at 228 Montrose Drive.

Wesley was employed at Zeigler No. 9 Coal Company from 1970 until it closed in 1979. Following his employment at Zeigler, he worked as a Security Guard at the York Borg Warner Plant from 1979-1987. He is currently employed as a Security Guard at the General Electric Plant.

Deloris worked at the Child Care Center at the First Church of God from 1973-1975. In 1975, she began employment with the Hopkins County Senior Citizens Center. In 1979, she was promoted to Director of the Center. In 1985, the Regional Senior Citizens Center was built and dedicated. In 1985, Deloris received her Bachelor of Arts Degree from Gulf Coast Bible College in Houston, TX. In December of 1986, Deloris was hired as Senior Services Manager of the Regional Medical Center.

The Padgetts have been very active in the First Church of God. They have both served on various committees and boards and sing in the church choir. Deloris received the Madisonville Lions Club Woman of the Year Award in 1986. She has served as a Section and Division Chairman of the United Way, member of the Red Cross Board, Community Improvement Foundation, Christian Food Bank of Hopkins County, Intra-Agency of Hopkins County and on a National Task Force on Aging for her Church.

The Padgett's daughter Ruthann is married

to David Wells. They have a daughter, Melanie Alicia Wells.

The Padgett's son, Russell is still in school and living at home. - *Submitted by Deloris Padgett*

PADGETT-WRIGHT

Wesley S. Padgett was born on July 6, 1912, in Linton, IN. Dorothy Wright was born on Dec. 15, 1917, in Linton, IN. They were married on July 4, 1935, in Linton, IN. Mr. Padgett is a Navy Veteran of World War II. Wesley and Dorothy had four children. Their children are Elaine, Darrell, Wesley Jr. and Brenda. In 1951, the Padgett's moved to Madisonville. Mr. Padgett was employed at the Oriole Mine on outer Laffoon Trail. He worked there until 1967, when he received disability due to a mine injury. The Padgett family lived on S. Scott St., Harrig St., the Stinnett Farm, and Nisbet Street. They now reside in Elk Creek Mobile Home Park. The Padgett's are members of the First Church of God.

Their daughter Elaine married Johnny Baggett. The Baggetts reside in Fayetteville, NC. They have two children Bradley Baggett and Crystal Simpson. There are three grandchildren:

Darrell Padgett married Greta Hale. They have four children; Barry Hale, Terry Hale, Randy Hale, and Sandy Hale. They have three grandchildren. Darrell and Greta reside in Madisonville.

Wesley Jr. married Deloris Ratzlaff. They have two children; Ruthann Wells, and Rusty Padgett. They have one grandchild. Wesley and Deloris reside in Madisonville. (See Padgett-Ratzlaff)

Brenda married Tom Gibson. They live in Fayetteville, NC. They have six children; Jill, Diane, Robin, Nadine, Nancy, and David Hopkins. - *Submitted by Deloris Padgett*

PAGE

As far as can be ascertained, John Page of Virginia was the founding ancestor. He was born 1766, and married Cecilia Douglas, also of Virginia, sometime before the 1800 Fed. Census was taken. He is listed as having two children at that time, Jacob and Barnabas, both born before 1800. These two brothers married sisters, daughters of Hezekiah Allen and Martha, a full-blood Cherokee Indian. Jane Allen, born 1804, in North Carolina, married Jacob. Mary Allen, born 1797, North Carolina, married Barnabas in 1819. Barnabas and Mary Allen Page settled in DeKalb Co., TN, near Smithville, the county seat. Barnabas was a tenant farmer. He died Feb. 18, 1866, and is buried in DeKalb Co., TN. Mary Allen Page died Dec. 27, 1865 and is also buried in DeKalb Co., TN. They were the parents of ten children listed thus:

1. James, born Feb. 23, 1820; died Mar. 2, 1880, married Mary Jane Lee 1841.
2. Hugh, born Sept. 25, 1822; died August 1890, married (1) Elizabeth Baldwin, (2) Gemima Atnip, from Switzerland.
3. Mahaley, born 1824; died ca. (1850-1860), married James T. McIntire.
4. Andrew, born Oct. 7, 1825; died Aug. 24, 1871, married 1848, Kizanna Irene Lawrence.
5. Martha, born June 17, 1826; died Nov. 20, 1885, married Aug. 6, 1847, John Bethel Taylor.
6. Lourany, born Mar. 17, 1829; died June 27, 1906, in Texas. Married Sept. 16, 1847, Daniel Hale.
7. Seburn, born Dec. 27, 1830; died May 18, 1901, Van Buren Co., AR. Seburn had three wives and fathered 14 children. More about him later.
8. Louisa, born 1833; died Feb. 2, 1865, married Oct. 20, 1853, Hezekiah Allen, (probably a cousin).
9. Mary (Polly), born 1835, married Dec. 29, 1855, John Allen, a first cousin.
10. William, mentioned in his father's will, no further data.

SEBURN PAGE is the direct ancestor of the Pages of Hopkins County. He was born Dec. 27, 1830, in DeKalb Co., TN; died May 18, 1901, in Van Buren Co., AR at age 71. According to the HISTORY OF VAN BUREN COUNTY, ARKANSAS, River Road Press, 1976, Seburn was first to be buried in Crabtree Cemetery, near Clinton, AR. Seburn was active in the Civil War. He has a war marker at his graveside which reads: Sergt. Seburn Page, Co. F, Tenn. Mtd. Inf.

SEBURN PAGE was married three times and fathered 14 known children. His first wife was Louisa Trammel, born 1834, and daughter of Shadrick and Elizabeth McIntire Trammel of DeKalb Co., TN. Marriage date was May 12, 1850. Issue: John Jefferson, who wed Sarah E. Lee of DeKalb Co., TN and later settled in Hopkins Co., KY. (This is great grandfather of Sheriff John Beau Summers); William F., married and settled in Daviess Co., KY. No further data; Nancy, only 6 months old in 1860. She is listed on Daviess Co. KY Fed. Census 1880, as age 20; single. No further data.

SEBURN PAGE wed second time Elizabeth Hill, Smith Co., TN, Nov. 1, 1863. They had two children born in Tennessee: Thomas A. and Harrison Seburn (more on him later). Sometime between May 1868, and March 1869, SEBURN and his family left Tennessee and emigrated to Texas, settling in Tarrant County. Evidently SEBURN bought land in that area as the 1870 Fed. Census of that county list him as having real estate valued at $500. While living in Texas, daughters Louisa S. and Polly were born.

Between the years 1870 and 1873, SEBURN PAGE and family removed from Texas to Daviess Co., KY. He purchased a small farm (48 acres) from James L. Vanover Sept. 6, 1873. While living in Daviess County, daughters Sami, Amanda and Eppey were born. Elizabeth Hill Page, born 1842, in Tennessee, must have died soon after child Eppey was born in 1879, because the 1880 Fed. Census of Daviess County does not list SEBURN as having a wife. Elizabeth Hill Page is believed buried in Daviess County but time of death and burial place has not been ascertained.

SEBURN PAGE was married third time Mar. 16, 1881, to Mrs. Mary Watts of Daviess Co., KY. She was born Dec. 18, 1852. According to family reports, SEBURN took the youngest children and returned to Texas in 1890. It is a known fact that four of his older children remained in Kentucky. John Jefferson and William, who were already married and living in Daviess Co. at that time, and Louisa S., who married Horatious Seymour Lamb, in 1890 and lived the remainder of her life in Daviess Co., and Harrison Seburn, who settled in Hopkins County and married Miss Mary Elizabeth Lipscomb, daughter of J.J. Lipscomb July 17, 1889.

While living in Daviess Co., KY, Mrs. Mary Watts Page presented SEBURN with two sons - Gardiner S., born Jan. 29, 1882; died Oct. 14, 1950, wed Gertrude Williams of Van Buren Co., AR. Both are buried in Crabtree Cemetery, near Clinton, AR; Floyd S., born November 1883, no further data.

It is unknown just where the much traveled SEBURN PAGE and family were between the years 1887, and 1888. If he returned to Texas, he only remained there a short time, for he had a daughter, Ruth A., born April 1888, in Arkansas and another daughter, Anna B., born May 1891.

SEBURN PAGE died May 18, 1901 at age 71. He is buried in Crabtree Cemetery, Van Buren Co., AR. Mary Watts Page, born Dec. 18, 1852; died Aug. 8, 1936 and is buried beside Seburn in Crabtree Cemetery. - *Submitted by Louise Page Fleming*

HARRISON SEBURN PAGE

HARRISON SEBURN PAGE, born May, 1868, in DeKalb Co., TN, son of Seburn Page and his second wife, Elizabeth Hill Page. When quite young he emigrated to Texas with his parents, living in Tarrant County, near Fort Worth. Later the family emigrated to Kentucky, living on a 48-1/2 acre farm in Daviess County, near Owensboro.

On July 17, 1889, HARRISON SEBURN married Miss Mary Elizabeth Lipscomb, daughter of J.J. Lipscomb of Hopkins Co., KY. The wedding was performed by Wilford Morgan, M.G. and recorded in Hopkins County Marriage Book 1885-1890, page 250-251. He was age 22, she age 20, first marriage for both.

Mary Elizabeth Lipscomb Page drowned in a farm pond in 1917, and is buried in the Pleasant View Cemetery, Hopkins Co., KY. Before her death she bore Harrison Seburn six children listed below.

HARRISON SEBURN PAGE married second time, date unknown, Mrs. Dovie Allen, daughter of James William and Eliza Heflin Overton of Christian Co., KY. She had son, Jewell Allen, by previous marriage.

HARRISON SEBURN PAGE died Oct. 21, 1944, at age 76 and is buried at Pleasant View Cemetery, Hopkins Co., beside his first wife. (Death Cert. #22461, Vol. 45) Dovie Allen Page, died Aug. 27, 1967, age 83, and is buried Barnsley Cemetery, Hopkins Co. (Death Cert. #20991, Vol. 42).

ISSUE OF HARRISON SEBURN AND
MARY ELIZABETH LIPSCOMB PAGE

1. VERDIE-born Sept. 29, 1890; died Aug. 5, 1968, age 77. Buried Providence Rural Methodist Cemetery near Hanson, KY.

1st husband-John Bowley, born 1890; died 1916, buried Old Salem Cemetery, Hopkins Co. Issue: Alton, Carl, Willman Harrison.

2nd husband-wed 1921, George Martin, Sr.

(born 1870; died 1939; buried Providence Rural Methodist Cemetery, near Hanson, KY). Issue: Grace, George, Jr., William (Billy).

3rd husband-married Nov. 16, 1950, Benjamin Franklin Scott, born 1880, died July 4, 1965, age 85. Buried Equality Cemetery, Ohio Co., KY. No issue.

2. JAMES BLANTON-born Dec. 21, 1892, died Feb. 4, 1967, age 74. Buried Pleasant View Cemetery, Hopkins Co., KY. Married Nov. 26, 1919 Virgie Mabel Roddy, daughter of James Roddy and the late Carrie Osborn Roddy, of rural Union Co., KY. Virgie Mabel Roddy Page, born Nov. 28, 1892, died September 1981, buried Pleasant View Cemetery, Hopkins Co. Issue: Mary Cain, Thomas Cebern, Effie Isobel, Anna Catherine, Virgie Louise, James Delano.

3. SUSIE ISOBEL-born April 1895; still living 1987. Wed Mar. 18, 1918, James Lacy O'Bryan (born Aug. 7, 1857; died May 30, 1944, buried Grapevine Cemetery, near Madisonville, KY). Issue: Lucian (early deceased), Herschel, Travis, Finley Ray.

4. JOHNNY-born October 1897, killed in France during World War I.

5. CHESLEY, born 1899, died 1968 in Detroit, buried there. Wed Feb. 28, 1923, Virgie Sigler, daughter of Walter and Lula King Sigler, Providence, KY. Issue: Lucille, Frances, Juanita, Sonny.

6. NORMAN-born 1901, died 1985 Cleveland, OH, buried there. Married 1st Opal Sigler, daughter of Walter and Lula King Sigler, Providence, KY. Issue: Gloria Fay. Divorced. Wed 2nd, Vicky ? of Cleveland, OH. No further data.

- *Submitted by Louise Page Fleming*

JAMES BLANTON PAGE

JAMES BLANTON PAGE, born Dec. 21, 1892, rural Hopkins Co., KY, was oldest son of Harrison Seburn and Mary Elizabeth Lipscomb Page. James Blanton received his education in the common schools of rural Hopkins County and was employed as both farmer and coal miner. He was a veteran of World War I, and an ordained deacon of the Southern Missionary Baptist faith for over half a century.

James Blanton and Virgie Roddy Springfield Page

On Nov. 26, 1919, he wed Miss Virgie Mabel Roddy, daughter of James Roddy and the late Carrie Osborn Roddy, both of rural Union Co., KY. They were wed in Methodist Church at Madisonville, KY, by minister Rev. G.P. Gillon. Virgie Mabel Roddy was born Nov. 28, 1892, in Union Co., KY, but was adopted by prosperous farmer Thomas and Beulah Cain Springfield of Hopkins County at the age of two years, when her mother died at age 29 of a heart attack at the supper table.

JAMES BLANTON PAGE died Feb. 4, 1967, and is buried at Pleasant View Cemetery, Hopkins Co., KY. Virgie Mabel Roddy Springfield Page died Sept. 25, 1981, and is buried beside James Blanton in the Pleasant View Cemetery on lot with her adopted parents. Before her death she bore six children listed below:

1. MARY CAIN, born Oct. 12, 1920. Unmarried at this time, lives in Madisonville, KY.

2. THOMAS CEBURN, born June 9, 1922. Married (1) Mar. 15, 1944, June Berry, daughter of Walter and Cecil Berry of Evansville, IN. Issue: Thomas Ceburn II, Judith Gail, Pamela June. Married (2) Wanda Pate of Evansville, IN. No issue. THOMAS CEBURN was a veteran of World War II and Korean War. He retired with rank of Sergeant-Major after being in army twenty years. He lives in Colorado Springs, CO.

3. EFFIE ISOBELLE, born Feb. 25, 1925. Married Sept. 1, 1942, Joseph Edward Veasey, son of Tommy and Amy Faucett Veasey, of Hopkins Co., KY. Joe served in army during World War II, stationed in Texas. He died Oct. 28, 1986, of heart attack and was cremated. Effie Isobelle lives in Clarksville, IN. Issue: James Edward, Virginia Lee, and Richard Earl.

4. ANNA CATHERINE, born Aug. 5, 1926. Married Apr. 21, 1956, Parl Thornton Givens, son of George and Josephine Hicks Givens of the Government Bend Community of Hopkins County. Parl is a veteran of World War II, serving in the European theatre. He and Anna live in Madisonville, KY. No issue.

5. VIRGIE LOUISE, born Jan. 16, 1929. Wed Oct. 27, 1956, Steve Alvin Fleming, son of Henry and Dona Hancock Fleming of Webster Co., KY and great grandson of the prominent family of Louis and Sarah (Sally) Bradshaw Hancock of Webster County. Sally Bradshaw was cousin to Gen. Robert E. Lee of Civil War fame. Steve is a veteran of Korean War. Issue: Anna Lisa, married to Jim Lee Kennedy of Kirkwood Springs community, and Julie Page, married to Martin (Marty) Walters of Louisville, KY.

6. JAMES DELANO, born Mar. 1, 1934. Wed Feb. 11, 1954, Rosie Bell Davis, daughter of Nolen and Edra Morphew Davis of Muhlenburg County. James and Rosie reside in Madisonville, KY. They have one son, James Nolen, unmarried at this time. - *Submitted by Louise Page Fleming*

PALMER-GRACE-TYSON

Jeremiah Palmer was born in 1792, in South Carolina and died after 1870, in Hopkins Co., KY. He was the son of John and Susannah (Dailey) Palmer. John was born in New Jersey. He fought in the Revolutionary War and received land in Wilks Co., GA, for his war service. John and his family moved to Henderson Co., KY, by 1810. He lived there twelve years and then moved to Henry Co., TN, where he died in 1834. Susannah must have come back to Hopkins Co., KY, as Jeremiah settled her estate. The Palmers are from Southwork, England.

Jeremiah Palmer married on Apr. 6, 1837, in Hopkins Co., KY, to Mary Ann Oran, who was born in 1814, and died Jan. 12, 1907. She is buried in Henderson Co., KY. Their children were: Susan, Mary Jane, John W., James K., Jeremiah M., Martha E., and Sarah Ellen Palmer.

Jeremiah was first married to Sarah Cates. One child from this marriage, Cynthia Palmer.

Mary Jane Palmer was born Aug. 22, 1840, in Hopkins Co., KY, and died Sept. 22, 1915, in Christian Co., KY. On Feb. 6, 1866, in Hopkins Co., she married David Crockett Grace, who was born Apr. 24, 1843, and died in 1921. David C. served three years in the Union Army in the war between the states. He and his wife Mary Jane settled in North Christian Co., KY. Their children were: Mary Bell, Delia R., Chess Ellen, Maggie Healing and Eva Alice Grace. David C.'s parents were Ervin and Nancy (Lewis) Grace. The Grace line goes back to Solomon Grace of Maryland.

Eva Alice Grace was born Mar. 22, 1876, and died June 8, 1959, in Ferndale, MI, and is buried in Crofton Cemetery. She married Wiley Mason Tyson who was born Mar. 15, 1868, and died Apr. 13, 1902, of pneumonia in New Baden, IL. His body was brought back to Hopkins Co., KY, and buried at the Odd Fellows Cemetery at Madisonville, KY. Their children were: Basil, Baylas, William Bartram and Rily Tyson. Eva Alice was married a second time to John Renshaw of Crofton, KY. No children.

Wiley Mason Tyson's parents were Silas Tyson (born 1837-died 1910 and is buried near White Plains, KY), and Martha (Uzzel) Tyson. Silas was in the Union army for three years during the war between the states, Co. K, Reg. KY Inft. Their children were: Wiley, Thomas, James and Jason Tyson.

Silas Tyson's parents were Thomas and Rebecca Elizabeth (Mercer) Tyson. His parents were Ezekiel and Nancy Jane (Mercer) Tyson. These families lived in Muhlenberg Co., KY.

For other lines to this family, see Warner-Stevens-Crunk. - *Submitted by Sylvia G. Burke*

DAVID "PEWEE" PARISH

David A. "Peewee" Parish was born Nov. 28, 1899, in Madisonville, the son of Rufus Lee and Martha James Parish. He had a brother, R.J., and two sisters, Martha Lou Parish and Helen Parish, who preceded him in death. His ancestors were Scotch-Irish and he could trace his ancestry to Dr. Benjamin Rush, one of the signers of the Declaration of Independence.

David "Pee Wee" Parish

He attended West Broadway School and attended high school at Waddill Avenue School. After high school, he attended the U.S. Naval Academy at Annapolis, MD, and later went to McDonald Pharmacy School and became a registered pharmacist. On Nov. 15, 1932, he bought the drug store at 5 E. Center Street, where he had previously worked. The drug store was a local gathering place for years. It closed in 1980.

In 1946, he became Mayor of Madisonville. He held this position for the next 28 years. Under his leadership, Madisonville experienced a lot of change and growth. Some of the most notable that he played a large part in are: Enro, General Electric, American Mine Tool, Speed Queen, Goodyear, York, Mid-American Canning, National Can and Versnick Manufacturing industries locating here; a new wing was added to Hopkins County Hospital; a new National Guard Armory, Rizpah Shrine Temple and Army Reserve Center were built here; the city purchase of Odd Fellows Cemetery for $1.00 with the promise to retain the lodge's name; and the solving of the city's water problems in 1951, by the digging of a lake, later named Lake Pewee in his honor.

Pewee was a supporter of both the young and the old. He served as president of the Hopkins County Youth Center for many years and served on the board of directors of the Hopkins County Senior Citizens Center. He was a member of the Madisonville Benevolent and Protective Order of Elks, York Rite, Scottish Rite, Past Potentate and trustee for 12 years of Rizpah Temple; 33rd degree Mason receiving his degree in Washington, D.C.; served as past president and director of Madisonville Community College Board; past president of Madisonville Hospital Corporation; a director of Trover Clinic Foundation; director of the Chamber of Commerce; past president of Madisonville Country Club; president of Hopkins County Development Corporation; was Democratic chairman in Hopkins County for 12 years; member of the 100 Million Dollar Club/Shrine Crippled Children; Lions Club Man of the Year in 1950; was listed in Outstanding Personalities of the South (1967) and was a longtime member of the First United Methodist Church of Madisonville.

No one can ever talk about the history of Madisonville for more than a few minutes without the name of David "Pewee" Parish coming to mind.

Pewee died Mar. 14, 1987, in Clinic Convalescent Center in Madisonville. He was buried at Odd Fellows Cemetery. - *Submitted by: Debbie Knight Hammonds*

PARISH-DUNCAN

Ruby Irene Duncan and Virgil Lee Parish were united in marriage Jan. 3, 1939 in Dixon, KY.

Ruby (born May 26, 1919) was the daughter of Doc Roscoe Duncan and Cassie Jane Harris Duncan. Her paternal grandparents were Elizabeth Brinkley Duncan and George Duncan. Her maternal grandparents were Nancy Ann Durham Harris and Bill Harris. Ruby has

Ruby and Virgil Parish

three sisters: Verlie Parish, Edna Fuson, and Annie Winstead.

Ruby enjoys quilting and working in her flea market business

Virgil (born Feb. 5, 1921) the son of Ruby Ethel Duncan Parish and Lee Anderson Parish. His paternal grandparents were Joe Parish and Molly Walker. His maternal grandparents were Macey Nichols Duncan and Jeff Duncan. Jeff Duncan was the son of George Duncan. (See Duncan-Parish). Virgil has two brothers: Nobel and Howard Parish.

Virgil has been a "jack of all trades". He has worked in construction, trucking, farming, coal mines, and the flea market. His hobbies include cooking. Virgil is well known for his fried apple pies and delicious cornbread.

Virgil and Ruby grew up together. They have resided in the Coiltown, Nebo, and Manitou area their entire life. They attended Browns School and Concord General Baptist Church together. Virgil has been a deacon in the church thirty-eight years and Ruby sings soprano in the church choir.

Virgil and Ruby courted in a 1928 Model A Ford Sedan. They double dated often with Carrie Duncan and Archie Carnal, and Lavena Rhew and Edward Duncan. (See Duncan-Rhew). The dates consisted of attending church and going to square dances in the country homes. At the square dances, all of the furniture was moved out of one room to allow space to dance. Music was furnished by country folks playing guitars, fiddles, and "tator bugs", as Virgil laughingly recalls. Pie suppers at school were also a source of entertainment. The girls baked the pies and the boys bid on them in order to eat the pie with the one who baked it.

In those days there were three consecutive two week revivals at Concord, Oakley Home and Star Hope. Reverend Oscar Duncan was either the pastor or evangelist of the revivals. Ruby and Virgil, along with other members of Rev. Duncan's family would load up in a hay wagon with quilts and attend all the meetings.

Ruby and Virgil have now been married forty-nine years. God has blessed their marriage with four children: Patsy Faye Stone (Feb. 12, 1940), Judy Ann Moore (June 25, 1943), Jerry (Apr. 5, 1947), and Dwight (Apr. 23, 1957). They also have four grandchildren, two great grandchildren, and seven great stepgrandchildren. *Submitted by Retha Duncan Tarter (Tarter-Duncan)*

PARKER-CANSLER

Ebert James Parker and Beatrice Sterling Cansler were married Apr. 25, 1934.

Beatrice was born Feb. 22, 1919 in Christian County, the daughter of Thurman Cansler and Cynthia Jackson Cansler. Thurman and Cynthia were both born in Christian County and were the parents of three other children: Estoil Cansler Menser, Virginia Cansler Haley, and Thurman LaRue (T.L.) Cansler.

Beatrice is now retired. She worked at Arvin's Factory for almost ten years. She has also worked at Ben Franklin and Pennyrile State Park. In her spare time she enjoys shopping and bowling.

Ebert was born Feb. 24, 1913 in Christian County. He was one of two children of Hiram Parker, born in Christian County, and Laura Jenkins Parker, born in Tennessee. Hiram and Laura's other child was a son, Thurman Parker, who is now deceased.

Ebert is currently retired. His last job was as a car salesman. He sold cars for Jennings Chevrolet and DeHaven Chevrolet for 18 years. He also worked as a surveyor for TVA for three years and was an engineer for the United States Corp of Engineers for 12 years. Ebert now enjoys fishing, gardening, and bowling in his spare time.

Ebert and Beatrice have three children, six grandchildren, and two great grandchildren.

Linda Wyvonne Parker Grimes is Ebert and Beatrice's only daughter. She is also the oldest of the three children and was born Aug. 9, 1937. In 1952, she married Wesley Grimes. They have two children, Rhonda Lynn Grimes Smith and Wesley Markal Grimes. They reside in Hopkinsville, KY.

Rex Dale Parker is the middle child. He was born Feb. 22, 1942. He married Sandra Kay Hopper on Feb. 24, 1960. They have one child, Lori Michele Parker, and reside in Dawson Springs.

Ebert and Beatrice's youngest son is Phillip LaRue Parker. He was born Oct. 29, 1947. On Dec. 27, 1964, he married Donna Kay Thomas. They have three children, Stephanie Lynn Parker, Steven LaRue Parker, and Melissa Kaye Parker. They reside in Dawson Springs.

Ebert and Beatrice have lived in Hopkins County almost all of their married life. They currently reside at 1014 Hospital Road, Dawson Springs.- *Submitted by Stephanie Parker*

PARKER-CARLISLE

George E. Parker Sr. (1879-1976), and Leslie Carlisle (1883-1970), had early "ancestral roots" in Hopkins County. His ties began in 1837 when great-grandparents Jonas Parker and Ruth Tapp removed their family from Person Co., NC, to their farm in Hopkins-Henderson Counties (area of present Dixon, KY). In 1838-1840, his great-grandparents, Willis L. Gooch and Rachel Cozart and great-great-grandparents, Thomas Gooch and Jemima Hester "sold out" in Granville Co., NC, and settled in Hopkins Co., west of Hanson.

Leslie Carlisle Parker's "ancestral ties" were: Arthur Porter Slaton, William Lewis Hancock and Sarah Bradshaw from Goochland Co., VA; Alexander Ashby and Ann Browning from Culpepper Co., VA; Edward Orton (son of Robert), and wife Anna Neale (granddaughter of Revolutionary War Capt. Stephen Ashby); George Fugate and Martha

Howell of counties in northern Virginia; Richard Dunville and Elizabeth Adam, Kershaw Co., SC; Thomas Carlisle and son John Milby Carlisle, Mary Rust Jackson Carlisle and son Charles King Jackson of Sussex Co., DE.

George was the oldest child of Willis Jonas Parker (b. 1850, Hopkins Co.), and Lucinda Isbell (b. 1851, Newton Co., MO). His parents lived during the Civil War and World War I. They raised their family in the Belcourt-Breton area, Webster Co. Lucinda's father, George Isbell (b. 1807, Halifax Co., VA), died in 1888 in the home of Willis and Lucinda Parker. He is buried near them at Zion "Brick" Baptist Church, in Hopkins Co. near Slaughters.

Leslie was the oldest child of Lee W. Carlisle and Blanche Eleanor Jackson of Belcourt-Sassafras Grove area of Webster Co. Her parents removed to McLean and Ohio Cos., KY. Before her marriage (1904), Leslie taught in Hopkins rural schools: Hawkins near New Salem Methodist Church and the Pritchett school east of Hanson.

Late in 1910, George and Leslie with their young family removed to the newly purchased farm homeplace on the Island Ford Road, south of Otter Creek, in the Vandetta community. Their children attended Howell School (the only two-room graded rural school in NE Hopkins). The older children attended Slaughters High. In 1935, Hopkins school board established bus transportation for high school pupils. Thus, Mahlon and James (Buddy) attended Hanson High.

The Vandetta community had three churches: Howell Methodist Episcopal South (1872), Emberry Methodist Episcopal (1876) ("Northern" Methodist) and Qualls Chapel Christian (1907), with a pastor's appointment one Sunday per month. Each maintained a Sunday School. The popular Vandetta Choir, with members from each church, participated in singing conventions in Hopkins.

George and his six sons did diversified farming with considerable skill and management. They welcomed the KY Extension Service and Farm Agents. They forged themselves ahead of the average in using better livestock (prior to tractor era), crop rotation, thorough preparation of seed beds and better seeds, judicious use of fertilizers, soil conservation and good home gardens.

Leslie and daughters were active in the Vandetta Homemakers Club, organized ca 1930. In 1925, the 4-H program expanded to include summer camp at Slaughters Lake for high school 4-H'ers of Hopkins-Webster counties. Evadine was one of the "pioneer" campers! Blanche and Dorothy won honors with 4-H projects. Hoyt, Bernice (B.C.), Mahlon and James won trips to Kentucky State Fairs in Louisville and to lamb shows/sales in Lexington.

Depression years caused Carlisle and Edwin to return from Michigan to Kentucky farm life for a few years.

Leslie worked with quilt-making about seventy of the eighty-six years of her life. She did all her piecing "on her fingers", making neat even stitches to assemble the pieces into colorful blocks.

Many, many visitors enjoyed the splendidly cooked food and other hospitalities.

George and Leslie observed their 50th wedding anniversary, Dec. 24, 1954, in their home. Their nine children with spouses and grandchildren were with them for their special day. Their children were: Willis Carlisle, George Edwin, Leslie Evadine, Hoyt Ruby, Bernice Clyde "B.C.", Blanche Katherine, Dorothy Frances, Mahlon Ross and James M. "Buddy".

The home-place is no longer owned by family members. The children and grandchildren have many pleasant memories of George and Leslie and their home-place. - *Submitted by: L. Evadine Parker*

WILLIAM PARRISH, SR.

William Parrish, Sr. was born 1801, in North Carolina and migrated to Hopkins Co. in 1851 from the Granville Co./Orange Co., NC area. Research indicates that his father was probably Claiborn Parrish.

In 1820, William married Mary (Polly) Jones, daughter of Edward Jones, Sr. Children of William and Polly were: Jane, born ca 1821, wife of John Veasey; Henry S., 1825; William S., 1827; Jefferson J., 1829; Rebecca, 1831, wife of Joseph A. Hobgood; Alice, ca 1834, wife of Carrington Cozart; and twins Allen and Alfred, born 1840.

In 1847, William Parrish Sr. married widow Charlotte (Madison) Roberts. Their children were Nicholas Jasper, 1850; and George, 1852 (died young). William Parrish Sr. died in 1876 and is buried in Johnson Island Cemetery.

Henry S. and Jane (Hester) Parrish

Henry S. Parrish married Emily Jane Hester, daughter of Benjamin Hester, in Orange Co., NC, in 1847. Their children born in North Carolina were: Francis Marion, 1848; Volney B., 1850; and Nancy E., 1852, wife of David Martin. Those born in Hopkins Co. were: George Thomas, 1854; Winfrey H., 1856; Luetta, 1859, wife of Buck Madison; Jefferson Davis, 1861; William B., 1864 (grandfather of Harold Gooch of Evansville, IN and Rev. James E. Gooch of McVeigh, KY); Tametia, 1867, wife of James T. Madison; Robert Lacy, 1869; Charles Cornelius, 1872 (died age 12); and Flora, 1875, wife of Will Thomas (grandparents of Wayne Thomas of Hopkins Co.) Henry S. Parrish died 1899, and Emily Jane died 1900. Both are buried in Olive Branch Cemetery. Their farm was near Buntin School.

Robert Lacy Parrish and Delora Jones (daughter of Doctor Hill Jones and Isadora Barron) were married in 1890. He died 1939, and she in 1941, buried at Olive Branch Cemetery. Their farm was on the Johnny Thomas

Robert Lacy and Delora (Jones) Parrish

Road. Their children were: Cayce B., (1891-1973); Dessie, (1894-1984); Norman Bryan, (1896-1961); Dorothy, (1899-1941); and Carlos and Dora Jane, who died in infancy.

Cayce B. Parrish married Magalee Rice and their children are C.B., Jr. of Texas, and Margaret Kenecht Hudson of Florida.

Dessie Parrish married Homer Mullennix and their children are (1) James Lacy Mullennix of Paducah, KY, whose children are James P. of Colorado, and Mary Warren (deceased), and (2) Evelyn Cox Jenkins of Gilbertsville, KY, whose daughters are Lee Ann Cox Runyon of Paducah, and Marie Cox (Mrs. Wayne) Brown of Madisonville. (Evelyn C. Jenkins died Dec. 20, 1987).

Norman Parrish married Goldie May Logan and their daughter is Mary Louise, (born in Hopkins Co.), wife of James M. Bevers of Evansville, IN. The Bevers sons are David, 1953; Michael, 1963, and Daniel, 1973. David married Candace Gilmore and their children are; Chad, Casey, and Kelsey Nicole. Michael married Joan Marie Shrawder. All live in Evansville.

Dorothy Parrish married Lacy Gammon. Their daughters: (1) Iva Lou (deceased), wife of William Jarrell of Nebo, whose children are Charles Judson Jarrell of Nebo, and Teresa (Mrs. Duane) Burden of Manitou; and (2) Helen, wife of Billy Page of Madisonville, whose children are: Nena, wife of Denny Matheny, of Hanson; and Nanette of Owensboro and Madisonville. - *Submitted by Mary Louise Parrish Bevers*

THE PAYNE FAMILY

Cornelius Payne was born in Virginia about 1788, and married Louisa Ann Walton, daughter of William Walton and Sally Ward, in Pittsylvania Co., VA, in 1817. A few years later they moved to Maury Co., TN, where he taught school and farmed. Later, they moved to Logan Co., KY, for a few years and then moved to Hopkins County about 1850 and bought a farm near Nebo. In addition to farming, Cornelius was also a merchant and a Baptist minister. Cornelius and Louisa Ann died on the same day, Sept. 19, 1876, and were buried in the family cemetery near Nebo. They had eleven children: William Cornelius, Robert, Harriet, Eliza, Mary Louisa, James M., Joseph, Ann, John Lee, Paralee Tennessee and Thomas Buford Payne. The eldest child was born in Virginia and the others in Tennessee.

Mary Louisa Payne married Joseph Misher Cunningham in Williamson Co., TN, in 1845. They moved to Hopkins Co., KY, in 1850 and had a farm near Nebo. Joseph, a noncombatant, contracted small pox in a Yankee

Cornelius and Louisa Ann Walton Payne about 1860.

prison in Hopkinsville and died in 1863. Mary Louisa died in 1868, and their minor children were reared by their uncle, "Bufe" Payne. Their children were: John Cornelius, James, William Lee, Mary Louisa, Susan, Roenar, Misher Izora, Anna Elizabeth and Thomas Jefferson Cunningham. John was in the Confederate Army and survived long imprisonment at Camp Douglass, IL. William Lee's son, Jefferson Davis Cunningham lived in Coiltown. Mary Louisa married Benjamin Gratz Smith and their son Robert Lee Smith was reared by his aunt, Misher Izora, and her husband, Gustavus Adolphus Bassett. Lee's son, Robert Lloyd Smith, was born in Madisonville and became a prominent business man in Chicago.

James M. Payne married Elizabeth Lunsford in 1855. He was in the Confederate Army and was in the battle of Burnt Mill, Vanderburg, purportedly the first Civil War action in Kentucky. The children of James M. and Elizabeth were Kansas B., Ada, William McNary, David Whittinghill, John Gammon, Louisa Ann and Ethelbert. David Whittinghill "Whit" Payne married Sallie Baker and was a merchant and Mayor of Providence.

John Lee Payne married Josephine Gooch in 1860, and their children were; Coralee, Dixie, Cornelius, Willis Brown, Sybil, Lelia, Ethel Goochye, Buford, Robert Lee, Mildred, Mary Elizabeth and Reginald. John Lee served in the Kentucky Legislature, as Postmaster of Nebo and was one of the founders of Union Cemetery. His grandson, Claude Brown Payne, was one of the founders of the American Legion after World War I.

Paralee Tennessee Payne married Radford B. Tapp, in 1857. They were known as uncle Rad and Aunt Paz and had a large farm near Manitou. Their children were; Menemma Captola, Minera Vineras, Manorah, Menalis Nevalis, Metura Idalia, Lona Adams, Ezra Gooch, Myrtle Buford and Aubie H. Tapp. Minera Vineras married Joseph Lawrence Rogers, a prominent merchant and farmer in Nebo.

Thomas Buford Payne married Isabella Herrin in 1864. He was a merchant in Providence and owned and operated a tobacco stemmery. Their children were Annie, Strother, Neal J. and Thomas Buford, Jr. - *Submitted by Wm. Kerr Bassett*

PENDLEY-DUNCAN

Lesia Arleen Duncan and Douglas Paul Pendley were united in marriage May 9, 1980, by Reverand Oscar Lee Duncan, at Concord General Baptist Church near Manitou, KY.

Lesia was born June 4, 1959. Her parents are Edward Lee Duncan and the late Lavena Mae Rhew. (See Duncan-Rhew). She attended West Broadway, Seminary, Madisonville Junior High, and graduated from Madisonville North Hopkins in 1977. Lesia worked as an assistant for Dr. Ivy, accounts receivable clerk for Overnite Transportation, and a contractor pay specialist at Ligon. She is presently employed by the Hopkins County Board of Education as a school bus driver for Nebo and West Hopkins. Her hobbies include; sewing, quilting, embroidery, and bowling.

Douglas Paul and Lesia Duncan Pendley

Doug is the son of Dixie Lee (Ruthe) Kistner and the late Jewell Willard Pendley. (See Pendley-Kistner). He was born Sept. 21, 1959. He attended school in Hopkins County. Doug is employed by Big Rivers Electric Corporation at the Green Station in Sebree, KY, as an auxiliary operator. His hobbies include; collecting record albums, playing the drums, and working in the yard.

Lesia and Doug have two children: Neal Douglas (Sept. 2, 1982), and Nicole Marie (Dec. 20, 1983). They reside in Manitou, KY. - *Submitted by Lesia Pendley*

PENDLEY-KISTNER

Dixie Lee (Ruthe) Kistner and Jewell Willard Pendley were united in marriage June 23, 1945.

Ruthe was born Oct. 1, 1923, in Hopkins County. Her parents were Lillie Bell Oliver and Claude Kistner. Her maternal grandparents were Lucy Jones and Nathan Oliver. Her paternal grandparents were Archie Green and Charlie Kistner. Ruthe had four brothers: Ross, Lawrence, Cline, and Paul. She had one sister Claudie.

Ruthe and Jewell Pendley

During World War II Ruthe worked at the S.J. Campbell Parachute Company, in Madisonville. She enjoys; fishing, quilting, crossword puzzles and reading.

Jewell was born May 20, 1911, in Christian County. His parents were Virginia Blades and Andrew Jackson Pendley. Jewell had two brothers: Edgar (a judge in Louisville) and Roy. He had three sisters: Clara Smith, Edith Smith, and Vera West.

Jewell was ordained as a Baptist minister at the age of twenty-one. Reverend Pendley preached in the surrounding counties and in the General Baptist Church in Dawson Springs. He worked at the Kentucky Utilities in Earlington, KY. After the Earlington plant closed, he worked for the Green River Generating plant in Central City as a control room operator. His hobbies were carpentry and mechanical work. His dream was to one day have his own carpentry shop.

Jewell was married first to Irene Rector. They had four sons: Earl, Clyde, Cleatus, and Ronald and one daughter, Wanda Villines. After Irene died, Jewell married Ruthe.

Jewell and Ruthe had two sons: Dennis Ray, and Douglas Paul (See Pendley-Duncan) and one daughter Dixie Ann Suthard. (See Suthard-Pendley).

After Jewell's death, Apr. 1, 1970, Ruthe married Eddlee Thomas Pendley on Oct. 5, 1973. They reside in Dawson Springs, KY. - *Submitted by: Lesia Pendley*

PENNINGTON-GAMBLE

Shelia Ann Gamble (b. Jan. 23, 1950), and George David Pennington (b. Nov. 26, 1946), were married Jan. 16, 1971, at New Salem Baptist Church, in Nortonville, KY. They have two children, Christina Janel (b. July 3, 1973), and Jared Ross (b. Aug. 14, 1975).

Shelia is the daughter of Leamon Ross Gamble (b. May 3, 1929), a coal miner and owner of Terry's Termite Control, and Geneva Nell Cook Gamble (b. Jan. 8, 1931), married Dec. 15, 1948. She has a sister, Deborah Kay Back (Debbie) (b. Mar. 25, 1954), and married to Donald Wayne Back (b. Jan. 10, 1942). They have four children: Donia Kay (b. Nov. 9, 1971); Melissa Dawn (b. Dec. 14, 1973); Jennifer Leigh (b. Jan. 10, 1977); and Matthew Scott, who was born in Seoul, Korea, Dec. 19, 1984; and came to Nortonville on Mar. 25, 1985. Matthew will be getting a brother, Timothy Jordan (T.J.) (b. July 4, 1987), from Korea in a couple of months. Sheila's brother, Terry Lee (b. Nov. 5, 1960), is married to the former Peggy Lynn Brackett (b. Feb. 10, 1961). They have two boys; Dustin Lee (b. June 30, 1978), and Eric Lynn (b. Sept. 29, 1983).

Sheila is a graduate of South Hopkins High School and worked as a Pharmacy Clerk at Hopkins Co. Hospital for two years. She is now a loan secretary at Peoples Bank & Trust Co. at the Nortonville Office, where she has been employed since 1972. She is the treasurer for the Professional Secretaries International Madisonville Chapter. She is a Sunday School teacher at New Salem Missionary Baptist Church where she has been a member since 1961, and is also on the Financial Committee there.

She is the granddaughter of the late Solomon Ross Gamble (b. Jan. 13, 1909-d. Sept. 2, 1982), and Mona Mable Jackson Gamble (b. Aug. 15, 1910). Her maternal grandparents are

Johnny Edward Cook and Rosie Olive Cornell (July 30, 1915).

George is the son of Emmett Clair Pennington Sr. (b. Aug. 9, 1912), and Edna Davis (b. Jan. 20, 1920), of Liberty, KY. George was born in Casey Co. home of the world's largest apple pie, where he graduated from Casey Co. High School as Valedictorian. He is an honor graduate of Western KY University. He came to Hopkins Co. in the fall of 1968, when he began teaching at Madisonville Jr. High. He is now in the Math and Science Dept. at Madisonville North Hopkins High School. He is a Sunday School teacher and Deacon at New Salem Missionary Baptist Church, where he has been a member sine 1970. His ancestors are from Virginia. - *Submitted by George and Shelia Pennington*

PERRY-HAMBY

Eudenah Hamby and Laban Littleton Perry were married June 3, 1934, in the First Christian Church of Dawson Springs, KY.

Eudenah was born Nov. 12, 1910, in Hopkins County, near White Plains. She is the daughter of Zorah Lamb and Golden Ezekiel Hamby (see LAMB-HAMBY).

Laban L. and Eudenah Perry

Eudenah attended school in Dawson Springs, graduating in 1928. She graduated from the U. of Kentucky in 1932, with a B.S. degree in Home Economics. She taught school in Milton, Fredonia, and Dawson Springs, all in Kentucky.

In 1951, she was employed as Educational Therapist at Outwood V.A. Hospital, and in 1958, became employed as Home Economist with the Kentucky Utilities Company, from which she retired in 1972. She has been a member of the First Christian Church, Dawson Springs, KY, since age nine, and is Organist and Elder Emeritus. She has been active in various civic organizations and church-related activities.

Other ancestral names are Smith, Glass, Woolf, Jennings, Scott, Rogers, Clayton, Wilson, McKnight, and Thompson.

Laban was born Jan. 30, 1907, in Caldwell County, to Autha Ella Dearing and Robert Littleton Perry. He attended school in Caldwell County, and graduated from Dawson Springs High School in 1927. In 1928, he was employed by the United States Postal Service, from which he retired in 1970, after forty-two years of service. He then worked for the Commercial Bank of Dawson Springs until 1972, and his second retirement. He has been a member of the Dawson Springs Christian Church since 1930, and is now Elder Emeritus. Laban has been active in Rotary International, N.A.P.S., N.A.R.F.E., and many civic affairs, and served one term on the Dawson Springs City Council. Other ancestral names are; Crowe, Hopper, Bishop, Jenkins, Nichols, Rhodes, and Tandy.

Laban and Eudenah have one daughter, Susan, and one son, Kenneth Littleton. Susan married James Mestan, of New York, and teaches Art in the Caldwell County School System. James works at the Regional Medical Center, and they own a business in Princeton, KY. They have two children, Sheri Lynn, of Arlington, VA, and Sean, of Murray, KY. Kenneth married Sharon Thomas, of Caldwell County, and teaches for the U. of Kentucky Community College System. Sharon is employed with the Department of Human Resources in Frankfort. They have one son, Brian Littleton, and reside in Versailles, KY. Sources: Family records. *Submitted by Laban L. Perry*

PEYTON-FOSTER

William Thomas Peyton (b. Dec. 29, 1883-d. 1964), son of Calvin Radie Peyton (b. Jan. 18, 1856-d. Feb. 22, 1921), and Lucretia Whitfield (b. Nov. 21, 1863-d. June 15, 1914), married Ruby Foster (b. Aug. 27, 1885-d. 1954), the daughter of Judge Palates Foster (b. July 6, 1852-d. July 14, 1909), and Elizabeth Mills Minter (b. Mar. 28, 1864-d. Dec. 11, 1938). Judge Palates and Elizabeth Foster had four children: Eugene (b. Sept. 9, 1887-d. June 21, 1924), never married. He is buried at Oakwood Cemetery, Earlington; Otho M. Foster (b. 1894-d. 1946), was married to Myrtlee Rogers, and they are buried in Odd Fellows Cemetery; Mamie Foster, who died young; and Ruby Foster who married Wm. Thomas Peyton.

Lois (Peyton) and Edward Warren

William Thomas and Ruby lived in Earlington for many years. He was a Supt. Mining Engineer. They are buried at Sturgis, KY. They had four children as follows:

Lois Virginia Peyton, b. June 18, 1906, at Earlington, married Farleigh Edward Warren (b. Aug. 3, 1902), son of Thomas Marion Warren and Dovie Emma Jordan. (See ASHBY-WARREN) Edward is a retired Insurance Underwriter with Metropolitan Insurance Co. They now live in Louisville. They have one son, William Edward "Eddie" Warren (b. Jan. 31, 1925), in Earlington, KY, who married Margaret Frances Brownell (born Jan. 23, 1925), dau. of Norman Wetherby Brownell and Margaret Frances Denson, of Louisville. Eddie is a retired executive personnel manager with Union Carbide Corp., Victoria, TX, where they now reside. Their son, Douglas Edward Warren (b. Aug. 3, 1959), is married to Laurilyn Forsythe, on Apr. 25, 1987. Doug works for Vistron Corp., in Victoria, where they reside.

David Foster Peyton Sr. (known to most as "Tip"), born Oct. 2, 1910, married Trudie Matheis (born Apr. 25, 1907). He was an executive with Union Carbide Corp., Victoria, TX. Trudie died in 1986, and Tip died Apr. 15, 1987. Their son, David Peyton II (born Nov. 1, 1941), who married Jerry Bell Hall, is Executive Vice President, Building and Loan, Victoria.

William Dudley Peyton, b. Aug. 19, 1914, married Lillie Kuykendall, a school teacher at Sturgis, KY. Later, he married Joy Freer, and they lived at Princeton, KY. They had a son, William Dudley Jr., b. Jan. 27, 1969. Dudley died Sept. 22, 1969, in a tragic car accident, and is buried at Sturgis. Joy and Dudley Jr. continue to reside in Princeton. Dudley Jr. is a student at Western Kentucky U.

Thomas Gene "Tom" Peyton, b. Jan. 4, 1924, married Mary Metcalfe (b. Jan. 1, 1927), of Madisonville. Tom is Administrator at McPherson Memorial Hospital at Durham, NC. Their children are: Ann Lee Peyton (b. Aug. 14, 1953), who is a Resort Food Service Director, Dillon, CO; and William Dudley Peyton (b. Oct. 20, 1955), who is Vice President and Trust Officer of a bank in Raleigh, NC. - *Submitted by Lois Peyton Warren. Written by Rella G. Jenkins*

PEYTON-HART

John Milton Peyton, born Mar. 31, 1921, son of Elmer Bernard Peyton (1898-1960), Hopkins, son of John D. and Mary Cassandra (Toombs) Peyton, (F/M) Sumpter and Virginia Toombs, (4) George and Jane Hill Peyton, KY pioneers. Elmer traveled with carnivals as a mechanic until his retirement. Elmer married, 1920, Caldwell Co., KY, Lillie Beatrice Melton (1904-1973). Married 2nd Clarence Grubbs, AL. Lillie was the daughter of Millard (Melton) Milton and Mahalie Capps, whose parents were, George and Martha Capps. (3) Obedire Melton, married Martha Eliz. Tines, daughter of Lawrence Tines and Amanda Orange, Logan Co., KY, daughter of Zephania, Caldwell Co., KY, son of William Orange (b. Virginia, married Elizabeth Melton, settled, Smith Co., TN). (4) Thomas Melton, b. Virginia-d. Logan Co., KY.

John Milton, married 1939, Caldwell Co., KY, Helen Elvoree Hart (b. Sept. 10, 1921), their daughter, Betty June was born in 1940, in Hopkins County. Daughter, Patricia Helen, b. 1947, Chicago, IL, married 1975, to Robert Karl Johnson, Ph. D. (b. 1944, Minnesota), Director of Grice Marine Biological Laboratory and Professor at the College of Charleston, SC.

John M. lived with his grandfather, Millard (Melton) Milton. He attended school in both Caldwell and Hopkins Counties. In November of 1940, John M. moved his family to Har-

John M. and Helen E. Peyton with daughters Betty J. and Patricia H. in 1959

Absalom Phelps and daughter Rebecca Jane

lan Co., KY, for six months, then to Chicago, IL, returning to Kentucky (1952-1956). During WW II, John M. served in the US Army (1944-46), in the South Pacific, earning the Campaign Medal, Asiatic-Pacific Medal w/2 Bronze Battle Stars, the WW II Victory Medal, 2 Overseas Service Bars, and the Philippines Liberation Ribbon w/1 Bronze Star. He worked many years for International Harvester Company in Illinois and Evansville, IN. In 1961, he joined the work force at Landon Cartage Co. in Chicago, where he served as dockman and foreman until his retirement in 1982. He is a member of Teamster's Union Pioneer Club, and Family Motor Coach Association; he enjoys fishing and traveling the US in his Allegro Motor Coach.

Helen Elvoree is the daughter of William Benjamin Hart (1875-1931) and Pernecia Helen Franklin (1881-1981) both of Hopkins Co. The Hart family is descended from John Solomon Hart, early pioneer of Hopkins, died 1821, Union Co. The Franklin family is descended from James Franklin Jr. from South Carolina, settled in Hopkins Co. by 1805. Besides rearing two daughters, Helen E. served the WW II effort by working defense; she later worked for 18 yrs. as a winder making air craft and automotive parts, returned to school for two years at Moraine Valley Community College, Palos Hills, IL, studied writing from The Institute of Children's Literature, CN. She enjoys magazine article writing, traveling, doing family research, author of "Some Early Pioneers of Western Kentucky, Their Ancestors and Descendants"; presently preparing manuscript for a 2nd printing, a member of the Daughters of the American Revolution. In religion, the Peyton's are Apostolic Pentecostal; in politics, Democrats. - *Submitted by Helen E. Peyton*

PHELPS-COATS

The parentage of Absalom Phelps is uncertain. He was born in Hopkins Co., in the Dalton-Beulah area, on June 1, 1844, and was brought up in the household of Nancy Phelps. He took the name Phelps when quite young. On May 27, 1862, he married Mary Jane Coats (b. July 14, 1844), daughter of John and Mary (Womack) Coats. He served in the 48th Kentucky Mounted Infantry (Union), 1863-64, and was plagued all the rest of his life by health problems incurred during his term of service.

He was engaged in farming in Hopkins Co. for most of his life, and he and his wife raised a large family: Mary Elizabeth, b. July 7, 1863 (d. young); Rebecca Jane, b. June 30, 1865; Mary Jeems, b. Aug. 18, 1867 (d. young); Henry Absalom, b. June 1, 1869; William Wilson, b. Feb. 28, 1872; John Leeper, b. Jan. 28, 1874; Albert Marion, b. Apr. 2, 1876; Sarah Nora, b. Feb. 15, 1878; Riley Edgar, b. July 11, 1880; Thomas Kelly, b. Oct. 26, 1882; and Cora Adeline, b. Mar. 25, 1886 (d. young).

In 1887, with his brother-in-law Wilson B. Coats and his son-in-law George Whitson Etheridge and their families, Absalom took his family to Colorado to stake out a homestead and begin a new life. Shortly after their arrival, however, Absalom was taken sick with pneumonia in a snowstorm and died on Dec. 29, 1887. Mary Jane succeeded in bringing up their large family. She died on Dec. 22, 1932, in Wheatland, WY, leaving many descendants in Colorado and Wyoming and other parts of the west. - *Submitted by Sanford G. Etheridge*

RICHARD V. PICKERING JR.

In the year 1946, Richard Vance Pickering Jr. was born at the Caldwell County Hospital. Richard's father is Richard Vance Pickering Sr. and his mother is Elizabeth Michelle Pickering.

Richard was reared in the southwest part of Caldwell County on a 300 acre farm. Richard lived there until his family's house burned in 1963. They moved to Princeton for four months while a new home was being built. In early 1964, Richard and his family moved into their new home, which was located in the same place as his old home.

Richard went to school in Caldwell County. After graduating, he moved to Murray, KY so he could attend college at Murray State University. Richard graduated from Murray State with a degree in Business and Agriculture. After leaving Murray State, he moved back to Princeton and married Wanda Hale in February of 1967. They lived in Princeton while Richard worked at the state penitentiary at Eddyville. After four years at the state penitentiary he worked at Browning Springs Middle School. He then went to work at Ottenhiemers for two years. While working at Ottenheimers, he moved to Dawson Springs. After being laid off, he started work at Island Creek Coal Mines in Hopkins County. Richard worked at Island Creek for four years. He then went to work for Pyro mining where he is presently employed.

In 1969, Richard's wife gave birth to their first child, Dawn Michelle Pickering. Michelle went to school at Dawson Springs and is presently going to college at Hopkinsville Community College.

In 1970, Richard's wife gave birth to their second child, Richard Vance Pickering III. Vance is presently enrolled at Dawson Springs High School. - *Submitted by Vance Pickering*

POLLARD-KNIGHT

Mary Pauline Knight and the late Joseph Andrew Pollard were married on Mar. 23, 1940, in Dawson Springs. Mary is the daughter of the late Willie Enlo Knight and Retta Antonette Lacy Knight of Decaturville, TN. Joe was the son of Thomas Henry Pollard and Nancy Mildred Metheny Pollard of Christian Co., KY.

Back l to r: Dale, Burniece, Donna, Kenneth and Joe. Front l to r: Brenda, Mary, Debbie and Johnnie

Their children are: Joyce Faye, Willie Berniece, Johnnie Lynn, Brenda Darlene, Kenneth Ray, Dale Glenn, Debra Jean and Donna Gale Pollard. Their oldest daughter, Joyce Faye, died at the age of four and one half months with whooping cough and is buried at Rosedale Cemetery in Dawson Springs, KY.

Burniece is married to Gene Workman. They have two boys, Monte Gene and Gregory Shane and live in Charleston, KY. Johnnie is married to Linda Walker. They have one son Scott Earl and live in Snellville, GA. Brenda is married to Richard Dale Sheppard. They have two sons, Richard Wayne and Brent James and live in Hopkinsville, KY. Kenneth has two children from a previous marriage, Melissa Ann and Joseph Ray. Kenneth's second marriage is to Wilma Mallory and they have one son, Jeffery Allen, and live at Richland, KY. Dale married Linda Etta Eaves and they have two children Stephanie Lynn and Bryant Dale and live in Dawson Springs. Debbie married Robert Tilman Dearing and they live in Princeton, KY. Donna married Darrel Wayne Fox and they live in St. Charles.

The late Joseph Andrew Pollard was a coal miner and worked for Dawson Daylight for 31 years. Joe died on Nov. 22, 1966, and is buried at Rosedale Cemetery. Mary has been employed at Ottemheimers, as a operator and is currently working for Dawson Springs Manufacturing as an operator and lives in Dawson Springs. - *Submitted by Gene Workman*

POLLEY-JONES

Sallie Lee Jones married Carlos Burell Polley, b. 1905, in Hopkins County. Sallie born 1887 and died 1968, in Hopkins County, a daughter of Wash Jones and Loucrisa Newton (see Washington F. Jones). She attended schools in Hopkins County. The Polley yard and vegetable garden was a show place of beauty. Sallie's love of wood crafting and carpentry, interior decorating and sewing made her equally at home with hammer, nails, and saw, milking cows, hunting the guinea's nest, plucking geese, or baking pie for Sunday dinner. Her clear high soprano could be heard as she worked or from Oakley Home Church, (Highway 630) where she attended. Neighbors called for her help at births and deaths. Sallie left a legacy of beautiful poems and hymns she wrote through the years. A song written just after the death of Carlos was put to music by a granddaughter, Dorothy Miller Shoulders and sung at Sallie's funeral. She loved to travel and did so, covering the U.S. and Canada after the death of her husband, Carlos.

Spring 1938-Standing l to r: Kathleen and Huston Vanvactor, Annie and Arthur Miller and Opal and Thomas Wilson. Seated: Sallie holding Wanda Miller and Carlos Polley. Bottom: Dorothy Miller and Carl Wilson.

Carlos, born 1886, and died 1957, a son of Peter Polley and Katie Cobb of Webster County. Reared a farm boy, he enjoyed the work and closeness of nature. His light baritone was easy to hear at church or while plowing. He had a deep sense of humor and loved a good joke or prank. Carlos owned a farm just off highway 630, in the Cox's Store community until he retired and moved to Grapevine in the late 1940's. Carlos's brothers: Leslie, Ivy, Laffe, Ben and Dennis; sisters: Allie and Illy. Sister Illy outlived them all, reaching over 101.

Their three children pictured 1938; Kathleen (youngest), married Huston Vanvactor of rural Hanson, where they still reside. Kathleen's son, Dean, married Betty Nance and died in 1978. Their sons: J.B., married Penny Prez and lives in Florida. Tracy lives in Hanson, KY. Kathleen's daughter, Linda of Hanson has worked for Pleasant View Green House for 15 years. Annie (oldest), married Arthur Miller, both now deceased, had three living children, only two shown here. A son, Arthur Jr. (Sonny), married Catherine Wilson of Onton. Sonny has a farm near Nebo. His two sons, Allen Dale also of Nebo, married Becky Laffoon and has a daughter, Christy Amber; the other son Randall Arthur is at home. Opal (2nd oldest), married Rev. Thomas Wilson, has two living sons. Opal, now widowed, lives next door to her youngest son, Wallace, on McLeod Lane. Wallace married Betty Walters; has a teenage son, Jeffery. In Sallie's lap is Annie's Wanda Fraye, now married to Steven Jennings of Grapevine, where they still reside. Wanda's son Brent, married Sharon Reynolds and he is a security guard for local mines. Her daughter Lynn Anne is at home. In front of Sallie is Annie's Dorothy (see Miller and Shoulders). In front of Carlos is Opal's Carl (see the Wilsons).

The house behind the Polleys still stands abandoned and decaying but the memory of laughter and music remains: A guitar still played by a granddaughter, the singing of a great granddaughter, the piano music of two great-great-grandsons, and that funloving sense of humor. - *Submitted by Dorothy Shoulders*

POOL-CARNAL

Millie Victoria Carnal, daughter of Melvina Caroline Beckham Carnal and Alfred J. Carnal, and Jasper Pool, son of Nancy Jane Gooch Pool and Francis Marion Pool, were united in marriage, Nov. 1, 1924, at Madisonville, KY. The Reverend Will Winstead performed the ceremony at the home of the bride's sister, Mrs. Ada Edwards. The wedding attendants were Laura and Tom Pool.

Jasper and Millie Pool on their 50th wedding anniversary

Millie and Jasper lived their entire lives in Hopkins County in the West Hanson area.

Millie and Jasper were active in the Olive Branch Baptist Church. Millie taught Sunday School and worked with youth groups in the church for fifty (50) years. Jasper was a deacon in the church from 1947, until the time of his death.

Both Millie and Jasper have been active in the community. They contributed to the schools, The United Way, The Senior Citizen Association, The Hopkins County Historical Society and benevolent organizations.

Jasper was a musician. He could play any instrument and play any type of music. "Kentucky Blue Grass" and hymns were his favorites.

Millie's hobby was sewing. For the past several years, she has worked with ceramics. She has made many beautiful things. Millie's greatest interest has been and is her family.

The family of Millie and Jasper are: Marquerette, daughter; Raymond James, son-in-law; Carolyn Harshbarger, granddaughter; Marilyn James, granddaughter; Jacob James, grandson; Jessica James, great granddaughter.

Marilyn and Jessica James, granddaughter and great granddaugher and Jacob James, grandson of Jasper and Millie Pool.

Carolyn James Harshbarger earned a bachelor of arts degree from the U. of Chicago. Her master of arts in education was earned at Oberlin, OH. She taught in Poway School District in Poway, CA. At the time of her death in 1977, she was a realtor in Henderson Co., KY.

Marilyn James attended the Brooks Women's College in Long Beach, CA, and the Palomar College in San Mareds, CA. She is presently employed at Trover Clinic.

Jacob James lives with his parents, is attending Hanson School. He is interested in music and baseball.

Jessica James lives with her mother and will be attending Christ the King enrichment program in August.

Jasper Pool died Nov. 9, 1977.

Millie Pool lives at the home place, The Jackson Stage Stop House. - *Submitted by Marquerette J. James*

POOL-GOOCH

Nancy Jane (Nannie) Gooch, daughter of Alonzo and Susan Gooch and Francis Marion Pool, son of William and Malinda Pool, were united in marriage.

Nannie and her parents moved to Hopkins County, from Granville Co., NC, just after the Civil War.

Marion's family moved from Person Co., NC, before 1860.

During the early years of their marriage, Nannie and Marion lived in Webster County near Dixon. In 1895, they moved to a farm in the west Hanson area. The farm is located west of what is now Highway 1069.

Eleven children were born to these parents; 1-Ayer, 2-Orah, 3-Hester, 4-Dudley, 5-James, 6-Bettie, 7-Frances E., 8-Jackson, 9-Thomas L., 10-Lawrence, 11-Jasper.

Marion was member of the Antioch Primitive Baptist Church. Nannie was a member of the Olive Branch Baptist Church. The family life was governed by the strict rules of the Baptist church.

Because each member of the family either played a musical instrument or sang well, the house was filled with music, hymns, Kentucky folk music, classical music. However, on Sundays, only hymns were sung accompanied by one of the sisters at the organ. There was no folk music, no classical music on the "Lord's Day". The stringed instruments were not played on Sundays.

Nannie, having been a semi-invalid for

more than a decade, died Apr. 10, 1918. Marion, while walking on his farm, died of a heart attack on Feb. 25, 1922. After the death of their parents, each child contributed to the family.

Hester and Frances (Fannie) were nurses. Betty and Dudley were school teachers. Dudley conducted neighborhood singing schools. James, Jack and Lawrence operated a wheat thresher during the summer and a sawmill in winter. Ayer, Thomas (Tom) and Jasper were farmers. Orah was an insurance broker and a farmer in Webster County. Frances E. Arnold (Fannie), is the only surviving child of Nannie and Marion Pool. - *Submitted by Marquerette J. James*

POOLE-GIBSON

Flora Mae Gibson was born on June 26, 1901, near Greenville, KY. She was the daughter of Wade Gibson and Lottie L. Cunningham Gibson (born Oct. 23, 1878). Lottie was the daughter of James Washington Cunningham (born Aug. 1, 1848), and Zellis Netta Moore (born Oct. 14, 1848), who were married Apr. 9, 1868.

W.B. and Flora Poole on their 50th wedding anniversary

Flora's mother died on Aug. 29, 1901, soon after Flora was born. She was reared by an aunt, Sophia Jane Cunningham (born 1870), with whom she lived until her marriage to Wallace B. Poole. Flora worked as a telephone operator for a while and also at the Cigar Factory in Madisonville, KY. Flora died on Mar. 28, 1984, and is buried at Forest Lawn Cemetery in Madisonville, KY.

Wallace Beckham Poole was born Sept. 21, 1900. He was the son of Andrew Johnson Poole (born May 1, 1866), and Manolia Alice Bowles Poole (born May 28, 1872), who were married in Hopkins County, on Oct. 13, 1886.

The Beckham Pooles lived in the White Plains and Hanson areas before moving permanently to Madisonville, KY. Beckham Poole engaged in farming for a short time, but soon after marrying started barbering. He was a barber in Hopkins County for almost fifty years. The last shop he owned was "The Hub Barber Shop", located on the corner of Center and Main Streets in Madisonville. He was well known for his fiddle playing and won many prizes at Old Fiddlers Contests. He was also well known for his Bar-B-Queing, especially at Barber Union picnics. "Beck", as he was known to his many friends, died on Oct. 28, 1968, and is buried at Forest Lawn Cemetery in Madisonville, KY.

Wallace Beckham Poole and Flora Mae Gibson, both of White Plains, were married in Clarksville, TN, on Apr. 24, 1918. The Poole's were the parents of two daughters; Edythe Poole (born Feb. 22, 1919), and Eva Nell Poole (born Apr. 21, 1925).

Edythe was married to James C. Barnhill, Jr. of Providence, KY. They had two daughters; Carolyne Ann, who married David Roehrenbeck, and Jane, who married John Cullen. Edythe and James C. Barnhill were divorced in 1973. Edythe worked for Ruby Lumber Company, Hart Lumber Company and First Federal in Providence, KY. She now lives in Lexington, KY where she is House Director for the Delta Zeta Sorority at the U. of Kentucky.

Nell was married to Roy Lee Brinkley on June 23, 1945. They had one son, Joseph Michael Brinkley (born Aug. 29, 1951), who married Roberta McGuyer of Madisonville. Nell and Roy Lee Brinkley were divorced in June of 1955. Nell worked as bookkeeper for Pride Ice and Coal Company and for the Ben Franklin Stores in Madisonville for 13 years. Nell married Ralph L. White of Providence, KY, on June 11, 1969. They moved to Cary, IL. Nell now works as accountant for Brock Equipment Company in Crystal Lake, IL. - *Submitted by Nell White*

BRADFORD PORTER

Bradford Lawrence and Martha Porter bought 830 acres of land just south of Manitou in 1838, with gold they had earned teaching in a government school on an Indian reservation in Iowa. Since that time five generations of Porters have lived on that farm.

The five sons of Thomas and Kathleen Porter are pictured holding the leather box which contained the gold brought from Iowa and used to purchase the Porter farm. From l to r: Tom, Claud, David, Robert and John holding the box, 1966.

Bradford Porter was a well-known citizen of Kentucky, serving as a member of the Kentucky House of Representatives. His son, Herschel Fillmore, was born in 1847, in the house which still stands on the farm and where his grandson, Thomas H. Porter, Sr. now lives. Herschel Fillmore served as a magistrate in Hopkins County. His only brother, Thomas Bradford, built a brick home across Highway 41A from the original farmhouse. Some of the walls are still standing. Herschel Fillmore had two daughters and one son, Claud, who was vice-president and cashier of the Nebo Citizens Bank until its liquidation in 1937. Claud married Eva Bell and from this union four children were born: Mary D., Emma Bell, Lora Lillian and Thomas Herschel.

Thomas Herschel now owns and operates the original farm and lives in the farmhouse built in 1838. He married the former Kathleen Bealmear, a descendant of Paddy Christian, who was with George Washington during the Revolutionary War. (Christian County was named for Colonel William Christian, Paddy's son.) Thomas and Kathleen have five sons: Claud Fillmore, Thomas Herschel, Jr., Robert Christian, John Bealmear, and David Allen. - *Submitted by Kathleen Porter*

PATRICIA PORTERFIELD

Patricia Lee Porterfield was born July 22, 1939, in Madisonville, KY. The only child of Frank Edward Porterfield of Wayne Co., IL, and Janelle Bond Durham of Edwards Co., IL. Frank Porterfield was the son of Oscar F. Porterfield and Ona Mae Borah of Wayne Co., IL. Janelle Durham is the daughter of John Y. Durham of Hopkins Co., KY, and Alma Bond of Edwards Co., IL.

On July 16, 1956, Patricia Lee Porterfield married Alvin Lee "Bud" Brock of Edwards Co., IL. He is the only son of Virgil G. Brock and Edna Alice Stennett both of Edwards Co. Bud is the fourth of five children born to his parents. Brothers and sisters are: Paul Verdane, Ivan Leroy, Nettie Lou Brock Ile and Ruby Elaine Brock Wiles.

Pat and Bud Brock are the parents of three sons. Andrew David born Nov. 8, 1959 and married Aug. 30, 1980 to Teresa Kay Pearson of Illinois. Andrew has a degree in Welding from Olney Central College and is employed in electrical maintenance at Public Service of Indiana. The second son is James Frank Brock born May 12, 1964. He has a degree in welding from Olney Central College and a Certificate in auto/diesel mechanics from Oakland City College, in Indiana. He is employed at Champion Laboratories in the maintenance department. John Patrick Brock was born Aug. 15, 1966 and has a degree in Radio/TV broadcasting and communications from Wabash Valley College. He is presently employed at Fairfield Radio Station.

Patricia Lee Porterfield Brock graduated from Edwards Sr. High School in 1957 and in 1970 enrolled in Olney Central College and received a degree in Nursing. She is presently employed at Fairfield Memorial Hospital as an RN and also Utilization Review Coordinator. Bud is a mechanic and owns and operates his own business at their home on Rt. 1, in Albion, IL. - *Submitted by Pat Brock*

POTTS-GUGE

Rita Juanita Guge and Ellis Orian Potts were married Jan. 21, 1955 in the First Church of God, Madisonville, KY.

Juanita was born Aug. 25, 1937, in Madisonville, Hopkins Co. She is the daughter of George Linsey Guge and Mary Florence Franklin. Juanita attended Waddill and Hall St. Grade Schools and graduated from Madisonville High School in 1955. She is presently employed by Birmingham Bolt Co.,-KY Div. She attends the First Church of God and has served as treasurer for approximately 25 years. Juanita is a member of the Hopkins Co. Genealogical Society and the Hopkins Co. Historical Society.

Juanita and Ellis O. Potts

Ellis was born June 4, 1935, in Union Co., KY, to Johnnie Meredith Potts and Mary Virginia Springer, she being the daughter of Herman Ellis Springer and Susan Elizabeth Roberson. Mary Virginia was born Oct. 12, 1909. Johnnie Meredith was born Aug. 24, 1910. He is the son of Alfred Orian Potts and Dora Etta Kelley. Ellis has four sisters: Dois Jones, Marcella Morris, Etta Fahning and Virginia Starr. Ellis attended school in Madisonville. Ellis joined the KY National Guard in 1952. He served in various jobs before attending Officers Candidate School receiving his Commission as 2nd Lt. in 1963. He served as Commander of the Madisonville and Hopkinsville Units before retiring in 1974, as a Major. Ellis worked at the Shoe Box, Fowler Turner Lumber Co., as a self employed Building Contractor for 13 years, he then opened E.O. Potts Custom Marble and E.O. Potts Sports Headquarters, later changing the operation to his present business E.O. Potts Marine Sales & Service.

Ellis and Juanita have two daughters: Tijuana Leigh Rickard and Tonia Renee Gibson. Tonia married Michael Lawrence Gibson May 16, 1981. They have four grandchildren: April Nicole Rickard, Micah Kern, Kalen Ryan, and Bryce Linsey Gibson. Tijuana is employed at Birmingham Bolt Co.,-KY Div. Tonia is a Radiologist at Trover Clinic. - *Submitted by Juanita Potts*

PRATHER-WHALEY

Alva Preston Prather was born Apr. 17, 1892, in Winchester, KY. He was of Welsh descent. His ancestors from Wales settled first in Mason County and then in Robertson Co., KY. His grandfather gave land for the first church and school in Mt. Olivet, KY.

A.P. graduated from high school in Mt. Olivet. His college days were spent at Eastern State College and the University of Kentucky. During the summers of 1924-1929, he did graduated work at Columbia University, New York, NY, where he received his Master's Degree in Educational Administration.

His first job was as helper in a drug store in his hometown. He became principal of schools there. He was in school work in Crittenden Co., KY, later principal of Columbia High School in Columbia, KY. In 1924, he came to Earlington where he served as Superintendent of schools until his retirement in June 1962.

In July 1919, he married Nancy Whaley. She was born Jan. 11, 1893, in Bath Co., KY. She was a graduate of Millersburg Female College in 1911, and from Eastern State Teachers College in 1913. She taught school in the Louisville system for five years, one year at Millersburg, four years at Columbia, KY, and for 38 years at Earlington before retiring in 1963.

A.P. was a member of the First Christian Church in Earlington where he was an elder, deacon and taught the men's Sunday School class for many years. He was a Mason and a leader in civic affairs.

Nancy was a member of the Earlington Methodist Church where she taught a Sunday School class for a number of years.

Nancy Prather died Dec. 13, 1965. A.P. Prather died Nov. 4, 1977. The following is on their tombstone in Oakwood Cemetery in Earlington:

"They were teachers. They found their greatest happiness in looking into the faces of children, illuminated with the joy of learning, and watching the eyes of those children shine with the light of understanding." - *Compiled by Debbie Knight Hammonds and James W. Larmouth*

JOHN PRATHER

The Honorable Thomas Prather, born 1760-1770, was a son of John Hunt Prather and Elleanor Turner. In 1787, in Mercer Co., KY, he married Anne Ashby, daughter of Captain Stephen Ashby, Revolutionary War soldier.

Thomas and Anne came to the Hopkins Co. area very early with Anne's brothers; Col. Daniel Ashby, Absalom, John, "General" Stephen, and Enos Ashby, and her sister Rosie, who had married Capt. George Timmons, another Revolutionary War soldier.

John Prather

On May 25, 1807, Thomas Prather took the oath of Assistant Judge of the Hopkins Circuit Court. Anne had died about 1822, and Thomas married Jemima Ashby, widow of his brother-in-law Enos Ashby, in 1823. In 1834, Thomas married Phebe Barr, widow of George Barr. Thomas died in 1839, and is buried in the Old Ashby Cemetery.

Children of Thomas and Ann were: James, Stephen, Rebecca (married Nathaniel Ashby), Eleanor (married Joseph Crabtree), Letty (married Charles Murphy), Philip, John, Rosie (married William Crabtree), and Washington Prather.

Son Stephen was born Nov. 24, 1789, in Mercer Co., KY, and in 1810, married in Hopkins Co. Elizabeth Ashby, daughter of Henry Ashby (1745-1817), and Judith Shumate. Stephen died in 1856, in Hopkins Co. and Elizabeth died after 1871.

Children of Stephen Prather and Elizabeth were: Henry A., Ann (married James Ashby), Thomas, John, Sarah Jane (married Wm. A. Hall), Elizabeth (married Isaac Coffman), and Letitia (married Joseph Crews and was living in Sanders, NB in 1871). All the others were still in Hopkins and Webster Counties in 1871. (Ref: Hopkins Co. Deed Bk. 32, p. 214).

John Prather, son of Stephen and Elizabeth, was born Oct. 9, 1823, and in 1846, married Louisa Branson. Their children were: Columbus, 1847; William A., 1849; and James F., 1851 (all three died in 1852); Stephen Henry, 1854; Mary Elizabeth, 1856 (married Joe Gooch); Sarah Isabell, 1858 (married Paul McKenzie Gooch); Louisa, 1860 (married Edward Flemming); Emma F., 1862 (married J.M. Chandler); and Priscilla Frances (Fanny) 1864 (married Willis Brooks).

Louisa died in 1867 and John married Louisianna Branson Pidcock, widow of Madison Pidcock, in 1869. Louisianna died in May, 1870, and that October, John married 20 year old, Verrilda Kenyon, daughter of Lucius Patrick Kenyon.

Children of John and Verrilda were Laura Lee, 1872; John, 1874; and Alonza E., 1876. John and Verrilda lived briefly in Missouri, but returned to Hopkins Co. where John died on Dec. 14, 1877. Verrilda then married Clevarious Brown in 1884 (a widower with five children), and they had three children; Lillian, Emma (married Julian Day) and Whitson Brown. Verrilda later reared an orphan granddaughter—thus making her "mother" to two sets of step children, two sets of her own, and a grandchild—a total of 18 persons. She moved to Evansville about 1926, where she died in 1936.

Of the three children of John Prather and Verrilda, (1) Laura Lee married Filson Matthew Logan (see John Blue story for their descendants); (2) John married Bess Balentine and had sons Paul, who died in Evansville in 1969, and Jack, who lives in Arizona; and (3) Alonza died in 1900, unmarried. - *Submitted by Mary Louise Parrish Bevers*

THOMAS PRATHER

Thomas Prather was born ca. 1768. He died after Oct. 25, 1831 (date of his will), in Hopkins County. His parents are unknown.

Thomas settled in Hopkins County in the early days, coming from Mercer County. He appears in the 1795 list of taxable property of Mercer County and in taxable property list in 1799, of Henderson County as having 320 acres on Otter Creek. Thomas was one of the early judges of Hopkins County. He is buried in the Old Ashby Cemetery east of Providence. His marker is of rough sandstone slab, with only his name, no date of death.

Thomas married Anne Ashby on Mar. 6, 1787. Anne was born 1770, and died 1822. She was the daughter of Captain Stephen Ashby. The second child born to Thomas and Anne was Stephen, born Nov. 24, 1789, in Mercer County. He died June 23, 1856, in Hopkins County. Stephen married Elizabeth Ashby July 16, 1810, she was the daughter of Henry Ashby and Judith Shumate. Elizabeth died after 1870. Stephen was a farmer as were most Prathers.

Other children of Thomas and Anne (Ashby) Prather were James, born 1788 in Mercer County, died Oct. 23, 1853; Rebecca, born 1794, married Nathaniel Ashby; Ellender, born 1795 married Joseph Crabtree; Letty (Betty), born 1799, married Charles Murphy; John; Phillip, born Feb. 7, 1803, died Dec. 26, 1868, married Sarah Ashby July 5, 1826; Washington, born 1816, married Hester Reynolds, who was the daughter of Thomas Reynolds; Rosa, born 1823, married William Crabtree.

Thomas married the second time to Jimimah (Jemima) Ashby (maiden name unknown), July 4, 1823. (This wife is mentioned in his will.) In 1834, Thomas married wife number 3, Phebe Barr (maiden name unknown), widow of George Barr. Phebe was born 1782, died Oct. 9, 1856.

Henry A Prather was the oldest child of Stephen and Elizabeth (Ashby) Prather. Henry was born ca. 1810, in Hopkins County. He married Mary E. Reynolds on Mar. 15, 1832. Mary was born Oct. 12, 1816, the daughter of Thomas Reynolds, (mother unknown). She died Aug. 14, 1875. Other children of Stephen and Elizabeth Ashby Prather were Anne, born Oct. 28, 1811, died October 1829, married Thomas Prather; Thomas, born Jan. 7, 1816, married Pricilla Ashby; John, born Oct. 9, 1823, married Louisa Branson; Sarah Jane, born ca. 1825, married William A. Hall; Elizabeth J., born Sept. 13, 1829, married Isaac Coffman.

Henry Clay Prather was the third of six children born to Henry A. and Mary E. Reynolds Prather. Henry Clay was born Nov. 9, 1842, died May 21, 1810, in Webster County, married Dica Ann Pritchett Dec. 14, 1862, in Hopkins County. Dica was the daughter of Robert P. and Jemima Ashby Pritchett. Dica was born June 10, 1843. - *Submitted by Emmalou Prather Anderson*

PRESTON-WHITFIELD

Myra Eugena Whitfield and Basil Roberts Preston were married Dec. 12, 1925, in Clarksville, TN, and moved to the Anton community, where Basil owned Preston's Garage, which he still operates. They have been members of Bethlehem Christian Church for sixty years.

Myra was born Apr. 7, 1909, the daughter of Maggie Mae Oates and E. Pratt Whitfield and has one brother O. Gay Whitfield, Fowler Road, Madisonville, KY.

Maggie was the daughter of Dr. R.M. (Dick) Oates, who was born in 1851, and married Jenny Murphy in 1881. Descendents of Jessie Oates, who came from England in the 1700's, settled in South Carolina, coming to Hopkins Co. (then Muhlenburg Co.) in the early 1800's. Maggie is related to the Earles, Winebarger, Slatons, Murphys, Dillinghams and many others in Hopkins and Muhlenburg Cos.

Pratt is the son of William Henry Whitfield and Floressa Matelin Graddy and had three brothers and three sisters all deceased. His grandfather, Isaac Whitfield, came to what is called Whitfield District near White Plains from Tennessee in the early 1800's. Relatives are Page, Furgerson, Moore, Hunt, Fox, Graddy, Denton, Rodgers and other in Hopkins and surrounding counties.

Basil is the oldest son of Ida Maud Rodgers and Ernest B. Preston and has six brothers and three sisters. Homer (deceased), B.E. (Dick), Roy W. (Jim), and Gerald of Madisonville, West and Edwin (Bud) of Michigan, Nannie Mae Crowell of Goble, MI, Jessie I. Thomas and Bertha Marie Scott of Madisonville. Ida, his mother, was the daughter of David Rodgers and Nancy Robertson, lived on what is now Highway 70 and 85E near East Diamond Mine. She had three brothers and four sisters. Relatives are Rodgers, Cardwells, Bowles, Bennett, Hendricks, Friday and Robertson.

His father, the son of P.H. Preston and Ophelia Ellen Roberts moved to Hopkins County in 1849, from Calhoun, KY, and from Illinois in the early 1800's; he lived on Pond River Colleries Road. He had three brothers and a sister all deceased.

The Prestons have three children: Basil Roberts Preston Jr., who married Joyce Ann Adams in 1947, Panama City Beach, FL, and Ernest Eugene Preston of Bowling Green, KY, and Judith Gayle, who married Donald Gamblin in 1967, of Earlington, KY.

They have three grandchildren: Sandra Ann Sanders of Headland, AL; Steven Roberts Preston of Panama City, FL; and DeAnna Lynn Gamblin of Earlington, KY. There are also our great grandsons, two great granddaughters and one great-great grandson. - *Submitted by Myra E. Preston*

ROBERT SILAS PRIDE

Robert Silas Pride was born Dec. 1, 1879, in Bordley, Union Co., KY, to James Shields Pride (Dec. 10, 1810-Jan. 24, 1886), and Harriet Frost Hardy (abt. 1845-abt. 1884). His father had three wives and twenty-one children. His first two wives were Annie Crawford and Pithy Porter. Robert Silas Pride was the fifth of six children born to this marriage and he was conceived when his father was approximately seventy years old. His other brothers and sisters were: Lillie, Tilatha, Paul, Cordelia "Deala", and Drucilla (died very young).

His father and mother died when he was about seven years old. He was raised by his half-brother, "Uncle Jim",—James Pinkney Pride (Jan. 5, 1853-unknown), who married Mary Isabelle Christian. It is said that he ran away from home at age ten and worked on a riverboat. He went to school through the third grade; however, his daughter, Freddy, remembers his helping her with high school algebra. He found Thomas Edison fascinating and taught himself about electricity. He finally teamed up with Frederick Gilbert, and the two of them built a small power plant near Morganfield. They strung their own wires and sold electricity to the area. When Kentucky Utilities started buying up the small power plants over the state, they sold out to K.U., and Robert Silas went to work for K.U. as an engineer. He became a district manager which lasted twenty-one of his thirty-three years with the company.

After retirement from K.U. in 1938, he rented the K.U. ice plant in Madisonville, and started Pride Ice and Coal Company. The business was managed by his daughters, Jane and Freddy, after his death in 1942.

Robert Silas was married twice. The first marriage was to Bettie Wright and to them three children were born: Irma Lydia (abt. 1914-Nov.5, 1987), Paul Forrest "Buddy" (abt. 1915-Aug. 15, 1970), and Helen (abt. 1916-Mar. 3, 1969). Bettie died when Helen was about six weeks old. Within a year he remarried Cyrena Helon Jagoe (Apr. 26, 1882-June 5, 1972), the daughter of Alonzo Livermore Jagoe (Jan. 5, 1858-Jan. 14, 1936), and Cyrena Jane Davis (Nov. 19, 1856-Aug. 19, 1930), on Nov. 12, 1916. Robert Silas and Helon had two children: Jane Lillian Pride, (Aug. 21, 1917-Mar. 3, 1986), and Mary Frederica Pride, born Mar. 30, 1925.

Next to his business, Rizpah Temple Shrine, was closest to his heart. He served as Potentate one term in 1935, and as a member of the official family for many years. He was also chairman of the crippled children committee continuously after the death of Dr. E.B. Hardin, his predecessor.

He served as master of Madisonville Lodge, Free and Accepted Masons, was a member of the Elks Lodge, the Kiwanis Club, the Madisonville Country Club and was active in most civic affairs. He was a long-time member of the First Christian Church of Madisonville. He died of cancer on May 6, 1942. He is buried at Grapevine Cemetery. - *Submitted by Robert P. Moore*

PRIEST

The Crest, adopted by the Priests was a martlet and was displayed in various forms. It was usually a fanciful bird, its legs cut down to mere stumps, without feet, as a mark of distinction of younger sons, to remind them that they must rise by wings of virtue and merit, not trusting to their fee, since they had little to stand upon. The martlet is the bird of good news.

Peter Priest settled in Virginia 1720, his widow, Sarah, was living in 1781.

About 1730, three brothers by the name of Priest emigrated from North Wales and settled in Virginia. One died shortly after landing, a second went to South Carolina or Georgia and reared a family there. The third remained in

Basil and Myra Preston and family at their 50th wedding anniversary Dec. 12, 1975.

Amy Lee Priest

Virginia and reared a family of five sons and one daughter. They were: Thomas, John, George, Peter, William and Elizabeth.

A Defory Priest came to America on the Mayflower; he was the 29th signer. His wife and two daughters were to arrive later. From a sketch of Plymouth Village in the November 1963 D.A.R. Magazine, his was the third house from Myles Standish. He died the 2nd year. His branch was not in the direct line of descent.

The Priest line of my husband (Maxey Hill Priest, Jr.), has been traced back to 1812, the year <u>Thomas Hardin Priest</u> was born. He died in 1893. His first wife was <u>Nancy Merritt</u> (married Sept. 3, 1835 by Moses Gocey), born 1851, died 1856. Children (9) were: Sara Ann Priest, b. 1836; James M. Priest, b. 1838; Thomas R. Priest, b. 1841; Mary E. Priest, b. 1845; Carylin L. Priest, b. 1847; Susan M. Priest, b. 1849; Charles Knot Priest, b. 1851; <u>Robert Allison Priest</u>, b. 1853; and William Samuel Priest, b. 1856. The above information taken from the Priest Bible. (The name of the second wife unknown, no issue). All were born in Spring Hill, TN. Thomas Hardin Priest was a coffin maker for Maury Co., TN. Coffins sold for $32.50.

Priest Bible certifies that "<u>Robert Allison Priest</u> and <u>Laura Jordan</u> were solemnly united by me in the residence of M. Jordan Allison on the 24th day of Dec. 1874, in the presence of family" Signed, Rev. John M. Jordan, minister, Spring Hill, TN.

Of the seven children, Margaret Priest Foster (Mrs. Frank) is still living in Nashville, TN, in a nursing home.

<u>Maxey Hill Priest (Sr.)</u>, the 5th child, died in 1964. He and <u>Myrtle Mae Griffin</u> of Earlington, KY, were married in Evansville, IN, in 1908. Myrtle died in 1967. He was named for a Methodist minister, Rev. Maxey Hill of Tennessee. Myrtle was the daughter of John Riley Griffin and Louisa Warner. John and Louisa were married by this writer's grandfather, Rev. George Washington DeMoss. Maxey Sr. retired from the L & N, in 1954. He was transferred from Earlington to Howell, IN, in 1927. Their two children were: Maxey Hill Priest, Jr., and Evalyne Louisa Priest (Heil, Mrs. Patrick), who lives in Evansville. She has three children and grandchildren.

<u>Maxey H. Priest, Jr.</u> married <u>Irene DeMoss</u>, daughter of William Lee DeMoss and Mary Ferdie Jackson DeMoss of Madisonville, by the Rev. M.H. Stroud, Methodist minister, in Greenville, KY, Thursday, Dec. 24, 1936.

They have one son, <u>Maxey Hill Priest III</u>, married <u>Barbara Musgrove</u> in 1969. They reside in Madisonville. Their children are Russell Edward Priest, Ronald Wayne Priest and Amy Lee Priest. Sources: Genealogy of the Priest, Harris, Stubblefield Families. Tennessee Archives, 1962. - *Submitted by Irene DeMoss Priest*

PRITCHETT-BISHOP

Mary Ann Bishop, born June 1842, married Doctor James William Pritchett in 1865. Dr. Pritchett was a very popular physician and was called, "beloved physician". He had a large practice extending over most of the county and in those days a doctor's life was a hard one; he never refused to go where called, regardless of weather conditions, money, or his health. After several month's illness from bronchial trouble, he died in 1883. They resided at 106 North Seminary St. Mary Ann, called "Molly", had five children to raise. She died in 1927. The children:

<u>Sallie Pritchett,</u> born 1866, married James Fleming Gordon, a prominent attorney, and later Circuit Judge. She died in 1912. <u>William Woodson Pritchett</u> called "Aunt Willie", born October 1869, married Frank Wake, who was from Lyon County and was interested in tobacco business and banking. Aunt Willie was an active member of the American Legion Aux., and spent many years helping disabled veterans in Outwood Hospital at Dawson Springs. She and her husband were among the first members of St. Mary's Episcopal Church and she played the organ there for many years. <u>Orlean Pritchett,</u> born 1874, and on June 1898, he enlisted in the 3rd KY Infantry to U.S.A. Volunteers during the Spanish American War and WW I. He retired as Lt. Colonel, came home and later married his childhood sweetheart, Kate Durrett of Hopkinsville, and they lived there the rest of their lives. <u>James Clift Pritchett,</u> born 1878, was prominent in church work and a talented musician. He played the organ at the Methodist church for many years. He married Nell Rees of Fayetteville, TN, and they had one son, Rees. They lived at 106 N. Seminary, Madisonville. Clift was with Dulins Store for a few years and when Rees was five years old, they moved to New York City. Mr. and Mrs. Pritchett died there and were brought back to Madisonville for burial. Rees is a doctor in New York—he married a nurse Jane and they have a daughter, Susan. She is married and lives in Alexandra, VA. <u>Ada Marvin Pritchett,</u> born 1872, died 1950. She married John Edward Arnold, son of a pioneer Hopkins Co. family. Many of his ancestors were interested in politics, including William R. King, Vice President of the U.S. in 1853. Ed Arnold had a grocery store across the street from the Post Office and his name is still in the sidewalk there. Mr. and Mrs. Arnold had four children and they lived next to her mother at 211 N. Seminary. The Arnold children are:

<u>James Hunter Arnold</u> born 1900, married Frances Norton of Birmingham, AL, in 1924. They had one dau., Nell Norton Arnold. James worked at Dulins Store; later he got into the gasoline business and moved to Gadsden, AL. Nell married Jack Winter and moved to Baltimore. They had one son. James died in 1967. Frances lives in Gadsden. <u>Lucy Gordon Arnold,</u> born 1903, married Hillyard Jackson in 1923. He worked at Farmers Bank for many years. They spent a short time in Florida, but returned to live with her mother, who was an invalid. Jack was connected with U.C. Milk Co. Lucy died 1957 and Jack in 1981. <u>Nell Wade Arnold,</u> born 1906, after graduation from H.S., went to Louisville Conservatory of Music. She married Carr H. Trathen in 1937. He worked for Williams Coal Co., and died in 1951.

The Woodson and Bishop heirs (many lived at Browning Springs which is now the school and grounds on West Arch St.), gave six acres of land to Oriental Lodge of Odd Fellows in Madisonville on Mar. 23, 1860, for a cemetery, reserving a section for their heirs. This cemetery is now known as Odd Fellows Cemetery.

Ada Bishop was born 1849, and died in 1934. She married James A. Ramsey in 1888, and he died in 1899. Her sister is Mary Ann Bishop in this story above. James was very successful in the tobacco market and she was a devout Methodist. Her Sunday School class went on for years, and she made many things possible for the church with her financial support. - *Submitted by Nell Trathen*

PROW-IVEY

A Tennessee belle named Helen Ivey moved to Madisonville with her parents, Samuel C. Ivey and Nora (Taylor) Ivey, in 1921, at the age of eight, and there she later met her fate.

Aubrey Prow was born in Webster County Sept. 13, 1906, and moved to the Madisonville area in 1910. Aubrey became a plumber and went to work for Helen's father, Samuel in 1923. His parents were B.L. Prow and Nettie Ann Neisz Prow, now both deceased.

Helen and Aubrey Prow in 1927 about a year before they married

Helen, born Aug. 24, 1913, and Aubrey were married on Dec. 11, 1928. This union has been blessed with four children.

Joy Elaine (Mrs. Kenneth Sisk), born in 1935, whose issue are Dennis and Mark, who each have two children. Dennis married Beverly Powell and their children are Constance and Lindsay. Mark married Kim Lemon and their children are Jamie and Katy.

Kay Sharon (Mrs. Charles Crafton), born 1937, has two children, Laura and Barbara.

Shirley Ann (Mrs. Joel Utley), born 1942, has three children; Stacey, Craig and Brian.

Russell Prow, born 1944, married Anne Vaughn and they have two children; Sheri and Jennifer.

This family of four great grandchildren, nine grandchildren, and four children look forward with great joy to the celebration of Helen and Aubrey's 60th Wedding Anniversary in December of 1988.

Helen's sisters are Beatrice Ivey Prow, married E.L. "Doc" Prow, a brother to Aubrey; and Sarah Reynolds, married Leonard Reynolds.

Aubrey has one living sister, Bertha Cobb, who was married to Clarence Cobb, deceased. Out of 13 children in this Prow family, only Aubrey and Bertha remain. - *Submitted by Helen Prow*

PRUITT

Julie Ann Marcum and James Lockett Pruitt were married in Springfield, TN, on May 13, 1977.

Julie, born Feb. 26, 1947, in Tuscaloosa, AL, is the 2nd daughter of Cledith Marcum and Louise Boothe. Her sisters are Joyce Marcum and Marie Towl, both of Alabama. Other ancestral names are Channell and Lindsey and American Indian.

The Pruitts l to r: Bobby, Jim, Nancy, Julie and Bo.

Julie attended grade school and high school in Alabama. Children of a previous marriage are Micheal Tingle, Randall (Bo) and Pam Huffenstufer. Randall, 14, now lives with his mother. After moving to Madisonville, Julie worked as a waitress, department store clerk and a nurse's aide. She has enjoyed working as a dealer for various home products for over 10 years. She has worked for Avon, Tupperware, Watkins, Stanley, Amway and Shaklee. An excellent southern cook, Julie enjoys working with the youth and V.B.S. at Concord General Baptist Church, where she and her husband are active members. She also works as a part-time teacher's aide at Madisonville Life Christian Academy where her two younger children attend.

James, better known as Jim, was born Apr. 1, 1939, in Henderson Co., the oldest son of Robert Pruitt and Frances Gregory. He has a brother William of Henderson Co. and a sister Martha Helen Smith of Louisville. Other ancestral names are Tillison and Newmen.

Jim attended Henderson Co. schools graduating in 1955. He has been an engineer for C.S.X. Railroad for 21 years. He received his real estate and auctioneer's license in 1986-87, respectively. He is affiliated with Riden Auction and Realty of Providence and Key Associates. Other interests are carpentry which was put to good use when his trailer home burned. With a bit of help from neighbors, he designed and built their beautiful hillside home on 630 near Manitou. Jim learned quickly to work with heavy equipment and with a friend's bulldozer, constructed a lake on his property for family fun of swimming and fishing. His newest endeavor, an auction barn he and Julie have opened in Madisonville. Jim is also an accredited chimney sweep. He has been a member of the Masonic Lodge since 1960. Jim has four children from a previous marriage: Kathy Greenwell, Rebecca Smith, Judy Baxter and Robert (Bobby) Pruitt still at home.

The Pruitt's have one daughter, Nancy, age 9. A talented youngster, she has been singing for community gatherings and churches since she was 6. Nancy's most exciting accomplishment was singing with the well-known gospel group, The Kingsmen. She and her brother "Bo" enjoy swimming and playing their organ and keyboard.

Julie and Jim's grandchildren are: Jessica of Alabama, Melessa, Angie, Beth Ann and Mathew. Step grandchildren: Josh and Clayton of Henderson Co. - *Submitted by Dorothy Shoulders*

PURDY

On Aug. 10, 1987, there were 50 registered voters in Hopkins County by the name of Purdy.

The Media Research Bureau in Washington, D.C. records the information that Francis Purdy immigrated from England to Concord, MA, about 1635.

Aaron Purdy of Massachusetts was a Lieutenant in the Revolutionary War. Aaron Purdy married Peachy Davenport of York Co., VA, in 1772, and was given a land grant when Kentucky County was still a part of Virginia. This farm land, located near Kirkwood Springs in Hopkins County, is still in the Purdy family, its owners being Newman, Glen, Dixon B. Jr. and Kenneth Purdy.

On the left, Arch Aaron Purdy (1893-1970), on the right William Wallace Purdy (1890-1967). Both are great grandsons of Aaron and Peachy Purdy.

Aaron Purdy and his wife Peachy had a son, Aaron. The second Aaron fathered 17 children, among whom was David Jasper, who fathered 10 children. There were many grandchildren and great grandchildren.

The Purdys have been active in the growth of Hopkins County vicinity for 200 years. The majority of them have been Democrats and Baptists. Through the years, their occupations have been in the fields of politics, business, education, medicine, farming and mining. - *Submitted by Louise C. (Mrs. Homer L.) Purdy*

ORA PURDY-ZAPARANICK

Mary McFarland Purdy gave birth to Ora Ruth Purdy on Dec. 26, 1941. Ora's father was Casey J. Purdy. Ora's maternal grandparents were Ulysses Grant McFarland and Ida Spears McFarland. Ora's paternal grandparents were Eldora Inglis Purdy and David Dennis Purdy, a direct descendent of Aaron Purdy.

Aaron Purdy was born in North Carolina in the 1780's. Aaron moved to Hopkins Co., KY before the 1820's and thus began a line of Hopkins County Purdys. Aaron's second wife, Elizabeth Nall, bore him several children, one of which they named Aaron. The second Aaron was born in 1815. This Aaron married Avey Chapell, the second of three wives, who bore him four children.

David Jasper was born to Aaron and Avey on Dec 23, 1853. David Japser married Mariah Dunbar who bore him ten children. Their oldest son, David Dennis, was born on June 12, 1877. David Dennis married Eldora Inglis and together they had four children. These chidren were: Elsie, Casey J., Dixie Mae, and a stillborn. None of David Dennis and Eldora's children are living.

Casey J. Purdy was born on Nov. 25, 1901. His first wife, Ruth McFarland, gave him one child, Mary Ann Purdy (Winstead). Casey's second wife, Mary Sue McFarland, married him in June of 1938. David Grant was born to Casey and Mary on Aug. 12, 1940 and a daughter, Ora Ruth, soon followed on Dec. 26, 1941.

Ora Ruth Purdy attended Lone Oak Elementary and George Rogers Clark Elementary. After her elementary graduation, Ora then became a student at Adah Brazelton Junior High and then at Paducah Tilghman. Ora played the violin in her fourth, fifth and sixth grade years. She played the French horn in her high school orchestra. Ora was also a National Honor Society member. Ora attended the University of Kentucky and graduated in December of 1964. Ora belonged to the Baptist Tabernacle Church in Paducah.

On July 11, 1964, Ora exchanged wedding vows with a young man named David Carl Zaparanick from Westfield, NJ. Soon after their marriage, Ora was baptized a Catholic. David and Ora's first-born, Tracy Leigh, was born on Nov. 25, 1965 in Lexington, KY. David Matthew soon followed on Nov. 17, 1967 in Logan, UT. Michele Lynn was born on May 9, 1970 in Elizabethtown, KY and Carl Travis was born on Sept. 15, 1978 in Madisonville, KY.

Currently, Ora enjoys her job as Director of Nursing at the New Dawson Nursing Home. In her free time, Ora enjoys reading, watching U.K. Wildcat basketball games, swimming, handcrafts and gardening. - *Submitted by Michele Zaparanick*

PURYEAR-HOWELL

Dorothy Howell and William Darriel

Puryear were married in Hopkins County in 1961.

Dorothy was born in Hopkins County in 1942, the daughter of Ida Hibbs and William Harlan Howell. Other children were: Anna Mae, widow of George Wood (who had four daughters); Mary Jane married Shelton (had two sons); and Sarah Katherine married Paul Wayne Polley (has one son and one daughter). Ida's parents were Liza Tucker and Lacy Hibbs. Harlan's parents were Myrtle Staton and Henry Edward Howell.

Dorothy (Howell) and William Darriel Puryear

Dorothy attended school at Hanson, KY, and graduated from high school in 1960. She was employed by the Board of Education for seven years as a Library Aide. She is a housewife, mother and is now employed as a receptionist at Show and Tell Want Ads.

Darriel was born in the Nebo area of Hopkins County in 1942, the son of Georgia Lee Mitchell and Samuel Forrest Puryear. Georgia's parents were Nancy Curneal and Clarence Mitchell. Forrest's parents were Effie Mae Clement and Paul Puryear. Other children of Georgia and Forrest: Wanda Jean married to Joe Lander (has three sons); Forrest L. married to Anna Lou McKnight (have three daughters and one son); and Janice Carol married Bill Cardwell (have three daughters).

Dorothy and Darriel have two children: William Brian, born July 20, 1963, married Jenny Thomas; and Sonya Dee, born Sept. 20, 1966. At this time all are enrolled at Murray State U. - Submitted by Rea Joyner Walker

PURYEAR-THOMAS

Jenny Lyn Thomas and William Brian Puryear were married December 20, 1986, in the First Baptist Church in Madisonville.

Jenny was born Mar. 4, 1966, the only child of Shirley Walker and Joe Thomas (see Thomas-Walker). Jenny attended Madisonville schools, graduating from Madisonville North Hopkins High in 1984. She was a member of various scholarship and social clubs and a member of the Maroons Marching Band for three years. She was chosen Miss Hopkins Co. of 1984. She attended Madisonville Community College, Western Kentucky U. and Murray State U. receiving honors at each school. She is a member of Nebo Christian Church.

Brian was born in Hopkins County in 1963, the son of Dorothy Howell and William Dar-

Jenny Lynn (Thomas) and William Brian Puryear

riel Puryear (see Puryear-Howell). When Brian was six weeks old, his parents moved to San Juan, Puerto Rico, on a work consignment which lasted for two years. The family then returned to Hopkins County to make their home. Brian attended Madisonville schools, graduating from Madisonville North Hopkins High in 1981. He played varsity football and was a member of various social clubs. After high school, he attended Madisonville Community College, receiving an Associate degree in Reclamation Technology. He also attended Western Kentucky U. and Murray State U.

Both Jenny and Brian are employed by Briggs and Stratton. - Submitted by Rea Joyner Walker

WILLIAM EDWARD QUALLS

W.E. or Ed Qualls, born Nov. 8, 1866, was the eldest of fourteen children born to James Gideon Qualls and Mary (Branson) Qualls. Seven of the fourteen survived the pitfalls, and childhood illnesses, to arrive to adulthood. Two brothers; Thomas Qualls, and Lonnie Qualls and two sisters; Clara (Qualls) Nance, and Alice (Qualls) Winstead, were all residents of Hopkins County, and two sisters, Hattie (Qualls) Ashby, and Lilly (Qualls) Campbell, were residents of Cocheese Co., AZ.

William Edward and Lizzie Velva (Crowley) Qualls about 1935

The Qualls family migrated to Hopkins County from Granville Co., NC, and when Edward, who was born in Hopkins County, reached adulthood, he and his brothers traveled to Bisbee AZ, where the big Copper Lode had been discovered. Copper was to be mined, and fortunes to be made.

Five years later, in 1894, with his little nest egg in pocket, Ed returned to Hopkins County, where he bought a 210 acre farm, 1/2 mile south of the intersection of State Roads #'s 254 & 862, just east of Brown Road. He built a house thereon, and married Lizzie Velva Crowley, of Madisonville on Nov. 13, 1894. Of course the road markings and names were not there at that time, but the above are current directions. The farm is still in the family, although divided to the four children or their survivors.

Times were hard, crops were bad. In 1897, Edward and his bride of three years went back to Bisbee again, and while they were out of state, Ed's sister Alice Winstead, and her husband Bee lived in the house that Ed had built, and during that time their son was born, at that house. He was given the name of Bailey Winstead, and this was the man who in 1936, coached the Nebo High School Basketball team to the state runner-up position, and I think should have won state title.

Edward and Lizzie were in Arizona for four years, during which time their first-born son arrived, and they named him James William Jasper Qualls. When Jasper was two years old they came home and returned to the old home place, never to leave again. In 1901, the second blessing came along in the form of a daughter, Delia (Qualls) Brooks, who is the mother of Hopkins County Clerk W.T. 'Bill' Brooks.

In 1908, Ed & Lizzie were blessed with another daughter Audry, who later married David Ashby, and they were blessed with four children; W.R. (William Roger) (deceased), Raymond Wesley, Shirley Ann, and Bobby Lee Ashby.

Another son was born to Ed & Lizzie in 1922, for a total of four children. This son was named Robert Jewel, who later married Marcella Moore, and they together had three children; Bobby, Linda, and Tommy. R.J., Delia & Audry and their descendents are all residents of Hopkins County.

Jasper (deceased) married Thula Bailey, and they had two children Albert G. of Evansville, and Sharon O'Dell, of Battleground, IN.

Ed Qualls was a community leader, worked in the Copper Mines while in Arizona, was a hard-working farmer, who later built two more houses on the farm, and helped establish the old, one room "Ditney" school in the area, where the farm is located, and went on to meet his maker, Mar. 22, 1945. - Submitted by Albert G. Qualls

RAMSEY

John Mansfield Ramsey, Sr. was born in Webster County June 17, 1937. He has lived in Hopkins County several years. He is the son of Agnes and Samuel Ramsey. Agnes Marie Shelton Ramsey was also born in Webster County on May 9, 1914. His father, Samuel

Pratt Ramsey, was born in Providence, KY Jan. 29, 1914. Agnes and Samuel have been living in Charleston, KY nearly 40 years. John has two brothers, William Samuel Ramsey and Earl Patton Ramsey, and one sister, Mary DeLaine Ramsey. William, Earl and Mary DeLaine are all currently living in Hopkins County.

John Ramsey is married to Lana Kay Binkley Ramsey. They have five children. Suzanne Alexis Ramsey Talerico, 25 years of age, is the oldest child. She was born Jan. 11. 1962. Suzanne attended college at Murray State U. She is also a sergeant in the United States Army Reserves. Suzanne is married to Peter Talerico and is the mother to one son, Chase Philip Talerico, born Nov. 18, 1985. She is now living in San Antonio, TX. Jay Dee Vaughn, who is the second oldest, is 20 years old and was born Sept. 15, 1967. He attended the University of Kentucky one year and then decided to join the United States Air Force. He is presently stationed at Clark Air Base in the Philipines. Next in line is Candra Kay Vaughn, a senior at Dawson Springs High School. She was born Aug. 4, 1970. Johnna JoNell Ramsey was born July 29, 1972. She is a 15 year old sophomore at Dawson Springs High School. Finally, John Mansfield Ramsey, Jr. is a 7th grader at Dawson Springs High School and was born Feb. 13, 1975.

John Ramsey, Sr. enjoys playing golf and riding trail bikes. From 1st to 7th grade (1943-1950), he went to school in Clay, Ky. During his 7th grade year, he moved to Charleston, KY and attended Charleston High School, where he graduated in 1955. He made the boy's varsity basketball team for four year. After he graduated, he went to Bethel College in Hopkinsville for two years and then to Murray State University another two years. John was also in the Army Reserves at this time and was on active duty for one year after he attended Murray State. In 1960, he taught 7th grade at Webster County Middle School. During September of 1962, John worked at Outwood Hospital for two months. In November of 1962, he started working for Kentucky Utilites Company in Earlington, KY. He spent five years in a line crew advancing to first class lineman. The next five years, he worked as a Commercial Service Advisor. He was transferred to Marion, KY and promoted to local manager of the Marion office. John was promoted to district manager at Dawson Springs in 1981, where he is currently employed. - Submitted by Candy Vaughn

RAMSEY-BROWN

Martha Narcissus "Matt" Brown (Apr. 28, 1871 to Jan. 24, 1927), married John Will Ramsey (Jan. 18, 1864 to Oct. 19, 1948), of the Government Section of Hopkins County near Dalton, KY. They were blessed with three children.

1. Carl Raymond Ramsey m. Marietta Milligan and they made their home in Lexington, KY. Children: Carl (no children); Martha Jane - three sons and one daughter; Halliene - three sons and one daughter.

2. Geoffrey, was burdened with a heart condition and never married.

The John Will Ramsey home in the government section of Hopkins County about 1905. Standing l to r: John Will, Ruth, Raymond and Martha (Aunt "Matt").

3. Ruth Gilliam Ramsey was born Nov. 15, 1902. She married Wash Ray Logan on Apr. 6, 1922. Ray was born Mar. 19, 1900, and died Sept. 15, 1951. They had one daughter, Dema Sue Logan, born Sept. 29, 1923, and made their home in Madisonville. On Nov. 6, 1944, Sue married Gordon Brown, who was born on June 7, 1920. They had one daughter, Martha Lee Brown, born Mar. 7, 1947, and made their home in Madisonville.

Martha married Paul Dean Hartwig (born Mar. 10, 1946), and lives in St. Louis, MO, with their two children; Benjamin Logan Hartwig (born Jan. 26, 1976), and Lesley Deneen Hartwig (born Sept. 21, 1981).

Ruth Gilliam Ramsey Logan remarried after Ray's death. She married Clint Ashby (Sept. 6, 1892 to Sept. 15, 1978), of Hanson, KY, on Oct. 10, 1967. They had no children and lived in Hanson.

Ruth is now residing in Kentucky Rest Haven in Madisonville, KY. She is 87 years old and enjoys company very much. (See Jones-Ramsey) - Submitted by Peggy Sullivan Waide

RAMSEY-DEVER

The first child of John Gilliam "Doc" and Louiza Gore Ramsey was a son, James Samuel, born Mar. 10, 1861.

The sectional debates and the fierce rumblings, which would become the Civil War, could already be heard, but Illinois was a northern state. Not everyone was directly involved, as was generally the situation below the Mason-Dixon line.

This little family would blossom to 12 children. James Samuel's clan would become the largest. When still young, he helped around the farm and assisted in raising the ever-growing family.

While still a boy, they left Illinois, and moved to Western Kentucky. They crossed the Ohio in a caulked, covered wagon.

"Doc" farmed, and with his father, Samuel Pratt Ramsey I, he made furniture. They also ran a sawmill, where James Samuel would work 39 years.

My grandfather, Ernest Delmar Ramsey, was a brother to James Samuel and the youngest of the 12 children. Uncle Sam was the eldest. I never met him. He passed on Apr. 26, 1926. I would not be—until Dec. 11, 1936.

I saw Aunt Emma on occasions. There were many Ramsey relatives. I didn't know them all, but I always enjoyed being with the older ones. They taught me, by relating their memories.

I remember Aunt Emma in longer than average dresses. Her granddaughter, Mary DeLaine Ramsey, has been invaluable to my research on this limb of the family tree. Her mother, Agnes, had kept the dates in a ledger and DeLaine sat and talked with her grandmother for hours, as a child.

The girl next door to the Ramseys was Mary Emma Dever (Oct. 30, 1880 to Oct. 26, 1974). Their father's farms met with a country lane between them.

Emma and Annie Ramsey were best friends and the same age, 19 years younger than Uncle Sam. Age wasn't important. They fell in love and planned their wedding day. Uncle Sam had a diamond ring he had let his sister "Sally" wear. He asked Aunt Emma if she would like that one or a new one. She chose the new one. He got a ring of solid gold, the ring was engraved SOLID GOLD, on the inside. She wore it always, even when it had worn down to a very thin piece.

They drove a buggy into Princeton to be married, on June 10, 1901.

They ran a small grocery store about a mile south of the home place. They also lived in Providence, ran a store, and built a house there.

Aunt Emma loved animals of every variety. She also pieced lovely quilt tops which are remembered to this day. She was to be loved, deeply, by her children and grandchildren.

Uncle Sam was not to have a lot of years with Aunt Emma. He passed on, Apr. 26, 1926, nearly 50 years ahead of her.

They had three sons: Felix Gilliam (Mar. 7, 1902 to Dec. 24, 1961); Henry Gordon (Apr. 23, 1907 to Apr. 23, 1985); and Samuel Pratt Ramsey II (born Jan. 29, 1914).

Felix married Stella Glendola Jones. Gordon married twice. First marriage was to Lillian Marie Johnson and the second to Goldie Mae Lynn. Samuel Pratt II married Agnes Marie Shelton.

I will divide this branch into three segments, due to size. (See Felix Gilliam Ramsey; Henry Gordon Ramsey; Samuel Pratt Ramsey).- Submitted by Peggy Sullivan Waide

RAMSEY-GARDNER

I'm sure if the entire family was assembled, I could come up with much more information concerning Aunt "Lizzie" and Uncle Joe Ramsey.

I remember them fairly well, as we attended many family reunions and I can also recall going to their home on Willow Street in Providence. Past these occurrences, I am very limited.

Uncle Joe was a great jokester. As a child, I did not always know how to take him. As an adult, I can see the paths they traveled and understand more clearly. Most clowns cover a multitude of tears behind that facadial mask.

Uncle Joe was a fine-looking young man. He was tall and straight of stature. Elizabeth O. Gardner lived in Crittenden County and was the daughter of John and Minnie Mae Gardner. She and Joe fell in love. They were married and had two children.

I had always thought they were twin sons. I was mistaken. The first was still born in 1906. The other, Frank Taylor Ramsey, died in infancy (1909-1910).

Uncle Joe was a farmer and owned a small coal mine. Aunt "Lizzie" was a housewife. They were Methodists by denomination.

Uncle Joe was born Feb. 27, 1876, and passed on Oct. 2, 1956. I have only Aunt "Lizzie's" year of birth, 1881. She died Dec. 12, 1966. They leave no direct heirs.

The family probably never knew the depth of their inner pain-albeit only a speculation on my part.

They are all buried in Traylor Cemetery in the Government Section of the Dalton area of Hopkins County. (See Minnie Edna Ramsey) - *Submitted by Peggy Sullivan Waide*

RAMSEY-JONES

Charles Crawford was the name chosen for J.G. Ramsey's fourth child. It was June 26, 1866. This son just missed the Civil War but would live through the Spanish-American, WWI, WWII, and Korean Conflict, sending sons to each of the world wars.

He was my grandfather's (Ernest Delmar Ramsey) brother. Uncle Charlie was fascinating. He could weave yarns, family tales — history, if you will. I knew him and loved him. He repaired sewing machines and guns. His services were sought far and near because he did excellent work.

Uncle Charlie married 3 times — nearly four. After WWII, my family went to Kansas. Uncle Charlie went too. His family never knew his purpose for the trip. I didn't know his destination but he was in high, good humor on the way. He was an accomplished whistler and he whistled from Kentucky on. We left him where he caught his bus. He had a hurried trip. He had known the lady in earlier years. Whatever they planned failed to materialize as expected. He nearly beat us home on another bus.

Left - Val Bernard Ramsey (1893-1964) only son of Charles Crawford Ramsey and Necie Mae Jones. Val served in the U.S. Army during W.W. I. Right- Elliot Walton Ramsey (1911-1986) only son of Charles Crawford Ramsey and Claudia Fortney Woodburn. Elliot served in the U.S. Navy during W.W. II. Both sons returned home

He buried three wives, lost children and grandchildren, but alway looked ahead-never back. Charles Crawford had fierce loyalty and a temper to match. He lived in Central City, KY most of his life.

Charles Crawford Ramsey (6-26-1866 to 8-6-1957) married first Necie Mae Jones. They were the parents of Val Bernard Ramsey (11-7-1893 to 4-6-1964). Val Bernard married Agatha Irene "Lady" Treece (3-3-1896 to 7-26-1968) of Central City and they were the parents of seven children (including twin sons), one girl and six boys. Only one survived, Necia Mae, who was named for her grandmother, albeit the spelling is different.

Necia Mae (10-8-1923) married Louis Freeland Frazier (11-20-1922) and they were the parents of: Louis Freeland II (1-29-1944), married Linda Loraine Kendall in Hugo, OK 6-23-1967 and they are the parents of Stuart Freeland (5-21-1974) and Lindsey Nicole (1-28-1978); Necia Anne (11-11-1947) married Herbert Daniel Averitt 6-14-1969; Joseph Daniel (8-1-1950) married Barbara Jane Boggess 5-4-1973 and they are the parents of Eric Daniel (2-7-1983); Tammi Sue (10-26-1959) married Michial Ray English 4-12-1986 and they have a son, Michial Louis Ray English (8-4-1987); a child still born; and Kimberley Jo (6-16-1961) married Jimmie Lee Wilbourn 4-18-1981, divorced 3-21-1983, and they have a son, James Louis Wilbourn (8-27-1981).

Charles Crawford Ramsey married second Cornelia Wyatt and they were the parents of twin girls who were stillborn.

He then married third Claudia Fortney Woodburn and they had a son, Elliott Walton Ramsey (9-30-1911 to 10-28-1987), who married Annie Elizabeth Lovell (? to 9-1-1973) in Central City on 9-26-1936. Their children are Elizabeth Ann and Nancy Sue. Elizabeth Ann (around 1941) married Thomas Carroll 8-25-1962. Their children are: Elizabeth Michele (4-1-1966) who married in 1986; John David (7-14-1967); and Andrew Michael (6-20-1973). Nancy Sue (1-17-1943) married Lewis Edward Chaney (10-21-1940) on 7-7-1957 and they are the parents of: Lewis Edward Jr. (3-25-1958) married Judy Mayes 10-18-1975 and they have a son, Michael Elliott (2-27-1976); Sherrie Lorene (1-17-1960) married Steve Stirsman (he had twin daughters, Jennifer and Amanda Stirsman); Cathy Sue (6-24-1961) married John Mallory and they are the parents of Sarah Elizabeth; John Steven (6-24-1965) is single; and Mary Elizabeth (8-20-1977). (See Henry Sanford Ramsey) -*Submitted by Peggy Sullivan Waide*

RAMSEY-LANGLEY

Franklin David Ramsey (1852-1914) on Dec. 20, 1882, married Jane H. Langley (1863-1951).

Frank descended from Dr. John Ramsey, who emigrated from Aberdeen Scotland in the 1740's. Frank's lineage includes Karr, Brown, and Hutchinson. Jane's lineage includes Cox, Winstead, Tapp, Sargent, Weir, Ballard, Clopton and Jarratt.

They had three children: Marie Langley (1884-1972); James Karr, II (1891-1958); and David Franklin (1896-1957). They had eight grandchildren, 28 great-grandchildren and 12 great-great grandchildren. Total issue 51, of whom 45 are living and scattered over ten states.

Frank was raised on a farm near Nebo. As a young man he entered the tobacco business

The Ramsey's. Front row l to r: Franklin D., David F. and Jane L. Back row l to r: Marie L. and James K.

with his brother-in-law, Minos R. Cotton. The firm of Cotton and Ramsey prospered and moved to Madisonville in the 1880's. Frank D. was an original shareholder in the Hopkins County Bank (chartered Apr. 7, 1890), and was for many years a director. The Hopkins County bank was located at 33 West Center until July 1910, when it moved into the Morton Bank Bldg. at 5 N. Main St. He was also active in the coal business in Webster County, where he and W.A. Nisbet founded the Providence Coal Mining Company.

After their marriage, Jane and Frank lived in Nebo for several years, and Marie was born there. In the late 1880's, they moved to Madisonville and lived on the northwest corner of Main and Noel in a frame house that presently stands at 34 West Noel Ave. Karr was born in this house. They then moved to a three-story brick house on the southeast corner of Main and Noel, and David was born there. Jane sold this house and lot in 1948, to the First Baptist Church which stands there now.

Marie L. Ramsey (1884-1972), married Stuart Raper Crockett (1879-1948), a Presbyterian minister on Sept. 7, 1907, and had four children: Howe T. (1908); Nancy J. (1909), Frank R. (1913-1922); and John S.R. (1926). Three of these children married and had issue as follows:

1. Howe T. Crockett II m. Ruth Summerow, and they had three children: George Stuart, Nancy Ruth (who had one daughter, Laura R. Phillips); and Howe T. III.

2. Nancy J. Crockett m. Hansford Mims, and they had three children: Julian L. III (who had Stuart Crockett, Julian L. IV, and Florende A.); Matthew H. Jr. (who had Clark and Nancy Gwynne); and Marie C.M. Meyer.

3. John S.R. Crockett m. Shirley J. Hobson, and they had four children: Nancy Elizabeth, Susan Marie, Carolyn Kent, and Cynthia Ruth.

James Karr Ramsey, II (1891-1958), married Frank E. Waller (1892-1939), on Aug. 17, 1917. Karr played football at Centre College and was all-Southern for three years, graduating in 1912. He served in W.W. I as an officer in the 369th Infantry Regiment, and later commanded the local National Guard, Hqs. Co., 3rd Bn., 149th Infantry Regiment. Late in 1940, he organized Hqs. Btry., 106th Bn. C.A.C., which went on active duty at Camp Hulin, Texas. He was given a medical discharge in 1941 because of hypertension. Karr was a Director of The Hopkins County Bank and The Providence Coal Mining Co. and was very active in coaching high school sports. He owned and managed the Shamrock Dairy Farm where he installed the first electric milking machines in Hopkins County in 1926.

"Miss" Frank graduated with honors from Georgetown College in 1914, and was active in local civic, church and club work throughout her life. She is best remembered as a high school English teacher from 1914 to 1939. They had three children; James K. III (1919), Jane Waller (1923) and Frank D. (1926), who had issue as follows:

1. James Karr III m. Marie J. Eba, and they had five children: James McD. (who had James William, Kathryn, and Rachel); Nancy J. (who had Elizabeth Ann Hasenmueller); Ella Lou; Suzanne K. Fello; and Clara Mae.

2. Jane Waller m. Davis S. Morgan and they had four children: D. Shannon; Frank R., Jane Leith (who had Helen Perez); and Martha Floy.

3. Frank D. m. Josephine Creekmur, and they had five children: Patricia (b & d 1953); Robin; Steven; Terrence (dec.); and Jane.

David Franklin attended V.M.I., served with the mobilized Home Guard on the Mexican Border, was an officer on the Tank Corps in W.W. I and was later active in the local National Guard, Hqs. Co., 3rd Bn., 149th Infantry Regt. David owned and managed the Star Buick Co. for many years. This Dealership was located at 31 N. Main St., the present locale of the downtown Dollar General store. He was active in civic affairs including the Masonic Order and the Shrine.

David married M. Julia Holloman on Mar. 6, 1923. Julia is the daughter of Ashley and Mary Williams Holloman and a granddaughter of Chesley S. Williams. They had one child, Mary Jane (1924), who married Harold Gordon Mullins on Feb. 22, 1947. They have four children; Jane Gordon (1947), Julia Lee (1950), Joe David (1961) and Janet (1964) and one grandson, Donald Blair Lowe IV. (See also Ashby, Waller) - *Submitted by James K. Ramsey, III*

RAMSEY-RASH

George Washington Ramsey and Mattie Rash were married in 1876. They were from Madisonville, KY. George was born in 1849 to James K. Ramsey and (?) Elmira. He was a tobacco farmer, lawyer, and tobacco exporter. He died in Louisville, KY, in 1928, and was buried in Cave Hill Cemetery there.

George's brothers and sisters were: Margaret, James, Nancy, Frank, and Lenard.

Mattie Rash Ramsey was born in 1858, in Madisonville, KY. Her parents were Stephen D. Rash (born 1816) and Eliza J. Wilson Rash of Madisonville. Mattie died in 1886 and was buried in Grapevine Cemetery, Madisonville.

George and Mattie had three children. Only one lived past infancy. He was Roy Rash Ramsey. He was born in 1880, in Madisonville. After his mother died, he and his father George moved to Louisville. There Roy met and married Dollie Piland of Monroe County.

Roy's infant sister and brother were Addie Desolee, born 1877-died 1878 and Lucien E., born 1883-died 1884. They are buried in Grapevine Cemetery.

Roy Rash Ramsey was a graduate of the U. of Kentucky (1899), in Lexington, KY, The School of Osteopathy in Franklin, KY, and The Louisville School of Pharmacy. He died of a heart attack in 1928, at the age of 47, and was buried in Cave Hill Cemetery.

Roy and Dollie Piland Ramsey had two children: Desolee Louise Ramsey, born 1915, and Roy Rash Ramsey, Jr., born 1925. - *Submitted by Louise R. Johnson*

RAMSEY-RINGO

Opal Vivian Ringo (May 25, 1895 to May 4, 1967), and Ernest Delmar Ramsey (Nov. 5, 1883 to June 7, 1976), were united in marriage on Apr. 29, 1913, in Springfield, TN. She was the daughter of Benjamin Franklin Ringo (1865-1962) and Florence Dye Ringo (1872-1905). He was the youngest child and the seventh son of John Gilliam "Doc" Ramsey and Louiza Gore Ramsey of the Government Section, in the far western tip of Hopkins County. They were my grandparents, my beloved, "Big Mama" and "Daddy Paw".

Opal and Ernest Ramsey at their home in Madisonville in the early 1940's.

Opal was a housewife and mother. Ernest, early on, was in the automobile business. He and Judge Joseph Hewitt, of Madisonville, owned the Oldsmobile - Cadillac - LaSalle Dealership.

During the depression years he was with the Metropolitan Insurance Company. He later operated a cheese factory where Ruby Concrete Company stands today. In the late 1930's, he started a trucking firm. At first hauling coal, then into trailer trucks, which carried the local tobacco sales to their destination, among other loads.

Upon retirement, he sold his company to Arnold Ligon, who built it into a nationally-recognized firm. He retired in 1953, and was a Kentucky Colonel. They had one child, Anna Margaret, born in Webster County, July 3, 1915. She married Eugene Sullivan (born May 24, 1914), of Marion, KY, on Aug. 3, 1935, in Shawneetown, IL. He was the son of Gideon and Percy Jennings Sullivan of Livingston County.

Eugene and Margaret met while he was attending college in Bowling Green, KY. He acquired the nickname of "Jobie" from his team-mates on the 1934 Western football team. He was an only child, but had one half-sister, Vera Pauline Sullivan and two half-brothers, Ray and Estle Sullivan.

Margaret and Jobie had one daughter, born Dec. 11, 1936. (The same night Edward the Eighth of England abdicated his throne.) She was named Peggy Ann, her mothers name in reverse. They lost one son, being stillborn in the summer of 1941. His name was Raymond.

The Sullivans and Ramseys lived together in those depression and war years, in Madisonville. In 1954, the Sullivans moved to the "Old Ramsey Homestead", where they lived twelve years.

In the fifties, Margaret worked five years at the old Coca Cola Bottling Company. "Jobie" was employed by S.J. Campbell & Company parachute factory during the war years. After the allied victory, the company made Pilgrim Brand shirts for Sears, Roebuck and Company.

In July of 1949, he was hired by West Kentucky Coal Company, from which he retired in July of 1977, after having worked at every mine they owned. He started as timekeeper at Old North Diamond and retired from Fies #11, under the Island Creek banner.

Peggy graduated from Madisonville High School in 1955. She attended Western Kentucky State Teachers College in Bowling Green. She worked two and a half years at Trover Clinic before retiring to be married in October of 1958.

All of the family were members of the First Methodist Church in Madisonville. Margaret and "Jobie" are now members of the Marion, KY Methodist Church. Peggy belongs to St. Mary's Episcopal in Madisonville.

"Jobie" is a Kentucky Colonel and enjoys golf with his old friends at Marion Country Club and various ball games. Margaret enjoys traveling, her family and going to auctions. She is also a Kentucky Colonel.

The Ramseys have passed on. The Sullivans live in retirement, in Marion. Peggy married Harry Doyle Waide of Providence Oct. 18, 1958. (See Sullivan-Ramsey). - *Submitted by Peggy Sullivan Waide*

RAMSEY-STEVENS-GORE

Knowledge of my mother's paternal ancestors is great, yet limited to names and dates, mostly. I will chronicle various families within the family, but without much insight past their names. Please note after each segment, I will list the next section in order of the 12 children (birthdays) of J.G. and Louiza Ramsey.

My great-great-grandfather was Samuel Pratt Ramsey I. He was married to Elizabeth Stevens (born 1806, we think in Virginia—died Sept. 10, 1895, in Hopkins County and is buried in Traylor Cemetery in Western Hopkins County). It is my understanding they came from Virginia or West Virginia. (He was buried in Caldwell Co. in a small cemetery.)

Their son, John Gilliam "Doc" Ramsey (Oct. 18, 1839 to Apr. 27, 1926), is my great grandfather. He married Louiza Elvina Gore on Dec. 21, 1859, at the home of her parents, James and Rejoina Traylor Gore, Sr. (Louiza had a brother James Gore, Jr., Aug. 23, 1838 to July 29, 1925), and a sister, Nancy Williams Gore (born Dec. 11, 1843-?). They were married by Thomas Young, D.D.

James Gore, Sr. was born Dec. 25, 1786 (or 1788), in Virginia. He was a farmer and mar-

The John Gilliam and Louiza Ramsey family in front of the "Old Ramsey Homestead" circa 1890's. One child, Mary Alice died in infancy. Standing from left to right: Helen Elizabeth, Ernest Delmar, Sarah "Sally"Isabel, Joseph Taylor, John Will, Robert Winfield, Minnie Edna, James Samuel and Annie Victoria. Seated l to r: Henry Sanford, John Gilliam "Doc", Louiza Elvina and Charles Crawford.

ried twice. He had seven children by his first wife, Elizabeth, who died Apr. 15, 1836, leaving him with seven children. Uncle Albert Gore's family Bible stated, Grandfather James Gore, Sr. was born in 1786 (but I mention 1788 as it was on some old papers). It is entirely possible that Louiza Elvina's name is really Elizabeth as it is recorded in some family records. James Gore, Sr. is recorded as dead on or about July 20, 1847. Another discrepancy is that Rejoina Gore is also spelled Regina, all according to which document, I presume.

Rejoina (I will use this spelling, the reader is invited to speculate) and James Sr. had three children, previously mentioned. Rejoina was born in Charleston, SC, in 1798 and moved to Kentucky when she was 12. There might also be cause to speculate, as Nancy Williams Gore does not seem to be listed elsewhere. However, a child named Mary is stated to have married John B. Fox, of Kentucky. They spent their lifetime in Illinois, presumably.

James Gore, Jr. was married Dec. 14, 1859, to Martha, daughter of John and Cynthia Leech. (Martha's birthdate Dec. 10, 1838).

James, Jr. sent his family and his mother Rejoina, to Illinois during the Civil War, while he served in "Co. I, 17th Kentucky Cavalry", from which he was honorably discharged in October 1865.

Rejoina lived about 30 years longer than her husband. She made her home with James, Jr. and Martha's family. While visiting her daughter, Elizabeth, wife of John G. Ramsey, in Kentucky, she died quite unexpectedly. (This record of Elizabeth's name instead of Louiza was copied from Uncle Albert Gore's old account book).

There are many Gores in Illinois today. Other names interspersed in the family are: Crowder, Travis, Drennan, Mathis, Wilbern, Houston, Barnes, Mace, Barton and Wise.

Continuing the Ramseys, J.G. Ramsey (Oct. 18, 1839 to Apr. 27, 1926), and Louiza Gore Ramsey (Feb. 8, 1841 to Oct. 10, 1913), moved to Kentucky from Elizabethtown, IL, possibly in the 1870's. They caulked a covered wagon and floated it across the Ohio River as the old family tales relate.

Their five daughters and seven sons are chronicled below.

James Samuel Ramsey, b. Mar. 10, 1861 died Apr. 26, 1926; Mary Alice Ramsey, b. Oct. 30, 1862 died Nov. 20, 1862; John Will Ramsey, b. Jan. 18, 1864 died Oct. 19, 1948; Charles Crawford Ramsey, b. June 26, 1866 died Aug. 6, 1957; Henry Sanford Ramsey, b. Mar. 13, 1868 died May 15, 1939; Helen Elizabeth Ramsey, b. July 23, 1870 died Sept. 4, 1940; Robert Winfield Ramsey, b. Mr. 19, 1872 died Feb. 24, 1931; Sarah "Sally" Isabel Ramsey, b. Mar. 24, 1874 died Nov. 24, 1958; Joseph Taylor Ramsey, b. Feb. 27, 1876 died Oct. 2, 1956; Minnie Edna Ramsey, b. Dec. 20, 1877 died Apr. 8, 1951; Annie Victoria Ramsey, b. Oct. 15, 1879 died Aug. 16, 1971; Ernest Delmar Ramsey, b. Nov. 5, 1883 died June 7, 1976.

The Ramseys also raised at least two more young people who just showed up at their house. They also educated them, far beyond what was expected in that day and time. One young man stayed until he was about 40. (See Ramsey-Dever). - *Submitted by Peggy Sullivan Waide*

FELIX GILLIAM RAMSEY

In continuing the Dever-Ramsey segment of Stevens-Ramsey-Gore, I am chronicling each son of Emma and James Samuel Ramsey, separately.

The oldest son was Felix Gilliam Ramsey born Mar. 7, 1902. Felix married Stella Glendola Jones (Aug. 24, 1907), on Feb. 2, 1929, at Judge Hall's home in Dixon, KY.

Felix was a miner and worked 41 years at Dawson Daylight mine near Charleston.

They made their home there and raised a family. The Ramseys were well known for teaching. Albeit, only Mary Rachel is still teaching at Charleston. Glendola related that she has had a child going to Charleston school for 50 years, either as a student or teacher, and that's a hard record to beat. In 1987, there were three generations of the family starting at Charleston. (A niece, DeLaine Ramsey, also teaches there).

Felix was to enjoy 42 years of family life before passing on, Dec. 24, 1961. He is buried in Odd Fellows Cemetery in Clay.

Glendola remained single and continued to keep their home in Charleston. Mary Rachel lives at home and Martha Lou next door.

Felix and Glendola's four children and heirs are:

A. James Gilliam (Nov. 22, 1930), married Ellen Joyce Buchanan (Aug. 5, 1934), in Sullivan, KY, on Aug. 1, 1953, at the Baptist Church. He started teaching school at 18 years of age, teaching two years at Anton, one at Munns, one at Menser and 29 years at Charleston. He retired in 1987, after 33 years in the profession. Joyce was and is a housewife, companion and the mother of their three children. 1a. James Duane (Dec. 10, 1955), married Rosetta Menser Jenkins, (Jan. 9, 1953), at the First Baptist Church in Dawson Springs, Dec. 20, 1979. Their children are: I. Kelly Renee' (May 14, 1981 to June 9, 1981); II. Rebecca Diane (Nov. 9, 1982); III. Jennifer Kay (June 7, 1984). James Duane is employed by the State of Kentucky and they live in Frankfort. 1b. Charles Anthony Ramsey (Aug. 20, 1957), married Lorrie Ann McAbee (July 11, 1957) at First Baptist Church in Dawson Springs, June 30, 1978. Their children are: I. Alysia Nichole (Apr. 28, 1979); II. Shauna Danielle (Dec. 2, 1981). Charles works for Island Creek Coal Company. They live on Mockingbird Lane, in Madisonville. 1c. Lewis Gilliam (July 29, 1964), married Sherry Foust (Mar. 10, 1962), at Walnut Grove New Covenant Church in Dawson Springs, Oct. 5, 1985. Lewis is employed by U.C. Milk Company in Madisonville. They live in Clay. No children.

B. Martha Lou (May 23, 1934), married George Mitchell (June 29, 1927), at the Presbyterian Church in Frankfort, KY, Sept. 24, 1955. They were later divorced. Their children are: 1a. Ann Kaye (Sept. 20, 1958 to Sept. 30, 1964). 1b. Mary Cordelia (Apr. 23, 1962), is single. 1c. Jonell (Apr. 13, 1965), married Donald "Beau" Raynor (Jan. 9, 1961), at Charleston Baptist Church, in 1985. They live in Clay. No children. Martha works for Russell Builders in Clay.

C. Mary Rachel (Mar. 14, 1932), is a school teacher. She started teaching at 19 and has taught at Charleston 37 years.

D. LaMona Ann (Aug. 12, 1936), married Gerald "Pedro" Russell (Aug. 26, 1936), at Charleston Baptist Church, June 19, 1955. They have Russell Builders in Clay and live there. Their children are: I. Rodney Gerald (Apr. 12, 1956), married Gina Cherry in 1986. She has two children by a previous marriage, Michael and Christopher Cherry. II. Lou Ann (Apr. 12, 1962), married Charles Ayres (Apr. 26, 1961), on Mar. 15, 1986. No children. (See Henry Gordon Ramsey) - *Submitted by Peggy Sullivan Waide*

HENRY GORDON RAMSEY

Henry Gordon Ramsey was the second son of Emma Devera and James Samuel Ramsey. He was born Apr. 23, 1907. I know so very little about Gordon, personally. I met him on various family occasions. I knew he was my mother's first cousin. In the Ramsey family, there is a multitude of cousins. I am indebted to his daughter, Sue, and various other family members for this information.

Gordon was a coal miner at Dawson Daylight Company, near Charleston. He married Marie Johnson on June 26, 1930 at Shawneetown, IL. They made their home in Charleston. On Apr. 1, 1933, they welcomed a baby daughter, Betty Sue, into the family. Lillian did not live to see Sue grown. She passed away in May of 1935. (I do not know her date of birth).

Uncle Sam had passed in 1926, so Aunt Emma helped Gordon, her middle son, during a trying time in all their lives. She stepped in and raised her granddaughter, Sue.

Many years later, Gordon married Goldie Mae Lynn (5-6-1922 to 12-9-1984) in Springfield, TN, July 4, 1958. He was to outlive her by five months. Gordon died April 23 (his birthday), 1985.

Gordon and Marie's daughter, Betty Sue, married Ezra McDowell, Jr. (6-26-1930) at the Leitchfield Methodist Church on Dec. 20, 1954 in Leitchfield, KY. They were married by the minister of the church. Ezra was the son of Myrtle and Ezra McDowell Sr. of Providence. He had one sister, Glendal Ovella McDowell.

A group of Ramsey heirs at the 50th wedding anniversary gathering at Dawson Springs, KY. Community Center July 18, 1986. Back row l to r: "Jobie" Sullivan, Sharon and Terry Ramsey, Ezra and Sue McDowell, Mary Ramsey, Frank and Pauline Larkin, LaMona Russell, Sue Logan Brown, and Martha Mitchell. Front row l to r: James G. Ramsey, Anna Margaret Sullivan, Glendola Ramsey, Samuel Ramsey II, Agnes Ramsey, Lou Gore Sigler Myers, Marion Joyce Davis and Joyce Ramsey.

Ezra and Sue had two sons and one daughter: Kent Allen (12-3-1962 to 11-23-1977); Ronald Keith (11-29-1956) who married Barbara Gene Mitchell in his sister, Theresa's, home in Providence in 1977 and they have Trent Allen (12-8-1977) and Cathie Lee (10-27-1982); and Theresa Darlene (2-27-1955) married Ricky Wayne Phillips (2-1-1955) at Victory Baptist Church in Providence on Aug. 25, 1974 and they are the parents of Heather Darlene Phillips (3-3-1978) and Heath Wayne Phillips (11-17-1980).

The children of Henry Gordon Ramsey and Goldie Mae Lynn are: Terry Wayne Ramsey (10-23-1959) who is single and Sharon Leigh Ramsey (6-21-1961) who married Larry Skaggs and is divorced with no children.

All the children live around Providence or Charleston. I do not know most of them. In these segments I have written on various parts of my family, I have felt a yearning to get the entire family together —so we might, at least, meet those who we, or time, have not allowed a chance encounter.

The old family reunions were fun when I was small. There was one a few summers ago, which I was unable to attend. I missed the last opportunity I would have to be with Elliot Ramsey, Uncle Charlie's son.

Time passes quickly and the important moments are lost. Let us hope—not all.

(See Samuel Pratt Ramsey,)-*Submitted by Peggy Sullivan Wade*

HENRY SANFORD RAMSEY

Fifth-in-line on the family tree of John Gilliam and Louise Gore Ramsey was a son, Henry Sanford Ramsey, born Mar. 13, 1868.

Uncle Henry never married and worked with his father and brothers on the family farm and in the family operated sawmill business. Some of the Ramsey men also made furniture, which would be classified by an antique dealer today as primitive antiques. There are very few pieces left that they made. When stores started to stock furniture on a regular basis, many a piece of homemade furniture found its way to the kindling pile. It never mattered if

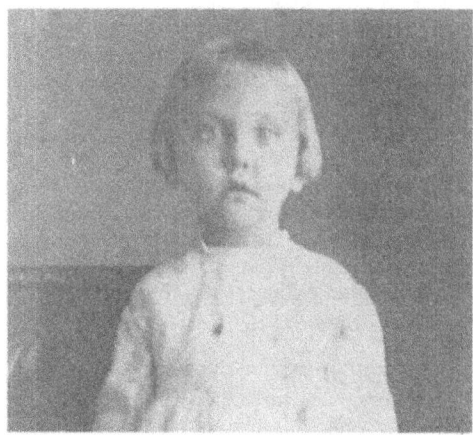

Anna Margaret Ramsey (Sullivan) at about three years of age, the daughter of Opal Vivian and Ernest Delmar Ramsey (brother of Henry Sanford Ramsey). Anna Margaret was Uncle Henry's favorite barber.

the wood was walnut, oak, cherry or whatever, much to our sorrow.

My mother, Margaret Ramsey Sullivan, loved to visit the homestead. Uncle Henry was one of the reasons why. They had a great relationship. He let her sucker tobacco and ride the horse. He was even known to allow her to shave him.

I can barely remember one encounter with Uncle Henry. He was visiting us in Madisonville. I was about three years old. I have no idea why I was crying so hard but Uncle Henry wouldn't let anyone reprimand me. Said Uncle Henry upon arriving home, "she was the best-behaved baby I've ever seen." Thanks, Uncle Henry!

He passed away May 15, 1939. (See Armstrong-Ramsey) *Submitted by Peggy Sullivan Waide*

MARY ALICE RAMSEY

Little Mary Alice Ramsey was born Oct. 30, 1862, and was the oldest daughter of John William "Doc" and Louiza Gore Ramsey of the Government Section of Hopkins County. She was to live only twenty days when she died on Nov. 20, 1862.

She would always be remembered as "Little Alice." She is buried in Traylor Cemetery in the Government Section of Hopkins Co., off Highway 293. (See Ramsey-Brown) - *Submitted by Peggy Sullivan Waide*

MINNIE EDNA RAMSEY

Dear Aunt Minnie, how do I write about a dear one, such as you? By explaining how welcome you always made a little girl feel when she stayed away from home? By relating your interest and taking time to explain the hows and whys of living on the old home place—from country bacon and cow's milk to lye soap. Never could I profile Minnie Edna Ramsey, without reliving many happy times spent in her company.

Aunt Minnie (born Dec. 20, 1877), never married. She stayed on at the home place and in a sense, picked up and carried on as Grandma would have done.

She was 36 when her mother died and grandpa outlived his wife 13 years. Minnie Edna was not the only one at home. Uncle Bob, Uncle Charlie, Uncle Henry, Uncle John Will and Aunt Annie would come and go, but Aunt Minnie was always there. This was a real family community, and somehow, Aunt Minnie was the thread which continued to keep it woven together.

She like to listen to the battery-powered radio of Uncle John Will's. I couldn't understand turning it off as soon as the show was over. Electricity hadn't made it to the Government Section yet.

Clothes were washed in iron kettles in the backyard with a big fire to keep the water hot. Many a morning's wash was done with heavy coats on and scarfs wrapped over nose and mouth, so as not to catch their death of cold.

These same kettles were used when making lye soap. I know it worked, but I still do not understand the art of making soap from grease.

The word that suffices, is discipline. One kept on keeping on. Life was rather narrow in most cases. People were buried pretty close to where they died, transportation being limited. Deep and abiding love, being there for each other, taking responsibility for the others. It worked, it was a good recipe—it works today, if applied.

Aunt Minnie was a diabetic and had other ailments. As she got older, she was really not able to manage but she always kept trying. Aunt Annie was living there with her and Uncle John Will until he passed away in 1948. They pulled together.

Her health steadily declined and on Sunday, Apr. 8, 1951, I was with her in Cardwell Clinic (hospital) in Providence. My family insisted I leave when part of the family was driving to Madisonville. I knew I'd never be with her again. She passed on two hours later.

There is nothing in the world any sadder than a down-home country funeral, in a church, where the coal stove was kindled 30 minutes before the service and all the furniture is still bone-chillingly cold.

All the same, funerals are really for the

living, and so was Aunt Minnie's. Services allow the living to do "something" for the departed ones. Whatever they believe they should—in their hearts.

When the piano starts the service (always out of tune), and the neighborhood assembled choir sings, "Beyond The Sunset", each one becomes an intregal part of the passing.

Thus it was at Aunt Minnie's service in the old Mount Olivet Methodist Church her father had built many years before. Aunt Minnie had fought the good fight and was laid to rest in Traylor Cemetery just a couple of hills over from the church. I was a flower girl—that was my thing to do.

I still have a rose from that day tucked in my old Bible—and I still love you, Aunt Minnie. (See Joyce-Ramsey) *Submitted by Peggy Sullivan Waide*

PAPPY RAMSEY

James Karr Ramsey II, born July 16, 1891, had several "nicknames" but is probably most affectionately remembered as Pappy, but more about that later. How can you do justice to the life of a man with such a broad range of interests and activities? College, football, history, husband and father, coaching, military and National Guard, business and agriculture.

James Karr (Pappy) Ramsey II

His parents were Franklin David Ramsey and Janie Langley. His lineage includes Cox, Brown, Karr, Weir, Winstead, Ballard, Tapp, Clopton and Sargent. His parents raised him and two siblings, Marie Langley R. (Crockett) and David F., on the southeast corner of N. Main and Noel Avenue where the First Baptist Church now stands. The progeny of these three give F.D. and Janie eight grandchildren, 27 great grandchildren and 12 great great grandchildren.

Dad loved to read, especially historical novels. From G.A. Henty's 110 volumes he got a very pro-British view of world history. He entered Centre College in 1908, played four years of varsity football, fullback on offense, tackle on defense and was All-Southern 3 years. There, he was associated with men of future prominence such as Fred Vinson, Louis and Bill Seelbach, Bill Duffy, etc., graduating in 1912.

Dad enlisted in WW I, was commissioned a 2nd Lt. from O.T.C. and on Aug. 17, 1917, made the smartest move of his life when he married Miss Frank Waller (see her story). This union produced three children; Jimmy, Jane Waller and Frank; 13 grandchildren and five great grandchildren.

Dad's business interests were farming (Shamrock Dairy Farm), banking (Hopkins County Bank) and coal mining (Providence Coal Co.). He had two avocations that were of great interest, high school football coaching and National Guard service.

His coaching during the 20's and early 30's led to a strong influence for good with young men such as Beverly and Clifton Waddill, Otto Corum and Carl Pate to name just a few. His work as Commanding Officer of the local N.G. Co. (Headquarters Co., 3rd Bn., 149th Infantry Regiment) led to further association with young men of Hopkins County from 1926, to his retirement for physical disability in 1941.

He was wild about his only daughter Jane Waller and here is how he got the nickname "Pappy". Mother taught Jane Waller to call him Pappy and it stuck. Dad was a very warm hearted, outgoing, jocular person and because of the fatherly interest he took in the young men he worked with, the nickname Pappy seemed a natural and it stuck.

Dad was very patriotic and a great believer in the importance of the role to be played by the "citizen soldier" in the National Guard and Reserve. His failure to qualify physically for service in WW II was one of the great disappointments of his life. Norvel Moore, Robert V. Hall, Tubby Brown, Al Mabrey, Bud Bone, and Lloyd Farmer are just a few of the many whose first military training under "Pappy" Ramsey led to distinguished service in W.W. II.

Pappy died on Dec. 10, 1958. - *Submitted by James K Ramsey III*

ROBERT WINFIELD RAMSEY

I know so very little about Uncle Robert. He was not a robust man, however, he lived to be nearly 60 years old. He was born Mar. 19, 1872, and died Feb. 24, 1931. He was my great uncle.

He was born with an asthmatic condition, which left him a bit weak, much of the time. However, he did work on the farm and helped in the sawmill some.

He was not the only single Ramsey to remain at the old homestead. Uncle Henry and Aunt Minnie remained single, also. Then there were times when one or another was left alone after the death of a spouse. They always could go back and live at the old homestead, and many did.

I remember, well, going to the farm in the late 30's, 40's and early 50's. Terrible roads! If it looked like rain, (this was in the 30's and early 40's), we had to hurry and leave, because the road into Providence would get muddy.

Aunt Annie Larkin and Uncle John Will were left alone and both returned to the home of their youth and made a home with Aunt Minnie, who never married.

The big job for the kids was to keep the flies shooed away from the table before meals. During my early years, they didn't have screens on the windows. That one thing was remedied pretty early in my childhood and with the advent of all those screens, I lost my flyswatting job.

I also remember time passed so slowly down home. Everyone went to bed about dark in the summertime, because they all got up so early.

One thing I never touched, but once, down home, and that was "cow's milk". They all loved to tease me, gently, about cow's milk but I remained adamant in my assumption that the milk at home was store milk. I wasn't about to drink anything from a cow. Albeit was lots of fun to be allowed a turn at the churn.

Time did move slowly for them and most of the world. It was a different time, a gentler time I treasure in my memory book. How blessed I was to know the ones I did. How blessed I am to be able to remember them so well.

Even though Uncle Bob passed on five years before my birth, he was a part of the life I knew "down home", as we called the farm. He was in many of the conversations, as were Grandpa and Grandma and all the others who passed before my arrival. How rich I am in all my recollections. Praise the Lord, I am blessed. (See Sigler-Ramsey) - *Submitted by Peggy Sullivan Waide*

SAMUEL PRATT RAMSEY

Samuel Pratt Ramsey was born on Jan. 29, 1914 in a small house in Providence, KY. His mother, Mary Emma Devor Ramsey, was born in Dalton, KY on Oct. 30, 1880. His father was born in the state of Illinois on Mar. 10, 1861.

Samuel had two brothers who were older: Felix Gilliam Ramsey born Mar. 7, 1902, and Henry Gordon Ramsey born Apr. 23, 1907. Both are deceased.

Samuel joined the Mt. Olivet Methodist Church as a young boy. He went to school at Clay Elementary, but dropped out at the fifth grade to make a living. At twelve years old, he worked on a farm and later at eighteen, he worked at the coal mines. After he left the coal mines, he had minor jobs such as working as an electrician, a motor operator, and at the shipyards. For 25 years, he owned and operated a small grocery in Charleston, KY where he also owned an independent trucking company.

Samuel enjoys gardening, carpentry, fishing and hunting. He also enjoys sitting in his "green chair" and looking out the bay window in his living room. Samuel is now a 37 year resident of Charleston, KY.

Agnes Marie Shelton became Samuel's bride on July 18, 1936. Agnes helped him with the store while Samuel was operating the trucking business.

Agnes and Samuel have four children. John Mansfield Ramsey Sr. was the first born. He was born June 17, 1937. His first wife, Donna Rebecca Ann Pague, was born on Mar. 28, 1938. John and Donna married on Apr. 22, 1961 and had their first child, Suzanne Alexis Ramsey, on Jan. 11, 1963. On July 29, 1972, their second child, Johnna JoNell Ramsey, was born. On Nov. 28, 1972, Donna died. On July 27, 1973, John married Lana Kay Binkley Vaughn. To this union, one son was born, John Mansfield Ramsey, Jr., on Feb. 13, 1975. John Sr. works for the Kentucky Utilities Company and some of his hobbies are playing golf, watching Nascar races, and watching sports on television.

Samuel Ramsey Family on their 50th wedding anniversary at the Dawson Springs, KY Community Center. Standing l to r: Lara Ramsey, Jay Vaughn, Jeannette and Kay Ramsey, Candy Vaughn, Kerry and John Ramsey Jr., Peter Talerico, Shirley, Walter, Edwin, Judy, and Johnna Ramsey. Seated l to r: Suzanne Talerico, Earl, DeLaine, Samuel, Agnes, John, (holding grandson, Chase Talerico), William, and Joy Ramsey. Photo courtesy of Peggy Sullivan Waide.

The second born was William Samuel Ramsey. William married Shirley Marie Bayer on Jan. 25, 1963. Their first child, Judith Carol Ramsey was born on June 15, 1964. Edwin Samuel Ramsey, their second child, was born on Mar. 21, 1967. Their youngest child, Walter Brian Ramsey, was born on Nov. 4, 1971. William works for the U. C. Milk Company driving a delivery truck. Some of William's hobbies are playing golf, working as a carpenter and watching sports on television.

The third son, Earl Patton Ramsey, married Barbara Jenette Thorp on Apr. 13, 1966. They have three children: Lara Gay Ramsey born Nov. 9, 1969; Joy Evon Ramsey born Oct. 14, 1972; and Kerry Patton Ramsey born June 9, 1976. Earl is the manager of the Dollar General Store in Dawson Springs, KY. His other source of income is raising pigs and cattle on his farm.

Mary DeLaine is the only girl and the youngest child. She was born on June 12, 1951. She is single and an elementary teacher for the Hopkins County School System. Her hobbies are reading books, watching television and playing with her dog, Rastus. -Submitted by Johnna Ramsey

RANDLE-GIVENS

FRANCES/FANNIE ABIAH GIVENS was born in Madisonville, at the home of her maternal grandparents, Benjamin Marston Clay and Abigail (Abiah) Frances McDowell Clay on Dec. 29, 1868. She died Dec. 11, 1948, in Wichita, KS. She was only five feet tall, gentle, kind, with great natural warmth and dignity; described by one of her cousins-in-law as a saint on earth.

Francis Givens Randle

She was descended on her mother's side from the Clays of Virginia and her father, NATHANIEL KARR GIVENS (1837 KY-1871 KY), was a descendant of the equally distinguished Christian-Givens families of Augusta Co., VA. (The BERRY, CHRISTIAN and GIVENS families are described elsewhere in this book). Fannie's father died when she was only two years old and her mother, SARAH ELIZABETH CLAY GIVENS (1848 Indiana-1925 Coats, KS), the granddaughter of Benjamin and Winney Berry - early Hopkins County settlers - married 2nd in 1874 Sherwood Hicks Woolfolk, a lawyer in Madisonville. Fannie came to Pratt Co., KS, Apr. 1, 1886, with her step-father and mother, a step-brother, Lilburn Magruder Woolfolk, and four half-brothers and sisters. Her half-brother, Sam, was born in Kansas in the fall of '86. The trip was made by train from Henderson to St. Louis, and then to Kingman, KS, where the railroad ended and Mr. Woolfolk met them with a buggy. Their life was a typical one of pioneer farmers on the prairie. She married in 1893, GEORGE SIMMONS RANDLE (1867 Logan Co., IL - 1957 Wichita, KS). Mr. Randle taught school and farmed in Pratt County until 1910, when they removed to Wichita, where his business was real estate and investments. In 1893, Fannie and her mother sold the Hopkins County Farm (Old Lutontown Rd near the intersection of Highway 109 and 814), which they had inherited from Nat Givens - 350 acres from his father, James Kerr Givens, and 100 acres from his mother, Elizabeth Christian Givens. This was not the end of their connection with Kentucky as they often visited back and forth. Fannie, like her mother in so many ways, was also extremely hospitable, so "company" was always welcome in both households. She and her husband, George, kept in close touch with their relatives, making frequent trips to western Kansas and two happy visits to Kentucky after their marriage.

FRANCES ABIAH GIVENS (1868 Kentucky-1948 Kansas) m. GEORGE SIMMONS RANDLE (1867 Illinois-1957 Kansas). Their children were: 1. Harry Karr Randle (1894 Kansas-); 2. KLON RANDLE; and 3. T.K. Randle (1905 Kansas-).

KLON RANDLE (1897 Sawyer, Pratt Co., KS-1983 Wichita, KS), m. Sept. 28, 1922, GENEVIEVE IRENE PARSONS (1899 Ft. Scott, KS-1965 Wichita, KS). Mr. Randle was a World War I veteran, pharmacist and owner of the Randle Drug Co. He was a director of the Kansas Pharmaceutical Association and served as president in 1937/8. His wife graduated with the first nurses' training class at St. Francis Hospital in Wichita, KS. Children: 1. PATRICIA JEANNE RANDLE; 2. Klon Randle, Jr. (1924 Kansas-); and 3. Corrine Randle (1927 Kansas-).

Patricia Randle Gillespie with her three granddaughters l to r: Ann Tearney Gillespie, Caroline Cooper Gillespie and Jane Givens Gillespie.

PATRICIA JEANNE RANDLE (1923 Wichita, KS-), m. 1950 WARREN BROWN GILLESPIE (1922 Wichita, KS-). Patricia attended Wichita University and graduated from Carleton College. Warren Gillespie is a graduate of Dartmouth College. They were divorced in 1960. One son:

JAMES PAUL GILLESPIE (1951 Kansas-), B.S.M.E. University of Kansas 1975 m. RUTH LOUISE BECKER (1951 Kansas-), May 25, 1974. Children: 1. ANN TEARNEY GILLESPIE (1978 Missouri-); 2. JANE GIVENS GILLESPIE (1981 Kansas-); 3. CAROLINE COOPER GILLESPIE (1984 Kansas-). - Submitted by Patricia Randle Gillespie

RASH-NISBET CHILDREN

James Rhea Rash, third child of Benjamin L. Rash and Agnes Jane Nisbet, born Apr. 5, 1853, married Louise V. Dillman, b. Nov. 5, 1853.

A son, F. Frank Rash, b. Sept. 1, 1876, in St. Charles, graduated from Boston Technical Engineering School, associated with St. Bernard Coal Co. Was Major Adjutant General of Third KY National Guard before going to the Mexican Border in 1916. After WW I was elected Vice-Commander of American Legion. Married Susan Atkinson of Earlington—one son, James Dillman Rash, a General in the Reserves after WW II. Now resides in Louisville, KY.

James Rhea died June 28, 1952, and Louise died Feb. 12, 1899. Buried in Grapevine Cemetery.

Mary Cordelia Rash, b. Dec. 30, 1860, married Roy Salmon, had two children: Benjamin Salmon, b. 1884 d. 1854, unmarried; Mary Agnes Salmon, b. June 12, 1890, married Dr.

Austin Flint Finley, b. Oct. 24, 1881. Their children: Agnes Finley, Mary Hart Finley, and Jane Rash Finley, who married James Glenn Bone. Their children: Flint Finley Bone, James Rash Bone and Mary Agnes Bone. Dr. Finley died Aug. 18, 1962, and Mrs. Finley died May 20, 1984.

George Waller Rash, b. Nov. 8, 1863, married Bessie B. Withers, one son, Edward Lewis Rash. Second, George married a Brasher. He died Sept. 8, 1917.

James Nisbet Jr. Children:

Mary Elizabeth Nisbet, fourth child of James Nisbet Jr., b. Feb. 11, 1827-d. July 18, 1847, buried at Grapevine Cemetery.

James Moore Nisbet, fifth child, b. Feb. 11, 1829, married Mary Jane Davis, b. Aug. 22, 1830, dau. of Benjamin Davis of St. Charles. James Moore Nisbet was Sheriff of Hopkins Co. and a farmer. He and Mary Jane had children: (1.) Mary Emma, b. Oct. 14, 1853, married John Wm. Patterson, b. 1849-d. 1905, who was public school teacher and manufactured "Patterson" road wagons. Children: William Patterson married Nannie Melton; Mary Emma married Richard Omer, rural mail carrier; Ernest Moore Patterson married Willie Ezell—children: James, Wm., Mary Ellen, Mildred and Sarah; (2) Benjamin Richard Nisbet, b. Dec. 6, 1854-d. July 13, 1899; (3) John Crittenden Nisbet, b. Aug. 23, 1856-d. Mar. 4, 1922, was deputy Sheriff under father, married Sarah (Sallie) Ella Wheatley, b. 1861-d. 1895, children: (1) Mary Wheatley Nisbet, b. Feb. 11, 1900-d. Jan. 1, 1920, married Charles Woodruff of St. Charles. Their children Nannie Love and Mary Elizabeth Woodruff. (2) Benjamin Louis Nisbet, b. Aug. 23, 1892, married Helen Lafferty, b. Feb. 9, 1892, was a lawyer, both city and county attorney for Hopkins Co. He was a charter member of the Sons of the American Revolution in KY. One daughter, Louise Nisbet, b. Apr. 21, 1919, who married Warren Roberts in London, England. Both are teachers. Benjamin L. died Sept. 14, 1958, bur. at Grapevine Cemetery. (See Woodruff-Nisbet family) - *Submitted by Rella G. Jenkins with approval from Mrs. Laura Suthard*

JAMES R. RASH

James R. Rash was born on Apr. 5, 1853, on a farm north-east of Madisonville. He was the third of five children born to Benjamin Louis Rash (1820-1912), and Agnes L. Nisbet Rash (1825-1877).

At the age of 17, he began working for $1.00 per day weighing coal for the St. Bernard Coal Company in Earlington. He received a series of promotions - clerk in the company-owned store, followed by manager of the new company-owned store at St. Charles, then to the post of superintendent of all company-owned stores. He later bought land for the company and became the company director. He held this position until his retirement in 1924, completing 54 years of working for St. Bernard.

Mr. Rash married Louise V. Dillman (Nov. 6, 1853-Feb. 12, 1899), of Owensboro. They were the parents of: Frank Dillman Rash (Sept. 1, 1878-Apr. 18, 1946), who is buried in Cave Hill Cemetery in Louisville; Jerry Black Rash (Nov. 2, 1880-Nov. 9, 1884), and Ben L. Rash (Nov. 18, 1885-Sept. 13, 1904), both who are buried in Grapevine Cemetery.

In November of 1903, Mr. Rash married Georgia J. Jones. They were the parents of one son who died Dec. 16, 1904, and is buried in Grapevine Cemetery.

Mr. Rash was a state senator from 1921-1924, and did not seek re-election. He was co-sponsor of the Rash-Gillion Act, the state's prohibition bill. He served as mayor of Earlington and was the first president of the Earlington Bank. He also served as a member of the board of directors of the Earlington Bank and the Kentucky Bank and Trust Co. in Madisonville. Mr. Rash was the first potentate of the Rizpah Shrine Temple in Madisonville and a past exalted ruler of Madisonville Lodge No. 738, B.P.O.E. He joined the Earlington Masonic Lodge in 1874. At the time of his death, he was the fourth oldest Mason in the world in point of membership and the oldest in Kentucky. Since boyhood he had been a member of the Earlington Christian Church.

Mr. Rash died on June 28, 1952, at the age of 99. He was buried in the family plot in Grapevine Cemetery. He left $21,000.00 in his will as a perpetual endowment for the maintenance of the cemetery. He also made many bequeaths to charitable organizations. Sources-Newspapers and cemetery records. - *Compiled by Debbie Knight Hammonds*

RATLIFF

William Harrison Ratliff (Mar. 19, 1836-Apr. 10, 1908), and Margaret Ann Hoagland (Oct. 2, 1840-Mar. 7, 1920), had a home in McLean Co., where they had: Mary (1863-?), wed Sim Tabor and had one son; James S. (Jim) (1865-1931), wed Ida Smith (1864-1944), had seven children: Melissa Jane (Kate) (June 2, 1867-Oct. 12, 1942), wed Sabastian (Boss) Troutman (Sept. 24, 1843-Dec. 11, 1917), had eight children; John Stonard (Jack) (Jan. 4, 1869-Jan. 5, 1959), wed Louania Hardwick Watts (Apr. 14, 1876-Dec. 13, 1960), had seven children; Charlie born 1872, died young; Joe (he made it clear that he was "Just plain Joe", not Joseph) (Mar. 23, 1870-1949), wed William Clyde Ashby (May 25, 1879-1959), had 11 children; Jake (Jan. 4, 1874-Feb. 12, 1907), wed Ada Smith (Aug. 29, 1869-Dec. 15, 1937), had three children.

Joe Ratliff wed William Clyde Ashby from Ashbyburg, KY. She was the daughter of William Harrison Ashby (note, name is same as her father-in-law) and Emmazetta Harding (it was said that she was part Indian and a midwife, who chose some unusual names for her children). The known Ashby boys were Lucian, Chesley and Church; while the girls were William Clyde and Queen Friday.

Following their marriage, Joe and Clyde Ratliff had several of their 11 children before moving to Hopkins Co., around 1905. One child died very young, name and dates unavailable; others were Arthur William (see later story), Ollie Belle, Minnie Lee, William Harrison, Stella Ellen, Frank Leslie, Lucian, Robert Brown, Raymond Strother and Joe Thomas.

Arthur William (A.W. to friends) (Nov. 29, 1895-May 10, 1967), wed Winifred Lee Gamblin (Aug. 10, 1898-Nov. 10, 1986), daughter of Sherwood Hickman and Sarah Ann Furlow Gamblin, native of Earlington.

One of the first places the newlyweds lived was Cat Town (near Madisonville). Their children were: William Ray (Bill) (Oct. 5, 1922-Jan. 3, 1987), wed Betty Jo Tabor, had six children then after her death, wed Anna Richie Ashby; Margaret Lee (Sept. 29, 1923), wed Leo Jarvis, had three children; James Darrel (Jimmie) (Oct. 12, 1925), wed Nora Lou Howton, had two children; Robert Earl (June 26, 1931-Dec. 13, 1985), wed Betty Jean Hurst, had four boys; Clyde Hickman (July 9, 1933), wed Betsy Dickson, had one son, divorced and later married Evadine Drevecky, had two children; Rudolph Wayne (July 26, 1935), married Sue Nell Faith, two children, divorced and later married Deloris Battey, had one child; Joann (Nov. 29, 1937), wed Douglas Eugene Hutchison, had five children.

Jimmie and Nora Lou (Mar. 25, 1928) (child of William Baxter Howton and Gladys Mae Asbridge Howton Harmon), wed after he served in the Navy in the Philippines and Australia during W.W. II. Married Dec. 7, 1946, at the Christian Co. Court House and soon moved to Madisonville. Born to them were Linda Lou (Dec. 16, 1947), and Darell Kent (May 11, 1954).

Linda wed Bowling Green, OH, native Michael Frank Gantt in the First Christian Church by Rev. Edward Coffman, Jr. on Dec. 16, 1972. The long-awaited grandchildren were Gabriel Baxter (July 25, 1979), Rebecca Lynn (Nov. 21, 1982), and Christopher Michael (July 13, 1985).

Darell was inspired by his grandfather A.W. to become a cobbler to repair and help fit special shoes to those who need them. A.W. had a clubbed foot and had a very hard time finding shoes that fit properly. *Submitted by Linda Lou Ratliff Gantt*

RATLIFF-HOWTON

James Darrel Ratliff, Oct. 12, 1925 (see stories on "Ratliff", A.W. Ratliff and Winifred Gamblin Ratliff), was born in Richland, the third of seven children. He attended the Henson school near the Henson Cemetery, then went to Dalton School.

James D. and Nora Lou Ratliff

He helped his dad in the coal mines, then was drafted in 1944. He served in the Navy and went to the Philippines where he helped airlift casualties. One of his bright memories was going "down under" for a while, not in a submarine, but to Australia where he felt almost home.

While Jimmy was away, he kept in touch with a special girl, Nora Lou Howton.

Nora (see stories on "Howton", Baxter Howton and Gladys Howton Harmon), went to school in Silent Run, Dalton, Charleston, Madisonville and back to Dalton to graduate in 1945. She then went to Nashville, to Draughn's Business School. Her father died a short time after she started, but she was able to finish school and two days after her 18th birthday she began at the V.A. Office in Nashville as a legal secretary.

Jimmy was back from the war and working at Boggess Chevrolet as a mechanic's helper. Nora and Jimmy had an understanding and she left Nashville to marry him on Dec. 7, 1946.

She worked at Madisonville's first radio station, WCIF as receptionist/bookkeeper, and Jimmy apprenticed for Owen Boone at his cabinet shop on Sharp Ave. near the Ratliff home. While working there, he was attending Madisonville Voc. Ed. Mechanics school and got his diploma.

Nora left the radio station for the birth of their first child, Linda Lou (Dec. 16, 1947). When the baby was about 6 mos. old, their neighbor Minnie Gunn kept her while Nora worked for the city Light and Water Office. Cates Motor Co. hired Jimmy the same year and that was where he continued until retiring in 1988.

May 11, 1954, was when their second child, Darell Kent was born. At that time they lived on Spring Street where Kent became friends with a serious little fellow, Paul Allen Summers.

Nora worked for G.E. in Owensboro for a year then returned to the Light and Water until 1956, when she began as a bookkeeper at Farmers National Bank. She continues as Head Cashier at Farmers Bank and Trust.

Linda is married and has three children who often are topics for many advice sessions.

Kent is a single man, who owns and operates The Kounty Kobbler shoe repair shop and often works weekends for WTTL.

He has training in many areas, including speech, theater arts, radio broadcasting, electrical repair and received his Orthopedic Shoe Technicians' certificate from Ball State U.

One thing Jimmy and Nora stressed to their children is diversification. If there is a problem, with God's help, there's a solution and they can find it if they are prepared. *Written by Linda Lou Ratliff Gantt*

A.W. RATLIFF

Arthur William Ratliff (Nov. 29, 1895-May 10, 1967), was born to "Just Plain Joe" and Clyde William Ashby Ratliff in their McClean County home. He was the first of eleven children and the only one to have a clubbed foot. His mother refused to have him operated on because she believed that God wanted it that way. What could have been a true handicap didn't daunt Arthur except when he wanted to help serve in World War I and wasn't ac-

A.W. Ratliff

cepted. Anyone who knew him long rarely, if ever, thought of his deformity.

A.W. as he was usually called, was a handsome man with a twinkle in his eyes, a quick wit and a love of books, as well as the outdoors. He worked in several coal mines, dug wells, farmed a lot and had some cash crops in tobacco and corn. He smoked pipes (Prince Edwards Cherry Pipe Tobacco lingered all through the house) and enjoyed collecting them.

Faith was intertwined throughout his life; he supported it as well as talked about it. Old Southards Church was one place he worshipped and it was there that he met his future wife, Winifred Lee Gamblin, an Earlington native, daughter of Sherwood Hickman and Sarah Ann Furlow Gamblin.

When "Gal" and Arthur married, they moved to Richland and began their family. First was William Ray (Oct. 5, 1922-Jan. 3, 1987); then Margaret Lee (Sept. 29, 1923); followed by James Darrel (Oct. 12, 1925); Robert Earl (June 26, 1931-Dec. 13, 1985); Clyde Hickman (July 9, 1933); Rudolph Wayne (July 26, 1935); and Joann (Nov. 29, 1937), was born on A.W.'s 42nd birthday.

Large families need plenty of care and direction, and for this, A.W. and Winnie relied again on their strong Christian bonds. When time came for A.W. to stop mining, he became a caretaker for the Richland Missionary Baptist Church; seeing to the outhouses, well water and grounds as well as to the general sweeping up and classroom preparations. If the church doors were open, he and Winnie were there. The AMEN corner was his favorite spot, while Winnie often sat closer to the choir.

After the children were all grown and married, the Ratliffs started taking little vacations. They would often take Margaret and Irene (Winnie's sisters) along, and took pictures of all the places they'd visit. The rest of the family would often get nervous because of Arthur's interest in the "less-travelled" roads, which he found interesting and would then explore. One trip to visit Clyde Hickman (they called him Hickey), and his wife in California made a real adventure for them, while all those left back home waited anxiously to hear from them. They made it fine.

A.W. was a man who enjoyed reading (his favorite topics were religion and history, mainly the Civil War), and working that garden. It was in the garden where he had a fatal heart attack; he was ready, but those left were not.

If he had any regrets, it was that he wasn't able to serve his country in the military, but his love of the country came forth in his sons. Bill served in the Army, while Jimmie, Bob and Rudy joined the Navy and Hick was in the Army and Air Force. Margaret Lee's husband Leo (Shotgun) was also in the Army. He had little reason for regrets. - *Written by Linda Lou Ratliff Gantt, granddaughter*

WINNIE GAMBLIN RATLIFF

Winifred Lee Gamblin Ratliff (Aug. 10, 1898-Nov. 10, 1986), was born in Earlington. Her father was Sherwood Hickman Gamblin (June 7, 1875-Jan. 2, 1938), son of Madison Gamblin, who was a well-to-do farmer before the Civil War, and Louann Franklin. Sarah Ann Furlow Gamblin (Feb. 9, 1875-June 20, 1974), Winnie's mother, was a child of French-born John Richard Lenore Furlow and his Christian Co. wife Eugenie Smith (father James Green Smith, Mother-Cordelia Florence Smith).

Winnie, as her family and friends called her, had seven brothers and sisters. They were: Irene Inez (Mar. 26, 1892-Dec. 15, 1975), wed Virgil Pratt Smith; Garth (Apr. 16, 1895-Sept. 25, 1924), wed Fannye DeMoss, he was later killed in a mining accident; Margaret Louise (Jan. 10, 1903), wed James Claude Grace and settled in White Plains; George (called himself Jack) (May 20, 1905-June 17, 1962), wed Garah Hankins; Thelma (Aug. 11, 1908), wed Wallace Cato; Cecil Archie (Aug. 29, 1912), wed Mary Rigney; Durwood Arthur (Dec. 23, 1915-Aug. 15, 1981), wed Maude Evelyn Brooks.

Religion played an important roll all through her life, in fact Winnie met Arthur William Ratliff (Nov. 29, 1895-May 10, 1967), at the "Old Southards" church. There were ice cream socials, revivals, baptizings and another favorite time, Homecoming. Winnie and A.W. were drawn to one another and after a rather long courtship, were married in a double wedding with her sister Margaret and Claude

Front row l to r: Durwood Gamblin, Virgil Smith holding Avanell Grace, Thelma Gamblin, Sarah Ann Furlow Gamblin and Sherwood Gamblin. 2nd row l to r: Margaret Gamblin Grace, Irene Gamblin Smith, Winifred Lee Gamblin Ratliff and James D. Ratliff. Back row l to r: A.W. Ratliff, Margaret Lee Ratliff, Billy Ray Ratliff and Cecil Gamblin at the Dawson Springs Caves about 1927/28.

Grace. It was Nov. 4, 1921, in the Hopkins Co. Court House where Judge Rev. Shane officiated.

Richland became "home" to the Ratliffs with the first place in a part called "Cat Town" near the over-pass bridge. He and "Gal", as he called her, soon moved to an area where the Richland Volunteer Fire Dept. is being built. Most of their seven children (See Ratliff) were born on that land

Quilting bees helped Winnie hone her skills and have fun while doing it. Many a good time was had when she and her family and friends would get together at one of their homes and let down the quilting frame (if you were really serious, you had one fastened to the ceiling, so during the quilting bees everyone could pull up chairs and have a place to quilt and finish-off in a very short time), and share in the latest news. Later, she used a large oval quilting hoop and gave lessons to several of her numerous grandchildren.

Handwork always seemed to draw Winnie, she enjoyed tatting lace edgings and doilies for her home and as gifts for others. Cross-stitching was another of her activities.

Winnie Ratliff

Gardening held a great interest for both A.W. and Winnie after farming became too much to handle and their fruits and vegetables were nearly as good-tasting as Winnie's flowers were abundant.

She had a vigorous life, filled with work, activity and most of all love, love of Jesus Christ, her family and friends, and it was returned. - *Written by Linda Lou Ratliff Gantt, granddaughter*

REID-PRICE

Hubert Reid was born in 1908 in Henderson County, KY, one of seven children of L. H. Reid (1877-1958) and Minnie Moss Reid (-1954).

Hubert attended school in Henderson County and when the family moved to Hopkins County in 1926, he graduated from Madisonville High School. He then attended the Kentucky College of Embalming in Louisville.

In 1928, Hubert married Edith Louise Price, the daughter of Paul Price Sr. (1875-1952) and Sue Burr Price (1879-1949). Paul Price was a veteran of the Spanish-American War. He was the second president of the Earlington Bank.

Edith graduated from Earlington High School and the University of Kentucky. She taught at the Earlington grade school for a few years. Upon her marriage to Hubert, she began the job of being his partner in business and life. In 1962, she was the recipient of the Earlington Civic Club "Woman of the Year" Award.

Until Reid Funeral Home was established in Earlington, funerals were handled by the St. Bernard and West Kentucky Coal Companys who employed a funeral director. Thus began one of the oldest funeral businesses in Hopkins County.

Hubert was well known by Hopkins Countians. He was active in Democratic politics. In 1958, he was elected to the position of county coroner, an office he held until 1966. From 1966-1970, he served as county judge. He was a founder of First Federal Savings and Loan in Madisonville and was a director emeritus of Peoples Bank and Trust.

Hubert was active in many organizations and civic affairs: member of the Hopkins County Fair Board; member of B.P.O.E.; past master of E.W. Turner Masonic Lodge No. 548 F&AM; member of the Madisonville Chapter No. 123 of the R.A.M.; past commander of the Earlington Commandery No. 27 KT; past potentate of the Rizpah Shrine Temple in Madisonville; Chairman of the Hopkins County American Red Cross for three years; past president of the Earlington Civic Club, receiving the Outstanding Civic Award in 1962. Hubert served four years on the State Board of Embalming, holding the office of secretary during that time; past president of both the West Kentucky Funeral Directors and the Kentucky Association of Funeral Directors.

Hubert and Edith were both members of the First Baptist Church in Earlington.

On Oct. 9, 1987, Hubert passed away. He is buried in Oakwood Cemetery in Earlington. Edith continues to reside in Earlington. - *Compiled by Debbie Knight Hammonds*

RHEA-EARLE

ROBERT RHEA was born 1795, in Greenbrier, VA, and died in Hopkins Co., KY, in 1847. It is believed that he came as a child before Hopkins County was officially a county.

He married ELIZABETH EARLE, whose parents came from South Carolina about 1800. Her father, Thomas Prince Earle, was one of the eight children of MAJOR BAYLISS EARLE, who brought their families and settled in this area. Hopkins County was then still a part of its parent county. Thomas P. Earle died shortly after coming to Kentucky leaving the one daughter, ELIZABETH, and his wife MARY (STALLARD), who later married SOLOMON SUMMERS.

ROBERT was a surveyor and in 1822, was commissioned to resurvey the town of Madisonville and make some changes. JOHN GORDON, the first surveyor of Hopkins County had laid out the lots and Public Square in 1807.

In 1822, as commissioned by the County Trustees, ROBERT RHEA widened Main Cross Street (now Center Street), and took some land from the Public Square in order to create the beginning of UNION STREET south of the now Center Street.

ROBERT and ELIZABETH were the parents of four (4) sons.

1. THOMAS PRINCE EARLE RHEA, who evidently died as a young man.
2. ROBERT HENRY CLARK RHEA located in Union County, and is recorded in their History Books as a prominent doctor and a poet of some renown.
3. WASHINGTON MILLER RHEA was a well-known farmer here in Hopkins Co. He was a dedicated member of Pleasant Grove Baptist Church, being a charter member. He was also noted as an enthusiastic Fox Hunter.
4. W.E. WILBUR RHEA the youngest settled in Webster County and may have descendents living there now. Sources: (Maps from Harold Ledbetter papers, Historical Society) - *Submitted by Helen (Henify) Wilcox*

RHEA-HIBBS

WASHINGTON M. RHEA, third son of ROBERT and ELIZABETH (EARLE) RHEA was born in Hopkins County in 1835. His father died in 1847 and WASH (age 15) was an apprentice farmer with John Lunsford in 1850 Census.

SARAH was born in 1840, daughter of WILLIAM and ELIZABETH (Aldredge) HIBBS. WASH and SARAH married in 1855, and were prominent Hopkins County farmers, having a farm on Rose Creek Road. They were the parents of fourteen children, seven surviving his death in 1911. SARAH lived until 1936, with only five children surviving. She was one of the County's oldest citizens at that time.

Washington M. Rhea

They were devoted members of Pleasant Grove Baptist Church, both being charter members. Wash was one of a group who in 1860, left Liberty Baptist church to organize their church. They are buried in the Church Cemetery along with a number of their children and grandchildren.

WASH was an enthusiastic foxhunter, raising fox hounds. He seems to have sold foxes and also a hound as far away as Texas (See- "OLD TROUBLE"-In Historical Society Yearbook 1984.)

Major Gordon mentioned WASH in his History of Hopkins County as a talented surveyor. He was also interested in genealogy, as he left a record of his maternal family for many generations. His father Robert came from Virginia and was also a surveyor. He is credited with making the second map of Madisonville in 1822, in which he added Union Street to the original lay-out by John Gordon.

Wash and Sarah Rhea were evidently fine folk, as they seem to have been well-respected and loved by those who knew them. I wish that I could have known them. - *Submitted by Helen (Henify) Wilcox*

RHEW-ARNOLD

Mamie Mae Arnold (Mar. 12, 1902-Mar. 22, 1959), and Benjamin Rashley Rhew (Jan. 29, 1894-Mar. 12, 1980), were united in marriage Jan. 13, 1917, in the home of W.S. Adams.

Mamie was the daughter of Susie Daniel and Thomas Arnold. Her maternal grandparents were Mary Yarbrough and Matthew Daniel. Her paternal grandparents were Lucy Dame and Issic Shelby Arnold. Mamie had eight brothers and sisters: Rufus, Herman, Irma Siria, Alice Siria, Oma Curneal, Johnnie, Ina Pearl Noel, and David.

Mamie Mae (Arnold) and Benjamin Rashley Rhew

Mamie was a faithful and active member of the Primitive Baptist Church. She enjoyed playing the piano and organ. She had a beautiful alto voice and loved to sing. Fond memories are of her sitting at the piano in her home with her daughters gathered around singing their favorite gospel songs.

Mamie was a very active person, with a glowing personality. She aimed for harmony among all people.

Benjamin (Ben) was one of eleven children born to Naomi Lutz and Robert Thomas Rhew. His maternal grandparents were Francis Winstead and Robert Franklin Lutz. His paternal grandparents were Jane and William Rhew. His brothers and sisters were: Callie, Girdie Rainwater, Rob, Edd, Levie, Vernie Utterback, Lessie Siria, Grace Webster, Versie Dement, and James Harvey.

Ben worked as a coal miner and farmer. He enjoyed fox hunting. Ben looked forward to fattening up a goat and having his friends in once a year for barbecued goat.

Ben was of a peaceful, gentle, loving, and even-tempered nature. However, if provided, "Watch out Katie!"

Fond memories are of Ben sitting under the shade tree, straw hat on his head, pipe in hand, watching his garden grow, and feeding his pet squirrel.

God blessed Ben and Mamie with six children: Pazzie Marie Wilson (July 23, 1918),;Lavena Mae Duncan (Oct. 7, 1920-Oct. 9, 1969) (See Duncan-Rhew); Arletta Lewis Parrott (Dec. 7, 1921); Edna Louise Duncan (May 12, 1927) (See Duncan-Rhew); Jessie Lee Putty (Feb. 14, 1930); and Benjamin Austin Rhew (Dec. 14, 1932-Dec. 28, 1982). - *Submitted by Granddaughters Retha Duncan Tarter (See Duncan-Tarter) and Lesia Duncan Pendley (See Duncan-Pendley)*

JUSTICE CALVIN RHODES

Justice Calvin "Pappy" Rhodes was born in Hopkins County on Dec. 7, 1919. His parents were James Spurlin Rhodes (b. 1885, Muhlenberg County d. 1970, Hopkins County), and Gordie Felty (b. 1893, Butler County, d. 1947, Christian County). From this union came nine children: Vivan Lawrence (b. 1912), James Harrison (b. 1915), B.L. (b. 1917), Justice (b. 1919), Gusta Mae (b. 1922), Willis Ray (b. 1925), Margaret Helen (b. 1928), and Elbert and Delbert (b. 1931). This family can be traced back to General Henry (Roth) Rhoads (b. 1739, Pennsylvania-d. 1814 Muhlenberg County), who fought with George Washington at Valley Forge. Henry Rhoads has been given credit for settling and naming Muhlenberg County.

At a friend's birthday party in June of 1941, Justice met Edna Jewel Smith (b. 1921, Florence, AL). Oct. 18, 1941, they became man and wife. From this union six children were born: Edna Marie (b. 1942); Linda Kay (b. 1947); Patsy Jane (b. 1950); Rebecca Lynn (b. 1952); Virginia Lane (b. 1955); and Justice "Jay" Walton (b. 1959). Jewel's parents were Leonard Oscar Smith (b. 1882, Humbolt, TN-d. 1963 Hopkins County); and Edna Mae Wallace (b. 1900, Port Gibson, MS-d. 1983, Hopkins County). This 1918 marriage produced nine surviving children: Edna Jewel; Martha; L.O. Jr.; Lena Katherine; Sara Jane; Walter James; Sophronie; George Wallace; and Barbara.

Justice Rhodes' main interest can be summed up in one word-people. He loved and enjoyed being around people. He was a man of many opinions on a vast number of life's situations. He was not shy about sharing these. In his early 20's he earned the name "Pappy", while working at Dunville's Garage. Many young (some still local) boys would ask for advice. "Pappy" gladly gave it to them.

"Pappy's" life was people-centered. His choice of careers enabled him to do what he loved best, to help and meet people. On May 1, 1947, he started driving a wrecker for Dunville's Garage. He went into business for himself and thus Rhodes Wrecker Service was born in 1954. He remained in this business until July 1983, when, because of declining health, he sold the wreckers. During his more than three decades in this business, there were many stories. I can remember when several teenage boys went out one night with one of the boy's family car. The car "jumped" into a ditch. Pappy pulled the car out, took the boys home, and talked to the boy's dad. He stayed there and talked until the dad was laughing about some of the things he did as a boy.

He worked 24 hours a day, seven days a week. This did not leave him with too much free time. I can remember only one family vacation. In 1964, for a three day trip, the family went to Hazzlehurt, MS. In the early 60's, he organized the Hopkins County Radio and Rescue Squad which worked with the police in search of lost people and in dragging for drown victims. He was a member of the Kentucky Colonels, and served as sixth ward councilman for two terms.

Sept. 14, 1983, at 4:12 a.m., my father died of lung cancer, which had spread to his spine. I would like to think that a little of "Pappy" Rhodes lives on through us, his children, and through his many friends he made. He loved this town and the people in it. I can remember him saying he could not understand why anyone would want to live or work anywhere else but in Hopkins County. Madisonville was the best town on earth to him because of the love, concern, hope and foresight of the good people who lived here. *Submitted by Rebecca Rhodes and Linda Rhodes (daughters)*

RICHARDS-FRAZER

Augustus Owen Richards was born Nov. 24, 1913, in Caldwell Co., KY, the son of William Joe and Dixie Hortense Logan Richards. They are buried at Beulah, KY. His grandparents were Zack Richards, who came to America from England, and Hortense Germarne Richards, who came to America from France. They are buried at Old Beulah. His other grandparents were Thomas Owen Logan and Dorothy Colene Jewell Logan. They are buried at Silent Run.

From l to r: Linda Bearden, A.O. and Nell Richards, Gayle Davis and Cindy Wright, June 1987

Nellie Green Frazer Richards was born Feb. 8, 1920, the daughter of William Alexander Frazer and Pearl Bird Wyatt Frazer. They are buried at Dalton. Her grandparents were Thomas Alexander Frazer and Mary Jane Lynn Frazer. They are buried at Beulah. Her other grandparents were George Green Wyatt and Autha Amamda Holloman Wyatt. They are buried at Dalton.

Augustus Owen Richards and Nellie Green Frazer were married June 5, 1937, in Dawson Springs. The officiating minister was John F. Culver. The attendants were Thornton Dever and Amanda Frazer. They have three daughters. The oldest, Linda Dale, teaches music in Hopkins Co. schools. She is married to James Thomas Bearden, who is principal of Pride Avenue School. They have two daughters; Robyn Carole, and Augusta Cheree. Their second daughter, Judith Gayle, is guidance counselor at West Hopkins High School. She is married to Jay Warren Davis, who is Materials Manager for Caldwell County Hospital. They have a son, Kelly Owen, and a daughter, Jayme Lauren. Their third daughter is Cynthia Wyatt, who is a reading teacher at Dalton School. She is married to James Beakley Wright, an insurance salesman. They have a son, Irvin Richards, and a daughter, Leah Janelle.

Augustus Owen had two sisters, Marie Hortense and Dixie Bell, both of whom are deceased. He had a brother, William Paul, who died in a military plane crash during World War II, and his other brother Zack Logan Richards, retired, resides in Madisonville.

Nellie has two sisters, Amanda Dever and Ada Peyton and a brother, William Rhodes Frazer, all of whom reside in Dalton, KY.

Augustus Owen, retired, taught school for forty-one years, beginning at age 17. The first five years were in the one room schools of Elam and Fiddlebow. He went to Dalton High School as principal in 1936, at 22 years of age. When West Hopkins High School was constructed he went there as principal in 1962, and retained that position until retirement in 1979.

Nellie is a homemaker, having raised her three daughters, she kept her husband in school and has kept her six grandchildren while their mothers taught school.

Mr. and Mrs. Richards have been married fifty years. They are members of the Dalton Missionary Baptist Church, where Mr. Richards is a deacon.

They reside on a farm, the homeplace of Mr. Richards' grandfather Logan, on Logan Road, Route 1, Box 364, Dawson Springs, KY 42408. - *Submitted by Augustus Owen Richards*

RIDENOUR-BURTON

Mildred Burton and Roy Allen Ridenour were married Nov. 14, 1936 in Macedonia Baptist Church in Breckenridge Co., KY.

Mildred, the daughter of Ira and Serenia Kerby Burton, was born Dec. 4, 1916 in Breckinridge Co. Ira was the son of Crittenden and Katie Harl Burton. Serenia was the daughter of William and Fanny Reece Kerby. Mildred's siblings: Beatrice, Frances, Clarence, Hubert and Earl.

Mildred attended her elementary grades in a one room school in Breckenridge Co. and her high school years at Livermore, KY. Years later she took several courses at Oakland City College in Indiana. Her hobby is working in all types of arts and crafts. This was put to good use in a craft shop she maintained in Manitou in 1974-75. Mildred's first love is quilting. Many beautiful quilts grace her home and those of her family.

Roy, the son of William and Edna King Ridenour, was born Aug. 22, 1915 in McLean Co. William was the son of John and Martha Sharp Ridenour. Edna was the daughter of Charles and Elizabeth Miller King. The family name, King, was shortened by ancestor Karl Koenig when he came from Germany.

Roy attended elementary school in a one room school in McLean Co. and high school in Livermore, class of '36. College years were at Oakland City College. In 1985, he was awarded an honorary doctoric of divinity degree. A carpenter by trade until entering the ministry in 1949, he has pastored seven churches in Kentucky. He was twice pastor at Concord General Baptist Church near Manitou.

Sharing Roy's love of carpentry, Mildred has drawn the blue prints for every building Roy has built during their 50 years of marriage. Their retirement home, on Hwy. 630 near Manitou, was Mildred's blue print and Roy's carpentry. Roy also built a country store type workshop nestled in the trees, called "Shakerag Shop", where he enjoys his hobby building things. Since 1975, they both have enjoyed oil painting. Both have won many prizes and have their paintings hanging in Regional Medical Center in Madisonville and the library at Livermore. They enjoy painting landscapes, old homes, barns and landmarks.

Roy and Mildred Ridenour

The Ridenour's, better known as Brother Roy and Sister Mildred, worked in the Home Mission field for over seven years, living in a small 19 ft. trailer while at building sites. There were seven churches built and the parsonage at the Indian Mission in Oklahoma was repaired. They averaged 60,000 miles a year for the three years they spent in evangelism work, filling pulpits for special services, visiting and speaking in denominational association meetings, working and teaching in youth camps, and helping to organize youth camps. They helped in D.V.B.S. at mission churches, Roy building, Mildred organizing the kitchen and teaching crafts. They helped organize and build a church in Florida. Other states they have been in are Colorado, Tennessee, Arkansas and Missouri. Roy has also taught home study classes to new ministers. Far from being retired, Brother Roy is pastoring at Green's Chapel Church near Greenville. Mildred has been active in mission work at the local level, organizing church women and guilds for the teenage girls.

The Ridenours have two children. Kerby married Howard Parish and they live on Hwy. 630 near Manitou. Kerby and Howard have two children, Allen Lee who is employed at U.C. Milk Co., and Lelia Yvonne who lives at home and is a student at Madisonville Community College. Both graduated from West Hopkins High School. Kerby is a teacher at Pride Ave. School in Madisonville. Hugh Allen Ridenour is married to the former Carolyn Duncan and they live on Hwy. 1069. Hugh and Carolyn are high school teachers. - *Submitted by Dorothy Miller Shoulders*

RIGGS-DAVIS

The Riggs' of Hopkins Co. are descended from two brothers, Joseph & Abraham. Joseph is the ancestor of the Riggs' in the Hanson & Nebo areas. Those Riggs' in and around Dawson Springs are descended from Abraham, whose lineage follows:

WILLIAM H. RIGGS m. a Miss Burdine of Wheeling, WV circa 1790. He moved to Washington Co., KY, and died there in 1814 or '15. Three of their sons came to Calhoun, KY, about 1810. (McLean Co. was then part of Daviess Co.) All three served during the War of 1812.

(1) Joseph, b. 1794, m. Mar. 10, 1818, to Lucy Elizabeth Dicken, b. 1797. Their children were LaFayette, Sally, Daniel, Lucy, Judy, William & Martha.

(2) Isaac B., b. 1804, m. 1st wife, children unknown except for Isaac Jr. & Hanison W., 2nd wife, Meary, only known child a dau. Lucy.

(3) ABRAHAM, b. 1796, m. Mary (Polly) Chamberlain in Washington Co., KY, Apr. 15, 1815. Their son,

WILLIAM B., b. 1817 m. June 1, 1837, to Alcy Scott in Daviess Co. Alcy, b. 1821, moved with her parents Benjamin & Mary Soueber Scott, to where Evansville, IN, now stands, when only one log cabin was there.

William & Alcy had 11 children, LOGAN THOMAS, James, Mary, David, Finley, David, Savilla, Eunice, Theodius (Thee), Jane, & Panehus.

LOGAN THOMAS, b. June 30, 1838, m. Elizabeth Jane Bryant, raised by Abraham & Polly Riggs, Logan's grandparents.

Logan & Eliza Jane moved to Attica, AR, near Pocahontas, about 1865. They had 14 children, some in Arkansas & some in Kentucky, Alcy, Ralph Rosie, infant girl, William Finis, Abraham (Ham), Eliza, Thomas, Sanford (Bip), James J., ALFRED the GREAT, Effie, Christina (Tina), & two other girls, names unknown to me.

Duessie Davis Riggs, about 1918.

ALFRED the GREAT, b. July 12, 1879, in Attica, AR, moved to Charleston, KY, in the 1890's. He m. July 1, 1900 to Mary Duessie Davis, b. Feb. 12, 1882, dau. of Sidney Stanton & Arcena Hudson Davis.

Alfred, called A.G., & Duessie bought a farm at Huckleberry & had four children, (1) Carl Clifton, July 6, 1901-Feb. 26, 1970, m. Edith Cansler, settled in Detroit, MI. They had one son, Gary.

(2) Erma Vada Aug. 1, 1904-Nov. 15, 1925, m. William Benson Hamby, settled near Hamby Station, they had four children; Lotus

Ruella, Frances Eveline, & twin boys, Alfred Jackson & Albert Great.

(3) Euen Finis (Buster) Dec. 19, 1908-Mar. 21, 1983, m. 1st wife ? had twin daus. Polly & Vada Louise. M. 2nd wife Mary Hightower, no children. M. 3rd wife, Edith Mae Boyd, settled in Uniontown, their children Allen Douglas, Phillip David, Michael Euen, Linda Susan, & Timothy Scott.

(4) Hazel Ruth, b. June 2, 1913, m. John Raymond Carter in 1932, & settled near Dawson Springs. They had three daughters, Gloria Diann, Jackie Rae, & Julia Kay. Raymond died in 1953, & Hazel m. Darrel Gray Sept. 12, 1955. The family settled in Owensboro.

Soon after Hazel's birth, Alfred & Duessie sold the farm & bought another on the Greenville Rd. near Crabtree (Ilsley). The large one story "L" shaped farmhouse still stands off the road at the "Y" of Hwys. 62 & 112. Their fifth child HENRY DOUGLAS was born in the front room Jan. 30, 1918. Duessie died Aug. 20, 1919, & was buried in Carter Cem. at Huckleberry.

Robert Fox in the wagon. Henry Riggs with the pipe. Taken on A.G. Riggs farm about 1921.

HENRY DOUGLAS RIGGS m. July 20, 1941, to Elizabeth Terzah (Terry) Adams of Belfountaine, OH, b. Mar. 2, 1919, in Kenton, OH. They have one dau. Sharon Kaye, b. Sept. 22, 1952, m. Sept. 1, 1972, to Ronald Wayne Johnston, b. Sept. 13, 1952. (See Archie D. Johnston) (See also: Riggs-Eli) - *Compiled by Sharon Riggs Johnston*

RIGGS-ELI

Alfred the Great Riggs, b. July 12, 1879, in Attica, AR, moved to Charleston, KY, in the 1890's. He m. Mary Duessie Davis July 1, 1900, and had five children, Carl Clifton, Erma Vada, Euen Finis (Buster), Hazel Ruth, & Henry Douglas (Buck). Duessie died in 1919.

Alfred or A.G. m. in 1921, to Barbara Allen Eli, b. Feb. 24, 1881. She had five children from her first marriage to James (Jim) Collins. They were Charlie Louis (died as a baby), Georgia, James Edna, Archie, & J.D.

A.G. & Barbara then had three children of their own, twin girls, Aminell & Estelle, b. Jan. 19, 1922, & a son, Alfred Ray, b. Mar. 21, 1925.

(1) Aminell m. July 5, 1941, to Richard Elmo (Rip) Morris, b. Mar. 14, 1919, son of Charle Amon & Sybil Bess Cobb Morris. Aminell & Rip settled in Dawson Springs & had one dau. Elaina Jo, b. Mar. 2, 1942.

Alfred the Great and Barbara Eli Riggs, about 1924 and Estelle and Aminell Riggs (twins) about 1930

(2) Estelle m. Jan. 17, 1944, to Lyndle Barnes, b. Nov. 22, 1921, son of Luther & Prudy Stallins Barnes. They had three children, Lyndle, Jr., b. Nov. 3, 1946, Janice Kaye, b. Jan. 28, 1950, Allen Wayne, b. Mar. 24, 1951.

(3) Alfred Ray m. July 28, 1946, to Vera L. Lyon, b. Aug. 23, 1920, dau. of Joseph & Elizabeth Sulu Morgan Lyon. They had two daus. Barbara Ray, b. Feb. 1, 1948 and Delores Kay, b. Aug. 25, 1951. Alfred Ray died June 27, 1987, & was buried in Rosedale Cem. Dawson Springs.

The Riggs' farm was on the Greenville Rd. near Crabtree (Ilsley). The house can still be seen about 500 ft. off the road on the northwest side of the "Y" intersection of hwys. 62 & 112. The last of the Riggs-Davis children, Henry Douglas (Buck) and all three of A.G. & Barbara's children were born in the front room of that farmhouse.

A.G. was a farmer & coalminer. He worked for the old Norton Mining Co. as a pump man at Top Pond near Crabtree & Magic Lake near Hamby Station just off of Union Temple Rd.

A.G. traded the house and section of farm on the north side of Hwy. 62, for a house & lot on Walnut St. in Dawson Springs, in 1931. It had renters at the time, so the family moved into a house on N. Main St. that Barbara already owned. A.G. still owned that portion of his farm on the south side of Hwy. 62. He was digging coal on the property at this time & built a log cabin to stay in. The family moved back to the "Y" and into the cabin to be with him. They lived there about a year, then A.G. was hired as a policeman in Dawson Springs.

While they lived in the cabin, the house on Main St. burned down & the renters moved out of the other house. So, in 1933, the Riggs' settled into the house they had traded for two years before.

A.G. was night policeman in town, he carried a pistol and a nightstick. It was his job to handle whatever trouble came up in the course of a night anywhere in town as Dawson Springs was rather rough in the '30's.

One night, in 1935, A.G. was patrolling on South Main St. when he heard a woman's cry for help. The sound came from behind the New Century Hotel. When he went around back, there was a black man and the woman who had called for help. The man had a knife & stabbed A.G. several times, and before fleeing, also slit the policeman's throat. They took A.G. to Madisonville to the hospital where he underwent surgery for his injuries, but because of a heart condition, the doctors couldn't use anesthetic. He did recover & lived to age 72. The man who attached A.G. was caught and imprisoned.

Barbara died May 6, 1949, & Alfred the Great Riggs died Mar. 5, 1952, both are buried in Rosedale Cem. Dawson Springs. (See also: Riggs-Davis) - *Compiled by Sharon Riggs Johnston*

RINGO-ARNETT

On June 4, 1926, Susie Kathleen Arnett became the bride of Ben Spaulding Ringo. They had courted for eight years and he knew the first night they met that she was the only one for him.

Why did they wait? Well, he was a little intimidated because her father was a physician and he was a farm bred lad. So—he worked diligently, in order to become able to provide as he felt he should.

From left to right: Curry Nichols (a Marion, KY cousin on the Dye side), Kathleen (Arnett) and Spaulding Ringo, circa late 1920's

Years passed and, indeed, he did make his mark on the city of Madisonville. He went into the tire business and also recapping with his brother-in-law, Chester Lloyd Seymour, who was also a local councilman.

Eventually, Spaulding bought Seymour out, but the name remained Seymour and Ringo. He had the Goodyear dealership for the first three years. He then acquired the General Tire franchise and represented that company for the next 38 years at 18 North Franklin in Madisonville.

Kathleen's parents were Dr. Boyd and Mary Arnett. They had two other children: Neveleen, who married Tom Ellis, of Rumsey, KY and (Bill) William, who married Betty Brown of Marysville, CA. The Ellis's live in Covington, KY, and the Arnetts in Yuba City, CA.

Neveleen ("Sal") was ten years younger than Kathleen and "Bill" was ten years younger than Neveleen.

The Ringos were not blessed with children but in many ways they were much into parenting roles with her brother and sister. That also included chaperoning a group of girls to the World's Fair in Chicago.

Spaulding had a great love for the land. His parents owned a large farm in Western Hopkins Co. on the banks of Tradewater river. His mother, Florence Dye Ringo passed away when he was nine, but he never forgot her gentleness and that she was a great lady. I have always heard the same from those who knew her, and I was interested, because she was my great-grandmother. My great-grandfather, B.F. Ringo, had three children when his wife passed. Leavy Novelist, Opal Vivian (my grandmother) and Ben Spaulding.

The role of caring for children as great in Aunt Kathleen's life. She was a school teacher for many years in Madisonville's elementary schools.

Three summers ago Uncle Spaulding ("Sugie", as we call him), felt he must make a change. He was in relative good health but did need to be in a one-story home. Aunt Kathleen had been in Kentucky Rest Haven for 3-1/2 years. He sold the house and moved across the street to a home on one floor and a neighbor, Mrs. Louise Renfro, who would attend to his needs.

He has lots of company, especially from First Baptist Church, where they attended for many years. He loves his church very much. "Sugie" was born Mar. 26, 1898. He is 89 and enjoys keeping up with things around him.

Aunt Kathleen (June 30, 1900 to Mar. 15, 1985), passed on and is buried in Hicklin Cemetery in Anton.

They were married 58 years, and to my knowledge, the honeymoon never wore off. It was worth the eight-year wait. (See Ringo-Dye, Ramsey-Ringo, Seymour-Ringo, Kennedy-Ringo and Mather-Ringo) - *Submitted by Peggy Sullivan Waide*

RINGO-DYE

My knowledge of my maternal ancestors is even less than the paternal. I write what I know only as a genealogical record.

My great-great-grandfather Ringo came from Virginia. My great-great-grandmother died in Kentucky. He remarried and lived near Wheatcroft, KY. (First name and burial sites unknown, albeit he may be buried near Wheatcroft with his second wife.) After he remarried, my great-grandfather, Benjamin Franklin Ringo (Poppa) left home at the age of 13 and worked on a farm for Worth Anderson, who gave him a home, near Blackford, KY. His father died shortly thereafter. Poppa had two sisters and two brothers. One sister later lived in Indianapolis, IN, and worked in management in the Woolworth Company in the 1930's.

On Jan. 1, 1890, Poppa married Florence Dye at Atley's Chapel. The minister was a Brother Gibbs. They had four children. Florence (Mar. 1, 1872 to June 12, 1907), died prematurely of a ruptured appendix.

Their first child, Leavy Novelist (Dec. 8, 1889 to Aug. 22, 1971), married Chester Lloyd Seymour (Mar. 27, 1887 to Oct. 20, 1958), on Feb. 23, 1910 (no children). Their second child was Leah Pauline (May 11, 1893 to Oct. 20, 1894). My grandmother was Opal Vivian (May 25, 1895 to May 4, 1967), wife of Ernest Delmar Ramsey and mother of Anna Margaret, my mother.

She married Eugene Sullivan of Marion, KY. They had one daughter, Peggy Ann, who married Harry Doyle Waide of Providence. This union produced three children. Suzanne Camille Waide, married Clay Neal Curb of Houston, TX, on Mar. 12, 1982. The Curbs have

Florence Dye Ringo, wife of Benjamin Franklin Ringo

two daughters, Hannah Jo, and Mary Mae Curb.

The Waides had two sons, Forrest Lynn "Ben" Waide and Kent, both single.

The Sullivans had one other child, a son, who was stillborn. His name was Raymond.

Ringo's fourth child was Ben Spaulding, who married Susie Kathleen Arnett of Madisonville on June 4, 1926, and had no issuance.

After Florence's death, B.F. married Lena Gertrude Sigler (Aug. 6, 1888 to Nov. 7, 1974), of Caldwell Co. They had two daughters. Alice Reba (b. Oct. 3, 1910), married John Kennedy, Providence, and had one son, James Franklin Kennedy. (John had one son by a previous marriage, Johnny).

Jimmy Kennedy married Lucinda Ruby, daughter of Edwin and Mary Comer Ruby of Madisonville. They divorced and he married June Ferris, Owensboro. They have one adopted child, John, 16. They were divorced briefly but remarried and live in Goldsboro, NC, as does his widowed mother.

B.F. and Gertrude's second daughter, Zeola Virginia (b. Nov. 12, 1916), married Robert Mather from Indianapolis and had one son, Ben. Virginia is widowed and still lives there.

Ben married Janet Imus and they had two sons, Eric Ian and Brett Mather. Ben and Janet divorced. She has the sons and never remarried. He is remarried to Kate Gerencer and has one son, Logan Holmes Mather (July 27, 1987).

The Ringos were of hardy stock and Christian by nature. I always heard what a Christian and wonderful woman my great-grandmother Florence was. Her children never ceased to revere her. B.F. Ringo (Aug. 17, 1864 to June 29, 1962), is buried with Florence and their infant daughter, Leah in Blackford Cemetery. Lena Gertrude Ringo is buried in Shady Grove Cemetery. My great-uncle, Spauling Ringo, is 89, and still resides in Madisonville. He was in the tire business 40 years, part of that time with his brother-in-law, Chester Seymour. It was called Seymour & Ringo.

He is very close to us and we call him, "Sugie". To my grandchildren he is, "Uncle Sugie", and indeed, he is that. (See Ringo-Ramsey, Ringo-Arnett, Seymour-Ringo, Kennedy-Ringo and Mather-Ringo.) - *Submitted b: Peggy Sullivan Waide*

ROBARDS

James Ercely Robards was the son of Dave Robards and Mary George Dockery.

James "Ercely" Robards, born Dec. 5, 1895, married Lena Howton born May 28, 1906, on May 23, 1918, in Cheatam Co., TN. He was twenty-two years old. She was eleven. She was to celebrate her twelfth birthday and the departing of her new husband into the army only five days later.

Ercely and Lena Robards on their wedding day, and Ercely during WW I

Ercely was sent to a camp in Kentucky and then moved to one in Louisiana. He wrote of the different towns they were traveling through and asked her to save them so he might trace his route later. He also sent words to a song he wanted them to learn. Both seemed to be anxious for the emergency to be over so they could begin their life together.

Lena was to busy herself for the next few months with quilting and other labors of love in the preparation for her own home. She also moved from home to home attending other members of her family who were sick; needless to say much of her time was spent writing letters.

Ercely was discharged a private of Supply Company, 5th Infantry on Mar. 10, 1919, by reason of demobilization.

After being discharged he made their livelyhood at farming as most other families did at that time. Later on he would be employed and retired from a job at Outwood Veterans Hospital in Dawson Springs, KY.

Lena delivered their first child at age 13. They were to have six children in all. Three died in infancy.

Florella, born Dec. 9, 1919, married Feb. 4, 1939, Bruce Towe, born June 22, 1909. They have six children: Norma, born Jan. 6, 1940; James William, born Apr. 20, 1941; Larry Bruce, born Feb. 29, 1948; Wanda, born Jan. 6, 1951; Carolyn, born Aug. 3, 1954; and Sandra, born Aug. 3, 1956. Bruce and Florella presently live at Route #1, Dawson Springs, KY.

Kate, born June 27, 1921, married June 3, 1944, William Ruby Utley, born Aug. 21, 1925. Their children are Michael, born Feb. 5, 1947, and Ruth, born Mar. 23, 1949. Kate married second Robert May. They presently live in Blakely, GA.

Norman, born Mar. 11, 1923, married Dec. 26, 1943, Roberta McMillin, born June 23, 1925. Their children are Ronald, born Jan. 22, 1945; Reba, born Nov. 22, 1951; and Barbara, born Oct. 10, 1953. Norman and Roberta presently live in Americus, GA.

James Hilton, born Dec. 5, 1928, died Dec. 9, 1928, buried at Lafayette Church Cemetery.

Marjory, stillborn Aug. 22, 1930, buried at Lafayette Church Cemetery.

Vurla Jean, born Mar. 26, 1932, died Mar. 29, 1932, buried at Lafayette Church Cemetery.

Ercely and Lena were to have only a short 33 years together. She died Mar. 11, 1951, at age 44, he in 1964, at age 69. Much was accomplished during this time with three children to raise and educate.

Many lives were touched in the west county areas of Beulah and Dalton as Lena became a midwife and delivered many babies during her short life.

James Ercely and Lena Howton Robards are buried at Lafayette Church Cemetery. (See Howton) - *Submitted by Norma Towe Cullen*

ROBERTS-ARNOLD

Betty Ruth Arnold, the daughter of James L. and Eldee Wilkey Arnold, and Rupert Owen Roberts, the son of Dolph and Alice Roberts, were married Sept. 19, 1949, in Columbia, KY. To this union one son, David Arnold Roberts, was born Nov. 19, 1956.

David married Rebecca Ruth Woods on Mar. 18, 1978, and they have two children: Benjamin Owen, born Dec. 14, 1981 and Nicholas Adam, born Mar. 3, 1984. They live in Mt. Juliet, TN. David is employed as manager of the meat department at Winn-Dixie in Nashville and Becky works for Gibson Guitars.

Betty and Rupert Roberts in 1950

Rupert worked for Tertling Brothers and then Peabody Coal Company before he died on Sept. 27, 1971. Betty remarried to Walter N. Martin, a farmer, originally from Louisville, on Aug. 17, 1978. They purchased a farm in Iowa and moved in April 1979. Walter died in November 1979 and Betty moved back to Madisonville. Betty went back to work at Rocket Oil, her previous employer.

Betty is a member of First Presbyterian Church, past president of the VFW Auxiliary Post 5480, and was active in PTA, while David was in school. Her hobbies are sports, needlework and flowers. - *Submitted by Betty A. Martin*

ROBINSON

The name Robinson is an old one in Hopkins County. My great-grandparents were Jesse and Milly (Dunn) Robinson. They resided in Hopkins County spending a portion of their lives in the Menser Community near Dawson Springs.

Jesse (1805-1853), and Milly (1810-1857), were married July 3, 1827, and were the parents of nine children: Alexander W. (1831-1904); Nancy Caroline (1833-1902); Benjamin Thomas (1837-1860); Julian Florenda (1839-

Willis White Robinson and Eva Lou Dunbar Robinson in 1917

1924); Martha Elizabeth (1842-1845); Jemima Frances (1844-1845); William McGilbra (1846-1926); Jesse Robert (1847-1924); and, James Jasper (1852-?). The parents died before some of the children were grown. My grandfather William McGilbra went to live with a Dr. and Mrs. Brown, who finished rearing him. Other siblings were reared in different homes, but they all kept in touch and continued to get together for visits even when they were old.

William McGilbra Robinson married Martha Frances Mount of Caldwell County in 1877. They were fondly called "Uncle Mack" and "Aunt Matt" by younger acquaintances. They were the parents of seven children; six of these lived to be elderly - some past 90 years of age. Their children were: Willis White, Susan Carolina, Lillian Malone, James Thomas, Rosa Tennessee Ann, and William Bert. Another daughter Hattie died as a small child.

William McGilbra was a farmer and railroader. He helped build the first railroad through Dawson Springs and later, he worked for the Railroad Company. As a teenager, he was in the Confederate Army, fighting in the Battle at Fort Donaldson.

My father Willis White Robinson was the oldest child of William McGilbra and Martha Frances. He was born Nov. 23, 1877. He was a farmer, a railroader, and then a barber for over 50 years. Willis married Eva Lou Dunbar of Caldwell County on Apr. 16, 1912. They were active in the Methodist Church and the Eastern Star; and Willis was a Mason. He served terms on the Dawson Springs City Council and was a Democrat.

I, Nola Evelyn Robinson Haley, was born in 1916, and am the only child of Willis White and Eva Lou Robinson. I married George Franklin Haley of Christian County (1913-1971), and have one daughter, Evvylu Alice, born Mar. 16, 1956, at the old Hopkins County Hospital.

We lived out of Hopkins County for several years due to our work, but returned in 1977, and are happy to be residents of the county again.

We are related to the Robinsons in Hopkins, Christian and Caldwell Counties. - *Submitted by Nola R. Haley*

ROBINSON-DAVIS

James Robinson (sometimes found as Robertson, as the family spelled the name both ways) was born May 8, 1841, the son of Vincent F. and Miranda Davis Robinson. On Oct. 1, 1871 in Hopkins County, James married Sarah Virginia Stokes. Sarah Virginia was born Oct. 17, 1851, the daughter of David A. and Susan E. Wright Stokes.

James and Sarah Virginia were the parents of Agnes, Alice, Lou, Eugenia, William Columbus (Lum), Cora, Clara, Myrtle, and Garland.

Agnes (1872-1937) married Lige Robinson and they had no children. Agnes is buried at Old Suthards Cemetery.

Alice (1875-1905) married Neal Summers. They were the parents of James, Oscar, Tom, Lizzie, Bertha, Goldie and Marie. Alice is buried at Union Cemetery.

Lou (1876-1949) married Neal Summers after the death of her sister, Alice. They were the parents of Luther and Geneva. Both are buried at Beulah Cemetery.

Eugenia (1879-1947) married Charles E. Baker. They had one child, Lucien. Eugenia married second Hugh Griffin and they had no children. Eugenia and Hugh are buried at Oddfellows Cemetery.

William Columbus (1880-1959) married Bertha Fowler. They had no children. Both are buried at Oddfellows Cemetery.

Cora (1882-1969) married Ed. Z. Smith. They were the parents of Carl, Gladys, Thurman, and Kathryn. Both are buried at Oakwood Cemetery.

Clara (1886-1978) married Taylor F. Hawkins Sr. They were the parents of Margaret Elizabeth, Ruth Helen, and Taylor F. Jr. Both are buried at Oddfellows Cemetery.

Myrtle (1888-1981) married Desmond Smith. They were the parents of Agnes and Mary Virginia. Both are buried at Oddfellows Cemetery.

Garland (1891-1953) married Minnie Lee Ratliff. They were the parents of Robbie Jo and Ronald Jackson. Both are buried at Oakwood Cemetery.

James Robinson died June 18, 1917 and Sarah Virginia died Sept. 21, 1941. Both are buried at Old Suthards Cemetery. -*Submitted by Taylor F. Hawkins Jr.*

See picture on page 33.

BEN T. ROBINSON

Ben T. Robinson, well-known druggist, and two-term mayor of Mortons Gap, was born in Wisconsin. He came with his parents to Christian Co., KY, when he was five years of age. In 1869, the family moved to Earlington, and it was there he obtained what little schooling he got, before he went to work at the age of thirteen.

In 1886, Ben T. Robinson moved to Mortons Gap and started in the drug business on the southeast corner of Main and Cross Streets. In 1911, he had the reputation of having been in business longer than any other firm in the town.

In his store was a complete line of drugs, patent medicines, perfumes, toilet articles, stationery, rubbery goods, paints, oils, varnishes, tobacco, and most anything else a customer could want.

In 1899, Mayor Robinson was elected to the state legislature in a strong Democrat county, and was a member of the general assembly at the time Governor Goebel was assassinated.

From the time of the town's organization in 1888, he was an officer in some capacity. He was police judge, trustee, and mayor, being elected mayor the last time without any opposition. He was also vice president of the Planters Bank and the Mortons Gap Mercantile Company.

In 1883, he married Miss Lizzie F. Harris, of Trigg County, KY, and to this union four sons were born: Roy, Lisle, Thomas, and Carlstedt.

He erected his first store in 1907. This building was later moved and made into houses. He built a handsome two-story building on the corner about 1914.

After Mr. Robinson went out of business, several different firms occupied the building, and made some changes in its appearance, but very few.

Today it is the City Hall of Mortons Gap, and also police headquarters. However, the city administration has hopes of erecting a new municipal building in the near future. - *Submitted by Margaret Berry*

DR. ROY F. ROBINSON

Dr. Roy Forrest Robinson was a practicing physician in Madisonville for more than 45 years. He was born in St. Charles, KY, on July 9, 1883, the son of Benjamin T. and Elizabeth Forrest (Harris) Robinson. (See BEN T. ROBINSON article.) Before attending medical school, he worked in the coal mines in Mortons Gap. In 1906, he graduated from the U. of Louisville Medical School, where he was valedictorian of his class. For several years he was an assistant physician at Western State Hospital in Hopkinsville before establishing a practice with Dr. W.M. Hammack in Madisonville.

Roy Forrest Robinson and Elinor Margaret Gardiner Robinson

He married Elinor Margaret Gardiner, daughter of Dr. Thomas Wright and Mollie Gardiner (see DR. THOMAS WRIGHT GARDINER article), on Aug. 2, 1912, and they had one child, Eloise Robinson.

In April of 1918, Dr. Robinson enlisted in the United States Army Medical Corps and served two years overseas. And in 1942, he again volunteered his services to the U.S. Navy, although he was not called. He was a member of the Veterans of Foreign Wars and Disabled American Veterans.

Dr. Roy F. Robinson

He served as a member of the Madisonville Board of Education for a number of years. He died Apr. 1, 1956. - *Submitted by Margaret Berry*

BEDFORD ROLAND

Bedford Roland was born circa 1795, in Virginia. He was in Franklin Co., GA, when he entered the War of 1812, and was assigned to Captain Garrett Sandidge's Company of Volunteer Riflemen. He was discharged in 1814, at Milledgeville, GA.

Bedford Roland returned to Franklin County, and married Martha "Patsey" Pruitt in 1816. She was born Aug. 4, 1798, the daughter of Japheth Pruitt, deceased. Her Uncle Samuel Pruitt was guardian of Martha and her brothers Phillip Pruitt, Tillman Pruitt, and Zachariah Pruitt. The first child of Bedford and Martha was Robert born Aug. 8, 1817.

By 1819, the Roland Family had settled in Hopkins County, KY. Other children were: Julia Ann, William Jasper, Tillman, Rachel, Nancy, and Lorenzo Jefferson "L.J." Roland.

Robert and Rachel (Slaton) Roland

On Dec. 20, 1838, Robert Roland married Rachel Slaton. The ceremony was solemnized by The Reverend R.G. Gardiner. Rachel was born Apr. 28, 1819, daughter of Edmund and Nancy (Allen) Slaton, who had owned land in Hopkins County since 1807.

In 1840, Philip Prewitt of Benton Co., AL, sold Bedford Roland 206 acres of land on Deer Creek, in consideration of $450. In 1841, John Newton and wife Mary deeded land to Bedford Roland. Joel Y. Trice deeded him land in 1849. Bedford and Martha Roland deeded land to John Lockbridge, Wm. Scott, and to their son William J. Roland.

About 1852, Bedford Roland contracted for land on the North side of Green River, in Daviess County (now McLean). This land joined their son Robert Roland's land. Martha Roland died there July 23, 1853. Bedford Roland died Mar. 23, 1855.

Lola (Roland) Dent, granddaughter of Robert and Rachel Roland

The above family history was given to me by my Mother Lola (Roland) Dent. She was a granddaughter of Robert and Rachel (Slaton) Roland. - *Submitted by Nadine (Dent) McCall*

CLAUDE L. ROSS

Claude L. Ross was born in Madisonville on Jan. 6, 1864, to James Bordley Ross and Sara ("Sallie") Bradley Ross, who had moved to Hopkins County from the town of Bordley in Union County, near Sturgis. Bordley, KY, was founded in 1821, by James' father, Charles Bordley Ross, and uncle, William Stuart Ross, upon their move to Kentucky from Maryland with their wives, Parthenia Dade and Ellen Dade, who were sisters.

Claude L. Ross home was located on the site of the present MESSENGER building

Charles and William, incidentally, were sons of Major David Ross, Revolutionary War officer and nephew of George Ross, a signer of the Declaration of Independence.

Claude carried on his father's grocery business, known as "Ross Grocery Company", on East Center Street in Madisonville. Upon his retirement, Mr. Ross sold the Center Street frontage of the real estate, where the store was located to J.C. Penney Co. It is presently occupied by the Municipal Offices of the City of Madisonville.

After his parents' death, Claude bought the interest of his younger brother, Preston Bradley Ross, who later was Vice President of the Kentucky Bank & Trust Co., in the family real estate located on the west side of South Main Street, one lot south of its corner with West Broadway. After James Bordley Ross' death in 1886, and until her death in 1892, their mother lived in a small house there, onto which Claude built a large two story residence in about 1900. The house stood until after Mr. Ross' death in 1958, at the age of 94. It was razed after the property was sold and later was bought by Madisonville Publishing Co., which built a new contemporary building, where "The Messenger" is published.

Claude married Mary Ellen Pinckard of Murfreesboro, TN, in 1896, and two children were born to this union; James Bordley Ross, II and Louise Pinckard Ross. James retired after working for many years for Ruby Lumber Co. and died childless in 1980.

Louise married Thomas Butler Spain, also of Murfreesboro, TN, in 1925 and to this marriage two children were born, Sara Ross Spain and Thomas Butler Spain, Jr. Louise Spain later married Richard A. Dunham of New York and they resided on Princeton Avenue in Madisonville.

Two sons were born of the marriage of Sara Ross Spain to Lawrence L. Smith, Jr. of Connecticut; Lawrence Thomas Smith and Jerry Alan Smith. Several years after the death of her first husband, Sara Ross married Donald B. Mills of Evansville, and a daughter, Kathleen Kay Mills, was born to them.

Lawrence Thomas Smith married Betty Erwin in 1971, and two daughters were born to them, Heidi Louise Smith and Christine Ross Smith.

Jerry Alan Smith and Jane Brown, both of Evansville, IN, were married in 1986.

Thomas Butler Spain, Jr. married Frances M. Jones of Lexington, KY, in 1954, and two sons were born to them, Edward Butler Spain and David Ross Spain. Edward married Carolyn Etheridge of Franklin, TN, in 1984, and David married Janice Newsam of Madisonville in 1986. (See "Thomas B. Spain, Jr.") - *Submitted by Judge Thomas B. Spain*

RUBY

The Ruby family history dates back to 1300 A.D. in Switzerland. For more recent times, John Brooks Ruby was born Apr. 1, 1782, in Virginia in what is now called Hardin Co., KY. He married Nancy Burrell, who was born Mar. 28, 1778, and died May 28, 1848. John was a surveyor and one of the earliest settlers in the Green River County.

John and Nancy had three children: 1. Edwin Ruby was born Aug. 13, 1808. Edwin was married (first) his wife's name was not recorded. They had three children: 1. Brickley J. Ruby; 2. Bushard Ruby; 3. Sarah Ruby. Edwin married (second) Fertina Winstead on Apr. 2, 1846. They had three children: 1. Nancy R. Ruby, born in 1847; 2. Aurelius Ruby, born in 1848; 3. John Edwin Ruby, who was born Sept. 3, 1849. He married Vaden Turner on Jan. 29, 1874, at the home of her parents in Princeton, KY. Her father was a judge in Princeton. She was born Jan. 5, 1850, and died Sept. 25, 1914.

Vaden and Turner, who was a man long before his time, operated a general store in Madisonville. Vaden also operated a ladies hat store. In the General Store one could buy anything. This later became Ruby Lumber Company, the largest and most complete building material store west of Louisville. Ruby Lumber Company became the parent company of Ruby Construction Company; Ruby Mining Company; Ruby Engineering Company; Earlewood Development Company; Ruby Precast Concrete Company and many others. Later on, Turner was joined in business by Laurel Ruby, Clyde Ruby and Lucien Ruby. As time went on John Edwin (son of Laurel), and Clyde (son of Clyde, Sr.), became involved in these businesses. Edwin and Clyde mostly in heavy construction, such as bridges and utilities work. Ruby Construction Company is still in business in Louisville even though there are no Rubys involved at this time.

John Edwin Ruby and Vaden Turner Ruby had six children: 1. Edwin Turner Ruby was born Dec. 29, 1874, and died Apr. 7, 1938. He married Alice Snell, who was born in 1876, and died in 1903. They had one daughter: Mary Snell Ruby, who was born Feb. 20, 1902. Edwin Turner Ruby is buried in the Odd Fellow's Cemetery in Madisonville, KY.

2. Laurel E. Ruby was born Dec. 20, 1878, and died in 1948. He married Mabel Callen. They had one son: John Edwin Ruby, who was born Aug. 4, 1905, and died Nov. 12, 1964. He married Mary Comer, who was born Apr. 15, 1907, and died Mar. 22, 1955. They had three children: 1. John Edwin Ruby, Jr., born June 1934; 2. Aldis Ruby, born in 1935; 3. Lucinda Ruby, born February 1939.

3. Walter John Ruby, Sr., was born Aug. 18, 1880, and died Jan. 26, 1926. He was an insurance executive and in 1910, became the President and Chairman of the Board of The Kentucky Bank & Trust Company in Madisonville. His son, Walter John Ruby, Jr., was a farmer and a breeder of fine cattle. Walter John Ruby, Sr., married Anna Grace Connor, Oct. 21, 1917. They had one son: 1. Walter John Ruby, Jr. was born Oct. 12, 1919. He had four children: 1. Walter Ruby; 2. Turner Ruby; 3. Laurel Ruby and 4. Anna Connor Ruby. Walter John Ruby, Sr., is buried in his Mausoleum in the Odd Fellow's Cemetery in Madisonville, KY.

4. Clyde Ruby, Sr., was born June 1, 1882, and died July 26, 1913. He married Aileen Morton on Oct. 16, 1906. She died in 1956. They had two sons: 1. Charles Everette Ruby, born July 21, 1907; 2. Clyde Ruby, Jr., born Oct. 14, 1913. Clyde Ruby married Lorena Dempster on Apr. 22, 1939. They live in Madisonville, KY (1983). They have one son: 1. Lucien Ruby, who was born Feb. 9, 1944. Lucien is a graduate in Civil Engineering from Duke University and has a Masters Degree in Business Administration from Harvard University. He lives in San Francisco, CA.

5. Henry D. Ruby was born Aug. 14, 1884, and died in 1915. He is buried in the Grapevine Cemetery in Madisonville, KY.

6. Lucien Ruby was born Sept. 14, 1886, and died in 1949. He married Hattie West of Hopkinsville, KY. They had one daughter: 1. Katherine Ruby, born and died in 1913. John Edwin Ruby died July 3, 1891, and is buried in the Grapevine Cemetery in Madisonville, KY. His wife Vaden Turner Ruby died Sept. 25, 1914, and is buried beside John Edwin. - *Submitted by Walter Ruby*

JAMES L. SALMON, M.D.

Dr. James L. Salmon, son of Thaddeus Robert Salmon and Lucy Alice DeMonbreum Salmon, was born Sept. 14, 1905, in Metcalfe Co., KY. His paternal grandparents were Sarah Jane Rodgers and James Marion Salmon. His maternal grandparents were Mr. and Mrs. Joseph Marion DeMonbreum.

Dr. Salmon and Ellene Ruth Reeves were married July 27, 1934, in Bowling Green, KY. Ellene Ruth, born Apr. 1, 1912, in Gainesboro, TN, was the daughter of Lois Choate and James Charles Reeves. Paternal grandparents were Donna and William Reeves. Maternal grandparents were Fatima Wells and Dr. John Choate.

Dr. James L. Salmon studied Pre-Med at the University of KY, and graduated from the Vanderbilt School of Medicine in 1932. He did his internship and residency at Nashville General Hospital, where he met Ruth, who was studying nursing, and she graduated in 1933. Dr. Salmon served as a colonel in the Third Armored Division during WWII. The Salmons moved to 208 N. Main St. on Dec. 5, 1945. A few months before, Dr. Salmon had begun his practice of general medicine and surgery in the old Doctors' Bldg. on the corner of Sugg and S. Main. He built the Salmon Memorial Clinic at 412 N. Kentucky, in 1964, and practiced there until his death in 1984.

Dr. and Mrs. Salmon had five children, all of whom graduated from the University of KY, before going on to pursue further studies elsewhere. They are: Dr. Lucy Ruth Salmon Crain, born May 3, 1940, is a pediatrician on staff at the University of California, San Francisco. She is married to Wm. Ray Crain, M.D., a dermatologist from Flemingsburg, KY. They have one son, Wm. Ray Crain, Jr. and one daughter, Sara Lois Crain. Mary Ellene Salmon Templeton, born Jan. 24, 1944, is an R.N. in the recovery room at George Washington Hospital in Washington, D.C. She is married to Alton Templeton from Princeton, KY. Sue Anne Salmon, born Nov. 7, 1948, earned a Bachelor of Fine Arts Degree from the California College of Arts and Crafts, Oakland, CA. Dr. James L. Salmon, Jr., born Aug. 15, 1950, is an otolaryngologist, practicing in Bowling Green, KY. He is married to Diane Bianchi from Harlan Co., KY. Their children are James Lewis Branen Salmon, Eric Joseph Salmon, and Elizabeth Ellene Salmon. Dr. Thaddeus Robert Salmon practices family medicine in Madisonville in the Salmon Memorial Clinic. He is married to Sarah Lee Floyd from Lexington, KY. Their children are Ainsley Elizabeth Salmon and Thaddeus Robert Salmon III. - *Submitted by Sally Salmon*

THADDEUS ROBERT SALMON, D.O.

Dr. Thaddeus R. Salmon was born May 30, 1954. He was the fifth of five children born to Dr. James L. Salmon and Ellene Ruth Reeves Salmon, born Apr. 1, 1912, in Gainesboro, Jackson Co., TN. James L. Salmon, born Sept. 14, 1905, in Cork, Metcalfe Co., KY, died Dec. 1, 1984, in Nashville, TN, moved into their home on Main St. in Madisonville, on Dec. 5, 1945.

Dr. James Salmon, Sr. began his practice of general surgery and medicine in October 1945. His office was initially located in the old hospital building, which became known as the Doctors' Building, on the corner of Sugg and Main St. in downtown Madisonville. He practiced there until 1966, when he moved his office to the Salmon Memorial Clinic, which he constructed at 412 N. Kentucky Ave. in Madisonville. He continued to practice there until shortly before his death in December 1984. He is survived by his wife and five children. He was a member of the First United Methodist Church. He is buried in Odd Fellows Cemetery.

The parents of James L. Salmon were Thaddeus Robert, died at age 78, in July, 1945, and Lucy Alice DeMonbreum Salmon, died age 79,

June 16, 1954. Parents of Ellene Ruth Reeves Salmon were James Charles Reeves, died at age 87, Apr. 22, 1953, and Lois Choate Reeves, died at age 73, Jan. 9, 1955.

The brother and sisters of Dr. Thaddeus R. Salmon are James L. Salmon, Jr., born Aug. 15, 1950; Dr. Lucy Ruth Salmon Crain, born May 3, 1940; Mary Ellene Salmon Templeton, born Jan. 24, 1944; and Sue Anne Salmon, born Nov. 7, 1948.

Dr. Thaddeus Robert and Sarah Lee (Floyd) Salmon and children Ainsley Elizabeth and Thaddeus Robert Salmon III

Dr. Thaddeus R. Salmon married Sarah Lee Floyd, born Sept. 17, 1954, on June 2, 1979. They were married in Maxwell Street Presbyterian Church, Lexington, KY. "Sally" is the daughter of James Neville Floyd and Sarah Frances Edmonds Floyd of Lexington, KY. Sally has one brother, James Allen Floyd, born Feb. 6, 1946. James Neville is the son of Orestes Foraker Floyd and Marietta Finley Cassady Floyd. Sarah Frances is the daughter of Eugene Allen Edmonds and Dorothea "Dolly" Taylor Battaile Edmonds. Sally's grandparents were also of central Kentucky.

Following their marriage in 1979, Thad and Sally moved to Kansas City, MO, where Dr. Salmon attended the University of Health Sciences, College of Osteopathic Medicine. After earning his D.O. Degree (Doctor of Osteopathy), they moved to Silver Lake, OH, while Dr. Salmon did his internship and Family Medicine Residency at Cuyahoga Falls General Hospital, Cuyahoga Falls, OH. Dr. Salmon became board certified by the American Osteopathic Board of General Practice on Feb. 17, 1986.

Thad and Sally moved to Madisonville in early July 1985. Their daughter, Ainsley Elizabeth Salmon, was born Sept. 17, 1982, in Shawnee Mission, KS. Their son, Thaddeus Robert Salmon III, was born Apr. 4, 1986, in Henderson, KY. The Thad Salmons belong to the First Presbyterian Church in Madisonville. Dr. Salmon's office is located in the Salmon Memorial Clinic, where his father had practiced for the preceding 19 years. (Dr. James L. Salmon practiced medicine in Madisonville for a total of 39 years.) - *Submitted by Sally Salmon*

SAMUELS-THORNHILL-LEWIS
Up from Slavery—Nov. 19, 1835. Our family originated from Trenton, KY, Todd Co. Later some settled in other states, such as Chicago, IL, and Hopkins Co., Madisonville, KY.

My great grandmother, Mary Thornhill, was asked for her hand in marriage, by Thomas Samuels, in 1835. Thomas Samuels was an Indian, and no Indians were slaves. My great grandmother lived on the plantation of the Thornhill family, who owned her. She took the name of the slave owner. When Thomas Samuels fell in love with great grandmother, the Thornhill's "Massah," said that the only way that Great Grandmother Mary could marry Thomas Samuels, would be he would have to buy her. Great grandfather had to work for many months, maybe years, to buy Great Grandmother. He worked until he had a hat full of money, but he could not read, write, nor figure, so he did not know how much he really had. The old Massah said it was not enough, so Great Grandfather Samuels worked until he had another hat full to the brim, and it was then that Great Grandmother became the bride of Thomas Samuels—Mrs. Mary Samuels. Mary Samuels was then a free woman.

Mary Thornhill Samuels wearing her second day dress after her marriage to Thomas Samuels

Amy Frances Samuels, my mother's mother, was the first child to be born. When she was five years old, the Civil War was ended and freedom came to all. Six children were born to this family, four daughters, and two sons. The daughters were: Barbara, Mary Ellen, Amy Frances and Rebecca; the boys were Roger and Thomas Mansfield.

All of the children grew up and married. Both of the sons became ministers. Mansfield Samuels lived in Hopkinsville, where he pastored a church. He had more than a $1,000 worth of books in his home library. He lived with his wife in Hopkinsville until he died. They had no children. Roger Samuels, the second son, also a minister, made his home in Madisonville. He married Mrs. Daisy Samuels, and they had six children. He and his wife are buried in Elliott's Memorial Gardens, Madisonville. Barbara Samuels was married to the President of Fisk University, Nashville, and they had three children. When her husband died, the family moved to Chicago, IL. My great grandmother Mary lived with Barbara and family, and lived to be 112 years old. She died in Chicago. Her daughter and two grandchildren are living in Chicago at present. The other three daus. were last known to be living in Guthrie, KY.

Amy Frances Samuels married Will Lewis, and they had twelve children. The birthdates are unknown, therefore they are listed at random order: Willie, a daughter; Edward; Roxie; Blanche; McKinley, son; Herbert; Carrie; Carl; Hattie; Emma; unnamed baby died in infancy; and Mary Bell, my mother who married Sanders Elliott. (See ELLIOTT-LEWIS) - *Submitted by Elizabeth Elliott Van Leer*

SATTERFIELD-MADISON
Hiram Satterfield was born Jan. 9, 1813, in Person Co., NC, to John (Jack) Satterfield (1786-1842), and his wife Polly Ann Cothran Satterfield (1790-1874). Hiram married Elizabeth Ann Madison in 1852, in Granville, NC. Elizabeth Ann was the daughter of Peyton Madison (1780-1847) and his wife Elizabeth Carey Madison (1784 in Scotland-1889 Hopkins Co., KY). Elizabeth Ann was born Oct. 1, 1828, in Granville, NC.

Hiram started teaching school at the age of nineteen and taught for over forty years. He was elected to the Legislature Aug. 4, 1842, from Person Co., NC and one of the first things he did was to present a bill to pay to General Jackson $1000, plus interest for a fine he thought was unjustly put on him in New Orleans, in the month of January 1815, while he was commander of the army. The bill passed on first reading.

Hiram and Elizabeth, with their first three children, moved to Sumner Co., TN, in October of 1857, and lived there until the fall of 1858. Then, with the addition of another child born while in Tennessee, they moved onto Hopkins Co., KY, by way of the Cumberland Gap. The Satterfields first settled on the Tucker School Road, a short distance from U.S. 41 North. Hiram taught school in a log school house on Judge Pratt's farm (Tucker School House) and in other districts in the Northwest part of the county. He did a lot of writing to the editors of the Roxboro, NC NEWS, and the MADISONVILLE TIMES, and he would caption his writings as "Shakerag, Ky. News." Part of Person Co., NC, had been called Shakerag from Revolutionary Days and to Hiram and so many other settlers from North Carolina, this section of Hopkins Co., KY, was a lot like Shakerag, NC.

In a letter to the editor of the TIMES, dated Mar. 12, 1883, Hiram describes the village of Manitou and how it had improved with the passing of the Iron Horse through it. There was a store, post office, grocery and saloon combined, photograph gallery and all of these were said to be doing a good business. Some of the proprietors he mentioned were: Messrs. Barnets, Swope, Massey and Wm. Yarbrough.

In another letter to the TIMES Editor, Hiram wrote with regard to "Hanson Notes." He tells how on a visit to the village after a lengthy absence, in one of the stores there they were waited on by a "handsome, genteel lady" in the capacity of clerk and salesman. He wrote that her polite and pleasant manners were prima facie, evidence of her fitness for the position. He apparently had no objection to the extension of the rights and privileges of women as advocated by Miss Susan Anthony (as he wrote).

In another letter he provides an interesting story of the origin of the name Shakerag. He states that the district once had a Captain William (Bill) Daniel, who gave the district the name Shakerag from the shabby appearance-apparel of his men. Captain Bill was supposedly a very popular captain with his men: his first word of command being "fall up in a lump".

The children born to Hiram and Elizabeth (Liza) were:

Walter C. Satterfield, b. May 16, 1853 in North Carolina, d. Jan. 23, 1928, in Hopkins Co., married Lucresa Boyd of Hopkins Co.

Corena M. Satterfield (twin sister to Walter), b. May 16, 1853, in North Carolina, d. Sept. 29, 1877 (of consumption a short time before she was to be married).

John Madison Satterfield, b. Nov. 18, 1855, in North Carolina, d. May 31, 1948, in Hopkins Co., married Janava Cates Dec. 21, 1879, in Hopkins Co.

James Bennett Satterfield, b. June 8, 1858 in Sumner Co., TN, d. Dec. 27, 1937, in Hopkins Co.

Polly Ann Satterfield, b. Feb. 19, 1860, in Hopkins Co., KY, d. Nov. 7, 1912, married Nathan Hibbs of Madisonville (no children).

Hiram Satterfield died Sept. 3, 1893, and Elizabeth Madison Satterfield died Feb. 9, 1917. Both are buried at Veazey Cemetery in Hopkins County.

The only child of Hiram and Elizabeth to have children was their son John M. and his wife Janava Melissa Cates Satterfield. Janava M. was born Aug. 31, 1864, in Hopkins Co., KY. She died Feb. 3, 1942, in Madisonville and is buried at Olive Branch.

Their children (all born in Hopkins County) were: Lola Monta Satterfield (Fryer/Carroll); Margaret Ann (Moore); Walter Clifton; Maude Lee (Long/Kirkwood); Vida Aileen (Scott); Annie Melissa (Utterback); Bessie Mae; Johnnie Celysa (Masoncup); Gladys Catherine; Boyd Gatlin; Fraulein Strother; and Wallace Gordon Satterfield. Wallace Gordon's wife (Mable Bell Morgan Satterfield), still lives and resides at this time in Madisonville. Sources: Family Diaries, Old Newspaper Clippings, and Vida Satterfield Scott's Scrapbook. - Compiled by Jan Jones (Mrs. Larry Wygal)

NOTE: Randa Bearden has in her possession a quilt pieced and quilted by Correna Satterfield while still a teenager. This quilt is approximately 117 years old. She also submits the following from a Hiram Satterfield discussion on SHAKERAG.

There have been many disagreements over the origin of the name of Shakerag. It seems that the argument isn't a recent phenomenon. According to the following letter it was being discussed as early as 1842. This letter was written to the editors of the paper in Roxboro, NC, and was reprinted in the Centennial Edition of 1983 of THE COURIER-TIMES.

"Messrs. Editors: It may be interesting to some of the present generation to learn something as to the history of Shakerag. How it acquired the name has always, to some extent, been a mystery. Tradition informs us that the district once had a captain by the name of William Daniel familiarly called, by his neighbors and friends, Stoker Bill Daniel. He gave the district the name of Shakerag from the shabby apparel of his men. His first word of command was "fall up in a lump"; he would then direct his Lieutenant to call the roll and when through he would make some excuse for not drilling, invite his men to the liquor stand, and treat them to as much as they would drink. We have heard some of the old men say they had rather muster under Capt. Daniel than anybody else—all they had to do was to attend the roll call and then repair to the liquor stand. I was at Hayneville, AL, in 1842, and had some business with a firm of law of intelligent gentlemen, and they inquired what county in North Carolina was I from. I told them Person. They asked me if that was the county called Shakerag. I told them it was. (It seems that the whole county at distance is known by that name.) They said they had often heard of Shakerag and asked me many questions in relation to its history which I answered much to their satisfaction and amusement. In my travels through Tennessee, South Carolina, Georgia, Alabama, and Mississippi, the name of Shakerag seemed to be as familiar as a household word, and here in Kentucky the people know as much about Shakerag as the people of Mt. Tirzah do."

Hiram Satterfield
Manitou, KY
March 8, 1887- *Submitted by Randa Bearden*

SCHMETZER

Martin Schmetzer married Christiana Calvert shortly after they arrived in the U.S. from Germany, sometime around 1850.

Christiana and her sister, Annie were 16 and 18 year old orphans when they crossed the ocean together. Annie married Henrey Gloss and they lived in Chicago.

Martin died shortly after they established a home in Hopkins County. Christiana raised six children to adults. They owned homes and farmed in Hopkins County.

John (1858-1888) operated a stage coach and blacksmith business in Chicago.

Lee Washington (1865-1942) married Cordelia Sisk, daughter of Victoria and Albert Sisk. No children.

Joel (1867-1952) married Annie Burton, daughter of Dolphus and Nannie Burton. Two children, J.D. (deceased) and Bonnie Lee Kirkwood.

Robert Martin (1868-1950) married Emma Craig, daughter of Denishe and J. Ingrim Craig. Two daughters, Christie Lee Payne (deceased) and Ann Elsie, single.

Julia (1863-1930) married Emmett O'Bryan. Two children, Martin and Oral (deceased).

Fannie (1871-1922) never married.- *Submitted by Ann Elsie Schmetzer*

SCOTT-SLATON

Benjamin Townes (B.T.) son of Thomas C. and Melinda Hill Scott, was born Sept. 27, 1913 in Hopkins Co., KY. He was born in the Bourland House, which is the site on which the First Baptist Church parsonage is now located. For several years he was a farmer, but most of his married life he was a coal mine mechanic. He was married to Lanna Slaton, Dec. 24, 1932. B.T. died Jan. 30, 1981. They moved to their home on Laffoon Trail, Madisonville, in 1944, and Lanna still lives there. They have two sons and one daughter.

B.T. and Lanna Scott

Their first son, Robert Carroll (b. Sept. 7, 1933), and his wife Joan (Cates) live in Providence, KY. They have five children. Susan Carol is married to Richard Mitchell of Clay, KY and they have two sons; Bruce and Phillip George. Patty Lynn is married to Ricky Householder. They live in Clay and have a daughter, Amelia. Richard Alan of Carmi, IL, is married to Vicki Northern (from Providence, KY) and they have a daughter, Leah. The fourth child, Lori Elaine is married to Mark Martin of Clay and has two sons; Matthew and Derek. The fifth child, a son Robert Townes is single and lives at home.

Their second son, James Marlin was born in Hopkins County, Sept. 7, 1938. He is married to Phyllis Harm of Owensboro. They live in Morganfield, KY, and have two sons and two daughters. First child, Cynthia (Cindy) is married to Jim Guess of Ft. Lauderdale, FL. Second child, Michael (Mike) is attending University of KY, as is third child, Timothy (Tim). Fourth child, Kelly is at Western KY U.

Their daughter, Jo Evelyn, lives in Madisonville. She was born in Madisonville, June 21, 1951. She is married to Douglas E. Brown, II, of Providence, KY, and they have three sons: Douglas E. Brown III, Graham Benjamin and Alex Christopher.

Lanna, born Apr. 30, 1911, in Hopkins Co., is the second daughter of James Edmond and Amelia Denton Slaton. She taught school for two years at Wilson (her home school) and was married to B.T. Since that time she has been housewife and mother and is now enjoying the children, grandchildren and great grandchildren, and like her grandmothers before her is an avid quilter. - *Submitted by Lanna Scott*

SEYMOUR-RINGO

Leavy Novelist Ringo (Dec. 8, 1889 to Aug. 22, 1971), was true to her name...she loved books. When widowed and alone, her books became her solace, especially scripture. While in her seventies, she needed her encyclopedia to "improve her mind".

She was my dear Aunt Leavy, who let me visit and taught me whatever I needed to

Standing l to r: Spaulding Ringo, Kathleen Ringo, Chester Seymour, Leavy Seymour, John Kennedy, Alice Kennedy, B.F. (Poppa) Ringo holding new grandson, Gertrude Ringo and Opal Ramsey. Seated l to r: Virginia Ringo and others unknown. Picture taken by Ernest Ramsey

know. She was my maternal grandmother's sister.

Chester Lloyd Seymour (Mar. 27, 1887 to Oct. 20, 1958), and Leavy Ringo were married Feb. 23, 1910, in Evansville, IN. She was 18 and he 22. Their parents were farmers. Her parents were Benjamin Franklin and Florence Dye Ringo. She was born in Blackford, he, in Hopkins County.

Aunt Leavy was a housewife, through and through, one of the world's truly great cake bakers. It was a toss-up who was the best cook, Aunt Leavy or Aunt Kathleen.

Chester had the opportunity to engineer an ICRR train and moved to Princeton, KY. They were there 10 years. In Akron, OH, he learned to vulcanize tires. He knew recapping was up-and-coming. They were in Akron five years. He had tire and vulcanizing businesses in Evansville, Owensboro, and Madisonville at various times.

One of my earliest memories is of Uncle Chester carrying me to the riverbank in Owensboro, so I might see a showboat.

The Madisonville shop was at 18 North Franklin. Aunt Leavy's brother, Spaulding Ringo, moved to Madisonville. He and Chester became partners around 1924. They named the business Seymour and Ringo. The name remained the same until Uncle Spaulding razed the building and built a new one in the mid-1960's.

The Seymours left Madisonville and opened their large store in Owensboro. I visited often and was there on V-J Day....what a parade! I had never seen so many people so excited, THE WAR WAS OVER.

Aunt Leavy was a strong Baptist and Uncle Chester was Methodist and a Sunday School teacher. In 1923, he was a member of the board, when the cornerstone was laid for the "big" Methodist Church on Center and Scott in Madisonville. He was also a councilman when the old fire station was built. Through it all he never forgot his love of railroads.

Aunt Leavy and Uncle Chester were constant and loving visitors to our home. They had no children, so my mother and I were theirs. I remember well two Sundays. One was when I was 11 and joined the Methodist church. He joined with me. The other was Pearl Harbor day, Dec. 7, 1941. I was four days short of five years old, but I remember it like yesterday. A pall was spreading over our world that Sunday. One that would never go away. Victory could not wipe out the knowledge of the Atom bomb which was to come.

I am most thankful for my parents, Margaret and "Jobie" Sullivan, my grandparents, Opal and Ernest Ramsey (whom I knew as "Big Mama and Daddy Paw"), my great-aunts and great-uncles, Leavy and Chester Seymour and Kathleen and Spaulding Ringo.

They were a constant in the midst of turmoil. As with most families of that period, we relied on the faith of our fathers. Each one of these dear ones made my world a bit calmer with their love, their time, but most of all, their consistency.

All of the older ones are gone now except my beloved "Sugie", my great-uncle Spaulding Ringo. God Bless them all. (See Ringo-Dye, Mather-Ringo, Ramsey-Ringo, Ringo-Arnett, and Kennedy-Ringo) - *Submitted by Peggy Sullivan Waide*

SHARKEY-LUTZ

Shellia Dianne Lutz and Lowell Gene Sharkey were united in marriage Aug. 30, 1969, in Tallahassee, FL.

Shellia was born May 24, 1949. Her parents are Mary Lou Duncan and the late Reverend Lona Ray Lutz. (See Lutz-Duncan)

Lowell and Shellia with children Jennifer Michelle and Jathan David

Shellia attended Nebo, Pride, Seminary, and Madisonville High School in Hopkins County. She graduated from Rickards High School in Tallahassee, FL, in 1967. She attended Florida State U. one year. She graduated from Tallahassee Community College in 1970, with an associate degree in Applied Science.

Shellia was employed by the State of Florida in the Vocational Re-Hab department for one year. She has also worked for Ryder Truck Rental in Florida and Indiana.

Her hobbies include: singing, playing the piano, making stained glass and crafts.

Lowell was born Oct. 4, 1949, in Lafayette, IN. His parents are Mary Alice Knochel and Ralph Roland Sharkey. He has one sister, Linda Sugimoto and one brother, Kenneth. He has one step-sister, Carol Ann McIntyre, three half sisters: Lisa, Carol, and Brenda Sharkey, and three half brothers: William G. McIntyre, David Christopher McIntyre (deceased) and Bobby Sharkey.

Lowell attended school in Kentland, Auburn, and Knox, IN. He also attended Leon High School in Tallahassee, FL. He graduated from Rickards High School, Tallahassee, FL, in 1967. Lowell attended Florida State U. and Purdue University Extension in Indianapolis, IN.

Lowell served two years in the United States Navy (1970-72). He was a radioman stationed at Jacksonville Naval Air Station.

Lowell's hobbies include flying, electronics, and mechanics.

Lowell and Shellia opened their own business, "Sharkey's Westside Service", in September 1979. They live on Wolf Hollow Rd., Manitou, KY, with their two children: Jennifer Michelle (Jan. 27, 1974), and Jathan David (Jan. 24, 1978). They are members of the Madisonville First Baptist Church. - *Submitted by Retha Tarter*

DOROTHY SHIPP

My grandmother is a very nice and sweet woman. Dorothy Shipp was born on Apr. 1, 1930 in Hopkins County. She was delivered at home by Dr. Johnson.

Dorothy went to school for about five years and had to quit to help her mother make a living. Her mother, Crill Sharp, was born on Oct. 29, 1912 in Lyon County and was a mother to six children.

Dorothy has five children. Bobby Clark was born on July 11, 1944 and is married to Donna Burris. They have two daughters, Melanie and Melissa. Sunnie Shipp was born Aug. 17, 1947 and he is married to Nancy Oldham. They have four children, Michelle, Jeffery, Chad and Elizabeth. Barbara is the oldest daughter and was born on Feb. 14, 1952. She is married to Robert Clifford and they have two sons, Jason and Eddie. Virginia Felker is the youngest daughter and has two daughters, April Shrum and Stephanie Walker. Neal Shipp, the youngest son, is married to Barbara Martin. They have two sons, Keith and David.

Dorothy went to school in Carbondale, KY. The school had only two rooms. She attended a Holiness Church and her hobbies are reading and embroidery.

Dorothy was employed at Buckhorn for several years, but is now unemployed. She likes to have a great time and many laughs. She lives on East Keigan Street in Dawson Springs. *-Submitted by, grandaughter, Stephanie Walker*

SHOULDERS-MILLER

Dorothy Lou Miller and James Odis Shoulders were married in her parents' home, rural Nebo, on May 10, 1947.

Dorothy was born Feb. 26, 1929, in Hopkins Co. near Madisonville, the oldest daughter of Arthur B. Miller and Annie Lue Polley. Arthur, born Dec. 5, 1906, in San Angelo, TX, was the only child of Isaac Miller and Fraye Smith. Arthur and Annie were married July 24, 1925, in Shawneetown, IL. Annie, daughter of Carlos Polley and Sallie Jones (see Wash Jones), was born Sept. 18, 1907, in Hopkins Co. Annie's sisters were: Opal Mae, married Rev. Thomas Wilson and Ily Kathleen married Huston Vanvactor. Other children of Annie and Arthur: Wanda Fraye Jennings, Arthur Jr.

James and Dorothy Miller Shoulders

(better known as Sonny), and two boys who died in infancy. Arthur Sr. died in 1951. In 1958, Annie married Regel Villines. She died in 1975.

Dorothy attended Greenwood School five years, 6th grade at Nebo, middle school in Chicago, IL, and returned to Nebo for High School, graduating in 1946. She took piano from Lillian Harralson and Grace Cox, local teachers and Mrs. Sullens in New Mexico and voice lessons from Tom Pate of the Conservatory of Music in Texas, Owen Egeberg, T.T.E.A. Music Division of Madisonville. Dorothy has taught music in local studios and privately for 25 years and is a charter member of the area chapter of Pennyrile Piano Teacher's Assoc. She and James have been members of Concord General Baptist Church over 25 years, where Dorothy is a choir member.

Ancestral names: Cobb, Newton, Sims, Lamb, Grand, Hawkins and Atkinson. From Ireland in the 1770's came the Millers. From England the Smiths to Illinois, who intermarried with the American Indians.

James, born Sept. 18, 1923, in Webster Co. to Ott Shoulders and Betty Jane Hopper born 1900, in Webster Co., daughter of John Hopper and Caroldone Cowan. Ott was born 1896, son of Joseph Shoulders of Tennessee and Marial (Molly) Murphy of Grapevine near Madisonville. James' brothers: Jack (deceased), Claude, George, William, and Joe. James' sisters: Lou Mabrey Johnson, Ora Mae Rodgers and Betty Ruth Osborn (See Osborn-Miller). Ancestral names: Reed, Sanders, Gregery (from Tennessee). From England: Prather, Ashley, Heiffey, Hibbs. Also Cherokee Indian.

James attended school in Webster Co., Vocational School on the G.I. Bill at Nebo, Adult Education in New Mexico. He entered the Navy in July 1944, serving in Puerto Rico, Cuba and Trinidad until June 1946. He bought a farm near Nebo soon after marriage. He worked five years as a concrete finisher, ironworker and welder in New Mexico and served as a deacon for the Free Will Baptist Church there. Since returning to Hopkins Co., he has owned and operated a bulldozer for over 20 years. He retired in 1986. He has been a member of the Nebo Masonic Lodge since 1953.

James and Dorothy adopted three daughters. Karen Anne Lindsey lives in Oklahoma and is a masseuse and amateur artist and has no children. Lola Marlene Mitchell lives in Nebo and is a nurse for a local Health Care Center and the mother of David, 13; Andrew, 9-1/2; and Cody, 2. Kimberly Jane Cunningham (See her story) lived in Madisonville and died in 1983. She was a Medical Secretary at Trover Clinic at the time of her death. Her daughter, Kayôna is now 10. - *Submitted by Dorothy Shoulders*

SIGLER-RAMSEY

Her name was Sarah Isabel Ramsey on the day of her birth, Mar. 24, 1874. She was to become "Sally" to her friends and family. She was my great-aunt, my maternal grandfather's (Ernest Ramsey) sister. She was one of five girls and seven boys in the Ramsey family. "Sally" was their eighth child and third girl. Little Alice, the first daughter, lived only 20 days.

James Gore Jr., brother of Louiza Elvina Gore Ramsey. He served in the 17th KY Calvary, I Co. in the Civil War. Honorably discharged in October of 1865

Being the baby gave her an enviable position with so man older brothers, for a few years, anyway. The Ramseys were to have 12 children. Aunt "Sally" was born nine years after the Civil War. While still a very small child, her maternal grandmother, Rejoina Gore visited the Ramseys for an extended time, not uncommon in those days.

There is some speculation that Nancy Williams Gore might actually be Mary W. Gore, who married a Kentuckian, John B. Fox. Mary is mentioned - more than once as a sister to Elizabeth, who married John G. Ramsey and lived in Kentucky. Aunt "Sally" remembered going shopping for material in Shady Grove and staying at Aunt Mary and Uncle John Fox's house. This would tend to disprove the claim that the Foxes moved to Illinois and spent the remainder of their days. (Taken from Uncle Albert Gore's old account book).

I have wondered how much Aunt "Sally" overheard. Children generally hear lots, if they are quiet and attentive. It is plausible that she heard the war stories about her Uncle Jim Gore (Aug. 23, 1838 to July 29, 1925), Louiza's brother. (He was in "I" Company - 17th Kentucky Calvary). He sent his widowed mother, Rejoina and his wife, Martha Leech Gore and family, to Illinois to wait out the war. His father was James Gore, Sr. (Dec. 25, 1786 to July 20, 1847). (This last material is from an old ledger of Uncle Albert Gore's).

Were they Confederate or Union sympathizers? I have no idea, but I intend to find out. It is also known that James did not come home, immediately. He was honorably discharged in October 1865, some six months later. This would indicate he had some duty to fulfill. I bring up these points of interest as they relate to a later action of Sally's.

Sally was very close to her parents, especially her mother, Louiza. The family was founded on Christian doctrines and Grandpa and Grandma, especially, lived their faith.

Sally met Robert Lee Sigler at Mt. Olivet Methodist Church. They were married in Morganfield, KY, on September 24, 1913, only 16 days before her mother succumbed to pneumonia, unexpectedly. They made their home three miles north of Providence, very close to Duvin Mine. They were farmers.

God granted two children, a son, stillborn, and a daughter, named Lou Gore, born May 9, 1915. In speculation I can see many ties to the Gores. Are these why this name was chosen? Her mother, grandmother, Uncle James, Aunt Mary, how much did the Gores really influence her life?

Aunt "Sally" was an invalid at a young age and was lovingly cared for by her husband and daughter. They moved to Providence and Lou Gore graduated from Providence High School in 1932. She became a seamstress and made her way while still being able to care for Aunt "Sally".

Uncle Robert was a quiet, kind man in my memory. He passed on Feb. 17, 1952.

Lou Gore and Aunt "Sally" lived on in Providence, until her death, Nov. 24, 1958. I lost a great-uncle, also, within a month and six days — the other was Chester Lloyd Seymour (of Providence), on Oct. 20, 1958.

Lou Gore later married Clebie Elbert Myers. She is now widowed and resides in Madisonville. (See Ramsey-Gardner) - *Submitted by Peggy Sullivan Waide*

NANCY J. SIGLER

Nancy J. Sigler was born Aug. 20, 1959 at Caldwell County War Memorial Hospital in Princeton, KY. Nancy's mother, June Son, was born Apr. 19, 1922 in Lyon County. Nancy's father, Bill Son, was born Apr. 18, 1918 in Caldwell County. Bill and June were wed Jan. 11, 1946.

Nancy has six brothers and one sister: Billy Son, 41; Randy Son, 40; Larry Son, 38; Richard Son, 34; Johnny Son, 26; David Son, deceased; and Sandra Thompson, 37.

Nancy attended Charleston Elementary School and West Hopkins High School, graduating in 1977. She graduated with a vocational business degree. While in high school, Nancy was in several clubs such as Future Business Leaders of America, Student Council, Teens Who Care, and the Pep Club. Nancy graduated with many music honors. She sang at graduation, weddings, banquets, competitions, and festivals. During Nancy's senior year, she was the Student Council Secretary. A few years after graduation. Nancy attended Madisonville Community College. She may attend Murray State University in a few years.

Softball is Nancy's main hobby. She has been playing this sport for about seven years and has played on several different softball teams.

Nancy was in a co-op program while in high

school. She got on-the-job- training at Trover Clinic in Madisonville, KY and worked in the medical records department. Nancy has worked as a switchboard receptionist at Mobile Traveler in Junction City, KS. She has also worked as a typist at the Hosiery Mill in Princeton, KY. Nancy is currently unemployed.

For six years Nancy has been a member of Southside Baptist Church in Princeton, Ky. She is very fond of this church and has been in the church choir for several years.

Nancy has one daughter, Emmaline Bree Hensley, born Oct. 4, 1981.

Nancy is expecting her second child sometime in late March or early April, 1988.

Nancy has lived out of Hopkins County for four years and is now living in Princeton, KY.- Submitted by Sherry Son

SIMONS-CUNNINGHAM

Hopkins County has been home to me all of my life. I am fifteen years old and I was born in Madisonville but my home town is now Dawson Springs.

My mom's side of the family and I attend First Baptist Church. This church has always been my home church. My father's side of the family attends the First Christian Church, but my father attends my church now.

My mother and father are Jennifer Ann Cunningham, Cunningham being her maiden name, and Scott Simons. My mother has two brothers and two sisters. My father has three sisters.

Jean Jackson, my maternal grandmother, has told me about how Dawson Spings was at one time. She said that Dawson was very dependent on the railroad for income. Railroad tracks once ran where the main road of Dawson now runs. Dawson has a reputation of having mineral water that is good for you. The mineral water is being sold again. When sales began the second time, the first jug was sold for close to a thousand dollars, but the price is currently under thirty dollars now.

Dawson had many hotels because of all the people coming in on the railroad, but for some reason all the hotels burned down. The seven hotels that burned were Niles Hotel, St. Earls Hotel, New Century Hotel, Hamby Hotel, Summit Hotel, Phillips Hotel, and the Arcadia Hotel.

Many people in Dawson, forty years ago, went to the Hamby's Well to have a soda and to eat. It had a pleasant atmosphere. It was built around a well, and that is why it is called Hamby's Well. But, unfortunately, it was torn down. The well is still standing though.

My father is a carpenter. He comes from four generations of carpenters. He was born in Caldwell County, but has lived in Hopkins County all thirty-three years of his life. He was born on Sept. 1, 1954. My mother was born in Hopkins County and has also lived her all of her life. She was born on Oct. 15, 1954.

My grandmother, Jean Jackson, had operated a beauty shop in Hopkins County for close to forty-three years. She has met many pleasant people over those years and has enjoyed living there.

Hopkins County is where my family history is and is a very pleasant place to have a future. It is a wonderful place to live.-Submitted by Greg Simons

SIMMONS-WHITFIELD

Jessie Elayne Whitfield and James William Simmons were married on June 21, 1938, at the home of her parents, Mr. and Mrs. A.C. Whitfield in Nortonville, KY.

James Simmons was born in Russellville, KY, on June 21, 1913. His parents were Laura Davis Simmons and Andrew Jackson Simmons. James had two brothers, Adrian Simmons and Andrew Simmons and a half sister Ira Simmons; all are deceased at this time.

James Simmons and Jessie Simmons

James was educated in Logan County schools, where he graduated from Russellville High School in 1932. He continued his education at Western Kentucky U. and the U. of Kentucky, where he graduated in 1936, with a degree in agriculture. He was employed by the U. of Kentucky Agricultural Extension Service as an assistant county agricultural agent for three years. He worked in Hopkins County, as an agent, during 1937. Later, he resigned this position to work with Farm Security Administration, until he was drafted into military service in 1942, serving three years in the U.S. Army.

In 1947, the family moved to Madisonville, KY. James worked with the VA for two years and later bought a Southern States farm store in Sacramento, KY, that he operated for fifteen years. After retirement he pursued a hobby of collecting antiques by owning and operating an antique shop on west Noel Avenue. It was known as Hickory Bill's Trading Post. James died with a heart attack on June 17, 1982, at age 69.

Jessie was born in Nortonville, KY, on Nov. 2, 1917. Her parents were Lonnie Denton Whitfield and Archie Cleveland Whitfield. A brother, Carl Cleveland Whitfield was born ten years later. He lives in Madisonville and is a pharmacist at Earlington Pharmacy.

Jessie graduated from Nortonville High School in 1934, and continued her education at U. of Kentucky, Lexington, KY, graduating in 1938, with a degree in home economics. She taught in the Hopkins County School system for thirty years and at the time of her retirement in 1976, she was department chairman of the Home Economics Department at Madisonville-North Hopkins High School.

James and Jessie met at a summer youth conference of the Christian Church in 1933. They became engaged in 1937, and married the following year. Before moving to Madisonville in 1947, they had lived in Independence, Scottsville and Morganfield, KY. While James was serving in the army in WW II, a daughter was born, Charlotte Ann Simmons. Her birthday was Mar. 26, 1943.

Jessie, James, and Charlotte became active members of the First Christian Church (Disciples of Christ). James served as an elder, chairman of the board and Sunday School Superintendent. Jessie has served as president of Christian Women's Fellowship and Sunday School teacher, as well as singing in the Chancel Choir. Charlotte was active in all youth activities of the church, which helped her to attend Transylvania U. in Lexington, where she graduated in 1965, with a degree in music and a major in piano. Charlotte has taught in Ohio, Hawaii, and Hopkins County schools, where she still substitutes. She is especially interested in arranging music for the piano and enjoys giving piano concerts in churches and civic clubs. She is married to William Kennedy Adcock, who is a teacher at Pride Avenue Elementary School in Madisonville. He graduated from Kentucky Wesleyan College in 1976 and holds an M.A. in Ed. from Murray State University.

The Adcocks have two children: Paul Kennedy Adcock, born Nov. 10, 1968, in Honolulu, HI and a daughter, Chasta Nicole Adcock, born Aug. 31, 1976.

James was an active member of the Madisonville Kiwanis Club; while Jessie is a member of the Twentieth Century Prosody Club, Hopkins County Retired Teachers Association and University of Kentucky Home Economics Alumni Association. She continues to be active as a member of First Christian Church, where she is now an elder. - Submitted by Jessie Elayne Whitfield Simmons

LENA SLATON SIMONS

Lena Slaton was born Mary Lee Slaton on Jan. 5, 1881, the daughter of Rev. Aurelius C. (A.C.) Slaton and Martha Jane Oldham Slaton. A day or so after she was born, Mrs. Slaton's best friend was visiting. While holding the baby, she asked if the Slaton's would name the baby for her! From that day forward, she was known as Lena.

Lena had one brother and two sisters. She attended the old White School that later became Pleasant View School.

On Dec. 20, 1899, Lena married Thomas L. Hewlett in her home in the Pleasant View community with Rev. Price E. Gatlin officiating. To this union three children were born: Raymond S. Hewlett (deceased), lived in Valparaiso, IN; Bonnie Hewlett Harris of Madisonville; and William D. Hewlett of Green Valley, AZ. There are four grandchildren,

Mary Ellen Boyd Oldham, Martha Jane Oldham Slaton, Mary Lee (Lena) Slaton Hewlett, and Bonnie Mae Hewlett

seven great grandchildren, and one great great grandchild.

Thomas Hewlett met an untimely death in March of 1924. He was working on the Grapevine bridge and stepped backwards, falling to the railroad tracks below. Death came two or three days later.

In 1946, Lena married Phil Simons who died in 1949.

A faithful Christian, Lena joined the Pleasant View Baptist Church at an early age. She was a member of the Presbyterian Church on Princeton Pike in Madisonville at her death. Lena enjoyed quilting, making many beautiful quilts, and crocheting bedspreads and also worked tirelessly in her flower garden. Her cooking specialties were jam cake and chess pie which she always had ready when her children and grandchildren came for a visit.

In 1978, Lena fell and broke her hip and had to go to the Kentucky Rest Haven. Not one to give up, she recovered quickly and was soon up walking and visiting others who were worse off than she. She took care of her own personal needs and was never bedfast. She had eye surgery when she was past 90 and continued to read THE MESSENGER every day until a week before her death.

Lena died Sept. 24, 1982 and is buried at Oddfellows Cemetery in Madisonville. See Hopkins County Centenerians. -*Information from Bonnie Hewlett Harris, written by Dorothy Miller Shoulders*

SISK-HILL

Margaret Hill was born in Lisbon, KY, on Sept. 14, 1883 and died Apr. 27, 1979. Margaret was the 3rd child of William Duane Hill and Louella Cole. They moved from Lisbon in 1884, to the country in Barnsley, KY.

As a young lady, she worked at the St. Bernard Store and the Post Office in Barnsley. Barnsley was a thriving community and she was kept busy selling dry goods, groceries and feed, etc., across the counter. Although her boss had given her instructions to throw away the broken pieces of cookies, cheese and crackers, Margaret saved them and gave the goodies to the poor children, whose parents could not afford to buy such extras for their children. Her kind heart was also a heart of fun. She often told of "Little Britches", who would visit her daily. He would fill up the pot belly stove with coal that sat in the middle of the room. The local men folk would surround the stove telling their stories, tipped back in their chairs. She laughed to herself as she gave "Little Britches" some black pepper to add to the coal as he filled the stove one cold day. Soon the fumes of the pepper sent the men elsewhere and Margaret slowly felt some heat drift back to her.

She married Thompson Hamby Sisk, born May 3, 1861, died Dec. 15, 1941. He was the son of the late Judge Andrew Jackson Sisk, "Little Andy". "Little Andy" rode horse back during all of his campaigns. He served as Constable four years, Deputy Sheriff four years, Sheriff four years, and Judge 18 years from Nov. 1, 1870 to Sept. 2, 1878 and also from Nov. 9, 1882 to Apr. 4, 1892. His grandfather was Andrew Jackson Sisk, "Big Andy", who served in the War of 1812, and fought at the Battle of Tippecanoe, and served in the Kentucky Legislature from 1829-1831 and in the State Senate 1832-1836. Thompson's mother was Narcissus Isabel Morton.

Thompson often told his children about the day he met their mother. "I saw her walking down the road by the railroad tract where I was sitting. She was dressed in a red satin (ankle length) dress with overlace. The sun was shining on her golden hair and she was the most beautiful girl I had ever seen".

Thompson worked at the Hopkins County road system. He drove a four horse team that graded the roads, etc. He also worked as a guard at the St. Bernard Store and worked inside the coal mines. After a coal mine accident, he retired and worked on his farm on Brackett Lane just outside Mortons Gap, KY.

To this union five children were born: A.O., Ida Blanche, Sister Margaret Siena (Laura Agnella), who is a Catholic nun in the order of the Sister of Charity of Nazareth, James O'Brien and Mary Capitola (Cappie). - *Submitted by Karol Durham Welch*

SISK-RODGERS

Madalyn Elizabeth Rodgers and Leonard Thompson Sisk were married Dec. 24, 1936, in Madisonville, KY. Madalyn was born Apr. 1, 1918, on the island near Pond River, in Hopkins County. She is the daughter of William Marion Rodgers and Mary Cummings Haley. Wm. M. Rodgers was born Jan. 30, 1897, in Hopkins Co. He celebrated his 90th birthday this year (1987), and is currently active with his vegetable garden. He married Mary Cummings Haley Apr. 4, 1917, daughter of Jacob Williston Haley and Martha Mariah (Mattie) Veatch. Mary Cummings was born July 10, 1898, in Utica, Daviess Co., KY. She died July 14, 1977, after sharing 60 years of marriage with William. They were for many years active in the Liberty Baptist Church. Madalyn has two sisters, Hattie Veatch (Peach) Staton and Marie Parkest.

William M. Rodgers was the son of J. Wm. Rodgers and Hattie Christian. Hattie was a native of Todd Co., and a descendant of Gov. James Garrard of Kentucky. J. Wm. Rodgers was born July 11, 1863, in Hopkins Co., and died Aug. 26, 1958. His early Hopkins Co. family lines were Robertson, Cardwell, Ashley and Egbert.

Leonard was born May 21, 1912, in Hopkins Co. to Morgan Lennox Sisk and Mary Della Coomes. She was a native of McLean/Daviess County line and a daughter of Leonard Benedict Coomes and Louisa Jane Sutton. Her family history follows the Catholic settlement of Kentucky. Morgan Lennox Sisk was born Sept. 7, 1886, in Hopkins Co., son of Thompson Hamby Sisk and Henrietta Morgan. Her father, Wm. R. Morgan was a native of South Wales. He married Sarah Fugate, daughter of Zachariah Fugate and granddaughter of George Fugate, pioneer settler of Hopkins Co. Other family lines include Wilson, Howell, and Lewis. Leonard has two brothers living, Mason Joseph Sisk and Woodrow Amplis Sisk and a sister Mary Harris.

Thompson Hamby Sisk, born May 3, 1861, died Dec. 15, 1941, the son of Andrew Jackson Sisk and Narcissa Morton. Judge Andrew served 33 years in public office, 18 years as County Judge. He was the son of Andrew Sisk Sr., born Mar. 15, 1790, North Carolina, and an early settler of Hopkins Co., having served in the War of 1812, and the KY Legislature. He was married to Polly Littlepage, Apr. 24, 1820. Her family settled in Hopkins Co. from Virginia.

Narcissa Morton, born May 6, 1834, died Dec. 25, 1864, was the daughter of Thomas Morton Jr. and Elizabeth Graddy, the granddaughter of Thomas Morton Sr. and Elizabeth Davis, more early settlers of Hopkins County.

Leonard and Madalyn made their home in Madisonville until 1954, ultimately settling in Clarksville, TN. With frequent visits to Madisonville, they have maintained close ties to the county. In December 1986, they celebrated their 50th Wedding Anniversary, with her father, Mr. William Rodgers in attendance. The event was sponsored by their only child, Doris Ann Rittenberry and their grandchildren, Thomas Wm. Diggs, Sabrina Ann Greenfield, and Regina Lynne Sargous. They have one great grandchild, Clayton Michael Greenfield, age three. - *Submitted by Doris Ann (Sisk) Rittenberry*

SISK-VANNOY

Barten N. Sisk was born in 1821, the firstborn son of Hezekiah and Anna Sisk Sisk. He married Dicey Vannoy in Hopkins County, in 1840. Dicey was born in 1824, the daughter of Jessee Vannoy.

Barten was a farmer and he and Dicey were the parents of thirteen children: Alla (b. ca. 1843); John M. (b. 1844); Hezekiah (b. 1846); Nancy (b. 1847); Martha (b. 1848); Alexander Logan (b. 1849); Eliza (b. 1852); Sarah (b. 1854); Irena (b. 1856); Henry Talbott (b. 1859); Joana (b. 1861); William D. (b. 1868); and Bartello (b. 1857).

In 1897, Barten died and was buried in the Dalton Cemetery. Dicey died in 1918 and is

Thompson Hamby Sisk and Margaret Hill Sisk with daughter Cappie

Madalyn E. Rodgers and Leonard T. Sisk

buried in the Odd Fellows Cemetery. - *Written and researched by Paula L. Morrow-Bentley*

A.J. SISK

A.J. Sisk, County Judge of Hopkins County, was born on Nov. 27, 1824, in Hopkins County. He was the son of Andrew Jackson Sisk, born in North Carolina, and his mother was born in Virginia. They were of English origin. A.J. Sr. served in the War of 1812, later served three terms in the Legislature and four terms in the State Senate. He died in the fall of 1857, at the age of sixty-seven.

Judge Sisk inherited his father's farm in 1857. He was elected constable in 1870. He was elected County Judge serving eight years and was elected again in 1882, and held this office honorably the rest of his life.

He was married to Martha Hampton, April 1848. His second marriage was to Narcissa Isabel Morton (sister of Bert Morton). She died leaving three children: Lizzie (who married a Edwards); Thomas; and Boyd. A.J.'s third marriage was to Mary Luck in December 1869. They had five children, three boys and two girls.

A.J. was the grandfather of Lula Hickman (see Hickman Story). - *Submitted by Mary Edna Harris*

BARNABAS SISK SR.

The Wilkes Co., NC, taxable list for 1791 thru 1794 shows the following Sisks: Josiah, Timothy, John Sr., Thomas, and Barnabas with various acres. In 1793, Wilkes Co. Deed Book 1, page 293, John Bourland sold to Barnabas Sisk 150 acres for 65 pounds on Swan Creek. Barnabas was born May 15, 1769, in Virginia or North Carolina, died in Hopkins Co., Sept. 6, 1841. The last record of Barnabas in Wilkes Co., NC, is Feb. 1, 1796, which shows a land sale of 150 acres to John Martin, land near wagon road, Deed Book D, page 156. The next record fo Barnabas, along with other Sisks, was in Pendleton Co., SC, in 1800 with six males and two females.

Mansel Meredith and Nancy Ellen Todd Sisk

May 1804, land grants were made to Barnabas for 200 acres along Clear Creek, Richland area of Hopkins Co. His children were: Meredith, Barnabas Jr., Patsy, Harrison, Pendleton (named for Pendleton, SC), and Gilly Sisk. In 1820, Barnabas Sr. married 2nd, Sally Woolridge. In 1824, he owned 200 acres on Flat Creek and another 112 acres in 1829, Deed Book 4 & 5, pages 320 and 344. In 1841, Barnabas sold his personal property to George Waetzel, who was married to his granddaughter Henrietta (Nettie) Sisk, Mortgage Book 9, page 329. Barnabas is buried at Flat Creek, but no stone has been located.

Barnabas Jr. (Oct. 8, 1812-July 1, 1887), married Mary Polly Howell (Jan. 11, 1810-Jan. 23, 1900), on Feb. 8, 1831. She was the daughter of Julson (Judson) Howell. Both are buried at Flat Creek Cemetery. Barnabas Jr. was a farmer and a jailer in the 1870, Census of Hopkins Co. He owned land at Flat Creek. Children: Judiah Carolina, married William Travis Laffoon; Hardin; Stinnett H., married Joana Suthard; Mansel Meredith, married Nancy Ellen Todd; Dorinda, married Lysander Todd; and Matilda, married Perry McCulley.

Mansel Meredith Sisk (May 5, 1837-Aug. 2, 1918), married Jan. 24, 1866, Nancy Ellen Todd (June 26, 1844-Dec. 28, 1910), the daughter of Garsh Todd. Their children: James Elliott; Laura Lee; Tolbert (Tol); Alice Jane; and William Marion.

James Elliott (Nov. 17, 1866-Feb. 20, 1946), married Dec. 12, 1886, Annie Edmonson Offutt (Dec. 13, 1863-Jan. 13, 1889), the daughter of John Sanford Offutt and Mary Waller Goodloe. They had one son, John McGowan (see his story). James Elliott married second Sallie Robertson. Their children: Tommie (Apr. 25, 1892-Nov. 24, 1912); Paul (Aug. 13, 1896-Feb. 2, 1907); Mattie (June 22, 1899-Feb. 18, 1907); Kenneth (June 6, 1908-July 3, 1908); Lloyd (born 1894, died in France in 1918); William, born Jan. 22, 1905, married Thula Morris and had one child Wilma; Ruth, born Mar. 10, 1912, married Elby Hampton and their children are Thula, Barbara, Granville and Aileen, deceased; and James Elwood (Nov. 3, 1914-Mar. 26, 1985), married Ruby Stearsman and had one son James Jr. (Aug. 27, 1946-Nov. 5, 1964).

Barnabas Sr. was in my opinion related to Robert Sisk, who lived at Plumb Orchard, probably an uncle, a brother to his father Daniel, who was killed in the Revolutionary War. Barnabas was a trustee for Madisonville, later constable, and a surveyor. He was a witness along with Timothy Sisk in 1803, when Flat Creek Baptist Church was constituted. Sources: Sisk Families by L.L. Sisk, The Offutt Family by Mrs. P.G. (Eunice) Brown and personal knowledge. - *Submitted by John A. Sisk*

HANSON RAY SISK

Hanson Ray Sisk was born in Madisonville, KY, in 1893. His was a life of accomplishment and adventure as a journalist, publisher, and civic leader. He left Madisonville as a young man and was hired by the El Paso (Texas) HERALD as a newspaper reporter. Soon he joined the ASSOCIATED PRESS and was sent into Mexico to cover the Mexican Revolution. His assignments included reporting on the exploits of the legendary Mexican general, Pancho Villa.

In 1914, he settled down as a reporter for the newly founded NOGALES DAILY HERALD in Nogales, AZ, which is on the Mexican border. In 1915, he married Dorothy Poole of Nogales. In 1918, at the age of 25, he purchased

Hanson Ray Sisk

the Nogales HERALD and began a career as a respected newspaper publisher. His daily column, "Views and Interviews," was widely read in Arizona, and Mexico.

Mr. Sisk hired a number of young journalists who later made a mark on their profession. Perhaps the best known was Robert Berrellez, who as a reporter, was sent to Cuba by the AP and was imprisoned by Fidel Castro for several months on trumped up charges. In 1963, Mr. Sisk, dean of the Arizona newspaper publishers, received the Arizona Newspapers Association's first Master Editor-Publisher Award for his nearly half century of contributions to journalism and civic affairs.

The Sisks had three children: Alvin Sisk, who succeeded his father as publisher of the HERALD; Mrs. William Graham Bell of Tucson, AZ; and Mrs. Rush W. Dozier of Madisonville. There are three grandchildren. One of these grandchildren was Rush W. Dozier, Jr., a 1972 Harvard college graduate, who at one time was an editorial writer and later city editor of the LEXINGTON HERALD newspaper of Lexington, KY.

Mr. Sisk died in Nogales in 1973. Mrs. Sisk died in 1986. In memory of Mr. Sisk, the citizens of Nogales created a small park next to the NOGALES DAILY HERALD building with a bronze statue of a newsboy. - *Submitted by Rush W. Dozier Sr.*

JOHN McGOWAN SISK

John McGowan Sisk was born Nov. 18, 1887, the son of James Elliott Sisk (see Barnabas Sisk), and Annie Edmonson Offutt. When John McGowan was two his mother died and he was taken in and raised by his grandparents Mansel Meredith and Nancy Ellen Todd Sisk.

On May 17, 1905, he married Flora Elizabeth Austin (Dec. 2, 1889-Aug. 28, 1972), the daughter of Mary E. Dame and Edward Nichols Austin.

John McGowan worked on various railroads (the LH&St. L and the L&N), retiring from the STL&SW RR in East St. Louis, IL, as round house foreman in 1946. He returned to Earlington, KY, where he lived until his wife Flora died in 1972. He then moved to Princeton, KY, where he lived until his death at the age of 90, on Jan. 10, 1978. He was a Mason and Shriner. Both John McGowan and Flora are buried in Grapevine Cemetery in Madisonville.

John McGowan and Flora Elizabeth were

John McGowan and Flora E. Sisk

Pearllie Abbie (Sizemore) and William Isaac Alexander

the parents of: Annie Mae; James Edward; Arthur M. (Jan. 12, 1910-Nov. 6, 1910); Hershel Lee (Sept. 29, 1912-Jan. 24, 1913); Mary Helen (Mar. 4, 1916-Mar. 3, 1917); Edna Alice; Gladys Elizabeth; John A.; and Raymond Eugene (Apr. 21, 1930-Jan. 18, 1961).

Annie Mae was born Mar. 19, 1906. She married Henry Brown and had one son, Henry Jr., who died June 17, 1923. She married 2nd Luther Ligon and had one daughter, Dorothy, who married James Oliver. Dorothy and James' children are: James Ronnie, Cathy and Roger. Annie married 3rd an Egbert and 4th Roy Koltinsky (Feb. 23, 1891-June 14, 1979).

James Edward (Feb. 29, 1908-Apr. 16, 1981), married Iva Jewell Barnett on Mar. 23, 1930, and had one daughter, Mary Arlene. Mary Arlene married Ronnie Gene Slinkard and their child, Ronda Jean Seabough lives in Cape Girardeau, MO.

Edna Alice was born Feb. 28, 1918. She married Clarence U. Smith Mar. 24, 1933. Their children: Clarence Edward, Billy Herman, Larry Allen, Bobby Ray, Danny Wayne, Barbara Ann, Dale Lynn, and Debra Leigh.

Gladys Elizabeth was born Aug. 9, 1919. She married Eugene Brooks on Jan. 20, 1940. Their children: David, twins Marsha and Marshall.

John A. was born May 28, 1922. He married Helene Bernice Sofranko on June 29, 1946. She was the daughter of William H. and Mary Durank and was born Nov. 6, 1919. They have no children. John was wounded in action in Italy on Oct. 13, 1944, and discharged from the Army on Dec. 6, 1945. Bernice was 2nd Lt. Army Nurse Core and was discharged in May 1946. John is a retired Agent with L&N Railroad. Bernice is a retired nursing home nurse. Sources: Sisk Families by L.L. Sisk, The Offutt Family by Mrs. P.G. (Eunice) Brown and personal knowledge. - Submitted by John A. Sisk

SIZEMORE-ALEXANDER

Born in Christian County, Aug. 16, 1888, the daughter of Westwood Bouden (Boud) Sizemore and Isabelle (Belle) Citira Gothard, my mother was named Pearllie Abbie, known in her adult years as Pearl. W.B. and Belle bought 140 acres of land near the old Gilliland School in the late 1800's. There they raised their family: William, Walter, La Rue, Theodocia, Foster and Pearl.

W.B. was born in Christian County, served two times in the calvary in the Civil War for the Union, being wounded when his horse fell on him during battle. His parents were William Sizemore and Unity Canaday of Christian County.

Isabelle was the daughter of Ira Gothard and Elinor Elizabeth Moultan. The father of Ira Gothard was Larkin Gothard, whom we are told married an Indian girl in Tennessee.

During World War I Pearl was married to James M. White, who died while in service of influenza in Michigan. In April 1922, Pearl married William Isaac Alexander in Herrin, IL. Their first child Edith Naomi was born there in 1923. About six months later they moved back to the old Sizemore farm near St. Charles.

William (Ike) was the son of James Washington (Bud) Alexander and Cordelia (Delia) Miller. Cordelia's father was Frank Miller, who was married about four times. Parents of James W. (Bud) Alexander were Moses H. Alexander and Nancy Dyer. Parents of Priscilla Parsons were William Parson and Lucretia Gunn. Lucretia was the daughter of Daniel Marks Gunn, who was the son of Thomas Gunn III, who was the son of Thomas Gunn II, who was the son of Thomas Gunn of England. - Submitted by Edith N. Butler

ESTEY MAYFIELD SKAGGS

Henry Skaggs I was the father of Henry Skaggs II, who was the father of Isom, the father of Martin, the father of William Skaggs. William Skaggs married Theodosia Williams. Their children were Asa Tilden, who married Mary Eliza Hale, Ella, John Thomas, Willis, Homer, Ada and Ermine.

Estey Mayfield Skaggs

Joseph Hale and Martha E. Hale were the parents of Mary Eliza Hale. They had five other children: John Lindsey, George, Grant, Ligon and Richard (Dick).

Asa Tilden Skaggs and Mary Eliza Hale were the parents of Estey Mayfield Skaggs, who was born May 1, 1904. He had three sisters: Donna (birth date unknown); Florence (Feb. 11, 1901); and Eva Marie (Apr. 27, 1916). He had four brothers: Joseph (birth date unknown); William Manford (Jan. 4, 1908); Edward Garfield (May 10, 1910); and Ernest (birth date unknown). Donna, the oldest, Joseph and Ernest all died of diphtheria.

Asa Tilden moved his family to Hopkins County, where he purchased a farm near White Plains, KY, next to the Concord Baptist Church. There he spent several years with the children after the death of his wife. His second wife, Pearl (Nov. 2, 1884), bore him no children.

Estey Mayfield married Ollie Gobel Cunningham and to that union was born two sons, Estey Murle Skaggs born September 1923, and Franklin Dee Skaggs, born March 1936. After Mayfield and Ollie married they moved to a part of Hopkins County near Madisonville known as Grapevine. Their children grew up there and attended the Madisonville City Schools. Ollie died of cancer in June of 1946. Murle had just married Betty Lovan and had spent a brief time with the U.S. Navy at Norfolk, VA.

After the death of his first wife, Mayfield married Arrie Lee Lovan in November of 1946. At this writing they are both living at 1825 Grapevine Road, Madisonville, KY.

The youngest son, Franklin Dee, married Betty Sue Buchanan (November 1935) on Sept. 3, 1955.

Estey Mayfield Skaggs spent most of his years as a coal miner. He was an employee of the Sunlight Coal Company and retired from the Grapevine Coal Company. He was honored by the Grapevine Baptist Church for more than 50 years as an active deacon. During his years of service at Grapevine Baptist Church, he served as treasurer for many years and also taught an adult Sunday School class for over 40 years.

Murle and Betty Skaggs had two children, Michael Lynn (1948) and Susan Jill (1955). They also have one grandson, Nathan Harrison Wright (1981).

Franklin and Betty Skaggs had three children: Terry Lynn (1959), Dee Ann (1962), and Connie Sue (1963). They also have two granddaughters: Lindsey Paige LeFan (1982), and Sarah Jo Evans (1984).

At age 83, Estey Mayfield Skaggs still enjoys telling stories of his life and remembers the good times he had with his brothers and sister, who have all preceded him in death except one, Edward, who lives in California.

Many have enjoyed the story about his name "Mayfield". His mother, Mary Eliza (as the story is told), realized the time of his birth was at hand. Recognizing the time was near, a decision was made to move her on a small bed to a house nearby. It was during the move that the baby was born in a field between the two houses. After the birth, the family doctor was called to the home to care for the mother and child. When time came for the birth certificate to be completed, the doctor asked if a name had been chosen. No name was given. The doctor, knowing the date and place of birth, recommended that he be named "Mayfield" and so it was. On May 1, 1904, Estey Mayfield Skaggs was born.

And now you know the rest of the story. His sons are honored to bear his name and proudly acknowledge him as "Dad"! - Submitted by Franklin D. Skaggs

SLATON-BREEDLOVE

John Marion Slaton and Alma Nellie Breedlove were married Nov. 27, 1937, in Madisonville, KY.

John (b. Feb. 3, 1914), and his twin sister Nannie Evelyn are the children of James Edmond and Amelia Denton Slaton.

Alma (b. Feb. 18, 1916), is the youngest of nine children born to William Monroe and Bernie Victoria Downs Breedlove (b. Aug. 5, 1878, d. Oct. 18, 1982).

John and Alma have resided in eastern Hopkins County since marriage. One location was called "The Island" because it was surrounded nearly every spring with backwater from Pond River. Their current residence is a 23 acre farm on the Browder Church Road south of Highway 85, where they have lived since Christmas Day 1946.

John and Alma both grew up on farms and continue to do farm work. They always shave a large garden, and have raised corn, hogs, chickens, tobacco and other farm crops with the help of their children. In addition to farm work, John worked in and around underground coal mines, including Kentucky Derby, which later became Pine Hill, Blue Valley, Flat Creek, Magnolia; Coiltown for 12 years and Pyro for 13 years, retiring from Pyro at age 65.

Their children are Edmond Monroe, b. Nov. 18, 1943. He graduated from Madisonville High School in 1961, attended Western Kentucky University, then transferred to Auburn University, where he graduated with a Doctorate of Veterinary Medicine in 1968. He operates the Madisonville Veterinary Clinic. Erma Mae, b. Sept. 11, 1946, d. Mar. 13, 1949. She died at age two years six months and two days of appendicitis. Marilyn Lee Slaton (Mrs. J.D.) Drennan, b. Sept. 17, 1950. She attended Madisonville High School graduating in 1968, then went to Spencerian College in Louisville. Alan Norris, b. Oct. 4, 1955. He graduated from Madisonville North Hopkins High School in 1973, and attended Madisonville Community College. He farms and works in surface mining.

John and Alma are active members of Liberty Baptist Church, where John serves as a deacon. John likes to hunt and fish. Alma enjoys quilting and growing flowers. They have eight grandchildren to share their love, knowledge and heritage with. - Submitted by Mrs. Norris Slaton

SLATON-CALLIS

Before the November 1955 general election in Hopkins Co., Hanson Slaton joined the Will Neisz ticket for sheriff, in anticipation of his becoming a deputy. The Neisz ticket won and on Jan. 1, 1956, Hanson Slaton, at age 28, began his career in county government, as deputy sheriff.

This was Hanson's first venture out after a long, serious siege of treatments and surgery for tuberculosis, lasting approximately two years.

Hanson Slaton, born Apr. 18, 1927, was the son of Clyde Slaton (b. Feb. 27, 1892 d. Oct. 8, 1969), and Addie Woodson (Walker) Slaton (b. Jan. 7, 1898 d. Dec. 3, 1962), of rural White Plains where he attended school. Clyde was a farmer and operated a service station in White Plains for 25 years. The parents are buried at

Judge-Executive Hanson Slaton

Concord Cemetery at White Plains. Clyde and Addie had four other children: Charles Herbert Slaton, deceased, married Charlotte Griffor and resided in Saginaw, MI; Liggett Bailey "Doc" Slaton, deceased, married Willie Mae Madden, lived in White Plains; Clyde A. Slaton married Ruth Kuehn and they live in Memphis, TN; Ada Slaton married Edward Mauk of Muhlenberg Co. and they live in Madisonville. (See MAUK-SLATON)

After the Neisz term of sheriff, Al Lantrip was next elected sheriff but died leaving one-half of his term, to which Hanson Slaton was appointed as the sheriff for the remainder of the unexpired term. In the next election Slaton was elected to a full term of his own.

Since 1968, Slaton has occupied the top executive spot of county govt. first as Co. Judge, exercising both judicial and administrative functions. With the re-organization of the Courts in 1977, the KY County Judge became the Judge Executive, with all duties administrative, and Hanson Slaton has remained in that same position since, administering county government. He's won every election in which he has ever run and is looking forward to 1988.

He enjoys his work and retirement has no appeal to him. This job as Judge-Executive gives him the best chance to get more things accomplished. Among projects under his leadership of which he is very proud are the county's Landfill Convenience Center System, second to none; the new, well-located and well-run Senior Citizens Center; the revamped County Welfare System in new quarters, as well as the local Disaster and Emergency Services Organization (DES) now under one roof, and many more progressive satisfactory steps during his career.

Hanson Slaton married Betty Callis, born July 18, 1924, dau. of Henry Callis, born Oct. 18, 1901, and Vaneta Timmons (b. July 4, 1901 d. June 26, 1951). Vaneta is buried at Providence Westlawn Cem. Henry Callis is presently married to Lucille Riley Callis, and they live on Route 1, Utica, KY.

Betty graduated from Hanson H.S. and Western KY State College. She taught at Hanson H.S. until consolidation in 1962, then went to Earlington H.S. as Counselor/Pupil Personnel Director for 13 years. She next was Pupil Personnel Director, and Director of Special Programs at Central Office until retirement in 1982. The Slatons live in Hanson in the former Timmons homeplace where Betty was born.

Betty Slaton's brother, Dr. James H. Callis, Owensboro, is presently married to Karen Sinclair, and their dau. is Mary Frances, age 5.

He was first married to Nelda Boggess. Their three children are Dr. James Timmons Callis, a cardio-vascular surgeon at Vanderbilt Univ., Nashville, married to Joanne Brown. Their dau. is Amy Elizabeth Callis, and they are expecting a son (already named James David) momentarily; Dr. William Casey Callis, a dentist in Owensboro, married Donna Dean Ballance; Dr. Amy Vaneta Callis is anesthetist at the Owensboro Hospitals. - Submitted by Judge-Executive Hanson Slaton. Written by Rella Jenkins

SLATON-DENTON

James Edmond Slaton (b. Jan. 17, 1879, d. Feb. 15, 1970), and Amelia Denton (b. June 4, 1884, d. June 17, 1974), were married Apr. 15, 1906.

James E. was the eldest son of Thomas Marion and Anne L. Wooten Slaton.

Amelia was the youngest daughter of John William Denton (b. July 2, 1831, d. Dec. 25, 1922), and Pamela McCarley (b. Feb. 17, 1839, d. Mar. 9, 1935), who married Feb. 15, 1868.

James E. and Amelia farmed east of Madisonville in the Wilson School District, until they retired in 1950 and moved to Madisonville. Their children are as follows:

Albert Edmond (b. July 22, 1907), who on Nov. 27, 1937, married Edna Offutt (b. June 24, 1906).

Nora Lee (b. June 4, 1909), who on Aug. 15, 1961, married Dr. Donald Anderson (b. Feb. 9, 1915, d. May 5, 1963).

Lanna Pearl (b. Apr. 30, 1911), who on Dec. 24, 1932, married Benjamin Townes Scott (b. Sept. 27, 1913, d. Jan. 30, 1981).

Nannie Evelyn Slaton (b. Feb. 3, 1914).

John Marion (b. Feb. 3, 1914), who on Nov. 27, 1937, married Alma Nellie Breedlove (b. Feb. 18, 1916).

Joseph K. (b. Dec. 28, 1916), who on Dec. 23, 1939, married Bonnie Mae Melton (b. Aug. 5, 1918).

James and Amelia were active members of Liberty Baptist Church. They are buried in Browder Church Cemetery. Next to their stone is one marking the resting place of "Infant Sons of James E. and Amelia Slaton", twins who died at birth, Nov. 2, 1912. - Submitted by Mrs. Norris Slaton

SLATON-FINCH

Alan Norris Slaton and Donna Marie Finch were married on Saturday, Mar. 3, 1979 in the James E. Slaton family home place, then occupied by Henry Flether and Stella Stum Slaton. The house was originally owned by Norris's paternal great-great grandfather. The ceremony was performed by Harold Ledbetter before an improvised altar in the parlor.

Norris is the son of John Marion and Alma Nellie Breedlove Slaton. He was born Oct. 4, 1955, in Hopkins County. He attended Anton Junior High and Madisonville North Hopkins high School and Madisonville Community College. He has been self-employed in agriculture since 1973, primarily in growing tobacco—from four to as many as twenty-three acres in a year. In addition he operated a custom lime/fertilizer hauling and spreading business for several years. In 1979, he was employed by Cimarron Coal Corporation and has been working in surface mining since that time; currently for Andalex Resources, Inc. Cimarron Division.

Donna is the daughter of Henry Finch Jr. (b. Feb. 11, 1922), and Thelma Mergen Cashon Finch (b. Aug. 19, 1926). Henry and Thelma married on Christmas Day, 1947. Donna was born June 4, 1953, in Fulton Co., KY. She grew up in western McCracken County attending Concord Elementary and Heath High School. She graduated 3rd in the 1976 summer graduating class at Murray State University with magna cum laude honors and was named Outstanding Library Science Major of 1974. She came to Madisonville in August 1974, to work as assistant librarian in the newly formed Hopkins County-Madisonville Public Library and was promoted to Associate Director in 1977. She was named Outstanding Young Careerist by NIKE BPW in 1980. She is a member of the American and Kentucky Library Associations. She participates in the following community activities: Historical Society of Hopkins County; Friends of the Hopkins County-Madisonville Public Library; Public Library Board of Trustees 1985—; Anton Homemakers; Madisonville Mothers of Twins Club. She left public work July 31, 1984, to become a full-time farm wife and homemaker.

Norris and Donna now reside on the family homeplace with their three children: Susan Marie, b. Mar. 25, 1984, and John Thomas and James Edmond, fraternal twins, b. Dec. 3, 1986. - *Prepared by Donna Slaton*

SLATON-HODGES

John Slaton was born Feb. 22, 1730, in St. Peters Parish, New Kent Co., VA, the son of Arthur and Rachel Slaton. He served as a 1st Lt. in the Revolutionary War. On Dec. 20, 1756, he married Susannah Hodges, daughter of Edmund and Nephana (Walker?) Hodges. Susannah was born 1734, in Goochland Co., VA, where her marriage to John Slaton is recorded.

They had these children: Sarah (b. Jan. 8, 1758), who married David Walker; James (b. Mar. 22, 1760), who married Martha Pigg; Rachel (b. August 1764), who married Isham Browder; Martha (b. Aug. 13, 1768), who married William Bourland; John Jr. (b. Sept. 12, 1773), who married Edith Hibbs; Edmund (b. Feb. 13, 1777), who married Nancy Rossner Allen; Arthur Porter (b. Apr. 20, 1780), who married Catherine Fugate. Susannah Hodges Slaton died sometime after the birth of Arthur. John Slaton then remarried, another Susannah. Children by his second wife Susannah Groom are as follows: Daniel Slaton (b. June 22, 1782), and Mary (Polly) (b. May 19, 1788), who married John Grant. - *Submitted by Beatrice Martin*

SLATON-WHITFIELD

John H. Slaton was born Feb. 20, 1867 in Hopkins Co., the son of James Oliver Perry Slaton (Sept. 30, 1837-Oct. 22, 1900) and Sarah E. Graddy Slaton (Feb. 25, 1829-Jan 11, 1906).

On Mar. 14, 1901, John married Florence M. Whitfield, (who was born Oct. 28, 1882) the daughter of Needham H. and Susan F. Lovan Whitfield.

Mr. and Mrs. John H. Slaton

John and Florence lived on a farm just outside of Mortons Gap until about 1948 when they moved into Mortons Gap. John was considered one of Hopkins County's champion tobacco growers, receiving top prize for his crop several times. He enjoyed hunting and fishing. John was very active in politics, with his first vote being cast for Grover Cleveland for president in 1888. John only missed voting twice in his life. In 1965, at the age of 98, he cast his vote for his great nephew Hanson Slaton (now County Judge Executive) in the race of County Sheriff.

Both John and Florence would tell the stories their fathers had told about their days in the Civil War. And John would relate how at the age of 13, he and his family made a trip to Arkansas in a covered wagon.

Florence took pride in her garden and flowers and loved to share both with family and friends. Relatives and friends would often visit and Florence would prepare delicious meals.

John and Florence were members of the Concord Baptist Church near White Plains. They were the parents of six daughters and two sons; with one daughter and one son dying in childhood. The daughters: Dixie Putman, Lucy Kyle, Pauline Roberts, Bonnie Langzell, Marga Cunningham; the son, Con L. Slaton.

Florence died Oct. 26, 1966. John died at the home of his daughter, Dixie on November 26, 1966 at the age of 99 years and 10 months thus just missing his ambition of living to the age of 100. Both are buried in Concord Cemetery near White Plains. -Sub*mitted by Bonnie Slaton Langzell*

SLATON-WOOTON

Thomas Marion Slaton (b. Mar. 24, 1854, d. Jan. 30, 1940), and Anne Liza Wooton (b. Jan. 16, 1859, d. Aug. 6, 1927), were married Mar. 1, 1877, at the bride's home by Brother Alexandra, with witnesses Alex Clark and David Fowler.

Thomas was the eldest son of James Edmond and Mary Wilson Slaton. Anne was the daughter of Jesse and Nannie A. Wooton.

The family Bible gives the following information about their children: James Edmond Slaton (b. Jan. 17, 1879, d. Feb. 15, 1970), married Amelia Denton on Apr. 15, 1906; Joseph Washington Slaton (b. Apr. 13, 1881, d. April 1882, 1 yr.); Lilla Slaton (b. Mar. 19, 1883, d. Dec. 19, 1902); Jessie Lee Slaton (b. Sept. 6, 1885, d. 1948), married Leonard N. Springfield (1873-1965), on Feb. 21, 1906; George Absalom Slaton (b. May 8, 1887, d. July 1888, 1 yr., 2 mo.); William Lloyd Slaton (b. Mar. 2, 1889, d. ?), married Modest McGregor on Sept. 28, 1910; Nannie Mae (or May) (b. July 19, 1891, d. Sept. 16, 1984), who married Robert Lear on May 5, 1943; Louis Rector (Rex) (b. Jan. 26, 1895, d. Dec. 17, 1984), who married Mary Ruth McGuyer on Jan. 28, 1933; Thomas Gardiner (Doc) Slaton (b. Nov. 25, 1896, d. Jan. 3, 1984), single; Ruth and Ruby Slaton (b. July 30, 1901, Ruth d. July 3, 1902, Ruby d. July 22, 1902).

Thomas and Anne farmed east of Madisonville in what was then the Wilson School District, less than a mile from his parents' homeplace. They are buried in Browder Church Cemetery. - *Submitted by Mrs. Norris Slaton*

AURELIUS C. SLATON

Aurelius Clendening Slaton, better known to family and friends as "Rill", was born Feb. 23, 1853, in Hopkins County, Pleasant View community. He spent his entire life in this community as a farmer and Baptist minister. He was licensed to preach August 1883, and was ordained as a minister September 1885, by the Pleasant Grove Baptist Church of which he was a member at that time. He later joined Pleasant View Baptist Church and was a member there until his death. He pastored several churches in Hopkins and Webster counties during his ministry. He influenced many lives during his lifetime on this earth and now his testimony still lives on through lives he influenced even though the Lord called him to be with him in Glory on Feb. 7, 1925, after a fruitful life on earth. He is buried at Pleasant View Cemetery as are several other members of his family.

A.C. was the sixth of fourteen children born to Arthur Walker Slaton and Polly Lee O'Bryan. He was the grandson of Edmund Slayden and Nancy Rossler Allan.

The earliest record of this Slaton family in Hopkins County is where Edmund Slayden took title to 200 acres of farm land Oct. 23, 1807. One record shows Edmund Slayden owned 200 acres of land on the Princeton Road west of Madisonville. This may have been the land he took title to in 1807.

Arthur Walker Slaton was born Dec. 28, 1810. Arthur married Polly Lee O'Bryan Aug. 25, 1840, and by October 1840, had moved into a one room, story-and-a-half log house, built by Arthur, which was their home the remainder of their lives as well as the birthplace and home of their fourteen children. This homestead was located in the Pleasant View community west of Madisonville on what is now known as the Hollis Slaton Road.

Brothers and sisters of A.C. were: Joseph Board, born Feb. 23, 1842, who served in the Confederate Army; Elizabeth Rossler, born Nov. 12, 1844; Clifton Hopkins, born Nov. 22, 1846, who served in Co. H, 1st Ky. Vol. Union Army and also served as Policeman in Madisonville and was killed while on duty; James Reddrick, born Jan. 29, 1849; Susan Emaline, born May 1, 1850; Emily Gipson, born Apr. 4, 1854; Benjamin Allen, born Dec. 25, 1855; Mary Walker (Mollie), born Nov. 2, 1857; Martha Frances (Mattie), born June 14, 1859;

Robert Pother, born Aug. 6, 1861; Charles Edmund, born Feb. 24, 1863; Ambia Ann, born July 9, 1865; Lucy Electra, born Mar. 17, 1871.

A.C. married Martha Jane Oldham, Oct. 18, 1875. He, as his father Arthur, built a log house on land adjoining the old Slaton homestead and he and his bride were soon housekeeping, where they spent their lives and reared their children: Lonnie, born Sept. 4, 1878; Lena, born Jan. 1, 1881; Hollis, born Apr. 7, 1890; Edna, born Sept. 20, 1893; Auburn, born Jan. 18, 1897.

The log room or house built by A.C. in 1875-1876, still stands in the Pleasant View community but it can't be recognized as a log house because in the early 1900's or earlier, additions were made to the log house making a six room house with hall and two porches.

After A.C.'s death, Hollis second son of A.C., bought the homeplace and lived there until his death Mar. 2, 1972.

The appearance of the house was changed but very little over that period of time. Since the death of Hollis, a new front porch has replaced the old one, the outside has been bricked and the inside renovated. After being in the Slaton family for almost a century, this homestead was sold outside the family in 1972.
- Submitted by Alline Slaton Polley

CLARA SCOTT-SLATON

Clara Bell Scott, born Sept. 10, 1888, in Hopkins Co., KY, died Sept. 22, 1978, was born to William Scott and Annie, born 1849, died 1901. She married Sherman Slaton, born Jan. 3, 1878, died August 1947, in 1906 and they made their home on her father-in-law's farm (Sam Slaton) on Dobbins Hill in White City, an area around Mortons Gap, KY. There, six sons were born of which the first died. Later, after a tragic fire that left them homeless, they moved to a farm in Madisonville on Brown Road, where five more sons were born. Three of their 11 children preceded her in death: Baby Slaton; Frankie James, born Apr. 4, 1919, died July 7, 1932; Abraham (Abe), born Nov. 5, 1910, died Dec. 2, 1972, and two have passed since her death: Amplis William, born Aug. 6, 1908, died Oct. 31, 1982, and Andrew Columbus, born Nov. 3, 1914, died Sept. 16, 1985. Six children yet live and reside in Madisonville, KY: Booker T., born Dec. 7, 1912; Rufus Sherman, born Jan. 15, 1917; Thomas Lester, born Dec. 9, 1922; Sylvester, born Aug. 30, 1924; Euramus, born May 30, 1927; and George Albert, born Apr. 1, 1929.

She had four brothers: William (Buck) Scott, born Jan. 31, 1877, died June 20, 1967; George, Abraham and Henry.

Clara had five sisters: (1) Liza Scott Johnson, whose children are Mary, Mitchell, Arthur and Estele. (2) Lucy Scott Moss, whose child was Willie V. Littlepage. (3) Vickie Scott Pritchett, born April, 1871, died November 1911, whose children were Georgia Pritchett Morris (her children were Reed Hughes Jr., born 1921, died 1921; Hilda R. Steppe, born 1924, died 1964; and Winifred Williams, born Apr. 6, 1922, died Apr. 5, 1967); Bud Pritchett, born Apr. 12, 1902, died Mar. 22, 1947 (his child was Jean); Mayme R. Pritchett Hayes, born Oct. 19, 1890, died Apr. 22, 1970 (her children were Helen Banks, Mertis, Willie Lee, Ernestine, Viola Drake, and Anna Ruth); Mabel Pritchett Sherrod, died

Clara Bell Scott-Slaton

1924 (her children were Walter H. Sherrod, born 1913, died 1983 and Francis Sherrod Woodbridge, born 1916, died 1980); Annie Pritchett, born Oct. 10, 1893, died Nov. 25, 1899; Fannie Pritchett; Lovie Pritchett, born Aug. 14, 1905, died Feb. 4, 1906; and Bertha Pritchett. (4) Nora Scott. (5) Cordie Scott Nichols, born 1874, died 1900. Her children were: Pete Nichols, died Nov. 12, 1936 (his children were: Effie Mae Buell, George William Nichols, John Henry Nichols, Lee Roy Nichols, James Columbus Nichols, Carlene Nichols, Annie Nell Nichols, Pete Nichols Jr.); Henry Nichols, born 1899, died 1967; Ruby Nichols Foster (her children were Carlene Baker and William Henry Baker); and Birdie Nichols Hall.

She had one uncle: Julius Scott, born Feb. 12, 1843, died Jan. 17, 1904. His children were Mader Scott Logan, born Feb. 14, 1884, died Sept. 21, 1944 (her children were Mattie Logan Snorton, Strother, born Apr. 29, 1910, died July 20, 1929; William Thomas, born Mar. 24, 1926, died Nov. 22, 1983; Ministers Eugene, born July 23, 1921, died Aug. 27, 1974; Press Logan, born 1915, died 1984, Anna Logan and Ola Logan Graham); Julie Scott Conner (her children were Venolia Conner, born July 11, 1906, died Apr. 22, 1969, Wardell and Parvin); Pete Scott (his children were Mary Elizah Savage, Mary Lucy Hayden and James Scott); Julius Scott Jr., (his children are Jerome and Juanita Scott); and Mance Scott. - Submitted by Evelyn Slaton Reynolds

JAMES EDMUND SLATON

James Edmund Slaton, born Mar. 22, 1825, in Hopkins Co., KY, was the tenth of eleven children born to Arthur Porter Slayden (Slaton) and Catherine Fugate Slaton, daughter of George and Martha Fugate.

Arthur Porter Slaton (born Apr. 20, 1780 in Goochland Co., VA; died Apr. 9, 1843 in Hopkins County) first came to Hopkins County in 1799, and took title to land on the Elk Fork of Pond River—at that time the area was part of Christian County as Hopkins County had not yet been formed. Arthur P. and many of his descendants to this day have lived in the Pond River area. Records show that he was active in the Methodist Church and helped organize Browders Methodist Church. He is buried in the Browder Church Cemetery as is James E. (died Feb. 22, 1916), and many of the other descendants.

The brothers and sisters of James E. were: Squire H., born Mar. 27, 1805; William Marcus, born Mar. 14, 1807; Martha Ann, born Nov. 2, 1809; Francis Hawkins, born Nov. 16, 1811; Lewis Swrader, born Jan. 23, 1814; Nancy Sla-

The James E. Slaton Home

ton, born Mar. 27, 1818; Sarah Ann, born Jan. 18, 1820; Mary Ann, born Dec. 17, 1823; George P., born May 8, 1829.

James E. married Mary Emily Wilson (born July 27, 1830, died Mar. 27, 1909), on Dec. 13, 1849. Their children were Nancy Catherine Slaton, born Oct. 9, 1852 died Jan. 12, 1853; Thomas Marion, born Mar. 24, 1854; George Squire Slaton, born Dec. 30, 1857; and Sarah Washington Slaton, born May 8, 1862.

James E. and family settled on a 395 acre farm in the Little Flat Creek area near Pond River, six miles east of Madisonville. The family home, built by James E., was begun in 1861, and finished circa 1864. The home still stands and is currently being renovated by John Marion Slaton (grandson of Thomas Marion), and his son Alan Norris Slaton, who along with Nannie Evelyn Slaton (twin sister of John M.),are the current owners of the farm. The land on which the house stands was purchased by James E. from his wife's family, the Wilsons. Previous to the Wilson's, the land was owned by Edmund Slaton, an uncle of James E.; therefore the land has been in the Slaton family for six generations and a seventh generation currently lives there, daughter of Alan Norris Slaton. Sources: The Slaton Book by Arthur J. Slaton, the Family Bible. - Compiled by Donna F. (Mrs. Alan Norris) Slaton

ROBERT LOUIS SLATON

Robert Louis Slaton was born in Hopkins Co., KY, June 25, 1941. He is the only child born to Louis Rector (Rex) Slaton and Mary Ruth Slaton (McGuyer).

Louis Rector Slaton was born Jan. 26, 1895, in Hopkins Co., KY, and died in Hopkins Co., KY, Dec. 17, 1984. He was the son of Thomas Marion Slaton and Annie Wooten Slaton.

Robert Slaton in the front yard of his boyhood home off Davis Well Road east of Madisonville about 1950

Mary Ruth McGuyer was born in Hopkins County July 30, 1911, and died Nov. 15, 1973.

She was the second of two children born to Thomas Theodore McGuyer and Eula Whitfield. Robert Harry McGuyer, her brother, was born Jan. 5, 1904, and died Jan. 4, 1922. Eula Whitfield was born in Hopkins County in 1874, and died in Hopkins County in 1959. She was the second of two daughters born to Mary Younger Kirkwood Whitfield and William W. Whitfield. Both her parents had been married previously, and as a result, Eula McGuyer had a number of half brothers and sisters. Mary Younger Kirkwood Whitfield was the daughter of Captain Willie Younger and Caroline Oates Younger.

Robert Slaton married Shirley Edwina McClaren in Charleston, MO, in 1962. There were two children of this marriage, Andrea Lynn Slaton, born Apr. 8, 1969, and Robert Lyle Slaton, born Aug. 16, 1971. The marriage ended in divorce in February, 1973. Robert Slaton married Maureen Daley Lyons, Feb. 15, 1974. Maureen Daley Lyons was born in Louisville, KY, Feb. 27, 1949. She was the daughter of Harry Pell Lyons and Helen Holland Lyons. There were three children of this marriage, Thomas McGuyer Slaton, born June 25, 1976, Daniel Lyons Slaton, born July 25, 1978, and Michael Holland Slaton, born June 11, 1981.

Robert Louis Slaton graduated from Western Kentucky University and the University of Louisville. He worked for Kentucky State Government in Frankfort for a number of years including two years as Commissioner of Health. He also served as an Administrator with Trover Clinic in Madisonville. - *Submitted by Robert Slaton*

SAM SLATON

Sam Slaton, born Oct. 17, 1843, in Hopkins Co., KY, (died Sept. 4, 1918) was a successful farmer and owned his own land on Dobbins Hill in White City, an area around Mortons Gap. His first wife was buried on the farm in their private family cemetery.

Sam Slaton

Sam later married Ellen N., born Sept. 4, 1859 (died Apr. 11, 1887). They had four children (three boys and one girl). Sam had two other children (Frank and Jordan) prior to his marriage to Ellen. Sam was hardworking and his trait passed down to his children and grandchildren. Their children were as follows:

Frank, who had four children: Jessie, Vera Mae Littlepage, Arthur and Auzie.

Jordan, who had two children: Ross and Cora.

Sherman, born Jan. 3, 1878 (died August, 1947), married Clara Bell Scott, born Sept. 10, 1888 (died Sept. 22, 1978), in 1906. They had 11 children: Baby Slaton; Amplis William, born Aug. 6, 1908 (died Oct. 31, 1982); Abraham (Abe), born Nov. 5, 1910 (died Dec. 2,1972); Booker T., born Dec. 7, 1912; Andrew Columbus, born Nov. 3, 1914 (died Sept. 16, 1985); Rufus Sherman, born Jan. 15, 1917; Frankie James, born Apr. 4, 1919 (died July 7, 1932); Thomas Lester, born Dec. 9, 1922; Sylvester, born Aug. 30, 1924; Euramus, born May 30, 1927; and George Albert, born Apr. 1, 1929.

Marion, born Mar. 6, 1881 (died March, 1956), married Mary (Maggie) Magland Fletcher, born Mar. 8, 1881 (died June 14, 1973). They had three children: Roy, born Dec. 25, 1906 (died June 14, 1961); Ruth Johnson, born Apr. 6, 1900 (died Sept. 20, 1964); and Helen Trice, born Nov. 4, 1909.

Hana, born Aug. 15, 1884 (died May/June 1917), married Samuel J. Ashby. They had five children: Roth, born Sept. 30, 1903, who married Mary Jessie Crump, born Feb. 28, 1899, in 1924; Goldie, born 1905, and now deceased; Marshall, born 1908; Samuel J., born 1910 (died 1974); and Robert, born 1914, and now deceased.

Tom, born June 1, 1886 (died Oct. 31, 1959), married Mattie Morton in 1907. They had one daughter: Roberta Ross, born Aug. 28, 1908.

Sam Slaton is buried, along with four of his sons (Frank, Jordan, Sherman, and Marion) and only daughter (Hana) in Browder Cemetery. Further history on some of Sam's grandchildren can be found under Sherman Slaton. Sources: Helen Trice and Booker T. Slaton - *Compiled by Evelyn Slaton Reynolds*

SHERMAN SLATON

Sherman Slaton, born Jan. 3, 1878 (died August 1947), was born to Sam Slaton, born Oct. 17, 1843 (died Sept. 4, 1918), and Ellen N., born Sept. 4, 1859 (died Apr. 11, 1887). He married Clara Bell Scott, born Sept. 10, 1888 (died Sept. 22, 1978), in 1906. They made their home on his father's farm (Sam Slaton) on Dobbins Hill in White City, an area around Mortons Gap, KY, where their first six sons were born of which the first died. After a tragic fire, in which their house burned down, they then moved to the farm in Madisonville on Brown Road where five more sons were born. Two of their 11 children (Booker T. and Euramus) yet reside on the farm. Their children are as follows:

BABY SLATON

AMPLIS WILLIAM SLATON, born Aug. 6, 1908 (died Oct. 31, 1982), married Fannie Mae Bowles, born Aug. 10, 1915 (died June 6, 1982). They had four children: (1) Ruby Nell, married Robert E. Lee and resides in Louisville, KY. They have four children: Anita Britt, Vanessa, Robert Jr. and William; (2) Gloria Yvonne, married Rufus Cox Jr. and resides in Madisonville, KY. They have two children: Anthony and Jeffrey; (3) Amplis William Jr., married Wanda Davis and resides in Madisonville, KY. They have three children: Antonio, Kerry and Amplis III; (4) Linda Louise, married Robert Chastine and resides in Huntsville, AL. They have two children: Robert Thomas Jr. and Melissa Telfare.

ABRAHAM (ABE) SLATON, born Nov. 5, 1910 (died Dec. 2, 1972), married Claudine Kirkwood. They had one child: James Albert, married Ophelia Cox. They live in Madisonville, KY, and have six children: Valveta White, Michael, Terry, James Kelly, Patricia and Aliysia.

BOOKER T. SLATON, born Dec. 7, 1912, has never married and lives on the farm with his brother Euramus.

ANDREW COLUMBUS SLATON, born Nov. 3, 1914 (died Sept. 16, 1985), had five children: Evelyn Louise, married James W. Reynolds, Jr. They live in Madisonville, KY, and have four children: Kenneth Tyrone and Leslie Floyd Murphy, Andrea Jean and Jamie Aleah Reynolds; Antionette (Mada) Gause, married Joseph Gause. They live in Madisonville, KY, and have three children: Amaja, Adrian and Joy; Andrew Alvin, resides in Earlington, KY, and has one child, Lamont. Timothy, married Sonya Smith. They live in Anchorage, AK, and have two children: Jason & Jessica. Tim serves in the U.S. Air Force, was recently ordained an Elder and is the Pastor's Assistant of the Prevailing Word Outreach Church in Anchorage; Rosemary, resides in Louisville, KY, where she attends Sullivan Junior Business College. Rosemary will graduate in March 1988 with an Associate Degree in Accounting. She is presently employed by Dr. Robert Skiles, D.M.D. as his Receptionist/Bookkeeper.

RUFUS SHERMAN SLATON, born Jan. 15, 1917, married Mabel Louise Lester. They had seven children: Rufus Jr., married Shirley Brewer. They reside in Ballejo, CA, and have five children: Rhonda, Stephanie, Rufus Sherman III, Randy and Shirley; Ann Elizabeth, married Harvey Langford. They live in Louisville, KY, and have three children: Lisa, William and Elizabeth Ann; William Andrew, married Deborah Davis. They live in Madisonville, KY, and have two children: Jeffrey Lynn and William Andrew, Jr.; Samuel Eugene, (b. Aug. 31, 1945; d. June 10, 1983), married Brenda Williams. They had three children: Christopher, Derick and Brandon. Brenda and the children reside in Madisonville, KY; Richard Lester, married Barbara Williams. They reside in Delray Beach, FL, and have two children: Robin and Bret; Kathy Teresa, resides in Louisville, KY, and works at First National Bank; Angela Elaine, resides in Madisonville with her father and works at Regional Medical Center as a Unit Resource Clerk.

FRANKIE JAMES SLATON, born Apr. 4, 1919 (died July 7, 1932).

THOMAS LESTER SLATON, born Dec. 9, 1922, married Effie Lee Kirkwood. They reside in Madisonville, KY, and have four children: Thomas Jr., married Margie Bowman. They live in Madisonville and do not have any children; Barbara Cecilia, married Kenneth Avery. They reside in San Pedro, CA, and have two children: Chauston and Amanda; Saundra Lovella, married Jeffrey Moseley. They reside in Louisville, KY, and have two children: Stephanie and Jason; Claire Cornelious, married Toni Smith. They reside in Madisonville,

KY, where Cornelious has a practice in Oral and Maxillofacial Surgery. His office is located in the Salmon Memorial Clinic. His wife Toni is his Assistant and Office Manager. They are expecting their first child on Oct. 31, 1987.

SYLVESTER SLATON, born Aug. 30, 1924, and has three children: Sylvia Marie, married James Clark. They live in Madisonville, KY, and have two children: Stanford and Aubree; William Scott, resides in Madisonville, KY, and is to marry Dorain Johnson this year on November 7th; Cynthia Elaine, resides in Madisonville, KY, with her mother and works at General Electric.

EURAMUS SLATON, born May 30, 1927, has never married and resides with his brother Booker T. on the farm.

GEORGE ALBERT SLATON, born Apr. 1, 1929, married Evelyn Ruth Kirkwood. They reside in Madisonville, KY, and have one child: Mary Ruth, married Tracy Logan and they live in Madisonville, KY. They have two children: William Earl Drake III and Quinton Johnson.

Sherman Slaton

Sherman Slaton worked hard in the hot fields as a farmer to provide for his family as his wife, Clara Bell, a quiet, soft-spoken woman tended daily chores and labored daily over a hot, coal cookstove to ensure meals were ready when her husband and sons came in out of the fields. Truly, Psalms 1 and 3 speaks for their life.

...And he shall be like a tree planted by the rivers of water, that bringeth forth his fruit in his season: His leaf also shall not wither: And whatsoever he doeth shall prosper...Psalms 1:3 - *Submitted by Evelyn Slaton Reynolds*

SMITH-ALEXANDER

Vernon Clay Smith and Retta Mae Alexander of St. Charles, KY, were married Mar. 14, 1936, at Shawneetown, IL. Their witnesses were Lucille Smith and Tommy Adams. Tommy is deceased.

They have five living children. The eldest, a daughter, Doris Josephine, was born Oct. 29, 1937, and died Sept. 13, 1938.

Yvonne was born Oct. 8, 1939. She is married to Kenneth Fuller. They live in St. Charles and have five children: Reda Rambo, who has two children and works at the Trover Clinic in Madisonville; Monty, who has two children and is employed with the Goodyear Plant in Martin, TN; Joy is single and works at the Earlington Pharmacy; Kimberly Orten is employed at the Walmart Store in Madisonville; and Cheryl, who is eleven years old and attends the St. Charles Elementary School.

Joanne was born Nov. 16, 1941. She is married to Rev. Paul Fuller Sr. They live in St.

Retta Mae and Vernon Smith

Charles and have three children: Paula Abbott, a housewife and mother of three; Paul Jr. has two children, lives in Dawson Springs and is employed at Davis Best Way Store and is also a Pentecostal minister; and Roger who has one child, works for the Hopkins County Board of Education and lives at Grapevine in Madisonville.

Shirley was born Oct. 17, 1944, and is married to James Hanks. They live in Earlington with their two children. Shirley works for Steele, Hoodenpyle and Roberts Insurance Company. James is employed with Island Creek Coal Company as a diesel mechanic.

David (Mike) was born Dec. 9, 1950, and is married to Yvonne Lynn. They live in Madisonville. He has three children by a previous marriage. He is employed by the Green River Coal Company in Madisonville.

Freddy was born Oct. 14, 1958, and is married to Mary Ann Winters. They have two children and live in St. Charles. He is employed at Speed Queen in Madisonville.

Vernon has worked on the farm, for the Works Progress Administration and is a retired coal miner. He has put in over forty years in the mines, having retired from the Island Creek Coal Company. He worked his last shift at the Fies No. 9 Mine at Madisonville.

Retta has been a housewife and mother. She has a "St. Charles Neighbor's" column which is published weekly in THE MESSENGER. Her first writing was for a small paper, THE NEWSCENE/PENNY PINCHER, in Madisonville. She has dabbled around with some poetry, but is still undiscovered. She has had several poems published but only one has won recognition. The name of the poem was "A Mountain of Love". It is dedicated to the Lord, as is all of her work.

The Smith's live in St. Charles and go camping or fishing whenever they are able. They are both members of the Lake Grove General Baptist Church near their home, where Mr. Smith is a deacon. - *Submitted by Retta Mae Smith*

SMITH-DAVIS

After Richard (Dick) Smith (1863-1920), married Sarah Marie Davis (1866-1951), who came from Texas to the New Salem area near Nortonville, they settled on a 200 acre farm in the Sunlight community (past Grapevine) and raised most of their eight children there. Richard, who furnished farm products to nearby stores, came to be known as "the Mayor of Punkin Center". After the children were grown, they bought the property at the corner of Kentucky and Hall St. in Madisonville, after which a series of tragedies came within two years. Richard became despondent and shot himself (1920), a son Bill, at 30 years old, was killed in Chickasaw Mines near Sunlight (1921) and Sarah's mother, Mary Davis, who had been brought from Texas, died (1921). Sarah then became the matriarch of the family and bought the property at the northwest corner of South Main and Lake where she lived for 31 years, until her death at 83.

The children of Richard and Sarah were: (1) James Claud (Nov. 29, 1885-Apr. 10, 1977); (2) Annie (Audie) Offutt and daughter Martha from E. Broadway; (3) Myrtle (Walter) Robinson (Barney) Adams from Anton and E. Hall St. had Alma, Joyce and Bud; (4) Maymie (Les) Davis (Roy) Wilkerson lived on Hall St. with one daughter, Dorothy; (5) J.W. "Bill" (Dessie Littlepage) (1891-1921) Madisonville, had one daughter, Sarah; (6) Kate (Everett) Uzzle (1900-1986) lived in Mortons Gap with son, Don; (7) Edward of Madisonville and Mortons Gap (died August 1980), unmarried; (8) another child died in 1909, with typhoid fever. Most of the offspring lived to a ripe old age. Maymie is the sole sibling survivor, living in Evansville at the time of this writing.

James Claud Smith, oldest son of Richard and Sarah, started working in the coal mines at an early age and spent over 50 years with such mine companies as White City, St. Bernard, Sunset, Blue Valley, Trio, Ross, Kentucky Derby and Redbud. In 1923, he bought a mine located left of Sunlight and furnished coal for equipment to run construction of the Illinois Central Railroad through Hopkins County. James C. married Luvenia Marks (Webster County), who died of tuberculosis at the age 25, leaving sons Cecil (age 6) and Roy Martin (age 4). He married Kate Gunn (1888-1968), who gave him four sons and two daughters: Marvin, Hazel Young, Roxie Fridy, Calvin, Herschel, who was killed in a haying accident (1922-1935), and James.

The two sons of James C. and Luvenia were raised by their grandmother Sarah and both followed their father's occupation of mining. Cecil (Marie Dossett) settled in the Briar Creek community in Muhlenberg Co. and had children Charles and Anna Ruth, grandchildren and a great-grandchild. Roy (Modest Harris) (Barbara Sutton) lived in Detroit and Madisonville and raised three daughters, Eloyse Jean Merrell, Wilma Sue Phillips and Carolyn Uplinger, and has grandchildren and great-grandchildren. - *Submitted by Jean Groves Merrell, granddaughter*

SMITH-DENNIS

Henry J. Smith was born circa 1820, in Kentucky. He married Rebecca Dennis on Apr. 1, 1841, in Butler Co., KY. Rebecca was the daughter of Nathaniel and Sally Childers (Childress) Dennis and was born circa 1820, in Butler Co. Records indicate that Henry's parents may have been Austin P. and Elmira Sisk Smith of Hopkins County.

Henry and Rebecca began married life in Butler Co., but later settled down in Hopkins County where Henry farmed.

Sometime in 1856, Henry died leaving his widow with seven children. In 1857, one daughter died. In 1858, Rebecca married Allen Gunn in Hopkins County. Allen had five children and thus Rebecca had 11 children ages 2 to 16 to raise.

Henry and Rebecca's children are as follows:

Nathaniel J. Smith was born Apr. 28, 1842. He married Mary J. Martin in 1866, in Christian Co., KY. They had six children: Sarah E., Annie L., Rebecca E., Storey (Henry ?) S., James D., and John F. Nathaniel died in 1897, and is buried in the Simpson Cemetery in Christian County.

Myra (Muriel) E. was born in Butler County circa 1843. She died in Hopkins County on Sept. 17, 1857.

Augustine P. was born circa 1845.

John J. was born circa 1847.

Robert A. was born in 1848, in Hopkins County. He married Amanda Oldham in Hopkins County in 1869, and raised his seven children there: William, Henry H., Thomas M., Nolie Etta, Maude, Betty and James R. He died in 1910, in Hopkins County and is buried in the Grapevine Cemetery.

Sarah was born circa 1851.

Henry was born circa 1857. - *Written and researched by Paula L. Morrow-Bentley*

SMITH-OLDHAM

Robert Alexander Smith was the son of Henry J. and Rebecca Dennis Smith. He was born on Mar. 23, 1848. When he was eight years old, Robert's father died. By age 10, his mother had remarried to Allen Gunn and thus he had a stepfather and step-siblings to grow up with. In 1869, he married Amanda Oldham in Hopkins Co., KY. Amanda was born Jan. 26, 1844, to Jessee E. and Nancy Shelton Oldham. Both Robert and Amanda were born, raised and died in Hopkins County.

In the beginning Robert was a farmer, farming the land in the Pleasant Run area, which he had inherited from his father. He later lived in Earlington and worked as a miner. He died on Nov. 25, 1910. Amanda died Sept. 18, 1924. They are buried next to one another in the Grapevine Cemetery. He and Amanda raised all seven of their children in Hopkins Co.:

William Smith born circa 1871, and as near as records can indicate married Elizabeth A. Wade in Hopkins Co. in 1889. They had at least three children, Everet, Edgar and Maude.

Henry H. Smith was born in November, 1873.

Thomas M. was born circa 1875. He moved to Randolph Co., IL, worked as a miner and married Mary Louise Mischke in 1899. They had at least three children: Ray, Ruth and Curtis. He died in 1931.

The Smith daughters l to r: Nolie Etta, age 19, Maude, age 18, and Betty, age 16

Nolie Etta was born on Jan. 23, 1878. She married John W. Davenport in Hopkins County in 1896. She had nine children: Carl, Mabel, Cil, Archie, J. Pauline, Lawrence, Nellie, Frank and John. She died of tuberculosis in 1915, and is buried in the Earlington Cemetery.

Maude was born on Jan. 26, 1879. She married Jack A. Rainwater in Hopkins County in 1899. She had eight children: Una, Curtis, James, Amanda, Mary Ellen, Paul, Robert and David T. When she died in 1916, only four of her children were living. She and her family are buried in the Oakwood Cemetery in Hopkins Co.

Betty M. was born April of 1883. In 1905, she married Dick Hankins in Hopkins County. She had two daughters (maybe three): Emma and Roxie. She died very young in 1909, and is interred in the Grapevine Cemetery.

James R. was born Jan. 8, 1887. He married Hazel Hale. James died in 1960 and is buried in the Grapevine Cemetery. - *Written and researched by Paula L. Morrow-Bentley*

SMITH-WOODRUFF

George David Smith (b. Nov. 20, 1890 d. Dec. 24, 1953), son of John Ross Smith and Nannie (Carroll) Smith, married Cora Mae Carroll (b. Oct. 7, 1892 d. September 1984), daughter of David Demanuel Carroll and Molly (Greer) Carroll.

The George David Smith family. Back row l to r: Geneva (Smith) Howerton, George David Smith, Cora Mae Carroll Smith, Joyce (Smith) Oglesby and J.C. Smith. Front row l to r: Aubrey Smith, Troy D. Smith and Orvil Smith

George and Cora Smith had seven children: (1) Arles Huston Smith (b. Feb. 9, 1909), and died when he was six years old (Mar. 15, 1915); (2) Aubrey Lee Smith (b. May 19, 1911 d. Jan. 2, 1954), married Bessie Vandiver, no children; (3) Geneva Smith (b. Apr. 9, 1914), is married to Bill Howerton, and they live in Louisville. She has five children by a former marriage; (4) Orvil Elwood Smith (see below); (5) J.C. Smith (b. July 23, 1924), married Peggy Thomas Reed. They are retired merchants, living in Paducah. Peggy and J.C. have two children, and Peggy has three by a previous marriage; (6) Troy Dean Smith (b. Mar. 15, 1930), married Maxine Davis, retired school teacher. Troy works in the mines, and they operate S & S Laundry. They have one daughter, Christy, and two granddaughters; (7) Joyce Helen Smith (b. May 24, 1932), married A.C. Oglesby. They have three children, live in Madisonville.

Richard David Dixon (D.D.) Woodruff (b. 1857), married Laura Catherine Nisbet (See Woodruff-Nisbet family). One son, John Clay Woodruff, (b. Apr. 29, 1887 d. Sept. 15, 1930), married Willie Mae Jenkins (b. Nov. 23, 1889 and d. Apr. 26, 1964), daughter of Wm. Costello Jenkins and Annie King (See Jenkins-King family). Clay operated a general merchandise store in St. Charles and owned partnership in a coal mine. Clay and Willie are buried at Christian Privilege Cemetery, St. Charles.

Orvil Elwood Smith (b. Oct. 15, 1917), married Hilda Mae Woodruff (Mar. 26, 1921) daughter of Clay and Willie. Orvil is self-employed, operating Smith's Diesel Repair at his home in Eddyville. Their children are:

(1) Shirley Ann Smith (b. Mar. 8, 1939), at St. Charles, married Billy Franklin Bridges (b. Jan. 15, 1937), son of Albert Claud Bridges (b. 1895 d. 1964), and Ethelene Bonner (b. 1900 d. 1970). Billy works at General Analine Film at Calvert City and Ann is an EMT with Lyon Co. Ambulance Service, in Eddyville. They have two sons, Mark Wayne Bridges (b. Mar. 30, 1964), who married Carol Elaine Williams (b. Dec. 2, 1967), on July 18, 1987. She is the daughter of Bobby and Donna (Gray) Williams, Eddyville. Mark works at LWD, Calvert City; Garrett Kyle Bridges (b. Sept. 20, 1968), single, works at KY, Lake Sales, Grand Rivers, KY and has attended Paducah Community College.

(2) Richard David Smith (b. Feb. 25, 1946), married Dorothy Nell Holsapple (b. Oct. 9, 1946), daughter of Willie Glen Holsapple Sr. (b. 1921), and Dorothy Louise Yates (b. 1922). Their daughter is Michelle Lyn Smith (b. Nov. 2, 1972). Dick is a Safety Officer, Air Products and Chemicals, Calvert City, and Nell is secretary/bookkeeper for H & G Construction Co., Kuttawa. They live in Eddyville.

(3) Howard Woodruff Smith (b. May 21, 1955), is a partner with his father in Diesel Repair, Eddyville. He married Verena Ann Hall (b. Nov. 22, 1963), on Mar. 29, 1986. Her parents: Raymond and Janice Hall, Kuttawa.

Hilda Smith died June 14, 1984, of a heart attack. She was cremated and the memorial urn is in Eddyville Cemetery. - *Submitted by Rella G. Jenkins*

ALBERT WESLEY SMITH

Albert Wesley Smith was born Apr. 9, 1885, died March 1964. He was the third child of Joe C. Smith and Nancy M. Woodruff of Hopkins County. Joe was born in 1862, died March, 1936. Nan was born 1853, died 1918. Albert's grandparents were Levi Woodruff, born in Palmer, Hopkins Co., KY, died Sept. 24, 1980 in St. Charles and Elizabeth (Betsy) Laffoon, born May 19, 1818, year of death uncertain. Paternal grandparents were Rile Smith and Lindy Laffoon. Rile owned a grist mill in Olney, KY. Their births and deaths are unknown.

Albert had four siblings: Lee, Laura, Florence and Benjamin, all deceased.

Albert married four times. All four wives preceded him in death. He married Lorettie Chaney, daughter of Rev. Jim and Lucinda Chaney, June 7, 1905, at the local county courthouse, by J.W. Wilson. Witnesses were Charles Caldwell and Walter Corneal. They had one child, Clifford, who died in infancy. Lorettie died soon after Clifford. The time of her birth and death is uncertain.

He then married Josie Carroll, daughter of

Scott Carroll and Molly Greer. They too married in the local County Court Clerk's office, with J.W. Wilson officiating on Dec. 24, 1908. Witnesses were N.M. Simms and W.F.S. Bailey. They had a son, Ellis (Peck) Smith. He was born October 1909 and died August 1977.

The Smith family - Albert Wesley, Lellar Josephine, Ellis (Peck), and Justine about 1914/15

On Nov. 16, 1911, he married Lellar Josephine Sneed, daughter of Jesse Sneed and Lou Butler, in her parent's home in St. Charles. The ceremony was performed by Rev. W.N. Teague. Witnesses were Froge Butler and Jesse Sneed. Benjamin Smith, Albert's brother, and Lucy Sneed, Lellar's sister, were married under the same ceremony. Lellar died in 1925. They had five children, all surviving: Justine Vandiver, Vernon Smith, Roberta Franklin and Dorthy Nell Franklin.

He then married Martha Hoard Franklin on June 23, 1931, at Earlington, by Rev. C.J. Carroll. Witnesses were Ernest Carroll and Mona Carroll. She died in the spring of 1953. They had no children.

Albert was a coal miner, losing his job at St. Bernard Coal Co. when he joined the Union. He then farmed for awhile. He was a deacon of the Lake Grove General Baptist Church at St. Charles, leaving said church in the late thirties to start Sunday School in the Gilliland school house on the St. Charles Route. Later, he founded a church there, now known as the Gilliland Ridge Independent General Baptist Church, which is pastored by Brother Jim Camplin. When necessary, he filled in for ministers and performed rites at funerals; one being for Dellar Camplin at her request. She was Brother Jim Camplin's mother.

Gilliland Ridge General Baptist Church founded by Albert W. Smith

Next to God, he loved his family. He was a very kind, considerate man. He is buried at the Lake Grove Cemetery at St. Charles with his first three wives and deceased children. Martha was buried at the Cranor cemetery by her first husband, Earl Franklin. - *Submitted by Retta M. Smith*

CALDWELL SMITH SR.

Caldwell Smith Sr. was one of seven children, being the fourth child born Apr. 3, 1913, to Luther T. and Irene McGregor Smith of Earlington, KY, Hopkins County. Both were Tennesseans who came to Hopkins County in the early 1900's, making this their final and permanent residence.

Caldwell Smith, Sr.

Caldwell's early life was spent in Earlington, KY, where he attended grade school and later in 1932, graduated from J.W. Million High School. His ambition and motivation inspired him to further his education. With this ambition and encouragement from family and teachers he literally made his way to Frankfort, KY, where he enrolled in Kentucky State College, and after completing the four years course of study he received his B.S. degree in 1936.

Smith's teaching career began at Rosenwald High School, now the Learning Resource Center on North Kentucky Avenue. He came to the school in 1938, as a Science instructor and Varsity Basketball Coach. A stint in the United States Army from June 1941 to August 1941 was fulfilled and Caldwell was discharged. He was then elected as Varsity Coach and instructor at Lincoln Institute at Simpsonville, KY.

On Nov. 1, 1941, Caldwell was united in marriage to Mary Ruth Shelton, daughter of Rev. & Mrs. Daniel A. Shelton. Two sons, Caldwell Smith Jr. and Shelton T. Smith Sr., were born to Caldwell Sr. and Mary Ruth Smith. They have three grandchildren, Shelton T. Smith Jr., Margra S. Smith and Caldwell Smith III. Daughters-in-law and mothers of the grandchildren: Caldwell Jr. married Sharon Lee Taylor, mother of Margra and Caldwell III; Shelton Sr. married Carolyn Scisney, mother of Shelton Jr.

After the Pearl Harbor attack, Dec. 7, 1941, Caldwell was recalled to active service in the U.S. Army, making his entire military service of 56 months. He saw action in the Pacific Theater. His discharge was January 1946.

Upon completion of Caldwell's military service, he resumed his teaching and coaching

The Caldwell Smith Sr. family at Kentucky State College in 1966 for Caldwell Jr.'s graduation

position at Rosenwald High School, where his influence as coach brought lasting recognition to Rosenwald in the field of basketball.

Caldwell's education was furthered as he attended sessions of summer school and in 1963, he earned a Master's degree from Western Kentucky State University at Bowling Green, KY.

After the death of Mrs. Pearl M. Arnett, late principal of Rosenwald, Smith was elected principal and served from 1963-1966, when integration was implemented within the Hopkins County School System.

From 1966-1972, Caldwell was School Social Worker for the Hopkins County School System.

In 1972, Caldwell was appointed Assistant Principal at Madisonville North Hopkins High School, being the first black to hold that position in Madisonville. Here he served until his retirement in June 1978. A total of 40 years in the school system.

Caldwell Smith's life was a full one in many areas. Each phase of his life gave prestige to his name as a faithful Christian, loyal citizen and a wise counselor.

Upon retirement, Caldwell answered the call to the ministry of the Gospel and fulfilled the requirements of study and became an ordained Elder in the church of his choice, the A.M.E. Zion Church of the Kentucky Annual Conference under the presiding Episcopacy of the Rt. Rev. J. Clinton Hoggard, who appointed him as pastor of Hayes Chapel, Nebo, KY and Ross Chapel, Providence, KY. He served well these appointments until his health failed and he asked to be relieved.

Caldwell's love for God and his fellowman led him to serve faithfully in Zion Temple, A.M.E. Zion in several offices in the period of his membership of 46 years, until his "Home Going" on July 21, 1985. - *Compiled by Mary Ruth (Mrs. Caldwell Smith Sr.) Smith*

HENRY CLAY SMITH

Henry Clay Smith, (1843-1922) was red-headed and barely twenty years old working in the fields in Kirkwood Springs in 1863, when part of Company C of the 6th Ky. Calvary approached him. Through a combination of intimidation and an appeal to his spirit of adventure, he was recruited to fight the Confederacy. He kissed his young wife, Florence Howton Smith and infant daughter, Media, and left that very afternoon and did not return for two years. He fought all across the South as part of General Sherman's army. He was part of the famous drive across the South in which Sherman drove to the seacoast and in the process captured Atlanta, GA.

In 1865, after the surrender of the Confederacy, he found his wife gravely ill with pneumonia. She was racked with fever and hardly recognized him at first. She died a few days later - leaving Henry to care for their three-year-old daughter.

Shortly, Henry met Serena Purdy. She was younger than he and half Cherokee Indian. However, she had a fair complexion and looked like her European father. Serena was not permitted the luxury of attending school like her brothers. Because she was a girl, she had to help with the crop, attend to chores and family needs. She never stopped resenting her family for this imposition and eventually totally broke off any relationship with her family.

Falling in love with Serena was not difficult. She was extremely lovely, in spite of her rough hands and worn clothing. She was kind to Media so they married soon thereafter.

After years of cultivation and the quality of crops getting worse, they moved to Earlington, KY, to mine coal. He built a small house at 514 Robinson St. - most all homes were owned by the St. Bernard Coal Company. Some of their descendants haven't moved over a stone's throw from the Robinson Street area in a hundred years.

In her late teens, Media (Mee-dee) married Lou Egbert, producing Cora and Ed Egbert. Later she married James Hankins, producing Aggie Hankins.

Henry and Serena produced France, Dixie, Laura, Whit, Ida and Betty Ann Elizabeth.

Back row l to r: Ida Stokes with Herschel and Harry Stokes, Pearlie, Serena Smith, Henry Clay Smith, France and Harpie. Children front row: Mabel Lamb, Clara Stokes, Kenneth Walton, Margaret Walton, Katie and Clifton Smith

France married a man named Graham and had Raymond, Willie and Pearl.

Dixie became known as Harpie. She married Amos Phelps and had Ellie May. Ellie married Elgie Smith. Later Harpie married Emerson Almon, divorced, and married for the third time to Will Lamb producing Henry, William Earl, Mabel, Edward and Dorothy Jean.

Laura married Luther Phelps and had Mamie and Bill.

Whit married Janie Young and had John Henry, Clifton Pratt, Katie, Edith, Ola Belle, Margie Ann and Mabel.

Ida married Taylor Stokes and of their children, the only one known is Clara.

Betty Ann Elizabeth or "Aunt Betsy" married Walter Almon. - *Submitted by Don Almon*

WHIT SMITH

Whit was born Oct. 8, 1882, in Kirkwood Springs, KY, and died June 24, 1965. Out of six surviving children, Whit was the only son born to Henry Clay Smith and Serena Purdy Smith.

Whit often told about his mother taking him to the front door at the school house and he promptly exiting through the back door. He wanted his children and grandchildren to go to school because he was always sorry that he couldn't read, although he could write his name and figure numbers and money.

Whit and Janie Smith with granddaughters Karol Durham Welch and Linda Durham Lam, 1956

Whit met Janie Young and in time they drove by horse-drawn buggy to Nortonville to be married. Janie was born Dec. 30, 1886, and died July 29, 1978. They had seven children who survived: John Henry, Clifton Pratt, Katie, Edith, Ola Belle, Margie Ann and Mabel. They lived on Robinson Street in Earlington until Whit's father died in 1922. Times were hard, but Whit managed to buy a 89 acre farm on the Barnsley Loop from the money had made coal mining from the St. Bernard Coal Company and the railroad. All the family moved to the farm, except the oldest, John, who stayed to take care of Granny Smith.

Buying the farm was a wonderful idea, the kids could hardly wait to load up in the wagon for the big move to the country. Long hours, hard work and many hands were needed to help feed the family in the rough years that followed.

Whit loved to have Janie read the Bible and newspapers to him. He was very soft-hearted and offered his home not only to relatives when they were homeless and hungry, but to friends and total strangers. Several people lived in the family home or in the small two and three room houses that were on his land. These families would help work the fields in exchange for their lodging and sometimes meals, if they were not married.

Everyone loved to visit Uncle Whit and Aunt Janie, especially on Sundays. They knew Aunt Janie would kill a chicken and seem to make a big meal out of thin air, since grocery shopping was done only twice a year. After killing the hogs and selling the meat they would then have enough money to buy staples like sugar, flour, etc. They also would buy groceries a month or so before Christmas so the children could get fruit and candy, which was a rare treat.

There are many families who still tell of their visits and nights spent with the family. If the garden was in, the visitors would leave with a wagon, or in later years a car, filled with fresh grown vegetables, fruit and nuts. They will also recall sitting around a glowing fireplace with all the men folk telling stories of the past and sometimes stories that had been told to them, but you always knew that you were always welcome at the farm. - *Submitted by Karol Durham Welch*

THOMAS NELSON SNEED

Thomas Nelson Sneed was born in Hopkins County, on Dec. 9, 1935, to Elnora Killough and Clarence Nelson Sneed. When his parents moved to Baltimore, MD, in 1943, he stayed in Madisonville and lived with his maternal grandmother Susie M. Cobb Killough. With the exception of two years spent in the U.S. Army 1956-58, Tommy lived all of his life in Madisonville. He graduated from Madisonville High School in 1954, and worked for Kroger for 16 years. On June 9, 1965, he married Joanne Lawson (Aug. 16, 1940), an elementary teacher from Barren Co., KY. On May 2, 1972, their only child, Thomas Nelson Sneed II was born. After working at Kroger, Tommy worked for the Kentucky State Department of Education. Tommy was fatally injured in a head-on collision with an eighteen wheeler near Memphis, TN, on May 22, 1986, while traveling as a property screener of government surplus property.

Tommy Sneed family, 1982

Tommy's maternal grandparents were Susie M. Cobb (Jan. 6, 1883—Feb. 17, 1970), and David Shelby Killough (July 31, 1865—Jan. 26, 1941). They moved to Hopkins County in 1917, from Webster County and lived in Earlington. In 1922 they moved to Coiltown, where David Killough worked in the coal mines. In 1929, they moved to Madisonville. Their children were Willie, Vernon, Annie Mae, Ernest and Elnora (June 1, 1910).

Tommy's paternal grandparents were Mamon Elizabeth Price (Mar. 31, 1889—Nov. 3, 1976), and Mack Donald Sneed (June 19, 1887—May 1, 1970). They were both born in Jackson Co., TN, and married Nov. 18, 1907. A man named Clarence Nelson loaned them a buggy so they could go get married. They named their first child after this man—Clarence Nelson Sneed (Nov. 24, 1908). Their other children were Ethel, Clara Isabel and Maxie Eugene. They came to Hopkins County in 1921, and lived in a section house off West Broadway. Mack Sneed worked for the L & N Railroad.

Tommy's wife, Joanne Lawson Sneed is a first grade teacher at Pride Elementary School and writes children's books. Joanne's latest book, BUFORD TALES—A COLLECTION OF SHORT STORIES is dedicated to the memory of Tommy Sneed. The Tommy Sneed Memorial Scholarship for elementary teachers has been endowed at Freed-Hardeman College, Henderson, TN, by Joanne and Thomas II. Tommy was a member of the Church of Christ and is buried at Odd Fellows Cemetery. - *Submitted by Joanne Lawson Sneed*

SOUTHWORTH-ASHBY

Annie Ashby was born May 12, 1878, near Madisonville. She was the daughter of William Emsley (1841-1918), and Vitula Wilson Ashby (1852-1943). She had three sisters: Mildred W., who married Nicholas Toombs; Elizabeth, who married William Burgess Wise; and Nancy "Nannie", who married Amplias O. Sisk (M.D.).

Miss Annie, as she was known all her life, moved to Earlington at the age of six with her family. She went as far as she could in school as there was no high school in Earlington at that time. At the age of 16, she went to work for the EARLINGTON BEE newspaper. Later, she was bookkeeper for the St. Bernard and West Kentucky Coal Co. stores from which she retired at the age of 62.

Miss Annie did not marry until she was 45. On Feb. 14, 1932, she married Brick Southworth.

Brick was born July 1, 1879 at St. Charles, the son of William (1847-1887) and Delia (1859-1955) Southworth.

Brick was a cashier and paymaster for the St. Bernard and West Kentucky Coal Co. He served for many years as a 1st Lieutenant in the local National Guard Company and was an Earlington City Clerk for many years. In 1951, he was honored by the Chief of the U.S. Weather Bureau for 40 years of volunteer work as a weather observer, never missing a day.

Miss Annie was a charter member of the EARLINGTON Methodist Church, organized in 1894, and received a plaque for this. She taught Sunday School and sang in the choir. A missionary circle at the church was named for her. She was active in all civic organizations and was named Earlington's Woman of the Year in 1967. She was a regent of the Daughters of the American Revolution and the local chapter was named for Capt. Stephen Ashby, one of her ancestors.

Dancing was something Miss Annie and Brick loved to do. For many years, they were invited to attend the Earlington High School prom where everyone would watch them dance.,

Miss Annie and Brick never had any children. Brick died on Apr. 8, 1962 and Miss Annie died Sept. 12, 1977. Both are buried at Odd Fellows Cemetery in Madisonville.

Miss Annie never lacked appreciation of the earth's beauty or failed to express it. The residents of Earlington will always remember fondly Miss Annie's sharp wit and keen sense of humor. - *Submitted by Irene Priest and Debbie Hammonds*

THOMAS B. SPAIN, JR.

Thomas Butler Spain, Jr. was born in Madisonville on Nov. 5, 1928, the son of Thomas Butler Spain of Murfreesboro, TN, and Louise Pinckard Ross of Madisonville. Like his older sister, Sara Ross Spain, and his mother, Spain was born at the family home of his maternal grandparents, Ellen P. Ross and Claude L. Ross (located on the west side of South Main Street, one lot south of its intersection with West Broadway, where THE MESSENGER office now stands). (See "Claude L. Ross Family")

Judge and Mrs. Thomas B. Spain

Spain attended public schools and was graduated from Madisonville High School in 1946. He attended Western Kentucky University and was graduated from the College of Law of the University of Kentucky in 1951. While at UK, Spain met Frances Mitchell Jones of Lexington, who also was graduated in 1951 from the College of Home Economics, and they were married on Jan. 9, 1954, upon his return from service in Korea with the U.S. Army. During his absence, Miss Jones, daughter of Edward Stewart Jones and Jeannette Rice, interned in dietetics and served on the staff of Christ Hospital in Cincinnati.

The Spains returned to Madisonville in 1955, upon Lt. Spain's discharge from the U.S. Army after four years of active duty. Spain joined the law firm of Gordon & Gordon & Mills and later was a partner in the firm of Mills, Spain, Mitchell and Turner. In June of 1973, Spain was appointed Circuit Judge of the Fourth Judicial Circuit by Gov. Wendell Ford. He continues to serve in that office. He is past president of the Kentucky Association of Circuit Judges, was selected as Outstanding Judge for 1985 by the Kentucky Bar Association and received the Outstanding Trial Judge Award for 1983 from the Kentucky Association of Trial Attorneys. He is past president of the Kiwanis Club of Madisonville and the Audubon Council, Boy Scouts of America, who bestowed on him the Silver Beaver Award.

Mrs. Spain is a Registered Dietitian and retired after 21 years' service with the Hopkins County Board of Education as Food Service Director. Both Judge and Mrs. Spain are Elders and teachers of Adult Sunday School classes in the First Presbyterian Church of Madisonville and serve on committees of the Presbytery of Western Kentucky.

Two sons were born of this marriage, Edward Butler Spain in 1956, and David Ross Spain in 1958. Both were graduated from Madisonville-North Hopkins High School and both are Eagle Scouts.

Edward attended Centre College and was graduated from the University of Kentucky in 1978 with a Bachelor's Degree in Business Administration. He subsequently received an Associate Degree in Computer Technology from Nashville Technological Institute and is employed as a computer engineer with National Semi-Conductor Corporation. He and his wife, Carolyn Etheridge of Franklin, TN, reside in Tampa, FL.

David received his Bachelor's and Master's Degrees in Geology from Murray State and Vanderbilt Universities and is employed as Senior Petroleum Geologist by Amoco Production Company in Houston, TX. He and Janice C. Newsam of Madisonville married in 1986. - *Submitted by Judge Thomas B. Spain*

SPRINGFIELD

George William Springfield was born Jan. 25, 1806, in Roxboro, NC. His father was Moore Springfield, who died in Hopkins Co., KY, on Oct. 28, 1843. He married Rebecca Davey Mitchell on Dec. 29, 1825, in Person Co., NC. George William died on Feb. 15, 1856, and is buried near Slaughters, KY.

Rebecca Davey was born May 16, 1798, in Person Co., NC, to Gabriel Davey, Jr. of Person Co., NC. Gabriel's father was Gabriel Davie Sr., who was a soldier in the Revolutionary War. He was born around 1735 to William Davey and Lady Mary Ashburne. He married Elizabeth Bumpas, who's father was Robert Bumpas and who's mother was Sarah S. Gabriel Sr. died in 1792, Person Co., NC, and Elizabeth died in 1791, Person Co., NC. Gabriel Davey Jr. is supposed to have died in Tennessee. Rebecca Davey died on July 15, 1874, in Hopkins Co., KY. She is buried with George William.

George and Rebecca had four children: George Gabriel was born on Aug. 10, 1823, in North Carolina, married on Feb. 1, 1849, in Hopkins Co., KY, to Rebecca Day (Sept. 24, 1826-July 23, 1889), died on Jan. 24, 1893, and buried in the Day Cemetery on Highway 630; Rebecca was born 1831, in North Carolina, married W.T. Jones; Frances was born 1836, in North Carolina and died 1918; Benjamin Franklin was born on May 2, 1838, in North Carolina, married on Oct. 12, 1863, in Hopkins Co., KY to Henriette Jane Steen (Aug. 1, 1838-Dec. 12, 1917), died Sept. 24, 1900 and is buried at Liberty, KY, at the Star Hope Cemetery. - *Submitted by Sandra Donaldson*

SPRINGFIELD-STEEN

Benjamin Franklin Springfield was born on May 2, 1838, in North Carolina, to G.W. and Rebecca Springfield. He was married to Henrietta Jane Steen on Oct. 12, 1863, in Hopkins Co.,

KY. They lived on a farm that was located in north Nebo. Everyone knew B.F. as "Doc", who had had some training in medicine. Henrietta was born on Aug. 1, 1838, in Hopkins Co., KY, to Wilkerson and Synthia Steen. Doc died on Sept. 24, 1900, and Henrietta died on Dec. 12, 1917. They are buried at Star Hope Cemetery in Liberty, KY.

B.F. and Henrietta (Steen) Springfield

They had five children: Florence Marshall was born on Aug. 1, 1864, married 1st George Killough, 2nd Wilbur Forest Curtright and Hugh Almon, died May 17, 1950, and is buried at Star Hope Cemetery at Liberty, KY; Montgomery Davey was born Sept. 28, 1866, married Minnie, died Dec. 23, 1964, and is buried at Star Hope Cemetery in Liberty, KY; Thomas Lee was born Jan. 28, 1869, married Beaulah C. and died on Apr. 22, 1951, in Lamarr, MO, and is buried at Star Hope Cemetery in Liberty, KY; Sam was born on Oct. 4, 1872, and died Dec. 10, 1944; Valeria Helen was born Oct. 1, 1875, married Willie Mooney on Dec. 26, 1894, died in Denver, CO, and is buried at Star Hope Cemetery in Liberty, KY.

Florence Marshall married first George Killough and they had one daughter Clara Vaden (Veasey). Vaden had one daughter, Odette Veasey (Brown). Second she married Wilbur Forest Curtright and they had two daughters, Grace (1892-1970), and Hattie (1895-living). Grace married A.H. Townsend and they had one daughter, Thelma Geraldine (1910-living). Hattie married twice and had two sons; Davis Howard Crowe and Eugene Dame.

Montgomery Davey married Minnie from Perry, OK, late in life and didn't have any children. He lived in Little Rock, AR, but also owned property in Oklahoma and Kentucky.

Sam lived in Little Rock, AR, and never married. In 1944, he was killed by a man trying to rob him.

Valeria Helen married Willie Mooney and had one son, Guy and one daughter, Lelia.

Thomas Lee was married and had several children. *Submitted by Sandra Donaldson*

STEELE-CARY

Edward Mitchell Steele and Mary Grace Cary of Greenville, KY, were married Dec. 19, 1948. They moved to Madisonville in March 1954. They are the parents of two sons and one daughter, all born in Hopkins County.

Mitchell Wesley was born Nov. 10, 1954. He married Dorothy Marie Hayes of Nebo. They have one daughter, Rachel Marie age 8. They live in Dalton and Wesley is employed at Providence #1 mine. Dorothy is employed at Calvert & Moore, Attorneys at Law.

Mary Grace and Edward Steele

Robert Edward was born Mar. 12, 1956. He married Karin Schmitt from West Germany. They have two living sons, Michael Robert, age 6 and Kevin James, age 4. Their first son Jason Edward was born June 19, 1979, and died Jan. 20, 1982. Robert is employed by American Mine & Tool. They live in Hanson.

Christine Elaine was born July 13, 1964. She married Robert William Osborne. She is in the student nursing program at M.C.C. Robert is employed by United Parcel Service. They live in Madisonville.

Ed has been in the insurance business over 30 years in Hopkins County. He has offices in Nortonville and in Earlington. His hobby is playing golf.

Mary Grace keeps busy being a wife, mother and grandmother.

The Steeles live on Country Club Drive in Madisonville and are members of the First Baptist Church of Earlington. - *Submitted by Mary Grace Steele*

STEVENS-TEAGUE

Dewey Nelson Stevens, born Jan. 24, 1905, son of Tom and Ollie Crunk Stevens of Christian Co., KY. Dewey grew up and worked on the farm with his dad until he came to Nortonville and went to work in the coal mines. He married Helen Geneva Teague, b. Mar. 24, 1913 the daughter of George Anderson and Effie Rachel Lyell Teague.

Dewey Nelson and Helen Geneva (Teague) Stevens

The doctor advised Dewey to leave the mine due to his health. They moved to Detroit, MI, where Dewey was employed by Seal-Test for approximately 25 years, retiring in 1963, after his first heart attack. They came back to Kentucky in 1969, and Dewey died in 1979. He is buried in New Salem Cemetery, Nortonville.

Helen grew up and attended grammar and high school in Nortonville. She was a housewife and mother. She is active in the Trinity Gospel Tabernacle of Nortonville.

Their children:

Loretta, b. Jan. 12, 1934, married Mervin Stringer. Loretta is Secretary in Engineering for Michigan Bell Telephone Co. Mervin is a retired Special Insurance Adjustor for Engineering at Michigan Bell. They make their home in Livonia, MI. Loretta has a son, Michael McGowan, by a former marriage. Mike married Deidra Baker. They make their home in Nortonville with their children Crystel Ann Rachel and Matthew William. Mike is employed by Lewis' in Nortonville.

Jimmy Nelson, b. Oct. 28, 1938, married Priscilla Martin, b. Sept. 2, 1941, the daughter of Mr. & Mrs. John Martin of Detroit, MI. Jim finished grammar school at Tildon High, graduated from Cass Tech. in 1958. He has been employed by Prompt Pattern Co. approximately 24 years. Priscilla is a housewife and mother and is employed in the office at K-Mart. Their home is in Uttica, MI. Their children: Ann Marie Stevens, single at this date, is a Sales and Marketing Coordinator of General Motors Accounts, lives with her parents; James Nelson Stevens married Bobby McMillan. Jim is employed by a car pattern company. They reside in Oxford, MI; and Laura Ann Stevens, single at this date, attends college and works part time in San Diego, CA. - *Submitted by Agnes Teague Cunningham*

STEWART-LACY

WILLIAM LYALLS STEWART was born in St. Charles, KY, on Feb. 13, 1906, to MERRITT OMER STEWART AND EULALIA JANE JEFFREY. He attended elementary school in St. Charles and high school in Lexington, TN. He worked as a bookkeeper for the St. Bernard Coal Company, as an assistant druggist and owned and operated a coal mine, all in St. Charles. Then he moved to Los Angeles, CA, where he worked for two years before returning to Kentucky and settling in Madisonville.

Lyall and Carrie Stewart

On Apr. 24, 1937, in Mortons Gap, KY, he married CARRIE ELIZABETH LACY, daughter of Edd Lee Lacy and Helena Emilia Miller. He sold cars for Kelly Jones Motor Company and Scott-McGaw Motor Company before opening Lyall Stewart Auto Sales on Federal Street in June 1943, later moving to 795 South Main Street to continue his auto sales business, until retirement in January 1971.

Lyall served as Central Tire Inspector for Hopkins County under the WPA during World War II. Lyall is a fifty-year Mason and lifelong member of the Christian Church, serving the First Christian Church of Madisonville as a deacon and elder for ten years, during which time he was elected chairman of the board for one term. He was an avid hunter and fisherman, until he retired.

CARRIE ELIZABETH (LACY) STEWART, daughter of EDD AND HELEN LACY was born in Glasgow, KY, on Oct. 13, 1913, but moved to Madisonville shortly thereafter. She attended schools in Madisonville, graduating from Madisonville High School in 1931. Carrie's two major interests, aside form her family, are education and volunteer work in her community. She has attended Western and Murray State College extension courses and Evansville College. She served as Madisonville High School PTA President, 1952-53; PTA Council President, 1955-57; President of the Young Woman's Homemaker's Club; Secretary and President of the Homemakers' Extension Council, September 1963-65; elected PTA life membership in Hopkins County Council of PTA in 1957; served on Mental Health-Retardation Board 1965-68; served 1968-72 as Volunteer Coordinator for Mental Health, which merged with nine county Pennyroyal Mental Health Association; represented Kidney Foundation of Kentucky for all of Western Kentucky 1972-74; cooperated in organizing GFWC Woman's Club of Madisonville in January 1969, serving as president from August 1969 to May 1971, and again from May 1984-86. In 1951-52, Carrie Stewart and A.O. Johnston, cooperated in establishing the Hopkins County Youth Center, which was operational until the summer of 1987.

Lyall and Carrie moved to the family residence at 155 West Lake Street, Madisonville in 1943. They have three daughters: CATHERINE EULALIA (LAYLE), born in Madisonville June 2, 1939, married to Jackson Ralph Luckett in Washington, D.C., on June 23, 1967; SANDRA LYLE (SANDY), born in Madisonville May 6, 1943, married to Millard John Morgan in Beaufort, SC on Oct. 8, 1966; and CARRIE ELIZABETH II (LIBBY), born Sept. 14, 1949, in Hopkinsville. Refer to: Merritt Omer Stewart, Edd Lee Lacy, Emil George Miller, Catherine Eulalia Stewart Luckett, Sandra Lyle Stewart Morgan, Carrie Elizabeth Stewart II. *Submitted by Mrs. Lyall Stewart*

CARRIE E. STEWART II

CARRIE ELIZABETH (LIBBY) STEWART II, the youngest daughter of LYALL AND CARRIE STEWART, was born on Sept. 14, 1949, in Hopkinsville, KY. She began dancing lessons at age three and continued lessons in swimming, piano, tennis, golf, bridge and art. She was active in Brownie, intermediate and

Libby Stewart

senior Girl Scouts and was a member of the Hopkins County Youth Center.

Libby attended kindergarten through the third grade at Immaculate Conception School, in Earlington, KY, during which time she joined the First Christian Church in Madisonville. The rest of her elementary schooling was spent at West Broadway School, then on to Madisonville Junior High (now Browning Springs Middle School), and Madisonville-North Hopkins High School. For her last two years of high school, Libby went to Stuart Hall in Staunton, VA, graduating in June 1967, at which time she received the School History Award.

Libby was honored with a scholarship to Randolph-Macon Woman's College in Lynchburg, VA, where she completed two years of college before transferring to the University of Kentucky, where she became a member of Alpha Theta Chapter of Delta Zeta Sorority. She received her BA degree in history and political science in May 1971. In addition, she took courses at Evansville College and Kentucky Wesleyan in Owensboro. In the summer of 1970, she joined the Randolph-Macon Foreign Study Program in Europe, studying in England, France, Belgium, Italy, Austria, Holland and Yugoslavia.

Libby held summer jobs at Pennyrile State Park and in the offices of the Hopkins County Court Clerk and the County Tax Office.

Her first employment following college was with the Kentucky Legislative Research Commission in Frankfort, KY. In 1973, she moved to Louisville where she accepted a position as the assistant to the operations manager of WAVE Radio, later moving to WAVE-TV in the research department of Orion Broadcasting. While at WAVE, she became an officer of American Women in Radio and TV and Joined the Third Century Club of Louisville.

In September 1979, Libby moved to Shelby, NC, to work as sales representative for Container Corporation of American, a corrugated box company. In 1985, she transferred to Chesapeake Display Packaging of Winston Salem, NC. She is currently working for Chambers Container of Gastonia, NC, representing the same type of product.

In 1985, Libby traveled to Oberammeragua, Bavaria, West Germany, to see the famous Passion Play, which is presented by the villagers only once every ten years, this one celebrating 350 years of production. She also visited, France, Italy, Germany and Switzerland.

Her hobbies are golf, collecting shells in Florida, and her vast collection of novelty boxes.

Libby continues to live in Shelby, where she is a member of the Presbyterian Church. Refer to: Edd Lee Lacy, Emil G. Miller, M.O. Stewart, William Lyalls and Carrie Stewart. - *Submitted by Mrs. Lyall Stewart*

MERRITT OMER STEWART

MERRITT OMER (MED) STEWART (born Sept. 3, 1867 and died Nov. 1, 1949), married EULALIA JANE JEFFREY (born Feb. 5, 1873, and died Nov. 23, 1942). Both Merritt Omer and Eulalia Jane died in St. Charles, KY, and are buried in Christian Privilege Cemetery in St. Charles, KY. Merritt was the son of WILLIAM STEWART AND MARTHA ANN DAVIS GREGORY.

Merritt Omer (Med) and Eulalia Jane Jeffrey Stewart

MARTHA ANN DAVIS GREGORY was the daughter of CAPTAIN BEN DAVIS, of Civil War fame, who fought for the Confederate Army, then settled on his farm in St. Charles, KY. He was married to ? LIGON of Hanibel, MO. Captain Davis always said he "ran Sherman to the sea — he was about one hundred yards in front of General Sherman". Captain Davis' daughter, MARTHA ANN DAVIS, was first married to CHARLES GREGORY, SR. They moved to Shawneetown, IL, where they operated a variety store. They had two sons, CHARLES, JR., AND WALTER.

Charles Sr. was killed by a drunken soldier, so Martha Ann moved back to the Davis family home in St. Charles with her sons, where she later married WILLIAM STEWART, who died in 1904, and is buried in the Christian Privilege Cemetery in St. Charles. They had two more sons, MERRITT OMER STEWART AND FRANK STEWART, who died in 1954, in Lexington, TN.

Merritt Omer and Eulalia Jane Stewart lived on the St. Charles farm, later known as the Stewart Place. They had four children:

1) MABLE CATHERINE (born Feb. 4, 1894), married JACK DENNISON from Lexington, TN, where they made their home. They had two sons, LEONARD AND JAMES. Jack Dennison was an engineer for the C&I Railroad. Mable died in Lexington, TN, in April 1931. Jack died in March 1937. They are both buried in Lexington, TN.

2) GLADYS STEWART (born on Aug. 24, 1896, and died in St. Charles, KY, in October, 1970), was married to George Cheek. George worked for the St. Bernard Coal Company, then operated his own grocery store, Cheek's

Grocery, in St. Charles, for many years. They had two sons and a daughter: HAROLD STEWART CHEEK, currently residing in Bowling Green, KY; FRANK ARNOLD CHEEK of Madisonville; and MABLE DORIS CHEEK, currently residing in Owensboro, KY. Gladys and George Cheek are both buried in the Odd Fellows Cemetery in Madisonville.

3) JAMES LEON STEWART was born on Apr. 20, 1900, and died on July 3, 1951. He is buried in the Christian Privilege Cemetery in St. Charles, KY. He was married to Arietta Sisk.

4) WILLIAM LYALLS STEWART (born on Feb. 13, 1906), married Carrie Elizabeth Lacy (born Oct. 13, 1913), on Apr. 24, 1937. They had three daughters: CATHERINE EULALIA (born June 2, 1939), currently residing in La Jolla, CA; SANDRA LYLE (born May 6, 1942), currently residing in Lompoc, CA; and CARRIE ELIZABETH II (born Sept. 14, 1949), currently living in Shelby, NC. Refer to: William Lyalls and Carrie Elizabeth Lacy Stewart, Edd Lee Lacy, Catherine Eulalia Stewart Luckett, Sandra Lyle Stewart Morgan, Carrie Elizabeth Stewart II. *Submitted by Mrs. Lyall Stewart*

ERNEST LEE STOKES

Ernest Lee Stokes (1869-1941), born at Port Royal, TN, was five years old when his parents came to Earlington from Crofton, KY. He became a skilled carpenter, craftsman and cabinet maker and built his home next to his father's. He was a carpenter for the St. Bernard Coal Co. and West Ky. Coal Co., until his retirement because of ill health. He was a fifty-year Mason and Past Master of the lodge; from early youth a member of the Methodist Church. In 1896, he married Nancy Ann Robertson (1870-1939), born in Bowling Green, KY. At age one, her parents moved to Tennessee and as a young lady she came to Earlington to live with her brother Joe Robertson. Ernest and Annie had five children: Fern, Malcolm, Julia, Joseph and Frank.

Annie (Robinson) and Ernest Stokes

Fern Stokes, born 1897, still lives in the family home. She taught school 52 years and was also a Sunday School teacher at the Methodist Church in Earlington. She was very active in all school, church and civic activities until bad health prevented.

Malcolm (1899-1965), was an electrical and building contractor, moved to Florida and entered the real estate business. In 1930, he married Jessie Halsall in Florida. She lives in West Palm Beach, FL, where Malcolm is buried. They had one child, Ernest Malcolm, who lives in Georgia. Julia was born May 23, 1903, and died Sept. 4, 1903.

Joseph died at seven months of age.

Frank (1904-1947), was a twin to Joseph. He lived all his life in Earlington, was a skilled baseball player, worked as electrician for West Ky. Coal Co., then as a mine mechanic and lost his life Christmas Eve in 1947, in the East Diamond Mine fire. He was married to Frances Wyatt of Earlington and they had three sons: Bill, Joe and Jim Stokes, who all played basketball for Earlington High School.

Dr. William Stokes now lives in Miami, FL, and is Vice President of South Campus, Miami Dade Community College.

Joseph Stokes M.D. is a Radiologist in Greenville, KY.

James Stokes lives in Ft. Collins, CO, and is County Director of Information Management for Larimer County, CO.

Ernest Lee Stokes was the son of Andrew Jackson Stokes, born in Trigg Co., and Fannie Farmer born at Port Royal, TN. Andrew was a Civil War Veteran and eighteen months a Union prisoner at Rock Island Prison. He was the first Police Judge of Crofton, KY, and came to Earlington in 1874. He built his own home and was employed by Mr. J.B. Atkinson as a carpenter. He served 15 years on the school board, was a magistrate of the second district, 1883-1884 was Master of E.W. Turner Lodge F & AM. He joined the Masonic Lodge in Tennessee before the War. There were ten children: Olive, who died young; Mrs. Ernest Newton; Mrs. Elmo Shaver; Mrs. Albert Keown; Mrs. Ed Trahern; Mrs. Chester Hutchinson; Miss Effie Stokes; Jack Clay Stokes; and Ernest Stokes. - *Submitted by Francis Blais*

STROTHER-WILLIS

Dr. Fred Price Strother came to Madisonville, KY, following graduation from University of Louisville Medical School in 1903, and practiced medicine here for 55 years before his death, June 18, 1961.

He was born in Butler Co., KY, May 19, 1875, son of Dr. John French Strother a native of Virginia and Mollie Chauvin Strother of Franklin, KY. He was the fifth of seven children (Fannie, William, Clarence, Gertrude, Fred, David and Jesse), and received his early education in Rochester, KY, and Morgantown schools. He and Fannie May Willis of Rochester were married Oct. 6, 1898. They had two children: Mary Ruth and William Frederick.

He first formed a partnership with Dr. Will P. Ross of Madisonville, then later opened his own office. Dr. Jesse Strother subsequently moved to Madisonville and was in partnership with his brother for twelve years before moving to Henderson, KY. Jesse was married to Martha Kittinger and they had one son, John William, born in 1916, in Madisonville.

Fred Price and Fannie May were active members of First Christian Church. He was a Mason, a member of the American Medical Assn., Hopkins Co. Medical Society, a director of Kentucky Bank and Trust Co. for over 25 years, Vice-President of Madisonville Building and Loan Assoc. and member of Madisonville Civil Service Commission. During World War I, he served as captain in the Medical Corps stationed at Ft. Oglethorpe, GA.

Fannie Mae (born Apr. 6, 1876 in Rochester died Jan. 13, 1968 in Madisonville), was the daughter of William and Phoebe Brewer Willis. She was the second of six girls, attended school in Rochester, then later South Kentucky College in Hopkinsville. She was a member of the first Board of Directors of Madisonville Public Library, President of the Madisonville Woman's Club and taught Sunday School Class-14 at the First Christian Church for thirty years.

Mary Ruth, born Dec. 30, 1905, in Madisonville, graduated from Madisonville High School, Ward-Belmont College and Vanderbilt University. She was married to Karl Berlin Matthai of Nashville, TN, May 13, 1934, and resides in Nashville. He died Nov. 16, 1970.

William Frederick (born Oct. 17, 1909, died May 15, 1975), was a graduate of Madisonville High School and attended Transylvania College. He was a Madisonville Funeral Director, owner of Barnett-Strother Funeral Home, member of Madisonville First Christian Church, Masonic Lodge, Elks Lodge, Rizpah Shrine and Scottish Rite. He was married to Artie Mae Stanley Feiler of Paducah, KY. - *Submitted by Mary Ruth Strother Matthai*

SULLIVAN-RAMSEY

Opal Vivian Ringo and Ernest Delmar Ramsey had a short courtship. She was engaged to Ross Fox, across Tradewater river in Caldwell County. Ernest finished Business College in Evansville and lived in East St. Louis, IL. He managed the American Cigar Store there. He also went to the St. Louis World's Fair in 1904, and was marooned on top of the ferris wheel for some hours. It was a cage, one stood in; they didn't have the seats yet. When the river froze everyone walked, so they could say they walked on the Mississippi River.

He, too, had a great love in St. Louis. For some reason, he came home. He was the family's baby at 29. The Ringos were new in the neighborhood, Opal was 17, and Ernest started courting her. Tradewater river rose and stayed up for three months. Ross couldn't get across and Ernest didn't go back to St. Louis — so, they eloped. Yes, out of the window!

They were married 54 years and had one daughter, Anna Margaret, born July 3, 1915. She was the apple of his eye. He was nearly 30 and was wild about his daughter. She attended Madisonville schools and even vacated some. The old school house on Broadway and Scott was where she started. Ernest took her and was talking with the teacher. She didn't want to go to school, so she jumped out the window and ran home. After a number of times, she finally gave up. She also attended Waddill Avenue, which was "out in the country".

Visiting cousins in Marion, she met Eugene "Jobie" Sullivan, from Livingston County. His father was Gideon Sullivan and his mother, Percy Jennings Sullivan, died while he was an infant. He had one half sister, Vera Pauline Sullivan (married Guy Guess, Marion), and

Eugene "Jobie" and Margaret Sullivan at their 50th wedding anniversary open house, Aug. 11, 1985, in Marion, KY

two half brothers, Estle and Ray Sullivan. Pauline had five children; Estle 2; Ray 1.

"Jobie" and Margaret wrote while he was in school. In later years, I would live rough (deservedly so), over those letters I read to my class before the teacher came in.

They were married Aug. 3, 1935, in Shawneetown, IL, and made their home in Madisonville. They had two children, Peggy Ann, born Dec. 11, 1936, and one son, stillborn in August of 1941. His name was Raymond.

Peggy was not the healthiest child. She was the first known case of viral pneumonia in Hopkins County. On Dec. 11, 1943 (her birthday), she slipped into a coma and was not expected to survive. Dr. James L. Salmon was new in Madisonville. He procured some sulpha, which was being tested by the U.S. Army.

The drug was administered. As with all happy ending stories", she awoke on Christmas morning. (Barry Fitzgerald and Bing Crosby have to be in there, somewhere). Opal died May 4, 1967, and Ernest on June 7, 1976.

Peggy married Harry Doyle Waide, Oct. 18, 1958. They have three children and two grandchildren.

"Nana" and "Dodie" as their grand and great-grandchildren call them, are retired in Marion, KY. They celebrated their 50th anniversary in 1985. (See Waide-Sullivan, Ramsey-Ringo) - *Submitted by Peggy Sullivan Waide*

SUMMERS-AUSENBAUGH

More than 30 years ago John Wayne (Beau) Summers became interested in politics when he was associated with J.B. Daniels in an unsuccessful race for sheriff in the early 1950's. Although he did not become a deputy sheriff as he had hoped, he never entirely gave up the idea.

John Wayne (Beau) Summers was born Feb 12, 1930, to Luther and Verda Mae (Laffoon) Summers of the Fiddle Bow community of Hopkins Co. (See SUMMERS-LAFFOON). He attended Dalton High School and in 1948, after high school, he had jobs with Dunville Motors and Gulf Refining Co., until he went into the Army in 1951, during the Korean War, as a member of the 1st Cavalry Division's 70th Tank Battalion. After serving six months in Korea and 14 months in Japan, he was honorably discharged as a sergeant in February, 1953.

Sheriff Beau Summers

After the service, for two years he again drove a truck for Gulf in Owensboro, operated his own business, South Main Marathon, for a few years, and worked for Firestone Tire and Rubber Co., in Daytona, FL, for a time. After the family's return from Florida, Beau and Clint Cullen bought an auto parts business, which became known as S & C Auto Parts at Arch and Franklin streets. Beau later became sole owner and is to this date.

In 1955, John Wayne Summers married Jean Ausenbaugh, born June 20, 1932, dau. of Ernest Ray and Stella (Ratliff) Ausenbaugh of the Richland community. He had acquired the name "Beau" while he was in H.S., when his girlfriend, Jean, gave him the French spelling of her "sweetheart", and it became semi-official during his campaign for sheriff in 1985. Beau and Jean are parents of two daughters, Patricia Jane Summers born Apr. 13, 1957, who works at South Central Bell in Owensboro; and Tracy Lynn Summers, born Feb. 15, 1961, married to Mark Allen Clayton, born Sept. 22, 1956. Tracy is a secretary at KY Bank and Trust Company. They have a daughter, Rachael Nichole Clayton, b. Dec. 9, 1983.

Beau Summers served first as a deputy sheriff for a short time for Sheriff Ronald Eastwood, but Summers, along with deputy Jim Lantrip, left the office before Eastwood's term ended, because of differences on several issues.

In May 1985 primary, Summers opposed Ronald Eastwood for Sheriff but because of ill health, Eastwood withdrew and threw his support to Jim Kennedy, his deputy. It was a hotly contested race, but Beau Summers won solidly the office of Sheriff. Soon after the primary, Eastwood died, and Summers was appointed in July 1985 to fill the remaining six months of the term. In January 1986, Summers was sworn in for his own four-year term as Sheriff, and his 30-year dream had been realized.

As Sheriff, Beau Summers now has a desire to build a modern sheriff's office to include a new radio system and an in-house computer system to be used for records keeping and data storage, and to enlarge his field staff to about double the present size.

Budgetary limitations and the pace of the "system" under which he must function prevents his ideal operational efficiency. But when the frustrations of the job get too numerous, he and Mrs. Summers sometimes take a day or two off and go to their houseboat on Kentucky Lake. - *Submitted by John (Beau) Summer as compiled by Rella Jenkins*

SUMMERS-LAFFOON

Neal Summers (b. 1870 d. 1929), from the Fiddle Bow community of Hopkins County, first married Alice Robinson. They were the parents of Tom, who married Jennie Rollins; Oscar, who married Bertha Lamb; Goldie, who married Perry Lyon of Morton's Gap; Marie (b. July 28, 1905 d. Sept. 22, 1985), buried at Odd Fellows Cemetery. She married Marlin Melton of Hopkins Co.; Bertha, who married Lloyd Wyatt; and Lizzie, who married Hutch Lamb.

Neal's second wife was Lou Robinson (b. 1876 d. 1949), a sister to Alice, and their two children were: Luther Summers (b. May 2, 1908 d. Feb. 24, 1979), and Myrtle Geneva Summers (b. Nov. 30, 1910 d. July 19, 1983), who was married to Ruby Jackson (b. Oct. 2, 1903 d. Jan. 16, 1984). They are all buried at New Beulah Cem.

Verda Mae and Luther Summers on their 50th wedding anniversary in 1977

Luther Summers married Verda Mae Laffoon, b. May 10, 1908, dau. of John Marcus Laffoon (b. May 20, 1875 d. Nov. 28, 1956), cousin to Ruby Laffoon, and Sarah Melissa Page (b. June 6, 1886 d. June 22, 1982), of Hopkins Co., who are buried at Odd Fellows. Verda Mae has one brother, Johnny Hardin Laffoon, b. Oct. 9, 1917, who was married to Bonnie Tucker (b. Apr. 13, 1899 d. Aug. 29, 1980). Johnny is Supt. of the county landfill of Hopkins Co. Verda Mae's sister is Letha Laffoon Perkins (Mrs. James Mangum), b. Sept. 25, 1910, who lives in Owensboro.

Luther and Verda Mae had four children: Paul Edward Summers (b. Mar. 19, 1928), first married Norene Grable, who lives in California. They had one son, Paul Allen Summers, born June 13, 1964. Paul E. later married Katherine Holt of Dawson Springs. He was fatally injured in a car accident on Nov. 27, 1968, and is buried at Old Beulah Cem. near Dawson Springs.

John Wayne (Beau) Summers, born Dec. 12, 1930, is married to Jean Ausenbaugh, born June 20, 1932, of Richland community. He is presently the Sheriff of Hopkins County. (See SHERIFF BEAU SUMMERS).

Donald Ray Summers, born Mar. 12, 1939, of Whitehouse, TX, was first married to Loudell Winstead of Hopkins Co. and their daughter is Gigi Denise Summers, first married to Andy Payne. She has a son, Anthony Travis Payne, and she is now married to David Martin of Calhoun, KY. Donald Ray is now married to the former Lottie Doss. Their dau. is Trina Volette Summers, age 20, a college student. He is a Federal mine inspector in Texas.

Glenda Gail Summers, born Dec. 11, 1945, was married July 3, 1964 to Ronald W. Ayers, born May 30, 1945, son of Wilburn Dixon Ayers and Idema (Dorris) Ayers. Ronald is employed by Advance Truck Lines, Nashville, TN. From 1977, Glenda worked as assistant Hopkins Co. Treasurer, until July 1981, when she was appointed to the position of Hopkins County Treasurer, which she now holds.

Glenda and Ronald have two daughters: Rhonda Gail Ayers, b. Sept. 19, 1967, married to C. Duane Burns, b. Jan. 9, 1964, on Dec. 16, 1983. They have two children, Brooke Ashley Burns, b. July 21, 1984, and Derek Mitchell Burns, born Aug. 27, 1987. The second daughter, Stacey Michelle Ayers, born Jan. 23, 1971, married Danny Ray Offutt, born Mar. 23, 1966, on Aug. 14, 1987. Michelle is a Junior at Madisonville-North Hopkins H.S.

At the time of Paul Edward Summers' death, his son, Paul Allen, age 14, went to live with his grandparents, Mr. and Mrs. Luther Summers in Madisonville. He is a graduate of Madisonville-North Hopkins H.S., attended Madisonville Community College, and is a graduate of Western Kentucky Univ. in 1976. After working several years in the Property Valuation Administration Office, Paul Allen was elected for six years the Circuit Court Clerk of Hopkins Co. in 1981. He is un-opposed for re-election this year, 1987. He is married to Karen Annette Smith, born Mar. 2, 1959, dau. of James Dewey Smith and Mary Rose (Allen) Smith of Nebo. They have two sons, Kyle Edward, born June 12, 1985, and Corey Travis, born Nov. 16, 1986. - *Submitted by Verda Mae Summers as Compiled by Rella Jenkins*

SUTHARD-DICKERSON

On Mar. 8, 1917, Morton Hailey Dickerson was born, the first son of James Arthur Dickerson and Hazel Earl Hailey Dickerson, on Route #4, Madisonville, KY. Mary Helen Suthard was born on Nov. 26, 1919, to Homer Suthard, Sr. and Mary Myrtle Hicklin Suthard, although she lived with her grandparents, Norman Enos Suthard and Stella Holland Greer Suthard from a very early age. Later, on May 17, 1941, Morton Dickerson and Helen Suthard were married in Clarksville, TN. They have two daughters, Vicki Jean Dickerson and Cathy Ann Offutt. They also have three grandchildren.

The oldest daughter, Vicki Jean, was born on Oct. 15, 1948. She married Jeff Thomison on July 25, 1969. They have two children, Andy Neal Thomison, born Mar. 30, 1974, and Amy Hailey Thomison, born Apr. 18, 1977. They live on Brown Road, Route #3, Madisonville. Jeff works for Peabody Coal Company, at River Queen Mines in Greenville, KY.

Cathy Ann, the youngest daughter married Terry Offutt, Oct. 27, 1978. They have a daughter, Hailey Beth Offutt, born May 26, 1984. Terry works for Austin Powder Company, and Cathy is employed in the County Court Clerks Office at the Hopkins County Courthouse. They live on Route #3 in Madisonville.

Morton and Helen were self-employed as welder and bookkeeper, owning and operating Dickerson Welding Company on Bassett Avenue for many years, till they retired in July of 1982. Morton also served during World War II in both theaters of operations. Morton is very active politically, as he was magistrate of the Third District for twenty years. They are both still very active in their community.

They live at 829 Brown Road and are kept busy by hobbies, old cars, refinishing furniture and traveling in their motorhome. They are members of Madisonville First United Methodist Church. - *Submitted by Vicki Thomison*

SUTHARD-PENDLEY

Dixie Ann Pendley and Clarence Truman Suthard were married June 15, 1963.

Dixie was born Sept. 24, 1946. Her parents are Dixie Lee (Ruthe) Kistner and the late Rev. Jewell Willard Pendley. (See: PENDLEY-KISTNER) Dixie attended school in Earlington and graduated from Earlington High School in 1964. She has been employed by West Kentucky Coal Co., Enro Credit Union, and People's Bank and Trust Co. She is currently a housewife. She enjoys sewing and quilting. She is a member of the Salem Missionary Baptist Church at Mortons Gap. She enjoys her duties as a Sunday School teacher and church clerk. She is also the Chaplain for the Gideon Auxiliary.

Dixie and Truman Suthard

Clarence (Truman) was born Mar. 27, 1942. He is the son of Helen Juanita Fox and Clarence Lacy Suthard. Maternal grandparents were Julie Florence Page and Ennis Wesley Fox. Paternal grandparents were Lora Bell Allen and Claude Lacy Suthard. He has one sister, Helen Joyce Kennett.

Truman attended school in Mortons Gap and graduated from South Hopkins High School in 1960. He has been employed by Pratt Moore's Store and Enro Shirt Factory. He is currently the Safety and Training Co-ordinator at Big Rivers Electric in Sebree. Truman enjoys restoring old cars. He is also a member of Salem Baptist Church, where he serves as a Deacon, Trustee, and Sunday School teacher. He is a member of the Gideon ministry.

Dixie and Truman have two daughters: Trina Michele (Jan. 1, 1966) and Kristi Lee (June 15, 1968). Trina graduated from Madisonville North in 1983 and will be a senior at Western Kentucky University in 1987. Kristi graduated from Madisonville North in 1986. She attends Madisonville Community College.

Dixie and Truman now reside in Hanson, KY. (See PENDLEY-KISTNER) - *Submitted by Dixie Suthard*

SUTHERLAND-CHESHER

Henry Norton Sutherland and Avanell Chesher Sutherland came to Madisonville in June 1967, from Salisbury, MD.

Henry Sutherland was born near Bardstown in Nelson Co., KY, on Nov. 25, 1932, the son of Archibald Cameron Sutherland and Effie Gertrude Brown. He has one brother, Fred Sutherland, and one sister, Ina Fay Reeb. The Sutherlands, originally from Scotland, came to Nelson County in 1780. Other direct ancestors are Cameron, Aydelotte, Read, Price, and Miles. The Brown family was in Nelson County in the early 1800's or earlier. Ancestors in the Brown family were named Smock, Buckler, Cox, and Wood.

Henry and Avanell Sutherland and daughters Diane and Carol

Avanell Sutherland was born in Louisville, KY, on May 7, 1934, the daughter of Ollie Leonard Chesher and Louise Douglas Moss. She has one brother, Ollie Chesher, and one sister, LaVerne Drane. The Chesher family is from Shelby Co., KY. Chesher ancestors were Brumley, Walker, Burns, Brooks, Hackley, and Taylor. The Moss family is from Perryville, KY. Family names were Graham, Feathers, Rainey, Hart, and Young.

Henry and Avanell Sutherland were married in Louisville, KY, on Oct. 26, 1956. They are the parents of two children. Diane Elizabeth was born June 29, 1961, in Louisville, KY. Carol Ann was born Nov. 8, 1965, in Ashland, KY. Both Diane and Carol are graduates of Kentucky Wesleyan College in Owensboro, KY. Diane was married on June 22, 1985, to Jerome Eric Luczaj of Columbus, OH. Eric is also a graduate of Kentucky Wesleyan College.

Henry Sutherland graduated from the University of Louisville in 1954, with a major in History. He served as an officer in the U.S. Navy from June 1954 to June 1959. He had two years of sea duty, serving on the USS Pittsburgh (CA 72) and on the USS Franklin D. Roosevelt (CVA 42). From June 1957 to June 1959, he was assigned to duty as Associate

Professor of Naval Science at the University of South Carolina. In June 1959, upon his release from the Navy, he was employed by the Social Security Administration. After assignments in Lexington, Louisville, and Ashland, KY, and Salisbury, MD, he was transferred to Madisonville in June 1967, as manager of the newly opened Social Security office.

Avanell Sutherland graduated from the University of Louisville in June 1956, with a major in Sociology. She was employed by the Social Security Administration from June 1956 until January 1960. She is currently employed as a hearings reporter and test examiner for the United States government.

Henry and Avanell Sutherland are currently residents of Madisonville and are members of the First Baptist Church. - Submitted by Henry N. Sutherland

SUTTLE-RUSSELL

Wanda Sue Russell and Donald Ray Suttle were married May 4, 1966. They remarried May 4, 1976.

Wanda, the proud daughter of Mrs. Rose Floyd Nash and Mr. Kelly Russell from Tennessee, became the first New Year's child in 1942 in Madisonville, KY. Wanda is presently employed at Dawson Springs Health Care Center as a nurse's aid. In Aug. of 1988, she will have dedicated ten years of hard work to this avocation.

Wanda attended the Richland Elementary School in Richland, KY and succeeded only to the seventh grade. She is one of four children Mrs. Rose Russell reared. She has two sister, Norene and Lynda, and one bother, Johnny.

Norene's family, who lives in Dixon, KY, includes her husband, Humphrey Stone, and her four children: Debbie, Carolyn, Charles (Chuck), and Wesley. Lynda who resides in St. Charles, KY, reared five children: Stacy, Gary, Beverly, Donnie and Brian. Lynda's only spouse has been deceased for six years now. Wanda's only brother, Johnny, lives in Richland, KY with his beloved wife, Helen, and their three elegant children: Rhonda, and the twins, Tammy and Johnny.,

On Mar. 21, 1959, Wanda married her first husband, Willie Ray Plunkett. Their marriage ended in 1963. The unsuccessful marriage ceased with a divorce but resulted in four beautiful children.

(1) Lisa, born Mar. 4, 1960, married Terrry Settle and became the mother of two children, Amy and Travis. Amy was born to Lisa and Jimmy Earl, her first husband. (2) Donna made her way into the world on Mar. 4, 1961. In 1979 she became the first child to graduated from Dawson Springs High School in Wanda's family. She recently married Roger Wayne Simms. (3) Born on June 9, 1962, Teresa made her vows at the altar to Kenneth Darrell Bennett and became a mother to daughter, Heather Dawn Bennett. Teresa has two other children, Sundie and Michael from her first love, Danny Vandiver. (4) The only son, Johnny, was born July 14, 1963, and he is presently dating Becky Haile. He also has a son, Jedidiah Dewayne Plunkett, from his marriage to his former wife, Angela Driver.

Donald Ray Suttle was born Oct. 14, 1940 in St. Charles, KY to Mrs. Rose Dimple (Greer) Suttle and the late Mr. Elvie Suttle. He attended Gilliland Ridge Elementary School through the 3rd grade. Education ceased for his subsequenting years in school. Donald is formally employed with Deer Creek Coal Company under two supervisors, Buck and Louis Vandiver. His present address is General Delivery, St. Charles, KY.

Besides Donald, Mrs. and Mr. Elvie Suttle also reared six other children: Harley, Gilbert, Thama, and Shirley. Those children who are deceased are Harold and Wayne.

Wanda and Donald have two daughters. Kathy, born on Sept. 20, 1966, resides in Marietta, GA. Lori, born on Aug. 26, 1970, attends the 12th grade at Dawson Springs High School. Submitted by Lori Suttle

TAPP

The Tapps were descendents of Eli Tapp, who came to Hopkins County from Person Co., NC, in about 1833 and purchased land in the Slaughters area.

Eli's son, Vincent Tapp, married Emily Orman Pritchett in 1851, in Hopkins County and they had two children:

(I) Laura Tapp, who married E.C. (wed) Brown, in 1875. Their children were: (1) Altha Brown, (2) John Vincent (Johnny) Brown, and (3) Alice Laura Brown.

W.R. (Bob) Tapp, died Nov. 29, 1979

(II) Robert Calvin (Bob) Tapp, farmer and one time Sheriff of Hopkins County, married Lula Jones in 1878, and their children were:

(1) Willis James Tapp, who married Sammie Bassett in 1909, and their children were: (1a) William Robert (Bob) - prominent attorney, Madisonville, KY, member of Kentucky House of Representatives in 1936-38. Served in United States Army 1943-48. Married Mary Eleanor Huston, 1937. Both are now deceased. (1b) Josephine Tapp, Deputy Property Valuation Administrator, Hopkins County, married Samuel James Baker in 1941 (deceased). One child, Lana Sue Baker (deceased). (1c) Margaret Tapp married Hugh Davis Noe in 1937. Their home is Somerset, KY. Their two children are Sarah Davis, Madisonville, KY, and Sam Noe, Jacksonville, FL. They have one grandchild Hugh Gordon Davis.

Betsy Tapp, W.C. and Lucy Tapp Hopkins

(2) Hal Jackson Tapp married Nina Bassett in 1913, and had two children: (1) Betsy Tapp of Louisville, KY. (2) Lucy Tapp married Walter Hopkins and their children are: (2a) Thomas Walter Hopkins of Anchorage, KY. (2b) Peggy Hopkins Landiai of Washington, D.C. They have two grandchildren: Bob Hopkins and Tim Hopkins. - Compiled by Margaret Tapp Noe and correlated by Lucy Tapp Hopkins

TARTER-DUNCAN

Retha Carol Duncan and Charles Alexander Tarter were united in marriage July 26, 1965.

Retha was born Aug. 13, 1948, in Hopkins County to Lavena Mae Rhew and Edward Lee Duncan (See Duncan-Rhew). She has three brothers: Jerry, Larry, and Casey. She also has two sisters: Brenda Brackett and Lesia Pendley. Other family names are: Parish, Brinkley, Walker, Arnold, Lutz, Winstead, Dame, Daniel, and Yarbrough.

Retha Carol (Duncan) and Charles Alexander Tarter with children Chamala Ann and Scott Alexander

Retha attended Nebo and West Broadway Elementary School. She also attended Seminary Junior High and Madisonville High School. She played the trumpet in the Madisonville High School Band and sang in Glee Club. After her marriage to Charles, Retha continued school in Oregon and graduated from La Grande High School in La Grande, OR.

Like her mother and grandmother before her, Retha enjoys playing the piano and singing alto. Retha belongs to the "Monday Night Bridge Club". She is also an active member of the Hopkins County Republican Party.

Retha is a Certified Dental Assistant. She has served all offices in the West Central Dental Assistants Society. She is a member of the Kentucky Dental Assistants Association of which she has served as First and Second Vice President, President-Elect and President. She was named Kentucky Dental Assistant of the Year in 1982.

Charles (Chuck) was born Apr. 1, 1944, in La Grande, OR. His parents are Phyllis Jane Hancock and Victor Lloyd Tarter of La Grande, OR. He has one brother: Nels Victor Tarter of Seattle, WA. Other family names are: George, Thornsberry, and Hill.

Chuck graduated from La Grande High School, La Grande, OR, in 1962. Chuck was a member of the football, wrestling and ski team.

Chuck met Retha while he was serving with the 101st Airborne Division at Fort Campbell, KY. He is presently employed by the CSX Railroad as a brakeman-conductor.

Chuck is a member of the Hopkins County Republican Party and the Hopkins County Bass Club. His hobbies include bass fishing, repairing and making fishing equipment, deer hunting, gardening, and working with wood and metal. Retha and the children say he is an excellent cook.

Chuck and Retha have two children: Chamala Ann (Mar. 6, 1966), and Scott Alexander (Jan. 3, 1969). They reside in Madisonville, KY. - *Submitted by Retha Tarter*

JAMES HENRY TAYLOR

James H. Taylor was half Cherokee Indian, born Feb. 3, 1838, Henderson Co., KY. It is believed that he came to Hopkins Co. from Henderson Co., between 1870 and 1874. He was the fourth of fourteen children born to Wilson F. Taylor, a full-blooded Cherokee Indian, and Mary K. Pickens, daughter of George Pickens and Catherine Marks.

James Henry and Sarah Jane (Clayton) Taylor

Wilson F. Taylor, born ca. 1808, in Kentucky, married Mary K. Pickens (born ca 1816, Loudoun Co., VA), on Aug. 15, 1831, in Henderson Co., KY. The brothers and sisters of James H. are as follows: Margaret, born ca 1833; William, born ca 1835; Mary Elizabeth, born ca 1837; David D., born ca 1847; Lucy C., born ca 1848; John Peter, born ca 1849; Elzena C., born ca 1854; Frances E., born ca 1855; Judy A., born ca 1856; and Mary Adelaide, born ca 1860. Wilson F. Taylor married second Lurilla Ann Way on Feb. 17, 1875, at the home of the bridegroom in Henderson Co., KY.

James H. married first Martha Caroline Fuller (born ca 1843-died before 1870), on Feb. 14, 1860, in Union Co., KY. Their children were: Mary Ella, born Aug. 29, 1863-died Apr. 11, 1921; Margaret Ann, born Mar. 10, 1867-died Feb. 18, 1946. James H. married second Sarah Jane Clayton (born June 1843 in Orange Co., NC-died Feb. 10, 1902), on Aug. 6, 1874, in Hopkins Co. She was the daughter of Solomon C. Clayton, Jr., and Alcie Yarbrough. The children of James H. and Sarah are as follows: Solomon David, born July 29, 1875-died June 14, 1958; Susan Frances, born Aug. 9, 1877-died Feb. 20, 1959; Elsie Annie, born July 17, 1881-died Oct. 2, 1962; Nancy Catherine, born August 1885; Eura Jane, born Jan. 25, 1889-died Nov. 8, 1924; and Clementine, born Jan. 14, 1890-died Nov. 30, 1980.

James H. is best remembered in a photograph taken when he was about 90 years old by his granddaughter, Ollie Spicer Breedlove. He was living at the home of his daughter, Clementine and Carlos Littlepage in Hopkins Co. The photograph best describes him in his later years as having a long white beard and using a walking cane. His grandson, William F. Winstead, recalls when James H. stayed at his home in Hopkins Co., he would groom his long white beard with a comb. Nell Littlepage Yarbrough tells that due to his failing eyesight he would take the crook of his cane and tap the children with it if they annoyed him too much.

James H. died Feb. 25, 1923 at his daughter's home in Hopkins Co. He and his wife are buried in separate cemeteries in Hopkins Co. in unmarked graves—James H. at Pleasant View Cemetery and Sarah Jane Clayton at Clayton Cemetery in Shakerag. - *Compiled by Mary Louise Winstead Wells*

TEAGUE

Edward Teague b. ca. 1660, transported into the providence of Maryland in 1675. In Cecil Co., MD, in St. Mary Ann's Parish in the vicinity of the Rising Sun, there are tombs of William and Elijah Teague, one of whom may or may not be the father of Edward.

Edward married Susan ? and there are records of three children: Catherine; William, b. 1693; and Ann. Edward died in 1697.

William, b. 1693, married Isabelle ? and there are records for nine children: Edward, b. 1716; Moses, b. 1718; Abraham, b. May 5, 1720; Charity, b. Dec. 11, 1722; Elijah, b. May 1, 1726; Susanna, b. Jan. 30, 1730; Joshua, b. 1732; William, b. July 31, 1733; and Rachel, b. 1735. William and his family left Maryland, moved to Virginia and on into the Carolinas.

Edward, b. 1716, married Luranna Van Swearingen and there are records of six children: Van Swearingen, b. ca. 1744; Edward; John; Rebecca; Luranna; and Isabelle. On July 31, 1949, a memorial address was delivered at Mondy's Cemetery in Alexandria Co., NC, by Rev. L.W. Teague to the memory of the great Pioneer Preacher, Rev. Edward Teague, b. 1716.

Van Swearingen Teague married Mary ?. He and his family left North Carolina and were in Madison Co., KY, in 1792, later located in Christian Co., KY, in 1797. Records for five children: William, b. Sept. 12, 1769; Jacob, b. 1771; Van S., b. Mar. 10, 1773; Abel, b. 1775; and Elizabeth, b. 1777. There were four children in the early court records who are believed to belong to this family: John, Burtha, Joshua and Thomas.

An American War Record was found in North Carolina for Van Teague. A government marker has been placed in the family burial plot in a pine grove behind the home of the Alton Hunts' in Petersburg, KY, (now called Mannington). It is believed the Teague's founded Petersburg.

William, b. Sept. 12, 1769, married Mary Metcalfe, on Sept. 24, 1792 and had 13 children: Edward, b. 1793; William, b. 1797; Elizabeth, b. 1799; May or Mary, b. 1799; Hester, b. 1801; Gracie, b. 1803; James M., b. 1805; Van S., b. 1807; Abel, b. 1809; Jacob, b. 1811; John P., b. 1813; Manerva, b. 1816; and Isaac, b. 1819.

James M., b. 1805 married Dorcus Stanley, b. 1804 in North Carolina. Their children: William (Bill), b. 1828; Mary Jane, b. 1830; Moses and James (twins), b. 1832; John E., b. 1835; Nancy Hester, b. 1837; and Joshua, b. 1839.

Bill married Sara Croft. Their children: William Guiery, b. Aug. 12, 1849 (see his story); Elizabeth, b. 1850; Dorcus, b. 1852; Martha, b. 1858; and Willie, b. 1870. Bill served in the Civil War and has a Civil War marker erected to his memory on the old Croft farm above Empire, KY. Source - The Teague Book - *Submitted by Agnes Teague Cunningham and Wetona Franklin Cotton*

TEAGUE-DENTON

Able Teague, born June 19, 1809, died Dec. 22, 1891, grandson of Van Swaringen and Mary Teague, was the ninth child of William and Mary Metcalfe Teague. This family came into Christian Co., KY, in the late 1700's from Madison Co., KY.

Mary and Able Teague

Able Teague married Mary Jane Denton, Jan. 22, 1833. The children born to this union were:

Jessee Edward Teague, born Apr. 2, 1834; Mary Elizabeth Teague, born Dec. 27, 1835; William Harrison Teague, born Aug. 31, 1837; Daniel Franklin Teague, born Sept. 20, 1839; Sarah Isabelle Teague, born Apr. 25, 1843; Nancy Eveline Teague, born Aug. 15, 1851; Able DeBunyon Teague, born June 2, 1858.

Able Teague and Mary Jane Denton Teague are buried at Petersburg Cemetery, Christian Co., KY. (See Teague story by Agnes Cunningham) Sources: History and Genealogy on Teague Pioneers of Christian County, Kentucky, by Agnes Teague Cunningham. - *Compiled by Iretta McGregor*

TEAGUE-HOWELL

Wm. Guiery Teague, b. Sept. 12, 1849-d. Sept. 10, 1934, son of Bill and Sara Croft Teague, married June 21, 1867, to Anna Howell, b. Apr. 13, 1854. Guiery's father served in the Civil War. Guiery ran off, went to the camp where his dad was, but he was too young to fight, so they let him cook. It is believed the camp was located in Bowling Green. On a senior trip in 1935 to Western College, our H.S. Principal, Mr. A.L. Skaggs, Sr. called our attention to the shallow trenches on the campus that the soldiers used during battle. Guiery's occupation was a miner and a farmer. He was a Christian minister; I was told he preached 35 years. Buried in Petersburg Cemetery, Christian Co., KY. They had nine children, two died in infancy.

William Guiery Teague, minister of the gospel, with wife Anna Howell Teague and grandson Evan Brasher

Other children are: George Anderson Teague, b. Nov. 26, 1874 (See TEAGUE-LYELL); James Teague, b. Nov. 15, 1877-d. May 24, 1944, married Margaret Trotter, b. 1880-d. 1949, 3 children: Anna Rosa, b. July 1, 1913-d. July 5, 1913; Jerold, b. May 4, 1916-d. Nov. 14, 1916; Thelma Jaynet (Baby) Teague, b. May 4, 1916-d. June 10, 1968, twin to Jerold. Thelma attended school at Goodhope, graduated from Nortonville High School in 1935. Worked in Michigan, came home to care for her parents. After their death, enlisted in WAF—weather division, served over 18 years. Died in Walter Reid Hosp., buried Petersburg Cem.

Ina Teague, b. Aug. 15, 1879-d. June 15, 1963, married Charley Murphy. Baptist faith. They made their home in Herrin, IL. One son, adopted, Huston. Married Clestel Smith, they have three sons: Harold Gene, Robert, and Jack Murphy.

Katheryn Teague, b. June 8, 1886-d. 193?, married Riley Brasher, one son, Evan Brasher, who married Bonnie Faughender. They have six children: Willis Elfridge, Wanda Louise, James (Jimmy), Don Lindell, Lee Anthony, and Larry Joe. Evan and Bonnie reared their children in Nortonville. Katheryn 2nd, married Porter Woosley, they had six children: Irene, Ilene, Aubry, Elean, Ruby, and Inez. This family moved to Decatur, AL, where some members still live.

Albert Teague, b. Apr. 30, 1888-d. May 6, 1934, married Ollie Butler, b. July 3, 1888-d. Jan. 30, 1933. Children: (1) Kathleen married Glenn Trover, seven children: Mary Anna, Charles Wayne, Wetona Mae, Bobby J., Jo Nell, Lana Faye, and Jerry Trover. Kathleen and Glenn reared their children in Earlington. (2) Imogene, married Clarence Blankenship, one son, Richard Lee married Mary Grace Smith—two children: Mary Roseland and Rickie Lee. Clarence is deceased. Imogene makes her home in St. Charles, KY. (3) Infant deceased. (4) Eugene married Mable Walker. Eugene is retired, they reside in St. Charles. Two children by a former marriage are, Sharon and Larkin Teague. (5) Lawrence married Agnes Alexander, they have one son, Gayle. Since Lawrence's death, Agnes and Gayle make their home in Dawson Springs, KY. (6) Annalean married Paul G. Denton; they have three children: Peggy Lou, Billy Clark, and Vickie Ann. Paul and Annalean make their home in Brandenburg, IN. (7) Doris married Albert Walker; they have five children: Jane Caroline, Janice Gaye, Janet Debra, infant deceased, and Ronnie Neal Walker. Doris and Albert made their home in Indiana. Doris is deceased, died in the sixties, burial at Lake Grove Cem., St. Charles.

Della Teague, b. Sept. 2, 1889-d. Dec. 27, 1957, married Will Brasher. They had one dau., Rosa, died in infancy, (2) Howard Wisks, occupation coal driller; well-known in the county working for numerous coal companies. One adopted dau., Ora Mae, married W.P. Davis, one son Phillip, dau.-in-law, Lyn, and two granddaughters, Cheryl and Lisa. Ora Mae and Pershing reside in their home in Tucker, GA. Howard and Della buried at Petersburg Cem.

Rosa Teague, b. May 21, 1892-d. Apr. 21, 1908, married Fred Whitfield. A child bride, died when expecting her first child. Burial, Petersburg Cem. - *Submitted by Mrs. C.L. Cunningham*

TEAGUE-LYELL

George Anderson Teague, b. Nov. 26, 1874-d. Feb. 27, 1928, son of Wm. Guiery and Anna Howell of Christian Co., KY, married Apr. 25, 1897 to Effie Rachel Lyell, b. Apr. 2, 1883, dau. of W.C. and Amanda Crick Lyell. He was a miner and a farmer, belonged to Christian Church. He had high blood pressure and died at age of 53, and 3 months. He was buried at Petersburg Cem. in Christian Co. Effie managed with the help of her son to keep the family together. She married second time to Otho Martin. He died and she continued to live alone until her death, Sept. 27, 1968. Burial at New Salem Cem., Nortonville. Her seven children were:

(1) Orva Leamon Teague, b. Sept. 17, 1898. (See FRANKLIN-TEAGUE)

(2) Earl Teague, b. Mar 3, 1901-d. Mar. 5, 1977. He was a miner/farmer. Married Grace Johnson late in life. Grace only lived a few years, and Earl continued to live alone. He belonged to First Christian Church, Nortonville. Buried at Petersburg Cem.

(3) Charley Wm. Teague, b. Sept. 5, 1903-d. May 18, 1968. Married Cora Browning, b. Apr. 7, 1909-d. Dec. 6, 1983. He was a coal miner. A

George Anderson Teague

member of First Christian Church, Nortonville. Buried at New Salem in Nortonville. One dau., Thelma DeLois, b. Sept. 12, 1924, married Justice Uzzle. One son, Regional Aron Uzzle, grandchildren Keith and Terri. Thelma is an LPN and works at St. Elizabeth Hospital, Belleville, IL.

(4) George Ancil Teague, b. May 3, 1906-d. Nov. 9, 1983, married Helen Rogers, b. June 2, 1911-d. Sept. 26, 1945. He was a heavy equipment operator and miner. Ancil remained single after Helen's death; lived his last few years in the home of a son, Doug. Buried at Ridge Top Cemetery, Crofton. Ancil's three children: Marjorie June, b. June 21, 1930, married Lester Hopper, b. May 22, 1916-d. Dec. 5, 1980; he was a coal miner; buried at Ridge Top Cem. June, a housewife and mother, member of Castleberry Baptist Church, had six children: (a) Lester Alan married Jackie Rose; he works at Goodyear Tire and Rubber Co., member of Assembly of God, Crofton, and is a minister of the gospel. Their 3 children: Gil, Clint and Amanda. (b) Lindsey Farrell married Diana Stokes, he works for Peabody Coal Co., and Diana works at the Dawson Mfg. Co. Lindsey and Diana are members of Crofton Assembly of God. They reside in Mannington. Have two daughters, Crystal and Summer Hopper. (c) Gill Hopper married Jo Ann Burchfield—divorced—He works at Goodyear Tire and Rubber Co., is a member of Crofton Baptist Church. He lives in Petersburg, KY. Two children: Jason and Michelle Hopper. (d) Loretta Gwyn Hopper, b. June 16, 1955-d. Dec. 8, 1972, while a Junior at South Hopkins High School from kidney failure. She was a member of Castleberry Baptist Church. Buried at Ridge Top Cemetery. (e) Joy Lynn Hopper married Terry Bullock, who operates The Crofton Wood Shop. Joy works at People's Security Finance Co., Madisonville. They are members of the Castleberry Baptist Church, live on Rural Rte., Crofton. (f) Thad Lee Hopper married Kathleen Young. He works at the Crofton Wood Shop. They are members of Crofton Baptist Church. Thad has a dau. by a former marriage, Tana Hopper.

Ancil's 2nd child: Henry Douglas Teague, b. Dec. 25, 1931, married Dorothy Jean Lewis, b. Apr. 18, 1931. Douglas is retired from Peabody Coal Co. Dorothy is a housewife and mother. Three children: (a) Kerry Douglas Teague married Cindy Groves. He works for Peabody Coal Co. Two children by a former marriage,

Angie and Kasey Teague. (b) LaDonna Jean Teague, married Glenn Robinson. He is employed at Wriggley's Gum, and attends a trade school in Chicago, IL; their one dau. Shawn Robinson. LaDonna has a dau., Lisa Dulin, by a former marriage. (c) Jane Ann Teague married Lincoln Davis, who is employed at a chemical plant in Hopkinsville. Two children are April and Jacob. Jane has a son by a former marriage, Charles (Chuckie) Allen. Ancil's 3rd child: Larry Ray Teague, b. May 17, 1943, graduated from Christian Co. H.S. Served in the U.S. Army, with one year in Germany. Married Tina Thomas. Larry and Tina are employed at Thomas Industries in Hopkinsville. They reside in Crofton. Larry has two sons Robert and Darrin, by a former marriage.

(5) Thelma Pearl Teague See EVANS-TEAGUE.

(6) Helen Geneva Teague See STEVENS-TEAGUE.

(7) Agnes Teague See CUNNINGHAM-TEAGUE. - *Submitted by Agnes Cunningham*

TEAGUE-WOODRUFF

Charley McClelan Teague and Mary Lee Josaphine Woodruff were married Apr. 14, 1887.

Charley McClelan was born Feb. 5, 1864, and died Feb. 21, 1936 of double pneumonia. He was the second child of Daniel Franklin Teague and Margaret Evelyn Williams. See DANIEL FRANKLIN TEAGUE story.

From l to r: William Kenneth Teague, Benjamin Franklin Teague, Charley McClelan Teague, Annice Lee Teague, Earl Clayton, Julian Ellwood Teague, Mary Lee Josaphine Woodruff Teague and Jesse McClelland Teague

Mary Lee Josaphine Woodruff was born May 3, 1867, and died June 9, 1920 of cancer. She was the daughter of Benjamin Bayless Woodruff, born July 4, 1827, died Mar. 15, 1920, and Sarah M. Denton, born 1843, died 1885. Benjamin Bayless and Sarah Denton Woodruff are buried at Christian Privilege Cemetery at St. Charles, KY. See WOODRUFF story.

Charley and Mary Woodruff Teague had eight children as follows:

(1) Theodocia Eveline Teague Worthington Clark, born Jan. 27, 1889, died Oct. 31, 1918 of flu.

(2) Benjamin Franklin Teague, born July 9, 1891, died Sept. 6, 1967 of heart attack.

(3) Byron Alvyn Teague, born Sept. 21, 1893, died July 21, 1909, Sawmill accident—slab of lumber into abdomen.

(4) William Kenneth Teague, born Feb. 22, 1896, died Apr. 2, 1970 of heart attack.

(5) Jesse McClelland Teague, born June 5, 1889, died Oct. 12, 1932, cutting timber—tree fell on him.

(6) Victor Adison Teague, born Jan. 28, 1901, died July 11, 1901, Unknown infant disease.

(7) Julian Ellwood Teague, born May 25, 1902, died August, 1978 of heart attack.

(8) Annice Lee Teague Earl Clayton, May 8, 1905, presently living in Sesser, IL.

Ben Teague (seated) and Kenneth Teague, brothers, 1918

Charley McClelan Teague was a farmer and operated a saw mill and grist mill in the St. Charles area of Hopkins County. He and his family were of the Universalist Faith and attend church at Good Hope Universalist Church. He and Mary Woodruff Teague are buried at Good Hope Cemetery. - *By Iretta McGregor*

DANIEL FRANKLIN TEAGUE

Daniel Franklin Teague, born Sept. 20, 1839, and died 1908, was the fourth child of Able (see his story) and Mary Jane Denton Teague.

He married Margaret Evelyn Williams, born 1841, died Nov. 23, 1874. Marriage is recorded in Hopkinsville, Christian Co., KY. Burial for Margaret Evelyn Williams Teague—Petersburg Cemetery, Christian Co., KY.

Daniel Franklin Teague

Children born to this union: Walter Teague, born 1862; Charley Teague, born 1864, died 1936; Parlee Teague, born 1866; and Viva Teague, born 1874.

Daniel Franklin Teague's second marriage was to Ann Denton, married June 2, 1875.

Children born to this union are: Dennie Teague, born July 14, 1881; and Lawrence Teague, born 1891.

Daniel Franklin Teague and Ann Denton Teague are buried at Good Hope Cemetery. - *Submitted by Iretta McGregor*

WILLIAM KENNETH TEAGUE

Cora Lee Denton and William Kenneth Teague were married Sept. 30, 1919, at Madisonville, KY.

Cora was born Feb. 3, 1896, near Daniel Boone in Hopkins Co., KY. She was the youngest child of Thomas Jefferson Denton and Una Rosaline Earl Denton. Her childhood homeplace joined her grandfather, John Orville (Jack) Earle's farm. She attended school at the Norton School House between her home and Daniel Boone. Her father was a farmer in that area.

William Kenneth Teague, 1918 and Mr. & Mrs. Kenneth Teague, 1960

William Kenneth Teague was born Feb. 22, 1896, to Charley McClelan Teague and Mary Woodruff Teague. (see Teague-Woodruff) He grew up on the Able Teague farm just south of the Jack Earle farm. He attended school at Good Hope School and his family attended church at the Good Hope Universalist Church.

He was in the Army during World War I and was sent to France and Germany but the Armistice was signed before he reached the front lines. Food was scarce at times because the supply lines could not get through, so he knew what it meant to be hungry. He never complained whatever food was prepared and placed before him.

He was a farmer and coal miner in the St. Charles, Daniel Boone area and lived on the farm there until 1938. At that time the family moved to St. Charles, where he and Cora lived until their deaths.

Kenneth and Cora had two daughters: Gladys Marie Teague Mabry, born Sept. 12, 1922, and Mary Iretta Teague McGregor, born Aug. 30, 1926.

They celebrated their 50th Wedding Anniversary in 1969, and Kenneth Teague died Apr. 2, 1970. Cora died Aug. 7, 1977. They are buried at Good Hope Cemetery. - *Submitted by Iretta McGregor*

THOMAS-BRATCHER

Barbara Ann and William Dallas Thomas are my parents.

Barbara Ann Bratcher Thomas, born Mar. 10, 1950, was the first daughter and fourth child of Mr. & Mrs. Beedie Bratcher, Sr. She had three brothers and one sister. Her three brothers were, from the oldest to the youngest, Beedie Ellis, Jr., James Alfred, and Earl Wayne Bratcher. Her sister is Mary Alice Bratcher. All of these children were born and raised in the same house, on what is now Highway #109, beside the Dunn Church and Cemetery.

Beedie Ellis Bratcher, Sr. was born Mar. 24, 1917 in an old farm house in Butler County. The town was Caneyville, KY. Mary Annis Burgess Bratcher was born on a farm in Livingston County, near Smithland, KY on Oct. 4, 1917.

Dallas was the third son and fourth child of Mr. and Mrs. Harley Thomas. He had two brothers and one sister. His brothers were, from the oldest to the youngest, Norman Evan and James Elvin Thomas. His sister, the oldest child, is Marian Louise Thomas. These children were born in southern Indiana. The birth place of William Dallas Thomas was in an old farm house on the banks of Oil Creek, in Branchville, IN. The date of birth of Dallas was May 4, 1948.

Dallas' mother was Ida Irene Fulton Thomas, who was born Dec. 1, 1912 in Spotsville, KY, on the Ohio River. Harley Evans Thomas was born June 22, 1909 in Caldwell County, near Dawson Springs, on what is now known as Cadiz Hill.

Considering the amount of education that Barbara's and Dallas's parents had, which was grade school level, they got their children through high school. Dallas's mother and father had a sixth grade education. Barbara's parents had a fourth grade and eighth grade education. All four parents were very intelligent and self-taught.

Barbara went to Charleston in her elementary years and then to West Hopkins High School, She also has some college hours earned at Madisonville Community College.

Dallas went to a little country school in Indiana until the fourth grade. Then his family moved to the city, where he went to the Tell City School in Indiana until his move to Dawson Springs. Dallas attended high school, 9th through 12th grade, at Dawson Springs. After graduation, he went to Barber College in Henderson, KY.

Barbara and Dallas and family now live at 401 W. Arcadia Avenue, Dawson Springs. They were married in Dawson Springs and have lived here ever since. They have a business in town and have no intentions of moving away from this area. - *Submitted by Brian Thomas*

THOMAS-WALKER

Shirley Faye Walker and Joseph Wayne Thomas married in 1965, have lived in Hopkins County all their lives. Shirley, born in 1946 to Rea Joyner and James Howard Walker (see Walker-Joyner), has an older sister, Barbara June, who married Phillip Landrum (see Landrum-Walker).

Shirley lived on the family farm near Nebo, until 1956, when the family moved to Madisonville. The farm was the home place of her great-grandparents, Virginia Lee Watson (b. 1865), and W.D. "Pete" Winstead (b. 1854). Their children were: Bessie, Anna Lou and Givins. Anna Lou (b. 1891), and husband,

Joseph and Shirley Walker Thomas

Emmon E. Walker (b. 1891), later purchased the farm. Their only child, James Howard and wife, Rea, lived with them their first two years of marriage.

After moving to Madisonville, Shirley attended West Broadway and Seminary and graduated from Madisonville High School in 1964. She also attended Madisonville Community College and Western Kentucky U. The couple's only child, Jenny Lyn, was born in 1966, and married William Brian Puryear (see Puryear-Thomas). Shirley was employed at the Kentucky Bank and Trust Company in 1967, and was elected Vice President and Trust Officer in 1987. Other memberships and civic activities include Nebo Christian Church, Lioness, American Heart Assn., United Way, Kentucky Colonels and one-term on the Hopkins County Board of Education.

Joseph Wayne Thomas was born to James Dowell (b. 1914), and Jessie Irene Preston (b. 1914), in 1942 in Hopkins County. James served in the U.S. Navy during WW II. Joe has one sister, Elizabeth Sharon, who teaches school in Hopkins County.

Joe began his education at Anton School graduating from Madisonville High School in 1961, and received a BS (1965) MA and Rank I degrees from Western Kentucky U. He played varsity basketball in high school and coached basketball at Mortons Gap and at Graham (Muhlenberg County). He began teaching in Hopkins County in 1965, later serving as assistant Principal and is currently the Director of Federal Programs and of Food Services. His interests include antiques and classic automobiles. After purchasing the former Claude Denton home at 308 N. Main Street, Joe and Shirley spent 18 months restoring their home to it's former Victorian style. In 1978, the Hopkins County Board of Realtors and the Historical Society of Hopkins County awarded the Thomas' the year plaque for a residence of 50 years.

The genealogy of James Thomas includes: Rosa Pereal Martin (b. 1893), and Rufus Dowell Thomas (b. 1886); Margaret Emuline Anderson (b. 1845), and Henry Thomas; Sarah Elizabeth Jones and Presley Obanion Martin.

Jessie Thomas' genealogy includes: Ida Maude Rodgers (b. 1877), and Ernest B. Preston (b. 1873); Nancy Robinson (b. 1839), and D. Jack Rodgers; and Ophlia Ellen Roberts and Henry Preston. Other family names include Cardwell. - *Submitted by Rea Joyner Walker*

IMOGENE JONES THOMAS

Imogene Jones Thomas was married to Guy David Thomas, who is now deceased. Imogene was born Jan. 21, 1921 in Caldwell County and now makes her home at 200 Hall Street, Dawson Springs, KY.

Imogene's mother was Hester Egbert Jones who was born in Caldwell County, July 12, 1880. Hester died on Feb. 21, 1963 at the age of 83. Imogene's father was Charlie Jones who was born Mar. 25, 1867 in Caldwell Co. Charlie died June 12, 1943 at the age of 76. Hester and Charlie married on Jan. 20, 1897. Hester was 16 years of age when she married and Charlie was 30 years old. Exactly 24 years after their marriage, Imogene was born. Hester and Charlie had a considerably large family. Imogene had 13 brothers and sisters. Imogene's seven brothers, from oldest to youngest, were: Jack, Ernest, Cecil, Rufus, Guy, Eugene, and Earl. Her six sisters, also in order, were: Ruby, Beulah, Lelia, Bertha, Ruthaleen, and Minnie. Imogene is the fraternal twin of her brother, Eugene.

On Dec. 9, 1944, at the age of 23, Imogene Jones became Imogene Jones Thomas when she married Guy David Thomas. Two years later they had their first child, Donna Faye Thomas. Imogene and Guy had two other children, both girls. The second born was Dianna Kaye, and the last was Kelly Lynn.

Donna Faye was born Feb. 13, 1946. She married Phillip Larue Parker at the age of 18 and has three children: Stephanie, Steven, and Melissa. Stephanie, who is now 17 years old, was born July 23, 1970. Steven was born Mar. 16, 1972 and is now 15 years old. Melissa, now age 8 was born Sept. 29, 1979.

Dianna was born Oct. 18, 1949. She married Warren Terrell Coates and had three children: Greg, John, and Jolie. Greg, the oldest, was born Sept. 7, 1972 and is now 15. John, 13 years of age, was born July 9, 1974. Jolie was born Nov. 12, 1977 and is now 10 years old.

Imogene and Guy's last child, Kelly, was born Oct. 19, 1964. She is not married at this time.

An interesting fact about Imogene is that she and her husband, Guy, were born in the same house, the same month, but one year apart. A special skill or hobby of Imogene's is quilting. She has made some beautiful quilts, and the best part is that she loves to do it. - *Submitted by grandson, Steven Parker*

THOMPSON

Larry Wayne Thompson is the oldest son of Joe and Mary Lou Thompson. Joe and Mary Lou have lived in Earlington, Ky all their married life. On Mar. 17, 1988, they will have been married 48 years. They are also the parents of a daughter, Kay Thompson Benton, and four sons, Gilbert, Darrell, David, and Johnny.

Larry and Sonya Richards met on Apr. 22, 1963 on their first date. It was a blind date, they were introduced by friends, and after dating less than six months they were married on Oct. 19, 1963.

Sonya was the daughter of George and Ammie Richards. Sonya has three older sisters, and two sisters and one brother younger than she is. Sonya's father died when she was three years old. Her mother died when she was nineteen.

Larry and Sonya are the parents of three chidren: Sherry born Aug. 26, 1964, Richard born May 13, 1966 and Preston born Oct. 7, 1971. All were born in Hopkins County. Before the birth of Preston, the family lived in Evansville, IN for five years. They moved to Evansville in September of 1966 because Larry was working for L&N Railroad. He was transferred back to Madisonville in August of 1971.

From 1973 to 1982, Larry worked in the coal mines. He was laid off for three years. In June 1985, Larry got a job at General Electric in Madisonville. Sonya works in the lunch room at South Hopkins High School where she has been working for five years.

Sherry and Richard are both graduates of South Hopkins High School and are both married. Sherry is married to Rocky Head and they both work at Regional Medical Center in Madisonville. They live on Main Street in Nortonville. Richard is in the U.S. Air Force, stationed at Scott Air Force Base in Bellville, IL. He and his wife, Joan, live in an apartment in Belleville. Joan works in a bank. Preston lives with his mother and father and attends Dawson Springs High School. He has just started attending this school and like it very much. Preston enjoys watching U.K. basketball. His biggest hobby is playing basketball. He has been playing basketball since the age of seven.-*Submitted by Preston Thompson*

REV. CLARENCE L. TIMBERLAKE

Rev. Timberlake was an educator not only because such a course is a worthy life for any man, but also because as he put it "It is fun—it is my hobby. I enjoy every moment of it." His actions testify to the truth of his words.

Rev. Clarence L. Timberlake

Rev. Timberlake was no stranger in Kentucky. He was born in 1885, at Nepton in Fleming County, the son of Joseph and Melinda Timberlake. He received his early education in the public schools, later entering Kentucky State College (then Kentucky Normal and Industrial Institute). He completed a course in agriculture. Continuing his college work, he received his AB degree from Simmons University in Louisville. He did his graduate work at Hampton Institute and the University of Cincinnati.

The Rev. Timberlake was one of the oldest black educators in the state of Kentucky. He served as principal of Kentucky schools in Pembroke, Greenville, Morganfield and Madisonville and was president of West Kentucky Vocational School in Paducah, KY. At Pembroke, he organized the Teacher Training School and conducted Summer Normal at Greenville, starting the trade and industrial courses in both schools. While principal at Morganfield, he was instrumental in purchasing 26 acres of land upon which was built a gymnasium and recreational building. In Madisonville, he organized the first black four-year high school and extended the school term from seven months to nine. In 1923, he had the first high school graduating class consisting of 11 students.

In 1926, he wrote and sponsored a bill through the Kentucky Legislature to appropriate $35,000.00 to establish a State Trade and Training School for Negroes in Western Kentucky.

Aside from his educational work, he took an active part in civic, social and religious organizations and received citations for service rendered. He made the school a community center. In the communities where he worked, he organized the entire county and successfully conducted the Farmer's Conference and Industrial Exhibits.

Governor William J. Fields appointed Rev. Timberlake to represent the State of Kentucky at the 27th Annual Convention of the National Negro Educational Congress which met in Kansas City, KS, and he was elected Vice President of this meeting.

In 1945, he was awarded a certificate for Meritorious Service in U.S.O. war work. In 1949, he was the first Negro to be appointed on the State Text Book Commission; while in this capacity he succeeded in getting two books on Negro History adopted as text books in the public schools of the state. In 1955, he was appointed by Governor Lawrence W. Wetherby to the State Public Health Committee and received an award from the Kentucky Teachers Association (K.E.T.) for developing the West Kentucky Vocational School in Paducah. In 1956, he was appointed as a Delegate to the Governor's Conference on Education. He was awarded a certificate of recognition by the National Urban League and Alumni Award for Distinguished Services of the Class of 1904 of Kentucky State College. In 1957, he received a "Key to the City" from Paducah Mayor George Jacobs.

Rev. Timberlake served on the advisory board of the old Hopkins-Muhlenberg Community Action Agency 1966-67, and was helpful in organizing Madisonville's first child care center, which was sponsored by the Community Action Agency. In 1974, he received the "Duke of Paducah" award from Mayor Dolly McNutt.

Rev. Timberlake was a Kentucky Colonel; member of Merriweather Masonic Lodge No. 42; member of the East View Baptist Church of which he was the teacher of the Men's Sunday School Class; Vice President of the Humane Society; and a member of the Board of Directors of the Historical Society of Hopkins County.

Rev. Timberlake married Augusta Turner. Augusta was a school teacher and a very brilliant educator. She taught at Madisonville's first black high school. They were the parents of one daughter, Dorothy, who married Aubrey Weir. Aubrey Weir resides in Madisonville in the former Timberlake home.

Rev. C.L. Timberlake lived a long and resourceful life and was a very active and courageous man. He died Feb. 24, 1979. Rev. Timberlake is "gone but not forgotten". His educational achievements and contributions will always be remembered. - *Submitted by Winola Mimms*

HELEN MASON TINSLEY

Helen Keith Mason Tinsley is the daughter of Ernest Sr. and Mayme (Starks) Mason (see Ernest Mason Sr. story).

Helen graduated from Rosenwald High School in 1963. She then attended Western Kentucky Beauty School in Paducah, KY, graduated, and is a licensed Cosmetologist. She resides in Madisonville and is presently employed by the State Employment Service as an Employment Placement Interviewer.

Helen has two sons: Tery, 20, who is attending Fort Valley State College in Fort Valley, GA, and Micheal, 14, who attends Browning Springs Middle School in Madisonville. Helen and her children are members of Wesley Chapel C.M.E. Church in Madisonville. - *Submitted by Mayme L. Mason*

TODD

Jesse L. Todd and Mary H. Jackson born and raised in Hopkins Co., KY were married Sept. 3, 1946, in Hopkinsville, KY.

Jesse spent three and one half years overseas in World War II, serving with the 25th Division in Hawaii, Guadalcanal, Northern Solomons Islands and the Philippines. He was wounded January 1945, on the Island of Luzon and was honorably discharged, Sept. 16, 1945. He was a recipient of the Purple Heart and the Bronze Star.

Jesse and Mary Todd

Jesse went to work in the lumber industry, the railroad, theaters, and factories until his retirement in 1985.

Jesse and Mary were the parents of six children: Deloris J. Howard, Diana L. Bowles, Ronnie W. Todd (served a tour of duty in Germany and was honorably discharged),

Stephen C. Todd (served tours of duty in several countries including Southeast Asia, honorably discharged), Shirley D. Westby and Alan K. Todd.

From these six children, there were born 14 grandchildren: Angela K. Howard, Kimberly D. Bowles, Timothy W. Howard, Kristie D. Bowles, Stacey L. Howard, Adrea L. Todd, April D. Westby, Amber P. Howard, Jeffery S. Westby, Sean D. Todd, Robin A. Todd, Stephanie N. Todd, Veronica Todd and Shawn M. Todd. There are also four great grandchildren: Jeramie Dame, Johnathan Bowles, Devon B. Howard and Tara Dame.

The Todd ancestory is as follows: Paternal - Dave Todd, father; Frank James Todd, grandfather; and Mary Ann Carter Todd, grandmother. Maternal - Margie Adcock Todd, mother; Roland Adcock, grandfather; and Fannie Masoncup Adcock, grandmother.

Frank James Todd and Roland Adcock both fought for the Confederacy during the Civil War. - *Submitted by Jesse L. Todd*

TOMBLINSON

The first Tomblinson, who came to Hopkins County, was Hambleton T. He was born in Virginia, June 6, 1795, and arrived in Hopkins County sometime prior to 1835, as he married Margaret Reynolds here, during that year. Nine children were born to this union, one of which was James P. Tomblinson (Aug. 28, 1852-Jan. 17, 1915).

James P.T. married Elizabeth Ashby Sept. 2, 1879, and fathered ten children: Benjamin Edmon, Ernest, Bertha, Viola, Blanche, Homer, Arnold, J.C., Wilda Reed and Mary Sue. Benjamin Edmon, the oldest of these children graduated from Dental School at the University of Tenn. He practiced dentistry in Calhoun and Ashbyburg, where he also operated a general store and was appointed postmaster of that fourth class post office in 1920 (there is no post office there now). On Dec. 13, 1902, he married Ethel Corum (July 12, 1885-May 26, 1982), and was associated with her brothers Arthur, Ashby and John in business ventures. He died in Colorado in December 1921, and Mrs. Tomblinson brought their four children back to Madisonville: Carnille (Apr. 20, 1904), who married Roscoe Triplett; Lucella (Apr. 20, 1912-Mar. 16, 1986) (Mrs. Howard Williamson); Jetrue (Aug. 22, 1915) (Mrs. Herschel Ben Robinson, now residing in Beaver Dam, KY); and Ben E., Jr. (Feb. 28, 1919). Carnille and Roscoe Triplett have one son, John Roscoe Triplett (Feb. 16, 1915) who married Hazel Larkin in June 1943. They have two sons: Tony (Oct. 14, 1951) and Tandy (Mar. 8, 1956), and now live in Louisville, KY. The Williamsons have one son, Howard Edmon (May 23, 1933), who married Joan Hines (June 12, 1958) and are parents of two children: Denise (May 3, 1967), and Gary (Oct. 31, 1971). They live in Peoria, IL.

Ben E. Tomblinson, Jr. graduated from Madisonville High School in 1939, and attended Western Ky. University for two years. He served during World War 2 with the Signal Corps attached to the Fifth Air Force in the South Pacific theater—New Guinea, the Philippines and Japan. Upon returning from Service he continued with his electrical interests, beginning his own business in 1960. In 1967, he bought R. & D. Electric company and is active in that business at the present time. In 1941, he married Jeane Myers (daughter of B.J. Myers), and they are parents of two sons: Ben E. III (Nov. 19, 1946), and Michael Myers (Dec. 14, 1949).

The Ben E. Tomblinson II family

Ben Tomblinson III graduated from W.K.U. in 1969, and now resides in Bowling Green, KY. He married Rebecca S. Parker in 1968, and they are parents of Angela Jeane (July 11, 1971), and Ben E. IV (May 29, 1975).

Michael graduated from W.K.U. in 1972, and became associated with R. & D. Electric Co., where he is now co-owner and General Manager. He married Maureen Ray of Pensacola, FL, Feb. 10, 1973, and they are parents of Jacob Michael Tomblinson (July 19, 1980). - *Submitted by Ben E. Tomblinson 2nd*

RODERICK J. TOMPKINS

Roderick J. Tompkins, Hopkins County, was born Feb. 4, 1940. His earliest record of the Tompkins family in Hopkins County, (formerly Henderson County) KY, begins in the summer of 1799, when James Tompkins assisted in the capture of Big Harp and Little Harp. James' horse, Nance, was ridden by John Leeper who was the member of the possee that overtook the Harps and killed Big Harp. The story is told that Leeper also used Tompkin's gun that fired the fatal shot. The powder for the gun was given to Tompkins at an earlier date during a visit by the Harps at Tompkins farm. Thus, Big Harp died by his own gun powder. James died in 1833. At the time of his death, he had forty-two slaves that were divided among his eight children.

Thomas Tompkins, son of James, was born in approximately 1800, and died in 1879. He was referred to as "Tiger Tom." He married Emily Mansareth Hicks and they had four sons and three daughters. Joseph, son of Thomas, was born in 1844, and died in 1879. He married Leslie Hampton and they had four sons. Joseph was the father of Roderick's grandfather, Finis. At Joseph's early death, in 1904, his sons inherited the farm. Due to their young age, the sons were sent to live with relatives and friends. When Finis became an adult, he returned the family to the farm to live. One brother, Jessee, died in 1912, at the age of twenty.

Finis was born in 1890, and married Grace Hobgood. They had six sons and four daughters. Finis, in addition to farming, operated a general store in the Mt. Gilead community and later in Slaughters for approximately thirty-five years, ending in 1955. At Finis' death, his farm was sold outside of the Tompkins family. It is said that this sale represented the first disposal of family farmland since James Tompkins acquired the land in the 1700s. Joe Tompkins, father of Roderick, was born in 1912. Joe married Cosby E. Todd in 1934. They had two children, Roderick J. and Jarrett. Joe farmed and was in the grocery business in Evansville, IN, and Slaughters until retirement in 1975.

Roderick's wife, the former Brenda Sisk, born Apr. 29, 1941, is a native of Hopkins County. They had two daughters and one son. Teresa K. Tompkins was born Mar. 8, 1963; Roderick J. Tompkins, Jr. was born Feb. 27, 1966; and Lori A. Tompkins was born Nov. 15, 1967. Roderick is a 1961 graduate of the University of Kentucky and a Certified Public Accountant, practicing in Madisonville. In 1986-1987, he served as president of the Kentucky Society of Certified Public Accountants.

This historical account follows his genealogy from late 1700 to 1987, in Hopkins Co., KY. As mentioned previously, in 1987, members of the Tompkins family reside on family farms, located three miles west of Mt. Gilead Church on the old Madisonville-Henderson Road (now Webster County), which have been family-owned since the late 1700s. - *Submitted by Roderick J. Tompkins and Brenda Sisk Tompkins*

W.A. TOOMBS

Sometime during the 1770's, Hull Toombs came to America from England and settled in Virginia, where he married an Indian girl of the same tribe as Pocahontas. They had one son named George, who served as a sergeant in the War of 1812.

When George Toombs married, he and his wife had four sons: George James, Arch, Robert and John. Arch eventually located in Iowa; Robert was killed at a house-raising near Castalian Springs, TN; John was married to Jeannie Todd; and George James Toombs, who married Sallie Holt (daughter of Billie and Nancy Hughes Holt), moved to Tennessee and settled in Sumner County.

George James and Sally had seven children and in time all of them moved to Kentucky and made their homes Hopkins, Webster and Union counties.

They were: Robert Sumpter moved to Union County and married Mattie Wade. Their children were Robert, Cassie, Lanie, Maggie, Jack and Albert; Archibald Frank, John and Sarah Ann, all moved to Hopkins and Union counties, but were never married. Jimmie Toombs, living in the Webster County area, married a girl named Melissa (?); and Caroline married Dan Roland and had two children, making their home in the Nebo-Coiltown area.

The other son of George James and Sallie was William Albert. He was born in Castalian Springs, TN, in 1851—came to Kentucky in 1867, married in 1878, and came to Earlington in 1881.

Before William Albert (better known later as Col. Toombs), came to Earlington he had been working as a carpenter in Nebo and Sebree. He was hired by St. Bernard Mining Company as a mechanic and carpenter. He invented and constructed a model mine ventilating fan which was shown at the State Fair, Owensboro, and later on, a fan made from this model, was installed at Fox Run Mine. He was part owner and contributor to Earlington's early newspaper, "The Bee" and was an active member of the Masonic Lodge for over 50 years.

Col. Toombs was married to Rebecca Hibbs, one of eleven children born to Joe and Margaret Osborne Hibbs of the Mortons Gap community.

Children of William Albert and Rebecca Toombs were:

Grace and Lena, who died in childhood; Lillie, who was married to Henry Byrun and had three children—Carlos, Claude and Martha; Harold ("Cheek"), who was married to Joanna Brown of Hanson were the parents of seven children; and Ada, who was married to George Armstrong in 1910. They had four children—Karl (deceased), George Jr. and Bill, now living in Nashville, TN; and Elinor, who is married to Robert Rich and living in Earlington. They have one child, Lynda, who is married to Huston Hartline, and they are the parents of three children—Jennifer, married to Ricky Franklin; Wesley, married to Lisa (Wright); and Amy, married to Troy Bratcher. The Bratchers have one daughter, Emily Christin, and they are living in Dawson Springs.

This covers eight generations of the family of Col. W.A. Toombs. - *Submitted by Elinor Rich*

GRACE C. TOWNSEND

Grace Curtright was born Jan. 26, 1892, to Wilbur Forest Curtright (1860-1921) and Florence Marshall Springfield (1864-1950). She was reared and educated in the Nebo area. She met Aaron Hubert Townsend (1890-1979), of Liberty, KY, son of Rolland Gooch Townsend (1868-1919), and Sally Evelyn Clayton (1871-1960), and married him on Nov. 16, 1907, in Webster Co., KY. They had one daughter, Thelma Geraldine Townsend, born Apr. 28, 1910, in Webster Co., KY. They were married for five years and then divorced. Grace returned to Nebo with her daughter to reside, until her death on Jan. 27, 1970. She bought land and started farming in 1919. Her first purchase was a 176 acre tract, which was where she built her home.

The homestead is now the home of her granddaughter, Sandra Grace Donaldson and family. The older home has been replaced by a new house but still on the original spot. She was a very enterprising lady of her time. Some of her endeavors were: farming, running a dairy, raising chickens (10,000 at a time), for which she had a contract with the Outwood Hospital for eggs and fryers. She owned school buses that she ran for the Hopkins County system, her first children were transported in a station wagon. She had a bus contract, starting in the late 1940's until her death in 1970. She was an astute politician and a 'dyed in the wool' Democrat. When election day came, she would transport voters to the polls. She helped many people throughout her life by donations

Small girl-Odette (Veazey) Brown. Seated-Florence (Springfield) Killough Curtright Almon. Standing l to r: Vaden (Killough) Veazey, Grace (Curtright) Townsend and Hattie (Curtright) Crowe Dame Rhew.

of food, clothes, transportation and money for education.

In 1947, she bought her first apartment and continued buying and building apartments until her death. She was awarded many honors in agriculture. In the early 1950's, she was recording corn yields of 115 bushels per acre. She never asked a person to do any work that she wouldn't do. You could see her everyday out in the fields with the men and women. She always traveled to Arkansas and Oklahoma twice a year to see about her uncle, M.D. Springfield. She died in 1970 of the Lou Gehrig Disease, "A woman among men, who succeeded". - *Submitted by Sandra Donaldson*

VILLA MAY TOWNSEND

My grandmother is a very interesting person. I like to be around her and spend time with her. Her full name is Villa May (Laffoon) Townsend. She was born on July 3, 1926 in Greenup, IL. I think she is very important because she didn't have very much when she was growing up, and she eventually came to Hopkins County to be a nurse.

She was one of seven children and was approximately twelve years old when her parents divorced. The children were split, and she went to Georgia for a year. When she was thirteen years old, she wrote the Robards family whom she previously knew, to request permission to live in Dawson Springs with them. She worked in a grocery store in Georgia to earn money to come to Dawson Springs. She earned enough money and moved in with the Robards family on their farm and worked to help their family. She lived with them until she graduated from high school.

She attended Madisonville High School in seventh grade, Charleston in the eighth and ninth grades, Madisonville in the tenth grade, and Dawson Springs High School for the eleventh and twelvth grades. She was a cheerleader during the eleventh grade. She graduated with honors.

She attended Welborn Baptist Hospital School of Nursing, where she graduated when she was twenty-one years old. She then began practicing nursing and worked at several different hospitals. She has attended Murray State U., Western State U., and the U. of Kentucky working towards a degree in Vocational Education.

While she was a senior at Welborn Baptist School of Nursing, she met Eugene Brown Townsend, my grandfather. They were married Apr. 30, 1948 in a Baptist Church in Evansville. They moved to Madisonville in July of 1974 because she was offered a job working in a hospital and for other personal reasons. She is currently the Clinical Instructor in surgery at Regional Medical Center of Madisonville.

She has many hobbies and interests. Some of them include collecting mini-castle homes from England, collecting oriental ginger jars, gardening, tennis, traveling, especialy in foreign countries, and she also likes her job.

There are many fascinating things abut her, and she has won many awards. She is on the Board of the Professional Organization, a member of the Association of Registered Nurses (AORN) and will soon be attending the national conference in Dallas, TX as a delegate in 1988. She was suggested by her only daughter, Jeanne Knapp (born Feb. 10, 1948), to be deserving of the Kentucky Colonel Award and was accepted as of 1987. She carried a torch in the Special Olympics in 1985. She was PTA president for two years in California, chosen as Nurse of the Year in 1987, and was also chosen as Vocational Instructor in 1983. Another interesting fact is that her grandfather was the brother of the former governor of Kentucky, Ruby Laffoon.

My grandmother had much determination to go from a destitute childhood to make herself helpful to our community.-*Submitted by Carole Knapp*

JABEZ HEADLEY TRATHEN

Jabez Headley Trathen, b. Dec. 10, 1845,-d. July 6, 1921, and his brother John, b. Nov. 22, 1847,-d. Sept. 22, 1913, came from Mousehold, Cornwall, England, where they were born, to Kentucky in the 1860's. Together they introduced shaft mining in Hopkins County in the Hecla area. John went on to Colorado to prospect in gold and silver. Their parents, Mary Ash and John Edwin Trathen, m. Oct. 13, 1844 in England.

Jabez married on Sept. 16, 1872, Cordelia Ann Littlepage, b. June 29, 1852-d. Aug. 10, 1932, daughter of Hilliard Hobson Littlepage, b. Dec. 21, 1825-d. Aug. 25, 1878, and Mary Jane Fugate, b. Nov. 17, 1832-d. Dec. 4, 1910, all of Hopkins County. They were married Oct. 1, 1851. Parents of Hilliard Epps Littlepage and Nancy Forkner, and grandparents: John Littlepage and Amy Scott. Mary Jane's parents: Zachary (Zachariah) Fugate and Elizabeth (Betsy) Wilson.

Jabez and Cordelia's nine children, all born in Hopkins County, were: William Headley (1873-1949), m. Robert Jessie (Bob) Lovan (b. 1884); Cordelia Ann (1874-1963), m. William Henry Hall (1874-1901); John Hilliard (1876-1914) m. Minnie Pearl Ries (1879-1937); Charles Bert (1879-1960), m. Nannie Lee Wilkins (1883-1960); Mary Gertrude (1880-1946), m. James Christy Scobee (1870-1939); Robert Hanson (1882-1935), m. Ella Mae Tipton (1883-1956); Zachariah Frederick (1884-1969), m.

Evelyn Brown (1883-1956); Everett Edwin (1886-1887); and Fannie Mae (1889-1970), m. John Carr Wilkins (1885-1927).

Headley and his ten children settled in the Washington, D.C. area, where he was clerk in the office of the Adjutant General. Only one child, Edwin Jabez (b. 1918), lives in Madisonville, and is married to Naomi Franklin.

Cordelia had four children, one of whom was Mourning Cordelia Hall (1897-1961), m. Thomas Harvey Barnett, who with Mourning founded what is now Barnett-Strother Funeral Home. Their daughter Elizabeth Jane (Betty) lives in Madisonville and is married to Roy Schmetzer.

John Hilliard, a mine superintendent, was killed in a mine accident in Drakesboro, KY. He and Minnie had two children: Jabez Ries (1898-1962) and Anna Louise (1900-1976). Ries married Mildred Goebel Kington (1899-1953). Their eldest daughter, Eva Lloyd, married Maurice Peel Caruthers; Mary Jean Marquis and James Ries Trathen live in Nashville, TN, and each has two sons. Anna Louise Trathen married Roy Melvin Gabbert, and three of their children live in Owensboro, KY, and one in Richmond, VA.

Charles had an insurance business in Madisonville until his death, and his son Carr Hilliard Trathen's widow is Nell Arnold Trathen of Madisonville.

Mary's daughter Jane B. French lives in Louisville, KY.

Robert (Bob) was killed in an auto accident. His daughter Elizabeth Harrigan also lives in Louisville.

Fred's daughter Virginia Brown McDowell lives in Muhlenberg Co., KY, and his son Fred Haywood lives in Texas.

Fannie's daughter was Mary Frances Wilkins, who married Nathaniel Travis, was a legal secretary and court reporter in Madisonville. - *Submitted by Eva Lloyd (Trathen) Caruthers*

TROOP

William Troop, the suspected progenitor of the Troop family of Hopkins County, was born in 1833, in Lincoln Co., TN, and migrated to Hopkins County prior to 1850.

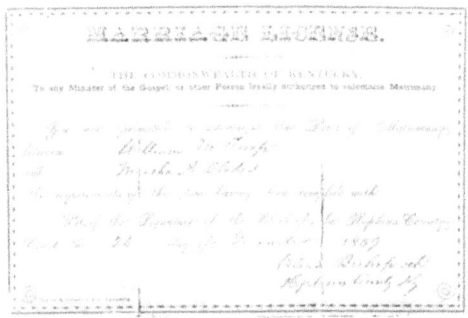

1859 Marriage record

William married on Dec. 26, 1859, in Madisonville, Martha Ann Blades, born in Tennessee around 1838/39, the daughter of James T. Blades and his wife Pritta. It has been said that Pritta was a full-blooded Cherokee Indian and the succeeding generations of Troops reflect this Indian heritage characterized by straight black hair and high cheekbones.

William served in the Kentucky infantry of the Union Army during the War between the States and after spending time in various hospitals with various illnesses, evidently decided the Kentucky farm was a healthier place to be, and was Absent Without Leave on several occasions. He died as a young man, in 1868, most likely of the lingering effects of the smallpox he contracted while in the army and is buried in Oddfellows Cemetery in Madisonville.

Martha Ann Blades Troop became the sole support of her five children and on Nov. 20, 1872, married Dan Kiethler and was known until her death in 1932/33 as Granny Kiethler. She is also buried at Oddfellows Cemetery in Madisonville next to William.

The children of William and Martha became well-known farmers in the Madisonville area controlling several hundred acres off the road known as Happy Lane. These children were:

Walter Jerome Troop, born Sept. 22, 1860, married Sept. 12, 1888, Annie Lewis Simms, born Aug. 18, 1867, the daughter of John Lewis Simms and Susan Verdonia Lawson. Walter died Jan. 4/5, 1940. Annie died Jan. 10, 1930. They had eight children; five that reached adulthood:

Mattie Mae Troop Averitt, John Will Troop, Walter Huffman Troop, Beckam Troop (died age 9), Pete Bradley Troop (authors father), Dixie Hady Troop, Ruby Troop (died in infancy), and Anna Troop (died in infancy).

Ella S. Troop, born 1861, married Jan. 4, 1877, R. Thomas Wingo, born in 1844. Ella died in 1898 and R. Thomas died in 1924. No children of this union have been found to date.

Pete Sigler Troop, born Feb. 22, 1863, married 1) Francis Penelope Simons, born around 1866, died Aug. 15, 1926; 2) Minnie E. Reynolds. Pete and Minnie both died Oct. 18, 1931. Pete and Francis had twelve children, eleven of which reached adulthood:

Ada Bell Troop Griffey, George Lafayette Troop, Agnes Maude Troop Shoemaker Dalton, Daniel Boone Troop Sr., Carrie Kell Troop Starks, Tommy Bishop Troop, Hop Holeman Troop, Annie Goebel Troop (died age 5), Euria Pete (Jack) Troop, Mary Francis Troop Bruce, Helen Marie Troop Weir and William Chesley Troop.

Mandlebert (Bert) Troop, born 1866, married 1) Alice Simms, a sister to Annie Simms; 2) Lizzie Pate, born 1876. Mandlebert and Alice had seven children. Mandlebert and Lizzie had two children:

By Alice Simms: Charles Troop, Alvis Troop, Jesse Troop, Louis C. Troop, John Emmett Troop, Lela Troop Wright and Birdy Troop Vaughan.

By Lizzie Pate: Lurie (Lessie) Troop (died in infancy), and Annie Lee (Ilene) Troop (died age 4-1/2).

Sarah J. (Sallie) Troop, born 1868, married Mar. 3, 1886, Nathan A. Hibbs Jr. Sarah and Nathan had two children:

William Hibbs and Pete Harvey Hibbs.

Many Troops still live in Hopkins and the surrounding counties and the known descendants of William and Martha Ann number over 125. - *Submitted by Ralph Payne Troop, great grandson of William Troop*

BARTON C. TROVER

Barton Crutchfield Trover, born Dec. 3, 1886, at St. Charles, KY, was the son of Zedekiah Frances Trover and his wife, the former Mary Melvina Sanders born in 1863, the daughter of William Riley Sanders and Jane Vickery of Caldwell County.

Left-Joseph Basil Hibbs. Right-Barton Crutchfield Trover singing with a quartet at Suthards Church

In 1910, he married Ruth Hibbs, born in 1892, the daughter of Joseph Basil Hibbs and Mary Anne Faull. They were married in a buggy by a Justice of the Peace in Hopkins County. After living with his parents for a few months, they moved to their farm which was located on the old road from St. Charles to Madisonville, between Suthards and Carbondale.

To the couple, three children were born: Mary Kathleen on June 18, 1912; Loman Crutchfield, Aug. 30, 1915; Faull Sanders, Feb. 18, 1918.

After the end of World War I in November 1919, when the state had cut a new highway through the farm, transporting their young daughter to school at Carbondale was difficult and they sold the farm and moved to Earlington, which was a booming small town of 3,500, due to mines and the L&N Railroad. They spent the remainder of their lives there, sending the three children through high school and then to Transylvania College in Lexington, KY.

Mary Kathleen married a young minister of the Disciple of Christ Church, Harry McCuan Davis, whom she met at Transylvania, in 1933. Loman Crutchfield graduated from Transylvania, as did Faull Sanders and then the University of Louisville Medical School. Loman married Helen Wash in Louisville in 1948. They live in Earlington and have reared six children: Stephanie, Kathleen, Philip, Michael, Regina, and Lorraine. Faull married Betty Hailey, from San Antonio, TX, in 1950. Their children are Faull Sanders, Jr., Barton Crutchfield, Marguerite Hailey, and Anne, all of whom live in Madisonville, except Marguerite.

Mary Kathleen and Harry Davis had two daughters, Jane Anne and Nancy Trover. Harry Davis died in 1984 after serving fifty years in the ministry. He is buried in Oakwood

Cemetery on the Trover plot. They had purchased a home in Earlington after semi-retiring and Kathleen still occupies their home. - *Submitted by Kathleen Trover Davis*

WILLIAM HARVEY TROVER

John Trover (the name probably is from the French "trouver") was born between 1750 and 1760 in Pennsylvania, but was living in Rockingham Co., VA, now Harrisonburg, WV, when in 1779, during the Revolutionary War he enlisted as a private soldier for the term of two years in the Regiment commanded by Col. Joseph Crocket. He served out his term in Capt. John Varney's company of the western battalion raised for the defense of the western frontier of Virginia and was discharged entitled to the benefits thereof of Virginia, Dec. 21, 1781.

He resided in Rockingham Co., VA, until moving to Christian Co., KY, in 1812. His family including Caty (who had married William Brown in 1804), William S. Trover (born in 1802), and Peggy (who married Edward Shanklin in 1821), moved with him. William S. married Elizabeth Overshiner (born in 1803), in 1825, whose father was the lawyer Gideon Overshiner, a prominent man in Hopkinsville, along with his brother Alexander Campbell Overshiner. They were all from Rockingham Co., VA, settling on Little River.

William Harvey Trover said he was Irish, but the name is a familiar one in Wales. They probably arrived in the British Isles with the Norman Invasion.

John Trover lived in Christian County at Hopkinsville until his death in May 1832, and is buried there. In 1832, an act was passed by Congress providing for benefits to Revolutionary War soldiers. William S. Trover and Daniel S. Hays, executors of John Trover's estate, reinstated the request for a pension that John Trover had filed in April 1818. Several prominent Hopkinsville men attested to his character and veracity "for he was universally witnessed a strictly honest, truthful and upright man by every person who knew him". They received an original land grant in Christian Co., KY, Nov. 18, 1844.

There are several legal transactions in the Christian County Court records for William S. Trover between the years of 1833-1849. He served on a jury in 1833. William Harvey was born in 1829; two other boys were born later; then Ed Trover in 1840 and Elizabeth in 1847.

William Harvey married Henrietta Nixon (born in 1826 at Hopkinsville), in 1849. Shortly afterwards the tobacco crops failed, the slavery issue began to ferment, and a number of Hopkinsville residents moved on further west. All of the Trover families sold their land and left for Missouri. They settled in Macoupin County, but in 1858, moved into Illinois where William S. is listed as a carpenter in the 1860 census, living at Carlinville.

To William Harvey and Henrietta were born five children: Margaret Elizabeth in 1856, twins Zedekiah Frances and Laura W. in 1857, Florence Alice in 1863, and George in 1865. Henrietta died about four months after the birth of George and is buried at Carlinville. Ben Nixon (Henrietta's brother) invited William Harvey to bring his young family back to the homeplace, a log home in the Huckleberry area in Hopkins County. During the Civil War, the man, four young children and a young baby made the hazardous trek in a covered wagon, fording streams and a river.

In 1867 in Hopkinsville, he married Susan Fox, with Z.F. Nixon posting the bond for the marriage. Later, he moved to the Will Sisk farm in the Carbondale area, but eventually to St. Charles where he worked outside the mines until his death. Burial was in Christian Privilege Cemetery.

All of his children, except Zedekiah, lived at home until they died, two, Alice and George, returning to the homeplace after their spouses died. Betty and Laura also reared George's three young children after their mother's death. He did not remarry. The children were William, Glenn and Bessie (who married Dr. Morse after working for a number of years in the St. Bernard Mining Company's store or office). - *Submitted by Kathleen Trover Davis*

ZEDEKIAH F. TROVER

Zedekiah Frances Trover (born Sept. 28, 1857), married Mary Melvina Sanders (Molly) in 1880 (born June 3, 1863). She was the daughter of William Riley Sanders (1838), and Jane Vickery (1836), of Caldwell Co., KY. Riley Sanders died in a sawmill accident before his youngest of three daughters was born. Jane (Tinsey) then married John Laffoon and raised a large family in the Suthards area. Nan wed Burnett Todd.

Zedekiah Frances and Mary Melvina (Sanders) Trover

Zed and Molly had eight children: William Everett born in 1880, Letcher Lee in 1882, Lela May in 1885, on a farm in the County, Barton Crutchfield in 1886 in St. Charles, Ethel Jane in 1893, Helen Ruth in 1895, and Amma Lillian in 1897, each in the County where they had moved back to a farm when Barton was three. Charlene had died when she was four years of age.

Zedekiah had worked around the mines, outside, but had moved on the Dr. Thomas Finley farm in the Huckleberry sector, then purchased 100 acres, the old Lynn farm from Tom Finley. Later, they added an adjoining 50 acre Brown farm for Letcher and the 50 acre Bass Hibbs farm for Barton. Everett's wife, Lena Suthard, inherited a 50 acre farm from her father. The brothers worked together to build houses, barns, and other buildings.

Letcher married Viola Howell; Lela married Garfield Oldham; Barton married Ruth Hibbs, daughter of Basil and Mary Anne, in 1910; Ethel married Sam Clark in 1915; Helen Ruth married Elmer Todd; and Amma married Ray McCully.

In 1919, a state highway was cut through the Barton Trover farm after World War I ended, Nov. 11, 1918. Difficulty in transporting children to school and undoubtedly other factors prompted several members of the closely knit family to sell their farms, purchase a livery stable on Main St. from Charlie Barnett, and move to Earlington in 1920. Each family, including Zedekiah and Melvina, had purchased a Ford car soon after the war ended. But, so had other people and the livery stable did not prove to be lucrative enough to support them. After a few years, they found other work in lumber, road building, still farming, mines. Elmer became Chief of Police, the Clarks and McCulleys moved back to the country. Everett's family remained in their home near Suthards Christian Church until after he died in 1949. Then his family moved to Madisonville. Everett and Laura were buried in Suthard's Cemetery, as were Amma and Ray McCulley.

Zedekiah (Zed) died at their home in Earlington in 1936, and was buried in Oakwood Cemetery. Molly died in 1941. Ruth had died of pneumonia in 1933. - *Submitted by Kathleen Trover Davis*

UTLEY

The surname Utta is over 1000 years old. A man named Utta once lived just north of the present day city of Leeds in the scenic Aire River valley of England. The site was originally called Uttaleah (Utta's forest clearing). By the 1600s the site was known as Uttley or Utley.

The Francis Wayne Utley family

The first Utleys in America were part of the Jamestown Colony. In the 1620s, Ensign John Utley was living at Hog Island on the James River. As the Jamestown Colony grew, the Utleys migrated westward and by 1740, they had settled in Goochland City, VA.

In the 1790s, a portion of the Utley clan migrated to Kentucky and settled in the Lexington and Harrodsburg areas.

In the 1820s the families of Royal, Obediah, George and David had settled in the Clear Creek area of Hopkins County. George and Mary Utley had five children; Redmon Royal, William, John, Sarah and Theodore.

Redmon Royal became a blacksmith and on Mar. 19, 1862, married Fredonia Larentine Kirkwood. They had four children: Mary Florence (Molly) born Jan. 7, 1863; Robert Lee, born Mar. 29, 1864; Lumira C. born Oct. 16, 1865 (died Feb. 10, 1889) and Francis Wayne born July 31, 1870.

On May 14, 1922, Francis Wayne Utley (Franc) and Nellie Maude Bruce were married. Nellie, born Jan. 1, 1896, was the daughter of John Richard and Laura J. Bruce. They made their home on the Pleasant View Road in the house Franc inherited from his parents.

Their first child, Bonnie Magdaline, was born Mar. 28, 1923. She was married to Thomas Alvia Killough. She had two children, James Harold, born Apr. 27, 1939 and David Earl, born Mar. 15, 1943. She died on Mar. 1, 1950.

Franc and Nellie's second child, Maurice Wayne, was born Feb. 28, 1925. He was first married to Jonell Lamb and had one child, Carma Belinda, born Aug. 3, 1949. He later married Sylvia Berry and had four children: Maurice Wayne, Jr. born Oct. 22, 1960; Rebecca Ann, born Mar. 5, 1963; Berry Dupree, born Aug. 6, 1965 and Donald Ryan, born Jan. 25, 1968.

Their third child, Mary Elizabeth, was born June 20, 1927. She married Wendell Finley Wright. She has five children: Mary Helen, born Feb. 7, 1944; Doris Jean born Mar. 4, 1945; twins Brenda Lou and Linda Sue, born May 8, 1947 (Linda Sue died Mar. 20, 1948); Patricia Ann, born Dec. 10, 1948 and Wendell Finley, Jr., born Apr. 26, 1958.

Their fourth child, Redmon Lee, was born Oct. 31, 1929. He married Virginia Louise Oldham. He has two children: Gregory Lee, born Mar. 8, 1956 and Terry Leon, born Aug. 2, 1961.

Their fifth child, William Edward, was born Mar. 2, 1934 and died in 1935.

Mary Kirkwood, Franc's grandmother, and Fredonia Larentine, his mother, gave trees from the family farm to help build Pleasant View Baptist Church. Franc hauled the logs to the mill and helped to build the church. Church discipline in the 1800s was very strict and Franc and others were "turned out" for the sin of dancing.

Francis Wayne Utley died on Feb. 15, 1951. Nellie Maude Bruce Utley died July 13, 1984. They are buried in Pleasant View Cemetery. *Submitted by J. Harold Utley*

RICHARD V. VAN HOOK

Richard Valentine Van Hook, born Feb. 14, 1899 in Hopkins Co., KY on Valentine's Day, was the youngest of seven children born to John Wesley Van Hook and Emily Lynn (Vaughn) Van Hook.

Thru checking the Van Hook family history one can see they truly had a Pioneering Spirit. Some old letters in Texas disclose that Arent Isaacszen Van Hoeck (Van Hook) sailed to this land on the "Half Moon", a flagship of the Henry Hudson expedition which was several years before the Mayflower sailing.

They came from Holland to England to New York, to New Jersey, Pennsylvania, and North Carolina to Tennessee, then on to Nebo, KY around 1897. In Nebo they tilled the soil for a living.

Richard V. VanHook's daughter Mary Rose, captures a life time of memories on a patchwork quilt

Richard Valentine was born in Nebo, then moved to Evansville, IN at the age of seventeen, where he met and married Susie Catherine Sears (b. Apr. 18, 1902) of Reed, KY on July 1, 1918. They sailed on the Delta Queen to Owensboro, KY for their special day. They had a total of eleven children, of which five were reared to adulthood. Four sons: John Wesley (b. Feb. 13, 1921); Raymond Otis (b. Mar. 22, 1925); Richard Jr. (b. Mar. 13, 1927); Jack Lowell (b. May 13, 1932); and their last child a daughter, Mary Marie (nick-name, Mary Rose) (b. July 1, 1934) was born on their Sixteenth Wedding Anniversary.

In 1955, Richard Valentine Van Hook and wife Susie Catherine continued pioneering as they moved West to Redondo Beach, CA where he retired. Richard died there in 1970 at the age of 71.

His daughter, Mary Rose, married George Richard Pierson (b. Mar. 28, 1934) of Union Co., KY on May 9, 1952 in Evansville, IN. This marriage produced five daughters. As of 1987 they reside in Hanson, KY with their youngest daughter, Sandra Gail Pierson (b. Aug. 28, 1976). Karen Sue Pierson (b. Feb. 22, 1953) lives in Idaho and is married to Terry Mark West (b. Jan. 13, 1955). Karen has three children by a previous marriage. They are Melissa Lynn Mills (b. Mar. 3, 1973), Jason Michael Mills (b. Jan. 21, 1976) and Mitchell Ryan Mills (b. Nov. 29, 1977). Donna Marie Pierson (b. Sept. 17, 1958) married Douglas Wayne Wilson (b. Mar. 23, 1955) and they located in California. Their three children are, Amanda Marie Wilson (b. May 24, 1983), Jonathan Paul Wilson (b. Dec. 7, 1985) and Kristina Marie Wilson (b. Aug. 11, 1987). Cheryl Ann Pierson (b. July 16, 1959) married Martin Evan Richey (b. Apr. 17, 1961) and they settled in Ohio. They have one daughter, Heather Nicole Richey (b. Apr. 11, 1987). Lisa Kay Pierson (b. Nov. 30, 1963) married Michael John Emanuel (b. Jan. 27, 1953) and they reside in Florida. They have one son, Michael Aaron Emanuel (b. Mar. 24, 1985).

As you can see Richard Valentine Van Hook's granddaughters, each one living in a different time zone in the United States, still possess that Pioneering Spirit which was so essential in the making of our great Country. Sources: The Van Hook Book by Bernice Hubbard Keister and the Family Bible. - *Compiled by Mary Rose (Van Hook) Pierson*

VAN LEER-ELLIOTT

Robert Garfield Van Leer, son of Marion and Ella Noel Van Leer, and Elizabeth Elliott, daughter of Sanders and Mary Bell Elliott, were married in the home of the bride July 6, 1944, by Rev. F. S. Jones. Both Robert G. and Elizabeth were born in Madisonville, Hopkins Co., KY.

Robert G. graduated from Rosenwald H.S. and enlisted in the U.S. Navy in 1938, where he trained for his future career of mass food preparation. He was honorably discharged in 1946. In 1949, Robert G. received a Certificate of completion of a course from the Chicago School of Shoe Rebuilding and Hat Blocking, a career he pursued in Madisonville for a time. For the last 8 years, Robert G. has been a minister, being pastor of Christ Church Holiness in Providence for six years, and is the associate pastor at present.

Elizabeth Elliott Van Leer is a graduate of Rosenwald High School, Western Kentucky Beauty College, Paducah, and is a licensed Cosmetologist for Kentucky. She is a licensed funeral director for Kentucky and has taken business courses at Madisonville Community College and Health Occupation School. She is a gospel soloist, singing since she was about four years old.

Robert G. and Elizabeth have five children: Robert Lewis Van Leer, born May 3, 1946. He graduated from Madisonville High School and attended Eastern KY State College, Richmond, for two years. He is married and has five children. (See ROBERT LEWIS VAN LEER)

James Martin Van Leer, born Oct. 27, 1947. He graduated from Madisonville H.S. and Murray State U., with a B.S. degree in social work and an A.S. degree in theatre arts. He is married and resides in Evansville. (See JAMES MARTIN VAN LEER)

Myron Dale Van Leer, born Feb. 17, 1955. He graduated from Madisonville North Hopkins H.S., and attended Murray State University for two years. He is single, and is presently employed by the Madisonville Street Dept. From first grade through high school he would never seek help from anyone with his lessons. In 1986 Myron took a C.P.R. examination and passed the written test without having attended the training class or reviewing the class material. C.P.R. is Cardio Pulmonary Resuscitation.

Gloria Darneaih Van Leer born Nov. 20, 1958, graduated from Madisonville North Hopkins H.S. and attended University of Louisville. She is a certified optician from the American Board of Opticianry, and is em-

The Van Leer Family in June, 1987. L to r: James, Myron, Joan, Darryl, Gloria (Van Leer) Williams, Harold Williams, Robert L., his daughter Yolanda, Elizabeth and Robert, and Robyn, Robert's daughter

ployed by the Southern Optical Co. of Louisville. She is married to Harold Williams, graduate of the University of Louisville, a Certified Public Accountant. They are expecting their first child in November 1987.

Darryl Edward Clarence Van Leer, born Oct. 31, 1960, graduated from Madisonville-North Hopkins H.S. and Western Kentucky University with Associate in Science and Bachelor of Arts degrees. He is presently single, but engaged. He is employed by the National Publishing Board, Nashville, TN, and is a photographer for Bobby Jones of the TV Gospel Show, Nashville. Darryl has made speeches during Black History Week, traveling to various cities, commemorating Dr. Martin Luther King, and has led marches in Indiana, Kentucky and Tennessee with his brother James Martin Van Leer, doing the same.

Elizabeth Elliott Van Leer's many first steps as a black woman are: One of the first black women in Madisonville to do commercial radio broadcasting on WFMW for Jerri's Clothing Store and the Confectioner's Candy Store; first black singer over Channel 13, Bowling Green; the first black candidate for the Board of Education; first black chairman of a Christmas parade; first black woman in the Footlight Players in the production "Once Upon a Mattress"—was in the chorus line; the first black woman to begin a nursery school for children ages two and over; and is the first licensed black Cosmetologist in Madisonville. - Submitted by Elizabeth Elliott Van Leer

VAN LEER-HOLLOWAY

Martin Van Leer was born in Tennessee and was 12 years old when he was freed from slavery. Ellen Holloway was born in Caldwell Co., KY. Marion Van Leer was born to Martin Van Leer and Ellen Holloway on Dec. 1, 1878.

To the union of Marion Van Leer and Ella Hayes Noel, six children were born. They were Isadore, Lucille, Edgar, Carretus (d. July 13, 1987 in Chicago), Marion, and Robert G. All but Robert G. settled in Chicago, Toledo, and Detroit. Carretus is survived by his wife, Olivia Van Leer and a son, Carretus Jr. of Chicago.

Ella Hayes Noel received her education at Atkinson College in Madisonville. She taught school in the Christ Church Holiness educational system in Madisonville. She also took in washing and ironing and canvassed (door-to-door sales) for a few years.

Ella had three brothers, Robert Noel, John Noel, and Joe Noel, an adopted brother. Robert and wife Charlie Noel had two boys and one girl. The only survivors of Robert's family are John Noel Jr. who lives in California and some cousins in Providence and Earlington, KY. John and Joe had no family.

Robert G. Van Leer is the only survivor of his brothers and sisters. Upon graduation from Rosenwald High School in 1938, Robert G. enlisted in the U.S. Navy, serving eight years on various ships and Naval bases, including Pearl Harbor and Iwo Jima.

Robert continued in public life the training of mass preparation of food which he had received in service. Leaving the Navy honorably discharged, Robert G. pursued a course in shoe rebuilding and hat blocking, and worked at this trade for some time in Madisonville.

Robert G. Van Leer married Elizabeth Elliott on July 6, 1944. Elizabeth is the daughter of Sanders Elliott and Mary Bell Lewis Elliott. (See Elliott-Lewis and Van Leer-Elliott). - Submitted by Robert G. Van Leer

JAMES MARTIN VAN LEER

It was 1956 and with the Supreme Court decision on integration, the Federal Courts found it necessary to enforce this decision, which in turn affected all grades of the Hopkins County school system.

For eight years Mrs. Elizabeth Van Leer had been the President of the local chapter of the N.A.A.C.P. Through a survey made of the Hopkins Co. schools, it was learned that the students of Rosenwald High School, the all-black school, were offered only 16 subjects from which to choose, while the Madisonville High School (all white) offered double that number to its students, which gave them an advantage in meeting the standards of education in entering colleges and universities. It was realized by the black community that the only way their children would have the advantages of higher standards of education was for them to prepare for their children to enter the all-white school where more subjects were offered, with more advantages for college entrance. Many names were placed on a list for their children to enter the Madisonville High School on the morning of integration, but the parents later withdrew their names.

The Rev. Robert G. and Elizabeth Van Leer, the parents of James Martin Van Leer, were the only parents who left their children's name on the list, because they believed that one black child could bring about the success of the integration process. Opposition and harassment such as crosses burned, mother's home set afire, relations threatened, and threatening phone calls was experienced for months, reported Mrs. Van Leer.

The integration case was won through the Federal Court in Owensboro, with Attorneys James Crumblin of Louisville, and Attorney Greenburg of New York, handling the case, supported by the N.A.A.C.P. The MESSENGER of Madisonville reported the decision in headlines on the front page.

James Martin Van Leer, age nine, was enrolled in Grade 4, in Waddill Ave. Elem. school in September, 1956, accompanied the first day by his mother Elizabeth Van Leer, his brother, Robert Lewis, and his aunt, Willie Mae Elliott. It was a quiet morning with no incidents, with the principal, Miss Dixie Lois Logan, keeping things going very smoothly. For three years James was the only black child in the schools that had been previously all white.

Waddill Elementary School as it looks in 1987. It was the first school to admit a black student, James M. Van Leer, in 1956

James' school days began to be happy ones, and he made many friends. In 1967, James Van Leer was graduated from Madisonville High School. He and his mother were the first blacks to perform in the Footlight Players community theatre.

James Martin Van Leer was graduated from Murray State University with a B.S. degree in Social Work, with an A.S. degree in theatre arts. He went to Evansville where he worked in a Federal program for Offender Aid Restoration, where he wrote the TV commercials and acted in the TV announcements. He has worked as supervisor and counselor for Federal prisoners in the Second Chance half-way house. He has written plays for some students at Evansville University. He continues his training and interest in theatre arts through community theatre in Evansville. He is presently employed at the Private Industry Council, doing counseling to persons 55 years and older in Evansville.

James M. Van Leer

During Black History weeks, James has traveled to make speeches to gatherings commemorating Dr. Martin Luther King, and has led marches in Indiana, Kentucky and Tennessee with several hundred followers. He has also spoken to groups in Madisonville, his home town.

James is married to Dorothy Thomas, dau. of Mrs. Johnnie Butler and Sammie Butler of Evansville. She attended Lockyear College, and is a data control clerk at Meade Johnson and Co. James has two step-sons, Jeffrey and John L. Thomas Jr.

Many thousands have been and will be benefitted by the integration program. The N.C.A.C.P., friends, relatives, and certainly the Van Leer family thanks God for the blessing. - *Submitted by Elizabeth Elliott Van Leer*

ROBERT LEWIS VAN LEER

In 1960, Robert Lewis Van Leer, oldest son of Robert and Elizabeth Elliott Van Leer of Madisonville, was the first black student, when a freshman, to attend an all-white Madisonville High School. His brother, James Martin Van Leer, was the first black student to walk through the doors to enroll at the all-white Waddill Ave. grade school.

The Browning Springs Middle School in 1987, was the Madisonville High School in 1960 when it admitted the first black student, Robert L. Van Leer, age 14, as a freshman.

Some trouble signs had cooled down and the weather was pleasant. On the first day of school, Robert Lewis was accompanied by his mother, Mrs. Elizabeth Elliott Van Leer, and his aunt, Miss Willie Mae Elliott. The faculty and student body had assembled in the auditorium and the devotion was in progress, and they paused in the center of the auditorium until it was finished. With mixed feelings of joy and worry, they proceeded down the aisle to find a seat, with some questionable glances from some students following them. Robert Lewis was a healthy, robust teenager, age 14, who looked like a good candidate for the high school football team. He did play guard on the MHS team.

After a few days, Robert learned on the playground that some few students might be planning to do him some bodily harm. He and his mother went to the Principal Mr. Weldon Hall who assured them they need not worry, that he would take care of the situation, which he did.

Since Robert Lewis was in the 5th grade at Rosenwald School, on Kentucky Ave., he had taken music and saxophone lessons from Mr. Danny Crow, and later from Mr. Orange Franklin, competent music teachers at Rosenwald. The parents were pleased with his musical progress. Thus, because of his musical knowledge, Robert Lewis was the first black student placed in the MHS all-white band, by the band director, Mr. Dean Dowdy. Mr. Dowdy took Robert "under his wing", and later said that he was a credit to the band.

Robert Lewis graduated from Madisonville High School in 1964. He enrolled in Eastern Kentucky State University with a major in music. While he served in the U.S. Air Force, he was a musician, and to the present, he continues to broaden and develop his music. He can play any instrument in a band, and he repairs instruments for school children through the music shops of Hopkins County. At one time, Robert was asked by the coordinator of the Fats Domino Band if he wanted to become a member of the band, but because of family responsibilities, he would not accept the offer.

Robert L. Van Leer

For a time Robert L. was the assistant manager of Time Finance Co., but is now employed as a mechanic in the mines. He is also a general assistant, licensed as Emergency Medical Technician, on the staff at Elliott Mortuary. He too, is blessed with an inventive mind inherited from his grandfather, Sanders Elliott, and his uncle, Durwood Elliott. He is talented in sciences, and often advises students who are preparing for the school science fairs. And, he inherited his musical talent from his mother, Elizabeth E. Van Leer, who has been singing gospel music since her early childhood.

Robert Lewis is married to Joan Haun whom he met at Eastern Kentucky University. They have five children: Robyn Yvette, age 18, a freshman at the University of Kentucky; Yolanda Lateche, age 15, 10th grade at Madisonville-North Hopkins H.S.; Latasha Lucinda, age 13, 8th grade at Browning Springs Middle School; Charlotta Fine age 12, 7th grade at Browning Springs; and Robert Lewis, Jr., age 11, 5th grade, Waddill Ave. Elementary. - *Submitted by Elizabeth Elliott Van Leer*

VANNOY-WILSON

Roy Logan Vannoy was born in Madisonville on Oct. 19, 1888 to Benjamin Franklin "Frank" Vannoy and Lina E. Shackelford Vannoy. He had one brother, Felix Ross Vannoy, born July 4, 1896. Roy's father died May 2, 1910. Lina died Nov. 16, 1945. Lina was a scriptorian and taught Sunday School for many years in the Presbyterian Church. The Lina Shackelford Vannoy Sunday School Class is named for her. Lina and Frank are both buried in Odd Fellow Cemetery.

Roy Logan Vannoy and Elsie Mae Wilson Vannoy

On Sept. 27, 1913, Roy married Elsie Mae Wilson in a ceremony conducted by James Vernon in Henderson, Henderson Co., KY. Elsie's brother, William Elmer, served as one of the witnesses. Born on Dec. 23, 1887 in Webster County, Elsie was the seventh of fourteen children born to William S. Wilson and Samantha Ann Wise Wilson. The Wilsons moved to Madisonville in 1905 to give the children an opportunity to obtain an education. Elsie combined her love of learning and her love for children to become a school teacher.

Roy and Elsie had two children. Frank Wilson Vannoy was born Nov. 26, 1915 and married Agnes Loretta Sutton on Mar. 19, 1944 in Honolulu, HI. Ann Cathryne Vannoy was born Dec. 8, 1917 and married Hugh Blanchard, Jr. on Apr. 12, 1944 in Red Bank, NJ. Elsie died tragically on Nov. 11, 1919 of complications from typhoid fever. She is buried in the Wilson Plot in Odd Fellows Cemetery.

Roy was office manager for Gulf Refining Company when he died on Sept. 12, 1955. He had been associated with Gulf Oil for 19 years. Prior to that, he was associated with the former Madisonville Milling Company. He is buried in the Staples/Vannoy Plot at Odd Fellows Cemetery. They were members of the Christian Church. Sources: Wilson Family Bible; Marriage Bond and Certificate; Death Certificates; tombstones; obituaries. - *Submitted by Ann Wilson Blanchard Peralta*

VICE ADMIRAL FRANK WILSON VANNOY (USN-RET.)

Frank Wilson Vannoy, born Nov. 26, 1915 in Madisonville is the elder of two children born to Roy Logan Vannoy and Elsie Mae Wilson Vannoy. He graduated as valedictorian of his class at Madisonville High School. He spent one year at the University of Kentucky and then received an appointment to the U.S. Naval Academy. He graduated with distinction and was commissioned an Ensign on June 1, 1939, and assigned to the USS Mississippi. He was on board the Mississippi in Iceland when Pearl Harbor was bombed and the United States entered World War II. During the war, he participated in most of the major amphibious operations in the Central Pacific and was awarded the Legion of Merit with Combat "V".

Vice Admiral Frank Wilson Vannoy (USN-Retired)

After World War II, Vannoy served in a variety of positions, from the Staff of Command Amphibious Force, Pacific Fleet, to Navy Special Weapons Unit 471 to the 8460th Special Weapons Group. Later, he served as Operations Officer on the USS Des Moines and commanded the USS Watts. He then attended the Naval War College and was kept on to serve on the Staff in the Strategy and Tactics Department until mid-1957. Following service as the Commander of Mine Division Eight, Vannoy was assigned to the office of the Chief of Naval Operations, where he headed the Special Weapons Plans Branch in 1960 and 1961. He commanded the USS Vermillion and then became the Commander of Amphibious Squadron Ten in 1963. In 1964, he returned to the Office of the Chief of Naval Operations as head of the Joint and International Plans Branch. While there, he was awarded a Gold Star in lieu of a second Legion of Merit.

In 1965, Vannoy served as commander Amphibious Training Command, U.S. Atlantic Fleet and then assumed command of Amphibious Groups One and Three. In 1967, he was awarded a second gold star in lieu of a third Legion of Merit while serving as Commander Task Force Seventy-Six. May 1968, found Vannoy assigned to the Joint Staff Office, Joint Chiefs of Staff as Chief of the Far East Division, and later, as Deputy Director of Plans and Policy. Vannoy returned to the Office of the Chief of Naval Operations in July 1970 as Assistant Deputy of Naval Operations (Plans and Policy). In July 1971, he was named Deputy Chief of Naval Operations (Plans and Policy). He advanced to the rank of Vice Admiral in July 1971, and on Oct. 31, 1973, was named Commander Amphib. Forces, Atlantic. He retired as a Three Star Admiral.

Frank Wilson Vannoy married Agnes Loretta Sutton on Mar. 19, 1944 in Honolulu, HI. The Vannoys have two daughters (Carol Jean Vannoy Burgess and Sandra Gail Vannoy) and two grandchildren (Michael Burgess and Stacy Burgess). The Vannoys are active members of their Episcopal Church in McLean, VA. Sources: Wilson Family Bible, Military Records, Newspaper articles. - *Submitted by Ann Wilson Blanchard Peralta*

VEAZEY-CAVANAH

The history of the Lee and Lula Cavanah Veazey family is simple, loving, and cherished. Mama and Papa met in Madisonville while preparing to teach in Hopkins County schools. Papa came from west Hanson, known as Shakerag, which is a vast area without charter, deed, or title; therefore, it's boundaries can't be defined. Other prominent names in Papa's ancestry are Waller and Roberts.

Wedding picture of Lula and Lee Veazey, 1906

Mama, daughter of Tom and Emma Melton Cavanah, came from near Richland. Before marriage in 1906, she taught at Cavanah and Munn's School while Papa taught in Shakerag.

In 1906, they bought a farm where we now own and live; thus our farm has been in the family eighty-one years. Rupert arrived in 1907; while yet unnamed, Papa had it announced in the paper that they were the parents of a fine young Democrat. Rupert was rare, being both academic and practical. His vocations were teacher, electrician and letter carrier. He succumbed to a heart ailment in 1968. Married to Anna Katherine Marks, they had one son Bob who married Joan Scott. They had a son Scott and a daughter Lee Ann who are married with a son and daughter each.

Erline, born in 1909, like the rest went through the grades at Buntin School. She roomed and boarded at Hanson during high school. Meeting her husband, Walter Hughes, in college, they then taught in Muhlenberg County. After W.W. II he was employed by the Air Force. Today, they are retired among friends in Madisonville.

Durwood arrived in 1915. As a teenager he took much responsibility as Papa's health declined. Durwood was muscular and delighted in using farm machinery. Heat or cold never deterred him from his farming duties. Married to Blanche Oakley in 1935, they have one son, Dwight, who farms and is a racing enthusiast.

Emmagene, born in 1918, I do not remember for she left for her heavenly reward at the age of four, when I was two. The mention of her name evokes family tears even yet.

My entry was in 1920. In my second year Papa built the house, which after remodeling, is our home today. Fruits, vegetables, meat, milk, and eggs were farm produced; they were also exchanged for sugar, salt, kerosene, gingham and calico. My family saw the automobile enter and horses exit. I rode a mare five miles to high school before buses were used.

My father's death in 1936 was a hard blow for me at age fifteen.

In 1941 I went to California, working briefly for an uncle until W.W. II. During Navy days I married a precious W.A.V.E., Eleanor Depue. After the war we settled in San Diego where David was born in 1948. We returned to Kentucky in 1950 just before Carl arrived.

In Kentucky I have been farmer, life underwriter, and postman, Bible teacher and deacon. David and Carl obtained degrees from Murray State and Western State respectfully. David is employed in the health field in Florida and Carl in the postal service here. Both are married with a precious son and daughter each.

Mama entered her eternal abode in 1973 at age 91.

Eleanor and I are very happy in retirement, traveling by donkey, steamship, plane, Greyhound, Amtrak and automobile.

Thank the Lord for retirement days among friends. - *Submitted by Leroy Veazey*

VEAZEY-YEANEY

David L. Veazey and Nancy J. Yeaney were married on Jan. 7, 1978 at St. Mark Methodist Church in Galion, OH.

David was born Dec. 19, 1948 in San Diego, CA, the elder son of Leroy Veazey and Eleanor Depue. He was raised in the Shakerag area of Hopkins County and attended Hanson Elementary School and Madisonville High School. He graduated from Murray State University in 1970 and entered the Air Force the same year. David spent his service in Langley Air Force Base in Virginia and was discharged from there in 1974. He also earned his Master's Degree in Education from the College of William and Mary while in service. He returned to Hopkins County and worked as a Probation and Parole Officer. David joined ServiceMaster Industries in 1977 and moved to Galion, OH where he met and married Nancy.

Nancy was born Dec. 14, 1952 in Bradford, PA, the daughter of George Yeaney and Marie Wells. She attended Bradford area schools until her senior year of high school when she and her mother moved to Galion, OH, after her father's death. After graduating, Nancy spent three years in a nursing program in Columbus, OH and Asheville, NC. She became a registered nurse and went to work in Galion Community Hospital where she met David.

After marriage, David and Nancy lived in Galion, in Carey, OH, and in Elizabethtown, KY, before moving to Ocala, FL in 1983. David

David Veazey and wife Nancy with children William and Kristen

is the manager of Environmental Services at Marion Community Hospital in Ocala and Nancy is a hemodialysis nurse. They have two children, Kristen, 6, and William, 2. - *Submitted by David L. Veazey*

WADE-BARKER

Caleb WADE and brother Joshua were early settlers from South Carolina. Joshua, in January 1806, claimed 200 acres "for settling and improving the vacant lands of this commonwealth lying on the waters of Lick Creek a branch of Clear Creek beginning..at corner of Jacob BARKERS 400 acre survey.." (Land Warrant Bk 1, p 36). Caleb WADE married Rachel BAKER/BARKER, possibly a daughter of this Jacob. The Land & Tax Book of 1807 records Caleb purchased 100 acres from Rhea ALEXANDER and 100 acres from John WILSON. John WILSON also sold 100 acres to an older gentleman, Zachiriah WADE (b. 1760/70), that same year. In 1822, Zachiriah sold 50 acres to Issac CONNER for $100. It isn't clear what kinship this Zachiriah, whose son John was killed in the War of 1812, had to Caleb and Joshua.

John Wesley Wade 1846-1926

Caleb (1780/90-1840+) had two children, Elizabeth (who married John GARRIS in 1832; no issue) and Joshua P. (1809-1882, married Dorcas Campbell RICHETTS, no issue; Posey Co., IN will, Bk 1, p 22 names siblings), before moving to Rutherford Co., TN where six more children were born: (1) Zachariah (1811-1877), m. Elizabeth HAYES, died Edwards Co., IL (2) Sarah (1814-before 1870) m. Alexander McKINNEY in 1848, Posey Co., IN (3) John F. (1815-before 1882) m. Sarah Ann LOCKRIDGE in 1835, Pope Co., IL (4) Caleb D. (1817-before 1899) m. Nancy FLEEHART in 1839, lived Posey Co., IN 1850-80 (5) Thomas G. (1819-late 1860's) m. Hannah McKINNEY Jan. 4, 1841 in Hopkins Co., moved to Posey Co. in 1850's and Wayne Co., IL in 1870-80's and (6) Braxton (1821-Apr. 30, 1884) m. Sarah CAMPBELL Dec. 30, 1844, he died in Posey Co., IN.

Caleb returned to Hopkins Co. for the birth of his ninth child, Lexinia, who married Jonas/James BRADLEY Nov. 10, 1850 and Catherine, his tenth child, born in 1825, who married Joseph C. ALEXANDER (children: Sarah & Zack). He is counted in Hickman County in the 1830 census but is back in Hopkins County leasing land from Noah FOX in 1837. It was probably at this time that he moved on to Posey Co., IN. His brother Joshua and wife Polly Connors WADE had also moved to Posey Co. with their eight children. In 1851 the city of Wadesville was laid out in that county to honor the pioneering WADE families from Hopkins Co., KY! - *Submitted by Karen Kerr Jensen*

WADE-CONNOR

The date and place of birth of Joshua WADE (1760/70-1844) and Polly CONNOR (1775/80-1848) is not known. It is certain they were living in Chester Co., SC before migrating to Kentucky. In the land records of Chester Co., 1766-1786, there is a John WADE county D.S. No other record has been found on this John WADE.

The 1790 census of Chester Co., SC has Isham and John CONNOR. The 1800 census has Zachiriah WADE, Isam and Thomas CONNOR and ? BAKER. By 1806 Joshua WADE has purchased land in Hopkins Co., KY. It is not known if his family was with him at the time. His son, Issac Murphy WADE, stated "I was born 1807 in Tennessee when my parents were on their way to Kentucky". By 1808, we find Zackiriah, Thomas, Caleb and Joshua WADE, Issac and Isham CONNOR and Jacob BARKER in Hopkins Co. Associations among these people are recorded in land and minute books of Hopkins Co., though their relationship has not been established. Joshua WADE was appointed surveyor in Hopkins Co. in 1815. By 1817 he moved to Posey Co., IN. He purchased 400 acres of land and in 1817-20 was elected inspector and constable of Robb Twp.

Very little is known of Joshua and Polly; we can only guess they migrated from the seaboard in search of a better life for themselves and their children. Joshua was a forward-looking man and very early worked for the establishment of a school system in Posey Co. His son Zackiriah was the first school teacher in 1820 as well as Col. in the Indiana Militia.

There are indications that Joshua may have had eight children, only seven lived to share his estate settlement in 1844. Polly is believed to have died before 1850. Their children were: (1) Zachiriah WADE b. ca 1794/7 m. Nov. 5, 1817 Nancy Harriet UNDERWOOD: m. 2nd July 26, 1835 Margaret AXTON-he was father of eight sons and three daus., (2) Thomas WADE b. 1800 South Carolina m. May 22, 1824 Mary CAMPBELL and had six sons and five daus., (3) Davis/David WADE b. ca 1805 South Carolina m. May 21, 1831 Elizabeth CAMPBELL and had four sons and two daus., (4) Issac Murphy WADE, b. ca 1807 Tennessee m. Jan. 2, 1828 Sarah WILSON and had five sons and six daus., (5) Lucinda WADE b. 1811 Hopkins Co. m. Jan. 16, 1834 David G. WATSON and had five sons and three daus., (6) John W. WADE b. 1815 Hopkins Co. m. May 28, 1837 Susanna BROWN and had one son and three daus., (7) Joshua Carter WADE b. 1817 Indiana m. 1839 Polly BENNET, m. 2nd Mary ROBINSON and had one son and two daus.

My husband Robert P. GARRETT is the son of Purl and Eva Wade GARRETT; grandson of Joshua C. WADE and Amanda HOLLAND; great-grandson of Zachkiriah WADE and Nancy Harriett UNDERWOOD and great-great grandson of Joshua WADE and Polly CONNOR. - *Submitted by Jeanne Garrett*

WADE-LOCKRIDGE

John F. WADE was the fifth child of early Hopkins Co. settler Caleb WADE. He was born in Rutherford Co., TN about 1816 and came to live in Hopkins Co. at age five. His family lived briefly in Hickman County when he was fourteen and then returned to Hopkins Co.

In the mid 1830's, his father and uncle Joshua were intent on immigrating to Posey Co., IN with their 18 children! John proposed marriage to Sarah Ann LOCKRIDGE, daughter of Sarah THOMAS and the deceased Andrew LOCKRIDGE (1770/80-1833); they were married in Golconda, IL, a large river settlement not far from Posey Co., IN, on Sept. 16, 1835. A number of Sarah's siblings also came to Posey Co. (see Andrew LOCKRIDGE bio. which also lists children of John and Sarah).

Sarah Caroline Wade with granddaughter Eleanor Wade Moseley, about 1918

By 1857, John and 2nd wife Mary COLEMAN lived in Wayne Co., IL and, at the close of the Civil War, his son John Wesley WADE married Lenora RICE, daughter of former Kentuckian William Rice, a wagon maker, and Carolina CROW who lived nearby. They had eleven children: (1) Sarah Caroline (Sept. 3, 1865-Sept. 5, 1942), (2) Martha (1868-alive 1942 in Granite City, IL) married Frank TAYLOR, issue: Maude died young, Hershel (3) James C. (January 1871-alive 1942) m. Nov. 18, 1893 Lucinda F. CHRISTMAN, Edwards Co., IL, issue: Flossie m. Harold RIGG, Bulah m. Chicago banker Benjamin SCHWARTZ, Mable OSGOOD, Verdin C. WADE has son who works at U of IL, (4) William (1872-1882) died of typhoid, (5) Nancy Lucinda (1874-alive 1942) m. John JOHNSON, issue: Raymond, Orville, Henry; m. 2nd Jacob WEBB, issue: Jacob, (6) John (1876-alive 1942) m. Apr. 5, 1891 Lucy ACKLEY, moved to Sioux City, IA, (7) Francis Lee (1879-alive 1942 in Palatine, IL) m. Luke STANLEY, issue: Hurbert, Bessie, Estella, Myrtle, (8) Mary WILLIAMS (1880-1898), issue: Mamie, (9) Adolphus (Apr. 27, 1881-Sept. 14, 1965) m. Bertha MAUMEE, Wabash Co., IL; issue: Howard, Mary Lee, Dorothy LOREAN, (10) Emma (Feb. 4, 1884-Oct. 17, 1884); (11) Hattie (Oct. 3, 1885-Aug. 26, 1891).

John Wesley's daughter Sarah Caroline Wade, pictured here, married Joshua KIMBRELL, a young man she met at the Christian Church with the best disposition and singing voice, on Aug. 1, 1888. They gave up farming and moved to Massac Co., IL with Leonard's Mill. Their family included: Ella May MOSELEY (1889-1960), Roy (b. 1891), Delbert (1893), Loyd (1895), Raleigh (1898-1984), Sterling (1905-1961), and Gilbert (lives Florida). - *Submitted by Sarah Caroline WADE's great granddaughter, Karen Kerr Jensen, Decatur, IL*

WAGONER-PARKER

John D. Wagoner (Wegener) (1848-1893) was born in Luxonborg, Germany in 1848 and came to the United States in 1861 at the age of 13. The ship search shows that he sailed by way of Rotterdam to Pennsylvania, having relatives there. He began his mining career at an early age, working in Pennsylvania and Illinois. He came to Hopkins County in 1883 with the first Reinecke coal operators. He helped to open the Reinecke Shaft Mines.

John D. Wagoner and Martha Parker Wagoner

In 1888, he bought a house and lot on the corner of Arch and Seminary Streets. He acquired a tract of land containing 10 acres located in the west part of Madisonville. The last part of that property was sold by is grandchildren to Madisonville Housing Authority in November of 1982, when Wagoner Street was closed by the city of Madisonville.

On Mar. 29, 1896, he married Martha Parker (1855-1896) from North Carolina, being of Indian descent.

John D. Wagoner died Oct. 1, 1893, leaving two small children, John Wagoner, age 2, and Margretta Wagoner, age 5. He is buried at Oddfellows Cemetery.

Martha died in 1896, leaving John, age 4, to be reared by the Wiley Hobgood family. Margretta was taken in by a Qualls family near Sturgis, KY. At age 16, she married the owner of the Sturgis Milling Company, Arthur Smith. Sources: Courthouse records and Family Bible - *Submitted by Pansy E. Ashby*

WAGONER-WIAR

Ida Mae Wiar (1895-1979) and John Wagoner (1891-1980) were married Jan. 10, 1915 in Hopkins County at the home of the bride's parents, near Manitou.

Ida Mae was born on June 17, 1895 in Webster County, the daughter of John Cox Wiar and Celia Elizabeth Carnal. Ida May had three sisters: Gertie, Grace and Beulah and two brothers: Johnny and Fred. Of these, Johnny and Gertie are still living.

John and Mae Wagoner on their 60th wedding anniversary

Ida Mae attended Pleasant Grove School through the sixth grade. She joined Pleasant Grove Church at an early age, and later Liberty Church, then Crofton Baptist Church.

John was born on Aug. 27, 1891 in Madisonville, KY the son of John D. Wagoner and Martha Parker. He had one sister, Margretta.

John, orphaned at four years old, lived with the Wiley Hobgood family until 1915, doing county road work and farming, but receiving no formal education.

In December of 1912, he sold the house and lot on Cemetery Street that he inherited from his father. On Dec. 22, 1917, he bought a 75 acre farm with the coal and mineral rights in the Flat Creek area from J.W. Parrish. David Well, containing mineral water, and from the Davis Well Road derived its name, was located on this farm.

In 1920, John discovered coal and opened the No. 12 vein, from which he sold country coal for three years. On Apr. 25, 1924, he sold the 75 acre farm with the No. 12 and No. 11 veins of coal to Audie Offutt. On Oct. 10, 1925, he sold the 75 acres of No. 9 and deep vein coal to Kentucky Royalty Company.

On Apr. 5, 1924, John bought 149 acres in the Pond River area from the Murphy heirs. Here he raised corn, tobacco, wheat, stock peas, sorghum and tomatoes.

In 1926 and 1927, he was involved in the timber industry with Scott Brothers in Muhlenberg Co. In 1928 and 1929, he was a partner in the Derby Mines, an unsuccessful venture, for in 1929, he sold six acres of tobacco for $24.

In 1943, John raised hemp for the government. Also, while owning this farm, he had a dairy herd of 15 to 20 cows and built an underground silo for feed storage.

On Apr. 19, 1949, he sold his 149 acres of land to Justin Potter, a coal operator, but retained the oil rights.

On Sept. 9, 1950, John bought a 209 acre farm in Christian Co. from Paul Terry. On Apr. 16, 1980, he formed the Wagoner Oil Trust, including all oil and mineral rights in both counties for his children.

John and Ida Mae were hard-working, happy people, married 64 years. They had four daughters and three sons: Pansy, Nevaline, John Ray, Pearline and Earlene (fraternal twins), Bobby and Joyce. All are still living.

A poem, written by one of his daughters, was read at John's funeral as a poignant tribute to a remarkable man:

At the tender of age of four,
I had a look at death's door,
When Mother's eyes were closed
Not to open anymore.

When the coffin lid was closed,
My heart broke right in two,
For I didn't know then
What I'd ever do.

Came a pat on the head
And a gentle voice said.
Hang onto your faith
And you will get ahead.

Your feet may be bare
And your hands may be cold.
Keep your heart warm with love
And a light in your soul."

The first years were hard;
I was hungry and cold.
I kept my heart warm with love
And a light in my soul.

The years have been long,
Have been good to me, too.
Twlight is here
And sunset is due.

When the death angel calls
And the gates open wide,
Mother will say "John,
Come on inside."

My feet may be bare
And my hands may be cold,
But I will have a heart warm with love,
And a light in my soul.

Ida Mae and John are both interred at Forest Lawn Mausoleum in Madisonville. Sources:

Courthouse records and Family Bible - *Submitted by Pansy Ashby*

WAIDE-SULLIVAN

On Oct. 18, 1958, Peggy Ann Sullivan of Madisonville, KY and Harry Doyle Waide of Providence, KY were married at "The Old Ramsey Homestead" in the Government section of Hopkins County. The Rev. William James, First Methodist Church, Madisonville, performed the ceremony.

Peggy and Harry Waide, 1987

Their parents are Margaret and Eugene Sullivan and the late Shirley Price Waide Hall of Providence and Denver Waide, Sr. of Henderson.

Harry was employed by Ruby Lumber Company in Providence, so they made their first home there.

Their first child, Suzanne Camille was born at Hopkins County Hospital on June 15, 1960, while they lived in Providence.

In 1961 the Waides moved to Madisonville when Ruby's in Providence closed. With the death of Edwin Ruby the company ceased to exist as it had been for many years. Their motto was "We Served Your Grandfathers".

Clyde Ruby then moved his operation to Ruby Concrete Company on Dempsey Street, where the old cheese factory once flourished. Harry moved with the company. He later purchased stock in Rubys and is now principal owner and President. He is commissioned a Kentucky Colonel.

Peggy is a real estate broker and owns Peggy Waide Real Estate in Earlington, KY. She received her GRI designation in 1974 and the CRS designation from the National Association of REALTORS in 1978. She is also commissioned a Kentucky Colonel.

She is a housewife and mother of three children and two grandchildren.

Two sons were born after the family moved to Madisonville. Forrest Lynn "Ben" Waide was born on May 17, 1963 and Kent Waide on May 26, 1964.

Suzanne married a young man from Houston, TX, Clay Neal Curb. He is the son of JoNell Swanzy Curb and Wayne Grayling Curb, Fort Worth, TX. They were married in St. Mary's Episcopal Church in Madisonville, KY, by Rector Robert A. King and First United Methodist Pastor, Dr. Wallace Thomas.

They have two daughters; the oldest was christened Hannah Jo Curb on Dec. 24, 1982. The youngest, christened on Dec. 24, 1984 is Mary Mae Curb. Both were christened by Rector King and blessed by their Creator, Lord of us all. Both Christmas Eve services were held in St. Mary's Episcopal Church in Madisonville.

God-Parents for the girls are their maternal grandparents, Peggy and Harry Waide and great-grandparents, Margaret and Eugene Sullivan.

"Ben" and Kent are single.

The entire family have been members of the First Methodist church in Madisonville and Marion until the girls were christened at St. Mary's.

On Dec. 7, 1986, Peggy Waide and her son-in-law, Clay Neal Curb were confirmed as Members of St. Mary's Episcopal by the Rt. Rev. David Reed, the Bishop of the Episcopal Diocese of Kentucky. Rector Robert A. King is St. Mary's minister.

The Sullivans have retired to Marion, KY; the Waides live in Earlington, KY and the Curbs are the only family members left in Madisonville except for Margaret Sullivan's uncle, Spaulding Ringo, who resides on Hall Street. He is 89.

Peggy Waide is profiled in the following publications:

A) Dictionary of International Biography, London, England, 1973, 1975, 1976, 1978.

B) International Who's Who of Intellectuals, London, England, Volume I, 1978.

C) Outstanding Young Women of America, 1972.

D) The World Who's Who of Women, 3rd Edition and 4th Edition, 1976-77, 1977-78, London, England.

E) Notable Americans III Edition, 1981.

F) Personalities of the South, 1973, 1974, 1975, 1976.

G) Community Leaders and Noteworthy Americans, 1975-76, 1976-77.

H) International Who's Who of Professional and Business Women, 1st Edition to be printed in 1988.

Harry D. Waide is profiled in the following publications:

A) Who's Who in Kentucky, 1974.

B) Who's Who in Finance and Industry 1975-76, 1977-78.

(see Curb-Waide, F.L. Waide and Kent Waide) - *Submitted by Peggy Sullivan Waide*

FORREST LYNN WAIDE

Forrest Lynn "Ben" Waide is the son of Peggy Sullivan Waide and Harry Doyle Waide. He was born in Hopkins County Hospital in Madisonville, KY on May 17, 1963.

He attended Madisonville city schools and in 1981 graduated from Madisonville North Hopkins High School, where he lettered three years in swimming and two years in band.

"Ben" was on the first swim team MNHHS outfitted and his best times were in breast stroke. His coach, Lairy Nofsinger, was also his coach on the Madisonville Country Club team where he was team captain in 1981.

He was voted "Best School Spirit" by the senior class of 1981; was the reorganizer and president of the Big Maroon Fan Club; member, M-Club; member, Hi-Y, and at the 1979

Forrest Lynn "Ben" Waide

Kentucky Youth Assembly, served as President of the Security Council at KUNA. In 1980 Kentucky Youth Assembly, he served as a Supreme Court Justice; was on 1980-81 Student Council at MNHHS; member of MNHHS band where he played drums.

"Ben" attended four years at Murray State University He majored in pre-physical therapy from August 1981-May 1985. "Ben" was voted "Mr. Murray State University" his junior year. He was a member of Pi Kappa Alpha social fraternity-Lambda Epsilon Chapter and was fraternity chaplain. He received the University Housing Senior Progress Award.

In his senior year, he and Miss America 1981, Cheryl Pruitt-Blackwood emceed the "Mr. Murray State" contest and entertained with a number of vocal solos and duos.

He was coach and swimmer of Murray's Intramural Swim Team Champions; member, Concert Committee; member, Student Senate; member, University Housing Association, Hall Council and Resident Advisor; Calloway County Physical Therapy Volunteer; Kentucky Special Olympics volunteer; member, Red Cross Society volunteer, CPR instructor and volunteer lifeguard instructor; Student Government Association officer; YMCA volunteer; member, Wesleyan Student Campus Organization; member, First Methodist Church, Madisonville and youth minister for 1-1/2 years at First United Methodist in Marion, KY.

At University of Louisville, "Ben" received AMBUCS scholarship for 1986; was member of U. of L.'s Student chapter, A.P.T.A., served as By-Laws committee Chairman; member, Student Senate; member, Student Organizations Board; was chairman of Southern Association of Colleges and Schools Self Study on Housing; member; Provosts Year End Appropriations Committee and President, Allied Health Council of Student Government Association for University of Louisville 1986-87. He was nominated by University of Louisville as one of ten outstanding students for BUSINESS TOMORROW XIII, held by Princeton University.

He was awarded the "Outstanding Contribution to Student Government Award" for 1987. Was an "Outstanding Young Man of America" recipient in 1986; listed in International Directory of Distinguished Leadership, 1987; profiled in Who's Who in American Universities and Colleges, 1987 and was commissioned a Kentucky Colonel by the

Governor of Kentucky, the Honorable Martha Layne Collins in 1987.

He graduated Aug. 16, 1987, receiving a Bachelor of Health Science degree in physical therapy from U. of Louisville. He also attended Harlaxton College in Grantham, England in 1987.

He enjoys golf, swimming and is envied by all family golfers. He played at St. Andrews old, celebrity championship course in Scotland.

"Ben" has held many jobs. In college years he was employed by Ruby Concrete Company; the City of Madisonville; YMCA of Madisonville; First Methodist Church, Marion, KY and Jewish Hospital, Louisville.

He is presently employed by Regional Medical Center in Madisonville. - *Submitted by Peggy Sullivan Waide*

KENT WAIDE

Kent (no middle initial) Waide is the son of Peggy Sullivan Waide and Harry Doyle Waide. He was born in Hopkins County Hospital in Madisonville, KY on May 26, 1964.

He attended Madisonville city schools and in 1982 graduated from Madisonville North Hopkins High School where he lettered four years in swimming.

Kent Waide

Kent was on MNHHS's first swim team. His best times were in breast stroke, although he was also quite adept at butterfly. His coach, Lairy Nofsinger, was also his coach at Madisonville Country Club. Coach Nofsinger, in a <u>Madisonville Messenger</u> column in 1986, called Kent Waide "the best swimmer he had ever coached".

Kent was Swim Team Captain in 1982. He followed family tradition and was the second President of the re-organized Big Maroon Fan Club in its second year; member of the M-Club; member of the Biology Club; member and helped organize Fellowship of Christian Athletes; voted "Best All Around" by his senior class; King of the Senior Prom; was a Hi-Y member and attended the 1979 and 1980 Kentucky Youth Assembly, serving as Vice President of the Security Council at KUNA in 1981. He also served as Chaplain of Hi-Y, was Sergeant of Arms for class of 1982; President of Methodist Youth Fellowship and was the 1982 recipient of the prestigious Waskon Award.

Kent's collegiate career entailed one year at West Ark Community College, Fort Smith, AR, one semester at Murray State University and three years at Oral Roberts University in Tulsa, OK.

While in college, Kent worked in a Wyoming auger mine; at MPSI, an internationally-based company in Tulsa, in demographic science; Jewish Community Center, Tulsa; Southern Hills Country Club, Tulsa; swim coach, Broken Arrow Marlins; assistant swim coach, Madisonville Country Club; coaching Special Olympic entrants and employment at ORU.

While in college, Kent swam on Oral Roberts first NCAA Swim Team. He competed in three Mid-Western Collegiate Conference NCAA meets and one in Southern Methodist University National Invitational meet in Dallas, TX, where he placed 7th in breast stroke. He held a number of records upon finishing his ORU swim career and was Team Captain his senior year. He was approved to try for the 1988 Olympics.

Kent served as co-ordinator for ORU's Shalom program, where would-be students and their parents visit the ORU campus; member, Administrative Management Society; Senior R.A. in Wesley Luering Dorm which housed 250 members; was named an Outstanding Young Man of America in 1986; listed, International Directory of Distinguished Leadership, 1987; profiled in Who's Who in American Universities and Colleges, 1987 and was commissioned Kentucky Colonel by the Governor of Kentucky, the Honorable Martha Layne Collins in 1987.

On May 2, 1987, Kent graduated Cum Laude and received a Bachelor of Science degree in Business Management from ORU, where he was nominated as an Academic All-American.

He is single and enjoys swimming, golf and church activities. He is a member of First United Methodist in Madisonville. He looks forward to the time coming, when he will work toward his Masters degree. He has been interviewed for same at Notre Dame.

Kent is employed as Vice-President and manager of Star Construction Company in Madisonville. (See Waide-Sullivan; Curb-Waide; F.L. Waide; Ramsey-Ringo; Arnett-Ringo; Sullivan-Ramsey and Ramsey-Stevens-Gore) - *Submitted by Peggy Sullivan Waide*

WALKER

Aubrey (A.D.) Walker, born Feb. 22, 1893 to James (1872) and Ida Bell (1877-1953), was the oldest of six children; Louisa, Commadore, Charles, Marion, and Amy. He served in the army during World War I. Shellie McKinsey (Dec. 1, 1899-Mar. 21, 1983) graduated from Madisonville High School in 1919 where she became the first of three generations to be voted wittiest of her class. On Jan. 25, 1922 A.D., now a farmer, married Shellie, a teacher. They lived in Vandetta and owned a grocery store.

Their first child, Nell (Apr. 28, 1925) has a love for music that began in the Hanson marching band. Nov. 22, 1945 Nell married Richard Tapscott, a minister in the Southern Baptist church. He has served churches throughout Kentucky and Tennessee. Nell pursued a career in banking, in addition to her

From l to r: Aubrey Walker, Calvin Walker, Nell Rose Walker, Shellie Walker and Carroll Walker

commitment to her husband's churches, where she plays the organ. They had two children, Thomas (Aug. 16, 1946) and Janet (Jan. 1, 1958-Jan. 26, 1983). Tom married Peggy Floyd Aug. 17, 1969. They live in Bellville, IL where he owns a music store and she is a teacher and counselor. Janet was working as a secretary/receptionist when she married Noah Eastman Jan. 3, 1982. They were married just one short year before Jan's untimely death.

The Walker's first son, Calvin (Apr. 8, 1931) attended Western Kentucky University before serving with the Second Infantry Division on the front lines in Korea. He was decorated for excellent performance of duty under fire. Discharged in 1953, Calvin returned to Madisonville to work as a coal miner at Walker and Son Coal Company, later transferring to Peabody Coal Company. On Dec. 26, 1958 Calvin married Evelyn Hoskins. Alternating her time between home and school responsibilities, Evelyn earned undergraduate and graduate degrees in English and raised two daughters, Vicki (Sept. 24, 1959) and Susan (Sept. 3, 1963). On June 4, 1983 Vicki married John Eshelman III. they reside in Newark, OH where she is a Minister of Christian Education and he is a United Methodist minister. Susan spent a year in the Fiji Islands with the Peace Corps and is now a Children's Librarian in Indianapolis, IN.

A.D. and Shellie's third child, Carroll ("Budgie") was born Feb. 5, 1934. The family later moved to Madisonville where A.D. worked for the Kentucky Department of Transportation. Budgie was well known for his love of cars and could often be found at the Madisonville Speedway. Ironically, the summer after his high school graduation he was hit by a drunk driver and tragically killed in an auto accident Sept. 2, 1952. Three years later, A.D. died of a heart attack, leaving Shellie to live alone the next 28 years. Her deep faith in God sustained her through these years, and thus she served as an inspiration to many people. After her death, the First United Methodist Church dedicated a stained glass window in her memory. This symbolic act memorializes the significance of Christ in her life. Sources: The Walker Genealogy by Janet Tapscott Eastman, Interviews with family members - *Compiled by Vicki Walker Eshelman and Susan Walker*

WALKER-JOYNER

James Walker was born in Evansville, IN in 1916, the only child of Anna Lou Winstead and Ernest Emmon Walker. Anna was the daughter of Virginia Lee Watson and William Dabney (Pete) Winstead. Emmon was the son of Mary Alice Curneal and Robert Walker. Robert's parents were Francis Buntin and Polk Walker. Francis's parents were Betsy and Billy Buntin.

James' early years were spent in Indiana, Kentucky and Michigan as his father was an L&N employee and was transferred often. In 1929, they moved to the Winstead farm near Nebo. James graduated from Nebo High School in 1934.

Rea (Joyner) and James Walker

James married Rea Joyner in Madisonville in 1937. Rea was the daughter of Callie Lee and William Bennett Joyner (see Joyner-Day story). Rea attended a one-room school near Nebo called Porter-Payne with a young Auvergne Crowe teaching all the students. She later taught at Nebo High School and was Rea's teacher at graduation time.

James and Rea lived in the house the grandparents had raised their children in. James and Rea's children are: Barbara June and Shirley Faye.

Barbara June was born in 1940. She married Phillip Landrum. (see Landrum-Walker) Their children: Bret David (married Gaylynn Deveraux and has a son, Bret Ryan) and Lisa Lyn (married Karl Parcher and has a daughter, Britney Aaron). Barbara June and Phillip live in Austin, TX.

Shirley Faye was born in 1946. She married Joseph Thomas (see Thomas-Walker). Their only child, Jenny Lyn, married Brian Puryear (see Puryear-Thomas). Shirley and Joe live in Madisonville.

James farmed until 1957 when he and Rea bought into Grant's Motel and moved to Madisonville. James retired from the Postal Service in 1976 after holding the position of Postal Foreman.

Rea was employed by Kentucky Bank and served as Deputy Clerk at the Hopkins County Court House under Reba Free. Rea wrote a small novel entitled "Hillbilly Heritage" that was filled with events that her mother told of the time she lived in the Shakerag area. The book suggests that if we better understand one's heritage, we will better understand the person.

James and Rea are members of the Nebo Christian Church with James serving as Deacon, Elder and Bible teacher. - *Submitted by Rea Joyner Walker*

WALLER

The Waller family traces to Alured de Waller of Newark County Nottingham, who came to England with William the Conqueror and settled in Kent. His issue trace to Dr. John Waller of Newport Pagnell, England (1645-1723) and his son, Col. John Waller (1674-1754) was the first Waller emigrant to America about 1693 or 94 and settled in Spotsylvania Co., VA.

Col. John Waller's great grandson, Zephaniah Waller (1744-1797) received a land grant in Granville Co., NC on Nov. 13, 1788, for service in the Revolution and moved there about that time.

His son, Zephania Waller, Jr. married Nancy Forsythe on Dec. 18, 1804 and raised six children: Lucy, James, Squire, Lively, Barbara and Elizabeth.

My great-grandfather, Squire Waller was born Feb. 11, 1809. He married Feribah (or Feralda) Forsythe of Georgia on Dec. 2, 1832. They lived on the family farm in Granville Co., NC until about 1850 or 51, when they moved to Hopkins Co., KY where they settled on a farm in the Shakerag area near Olive Branch Church.

Squire and Feribah had ten children, six of whom were born in North Carolina: James (1836-1864), Lucy (1838-1870), Gillie (1840-?), Mary (1842-?), J. Smith (1846-1914), and Enoch (1849-1853). Their last four children were born in Kentucky: Nellie (b & d Oct. 5, 1853), Taylor (1850-?), Frances (1852-after 1880), and E. Frank (1855-1891).

James Waller was a C.S.A. volunteer, was commissioned a First Lt. and was killed near Canton, KY in 1864. His mother took a wagon and servant and brought his remains home for burial at Olive Branch Cemetery.

Gillie married Bartlett L. Gooch on Feb. 7, 1867. They had at least three children as shown in the 1880 census: James 10, George 9, and Cordia 4. James Gooch had at least three children, Bettie, Gillie, and Bartlett, but I am unable to trace them farther.

J. Smith and E. Waller both became physicians and practiced medicine in Hanson, KY from the late 1870's until their deaths.

Smith Waller married Bettie Ashby in 1882, and they had five children: Annie (1883-1899), Burnice (1885-1927), Dot (1889-1978), Lamont (1892-1983), and Ashby (1895-1972). Dot married Chesley W. Holloman and they had one son Chesley, Jr. who married Janet Wise. They have three children, Steven, Catherine and David.

E. Frank Waller married Rose Ashby (1865-1941) on Jan. 31, 1887. They had two children: Willoughby Forsythe Waller (who died as a child) and Miss Frank E. Waller (1892-1939). There is an interesting family story about this baby. Her father died of pneumonia several months before her birth. Roe was devastated over her young husband's death and swore to name the baby for him. The newborn was a female but got the name Frank anyway.

Miss Frank graduated from Georgetown College, married James Karr Ramsey II, and raised three children: J.K. III, Jane Waller, and Frank D. Frank Waller Ramsey is best remembered as a lifelong teacher of English in Madisonville High School and her public spirited civic, church and club work. Her husband is best remembered as a football coach and National Guard officer. They had three children, fourteen grandchildren, and five great grandchildren. (See Ramsey-Langley family for names)

Squire and Feribah Waller's issue thru the fifth generation number at least fifty, of whom at least twenty-four are living in six different states, but none carry the surname Waller. - *Submitted by James K. Ramsey, III great-grandson*

MISS FRANK WALLER

Why did Frank E. Waller, a female born Aug. 27, 1892 carry a man's name all her life? She was named for her father, a doctor who died of pneumonia, contracted tending and nursing his patients, at the age of 37 before mother was born. Mrs. Waller (nee Pernettia Ross "Rose" Ashby) swore to name the child she carried for her beloved late husband, and when a female child arrived she did just that. Almost 47 years later, Frank Waller Ramsey died of kidney failure Aug. 2, 1939. A life that began on a note of sadness and ended in a tragic untimely death, was nonetheless one of great service and benefit to humankind and of great fulfillment to her.

Miss Frank E. Waller

This is the story of the life of a very intelligent, energetic, compassionate woman who was a great teacher and a stalwart friend, a person who gave light and understanding to every life she touched.

Her grandparents were: P-Squire Waller and Feribah Forsythe, M-Josiah Jackson Ashby and Sarah Wheaton Ross. Her lineage includes Morton, Bordely, Dade, Davis, Henley, Strawbridge, Nelson and Boysman.

Miss Frank graduated with honors from Georgetown College in 1914 with a major in English Literature and began a teaching career that, except for time out for childbearing, lasted the rest of her life. In her almost 25 years of teaching she exerted a positive and beneficial influence on many hundreds of young people. Many of her students pursued teaching careers themselves, no doubt inspired by her example.

She was very active in civic affairs. In 1919, she wrote the constitution for the newly formed P.T.A., an outgrowth of the mother's club. She was a lifelong member of the First Methodist Church. She was an active leader in the Women's Club and in the American Legion Women's Auxiliary.

On Aug. 17, 1917 she married James Karr Ramsey II and of this union bore three children: James K. III born April 1919, Jane Waller born June 1923, and Frank D. born 1926.

James K. III married Marie Eba and had five children: James M., Nancy, Ella, Sue and Clara. They also have four grandchildren.

Jane Waller married Davis S. Morgan and had four children: Shannon, Frank, Leith and Martha. They also have one grandchild.

Frank D. married Josephine Creekmur and had five children: Patricia, Robin, Steven, Terrence and Jane. He and his present wife, Betty, have no issue. (See also Ramsey) - *Submitted by James K. Ramsey III*

WALLER-PETSCH

Eddie and Emelia Waller came from Guthrie to Hopkins County about 1900. He worked for the L & N Railroad in Earlington until the strike in the early 1920's.

Edward Elmo and Emelia Eliza (Petsch) Waller about 1930

EDWARD ELMO (1867-1932), born in Montgomery Co., TN, was descended from the Virginia Waller's who came from England in the mid 1600's. His father John W. born in Tennessee, married Fredonia Neblett, daughter of Jordon and Mary. His Grandfather, Alfred from Virginia married Rebecca Parham in Todd Co., KY. Alfred taught school in Todd County about 1830.

EMELIA ELIZA (1872-1934) was born in Wisconsin of parents from Germany. Her father, Ferdinand Petsch came with his parents at age two in 1845. Louisa (Rex) came in 1855 at age eleven. (A younger sister died on the trip and was buried at sea.) Both families settled in Wisconsin. Ferdinand served with the Volunteers of Lebanon in the Civil War. In 1885 he brought his family to Christian County. Emelia was then thirteen, third in the family of nine. One brother died in Hopkinsville at age nine.

Emelia and Eddie were married in Hopkinsville in 1894, but lived most of their adult life in Earlington, (Hopkins County), KY.

Eddie and Emelia raised five children and helped raise six granddaughters.

1. AURELIA ELIZABETH (1895-1966) m.- John W. Henify (1886-1952) A. John Edward Henify (1913-1914) (died at 13 months) B. Helen Louise Henify (1916-) m. Charlie Eugene Wilcox (1910-1954) a. Charles Eugene (1943-) b. David Edward (1949-) C. Norma V. Henify (1921-) m. Francis Bernard Weakley a. Gerald Bernard (1946-) b. Susan Elizabeth (1949-).

2. JOHN FERDINAND (1898-1973) m. 1- Lallah Atkinson, 2-Jackie Malaier A. Frances

Back row l to r: Frieda Louise Waller, Emelia (Mammaw) Waller, Norma V. Henify and Sarah Emelia Waller. Front row: Helen Louise Henify, Hilda Lee Waller and Mary Elizabeth Waller

Winiferd (1919-one day)

3. WILLIE EDWARD (1899-1929) m. Ethel Mae Greer (Willie was killed in a mine accident February 1929) A. Frieda Louise (1919-) m. three times. a. David Edward b. Angela Carol c. William R. (twin) d. Robert W. (twin) e. Jacqueline; B. Sarah Emelia (1920-) m. three times a. Roberta Jean b. Frances Lynn c. Wayne E. d. Crystal e. Anita f. Kenneth; C. Mary Elizabeth (Libby) (1922-) m. Carl Baker, Tracy Humphrey a. Jack Elvis b. Mary Alice c. William E.; D. Hilda Lee (1924-) m. Joe Simpson a. Deanna Lee b. Dennis Earl c. John Daryl.

4. CHARLIE THOMAS (1901-1965) m. Flora Lee Hale A. John Elmo (1931-one day); B. Janet Lee (1933-) m. Myron Baker a. Sarah Janelle (1972-); C. Charles Hale (1938) m. twice a. Jeffery Scott b. Jennifer Lynn c. Christina; D. Robert Thomas (1949-) m. twice

5. ARNOLD ELMO (1907-1983) m. Evelyn Conyers A. Emelia Thomas (1940-); B. Patsy Arnold (1942-).

Edward and Emelia were members of the Christian Church in Earlington, and were honorable citizens, loved by relatives, friends and neighbors. Some of Emelia's nieces said their ambition was to be like "Aunt Emelia". I can also think of no higher compliment.

Emelia was "Mammaw" to six beloved and loving granddaughters, as she and Granddaddy did not live to enjoy the later grandchildren. Many were the times they had some or all of those six little girls in their charge.

As a loving memory those girls, (now Mothers and Grandmothers) have memories of times with "Mammaw and Granddaddy". There were lessons learned, German jingles, small chores, stories told and lots of HUGS and KISSES. Few punishments can be remembered, but Granddaddy was held in a bit of "AWE".

"Mammaw and Granddaddy" will live in memory as long as those girls live, hopefully they will have passed on to their children and grandchildren some of those joyous times when they were little girls. - *In loving memory Helen L. (Henify) Wilcox*

WALTON-BURTON

William Walton was born in Barnsley, Yorkshire, England in 1847, came to America and settled in Hopkins Co. He worked in the mines in and around Hopkins Co. William suffered a very serious injury to his eyes in a mine explosion in Newburgh, IN. As a result he could not blink or close his eyes, so he wore goggles. After the mine explosion, he returned to England in 1868 expecting to go blind. But he returned to America and did not let his injury defeat him. The average man would have given up, but not him. He went on to own his own coal company in Walton City, later to be named Barnsley, KY after the city he came from in England. He owned Waltons Bitters in Earlington in 1877. William was a sheet organ player as well as a concertina player. He died in 1903 in Earlington, KY and is buried in Oakwood Cemetery.

William Walton in Japan in 1882

His most remarkable feat was taking a trip around the world in 1882. Not many people in that day and age could claim this. In 1879 he had the idea to go around the world. In 1882 he started and as he was getting ready to leave Earlington an American flag was given him as a tourist flag and he carried and unfolded it in every country he was in. He went by train to San Francisco, CA and took a ship to Japan. He met and traveled with a Mr. Blackleigh from Philadelphia, a religious man that was traveling for a religious society. I wish I had room to tell about his travels, people, their way of life, things he saw and what he endured in his travels. One time he went for a swim and returning from the water someone had stolen his money and his hat was full of mud. He was given two nails by two Jewish friends to drive in the walls of Solomon's Temple. Mr. Bingham, the American Minister of Japan presented him with a Japanese flag and a ticket from Mocado to visit the Empress private park. This pass was considered sacred as it was from the hands of Macado. William returned to Earlington, KY in 1883 and kept a journal of his travels that is now being put together by his granddaughter, Nina Walton Laffoon Dunn.

William married Amelica Catherine Burton on July 30, 1872 (born Sept. 15, 1844 and died Sept. 12, 1885). They had two children, William Henry and Thomas and one adopted son Oscar Riley. Thomas died in 1879, Oscar was killed in Montana in 1907. William Henry lived in Earlington and Barnsley. William then married Margaret Lantrip on Apr. 2, 1886. Their children were, Bernard (born 1888) and Catherine (Kate) (born 1892). Kate is still living in Kissimmee, FL.

William's oldest son, William Henry, born 1872, worked for the mines as a night watchman until the 1930's. He married Edna Green

William and Amelica Burton Walton

in June 1893. She died Feb. 1898. They had one son, Johnny born Sept. 30, 1894 and died Oct. 25, 1957.

William Henry then married Cannie Burns on July 5, 1909. She died Dec. 25, 1942. They had ten children, five are still living: Arnold (b. 1911), Nina (b. 1921), Magadlene (b. 1923), Hazel (b. 1930) and Earnest (b. 1933).

William Henry died in Madisonville, KY Jan. 28, 1958 after working and living a lifetime of memories of his father coming from England and of joys and defeats in Earlington and Barnsley, KY. He is buried in Oakwood Cemetery in Earlington. - *Submitted by Nina Walton Laffoon Dunn*

JOHN BIVEN WALTRIP

My grandfather, John Biven Waltrip, moved to Hopkins County about 1885, and purchased a farm. He was born Sept. 1, 1840 in McLean Co., the second son of James and Martha Biven Waltrip. His older brother, James Madison, was a Civil War soldier, but John stayed home, took care of the family farm, his aged father, step-mother (Lucy Wall) and half-sisters, Mary and Martha. Older sisters - Sophia Ann married Bob Brown, lived in Hopkins Co. and Delila married Clayton Steffy, lived in Henderson.

John Biven Waltrip

John B. Waltrip and Elizabeth S. Bidwell were married in McLean Co. Nov. 22, 1865 at the home of her parents, John and Mary Vickers Bidwell. They lived south of Rumsey, farming and raising their large family, until the move to Hopkins Co. Sadly, they left six small graves behind. Their children were Martin Alonzo born Nov. 22, 1866; James Madison born June 15, 1868; William G. born Mar. 13, 1870; Mattie born Sept.20, 1871; Robert born Sept. 20, 1873; Mary Elizabeth "Mollie" born Jan. 23, 1875; Luke born July 2, 1877; Rufus born Dec. 13, 1879; Ruth born Aug. 20, 1881; Florence born Aug. 13, 1883; Worth born Oct. 22, 1884; Walter born Oct. 7, 1886; and (my father) John Bidwell born Feb. 22, 1889. Of these, Mollie (only girl), the three oldest sons, Lon, Jim, Will and the three youngest sons, Worth, Walter, John lived to maturity.

World War II soldiers, an Ohio Co., KY Company 1) Bell 2) John Bidwell Waltrip of Madisonville 3) Hardin 4) Tichenor and 5) Carter

During the early farming years, the family attended Rose Creek Baptist Church. Sometime before 1900, they moved to Madisonville and built a home on Broadway. Grandfather opened a grocery store and ran it about 27 years, until he was in his 80's. The oldest son, Lon, who had always worked in the store, continued in the grocery until retirement.

Lon married Leslie Edwards, had Ancil Edwards who married Josephine Clark. Jim married Sallie Bailey, had Frank, Horace, Davis, Hewlett, and Elizabeth. Jim married 2nd to Alberta Waltrip Horton. Will married Vaden Hanner, had Ruth who married Dr. Wm. Garrot. Mollie married James H. McFarland, had Richard Owen, Roscoe and John David. Worth married Emma Wilson, had Russell and Marjorie. Walter married Coralee Payne, Nebo, had Mildred, Louis and Walter Claude. John married Versa Hart, had Betty and Mary Ann, lived in Louisville.

Grandfather was an interesting man, who loved to tell a good story. When older, his hair and flowing mustache were white as snow. He would talk of his youth saying that his hair had been as "black as the raven's wing". Waltrip men were dark-skinned and black-headed, denoting their Welsh ancestry. He declared Waltrips back in Wales had been "Black Catholics", but no explanation of this is known.

John Biven Waltrip died Apr. 6, 1932 and was buried in Odd Fellows Cemetery. "Bettie" Bidwell Waltrip was born Jan. 19, 1847 and died Feb. 18, 1914, and lies buried by her husband's side.

The following poem was written in memory of John Biven Waltrip by his daughter-in-law, Mrs. Worth Waltrip.

GRANDPA
by Emma Wilson Waltrip

They speak of him softly, they say that he's gone,
They carried him out at the door,
And buried him low in the valley so still,
He'll never be there any more.

But how can he be gone yet move as before,
Now hither, now yon through each room?
Revealed he at night by the fire as of yore?
I sit with him there in the gloom.

Together we walk down the path to the barn.
Or tarry awhile at the well.
His dimming eyes kindle as always they did,
When some bit of nonsense I'd tell.

At morning, in springtime, he's evident too,
As out in the garden he plods,
And later at ease in the rocking chair tall
Where over a paper he nods.

Now humble, with bowed head he tenders his thanks
For blessings, allotments of food.
E'er sighing or frowning of sorrowing, glad
He lingers, disclosing each mood.

And so I just smile when they say he is gone
Lies low in the valley so still.
He hovers and potters there round the old place.
I know, I'm there with him at will.
- *Submitted by Betty Waltrip Irwin (Mrs. W. Fred)*

PEARL GENEVA WARINNER

Pearl Geneva Warinner, born Feb. 1, 1889 in Madisonville, was the fifth of seven children born to George W. Warinner (Jr.) and Susan Mariah Lutz. George Warinner (Jr.), born Sept. 19, 1857 in Russell Co. was the son of George W. Warinner (Sr.) and Mary 'Polly' Jones. Susan Lutz, born Sept. 5, 1860 in Hopkins County was the youngest child of Jacob Lutz (Jr.) and Matilda Osburn, both born in Nelson County. Matilda was the first child of Isaac Osburn by his first wife, Jane Threlkile. Jacob Lutz (Jr.) was the son of Jacob Lutz (Sr.), native of Pennsylvania and Mary Catherine Mathis of Maryland.

In 1845 Isaac Osburn sold his properties in Nelson County, gathered up most of his children, including Matilda and her husband Jacob Lutz, their families, and moved to Hopkins County.

About 1877 George Warinner (Jr.) and his brother James came to Hopkins County, bought land and raised tobacco. George was also a carpenter and butcher.

On Nov. 25, 1878 George eloped with Susan Lutz to Shawneetown, IL, where they were married. During the next eleven years George opened his first meat market called The White House Market, and built a home for his family at 730 Hanson Road, Madisonville. He later

Sitting: Geo. W. Warinner and wife Susan M. (Lutz), Thos. Everett and wife Nina and daughter Gladys. Standing: Roxie J., Esmer A., Docia M., Pearl G. and Grace M., 1905

opened another meat market called G.W. Warinner & Son. Susan died Oct. 27, 1925. George died Jan. 31, 1940. Both are buried in Odd Fellows Cemetery, Madisonville. Their children were: Thomas Everett, Grace Madeline, William George, Docia Marie, Pearl Geneva, Roxie Jane, and Esma Ann.

On June 15, 1906 in Nashville, TN Pearl Geneva Warinner married Roy Leslie Browning, son of Columbus M. and Georgia (Patterson) Browning of Earlington. Their daughter Louise Alcott was born Apr. 15, 1907 in Earlington. A dispute arose causing a divorce. Pearl and Louise lived with Pearl's parents. Pearl helped her father with his bookkeeping and banking, plus she was an excellent dress designer and seamstress, making beautiful dresses and hats, which earned her a comfortable living.

In 1915 she met Iver William Wahl, a native of Sweden. They were married Nov. 1, 1915 in Memphis, TN, making their home in Greenville, MS where their daughter Ruth Evelyn was born Aug. 16, 1916. Iver enlisted in World War I. When he returned home he found Pearl's health ailing, so moved his family to Denver, CO where the air was beneficial to Pearl's health. Their son, Iver William II, was born Aug. 23, 1923. A year later they moved to Colorado Springs where their son, Karl Gene, was born Sept. 20, 1925.

Pearl and Iver lived in Colorado Springs the rest of their married life. Iver died May 10, 1960. Pearl Geneva lived alone until 1972 when she moved to Boulder, CO to live with her son Iver and his family. She died there Oct. 27, 1972. Both are buried in Evergreen Cemetery, Colorado Springs.

Pearl Geneva's descendants now total seventeen. Four children: Mrs. Louise Umfress, Mrs. Ruth Laughlin, Iver Wahl II, and Karl Wahl. Five grandchildren: Raymond Haig, Mrs. Norma Rinck, Michael Wahl, Mrs. Eileen Gardner, and Mrs. Stephanie Heulitt. Eight great grandchildren: Michael & Suzanne Rinck, Kol Wahl, Sean McCullough, Rebecca Gardner, Heidi, Jonathan, & Jason Gamer. - *Prepared by Mrs. Ruth Wahl Laughlin*

WARNER-STEVENS-CRUNK

Henry Warner was born Mar. 31, 1835 in Tennessee and died Aug. 19, 1904 in Hopkins Co., KY. He married Sarah Jane Putman, who was born Aug. 22, 1838 in Tennessee and died Sept. 18, 1905 in Hopkins Co. They were married in Tennessee and came to Hopkins Co. after 1860. Sarah Jane was the daughter of William and Anna G. Putman. The children of Sarah Jane and Henry were: Tabitha, Sarah Jane, John Henry, William D., Dorcie, Dovey, Nora and Beth Warner.

Sarah Jane Warner, born Mar. 4, 1860 in Tennessee and died June 3, 1942 in Indianapolis, IN, married Dec. 18, 1874 in Muhlenberg Co., KY to Franklin Green Stevens. He was born in 1849 in Tennessee and died in 1888. He was the son of Thomas and Mary (Little) Stevens. The children of Green and Sarah Jane were: Henry Thomas, Ida Bell, Forest and Green Franklin Stevens Jr.

Sarah Jane married second Thomas Hogan on Mar. 12, 1889. Their children were: Effie, William, Hanson and Myrtle Hogan.

Henry Thomas Stevens, born Sept. 16, 1875 died Dec. 23, 1939, married Ollie Frances Crunk, born Mar. 9, 1881 died July 7, 1951. Her parents were Nicholas and Sarah Jane Temperance (Patterson) Crunk. The children of Henry and Ollie were: Pearl, Vitula, Lelear, Maude, Nelson, Tiney, Grace, Henry, Irene, Flody and Chester Stevens.

Children of Nicholas and Sarah J.T. (Patterson) Crunk were: Dora, Nancy, James William, Ollie Frances, Frank and Rosie Crunk. This family is a descendant of the very early families of Knowles, Giles, Perkins and Scales of Virginia.

Nicholas Crunk was first married to Adaline Boyce. Their children were: George M. and Mary E. Crunk.

Pearl Stevens was born Dec. 13, 1896 and died Sept. 3, 1951 in Christian Co., KY. She married Basil Tyson who was born Apr. 11, 1894 in Muhlenberg Co., KY and died Oct. 13, 1966 in Christian Co., KY. He was the son of Wiley Mason and Eva Alice (Grace) Tyson. Children of Basil and Pearl (Stevens) Tyson were: Hershel (dec'd), Altabee, Frances, Ozella, Dorothy, Esmarelda, Sylvada, Osbyron, Germaine, Donald and Terra Tyson.

Sylvada Tyson was born in Christian Co., KY. She married Jim Burke who was born in Trigg Co., KY. They are the parents of three children: James Steven Burke married Aug. 4, 1979 to Sherrill N. Barber of Graves Co., KY. They have one child, Steven Scott Burke age five, and are expecting another one in January of 1988; Janet Allyson Burke married Feb. 12, 1980 to Michael A. Green. They have one child, Shelly Yvette Green and live in Waco, TX; Sylvia Gaye Burke who just finished high school and lives at home.

For more on these family lines see Palmer-Grace-Tyson. - *Submitted by Sylvada T. Burke*

GEORGE L. WEATHERLY

George Lawson Weatherly was born Nov. 7, 1815 in Philadelphia, PA. He was one of seven children born to David Weatherly, who was born in Scotland, and Mary Lawson Weatherly, who was born in Maryland.

In 1848, George came to Hopkins County. On May 14, 1849, he married Mary Elizabeth Lynn. They were the parents of a daughter, Mary E., born June 26, 1853 and who died in infancy. The date of the death of Mary Elizabeth, the mother, is not known.

George Lawson Weatherly

On Dec. 3, 1856, George married Lorenda C. Bone (Apr. 11, 1828-May 2, 1858). They were the parents of a son, George, who died July 20, 1858 at the age of 9 months. Lorenda and the son are buried at Union Cemetery in Nebo.

On Oct. 4, 1859 in Logan Co., KY, George married Henrietta Johnson (Mar. 17, 1837-Dec. 10, 1873). Henrietta was born in Logan County, the daughter of William L. Johnson (1797-1860) and Nancy Ann Johnson (1820-1872) who were married in Logan County on Jan. 21, 1819. William and Nancy are buried in the William L. Johnson Cemetery in Logan County.

The children of George and Henrietta were: Mary (1860-1944) who married Thomas Wright Gardiner on Apr. 13, 1886 in Hopkins County (see Thomas Wright Gardiner article); Isabel (Belle) (1862-1933) who married John B. Harvey on Mar. 28, 1878 in Hopkins County (see Harvey-Weatherly); Willie (1865-1868); Ellen (Ellie) (1867-1933) never married; and Sherman (1868-1947) who married Corey Jurey of Pee Wee Valley, KY, he was an L & N employee for 50 years working his way up from messenger boy to Superintendent of Perishable Freight, and had one child, Elizabeth, who married but had no children.

George was a grocer in Madisonville and was a member of the Odd Fellows Lodge.

On Friday, Mar. 17, 1882 at approximately 8 p.m., as George was on his way home from his business, someone came up from behind him and hit him on the back of the head. Being found by some citizens of Madisonville, he was taken to his home and Drs. Gardiner and Ross were summoned. He died at about 10 p.m. His murder remained unsolved but the motive was thought to be robbery.

George and Henrietta and their three daughters are buried in Odd Fellows Cemetery in Madisonville. Sources: Vital Stats of Hopkins Co., KY; marriage records; Obit. of George L. Weatherly; and information from Margaret Berry. - *Submitted by Margaret Berry, written by Debbie Knight Hammonds*

WELCH-SISK

Ida Blanche was born in Barnsley, KY on Apr. 15, 1918. She is the 2nd child of Margaret and Thompson Hamby Sisk. She is a member of the Immaculate Conception Church and attended the Immaculate Conception School until the 5th grade. Then she transferred to St. Vincent Academy in Waverly, KY where she graduated.

Thomas and Ida Blanche Welch with children Thomas James, Margaret and Willie

In 1940, she met Thomas Felix Welch at the Nortonville bus station ticket window where Thomas was working as a ticket agent. Ida Blanche was buying a book of tickets for that month's fare. Although she was with several other young ladies, Thomas directed all of his conversation to her. The girls tried to tell her that Thomas was interested in her, but Ida Blanche didn't really think so until he sent a friend, Carl Barnes, to tell her that he wanted a date with her that Sunday. Even without an invitation he came that Sunday. After a year of steady courtship, they were married at Immaculate Conception Church rectory with the Rev. George Boehmicke officiating on Apr. 20, 1941. To this union three children were born: Thomas James, Margaret Elizabeth, and William Augustus.

Thomas Felix Welch was born in Daniel Boone near St. Charles, KY on Oct. 23, 1904. He was the 5th child of George Irvin Welch born in Nortonville, KY and Elizabeth Jane Price born in Duquion, IL. Thomas was thin, about 5 feet 4 inches, ruddy complexion with beautiful blue eyes and thin brown hair. He always wore a long sleeved grey shirt, that he would turn up two times in the summer because of the heat and brown pants with suspenders. In the winter he added a corduroy sports coat to his attire. He wore a brown felt hat year round that provided shade for him in the summer and warmth in the winter.

Thomas went to work at a country mine at the young age of fourteen to help support his mother after his father's death. He later worked at a restaurant and Norton Coal Mines in Nortonville and West Kentucky's East and North Diamond mines near Madisonville.

Thomas loved his children and to their delight, he would buy them a hamburger and soft drink every Saturday and maybe a trip to the movie at the Earl. One cold day, the children insisted upon shooting a roman candle. Thomas figured the best way to keep warm would be to open a window and shoot the candle from inside the house. A great plan, but when the grass caught on fire, he had to go outside anyway to put out the fire. One Christmas Day, Thomas sat smoking his pipe in front of the fireplace. Thomas James with his new drum, Willie, Margaret and cousin Nadie were marching around Thomas playing. How Thomas enjoyed watch the children play, not just on Christmas but everyday.

After Thomas' death, Ida Blanche raised the three children by working at the Immaculate Conception rectory for many years. - *Submitted by Karol Durham Welch*

JESSE C. WELLS

Many hot summers ago, as was the custom when neighbors got together to cut wheat, Frances Woodward and a friend were sent to the fields with a bucket of cool water for the workers. Jesse Wells, a good-looking young lad, lay on the top of a stack of bagged wheat taking a short rest. When Frances saw him she decided she wanted a better look so she pulled on the wheat bags and they cam tumbling down and Jesse too. Thus began their acquaintance and their courtship. Five years later they were married and have resided in Morton's Gap for the past 45 years.

The Jesse Wells family

They have one son, Ed, who lives in Princeton, KY with his wife Ruthie, a son Jesse Ray, 24, who is a member of the rock band "Gun Runners" and a daughter Tammy who is a freshman at M.S.U. Ed is Vice-President of Hicks Dollar General Corporation.

They have four daughters: Melinda Smith, who lives in Nortonville with her two sons, Trent age 13 and Mark age 11. Melinda, nicknamed "Skeeter", is the school bus driving instructor for Hopkins County Board of Education.

Joy, married to Rev. Mark Whicker, is a housewife and the mother of two sons, Jason 5 and Joshua 3. They reside in Beechmont, KY where her husband pastors Beech Creek Baptist Church.

Delena, married to Tracy Daves, has one son Brandon age 4 and lives in Madisonville. She is on the executive staff of the Hopkins County YMCA where she is Associate Program Director.

Dianna, who is a twin to Delena, is single and lives at home with her parents. She is also employed at the Hopkins County Family YMCA.

Many years have passed since that hot summer day in the wheat field and God has richly blessed our family. Jesse is now a retired coal miner and he and Frances attend Salem Missionary Baptist Church in Morton's Gap. - *Submitted by Melinda Smith*

WHITFIELD-ASHBY

Phinie Ruby Whitfield, Sr. was born Sept. 18, 1888 and died Apr. 5, 1949. He married Naomi Irvin Ashby on Dec. 25, 1910. Naomi was born Dec. 12, 1890 and died Nov. 3, 1982. Rube was a carpenter and one of his last jobs was helping his son, P.R., build his home in White Plains, KY. Naomi was a school teacher. She lived in Hanson and rode the train from Madisonville to Nortonville to teach at the Dillingham School, Mt. Carmel School, Bailey School, and Whitfield School, all in the Nortonville and White Plains area. While teaching she met and married Rube. She continued to teach until about 1918. Rube and Naomi were members of the First Baptist Church in White Plains, KY. They are buried at Concord Cemetery.

Their children are: Etoile, born Oct. 17, 1911; Loyce, born Sept. 7, 1913 and died Nov. 21, 1918; Phinie Ruby, Jr. (P.R.), born July 3, 1918; Mary Elizabeth, born Mar. 8, 1924; David Cole, born May 28, 1925 and killed while serving in the Navy during World War II on Feb. 21, 1945; and Carroll, born Feb. 12, 1934. Etoile married Melber Moore, born Mar. 30, 1912, died Dec. 11, 1978. They had children: Thomas, who died at birth, Bobby, Carolyn, and Patricia. P.R. married Agnes Putman, who was born Apr. 13, 1920. They have two daughters, Henrietta and Pamela. Mary Elizabeth married Robert Knowles, born Dec. 22, 1923. They have one son, Larry. David Cole married Ramona Bedwell, born June 13, 1926. They have a son, Ronald. Carroll married Laurel Grace, born May 25, 1933. They have two daughters, Belinda and Tina.

Rube was the first-born child of Needham Whitfield and Harriet Dillingham. Needham was born June 28, 1863 and died Dec. 11, 1935. Harriet was born July 22, 1867 and died Feb. 20, 1936. Their children were also: David, married Mamie Ashby, sister of Naomi; Helen, unmarried; Elizabeth, married L.H. Cavanaugh; Jackson, married Renna Moore Latham; Ruth, married Fred Mercer; Welby, married first Ethel Gray, second Ruth Smith; Ollie married W.E. Roberts; and Thomas, married first Hazel Fowler, second Elizabeth Guge Gibson, and third Gladys Murfin West.

The Whitfield family can be traced back to William Whitfield who was born in England in 1688. He travelled in his own ship, "The Providence", to Nansemonie, VA where he settled in the early part of the century.

Naomi was the daughter of Junius Ashby and Vida Blanche Ashby. Junius was born Oct. 4, 1857 and died Mar. 30, 1897. Vida was born Aug. 27, 1871 and died Feb. 12, 1902. Their other children were: Hershel, married Charlie Howard Barr; Mamie, married David Whitfield; and June, married Jack Pressley. Junius first married Celest Ashby, born Dec. 20, 1866 and died Dec. 10, 1884. They had a son Garnett, who married Anna Lewis Hayes. Celest and Vida were sisters, daughters of Prather and Celia Ashby.

Naomi descended from Thomas Ashby, born about 1680 and died 1752 in Frederick Co., VA. - *Submitted by Laurel Whitfield*

WHITFIELD-JACKSON

Otho Gay Whitfield and Mary Alice Jackson were married Apr. 9, 1938, in the home of Rev. E.S. Moore in Sebree, KY. Mary is the daughter of W.M. Jackson and Lula Mae Bloomer. All three were born in Trigg Co., KY.

Their only child, Anthony Gay (Tony)

Tony and Otho Gay Whitfield

Whitfield was born in Hopkins County Hospital Feb. 26, 1941. He is a Georgetown College Graduate and has served as Minister of Music and Youth in four different Baptist Churches in Evansville, IN, Louisville, KY, Knoxville, TN and Lone Oak Church in Paducah, KY. He is now a professor in the Music Department at Georgetown College. He was married to Georgann Hamrick in Frankfort, KY, Dec. 22, 1961. They have two children, Alice Catherine Wright and Anthony Gay Whitfield, Jr., who is in the U.S. Navy stationed aboard U.S.S. San Diego Aircraft Carrier. Alice was married to Joe Wright in Paducah, KY. They have one daughter, Catherine Ann Wright, and now reside in Arnold, MO.

Georgann, Otho Gay, Mary Alice, Tony Jr., Alice, Joe and Ann

Otho Gay's sister is Myra Preston and their parents were E. Pratt Whitfield and Maggie Mae Oates who were married Mar. 16, 1904. Maggie's parents were Dr. Richard M. Oates, born Apr. 8, 1851, died Aug. 3, 1899 and Virginia Murphy, born Feb. 28, 1861, died Nov. 17, 1891. Maggie was born in Granbury, TX, Sept. 14, 1884, died in Nortonville, KY, Oct. 15, 1933. E. Pratt Whitfield born Jan. 6, 1883, died Sept. 13, 1942. His parents were W.H. Whitfield, born May 19, 1849, died Aug. 23, 1924 and Maggie M. Oates, born Dec. 23, 1853, died Jan. 8, 1931. W.H. Whitfield's parents were I.K. Whitfield, born Apr. 15, 1822, died Sept. 28, 1900, and Narcissus Whitfield, born Feb. 28, 1826, died Sept. 28, 1905. They moved from North Carolina to White Plains, KY, Route #1 and bought several hundred acres of land at the above address and left each child they had a farm. They also gave land and a wrought iron fence for Whitfield's Cemetery and built Whitfield's Schoolhouse which does not exist now. This area was known as Whitfield's Settlement. *Submitted by Otho Gay Whitfield*

JOSEPH E. WHITFIELD

Joseph Edwin Whitfield was born Mar. 18, 1856. He was the fourth of nine children of Lewis B. Whitfield and Charity Outlaw Whitfield who were some of the earliest settlers of Hopkins County from North Carolina.

Joseph Edwin and Mary Ollie Whitfield

On Jan. 22, 1880, in Hopkins County, he married Mary Ollie Blades. To this union were born eleven children: James Edwin born May 3, 1881, Leonard Lewis born Nov. 29, 1883, Willie Pearl born May 30, 1886, Tommy Clarence born May 9, 1888, Myrtle Alice born Dec. 11, 1896, Elmer Bryan born Jan. 18, 1899, Rev. Iley Melton born Mar. 22, 1904, Alice M. born in 1896, Arnold Jewel born Aug. 18, 1890, Effie May, and Dr. Fran born in 1894.

Records show that Joseph Whitfield owned land on Drakes Creek. He was a farmer in Hopkins County for many years. He suffered several personal losses, the first being when his first-born James Edwin died five months after birth. His son Tommy Clarence died at age one and daughter Willie Pearl died at age four. After 24 years of marriage, his wife Mary Ollie died on Apr. 4, 1904. She was buried in New Salem Cemetery in Nortonville next to their three children who preceded her in death.

On Sept. 28, 1907 he married Geneva Smith of White Plains, KY. To this union was born one daughter, Aubrey.

Joseph E. Whitfield died on Mar. 5, 1931 and was buried in Concord Cemetery near White Plains. Joseph's will was probated on Apr. 6, 1931. All of the property was bequeathed to his wife Geneva. The mineral and oil rights, under said property were divided equally between all his children. - *Submitted by Craig A. Whitfield*

GEORGE W. WHITSELL

George Williamson (G.W.) Whitsell, was born May 5, 1853, in the Slaughtersville area of Hopkins County that in 1860 became a part of Webster Co., KY. He was the oldest of ten children of William George Whitsell (b. Oct. 13, 1826, Oglethorpe Co., GA) and Margaret (Margy) Frances Crews (b. July 9, 1835; d. Oct. 23, 1931).

His paternal grandparents, Elizabeth and George Whitsell, came to Kentucky from Oglethorpe Co., GA in 1830. The Whitsell family is of German ancestry. His maternal grandparents, Margaret Marks and Williamson Crews, also came from Oglethorpe Co., GA. His brothers and sisters were: John, Monroe, Margie, Sallie, David, Nancy, and Martha (d. infancy), Henry Powell and Andrew Jackson, who both died young.

As a youngster, G.W. began farm chores. He

George W. Whitsell, 89 and great grandson George Louis Oates III, 3 on their birthday May 5, 1942

often spoke of seeing Civil War soldiers running through the field he was plowing when he was 12 years old. As an adult, he continued farming.

On Sept. 2, 1875, he married Laura Coffman, who died circa 1876, after their daughter Inez Mabell Whitsell was born. Inez lived with her maternal grandparents. On Mar. 2, 1881, G.W. married Mary Catherine (Cannady) Jennings, a widow with two sons, Wiley and Kelly Jennings. She was a daughter of David Cannady (b. July 11, 1829; d. at age 104) and Sarah Ann Price. G.W. and Mary Catherine had six children: s. Jessie Forrest and d. Effie Marie, twins; sons James David (J.D.) and George Herbert, and daughters Ida Belle and Lula Catherine "Kate".

About 1906 the family moved to Hopkins Co. In 1911 G.W. bought 25 acres on Brown Road and lived there until January 1916, when he purchased a farm on Frostburg Road along Pond River and moved to the main dwelling and George Herbert (b. Apr. 8, 1894; d. Jan. 25, 1950) who still worked for his father after he married (Oct. 7, 1915) Mattie Mae McGary (See W.T. McGary Family) lived in a smaller house. Here their first daughter, Mary Nell Whitsell, was born July 10, 1916. Herbert had left the farm and was a miner when the other daughter, Mildred Louise Whitsell, was born Aug. 4, 1919, in Webster Co.

In 1920 G.W. disposed of the Frostburg Road property and bought several acres in the Maple Grove sub-division south of Madisonville, on Earlington Pike. There he had an apple orchard, a large grape arbor and good crop land. His wife, Mary Catherine Cannady (b. Dec. 27, 1853) died there Aug. 28, 1921. Following her death, Herbert and family lived with his father until after Mary Nell started to school in 1922.

G.W. then married Florence Wilson, Grayson Co., who shared his love for farm life. As the population grew toward Earlington, he sold part of his land and disposed of his livestock, but continued to raise a large vegetable garden until he was 90 years old. He died June 8, 1944, age 91. "Miss Florence" lived in the homeplace until shortly before she died July 22, 1959.

Their garden spot was where Imperial House restaurant now stands and The Exotic Florist occupies their two-story dwelling.

A tradition remembered by grandchildren was the family reunions each May with basket dinners in the shade of the four maple trees on the front lawn.

George Williamson Whitsell, a member of Salem Primitive Baptist Church, Madisonville, was buried in Odd Fellows Cemetery. Source: Family records, Oral history and Public records. (See Oates-Whitsell) - *Submitted by Mary Nell (Whitsell) Oates*

DAVID WHITTINGHILL

David Whittinghill was the son of John and Elizabeth Cooper Whittinghill. He was born June 9, 1819 on his parents' farm in Ohio Co., KY. He spent his childhood on this farm, attending schools in the area.

Margaret Phillips Whittinghill and David Whittinghill

On Feb. 19, 1843, in Ohio Co., KY, David Whittinghill married Margaret Phillips, daughter of Solomon and Juda Cooney Phillips. Margaret was born Mar. 20, 1821. She died Apr. 7, 1881 and is buried in Odd Fellows Cemetery on West Center Street in Madisonville.

After David and Margaret were married, they lived for several years in Hancock Co., KY.

In 1856 David was licensed to preach by the Panther Creek Baptist Church. On Nov. 31, 1857, he was ordained to the ministry.

The Whittinghills moved to Hopkins Co., KY in 1864 and purchased a farm near Manitou. During the years of 1864-1868 David Whittinghill served as pastor of the Pleasant Grove Baptist Church on Rose Creek Road in Hopkins County. In 1868, the Whittinghills moved to Henderson, KY, where they resided for three years.

In 1871 the Whittinghills returned to their farm near Manitou. David served as pastor of the Liberty Baptist Church in Hopkins County in the years 1872 and 1873. During the years 1874 and 1875, David served as pastor of Madisonville First Baptist Church.

After Margaret died, David Whittinghill married Martha Haden Carpenter on Mar. 14, 1883 in Union Co., KY. Martha was born in 1830, in Oldham Co., KY.

David Whittinghill was pastor of Liberty Baptist Church at the time of its reconstitution in 1883, serving until 1889. He was also pastor of Liberty from 1895 through 1898. Among other churches that David Whittinghill served as pastor were Slaughtersville Baptist Church, Richland Baptist Church and Harmony Baptist Church. Records show that he was still preaching as late as Mar. 31, 1900.

David and Margaret Phillips Whittinghill were the parents of eleven children: Silas W. born in 1845; Josephine born Aug. 24, 1846, married (1) Solomon Lyons and (2) I.T. Osburn; John Solomon born May 8, 1848, married (1) Genoa Gooch (2) Florence Lyle and (3) Mrs. Amelia Lindsay; James W. born Jan. 22, 1850, married Mary Harrington; Vitula (Vida) born 1852 married James N. Kosure; David Cicero born Mar. 18, 1854; Charles P. born 1856 married Mary (Macy) Givens; Rufus T. born 1858 married Mary Adams; Dudley B. born 1860; Dexter Gooch born 1866 married Susan Taylor (They were Southern Baptist missionaries to Italy for thirty eight years.); and Robert C. born 1868 married Melissa Polk.

David Whittinghill died July 7, 1901 and is buried in Odd Fellows Cemetery on West Center Street in Madisonville, KY. - *Compiled by Beverly H. Dockrey*

WILCOX-HENIFY

CHARLIE EUGENE WILCOX was born Aug. 15, 1910 in McHenry, Ohio County, and died Nov. 5, 1954 in Madisonville, KY at age 44. He was the son of Daniel S. and Ola (Raley) Wilcox.

Charlie Eugene Wilcox and Helen Louise Henify Wilcox

Helen Louise (Henify) Wilcox was born in Earlington on June 7, 1916. That day was so cool her grandmother had a fire built in the fireplace. Her parents were John W. Henify (1886-1952) and Aurelia Elizabeth (Waller) Henify (1895-1966) who were married in Tennessee and had two other children.

John Edward Henify (September 1913-October 1914) age thirteen months.

Norma V. Henify (June 27, 1921) who married Francis B. Weakley and they now live in Arizona. They have two children, Gerald B. and Susan Elizabeth.

John W. Henify was descended from the Earle's who came to Hopkins County in early 1800's. His grandfather was Wash M. Rhea whose parents were Robert Rhea and Elizabeth Earle, daughter of Thomas Prince Earle.

Aurelia's father, Edward Waller, was descended from the Waller's of Virginia. Her mother's parents came from Germany as small children.

GENE WILCOX and HELEN HENIFY were married Apr. 21, 1937 at Dixon, KY. They lived most of their married life in Earlington where Gene was a partner with his brother Freddie Wilcox in business in the late 1940's. Together they managed The Standard Oil Service Station and Wilcox Home and Auto Supply, both located on South Railroad Street. Freddie Wilcox served overseas in World War II in Patton's Third Army and Gene served on the Home Front looking forward to his brother's return. The last five years of Helen and Gene's life together were spent in Madisonville where Gene worked for West Kentucky Coal Company. They were members of First Christian Church in Earlington and in Madisonville, KY.

Since February 1980 Helen has worked at The Historical Library and Museum at 107 Union Street.

Wilcox Family, 1984 back l to r-Barbara, David, Helen, Charles and Susan. Front-Elizabeth (Beth) Wilcox and Alan D. Whittington

Gene and Helen Wilcox are proud parents of two sons: Charles Eugene Wilcox - born Mar. 3, 1943 and David Edward Wilcox - born Sept. 22, 1949 (see Wilcox -Wyatt).

CHARLES EUGENE WILCOX (Mar. 3, 1943) older son of Charlie Eugene Wilcox and Helen (Henify) Wilcox married Susan Orange Brown on Mar. 3, 1970 at Gallatin, TN. Sue's parents are Gusta (Mastin) and Estil Orange of Morgantown, KY.

Charles attended school in Madisonville (one year in Earlington) and graduated from Madisonville High School May 1961. He graduated from Western Kentucky University at Bowling Green, KY May 1966 and spent another year in graduated work there.

During his High and College years he worked for The Kroger Company. After college he continued in their Management Program, spending some time as Co-manager before advancing to the Personnel Offices in Nashville. Presently he is Personnel Director for Kirby Building Systems at Portland, TN with Headquarters in Nashville, TN. Charles and Sue live in Nashville, TN. - *Submitted by Helen Wilcox*

WILCOX-RALEY

DANIEL and OLA LEE WILCOX moved with their three children to Earlington, KY on Valentine's Day 1929. They had previously lived in Crofton, White Plains, and Morton's Gap. They originally came from Muhlenberg and Ohio Co.

Dan was the youngest of eleven children born to William Stites and Sarah Jane (Thompson) WILCOX, who were married in Hopkins County Mar. 16, 1859. Dan was a blacksmith by trade and worked in his later years for West Kentucky Coal Company. Ola Lee (Raley) Wilcox was the daughter of James E. and Martha Elizabeth (Stewart) RALEY. She had a twin brother, Oda Dee Raley and a brother Jay Raley. Dan was born Oct. 25, 1885 and died Mar. 25, 1953. Ola was born Feb. 2,

Ora Lee (Raley) and Daniel Stites Wilcox

Dan was the youngest of eleven children 1890 and died Dec. 25, 1974. Both are buried in Oakwood Cemetery, Earlington, KY.

They were married June 19, 1907 and were the parents of five children, two (Clara L. and James) died as infants.

Three of their children lived to adulthood:
1. CHARLIE EUGENE WILCOX (Aug. 15, 1910-Nov. 5, 1954), married Helen Henify at Dixon, KY Apr. 21, 1937. They have two sons: CHARLES EUGENE WILCOX and DAVID EDWARD WILCOX.

2. LOTTIE WILCOX married Roy Welch in 1935 and they had one daughter: DANNI ROYCE (PENNY) born July 9, 1954. Roy died 1977 and Lottie 1986.

3. FREDDIE LEE WILCOX (May 19, 1919) married Wandene McCormick, Feb. 23, 1946. They are the parents of two children: THOMAS WAYNE WILCOX (May 1, 1952) married Cathy (Smith) September 1972. They have a son Thomas Wayne Wilcox, Jr. JERRI LOU WILCOX (Aug. 1, 1958) married Don Sanders January 1977. They have two daughters: DANA MICHELLE SANDERS and LAURIE DEANNE SANDERS. - *Submitted by Helen Wilcox*

WILCOX-WYATT

David Edward Wilcox was born Sept. 22, 1949, in Madisonville, KY. David graduated from Madisonville High School in 1968. He graduated from the Madisonville Vocational Technical School. David is employed by Ronald R. Johnson and Associates, of Madisonville. David is a state-certified building inspector and serves as Inspector for Hopkins, Muhlenberg, and Webster Counties. David is a member of the Kentucky Association of Code Administrators.

Barbara and David Wilcox and Elizabeth Anne "Beth" Wilcox

On Oct. 20, 1973, David and Barbara Jean Wyatt were married at the Pleasant Valley Missionary Baptist Church, near Providence. Barbara is the daughter of Lester Givens Wyatt and Virginia Regina (Jena) Gold Wyatt who reside near Providence.

David and Barbara are the parents of one child, Elizabeth Anne Wilcox, who was born June 7, 1976, in Madisonville. Beth is a 6th grade student in Dixon Elementary School.

Barbara is employed by William E. Mitchell, the owner of the law firm of Miller and Mitchell, in Dixon, KY, as secretary to Mr. Mitchell who is the Assistant Commonwealth Attorney for the 5th Judicial District as well as being in private practice.

David, Barbara and Beth are members of the Pleasant Valley Missionary Baptist Church, near Providence. - *Submitted by Helen Wilcox*

WILKES-YANCEY

Curtis B. Wilkes and Opal Lavern Yancey of Earlington, KY were married Jan. 12, 1942. They have seven living children. The youngest, a son, Cletus Boyer Wilkes, was born Mar. 1, 1965 and died May 9, 1983.

Marilyn Linda a Behavior Specialist with Expectation Inc. was born Mar. 15, 1942. She is married to Henry Saterfield. They live in San Bernardino, CA and have six children: Henry Jr., Kevin, Keith, Renee who has one son, Cheryl who has one son and Karlene who is still in high school.

Ina Lois a computer programmer with The Computer Company, was born Aug. 3, 1944. She is married to Nathan Williams. They live in Indianapolis, IN and have three daughters: Felicia, Tamika and Danika.

Clifton Boyd a Baptist Minister was born Oct. 20, 1948. He is single and is the Assistant Director of School Services at Utah State U. in Logan, UT.

Patricia Louweldyn a Technology Leader for Administrative Services in the Process Systems Technology Directorate at Procter and Gamble was born May 17, 1951. She is married to Johnny Stone. They live in Mason, OH and have one son-Jonathan.

Clayton Banvoid, a Sergeant in the United States Air Force, was born Sept. 23, 1957. He and his wife Randine are stationed in Germany and have three children: Toby, Mervin, and Summer.

Curtis Barry employed by the Goodyear Plant in Danville, VA, was born Mar. 14, 1958. He is married to Phyllis Greene and they have one son, Curtis Boyer.

Beverly Loray a minister in the United Methodist Church, was born July 23, 1959. She is attending St. Paul School of Theology in Kansas City, MO. She is also a Second Lieutenant in the Missouri National Guard and she is single.

Curtis B. worked for the Roberts' Bros. Coal Company for more than 25 years. he retired on Oct. 27, 1977. Curtis is a deacon at the Pleasant Grove Baptist Church in Hecla. He enjoys gardening, singing and working for the Lord.

Opal has been a housewife, mother, and housekeeper. She serves on the Mother's Board at the Pleasant Grove Baptist Church. She is also active in Circle No. 1 of First District. She has been the kind of mother that her children call her blessed.

The Wilkeses enjoy visiting their children and playing with their grandchildren and great-grandchildren. - *Submitted by Mrs. Curtis Wilkes*

CHESLEY S. WILLIAMS

Chesley Simpson Williams (1834-1905) was born in Perry Co., IL, to Simpson Williams and Margery Dixon Williams. To this union were born two children, Chesley in 1834 and Elizabeth (m. Charles Harrison) in 1836. In 1837 Simpson Williams died and Margery Dixon Williams, at age 22, with her two small children came to Christian Co., KY, to live with her father-in-law, William Williams.

Williams homeplace on Drakes Creek about 1890. Shown in picture are Chesley and Missaniah with children Ruby and Mary Majorie Williams Holloman (in background)

In 1851, when Chesley was only 17 he was an entrepreneur doing for himself, farming, teaming and various other types of employ for several years and putting his money into farm land and real estate. He initially bought 200 acres in Christian County and in several years had increased this to 800 acres.

In 1864, at age 30, Chesley married the daughter of a very prominent Hopkins County family, Missaniah Jane Davis who was 17 years of age. To this union four children were born, one dying at the age of 16. The other three were: Mary Marjorie (b. 1865) who later married a prominent tobacco farmer, Ashley Holloman, from Dalton, KY; Chesley Simpson (Dink) (b. 1870) who married Eva Foster from Illinois and Ruby (b. 1886) who married Artie Cummings from Indiana who, upon his death in 1979, bequeathed $300,000 of his estate plus some farm property to the City of Madisonville Community Improvement Fund.

Chesley S. Williams came to Hopkins County with his family in 1868 and he and his mother, Margery, purchased 1300 acres near Mortons Gap on Drakes Creek from the Bank of Hopkinsville. As he prospered he purchased 118 acres on Pond River and property in Earlington and Madisonville. In 1877 he owned one-half interest in Williams and Dulin Mill property and in 1884 bought one-half interest in the Williams-Drake coal operation. Chesley Simpson bought, or built, for his three children large homes on South Main Street in Madisonville. He also owned several downtown Madisonville store fronts on Main Street and Center Street which included the building now occupied by the Kentucky Bank and Trust Company and the "Hustler" building now occupied by Howard Happy. He also owned several lots on Sugg Street and several on East

Broadway, one of which is still occupied by a granddaughter, Missaniah Julia Holloman Ramsey. Other of his grandchildren and their families still residing in Hopkins County are the J.C. Riddles.

Dr. Herbert Chaney of Dawson Springs was the husband of a great granddaughter Betty Jane Williams, now deceased, and he still owns the original Chesley Williams farm and homeplace which still stands on Highway 813 near Mortons Gap.

Chesley Simpson Williams was a Master Mason belonging to the Orphans Friend Lodge 523 at Mt. Carmel Church. He, his wife and most of his family are buried in Odd Fellows Cemetery on lots 263 and 264. - *Submitted by Mary J. R. Mullins*

NOAH DWIGHT WILLIAMS

Noah Dwight Williams Sr., born Aug. 11, 1958 in Hopkins County, was the second of two children born to Noah and Blonnie Mae Williams, daughter of Dave and Margie Todd. The first Williams child was born dead, but there is a half brother William Lee Shadrick.

Noah Dwight Williams age 17

Noah Williams, born Aug. 10, 1894 in Hopkins County died Aug. 28, 1961 in Hopkins County, was the son of William A. and America C. Williams. He was a veteran and is buried at Browder Cemetery.

Blonnie Mae Williams, born Oct. 27, 1917 in Hopkins County, is still living and remains a widow.

Noah Dwight Williams Sr. married Vicky Lynn Brown, the daughter of Edgar and Betty Brown of Nortonville, KY, on Feb. 1, 1977. Two children resulted from the marriage: Noah Dwight Jr. born Dec. 8, 1977 and Tammy Lynn born Apr. 16, 1980. Both children were born in Hopkins County.

William A. Williams came from Illinois in the late 1800's and met and married America C. Shanks from Muhlenberg County. They married on Oct. 19, 1893 and settled in Hopkins County. They were the first of this generation of Williams to settle in Hopkins County.

Music surrounds the Williams family and has for years. Noah Williams was a musician. Blonnie Mae Williams is known as one of the great piano players in Hopkins County. Noah Dwight Williams Sr. is a singer, songwriter and musician.

Other ancestral family names are Whitmer, Shanks and Massey. - *Submitted by Mae Williams and Noah D. Williams*

PEARL C. WILLIAMS

Pearl Chester Williams, born in Crabtree Coal Camp, Ilsley, Hopkins Co., KY on Nov. 19, 1886, was the only child of Andrew Johnson Williams and Ell Vira Goodaker Williams. Andrew Johnson was the son of Andrew Williams and Martha Evans Williams who came from North Carolina. Ell Vira Goodaker was the daughter of Sam Goodaker and Rachel Franklin. Andrew was born in Hopkins County Sept. 26, 1863, married Ell Vira on Feb. 25, 1886, and died on July 6, 1921. Ell Vira was born Sept. 11, 1862 and died Aug. 22, 1912. Both are buried at Oddfellows Cemetery, Madisonville, KY.

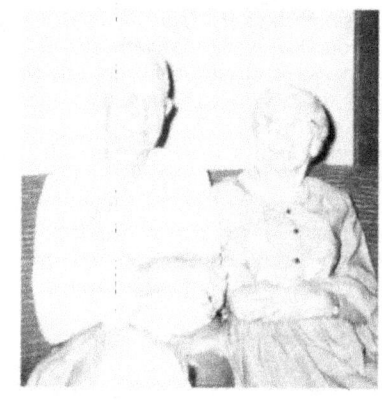

Pearl Chester and Nettie Miller Williams on their 50th wedding anniversary, May 14, 1961

Pearl Chester (P.C.) moved to Dawson Springs at an early age. His father, Johnson, was a City Policeman and Security Guard at mines in that area. P.C. went to school in Dawson and later in Madisonville he graduated from the eighth grade at the old West Broadway School. He owned and operated the Home Restaurant at 122 Sugg Street - where a meal ticket for twenty-one meals was advertised for $3.50 - until 1913. He married Adeline Nettie Miller on May 14, 1911, with Judge R.B. Bradley officiating.

P.C. later worked for Reinecke Coal Company from 1913 until 1921 as an electrical foreman. About 1921 he went into business as an independent electrical contractor and also owned and operated a grocery at 700 West Broadway until 1930. He discontinued his electrical business in 1941 and became an electrical inspector on the construction of Fort Campbell and later at S.J. Campbell Parachute Factory in Madisonville. After World War II he was an electrical inspector for the City of Madisonville until he retired because of illness in the spring of 1961. He died on Oct. 3, 1961. He was a member of First Methodist Church, F & AM Lodge No. 143 and Woodmen of the World. He is buried at Oddfellows on the Williams lot.

Nettie Miller was the daughter of Emil George Miller and Catherine Roehrig Miller who moved to Madisonville from Evansville in May 1903. (See Miller) She was born in Evansville Apr. 13, 1886. She helped her parents in the operation of a hotel and restaurant until her marriage, after which she became a housewife. She died Sept. 4, 1976 at the age of 90. She was an active member of First Methodist Church, a charter member of Order of Eastern Star No. 390 joining in March 1924 before the charter was granted in October 1924. She held many offices and was Worthy Matron in 1936-1937. She was also a member of the Woodmen Circle. She is also buried at Oddfellows.

Children of Pearl C. and A. Nettie Williams:

1. Elvira Catherine - born Aug. 6, 1912. Married James Blanks Thomas (Sept. 26, 1910-Feb. 19, 1956) on Aug. 18, 1951. Married Thorton Timmons (b. Apr. 19, 1914) on May 15, 1971. No children.

2. Thelma Louise - born Jan. 1, 1915. Married Edward Glenn Coffman (Mar. 20, 1909-Dec. 2, 1967) on Oct. 27, 1932. Children: Edward Glenn, Jr. born Nov. 29, 1933 and Malcolm Arvin born June 27, 1939.

3. Emil Johnson - born Nov. 23, 1916. Married Mildred Gertrude Tomblinson (b. Feb. 8, 1920) on June 5, 1938. Children: Emily Jane born Oct. 21, 1939 and Betsy Luck born Oct. 6, 1943.

4. John Edmund - born July 5, 1919, died Nov. 25, 1955. Buried at Oddfellows. Married Elizabeth Sisson on May 16, 1948. One child - Chester Franklin born July 4, 1953. - *Submitted by Elvira W. Timmons*

WILLIAMSON

Brother Lawson Williamson was born Dec. 3, 1933 in Gipson County, TN. He is the son of Mr. and Mrs. Roy Williamson of Gipson County and is one of six children. He has two sisters and three brothers. His mother, Esther, ironically was a Williamson before she married. Her husband, Roy, was born June 23, 1900 in Gipson County. Lawson's sisters are Lorene and Linnie. Lorene, now Lorene Croker, was born Apr. 2, 1921. She has one son, Jeffory Croker. Linnie, now Linnie Walden, was born Oct. 28, 1939. She has two children, a son Steve Walden and a daughter Stacy Walden. Lawson brothers are: Leamon, born Apr. 26, 1919, Lester born Jan. 17, 1937, and Lindel. Lester has two sons, Levelle and David Williamson.

Lawon Williamson attended Milend High School in Benton County, TN. He attended Union College in Jackson, TN and Bethel College in McKancie, TN.

Lawson married Gladys Williamson. She was born Mar. 31, 1938. They are the parents of two daughters, Pam and Beth. Pam was born Oct. 20, 1959 and is married to David Bowles. They have one son, Deven, who is four years old. Beth was born Feb. 26, 1967. She is married to Scott Pendly and they are expecting their first child. Both David and Scott are in the service. David is in the Air Force and Scott is in the Army. Oddly enough, they are stationed within miles of each other.

Lawson and his family moved to Hopkins County on Jan. 1, 1979. They have lived in Dawson Springs for nine years. Lawson is employed by the First Baptist Church of Dawson Springs. His hobbies include traveling and the outdoors. As Lawson's relatives are all in Tennessee, he visits as often as he can, mostly on holidays and other special occasions.-*Submitted by Mike McAlister*

WILSON

Eva Irene Skaggs and Carl Edward Wilson were married in his parents home in Grapevine by his father, Rev. Thomas Wilson, Feb. 17, 1950.

Eva was born Feb. 29, 1932 in rural Calhoun, KY, the daughter of Walter Skaggs and Georgia Viola Ruby. Walter was born in 1898 in Butler Co. the son of Pete Skaggs and Josie Cowans. They had two children, a son James Arthur now living in Madisonville, and Eva. They were divorced in 1943. Walter died in 1982. Viola was born in 1907 in Hopkins Co., the daughter of George Ruby and Alice Oakley. Viola remarried Hickman Kirkwood. Viola's grandmother Oakley's maiden name was Presley, a relative of the father of Elvis Presley. In 1938, at a Presley family reunion in Webster Co., everyone enjoyed three-year-old Elvis playing his guitar and singing, a cherished memory after he became famous. Eva's half-sister, Anna Pearl Pattie lives in Indiana.

Carl Edward, Eva Irene and Sarah Elizabeth Wilson

Eva attended her high school years at old Madisonville High, what is now Browning Springs Middle School. Her hobby is interior decorating. She has helped in restoring some of Madisonville's oldest homes. Eva and Carl have been active in their church more than 30 years.

Carl was born Aug. 16, 1930 in Hopkins Co. the oldest son of Rev. Thomas Wilson and Opal Mae Polley, born 1909 (see Wash Jones and Shoulders-Miller). Rev. Wilson, born 1906 died 1986, was the son of James (Jim) Wilson and Retta Murphy. Brother Tommy as he was known served the General Baptist churches for 53 years. He was Chaplain at Ky. Rest Haven for 14 years. Carl has a brother, Wallace, who lives with his wife and son in Grapevine.

Carl attended his first school at Cox's Store, Hwy. 630, 3rd grade at Nebo with teacher Sarah Barron. He shares with Eva the love of interior decorating, making it a working hobby besides his regular job. Carl now works for Dawson Springs Health Care Center as head maintenance man. His love of music has served well in his church, as he plays what is called an Invisible Harp, the ability to cup his hands over his mouth and make music. It sounds like a French Harp being blown into.

The Wilsons are parents of: Micheal who lives in Madisonville; Eddie who lives in Evansville, IN; and twins, Ronald Thomas who lived with his wife and child until his untimely death from a motorcycle accident in 1976 and Donald Walter who lives with his family in Evansville; and Sarah Elizabeth who is 13 and a 7th grader in Dawson Springs at this writing. Sarah shares her father's musical talent. She has been singing in churches and at family gatherings since she was very small. Daddy Carl accompanies her on his Invisible Harp.

Wilson grandchildren: Tracy, Laurie, Christopher, Chasitity, Charity, Julie and Brandie and a step-granddaughter, Heather. - *Submitted by Dorothy Shoulders*

WILSON-WISE

William Silas Wilson was born May 20, 1857 just north of Madisonville in Hopkins County to William A. Wilson and Nancy L. McGary (daughter of Toliver McGary and Elizabeth Dorinda Young McGary). William Silas' brothers and sisters include: Elizabeth R., Theodore, Nancy J. (Nannie), Sallie, Vitula, James Shackelford and George. William A. Wilson served as Sheriff of Hopkins County and died Nov. 19, 1866 at the age of 45 years, reportedly murdered by renegade Union soldiers. Nancy died in September 1883. Both are buried at Stevens Schoolhouse Cemetery in Madisonville.

William Silas Wilson family. Front l to r: George L., Samantha, William Silas and Cathryne. Back row: Herschel A., Roy S., Hattie D., W. Elmer, Aubra L., Elsie and Daisy D.

On Nov. 7, 1876, William married Samantha Ann Wise (born Dec. 22, 1858 to Henry Hardin Wise and Abigail Orsburn) at her parents' home in Webster County. Samantha was the oldest of seven daughters and one son. Fourteen children were born to William and Samantha: Ellis, Hattie D., Aubra L., William Elmer, Roy Silas (Buzz), Ivy H., Elsie Mae, Herschel A., Daisy Dell, Pauline E., Cathryn D., George L., and twin boys who died at birth.

After marrying, William and Samantha lived in Webster County and then near Robards, Henderson County. William was a strong believer in education, serving on the school board in Webster County and moving his family into Madisonville in 1905 so that all of the children could obtain an education. Five of the Wilson children became school teachers. The Wilson's first home in Madisonville was the big brick house across from West Broadway Elementary School. They later lived for many years on East Noel Avenue.

William was a large man (he stood over 6 feet), and his courage earned him the nickname "Tige". On one occasion, after being shot in the back, William calmly turned, shot his assailant through the head and walked home before seeking medical care. In the late 1930's, he was called out of retirement to guard the Kentucky Bank when rumor designated Madisonville as the possible target of bank robbers. He was long associated with the Madisonville Police Department and served as Chief of Police from 1914 to 1918. He was also employed by various coal companies and by the Louisville and Nashville Railroad for many years as a railroad detective and security guard.

William and Samantha belonged to the Madisonville Christian Church. Samantha died Feb. 3, 1945 at the age of 86. William followed her less than 11 months later, dying Dec. 31, 1945 at the age of 88. Both are buried in the Wilson plot at Odd Fellows Cemetery. Sources: Wilson Family Bible; Marriage Bonds and Certificates; Death Certificates; 1860 Census of Hopkins County; Will of Toliver McGary; Battle's "Kentucky: A History of the State"; Obituaries; tombstones in Odd Fellows Cemetery, Stevens Schoolhouse Cemetery and Grapevine Cemetery. - *Submitted by Ann Wilson Blanchard Peralta*

ROY SILAS WILSON

Roy Silas "Buzz" Wilson was born near Poole in Webster County on Mar. 24, 1884, the fifth of fourteen children born to William Silas Wilson and Samantha Ann Wise Wilson. In 1905, William and Samantha moved with their family to Madisonville so that the children could obtain an education. Buzz took seriously his parents' interest in education, being trained as a teacher as a young man and later working tirelessly for better education as a community leader. Working tirelessly was what Buzz did best. In 1913, he entered the insurance business with Sam D. Langley. This was the beginning of a successful career. The firm was known as Wilson and McPherson Insurance Company. As a life underwriter, Buzz frequently led the state of Kentucky in insurance sales.

The Roy S. Wilson family - William Robert, Josephine Doyle, John Doyle, Roy S. (Buzz) and Jo Ann

His exertions on behalf of his community and state were no less dedicated than his efforts on the job. In 1913, he served a term as Hopkins County's Representative in the Kentucky General Assembly. From that time on, Buzz took an active interest in Democratic politics and was called friend by a number of Kentucky governors. Buzz's energies were not only directed toward political matters. During World War II, he served as chairman of Hopkins County's Ration Board. At the time of his death, "The Madisonville Messenger" ran an article stating, in part, that Buzz Wilson was "a civic leader and participant in virtually every civic project here in the last fifty years". One of his proudest achievements was the construction in the 1930's and subsequent enlargements of Hopkins County Hospital. He and former "Madisonville Messenger" Editor Edgar Arnold Sr. directed the first subscription drive to raise funds to start the hospital and were instrumental in later expansion drives as well. An avid golfer, he was a charter member of Madisonville Country Club, serving as its president and numerous times on its board of directors. He was a charter member and president of Madisonville Kiwanis Club; a director of the Madisonville Chamber of Commerce; and a member of the board of Hopkins County Hospital Corporation.

Whatever Buzz achieved in the business world and in community service, his main focus was family. On Nov. 14, 1931, Roy Silas Wilson married Josephine Thomas Doyle. Four children were born to this union: Roy S. Wilson, Jr., John Doyle Wilson, William Robert Wilson, and Jo Ann Wilson. He quite simply adored his wife and children and extended great love to his parents, sisters, brothers, nieces and nephews as well. Being "family" meant something special to Buzz. Buzz died Apr. 13, 1964 at the age of eighty. He is buried in the Wilson Plot, Odd Fellows Cemetery. Sources: Wilson Family Bible; Death Certificates; Newspaper articles; tombstone. - *Submitted by Ann Wilson Blanchard Peralta*

SAMUEL J. WILSON

Samuel J. (S.J.) Wilson, born Feb. 21, 1896 in Cannon Co., TN, the oldest of ten children of Mike Wilson (son of Sam Wilson and Nancy Higgins) and Fannie Alexander (daughter of Dee Alexander and Susan Davenport). Mike and Fannie and their year old son, S.J., moved to Webster Co. near Slaughters in 1897.

S.J. and Pearl Wilson

S. J. Wilson and Pearl Mae Hawkins (daughter of Louis Daniel Hawkins and Nancy Owen) were married Oct. 14, 1914 in Webster Co. Pearl Mae was born Sept. 8, 1898 near Dixon, KY. Their children: James Paul (J.P.); Raymond Lee; Narvle Louis and Imogene. They moved to a farm in Hopkins Co. near Nebo in 1927. The children graduated from Nebo High School in the years 1935, 36, 37 and 39. S. J. was engaged in farming in the Nebo-Manitou community until his death Nov. 10, 1969. S. J. and Pearl were members of Mt. Gilead General Baptist Church and later joined Concord Church near Manitou. S.J. was ordained a deacon in 1931 and served in that capacity until his death.

J. P. (Dec. 14, 1915-Oct. 25, 1986) married Lucille Rainwater, daughter of Charley Rainwater and Elsie Railey of Manitou. Their son, James Lynn, is a CPA with Freeman Properties Inc., in Nashville, TN. Lynn married Janine Ellis of Nebo. They have a son, Chase Ellis. J.P. was a farmer, coal miner and operated a school bus for Hopkins Co. School System for twenty years. He attended Concord Church and was a member of the choir.

Raymond (born Mar. 7, 1917) married Pazzie Marie Rhew, the oldest daughter of Ben Rhew and Mamie Arnold, on Apr. 17, 1937. Their children: Gale Hobgood and Sharon Pittman. Gale is employed in Hopkins Co. as a teacher at Grapevine School. She married Morris Hobgood and has a son, Dirk, who attends Murray University They attend Nebo Christian Church where Gale is the organist. Sharon married James Pittman of Wickliffe, KY. Their children: Warren and Wilson. Sharon is employed as a teacher at Ballard Memorial School and is active in the First Baptist Church. Raymond and Pazzie attend Mt. Gilead Church near Slaughters, where he serves as deacon. They live on a farm near Manitou and raise registered Hereford cattle.

Narvis Louis, born Feb. 18, 1919, married Ona Evelyn Melton, daughter of Essel Melton and Pearl Cox. Their children: Eva Hill; Joyce Daniel; Jean Staser and Wade Wilson. Eva, secretary for Northwest Vocational School in Cincinnati, married Robert (Bob) Hill a former teacher at Nebo High School. Their daughter, Debbie Hamilton, is a Special Education teacher. Joyce, works at Clay Drug Store in Clay, married Gary Daniel. Their daughter, Tammy, attends Madisonville Community College. Jean, a bookkeeper at Cole's Office Outfitters Inc., married David Staser of Providence. Their son Chad attends Nebo School. Wade, a farmer and truck driver, married Terri Moore. Their children: Holly (the New Year Baby for 1986) and Brian (attends Nebo School). Louis worked on the farm all his life and at Farmer's Cooperative Inc. in the winter months until retiring in 1981.

Imogene, born Jan. 1, 1921, married George W. Russell son of Floyd Russell and Blanche Pearl Haleman of Richland on Nov. 9, 1945. Their son, George Wayne Russell, a Madisonville policeman, married Cecilia Wheeler of Greenville. They have twins, Tyler Wayne and Lauren Wheeler. Imogene attends Concord Church near Manitou and is a member of the choir. - *Submitted by Imogene Wilson Russell*

THOMAS KARR WILSON

Thomas was born Jan. 20, 1906 in Hopkins County, the son of James (Jim) and Retta Murphy Wilson. Thomas had two sisters, two brothers and three half-sisters.

Thomas attended Munns School located on Pleasant View Road. Like so many young men of his day, that was all of the formal education he received until years later. He then took several courses by mail and with private tutors.

While attending Munns School, he met Opal Mae Polley (see Polley-Jones). The couple had a unique, or at least different, wedding. As customers and clerks watched, they were married in February of 1926 at 12 noon in the front foyer of the Baker & Hickman Store in Madisonville. Using the glass front between

Rev. Thomas and Opal Wilson

the two double doors as an alter, they were married by the Rev. W. H. Moore, pastor of the Grapevine Christian Church. Their witnesses were John H. Vannoy, friend of the groom, and Arthur B. Miller, brother-in-law of the bride.

Thomas worked in the mines at Earlington and also the Redbud Mine at Grapevine. Brother Tommy, as he was known when he was ordained for the General Baptist ministry, served in over 32 churches in Hopkins, Muhlenberg, Todd, Christian, Webster and Crittenden Counties. He conducted over 75 revivals, more than 100 funerals, and married 60 or more couples.

Living at Manitou in the beginning of his ministry, he walked 36 miles round trip to hold weekend services near Nortonville. He continued this for 10 months, catching a ride when he could, until he could afford a car. To care for his family during those early years, he worked on a farm, at a local furniture store, drove a school bus and was the janitor at Grapevine School for about 20 years. Brother Tommy held Christian services at local rest homes and was the chaplain for over 11 years at Kentucky Rest Haven until cancer forced his retirement about six weeks before his death.

The Wilson's first child, Annie Ethel, was born in 1928 and died nine months later from a liver ailment. Their second child, Carl Edward (see Wilson story), was born in 1930. Their third child, Henry Wallace, was born in 1942 and lives with his wife and son in the Grapevine area.

Rev. Wilson was pastoring a small country church near Greenville at the time of his illness. He underwent surgery for the removal of a cancerous kidney in April of 1982. As soon as he was able, he continued his pastorate, counseling sessions, services at the rest home, conducting funerals, and married a grandson. Continuing to drive his car, he used a cane to aid his walking.

In spite of treatments for the cancer, it returned in 1985. He died Sept. 5, 1986. At his funeral, four of his close fellow ministers gave a tribute. The theme of each short message was "I remember a man". Rev. Wilson was buried in Oakley Home Church Cemetery on Highway 630, north of Manitou.-*Submitted by Dorothy Miller Shoulders*

WINDERS-FAULK

Dorthy Elizabeth Faulk and Oscar Albert Winders were married on Jan. 13, 1930 in Madisonville, KY.

Dorthy was born July 8, 1914 in Mortons Gap. She is the daughter of Omer R. Faulk and Dovie U. Mason. Oscar is the son of Roy Maynard Winders and Joni Bell of Todd Co.

Oscar A. and Dorothy E. Winders

R. Maynard was born in Todd Co. He was the son of Licugus E. Winders and Nanny Marshall. Licugus was born in 1856, the son of John Winders (born in 1826) and Emily Winders (born 1832). R. Maynard served in the U.S. army in Germany in WW I. He was well-known for his musical abilities. He was offered a position playing banjo at the Grand Ole Opry in Nashville, TN, but refused, to stay in Todd Co. with his second wife Nellie and his children. Maynard's family came from North Carolina to Kentucky.

Oscar an Dorthy Winders had the following children: Roy Wallace (Oct. 9, 1931), Wilda Elizabeth (Nov. 5, 1933-died March 1935, buried at Old Salem Cem. in Mortons Gap), Jackie Lee (Jan. 2, 1936), Bobby Glenn (Feb. 3, 1939), Linda Lou (June 18, 1940), Phyllis Ann (July 29, 1950) and Vickie Lane (Mar. 12, 1957).

Oscar was a coal miner for 50 years. He and Dorthy belong to the Mortons Gap Independent Methodist Church. They are the oldest couple in the church. Both have served as officers and trustees for the church over the past 50 years. Oscar helped to rebuild the present day church structure on Crooked St., after the original Methodist Church on Cross St. burned in the 1930's.

R. Wallace and Jackie L. graduated from Mortons Gap High School in the early 1950's. Both were well-known for their basketball playing; on several occasions both held state records. Wallace became a coal miner and belongs to the Mortons Gap Independent Methodist Church. Jackie served in the U.S. Army for two years. Jackie then graduated with a B.A. from Austin Peay University (Clarksville, TN) and a M.A. from Murray State University, Jackie has two children: Sabrina Leigh (May 30, 1968) and Christopher Darren (July 7, 1974).

Bobbie graduated from South Hopkins High. He was an outstanding athlete too. He was on the team that went to the state tournament. He graduated from Austin Peay University. He has two daughters: Kimberly Dawn (Dec. 2, 1963) and Stephanie Leigh (Aug. 20, 1965).

Linda graduated from South Hopkins and Ky. Wesleyan College in Owensboro, KY. She teaches kindergarten at White Plains and St. Charles Elem. Linda married Larry D. Knowles on Nov. 22, 1962. They have three children: Rickey Lynn and Mickey Glenn (twins - Feb. 17, 1963) and Crystal Beth (July 15, 1969). Linda belongs to the Independent Methodist Church.

Phyllis and Vickie graduated from South Hopkins and Murray State University Both received B.S. and M.A. degrees. Phyllis married Terry L. Bowman on July 4, 1970. They have four children: Misty Michelle (Feb. 8, 1977), Amy Lane (Nov. 11, 1979), and Sarah Elizabeth & Emily Maria (twins - May 1, 1984). Vickie married Barry Fox on Aug. 13, 1979. They have one son Joshua Aaron (May 16, 1985). Both Phyllis and Vickie's families belong to the Independent Methodist Church.

The Winders have lived, worked and contributed to Hopkins County all their lives. They presently live in their original home on Flat Creek St. in Mortons Gap. - *Submitted by Terry and Phyllis Bowman*

WINSETT

Eunice Bailey Winsett was born Dec. 4, 1904 the daughter of Charlie Winsett and Sallie Jane McCracken. On Nov. 22, 1922 she was married to Ruby Whitson Carlton the son of Jeptha D. Carlton and Annie E. Keith. Eunice and Ruby were the parents of seven children: James Charles (Duck) Carlton m. Willa Dean Choate, Geneva Irene Carlton m. Howard E. (Bill) Wilson, Arbie O'Bryant Carlton m. Janice Louise Butler, Laveta Corinne Carlton m. Jesse Willard Murrah, Rodney Wayne Carlton m. Ruth Ann Smith, William Whitson and Edward Lynn Carlton died in infancy. Eunice passed away on Jan. 5, 1965. She was buried at New Salem Cem.

Sallie Jane (McCracken) and Charlie W. Winsett

Charlie William Winsett was born Apr. 21, 1877 the son of Silas Jackson Winsett and Celia Jane Keith. On Nov. 14, 1903 he married Sallie Jane McCracken b. Sept. 4, 1882 the daughter of John Aaron McCracken and Susan E. Patterson. To their union were born seven children including Eunice. They were: Charles Winsett, d. at 9 days; Mary Elizabeth Winsett; Carrie Autense Keen Cook; Walter Jackson Winsett m. Hazel McIntosh; Toy West Winsett m. Sarah Simpson; and Assie Pearl Cavanaugh. Charlie Winsett died Sept. 9, 1949. He was buried at New Salem Cem. Sallie died on Oct. 20, 1956. She was laid to rest by his side.

Silas Jackson Winsett was born Apr. 4, 1849 the son of Josiah Floyd Winsett and America Evergreen Jackson. On Jan. 29, 1874 he married Celia Jane Keith, b. Jan. 29, 1850 the daughter of William Keith and Rebecca Summers. Silas and Celia were the parents of three other children besides Charlie: Dolly Frances Manire, Cordelia Dukes, and Edna Skeens. Silas died on Dec. 22, 1914. Celia died Nov. 22, 1932. They were buried at Rock Bridge Cem.

John Aaron McCracken was born in 1846 the son of Joseph and Betsy McCracken from Tennessee. He was married to Susan E. Patterson b. 1850 Tennessee the daughter of Aaron Patterson and Priscilla Davis. Both families moved to Kentucky in the 1850's.

Josiah Floyd Winsett b. Mar. 16, 1825 was the son of Silas Winsett and Sarah Freeman. He was first married to America Evergreen Jackson b. 1825 the daughter of Thomas Jackson and Ruth Hendrix. Josiah and America Winsett were the parents of four other children besides Silas: Ellen Mary Jane Stanley; John Winsett; George W. Winsett who died at age 10 mos.; and an unnamed infant who died along with its mother America on Oct. 28, 1857. After his first wife's death during childbirth, Josiah married Sarah Batts on Dec. 16, 1857. Josiah Floyd Winsett died Feb. 27, 1902 in Christian Co., KY.

The Winsetts and related families came from such varied places as Virginia, North Carolina, South Carolina and Tennessee to settle in Kentucky. Their many descendants live here still. - *Submitted by Willard, Corinne, Mike and Lou Ann Murrah*

WINSTEAD

Ivy Ernest Winstead married Jessie Manora Adams on Feb. 16, 1917. Six children were born to this couple, five of whom are still living. The children are: Anna Mae (1917-), Elsie Ree (1920-1922), Iva Ray (1924-), David Leon (1931-), Earl Franklin (1935-), and Sarah Grace (1940-). A total of five grandchildren and three great-grandchildren were produced by the group of siblings.

Ivy Ernest Winstead was the son of Manley William Winstead (1845-1933) and Elizabeth T. Winstead (nee) (1847-1900). Both Manley William Winstead and Elizabeth T. Winstead were direct descendents of Mandley Winstead (1760-1846), who moved to Hopkins County from North Carolina in 1818. Mandley Winstead was a veteran of the American Revolution, and will be discussed in detail shortly.

Manley William Winstead was a Union veteran of the Civil War, and fought at the Battle of Shiloh in Tennessee.

Elizabeth T. Winstead was the daughter of Alexander Taylor Winstead (1817-1887) and Priscilla Ann Trice Winstead (1817-1883). Alexander Taylor Winstead was the last of ten children born to Mandley Winstead.

Manley William Winstead was the son of Bushard D. Winstead, Jr. (1824-?) and Polly Ann Cox Winstead (1825-?).

Bushard D. Winstead, Jr. was the son of Bushard D. Winstead (1790-1843) and Susannah Cox (1789-1849). Bushard D. Winstead, Sr., died in 1843, while delivering tobacco, and was buried on the banks of the Mississippi River.

Bushard D. Winstead, Sr., was the fourth child of Mandley Winstead and his first wife, ? Tapp.

Mandley Winstead was born on Oct. 29, 1760, in Northumberland Co., VA, and was the son of Samuel Winstead III. (Samuel Winstead I and II were also residents of Virginia).

In 1776, Mandley Winstead moved to Caswell Co., NC, and was drafted into the North Carolina militia.

Mandley Winstead was married first to ? Tapp. In 1809, Mandley married Elizabeth Cox in Person Co., NC. Mandley had seven children by his first wife and three children by his second wife.

In 1821, Mandley married his third wife, Amy Brown Hutcheson. There were no children from this marriage.

In 1832, Mandley Winstead applied for and received a Revolutionary War Pension in Hopkins Co., KY. - *Submitted by Jack Lynn Branson*

WINSTEAD-MORROW

William Winstead Sr., bc. 1765 dc. 1828 will probated in Person Co., NC and re-recorded in Hopkins Co. in 1843 and wife Sarah (maiden name unknown) bc. 1765 dc. 1831 (will date). Their children as follows: Nancy married David Wilkerson Apr. 7, 1809 Person Co., NC., Lumpkin married Martha Williams Jan. 5, 1818 d. Sept. 25, 1829, *Patsy bc. 1791 married William Wilkerson Feb. 7, 1817 Person Co., *William bc. 1794 dc. 1862 married Sarah Morrow Sept. 18, 1816 in Person Co. (See Morrow-Winstead article), *Mary (Polly) bc. 1811 m. John Morrow in Person Co., Jean or Jane, Sally, Lucy, *George T. married Mary (Polly) Morrow. (Asterisk denotes those who came to Hopkins Co., KY)

William Winstead Jr., and Sarah Morrow came to Hopkins Co. ca. 1838. Sarah was deceased by 1846 as William remarried Elender Mitchell widow of Matthew Mitchell. Elender was deceased by 1857 as he remarried Rebecca Chandler. Their children as determined at this time are William H. Winstead b. Apr. 12 or 19, 1824, dc. 1895 buried in Morris Cemetery, Farmersville, Caldwell Co., KY. He married Alafar Hibbs dau. of William Hibbs and Betsy Arledge, b. July 17, 1829, d. June 6, 1914 buried McNeely Cemetery. John C. Winstead, bc. 1837 married Roena Stiles in Hopkins Co. September 1857. Probably a son named Alexander.

William Winstead married Alafar Nov. 6, 1845 in Hopkins Co. They lived near Vandersburg (now Webster Co.) and his occupation being a carriage maker. They apparently were active in the Harmony Missionary Baptist Church, he having preached there one or more times. One daughter Denolas Caldonia was born in Prairie Co., AR. It is unknown why they were in that area at that time. He deeded in 1891 a farm owned in Wayne Co., MO to this same daughter for his "love and affection for her".

At various times from 1870 until his death he owned and operated a sawmill, then a coal mines in Union Co., KY, probably near Boxville and Chalybeate Springs.

Children of William H. Winstead and Alafar Hibbs are, Almedia Francis, b. Jan. 13, 1846 Hopkins Co., d. Feb. 27, 1934 at the home of her dau. Nimma Beeny, was married Oct. 10, 1866 to Robert Franklin Lutz. Fanny was a member of Pleasant Grove all her life. She is buried at Olive Branch beside her husband. He was raised in the Lutheran faith and wasn't known to be a member of any local Church. (For children see article Lutz-Winstead) Mary E. bc. 1852, m. 1866 to W.T. Mangum may have gone to Texas. Nothing further known. William R. "Billy" bc. 1853 m. Julia A. Mitchell a maternal cousin. Their known children are Cora bc. 1873, John bc. 1878, and Wm. T. bc. 1879. Denolas Caldonia b. September 1858 Prairie Co., AR married Feb. 12, 1877 in Union Co., KY to David Joseph Parris. Lockie Anne bc. 1859 married Aug. 28, 1873 in Union Co., KY to John W. Mercer buried Bismark, St. Francis Co., MO. John Munroe "Bud" b. Feb. 20, 1862 d. Nov. 10, 1897 buried Morris Cemetery, Farmersville, Caldwell Co., KY, married Johnnie Irvin in Union Co. in 1889. Robert Marrion "Bob" bc. 1865 married Ida Irvin and he is buried in Springfield, MO. One son named Piffer. Charles Aloras b. 1872 d. 1918 buried McNeely Cemetery, near Kirkwood Springs, Hopkins Co. He married Kate McNeely. - *Submitted by Randa Bearden*

WINSTEAD-RAPPOLEE

Robert and Elta met in Paducah and married May 9, 1931. She was born at Birdsville, Livingston Co., KY. Her parents were Frederick Roland Rappolee (1875-1948) and Alice Warren Rappolee (1878-1962). She attended Livingston Co. High and Tilghman High and graduated. She was former head cashier, Meacham's Chain Store, Paducah. She encouraged her husband to accept call of Civil Service in 1936 and was a prime mover and strong supporter to husband to finish college. Her paternal grandparents were Flavius Josephus Rappolee (1828-1901) and Sarah Emaline Latimer Rappolee (1836-1917). Paternal great-grandparents were Thomas Warren (1846-1916), Civil War Soldier, and Isabelle Emery Fires Warren (1846-1934). Her maternal great-grandparents were William W. Warren and Nancy Jane Roe Warren (1823-1857). Other ancestors: John Fires (1799-1881) and Eunice Daniel Stilwell Fires, their parents D.F. and D.A. Fires and grandparents William Fires (1760-1837), Rev. Soldier and Julian Flagan Fires.

Robert and Elta Winstead

Robert Allen was born at Glennville, KY to Robert Edward Lee Winstead (1884-1977) and Mary Oma Dempsey Winstead (1887-1977). He first attended Sacramento school and graduated from Livermore, KY High, 1928, Draughon's College, Paducah, 1931, attended Murray State, graduated American Univ. 1946, 1948, graduate work Univ. Va. His first public employment was at Madisonville in 1929. He was chain store manager, Paducah and served nearly 40 years in USDA, Wash., D.C. as principal marketing specialist with ASCS. His paternal grandparents were Robert Allen Winstead (1862-1940) and Elizabeth Frances Brown Winstead (1862-1948). Prior Brown ancestors: Andrew Jackson Brown (1830-1888), Austin Brown (1786-1861), Peyton Brown (1764-1833), Rev. Soldier. Prior Winstead ancestors: Thomas Shelton Winstead (1833-1911) Sarah Elizabeth Cox Winstead (1838-1897), Matilda Winstead Clark (1815-), (husband unknown), Custance (Coutance) Winstead (1784-) and Susannah Winstead (ca. 1790-), Custance Winstead (ca. 1755-) and Katherine Hall Winstead, Samuel Winstead, III and Elizabeth Coutance Winstead, Samuel Winstead, II (1701-1774), Samuel Winstead, I (1650-1726). His maternal great-grandparents were Rev. Dr. William Dennis Dempsey (MD) (1814-1864) and Martha Comfort Richardson Dempsey (1831-ca. 1865). Prior Dempsey ancestors: Dubartes Dempsey (1790-1839), William Dempsey, Sr. (1730-1799), Rev. Soldier. A brother of Dubartes, Rev. Absolum Cornelius Dempsey (1787-1872) pastor 46 years, Mill Creek Baptist, Fincastle, VA.

Their son, Dale Eric Winstead born 1945 Alexandria, VA, graduate of Murray, KY Univ. is Sr. Communication Specialist with Military. His children are Dale Eric, Tina Jo and Chad (age in 1987) 17, 15, 9.

Robert and Elta became Christian Baptists: he in 1923 at Woodwards Valley, Ohio Co., she in 1927 at Dyers Hill, Livingston Co. They were prime starters and charter members of Gunston Baptist, Lorton, VA, constituted 1958, charter members Berkeley Spring, WV Baptist, constituted 1971. Both were appointed Ky. Colonels by the Governor. - *Submitted by Robert A. Winstead and Elta Winstead*

FREDERICK A. WINSTEAD

Frederick Alonzo Winstead, born Feb. 9, 1886 at Rangers Landing on Green River near Niagara, McLean Co., KY was the third of nine children born to Robert Allen Winstead and Elizabeth Frances Brown, daughter of Andrew Jackson Brown and Lucy Magolina Fulkerson. It is believed he came to Hopkins Co. from Henderson Co. between 1905 and 1908.

Robert Allen Winstead (born Feb. 16, 1862; died Jan. 5, 1940 in Hopkins Co.) married Elizabeth Frances Brown (born Apr. 22, 1862; died Oct. 3, 1948 in Hopkins Co.) on Jan. 4, 1882 in Henderson Co., KY. The brothers and sisters of Frederick A. were: Ella Marie, born Sept. 27, 1882 - died Mar. 24, 1967 in Pike Co., MS; Robert Edward Lee, born May 8, 1884 - died 1977; William Alvis, born Oct. 12, 1887; Virgie Ann, born Dec. 20, 1890 - died Apr. 3, 1968; Henry Boston, born May 12, 1892 - died Aug.

19, 1940; George Hermon, born Nov. 24, 1894; Hugh Nunn, born Aug. 16, 1899 - died Mar. 29, 1979; and Roy Rivers, born June 19, 1902 - died Sept. 13, 1981.

Frederick Alonzo Winstead and Eura Jane Taylor

Frederick A. married Eura Jane Taylor (born Jan. 25, 1889; died Nov. 8, 1924 in Hopkins Co.) on Aug. 23, 1905. Their children were: Oscar Eldridge, born Sept. 19, 1908 - died Sept. 25, 1964 in New Orleans, LA; Olga Pauline, born July 17, 1910; Margaret Nevelyn, born May 19, 1912; James Allen, born Sept. 20, 1913; William Fred, born Dec. 10, 1917; Thelma Louise, born July 9, 1919; and Alonzo Clarence, born Sept. 25, 1921.

Frederick A. and his family lived for a time on what was then known as the Old Ethel Wylie Place in the vicinity of Anton. He later built a home in the Grapevine Community which no longer stands today due to it burning. Frederick A. and Eura Jane were members of the Pond River Baptist Church.

Frederick A. worked for the Sunlight Coal Co. as a miner until his death on Mar. 13, 1927. The mining accident which caused his death occurred when a spark ignited 10 kegs of black powder. Frederick received powder burns over 75% of his body from the explosion. He is buried in Grapevine Cemetery.

Other ancestral names are: Taylor, Brown, Fulkerson, Cox, Tapp, Yarbrough, and Clayton. - *Compiled by Mary Louise Winstead Wells*

MANLEY WINSTEAD

Manley Winstead was born on Nov. 29, 1760 in Northumberland County, in the state of Virginia to Samuel and Elizabeth Winstead. At the age of sixteen or seventeen years of age he removed to Caswell County in North Carolina where he was drafted for a tour of six months. He was mustered into service under Captain George Moore in Colonel James Saunders' regiment of North Carolina Militia. He rendezvoused at Hillsborough, marched thence to Salisbury, thence to the neighborhood of Charleston in South Carolina, thence to Pluersburg (or Plurisburg) on the Savannah River and was stationed for sometime at a place called the Two Sisters on the Black Swamp. He was in hearing of the battle at Brier Creek in Georgia, was in the act of crossing the Savannah to reinforce the Americans when he was met by General Nash retreating, the Americans having been defeated. His commanding officer at that time was General Rutherford of North Carolina. He was then discharged and returned home having served out his full term of six months.

He was later drafted for three months in the county of Caswell and served under Captain James Greenwood in the militia Light Horse commanded by Colonel Lock and General Pickens. He marched to Salisbury and Camden, was in hearing of the battle on Catawba River where General Davidson was killed. He saw Generals Green and Morgan on this tour at Morgan's Camp having been a dispatch to the first from General Pickens the night before Davidson was killed and returned about the time he was killed with Green's answer. He was then marched to the neighborhood of South Boston on the Dan River and was discharged and sent home having served out his full term.

He married around 1793 to Miss Tapp (Nov. 6, 1799-died before 1809) daughter of William and Elizabeth Tapp. Manley and Miss Tapp had the following children: Manley, Jr. who married Catherine Coleman; Anna (1789-Nov. 1, 1854) married before 1807 in Person Co., NC to William Yarbrough; Bushard (1795-1843) married Apr. 11, 1811 to Susanna Cox; Jane (May 7, 1795-Aug. 4, 1862) married Mar. 26, 1816 to Eli Cox; Elizabeth married Weir; Sally G. (Nov. 6, 1799-Nov. 21, 1861) married Feb. 6, 1821 to Champion Samuel Cox; Charles Taylor (May 2, 1802-Sept. 10, 1862) married Ann Childs Brown.

Miss Tapp died in Person County before 1809 and Manley married on May 17, 1809 Elizabeth Cox (1794-1819) in Person Co., NC. She was the daughter of Samuel Cox and Temperance Bailey. Their children were: William Manley married on July 10, 1829 to Elizabeth Henry; Pleasant Bushard married on Apr. 23, 1833 to Sarah A. Wickliffe; and Alexander T. married on Feb. 12, 1838. Manley moved his family in 1818 from Caswell Co., NC to Hopkins Co., KY. Elizabeth died in 1819.

Manley married Amy Hutcheson on Apr. 14, 1821 in Hopkins Co., KY. They didn't have any children. Manley died on Dec. 26, 1846 and Amy died July 28, 1857. They are buried together on the Old Winstead Farm, North of Nebo, KY - *Submitted by Sandra Donaldson*

WILLIAM FRED WINSTEAD

William Fred Winstead was born Dec. 10, 1917 in Hopkins Co., KY. He was the fifth child of Frederick Alonzo Winstead and Eura Jane Taylor. He was born during a snowstorm just before Christmas in 1917 at the Lonnie Littlepage home on Grapevine Road. Since his mother, Eura, had not yet chosen a name for him, the attending physician, Dr. Fred Strother, suggested the newborn be named after him. That's how William Fred got his name.

William F. attended several schools in Hopkins Co.: Grapevine School, Ball School, Todd School and Wilson School at the time the Illinois Central Railroad was being built.

William F. was only 6 years old when his mother died in 1924. Three years later, his father died from injuries sustained in a mining accident. So Fred (as he was called) went to live with his father's sister, Ella Marie Winstead Spinks, in the Terry's Creek Community near Magnolia, MS.

William F. was 18 years old when he mar-

Ida Belle (Williams) and William Fred Winstead

ried Ida Belle Williams (born Mar. 15, 1918), daughter of Dudley Williams and Clara E. Wilson, on Dec. 8, 1936 in Pike Co., MS. He lived and worked in Terry's Creek as a farmer, logger and saw-mill worker. William F. was working for American District Telegraph Co. in New Orleans, LA just prior to the Army drafting him in 1942. During World War II, he served as a Private in the 398th Field Artillery Battery B, called "The Thundering Herd". He did his basic training at Fort Bragg, NC and shipped out for overseas duty from New York. William F. received five combat stars.

In 1948 he moved his family to Houston, TX. There he took a refrigeration course at the University of Houston. In 1950 he again moved his family to New Orleans, where he lived for over 35 years. William F. worked for the Dixie Plastics Company as an extruder operator until his retirement in December 1982. Upon retirement, he moved back to Terry's Creek, MS, where he and his wife, Ida Belle, now reside.

The children of William F. Winstead and Ida Belle Williams are Mary Louise, born Sept. 1, 1937; Fred Allen, who died in infancy; and William Richard, born Dec. 7, 1948.

Mary Louise married Jesse Lewis Wells Nov. 5, 1955 in New Orleans, LA. They have two daughters: Debra Ann, born June 14, 1956 and Cynthia Kay, born June 23, 1964.

Debra Ann married William James Bartlett on Sept. 28, 1974 in New Orleans, LA. Their children are: Keith Alan, born May 18, 1976; Dana Lynn, born Jan. 5, 1978; James Neil, born Aug. 3, 1979; and Lisa Janell, born Aug. 6, 1982.

William Richard Winstead married Catherine Lynn Dobbins on July 1, 1967. Their children are: Carolyn Kay, born Aug. 16, 1968; Mirian Lynn, born Apr. 17, 1970; and Kirstin, born Sept. 1, 1974. William R. married second Mary Frances Oates. They have one child, William Michael, born Nov. 12, 1980. - *Compiled by Mary Louise Winstead Wells*

WITHERSPOON

Granville Scott (1842-1908) and Mary Cornelia Witherspoon (1845-1924) came to Madisonville from Vanderburg Co., IN in 1886 and settled in this house on Gordon Ave. which was already in the Witherspoon family. It was the only house on a 296 acre tract of land that bordered on the west by Greasy Creek.

Mary Cornelia was the daughter of Mary M.

(died 1883) and William Kinney from Pennsylvania. Mary M. and William are buried at Odd Fellows Cemetery in Madisonville.

Mary Cornelia and Granville Witherspoon had eight children: Jesse, Elmer, Bishop, Martin Louis, Elizabeth May, Dora and the twins Edith and Ethel.

Elmer married Inez Dean and they had one son, Eugene. Elmer and Inez are buried in Odd Fellows Cemetery in Madisonville. Elizabeth May (1873-1918) married Charlie Murphy (1869-1919) from Anton. They are buried in Hicklin Cemetery in Anton. They had six children. Edith married John Gough and they had one son John Orville.

Dora was never married; she is buried in Odd Fellows at Madisonville. Jesse married Ellen Gianimma and they are buried in Evansville, IN.

Edith and Ethel are buried in Ft. Lauderdale, FL where they last lived.

Martin Louis (1879-1922) was married to Viola Pearl Owen (1890-1974) in 1916. She was the daughter of Martha Jane (1857-1936) and William James Owen (1858-1931) of Hopkins Co., KY. They are buried in Odd Fellows Cemetery at Madisonville.

At the time of marriage Martin Louis and Pearl were both working for the telephone company. He as a lineman and she as a telephone operator. Later they operated what was known as The Home Telephone Office. It was located upstairs over what is now Baker and Hickman.

Martin Louis (Marty, as he was called) belonged to the Woodman of the World and Pearl to the Woodman Circle. They are buried at Odd Fellows in Madisonville.

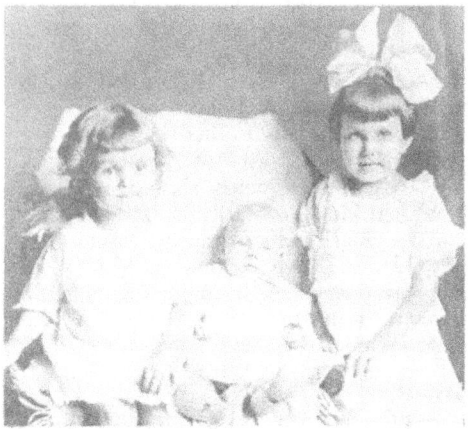

Martha, Katherine and Martin Louis Witherspoon in 1922

Pearl and Marty had three children; Martin Louis II, Anna Katherine and Martha Cornelia. Martin Louis lives in Beaver Dam, KY. He had one daughter Janet. Anna Katherine married Howard Cates and had three children: Howard Wayne, Robin and Anna.

Katherine (1919-1974) and Howard (1917-1980) are buried in Odd Fellows in Madisonville.

Martha Cornelia Witherspoon married James Cromer Daves August, 1936 at Mt. Vernon, IN. They have three children: James Ronald, Yvonne and Patsy Gail.

Ronald married Betty Hobgood of Nebo. They have three children: Tracy, Troy and Ronda. Ronald is with Texas Gas in Owensboro, KY. They have one grandson.

Yvonne has three children: Sherri, Carri and Eddy. She is married to Jack Whitfield. They live at Anton, KY. She has three grandchildren.

Patsy is married to Donnie Crawford. They live at Anton and have three children: Kathy, Donnie II and David and three grandchildren.

Martha Cornelia Witherspoon Daves and her family are the only known descendents of Granville S. and Mary Cornelia Witherspoon living in Hopkins Co., KY. - *Submitted by Martha C.W. Daves*

WILLIAM F. WOLFORD

William Franklin Wolford was born in Linton, IN, on May 17, 1920, to Charles L. Wolford and Esther Mott. He attended Purdue University before being drafted into the Army on May 27, 1942. He made thirteen round-trip voyages across the Atlantic as First Lieutenant, Transportation Officer. His ships departed mostly from New York or Boston harbor carrying cargo to England and France. He was honorably discharged from the Army Apr. 16, 1946. While in the service, Mar. 16, 1944, he married Lou Ann Phillips of Linton, IN, the daughter of Paul Phillips and Gladys Wallace. Lou Ann was born on July 8, 1923, in Rushville, IN. She attended the University of Illinois. They came to Madisonville in May, 1948, where Bill worked at Bell and Zoller Coal Company as surveyor. In 1968 after almost twenty years with the underground mine, he left to work for Dee R. Hogart. He worked for Hogart Excavating as an engineer until his death on Jan. 7, 1982.

From this union two sons were born: James William, Nov. 6, 1950, and Michael Douglas, Jan. 12, 1954. Both boys graduated from Madisonville High School.

From l to r: Phillip, Charles, Scott and Patrick Wolford

Jim was in the Army Reserve from December, 1972 to December, 1978. He attended Murray State University and graduated from the University of Oklahoma in 1975 with a degree in environmental science. On Dec. 30, 1978, he married the former Barbara Woodson, born Aug. 6, 1953, of Greenville, KY. She is the daughter of Dr. and Mrs. Hylan Woodson, Jr. She has a degree in business administration from Murray State University. They have three sons: Charles William, June 12, 1980; Phillip Woodson, Aug. 16, 1982; and Patrick James, May 28, 1986. Jim is working for Texas Gas as manager of gas storage operations; they live in Owensboro, KY. Jim enjoys photography and gardening, and Barbara likes to cross-stitch, coaches soccer, and teaches Sunday School.

Mike enjoyed track while in high school. He attended Eastern Kentucky University and graduated from Delta State university in Mississippi with a Master's Degree in health, physical education, and recreation. On May 15, 1976, he married Susanne Sbravati, born on July 9, 1955, of Lambert, MS. She is the daughter of Mr. and Mrs. Anthony Sbravati. Susanne received a Bachelor's Degree in English education from Delta State University and a Master's Degree from Murray State University. They live in Madisonville. Mike teaches health and physical education at Browning Springs Middle School, and Susanne teaches English at South Hopkins High School. They have one son, Michael Scott, born on Oct. 14, 1979. Mike enjoys running and golf; Susanne enjoys golf and sewing. - *Submitted by Lou Ann Wolford*

WOOD-NIXON

Mary Thelma Nixon was born June 24, 1912 the daughter of John Henry Campbell and Mary Etta Blackburn Nixon. She married Olus Vance Wood, born July 25, 1906 in Caldwell Co., on Nov. 21, 1927 in Caldwell Co. Olus Vance was a mechanic by occupation. He worked as a cook at Outwood Hospital during the 30's; then for Illinois Central Railroad; Arnold Ligon Truck Lines; Claude P'Pool Tractor Inc. and a number of years for Cedar Bluff Stone Co. He died of a stroke at Lourdes Hospital in Paducah, KY on Apr. 15, 1985 and is buried at Cross Roads Cemetery in Caldwell Co. Thelma is living with their son, Ralph Douglas in Caldwell Co. Their other children are: Mitchell Olus; Lewis Alton; Mary Frances (see Jackson story); Jo Ann; Nellie Sue (see Clouse-Wood story); Barbara Fae and Mildred Marie.

Mary Thelma (Nixon) and Olus Vance Wood

Mitchell Olus was born Apr. 13, 1929 and married Dorothy Jean Hobgood on Oct. 10, 1951 in Piggott, AR. They have one daughter, Karen Joyce, who was born in Hopkins Co. on July 3, 1962.

Lewis Alton was born and died May 8, 1930 and is buried at Cross Roads Cemetery in Caldwell Co.

Jo Ann was born June 25, 1943 and married

Ralph Hillyard in Louisville on Apr. 11, 1964. Their children: Kelly Joe (born and died Aug. 7, 1964, buried in Meeks Cemetery in Caldwell Co.); Lori Ann (born Feb. 22, 1966, married James Gregory Noel Mar. 4, 1984 in Caldwell Co.) and Jerry Pat (born Nov. 30, 1971 in Caldwell Co.).

Barbara Fae was born Dec. 26, 1946. She married Ronald Lee Clark on June 10, 1967 in Shawneetown, IL. Their children: Connie Faye (born Dec. 28, 1967 in Caldwell Co.); Ricky Lee (born July 11, 1970 in Caldwell Co.) and Matthew Kent (born Jan. 17, 1982 in Caldwell Co.).

Mildred Marie was born Sept. 23, 1949 and married Rudy Raymond Adams on Mar. 14, 1970 in Caldwell Co. Their children: Kimberly Carol (born May 3, 1975 in Caldwell Co.) and Jacqueline Lea (born Sept. 8, 1983 in Caldwell Co.).

Ralph Douglas was born May 30, 1951 in Caldwell Co. and is not married. - *Submitted by Mary Frances Wood Jackson*

WOODRUFF

Nathaniel Woodruff (1740-1822) with wife and son, Samuel Woodruff (1766-1845) came to Kentucky from Spartanburg, SC ca. 1812. Samuel married Mary Dinsmore and had David (1789-1841), Mary K. (1792-1852), John Willis (1793-1864), Virginia ca. 1800, Hiram (1805-1865). Samuel married a second time and had Robert (1809-1885), Nancy (1812-1900), Levi (1815-will filed Nov. 10, 1890), Mildred (1819-), Parthana (1824-1891), Sarah E. (1829-1919). He had a dau. Annie who died before Dec. 14, 1814, believed to be the first person buried in Christian Privilege Cemetery, with her body preserved in alcohol until burial.

David married Elizabeth Jones (1793-1869). She was married Dec. 9, 1842 to William Davis (1789-1848). She married 3rd time Hezekiah Puryear on Dec. 20, 1849. She is buried at Grapevine Cemetery as Elizabeth Puryear. Their children, Dinsmore (1808-1904), William P. ca. 1817, Dicie (1820-1908), Nancy Jane ca. 1832-1881.

Mary K. married Joseph Woodruff and had Rhoda, Nancy, Emily, Mahala Jane, Pickney, Louvincy, Susanna, Nathaniel Samuel, and Martha.

John Willis married Jan. 22, 1818 to Frances Elvira Davis (1799-1870). Their children: Nancy Elizabeth Tolbert (1819-1910), Charles Davis (1821-1904), Israel D. (1823-1906), Hiram Petilla (1825-1862), Benjamin Bayless (1827-1920), David Dickson (1830-1857) and Willis Wills (1832-1921).

Virginia/Jennie married John/Jack Keyser on July 21, 1817. Their children: James L.M. ca. 1822, William Samuel ca. 1824, Mary Eliz ca. 1829, Jane 1833, John E. 1836, and Nancy M.D. (1840-1841). Part of this family went to Jacksonville, IL.

Hiram married July 16, 1829 Eliza/Lydia Fox ca. 1815. He moved to Caldwell Co. in 1833. Their children, Lydia A. 1830, David, 1832, Eliza Jane (1834-1853), John W. (1835-1926), Cynthia A. ca. 1837, Mary Evelyn ca. 1839, Nancy Eliz. (1841-1900), Martha E. (1843-1923), Wm. C. ca. 1845, Thomas D. (1847-1920), Joseph W. (1849-1880) and Josephine B. ca. 1851, Victoria ca. 1853, George Lewis (1855-1920).

Robert/Robin married July 16, 1829 to Sarah Davis (1808-1853). Their children: John L. (1830-1843), Nancy Catherine (1831-1909), Elvira Malvina (1834-1865), Frances Emily (1836-1864), Charles Hampton (1838-1903), Wm. J. ca. 1840, Sarah S. (1844-1845), Thomas N. (1847-1879), Martha E. (1849-1909). Martha was actually born 1842.

Nancy married Feb. 14, 1833 to Thomas Robinson (1798-1856). Their children: Robert (1834-1917), Sarah E. (1836-1856), Jesse D. (1839-1910), Mildred Eliz. ca. 1840, Serena Jane (1842-1866), Dicie (1846-1881), Wm. T. ca. 1849, John Campbell (1852-1932).

Levi married Dec. 24, 1833 to Elizabeth Ann Laffoon (1818-). Their children: Thursy ca. 1834, Wm. Milton (1835-1910), Sarah Cynthia Jane (1840-1914), Benjamin T. (1842-1919), Mahala Ellen (1844-1917), Robert W.B. (1846-1864), Ambrose Gordon (1848-1919), Nancy M. (1850-1918), John Ray (1852-1914), Parthena Frances (1856-1929), Preston Norsworth Bradley (1857-1950) and Henry Briton (1861-1946).

Mildred married May 12, 1841 to John A. Ezell (1820-1879). Their children: Sarah E. (1842-1915), Nancy J. (1846-1862), Tabitha (1851-1923), William R. (1850-1850), James Thomas.

Parthena married Mar. 25, 1841 to Wilkerson Bestic Laffoon (1821-1904). Their children: Travis N. (1845-1863), John Rutherford (1848-1928), Nancy Eliz. (1853-1854), Mahala Catherine (1861-1924), Martha Mildred (1863-1935), Dillard Lee (1866-1920).

Sarah E. married Sept. 8, 1845 to John Nash Laffoon (1826-1899). Their children: Thomas N. 1846, James H. (1848-1931), Allen W. (1850-1928), Manthis Eliz., William Dixon (1866-1945). - *Submitted by Dorothy Abbott*

WOODRUFF-DAVIS

These are descendants of John W. Woodruff and Frances Elvira Davis, daughter of John Davis and Elizabeth Tolbert.

Nancy Elizabeth Tolbert married June 4, 1865 to Aurealis R Gipson, no issue.

Charles D. Woodruff on Mar. 23, 1846 married Cynthia Caroline Davis, (b. Apr. 3, 1830 d. Nov. 6, 1909), dau. of Thomas C. Davis and Elvira Fox. Their issue: Victoria Josephine (b. Nov. 16, 1848 d. Sept. 27, 1917), Theadore Petilla (b. Sept. 17, 1849 d. Feb. 17, 1925), Frances Elvira (b. Dec. 3, 1852), Elizabeth C. (1855-1859), Richard David Dickson (b. Aug. 20, 1857 d. Sept. 22, 1931), Rufus (b. Sept. 14, 1859 d. June 1, 1916), Margaret Ann (Apr. 12, 1861 d. Nov. 11, 1926), William Rodgers (Feb. 8, 1964 d. July 4, 1924), Melissa (1866-1922), Lewis Waller (b. Dec. 21, 1868 d. Feb. 11, 1882), Thomas Willard (June 15, 1870 d. Oct. 28, 1875), Minnie Lou (b. Apr. 27, 1873 d. Jan. 4, 1900).

Issue of Israel D. Woodruff married Mary Elizabeth Keyser (m. April 1827 d. Sept. 22, 1879): Theadocia Melissa (b. Nov. 28, 1850 d. Aug. 21, 1936) (dau. of John Keyser and Virginia Woodruff).

Issue of Hiram Petilla (m. Feb. 21, 1851) and Lounicy Crabtree (b. 1834 d. Nov. 11, 1855): John Isiah David (b. Jan. 3, 1852), James Benjamin (b. May 1, 1853 d. Mar. 5, 1887), Lounicy York (Oct. 28, 1855) dau. of Isiah Crabtree and Ruth Lindley. Hiram married 2nd to Mary J. Wright (b. Feb. 19, 1832 d. Jan. 3, 1908). Issue: Elizabeth Wills (b. Nov. 4, 1857 d. June 17, 1872), Lenora Ann ca. 1859-1861, Francis Petilla (b. Apr. 18, 1862 d. Apr. 26, 1914).

Issue of Benjamin Bayless married on May 31, 1855 to Mary Ann B. Croft (b. Aug. 31, 1834 d. July 3, 1862) dau. of William G. Croft and Elizabeth McKinney: Melissa (1856-1859), Richard died 18 mo., Willis Byron (b. Feb. 17, 1859 d. Jan. 7, 1940), Misseniah Frances (b. Dec. 15, 1861 d. May 6, 1888) and Elizabeth Charles (1863-1951). Benjamin married 2nd Sarah M. Denton (1843-1885) on Apr. 14, 1864. Issue: Theadocia Ann (b. Jan. 24, 1865 d. Feb. 3, 1911), Mary Lee Josephine (b. May 13, 1867 d. June 9, 1920), John Patrick David (1870-19—), Myrtle (1872), Iva W. (1874), Daisy E. ca. 1877, Matilda Catherine (b. Aug. 3, 1879 d. June 15, 1956), Benjamin Vickers Oct. 15, 1881.

Issue of William W. married Josephine Darnell on Apr. 5, 1871. She died Oct. 7, 1885. Altha F. Mar. 13, 1873..will brought in and recorded on Oct. 2, 1939. - *Submitted by Dorothy Abbott*

WOODRUFF-GAMBLE

William Thomas (W.T.) Woodruff, son of Boyd and Mary Sweeney Woodruff, married Alma Louise Gamble, daughter of Carl and Myrtle Wilson Gamble, on Jan. 16, 1942. They were all of St. Charles, KY. They were blessed with four children:

W.T. and Louise Woodruff

Darrell, born June 13, 1945, once served in the Air Force and married Theresa McKnight of Rt. 2, Dawson Springs, KY. They have two children: Darla, who works at the Wal Mart store in Madisonville, and Darren who is presently serving in the Air Force. The family's home is at Rt. 2, Dawson Springs.

Marilyn, born Feb. 8, 1947, married Joe G. Huddleston of Rt. 2, Dawson Springs and they have two children: Anthony who is now in the U.S. Marine Corps and Amy who still resides with her parents at their Rt. 2, Dawson Springs home.

Karen, born Oct. 5, 1951, married Larry Joe Geary of Ohio County and they have three children: Kimberly, Kenneth and Jason, all still at home. They live at Rockport, KY.

Kenneth, born Jan. 17, 1956, married Suzzane Helton of Middlesboro, KY. They have one 8 year-old daughter, Chrystal, and live in East Bernstadt, KY.

W.T.'s father died in 1972 and his mother died in 1976. He has three sisters: Mary Sue Devault of Gallatin, TN; Coleen Daniels of Ashville, NC; and Thelma Allen of Independence, MO. His younger brother, Ray, also died in 1972 and his widow, Elizabeth and their youngest son, Scott, live in Madisonville. Their oldest son, Greg, is married and works for Boyd Funeral home in Salem, KY where they make their home.

Louise's parents live in Belleville, IL near her two brothers, Larkin and Donald Gamble.

W.T. served four years in the Army. When he was discharged, he returned to the coal mines in Hopkins County. He was later transferred to Ohio County. They lived there until he retired from Peabody Coal Company and then moved back to the St. Charles area.

They attend the Assembly of God Church in Earlington, KY. - *Submitted by Louise Woodruff*

WOODRUFF-NISBET

Laura Kate Nisbet, 4th child of James Moore Nisbet (1829-1915) born Dec. 3, 1857, married David Dixon Woodruff b. 1857, of St. Charles, KY. He was connected with St. Bernard Coal Co., operated a livery stable, operated a meat market, and engaged in general commercial welfare of the community. They attended the Old Christian Privilege Christian Church, the first Christian church in Hopkins County. They had five children:

Laura Catherine Woodruff b. December 1884, married William Graham, a coal miner. Their children were: William David Graham b. Apr. 2, 1915, who married Ruth Agnes Newbold b. Feb. 9, 1927, and they have one daughter, Sheila Ruth Graham b. Feb. 4, 1952. She married John Maretich b. Oct. 14, 1952, their son is David Ethan Maretich b. Apr. 30, 1986. They live in Chattanooga, TN. The second Graham child: Harriett b. Apr. 2, 1918, married Ralph Kavanaugh, no children. They live in Dawson Springs.

Clay Woodruff b. Apr. 29, 1887 married Willie Mae Jenkins b. Nov. 23, 1889. He was a merchant and a coal operator at St. Charles. They had one dau. Hilda Mae Woodruff b. Mar. 26, 1921, married Orvil E. Smith. (see Smith-Woodruff family)

James Woodruff b. September 1888 married Mabel Cook. He owned and trained race horses and owned a coal mine. Their children: Farris Woodruff b. Apr. 13, 1912 married Hazel Maddox b. May 21, 1911. Farris and Hazel live at Nortonville. He is coal trucker and she is retired elementary teacher. They have one daughter, Anna Carol Woodruff b. Nov. 19, 1947, married Triston Kington b. Sept. 27, 1946, teacher and basketball coach at Union Co. H.S. They have two children: Amy Celeste b. Aug. 10, 1966, in college, and Derrick Scott b. Sept. 7, 1978. James (Jimmy) Woodruff b. Nov. 28, 1922 married Odenia Kirkpatrick b. May 12, 1929. Their son, Jamie Woodruff Aug. 31, 1953 presently married to Debbie Girten b. Jan. 31, 1961. One son, Brandon b. Sept. 7, 1976. Jimmy is a retired coal miner and Odenia teaches at South Hopkins High School. They all live in Nortonville.

Fannie M. (known as "Doll") Woodruff b. April 1890, married A.H. Kelley, a coal operator at Daniel Boone and St. Charles, no children.

Charlie B. (girl) b. Jan. 1, 1893 married George Bartholomew Jenkins b. Sept. 21, 1893 of St. Charles. Both died two days apart in the 1918 flue epidemic. They left a son, Richard Costello Jenkins b. Mar. 18, 1918, was a pharmacist at Old Eddyville, d. Oct. 13, 1972, buried with his parents at Christian Privilege Cemetery, St. Charles. - *Submitted by Rella G. Jenkins with approval from Mr. and Mrs. Farris Woodruff, Mr. and Mrs. Jimmy Woodruff, Mr. and Mrs. David Graham*

CARL EDWARD WOOLFOLK

CARL EDWARD WOOLFOLK, son of Thomas Lewis Woolfolk and Nannie T. Boulden, was born Nov. 25, 1876 and died Aug. 5, 1960. He never married. He is buried in Odd Fellows Cemetery, Madisonville, KY. - *Submitted by Ruby R. Shaw*

CLAY WOOLFOLK

CLAY WOOLFOLK, son of Sherwood Hicks Woolfolk and Sarah Elizabeth Clay Givens, was born Feb. 11, 1882 at Providence, KY. At the age of four he moved with his parents and family to Pratt, KS, where he grew to manhood. He married Ethel A. Reed on Dec. 25, 1907.

A son Glen was born Nov. 30, 1909. In 1914 Clay, Ethel and Glen moved to Comanche Co., KS. He managed the Lemon-Barbee Ranch for several years, then was able to buy land of his own in 1918. He was a successful farmer and cattleman. In 1943, they retired and moved into Protection. Their son Glen managed the farm. Ethel passed away Jan. 2, 1964 and Clay on Aug. 25, 1969.

Glen married Bernice Lindsay on Apr. 12, 1930. They lived on the farm raising wheat and cattle. They retired to live in Protection about 1964, leaving the farm work to their children. They had three children;

1. Raymond Wayne born May 8, 1932.
2. Orvid Delane born May 9, 1934.
3. Neoma Lea born May 8, 1936.

Bernice and Glen have nine grandchildren and 17 great grandchildren. Glen Woolfolk passed away June 3, 1987. *Submitted by Ruby R. Shaw*

JOHN LEWIS WOOLFOLK

JOHN LEWIS WOOLFOLK, son of Thomas Woolfolk (1765-1847), was born Jan. 11, 1806 in Woodford Co., KY. He moved with his father and family to Hopkins County about 1820. He died Aug. 22, 1884 in Madisonville, and he is buried in Odd Fellows Cemetery. He was past 78 years old. He was a blacksmith and gunsmith. He was married three times.

His first wife was Margaret Jane Bailey, born about 1816. Her parents were Richard R. Bailey (1770-1823) and Anne Nancy Brown. John Lewis and Margaret Jane were married July 22, 1830. She died July 20, 1842. they had seven children:

1. Sarah Catherine Woolfolk born 1831 and died 1877, married John Baylis Earle. (See her story.)
2. Willis West Woolfolk, born 1833, death date unknown.
3. Richard Runand Bailey Woolfolk, born 1834 and died 1838, four years old.
4. John Peter Woolfolk, born 1835, died at seven months.
5. Sherwood Hicks Woolfolk, born 1837 and died 1920. (See his story.)
6. Coanzay Woolfolk, born 1839, died 1840, at one year old.
7. Charles Lewis Woolfolk, born 1841, killed by lightening 1859.

Second wife of John Lewis Woolfolk was Sarah Russell Browder born 1826 and died Sept. 29, 1855. Her father was John Browder. They were married July 26, 1843. They had six children.

1. John Browder Woolfolk, born Mar. 13, 1845. He enlisted in the Confederate Army Sept. 20, 1862, at Madisonville, KY in Company I 10th Regiment Kentucky Cavalry under Gen. Adam Johnson. He was captured at Salem, IN on July 10, 1863 and imprisoned at Camp Morton, Indianapolis, IN. He escaped Feb. 11, 1864 and rejoined the 8th Kentucky Regiment, as most of the 10th were scattered, dead or imprisoned. He was shot and killed Apr. 28, 1865, by a Union soldier, at Paris, TN, while on leave from his base.
2. Edward West Woolfolk, born Aug. 29, 1846 and died two months old.
3. Mary Ellen Woolfolk, born 1848 and died 1880, married Burr Franklin Young Apr. 30, 1866. (See her story.)
4. Thomas Lewis Woolfolk born Dec. 31, 1850 and died Apr. 14, 1879, at Welaka, FL. He married Oct. 15, 1870 to Nannie T. Boulden. Their son, Carl Edward Woolfolk, was born Nov. 25, 1876 and died Aug. 5, 1960. (See their story.)
5. Frances Ellen Woolfolk, born Sept. 24, 1852 and died Nov. 21, 1852 at two months.
6. Laurel Russell Woolfolk born Feb. 20, 1855 and died Mar. 25, 1932. On Sept. 9, 1881 he married Mrs. Nannie T. Boulden, widow of his brother Thomas Lewis Woolfolk. Their daughter was: Vera Russell Woolfolk born 1884 and died 1955, married Charles W. Lindsay Dec. 4, 1902. They had 2 sons.

The third wife of John Lewis Woolfolk was Pauline J. Harvey married Aug. 14, 1857. She was born Nov. 20, 1810 and died Mar. 9, 1890. No children. - *Submitted by Ruby R. Shaw, great granddaughter*

LAURAL R. WOOLFOLK

LAURAL RUSSELL WOOLFOLK, son of John Lewis Woolfolk and Sarah Russell Browder, was born Feb. 20, 1855 and died Mar. 25, 1932. He married Sept. 9, 1881 to Mrs. Nannie T. Boulden, widow of his brother Thomas Lewis Woolfolk.

They had one daughter. Vera Russell Woolfolk was born Dec. 6, 1884 and died 1955. She married Charles W. Lindsay Dec. 4, 1902. He was born Nov. 5, 1881 and died Dec. 13, 1940. They had 2 boys: Charles W. Lindsay, Jr. and Laurel Tandy Lindsay. Both died as young boys.

Laurel R. Woolfolk married a second time to

Mrs. Cordelia Pritchett about 1926. She died about 1932. Both are buried at Madisonville, KY. - *Submitted by Ruby R. Shaw*

LILBURN M. WOOLFOLK

LILBURN MAGRUDER WOOLFOLK, son of Sherwood Hicks Woolfolk and his first wife Mary Eliza Magruder, was born Mar. 4, 1867 at Madisonville. His mother died at his birth. She is buried at Louisville, KY. Lilburn was cared for by his Aunt Belle Reynolds, of Goshen, KY for a few years. After his father married Mrs. Sarah Elizabeth Clay Givens on Jan. 23, 1874, he returned to Madisonville to live with his father and step-mother. Sally, as she was called, was a widow and had one little girl, Fanny, about the same age as Lilburn. They had many happy days together. Maggie Mae arrived in 1875; Mary Fern 1877 and Clay in 1882. (Their stories are elsewhere in this book.)

In 1885 they decided to move to Kansas. S.H. and Lilburn arrived in time for the terrible blizzard of January 1886. They bought land near Pratt, KS. Sally and the rest of the family arrived in April 1886. They built a house and barn on the farm and moved into it.

At age 21 Lilburn returned to Kentucky to care for the land he had inherited from his mother. He built a house and married Mary Pierce. They had two children:

Mary Belle Woolfolk was born November 1893 and died March 1898; John Pierce Woolfolk was born May 9, 1895.

Lilburn Magruder Woolfolk passed away May 27, 1903.

John Pierce Woolfolk continued to live on his father's farm. He married Laura Lang on Mar. 4, 1925. She died Nov. 5, 1977. Pierce married Tess Quinlan on Feb. 10, 1979. They still live on the same place, now called "Twelve Acres" near Goshen, KY. - *Submitted by Ruby R. Shaw, a cousin*

MAGGIE MAY WOOLFOLK

MAGGIE MAY WOOLFOLK, daughter of Sherwood Hicks Woolfolk and Sarah Elizabeth Clay Givens, was born Jan. 23, 1875 at Madisonville, KY. In 1886 she moved with her family to Pratt Co., KS. Maggie was eleven years old at that time and bitterly objected leaving "green Kentucky" and coming to "barren Kansas" saying; "I guess we'll just grow up with the Indians and I so wanted to go to school and be a teacher." Dreams do come true - Maggie finished grade school and went to Pratt Normal College for two years to prepare to become a teacher. She taught school for eleven years at various country schools in Pratt county.

She married George Armor Patterson on Jan. 19, 1910, at the home of her parents. They traveled by train to Protection, KS, where George had bought a quarter of land and built a house and barn on it. George was a successful farmer raising wheat, horses and mules. They purchased another quarter of land. Both these quarters still belong to the family.

George passed away Mar. 9, 1930 and Maggie on Feb. 8, 1963. Both are buried in the Protection Cemetery.

They had three children: Vella Mae Patterson was born July 12, 1911; Ruby Rose Patterson was born Jan. 11, 1913; and an infant son, who died soon after birth in January 1918.

Vella graduated from Protection High School and Wichita Business College. She attended Alva State Teacher's College where she met her future husband, Lloyd H. Wilhite. They were married Dec. 29, 1937. He died Apr. 13, 1942. He was employed at Boeing Airplane Company at this time. After college Vella worked for a Newspaper Publishing Service and traveled extensively throughout the United States. After the death of her husband she was employed by Cardwell Manufacturing Company for 15 years, until they closed. She then was employed by Energy Reserves Group Oil Company for 17 years.

Vella Wilhite or "Pat" as she is better known, has been very active in club work, she has served in all the various offices and has been past State President of the Kansas Federation of Business and Professional Women's Clubs and of Kansas Council of Women, a past-president of Pilot Club, Inter-Club Council, Oil Secretaries Association, Gamma Sigma Chapter of Epsilon Sigma Alpha, Desk and Derrick Club and Toastmistress Club, all of Wichita. She still lives in Wichita.

Ruby married Lloyd Ervin Shaw on Sept. 2, 1931 and they moved to the Patterson farm. Ervin enjoyed farm work, raising wheat, maize and feeding cattle until his death on Feb. 28, 1956. Ruby moved to town and was employed by the Protection Co-Op Lockers for the past twenty-five years.

They had three children:

Patricia Rose Shaw born Apr. 8, 1938 who married Austin Hunter Callison III on Sept. 30, 1956. They have two sons:

1. Scott Hunter Callison born Sept. 22, 1958 and married Marci Spradlin on Mar. 7, 1986.

2. Jeffrey Alan Callison born July 24, 1960 and married Lori Kotch on Jan. 15, 1983. They have Zachary Alan born Aug. 27, 1983 and Christopher Tyler born Sept. 26, 1986.

Harvey Allen Shaw born Jan. 8, 1942 and married Karen Kay Breit on June 12, 1962. She was born June 8, 1944, and passed away Dec. 17, 1980. They had two children:

1. Paul Allen Shaw born June 28, 1963.

2. Stephanie Kay Shaw born Feb. 15, 1966.

Myrna Mae Shaw born Aug. 8, 1949 married Richard Leroy Beck Nov 7, 1970. They have three children:

1. Sonya Michelle Beck born May 13, 1974.

2. Lynel Christina Beck born Jan. 26, 1976.

3. Richard Ryan Beck born Oct. 8, 1980. - *Submitted by Ruby R. Shaw*

MARY ELLEN WOOLFOLK

MARY ELLEN WOOLFOLK, daughter of John Lewis Woolfolk and Sarah Russell Browder, was born Oct. 9, 1848 Hopkins Co., KY and died May 4, 1880. She was married to Burr Franklin Young on Apr. 30, 1866. He was born Feb. 9, 1843 and died Oct. 23, 1928 at the age of 85. Both are buried Odd Fellows Cemetery Madisonville, KY.

One of their children was Ida Mary Young, born Oct. 4, 1874 and died Jan. 9, 1970. She was married on June 26, 1901 to Francis John Whitfield. He was born Dec. 11, 1876 and died Mar. 7, 1956. Both are buried at Grapevine Cemetery, Madisonville. They had a son Robert Marvin Whitfield, born Feb. 21, 1903 and died June 6, 1983. He was married Apr. 2, 1958 to Sory Stinnett. She still lives in Hopkins County.

Ida Mary Young Whitfield became blind in later years and was lovingly taken care of by her son Marvin and his wife Sory for many years. - *Submitted by Ruby R. Shaw, a cousin*

MARY FERN WOOLFOLK

MARY FERN WOOLFOLK, daughter of Sherwood Hicks Woolfolk and Sarah Elizabeth Clay Givens, was born Mar. 7, 1877 in Madisonville, KY. She moved to Pratt, KS, with her parents and family, arriving on Apr. 1, 1886. They lived on a farm. Fern attended Pratt Normal College and taught school for several terms. She married George David Miller, on Mar. 16, 1897. He came from Cass Co., MO. He was a farmer and cattleman.

They had four sons: (1) Marion born Jan. 5, 1898; died Aug. 9, 1973; (2) Percy born Nov. 28, 1902; (3) George Junior born June 2, 1907 and (4) Loyce born July 24, 1909.

George David Miller passed away Oct. 28, 1954 at Sawyer, KS where they lived. Fern passed away Jan. 30, 1971. Both are buried in the Coats Cemetery. - *Submitted by Ruby R. Shaw, a niece*

SAMUEL S. WOOLFOLK

SAMUEL SNOWDEN WOOLFOLK, son of Sherwood Hicks Woolfolk and Sarah Elizabeth Clay Givens, was born Nov. 8, 1886, after his parents had moved from Hopkins Co., KY. He took up wheat farming, first helping his father on his farm and then purchasing land for himself. He married Inez Viola Yoho on Oct. 14, 1909. Sam and Inez lived on the farm for the rest of his life. After his death Inez moved into Pratt, KS, and the boys took over the farm.

They had seven children: (1) Ruth Elizabeth born Aug. 6, 1910; (2) Beula Ivy born Jan. 5, 1914; (3) Clay David born Feb. 11, 1916; (4) Pearl Alice born June 25, 1918; (5) Paul Samuel born Aug. 15, 1920; (6) Dora Helen born Sept. 8, 1923; and (7) Clyde Richard born Apr. 21, 1925.

Samuel Snowden Woolfolk passed away Feb. 7, 1938 and Inez Viola on June 3, 1979. - *Submitted by Ruby R. Shaw, a niece*

SARAH C. WOOLFOLK

SARAH CATHERINE WOOLFOLK, oldest daughter of John Lewis Woolfolk and Margaret Jane Bailey, was born Apr. 21, 1831 and died Jan. 20, 1877. She lived all her life in Madisonville, KY. On Oct. 1, 1843 she married John Baylis Earle.

He was the son of Samuel Baylis Earle and Jane Woodson. He was born Jan. 3, 1823 and died July 8, 1906.

They had seven children, two died in infancy and the remaining are: (1) Lucian, born 1854 and died 1927. He married Oct. 9, 1884 to Belle Larimire at McPherson, KS, where he practiced law. They had one son, Basil Earle, who moved to California; (2) Luella, born 1856, died 1929; (3) Sarah, born 1858, died 1948; (4) Poritia, born 1860, died 1943; and (5) Augusta, born 1872, died 1960 at 88 years old. The four girls never married. They took care of their father until his death. The girls taught school and gave music lessons on a piano with solid ivory keys, which had been brought to Hopkins County from Pennsylvania by their Grandmother Earle in a covered wagon.

John Baylis Earle was brought up on his father's farm, attended school in a log school house. He became a well-educated man by his own individual efforts. At age twenty he taught school, later was appointed assessor of Muhlenberg Co., KY. Upon leaving this office he studied law and after two years of schooling he was admitted to the bar and began practice in Madisonville. In 1885 he was elected County Attorney of Hopkins County, serving four years. He practiced law at the Hopkins bar for fifty years.

In 1869 he opened the first coal mine in Hopkins County - the #11 Mine of the Bernard Coal Company near Earlington. The town of Earlington was named for him. His picture was still hanging in the Earlington High School in 1966.

The old Earle home on North Main, Madisonville, was the first home with running water. When the old house was torn down, the water pipes were still intact. They were made of wood.

John Baylis Earle led a useful life, never failing to extend a helping hand to the poor and oppressed.

Both are buried in Odd Fellows Cemetery in Madisonville, KY. - *Submitted by Ruby Shaw*

SHERWOOD H. WOOLFOLK

SHERWOOD HICKS WOOLFOLK, son of John Lewis Woolfolk and Margaret Jane Bailey, was born Apr. 13, 1837 at Madisonville, KY. At the age of 17 he entered Transylvania College for the study of law.

In 1861 he enlisted in the Confederate Army at Madisonville in Company I 10th Kentucky Regiment as a Lieutenant under General Adam Johnson. He fought in battles at Madisonville, Hopkinsville, Panther Creek, Elizabethtown, Lebanon, Uniontown, Green River Stockade, Muldraugh's Hill all in Kentucky; at Liberty and Snowhill in Tennessee. He was on Morgan's Raid into Indiana, was captured at Chesher, OH, on July 20, 1863. He was imprisoned at Camp Chase, OH. He was released Jan. 4, 1865. While in Camp Chase the men amused themselves by writing letters, enclosing them in sealed bottles, and throwing them into the river in hopes someone finding them would send an answer. S.H., as he was called, was lucky. He received an answer from Mary Eliza Magruder. They carried on a correspondence and when released, he hunted up Mary. They fell in love and were married Apr. 26, 1866. They made their home in Madisonville, where S.H. was admitted to the bar and practiced law there. Their son Lilburn Magruder was born Mar. 4, 1867. His mother passed away at his birth. She was buried at Louisville, KY. Her little son was cared for by his Aunt Belle Reynolds for a few years, at Goshen, KY. S.H. returned to his law practice and was elected County Attorney of Hopkins County for several years; was elected to the House of Representatives for a two year term 1871-73.

On Jan. 23, 1874 he married Mrs. Sarah Elizabeth Clay Givens. She was the daughter of Benjamin Marston Clay and Abiah Frances McDowell. Sallie, as she was called, was the widow of Nathaniel Karr Givens, of Providence, KY. He died Oct. 30, 1871. They had one daughter Francis Abiah (Fanny) Givens born Dec. 29, 1868. Thus S.H. and Sallie had a stepson and a step-daughter. On Jan. 23, 1875 a daughter Maggie May arrived, followed by Mary Fern, born Mar. 7, 1877, Aganes, born Apr. 5, 1879 but died at six months of age, and Clay, born Feb. 11, 1882. After the death of S.H.'s father, John Lewis Woolfolk, the family decided to move further west. S.H. and son Lilburn arrived in Pratt, KS just before the terrible blizzard of January 1886, when so many cattle were frozen to death. They bought land southwest of Pratt and Sallie, Fanny, Maggie, Mary Fern and Clay took the train to Kingman, KS, the end of the railroad and were met by S.H. and Lilburn. They were happy to be together again, but saddened by leaving Kentucky and moving to a strange land. They stayed in Pratt for a while running a boarding house on South Main until September 1886 when their new house on the farm was completed and they moved into it. On Aug. 11, 1886 another son, Samuel Snowden was born. When Lilburn was 21 he returned to Kentucky to take care of his land inherited from his mother. S.H. and Sallie farmed for a number of years until most of their children were married and the boys took over the farm work. They retired to Coats, KS, where S.H. passed away June 4, 1920 at age 83. Sallie died May 11, 1925 at the age of 78. They are buried at Coats, KS.

(The stories of their children are elsewhere in this book.) - *Submitted by Ruby R. Shaw, a granddaughter of S.H. and Sallie and a daughter of Maggie May Woolfolk*

THOMAS WOOLFOLK

THOMAS WOOLFOLK, born 1765 in Virginia, moved to Hopkins Co., KY around 1820 at about the age of 45. He is listed in the 1790 tax list in Woodford County; the 1810 Census of Fayette County; and in the tax list of Hopkins County in 1821. In 1839 Thomas Woolfolk frees a slave, Mini, Hopkins County Deed Book. He had a son John Lewis, born 1806 in Woodford County; a daughter Narcissa, born 1807 in Fayette County; a daughter, Elizabeth (Eliza) married in 1815 to John Shore in Fayette County. Thomas was living with his son, Edward W.R. in 1840 in Providence, KY, but died at the home of his son, John Lewis, in Madisonville, in 1847 at the age of 82. His wife's name, birth, death or burial place is unknown.

His children were:

1. Elizabeth (Eliza) who married John Shore on May 4, 1815 in Fayette County, Marriage bond signed by Thomas Woolfolk.

2. Caroline married William Bacon; their children were - Edward, Judith and Mary Ann.

3. Edward West R. married Lackey H. Noel on Jan. 25, 1828, Madisonville. His will signed 1841 still in probate in 1858. John Lewis was named administrator and guardian to his son, George. Edward lived in Providence and was a merchant and store keeper.

4. John Lewis, born Jan. 11, 1806 in Woodford Co., KY. He died Aug. 22, 1884; buried in the Odd Fellows Cemetery, Madisonville, Hopkins Co., KY. He married: 1st Margaret Jane Bailey, 2nd Sarah Russell Browder, 3rd Pauline J. Harvey. (See John Lewis Woolfolk's story elsewhere in this book.)

5. Narcissa, born 1807, Fayette Co., KY; died Sept. 11, 1854 Hopkins County. She married: 1st Fredrick Mandred Ashby, 2nd Thomas Berry.

6. Maria married Feb. 4, 1829 to Charles Henry Ashby.

7. Sarah married Sept. 5, 1831 to David Dunkerson.

Marriage Bonds for Edward, John Lewis, Narcissa, Maria and Sarah all signed in Hopkins Co., KY.

Thomas Woolfolk died July 12, 1847. - *Submitted by Ruby R. Shaw, a great-great granddaughter of Thomas Woolfolk*

THOMAS LEWIS WOOLFOLK

THOMAS LEWIS WOOLFOLK, son of John Lewis Woolfolk and Sarah Russell Browder, was born Dec. 31, 1850 at Madisonville, KY and died Apr. 14, 1879 at Welaka, FL. He was a dentist.

He married Oct. 15, 1870 to Nannie T. Boulden, she was born Feb. 19, 1852, and died May 11, 1920.

Their son, Carl Edward Woolfolk was born Nov. 25, 1876 and died 1960. He never married. - *Submitted by Ruby R. Shaw*

WOOTON

Thomas Pryor Wooton (1859-1951), was born in Kentucky, the son of J.E. Wooton, Sr., who was born in 1829 in North Carolina. The mother of Thomas Wooton was Mary Jones (1841), daughter of Thomas E. Jones and Melvina Jones.

The Jones' were married in 1839 in North Carolina and came with a band of folks from Granville Co., NC about 1846. They made the long trek over the mountains seeking new homes in Daniel Boone country. Thomas E. Jones 'took up' a section of land on the borders of Otter Creek near the area that became Hanson and made a home for his family which included three children, namely William, Mary and Lucy. They were born in North Carolina. William was lost in the Civil War. Lucy married Allen Parish. Mary married James E. Wooton I and had eight children - John F. 1857, Thomas 1859, William 1865, Benjamin 1867, Americus (called Meck) 1868, Mellie 1869, Maggie 1875 and James Ord 1877. Their mother, Mary, died about 1882 and the youngsters came back to Grandma "Viney's" home. She was a good practical doctor and midwife, who made her own medicines from herbs and barks she gathered from nature. The little Maggie was adopted by Given and Letitia Rothrock in Hanson and later became the wife of J.O. Edge, the hardware Merchant of Hanson.

The family home of James E. and Melvina Wooton was near the present Olive Branch area and others of the North Carolina emigrants settled round about. They had agreed to stay in contact and have "Granville County" carved on their tombstones in the Olive Branch Church Cemetery and those words are seen on many of the stones today.

Thomas Pryor Wooton married Ella Combs in Springfield, TN on Easter 1887. Ella was born in Kentucky in 1867, the daughter of John Henry Combs (1839-1909) and Mary Virginia Slaton Combs (1842-1921). John Henry Combs was the son of William, who was the son of John Combs I and Nancy Anne Adams. Nancy Adams was a near relative (niece?) of John Quincy Adams, sixth president of the United States. This was a tradition held with pride down through the years.

Thomas and Ella Combs Wooton had eight children: Murris 1890, Homer 1895, both died young, Mary 1892, Noel 1894, Thom Burr 1899, Nellie 1901, Georgia 1904, and James 1908. The sons served their country in the army; the youngest, Captain James Wooton gave 45 years to military service and was buried in 1986 in Arlington National Cemetery.

Carrying the Wooton family history farther- to the next next generation:

Mary Wooton married Z.T. Wilson and had Rudy, Margaret and Maxine.

Noel Wooton married Irma Frank and had Jack, June and Joanne.

Burr Wooton married Connor Sheckels and had Thomas C.

Nellie Wooton married Ora Mills and they had Billy-who was lost in the navy at Okinawa in W.W. II, Richard, Robert, Doris, Melvin, and Sharon.

Georgia Wooton married Billy Brown and they had Dorothy (Farmer). James Edgar Wooton II married Aleen Zynda and they had Carol Ann, James E. III, Roger, Brian and Mary Leslie.

For over one hundred years, some member of the Jones-Wooton family had lived in the old farm home (a story and a half frame house). Much of it was finished by hand plane and was one of the oldest in the community. It was sold when the Mills family moved to Hanson in 1946 and about ten years later burned to the ground. - *Submitted by Sharon Mills Thomson*

WOOTON-JACKSON

The wedding of Margaret Ann Jackson and James Lester Wooton on Feb. 23, 1947 was the first known wedding to take place in the old historic Grapevine Christian Church. Margaret, the youngest of five children born to Mary Belle Todd Jackson and Herman Franklin Jackson of 526 East Broadway in Madisonville, KY, was born at the home place on Aug. 20, 1927 and lived there until her marriage. Soon after graduation from Madisonville High School, she went to work for Ruby Lumber Company where she was employed until 1948. In 1952, Margaret was employed by The Kentucky Bank and Trust Company where she is now supervisor of the bookkeeping department.

James, the only child of Cassye Whitson King Wooton and Ovie Lester Wooton was born May 6, 1924 in a house on his grandfather Wooton's farm near Slaughters, KY in Webster County. Later he and his family moved into his grandfather's home where he lived until he married and moved to Madisonville. After

The James Wooton Family. Back row l to r: John Green, Joyce Green, Lois Green and Tom Green. Middle row l to r: Karen Green, James Wooton, Margaret Wooton and Johnna Green. Front row l to r: Joann Green, Samuel Green and Jennifer Green. Taken in August 1987

graduation from Slaughters High School, James worked in Evansville, IN as a welder at International Steel, a sub-contractor for the Evansville Shipyards making LST's for the Navy. Later he worked as a service station attendant and as a wood finisher. In 1947 he went to work for the Coca-Cola Bottling Company of Madisonville, which later became Mid-America Canning Corporation where he was employed as purchasing agent when the plant closed in January 1987. He is now employed by R. E. Moore Decorating Center on East Broadway.

James and Margaret lived in apartments and with his parents on West Broadway until 1955 when they built a home on Hipple Street where they still reside.

Identical twin daughters, Joyce Faye and Lois Ann were born to Margaret and James on Jan. 13, 1949. They graduated from Madisonville High School and Murray State University with honors and Lois received her master's degree from the University of Kentucky.

Lois married Thomas Lee Green of Hickory, KY on Aug. 23, 1970 at Grapevine Christian Church. Tom is one of triplet sons of Amy Lois West Green and Joe B. Green who live on a farm near Mayfield, KY in Graves County. One year later, on July 17, 1971 Joyce married one of Tom's triplet brothers, John Allen Green, their wedding also taking place at Grapevine Christian Church.

John is a dairy farmer in Graves County and he and Joyce have four daughters: Julie Ann, Jan. 11, 1974; Jennifer Faye, Mar. 8, 1976; Joann Elizabeth, Mar. 24, 1978; and Johnna Joyce, Aug. 9, 1980.

Tom, and obstetrician and gynecologist is a partner in the Murray Woman's Clinic at Murray, KY. He and Lois have two children: Samuel Thomas, Aug. 22, 1976 and Karen Ann, July 11, 1978.

Lois and Tom's family are active members in their church, Christian Community Church of Murray, KY, as are Joyce and John's family at the Highland Christian Church in Mayfield, KY.

James and Margaret are members of Grapevine Christian Church where James serves as an elder and Margaret is a Sunday School teacher. - *Submitted by Margaret Jackson Wooton*

WORKMAN-CHAPEL

Anna Bell Chapel was born Sept. 16, 1897 and died Apr. 21, 1965 in Hopkins Co., KY. She was the daughter of Alonzo B. Chapel (who was born May 17, 1840 and died July 12, 1921 in Hopkins County) and Mary Sophoronia Williams-Chapel. Alonzo is buried in Carter Cemetery on Huckleberry Road in Dawson Springs beside his mother and brothers and sisters. Alonzo's wife remarried Mr. William Stokes after her husband's death and moved to Jacksonville, FL where she died. Maternal grandparents of Anna Bell Chapel were Francis Williams and Susan Jones-Williams. Paternal grandparents were Thomas Chapel and Mary Bishop-Chapel (born Feb. 18, 1820; died Feb. 28, 1899). Mary is buried in Carter Cemetery in Hopkins County.

Anna Bell Chapel-Workman and Lester Volney Workman

Anna Bell married Lester Volney Workman, son of James William Workman and Orlena McNary Calvert-Workman of Hopkins County. Lester was born Apr. 1, 1897 in Lyon Co., KY and died July 29, 1976 in Hopkins Co., KY. Lester's ancestry has been proven back eleven generations to Lord Baltimore Calvert who was the founder of the colony of Maryland in the early 1600's. Lester's paternal grandparents were Isaac Newton Workman and Martha Ann Jenkins-Workman of Caldwell Co., KY. His paternal great-grandparents were Martin Workman and Martha Head-Workman.

Anna Bell and Lester made their home in the Charleston area of Dawson Springs and had six children. The first child was born May 31, 1918 and died the next day (June 1). She was named Audrey Dorris and is buried in an unmarked grave in Walnut Street Cemetery in Dawson Springs. She was born with six fingers. Their third child and oldest son, John Wood Workman (born July 10, 1922) was killed July 1944 in Normandy, France during World War II. Anna Bell and Lester never got over this tragedy. They kept a picture of John Wood on the living room wall the rest of their lives and kept a tradition of placing a new "poppy" in the edge of the frame each Veteran's Day.

Other children of Anna Bell and Lester are Virginia A. Workman-Lamb, Lora Mae Workman-Johnson, James Raymond (J.R.) Workman, and Ralph Newton Workman. (See Workman-Harris story).

Lester and Anna Bell are buried in Dunn Cemetery in Dawson Springs as are two of their children, Virginia and Ralph. - *Submitted by Kathy Annette Workman*

C. WORKMAN-FURGERSON

Charles Leonard Workman was born on Oct. 8, 1893 and Susie Henrietta Furgerson was born on Nov. 12, 1903. They were united in marriage on Nov. 25, 1922 in Clarksville, TN. Susie is the daughter of the late James William (Willie) Furgerson and Ada Elizabeth Hughes Furgerson. Leonard was the son of James William (J.W.) Workman and Orlena McNary Calvert Workman of Charleston.

Front l to r: Lena Elizabeth and James Carlton. Back: Charles Leonard and Susie Henrietta Workman

To this union were born two children. James Carlton Workman was born Feb. 4, 1924 over the B.F. Franklin Store and died on Feb. 9, 1957 and is buried at the Dunn Cemetery. Lena Elizabeth was born on July 10, 1925 in Susie and Leonard's new two room house. Lena married J.C. Stewart of Graham, KY on Sept. 7, 1942. To this union were born three children: James Charles, Larry Richard, and Shelia Kay Stewart.

Leonard came from a large family. He was the oldest boy of seven brothers: Lester Volney, Lexie Melon, Erbie Allen, James Ford, Infant Workman, and Isaac Newton. Leonard worked with his dad in the coal mines after moving to Charleston from Dawson Springs.

After Susie and Leonard married, they bought a new two room house in Charleston and they bought a new Chevrolet for $600. When their house burned, they sold their car to Ford and Lucy Workman in order to rebuild their home.

Leonard was in the Army during World War II. While in basic training, all he had to eat was rice with salt. He was in the service for six months before the war was over. Leonard died on July 5, 1934 and is buried at Dunn Cemetery.

Susie also came from a large family of ten brothers and sisters: Virgie Dewessey, Idella Mae, Ruby, Gutherie, Cecil Taylorsmine, Woodrow, Edna Tessabell and Violet Louise Furgerson.

Susie worked in the coal mines with her husband. She walked five miles each way to Dawson Springs to work at a sewing room, a paint factory over Purdy Grocery Store. She also worked for Jimmy and Halley Hamby at their restaurant and for a veterinarian, Wash Beshears, at a sewing room under the New Century Hotel, and for the W.P.A. After Leonard died, Susie took in washing. Susie and Carlton carried water from Jim Workman's spring or the Old Charleston Depot. Lena would deliver the clean clothes. The whole washing was done for fifty cents and all the washing was done on a wash board.

Leonard and Susie have the following great grandchildren: Keith Shannon and Kay Michelle, children of James Charles Stewart and Judy Gayle Wyatt Stewart; Steven Richard and Elizabeth Lee, children of Larry Richard Stewart and Debrah Kay Hanks Stewart; Leslie Marie and Lorie Ann, daughters of Shelia Kay Stewart Densmore and David Wayne Densmore. - *Submitted by Gene Workman*

E. WORKMAN-FURGERSON

Erbie Allen Workman was born Dec. 7, 1902 and was the son of James William and Orlena Calvert Workman. Susie Henrietta Furgerson was the daughter of James Willie and Ada Elizabeth Hughes Furgerson. She was born on Nov. 12, 1903.

Erbie Allen and Susie Henrietta Workman with children Joseph Allen, Rita Ann and Harlan Gene

Erbie and Susie were married in 1940 in Dawson Springs, KY. After their marriage, they moved to Evansville, IN where Erbie worked for his dad, J. W. Workman, in the coal mines.

To this union were born three children: Harlan Gene, born June 9, 1941 in Yankeetown, IN; Joseph Allen born Jan. 16, 1944; and Rita Ann born Aug. 5, 1945. Both Joe and Rita were born at Charleston, KY.

Erbie worked in the coal mines as a mine foreman, as a block layer and as a carpenter. He only had a third grade education. He and his brothers had to work hard when they were growing up. Erbie died Sept. 18, 1984 and is buried at the New Beulah Cemetery in Beulah, KY.

Harlan Gene married Willie Burniece Pollard on June 18, 1960. Joseph Allen married Nancy Mae Young on Mar. 23, 1963. Rita Ann married Gayle Nelson on Nov. 14, 1963.

Grandchildren of Erbie and Susie are: Monte Gene born Dec. 16, 1961, Gregory Shane born Jan. 9, 1970, Timothy Paul born and died Aug. 7, 1973, boys of Gene and Burniece Workman; Cynthia Mae born Jan. 17, 1966, Teresa Jo born Dec. 22, 1969, Krystal Susanne born Aug. 3, 1974, daughters of Joe and Nancy Workman; Reginia Ann born Aug. 29, 1964 and Felicia Renee born Oct. 17, 1966, daughters of Gayle and Rita Nelson. One great granddaughter, Ashtin Brooke born Feb. 27, 1987, the daughter of Rick and Renee Childress.

Susie's maternal grandparents were James Obadiah Hughes and Henrietta Jones Hughes and her paternal grandparents were William Buck Furgerson born Sept. 27, 1856 and Martha Ellen Franklin Furgerson born June 15, 1860 and buried at the New Beulah Cemetery, Beulah, KY.

Erbie's maternal grandparents were William Mansfield Calvert born Dec. 4, 1834 and Orlena McNary Sigler Calvert born Jan. 18, 1837. They were from Caldwell County and are buried at the Calvert Cemetery in the Sugar Creek community of Caldwell County. Erbie's paternal grandparents were Isaac Newton Workman born Jan. 12, 1847 and Martha Ann Jenkins Workman born Jan. 31, 1849. She was from Tennessee. Both are buried at the Liberty Cemetery in Lyon Co., KY. - *Submitted by Harlan Gene Workman*

WORKMAN-HARRIS

Mary Elizabeth Harris is the oldest child of Rosa Lee Miller-Brown-Harris and Rosa's second husband Robert Dewey (Dock) Harris. Mary was born Sept. 28, 1934 in Hopkins Co., KY and was raised by her grandparents Mary Easter Howton-Miller-Coulter and Jim Coulter. (See Coulter story). Mary graduated from Dawson Springs High School in 1953.

Back row-Mary Harris Workman, Ralph Newton Workman. Front row-Mary Easter Coulter, James Garfield Coulter, Kathy, Mary Harris and Ralph Newton Workman

Mary met Ralph Newton Workman in the spring of 1953 at the Strand Theatre in Dawson Springs when during an exciting part of the movie Ralph tapped her on the shoulder (to ask if he could sit by her) and she screamed. Ralph later apologized for scaring her and walked her home.

Six months later they married (Nov. 9, 1953) in Springfield, TN.

Ralph Newton Workman is the youngest child of Lester Volney Workman and Anna Bell Workman-Chapel (See Workman-Chapel story). Ralph was born Feb. 24, 1930 and died Sunday, Mar. 17, 1974. During his childhood he was stricken with rheumatic fever and nearly died. This left him in bad health with a heart disease. Ralph grew up in the Charleston area of Dawson Springs and graduated from Charleston High School.

Coming from a large family, Ralph wanted a family but Mary refused to marry him unless they stayed with her grandparents (Mr. and Mrs. Jim Coulter) because they were elderly and sick. Ralph and Mary made their home with the Coulters on Walnut Street in Dawson Springs.

At 7:15 a.m. Monday, Mar. 26, 1956 their daughter Kathy Annette was born in Anderson Clinic at Madisonville, KY. She weighed 4 lbs. 14 oz. Mary nearly died giving birth and the baby, too, nearly died, therefore they never had another child.

When the baby was 18 months old, while watching the baby play Ralph commented "That baby needs to be in Sunday School". Mary began attending different churches in the area and after months of searching began attending the Methodist Church in Dawson Springs. She later decided that since they went to visit Ralph's parents (who lived next door to the Charleston Baptist Church) every Sunday, it would be more convenient to attend Charleston Baptist Church. Eventually, they all three became members there.

Ralph got a job working for Kentucky State Highway Department and worked there until a couple of months before his death. Prior to this he had worked at Ben Franklin Five and Dime Store and Fox's Meat Market.

After the deaths of Mr. and Mrs. Coulter, Mary and Ralph sold their home on Walnut Street and moved to the Charleston area of Dawson Springs. Kathy attended first and second grades of school at Dawson Springs Elementary School and third through eight grades at Charleston Elementary School. Kathy graduated from West Hopkins High School 2-1/2 months after her father's death in 1974. - *Submitted by Kathy Annette Workman*

WORKMAN-POLLARD

Willie Berniece Pollard was born on May 11, 1942 in Decaturville, TN. She is the daughter of Mary Pauline Knight Pollard and the late Joseph Andrew Pollard. Harlan Gene Workman was born on June 9, 1941 in Yankeetown, IN and is the son of Susie Henrietta Furgerson and the late Erbie Allen Workman.

Monte Gene, Harlan Gene, Willie Berniece and Gregory Shane Workman

Gene and Burniece were married on June 18, 1960 in Shawneetown, IL. Their oldest son, Monte Gene, was born on Dec. 16, 1961 at Baptist Hospital in Nashville, TN. Their second son, Gregory Shane, was born on Jan. 9, 1970 at St. Francis Hospital in Columbus, GA. Their third son was still born on Aug. 7, 1973, his name Timothy Paul Workman. He is buried at Dunn Cemetery, Dawson Springs, KY.

Maternal grandparents of Burniece are the late Willie Enlo Knight and Retta Antonette Lacy Knight of Decaturville, TN. Paternal grandparents were Thomas Henry Pollard and Nancy Mildred Metheny Pollard of Christian Co., KY.

Gene's maternal grandparents were James Willie Furgerson born Apr. 24, 1877 and Elizabeth Hughes Furgerson born Dec. 31, 1880 and are buried at Dunn Cemetery in Dawson Springs. His paternal grandparents were James William (J.W.) Workman born Sept. 20, 1875 and Orlena McNary Calvert Workman born Sept. 18, 1897 of Charleston, KY and are buried at Dunn Cemetery in Dawson Springs.

Gene and Berniece make their home in Charleston, KY. - *Submitted by Gene Workman*

WORKMAN-SMITH

Flora E. Franklin was born July 10, 1892 and was the daughter of Henry Franklin born 1864 and Robinett Franklin born 1866. Erbie Allen was born on Dec. 7, 1902 and was the son of James William and Orlena McNary Calvert Workman. Flora was first married to Tom Smith from the Nortonville area. They had one son James Orville Smith born on September 1, 1918. He served in World War II entering about the time it was over. He died on Aug. 19, 1968 and is buried at the New Beulah Cemetery, Beulah, KY.

Erbie Allen and Flora E. Workman and child Lois Raye

Flora had two brothers, Newman and Curtis Franklin. Newman was married to Netta May Workman and Curtis was married to Rusha Franklin Hickman who now resides at Browns Rest Home in Madisonville, KY.

Flora attended Browns Academy in Providence, KY. She then went to Western University in Bowling Green, KY to take her teachers exam. She taught several years in Hopkins County schools including Munn and Fiddlebow, both one room schools.

After the death of her first husband, she married Erbie Workman. To this union was born one daughter Lois Raye Workman born Aug. 15, 1925 in Dawson Springs. They moved to the Charleston area in the early thirties.

Lois married Harry C. Howard on Aug. 18, 1945. One son, Perry Wayne Howard was born Dec. 10, 1946 in Providence, KY. Lois operated a restaurant in Providence. She worked for various doctors and later went to Madisonville Community College to receive an Associate Degree in Nursing. For several years she has been employed as Director of Nurses for National Health Corp. in Madisonville. Perry Wayne Howard married the former Donna C. Hibbs and they have one daughter, Tracie Leigh.

Harry C. Howard still resides in Providence. - *Submitted by Gene Workman*

WRIGHT

John Walter Wright and Augusta Jackson were married Aug. 25, 1935. They have two children: Mary Lu, wife of Wade Treutlen Mitchell and mother of Wade Wright and Catherine Wright; and John Walter Jr., husband of Joanne Lockhart Werner and father of Mary Elizabeth Wright Westbrook, John Walter III and Charles Werner.

Augusta Jackson Wright and John Walter Wright Sr.

Augusta J. Wright, whose ancestors were among Hopkins County's original settlers, is the daughter of Robert Lee Jackson and Lu Addie Fugate.

Robert Lee Jackson was the son of William Harrison "Hal" Jackson and Sarah Pritchett. Hal was the son of Beckley Jackson and Martha Brown. Beckley, son of Matthew and Elizabeth Jackson of Mecklenburg Co., VA, came to Hopkins County by 1815. He had a farm about nine miles north of Madisonville, where he also provided fresh horses and a mail distribution point for stage coaches traveling between Hopkinsville and Henderson. A state historical plaque in front of Beckley Jackson's house, built in 1830 of handmade brick and still occupied, marks the site of the Jackson Stage Stop. (Highway 1069)

Lu Addie Fugate was the daughter of William Lewis "Luke" Fugate and Nancy Susan Hanner. Luke was the son of Lewis Fugate and Nancy Ashby, whose parents were Stephen Ashby Jr. and Elizabeth. Stephen Ashby Jr. was present at the organization of Hopkins County in 1807 "dressed in his faded regimentals and topped with a coonskin cap with a tail." (M.K. Gordon) He was one of the first Justices of the Peace and founded the first town in Hopkins Co., Ashbyburg, on the Green River. His father, Stephen Ashby, from Prince William Co., VA, a captain in the Revolutionary War, was the son of Captain Thomas Ashby. Nancy Susan Hanner was the daughter of a Methodist minister, Reverend William Hanner, who was the son of Reverend James Hanner from Raleigh, NC. Her mother was Julia Ann Harrison, daughter of William Harrison.

Walter Wright came to Madisonville in 1928, at age 24, from Ripley, TN, to study coal mining at the Trio Mine, east of town. In 1930, when management problems forced Trio into bankruptcy, his employer, Kirkpatrick Coal Company of Memphis, asked him to take over as general manager, with responsibility for 165-180 men. He reorganized Trio Mine as Wright Coal Company and ran it until 1950.

Through the years Walter Wright and his partners bought or leased other mines, both underground and strip. These mines were Pine Hill Mining Company, renamed Derby Coal Company, east of Madisonville; Rutstein Coal Company and Long Davis Coal Company at Richland; and in Muhlenberg County, Caney Creek Coal Company, renamed Kirkpatrick Mining Company, a limited partnership, and Genet Huffstetler Coal Company, renamed Wright Coal Company.

Walter Wright served as President of the Western Kentucky Coal Producers Association for a number of years. He also was President of the Kentucky Coal Agency, was elected to the Madisonville Board of Education and is currently a director of the Farmers Bank and Trust Company. In 1986, at age 80, he received the Coal Miner of the Year Award from the West Kentucky Coal Association. - *Submitted by Mary Lu Wright Mitchell*

DAN, WILLIAM, AND FRANK WRISTEN

Daniel W., William, and Francis (Frank) Wristen were born in Hopkins Co., KY, near Madisonville, where they lived until ages 12, 9, and 8 before their family "Hit the Texas Trail" about 1851. After a brief stay in New Madrid Co., MO, they grew to manhood near old Irby and Mount Nebo, Parker Co., TX, during wild Comanche and Kiowa days. After about 1856, they worked as cowboys on the larger ranches and later as freight teamsters.

Daniel joined the 5th Texas Mounted Volunteers, CSA, in 1861 at Weatherford, TX. Not recorded in General Sibley's ill-fated New Mexico expedition, he was in Weatherford early in 1862 to recruit Company E, 19th Texas Cavalry. While back in Weatherford he married Mary J. Moore of Parker County. Back with the 5th Texas at Galveston, Jan. 1, 1863, Dan helped capture the Harriet Lane, a Federal Gunboat posted in Galveston Bay. Through 1864-April 1865, the served as First Sergeant along Red River in hard skirmishes then battles at Mansfield and Pleasant Hill, LA.

While with Co E, 19th Texas Cavalry, in Missouri and along White River in Arkansas, William died at Des Arc, AR, 1863. Frank joined Ben McCullogh's 1st Texas Mounted Volunteers (later named Taylor's Battalion, 8th Texas Cavalry) in 1861 and served in Arkansas, Tennessee, and Mississippi through the war.

After the War, Dan and Frank worked cattle, freighted with wagons, and made cattle drives "Up the Trail" to Kansas. Then with Robert E. Davis, they acquired a flour mill, cotton gin, and store in Balch, Parker County, about 1876. Dan and Frank sold out in 1879 and moved to Taylor Co., TX, kept store near Buffalo Gap and when Texas and Pacific Railroad built through, helped build Abilene in 1880-1881. Daniel served eight years as Abilene's Mayor then both moved to Baird, Callahan County, about 1900. Daniel and Mary had raised ten children before Mary died in 1900. By then 63 years old, Daniel married Nettie Thornton of Illinois in 1902. Frank was twice married and raised a considerable family. Daniel and Frank Wristen were typical pioneers and merchants who have many descendents in West Texas. REFERENCES: U.S. CENSUS, 1850, 1870, 1880, 1900, 1910; Callahan, Parker & Taylor County, Texas Records; Mamie Yeary, "Reminiscences of the Boys in Gray", 1861-1865 (Texas Archives, Austin, Texas); "History of North and West Texas" (Texas Archives) - *Submitted by Sam & Wilhelmina Andrew*

ELIJAH WRISTEN

Elijah Wristen (old spelling: Riston), the fourth son of Elisha and Nancy Wristen of Prince George Co., MD, was born in Virginia, 1807. He accompanied his parents to Christian Co., KY, about 1809, became a farmer, and married Leona Sisk in Hopkins County, Oct. 11, 1832. They lived the next eighteen years along Pond River, and their children were: Martha, 1834; Margaret Ellen, 1836; Daniel W., 1839; William, 1842; Francis (Frank), 1843; John, 1846; Mary, 1848; and Rufus, 1850. Leona died soon after Rufus was born, and Elijah married Nancy Sisk Davis, widow of Jacob Davis with sons Robert Earle, William, Charles H., and Hezekiah Butler, Nov. 24, 1850, a large family considered appropriate for a farmer.

Elijah and Nancy moved to New Madrid Co., MO, in 1851, where their daughter, Cynthia Emily, was born June 10, 1853, then moved to Texas about 1854, later settling in Irby Community on Spring Creek, Parker County, 1855, while Comanche raids could be expected every full moon. After Nancy died in 1856, Elijah married Mary (Brown?) and began a third family while the other children were approaching adulthood in pre-Civil War days.

We have not located Elijah during the Civil War, but from 1866-1874, he lived in Scott Co., AR, and returned to Parker, then Jack Co., TX, where he appeared on the 1880 Census with a new family. Cynthia Emily had married George Miller in 1873 and lived in Jack County until she died in 1923, survived by many children. Elijah's death date and burial site are unknown. Did he die in Texas or make the Sooner rush into Indian Territory? In 1900, his older sons, Daniel and Frank, lived in Taylor and Callahan Counties, TX, but his widow, Mary, and their sons: Albert V., David, and Joseph were living in Osage City, OK. Elijah Wristen seems to have loved the fringes of civilization. REFERENCES: Hopkins and Christian County Records; Parker County, Texas, Records; U.S. Census, 1850, 1870, 1880, 1900 - *Submitted by Sam and Wilhelmina Andrew*

WYATT

Henry, George and James Wyatt, early settlers of Earlington, were born in the Beulah section of Hopkins County, the sons of Colby and Amanda Dockery Wyatt, grandsons of George Wyatt Sr.

George Wyatt Sr. came to Hopkins County with his brothers Charles and Thomas. Perrins' History of Kentucky, 1885, states Charles Wyatt SC 1798 removed to Warren Co., KY, 1800 to Hopkins then Henderson County, one of its first settlers, "There not being more than 8 or 10 persons before him." George left for awhile. He married in Warren County, Delilah Nations born in North Carolina. He died in 1855 and was buried on his land in "Wyatt Cemetery". He had 13 children.

His son Joseph married Elizabeth, sister to Amanda. They were the daughters of Richard Dockery. Their son John, a Civil War Veteran, was the grandfather of John Wyatt (decd.), former Mayor of Earlington.

Colby, a carpenter, was killed by lightning in August 1871. Amanda and their oldest son had died before 1860. After Colby's death, his sons walked from Princeton, KY to their cousin's (Joseph's daughter) Mrs. Riley Brown's home, where Brown Meadow Lake is now. They settled in Earlington, married, raised families, became mine foremen, were prominent in mining circles, lodge and church activities and were charter members of the Earlington Christian Church. They were devoted brothers. After retirement, George and James visited almost every day and weather permitting would go for long walks. All three are buried in Oakwood Cemetery.

Henry S. (1853-1918) married in 1876 Do-

J.B. Wyatt family, 1899

ratha Mitchell, in 1896 Emma Brooks and 3rd Sallie Davis. All of his children left Kentucky.

George W. (1855-1945) married Sarah Oldham and had daughters Agnes and Georgia. Agnes married Henry Browning and their daughter Mrs. Helen Fisher lives at Kentucky Rest Haven. Georgia died at age 95. She was married to John Long, proprietor of Long's Bakery in Earlington.

James B. (1857-1940) went to Indian Territory, returned and married in 1884 Blanche Yates. They had eight children with two dying in infancy. His sons were life-long Earlington residents, all members of the Masonic Lodge. His four grandsons were in World War II. Children of James B. and Blanche were: Ruth, Hardy, Omer, Audrey and Creel (twins) and Ermitt.

Ruth married C.R. Bowman and moved to Evansville, IN.

Hardy and Omer worked for the L & N Railroad. Hardy married Ethel Oldham, their son Kenneth is deceased. Omer married Mary Parker and their son, William, lives in Newburgh, IN.

Audrey and Creel were miners. Audrey was magistrate for 22 years and married Aileen Fox. Their children: James Hudson (deceased) and Doris (Mrs. G.W. Evans) who lives in Madisonville. Creel married Adeline Favors and she still lives in Earlington. Their son, Robert, lives in Madisonville.

Ermitt was mine foreman for St. Bernard nd Superintendent for 22 years for West Ky. Coal Co. He married Carrie Coyle and they divorced. They were the parents of four children: twins who died, Mrs. Erma Hicks who lives in Earlington and Mrs. Frances Blais who lives in Florida. Ermitt married second, Nell Robinson.

Charles and George Wyatt Sr. have many descendents in Hopkins County. Thomas, in 1819, was killed by Indians. His widow and three children moved to Illinois.

These Wyatts, Norman-French origin, are of the Virginia Wyatts from Kent County, England. The family came to England with William the Conqueror. - *Submitted by Francis Wyatt Blais*

WYATT-BEARD

In 1926, a baby was born on Jan. 1, by the name of Gladys May Beard. The parents of this baby were Jake and Veda Beard. Gladys was born in Hopkins County in a house, not a hospital.

Gladys May Beard has two brothers and two sisters. Her brothers are James Thomas Beard and Melvin Beard, and her sisters are Opal Kay Tirey and Mary Louis Carlton. While Gladys and her brothers and sisters were growing up in Hopkins County, they did not have all the necessities that there are now. Gladys and her brothers and sisters did not have a lot of money growing up, so when it came to buying shoes, they only got one pair a year. But they always had a lot of food because Gladys and her brothers and sisters lived on a farm with farm animals that provided food.

Gladys attended school at Charleston from kindergarten to the eleventh grade. She had to walk at least five miles to shcool and five miles back every day. The main reasons Gladys only went to the eleventh grade are that she had to walk so far and she could not catch on to Algebra.

On the 19th day of September in 1942, Gladys married W.E. Wyatt. Her husband went off to war and on Dec. 31, 1943, they had their first child. Gladys gave birth to Janice Ann in her mother's house in Hopkins County. Then Gladys had her second and last child, Everett Raymond Wyatt born Feb. 22, 1950 in Madisonville. Gladys and W.E. reared their children in Hopkins County until they packed their bags and moved to Michigan. Gladys and W.E. and the family lived in Flint, Michigan for 22 years. During those 22 years, Janice Ann was married twice and is now living in Tawas City, MI. The youngest of Gladys's children, Everett, married a woman by the name of Pamela Berke and had four children: Richard John Martin Jr., James Michael Wyatt, Chad Everett Wyatt, and Lori Lynn Wyatt.

Gladys returned to Hopkins County in 1986. She now resides in Dawson Springs with her grandchild, James.- *Submitted by James Michael Wyatt*

GEORGE WYATT, SR.

George Wyatt, Sr. was born circa 1775-1785. It is believed that he was born in South Carolina.

George Wyatt married Delilah Nations on Feb. 2, 1804 in Warren Co., KY. George and Delilah moved to Hopkins Co., KY circa 1807. They were the parents of thirteen known children: Elizabeth Wyatt born in 1804 and married Jacob Jackson; Joshua Wyatt born between 1804-1810 and married Mary (Polly) Clark; Mary Ann (Polly) Wyatt born 1806 and married Jefferson Washington Fox; Delilah Wyatt born 1808 and married Ewell Fox; George Wyatt, Jr. born 1810 and married Louanna Fox; Joseph P. Wyatt born 1814 and married Sarah Elizabeth Dockery; Talitha Wyatt born 1815 and married James Knox; Matilda (?) Wyatt born between 1820-1825; Christopher Wyatt born 1822 and married Isabel Edmiston; Sydaham Wyatt born between 1825-1830 and married Elizabeth White; Colby S. Wyatt born 1828 and married (1) Amanda M. Dockery and (2) Rachel A. Southard; plus one daughter and one son whose names are unknown.

George Wyatt was engaged in farming all his life. He died in Hopkins Co., KY on Oct. 29, 1855 and is buried in Hell's Half Acre Cemetery near Beulah, KY. Hell's Half Acre Cemetery is located on land that was once owned by George Wyatt, Sr. - *Compiled by Daniel W. Dockrey*

Center St. in Madisonville looking east about 1900.

The St. Earl Hotel in 1911 in Dawson Springs

Geder and Mrs. Sisk in Dalton area

Fiddle Bow school group in 1931 - Mary Jones, teacher

The rear view of the old TB Hospital (1941-1974)

The north side of East Center St. in Madisonville in 1924

Construction during rebuilding of the Loch Mary Dam at Earlington

School History

Bonnie Hewlett dressed as The Statue of Liberty at West Broadway School about 1916

Silent Run School-A.J. Wyatt, Teacher-1900

I Heard It Through The Grapevine

Talking with Hopkins County senior citizens gives us insight into an era gone by, one that is fast fading into textbook memory. Not realizing the importance of keeping detailed records and with many of the older ones gone and what few written records there were being lost in home fires, even our county school offices have very few dusty old books with census taken only every so many years. The one or two room schools that once dotted the country side are now only memories. A few foundation rocks, an old well or cistern left to mark the spot. A rarity, but a few of the school buildings still stand being used as a farm out-building or even rarer, a dwelling. Some have served as churches, missions or a civic building.

Trails became roads, country roads became highways, giving an opportunity for further travel in half the time. With travel easier, the tiny country churches with few members began to look to the larger community church. Some closed their doors or lent their buildings to union churches or for community affairs. Some sold or tore their buildings down and their members disbursed to larger churches of like faith. Home fires destroyed church clerk records as it had the school records. Many a little church has faded from memory with only a dot on an old hand drawn surveyors map to mark its spot.

Schools began to consolidate, giving youth a chance to attend high school. That in turn gave even the remotest and less fortunate student a change to excel.

The following recollections, with a rare picture or document, has not been a matter of written record before, but was heard through the grapevine! People gave from their storehouse of memories. They are retired teachers and former students of old schools, while others are descendants of pastors or members of the long ago country churches. A lot of our heritage has been lost, but with tireless groping and listening the mist has cleared here and there.

There will be a few dates and facts unclear, but we have been as accurate as possible. We have pulled as much fact from what was buried deep within memory as was humanly possible. We are sorry if we missed your school, favorite teacher or old church, but remember—we only heard it through the grapevine.

History Of Black Schools

The Beginning - The first black school in Hopkins County was opened in Madisonville on June 1, 1866 and was taught by Mrs. Rosa Clark, a black woman who had managed to pick up a little education. School was taught in a horse stable that was owned by William Harris. The school term was for three months and Mrs. Clark received $15.00 per month for her services. In 1867, she was reemployed and taught for six months in the same location. During this year, the Freedmans Bureau paid $10.00 per month toward the school while patrons were to make up a like sum. Mrs. Clark continued to teach in Madisonville until 1879 when she taught one year at White Plains.

In 1876, B.P. Lee taught in Hopkins County District 1 receiving $22.00 for the whole term while Henry Morton taught in District 4 receiving only $10.32. In 1877, there were black schools in Districts 1, 2, 5, and 7. By 1882, black schools were in twelve of the thirteen districts.

John B. Atkinson College

John B. Atkinson College was named for John B. Atkinson of Earlington, whose generosity helped maintain the school. The

The first Atkinson College in 1894

The Atkinson College after it was rebuilt on West Broadway

school was founded 1892 and was a school of higher education for blacks of the surrounding communities. It was located on the west corner of South Seminary and Lake Streets in Madisonville until fire destroyed the buildings on Feb. 22, 1903. Land was purchased on West Broadway and two two-story buildings were built for dormitories. Some of the teachers were Mae Morton Wilson, Corrina Woodson Pettus, Naomi Morton Parks and Verdie Orton McCain. Due to financial difficulties, the school closed in 1932.

Barnhill Or District M

Little is known about this school as it went by more than one name. The tiny black community near the white Pleasant Ridge School was nicknamed Ho-Cake Corner and was located on what is now called the Old Dalton Road, near Providence. The school was on the Barnhill Farm, back on a lane, thus giving it that name according to Hopkins County records. Mrs. Margret Woolfolk says the school was just inside the Hopkins County line and served the tiny farming community in both Hopkins and Webster Counties. Mr. J.C. Barnhill, still living in the area, recalls his father talking about the school and that it was one of the early schools. Since the school was about two miles south of the Shamrock Mines, it is believed to have closed in early 1900 with the children going to Midway School, 2 1/2 miles to the north. Only two teachers are known, Mrs. Hennie Mitchell and L.A. Harrison. There are no known teachers after 1908. The county records show this school and Midway as the same, but Mr. Barnhill says that was impossible as the schools were two or more miles apart and that the well of the old Ho-Cake Corner or Barnhill School was still in use until a few years ago when the old dwelling nearby was torn down.

Barnsley Black Elementary

Barnsley Black Elementary was located on the second floor of a church on the Barnsley Loop Road, just south of Earlington. In its early years, it was known as District Q. Known teachers: Golden Winstead 1903, Sadie Anglin 1904, Malissa O'Brien 1905, Lula Grady 1906, Sadie O'Brien 1907, and Bessie Walker 1908-1910. In 1920, the district was renamed District B. The 1927 teacher was Mary Pritchett, 1928 Miss Jessie Cargile, 1932 Nettie Cargile Ringold. Mrs. Ringold remembers her classes were for the first four grades and hardly had the bare necessities. School closed for lack of funds and too few students and consolidated in the mid-30s with Earlington.

A story about this school was told by Mrs. Ruby Stearman Sisk, who taught at the white Barnsley school. Her father, J.A. Stearman,, a very education minded man became a trustee for the black school. It was his job to visit the school about every six weeks. Since he worked ten hours a day, many times his wife would make the visits for him. Ruby was a child of four or five, so she would accompany her mother on these visits. In later years, when Mrs. Sisk was also a teacher, she would go to the school to pick up their list of needs to take to Madisonville along with her own list. The children were using small rags to clean the blackboards and writing with chalk worn to less than an inch. They were getting by as best as they could, their young teacher said. Needless to say, Mrs. Sisk returned with plenty of chalk and erasers to last the remaining term.

Branch Street Elementary

Branch Street Elementary School was originally named ROSS-DELMONT HIGH SCHOOL, located on Branch Street. The Ross-Delmont High School was named to honor Mrs. Nora B. Ross who served as principal of the school and Mr. Delmont Utley, Chairman of the Board of Education at that time.

When the ROSENWALD HIGH SCHOOL was built on Kentucky Ave. in 1931-32, they then changed the name of the Ross-Delmont High School to the Branch Street Elementary School. More classrooms were needed to accommodate more students in a growing community. The two schools occupied a five acre tract and shared the activity field and lunchroom.

The principal of the Rosenwald High School also served as the principal of the Branch Street School. The principals are as follows: Mr. William E. Lee 1932-37; Mrs. Pearl (Patton) Arnett 1937-63; and Mr. Caldwell Smith Sr. 1963-66.

Some of the most cherished memories of the students introduction into the education process began at the Branch Street Elementary School. During the years 1932-1966, the very dedicated teachers whose chosen careers testified that they were indeed proficient in the art of molding and opening new and everlasting impressions on young needs were: Ms. Mabel Jackson, Mrs. Jaunita (Wheeler) Talley, Mrs. Ora Bell Clemons, Mrs. Vaden P. Stum, Mrs. Mabel Lester, Mrs. Mayme L. Parker, Mrs. Vivian R. Hocker, Mrs. Hattie L. Arvin, Mrs. Nettie Ringold, and Mrs. Jessie Cargile.

All of these teachers opened the imagination and allowed any child to grow in wisdom and knowledge to the furthermost extent of their capabilities. As in most cases of nostalgia, there are some events that seem to fade with the passing of time. But there will always be many occasions to recall these all important formative years spent under the care and supervision of those dedicated instructors who taught at the Branch Street School until the Hopkins County School System was integrated. - *Written by Mary L. Shelton*

Clack School

Clack School was established in the late 1800's. It was located in the northwest part of St. Charles, at the north end of the spur track through town, in a section called Allentown. The colored Methodist Church and houses were also in this section. The earliest known teacher was James O. Simpson who taught in 1889.

Mr. John Alvis, a native of St. Charles, was born in April of 1904 and recalls his school days as the happiest time of his life. One of his memories stands out above all others. It was the custom to allow the younger children out of school thirty minutes before the upper classes dismissed. "To keep us out of trouble with the big boys", he laughs. "The big boys from the white school and the black school used to meet near the creek and have mock battles. Not really hurt each other like now-a-days," Mr. Alvis explains, "just for fun and to see who dodged best." Being one of the small boys, Mr. Alvis and two of his friends hid under the bridge to watch. The next day, the teacher asked for volunteers to get switches. The three little boys not only went for the switches, but peeled the bark off and dragged them through the mud to make them hurt more. Since they had only watched the big boys at the creek, they felt self-righteous. The big boys got their switching, but so did the little watchers. And with their own switches too! "Last time I ever volunteered for anything." Mr. Alvis laughed.

Teachers remembered by Mr. Alvis are Herbert Kirkwood, Rev. Debandy, Vera McCain, Bea Cunningham, Professor Moses Hawkins and J.B. Coleman. Another teacher was Miss George L. Peyton. The school closed in the mid 1930's.

Dalton Black Elementary

Dalton Black Elementary School was held in a church located 1/2 mile east of Dalton on the Old Cemetery Road. The 1885 teacher was Dorinda Lamb. Just when the school came into being is not known. Other teachers were Frances Scott, Emma L. Bell, Blanche M. Nelson, Josephine Bass, Hurbert Kirkwood and Mary Oma Pryor. The school closed sometime in the early 1930's. The large globe that hung from the ceiling was donated to the nearby Jennings white school that was still in session at that time.

Ilsley Colored School

Ilsley Colored School was built in the 1800's by the Crabtree Coal Mining Company. It was located on a hill called Tukie, past the Crabtree house, near the church and cemetery. Some of the teachers were: Eliza M. Smith 1903-1904, Cornellia Steel 1904-1905, Ora Buckner 1905-1907, Ora Buckner and Pearl C. Bass 1907-1908, Ann Bradley 1908-1909, Jessie B. Miller 1909-1910, Ella M. Casey 1910-1911, W.R. Broxton 1911-1912, Ella M. Casey 1912-1913, L.A. McReynolds 1913-14, James H. Browley 1914-1915, Mayme Good 1915-16, Nathaniel C. Casey 1916-17, Ethyl C. Wright 1917-1919, Charlie B. Welch, 1919-20, Ethyl C. Tyler 1920-1922, Beatrice Cunningham 1922-1923, Emeline Mitchell 1923-1924, Maybelle Bowling (1/2 term) 1924-1925, Ida McLeod, Pearl White, Ola Crowley, and Martha Brown Finch 1930-1934. The school closed in 1934.

Kimblus Chapel School

Kimblus Chapel School (See Church Section)

MIDWAY SCHOOL

Midway School was located just north off the old Dalton Road (now 109) Barely inside the Hopkins County Line, it was the counterpart of the white Lutontown Camp School. It was built for the children of the black employees of the Shamrock Mines and a few scattered farm families. The school was named for the Midway Camp.

A former student, Garfield Gales of Providence, remembers his school days there while his father was working in the mines. Some of the teachers were: Devorah Couch Woolfolk 1919, Mr. Willie T. Brooks and Virgil L. Moore 1925, Herbert Kirkwood 1927 and his sister Virginia Kirkwood Springfield who was widowed and later remarried a Calbert, another sister Mary Orma Kirkwood Pryor, and Lizzie Duckett Lee. The old school closed about 1937 and was later used as a dwelling. The old mines worked out, families moved away and the Midway Camp was torn down and the land sold

J.W. MILLION SCHOOL

J.W. Million School, the first black school in Earlington was located behind the lake where A.M.E. Zion Church now stands. School was in session there in 1905 or 1912 when St. Bernard Coal Company built the brick building on North McEuen. In the beginning, Earlington white and black schools were under the same board or trusteeship. In 1922, the black board of education was organized with the assistance of J.W. Million, pastor of Zion Baptist Church. He launched the board with a $100.00 donation. When the gymnasium was built in 1935, the school was named in his honor.

The J.W. Million School

Professor Williams was the first superintendent of the Earlington black school system. Lester Mimms came to Million in 1935 as a teacher and basketball coach. In 1943, he became principal and coach, a position he held until the school closed at the end of the 1963-64 school year. The students entered Earlington High School in the fall of 1964, thus integrating the district.

MORTONS GAP BLACK ELEMENTARY SCHOOL

Mortons Gap Black Elementary School began around 1888 and was located in a dense woods called Goose Hollow, one mile southwest of Mortons Gap. It was a one room wooden frame building with a pot-bellied stove for heat. The school had thirty to forty students in nice weather. There was a lot of love between teacher and students. The school was for fun as well as learning. Hunters often used the path by the school and they would hunt small game in the woods. One incident remembered by all was the day a hunter shot a large snake out of the tree near the school. One brave girl, Rosa Torian, cut the snake open with a razor blade she had in her school desk. Lo and behold, a young squirrel was still alive and was able to scamper away! Miss Rosa now lives in a local nursing home. The favorite game at recess was tug-o-war with the boys against the girls. The parents were concerned about fire and finally had the school moved away from the woods to a lot across from the Jim Murray home. Later the school was moved to a location beside the Frank Campbell home. A new school was built on the east side of Highway 41, north of Mortons Gap. In the 1950's, this building was sold and students were bussed to Madisonville and Earlington until integration. The building was used as an American Legion Hall and two rooms were added. It still stands. Some of the teachers were: in 1888-89 S.D. Simpson, Prof. Moses Hawkins, Grace Smith 1925-1932, Ida King, Mary Pritchett, Ida McLeod, John Coleman, Lizzie Hall, and Deborah Woolfolk. Elizabeth Hamilton Willoughby furnished the information on this school.

NEBO BLACK ELEMENTARY SCHOOL

Nebo Black Elementary School became District 4 of the Hopkins Common Schools. The school was formed in 1894 with the ground given by the A.M.E. Zion Church on the northeast side of Nebo. Among the early teachers were James Cargile and a Professor Richards. Mr. Cargile had lost his wife after a little less than fifteen years of marriage. He then lived on a farm with his father north of Nebo. Mr. Cargile was the father of two girls and four boys who needed an education. The elder Cargile sold his farm and bought a beautiful home on the east end of Nebo on Highway 41-A, formerly owned by Dr. Tilford. Now his grandchildren could walk to school. James Cargile attended elementary school at Woolfolk down near the Matt Hearon Bottoms, just off of Weir Creek Levee on Highway 41-A North. He attended college at Berea, KY. His oldest daughter, Jessie born in 1902, attended Nebo Elementary and Kentucky State College and returned to teach in Nebo. Other teachers remembered by Miss Jessie were John Coleman, Hennie Mitchell, Radger Colbert, Louise Davidson, and Louise Black. The Nebo School was moved from the Methodist Church site to near the Holiness Church about two blocks west in the 1930's. Miss Cargile closed the school in 1951-52.

NORTONVILLE COLORED SCHOOL

According to Mrs. Sally Belle Hopson, the first black school in Nortonville, the Nortonville Colored School, was taught in the Methodist Church on Bass Hill. Shortly afterwards, a new building was constructed up the road from the church. The last building was built east of Highway 41 on a hill behind Lively Stone Church. Families who attended the school were Lovan, Johnson, Cash, Bass, Cushionberry, Dulin, Rice and Sams. Some of the teachers were M.V. Mitchell, Elenor Cherry, Hennie Mitchell, David E. Hall, Deborah Cash, Grace Smith, Lelia Littlepage Johnson, Mattie Ribers, Nettie Bass, and Madeline Taylor who was the last teacher. The school was consolidated with Nortonville and South Hopkins in 1965.

PLEASANT VALLEY SCHOOL

Pleasant Valley School was in session in 1908 for seven families in the Hanson Community. The families were originally from Henderson County and had fourteen children attending this school.

The school was located on the Charlie Blue Road. This information was given by Marvin Blue of Hanson. Mr. Blue does not remember when the school opened or closed. The year 1908 was his earliest memory of the school.

POND RIVER COLLIERS RD. SCHOOL

There was a black school on Pond River Colliers Road, just off Highway 85, on the farm owned by Shelley Moore. We have not been able to pin-point a name or any other information about this school.

PRITCHETT SCHOOL

Pritchett School was located in Anton on land that belonged to George Pritchett. The school began in the mid 1800's and was a log building heated with a pot-bellied stove. There was a shelf on the back wall for the water bucket and the children drank out of a gourd dipper or they brought their own tin cups. The benches were of rough planks. Georgia Pritchett Morris's father Walter, a brother to George, dug the well for the school. About 1906-1908 the log building was torn down and a one room white frame building was erected. Eldora Buckner of Madisonville remembers starting school at Pritchett at the age of four. The classes were divided, each in a different corner of the room. The children learned the alphabet from a chart. Mrs. Buckner's teacher was Mary Mitchell Pritchett with 25 children attending. Helen Slaton Trice attended in 1919. The school was in session from September through December and was for grades 1-5. Mrs. Trice walked to school, four miles each way. Her best friend was a Cardwell girl. They would walk to school together until they came to a Y in the road. They then went their separate ways to the white and black schools. The school closed about 1920-23. George Pritchett was by now deceased. The school building was used for a dwelling until the land was sold for the airport construction.

Madisonville Public School which was torn down for construction of Rosenwald School

Rosenwald High School

ROSENWALD HIGH SCHOOL

The site of Rosenwald High School was at one time the foundation for a two story frame building. Rosenwald was the first consolidated Negro public school to house grades one through eight. No county school was open to the grade school graduates until years later, when the late C.L. Timberlake became principal of this frame building. Under his administration, a three year high school was legally established with the elementary pupils in the lower section of the building and the secondary department in the upper section. Years later he resigned and Nora B. Ross became principal. By then Branch Street School had been erected and the high school department was named Ross-Delmont High, which existed until 1931.

In the fall of 1931, the present brick structure was begun, being funded by the Rosenwald Foundation - hence Rosenwald High School was established to serve Negro students throughout Hopkins County. In the year 1932, with accommodations and a well-equipped building, the school was opened with William E. Lee as its first principal. Under his leadership, Rosenwald soon received state rating as a four year high school.

Rosenwald High School and basketball soon became recognized throughout the state. John Banks served as coach of the Tigers, as the team was called, and along with other competitive basketball teams the Tigers soon became formidable foes. The Tigers won their first State Championship in 1936 and also competed in the National Tournament.

Rosenwald developed a strong academic program, including Business, Home Economics, Music, Shop and Library Science, which made the school more adequately comparable to other Kentucky High Schools. As time passed, William E. Lee resigned and Pearl McNary (Patton) Arnett was elected principal in 1937. During the time Mrs. Arnett was principal, the school saw 26 years of progress both in academics and sports. The Business Department flourished. New typewriters, books and other items were secured. The school had a very strong Parent-Teacher Association.

A Rosenwald School Marching Band was organized in 1952 by Mrs. M. H. Neal, a teacher, who became the first band director. Dean Dowdy and other community leaders helped with the organization and structure of the band. Mrs. Neal resigned and Evelyn Carter directed the band for a short time. Harold D. Crowe was hired as director in September of 1954. During that time, the school finally raised enough money to purchase uniforms for the band. When the band marched in the Christmas Parade that year, it was a joyous time for the school and surrounding communities. Harold Crowe resigned in May of 1958. Orange Franklin was hired as band director in September of 1958 and remained Director until the schools of Hopkins County integrated.

In sports, the Rosenwald Tigers won many district and regional tournaments during those years. Caldwell Smith Sr. began coaching the team in 1937. Robert Barlow was coach during the time that Mr. Smith served in the United States Army. In 1946, under Coach Barlow, the Tigers won their second State Tournament and went on to compete in the National Tournament. When Mr. Smith returned he resumed his coaching job. During the time that James Henry was his assistant coach, they were given the name "The Winningest Coaches in Kentucky".

Mrs. Arnett died in 1963. After her passing, Caldwell Smith Sr.

was elected principal. James Henry became coach of the Tigers with Eugene Hodges as his assistant coach. James Henry was named "Coach of the Year" in 1965 after leading the Tigers to the State Tournament. Being one of the "Sweet Sixteen" teams was the crowning point for them in 1965.

Caldwell Smith Sr. also introduced the latest methods of educational features, which inspired and influenced many of the graduates to seek higher learning which in turn led them to their professions and vocations and to becoming solid citizens.

Rosenwald High School served Negro girls and boys of Hopkins County for a total of 34 years. In the stream of time 34 years pass unnoticed often times, but in the lives of men 34 years can be a long time. Years ago who would have dreamed that Rosenwald as a high school would be no longer. Integration implementation came sooner than expected. But memories and the spirit of Rosenwald remain alive in the hearts of its constituents, hundreds of graduates from various communities of Hopkins County. - *Submitted by Ola M. Crawley, a retired Rosenwald High School Teacher.*

WOOLFOLK SCHOOL

Woolfolk School was called a county line school. It was located on Albert Woolfolk's farm just off of what is now Hwy. 41A, near the 41A cutoff to 109. At the time of the school, Hwy. 41-A was then known as the Dixie Bee. It curved to the left going north, therefore putting the school just over the county line in the newly formed Webster County.

The forming of Webster County in 1860 split the old Woolfolk farm. Albert's home and school were just inside of Webster County but the school was attended by Hopkins County students as well. Mr Woolfolk was born in 1847 and fathered thirteen children. Seeing the need for education for his growing family, Albert gave the use of an unoccupied building to be used as a school. As far as is known, this building was used for at least twenty years or more. Albert's eldest son, Edward Larnce Woolfolk, was the last teacher in 1902 when the school closed after he accepted another teaching job. From an old grade and record book of 1899, we learn the school was called District D and had 40 students enrolled. The youngest of Edward's brothers, Lewis at age 6, to the oldest student, brother John age 19, attended this school in 1899. All of the younger brothers and sisters were his students at one time. One of his former students, Annie Barnhill, later became his wife and they had eleven children. Most of Edward's line of Woolfolk still live in and around Providence.

The information on this school was furnished by some of those descendants and the widow of Lewis Woolfolk, Margret Couch Woolfolk of Madisonville.

PUBLIC SCHOOLS

ANTON SCHOOL

Anton School was first a two-room frame building in 1929. It was located on what is now Highway 85. As enrollment grew, additional rooms were added. In 1949, a new concrete building was erected after the consolidation of Baugh, Liberty, and Medlock with Anton School.

Children were able to complete high school in this new building. The building is still used today as an elementary school. Some teachers remembered: Mrs. Eunice Offutt Brown, Mrs. Mable Nisbet, Mary Vannoy, Merrill Speck, Lizzie Ross Vannoy, Audrey McCulley, Eleanor Batsel, Grace Phillips, Shirley Sisk, Mrs. Catharine Gantt, Mrs. Holland Francis, Jean Preston, and Dixie Martin.

ASHBYBURG SCHOOL

Ashbyburg School was built on the highest hill in Ashbyburg, overlooking the Green River. In 1890, W.K. Wall was the teacher before the second room was added, angled to the first. Being well above the high water level during the great flood of 1937, it was used as a shelter for the homeless. Soon after, a new two room, red clay tile building was constructed further down the hill. Other teachers were Grady H. Gentry and Miss Florence Tomblinson. After 1949 and consolidation, the building was sold and used as a dwelling but now no longer stands.

Ashbyburg School-(1905-1910) Front Row L. to R.: Unknown, Tom Corum, Elbridge Cobb, Twins Rudy & Ruby "Jim" Sutton with their sister between them. Second Row: First six unknown, Cora Baldwin, next seven unknown, Brian Cobb, next four unknown and Henry Ashby. Third Row: brother Jim Hartford-Teacher, Unknown, Rachel (Coffman) Oldham, Cora Tomblinson with Alma Friday in back, Unknown, Flora Hayden, Ronie Henry, Lockey Brown, Next two unknown, in front Beulah (Cobb) Allen, in back unknown, Lizzie Allen, in back Susie Henry, Dollie Tomblinson, unknown, Marvin Cobb, and next two unknown. Back row: Unknown, Unknown, Emma Corum, Lesbie Cobb, ____ Dodson, Laura Chastine, Egbert Allen, Clara Crabtree, C.D. Cobb, Charles Henry, Unknown and Unknown

ASHLEY CONCORD SCHOOL

Ashley Concord School was located just off of what is now Apple Lane on Hwy. 630, near the foot of Burton Hill, two miles north of Manitou. It was first located near the crest of the mile long Burton Hill in 1866 and was known as Concord. It was a small log cabin in which the Concord General Baptist Church was organized. It

Ashley Concord School, 1944-1945. Front Row L. to R.: Aubrey Wayne Walker, Dean Duncan, Wanda Cates, Hilda Duncan, James Whitfield, Jimmy Walker, Harold Coleman Clark, and Carroll Lutz. Second Row: LaMoine Owen, Cecil Mercer and Bobby Winstead. Back Row: Imogene Duncan, Anna Beth Carneal, Teacher Elois Kirkwood, Gene Clark and Richard Clark

was decided the church would build on the site, so the school was moved to the foot of the hill. A white frame building was built on land given by John Richard Burton. The school was renamed since the church had the same name of Concord. Mr. Burton named it Ashley for his wife's maiden name. In 1888 and 1889, N.A. Hibbs was the teacher. In 1890, the teacher was Miss Millie Brown. In 1906, Lula Cavanah Veazey rode several miles side saddle (the old fashion way) on a horse to teach. Other teachers were Nettie Lutz, Nora K. Crumbaker Brown, Cecil Clayton, Ina Pearl Arnold Noel 1932, Mildred Ashley Qualls, Claud Cates and Elois Kirkwood Duncan. In 1944-45, "Miss Elois", as everyone called her, had mostly Duncan or Duncan related children. Within a year, she became a new aunt to most of her students. One of the last schools to consolidate with Nebo, it closed in 1952-53.

JOHN B. ATKINSON SCHOOL

The John B. Atkinson School, first named the Earlington Public School, was completed in 1903 at a cost of $17,000. The school was a three story brick building erected by the St. Bernard Coal Company. The faculty for the first year was Miss Minnie Bourland, principal; Misses Mary Mothershead and Nellie Carlin, all of Earlington; Mr. Gilbert D. Deere of Indiana; and Mrs. Pearl Miller of Madisonville. The building was later named for John B. Atkinson who was then president of the mining company.

John B. Atkinson School, first grade about 1907-08, Miss Mary Mothershead-Teacher

J.B.A.M.G.S. closed in 1964, at which time the new Earlington High School (now the Earlington Elementary School) was completed on Pasture Hill and the grade school students were moved to the old high school. The school was razed in 1965.

BAILEY SCHOOL

Bailey School was first located on a hill on the George Lantrip place where it joined Phillip Pendley's and William Rodgers. It was named Bailey after a former owner of the property.

The school was constructed about 1890 with the teacher being Miss Lon Gatlin. The building was log with one door in the center. The seats were also built by the people of the community. Since children at that time carried their lunch pails, shelves were built on the wall to hold their lunch pails. The building was heated by a large coal stove. It was not uncommon at that period of time for children to walk as much as three miles to school. Later, a new building was constructed about one-half mile north on Pleasant Hill Road. It was a neat weatherboarded building painted white and had nice large windows.

John B. Atkinson School

Bailey School

Grades 1-12 were housed in this building. A complete graded and high school curriculum was steadily developed prior to the establishment of the Earlington Independent School District and an accredited four year high school in 1912. The first graduates from the four year high school occurred in June 1913. The school was razed in 1965.

When the first High School was built in 1927 (see Earlington High School), this school then became the John B. Atkinson Memorial Grade School, named for Mr. Atkinson who was president of St. Bernard Coal Company. Some of the later teachers were Mrs. Alice Hightower, Miss Anna Vanada, Mrs. Nancy Prather, Mrs. Mary E. Robinson, Mrs. Mabel Boyd, and Mrs. Emily Buntin.

Families who lived in the community were Shelton, Rodgers, Smith, Davis, Vandiver, Thomas, Lantrip, Choate, and Whitfield. Some of the teachers were Allie Campbell, Bell Berry, Lillian Crick, Lula Allen, Wheaton Orten, Virginia Tutt, Bonnie Langzell, Newton Oates, Edward Atkinson and Hazel Gladdish. Mrs. Gladdish was the last full time teacher in 1939-1942. The school was consolidated with Nortonville in 1943.

BANG DOODLE SCHOOL

Bang Doodle School was located on the west side of Hopkins County near Olney. It was built on the Henry Howton farm on

Pieburn Creek near Happy Hollow. The school was in session during the Civil War and Josh Harris taught there. Anyone wishing to send children there to school, would pay 50¢ per child for the four month term.

Sometime after the Civil War, the school was moved to what is now known as Lafayette Missionary Baptist Church. (see Lafayette-Freedom-Yellow School)

Mr. Leon Howton furnished the information on this school from his family records.

BARNSLEY SCHOOL

William Walton came from England and settled in the south end of the county. The small community was known as Walton City, located south of Earlington. At some time, the community became known as Barnsley, the name of the birthplace in England of William Walton (see Walton-Burton Story). In 1894, the community was populated with employees of the Cooperative Mining and Manufacturing Company. The first known school was in session in 1888 with the teacher being G.J. Long. The school was held on the ground floor of the Woodmen of the World Lodge. The 1889 teacher was M.A. Pratt and in 1890 there were two teachers, R.P. Brown and Miss Sallie Lovan. The school may have been held in two sessions, September through December and then spring school for six weeks in March and April, as many were at that time. This writer had a maiden aunt that taught spring school in the north end of the county. She told how spring school was usually held for the 1st through 3rd or 4th grades, those too young to help in the fields. The upper grades were only girls who hoped to get enough education to become teachers themselves.

In 1906-1907, Mr. Carl Stearman, still living in the area, remembers the lodge school house and his teacher was Georgie Arnett. "She used to catch me everytime I ran away", he recalls with a chuckle. " I was in the first grade and hated school, so I slipped off every chance I got." Once he got use to school, he did come to enjoy it. The Stearman family was very education minded. Three generations have had several teachers. Carl's sister, Ruby Stearman Sisk, was an alumnis of Barnsley and later returned to teach there. A new school was relocated near Highway 41-A behind Millton Grocery, just north of the middle of Barnsley. Records of the Board of Education show they bore a well in 1909. The 1912 teacher was Miss Mattie Shaw. Mrs. Sisk remembers these teachers: Ophelia Davis, Lula Allen, Linnie Hampton, and Mrs. Sisk was the 1932 teacher. Just when the Barnsley School became a two-room school is not known. However, Mrs. Fairy Lovan Egbert, now a resident of Clinic Convalescent, remembers that she and Helen Campbell Perkins (later Harralson) were the teachers in 1935. The school closed in 1937, consolidating with Mortons Gap. The building was sold to Bryan Fox for $301.00. *Written by Dorothy Shoulders*

BAUGH SCHOOL

Baugh School was located about one mile north of Anton. The 1890 teacher was Mrs. Wesley Speed. There were two buildings over the years, both in the same location. According to Mrs. Paul Dexter, who attended school in the second building, the building was a one-room frame with a pot-bellied stove. There was a board well with a pump, but water was later carried from a local dwelling to the school. Mrs. Dexter said that the school always had a cedar tree at Christmas, but one year it was decided to decorate the arch over the stage with cedar and candles. The decorations caught fire and some of the older boys put out the fire with no real damage except for smoke on the walls. Teachers remembered by Mrs. Dexter were: her brother Roy Woods, Mary Ellen Fox, Beatrice Cardwell, Mondra Sights, Eva Warren Adams, Katty Stodghill, Owen Stinnett, and Martin Roberts. The school consolidated with Anton School in 1949. The building was torn down and today the site is owned by W.C. Brown.

BEULAH SCHOOL

The land for the Beulah School was deeded by Jonathan Jackson Wilkey in 1877. A log building was built on the property, which is where the Beulah Pantry now stands, in the southeast corner of the intersection of Highways 109 and 70. The 1888 and 1889 teacher was William P. Scott and the 1890 teacher was Miss Althea Logan. On July 22, 1909, a number of old county schools were slated to have new buildings, Beulah was one of them. A new one room frame school was built beside the log structure.

Beulah Log School, circa 1909, Front Row L. to R.: Laurel Hicks, Wick Clark, Rulith Franklin, Clora Brown Lantaff, Chester Wilkey, Unknown and Hubert Wilkey. Second Row: unknown, Ollie Clark Hibbs, next three unknown. Third Row: Unknown and Mack Fitzsimmons. Fourth Row: Clora Howton, Floyd Wilkey, Wallace Hicks, Pearl Sisk-Teacher, Unknown, and Espy Brown. Top Row: Verba Clark Hunt, Bertha Dillingham Summers, Gusta Clark Franklin, Vera Lantaff Robards, Unknown, Lelia Hicks Sisk, and unknown

Some of the teachers were Ben Hardrick, Hubert Wilkey, Flora Wilkey 1910-11, Bonnie Wilkey Hopson, Robbie Morgan 1911-12, Justin Logan, Miss Lois Howton 1932, and Mildred Furguson 1944. According to Beulah Lewis, granddaughter of Jackson Wilkey, the old log school made a good playground. At recess, the pupils would invade the building, laughter would ring throughout as the children jumped from sill to sill and played games. The log building was torn down, perhaps folks thought it was too dangerous for the children to play in. A third school building was constructed about 1925 on the Hill just south of the old site, where the James Lewis home now stands. Beulah School was abolished circa 1950.

BLUE SPRINGS SCHOOL

Blue Springs was located just off the Pleasant View Road on the J.H. Porter farm. Access either way to the school has been sold to and closed by P&M Coal Company. Known as Kirkwood in the 1800's, the name was changed for a large spring that supplied the school with water. Calvin Martin went to school his first grade year at Blue Springs in 1918. In fact, all his eight grades were there. His teacher that first year was Helen Osborn who boarded with Calvin's parents, John Robert and Loucrisy Byrum, known as Bob and Lou. Mr. Martin recalls his teacher gave him more than one spanking for being naughty. He never once told his parents for fear of receiving another at home. The 1890 teacher was J.T. Ligon. Rosella Daniels Myres says the school was also called Tick Ridge. The Blue Springs school closed due to a lack of students. The exact date of closing is not known.

BONIFIDE SCHOOL

Bonifide School was first known as Schmetzers in the early 1800s. The large family of Schmetzers owned farms on both sides of what is now Highway 41-A, north of Nebo. On what is called Schmetzers Crossing Road, south of 41-A and near the railroad tracks, was a log school. Like so many others, it burned in the late 1880's. As the number of students had dwindled, a new location was sought. In his 90s, Mr. Raymond Cates remembers the new school was located just off Highway 41-A, two miles north of Nebo on the Hayes-Daugherty Road. The new school, Bonifide, began in the late 1890's. In 1910, the school was repainted.

Former student and later teacher, Mildred Cates Crowley, lists some of her teachers when she was a student: Leona Kington (1918), Dixie Harkins McCoy (1919), Gwendoline Clayton (1920-21) before she became Mrs. Sam Harralson who now lives in Madisonville, Euel Morgan (1922-23) who later became the post master at Nebo, and Robbie Townsend (1924-25).

Other teachers she remembers were two of her graduating classmates at Nebo, Gladys Lucas Landson (1930-31) now deceased and Sarah Barron (1931-32) who still lives in Nebo. Virgil Myers, a friend from the class of 1930, also taught at the school. Mrs. Crowley closed the school in February of 1937. The '37 flood had prevented all but two or three students from attending. School was to have closed that year in March but closed two weeks early. Mildred remembers how the last class was on Thursday and her wedding was the next day.

BROWDER SCHOOL

Browder School was located close to the Browder Church on Highway 70 East. The land was conveyed by H.K. Browder in 1896. The building was a one room frame building with a coal stove in the middle of the room. According to Pansey Wagoner Ashby who attended the school, the school had a well but on occasion the teacher would appoint two boys to walk to Lawrence Spring at the foot of the hill, below Browder Church, to get spring water. Teachers remembered were Emmitt Ashby, Lillie Hanner, Corine Pittman, Christine Webb, Louise Ramsey, Jessie Frances Jennings, Nevelyn Sisk Adams and John R. Thomas. The school closed around 1941. Today, the new church sits on the approximate site of the school.

BROWNS SCHOOL

Browns School was located on the Morganfield Road between Highways 630 and 502, across the creek on the south side of the road, that end of the low lands known then as Pratt's Bottoms. Two of the Duncan sisters attended here in 1919-20, Carrie Carnal and Anna Laura Walker. Mrs. Carnal told of their teacher making the naughty ones stand on one foot in front of everyone for punishment. Mrs. Walker was in awe of and feared their teacher, Harold Cox. "I just knew he didn't like me." Then at Christmas that year, he gave the students brightly colored toothbrushes. A smile lingers as Mrs. Walker told that her toothbrush had "Teachers Pet" stamped on it. "Such a warm feeling to me, a shy little girl, to know I was really the teachers favorite." Other teachers remembered were Bessie Slaton Cox and Anna Cox (Harold's wife), Faye Morgan, Nellie Cobb and in its last years, Miss Sarah Barron. The school was consolidated in the late 1930's.

BUNTIN SCHOOL

Buntin School was located on the north side of Hanson's Cox's Store Road. As was quite common, the school was named for the man who donated the land, William H. Buntin (1817-1901) who was a very prominent surveyor of the Shakerag hills area (See story on Shakerag by Leroy Veazey). In 1890 the teacher was Miss Willie Bone. Leroy Veazey believes his grandmother, Elizabeth Veazey (1851-1924), was a student at Buntin School as she taught some of the basics to his grandfather after their marriage. Mr. Veazey's father, Lee Veazey (1877-1936), and his brother, Rupert Veazey (1907-1968), taught in the second school building which was a frame building that was located across the road from the original log school. Other teachers were Beulah Whit Dowel, Tina Gooch Pugh, Nellie Wooten Mills, Mable Brooks Brown, Ina Pearl Noel and Miss Ruth Blankenship. Leroy Veazey, his sister and brothers, and countless others have the fondest of memories of Buntin School which closed in February of 1936 or 1937. The building burned in 1962 and according to Mr. Veazey, all that remains are the foundation stones, a few pictures and cherished memories.

Browder School-1927-28

Buntin School about 1906

CANE RUN

In 1909, the St. Bernard Mining Company deeded a 150' X 250' lot to the Board of Education. It was bounded by Mr. Fox and Mr. Webb's properties. The school, completed in 1910, was called Cane Run. The first teacher was Ethyl Kaiser Chappell in the 1910-11 school year.

It seems no one remembers what happened to the school or when, but a second school was built there later and called Carbondale. Mr. and Mrs. Isaac Lamb remember the school as being located just off Highway 112 on the Carbondale-Charleston Road. In the 1960s, there was a baseball field at the junction of the two roads and the school was just behind it. Both school buildings had just one room. Among those who taught were Anise Ashmore, Leslie Terry, Mr. L. Nisbet, Miss Jimmie D. Sisk and Miss Ruth Gailor in 1932, Porter Hudson, Miss Tinie Lutz 1928-29, Elmer Gamblin 1929-30, Mabel Clark 1944-45, and Owen Davis was the last teacher before the school closed.

CAVANAH SCHOOL

Cavanah School was appropriately named for W.W. (William Wallace) Cavanah (great grandfather of Leroy Veazey) who donated space for the institution from his farm to be used as long as needed and then would revert to his descendants. It was last used as a school about 1956.

Cavanah School about 1942

Mr. Cavanah not only performed a great service for the youth and neighborhood, but some fringe benefits for some of his descendants. Among the teachers were his son Tom Cavanah (grandfather of Leroy) who taught there in the 1885 era. About 1902, W.W.'s granddaughter, Lula Cavanah (Leroy's mother), taught there with some of the students fully grown and as many as 25 in number. Another granddaughter, Audrey Cavanah Phillips, who was the daughter of W.W.'s son John, taught there perhaps in 1913. Another granddaughter, Bethel Cavanah Nourse, daughter of W.W.'s son Elva, was a career teacher and taught there for a total of three years and elsewhere for 34 years. A great granddaughter, Erline Veazey Hughes, daughter of Lula Cavanah Veazey referred to above, taught there in the fall of 1928. Many honorable teachers have made a great impact upon hundreds of students who learned the three R's at Cavanah. The neighborhood was also known as Cavanah and even into the 1950's a column appeared in The Messenger entitled CAVANAH. Today the little parcel of land loaned to Hopkins County by W.W. Cavanah for educational purposes sits like a deserted island surrounded by nice farms. It is even yet legally in the hands of his descendants and Leroy Veazey states he is proud to be one of them. We are grateful to Leroy Veazey for contributing this information.

CHARLESTON SCHOOL

Charleston School began between 1870-73. A private school taught by Billy Hart, it was located for several years in an old store building. Later the school was moved to an old tobacco factory south of Charleston Colleries. The third location was a dwelling house. A school building erected in 1878 on land given by Thomas G. Chappell and Isaac M. Lynn. In 1924, a new building was built by joint contributions of the Dawson Daylight Coal Company and the Hopkins County Board of Education. A two year high school program was begun. In 1940, a new building was erected and this year was also the beginning of a four year high school program. Additional classrooms were added in 1946 and 1961. The 1961-62 school year was the last for a high school at Charleston, as the next year students attended the new West Hopkins High School. The school continues today, housing grades K-8.

Charleston School in 1987

Due to the long history of the school, it would take much space to list all of the school teachers. The following is a list through approximately the first 80 years of the schools history.

From 1879 to 1890: Ben F. Kendrick, Miss Flora Uierce, Mr. Isaac Wilkie, Mrs. Martha Jane Collins, Mr. Rance McIntosh, Miss Willie Lynch, Jack E. Day, Ruby Laffoon, W.T. Baker and his sister Ida, Miss Altha Logan, and W.H. White.

From 1890 to 1940: W.E. Castleberry, Miss Melza Alexander, Shelby Loving, Robert Martin, Uziah Earle, W.N. Stites, Charles G. Franklin, Will Miller, Tom Logan, J.H. Harralson, Miss Amma Fox, Dennie Teague, Brad Logan, Ruby Franklin, Frank Dunn, Herndon Townzen, Miss Cornelia Quinn, T.T. Piercy, Mrs. Bonnie Beshear Lee, Miss Marie Richards, Miss Lillian Mullens, Mrs. Flora Smith, Mrs. Mae Workman, Miss Grada Brown, Mrs. Connie Russell, Miss Mary Jones, Miss Sue Cavanah, Mrs. Kay Reed, Mrs. Nina Stevens, Mrs. Virginia Ervin, Miss Pauline Dillingham, Wilbur Branson, Regie Peyton, Miss Virgie Beshear, Miss Wanna Dixon, Mrs. Regie Peyton, Miss Dixie Lois Logan, Mrs.Weldon Brown.

A few of the teachers after 1940: Mrs. Bessie Beshear, Mrs. Kate Utley, Porter Hudson, Mrs. Blanche Calvert, Miss Ruth Poe, Jewell Logan, Ruby Jenkins, Gertha Hale, Ida Mae Good, Thomas Bradley Cox, Robert Hill and Ray Kirkwood.

We are grateful to Mary Ramsey for providing this article.

CHRIST THE KING SCHOOL

Christ The King School was built in Madisonville in 1978 after the closing of the Immaculate Conception School in Earlington. The school is located on Highway 41-A and is for grades K-8.

Christ The King School in 1987

CLEMENTS SCHOOL

Clements School was located near Highway 813 and Pennyrile Parkway, almost equal distance from Nortonville, Mortons Gap and White Plains. The ground on which it was built was donated by Chesley Williams. The school was named for William Clements, one of the older citizens of the community. Families who sent their children to Clements were: Almon, Littlepage, Morton, Slaton, Oglesby, Moore, Smith, Langzell, Clements, Givens, Tirey, Carroll, Williams, Cunningham, Kyle, Dickerson, Crick, Peterson, Graddy, Polley, Stankley, Stewart, Browning, Bilbro, Lovan, Oldham and Huggins. Known teachers were: Mrs. Sallie Cavanaugh in 1890, Hattie Morton, Sanna Bailey Bowling, Georgia Hamby Moore, Paul Dillingham, Bessie Slaton, Ola Cox Murphey, Lucille Fox, Lula Solomon, Nima Orange Hibbs, Mrs. Stodghill, Laura Suthard Jagoe, Bonnie Slaton Langzell, Lucy Slaton Kyle and Archie Jennings.

Clements School, Teacher Bonnie Slaton Langzell with a group of her students

The school was in session for over half a century when it was consolidated with Mortons Gap in 1937. The consolidation was largely protested by the community. Con Slaton, son of John H. Slaton, was one of the first students who rode the school bus on its first run to Mortons Gap. A few years ago, former students and teachers relived their school days at Clements with a reunion held near the site of the school. The reunion was begun by the ringing of an old school bell. The meal was a replica of the food carried in the lunch pails many years before. Thirty-six were present, representing many communities and states. The school building has been gone for several years. All that remains are the old well and precious memories of the residents, students and teachers who taught there.

COILTOWN SCHOOL

Coiltown School was located next to the Baptist Church, 1/4 mile through the little mining town of Coiltown, south on Highway 502. This school began around 1890 after the closing of the old CORBIN SCHOOL which was located further south toward Beulah. At that time, Highway 502 then made two consecutive L turns forming a square of land perfect for the school. Then in 1900 came two mining camps, facing each other on the crossroads of Rosecreek Road and Highway 502. With the mining workers came lots of children and a need for a large school. It was first one big room, then a smaller room added with a cloak room between, giving the building an L shape. Since Harold Cox was the big room teacher or principal several times, we will not mention him every time.

Coiltown School 1925, Front Row L. to R.: Harry Barron, Carmon Fortner, Wynon Peyton, Grace Hibbs, Odell Gaston, Agnes Byrum, James Royce Higdon, James Kirkwood, J.C. Tapp, Vivian Green, Myrtle Cox, Tapp Corbin, Willard Barnett, James Peyton, Johnny Engle, J.C. Allen, and Robert Nichols. Second Row: Gwendolyn Byrum, Wilma Allen, Helen Cunningham, William Jenkins, Tommy Barron, Lorene Jenkins, Zelda Fitzsimmons, George Corbin, Dorothy Barnett, Lloyd Peyton, Virginia Green, Ola Mae Nichols, Madge Hibbs, Wallace Peyton, Henry Engles, and Richard Peyton. Back Row: Ramy Higdon, Mildred Hyatt, Helen Byrum, Hugh Cunningham, Roy Fortner, Elizabeth Jenkins, Catherine Barron, Lorene Cox, R.P. Byrum, Jack Ligon, Teachers Norene Morrow Hill and Harold Cox, J.P. Edwards Nora Nichols, Lewood Watson, Mary Frances Byrum, Louise Allen, Opal Brinkley, and Mary Ellen Higdon

Some of the teachers were: Myrtle Mitchell 1903-04, Euel Morgan and Maude Wilkey, Mr. Dee Sisk and Mary Ellen Fox, Nevoline Cowan, Helen Osborn, Mary Nesbitt Minter and Norene Morrow later Hill also taught at other times, Opal Brinkley (a former student) and Margret Brown. The 1932 teachers were Hazel Wooten Fox and Mr. Harold Cox. In 1934-35, Tommy Arnold and Helen Walker Lewis taught. Mr. Arnold gave this interesting tidbit about the school. Coiltown has been known for its many sets of twins and triplets, but the year Mr. Arnold taught there were three sets of twins attending at one time. In the first grade were Emagene and Imagene Averitt, a little bit older were Lloyd and Louise Hibbs, and even a bit older were Coiltown's J.B. and J.D. Peyton, who by their own request were allowed to serve in the same unit in WWII. In the 1920s Mary and Sarah Frazer attended. Many years later, after Coiltown consolidated with Nebo, the Copely tripletts lived in Coiltown. One of the closing teachers was Josephine Parrish Wilhite about 1938. Information was furnished by former students Everett Hibbs, George Corbin, Lorine Cox Winstead, Michael Noel and Paul Bone.

COLUMBIA SCHOOL OR POSSOM COLLEGE

Columbia School or Possom College was located in the corner lot formed by the Manitou Road and Laffoon Trail. It was a small one room school at first a little further up the Trail. The teacher in 1890 was Mae Crabtree. No one seems to know how it got the name Columbia. In 1892 Widow Barnhill sold the land to the school board. The new building was moved to the corner of the lot and was enlarged. How it became known as Possom College was related by "old timers" as: One night in the fall of the year, some older boys of the community went hunting. They caught two gunny sacks of Opossums, brought them to Columbia School and turned them loose in the school building. The next morning, when the teacher and some of the children arrived, there were 20 (?) live opossum running about! The year 1909 was when Sam Morrow of Manitou began first grade. His teacher was Maude Fox. He remembers Ralph Cardwell as a teacher also. In 1911, $150.00 was spent on the school building for repairs and to add a new cloak room. Claude Porter was the teacher in 1912 when the school was closed for lack of enough students. It later reopened. Other teachers were: Miss Neely Hibbs, Linnie Johnson, Lloyd Jagoe and Mrs. Fannie Sisk. The year the school closed, Mr. Morrow recalls going to Pleasant Grove School. His younger sister, Lila Morrow Hibbs, recalls these teachers: Lena Pemberton (her first grade teacher), Vena Blue, Ruth Hall, Mary Thompson, Mrs. Jettie Osborn and daughter Sydney. Jonell Crowe was the teacher in 1929 when the school closed again.

In 1932 the teacher was Sallie Woodard. Later, former student Rosella Daniels Myers taught. The school closed for the last time in 1937 and the property was bought by a mine.

CONCORD SCHOOL

Concord School was located on what was called the Princeton-Greenville Road and is now called Concord Drive, one and one-half miles north of White Plains. The earliest known teacher was Charley Clark in 1890. According to Kermit Lovelace of White Plains, who attended this school, the school was a one-room frame building with the standard pot-bellied stove in the center of the room. Water for the school was hauled by the boys from a spring that was a quarter mile away. Mr. Lovelace says it was considered a privilege to be allowed to go get the water as you could dally along the way therefore avoiding class time. The Concord Church was close by and Mr. Lovelace remembers daytime revivals were held at the church. At least once during the revival, the teacher would line up the students and march them to the church to attend a revival service. Teachers remembered by Mr. Lovelace were: Myrtle Mercer Badger, a Mrs. Langley, Walter Simons, Newman Franklin, Mrs. Bertie Stodghill, Miss Lula Allen, Esther Oates Morton, Mrs. Mable Outlaw, and Mandolin Ryan. The school closed before 1937. The building still stands and is now a dwelling.

COPPERAS SPRINGS SCHOOL

Copperas Springs School was moved from northeast of Antioch Church on 1069 to a lot adjoining Olive Branch Church. In 1911, a new building was built at a cost of $394.00. In 1890 the teacher was Mrs. Nola Buchanan. Other teachers were Gusta James, who later married one of her older students (Luther Jones) in the mid 1910's, Betty Poole, Dudley Wallace Brown, Sallie Lynch Brown and J.L. Clayton. Elizabeth Rudd tells of the last year she taught there as does Waurika Clayton Nix.

COX SCHOOL

Cox School, known later as Cox's Store, was located on the corner of North Cox Road and Manitou-Dixon Road, now known as Highway 630. A small community called "Pull-tight", it had stores, churches, a blacksmith shop, and Veazeys Post Office. In 1890 the teacher was Stella Gregory. Other early teachers were Vera Mullenix, Rev. Pat Durham, Mrs. Mollie Crowe, Gusta James

Cox's Store School, 1942-43, Front Row L. to R.: Kenneth Lantrip, Harold Simms, Betty Lantrip, and James Oakley-Second Row: Ruth Oakley, Alfred Springfield, Jr., and Jonell Oakley. Third Row: Henry Louis Trice, Virginia Springfield, and D.B. Simms. Back Row: James Jones, Marshall Oakley (Deceased), Jenella Springfield, Sarah Allaway, and teacher Elois Kirkwood

Jones, Mildred Vannoy, Miss Linnie Jones who taught spring school and her sister Mrs. Gertie Morrow.

B.D. Nisbet closed the school, along with several others, for lacking 25 students. In July 1930, it reopened with Marjorie Crowe teaching her first year and boarding with the parents of Rev. Arvell Oakley.

In April of 1932, a spark from the chimney of a house nearby ignited the dry leaves in the attic vent of the house. The wind carried the fire over the wood lot between the house and the school. The school roof caught fire and both buildings were lost, as the men folk of the community were working in the fields. The school reopened in the unused store building, thus the name Cox's Store. A small white building was built in the late 30's. It still stands on the corner of Cox's Road and Highway 630, on the W.L. Carter property. It was used as a Holiness Church for a few years, but is now used for storage. Later teachers were Ruth Blankenship, Virgil Myers, Eloise Eastwood (now Duncan), and the last, Ora Villines. Due to illness, Mrs. Villines had to have Dorothy Miller Shoulders substitute in the fall of 1946 and 1947. In 1948, Helen Roberts Crook was the substitute. Mrs. Villines closed the school in 1951.

CRANOR SCHOOL

Cranor School was located about five miles southwest of St. Charles, on Buttermilk Road, not far past the Buffalo Creek Bridge. Through the years, there have been two buildings on the site. The second building is used today as a meeting house for various churches. The land was owned by George Terry and was deeded for the school in 1880 (Deed Book 39, page 415). The log school that was built, burned around the turn of the century and a new one room frame school was built by members of the community. The 1889 teacher was Mr. Rance McIntosh and the 1890 teacher was Davis Cranor. The children who attended, could go through the eighth grade. At that time, for most folks, this was enough schooling, but if you wanted to and had a way or people to board with, you could go to the high school in Nortonville.

Other teachers were Miss Edrie Robinson 1932, Mary Woodruff Terry, Alma Robinson, Anna Bell Wamos, an Indian woman that boarded with Mary Ellen and Cy Alexander, a Miss Crick from Nortonville, Rita Morris, Lena Melton, Myrtle Utley, and Floyd Howton. During its years as a school, Cranor was also a church. When the school board decided to close it down in 1940, the

Cranor School House as it is today

community wanted to keep their church, after all they had built it. But it was slated to be torn down, men came in and took the seats and other furnishings. Representing the community, Joe Cranor, Mary Utley, Ernest Dawson and Charlie Terry went to the Board and purchased the property. Those named above became the first trustees. Many of the folks living near the old school, contributed money and time to fix up and furnish the building as their church. One of the present trustees, Gaston Stewart, holds a copy of the deed and furnished this information. There are two other trustees at the present time, Jim Bennett and (Little) Noel Terry.

DALTON ELEMENTARY AND HIGH SCHOOL

Dalton was first known as Garnetville. The name was changed when it was learned another community had a post office already by that name. The first school was a tiny one-room log building near the Houston Harvey family farm. Mr. Harvey, born in 1823, was a teacher at the first school in later years according to his great granddaughter, Mrs. Beryl Peyton Hubbard. In 1875, a second school building was erected on a half acre tract of land given by R.J. McCulley.

Dalton School about 1921-22. Front Row, L. to R.: Ella May Morris, Hershel Sigler, Virginia Menser Harris. Woodrow Bryant, Marie Felker Madison, Tommy Bryant, Unknown, Imon Cullen Wyatt, Marion Dorris Carol Fox, Unknown, and Ruth Adkins Oost. Second Row: Amanda Dever, Huston Adkins, Ida Belle Mullins, Allie Morris, Anna Fancher, Hughston Peyton, Catherine Wiley, Thorton Dever, Olin Weir, Unknown Sylvia Sigler, Unknown and Geraldine Rhea. Third Row: Garland Sisk, Henry Rhea, Lois Cullen, Gertrude Herron, Florice Lester, Basil Perry Rich, Floy Howton, and Lula Perry Spencer. Fourth Row: Bonnie Church, Pauline Weir, Agnes Cullen, Brunette Johnston, Adeline Brown, Allie Bell Bryant, Sanford Peyton, Richard Morse, Paul Montgomery, and teacher Hugh Egbert

Early known teachers were: W.D. Davis and Miss Eliza Fox 1888, Prof. W.D. Davis and Miss Vi Wyatt 1889, and Will Wyatt 1890. By 1892, the school was expanded to two rooms. This building was replaced by a frame building. Around 1915-1917, a new two-room school was constructed near the site of the present location on Dalton Road. Other teachers were: a Mr. Shackleford, Will Miller, and Miss Charlie Sisk. A two-year high school was begun in 1923, with Beryl Peyton as principal. The 1924-25 principal was Earl Creasy and the 1925-1927 principal was R.E. Simons. In 1927, the 11th grade was added and in 1928, the school became a four-year high school with John R. Adams as principal from 1927-36.

In 1928, Mr. Adams married another teacher, Beatrice Norwood. Corine Dever and Basil Perry were the first to complete the four year high school course, but decided to wait and go through graduation exercises with those graduating in 1929: Frank Bell, Edgar Bell, Ollie Bryant, Roenah Chappelle, Mary Jones, Lula Perry, Retha Lovan, Ida Mae Parrish, Sanford Peyton and William Winstead.

Other principals at Dalton were: A.O. Richards 1936-43, B.D. Nisbet 1943-45, Arnold Hicks 1945-47, A.O. Richards 1947-51, John Fletcher 1951-52, Thorton Dever 1952-55, and A.O Richards 1955-1961.

Other teachers remembered: Ralph McGregor, Pauline Ferrell Peyton, H.W. Wilkey and Compton Crowe. The lunch room began in the late 1940's. Bura Brown was the first matron, with the food cooked at Mrs. Hubbard's home and taken to the school to be served. Dalton lost its gym to fire in 1949-50.

In 1950-51, a new gym and building were erected across the highway. The gym was never up to standard size, so games were played at Madisonville High School (now Browning Springs Middle School). Dalton High School consolidated into West Hopkins in the early 1960's. Over 466 graduated from Dalton High School from 1928 to 1962. The largest class of 33 members was in 1942. The smallest classes were in 1932 and 1957 with 6 each. Mrs. Thorton Devers (Amanda Frazer) a former student and now a retired substitute teacher still living in the Dalton area, helped with this information. The school is still used for elementary teaching today. - *Submitted by Dorothy Miller Shoulders*

DANIEL BOONE SCHOOL

Daniel Boone School was located off Highway 62 on what is now Highway 1687. It is not known exactly when the school was established. Some older Hopkins County residents say Daniel Boone School was once located about 1/2 mile east of its last location. In 1921, Mildred Toombs Adams was the teacher. There is a record of land given in 1922 by Carroll Patterson, who was the president of Stirling Coal Company. Mrs. Nevelyn Sewell Butler remembers that as a seventh grade student, the school was only

Daniel Boone School, Front Row L to R : First three unknown, Wilma Dean Adams, Joan Hale, and Willa Dean Knight. Second Row: Unknown, Melvin Miller, Charles Franklin, Aubry Miller, in front with Elwood Franklin in back, and unknown

one room. A short time later, the Norton School, which had already closed, was moved on skids and added on to Daniel Boone.

Other known teachers were: Mary Lou Matney Hibbs, Laura Pryor, Emmitt Ashby, Alva Lee Skaggs and later his daughter Margaret Skaggs, Louise Merrell, Sam Franklin, Artie Teague Moore, Artense Whitfield Cowan, James Suthard, Mr. and Mrs. Hobert Robertson, Mr. and Mrs. Luther Morse, Virgie Spickard Franklin, Iretta Teague McGregor, and Betty Wilkerson who is believed to have been the closing teacher in 1950 or 1952. Mr. Hobert Miller who attended all eight grades at Daniel Boone remembers a first grade boy who was not able to learn to count as quickly as the others. The youngster could not count to five. The teacher told the child to run five times around the school house in order to help him learn. Mr. Miller called himself and his brother "regular boys". He once received three spankings and his brother five, all in one day!

DAWSON SPRINGS SCHOOL

Dawson Springs School was built in the late 1870's on a site which is currently East Walnut Street, but at that time was outside the city limits of Dawson Springs. In 1885, a new school was built. The frame building had two stories with three rooms downstairs and two room upstairs. Woodburning stoves were in the middle of each room. The teacher in 1888 was Miss Annie Bradley of Princeton and in 1889, Prof. H.J. Carter and his wife and Miss Smyrna Blaine. In 1890, the teacher was H.J. Carter. In 1915, the citizens voted to build a new building. Students helped in digging the foundation by each removing a spade of dirt. A two-story brick building, the first floor held six classrooms and a large hall. The second floor had four classrooms, a study hall and a stage. Due to lack of money to finish the building, two classrooms were in the basement and both had dirt floors. Through fund raising activities of the PTA and women's clubs, the building was finished. For the next fifteen years, both elementary and high school classes were held in the new school.

Dawson Springs School

In 1929-30, a new building was built and used for the lower grades. Built on Alexander and Hickory Streets, it consisted of six classrooms and a gymnasium. In February of 1968, a new school facility was started. This building is still in use today as an elementary school. In the late 1970's, a new high school was built behind the elementary school. Dawson Springs still continues today as an Independent School System.

The above information was compiled from articles written by Jeannie Napier and Michael W. McAlister, Seniors at Dawson Springs High School.

DILLINGHAM SCHOOL

Dillingham School was located on the Dillingham School Road

Dillingham School

near White Plains. The land is currently part of the J.W. Orange farm.

On Feb. 13, 1892, Charles M. Pendley and his wife Liza gave a 1/2 acre tract of land to be used for school purposes which was to revert back to the owner when no longer needed. In 1908, the teacher was Naomi Ashby, the mother of Mrs. Eloile Whitfield Moore. Naomi Ashby married Mr. Whitfield in 1910. Other teachers remembered by Mrs. Moore were Lillian Fox Howton, Kate Bishop, Lillian Earl Fox, Miss Leafie Merrell, Chester Skillman, Mary Lester, Nimmia Orange Hibbs, Janice Craig, Mrs. Jenera Hanks, Lila Wright Tate, Gerald Lacy, Florence Curley Stanley, Fairy Lovan Egbert and Agnes Goad Greenfield.

Agnes Greenfield was a widow who married Earl Dawson. Mrs. Dawson closed the school in 1937. Mr. J.W. Orange has fond memories of Dillingham School. He remembers when Miss Agnes rode a pony to school and how it was his privilege to ride the pony home for lunch and to water it. As boys will do, as soon as he was out of sight of the school, he set the pony to running as hard as he could. One day the pony fell, throwing him. Nothing was broken, but it taught him a lesson. No more hard runs! Mr. Orange remembers playing ring-around-the-roses, pitching horse shoes, baseball, coo-sheepie (a form of tag), and Annie-over during recess. When the school closed in 1937, it was consolidated with White Plains and Nortonville.

DITNEY

Ditney #1 was built sometime in the mid 1800's and was located on the Wylie Roberts property, which is now called High Glory Hill. Marcella Griffin tells that it was first a log building that was later weatherboarded and her grandmother attended this school.

DITNEY #2 was located on the Ike Dearmond property on Brown Road. Marcella's mother attended this school (the girl holding the slate in the 1909 picture).

DITNEY #3 was on the Latt Rudd property now called Ditney Lane. In 1890, Miss Annie Foley taught at Ditney. Other teachers were Operah Hobgood, Audrey Eastwood, Willie Tirey, Charlie Cox, Gertie Fowler, Jim Ashby, Anna Lou Hatcher, Ila Mae Timmons, Margie Crowe and Miss Clemon C. Ashby. Marcella attended Ditney #3. It consolidated about 1940. The last school building is still in use as a corn crib. Near the school yard there are

Ditney School, Nov. 5, 1909. Front Row L. to R.: Cleo Rudd, Leota Stanley, Pearl Nance, William Katherine (Billie Boy) Wood, Ruby Dearmond, Delia Qualls, Vera Nance. Second Row: Bailey Nance, Guy Qualls, Jasper Qualls, Dewy Roberts, Coleman Qualls, Alford Wood, Ernest Campbell, Beckham Roberts. Third Row: Delbert Wood, Ethel Roberts, Annie Rogers, Unknown, Gertie Fowler, Ruby Rudd. Fourth Row: Charlie Cox Teacher, Leslie Roberts, Lena Roberts, Jenoah Campbell

Indian hominy holes, three small and a large one that is twenty inches deep.

DOCKERY-McGREGOR SCHOOL

The Dockery-McGregor School was located on the west side of Hopkins County. To reach the school site from Beulah, take Highway 70 west approximately two miles, then turn south on Fergusontown Road, go about 1 1/2 miles to the F.L. Dockery Road, turn right and go about 1/2 mile. From Charleston, take Niles Row Road to F.L. Dockery Road, turn right and go about one mile.

Some of the teachers at McGregor School were Luther Lawnzen 1903-04, Ira Cook 1904-05, Dixon Purdy 1905-06, A.H. Morgan 1906-07, and Iva Hicks 1907-08. The Dockery School was built in 1908 and some of the teachers were Constance Brown 1908-1910, Will Purdy, Clyde Wilkey, Essie Trent, Flora Wilkey Purdy, Archie Howton and Ruth Howton who was the last teacher.

Sometime after the school closed, it was torn down and Lexie Dockery used the lumber and other materials to build his home. The house is now owned by George Alexander.

The location and teachers names for Dockery School were furnished by Mr. Charlie Robards and Mrs. Bessie Lovell who both attended this school. The teachers at McGregor School were abstracted from records kept by the Hopkins County Board of Education.

MISS EARLE'S SCHOOL HOUSE

Only the following information was located about this school. The information was taken from the July 17, 1890 issue of the Hustler newspaper in Harold Ledbetter's possession. "The trustees of the Madisonville school have secured the graded building and Miss Mary Earle's house in which to teach the school this fall. Professor Thomas H. Smith has been chosen as superintendent of the whole. Professor C. M. Lutz is first assistant and will have charge of the Earle house in connection with Miss Mary Earle. Misses Flora Pierce and Mattie Daves will be the other assistants."

EARLINGTON HIGH SCHOOL

The first Earlington High School was erected in 1927. Built on the Evans homeplace, this was considered one of the finest school buildings in the area. A brick building, it had five classrooms, a large library, a science laboratory room and a combination gymnasium-auditorium seating about 700. The library was open for use by the citizens of the town as well as the students. Many basketball tournaments were held in the gymnasium. The school also contained separate office space for the Superintendent of Schools, who at this time was Mr. A.P. Prather. Mr. Prather came to Earlington in 1924 as Superintendent of Schools and remained Superintendent for 38 years until his retirement in 1962 at age 70.

Earlington High School, now Earlington K-8

In 1956, the people of Earlington voted upon itself a 25 year Special Voted School Building Tax that could be used only for new buildings. As a result of this tax, a new Earlington High School was built on property then called Pasture Hill and was occupied in February of 1964. This fulfilled a longtime dream of the Earlington people. James W. Larmouth was Superintendent of Schools at this time. He succeeded A.P. Prather in 1962 and remained Superintendent until the merger with Hopkins County School System in 1975. The Earlington schools were and are now a mirror of the people of Earlington, who gave great importance to education. Proof of this is found in the curriculum of the Earlington High School in the early 1930's: English I, II, III, IV; Latin I, II, Cicero, Virgil; Algebra I, II, Plane Geometry, Trigonometry; General Science, Biology, Chemistry, Physics; Civics, World History, American History and Democracy.

In later years the curriculum would be broadened to keep pace with the changing times and needs of students. Its faculty was always strong and dedicated to academic excellence. As a result, many prominent people graduated from this high school. Strong academics breeds strength in other endeavors and one example of this was the strong sports programs of the school. Turning out many outstanding teams through the years, basketball teams representing the school and community reached the State Tournament five times: the girls team of 1932 coached by C. Buford Webb; the first boys team in 1956 and the boys team of 1962, both coached by James Larmouth; the boys team of 1966; and the boys team of 1967, which fulfilled a long time dream of the school by winning the State Tournament.

The teams of 1966 and 1967 were coached by Bob Fox. Many fine athletes graduated from the school. Perhaps the most notable was Harry Todd of the class of '58. In addition to making all the All-State teams three years, he was a first team All-American player his senior year. All in all, it can be accurately said that the schools served the community well and the community served the schools well with great support. The schools were fortunate in that a strong, dedicated faculty was maintained down through the years with strong dedicated teachers and administrators being an absolute essential to good schools. A great school district in a great community. - *Submitted by James Larmouth*

East Broadway School

On Sept. 24, 1883, Professor Ernest McCulley purchased a lot on the corner of East Broadway and Baker Street (now Scott Street). The lot was 98' X 95' and was purchased from James W. Wilkins and his wife. The next year, Prof. McCulley and his associates built a private school. The school was named the Madisonville Normal School and Business College and was opened on July 15, 1884. Prof. McCulley taught math and business classes and also ran the school.

East Broadway School

On June 24, 1898, Paul Moore, as trustee of the Hopkins County College and Training School, bought the building for this type of school. Prof. Charles Stokes was one of the professors. On Sept. 4, 1906, the Madisonville Business College under the direction of the Scott Brothers opened in this building. The upper rooms were used for a dormitory for young men and the lower floor was divided into classrooms. The school was then bought by Munnel Wilson on Apr. 29, 1907. In May of 1907, George R. and Mary Lynn purchased the building and on July 3, 1907, the Lynns sold the building to the Madisonville Independent Board of Education.

East Broadway Public School was held in this building, housing grades one through four until crowded conditions required the building of the Hall Street School. On Aug. 30, 1924 the property was sold to Will L. Hall. At this time Hall Street School was in use and East Broadway School ceased to exist. The property was later bought by S.R. and Victoria Parker and converted into "The Parker Apartments". Today, after various owners, it is the two family dwelling of the James W. Cavanaugh and the Jim Allen families.

Elam School

Elam School was a little school about half way between Beulah and Kirkwood Springs Road, just a little northwest of Highway 70.

Elam School-Class of 1906

The closest landmark today is the natural gas storage area. The school was located a little way behind it. In 1889, the teachers were Mrs. Atha Campbell and Alice Brown. In 1890, the teacher was Miss Alice Brown. Other teachers were Ira Cook, ___Dunbar, Cleora Givins, Will Purdy, Beryl Peyton Hubbard, Cornelia Quinn, Floria Franklin Smith, Newman Franklin, Miss Florice Peyton 1928, Miss Mabel Hudson 1929, and A.O. Richards in 1932.

Elam closed when the bad flu epidemic struck during WWI, then reopened and held classes for a number of years. The school was closed permanently in or about 1935.

Eli School

Although Eli School was a little country school in Christian County, a number of it's students and teachers were from Hopkins County. To get to the site, take Highway 62 west, two miles from St. Charles, then turn south on Highway 1338, also known as Union Temple Road. The road is blacktop, has many hills and curves, and is quite a nice drive on an idyllic afternoon. Odell Hamby has a farm about four miles out on the right. About a half mile past his farm, up a hill, is a gravel road that turns off to the left. The school was back that road about 200 yards. The one room school was built sometime prior to 1925, on the Walter Lantrip farm.

Eli School, 1936, Front Row L. to R.: Hershel Lantrip, Odell Hamby, Dorothy Trotter and Opal Trotter. Second Row: Wanita Christopher, Catherine Cansler, Woodard Parker, Kenneth Parker and Johnny Cansler. Third Row: Herbert Lantrip, Elizabeth Christopher, J.T. Hamby, Calvin Collins, Vernon Parker and Kenneth (Cubby) Jackson. Top Row: Helen Cansler, Irene Gamble (teacher), Doris Collins and Arnold McKnight

Odell Hamby, who supplied much of this information, remembers the way they used to draw water from the well. Instead of the usual single bucket and crank, at the top of a framework support was a crank attached to a roller. Running over the roller, was a long sprocket chain that reached down into the well and back up to the roller again. Connected at regular intervals to the sprocket chain, were small scoops or buckets. As the crank was turned, one by one, the small empty buckets went down into the well and came up brimming with water. As the chain carried the buckets over the top of the roller, they poured the water into a slanted trough. The water then ran down the trough and into a large bucket, which was carried into the school for the day's drinking water. During the fall, usually on a Friday afternoon, when attendance was good and the pupils had learned their lessons well, the teacher would dismiss classes early and take the children walking in the woods. There they spent the warm, pleasant afternoon laughing and talking, as well as gathering the delicious brown hickory nuts which lay on the ground or fell from the tall trees as the wind moved the limbs overhead. Myrtle Utley, Lou Hamby, Maude Hudson Terry, Mary Rose Eli, and Irene Gamblin were among those who taught there.

Freda Parker taught the school's last session. Eli School closed about 1947. The building is gone, but those who attended or taught there bring the schoolhouse back to life, in fond memories of bygone days.

FIDDLEBOW SCHOOL

The land for Fiddlebow School was deeded to the Hopkins County School Board by A.F. (Doc) Burton in 1899. The school was built about 1900 and stood where Fiddlebow Road joins Highway 70, about 9 miles west of Madisonville. The area and the school were named for an oddly shaped tree that grew there. The school was in session as early as 1902.

Fiddlebow School in 1974

Some of the teachers were Catla Chandler 1903-04, Hugh Egbert 1904-05, O.L. McGregor 1905-06, W.L. Martin 1906-07, Ernest Lantaff 1907-08, Emma Fox 1908-09, Pearl White 1914, Mary Morse 1932, Ray Kirkwood 1943-44, Elmer Hicks 1944-45, A.O. Richards, Bethel Norse, Rachel Daves, Col. George (Bud) Bone, Arnold Hicks, Aubrey Inglis, Ira Cook, and Flora Wilkey Purdy. When Highway 70 was built in 1932, the Fiddlebow School building was moved up the hill about 300 feet. While these changes were taking place, that years school session was held in a house on Fiddlebow Road. The old school building can still be seen from Highway 70, just to the right of Fiddlebow Road. It is owned by Louis Gay and used for storage.

FRIDY SCHOOL

Fridy School was built on land given by George Fridy. Cecil Clayton remembers Mr. Fridy was a Yankee veteran. Cecil's grandfather was a Rebel veteran, but Cecil says the two men were good friends. Just after the Civil War, the people of Wolf Hollow and Shakerag built a log school on the north side of what is now called Leroy Veazey Road, just off Wolf Hollow Road. Years later, it was relocated with a better building on the south side of the road. Richard Dallas Clayton, known as Uncle Dick, gave use of several acres of woodland. The students had a very large area to play in. Some people think the school's name should have been changed to Clayton.

Teachers in 1888-90 were Mrs. Bessie Buchanan, A.T. Brown and Kate Sullivan. Others were Ernest Brown, Dudley Poole, Lee Veazey, Flora Kaiser and later as Mrs. Mike Swope, Gracie James, A.B. (Bernie) Clayton and J.L. (Jessie) Clayton, brothers of Cecil Clayton. The last teacher, Bonnie Capps, closed the school in 1941. A substantial building, it was torn down and moved to Hanson where it was added on to the school there for use as an agricultural building. The students at Fridy transferred to Hanson.

FRIENDSHIP SCHOOL

Friendship School was located on the Vandetta-Jewell City Road and was established in 1909. Sara Carrico of Hanson recalls her first teaching year in 1935, at Friendship. The school was perched just across the bridge on the banks of Otter Creek. Boarding with friends, she and the local children walked across the fields to school which made the walk shorter than walking along the road. They crossed the creek at a point dry enough to walk across in the dry season. In the wet season, a small boat would be tied in such a way for their use.

Another teacher was Bobbie Cates Vaughn. Bessie Lamarr, a student, remembers the '37 flood that washed everything away. The school closed never to reopen.

FURGERSON SCHOOL

Furgerson School was established around 1851, when one acre of land was conveyed by Thomas Morton. The teacher in 1889 was James W. Ferguson and the 1890 teacher was R.L. Furgerson. In 1910, Dick Ferguson gave land for the school. By trade, he received the old site near his home and he provided rough lumber for the new building. The new site was about 1 1/2 miles from the original site, on the Oak Hill-St. Charles Road between Highway 41 and Cross Roads. The school was frame with white weatherboard and was heated by a large coal stove. Families who lived in the community were Furgersons, Gill, Bryant, Aldridge, Satterfield, and Davis. Another known teacher was W.O. Farmer. The school was consolidated with Nortonville in 1940 with the last teacher being Mrs. Lillian Crick.

GILLILAND SCHOOL

Gilliland School was built south of St. Charles on Buttermilk Road. There is a fork in the road, near what is now Gilliland Church, the log school was built down the left fork about a half mile, behind the Hooper Camplin farm on John R. Gilliland's land. Mr. Gilliland and his wife deeded the lot for the school in 1882. The Gilliland's great grandson Gaston Stewart (father of the present Madisonville Postmaster, Terry Stewart), Retta Smith, both of St. Charles, and Nana Lou McGregor Powell formerly of St. Charles, supplied this information.

Gilliland School-Miss Anis Ashmore, Teacher

The little log school was used until the turn of the century, when a new plank building was constructed not far from its present site. The school was destroyed by fire about 1922 and rebuilt. In 1945 the school burned again and because Kentucky Store and Land Company wanted to mine the coal on the site, the school was not rebuilt. Area residents pressed to get their school back. Finally a site was selected and the families nearby built the school themselves. Meanwhile, classes were taught in a tenant house on the Will Davis farm.

Known teachers were Peter Ferguson 1889, R. McIntosh 1890, Tommie Terry who rode a horse all the way from Union Temple to the log school, Anise Ashmore, Docia Teague, Rivers Ashmore, Sam Franklin, Bailey Winstead, Nina Coffman Mitchell, Ruby Poe, Ellis Walker, Ralph McGregor 1928, Mary McGar 1929, Ragie Peyton 1930, Geneva Utley 1931, Hubert Robertson 1932, Owen Davis 1933, Elaine Davis, Porter Hudson during WWII, Nana Lou McGregor Powell who rode a horse from St. Charles and taught on an emergency certificate in the tenant house for about seven months while the new school was built in 1945, Don Smith, and Grace Fox who was the last to teach in 1947. Although the school closed in 1947, church services have been held in each school location since about 1934 to the present.

GOODACRE SCHOOL

Samuel Goodacre gave the land for the Goodacre School. His farm was just off of the Ilsley and Charleston Road, about half way between the two towns. The road that the school was on ran almost straight north and south from the Ilsley-Charleston Road to the Carbondale-Charleston Road. Ray Goodacre, who now owns his grandfather Samuel's farm, says that besides the school, there was also a blacksmith shop along the road. It isn't certain when the school was built, but Altha Logan taught there in 1888. Other teachers were Emma Wilson 1889-90 Erbie Earle 1903-04, Dona Ferret 1904-05, Tessia Phillips 1905-06, Ethyl Kizer 1906-07, and Vonia Beasle 1907-08. In 1911, the school board slated the school to be torn down and Huckleberry School was built to replace Goodacre. However, the school board was saved the trouble of razing the building, as it burned soon after the board's decision.

GOOD HOPE SCHOOL

Good Hope School was located about one and one-half miles west of Mannington on Pea Ridge Road, on land conveyed in 1893

Good Hope School, Front Row, L. to R.: Mack Teague, Lurman Teague, Julian Teague, Lola Denton, Lela Scrogins, Willie Franklin, Ronald Denton, Luke Parsons and next two unknown. Second Row: Unknown, Opal Thomas, Ruby Earl, Ruby Hayes, Unknown, Gobel Thomas, Unknown, Rufus Parsons, Lewis Teague, Opal Butler, Beulah Butler, Eunice Denton, Owen Denton and Edith Teague. Back Row: Unknown, Dick Teague, Elizabeth (Lizzie) Teague, Willie Earl, unknown, Pearl Thomas, unknown, Mr. Dennie Teague teacher, Fred Butler, Rufus Parsons, Lawrence Teague, Kenneth Teague and unknown

by D.F. Teague and his wife. Some of the teachers were Anna May Kiser, Lilly McGee, Pauline Glover, Edith Plank, Will Teague, Porter Hudson, Bell Berry, Helen Campbell, Lee Denton, Hazel Wilkerson, Margaret Curtis, Artie Teague Moore, Jewell Crowe and Virginia Plank. Barber Shelton was the last teacher and the school was consolidated with Nortonville in 1948.

Iretta Teague McGregor, a former student, recalls how school started in July. At this time, weather conditions would not allow the children to attend beyond Christmas. Iretta's father would drive his children to school in a wagon and would pick up other children along the way. Pie and box suppers were held at the school. The girls would decorate their boxes and the boys would bid for them, not knowing to whom they belonged. This was a way to raise money for school supplies and was a big community social gathering.

GOVERNMENT SCHOOL

Government School was located on Highway 293, just inside the Hopkins County line from Caldwell County. It is believed to have been called by several names when first organized. The student body moved from location to location. When settling on a permanent site, a name had to be chosen. At a community meeting there was a long and loud discussion held about who should have the privilege of the school name as it had been located on more than one persons land. At one time, it was located on or near the Mt. Carmel Church in a log cabin with a dirt floor. During the indecision, an old man asked to speak. When given the floor, he suggested to drop all family names and just call it "GOVERNMENT". The new name was accepted.

In 1888 and 1899 the teacher was Robert Dever. In 1890 the teacher was A.T. Wyatt. The community was growing, so in the early 1920's a new two room building was built. Other teachers were Raymond Ramsey 1932, Nell Talgloe, and Hugh Egbert. The last teachers were Vera Doris Prow and Huston Peyton. The school consolidated before World War II.

Information furnished by Bonnie Brown Hunt.

GRAPEVINE SCHOOL

Grapevine School has had various locations. In the mid-1800's, classes were held in the Grapevine Christian Church. Some parents chose to teach their children at home. The first state funded school in Grapevine was organized in 1898. Property was purchased from John J.B. and Helen Morton Hall and a one room school was built. This was just south of the Grapevine Christian Church.

About 1922 the school was moved to a three room building and by 1929, the building was five rooms. This school closed in 1955 with the opening of the school that is still in use today as

The Old Grapevine School

an elementary school. The teacher in 1890 was Sadie Lindle. Other teachers were Mrs. Kenton Slaton, Helen Hoffman, Eunice Offutt Brown and Miss Maude Wilkey.

GREENWOOD SCHOOL

As Hopkins County grew, boundaries moved and Webster County was formed. The farmland swelled with its youth that needed an education. Parents built a log school, a bowshot from what was to become the Webster County line. The school was named Compton. The teacher in 1889 was G.T. Northern of Webster County. In 1890, the school became known as Greenwood with B.F. Buchanan as the teacher. A square acre of land was bought in 1915 by the Board of Education from Mr. and Mrs. W.W. Hopewell for $40.00. A new weatherboarded building, with cloakrooms on either side of an entrance hall, fronted by a large porch, and a guttered filterbox, was built.

Greenwood School, 1919, with Gwen Clayton Harralson Teacher

Other teachers were: Bob Devers 1900, Monie Mae Morrow, George Sturgeon, Dr. Jack Harralson, Grace Cox, Garrett Withers, Hedon Harralson Sr., Nannie Porter, Helen Harralson, Cecil Neisz 1916, Delmar Salmon, Gwendoline Clayton Harralson 1918 and 1924, Beryl Peyton Hubbard, Nimma Ayers, Hortense Niswonger, Hazel Wooton 1933-34, D.B. Harralson 1934-36, Lillian Harralson 1936-38, and James Hunt 1938-39. Greenwood School closed and was bought by Finis Hinkle in the fall of 1939. Vandals burned the building on Oct. 30, 1974.

HALL STREET SCHOOL

Hall Street School was built in 1923 and is located on Hall Street in Madisonville. Some of the early teachers were: Thelma Gentry, Mrs. Carl Pate, Archilee Nuchols, Kathleen Ringo, Virginia Adams Fugate, Elizabeth Tooms, and Martha Grayson Johnson. The school is still an elementary school housing grades K-5.

HAMBY SCHOOL

The Hamby School was located on the southeast corner of the junction of Highways 62 and 1338 (Union Temple Road). The date it was built is unclear, but Andrew Jackson Hamby deeded an acre and a half to the school district in 1914. Porter Hudson, Riley Hudson, Leslie Terry, Annie Roberson, Nell Craig, Maude Hudson Terry 1928, Mabel Hudson 1929, and Melvin Robinson 1932, were among those who taught there. The school closed about 1932 and was torn down. Mr. Lee Hamby, son of Andrew Jackson Hamby, used the lumber and other materials from the old school to build his home on the same site, but a little closer to Highway 62. The house is still there and owned by Lee Hamby's granddaughter.

HANSON

On Apr. 7, 1853, trustees Samuel Adams, John N. Rudd, Fielding Prather, John Adams, and Solomon Jones purchased one acre of land for $5.00 from Rev. Roland Gooch, to build a new Methodist Church named Kyles Chapel South. This church was on a hill west of Hanson. It was also used for the first school in the area. The Civil War split the Methodist Church. Each Methodist Church in the Hanson area used the name Kyles Church with North or South added. Some of the members of Kyles Chapel South started a new church on the Slaughters Lake Road. After the Civil War, the North and South members became one church, the United Methodist Church. Tobacco factories were later used as school houses. The next school house was on the northeast corner across from the present Methodist Church. This is the location of where the former village blacksmith, S.A. Pool, lived. In 1897, the Hanson Independent School was dedicated. This building site was the same as the present school. It was a two-story building with two rooms on each floor and housed grades through the 10th. There was a basketball court outside and the ball team was called the Golden Eagles with their colors being gold and black. Some ball games were played in a downtown store building.

Hanson Independent School-1897

About 1927, the Hanson Independent School needed a larger building. The Hanson Independent School asked the county to take over and build a new school. The old building was torn down and a new school was built in 1928 with B.D. Nisbet as school superintendent and Hubert Wilkey as principal. This school had a gymnasium and the ball team name and school colors remained the same. During this, the H-W-H-U Tournament was held at the Hanson School. The counties participating were Henderson, Webster, Hopkins, and Union. In those days you could bring a chicken to exchange for a ticket to see all the games. This writer, F.W. Livingston, exchanged a Rhode Island Red Hen for a ticket. In 1936, Robert G. Wagner came to Hanson as a new coach, soon after the ball team's name was changed to Hanson Hunters. Up until WWII, the Hanson Hunters had an outstanding record.

A few years ago, most all of the 1928 building was replaced. Hanson now has a nice new elementary school with Bob Higgins as principal

HAWKINS SCHOOL

Hawkins School was on the Old Slaughters and Ashbyburg Road.

In 1889 Miss Coda Brown was the teacher. In 1890 the teacher was Jennie Hobgood. Marvin Blue, a very alert young 90 plus, remembers attending first grade at Hawkins in 1906. Later, Miss Westly Blue, his sister, returned to teach there. Other teachers were Ruth Orton, Egbert Allen and Elbert Brady. The last year for the school was about 1944-45.

HENSON SCHOOL

Years ago, the road that ends near Silent Run Missionary Baptist Church went through and connected with the Austin Powder Road near Pleasant View Church. The road that leads into Colonial Strip Mine, just west of Richland, intersected with the aforementioned road. It was near the intersection of these two roads, that Henson School was located. The land for the school was deeded from William Henson to the school district in 1869. Bonnie Kirkwood, who attended as a student, then later taught there, remembers that the school had no well, so water was drawn and carried from Onie McCormick's well, about a quarter of a mile away.

Henson School

Mrs. Ross Ashby lived about a mile from the school, toward Richland, and sold milk and butter in Earlington. On special occasions, the bigger boys would walk to her house and she gave them milk in buckets to make ice cream. The school needed fixing up from time to time, the children would carry the benches outside, while someone came to paint inside. Cornellius Hunt was one of those who painted the school and one of the boys found an empty hornet's nest to place in the classroom. There was a time in our history, and not too many years ago, when a classroom just was not complete without an empty hornets' nest. Some boys from school went to a junk pile and found some woven wire cables, brought them to school, and running them over the top of a wood pole frame, using short planks for seats, made swings. Some of the teachers were Miss Nora Lovell 1888-89, Lelia Daves 1890, Uel Fox 1904-05, Ernest Lantaff 1905-06, L.B. Adkins 1906-07, Ruby Wyatt 1907-08, Wm. W. Purdy 1908-09, Ruby Wyatt 1909-10, Essie Trent Barton 1917-18, Mae Workman, Aline Slaton Polley, Josephine Jones Maxwell, George (Bud) Bone, Mr. Hendricks, Audrey Chappell 1924-25, Mrs. Ross Ashby 1927, Miss Ruby Sisk, Cecil Clayton, Miss Josephine Clayton 1929, and Bonnie Kirkwood 1932.

Gus Willie Utley bought the school building and used the lumber in 1942 to build a house on Hwy. 109.

HOPKINS OR SEMINARY ACADEMY

On Jan. 31, 1818, an act of the Legislature was approved establishing what was then known as Hopkins Academy and later known as Seminary Academy. The site selected for the building was on the corner of Cross Main (now Center Street) and Seminary Streets in Madisonville and was deeded for school purposes by Joseph Fuquay. The first building erected was of brick. For an unknown reason, the building soon fell into decay and became too small for the needs. It was torn down and a two story frame building was erected. Not long after, this building burned and a brick structure approximately 22 x 45 feet, consisting of one room, was erected.

Ledger copies, in the possession of Harold Ledbetter, show that in 1886 six desks cost $3.00 and the cost of hauling the six desks was 25¢. Some people who were known to have attended this school were Gov. Ruby Laffoon, Clift and Ott Waddill, Judge H.F.S. Bailey and Aunt Lucy Brown, a colorful news reporter from the Piney Grove area. By 1880, public schools were beginning to attract students away from the private schools. The Academy was the only public school in Madisonville until 1887. The Academy will always live on, as Seminary Street was named for the school.

HOWELL SCHOOL

Howell was the name of the school at Vandetta. According to Minnie Howell of Hanson, in the 1800's the school was built by a Southern Methodist Minister named Perryman Howell who also gave the land for a church close by. In 1890 the teacher was Dollie Brown. There is no record of when the second room was added on. About November of 1925, the schools bad flue caught fire. With the fire raging out of control, the church also burned. B.H. Orton, still living in Vandetta, recalls the school beyond help and the church roof afire. A teenage boy, he climbed up on the church roof to help form a water bucket chain. He still laughs at himself when he remembers sliding off the roof, but was unhurt. Cecil Clayton of Slaughters tells of being principal there. Other teachers were Kathleen McGary, Miss Elizabeth Morgan, Isabelle Parker, and Miss Molly Ethel Kerr. The school was rebuilt after the fire and then consolidated in the late 1930's.

HOWTON-LIBERTY SCHOOL

Howton-Liberty School was built on the J.A. Howton farm, near Lafayette Church on the Tom Davis Road. Liberty School was built

Howton School-photo furnished by J.L. Fuller (taken Aug. 27, 1913) An unusual fact about this photo is that it contains three set of twins: Front Row: L. to R.: Bessie Purdy, Lottie Purdy, Lois Howton, Blondell Payton Hobgood, Ammanell Peyton Beshears, Archie and Walter Howton, Effra Howton, Clint Dunbar, and Willie Purdy. Second Row: Gerta McGregor, Everett Ausenbaugh, Basil Smith, Gullian Cook, Gertha Howton, Mable Brown, Alvie Howton, Turner Hankins, Ozellia Howton, Jessie Howton, Melvie Dunbar, Floyd Howton, Charlie and Henry Buntin, and Doc Harris. Third Row: Conbit Roberts, Paul Peyton, Harvey Harris, Dewey Cook, Ermon McGregor, Jake Purdy, Grace Hooker (teacher), David Poe, Chloe Howton, Ada Coats, Ollie Bell Robertson, Bertha Purdy, and Olla Howton. Top Row: Walter Simmons, Ersley Robards, Ruth Howton, Maude Poe, Bell Purdy, Bonnie Poe, Pricie Peyton, Shelly Poe, Dellie Purdy, Ardis Simons, Ocie Hooker, and Royce Simmons

on the north end of the farm and held classes from about 1898 to 1909. Ollie Fox was the teacher in 1901-02. In October of 1909, James Alfred Howton and his wife, Mary, deeded an acre on the south end of their farm for a new school. The new Howton School was a good, solid little school with tongue and groove board walls. Some of the teachers were Will Purdy about 1915, Miss Pauline Dillingham 1932, Opal Calvert 1936-37, Pauline Peyton, Flossie Calvert, Lawson Hale, Gertie Smith Hale, Marie Barnes, and Ruth Howton Harris who obtained an emergency teaching certificate and taught the 1940-41 term and was the last teacher. The school closed and the children began the next term at Union Grove School. The property was sold at auction in 1946. Leon Howton, son of James Alfred and Mary Howton, Mrs. Clint Dunbar, and Ruth Poe Purdy supplied most of this information

HUCKLEBERRY SCHOOL

Huckleberry School was located on a ridge, 2.7 miles west of Carbondale, on the Carbondale-Charleston Road. This small, one room school, with a well near one corner, was built to replace the Goodacre School that had burned down. During recess the children played ball, pull the sack (a game similar to tug-of-war, but using a cloth, potato or feed sack), and leap frog. When playtime was over, the pupils studied Arithmetic, Spelling, Reading, Writing and History. The children also had certain chores they did each day, some drew the drinking water from the well, some brought coal in for the stove, some erased blackboards, others got to take care of the teacher's horse. These chores were not really work, but a break in the normal routine and a welcome change. Audrey Cavanah rode a horse when she taught at Huckleberry, and Leonard Ramsey and Lester Crooks were the two pupils who took care of it for her. The horse could not eat hard corn, so they fed it either sweet feed or oats. Luke Price, who lived nearby, had a hen that always seemed to know when the boys fed Miss Audrey's horse and would get right under the horse's nose, eating almost as much as the horse. One day, so Leonard Ramsey tells, he got tired of trying to keep the hen out of the feed bucket, so he told Lester to hold the horse's head up out of the way, and picked up a good sized rock. When the chicken raised her head from the bucket, Leonard struck and killed her, then hid her in a brush pile.

Some folks wondered what happened to the old hen, but Leonard and Lester weren't talking. As far as they know, Luke Price never found out what happened to his hen.

Some of the teachers at Huckleberry, besides Audrey Cavanah in 1914, were Ethyl Kizer 1908-09, F.K. Beshear 1909-10, Mary Gamblin 1917, Audrey Chappell McCulley 1930-32, Ethyl Chappell, Lucille Dorris 1944-45, and Emily Sue Cavanah was teaching in the late 1940s when sparks from the stove pipe caught the roof on fire and the school burned down. The building has now been gone for many years and the schoolyard has grown up in woods. The well is still there, but hard to find unless you know where to look and the memories, they are there too, if you know where to look.

ILSLEY-CRABTREE SCHOOL

1894, R.M. Salmon and his brother, R.T., gave land for the first Crabtree School at Ilsley, named in honor of a Mr. Crabtree, the first settler there. A two room building, it was used for sixteen years. Some of the early teachers were Ruth Plain 1904-06, Erma Hill 1906-07, Pearle Miller 1907-08, and Edith Brewster 1909-10.

In 1910, a new school was built down on the main road, a few hundred feet from the Company Store. The land was donated by the Crabtree Coal Mining Company, owned and operated by Edward Ilsley and R.M. Salmon. The two room structure was divided, not by a wall, but by a curtain which could be pulled back to make one large room for plays or parties. The younger grades were taught on one side and the older children on the other. The school had no well, so water was carried daily from the Company Store pump. The filled bucket and dipper were set on a table. Pupils could then dip the water and fill their cups, which were either "boughten" collapsable cups or made from a folded leaf of paper. Two rooms were added in 1933, along with a two year high school which was discontinued in 1937.

Ilsley School about 1932. Top row from L. to R.: Hubert Robinson, Unknown, Unknown, W.D. Ladd, Joe Eades. Second Row: Glenn Sisk, Lola Fern Majors, Nevelyn Rae Alexander, Alberta Alexander, Audrey Lennings, Unknown, Fay Nell Alexander, W.D. Sisk, Euen Winn, John Lovan, Unknown, Unknown, Tom Dockery, Marshall Henley and Louis T. Hamby. Third Row: Unknown, Unknown, Unknown, Mabel Hudson, Dorothy Welch, Pauline Parker, Estell Riggs, Unknown, Unknown, Sonny Leasure. Fourth Row: Anita Carroll, Unknown, Margaret Carroll, Unknown, Unknown, Unknown, Unknown, Unknown, Orene Adcock, Josephine Sisk, Eula Laura Martin, Gladys Mansel, Unknown, Unknown, Unknown, Ishmael Parker, Harold Fox, Unknown, Unknown, Junior Lovan, Morris Sisk. Fifth Row: Unknown, Unknown, Unknown, Unknown, Unknown, Nell Allison, Irene Lennings, Valios Franklin, Aminell Riggs, Louise Fox, Willa Dean Townsend, Evelyn Carroll, Unknown, Unknown, Feda Martin, Unknown, Unknown, Unknown, Unknown, Unknown, Unknown. Bottom Row, kneeling: Unknown, James Morgan, Rex Alexander, Ernest T. Russell, Cletus Eades, Unknown Unknown, Unknown, Unknown, Louis T. Parker, Unknown, Unknown, Ray Riggs, J.C. Alexander, Unknown, Unknown, Unknown, Unknown, Unknown. Also in photo, Opal Martin and Joe Alexander

Huckleberry School about 1914. Front Row: L. to R.: Leonard Ramsey (standing), Melvin Clark, Leena Crook, Macy Ramsey, Audrey Chappell, Jewell Jenkins, Buck Reed, Euen Riggs, Lora Brown, Erma Riggs, and Algie Lamb. Second Row: Euel or Enos Brown, Euel or Enos Brown, Wick Clark, Clifton Riggs, Lee Crook, Bonnie Clark, Cliff Price, _____ Price, Ellen Ramsey, Thula Chappel, and Orva Clark. Back row: Hobert Jenkins, Margie Woodruff, Lora Utley, Verba Clark, Ollie Clark, Goldie Hibbs, Gertie Reed, Wallace Utley, Addie Price, Claude Jenkins, and Jerome Reed. Standing in back, teacher Audrey Cavanaugh

High winds during a storm on Labor Day of 1952, blew a large oak tree down on the school, collapsing the roof and most of the walls of the original two rooms and damaging the other two. By the grace of God, the storm came on a holiday. Classes continued in Ilsley's two churches, which flanked the school on either side, the Presbyterian on the south and the Holiness on the north. Reconstruction began with the clearing away of the older section and repairing of the damaged other half. Added were a kitchen and indoor restrooms, and a partial basement to hold a furnace and coal room.

The school had many teachers and several principals: Mr. Crosson 1920; Eva and Everett Creasey; Miss Willie Rasco principal and teacher 1925-27; Mrs. Neisbeth and Proctor Hampton 1927; Miss Ernestine Persley; Nell McGregor and Mrs. O.B. Russell 1932; Logan Richards, principal and teacher 1932-36 and his wife, Mary Bell Richards; Loella Lowery principal and teacher 1942-1944; Nannie Sue Wilkey and Elaine Davis 1944-45; Connie Russell; Docia Teague 1952-53; Josie Morrow 1957-58; Jack Haywood; Porter Hudson; Mabel Hudson; Billie McGregor; A.L. Skaggs principal; Geneva Hamby; Clyda Terry; Cleora Givins; Douglas H. Price; Mr. Camplin; Mr. Martin; Woodrow Purdy; Janey Craig, Hubert Robinson; Mrs. Ray Prather Robinson; Mrs. Linnie Hampton; Blanche Morgan; and Laura Jagoe Suthard.

Ilsley School's last session was the 1962-63 school year. Beginning in the fall of 1963, the children rode buses either to St. Charles or Charleston. The school building was torn down and the land is now the north end of Ilsley Cemetery.

IMMACULATE CONCEPTION SCHOOL

The Immaculate Conception School in Earlington began in September of 1875 with classes being held in the church. There were four teachers. In 1882, a two story brick school was built, later replaced by a wooden structure. In 1925, another two-story brick building was built. Different grades were taught over the years, with the school being closed in 1978 after it was condemned by the fire marshal.

JENNINGS SCHOOL

Jennings School was first located just off Highway 70 on what is now the Jewell Logan Road. In 1888 the teacher was B.F. Kendrick, in 1889 W.T. Baker, and in 1890 C.P. Kirkwood. In November 1897, the school burned because of a defective flue. The teacher was J.D. Sisk. The school was rebuilt on Highway 70, one half mile from the old site and south of the little community of Chalktown which was 16 miles southwest of Madisonville. A former student, Edith Richards returned to teach.

Some of the earlier teachers were Maud Fox 1908-10, Miss Cornelia Quinn, Essie Trent, Ida Peyton. During the big snow of 1917-18, Miss Cornelia rode her horse through the snow to break way for the children. With drifts that covered the fences and that was up to the horses belly, no child could walk to school. The first day, no one showed up. The 1932 teacher was Blanche Logan Calvert. The school closed about 1944-45.

JEWELL CITY SCHOOL

Jewell City School was located on the Vandetta Road near the community of Jewell City. It is not known when the school opened or closed. Cecil Clayton remembers teaching there in 1929-30. The school he remembers was near Pond River Road.

JOHNSON ISLAND

Johnson Island was located on a circle of roads forming a small ground island made by Rose Creek and Schmetzer Crossing Roads. In 1856, a twenty foot square log building was built on the George Banaugh property. The school had one door and one narrow window which extended the whole length of the building. The seats were of split logs with pegged legs and no backs. It was heated with a large fireplace, the chimney being of stick and dob mud. In 1878, it was torn down and replaced with a 24' x 30' building with three windows on each side, two doors and a blackboard. There were seats with writing desks and a pot-bellied stove in the center of the room.

Teachers during the years 1856-1890 were George Banaugh, C.N. Couch, Cam. Givens, Miss Cecil Gist, Miss Jennie Morton, J.W. Bowers, Rev. Cyrus Graham Sr., Charles Smith, Miss Mary Bradley, Miss Mary Bone, Miss Eliza Elder, James Graves, Mac Lynch, Miss Julia Peck, Mrs. Sue Knox, Miss Laura Head, Miss Ophelia Walker, Miss Frankie Parker, F.H. Bell, N.A. Hibbs, Robert Yarbrough, A. Rudy, J.Y. Brown, J.W. Davis, Willie Holloman, M.M. Wyatt, C.M. Lutz, Rev. Cyrus Graham Jr., Miss Lillie Johnson, and Mr. H.C. Bone.

In 1890 a new building was built. Teachers after 1900 were Vena Blue, Rodney Sisk, Faye Sisk Morgan, Dee Sisk, Tommie Arnold, and Sanford Bruce.

Karl Peyton and wife Helen Higdon Peyton recall their school days there. Helen tells how straight-laced Mr. Dee Sisk was. He would sit in the middle of the play yard reading, to enforce his rule of the boys playing on the one side and the girls on the other. Karl tells of Auvergne Crowe and her brother Compton. The big boys, for fun, had turned over the boys privy. Mr. Crowe, substituting for his sister, ordered the building uprighted. He then had each prankster march by him and bend over for a very heavy lick from "the board of education on the seat of understanding". The school consolidated with Nebo in 1938-39.

KIRKWOOD SPRINGS

Kirkwood Springs, a one room school, was built about 1900 on Jim Kirwood's land. To reach the old school site, take Highway 70 west from Beulah about four miles, then turn left on Kirkwood Springs Road. About a mile and a half back, a road turns to the right and goes back to the small community of Kirkwood Springs. Some of the teachers were Josephine Maxwell 1924-25, Fermon Lester 1925-27, Bill Winstead 1927-28, Elic Owen 1937, Arnold Hicks, Glenn McGregor who also attended school here, Ruth Howton, Marie Richards, Edith Richards 1944-45, and Edwin Martin. The school closed about 1946 and was torn down. The lumber from the school was used to build a house on the same site. Lillian Kennedy now lives in the house and tells that the girls, outhouse (privy) blew down in a storm a few years ago, but the boys' outhouse still stands in her backyard.

LAFAYETTE-FREEDOM-YELLOW SCHOOL

The history of Lafayette-Freedom-Yellow School, as well as Lafayette Church, are so intertwined as to warrant them all being written in the same article. The property belonged to Henry Howton, who deeded it to the school board in 1885, but the building was already there because records show that a church was organized there in 1878. The church and school were known as Lafayette until about 1896, when the board authorized the building of Freedom or the Yellow School. The old school was then known

Freedom School 1903, Maud Fox teacher

as Lafayette Missionary Baptist Church. The 1889 teacher was A.T. Wyatt and the 1890 teacher was N.S. Morgan.

The Yellow School (it was painted yellow), or Freedom, was constructed about three-quarters of a mile farther west, on the same road, at the junction of Lafayette Church Road and Kirkwood Springs Road. According to Leon Howton, who furnished this information and photograph, by 1906 the school was too small for the needs of the pupils and the decision was made to build a new school. The old building was torn down and Thomas Utley used part of the weatherboarding to build his own house. The new Freedom, still called the Yellow School because of its color, was built on the same lot as the previous one. Other teachers were Maude Fox 1903-04, Gainer Brown 1904-05, Jewel Logan 1905-06, Anna Logan 1906-07, Annie Clark 1907-08, Ruby Neisz 1908-10, John Paul Jones, and Ruby Richards (Miss Edith Richard's mother). The school closed about 1930 or 1935 and the land is now owned by Frank Stallins.

LEACH/LEECH SCHOOL

Leach/Leech School was first a log structure just off of Highway 879 behind Richard and Minnie Pressley's, on what is now Todd land. The earliest known teachers were J.G. Gatlin 1887-88, O.W. Lovan 1889, and T.C. O'Bryan 1890. From the Sept. 19, 1889 Hustler newspaper the following was found about the

Leach-Leech School, taken before 1919. Front Row L. to R.: Ruby Davis, Illene Messamore, Alton Davis, E. Hefflin, Bertha Watson, and Cecil Boyd. Second Row: Ray Ramsey, Dirt Dobber Hefflin, Opal Messamore, Maurice Ramsey, _____ Hefflin (boy with cap), Lillie Vincent, Susie Vincent, Sybil Boyd, Johnnie Watson, Raymond Davis, and Cinderella Brown. Third Row: Buster (Owen) Coffman (with cap), Gereline Reese, Ollie Utley, and Neveline Davis. Fourth Row: Verna Lee Utley, Gladys Vincent, Owen Brown, Macie Ramsey, Tina Watson, and Hazel Hefflin

school district, "A strange varmit was reported to be terrifying the women and children of this district."

The second building was a frame school built just a short distance from the first. It was located about a mile off of the Richland-Earlington Road, on the east side of Highway 879. The road that led by the school was, of course, dirt and when it rained the road became nearly impassable. A Baptist preacher named Siria, used to carry the mail and when his buggy or car, whichever he drove on that particular day, got stuck in one of the many mud holes, some of the boys from the school would go push him out. There was a cistern at Leach for a water supply, but by the time Minnie Pressley attended there, the cistern was dry and the children would throw leaves into it, in the fall of the year, and play in them. They constructed a crude ladder so they could climb in and out. Bob Hollis dug a well for the school, but struck mineral water. Some of the children did not like the taste of it, so carried buckets about a quarter of a mile away to the Gamblin house to draw water for the day.

Some of the teachers were Hattie Gamblin 1903-04, Lula Cavanah 1904-06, Grada Brown 1906-07, Cornelli Quinn 1907-08, Lelia Kaiser 1908-09, Audrey Cavanah 1908-10. Essie Trent 1912, Audrey Chappell 1925-28, Walton Calvert, Helen Calvert, Helen Campbell, K.D. Todd 1936, Mr. Walker, Mary Lou Nalls Gamblin, Cornellia Quinn, and Emily Sue Cavanah 1932. Leach School closed about 1940.

LIBERTY SCHOOL

Liberty School was located on Highway 85, where West Kentucky Welding Supply is now located. Lonnie Stum attended Liberty. The school had no well and the Stum family well, next door to the school, was used for the school water supply. All six children in the Stum family attended the school with three of the girls later teaching there. Mr. Stum says one of the things he remembers most was the day the circus came by the school on its way from Madisonville to Greenville. The teacher, Mrs. Mary Crabtree, dismissed school so the children could go out and watch the circus pass. Elephants were walking down the road and other animals were in cages pulled by horses. There was a calliope but it did not get steamed up to play until it was about 1000 feet past the school. Mr. Stum usually went home for lunch as he lived next to the school. Twice a year, as a big treat, his mother would fix his lunch and allow him to eat at school with the other children.

Teachers remembered are Stella, Eula Bell and Ola Mae Stum, Mary Crabtree and Mary Nola Shelton.

LUTONTOWN SCHOOL

Lutontown School was established in 1895 for the children of the miners of Luton and Shamrock Coal Company. Children of the local farmers also attended. One half acre of ground was bought from J.P. Harmon. The school was located on a circle of roads connecting 41-A and Old Dalton Road, now Hwy. 109. These roads have now been closed and the small mining town dissolved by a new mine, Providence No. 1. The earliest record of a teacher is Lelia Taylor for 1903-04. In 1919 Claudia Coffman Gipson, who now lives on 41-A near the spur Lutontown-Jones Road, recalls her first grade teacher was Otis Harkins. His sister, Dixie Harkins McCoy, also taught. Mrs. Gipson remembers her third grade teacher, Etha Davis Crook. Other teachers were Vena Blue and Jo Nell Teague.

In September 1923, Gwendoline Clayton was warned that the school was hard to teach with so many transient students. The school had a reputation of running off female teachers. She remembers how she went to work, stern and tough. She chuckles now when recalling how she earned the image of being a "typical sour old maid". There were 60 students enrolled the first week and

Lutontown School 1931-32. Front Row, L. to R.: ____ Witherspoon, Unknown, and Douglas Childers. Middle row: Gordon Morgan, brother and sister Hardwick, Charles Morgan, Unknown and Georgie Givens. Back Row: Thomas Earl Utley, teacher Tommy Arnold, Rosena Playl Martin, and Thomas Earl Thomason

Madisonville's North Hopkins High School

before school was out in February of 1924 there were 115 students moved in and out that term. Also, her image had changed. As weeks went by, even the hard to manage students had softened. In December, Miss Clayton married Sam Harralson of Nebo. Ten years later, the mining had curtailed and the number of students had dropped. Tommie Arnold, now living in Madisonville, had 12 or 13 students enrolled with an average attendance of nine, and graduated three from the 8th grade in 1932. Sanford Bruce of Nebo (now deceased) taught the 1932-33 term. Mrs. Ann Putman also taught there during the slow years. She kept hot soup on the pot bellied stove for her students in the winter months. The school closed in 1937 and was sold to Bryan Fox for $85.00.

McCord School

The land for McCord School was deeded to the Board of Education by T.F. McCord and his wife in 1882. The school was located southwest of Earlington, About a quarter mile east of the old Southard's Cemetery Rd., on or near what is now ALbert and Ruby Holzhauser's Land.

The only names for teachers at this school that could be found were the 1889 teacher, Miss Sallie Graddy, the 1890 teacher, Miss Minerva Wilson, and the 1908-09 teacher, Edna D. Boyd. In 1909 District 20 McCord was abolished.

McIntosh School

McIntosh School was located east of Highway 41, just south of the Christian County line. Families who lived in the community were Alexander, Cavanaugh, Davis, Gipson, Hunt, Kirksey, and Mosley. Some of the teachers were Allie Campbell, Lillian Crick, Lula Allen and Mrs. Georgia Hamby. The last teacher was Mrs. Bell Berry who taught there many many years. It was sometime referred to as Mrs. Bell Berry's School. Since there was no age limit for retirement at that time, Mrs. Berry was quite elderly her last school year. The school was consolidated with Nortonville in 1948.

Madisonville North-Hopkins High School

Madisonville North-Hopkins High School was constructed and ready for students in the fall of 1969. The first principal was Floyd Brown

Manitou

Manitou was a one room school in 1890 when J.W. Davis was the teacher. Sometime between 1918 and 1920 another room was added. Some of the teachers were Mr. and Mrs. Ralph Cardwell, Nora Higdon, Rolla Sisk, Mr. and Mrs. Claud Porter and Hazel Wooten Fox who now lives in Providence, KY. At one time, Dee Sisk and his daughter, Jimmie Dee, taught in the two rooms. With the little town of Manitou growing, a larger school was needed. Nebo was a short distance away with a new graded high school. Manitou consolidated in 1937-38. The school building is still in mint condition and is used as a dwelling with the present owners being Mr. and Mrs. Dennis Duncan.

Medlock School

Medlock School was located at Anton, just off the Hicklin Cemetery Road. The school was in session by 1889 with David Browning as the teacher. The 1890 teacher was Miss Annie Hicklin. Mr. and Mrs. Lonnie Clayton of Madisonville were both students at Medlock and Mrs. Clayton taught there from 1933-1941. The Claytons remember two school buildings.

The first building had one room. The second was built in front of the first and had two rooms with a partition, a pot-bellied stove and a shingle roof. The school had a well. As students, Bill Crumbaker and Lonnie Clayton got down in the well while it was being dug. Upon climbing out they were caught by teacher Mildred Sammons and her switch! While Mrs. Clayton and Mary Nola Shelton were teaching in the two room school, Mrs. Clayton smelt smoke and sent a student out to investigate. It was discovered that the shingle roof had caught fire. When Mrs. Clayton tried to quietly inform Miss Shelton, student Billy Perry over heard and began jumping up and down in his seat shouting "Fire!". Charles and Clarence Proctor were two of the older boys who helped form a bucket brigade and put out the fire. Only one day of school was missed. Mrs. Clayton recalls that as a teacher she not only had to walk a long distance to the school, she also had to sweep the floors and make the fire in the pot-bellied stove before the students arrived. When she first began teaching, her salary was $60.00 per month. During the depression years, her salary was about $43.00 per month. Other teachers remembered by Mrs. Clayton: A.B. Clayton (brother of Lonnie Clayton), Miss Ethel Jackson, Ruth Orton, Miss Charlie Ashby, Roy Stewart, Bertie Stodghill, Catty Stodhill, Mildred Jackson Moore. Frank Cox, Roy Woods, Mary Jackson, Stella Stum Slaton, and Miss Mary Louise Ramsey.

MENSER SCHOOL

The Menser School was a fairly large building, with folding doors across the middle to make two classrooms, grades one through four on one side and five through eight on the other. For special occasions the doors were folded back to make one large room. The school was located in the Menser community, about two and a half miles east of Dawson Springs, on the old Greenville Road. T.J. Ridley deeded this piece of ground to the Board of Education in 1904. The second Menser school was constructed near Hwy. 62, just east of the old Covington's Grocery. Some of the teachers were: Catla Chandler 1904-05, Clarence Hibbs 1905-06, Iva Hicks 1906-07, Nellie Davis 1907-08, D.W. Boitnott 1908-09, Ella Howell 1909-10. Elizabeth Lynch, Georgia Burris (for three years), Lucille McKnight, Mrs. Orbin Howton, Gretchen Stallins, J.R. Stevens, Chester Ausenbaugh about 1922 (his first teaching position), Donna Stevens about 1924, Docia Teague, Nina Stevens 1932-37, Estell Riggs taught the younger children and Mary Boitnott taught the older ones in 1942, and Mrs. Wylie Burse 1944-45. Estell Riggs Barnes furnished the school photograph and part of this information. Also furnishing information was Docia Teague and her sister, Bea Bedwell.

Mary Boitnott and Estelle Riggs at Menser School in 1942

MORGAN SCHOOLHOUSE

Little information is available about Morgan Schoolhouse. The land was deeded to the county school board in 1880 by N.P. Morgan and his wife and was located southeast of McNeeley Cemetery. The school, in session during the 1903-04 school year with Robert Howton teaching, closed soon afterward. Earlier known teachers were, in 1888, Mrs. Ammie Beshear, and in 1889, Miss Maude Bell, and in 1890, Miss Martha Rice.

MORTONS GAP SCHOOL

Mortons Gap School was held in a six room wooden building that was located on what is now Morton Street. Each room was heated with a pot-bellied stove. Concern about the possibility of fire caused the citizens of Mortons Gap to ask for a new building. Leading the concerned citizens was Rev. Thad Entzminger, pastor of the First Baptist Church of Mortons Gap. Land was purchased from Mr. and Mrs. Dave Kelley. The building was completed in 1937. A brick building, it contained ten rooms, a principal's office, gym and a library. Teachers and children brought their lunch, while those close enough, walked home for lunch. Years later a lunchroom and four rooms were added.

Mortons Gap School, Miss Ophelia Davis-Teacher about-1905-1906 Row #1: George Brewington, Thomas Robington, Unknown, Arthur Blair, Alvis Peyton, Paul Morton, Tom Blanks, Paul Jones, Wallace Jones, Earl Slaton, (Bub) Blanks, Willie Waller, Freeland Harris, Paul Slaton, Ferdinand Waller, Fred Hooker, Unknown, George Blanks, and Unknown. Row #2: Virgie Peyton, Goebel Kington, Naomi Hooker, Unknown, Bessie Hancock, Unknown, Carlin Smith, Selma Smith, Unknown, Rena Mae Kington, Unknown, Geneva Hart, Pauline Fields, Unknown, Lana Catlin, Jewell Catlin, and next 4 Unknown. Row #3: Mayme Durham, Whitson Jones, Unknown, Amplias Peyton, Dexter Hart, Oswald Kington, Unknown, Wallie Swope, Ruth Wilkes, Unknown, Carnie Jones, Edna Peyton, Edith Browning, Myrtle Goodloe, Ruth McGraw, Unknown, Fairleigh Slaton, Unknown, Leona Kington. Row #4: Bob Young, Carl Medlock, John Blair, Unknown, Clay Jones, Unknown, Willie Glenn Kington, Minnie Kington, Elgie Sisk, Lena Whitfield, Mattie Morton, Ethel Wright, Miss Ophelia Davis, Aurelia Waller, Unknown, Unknown. Back-Left Door: Unknown, Carlstedt Robinson, Mr. Charlie Sisk, Board Member and Michael Cain Morton. Right Door: Ila Peyton, Katherine Medlock, and Lila Jones. Those identified in this picture were remembered by - Mrs. Sibyl O'Bryant Henry, who says she should have been in this group, but must have missed that day

Some of the past principals and teachers are: Miss Ophelia Davis, Mr. Eberly Hammack, R.O. Edwards, Miss Mary L. Nisbet, Compton Crowe, Paul McGregor, Miss Fairy Lovan, Mrs. Ruby Graham, Mrs. Lela Tate, Roscoe Porter, and A.C. Ausenbaugh.

MOSS HILL SCHOOL

Moss Hill School was in the eastern section of Hopkins County, near the Concord-White Plains community of what is now White Plains, on a large steep hill called Moss Hill.

At the south end of Moss Hill, there was first built a one-room log school, where children trudged many miles and up the hill to reach the school during the six month sessions. The sessions began in July and ended the last week in January. In the 1880's, the first teachers were Mr. and Mrs. Shack Wyatt. The 1889 teacher was Marion Coleman and the 1890 teacher was J.W. Ferguson.

Later, in about 1900, Dr. H.D. Whitfield gave ground and lumber to build a two-room, weatherboarded school on the top of Moss Hill. This was a county school more centrally located for the children. In the early 1900's, Mr. Whitfield's oldest child, Loto Whitfield, taught one year there before she married Garnet Kington. I.J. Whitfield taught the Big Room, 5th through 8th grades, and Miss Lula Allen, daughter of Ampudia and Sally (Sisk) Allen, was the teacher in the Little Room, 1st through 4th grades. Miss Lula Allen taught many terms at Moss Hill. A few years later, Miss Autense Whitfield, later Mrs. Boyd Cowan, taught the Little Room, one year with 97 pupils enrolled, with Winford Kington teaching in the Big Room. Moss Hill school furnishings were four rows of double desks, a large coal burning, pot-bellied stove, a teachers desk, a bookcase, and a blackboard. Helen Allen Brown remembers that field trips were to Rock Lane, about 1/2 mile away from the school. Huge rocks about 500 feet long running parallel, formed a long lane. Large Huckleberry bushes grew there, and the children could climb on the rocks, and have a picnic perhaps.

In 1934-35, Miss Mildred Jackson taught. She roomed at the Ike and Eddie Moore home, where she met her husband Golden Moore. She taught the Little Room and John (Red) Thomas was principal and taught the upper four grades in the Big Room. She remembers some of the students were A.J. Moore, Ola Mae and Mary Ellen Fowler, and John Lloyd Harrison. Among others mentioned as early teachers were Frie and Pratt Bailey, a Mr. Key, Maggie Mitchell Henretty, Alice Mitchell Hightower, Leona Gentry Taliaferro, Mary Alice Robertson, Martha Mae Hawkins, Ruby Swan, LaRue Swan, Marie Barnes, Mary Louise Brown Quisenberry, Esther Oates Morton, Sybil Matheney, Demitt Kington, Phillip Jones and Martha Gooch.

Helen Allen Brown's father was a trustee and he bought the school building when, in the late 1930's, consolidation was started and the school was closed. He later sold it to Compton Crowe, who used the lumber to build a home on Island Ford Road.

Mt. Carmel School

Mt. Carmel School was located on Highway 813, about 1 1/2 miles southeast of White Plains, across the road from the Mt. Carmel Cumberland Presbyterian Church. In 1886, G.W. Putman gave a half acre of ground for a school. By 1899 he extended that to two more acres. The 1890 teacher was F.W. Rice and in 1903-04, L.R. Roy. Other teachers were Naomi Ashby Whitfield and Cora Grace Herring (mother-in-law of Mrs. Forrest Herring).

The Lee sisters, Mrs. Mary Young and Mrs. Flora Mae Elkins, remember teachers Lillian Fox (a resident of Senior Citizens Nursing Home), Lula Allen, Jenera Hanks, Mrs. Leonard (May) Young and Mabyn Higgens Oates. It is believed Mrs. Oates closed the school in 1932 with the children going to school in White Plains. Mary Lee Young remembers Mrs. Oates always walked 1 1/2 miles to school and how she built a fire in the winter with help from larger early arriving children. The other children took turns carrying water into the building for drinking, etc. Mrs. Oates was strict and had no trouble as "she knew what a paddle was used for", Mrs. Young laughed. "But we all loved her. She would get out at recess and play too." The one thing Mrs. Young best remembers about Mrs. Oates was the help she gave each of her 8th graders in preparing for the high school entrance test.

Mrs. Flora Mae Lee Elkins remembers the beginning of the school year of 1928. She was 13 and woke one morning with a terrible backache, so much so her mother told her to wait until noon before trying to go to school. Later, she was laying on a cot in the yard and decided to go into the house. When she tried to walk..."Its a terrible feeling to try to walk and find even though your eyes see a leg, you really don't have one." "Infantile Paralysis", the Doctor said. The children from school visited often and after a year she was able with the help of a brace, to go back to school. Another story related was that the church across the road had a second floor which was used by the Masonic Lodge. Children had heard from someone that the Lodge had a goat to ride. It brought a lot of smiles to hear how the children went over to the church but didn't find a goat. The Lee girls' uncle, Gable Lee bought the school and remodeled it for a dwelling. In later years, P&M Coal Company bought the property and the building was torn down.

Munns School

Munns School, District 19, was first a log building built in the early 1800's on the Hecla Road, somewhere near Clear Creek, across the present Princeton Pike Highway, and down the road from the present location. The one-room brick structure was built in the present location in about 1879, first of logs and bricked in 1905. There were about 50 students in the one-room school, with a pot bellied stove for heat, and Mr. Owen Stinnett was Bill Oldham's first teacher. In 1927 the second frame room was added to the back and it was called the "little" room which housed the first four grades.

Water was from a bored well. However, most of the time the teacher would let two of the boys go down the hill to a well and bring back a bucket of cool water for the students. Bill said, "We would take our time and sometimes we hid behind the hill and caught a little "smoke" before returning". The bucket set on a table, and each had his own drinking glass—usually a jelly jar of some kind.

The students received a basic education which helped them all through the years of their lives—many successful people were educated there. They sang "My Country 'Tis of Thee", recited the Lord's Prayer, saluted the American Flag, and studied things that upheld decency. They studied Geography and built such things as the Parthenon in the sand table. Bill says, "I never thought then that I would stand on the ground that I had studied about many years before, but later I had the privilege of seeing places that I had studied about. I have been to seven different countries in my lifetime, and I've never seen any of them come close to the American way of life. Roland Ledbetter and I were in Australia in the Army (WWII) and we sat for hours talking about Munns School and the community."

Richard Cates and Bill Oldham attended school at Munns and have continued to be good friends. Other names, among the many, were Hancock, Utley, Johnson, Sisk, Chappell, Hanner, Gatlin, Osburn, Brown, Polley, Cato, O'Bryan, Cates, Boyd, Stinnett, Rainwater, Messamore, Davis, Lewis, Crick, and Cartwright. Hundreds more also attended. (See A Short History Of Munns School in the Club section for names of many of the teachers).

Memories of Munns School from Bill Oldham, Written by Rella G. Jenkins.

Nebo Elementary And High School

The once thriving little town of Nebo with its stores, gas stations, banks, mill and tobacco factories, cannery, and post office, had a school that grew from one room to two rooms. In 1890, sisters Georgie and Roxie Eudaly were the teachers. Sarah Barron, a Nebo native, student and later third grade teacher, recalls that by 1916 there were more rooms and a football team. Home games were played in a field behind the Will Crowe home. The cheerleader was Ralph Cardwell, later the principal and much later a medical doctor. As a cheerleader, he wore whites and a multi-colored beanie. A large man with a "bay window", jumping up and down as he led students in a "2, 4, 6, 8," Who do we appreciate?, the beanie bounced too. When the ground was frozen, the boys played a game called "skinney", sometimes called "country boys hockey".

The high school was in the same brick building where Sarah began first grade. It had no cloak rooms, so the students folded their coats and sat on them. Miss Sarah, as she became known, remembers the pins and tacks hidden in the coats by the "bad boys". Then there would be debates on that subject. The hot pepper placed on the hot stove at recess "which nearly choked us", recalls Miss Sarah. There were also times when the stove pipe "accidentally" fell as a history book hit it and had to be fixed when Fess Harralson arrived to teach history. Miss Sarah well remembers the whole class standing outside in the snow having class after the third time the stove pipe had fallen. Needless to say, the pipe never fell again.

Nebo School, 1910. Front Row, L. to R.: Frank Cox, Unknown, Zelma Gipson, Unknown, Cora Gipson, next 5 Unknown, Roy Wheeler, Claud Payne, Edward Veazey, Herschel Barnett, Ray Winstead, and Morrow Cox. Second Row: Mary Sue Brinkley, _____ Corbitt, Katherine Cox, Floy Wheeler, next 3 Unknown, Willie Mae Cox, next 7 Unknown, Ruby Harris, Rice Cox, Dough Smith, Minus Cox, Joy Ligon, Johnnie Winstead, John Lee Crowe, Oswell Gipson, Harry Eudaley, Sam Crowe, and Delmar Townsend. Third Row: Lillian Cox, Myrtle Lee Rogers, Irene Brinkley, Unknown, Sidney Harris, Tommy Knox, Emmon Walker, Glen Eudaley, Ruben Crowe, Ross Cates, Wesley Crowe, Green Crowe, Claud Porter teacher, George Hill, next 2 Unknown, John Hoffman, Ross Cox, next 2 Unknown, Nannie Porter, and Helen Winstead. Fourth Row: Alsie Cox, Iva Ray, Alberta Barnett, Pauline Cox, Christ McCormick, Josie Payne, Hettie Daniel, Lisa Crow, Annie Townsend, Mary Crowe, Effie Veazey, next 2 Unknown, Allie Campbell teacher, Nora Cansler?, Sally Peyton, Hattie Townsend, Unknown, Susie Peyton, Unknown, Marion Cox, Cora Lee Payne, Unknown, and Marie Crowe

The basketball games were played on outdoor courts until the gym was completed only to burn in the fall of 1934. On senior "sneak day", it always seemed to rain. Dorothy Miller Shoulders says that on her "sneak day" it was blowing cold and icy riding in the back of a tarp covered truck and that most became sick.

1929 was the first year a class that attended a full four years graduated. Miss Sarah was one of thirteen in that class, with only seven still surviving and all of the teachers now deceased. Within ten years the one and two rooms were consolidating and the Nebo school was growing. 1962 was the last year for a high school graduating class. Today the school is Nebo Elementary School.

NEW SALEM

New Salem was located on Chicken Road near New Salem Missionary Baptist Church on land donated by Gregory Shelton.

New Salem School

Families who lived in the area were Clark, Smith, Key, Phillips, Davis, Scott, Wilkey, Vickery, Slaton, Hicks, Ashby and Adams. Some of the teachers were Allie Campbell, Lillian Crick, Elsie Crick, Sam Franklin, Mary Harris, Edith Teague, Mildred Toomes, Mary Wright, Mary Lester, Jack Suthard and Huston Gentry. The last teacher was Lloyd Whitfield. The school was consolidated with Nortonville in 1935.

NORTON SCHOOL

Norton School was a one-room school house located on a high hill in the Daniel Boone area of southern Hopkins County. The school was established on land given by the Eckstein Norton estate in 1896. Known teachers were: Lissie Teague, Ida Teague and Sam Franklin. Eunice Teague, of Madisonville, attended Nortons School for several years. She remembers how the children had to carry their water from home in gallon jugs. The favorite game at recess was baseball. It is believed this school closed sometime between 1917-20. The school building was later moved to the Daniel Boone School thus making it a two-room school.

Norton School. All in the first row are Unknown. In the second row, #11-Hazel Hanks, #12-Sybil Hanks, all others Unknown. Third row: Unknown, Ruby Earl, Willie Earl, next two Unknown, Grace Denton, Cora Denton, Unknown, teacher Miss Lissie Teague, Lewis Teague, next 3 Unknown

NORTONVILLE SCHOOL

Mr. W.S. Elgin had a large family of 8 or 9 children and he wanted them to have an education. In 1900, he bought land, built a school and hired a teacher. The school opened for public use in 1905 and was located were E.P. Saint now lives. About 1920, a new school was built on Oak Street, across from what is now the Christian Church. The school housed grades 1-8. Among the teachers were Betty Winstead, Mrs. Ruth Plain, Maude Wilkey, Helen Jackson, and Ruby Price. In the late 1920's, the people of Nortonville voted for a tax to build a high school. In 1929-30, while the high school was being built, classes were held in two houses near the grade school. The Nortonville High School was built on Main Street. The architect was C.W. Kimberline and the contractors were Fox Lumber Co. The St. Charles and Ilsley high school students began attending Nortonville in the mid-1930's. A primary wing was built in 1949. In 1955, Nortonville School became an elementary school when South Hopkins High School was built.

Past principals include David Edwards, James Suthards, A.C. Ausenbaugh, Judson Jenkins, James B. Kirkwood, C.R. Harralson, and Avah L. Skaggs Sr. and Jr.

Teachers at the school include Frank Dunn, Sue Ross, Mabel Fagan, Ruth Gailor, Oscar Lovan, Hazel Gladdish, Lillian Sisk, Lulu

Nortonville School-5th and 6th grades about 1926

Solomon, Docolia Franklin, Virginia Joiner, Allie Campbell, Mildred Furgerson, Jessie Simmons, Lanna Arnold, Mary Inglis, Hazel Wilkerson, Jeanine Stearsman, Ruby Sisk, Charles Sisk, Loella Lowery, Ruth Tucker, Kenneth Berry, Rella Jenkins, Ann Putman, Maude Murphy, May Gladdish Barnard, Billy Gene Welsh, Helen Lovelace, and Gertie Clayton. The school is still used as an elementary school.

OAK GROVE SCHOOL

Oak Grove School had two locations about a half a mile apart. The first, built about 1900, was off of Highway 62 between Dawson Springs and St. Charles on Union Temple Road (Highway 1338) in what is now Odell Hamby's pasture. The second building was constructed north of the other schoolhouse on W.H. Hamby and J.M. Cotton's properties. To reach it, you would turn west at the Union Temple Church, then left or south at the next fork. The school was only a few hundred feet beyond this fork. The first school, after it closed, served as a home for several couples just getting started, including Odell Hamby's parents Urie and Pearl Johnson Hamby.

The second Oak Grove School

When the second building was completed, the whole school group assembled at the old building, lined up, and marched to the new school to begin classes. Among the teachers were Leslie Terry, Maude Blane, Maggie Dunbar, Sadie Morse, Frank Dunn, E.D. McKnight 1903-04, L.B. McKnight 1906-08, B.F. Kendric 1908-09, Ida Teague 1909-10, Zilpha Barnes Jones 1925, and Clyda Terry in 1932. The school closed about 1938 and was then used for Holiness Church services for some time. It still stands, minus the front porch, and is now owned by Rupert and Ethyl Abbott, who use the building to store hay.

OAK HILL SCHOOL

Oak Hill was located on the top of a hill, between Russ Hill and Oak Hill, on land conveyed in 1902 by Chesley Williams. The school had two rooms. Late trustees of the school were William Teague and Wilson Sisk. Some of the teachers were Bell Berry, J.D. Perkins, Mabel Stodghill, Georgia Sisk, Lillian Crick, Ester Morton, Compton Crowe, Lelia Wright Tate, Laura Jagoe Suthard and Berdie Stodghill. The last teachers were Ernestine Parker and Compton Crowe. The school was consolidated with Nortonville about 1940.

OAKLAND SCHOOL

Oakland School was a log building in 1900. The school was located northwest of Hanson on the Joe Tippett Road, just off the Old Jackson Road, now 1069. In 1889, the teacher was E.S. Brown with over fifty students enrolled and in 1890 the teacher was J.D. Stodghill. Kirtley Buchanan of Madisonville says his mother, Minnie Tippett Buchanan, was a teacher there in 1926-27. The school closed in 1950-51 with the last teacher being Ruth Brown.

OAKWALL SCHOOL

Oakwall School was in session by 1890 with Lizzie Clift as the teacher. It was located on Highway 138 east of Slaughters. The school closed about 1937 with Mrs. Emory Blue as the last teacher.

OGLESBY SCHOOL

This school was in operation before 1875, and was a one-room log and frame school housing all eight grades. Mr. C.B. Herring went to school at Oglesby and at one time there were 103 pupils enrolled there in one room. It is located about three miles from White Plains toward the Muhlenberg county line, on Oglesby Cemetery Road. In about 1915-16 the Little room was added to the Big room. Mr. Herring's first teacher was Bob Deavers, and he remembers him as a very tough teacher. On Mr. Herring's first day the teacher whipped every one in the school in order to get punishment to the right one —except Herring, who had not attended the day before and he was not whipped because he had nothing to do with what happened the day before. Mr. Herring's father went to Oglesby school before him, and his uncle also attended Oglesby. Some of the teachers Mr. Herring remembers are Nell (McGregor) Bailey; Elizabeth (Teague) Skaggs; Mrs. Jim Blanks; Nora Lee (Crick) Pool; Miss Pearl Day, Cora (Grace) Herring and a Mr. Neisz. Some of the classmates of C.B. Herring were Verda Mae (Pearson) Johnson, Virginia Oates Neatherly, Mabyn (Higgins) Oates, Lillian (Earl) Fox, Forest Herring, and Buel Oglesby. The ground for the Oglesby school was donated by Buel Oglesby's great uncle and it burned to the ground in 1946.

PLEASANT GROVE

Pleasant Grove was near Pleasant Grove Baptist Church two miles west of Madisonville on Rose Creek Road near the railroad tracks and what is called Dead Mans Curve. It is believed the school began in February of 1889. The teacher in 1890 was Alice Mitchell. Arthur Crawford remembers his boyhood school days. His first teacher was Claud Porter in 1914.

Other teachers he remembers are Claud Cates, Sudie Harris, Mrs. Sallie Woodard, Vena Blue, and Mrs. Birdie Stodghill. Mrs. Stodghill drove a horse and buggy to school, leaving her horse at the nearby barn of Lee Harris. More than once, two of the older boys were sent to hitch her horse to the buggy and bring it to the school's back yard for her to drive home. The horse was spooked by the two delivery boys. Whatever they did, Mr. Crawford did not disclose. But when Mrs. Stodghill took the reins, the horse would bolt and run, leaving the students in gales of laughter.

The school closed in 1937.

PLEASANT RIDGE SCHOOL

Pleasant Ridge, also known as Barnhill School, was located on the Barnhill-Dalton Road, just inside the Hopkins County line with half of the students coming from Webster County. Mrs. Mary Barker Sisk, now living near Dawson Springs, talked about her old school, with the ground being given by her great grandfather, John Daniel Barnhill, in the 1880's. The 1889 teacher was Sallie Lisman and in 1890 Minnie Green.

The school was a small, weatherboarded log building with one door and window. In 1911, a new building was constructed for $397.50. Mrs. Eddie Barnhill Barker, Mary Sisk's, mother who lives in Providence, attended first grade here in 1903. Her teacher was Dan Dunbar. Later there was Claud Wilson, Vena Blue and Grace Cox. In 1919 Mrs. Barker was a teacher at her old school as was her sister, Sue Barnhill. The Barker children remember Robbie Townsend as the teacher in 1932 and also Aurelia Daniels, Mona Mae Newsom, Grace Richards and her sister Edith. Mary Sisk remembers the smells of the first school week. The pungent odor of freshly oiled wooden floors and waxed desks. Her favorite teacher "Miss Edith" Richards closed the school in 1939-40.

PLEASANT VIEW SCHOOL

Pleasant View School was first known as White's School as it was located on the White farm. The 1888-89 teacher was Miss May Crabtree and the 1890 teacher was Lula Arte. In 1912, the school was moved to be closer to a public road. The new site was the R.R. Graham farm on Pleasant View Road, near the Pleasant View Church. With the move, the school received its new name.

Pleasant View School, Front Row, L. to R.: George Lynch, Cecil Vickers, Horace Blades, Mary Barns?, and Emma Vickers. Second Row, L. to R.: J.D. Harris, Wedener Vickers, Laura Beth Slaton, Annie Vickers, Louette Morrow, Helen Locke, and Annie Lynch. Third Row, L. to R.: Loudell Lyons, Blanche Polley, Alline Slaton, Mary Frances Bourland, Arlon Harris, Bonnie Melton, and Cecil Polley. Fourth Row, L. to R.: Martha Lyons, Clayborn Locke, Myrtle Lenning, Joe Maxwell, Magaline Lenning, Roscoe Mullenix, Ruth McGuire, visitor Katherine and teacher Katholine Oldham

In 1920, Alline Slaton Polley began first grade at the school. Her teacher was Otis Harkins. The 1932 teacher was Robert A. Daniel. In 1934, Mrs. Polley returned to the school to begin her first year teaching. The first fire built in the stove in 1941 caused the school to burn. Students missed only one and a half days of school. Classes for the ten children were held in an old trailer. The school was closed in the 1940s with the children attending Munns School.

POND RIVER SCHOOL

Pond River School was established in 1911 by the division of the Baugh School District. A building was erected at a cost of $384.00. All of our efforts to locate someone with knowledge of this school failed. It is assumed that this school was not in session for long.

PORTER PAYNE

Porter Payne was on Highway 41-A, north of Manitou near Pond Creek bridge. In 1890, J.Y. Brown was the teacher. One of the older schools, it faded before consolidation, with the children going either to Nebo or Manitou. Sarah Barron says at the beginning of WWI Morris Taylor, the teacher, was drafted and there was no teacher available to finish teaching the school term. Mr. Taylor went to the Nebo School and asked for the smartest eighth grade student. After receiving permission from the school and her parents, Miss Jewell Inglis (later Reynolds) was allowed to finish teaching the school term for Mr. Taylor. Mattie Lou Brooks Butler, a retired teacher, remembers attending the fourth grade there. The school closed in May of 1925.

PRITCHETTS SCHOOL

Pritchetts School was on the north end of Brown Road. In 1890 the teacher was J.E. Crumbaker and in 1932 Mrs. Pearl Major. The school closed at the end of the 1941-42 term with Waurika Clayton Nix as the last teacher. Soon after, a church bought it and today it lives on as Pritchetts Chapel Church.

PROVIDENCE RURAL SCHOOL

Providence Rural School was near Providence Methodist Church. The teacher in 1890 was C.A. Eastwood. It is believed the school closed in 1932. The building was torn down and the site is now the cemetery for the Methodist Church.

RICHLAND SCHOOL

The hill where the Richland School was built, is on the northwest side of the railroad crossing, on the Richland-Earlington Road (Highway 1337). This school, as far as is recorded, has had two buildings, both located on the same site. The first, called the Lacy School, was in session in the 1800's. Only one teacher is known, Ed Morrow in 1890. It is not known for certain what happened to that building, but it was replaced by the Lovan School in 1894. Late in 1892, the people of Richland bought shares totaling $500 and in December of the same year, construction began on the new school. The building was to be a 24' x 40' frame structure, with 140 feet of blackboard and a student capacity of 80. Mr. Oscar Lovan, the teacher at Leech and a resident of Richland, was hired as principal. Oscar Lovan had a large home with five rooms near the school, and added three new rooms making a nice, convenient place for his pupils to board. By Jan. 5, 1894, Mr. Lovan's rooms

Richland School--1914-Wesley and Essie Barton, teachers

were ready and the school completed. Classes began Monday, January 8 at a cost of $1.75 for pupils in grade B and $2.00 for those in grade A. Several years later, Richland became part of the Hopkins County School District and continued for many years. Among those who taught were: A.T. Wyatt 1904-05, Catla Chandler 1905-06, O.L. McGregor 1906-07, B.F. Kendrick 1907-08, Vada Cates 1908-09, B.F. Kendrick 1909-10, Bro. Piercy (a Baptist Preacher) 1912, Essie Trent 1913-16, Mrs. Josephine Clayton 1928, Grada Workman 1932 and again in 1944-45, Walter Troop 1938, Charles Teague 1941, Bethel Nourse 1942-56, Mrs. Ruby Perkins 1951-52, Ruth Plain, Col. George (Bud) Bone, Ida Mae Goode, Margaret Brown, Mr. Slaton, Opal Calvert, Blanche Calvert, Mabel Fagan, Fermon and Florice Lester, Cressa Petyon, Mary Morse, Mr. Ragie B. Peyton and Josephine Maxwell. A two year high school was added and classes begun in 1936. While the addition was being built during 1935-36, the 8th and 9th grades met in a building on the site of what was later to be the Ratliff Grocery. When completed, the high school included the 9th and 10th grades. The first high school teacher was Gertrude Mahan.

Other high school teachers were Raymond Long, Frank Dunn, and Josephine Maxwell. Water for the school was carried from the cistern near Nourse's Grocery as the school had no well. Trent Barton drove the Richland school bus from 1949-1952. The school closed about 1955 or 1956 and the children then attended Dalton. The Richland Community bought the school after it closed for $300.00 for a meeting house-community center. The trustees were Trent Barton, Taylor Hawkins, Frank Nourse, and Herman Hancock. The school has been empty for a number of years and was sold at auction Oct. 17, 1987 to Robert Coleman for $6000.00. The early history of Richland School was extracted from the December 1893 and January 1984 issues of The Hustler newspaper. Other information was given by Frank and Bethel Nourse, Trent and Modell Barton, Josephine Maxwell, and Taylor and Betty Hawkins.

SALEM SCHOOL

Salem School was on the Vandetta Road and Eastwood Lane. B.F. Wilson was the teacher in 1889 and Miss Attie Beasley was the teacher in 1890. It is not certain if the old building burned as so many did, but it was a brick building by 1927. Mrs. Lorena Ashby Winstead was the teacher in 1932. After consolidation, a church group bought the building.

SHADRICK SCHOOL

Shadrick School was located on the Slaughters-Hanson Road. In 1889 Attie Beasley was the teacher and in 1890 the teacher was Miss Ada Brown. Mrs. A.J. Gooch also taught there. The Brown children, of which Ruth became a teacher, remember the road to the school as being long and dusty. A childhood illness broke out one year as school started. The Brown children were kept home for safety. Superintendent B.D. Nisbet visited to see why the children were not in school. When informed of the reason, he gave permission for them to attend Hanson. Ruth's brother, James T. Brown, recalls, the gravel road was much better and more traveled, so there were times they could hitch a ride with neighbors. Keith Brown, another brother, recalls the Shadrick School closing in the fall of 1936. The teacher was Sara Beasley.

SILENT RUN SCHOOL

Silent Run School was located just off of what is now Highway 502, near Highway 109. The ground was deeded from Francis M. Kirkwood and his wife, in 1864. A log school was constructed and used until about 1895, then a frame structure with painted plank siding was built.

The school was rebuilt again in 1910. This building was moved across the road, and became Silent Run Holiness Church in 1924 or '25. At the same time, a new frame school was built on the old school site. It consisted of one large room and three cloak rooms. Grades 1-8 were taught in the room until 1931, when the walls of two of the cloak rooms were removed and a partition set up to divide the room in half. The school then had two rooms, one for grades 1-4 and the other for grades 5-8. Up until this time, only one teacher was needed, now the school needed two.

Silent Run School, about 1918. Front Row, L. to R.: William Walker, Opel Franklin, Ruby Wyatt and James Walker. Second Row: Vannie Walker, Pearl Hill, Archie Utley, Chester Brown, Anna Pearl Kirkwood, Opel Franklin, Mary Grable, Bill Wyatt, Olene Sisk, Georgie Wyatt, Hurst Grable and Kirkwood Wyatt. Third Row: Ward Kirkwood, Rector Kirkwood, Goble Wyatt, Strother Wyatt, Douglas Utley, Clarence Adkins, Baxter Howton, and Ova Lee Maddox. Fourth Row: Josephine Clark, Alva Maddox, Ula Kirkwood, Johnnie Kirkwood, Mary Adkins, Ozie Franklin, Eveline Vandiver, Ellen Walker, Otha Adkins, Mary Walker Kirkwood and Pruitt Utley. Fifth Row: Talbern Martin, Bonnie Wyatt, Willie Utley, Dessie Grable, Hugh Cranor, Cecil Sisk, Connie Brown teacher, David Grable, Dulcie Clark, and Hustler Wyatt

There were many teachers at Silent Run School. Mr. and Mrs. Paul Bone and Modell Barton have supplied a nearly complete list: A.T. Brown 1888-89; R.A. Brown 1890; Lou Frazer; Maude Bell; Mae Yandell; Euel Morgan; Ben Kendrick; Roy Utley; Robin Cates; A.T. White 1900; Jewel Logan; Vena Blue; George Frazer; Myrtle Weir (Frazer); Noline Stewart; Hubert Wilkey; Georgia Purdy 1913; Flora Wilkey 1914; Archie Fox 1923-24; Thelma Pickens 1924-25; Josephine Maxwell 1925-26; Hugh Egbert 1926-27; Ina Hall 1927-29; and Bonnie Kirkwood 1929-30.

After the school was remodeled 1930-32, there were two teachers: Nannie Lansden 1931-32, younger class; George Bone 1932-34 older class; Corine Dever 1932-34 younger; Frank Bell 1934-36 older; Bonnie Kirkwood 1934-37 younger; Cleora Givins 1936-37 older; Edwin Martin, later principal of Dalton School, taught about 1938; Ada Bell Frazer Peyton 1942-43; Mary Nell Bone 1943-45 and Retha Daves.

Silent Run School closed about the time of World War II, when this district combined with Dalton. Richard Hamilton, a descendant of the Kirkwoods who deeded the land for the school, has built an A-frame home on the site of the school.

SISK RIDGE SCHOOL

Sisk Ridge School was also called PEA RIDGE SCHOOL. The land for this school was given in 1882 by Solomon Gamblin. The 1889 teacher was R.L. Furguson and in 1890 Etta Shaw. Other known teachers were Martha Gladys Allison in 1932 and Mrs. Fairy Lovan Egbert in 1934. It is not known when this school closed.

SMYRNA SCHOOL

Smyrna School was on the Rose Creek Road, 1/2 mile east of Coiltown off Highway 502. In 1890 the teacher was Sue Hoffman. Former students the Arivett sisters, Pauline and Cora Lee, and their brother, John, shared their memories of the school. Pauline, now a Barnhill, remembers in 1913 a Mr. Hendricks as her teacher. Other teachers were Dee Sisk and his wife Victoria, a cousin Rolla Sisk and Miss Vena Blue.

Smyrna School, 1920. Front Row: L. to R.: Maurice H. Perkins, John M. Arivett, Clara L. Arivett, Lorene Cox, Ruby McKnight, Vernard Young, Noble Hibbs, and Cora Lee Arivett. Second Row: Fletcher Hancock, Paul Barnes, Dan Simmons, Raymond Hibbs, George McKnight, Delia Peyton, Agnes Lucille Perkins, Edna Reynolds, Richard Peyton and William Eades. Third Row: Pauline Mitchell, Pauline Arivett, Miss Jimmie Dee Sisk (who later became a teacher), Jo Nell Crowe teacher, Opal McKnight, Dixie Troop, John W. Eades, Floyd Hill, and James Arivett

The old log building covered with weatherboard was badly damaged in a wind storm. It was knocked off two of the foundation rocks and the floor buckled. Mrs. Barnhill says it was repaired the best it could be until a new building was built in 1910. Cora Lee Parish (Pauline's sister) says the new school had one large room with small cloak rooms on either side of the entrance hall. Both sisters remembered Brother John receiving a spanking from teacher Harold Cox. Running home for comfort, he found none from Mother. He was sent right back to school. Jimmie Dee Sisk closed the school in 1930-31.

SOUTH HOPKINS HIGH SCHOOL

South Hopkins High School was constructed in 1955 on a 57 acre site. The school is located on U.S. 41-A South at Nortonville. The first principal was Charles Jenkins. The original building size has been expanded by additions in 1960, 1963 and 1968.

South Hopkins High School in 1987

STANLEY SCHOOL

Stanley School was located 3 1/2 or 4 miles from Madisonville and approximately one mile from the Sunlight Mine. Pontiac and Hamlet underground mines were also near the school. Body and Powell Mining Co. now have large strip mines in the area of where the school once stood.

The school was a large white weatherboarded building, built with the same general plan as other schools built in that time period. Grades 1-8 were taught at the school. As was the custom everywhere, the school began at 8 a.m. and was over at 4 p.m. Thirty minutes at 10 a.m. and 2 p.m. were allowed for rest and play. From 12 to 1 p.m., there was lunch and recreation. The little girls built playhouses and the small boys usually played marbles. The older boys and girls settled for ball, hide and go seek, sugar loaf town and similar games. There was a large cooler that was kept filled with water by the older boys. In the winter, the boys would carry in coal and sometimes one would arrive early and build a fire so the rooms would be warm when the students arrived. More often than not, it was the teacher who built the fire, swept the floor and made ready for school. There was a saw mill in the area. The students looked forward to the passing of a wagon filled with logs and pulled by two large oxen.

Families who lived in the area were: Lovans, Gatlins, Offutt, Whitfield, Fugate, Ledbetter, Moore, Favors, Wilson, and Sisk. Some of the teachers who taught there were: S.W. Story (1890), Emma Nesbit, Vi Watson, Ruby Sisk, Ollie Rodgers, Ruth Ashmore, Oscar Lovan, and Lethia Carrington. The school consolidated in the mid-30s with Mortons Gap, but a few went to Grapevine by choice. Nothing remains of the old school but strip gullies and memories of a time long gone.

ST. CHARLES SCHOOL

St. Charles School was built by the St. Bernard Coal Company. The school was located on College St., near the city hall in the southwest part of town. It was a big barn-like two story building near the sulphur pump used by the community as the water supply. The little room was used for grades 1-4 and the big room for grades 5-8. The 1888 teacher was Miss Sallie Brown, who was Hopkins County School Superintendent from 1900-1904. In 1889, Mr. J.W. Davis and Miss Fronie Murphey were the teachers with an enrollment of 104. E.J. Sisk was the 1890 teacher. Mrs. Opal

Jenkins, now residing in Madisonville, recalls Miss Flora Pendley as her teacher in the little room and Mr. Taylor Cranor as her teacher in the big room. She remembers the desks were one and two seaters with ink wells to the topside. Subjects taught were Grammar, Spelling, Writing, Arithmetic and Geography. According to Mrs. Jenkins, Mr. Cranor was a good disciplinarian and she remembers seeing one boy get whipped by a ruler, in front of the four grades, where the teacher made the dust fly out of his heavy wool britches. Most of the time, the teacher punished by keeping the student in at recess. Mrs. Jenkins remembers the girls playing on one side of the school yard and the boys on the other, playing games such as tag, softball and whip cracker where they would hold hands in a line and the "head" would start running and try to whip off the "tail" person.

Other teachers at St. Charles School were Compton Crowe, Walton Calvert, Miss Maudie Murphy, George Straight, Billy Ausenbaugh, and Miss Jane Robinson. In 1937 the building was sold and a new building was constructed. In 1942, this building caught fire. Not destroyed completely, the structure was rebuilt using some of the original walls. Classes were held in the nearby St. Bernard Company Store. Teachers who taught in the 1940's were Loella Lowery, Clyda Terry, Estelle Riggs, Maude Terry and Mabel Hudson. *For school picture please see page 349.*

STEVENS

Stevens #1 was a log building in a field on the Rob Stevens farm at the end of Stevens Lane. STEVENS #2 was built closer to the Stevens Lane. In 1890 the teacher was Miss Charlie Brown. STEVENS #3 was just off Island Ford Road where the Cross Creek Apartments complex is now located. A student remembers how she and friends had to sit in one recess time because they played too long at the creek and were late getting to class. Mr. and Mrs. Cecil Drake and Gilbert Fowler remember some of the teachers being Nannie Slaton Lear, Stella Stum Slaton and her sister, Eula Mae, Harley Rudd, Chesley Adams and Miss Kosia Crabtree. The school consolidated in the late 1930's.

STONEY POINT SCHOOL

Stoney Point School was located off Highway 109, one mile onto Highway 291. It was next to the Stoney Point Primitive Baptist Church, which is now located on Highway 109. In 1888, a new frame building was built to replace the old log building with Gus Brown teaching that year. The 1889 teacher was R.A. Brown and the 1890 teacher was A.T. Brown.

Still living near the old school site, Dolan Fox Edmiston recalls her happy times at this school. Her first teachers were Fanny Morgan and Miss Gordie Brown. Later teachers she remembers are Mr. Robby Morgan and Vena Blue whose younger sister attended the school and was a best friend of Mrs. Edmiston. The two girls enjoyed playing in the grove of trees behind the school. "Being 'tom-boys', she laughs, "we would climb those trees, grab a wild grapevine, swing out over the crest of the hill and let go. Then laughing, we would fall, tumbling down through the sage brush." About 1939-40, years after another room was added, the Edmiston children attended their early years at Stoney Point. The teacher in 1932 was Ida Mae Harris. Another teacher was Jessie Arnold Edwards, who husband owns Edwards IGA in Madisonville.

SUTHARDS SCHOOL

Suthards School was in session as early as 1888 with Miss Annie Knox as the teacher. The 1889 teacher was Miss Belle Graddy and the 1890 teacher was Miss Nora Lovell. It is known that there were

Suthards School in the fall of 1941 or spring of 1942. Front Row, L. to R.: Thomas H. Gamblin, Charles Epley, Bobby Clark, Ermitt Crook, Owen Ray Berry, Richard (Pete) Gill and Charles Long. Second Row: Iris Gill, Betty Gamblin, Verble Sue Long, Barbara Gamblin, Thelma Finley (behind Barbara Gamblin), Ruby Nell Lamb, Hilda Long, Rosetta Cummings, Faye Vincent, and Mary Shirley Stearman. Back Row: Elma Ray Keene, Opal Lee Long, Opal Thompson, Faye Long, Betty Gill, Ancil (Trover) King, William Ray Crook, Henry C. Cummings Jr., and the arm and shoulder of Gilbert Berry

at least two buildings and possibly a third. Suthards was a one room school with grades 1-8. Located near the junction of what is now Highway 879 and Suthards Church Road, Suthard Christian Church stands beside the old school site. The last school building and the church were built at the same time, with the same design, the only difference between them was that the church was built with a porch and the school without. Dr. Finley donated the timber from his woods for both buildings. The land belonged to Chester Laffoon. The half acre of ground was deeded to the school board in 1924, with the understanding that it would revert to the church next door, if or when the school was closed. Those who had a major part in building the school were Dr. Finley, Owen and Edgar Laffoon, and Ed and Ray McCulley. Suthards School operated for many years.

Among those who taught there where Nimma Ayers, Mrs. Wylie (Ruth) Burse, Sudie Harris, Ruby Woodis Graham, a Miss Ausenbaugh, _____ Oldham, Hellen Roberts Crook Sholar, John Henry Porter, Jack Parker, Mary Lou Nalls Gamblin, Miss Virgie R. Beshear 1928-29, Miss Lucy Stearman 1929-30, Edward Atkinson 1932, Linnie Hampton 1934, Audrey Chappell McCulley 1941-43, Virginia Brown 1944-45, and Vera Trover Lamb 1946. The school closed in 1951 and the Homemakers group met there for awhile. The building was torn down some years back and the property, as agreed, was titled to the church.

TODDS SCHOOL

Todds School was located on the Basil Todd family farm in the Anton area. The school was established circa 1900. Known teachers were: Lilly Molton 1906-07, Emitt Ashby, Maudie Murphy

Todd School, 1935-36, Tommy Arnold, Teacher

Pearce, Tommy Arnold and Nora Lee Slaton Anderson 1935-36, and Nannie Mae Slaton Lear taught in 1937 with the school consolidating with Anton the next year.

TRABUE SCHOOL

Trabue School is located in the vicinity of Old Salem Church, east of Mortons Gap. It is well over 100 years old, and within the last few years it has had some repairs, painting and a new roof, reported to have been done by Mrs. Autense Whitfield Cowan (Mrs. Boyd), in memory of her parents who donated the land and were teachers there.

Trabue School in 1987

Mrs. Mary Ellen Russell Cobb (Mrs. Will) is now 86 years old, and she attended Trabue throughout the 8 grades. She started when she was six years old and her first teacher was Miss Lula Allen. This school was a one-room frame building, and they had to carry water from the Page farm nearby for several years before a cistern was finally dug. Later, a side porch was built on the main room. They had many activities there including box suppers and queen contests for the festival on the last day of school. Mary Ellen Russell won one year and was crowned "Queen of Trabue School" over a contestant who was attending Clements School. Mrs. Cobb thinks maybe she had "more boyfriends" than the other girls did—anyway, it was a great honor to be "Queen of Trabue".

Other teachers Mrs. Cobb remembers are I.J. Whitfield, Loto Whitfield, Rossie Best, Miss Hallie Swope, and in later years, Mr. B. Dinsmore Nisbet. Mrs. Mabel Whitfield (Mrs. I.J.) also did substituting for her husband.

Some pupils remembered are Maggie Mitchell Henretty, Mrs. Peggy M. Brown Hughes, Vada Lovin Mitchell, Inis Lovin Moore, Tom Lovin, Maud Lovin Brackett and Alice Mitchell Hightower. Recently, before Christmas 1987, Mrs. Mary Ellen Russell Cobb had a luncheon for some of the "girls" who attended Trabue, and they had a wonderful time remembering things that happened there. The four who were the best of buddies at Trabue were Mary Ellen, Maggie Mitchell Henretty, Peggy M. Brown Hughes and Vada Lovin Mitchell. Other friends attending were Cybil Henry and Ava Cobb, although they did not attend Trabue.

TUCKERS SCHOOL

Tuckers School was just off 41-A, north of Madisonville and 1 1/2 miles north on Tuckers Schoolhouse Road on the right. Earl Tucker says his grandfather, Dudley Shackleford Tucker, gave ground for a log school in the 1880s. The 1889 teacher was Miss Millie Brown Howell and in 1890 the teacher was May Orton. The elder Tucker, beginning his own family, lived too far from a school and had the log building constructed but it burned in 1892. A larger weatherboarded building was completed at the turn of the century. It served the area well until the school consolidated with Nebo about 1937-38.

A former student, Cleroy Lutz, attended all eight grades at Tuckers and remembers some of the teachers as Web Brown and his wife Emma, and later in 1932 their son Glenvar (G.A.) Brown, Jessie Mitchell, James Hall, Jetty Osborn and later her daughter, Elouise. Ina Pearl Arnold remembers teaching there in 1930 as she married Mike Noel that year.

UNION GROVE SCHOOL

Classes were held in the Union Grove Church, located on the road by the same name, about two miles northwest of Dawson Springs. Sam McNeely helped to build the Church-School in 1901 or 1902. An agreement was made between the area residents and Jim Beshears, to build on Jim Beshear's land. A date was set for completion of the building. If it was not finished by midnight on the specified day, the land and the building reverted back to Mr. Beshears. Ollie Calvert Poe says that her grandfather, Sam McNeely, drove the nails in the last roof board, just before midnight.

About 1930, a new school was built to the west of Union Grove Church. Among the teachers were Fannie Morgan 1904-05, Wilson Howton 1905-06, Annie Brasher 1906-07, Georgia Purdy 1907-08, Dixon Purdy 1908-09, Flora Franklin 1909-1920, Lucille Duncan, Ruby Jenkins, Lucille McKnight, Pauline Dillingham, Ollie Calvert Poe, Mr. Franklin 1927, _____Neisz, Walton Calvert 1930, Connie Ligon 1932, Mary Boitnott 1940, and Ruth Poe 1941. The school was torn down in 1947 or early 1948, and a man (name withheld at daughter's request) bought the lumber and used it to remodel part of his home, as well as build his daughter a home. That house is now owned by Jasper Davis.

UTTERBACK SCHOOL

Utterback School in the late 1880's was a log cabin, like all schools at that time and like most it burned. It was rebuilt closer to the main road, 1069, known then as the Jackson Road which was an old stage coach route from Hopkinsville to Henderson. In 1890 the teacher was Miss F. Franklin. J.D. Buchanan remembers his uncle, E.T. Buchanan, taught in the log school. J.D. attended all eight grades at the new school and recalls three teachers: Cattie Stodghill, Jodie Gooch, both deceased, and Mrs. Mattye Lou Brooks Butler, still living, who remembers her seven years at the school. After the school consolidated in the late 1930s, the building was torn down and sold to make way for a dwelling.

WADDILL AVENUE SCHOOL

In 1911, Waddill Avenue School was built at a cost of $15,000.00. This became Madisonville's High School until 1923 when Madisonville High School on South Seminary was built. Waddill Avenue School then became an elementary school. Some of the early teachers were: Thelma Patterson, Miss Alice Solmon, Elizabeth Toombs, Edith Patterson, Louise Suggs, Mable Downey and Mrs. Robert Ray. The school still exists today, housing grades K-5.

WALNUT GROVE SCHOOL

Through the years, Walnut Grove School was in session in two different buildings. The propery for the first building was one acre, deeded to the Hopkins County School District by Madison Beshears and his wife in 1897. The first school was torn down and a second one built about 1933 on the same site. The school was located just a little west and north of the Highway 109 bridge over the Western Kentucky Parkway. The first building was just one room, but the second building had two, with a set of folding doors between them. The doors were opened for special days, such as school plays and parties. It was at Christmas time one year that Raymond Rambo got in a fight with one of the Calvert girls. Raymond's sister, June Rambo Baird, remembers the Christmas Tree had been cut and then trimmed in the school yard, cedar branches lay all around. Raymond Rambo and the Calvert girl started hitting each other with the branches and began to cuss. About that time, the teacher, Miss Bessie Beshear, came out and caught them. Miss Bessie sent them both home and said they couldn't come back until they had their mouths washed out with soap, by her. The way it was told was, the Calvert girl didn't come back, but Raymond did. He stood up in front of the whole school and Miss Bessie washed his mouth out with soap.

The 1889 teacher was Mrs. Ammie Beshear. Bessie Beshear taught from 1928-1930. Others who taught were Mamie Sisk Peyton 1930-31, Louis Good 1932, Woodrow Purdy, Arnold Hicks, Homer Purdy, Lucille Duncan, and Opal Neitz 1944-45. The school closed circa 1950.

WEST BROADWAY

In 1888 and 1889, discussion of a graded school for Madisonville began. School was held in various rented buildings. Until January 1904, Madisonville did not own a school building. At the end of 1903, a building was completed at a cost of $25,000.00. The building was located on West Broadway and was first called the Madisonville Grade School. The basement contained storage rooms, closets, and a playground area for use in bad weather. The high school classes were held on the second floor and the lower grades on the first floor. The newspaper, Glenn's Graphic, ran a contest form in the Nov. 12, 1903 issue for guesses of the number of boys and girls who would be attending the school. Prizes were offered. 1st place, one year subscription to the paper; 2nd place, a six month subscription to the paper; 3rd place, a school tablet and six pencils; and 4th place, a school tablet. The final total on opening day, Jan. 4, 1904, was 11 teachers and 449 pupils. The only student in the first grade was Miss Sarah Glazer. Tuition rates were grades 1-4 $2.00, grades 5-8 $4.00, and grades 9-11 $5.00. Some of the teachers during the first years were: R.B. Rubens, principal; L.R. Ray; Miss Pearl Eblen; Miss Nola Hill; Miss Goldie E. Walker; Mrs. Lillian Rudy; Miss Virginia Nourse; Miss Annie Plain; Miss Ada Morton; and Professor C.M. Lutz.

West Broadway School about 1914. Second Row, 5th from left is Carl Harris, 6th is Malcolm Smoot, and 7th is Lawrence Moore. Top row, third from right is Georgie E. Myers

By 1911, the school was being called West Broadway. In 1937, the school was razed to make way for a new building. The bricks from the first building were used in the building of Harper Gatton's home at 259 South Seminary in Madisonville. Mr. Gatton was the city school superintendent. Teachers who taught in this second building were: Mrs. Claude Allen, Esther Morrow, Mrs. C.I. Henry, Alice Wayne Hickman, Mrs. Trume Seymour, Lillian Cox, Pauline Magruder, Kathleen Arnett; Mrs. Lee Kosure, Hallie Ligon, Grace Barnhill, Elizabeth Utterback, Anna Lou Hatcher and Gladys Day.

The third building was erected in 1955 and is still in use today, housing grades K-5.

WEST HOPKINS HIGH SCHOOL

West Hopkins High School was constructed in 1962 on a 30 acre site. The first principal was A.O. Richards. An addition to the building was constructed in 1967.

West Hopkins High School in 1987

WHITFIELD SCHOOL

Whitfield School was located on the Red Hill Road between Nortonville and White Plains on land donated by Isaac Whitfield in the late 1800's. In 1890, the teacher was A.J. Fox. In the district, there were several different families of Whitfields, Rodgers, Smith and Stanley. Other teachers were Naomi Whitfield, Newton Oates, Florence Turley, Nora Lee Crick, Jackson Fox and Mattie Morton. The school was consolidated with White Plains and Nortonville according to the bus routes. The building was sold in 1937 to Bryan Fox for $76.00.

Whitfield School, student standing in front, Opal Shelton

WILSON SCHOOL

Wilson School was located in the Pond River Collieries area on Highway 1221, near Anton. The 1889-90 teacher was Miss Jessie F. Brown. The school was a one room frame building with a pot-bellied stove. Lunch buckets were kept on a shelf. A second room was later added.

Other teachers were: Nannie Mae Slaton Lear, Lanna Slaton Scott, James Suthard, Bethel Nourse, and Ann Childers Putman. The school closed about 1945 and the building no longer stands.

YARBROUGH SCHOOL

Yarbrough School was nestled at the foot of Yarbrough Hill on the Cox Store Road, just off the Morganfield Road. In 1890, W.E. Barron was the teacher. As early as 1883 Nila Cunningham, mother of Cecil Clayton, attended her first three years of school there. Mr. Clayton, a retired Hopkins County teacher and principal, recalls his mother telling of the storybooks she received for being an A plus student. Mrs. Mertie Sims Walker remembers attending as an eleven year old in 1920 with Euel Morgan as the teacher. "Mr. Morgan was the best teacher I ever went to", Mrs. Walker recalled. "I learnt more than from anyone else." Miss Faye Sisk also taught at Yarbrough and later became Mr. Morgan's wife. The school closed in or just before 1925.

MEMORIES OF A TEACHER

Miss Katholine Oldham was the teacher at Pleasant View during the 1925-26 school year.

Miss Katholine Oldham

I (Alline Slaton Polley) was a sixth grader that school year. I very much admired Miss Katholine for her neat appearance. During the warm months of the school year, she wore a fresh, starched dress every day. School started in July in the one-room country schools and closed in January. -*Submitted by Alline Polley*

St. Charles School, January 15, 1934. Front Row: L. to R.: First eight Unknown, ____ Morris, Naomi DeMoss, Unknown, Mabel Cheek, Helen Morris, ____ Hinton, Jack Knox, Jimmy Woodruff, Ray or Clay Smith, Cecil McDonald, ____ Woodruff, James Menser, Unknown, Unknown. Second Row: Unknown, Unknown, Polly Reynolds Merrill, next three Unknown, Linda Jackson Riley, next four Unknown, Kathleen Hoffman, next three Unknown, Melody Oglesby, Unknown, Calvin Smith, Douglas Trotter, Frank Cheek, next three Unknown, Ray or Clay Smith, Unknown, Hershell Riodan, Unknown, Unknown, ____ Walker, Taylor Adams, Unknown, Unknown, ____ Childers, Unknown. Third Row: Thelma Yandell, Marvin Davis Woodruff, next three Unknown, Dorothy Walker Sisk, Unknown, Velas Wright, Unknown, Unknown, Finas Oglesby, Elwood Reynolds, Tommy Lamb, Geneva McDonald Eades, Audrey Riodan Metherd McBride, Frances Margaret Hinton, Rupert Owen Phelps, teachers Compton Crowe, Mrs. Roberson and Miss Murphy. Back Row: Mabel Woodruff Teague, Unknown, Mary Elizabeth Allison, Isabel Bradshaw, ____ McClearn, Unknown, Doris Davis Boles, Jeanette Woodruff Qualls, Lucille Davis Bloodworth, ____ Franklin, Isabell McClearn, Hilda Woodruff Smith, Katherine Sue Knox, Beth Owen Berry Gatlin, Nana Lou McGregor Powell, Denzie Menser, George Henry Morris, Louis Chaney and Taylor Adams. Boys standing in back: Kenneth Alexander, Nick Woodruff, P.K. Nuckols, W.D. Berry and Frank Hoffman

Madisonville High School, 1913-14, 7th grade. The school is now Waddill Ave. Elementary. Front Row, L. to R.: Mary Hockersmith, Challot Scott, Lathe Hayes, Sarah Bacon, Ethel Greer, Ronney Williams, Ruby Siving, Mary Bassett, Mary Brown, and Ammie Thompson. Second Row: Sallie Cox, Unknown, Mary Thompson, Cynthia Utley, Grace Barnhill, Mary Ruby, Elaine Denton, Shiller Sharlite, Margrite King, Mary Hamilton, Elliane Brumley, Marie Myers, and Lila May Pritchett. Third Row: Louis Hammond, Clarence Parish, Raymond Bahlston, Clyde Watts, Robert Watwood, Frank Daves, Rufus Helsty, Griffin Howard, Rufus Parish, and Robert Gentry. Fourth Row: William Bailey, Lindel Bailey, James Arnold, Hopwell Thompson, Odis Thomas, Carl Bourland, Homer Martin, Clinton Staton, Orie Thomas, Jasper Davis, Clyde Demoss, James Jogoe, Carl Huff, and Ruby Weir

MADISONVILLE HIGH SCHOOL

In the year 1923, high school students began classes in a new building on South Seminary Street. Madisonville High School contained 16 classrooms, 2 large study halls and a large auditorium. Some of the early teachers were C.I. Henry, principal; Sam Pollock; Mrs. Carl Umstead; Mrs. J. Karr Ramsey; Lois Robinson; Catherine Pearce; Miss Gertrude Willis; R.E. Henry; and Miss Alma Miller.

In 1937, a WPA construction project for the new high school began at Arch and Spring Streets. The cost was $120,000.00. The building was completed in 1938 with expansions made in 1956 and 1962. Teachers remembered are Mrs. J.B. Moore; Alice Gatton; Dean Dowdy; Mr. & Mrs. Ray Ellis; D.O. Caywood; Mrs. William Morton; Helen Parish; Mary Hart Finley; Mary Evelyn Leasure; Eunice Bone; Mrs. Frank Brown; Hazel Grant; and Lennie McMurry Rash. In 1968, with the building of a new high school, this building became a junior high school. Today it is known as Browning Springs Middle School.

Nebo basketball team of 1946-47. From L. to R.: Neal Cates, Donald Lyons, _____ Stearsman, George Wooton, Frank Dorris, John H. Porter, Roy Skinner, Bill Barnwell, Jim Gooch, Curtis Melton, Jim Hankins. Front: Ernie Todd, Coach C.R. Harralson, and Brady Dorris

The Seminary Street building was used for junior high students for a number of years, closing in 1979. Today, after extensive remodeling, it is used for the offices of the Hopkins County Board of Education.

West Broadway School about 1916

Church History

Suthards Church, just after completion

A baptism near Mortons Gap

Ball's Hills Mission

Off of Highway 502N near Nebo, is a spur road called Ball's Hills. In the late 1940s and 50s, it was very narrow, not much more than a lane. Travel was possible by car only in the summer and frozen winter. As one traveled up each hill, a bit higher than the last, there was a farm, owned by Alonzo Jones, nested in the midst. With several families living in the hills, they had no church. Mr. Jones gave permission for the use of an old two room log cabin. The middle wall was removed, a makeshift pulpit and split-log benches were built. A beautiful setting, the children enjoyed Sunday School and the older people enjoyed the visiting speakers. As roads were widened and graveled, the little log house had served its purpose. In the harsh winter of 1951-52, the mission closed until spring. That spring, careless hunters caused a fire and the log mission burned. - *Submitted by Dorothy Miller Shoulders*

Bethany Methodist Church

Bethany Methodist Church was located on Rosecreek Road, west of the present Rosecreek Cumberland Presbyterian Church, and was organized sometime after the mid 1800s. As the mining camp and Coiltown grew, so did the church. Roads were not easily traveled and the building was moved closer to the congregation. A large beautiful edifice was built about 1900 or 1902. Mrs. Mayme Byrum Dorris of Madisonville remembers hearing the older people talk of the church. The new church was located on what is called Clark St., behind the Kennel Clark Company Store, in the middle of Coiltown. During the 1930s, the church became electric with beautiful brass fixtures installed throughout. A new, smaller building was built in 1943 or 1944 using the same brass fixtures. A new piano was purchased in the 1950s.

The first pastor Mrs. Dorris recalls was John Burton about 1915-17. A Rev. Perkins and Rev. Willie Blake were there in the early to mid 1930s. From 1938-40 the pastor was John L. Commer and from 1941-43, Bert Channelier.

The surrounding mines worked out, the school had consolidated, people were moving and the town was closing down. The congregation became smaller and there were a series of lay ministers between regular pastors. The small band of members were held together by Elder Grover Byrum Sr., Mrs. Dorris' father. Their last pastor, Harry Pullman, felt the church should close its doors. Elder Byrum had died in 1968 and his was the last funeral held in the church.

In our research, we find the same country church heartbreak. A big loophole in the original contract about when a church closes its doors and the fate of the church ground. After the building was razed, it is still not clear what happened to all of its contents. Its steeple bell, fixtured, and other furniture were lost to those that held them dear. *Submitted by Dorothy Miller Shoulders*

Christ Church Holiness

Christ Church Holiness was first organized in 1910 for the black families of Nebo. The church was located on North Hoffman Street and was originally called First Holiness. The founder was William A. Washington. The first woman pastor was Alice Bishop in 1932-33. In 1943, the church underwent a change and was renamed Christ Church Holiness.

Most of the members no longer live in Nebo and services are now held twice a month. The present pastor is Rev. O.C. Coleman. -*Submitted by Dorothy Miller Shoulders*

Christian Key Church

Christian Key Church was located east of Ball's Hills on the Cox-Yarbrough Road in the community known then as Pulltight, now called Cox's Store. It was centered in a wooded corner lot with a road running on either side. The ground for Christian Key was given either by Richard Key or his father in the early 1800s. Colonel Hazel Brooks of Nebo says Richard Key was his great grandfather. Col. Brooks remembers attending the church as a child and hearing the Elders speak of the church's beginnings. Ira Harris of Madisonville recalls his parents were members in the early 1900s. Services were still being held in the 1920s and 30s. Family reunions and homecomings were held in the early 1940s even though the membership had moved to neighboring churches. The old building was torn down in the late 1940s. The cemetery is still maintained by the descendants of its former members with burials still held there. - *Submitted by Dorothy Miller Shoulders*

Coiltown Baptist Church

Coiltown Baptist Church was located on Highway 502 South, 1/4 mile through the Rosecreek and Highway 502 crossing. The small church began sometimes around 1900. Rosecreek Coal Company sold the lot for the church. Four men were serving as deacons in 1916; J.B. Blakey, W.E. Utley, T.J. Baron and J.F. Hill, the father of John Hill of Nebo.

John Hill remembers attending the church with his parents. His stepmother, Ola Hill, played the old fashion pump organ which in later years was replaced with an up-right piano. As a teenager he recalls the ice cream supper and pie socials that were held during the depression years to help hold the struggling congregation together.

During the 1930s, people began moving away. John Hill had married a Coiltown school teacher, Norine Morrow, and they had moved to Providence. The Utley family had a son, Rupert. The now late Rev. Rupert Utley preached some of his first sermons at this church in the mid 30s recalls his widow, who now resides in Madisonville.

Mr. Hill remembers only two pastors from his childhood, a Rev. Gentry and a Rev. Staley. One memory that stands out above all others is how loud an Elder could shout when he rejoiced in a worship service.

There were not enough members to maintain the church and so the doors closed about 1936 or 37. The brick from the solid, very tall foundation was cleaned by community teens and used in the remodeling of the Baptist Church at Nebo during the summer of 1937 or 38. The pews and other usable articles were used in the Nebo Church and also in the rebuilding of Manitou Baptist. - *Submitted by Dorothy Miller Shoulders*

Coiltown Holiness Church

The Coiltown Holiness Church is located on what is called Peyton Avenue in Coiltown and is still occasionally used for summer revivals guest speakers, and Thursday evening services, weather permitting. Brother Romane Miller, now living on Tucker Schoolhouse Road near Madisonville, and his wife, the former Barbara Peyton, are caretakers and have been credited for preserving and remodeling the little church which has become a part of Coiltown's heritage.-*Submitted by Dorothy Miller Shoulders*

Concord General Baptist

Concord General Baptist Church is located on Highway 630, 2-1/2 miles north of Manitou, nestled at the crest of Burton Hill. The original log building was first used as a school called Concord. The school house was used for religious services on weekends. Sometime around 1866, the church and school decided to each build a separate building. The school was built further down the Burton Hill and renamed Ashley-Concord. The newly organized church built a small white frame building and kept the name Concord.

(Continued on page 363)

Church Of God Reformation

In 1909 a traveling evangelist named 'Bro. Blessing' came to Western Kentucky holding revival services. The converts that were saved as a result of his evangelistic efforts began to meet in brush arbor meetings during the summer and in homes during the winter. In 1913 a small chapel was built on property donated by Charles Adams. It soon became known as 'Whigs Chapel' as Mr. Adams nickname was 'Whig'. The church was located about 4 1/2 miles from Crofton. Converts from Pea Ridge (Cedar Hill area of Nortonville) came over in covered wagons to meet with the people from Whigs Chapel. George Dulin Morgan and James Suwell were active in the church at this time.

Several years later the Suwell and Morgan families moved to the Cedar Hill area and the converts began to worship at Cedar Hill. In 1922 the first church building was erected at Daniel Boone. James Suwell served the congregation as its first pastor. Willie Cox worked closely with him and later served as pastor. Families active in the church in these early days were: Lloyd Miller, George Franklin, Sam Franklin, Charles Franklin, Willie Morgan, Dall Wiley, Claude Denton, Walter Butler and Sam Butler. Early evangelists in the movement that came and held special services were: H.M. Riggle and E.E. Byrum.

During a revival service in April of 1940, a tornado struck the church. The church walls and roof were moved several feet away. No one was seriously injured. The congregation worked hard to rebuild and they were under roof before winter came.

In 1960 a decision was made to dissolve the church and worship with the Madisonville congregation. The property was sold and the money given to the Madisonville Church to pave the parking area.

The Church of God in Madisonville had its beginnings in a tabernacle on Arch. St. (where Lamb's Court now is) in 1945. Rev. Gilmore Earle and his brother Leroy Earle and their families lived in several rooms in the back of the building. The sanctuary had rough wooden pews and a sawdust floor. To raise money for a new church the congregation had a march of dimes every Sunday. Members would march by and dimes were dropped into a nail key at the front. Due to financial problems, the Earle's left, and several families began to meet in the Lloyd Smith home. In 1947 a lot was purchased on Park Ave. for $800.00. A tent costing $500.00 was also purchased. A church building was erected in 1948. Families active in the church during its early years were: Russell Starr, George Guge, Lloyd Smith, J.D. Phaup, Estell Starr, Holland Gray and Wallace Taylor. Four families from the church mortgaged their homes in order to borrow money to build the church. The amount borrowed was $5,700. A notation from the minutes states that in 1949 the Board of Trustees decided to pay the pastor $10.00 a week. Pastors at the Church on Park Ave. were: Rev. Leonard Norris, Rev. Jeff Webb, Rev. L.M. Acheson, Rev. Harry Frye (Associate), Rev. Samuel Betts, Rev. Gilbert Acheson, Rev. Silas Turnbow and Rev. Forest Robinson.

During the ministry of Rev. Forrest Robinson a new church at 617 S. Kentucky Ave. was built and the congregation moved in 1964. Dr. Dale Oldham spoke at the dedication of the new church and Doug Oldham sang. In 1967 a parsonage was built at 653 S. Kentucky Ave. Pastors who have served the church of S. Kentucky Ave are: Rev. Forrest Robinson, Rev. Charles Ridgway, Rev. John Paul Henning and current pastor Rev. Howard W. Sallee. The church is currently in a building program, adding a two story unit which will house a fellowship hall and classrooms.

The First Church of God

Earlington United Methodist Church

A few years after Earlington was settled in 1870, a Northern Methodist Church was built on Methodist Hill, later named Clark Street.

By 1890, Rev. Joe Love of Hanson assisted in the organization of a Southern Methodist Church. St. Bernard Coal Company donated the land on Sebree Street for the frame structure to be built. It was known as "Love's Chapel". When conferences took it over, the name was changed to Methodist Episcopal Church South (M.E. Church South). Rev. T.C. Peters were sent to preach one Sunday each month in 1892. He was the pastor for three years. The first Christmas cantata was in 1892.

In 1903, Rev. C.W. Hesson moved in the new frame parsonage.

In 1907, under the leadership of Rev. J.D. Fraser, plans were being made for a larger church, with much responsibility falling on Rev. W.C. Brandon who came to be pastor of the new brick church in 1909 which was still under construction on Moss and Robinson. It was Apr. 30, 1916 when the mortgage was burned; church dedicated by Rev. Frank Thomas. From a donation, the basement and kitchen was started and completed that year. Rev. W.A. Grant was pastor.

Down through the years, there were dedicated men and women who devoted their time and talents in their appointed capacity in His name.

By 1950, an electric organ had been purchased, and chimes as well. These added much to the spiritual development through music.

In 1953, a three bedroom brick parsonage was built on East Moss. It was dedicated May 6, 1956 by Rev. W.P. Gordon and Rev. Roscoe Tarter. The first occupants in the parsonage were Rev. and Mrs. Charles Hall.

June 10, 1959 was the ground-breaking ceremony for the educational building, by Dr. Leroy Baker and Rev. J.D. Morrow, pastor. The dedication of the annex was in 1969, by Bishop Roy Hunter Short and Rev. C.C. Cornelius, pastor.

In 1961, memorial stained glass windows were installed.

March 1, 1962, the choir-area and sanctuary pews were re-arranged, also a new electric organ (Baldwin 45-C) was purchased to replace the old one, Rev. J.D. Morrow, pastor.

In 1963, the first wall-to-wall carpeting and public address system was installed, Rev. A.L. Fraser, pastor.

April 1968, during the conference in Dallas, the name of the church was changed to United Methodist Church, Rev. C.C. Cornelius, pastor.

In 1969, the lot on the opposite corner was purchased for the purpose of making a parking lot. In 1971, air conditioning was installed through out. In 1972, it was officially announced that the Women's Society of Christian Service (of 1940) was changed to United Methodist Women. In 1974, the church purchased a new piano for the sanctuary, also new pews with cushion seats and kneeling pads. Rev. C.C. Cornelius, pastor.

In July 1976, Homecoming for the "Nations Bicentennial Celebration" was held with Dr. James S. Curry, guest speaker. Rev. Wallace Parker was pastor.

On Mar. 17, 1978, Rev. James R. Myers was ordained an Elder by Bishop Frank L. Robertson, assisted by Dr. James Curry and Rev. Walter McGee, with the laying-on-of hands. Rev. Myers received his parchment noting his ordination as a Elder. An impressive ceremony, and the first in this church. He was ill when conference was held, when the ordination was scheduled. He was pastor from 1977-1982. Through conference in 1981, he started the Ministers Pension Crusade program, the first crusade was in 1968. On Aug. 5, 1980, he organized the Convenant Prayer Group; Charter #2204 was received Oct. 1, 1980. Rev. Myers encouraged the Emmaus Walk, several responded.

Rev. J. Roger Dill had been here two months when he was promoted to Major, Dec. 11, 1982, in the Kentucky National Guard and on Sept. 1, 1986 he as appointed State Chaplain of the National Guard. On Oct. 17, 1983, he dedicated the new front entrance, including the ramp and steps. In 1983, the Centennial of the Woman's Society was celebrated assisted by the M.Y.F. and then in 1984, a Jubilee Celebration Tea for the Bicentennial of Methodism in America when other churches were invited. Also in 1983, the pastor's study was paneled, the fellowship class was carpeted, the children's department painted including the nursery. In 1984, a new carpet for the sanctuary was installed. In 1986, a parsonage garage was built and in 1987, new glass doors were installed at the front and side of the church and the parsonage was redecorated and some new furniture added. Earlier, a back-drop and a beautiful wood cross was fashioned behind the choir. All the carpentry was done under the leadership of Rev. Dill and his father Rev. James Dill, for which the church is grateful. As of this year, June 1987, Rev. Ray Brinegar is our pastor. We welcome him and his wife Carolyn and wish them well.

The church is very appreciative of the bequests that have been made by members in their wills. Also the memorials made by family and friends. We also celebrate the Bicenntennial of The Constitution, "We the people....."

Our Past Pastors: Joe W. Love 1890-1892, T.C. Peters 1892-1895, J.T. Cherry 1895-1898, S.H. Lovelace 1898-1899, R.M. Wheat 1899-1901, B.M. Currie 1901-1903, C.W. Hesson 1903-1905, J.E. King 1905-1907, J.D. Fraser 1907-1909, W.C Brandon 1909-1912, W.A. Grant 1912-1916, W.F. Cashman 1916-1919, W.H. Archey 1919-1922, D.L. Vance 1922-1924, M.M. Murrell 1924-1925, H.C. Napier 1925-1927, William Sneed Bolles 1927-1931, Kermith R. Dillon 1931-1932, W.H. Hickerson 1932-1935, J.A. Vire 1935-1940, W.H. Russell 1940-1945, Frank W. Cox 1945-1951, Roscoe J. Tarter 1951-1953, Charles Hall 1953-1956, W.P. Gordon (Interim) 1953, J.D. Morrow 1956-1962, A.L. Fraser 1962-1966, Calvin C. Cornelius 1966-1975, Wallace Parker 1975-1977, James R. Myers 1977-1982, James Roger Dill 1982-1987, Ray Brinegar 1987-, *By: Irene De Moss Priest (Mrs. Maxey H. Jr.)*

The Earlington United Methodist Church

East View Baptist Church

The East View Baptist Church of Madisonville, KY was founded in 1884 by Rev. Charlie Diggs. He baptized 47 candidates which constituted the original church membership. The first structure erected was a frame building on a lot on northeast Madisonville, corner of Halson and North Kentucky Avenue which was seated with rough plank, hewn from the trees from a nearby grove. Succeeding Rev. Diggs were the following: Rev. Cove McReynolds, Rev. P.S. Majors, Rev. William Dickerson, Rev. William Leavell, Rev. J.B. Anderson, Rev. W.M. Moore, Rev. L.C. Majors and Rev. R.P. Whiteside.

In 1907 a new sight was purchased under the pastorate of Rev. R.P. Whiteside. On this sight a brick structure was erected which contained modern furniture and a home for the minister was also purchased during this time. After 15 years of faithful service with us, Rev. Whiteside resigned to pastor the Greater Salem Baptist Church in Louisville, KY. Rev. Whiteside was well spoken of in an article in the Madisonville Messenger dated Apr. 5, 1924. He was known as a quiet and peaceable man, a man of ability, attended strictly to his own affairs, is a model pastor and stands well with his people.

His successor, Rev. A.F. Fox, saw the inadequacy of this structure to accomodate the growing membership and quickly arranged with the officers to erect the present edifice at the cost of $65,445.00. The reason this amount is given is because of the time frame in which such an undertaking was done. The struggle of liquidation was a hard one because of the days of depression. Rev. Fox resigned to accept another charge and Rev. W.H. Whittaker succeeded him. His stay was very brief, approximately nine months. Following him was the Rev. Jesse Darden of Clarksville, TN. On Nov. 1, 1942, Rev. F.S. Jones was called to take over the work of the church. He came with a determination to get the burden of payments off of the church. At his suggestion the church was reorganized and with his working with the members the entire debt was liquidated within 21 months and 14 days. On Apr. 14, 1950, Rev. Jones was suddenly taken ill and died within six hours in a local hospital.

Our membership was stricken beyond words to explain because of being so suddenly left without a shepherd. Knowing that God will make a way of no way, the church began seeking another minister to guide us. After having many ministers to visit with us, we called Rev. Erie Pullen. He accepted our call effective as of Sunday, Dec. 3, 1950. After twenty six and a half years of successful ministry, Rev. Pullen retired to his home in Paducah, KY. Rev. Pullen died in January of 1987 followed three months later by the death of his beloved wife, Mrs. Helen Pullen. In the fall of 1977 a call was extended to Rev. Phillip L. Hodge of Louisville, KY.

Though there are no survivors of the original church membership, there are off spring of that great group working together with others who sought refuge at East View Baptist Church to keep the spiritual flame burning as did the 47 original members. We thank God for such a wonderful guidance. -*Submitted by Rev. Phillip Hodge*

The East View Baptist Church

First Baptist Church

On Jan. 26. 1870 State Evangelist James S. Coleman, aided by Reverand John Gains and Elder Nicholas Lacy, conducted a meeting in the Cumberland Presbyterian Church for the purpose of organizing a Baptist Church in Madisonville.

Elder Coleman, acting as moderator, appointed Nicholas Lacy as Secretary. Thirty-two men and women became charter members of the new church and selected the name Madisonville Baptist Church (It wasn't until 1922 that the name First Baptist Church appears in church records.) The charter members were: Elder Nicholas Lacy, W.H. Hall, S.M. Furman, B.M. Clay, John Crawford, Lloyd Browning, John F. Browning, George A. Browning, Elder Wm. McLean, E.H. Baylus, J.C. Tailiaferro, Adaline Lacy, M.E. Kirkwood, Mary A. Kirkwood, E.G. Periman, Mourning Hall, Emma Young, A.F. Clay, G.A. Crawford, A.E. Pierce, R.F. Browning, E.A. Browning, Harriet McLean, Laura Ann McLean, M.W. Brewer, Bethany Wilson, M.J. Wallace, Sarah Osburn, Elizabeth Carbon, B.W. Bowers, E.H. Baylus and N.J. Collins.

At the second meeting of the church, William Henry Hall was elected church clerk; Lloyd Browning and B.M. Clay were appointed as the church's first deacons. Brother James Coleman Hopewell was elected by the congregation as the first pastor of Madisonville Baptist Church and he accepted the pastorate on May 14, 1870. The church continued to meet in the Presbyterian Church building on North Main and Federal Streets.

In 1874 the Baptist membership began meeting in the Methodist Episcopal Church on South Main Street. (In 1988 this building was torn down. It was located between First Federal Savings and Loan and the Chamber of Commerce building.) They continued meeting there until 1877 when the Baptist congregation moved into their own house of worship on North Main Street across from the present Madisonville post office. Since there was no baptistry in this building, baptismal services were held "in the waters of Spring Lake near Madisonville," even in the winter. By 1907 the Baptist Church was using the baptistry at the Christian Church for cold weather baptismal services.

The Baptist congregation had outgrown this first building by 1911. The old structure was razed in 1912 and construction was begun on a new building at the same North Main Street Site. During this construction the church members met in a frame tabernacle on the east side of North Seminary Street between Center and Arch Streets. The first service in the new buff colored brick building was held in the fall of 1913. An educational addition was built onto the back of this building in 1926.

When this structure was no longer adequate, the church purchased the F.D. Ramsey lot on the south east corner of North Main Street and Noel Avenue and construction was begun on the present church building. This building was completed under the leadership of the pastor, Harold D. Tallant and the first service was held on Feb. 14, 1954. To meet the changing needs of the congregation a special ministries building was constructed. This building occupied in June, 1975, contains an activities room, kitchen facilities, a fellowship room and offices for the church staff.

Throughout the years, First Baptist Church has given priority to missions. Early in the church's history, in October, 1888, the Madisonville Baptist Church assisted in the organization of the Earlington Baptist Church at the request of persons from Earlington. Several mission points have been established, two of which have become churches. One of these became the Second Baptist Church in 1947 and the other became the Park Avenue Baptist Church in 1972. First Baptist Church members took part in the Kentucky-Kenya partnership, with mission teams going to Kenya in 1986 and 1987.

The following men have served the First Baptist Church as pastor: James C. Hopewell, W.S. Adams, William McLean, John O'Bryan, David Whittinghill, J.F. Hardwick, John M. Peay, James S. Coleman, P.H. Lockett, John D. Jordan, T.N. Compton, Enoch Windes, Price E. Gatlin, J.M. Jones, J.A. Kirtley, W.J. Mahoney, A.F. Gordon, Maxwell E. Staley, Hollis S. Summers, Harold D. Tallent, Harold J. Purdy and H. Garrison Coltharp, present pastor, who came to First Baptist Church Oct. 1, 1981.

First Baptist Church has a resident membership of 1,714. The church staff consists of: Pastor Dr. H. Garrison Coltharp; Associate Pastor, Archie Oliver; Minister of Education/Administration, Rodney Vincent; Minister of Music/Youth, James W. McMurtie; Director of Activities, Mrs. Donna McMurtrie and Director of Children's Ministries, Mrs. Trace McCann. - *Written by Beverly Dockery*

The First Baptist Church

First Christian Church of Earlington
(Disciples of Christ)

The Earlington First Christian Church can trace its origin to the early 1870s when interested members from all over the community met in the two-story frame elementary school built by the St. Bernard Coal Company to plan an organization of their own. In this "Upper Room", the idea developed, and in a short time a few met in the home of Mrs. Tom McEuen, where the Rev. J.W. Higbee organized the church with elected elders J.B. Head and J.W. Day.

Ben Robinson and J.W. Day were members of the first building committee and W.A. Toombs was the building contractor. The entire building and church cost was $2000. The dedication service was conducted November 1889, with the Rev. Harry McDonald delivering the sermon, while Elder S. Sanders served as pastor of this church. The old bell which was in the original structure is still housed in the present belfry.

Fire destroyed the church in 1891, but another church was built within the year. In 1912 a parsonage was erected and the church was enlarged, brick veneered and redecorated. During this time, the church continued to grow.

During the ministry of Rev. J.S. Hawkins, the pipe organ was installed at a cost of $2750. Mr. W.K. Nisbet became the organist and served in that capacity for many years. Mrs. Roscoe Jackson (Jo Nell Oldham) is the present organist, having served for 50 years.

Rev. R.H. Stewart and his wife began a seven-year ministry in 1924. Their son "Dickie" was the first child born in the church parsonage.

Following the Stewarts, the Rev. and Mrs. M.J. Dick came and remained for 14 years of fruitful service. He improved the Sunday School program, continued Vacation Bible School and greatly enlarged the Boy Scout program. At the same time Mrs. Dick was busy with a program for the girls. Both the Rev. and Mrs. Dick are remembered as quiet and gentle folk who loved their work and their people.

Fire struck again on Mar. 11, 1943, gutting the upstairs interior at an estimated cost of $9000. The re-building committee, W.L. Phillips, Chairman; C.G. Trahern, Jesse Almon, Omer Wyatt and Ray Cobb, approved plans presented by A.F. Wicks, nationally known architect, who came from Indianapolis. On Easter Sunday, Apr. 9, 1944, the first services were held in the sanctuary, which was said to be one of the most beautiful of the smaller churches in Kentucky.

The Rev. and Mrs. Albert Stanley and son came for a ministry of nearly three years. The memorial windows were installed and dedicated during his ministry. In January, 1950, the Rev. and Mrs. Kenneth Hughes and two children came for two years service. For the next six years and the Rev. and Mrs. F.N. Wolfe served our congregation. The Rev. and Mrs. Oscar Jenkins were called in 1958 and came with their two children. They worked hard and built up a good youth program. The departmental type of organization within the church was begun under the ministry of the Rev. Houston Bowers, who came in 1965 and was our first bachelor pastor. Houston met and married Mary Knight of Madisonville while here. On Sept. 3, 1967, the Rev. Phillip Missick and family began their ministry with us for three years. Dr. and Mrs. R.T. Hunter and children served the church from 1970-75. Under his leadership, a new educational wing was added and the sanctuary was redecorated. On June 15, 1975, the Rev. John Lambert, his wife, Shirley, and daughter came from Monroe, GA, to serve our congregation. In March 1978, our new minister was the Rev. Larry McWilliams who came with his wife, Rita and children, Marty and Eric. In September, 1980, the Rev. Gary Edens and family were welcomed to serve our church. During Gary's ministry, the educational wing was paid in full, the kitchen remodeled, the Crusader's classroom was converted to a beautiful church parlor and the balance was placed in a savings account for a new church parsonage, all from the bequest of Mr. Leslie Boyd's estate. Our church parlor was named in his honor "The Boyd Room". The Boyd Room was furnished by the CWF's Christmas Bazaar Fund.

Our present pastor and wife, the Rev. William G. Pieper and Pam, came Nov. 1, 1983. Under his leadership, we have erected a new parsonage at 307 East Farren Avenue, at a cost of $93,000, which was paid in full when they occupied the new parsonage. Bill has reinstated our Sunday Evening Bible Study.

Some of the interim pastors serve our congregation when we were without a minster were: Dr. Herman Norton, Dr. Billy Williams, Dr. Byron Carlisle, Rev. Harry Davis, Roeland Ledbetter, Harold Ledbetter, Lairy Noffsinger and Johnny Matthews.

We have had two "Timothy's" to go from our church family in full time Christian service. Gwen Todd is a missionary presently serving in Vienna, Austria, and other parts of Europe. Kenneth Walker is a full time minister at the First Christian Church in Cheney, KS.

Our beliefs:
The Bible alone as our rule and guide
The Supremency of Jesus Christ
The Unity and liberty of all Christians in Christ
The two institutions of our Lord,
    Baptism by immersion
    The Lords Supper
We believe we are not the only Christians,
But we seek to be Christians only.

The First Christian Church of Earlington

The First Christian Church Of Madisonville

Christians, Cambellites, Disciples, what are we? All, it appears. Barton W. Stone led a Kentucky group calling themselves "Christians" and wanting greater religious freedom that held ideas very similar to the "Disciples" who followed the teaching of Thomas Campbell in Pennsylvania and West Virginia. In 1832 these two groups merged to form The Christian Church of the Disciples of Christ and their ministers spread the work westward with the frontiers.

The Christian Church of Madisonville came into being and their first preacher was a man named Roberts. They owned no building and so met in the Courthouse.

Fredrick Kelly, a wheelwright, and his wife Polly on February 16, 1846 deeded a 35' x 65' lot on the northwest corner of Main and Broadway Streets to the trustees of the First Christian Church; namely P. M. Robertson, James Nesbit, Horace Pritchett, Israel Davis and Thomas Campbell. This plot was the location of our congregation from its incorporation on November 7, 1849 until the great fire of July 5, 1975. For reasons unknown, this deed remained in the clerk's office until January 27, 1893 when it was delivered to Minos R. Cotton and B. L. Rash two of the church trustees.

Re. Orville Collins was called as the first pastor of the church. His ministry of almost 30 years and Edward F. Coffman Jr. of 20 years appears to have been two of the longest. If you count the Courthouse preacher Roberts and accept the listing of H.F.S. Bailey's 1922 church history then we have had 32 ministers, including James Mahoney, in our church history of some 138 plus years.

Should our history begin with official organization in 1849, or with Frederick Kelly's deed of 1846, or with the early meetings of the ad hoc congregation with preacher Roberts in the old Courthouse?

The first church built about 1850 was a fairly large frame structure which was also used as a school. In 1865, the church organized a regular Sunday School. This frame church stood until 1889 when it was replaced with a brick building costing $5,000.00 and said to be the finest Christian Church building west of Louisville. Its erection was supervised by a building committee made up of N. M. Holeman, C. J. Pratt and J. W. Pritchett. The minister at this time was J. W. Hardy. This building served the congregation for 21 years.

In 1910, we build a much larger church of mission finish brick with stone trim and a tile roof. It had many meeting rooms and very large auditorium and was completed at a cost of about $30,000.00. Sam M. Bernard was minister when this building was erected, John G. B. Hall was President Official Board. Wm. J. Cox, S. D. Langley, E. G. McLeod, C. J. Waddill and C. O. Osborn constituted the Building Committee.

In 1957, during the ministry of Rev. John M. Hardy, the church was completely redecorated and a much needed Christian Education building was erected on the south side of East Broadway.

First Christian Church-1910

On July 5, 1975 disaster struck when our church was completely gutted by fire and the masonary left standing had to be razed.

After consideration of all the factors involved it was decided to move the church, and property was purchased a the northwest corner of North Outer Main and College Drive. On Sunday, August 20, 1978, the contractors building proposal was accepted and ground was broken. The new church building was dedicated on March 23, 1980, almost five years after the fire. Ed Coffman's sermon that day was "A DREAM MADE REAL". This great achievement was possible because of the hard work and dedication of the entire congregation under the leadership of Dr. Coffman and the following committees:

Building Campaign Council: Jim Hammonds, Chairman; Beulah Cornette, Secretary; Dr. Edward Coffman, Minister; Mary Simms, Church Secretary; Joe Wagner, Church Secretary; Warren Kennett, Advance Gifts; Edwin McGary, Follow-Through; Jennie Stodghill, Publicity; Jewell Rodgers, Spiritual Life; Mary Beth Parris, Meals; James Simmons, Chairman of the Board; Harold Watkins, Guest Director; and W.W. McReynolds, Guest Director.

Building Committee: Bob Kik Chairman, Jim Ashmore, Cheri Bachman, Alan Cheek, Thurman Clark, Edward Coffman, Jr. Aubrey Cornette, Laurence Gordon, Paul Ireland, Edwin McGary, Bill Metcalfe, Catherine Mosely, Leon Peyton, Dixie Rakestraw, Clyde Ruby, Lorena Ruby and James Simmons.

First Christian Church in 1987

First Presbyterian Church

The First Presbyterian Church, Madisonville, KY was established in 1834 composed of 60 members at the corner of North Main Street and Federal Street. It was known then as "The Main Street Presbyterian Church".

The membership of the church continued to grow and in 1960 the construction of the present church building began.

On Sunday, May 14, 1961, the name the "First Presbyterian Church" was chosen by the congregation for the new church facility.

On Sept. 17, 1961 the first service and the special dedication service was held in the new church.

In 1972 the congregation having increased, a new addition was begun and a multi-purpose fellowship room or gymnasium, three classrooms, a large kitchen, restrooms and storage rooms were built. At this time the bell tower was built for the bell from the original church. In 1973 the special dedication for the new addition and bell tower was held.

The church facility provides Sunday School classrooms for children of all ages and grades. There are nine adult Sunday School classes. The church sponsors youth groups in various ages, several choir groups, including Bell Chime choirs, and a puppet group.

In addition to the regular choir there is a men's ensemble, "The Joyful Noise" who have recently cut tapes of their music.

The present membership of the church is 400.

The First Presbyterian Church has been honored of God through its varied ministry of the Word especially in that three of the young men from the congregation have made the decision to go into the ministry full time. One of these was ordained Oct. 18, 1987 and is now pastor of two churches in the state of Tennessee; one is pastoring in New Mexico; and one in his final year in a Theological Seminary in Ohio.

This church looks with faith and confidence toward the future, as it reflects the blessing of God in the past, and stands under its scrutiny in the present.

The members of the congregation of the First Presbyterian Church believe that the mission of the church is "to know Jesus as Lord and Saviour and make him known".

Pastor of the church is the Reverend John E. Pitzer.
Compiled and written by Grace Anderson.

The First Presbyterian Church

First United Methodist Church of Madisonville

First organized in 1828. It was a small log cabin near the center of town.

In 1836 the Methodists purchased a 35' x 55' lot one half block from the courthouse on South Main Street. It was on this lot that the first brick church was built. (1848). The second was built in 1870 and the third was built in 1901 and was the home of Methodist for 75 years.

The new church was on the corner of Scott and Center Streets, was built in 1926 and on Sept. 26, 1926 it was dedicated. Bishop James E. Dickey formally opened the Church Sanctuary.

The parsonage was built in 1950. Rev. Oscar Nichols and his family were the first family to use the new parsonage.

On Mar. 16, 1965 preparations were made and Ground Breaking Ceremonies were held for the new Education Building. All of the church was remodeled and air conditioning was installed. Rev. Harry Pullen, Jr. was the minister at this time. The Educational Building was completed and dedicated on Palm Sunday, Apr. 13, 1977.

In 1978 the members of First Church and friends celebrated the 150th birthday of the church.

Rev. Wallace Thomas was minister in 1977, Rev. James O. Thurmond followed Rev. Thomas. At the present time (1987) Rev. Glen Sowards is the minister. Gary Hughes is Director of Children and Youth Programs. Mrs. Leighton Thomison is the organist and Jonathan Baldwin is Director of the Music Ministry.

The Women in Mission of First Church have done much of the church work in the field of missions. Their purpose is to know God and to make Christ known throughout the world. They have also given vast amounts of money to the building fund and have furnished the fireside room as well as many other church projects.

Sunday School classes are held each Sunday morning for all ages. The teachers do a wonderful job in all classes. The classes have donated time, money and efforts to many projects for the church.

All in all, the entire membership of First Church continually worked together throughout the years to make it the great church it is today. As Paul in the scriptures stated, "We shall press forward to the mark of the high calling, which is in Christ Jesus our Lord."
- *Written by Eunice O. Brown*

The First United Methodist Church of Madisonville

Grapevine Baptist Church

On Sept. 3, 1933, a group of 15 Baptists met in the Grapevine School to organize the Grapevine Baptist Church. These 15 people were Uris and Ozelia Cartwright, Roxie Clayton, Mary Mounts, Fred and Rosa Cartwright, Gladys Cartwright, Pauline (Mrs. Tommie) Cartwright, Mae Egbert, Tennie Vaughn, Lula Belle Cartwright, Sammie and Lossie Ferrell, W.F. and Ruby Wilson. Eleven others united by letter or baptism that same day.

For the next three years, the church met in the homes of the members and the Grapevine School. In 1936, they bought some property on Old Hopkinsville, Rd., near the intersection of Grapevine Road and McLeod Lane and built a one room frame structure. Most of the labor was provided by the men of the church. At last they had a permanent place of worship, even though the first seats were nail keys with boards placed between them.

The church was organized by Rev. Rupert A. Utley and he continued to pastor the church until his death in February 1969. His ministry lasted for almost 35 years.

Rev. and Mrs. R.A. Utley in 1961

The church started with quarter time services, went to half time in 1941 and full time in 1946. Today, the church has a full program of organizations including Sunday School, Church Training, W.M.U., and Baptist men, Graded choirs and a Youth Ministry.

On Oct. 24, 1941, the church started a radio ministry which has broadcast weekly since that date. In 1986, the broadcast was expanded from 30 minutes weekly to 45 minutes. Presently, it is heard at 12:45 p.m. each Sunday on WFMW.

The small frame structure soon became too small and additions were made to accommodate the growing congregation. The first expansion was a basement which provided 14 Sunday School rooms. In 1951, a two story addition was added to the rear of the sanctuary that also included a baptistry. In 1954, the entire structure was remodeled and enlarged. Since then, the church has added more rest rooms, nurseries, pastor's study, church offices, youth director's office and a library. The entire building was air-conditioned. An activities building was built. The parking lot was paved. There is a softball field with bleachers on property at the rear of the church.

In 1969, a four bedroom pastorium was constructed on property adjacent to the church. A den, carport and other rooms were added in 1974.

The church has been served by four pastors. Rev. R.A. Utley, organizer and first pastor served from September 1933 until his death in February 1969. Rev. Bob Marine served from late in 1969 until 1972. Rev. Ralph Gill came in July 1973 and served until March 1983. Rev. Clark A. Brown was called to the church in October 1983 and continues to serve as Pastor.

Six men have been ordained to the gospel ministry by the church. A number of the men of the church have been ordained to serve as deacons. One missionary has gone out to serve with the Home Mission Board.

In 1970, the church began a Youth Ministry under the direction of Ray Hibbs as part-time leader. Steve Shirk came in 1983 as the first full-time Youth Director. Since then, Richard Barron, Frank Queen, Mark Gill and Anthony Wilson have served as Youth Directors. Anthony Wilson is the present Youth Director.

The church has a full time custodian, paid nursery workers and part-time secretary.

The church voted in 1986 to build a new sanctuary. Ground will be broken and construction will begin in the near future.

The Lord has blessed greatly in the last 54 years. Membership is now over 700 with an annual income of over $100,000.

The future of Grapevine Baptist Church is as bright as the promises of God and the church looks to Him for leadership in the years ahead.

Grapevine Baptist in the early 50's

The current Grapevine Baptist Church

GRAPEVINE CHRISTIAN CHURCH

The Grapevine Christian Church owes its beginning to meetings that were held in a brush arbor built near the site of the present church in the year 1818. Services were held in this brush arbor by different preachers until the year 1828, at which time Elder Washington Dunkerson came and preached regularly until the year 1834. The organization of the church took place on the 28th day of April 1834, with about 15 charter members. It was given the name of Christian Union, but because of the brush arbor and tangles growth of grapevines covering the hill it soon became known as the Grapevine Church.

The first building was of hewn logs and was about 15' wide x 30' long. It was in this humble log building that the great leader of the Disciples, Alexander Campbell, preached a sermon during a tour of Western Kentucky at some time near the year 1847. In 1849, the little log church was torn down and a frame building much larger was built to accommodate the increasing membership. This building was 40 x 60 feet but a little later 20 feet was added to the length indicating their rapid growth.

On Apr. 27, 1884, a great day dawned for the church, the celebration of its fiftieth anniversary. Elder D. M. Breaker preached the sermon. His text was Psalms 44:1 - "We have heard with our ears, O God, our fathers have told us, what work thou didst in their days, in times of old." Over 700 people attended that day.

With true pioneer spirit of ever pushing forward, in 1894 the old frame building was torn down and a brick one started. It was at this time that the last charter member of the church, Elder Horace Pritchett, died. The memorial service held, in the old building, over his remains was the last one ever to be held within its walls, for the very next day the men began to tear it down. The brick building was completed in 1895. Mr. Everett Morton was the architect. He designed the building after the Garfield Memorial Church in Washington.

Grapevine Christian Church-completed 1895

It was during the ministry of Clarence W. Thomas that the church celebrated its 100th anniversary. It was pointed out that the Grapevine Church was largely responsible for the formation of the Moss Hill, Madisonville, Mortons Gap and Bethlehem churches and many members had moved to other areas helping to make up congregations there.

On Mother's Day May 9, 1954, Jack L. Holt preached his trial sermon and became the 33rd and FIRST full-time minister of the church in June, 1954. He is the son of Gertrude and the late C.F. Holt of Mt. Vernon, KY. On Oct. 16, 1955, Bro. Jack and Julia A. Stinnett, daughter of Owen and the late Ruth Stinnett were married. They have two daughters, Rebecca L. Knight and Brenda H. Laskowski.

In September of 1963 a new forty by eighty building was dedicated and in April of 1974 an educational wing was added to it. Bro. Clarence Thomas, former pastor, brought the message for the dedication and 140th anniversary on April 28th.

Also in 1974 Grapevine began hiring Summer Interns to work with the youth. Rick Starr was the first then he was followed by Doug Newhouse, Becky Holt, Brian Lakin and Mike Brown. On Apr. 8, 1982, Don F. Hulsey son of Jane and Jimmy Hulsey of Madisonville, was accepted as full time Youth Minister. Don is a graduate of Johnson Bible College and married to the former Aleta Bliffin of Orange Park, FL. They have a son Joshua and a daughter Keri.

Grapevine Christian is non-denominational governed only by its elders who are elected by the congregation to oversee, shepherd and superintend. Christ its only head! It's members wear no other name than Christian according to Acts 11:26

Here, we have only hit the high spots of 153 years in the history of Grapevine Christian Church. We know that the future will hold joys and sorrows, successes and failures as we press onward toward the mark for the prize of the high calling of God in Christ Jesus. But the ultimate victory belongs to Christ. Matt.16:18

Grapevine Christian Church-Dedicated 1963

Concord General Baptist-Cont'd
(Continued from page 352)

Cecil Clayton of Slaughters says his grandparents, Mr. and Mrs. John Cates and Hugh and Jenny Cunningham, were charter members of the church. Mrs. Cunningham's brother, Rev. James H. Dame, was one of the first pastors. The oldest living pastor, Rev. O.L. Duncan (see Duncan-Parish story), is now in a local nursing home.

In the 1950s, a new building was erected. In the early 1960s, an addition was added and the church was bricked. In the late 1960s, an addition to the church was constructed and in the 1970s, the building and basement were again expanded with a complete remodeling of the inside furnishings. In 1987, a new and complete sound system was installed.

The present pastor is the Rev. Louis Baker. Rev. Baker, his wife Virginia and youngest son, Randy, came to Concord after serving as missionaries in Jamica. -Submitted by Dorothy Miller Shoulders

Elm Grove Methodist Church

Elm Grove Methodist Church is located at Anton. On July 17, 1893 William Melton Moore, a Methodist Minister also known as Uncle Billie, and his wife S.A. Moore deeded a two acre tract of land to the following trustees: John Murphy Sr., Dan L. Jameson, and Thomas Fugate. The timber for the building was given by Will Cardwell and John Murphy Sr.

Other early members were: Amos Whitmer, Miss Ann Hicklin, Mrs. Anne Murphy, Sam Barnard, Martha Murphy, America Hicklin, Charles Hicklin, Lula and Baker Jameson, Nealie and Annie Bet Webb.

Today, the original structure is still standing with an addition that was added onto the back. The present minister is Rev. Bill Lawson. -Submitted by Mary Edna Harris

Hayes Chapel Methodist

Hayes Chapel Methodist is the oldest church in the black community of Nebo. The church was organized in March of 1872 and was located on the third road to the right off North Hoffman Street, from High 41-A. A large cemetery for the community is to the north and east of the church drive. The first school for the community was located on an adjoining lot. The old building burned and was rebuilt under the leadership of Rev. J.A. Bard. Other ministers include William Yates, Caldwell Smith, and Marvin Poindexter. Since the death or moving away of most of its members, there are services held on the first and third Sundays of the month. The Rev. Joseph Hayes now serves as pastor. Marion Black Jr., the trustee, now lives in California. - Submitted by Dorothy Miller Shoulders

High Glory Church

High Glory Church was located on Island Ford Road, four miles northeast of Madisonville. A freeunion church, all denominations were welcome to hold services and summer revivals.

It is believed the church received its name for two reasons. The small church building was perched on a high hill and also a high bank from the road. The church held very spirited revivals. Even though it was called Free Union Church, it became known as High Glory.

Two stories are told that bring a smile. A young man, E.H. Rudd, after attending an evening service, missed the driveway and drove his horse and buggy down the very steep embankment from the church yard to the road. Nothing serious came of the incident and Mr. Rudd related the story some years later to his daughter, Mrs. Cecil Drake. Mr. Cecil Drake tells, the Drake family was attending an evening service. Since the service was lengthy, he as a small child fell asleep. The family was half-way home when it was realized Cecil was not with them. Upon a hurried return to the church, he was found asleep in a pew.

The land around High Glory has had several owners, Wilkersons, Asro Ellis, Cardwells, and now Cecil Holland. No one seems to know for sure when the church closed its doors or what happened to the old building. - Submitted by Dorothy Miller Shoulders

Ilsley (Crabtree) Presbyterian

In October of 1924, Bro. McKee Thomson, a Presbyterian missionary from Princeton, KY, came to do a survey and report to the Presbytery on the spiritual needs of Ilsley. He returned later that same month to organize a Sunday School, meeting in the school building. The first officers were Miss Willie Rasco, S.S. Superintendent (also principal and a teacher at the school) and Mrs. Pearl Franklin, secretary.

On June 1, 1925, Bro. Thomson, Bro. James T. Smith, another missionary from Smith Grove, KY and Rev. W.B. Strong, pastor of the 1st Presbyterian Church in Madisonville, started a Vacation Bible School and Evangelistic meeting, during which 20 professions of faith were made.

The church charter was signed June 7, 1925 with 22 members: Ressie Alexander Eades, Bessie Chappell Porter, Bertha Menser Alexander, Miss Mary Sandefur, S.L. Sandefur, Tressa Sisk Alexander, Nancy Jane McNeeley Beshear, Neicie Ausenbaugh Sisk, Iva Sisk Davis, John L. Walker, Mary Porter Franklin, Emma Downey Walker, Ryna Howell Jones, Mr. and Mrs. Claude Davis, Carlos Davis, Eula Brackett Majors, Acie Matheny, Lois Walker Matheny, J.I. McDonald, Nancy Browning McDonald, and P.W. Franklin.

It was decided to build a church and Jim Horn Beshears donated the land adjoining the cemetery. The trustees, W.B Strong, W.P. Scott, and A. Holloman, were appointed and the Dodge Bros. of Dawson Springs were contracted to build the church at an estimated cost of $2,650. The committee for subscribers of the building fund were Iva Davis and Eula Majors.

The cornerstone was laid July 12, 1926. A Holy Bible, hymn book, a Presbyterian Advance, July 10, 1926 issue of the Madisonville Messenger, a list of all subscribers to the building fund, and a copy of the building contract were sealed within. The building was completed in September 1926 (cost $2,905), the dedication was held October 17 at 2 p.m. Bro. James T. Smith gave the address, the key was presented by Louis Dodge, contractor, and accepted by W.P. Scott, trustee.

Listed below are Elders and Deacons with their date of ordination:

Elders: Carlos Davis and P.W. Franklin Aug. 30, 1925; J.I. McDonald ordained and installed as Ruling Elder Oct. 24, 1926; Alfred G. Riggs and D.M. Darnell Oct. 23, 1927; Dixon Ladd July 28, 1929; J.W. Houston Oct. 5, 1930; J.L. Nalls Oct 26, 1930; T.A. Petty Nov. 26, 1930; John C. Steeley and Major E. Barnes Feb. 5, 1950, Mrs. Jess (Bertie) Fox Jan. 27, 1952; Rufus Cotton and Andrew Bloodworth Mar. 4, 1956; E. Ray Woodruff Jan. 26, 1962, Ressie Alexander Eades Jan. 9, 1966, Amos J. Sizemore Jr. Feb. 26, 1967. Deacons: George Hardison Oct. 5, 1930; C.M. Turley and George E. Allen May 9, 1931; B.H. Walker Nov. 26, 1931; Elijah J. Steeley Apr. 15, 1956; Amos J. Sizemore Jr. Jan. 9, 1966.

Pastors were: Bro. W.B. Strong (father of Mrs. John Donan); Bro. Phillip Irvin; Bro. R.O. Garden; Bro. C.E. McClure; Bro. Edwin Kagin; Bro. Armen Trout; Bro. Doral Robling; Bro. Rufus Hickey; and Bro. Bill Williams. Bro. Irvin also served as supply pastor at times.

When the Presbytery decided to leave the church, the congregation was told they were welcome to go to Madisonville 1st

(Continued on page 365)

Lighthouse Pentecostal Church

The Lighthouse Pentecostal Church located at 2860 North Main Street was founded in 1948 on South Main Street in a building owned by Mr. R. M. Daniel and Mr. Wallace Sisk. Rev. Ellis Phaup conducted the services until he resigned in 1950 and Rev. James Russell assumed leadership.

In 1950, a small church building on Weldon Ave. was purchased and the congregation moved and started having Sunday School with nine in the adult class.

The next move was made after the purchase of six acres of land on Outer North Main St. Construction of the present church began in 1968 and was completed in 1969. Rev. Bobby Alvey became associate pastor in 1972. The church continued to experience growth and a wing was added to each side for additional Sunday School rooms.

In 1978, construction began on the Outreach Building and it was completed in 1979. Due to ill health, Rev. James Russell resigned and Rev. Ronald Hendricks assumed the duties of pastor in 1982 with Rev. Bobby Alvey continuing as associate pastor.

The Ladies Fellowship Circle is well known for their food, crafts and their many projects that are done in the Outreach Building. Separated from the rest of the building is the bus garage. Maintenance on the buses is a necessary part of providing the services that transports about 130 children to church on Sunday morning. Watching the children, faces aglow with happy expectations as they alight from their buses to step inside the warmth and welcome of their Sunday School rooms, we are made to realize our labor is not wasted or in vain.

The Lighthouse Church is committed to Apostolic Doctrine and worship with special emphasis on Bible teaching. The church continues to serve the community with three weekly services in Madisonville Nursing Homes.

The back hall shows the importance attached to sharing with others. On the wall is a growing number of pictures of missionaries the church helps to sponsor.

The mission of the church is to reach for this generation and to show forth the praises of Him who has called us out of darkness into His marvelous light. -*Submitted by: Ada Brown*

Lighthouse Pentecostal Church

ILSLEY (CRABTREE) PRESBYTERIAN-CONT'D.
(Continued from page 363)

Presbyterian Church, but it would be too far for most of the members.

The Disciples of Christ offered support for the little church. On Mar. 23, 1969, the church voted unanimously to become the Ilsley Christian Church. It remains so at present.

Sources: Mary Beth Eades McDonald, Bertie Fox, Mona Jones Mathews, Faye Nell Alexander Carroll, and Mrs. John Donan. Submitted by Sharon Riggs Johnston

KIMBLUS CHAPEL

Kimblus Chapel was located on Highway 85, east of Madisonville, and housed both a church and school. At one time a Rev. Driver was pastor. A Miss Lucille Van Leer was said to have been a teacher in the early 1900s. Miss Van Leer did teach at McNary Station around 1919 and later moved out of the state and married a Humphrey. Miss Van Leer was the older sister of Robert Van Leer of Madisonville.- *Submitted by Dorothy Miller Shoulders*

LITTLE FLOCK BAPTIST CHURCH

Little Flock Baptist Church in Nebo was organized in 1881. The church was first located between North Barnard and North Hoffman Streets. The church was rebuilt in 1963 on North Hoffman Street. The present minister in Walter L. Ellis. - *Submitted by Dorothy Miller Shoulders*

MANITOU CHRISTIAN CHURCH

Manitou Christian Church was located in Manitou on the corner of Highway 41-A and Manitou Road, going south towards Rose Creek Road. The church was built in the late 1800s. Micheal Noel, who still lives in the community, remembers Rev. Henry Moore was pastor in the early 1900s. Mr. Noel says attendance was good in the 1920's and the 1930's. As with most small churches, the membership dwindled. Rev. Gass was the last pastor. Even after membership was too small to afford another pastor's salary, they still had what is called Evergreen Sunday School with Mrs. Carrie Tapp and Mrs. Flora Swope teaching the classes for four or five years. The building was also used by young ministers just starting out, regardless of their denominations. The last funeral the Noels' remember at the church was Will Cardwell's, father of Manitou teacher and doctor Ralph Cardwell.

Around 1947, it was decided to have an auction and sell the church furnishings, building and lot. The Noels bought the two pulpit chairs. The rest of the furniture was bought by others in the community. The lot and building was sold to the late S.J. Wilson. He later tore it down and built a dwelling. The monies from the auction and sale were then divided evenly between the three local churches that the membership had joined: Nebo Christian, Madisonville Christian and Grapevine Christian. - *Submitted by Dorothy Miller Shoulders*

MT. ZION METHODIST CHURCH

The Mt. Zion Methodist Church was located on the Old Jackson Stage Coach Road, now Highway 1069. The church began in the late 1840s and served its community for nearly 100 years.

The white frame building had plain windows and was heated in the winter by a pot-bellied stove. In good times, there was a church, a school, and a burying ground. In sad times, the once flourishing congregation began to grow smaller and the number was not enough to have a pastor. The local men, feeling their church's need, were licensed to fill the pulpit. The District Conference of Henderson accepted the Hanson recommendation for the licensing of John Henry Fowler on Sept. 10, 1925 as lay pastor. Brother Fowler was the father of Gilbert Fowler now of Madisonville. The father of Cecil Drake, John Will Drake, also pastored and each did his part to keep the church on its feet.

When the depression years came, the little flock was finding it harder. The Drake and Fowler children married, and some moved away. In the late 1930s, Utterback School closed and so did the church. It was used as a community church for a year or so, before being sold to Deo Baldwin in 1939. Mrs. Baldwin remembers the building was torn down and stacked neatly. Its wide poplar planks were still like new. The Baldwins were living in what was then called the family "weaning house". It was 1944, two weeks before the birth of their daughter, when they finally moved to their new home, built from the Mt. Zion Church. Now once again, the building is to be torn down. Mrs. Baldwin hopes to attain some of the still beautiful poplar planks. Mt. Zion Cemetery is still in use. - *Submitted by Dorothy Miller Shoulders*

NEBO BAPTIST CHURCH

The Nebo Baptist Church is located on South Barnard Street and was organized around 1900. In 1913, the Presbyterian U.S.A. church closed its doors and the building was bought for $400.00 for the home of the Baptist church. In the 1930s, Coiltown Baptist Church closed and part of that church was brought to Nebo to use in remodeling. Donald Hunt of Nebo, remembers as a teenager helping in the remodeling. The building was strengthened by using iron rods connected to each side at ceiling level. The building has since been completely redone with brick and the addition of a Fellowship Hall and Sunday School rooms. The present pastor is Rev. Royce Dukes. - *Submitted by Dorothy Miller Shoulders*

NEBO BLACK CHRISTIAN CHURCH

In the late 1880s, the Christian Church was organized. The church was located near Highway 41-A, on the first road to the right on North Hoffman Street, sitting on the left side of the small road.

By early 1900, only a few families remained as members. Mrs. Nettie Cargile Ringo remembers Rev. J.E. Anderson was the pastor when she was a child. Her father, James Cargile, was a Sunday School teacher. The church closed in the early 1920s and the old building was torn down. With the closing of the church, the Cargile family began attending the white Christian Church in Nebo. - *Submitted by Dorothy Miller Shoulders*

NEBO CHRISTIAN CHURCH

Nebo Christian Church is located on North Barnard Street, on the right side from Highway 41-A. After the closing of the Old Republican Church on the Morganfield Road in 1884-85, the Nebo Church was built in 1885 within a month by its members. The ground was given by John Langley.

There was a revival that year (1885), held by Rev. J.F. Story, and 20 new members were baptized and received into the church. Sixty members from the old Republican Church joined, making it official that the two churches were now one. Much of the old church's furnishings were used also. Also, in 1885 several marriages took place in the new church with the first being the marriage of Eliza Cox and C.S. Hoffman.

In 1934, the church held a 100 year celebration in the wood frame Nebo School (the school burned in 1935).

The old building was remodeled at least once. In 1965 a complete new building with a fellowship hall and several Sunday School rooms was built. A new parking lot was added when the church purchased the adjoining lot.

One of the oldest churches in Hopkins County, it has served its people of Nebo as well as the surrounding communities for more than 150 years. The present pastor is Rev. George Carman. -*Submitted by Dorothy Miller Shoulders.*

NEBO CUMBERLAND PRESBYTERIAN

Nebo Cumberland Presbyterian Church was once at the location where the Baptist Church is today.

Anderson Presbytery met at Rose Creek Church Oct. 8, 1886. Rev. G.B. McDonald was Moderator. The opening sermon was preached by Rev. R.D. Smith from II Thes. 3:1. The following ministers were present: G.B. McDonald, G.W. Bone, J.T. Barbee, W.D. Blair, W.L. Caskey, Cyrus Graham, T.H. Mitchell, J.L. Price, R.D. Smith, W.W. Wynns, James Wilson and T.E. Young

Nebo was received as an organized congregation at this Presbytery.

In Hopkins County Court records, Deed Book 50, Pg. 602, Oct. 1, 1891 between Dr. W.R. McNary and Janie his wife of Hopkins County to Rev. Dr. James Gill of Elkton and others, trustees of the Cumberland Presbyterian Church, a lot in Nebo. This was a lot parallel to the existing church. In 1906, many Cumberland Presbyterian Churches merged with Presbyterian U.S.A. This was one of the merged churches. Later the church building was sold to the Baptist congregation and dedication services were held in the old brick school in Nebo 1913.

Mr. Sam Crowe remembers, as a very young lad, attending Sunday School at the Methodist Church in the morning and the Presbyterian Church in the afternoon, where a Mrs. Minerva (?) Hill was a teacher.

Sources: Taken in part from a brief history of Rose Creek Church from the 1906 Princeton Presbyterial records updated by the Rev. Chester E. Cannon and Elder Elmer Hill; and Hopkins County Court Records and personal interviews. -Submitted by Mrs. Betsy D. Bruce

NEBO METHODIST CHURCH

Nebo Methodist Church is located on Highway 41-A, about a block past the Barnard and Highway 41-A intersection. In 1815 the Crowe family moved onto the land between what became the Dixie Bee (Hwy. 41-A) and Old Madisonville-Morganfield Road (now Hwy. 502). The land settled, there was now a need for churches and schools. John S. Crowe, a layman preacher of Methodist faith, filled that need.

The first church building was located about 2 1/2 miles north of Nebo, turn west on the Crowe Cemetery Road, just off Hwy. 502. Mr. Sam Crowe, now living on Hwy. 502 one mile north of Nebo, remembers the Elder Crowe (his great grandfather) as a preacher of the First Methodist Church on his farm. The church was called Green Grove. Sometime in the late 1880s, the building was torn down and the church moved to Nebo. A larger building was built with a huge bell tower and beautiful cathedral type windows.

The great-great-grandson of Elder Crowe, John Henry Porter, does not know if the records show when the church changed its name.

In the late 1920's the church was remodeled with the huge bell tower removed and a plain steeple built in its place along with other changes. The land for the church has been provided on North Barnard Street by the Harris family. In the 1960s, it was decided to replace the old building and to also expand. The sons of Robert Harris Sr., Robert Jr. and Sidney, gave enough ground for the present location. The old building was sold to Clarence Morrow of Wicks Well and torn down. The choir and alter railings were so beautiful that Mr. Morrow used them around his stairwell in his home. The present pastor is Rev. Barnard Allen. -*Submitted by Dorothy Miller Shoulders*

PARK AVENUE BAPTIST CHURCH

In December of 1964, the First Baptist Church purchased the former Church of God property at 132 Park Avenue in Madisonville. At this location began a mission work, which became known as the Park Ave Chapel, with Rev. H.G.M. Hatler as pastor, and a starting Sunday School enrollment of 32. Bro. Hatler was assisted by the First Baptist Church members, who served as song leaders, Sunday School Directors and teachers. Besides Bro. Hatler, Bros. Woodrow Fountain, Gene Myers, and Marvin Freeman served as pastors, with Bros. George Park and Dr. C.D. Cole assisting as needed.

Bro. Marvin Freeman was serving as pastor when the Chapel was organized into a church on Aug. 20, 1972, with a membership of 128. As a gift, the First Baptist Church presented the property deed to the newly established Park Avenue Baptist Church.

The first song sung in the new church was "Blessed Assurance", and the first couple wed there was Miss Sharon Riggs to Mr. Ronald Johnston on Sept. 1, 1972.

The following have served as the church's pastors: Bros. Marvin Freeman (twice), Steve Hill, Wendell Rone (interim), Garry Miller, Hughlan Richey-past Director of Missions of the Little Bethel Assn. (interim), and at present Bro. Ralph Gill.

During it's history, the little church has ordained to preach, Carl Nelson and Clay Jones and licensed to preach, Kerry Smith, Carl Nelson, Kenny Parker, Randall Badger, and Terry Burden.

Those who have served as deacons are: Lanny Hillyard, Morton Summes, Charles Norvell, Clarence Berry, Rance Parker, Randall Bryan, Willis Kinder, Jim Alford, Ronald Johnston, Randall Badger, Hayden (sonny) Littlepage Jr., Tom Ellis, Terry Burden, Danny Gamblin, and David Corum.

Every year since the summer of 1971, the church has held a fish-fry potluck supper on the church grounds, much to the enjoyment of its' members and their guests.

Bro. Freeman, who helped start the annual fish-fry, was instrumental in the establishment of a building fund in the mid 1970s, as well as the ground breaking for the new building held May 11, 1986, and the realization of that work at the dedication on Mar. 1, 1987.

The first song sung in the new building was "Blessed Assurance", and the first couple to be wed in the new building was Miss Michelle Hillyard to Mr. John McCord on July 4, 1987.

With it's present membership standing at 261, the church continues to grow.

Since 1972, Park Avenue Baptist Church has had the distinction of being the youngest member church in the Little Bethel Assn. -*Submitted by Joyce Bell and Inez Ligon*

PLEASANT GROVE BAPTIST

Pleasant Grove Baptist Church, located on Rose Creek Road, was constituted in Hopkins County, KY, Feb. 11, 1860. Shortly before, 62 members of Liberty Baptist Church had been lettered out, 27 of these for the purpose of organizing Pleasant Grove Church.

A well established tradition is that in 1855 there was a brush arbor meeting near the present site of Pleasant Grove. A small log

(Continued on page 369)

NEW SALEM MISSIONARY BAPTIST
1845-1987

New Salem Baptist Church was constituted in 1845. Salem Baptist Church, Mortons Gap assisted in the organization. The meeting place was near Nortonville Lake in a log church, built by pioneers. It came into Little Bethel Association the year it was constituted. The pastor is unknown but our messengers were E. Ayres, J. Rhea and M.C. Cunningham. There were 28 members. In 1853 our membership was 30. G.W. Childs was treasurer. In 1856, the messengers were E. Ayres and J.C. Ayres. The minister was J. Roark. The membership was 21.

During the Civil War period, due to the unsettled conditions in the country, we sent no messengers. In 1885 the messengers were C.M. Pendly, D.F. Clark and W.N. Clark. Our membership continued small. Our discipline was very strict.

In 1888, a new log building was constructed on the site of the present church. James Madison Ezell was the first pastor. Some of the early members were Meredith Pendley, Francis Pendley, Aaron Clark and Charley Pendley. Ministers who have served the church during this period are J.M. Ezell, W.N. Clark, C.M. Pendley, B.A. Sisk, P.A. Thomas, J.D. Calvert, A.C. Slaton, T.T. Pierce and M.A. Utley.

New Salem Church assisted the people of White Plains in 1898 in organizing a Missionary Baptist Church.

From 1916 to 1922 New Salem was without a pastor and went through the darkest period of its history. During two of the years of that period only business meeting was held each year and that was on Homecoming Day.

In 1922 Rev. J.W. Elliott, having had a vision to restore New Salem Church, began his ministry and labored until 1926. During that period there were many additions to the church, both by letter and baptism. The church building was completely remodeled.

Continuing with our pastors, we had J.P. Clevenger, Willie Clark, E.G. Sisk, Fred Fox, W.T. Crumbaker, Gene Myers, Edgar Taylor, O. Kenneth Johnston, Dencil Lewis, Allen Jones, Tabor Best, Robert Ripley, and Roy D. Finley. Our interim pastor is Rev. G. W. Berry. He has served twice in that capacity. Each of these pastors have served us well and building additions, spiritual contributions, and growth in all organizations attest to that fact.

During the period from 1933 to 1936, a new building was erected on the same site as the second one. The building committee was S.B. Bilbro, L.R. Ferguson and John Miller. The work was done by members and friends. This period was a season characterized by great revivals and increased membership. After one revival 63 were baptized and 12 more that same year.

This building has been added to and renovated many times. Since 1980, we have constructed a new recreation building, added more Sunday School rooms, installed a sound system, added a library, black topped the parking lot, purchased a new van and made other small improvements. We have increased in membership and it was a period of growth in all departments and spirituality.

Since 1888, many dedicated man have served as Deacons. They are W.H. Pendley, A. Blythe, James Furgeson, A.L. Clark, P. Pendley, N.J. Whitfield, W.S. Miller, John Buchanan, Clint Almon, Chesley Lovan, Dan Cavanaugh, Edward Clark, Joe Tyson, Ruby Miller, Hardin Matney, Sam Bilbro, Wesley Newman, Monroe Scott and our present deacons, Otho Alexander, Norman Berry, Douglas Grace, Carmon Hight, O'Neal Lewis, George Pennington and Harold Vickery.

New Salem has ordained six to the ministry: W.J.T. Pendley, Billie Clark, Boyd Putman, Charles Pendley, B.A. Sisk, W.N. Clark, Virgil Brooks, Phillip Pendley, J.W. Elliott, David Phillips and Leslie Webster.

The church went to full time preaching in 1954, a Baptist Training Union was organized in 1945 and New Salem has had vacation Bible School since 1944. Mrs. Addie Cavanaugh, an active member of New Salem Church for 59 years, taught 40 years in Vacation Bible School and 28 years in Sunday School. A Women's Missionary Society was organized in 1958.

In 1987, we participated in the Kentucky-Kenya relationship. The church sent Glen Tyson as a representative.

Our present membership is 453 with a few non-resident members. The Choir Director is Norman Berry, pianist Pam Hight, organist Ramona Alexander, Sunday School Director Glen Tyson, Training Union Director Douglas Grace, WMU Director Sherry Tyson, Church Clerk Douglas Grace and our Executive Board Representative is O'Neal Lewis.

May we, as a church, be ever faithful to our Lord and the heritage that past generations have bestowed upon us. -*Submitted by Mrs. Herman Gladdish*

The New Salem Missionary Baptist Church of Nortonville

Providence Rural United Methodist Church

In 1831 God's Providence United Methodist Church was formed six miles north of Madisonville, KY and two miles east of Hanson, KY. Early settlers were using a round log building as a church and school. These settlers came from North Carolina, Virginia and other parts and settled near the waters of Elk Creek in Hopkins County. The site of this building consisted of approximately one acre. The property was deeded to the Trustees Mar. 23, 1844.

This first church proved too small as the community grew so they decided to build a better and larger building. This building was 30' x 40' and erected out of hand hewn poplar logs covered with boards. After the completion of this church the question arose as to what they should name it. Someone suggested that they let God provide a name. After prayer, adjournment and reassembling to worship at the church, they agreed in unison on the name "God's Providence". After struggling through the Civil War and enjoying four years of peace, this house was sold to negroes for a school house and moved.

In 1869 a contract was let for construction of the third church with dimensions of 32' x 52'. The main building was constructed of yellow poplar lumber. The rafters and connecting braces in the attic are put together with pegs. Inside the walls have what is believed to be the original wainscotting on lower portion.

In 1956 a full basement was dug and the church moved about 150' and placed over the basement. A lot of improvements have been made to the church since that time and the outside of the church brick veneered.

On September 9, 1980 ground was purchased near the church for a parsonage which was started January 26, 1981 and completed in May, 1981.

We welcome one and all to come worship with us at Providence Rural United Methodist Church near Hanson, KY.

The Providence Rural United Methodist Church

Pleasant Grove Baptist Cont'd

(Continued from page 366)

building was erected and was known as Jones Chapel. It appears that Pleasant Grove was organized in this building a few years later, and worshipped there until a larger and better building was completed in 1867.

The old deed for the original church was dated 14 of April 1862, between D.S. Jones of the first part and David Davis, B.D. Robertson and Washington M. Rhea, trustees of the church, as the second part. The next building was erected in 1899 and was replaced by a new brick veneer structure around 1947.

The first pastor called in the year 1860, by unanimous vote, was Elder Nicolas Lacy who served for three terms, lasting eight years. Several other pastors have served extensive terms lasting up to ten years. One pastor, E.G. Sisk, served 14 years.

Many outstanding pastors have served over the years. The present Don Lam and his family have now completed a year and one half of service.

The Pleasant Grove Congregation is a dedicated working fellowship, having served their Church and Community well over these many years. It is now a well established, healthy Church serving

Republican Christian Church

In the 1830s, there was a thriving community called Hoffmanville, a cluster of farm homes on what was called the Madisonville-Morganfield highway, nothing more than a winding dirt road connecting the two towns over 50 miles apart. Running parallel with the Dixie Bee (Hwy. 41-A), it meandered from farm house to farm house. The Dixie Bee had a straighter path, giving way for the smaller towns to locate and Nebo began to take shape. About three miles from Nebo, Hwy. 502 N merges with the Old Morganfield Road and this was the location of Hoffmanville. The church, built in 1834, was on the north side of the road. Why the church was called Republican, we aren't sure. But one definition of the word is: commonwealth or governed by a supreme power. The congregation was organized by the "Christian" denomination and lasted until the community began to move their small businesses to the larger Nebo. A Christian Church was then built at Nebo. Elder Giles Harralson (See Harralson story) was its last deacon. The old building was practically torn down and used for a dwelling on an adjoining lot. Some of the furniture was sold and some was given to the Nebo Church. John Harralson of eastern Kentucky, one of the two surviving grandsons of the Elder Harralson, inherited the communion table. With only the old flooring left, the Harralson boys enjoyed using it as a skating rink. Mrs. Gwendolyn Harralson, now of Madisonville, remembers when she married her husband Sam in 1923 only the foundation rocks were left. Her husband Sam told of skating on the floor as a child. -*Submitted by Dorothy Miller Shoulders*

Richland Missionary Baptist Church

During the 1830s, over a period of several years, the Highland Association of Baptists had become violently opposed to missionary effort and benevolent work, forbidding it's member churches to perform or participate in any such work and persecuted those who did.

In 1837, four members of the Richland community broke away from that body to form a new church which would more closely follow the guidelines set forth by our Lord Jesus Christ in the Holy Scriptures.

Reddick and Elizabeth O'Bryan and Isham and Sophia Slaton, with the help of two ministers, deeply founded in the faith, Bros. John Bourland and Timothy Sisk, wrote the new church constitution and founded Richland Missionary Baptist Church on Feb. 3, 1837.

The first pastor was Bro. John Bourland and the first deacons were Reddick O'Bryan and John Slaton. The first baptisms recorded were those of Emeline O'Bryan and Juliet Sanders and were administered by Bro. Richard Jones, the newly appointed missionary of the Little Bethel Assn. (founded the year before, 1836).

In 1838, F.D. Word and Hugh Kirkwood conveyed a tract of land for a church building site on the Richland-Carbondale Rd., to the trustees. The second building was constructed about 1862, with the Sunday School being organized in May 1885. The third and present building, located on Hwy. 70, was dedicated in June 1947. The church, in recent years has built an addition, bricked the outside, remodeled the interior, and blacktopped the parking area.

The pastors after Bro. Bourland: Joseph Board, James M. Ezell, *N.A. Hibbs, Wm. McLean, Lewis W. Bailey, *John O'Bryan, W.S. Adams, David Whittinghill, A.N. Whittinghill, U.J. Fox, J.H. Coleman, Wm. Banks, D.S. Edwards, C.M. Pendley, *E.B. Osburn, W.N. Clark, O.L. Weir, T.T. Piercy, J.P. Clevenger, R.W. Gentry, A.C. Slaton, M.E. Staley, W.T. Anderson, R.A. Utley, W.T. Crumbaker, George R. H. Gass, John W. Robison, J.C. Gunn (twice), John Boswell (twice), James Crowell, James Bishop, Albert Kemp, L.B. Wice (interim), Mike Neal, *Wm. (Bill) Clement, Larry Vincent, John Ashby-Director of Missions - Little Bethel Assn. (interim), and the present pastor, Chester Bobby (Bob) Tompkins. (*ordained by Richland Church) Others also ordained by this church were Major H. Utley, Raymond Davis, Laddie Pride, and Mike Hancock.

The present deacons are Loyd Ramsey, Chairman of deacons, Bill Troop, Maurice Ramsey, Ruby Vincent, Larry Bone, Trent Barton, Kenneth Presley, Dan Wilcox, and Ronald Johnston.

Richland is the oldest church in the Little Bethel Assn. continuously, under the same name and has aided in the founding of many of the Missionary Baptist Churches in our county.

Source: The History of Richland Church by Jesse Brown with additions by Sharon Riggs Johnston. Submitted by Sharon Riggs Johnston

Union Church

Union Church was organized in 1850. Composed of a part of the members of Rose Creek Cumberland Presbyterian Church sometime in 1816 to 1819 (1819 is the church's cornerstone date). Hugh Bone and family emigrated from Wilson Co., TN to Hopkins Co., KY Soon thereafter, some of the family connections removed to the same place. Among them were James Hill, Eli Lansden and others. A small society or church was established composed of these families.

Rev. William Harris was then called to take charge of the Rose Creek Church.

Rev. James Johnson was the next pastor through whose ministry God greatly revived his work and many were added to the church. Rev. Johnson lived in the Rose Creek settlement on what was known as the Cox farm. He took the young preachers Hugh Hill, M.H. Bone, Thomas Bone and others, instructing them in the Bible, theology and in literature. Some think Rose Creek was organized as early as 1817, the exact date is lost in obscurity. According to the minutes of Anderson Presbytery, Rose Creek was of sufficient prominence for this Presbytery to hold it's first meeting Apr. 5, 1822.

The elders of Rose Creek were Hugh Bone, Matthew Houston Bone, Eli M. Lansden, Harvey Graham, Isaac Gore, Thomas L. Hill and B.L. Porter. A brief history of Rose Creek Church records many camp meetings and great revivals in which God's blessings were poured out; great numbers were added to the church. From this church in 1850, Union Church was organized. Rev. J.W. Sharp was appointed to organize this church, but not being well, Rev. Thomas Bone officiated at the organization. The Union Church house was built about one mile east of Nebo, on top of knoll off the old Madisonville road (now 41 Alternate) at the Nebo Union Cemetery. The cemetery takes the name of Union from the old church. It is believed the cemetery was first called the Bone Family burying ground where many pioneers of the area are interred. Among the gravestones recorded, Hugh Bone Oct. 19, 1764-June 6, 1846, Mary wife of Hugh Bone, Apr. 16, 1762-Nov. 25, 1826. The earliest legible dates are: In memory of Elizabeth Lansden, consort of E.M. Lansden and dau. of Hugh and Mary Bone, Mar. 22, 1793-Aug. 23, 1824.

In Hopkins County Court records, Deed Book 27, Pg. 200-201, Apr. 4, 1866, William H. Winstead and Sarah Winstead his wife to Nancy J. Cardwell, Samuel N. Adams R.P. Henry and William Winstead as trustees of the Union Church burying ground of the counties of Webster and Hopkins and State of KY., for one dollar in hand, conveyed for burying ground. One square acre of ground in the Northwest corner of the tract of land known as the Andrew M. Bone Survey.

In Hopkins County Court Order Book 15, Pg. 69, Apr. 9, 1866, ordered that W.H. Winstead, Nancy J. Cardwell, S.N. Adams, R.P. Henry, he and they are hereby appointed trustees of the Union Church burying ground, near M.T. Winstead residence (Note: this is Manly Taylor Winstead whose residence was a large brick house across the road from the cemetery, in later years, the Ramsey Cox home.)

Union Church remained a separate congregation from Rose Creek until 1865. In 1850 to 1856, Rose Creek had no regular pastor. Rev. Thomas Bone preached and possibly, for short intervals, served as pastor. Rev. Bone was also pastor of Union Church most of the time, B.L. Porter, A.M. Bone, and R. H. Robertson represented Union Church in Presbytery until 1865. A.M. Bone represented both churches in 1854. Rev. S.B. Wade, Rev. Armstrong and Rev. W.G. McGehee pastored Union Church. Rev. W.H. Browning, William Roach and Adley Boyd preached for Union Church. During the Civil War, meetings were very irregular. As you walk through the Union Cemetery and gaze upon the dates of the gravestones, you can envision the struggle of the little church trying to survive. With the ravages of the Civil War and the natural passing of time taking many of their congregation and leadership. They were no longer able to support the church and remain a separate congregation.

R.C. Harris represented Rose Creek and Union in Anderson Presbytery at Canoe Creek in Henderson Co., KY, Mar. 30, 1865. On petition of these two churches they were reunited at Presbytery under the old name of Rose Creek Church.

Sources: Taken in part from a brief history of Rose Creek Church from the 1906 Princeton Presbyterial records updated by the Rev. Chester E. Cannon and Elder Elmer Hill; Hopkins County Court records; and personal interviews. - Submitted by Mrs. Betsy D. Bruce

White's Chapel Church

In the east rural Hanson area, about the mid-1800's, three men of the Methodist faith secured property for the building of a church and school. The three men were Mr. Graddy, Mr. White and Joe Hewlett. The church was organized as a A.M.E. Zion Church and was named White's Chapel. The building served as both a church and a community school. When families began to move out of the area, the church and the school closed. The ground was to revert back to the living heirs, but like so many others, it did not. As the church no longer had a pastor, all properties went to the Kentucky Conference. This information was furnished by a granddaughter of Joe Hewlett, Mrs. Caldwell Smith of Madisonville. *-Submitted by Dorothy Miller Shoulders*

Madisonville Baptist Church-First Building-1876-1912

Salem Missionary Baptist Church

Salem Missionary Baptist Church is located about seven-tenths of a mile east of Mortons Gap just off Highway 813.

Salem was organized Sept. 18, 1841, with 15 members. Bro. Gabriel Sisk was the first pastor.

Church services were held from house to house for several months, until a suitable place could be secured on which to build a meeting house. The first spot selected was donated by a Mr. Littlepage, but for some reason the title could not be obtained. A plot of ground was then donated by Mr. Rubin Loving at McDowell's Lick, where the first building was erected. The building was constructed of logs and did not have any heat for several years.

In October, 1868, a deed was received from Mr. Gabriel Lovan for the land on which to build the present church. It was completed the following year under the ministry of Bro. John O'Bryan. There have been many improvements over the years. The Sanctuary was completely renovated in 1984.

Our present pastor is Bro. Kenneth Johnston. Our average Sunday School attendance is 140. Our other ministries include an active youth department, training union, W.M.U., and Brotherhood. *- Submitted by Mrs. Dixie Suthard, Clerk*

St. Mary's Episcopal Church

St. Mary's Episcopal Church had its beginning over 100 years ago in the dream of a young woman who had become familiar with the Episcopal services while attending school in Louisville. Mary Belmont Morton interested three other young women in the church, and these four women took instructions under the Episcopal rector in Henderson. Then on Nov. 21, 1881, the first Episcopal service was held in Madisonville in the Christian Church. Bishop Thomas Underwood Dudley confirmed Mary Belmont Morton, Corine Browning, Ella Randall and Mary Weatherly.

Through the enthusiasm of these four communicants, in 1883 the Diocese of Kentucky purchased a lot (where West Broadway School now stands) as the site of a future church but this lot was sold four years later.

The records show only seven members being confirmed during the next 25 years. The handful of communicants and a few of their friends conducted Episcopal services from time to time in other church buildings and in their homes. Not until 1908 was interest in an Episcopal Church building revived when Francis Eugene Cordier, Edward Louis Rash, Harry Taliaferro, Mrs. Curtis B. Johnson and Robert Smith Dulin were confirmed. These people, together with Mr. and Mrs. Frank Wake and Dr. C.B. Johnson of the Episcopal Mission in Earlington became the foundation of the present church. In 1912 another lot, at 163 North Main Street where the church now stands, was purchased and two years later plans were drawn for the new building. In June of 1917, St. Mary's Episcopal Church was dedicated with the Rev. Clarence Buxton as the Deacon-in-Charge.

For the 11 years of the Rev. Clarence Buxton's residency, St. Mary's had a steady growth. But with his departure in 1927, a rapid decline in attendance and membership began. The Rev. R.L. Brown was rector from 1922 to 1929, and the Rev. Charles Wulf from 1929 to 1933. A number of members died or moved away from Madisonville during these years. With the arrival of the depth of the depression, St. Mary's became unable to be self-supporting. The Rev. Charles Wulf was the last resident rector for 20 years. Occasional services were held by ministers from Hopkinsville, but by 1949 only 10 communicants remained.

In 1947, the Rev. Ben Tinsley of Owensboro began holding services at St. Mary's on Sunday nights. St. Mary's began the long trek back. A vestry was formed and church officers elected. A Parish House was built behind the church to house Sunday School classes as well as business and social meetings. Training classes were held for acolytes; a men's Bible Class was organized; the Altar Guild was reorganized; a Hammond organ was installed; and the church underwent a general renovation. Christmas Eve midnight services were begun. The Rev. Ben Tinsley left St. Mary's in 1952.

By 1953, there were 40 communicants and 85 baptized members, enough to justify the Diocesan Department of Missions to send a full-time resident minister to Madisonville. In June of 1953, the Rev. Taylor Stevenson, Jr., a native of Owensboro who had just completed his training at the Virginia Theological Seminary, arrived in Madisonville with his wife and children. During the four years of the Rev. Taylor Stevenson's tenure, his emphasis upon lay evangelism resulted in an increase in communicant strength from 40 to over 100. An effort was made to make the church, even though small, a force in the community. A kindergarten was started to serve both member and non-member families. The AA group was invited to hold its meetings in the Parish Hall, and the rector served as an unofficial "Chaplain". An addition to the Parish House was built to house the growing church.

In the fall of 1957, the Rev. James M. Stoney, Jr., assumed the duties of rector. During his tenure, St. Mary's finally reached the end of the long trek back to self support. In 1960, St. Mary's was removed from Mission status and granted full Parish Status. There were 207 communicants and 261 baptized members. The Rev. James Stoney was followed by the Rev. Kimball Underwood who served as rector for nine months.

Then in May of 1963, the Rev. Custis Fletcher, Jr., who had been raised in Paducah, came to St. Mary's from Snyder, TX. Previously he had been rector of Holy Trinity in Gainesville, FL and had served as a foreign missionary in Brazil for 15 years. Under the Rev. Fletcher's leadership over the next 15 years, emphasis was placed on seeking Christian solutions to social problems of the day, and St. Mary's continued to grow. The Rev. Fletcher retired in November of 1978.

On Sept. 15, 1979, the Rev. Robert A. King assumed the duties of rector at St. Mary's. He came from Cleveland, OH with his wife and daughter. Since his arrival in Madisonville, the congregation has been challenged to new heights of lay evangelism. Many members have become involved in local and area retreats and renewal movements. They have been serving in many capacities, both locally and at the Diocesan level. Services have been more frequent at the hospital and nursing homes, as well as in the church building itself. A community support program for the chronically mentally ill meets at St. Mary's twice a week. It is sponsored by the Pennyroyal Mental Health Center. Regular Sunday Services are at 8:30 and 10:45 a.m. and a midday service is held at 12:10 p.m. on Fridays.

The rector is now being assisted by two deacons, the Rev. Sam Gilkey from Hopkinsville, and the Rev. Tom Mills of Madisonville (ordained June 14, 1987). Another member of St. Mary's, Eva Markham, is now studying to become a deacon in the near future.

A number of a recent remodeling projects have kept the church building modern and in good repair without destroying the beauty of the original building. For example, new stained glass windows designed by members of the congregation were installed and matching needlepoint kneelers were made by other members.
Submitted by Roberta Brinkley

St. Mary's Episcopal Church

The Ilsley Presbyterian Church group in September of 1926

Mortons Gap Methodist Sunday School Group 1924

The original Good Hope Church in 1908

The Nortonville Christian Church Group in 1923

Special Features

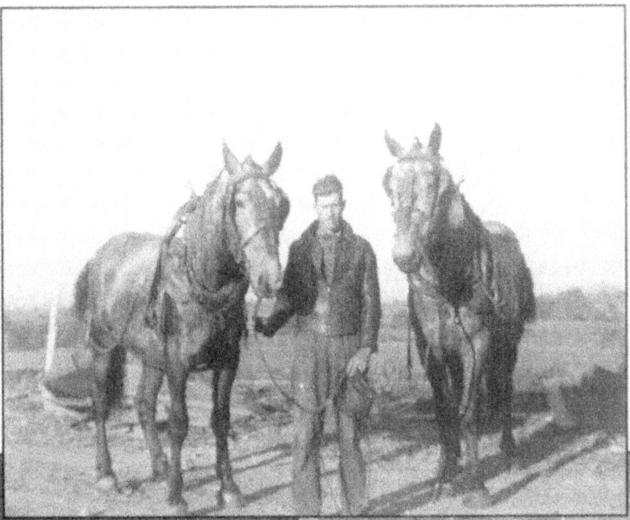

Louis Wilson and team, won the pulling contest at Hopkins Co. Fair in 1939.

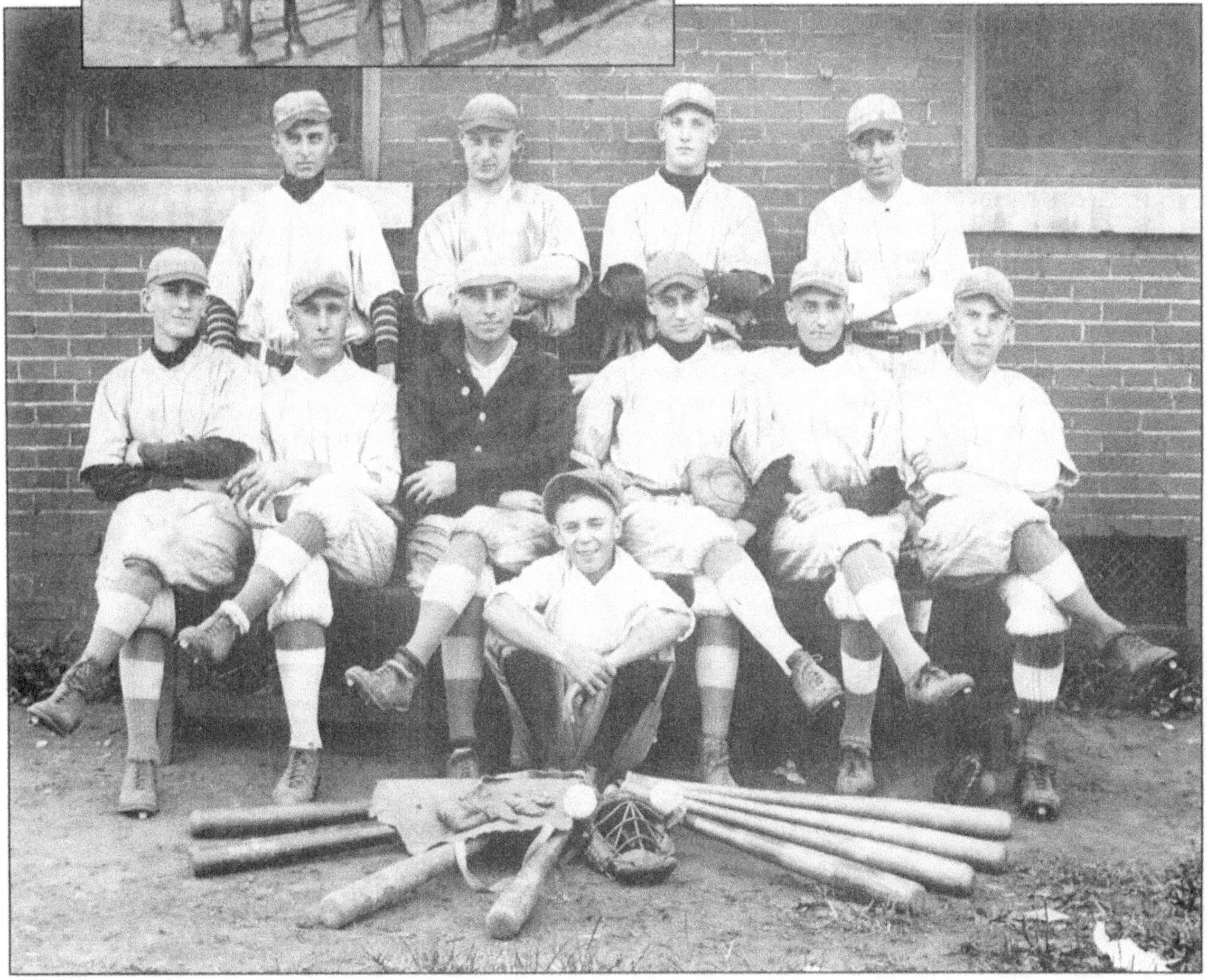

Earlington City Ball Team in the 1920's. Standing, L to R: Paul King, Gup Vinson, Harold Parnell, and Earl O'Bannon. Seated L to R: Rex Hamby, Dutch Deshon, Marvin Mitchell, Carl Umstead, Neal Spillman, and Tippy Foster. In front: Curtis Rule

THE BIG SNOW OF 1917-18

Mr. Marvin Blue of Hanson, who is 91 years old and will be married 70 years on Apr. 19, 1988, recalls the big snow of 1917-18.

The Blue family had just taken a large load of dark air-cured tobacco to Henderson, KY. On this the seventh night of December of 1917, the Big Snow started. The next day, the snow on the roads was too deep to travel. The driver of the wagon left the horses in Henderson and came back on a train. The horses stayed in Henderson about 10 days. Haden and Langley Blue rode to Henderson on the Little Dixie train and brought the team and wagon home.

Several days after the snow, the roads were still closed. Neighbors in the New Salem Community made a snow plow and hooked eight horses to it. With the help of about 25 men with scoop shovels, they cleaned out the road to Ashbysburg. The next day, they hooked up more horses to the plow and cleaned out from New Salem to Slaughters. The following day, the first mail was delivered from Slaughters and Ashbysburg.

Another weather-related incident recalled by Mr. Blue was in 1892 when he was about five years old. He tells that in January, the weather was so bad that rain and sleet formed a four inch thick sheet of ice. Some people drove nails into leather straps and tied them to their shoes. Mr. Blue said they had a steep hill behind the house. One afternoon, he slid down this hill on a plank. He made it to the bottom but couldn't get back up the hill. Laying down on the ice, he was found just before dark, about frozen.

Mr. Blue's father fastened ice shoes to his horses feet and they would haul a load of tobacco to market every day for several days.
-Submitted by Franklin W. Livingston

THE CONFEDERATE MONUMENT

On Sept. 22, 1904, the first movement to erect a monument to the memory of the Confederate war dead was begun by Mrs. Elizabeth Pearce at a meeting of the Second Kentucky Brigade held in Earlington, KY. Mrs. Pearce was the widow of Captain James W. Pearce who died at Shiloh. Others who worked with Mrs. Pearce were Major F.B. Harris, Captain L.D. Hockersmith, Adjutant H.R. Mills and Captain A. Tinder.

The unveiling was the climax of a two day reunion held in Madisonville on May 27 and 28, 1909. The big day began with a parade in the morning. Many former Confederate soldiers, Company E of Madisonville and Company G of Earlington, along with many prominent citizens marched with the United Daughters of the Confederacy.

A large reviewing stand was built in front of the courthouse. The main address at the ceremonies was delivered by General Bennett H. Young of Louisville before a crowd of 10,000. Mrs. Pearce presided at the unveiling of the monument.

The monument is located on the southwest corner of the courtyard. At a cost of $2000.00, it is 29 1/2 feet high from the base to the top of the statue and 9 1/2 feet square in circumference. The statue was made in Rome, Italy and stands 7 feet high. The Confederate soldier is standing at ease with his rifle at parade rest. The base was made in Warren County, KY and bears the inscription "Erected 1909 by U.D.C. of Hopkins County, to the memory of our Confederate dead 1861-1865".

Those who favored the Union Army approached the Fiscal Court for permission to erect a monument for the Union dead. They were given permission to do so on the northwest corner of the courtyard, but never did.

May 28, 1909-The Confederate Monument was unveiled on the Courthouse lawn

Years later, the rifle was struck by lightning leaving only the top of the barrel and the base of the butt. Today, the Confederate soldier still stands, with out his rifle, as a tribute to the Confederate dead.
Compiled by Debbie Knight Hammonds from Harold Ledbetter's notes. Photo courtesy of Harold Ledbetter

COURTHOUSES OF HOPKINS COUNTY

The first Courthouse in Hopkins County was built in 1807 at a cost of $329.00. The Courthouse was of logs seven inches thick, twenty feet square, eighteen feet high with a jointed shingled roof.

In 1825, the log Courthouse was replaced with a frame building.

On July 13, 1835, the Court deemed the Courthouse unsafe, ruling that it would "in all probability shortly fall and that the same is not susceptible of being repaired." The following men were appointed commissioners to draft a plan for a new brick Courthouse: Lawson Robertson, Samuel Morton, James Armstrong, Benjamin L. Todd, John M. Whobey, Burwell R. Bacon and Sam Woodson.

In 1840, a brick Courthouse was built and this structure stood until Confederate General Hylan Benton Lyon ordered his troops to burn it in December of 1864. The records were all saved as they were ordered removed from the Courthouse by General Lyon. The Courthouse was one of seven that General Lyon's troops burned in 23 days.

In 1866, a new brick Courthouse was built to replace the one that was burned. The county jail was located behind the Courthouse. Prisoners were known to yell obscenities at the people on the Courthouse square. So when the new Jail was erected in 1899, the location was moved across to East Center Street.

The 1866 Courthouse stood until 1892 when it was razed to make way for another structure that was completed the same year. It is the new structure built in 1892 that is used in the gold seal that embosses the front cover of this book.

Hopkins County Courthouse in 1910

A cistern was dug in 1897 on the front lawn of the Courthouse to furnish water for the downtown area of Madisonville. The cistern was twenty-five feet in circumference and thirty feet deep. It is not known when it ceased to be used. There was an iron fence around the Courthouse which was removed in 1912.

In 1935, officials again elected to build a new Courthouse. During the construction in 1935 and 1936, law offices and Court were located in the old cigar factory on the corner of West Center and Seminary Streets. This building is presently occupied by Todd's Furniture.

The 1935 structure, with few changes made, is still the Courthouse of Hopkins County today.

Source: Harold Ledbetter Collection, Compiled by Debbie Knight Hammonds

COAL MINING IN HOPKINS COUNTY

When the early settlers first came to Hopkins County, there was an abundance of wood easy to obtain for a fuel supply. If the presence of coal was noticed, there was no mention of it. The first known use of coal in Hopkins County was when coal was burned in a store operated by Weir and Wilkins on the north side of East Center Street opposite the north entrance of the courthouse. This coal was brought from Pittsburgh, PA in a barrel.

The first known use of Hopkins County coal was when in 1836, a local blacksmith, Jack Woolfolk, mined coal on Hunting Branch, located between Madisonville and Earlington, for use in his forge. In 1837, a survey of the geology of Hopkins County was conducted by the Kentucky Geological Survey that mentioned the presence of coal. In 1838, the first deed reservation of coal rights was noted. This was for a tract of 200 acres located on Sugar Creek.

On Jan. 11, 1856, the Hopkins Mastodon Coal and Iron Mining and Manufacturing Company was incorporated in Hopkins County with capital stock of $5,000,000,00. Shares sold for $100 each. The disturbance of the civil war suspended interest in Hopkins County coal.

When the American Contract Company completed the section of the Evansville, Henderson and Nashville Railroad into Earlington in 1870 interest in Hopkins County coal was renewed. A group of eastern capitalists, with interest in the railroads, organized the St. Bernard Coal Company. St. Bernard was named in honor of Bernard N. Farran, a member of the construction firm of Farran and Rutter. The first Board of Directors was Bernard Farran, Colonel E.G. Sebree, John B. Atkinson, George C. Atkinson, Henry B. Hanson, E.W. Hopper and W.H. Howe. Colonel Sebree was elected first president and John B. Atkinson was first secretary-treasurer.

In the summer of 1870, St. Bernard opened the No. 11 Mine in the north-west part of Earlington and in the fall the No. 9 Mine was opened. Combined production from these mines amounted to 3,864 tons of coal for which the company received $9,872.53 or $2.555 per ton. When the Elizabethtown-Paducah Railroad was completed, St. Bernard opened the St. Charles Mine in 1872.

The Diamond Coal and Mining Company opened their Diamond Mine at Mortons Gap in late 1872. Their holdings were acquired by St. Bernard in 1882. The Hecla Coal Company opened the Hecla Mine in 1873 just west of Earlington. The No. 9 coal seam was opened by a shaft, 50 feet deep. This was the first shaft dug in Hopkins County.

The Crabtree Coal Mining Company, in 1883, opened Crabtree Mine at Ilsley. This mine, by underground and stripping, continued in production until 1952.

The Clifton Coal Company opened their Clifton Mine near the Hopkins-Christian County line in 1883. Clifton Coal Company built 34 coke ovens and in March 1887, became the first coke producers in Kentucky.

In March 1886, a dispute over wages occurred between miners and the St. Bernard Coal Company at Earlington. A group of miners left and went to Barnsley where they formed the Co-Operative Coal Company. When the mine was opened, each miner working there owned a share in the company.

As the legend goes, Mr. Conrad Reinecke was on a train enroute to Tennessee to view coal property. When the train stopped in Madisonville, he got off and exclaimed "Eureka, I have found it"! In 1886, the Reinecke Coal Mining Company opened their Eureka

Mine by a shaft 382 feet deep to the No. 9 coal seam. This was the deepest shaft in the state at this time. The mine continued in production until 1939.

The Madisonville Coal Company opened the Madisonville Mine in 1891. This is more commonly known as the Victoria Mine. The mine was opened by a shaft 141 feet deep to the No. 11 coal seam and in 1894, the shaft was extended to 265 feet deep to the No. 9 coal seam. The mine was last owned by Brent Hart who closed the mine in 1937.

In 1892, the Oak Hill Coal and Mining Company opened the Oak Hill Mine south-east of Mortons Gap. This mine was subsequently operated by the Woodstock Coal Company, Oak Hill Mining Company and the Oak Hill Coal Company. The mine was closed in 1912.

The Carbondale Mine was opened in 1894 by the Carbondale Coal and Coke Company at Carbondale. A second opening was made in 1903 and both mines continued in operation until sometime between 1917 and 1919.

Sometime before 1898, the Kington-Wolfe Mine was opened by W.W. Kington on the west side of US 41-A at Mortons Gap. This mine operated until 1906.

In 1894, St. Bernard opened the South Diamond Mine which continued in operation until May 1926. The Barnsley Mine was opened in 1899 and continued until 1912.

The Arnold Mine was the last mine opened by St. Bernard before the turn of the century. It was in operation until 1929.

In 1902, the Nortonville Coal Company opened the Nortonville No. 1 Mine near the intersection of the Evansville, Henderson and Nashville Railroad with the Elizabethtown and Paducah Railroad at Nortonville. Later the company became the Nortonville Coal and Coke Company. In 1912 it was incorporated as the Norton Coal Mining Company and in 1925, it became Norton Coal Corporation. The No. 1 Mine operated until 1942. The Nortonville No. 2 Mine was started in 1904 and continued until 1921. The Nortonville No. 3 Mine in the No. 14 seam operated from 1920 until 1925.

The Rose Creek Mine opened in 1904 by the Rose Creek Coal and Mining Company was the first mine opened in the No. 14 coal seam. The mining in the No. 14 seam was discontinued in 1906 when a shaft to the No. 9 seam was started. This was completed in 1907 and mining in the seam continued until 1921.

The Buffalo Creek Coal Mining Company opened the Daniel Boone Mine in 1904 on the Elizabethtown-Paducah Railroad between Nortonville and St. Charles. The mine was subsequently owned by Daniel Boone Company, Sterling Coal and Coke Company and Sterling Coal Company. From 1920 until 1932, Sterling Coal Company operated the Seminole Mine in the No. 14 coal seam. In 1944, Sterling Coal Company became the Daniel Boone Coal Company and mining operations ceased.

The St. Bernard Coal Company opened their Fox Run Mine in 1904 to offset the decrease in production when they closed the St. Charles Mine. Fox Run Mine ceased operation in 1940. In 1913, St. Bernard purchased the Luton Mine which was opened in 1911. The mine operated until 1925. St. Bernard also opened their Nisbet and Sisk Mines in 1913. Both of these Mines closed in 1924.

In 1904, the Royal Coal Company opened the Royal Mine better known as the Sunset Mine. This mine was located on McCoy Avenue near the City of Madisonville Street Department building. The mine was purchased by West Kentucky Coal Company in 1924 and closed in 1932.

In 1907, Kington Coal Company opened the White City Mine. In 1920 Kington sold to Brent Hart in what was acclaimed the "biggest coal deal ever" in Hopkins County. The White City Mines were closed in 1940 and the Moss Hill No. 3 was opened in 1944 and continued operations until 1947.

The Nebo Mine was opened in the No. 14 coal seam in 1907

1907-Sunset Mine on South Kentucky in Madisonville

by the Nebo Consolidated Coal and Coke Company. In 1914, the mine was sold to the Nebo Coal Company and continued operating until 1916.

In 1911, the Coil Coal Company was incorporated and opened the Coil Mine. The mine was opened by a shaft 280 feet deep to the No. 11 coal seam. The mine was located north of the Hopkins County fairgrounds in north-east Madisonville. This mine was the site of the first major disaster in which five miners were killed by an explosion. In 1924, the mine was acquired by the West Kentucky Coal Company. It was closed in 1939.

After many years of promotion, the Grapevine Coal Company finally opened the Grapevine Mine in 1917. The mine opening was originally a shaft but a slope was dug later for easier access to the mine. It continued production until 1965.

In 1920, The Boyce Coal Company leased coal rights and one acre of surface rights from Horace W. Cox, et.al. In 1922, the assets of the bankrupt company were conveyed to the Finley Coal Company. Finley opened the Finley Mine by a shaft 280 feet deep to the No. 11 coal seam. In 1925, Finley Mine was the site of the second major disaster in Hopkins County when five miners were killed in an explosion. In December 1925, Finley Mine was conveyed to Trio Coal Company. The mine is best remembered as Trio Mine. The mine was closed in 1947.

On May 1, 1924, the St. Bernard Coal Company was sold to West Kentucky Coal Company of Sturgis, KY. The first mine opened by the new owners was the North Diamond Mine Complex consisting eventually of No. 1, No. 2 and No. 3. When No. 2 worked out, it was closed in 1950.

The Blue Valley Mine was opened by Blue Valley Coal Corporation in 1925. The last year of production for Blue Valley Mine was 1940.

In 1920, something entirely new in coal mining was introduced to Hopkins County when Sunlight Mine became the first strip mine in Hopkins County and Western Kentucky. Between 1920 and 1929, a total of eight strip mines were in operation in Hopkins County. These were: Sunlight at Grapevine, Western Collieries at Crabtree, Dempster east of St. Charles, Dawson Daylight at Charleston, Hawley-McIsaac at Carbondale and Coiltown, Boddie-Powell at Grapevine, Magic Collieries at Hamby Station and Midstate at White City. The stock market crash of 1929 brought a temporary end to strip mining.

In the time period from 1925 to present, Dawson Daylight opened three large mines, the North Opening (1928-1951), Dawson Springs Mine (1936-1961) and New Daylight (1951-1965). West Kentucky Coal Company opened Hecla (1941-1946),

East Diamond (1945-1972) (first mine in Hopkins County to produce one million tons of coal annually), Pleasant View (1948-1965), Justin Potter opened Williams No. 4 (1933-1972), Stony Point (1949-1957) and Fies (1950-1980). In 1955 Potter sold out to West Kentucky Coal Company.

Norton Coal Corporation opened the No. 5 (1926-1928) and the East Opening (1942-1952). In 1952 Norton temporarily ceased mining operations. However, in 1959, Norton reentered the mining picture with their mine the Bon Venture between Mortons Gap and White Plains. This mine was operated by Norton, Coy and Corder, Franklin Hunt and wound up as South Hopkins Coal Company. The mines at this location continued in operations until 1986.

The New Coal Corporation opened the New Coal Mine on the M H & E Railroad east of Anton in 1930 and continued in operation until 1949.

Than Rice, et.al. operated Charleston Collieries, Magnolia Mining Company and Coiltown Mining Company. Their mines were Morris No. 1 (1926-1945) Red Bud (1945-1958) Magnolia (1947-1955) Klondike (1952-1964).

In 1949 the Bell and Zoller Coal Company opened the Oriole Mine west of Madisonville in the No. 11 coal seam and in 1967, the slope was extended to the No. 9 seam. In 1971, a new slope on the north side of the Laffoon Trail was dug to the No. 9 coal seam. About this time Bell and Zoller was purchased by Zeigler Coal Company which continued mining until 1980.

In 1963, the West Kentucky Coal Company was sold to Island Creek Coal Company and became the West Kentucky Division. In 1968, the Providence No. 1 Mine was opened on 814 near the Hopkins-Webster County line. The mine is still in operation.

In 1973, the last attempt at mining the No. 14 coal seam was started by the Pittsburgh and Midway Coal Mining Company at their Drake IV Mine located off Rose Creek Road west of Madisonville. P&M briefly operated an underground mine in 1958 on an experimental basis at their Colonial Mine. The Drake IV Mine ceased operations in 1982.

In 1983, the Green River No. 9 Mine was opened east of Anton by the Green River Coal Company. The mine is in full production.

The last and most recent underground mine opened in Hopkins County was in 1986 when the Sextet Mining Company opened the West Hopkins Mine west of Coiltown near KY 109.

There have been numerous "local, wagon, or truck" mines, as they are called by the Kentucky Department of Mines and Minerals, in Hopkins County through the years. As they were not always under the jurisdiction of the State, their names and locations have been lost forever.

In 1936, Leslie Lofton opened a small strip mine west of Madisonville and Hopkins County re-entered strip mining. In 1937 his holdings were acquired by the Sentry Coal Company and large scale strip mining began. Sentry ceased stripping operations in 1947.

In 1940, Morgan Coal Company began stripping south of White Plains. This operation continued until 1954. Also in 1940, Young Coal Company started stripping operations which continued until 1949. Smith and Stokes began stripping near Blue Valley in 1941 and continued until 1948.

In 1943, the Badgett Brothers began strip mining operations in the North Diamond area. Their operations in this area continued until about 1965. Ruby Construction Company began stripping in the area between Earlington and the Blue Valley Mine. Their operations continued until about 1952.

The Industrial Coal Company began stripping in the Beulah area in 1943 and continued until about 1961.

In 1943 Mauger Construction Company began stripping in the Pond River area south-east of Madisonville. In 1946, this was acquired by Tertling Brothers, Inc. Peabody Coal Company bought Tertling Brothers, Inc. and changed the operation to the Pond River Mine. The mine operated until 1960.

In 1944 the Homestead Coal Company began mining in the Fox Run Hills between Mortons Gap and St. Charles. This operation continued until about 1955 when it was sold to the Peabody Coal Company. In 1956 Peabody Coal Company opened the White City Mine and gradually the Homestead operation was phased out. White City was closed in 1965.

In 1946, the Pittsburgh and Midway Coal Mining Company of Pittsburgh, KS acquired the extensive holding of the Lee Schmetzer estate from Kelly Bennett, et. al. and the Colonial Mine was opened. The mine has been in continuous operation now for 41 years.

In 1967 the Cimarron Coal Corporation started their Volunteer Mine in the Pond River area south-east of Madisonville. This mine is still in operation.

The last large surface mine opened in Hopkins County was in June 1978, when the Pittsburgh and Midway Coal Mining Company opened the Pleasant Hill Mine south of White Plains. This mine continued in operation until 1986.

As in the case of underground mines, there have been numerous small strip mines opened in Hopkins County and records of their existence do not remain. This is unfortunate but the memory of their existence will remain in the minds of those miners who toiled to mine the coal as they earned a living. -Submitted by J. Harold Utley

Crabtree Coal Mining Company

Thomas Crabtree organized the Crabtree mine in 1882 and began operation in 1883. The mine owned several thousand acres as Mr. Crabtree began buying large parcels of land along Caney Creek and Caney Fork in 1852.

The president of the company was Mr. A. Howell, a banker and prominent citizen of Clarksville, TN. He was also past Mayor of that city and instrumental in establishing a system of free public schools in Clarksville.

Edward Ilsley, a well respected banker and businessman from Philadelphia was Vice-President of Crabtree Coal Co. The community of Ilsley Station, Ilsley Post Office, and Ilsley itself were all named in his honor.

Two brothers, Richard M. (Dick) and John G. Salmon were among those to settle in Crabtree. They built and operated a store, which became the Crabtree Company Store. Dick Salmon, at the age of twenty eight, became the company's secretary-treasurer, as well as general manager. John Salmon, along with H.M. Eskridge became the company bookkeepers, and John Harlan was the mine foreman and also the school district representative.

The mine entrance was just northwest of Ilsley (Crabtree). In the mine's early days, the men used picks and shovels to dig the coal out and small rail cars pulled by mules to haul the coal out of the mine and to the tipple.

By 1903 the mine was using Harrison mining machines with a capacity of one thousand tons of coal per day and an H.K. Porter narrow gauge engine called a dinky, (John Benjamin Martin was engineer) to take coal to the tipple. At the tipple was a shaker screen that separated the coal into eleven different sizes, or grades. It was then loaded into standard size railroad cars and the mine locomotive (also called Dinky), with engineer Harley Adcock, would pull them two miles south down the spur track to Ilsley Station. (See Ilsley Station) The cars were then coupled with an Illinois Central Railroad train, to be delivered to buyers. Much of the coal was bought by the railroad to power the locomotives.

Crabtree Coal Mining Co. contributed a great deal to the growth and well-being of Crabtree.

1938-Harley Adcock (in overalls) was the engineer

The company built two schools, one white (see Ilsley School) and one black (see section on black schools), two churches one white and one black, and graded and maintained, without cost to the county, ten miles of road in and around Crabtree.

In 1923, Norton Coal Co. bought Crabtree Mine, as well as other mines in the county, such as Sunlight, Old Coiltown, Magic, Nortonville, and Carbondale. The Chairman of the Board of Directors was Monroe Linear, two other board members were Sterling Linear, and R.L. Schlottman.

Norton Coal Co. at Ilsley, operated until the late 1950's, then closed. - *Submitted by Sharon Riggs Johnston*

FORMER GOV. RUBY LAFFOON'S BIRTHPLACE

Ruby Laffoon was born Jan. 15, 1869 in a cabin in the country, four miles east of Madisonville, on what in that day was the Madisonville-Greenville Road. When KY 70 and 85 were built, this road was abandoned and is now grown over with grass and trees, with only a dip in the ground and an old fence to show where the road was.

Former Governor Ruby Laffoon

The family cabin was located on the farm of William Perry and his mother, Arcolia Perry, near the Liberty Baptist Church. The Perry's offered the cabin, the land it was on, and an entrance from KY 70-85 to the property to the Historical Society several times.

In 1987 the Historical Society voted to remove what remained of the old cabin to the vacant lot next to the Historical Society, 107 Union Street, Madisonville. Mr. Perry hauled the usable logs and all the chimney rocks for the Society, to their lot free of charge. The Society wrote letters and asked for donations to help restore the cabin as it was in Gov. Laffoon's boyhood. The response was overwhelming in money and items to place in the cabin.

Ruby was the son of John Bedlow and Martha Earle Laffoon and had two sisters older than him. His father was a Confederate soldier. When the war was over and he returned home, he found that the Union Army had burned his home. He proceeded to build this cabin, 18 x 38 feet with two rooms and a small attic, for his family. It was built around 1864.

We do not know how long the Laffoon family lived there after Ruby was born, but they owned the farm for several years after they moved to another place. From time to time the cabin was occupied by others, then it got in bad repair and Mr. Perry used it to store hay in. But it finally got so bad, Mr. Perry quit using it. It continually began to rot, until it was just a stack of rotten logs for the most part. Only 32 of the original logs were usable.

On Sept. 8, 1986, the Historical Society broke ground for the foundation of the cabin on Union Street, with Mrs. Martha Lou Robinson, Gov. Laffoon's daughter moving the first shovel of dirt.

Jess McGary and Harold Ledbetter oversaw the work, while Alfred Ross Miller of White Plains saw to the rebuilding, as he has built a lot of log cabins. Mr. Miller did a good job on the rebuilding, using what old logs were useable and then having to purchase new ones to replace those too rotten to use, including new hand made shingles for the roof.

By Mar. 12, 1987, the cabin was roughly together, however no mud had been placed between the logs and it was about half shingled. By June 18, the outside was complete except for windows and doors. Dec. 1, 1987, the cabin had been completely built on the outside and hundreds of items were donated to furnish it with, along with a few items which belonged to Gov. Laffoon.

The inside of the cabin is now being furnished and it is hoped that in two, maybe three, months it will be ready for public inspection. It will be as near like it was when Laffoon was a boy and lived there, and will be a wonderful historical show place of Hopkins County.

The restored cabin in which former Gov. Ruby Laffoon was born

Heretofore, the only recognition that we had given to the fact that Ruby Laffoon is the only Hopkins Countian to ever serve as governor, is a plaque placed in the courthouse yard stating this fact. It is too bad that we had to wait 52 years after he was governor to make his birthplace an interesting and important bit of history, showable in our county.

Ruby Laffoon was Governor of the Commonwealth of Kentucky 1931-1935. - *Submitted by Harold Ledbetter*

HOPKINS COUNTY JAIL

The Hopkins County Jail, the predecessor to the Hopkins County Detention Center, was built in 1899. The Fiscal Court awarded the contract to the Pauly Jail Building and Manufacturing Company of St. Louis, MO at a cost of $7500.00.

Hopkins County Jail is on the left-Madisonville City Hall on the right

The architect was W.C. Morton of Madisonville. The building committee was James Nichols, W.E. Jagoe and John G.B. Hall. The land, on East Center Street adjacent to the City Hall, was donated to Hopkins County by the City of Madisonville. Iron work from the former Jail was reused in this building. The Jail also included living quarters for the Jailer. The money to pay for the Jail construction was borrowed from the Hopkins County Bank.

In the early 1970's the Jail would not pass the state requirements and so a new Jail was considered. In 1975, bids were received for the new Jail to be erected at the rear of the Courthouse. Renshaw Construction of Madisonville was awarded the contract. Daniel W. Figert and Associates were the architects.

The new building, now called the Detention Center, was opened on Feb. 2, 1977 with 26 inmates being housed. The building cost $600,000.00 and was paid for with revenue sharing bonds. - *Compiled by Debbie Knight Hammonds*

THE KENTUCKY KARDINAL DANCE BAND

Mark Eastin of Madisonville believes his only "Claim to Fame" to have been his association with the "Kentucky Kardinal Dance Band". Mr. Eastin was the manager and played the banjo.

While cruising abroad, as members of the Complement of the Steamship President Arthur, in the summer of 1925, the band introduced "American Dixie Land Jazz" to the city of Jerusalem. The band was royally received and entertained by prominent Jewish leaders and the British Government (which was then governing Palestine), with much pomp, fanfare and enthusiasm.

Later in the cruise, the band also introduced Dixie Land Music in several other cities and countries along the coast of the Mediterranean Sea which had never before, at the time, had Dixie Land Jazz presented to them by an American Orchestra.

Other places the band performed were New York City; Halifax, Nova Scotia; Canada; Marseille, France; Monte Carlo, Monaco; Naples, Italy; Cadiz, Spain; Beirut, Turkey; and Alexandria and Cairo, Egypt.

The Kentucky Kardinal Dance Band with Mark E. Eastin Jr. on the far left with the banjo

OLIVE BRANCH CEMETERY

The Olive Branch Cemetery was first used in the 1850's, not long after the church of the same name was instituted. Sir names of those who were among the first to be buried there were Boyd, Springfield, Tapp, Buchanan, Waller, Bowles, Brown and others.

It was Elizabeth Springfield who suggested that the new church and cemetery be named Olive Branch in loving memory of the church and cemetery that they had left behind in Person County, NC prior to their journey by covered wagon into the wilderness of Kentucky, which had formerly been a county of (THE OLD DOMINION) Virginia.

By the time of the war between the states, the cemetery had become quite prominent and was considerably used. Dr. James Waller (1836-1864), a member of the Confederate forces, was mortally wounded while in the saddle at Canton, KY. A few days after the battle, his body was exhumed from the temporary burial and brought by oxcart to his native Hopkins County and laid to rest in the Olive Branch Cemetery. This sorrowful event is related in detail in "The Partisan Rangers" by Col. Adam R. Johnson, copyright 1904.

Another incident of which I am familiar is that of great great Aunt Jane Ellen Veazey (1820-1882). Her husband, John Comer Veazey (1809-1870), and numerous ones of their descendants were laid to rest in the Veazey Cemetery, Veazey, KY, which is about four miles north of Manitou. Aunt Jane had a problem. She had numerous gold teeth and grave robbers usually practiced their art in remote cemeteries like the one at Veazey. Her solution was for her to be buried in the more public cemetery at Olive Branch where the grave robbers would refuse to ply their trade. She was buried there in 1882 with no other family member. Her judgement was good, for her gold teeth were never disturbed in the cemetery at Olive Branch. -*Submitted by Leroy Veazey*

SHAKERAG

There are no two people who would give identical stories on the much debated area of Shakerag. The fact that there is no charter, title or deed to such a place has caused the subject to be most elastic. Some enthusiasts expand it to include their own property, but diminish it elsewhere to exclude someone elses.

I have it on what I consider good authority that the Revolutionary War soldiers from the North Carolina Colony (in what is now Person and Granville County) were of necessity quite shabby and near ragged in appearance as there were no uniforms or pay. Their commanding officer, a Mr. Satterfield, seeing how tattered their

What is left of the James Comer Veazey log home in Shakerag

clothing was, in compassion, referred to them as "my Shakerag boys". The name stuck and after returning to North Carolina, at the war's end, the public admiration for the "Shakerag Boys" caused the entire area to be called Shakerag. Before many decades, the march westward began and a goodly number of people from both Person and Granville Co., NC came by covered wagon through the Cumberland Gap and settled what is now North Hopkins County in the area west of Hanson. With fond memories, it was natural that our forebearers desired to transplant their Shakerag name here. It is also appropriate to state here that they also reused the name of Olive Branch Church also. My family and I have visited both Olive Branch and Shakerag in North Carolina. They are lovely people.

We found that the names Buchanan, Bowles, Compton, Poole, Jones, Clayton, Veazey and others that abounded in Shakerag here still do there also.

My great grandfather, James Louis Veazey, who lived in both of the Shakerags, lived to see Lincoln elected but died before he was inaugurated. His son, Noah Veazey, gave his life for the southern cause.

Of my 67 years, 54 of them have been spent in the hills and valleys of Shakerag. From great grandfather to two of my grandchildren, who live nearby, it is six consecutive generations of Veazeys to dwell here. Some of them, including my father Lee Veazey (1877-1936), spent all of their life here and some of us who left for a season were happy to return.

We love it. -Submitted by Leroy Veazey

TORNADO OF 1940

The following was taken from the "History of the Church of God in Hopkins County, 1909 through 1965 (Cedar Hill Church of God)" compiled in September of 1980.

On Apr. 30, 1940 (Tuesday) the Cedar Hill Church of God was conducting revival services. Bro. Rudolph was pastor at that time. Although there were reports of a storm, many went to church feeling that they would be as safe at the church as any place else. The evangelist, Bro. Houg, had just finished singing, "God Put a Rainbow in the Clouds", when the storm broke out. Sister Nevelyn Butler relates that the storm blew out all the windows on the south side first, and then came back around. The evangelist asked the congregation to get down in the middle isles. At that time the wind lifted the front end of the church up and completely took the wooden frame off the foundation. The floor, pews, pulpit and stove were all left standing intact. The piano was over-turned. No one was seriously injured. Most of the wooden frame of the church ended up on the Arnold Butler's front yard. His house was directly across the street from the church. Wood splinters from the storm remained driven into the front door of the Butler's house for many years after that. Bro. Lloyd Miller states that he was unable to attend the service that night, but three of his boys went. When the storm came up, one of his other sons came running to him and said, "Daddy, Daddy, the church is gone!" Since Bro. Miller lived next door to the church he grabbed a carbide lamp and started out the door. By this time it was pitch dark outside as the power was off all over. However, as the wind was still high, Bro. Miller could not go outside for fear of the lamp being blown out. One by one the boys came to the house, as did the entire church! Sister Butler relates that during the wind, the church bell started to ring. One lady became so frightened, she thought the second coming was at hand. Mattie Rodgers relates that her oldest son Harold, was hit by a piece of flying glass on his cheek, but the injury was not serious. Bro. Miller said that one of his sons who was attending the service, was picked up by the storm, carried over the entire congregation and let down in front of a utility pole. He clung to that pole until the storm was over. Bro. Arnold Butler was also unable to attend the service that night. He said that from across the street, the sight looked like a ball of fire. He ran into the house to protect his young son, Rodney, who was at home. The next day the neighborhood was amazed to drive by and see all the church furniture (pews, etc.) still in their proper places. It was truly a miracle!

GOING TO SCHOOL AT ILSLEY

What a wonderful place to go to school as a youngster. In these small schools, you had the feeling that you were special, that the teacher cared about you as a person. No matter what the problem, it seemed the teacher always had time to listen.

We learned the basics, the three R's, reading 'riting, and 'rithmetic. We learned to do math problems in our head and on the blackboard, not on a calculator. We learned to spell, and were tested in our skills in Spelling Bees. They usually took place on a Friday afternoon. We lined up around the room and were called on one by one to spell, when we missed a word, we had to sit down. The last one left standing, won.

Every morning we had exercises, if the weather permitted they took place outside, if not we did them inside. Then we "Pledge Allegiance To The Flag", sang the "Star Spangled Banner" and "America the Beautiful".

There was no indoor plumbing, but there was a "little house out back" for the girls and one for the boys. These were called privies. If you needed to "go" you raised your hand and asked to be excused. When you were thirsty, there stood a table with a bucket of water on it. A dipper hung on a nail nearby, we dipped the water and filled our cups, usually made from leaf paper. Some of the children from wealthier families, had a boughten collapsable cup.

At Thanksgiving time, we drew turkeys and put them up in the windows and on the blackboard. At Christmas, we had a large tree that we decorated, we drew names and exchanged gifts. We also put on a play and our parents would come and watch. On Valentines Day, each room (our school had three) had a large box covered with red and white crepe paper and decorated with hearts that had been cut-out and glued on. Anyone who brought valentines, put them in one of the boxes, at the designated time, the boxes were opened and valentines delivered.

School dismissed in time for spring planting so we could help at home. - *Submitted by Aminell Riggs Morris*

Captain Stephen Ashby Chapter, Daughters of The American Revolution

The Captain Stephen Ashby Chapter, Daughters of the American Revolution was organized in Madisonville, Kentucky, November 20, 1946.

The twenty-one charter members who obtained their own proof, honored the organizing regent, Mrs. Carl Polley, by naming the chapter for her ancestor, Stephen Ashby, who served as captain in the Revolutionary War. His children were among the first settlers in Hopkins County. Ashbyburg on Green River was named for his son, Stephen Ashby, Jr. The eldest son, Daniel served in the War along with his father and later became State Senator from Henderson County. Hopkins County was formed from Henderson, which was passed and approved by Gov. Christopher Greenup, December 6, 1806. This act was drafted by Senator Daniel Stephens and named for his colleague in the lower house, General Samuel Hopkins.

The objectives of the chapter are: EDUCATION, HISTORIC, PATRIOTIC.

Eighteen Revolutionary soldiers graves are located in Hopkins County.

By, Mrs. Maxey H. Priest, Jr.
D.A.R. Historian

CLUBS, ORGANIZATIONS AND MEMORIAL

Hopkins County Republican Headquarters

The Hopkins County Republican Party is a long standing organization of this county. It dates back to 1860 when the first meeting of the Republican Party of Kentucky was held in the Snowdoun House, which is now 533 Gordon Ave. That two story structure, having been built in 1824 of 16 x 24 inch logs, consisted of four rooms and a dog trot. Builder Snow was given the land in a land grant following the Revolutionary War. It is the oldest house in Hopkins County and of the city of Madisonville.

The H.C.R.P. is now headquartered at 47 North Main St. This is the first permanent headquarters the party has had, and is one of only several permanent headquarters in the state. The land was originally purchased from Kentucky Bank in 1904 by W. H. Arnold and Son. They built the existing building in that same year. The building has been bough and sold five times since 1904, and various businesses have operated there.

This building was acquired for the use of H.C.R.P. in the spring of 1985. It now serves as meeting place for regularly scheduled meetings of the Executive Board, the Republican Womans Club and the Young Republican Organization.

The Hopkins County Republican Organization continues to serve the community by helping people to register to vote, providing food baskets for the needy, sponsoring a fun run, as well as encouraging people to take an active part in local government.

The Hopkins County Republican Headquarters

Pennyrile Arts and Crafts Guild

Munns Schoolhouse is a Hopkins County landmark, located on the Princeton Pike, Highway 70, near Madisonville, which was restored by the Pennyrile Arts and Crafts Guild, through funds from Kentucky Heritage Council, a gift from the Community Improvement Foundation, Guild funds, and public donations of money, labor and gifts in kind.

The first school, located near Clear Creek, was constructed of logs in 1864, when Thomas G. Yates transferred on acre to the Hopkins County School Trustees. The original frame structure on the present site was build in the summer of 1879, and then replaced by the present brick building in 1906. In District 19, it was the first brick one-room school in Hopkins County. The second room was added in 1928. The school was named for Eleanor Munns from a prominent family in school affairs.

From 1879 to 1971 Munns School had been used as a community center for Sunday School, preaching and singing services, Boy Scouts, 4-H Clubs, soup suppers, pie suppers, Halloween parties, wedding showers, family and school reunions, and various other gatherings for the community area. The front room has been restored to a replica of the early school room, a museum for school groups and the general public to visit and enjoy. The back room is the Guild meeting room for programs, workshops, arts and crafts displays, and for the use of various groups and organizations to meet.

One of the first teachers at Munns was said to have been Mrs. Emma Shannon Gatlin. Later teachers mentioned include Delmont Utley (pupil of Mrs. Gatlin), Miss Minnie Dempsey, T. C. O'Bryan, Tom Ligon, Miss Kate Greer, H. F. S. Bailey, Miss Flora Pearce (1898), Mrs. Lizzie Hanks, Mrs. Lula Cavanah Veazey, Mr. and Mrs. Norman Hobgood (1900-01), Oscar McGregor, Miss Cattie Stodgill, Miss Nora Dame, Miss May Dunn, Mrs. Jettie Osburn, Mr. Owen Stinnett, Miss Helen Hoffman, Mrs. Nannie Love Woodruff, Miss Marion Ruby, Mrs. Ernie Todd (12 years), Mrs. May Workman, a Miss Sisk, Miss Maude Wilkey, Mrs. Era Dempsey, Mrs. Ed McCulley, Miss Sory Stinnett, Mr. John Paul Jones, Mrs. Olah Ray Murphey, Miss Mabel Fagan (10 years), Mrs. Aubrey Polley, Mrs. Mabel Nisbet, Mrs. Lennie Hampton, Mrs. Dorothy Teague, and Mr. James Ramsey who was the last teacher in 1955 when closed.

Munns School building was entered in the National Register of Historic Places in Washington, D. C. on August 30, 1983, which gives recognition that the site has historic, architectural and archaeological significance with the context of the community, state and nation. *Submitted by Rella G. Jenkins*

Munns School in 1984 during restoration

In Memory of

David A. Parish
1899-1987

Mayor of Madisonville
1945-1973

Business History

A service station on the Northwest corner of Arch and Main Streets in Madisonville

Employees of the St. Bernard Coal Company Store in Earlington, about 1940. Front Row, L. to R: Dillman Rash, Cammie Fox, Annie Southworth, Lena Hampton Fox, Miss Charlie Davis, Ruby Peyton, Ethel Evans, Ferd Waller, Curtis Rule, Miss Charlie Jennings. Back Row: Luther Lowe, John Coyle, Artie Jones and Otley Vannoy.

REGIONAL MEDICAL CENTER

HOME HEALTH
825-5237

...Surrounded by friends

Good Health care helps get people back home. That's why Home Health is so special. People who need short-term or continuing treatment can receive health care in their own homes. They have sound medical attention at reduced costs with increased convenience. Home is where the heart is. . home where the health is.

REGIONAL MEDICAL CENTER

MADISONVILLE

ALL THE HELP YOU NEED CLOSE TO HOME

Bandy Funeral Home

The history of funeral service in Nortonville can be traced back to the early 1920's. Mr. O. N. Beshear had the first funeral home in Nortonville. He used a horse drawn ambulance and later got a modern motor ambulance. The home was located on Main Street in the building formerly used by Dawson Store. Ligon Beshear became a partner with his father in the funeral business in 1932.

Mr. Bill Lively bought the funeral home from the Beshear's some time later. Mr. Sam Bilbro and son Sybert were also partners with Mr. Lively until they became the owners during the early 1940's. The business again changed owners in 1947 when Martin Gunn bought the funeral home and changed the name to Gunn Funeral Home.

Harold Bennett and Georgia Mary Allen Bandy, both from Greenville, bought the Gunn Funeral Home from Martin Gunn, December, 1951.

Harold graduated from the Kentucky School of Mortuary Science in Louisville, September, 1951. At this time Harold was the youngest funeral director and embalmer in the State of Kentucky to own his own business which was not a family inherited business.

The business operated under the name of Bandy & Gunn Funeral Home and was located in the J. N. Oates house on Main Street. After a short time Mr. Gunn left Nortonville and the funeral home then operated as Bandy Funeral Home.

Many years ago the funeral homes inherited the ambulance service business because their cars were large enough to transport the sick. So, we provided 24 hour ambulance service until December, 1976.

January, 1953 the two story W. G. Putman house on Poplar Street was converted into the funeral home with living quarters upstairs. This building provided a chapel that would seat seventy-five people or could be partitioned into two smaller chapels.

Georgia M. Bandy received her Funeral Directors license in 1955.

In 1956, James Floyd Allen, also of Greenville, Kentucky father of Georgia Bandy, came to work with the funeral home. Mr. Allen retired in 1976.

Realizing the need for a more modern building the Belcher property on Main Street was purchased and a new funeral home was built solely for funeral business. The building was completed May 1964. This funeral home had one chapel that would seat 175 people plus two smaller chapels, showroom, and a small apartment. This was first in the Nortonville area.

The oldest son Michael Bennett Bandy graduated from the Kentucky School of Mortuary Science and received his Embalmers and Funeral Directors license, July, 1972. Mike became a partner with his parents.

As the years passed the business grew and developed.

Across the street from the funeral home the Gatlin, Lena Fox, and Clarence Crane properties were acquired making space for a large paved parking lot. The twenty year old building was completely remodeled inside and out in 1984.

The Bandy's continue to serve the community with the help of their other children, Bobby, Linda, and Mary Beth whenever needed.

BARNETT-STROTHER FUNERAL HOME

Barnett Funeral Home, 108 S. Main St.-Madisonville

The Funeral Home in 1958 at 304 S. Main

2285 N. Main St.-Present location of Barnett-Strother Funeral Home, Inc.

The Barnett-Strother Funeral Home was founded in 1922 as the Barnett Funeral Home by Mr. Tom Barnett and Mr. Delmont Utley. This was the first funeral business in Hopkins County run strictly as a funeral home. The original building was at 109 South Main Street where the Masonic Building is now. In 1924 Mr. Utley sold his interest to Mr. Ben Slaton and the business was moved across the street to the W. A. Morton House at 108 S. Main St. This site is the present location of First Federal Savings & Loan Association. Mr. Slaton sold his interest to Mr. Barnett. Mr. Barnett died in 1931 and his widow Mrs. Mourning Hall Barnett continued to run the business. Over the next few years Mrs. Barnett, her stepson William L. Barnett and her daughters, Mrs. Elizabeth "Betty" Barnett Schmetzer and Mrs. Mary Jo Barnett Crumbaker, all helped in running the funeral home.

Mr. W. Fred Strother started the W. Fred Strother Funeral Home in July 1938 at 406 S. Main St. which was on the south corner of S. Main St. and Hall St. Mr. and Mrs. Strother closed the funeral home and sold all the equipment and the building in 1941 to go to military service. Mr. Strother was turned down for physical problems so they moved to Henderson, Kentucky and worked for Rudy-Rowland Funeral Home until returning to Madisonville in 1943. Mr. and Mrs. Strother bought the Barnett Funeral Home on May 11, 1949 from Mrs. Barnett. The name was soon changed to Barnett-Strother Funeral Home to distinguish between it and the William L. Barnett Funeral Service on E. Center St. run by Mrs. Barnett's stepson.

In 1955 Mr. and Mrs. Strother bought 406 S. Main St. from Mrs. Amelia Ruby and moved back into their original funeral home. The address has been changed to 304 S. Main St. The funeral home stayed here until June 15, 1969. The business was moved to it's present location at 2285 N. Main St. Mr. Strother died May 15, 1975 but Mrs. Artie Mae Strother continued to run the business. Today the business is owned by Mrs. Strother, Steve and Charlene Carson. Steve joined the business full time on July 15, 1969 and Charlene joined June 1, 1983.

The Barnett-Strother Funeral Home has been known for several firsts in the county. It had the first air conditioned chapel, the first permanent organ in the funeral home, the first straight ambulance and the first building built for a funeral home with it's present location.

Beshear Funeral Home, Inc.

Since 1909, in Dawson Springs, Kentucky, there has been a funeral firm operating continuously. This firm, first known as Clark, Beshear and Clark, has always had members of the Beshear family as owners and operators.

It began in a small building on Hunter Street. It's founders were Theodore Clark, Fred Beshear, and Denny Clark, son of Theodore.

In 1912, the firm moved to a new brick building on Railroad Avenue in downtown Dawson Springs. In those days, undertaking and furniture were companion businesses. This happened because furniture makers were also "coffin" makers. The many firms offering "furniture and undertaking", used the downstairs for furniture sales and the upstairs for casket sales and funeral work. In the earliest days it was a "take with you" type of business. Only the coffins were sold and the rest was up to friends, relative and neighbors. A few years later, this gave way to the "funeral director", who went in and did what obviously was very unpleasant to those previously mentioned.

Embalming was begun about the year 1914, by the firm. The original furniture store still thrives at the same location.

In the beginning, all funeral related transportation was by horse drawn hearse. The undertaking firm rented this important commodity to the deceased family for transporting the body to church and cemetery. Motor hearses came into use after World War I.

Fred Beshear, one of the founders certainly rated the title "One of the Fathers of Dawson Springs." Instrumental in locating coal mines near the city, he fought tirelessly and successfully for a U.S. Veterans Administration Hospital to be built at nearby Outwood, Kentucky. He also served two terms in the Kentucky legislature. He was bought out by Russell Beshear and Ligon Beshear in 1945, when he retired. That partnership lasted five years and was followed by a new partnership of Russell Beshear and younger brother Eddie Beshear and wife, Virginia. Eddie Beshear started with the firm in the fall of 1943. He married Virginia Madison, in 1947. Virginia is a descendant of President James Madison and was born near Madisonville. Eddie and Virginia had one daughter, Jenny Lynn Beshear Sewell, who with husband David C. Sewell are now affiliated with the firm. David and Jenny have a son, Gavin Lynn Sewell, born August, 1983.

The business was separated from the furniture store in 1952 and moved into a new location at 201 N. Main Street where it has been since that time. The name was changed at that time to Beshear Funeral Home. Two additions to the building and a complete renovation in 1975 made this one of the most modern funeral homes in Kentucky. The firm was proudly the first to install central air conditioning and a lounge in the area. It was definitely one of the first to make pre-arranged funerals in the modern norm used today. It served as sole ambulance service for the Dawson Springs area for fifty-five years. The firm is one of the oldest funeral firms in the state of Kentucky. It looks forward to the future with energy and creative foresight.

Left: David C. Sewell, Jenny Lynn Beshear Sewell, Gavin Lynn Sewell, Virginia Madison Beshear, Eddie M. Beshear

"Continuous Since 1909"

City Of Madisonville

Councilman James Gill - Ward 1
Councilman D. W. Riley - Ward 2
Councilman Rudy Stone - Ward 3

**The Honorable
O.L. Lantaff
Mayor**

Councilman Norman Suthard - Ward 4
Councilman George Moore -   Ward 5
Councilman Bob Simmons -   Ward 6

Madisonville is very proud of the new Police and City Council Complex

Madisonville Fire Complex houses the Communications, Training Facilities, and Dormitory area for our Fire Department

Coldwell Banker Terry and Associates

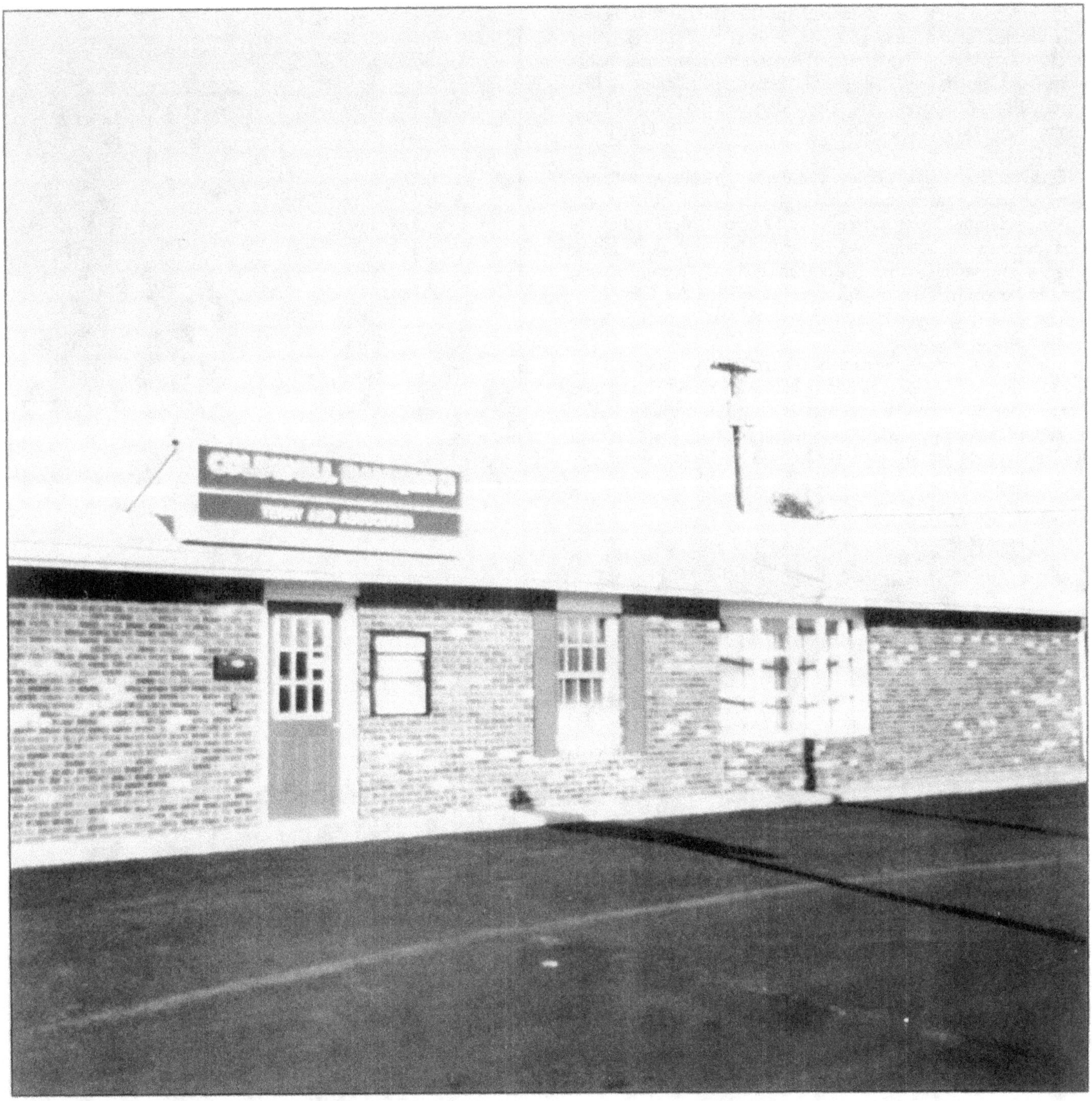

Terry Real Estate was founded in 1978 by Philip H. Terry. The first office was located at 507 S. Main Street, Madisonville, Kentucky.

In 1980, Allen F. Davis joined the firm and later became a partner in the business. By 1982, the company had grown to five people. A larger office was needed and the move was made to 1096 North Main Street in 1982. More sales people were added after the move.

In November, 1985 Terry Real Estate affiliated with Coldwell Banker and changed the company name to Coldwell Banker Terry and Associates. Within 1 year additional office space was needed due to the growing number of sales agents and the growing volume of business. The expansion added room for 3 additional sales desks, a waiting room, and a conference/closing room.

As of June, 1987, Coldwell Banker Terry and Associates has 10 active sales agents. Their hard work and dedication has made Coldwell Banker Terry and Associates one of the top listing and selling companies in Hopkins County.

Commercial Bank

Commercial Bank was established Apr. 20, 1907. The bank was built because of the rapid progress Dawson Springs was going through as a leading health resort. Among the first stockholders were Asa Harned, O.W. Likens, Eli Harned, J.C. Graham, R.B. Porter, Rhea Armstrong, I.N. Day, John R. Hoover, J.T. Day, James D. Meadows, E.H. Stanniger, W.D. Carter, A.E. Orten, and Mr. Hamby.

On Dec. 15, 1915, Commercial Bank consolidated with the Bank of Dawson to become the Commercial Bank of Dawson.

The bank moved from its location at 121 South Main to the new Commercial Bank building at 119 South Main in August, 1969, where it is presently located. The old bank building is currently being used to house the Dawson Springs Museum and Art Center.

The bank has enjoyed tremendous success, growing to its present size of $30 million.

In its 80-year history, the bank has had only five presidents. They are I.N. Day, J.C. Hayes, James H. Harned, Paul K. Turner, and Pete Turner. Mr. Pete Turner continues to serve as president today.

Todays directors include Louis Franklin, Jon M. Harned, Paul K. Turner, Pete Turner, Julie Banks, and Russell Beshear.

Old Commercial Bank Bldg.-Main St., Dawson

Present bank building

Farmers Bank & Trust Co.

Opening day, Nov. 18, 1907, of Farmers National Bank located on the northeast corner of Main & Center streets

On June 1, 1935, the bank relocated in the Mortons Bank building located at 5 North Main

On March 15, 1958, Farmers National Bank moved to the present location on the southwest corner of Main and Arch Streets. This was the first bank bldg. on this lot. While occupying this bldg., Farmers National Bank changed its name to Farmers Bank and Trust Co. in 1966

The remodeling of the present building was completed in July of 1981

FARMERS BANK & TRUST CO.
MADISONVILLE, KY. 42431

821-5150   Member FDIC

First Federal Savings

SERVING MADISONVILLE & HOPKINS COUNTY SINCE 1958

First Federal Savings
AND LOAN ASSOCIATION

HOME OFFICE
108 South Main
Madisonville

ALSO SERVING
Dawson Springs, Eddyville, Marion, Morganfield and Providence

Insured to $100,000
By FSLIC

Fugate Lumber Company

The Fugates have been interested in the growth and progress of Madisonville and Hopkins County since 1807. Yes, that's the year Vincent Fugate (one of Lawrence Fugate's ancestors) helped finance the first courthouse in Hopkins County. We're proud of the progress of our community since that time, and we feel that we have played a small role in making Madisonville and Hopkins County what it is today.

We started in business on Grapevine Road in 1947 and now, 40 years later we're proud to say we've expanded and relocated in order to serve our customers better. We thank all of you for your business through the years.

We're proud of our new building, located on Park Avenue, and we invite all our customers, old and new to come out and look over our modern facilities and fine selection of quality materials and products.

FUGATE LUMBER COMPANY, INC.

380 PARK AVENUE
MADISONVILLE
821-3183

SINCE 1947

"BIG ENOUGH TO SERVE YOU
SMALL ENOUGH TO NOW YOU"

GE MADISONVILLE

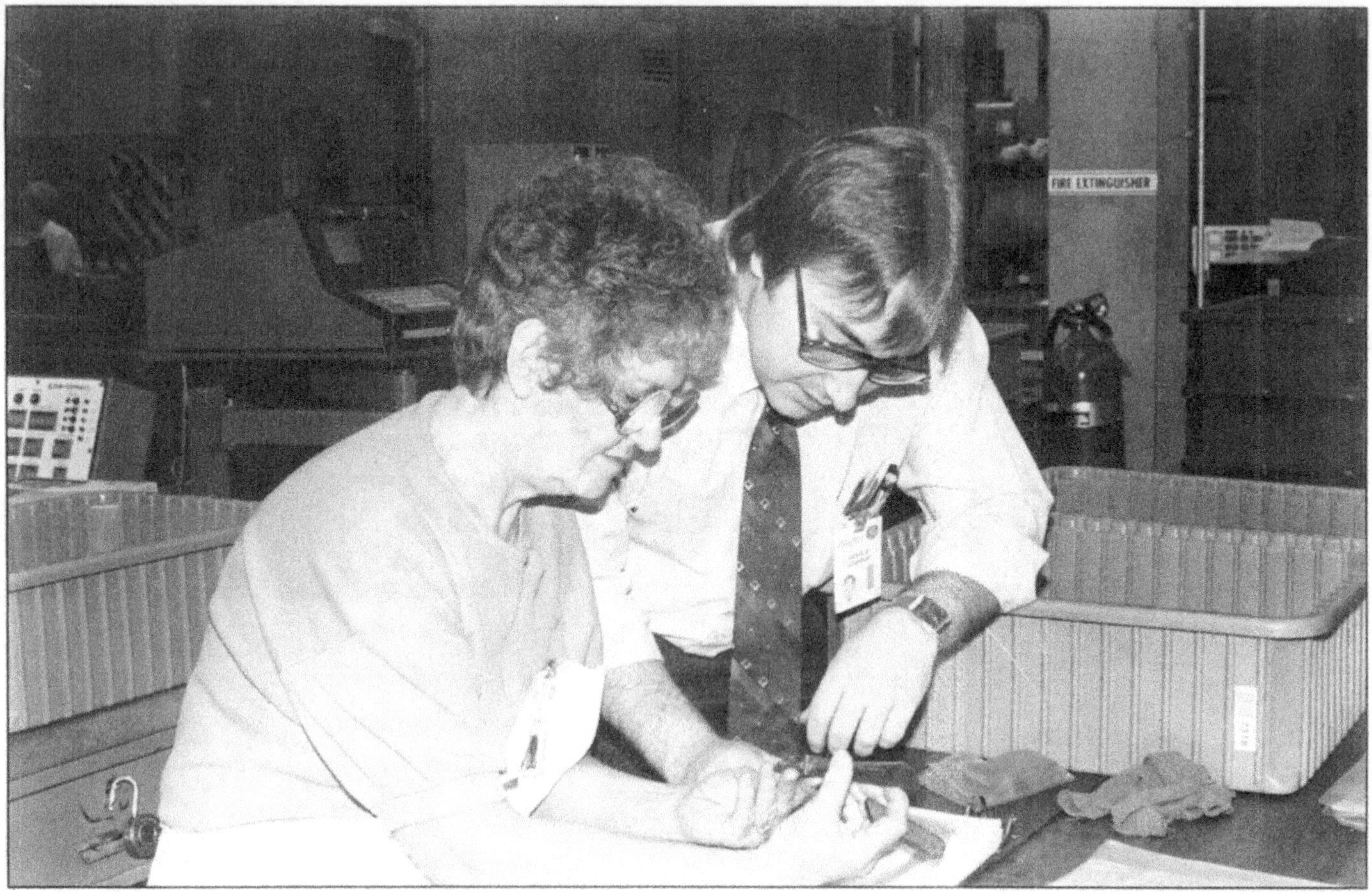

GE Madisonville: "Where people make the difference"

New horizons for an old friend.

"An Equal Opportunity Employer"

Aircraft Engine Business Group
U.S. HWY. 41A, RURAL ROUTE #2 • MADISONVILLE, KENTUCKY 42431

After several years of planning, GE's Board of Directors approved construction of a new plant in Madisonville, KY on Jan. 15, 1970. This new plant would manufacture fluorescent ballasts for the Ballast Department's Lighting Industry headquartered in Danville, IL. Footings and foundations were poured early April, 1970 for the initial construction of the 150,000 square foot building located in the Madisonville Industrial Park on US Hwy. 41A. Initial production from the new facility was expected by early 1971.

The first shipment of Madisonville GE Ballasts were sent out on Thursday, Mar. 18, 1971. This shipment represented the first Madisonville-assembled ballasts to be produced. On December 3rd of the following year, the first open house for employees and family members was held. Approximately 2,000 people toured the facility.

In late 1979, the GE Ballast plant was converted by the Aircraft Engine Business Group and production refocused to the manufacture of turbine airfoils (blades and vanes) for military and commercial aircraft jet engines and also for marine and industrial applications.

The blades and vanes produced here in Madisonville are shipped to larger plants in Evendale, OH or Lynn, MA for complete engine assembly. Today, the Madisonville plant is one of the most efficient plants in the GE Aircraft Engines' business.

Recognized as one of the most technically advanced airfoil manufacturing facilities in the world, this ultra-modern, high-tech plant features several automated systems including computerized materials handling and transportation, numerical controlled machinery, integrated quality inspection systems, computerized factory management, CAD/CAM and CIM, sophisticated laser hole drilling technology and integrated cell grinding and hole drilling systems.

Today, GE Aircraft Engines has invested over $80 million into Madisonville. The production output exceeds $150 million annually and the plant has expanded to over 300,000 square feet of floor space. In addition, employment is approaching 900 people.

The Madisonville plant exemplifies the committment to excellence that GE as a company has gained. When it comes to quality people performing a quality job and producing a quality, cost-competitive product, GE Madisonville ranks among the best.

Harris Funeral Home

Harris Funeral Home
INCORPORATED

MEMBER: NATIONAL FUNERAL DIRECTORS ASSN.
MEMBER: KENTUCKY FUNERAL DIRECTORS BURIAL ASSN.

Years of Distinctive Service
24 HOUR AIR - MOTOR AMBULANCE
•
134 NORTH MAIN STREET · TEL. (502) 821-6601
MADISONVILLE, KENTUCKY 42431

The Harris family and its associates have served the funeral needs of Hopkins County for many years. Sidney's father, Mr. Bob Harris, operated an undertaking establishment and casket shop in Nebo, Kentucky.

After working for his father and other funeral directors for several years, Sidney founded the Sidney T. Harris Funeral Home in Madisonville near its present location. Mrs. Harris, the former Eva Barnhill, has been active in the business since its founding.

Harley Stokes joined the Harris family in 1938 and remains very active in the management of the firm.

The firm prospered under Sidney's guidance until his death in May of 1970.

The firm was incorporated in June of 1960.

Tommy Craft and Eddie Wilson have been associated with Mr. Stokes and Mrs. Harris for many years.

Hawkins Motor Sales

Hawkins Motor Sales is the second oldest family owned automobile dealership in Hopkins County. Founded in 1932 by J. F. (Fount) and J. R. (Raymond) Hawkins, it has been serving the automobile needs for the people in Hopkins County and surrounding counties for over a half century. Hawkins Motors first location was in what was last known as the "City" maintenance department next to the old fire station. The maintenance department and old fire station were torn down in 1985 and the new "City Complex" built. A few years later the business outgrew that location and they moved to North Main Street where the Dollar General Store is now located. Sometime in the late thirties, they moved to Federal Street where the City Police Department was located before the new City complex was completed.

In 1941, the dealership closed because of the war since no cars were being built. After the war, the two founders came back to Madisonville and reopened their dealership on West Center Street where Todd's Furniture is now located. It was there that Fount's son, Douglas, returned from the war and assumed his father's interest in the dealership.

In 1953 they moved to the corner of East Center and Park Avenue. In 1968, Joe Hawkins entered the business and assumed his father's (Raymond) interest in the dealership. In 1972, Doug Hawkins retired from the car business and Joe became the sole proprietor of Hawkins Motor Sales. The business remained there until 1979. That year Hawkins purchased the Dodge, AMC, Jeep Agency from Purdy Motors. Hawkins Motor Sales merged the two dealerships into the location at 620 East Center where Purdy Motors was located.

In 1984, a new facility was built on the corner of South Main and McCoy Avenue where the agency is the authorized dealer for Chrysler, Plymouth, Dodge, AMC, Jeep and Renault. Being the newest car dealership in Hopkins County, the facility incorporates the most modern and efficient equipment to sell and service the vehicles it sells.

Hawkins Motor Sales is proud to be a part of the heritage of Hopkins County and is grateful to the people in Hopkins County whose patronage has made it possible for the firm to enjoy a long business history.

HILLIARD LYONS

The Hilliard Lyons Difference...

J.J.B. Hilliard,
W.L. Lyons, Inc.
22 North Main Street
P.O. Box 582
Madisonville
502-821-7990

Brokers

Sue S. Cumbee

William P. Munday

Michael W. Mefford

Burl F. Milligan

Hopkins County Fiscal Court

COUNTY JUDGE/EXECUTIVE - Hanson D. Slaton.. 1/78

- John W. Neisz - Deputy Judge/Executive
- Jessie N. Ashby - Executive Secretary
- Glenda G. Ayers - County Treasurer
- Dorothy A. Daves - Secretary/Co. Treasurer
- Ernest Champion - Road Foreman
- John H. Laffoon - Superintendent/Sanitation Dept.
- Ron Johnson - County Engineer

MAGISTRATES

- Dist. #1 - Karol Welch
- Dist. #2 - Bill Fugate
- Dist. #3 - Wayne Browning
- Dist. #4 - James T. Ray
- Dist. #5 - Glen Lynn
- Dist. #6 - Morton Jennings
- Dist. #7 - Trent Barton

COUNTY COURT CLERK... WILLIAM T. BROOKS.. 1/74

Grace Traylor	Sheri Brannon
Linda Hartline	Rhonda Burns
Donald Ethridge	Devra Heltsley
Cathy Offutt	Dru West
Sylvia Hamilton	Brenda Huddleston
Martha Clark	Kathleen Gardner
Beverly Gray	Caroline Davis

CIRCUIT COURT CLERK... Paul A. Summers... 11/81

Linda Wyatt	Becky Conyers
Anita Patterson	Lisa Jennings
Norma Ashby	Judy Gunn
Janet Winstead	Joyce Moore
Charlotte Spence	Rita McWilliams
Julia Hogan	Edna Clark
Dale Butler	Betty Leasure

DISTRICT JUDGE.... Charles Boteler
Carl Hurst
Charisse Richardson - Secretary

COUNTY ATTORNEY... W. Logan Calvert... 1/78

Assistant Co. Attorney... Robert Moore and Mark Little

Cheryl Armstrong	Pamela Jones
Debbie Myers	Sandy Messamore

COMMONWEALTH ATTORNEY... Al Spenard

Assistants.. Richard Hibbs and Vincent J. Eiden
Secretary... Jane Ann Jackson and Lisa Dame

Commonwealth Detective.. Vincent J. Eiden

CIRCUIT JUDGE... Thomas B. Spain

Secretary... Carolyn Polly

CORONER... John Walters

| Deputy Coroners.. | Mike Bandy | Steve Carson |
| | Charlie O'Neal | Harold Bandy |

D.E.S. DIRECTOR... Ed Teague

Deputy Director... W. R. Adams
Secretary.... Judy McGregor

ASSISTANCE CENTER DIRECTOR... Elizabeth Melton
Shirley Babineau

JAILER... Jim Lantrip

Alvis Wilson	Steve Morgon
Frank Chisholm	Phil Curtis
Dawn Curtis	Dianna Patterson

Larry Patterson

PROPERTY VALUATION ADMINISTRATION
Melvin Hicklin

Joe Bishop	Renee' Hicklin
David Gordon	Anna Samples
Helen Lamb	Tracy Couch
Lou Ann Ray	Margaret Brown

SHERIFF... John "Beau" Summers... 7/85

Gary Lee	Herbert Jones
Carroll Lutz	Linda Todd
Donald Buffington	Roxanne Foster
Raymond Jones	Robert Brown
Lita Krusinski	Gary Nance

Algia Morrow

EXTENSION OFFICE

Larry Mahurin
George Kelly
Jo Ann Pierce
Kitty Simpson
Sally Snyder

J. Craig Riddle Co.

J. Craig Riddle Co. was in the imagination of J. Craig Riddle, Sr. when he graduated from the University of Kentucky and after serving in the Army during World War I. When Craig returned to Madisonville, he joined the agency of Brooks & Corum. Later he bought Mr. Corum's interest and became a partner with Mr. Brooks. Upon retiring Mr. Brooks sold the agency to Craig Riddle. At that time J. Craig Riddle Co. was started. The agency was located on the second floor at 51 S. Main Street.

The companies that the new agency represented were AETNA INS. CO. which after fifty years we still represent SUN INS. CO. which was founded in 1710 and was the oldest in the world. The lines of business sold most frequently were fire, auto, windstorm and allied lines. We have in our office an automobile policy dated 1923 for a 1922 Ford coupe valued at $500. This policy is with AETNA INS CO. and the premium was $5.50 per year.

Craig moved his office to 9 East Center Street, located above Baker & Hickman Department Store. He had a secretary, Ms. Virgie Scott whom he gave a partnership until her retirement in 1940.

Craig saw the need in this area for commercial and industrial insurance and expanded his company to write this, also workmen's compensation and liability for coal mines. The agency became a branch office for Bitiminous Casualty, which was the largest compensation writer for coal mining operations in this state.

After graduation from the University of Kentucky and finishing his term of service with the Army Air Corps, Craig's oldest son, J. Craig Riddle, Jr. joined the agency in 1950. Craig, Jr. served his apprenticeship with Bitiminous Casualty in Louisville, KY and was well trained to handle the large amount of compensation business the agency handled for the coal mines in the surrounding area.

In 1954 Alice McCracken Jones was employed as bookkeeper/secretary. She is still with the firm.

Craig's other son, Chesley Riddle, Sr. joined the agency in 1956 after graduation from the University of Kentucky and serving in the U. S. Army.

In 1964, as the business grew, the Riddle's found a need for a larger office and relocated at 245 South Main Street. This property was the home of Chesley Williams, the parents of Mrs. Riddle (Amy Williams Riddle). The house was torn down and a modern building was constructed. The pear tree in the back yard was saved and still provides the employees with fruit.

In 1968 the Company incorporated and the name was changed to J. Craig Riddle Co., Inc.

Craig Jr.'s son, J. Craig Riddle, V (Chip) joined the agency in 1976 and was followed by Ches, Sr.'s two sons, Chesley Riddle, Jr. and James Lisle Riddle (Jimmy) in 1977. In 1984 Suzanne Riddle Wilson, Craig, Jr.'s daughter joined the agency.

It was a great loss to the family and the agency when J. Craig Riddle, Sr. passed away in 1981. Craig Sr. was the type of person that believed in hard work and through this belief, made his agency a successful one. Craig, Sr. also believed that advertisement by "word of mouth" was the best source. However, over the years, we have expanded our advertising to local radio stations and newspapers. The most recent addition to our advertising program is a large colorful hot air balloon. You may see this floating over Madisonville and the surrounding area.

The agency continues to operate from it's location at 245 S. Main; however, in 1986 they purchased the adjacent lot and expanded the building to nearly twice it's size.

J. Craig Riddle Co., Inc. continues to be a family operation with all of Craig Sr. descendants currently involved in the business.

Kentucky Bank

Current building

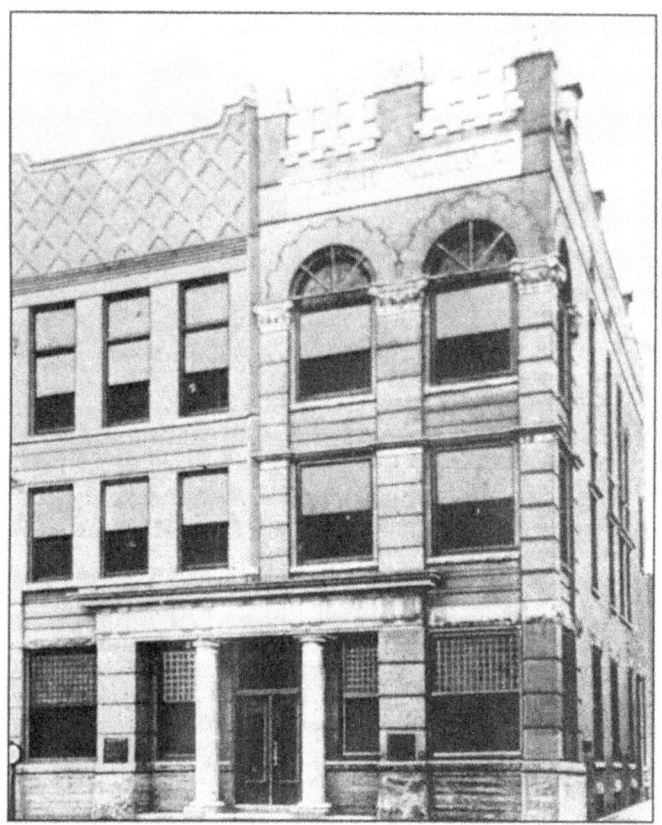

The early 1900's

The mid 1900's

The face of our BANK has changed over the years, but the principles of STRENGTH, SAFETY, STABILITY AND SERVICE upon which it was founded remain unchanged and a permanent part of our CORPORATE CULTURE. At KENTUCKY BANK our goal is basic, "PROVIDE THE BEST BANKING SERVICES AVAILABLE". Our growth and success go hand and hand with the growth and success of this community and its citizens. We are proud of our HERITAGE and the ROLE we have played and will play in the HISTORY and FUTURE of Madisonville and Hopkins County.

Knight & Son Monument Co., Inc.

"Western Kentucky's Fastest Growing Monument Co."

This company and its predecessor establishments have been in business in Hopkins County for more than 110 years. Wells and Rea, marble dealers, advertised in the Madisonville Times on August 29, 1877. They were succeeded in business by the Wells Brothers' Monument Company, which was sold to Knight and Son Monument Co., Inc. in January 1973.

Prior to acquiring Wells Brothers, Fred L. Knight and his father Charles, operated The Knight Monument Company located on South Main Street.

Since Fred's untimely death, the firm is operated by his heirs.

IN LOVING MEMORY

FRED L. KNIGHT

MAY 12, 1946 -
OCTOBER 7, 1987

Knight & Son Monument Co., Inc.
302 W. Center Street
Madisonville, Kentucky 42431
(502) 821-7553
"Western Kentucky's Fastest Growing Monument Co."

Madisonville Area Manufacturers Association

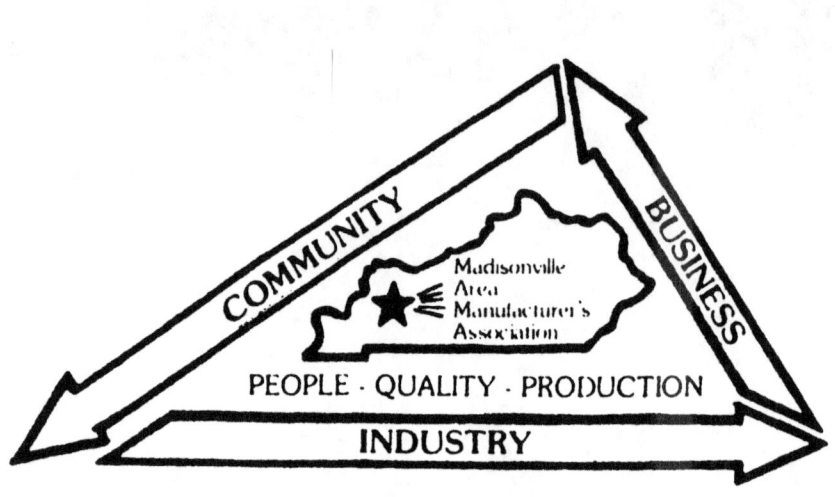

Madisonville Area Manufacturer's Association
The Morton House
140 South Main Street
Madisonville, KY 42431
(502) 821-3435

The Madisonville Area Manufacturers Association was begun in 1973 with Bob Welch and Karl Heyse as the motivating forces behind it's formation, along with Hubert Wells, Executive Vice President of the Chamber of Commerce. The original members of M.A.M,.A. were Birmingham Bolt, Huebsch Originators (now Speed Queen), Goodyear, York-Borg Warner (now York International), General Electric, American Mine Tool and Austin Powder Company.

The purpose of the Madisonville Area Manufacturers Association was to bring together management from the various manufacturing industries to share common interests, common problems, and to improve the working relationship between management, labor, education and the community.

The Association has now grown to 17 industries not only in Hopkins County, but outside of Hopkins County as well.

Local manufacturers producing goods for our community, the nation and the world. . . . .

American Mine Tool Company - The Company manufactures various mining tools and bits, with finished products being shipped to all parts of the world.

Birmingham Bolt Co., Inc. - The local plant manufactures mine roof bolts and plates used in the underground coal mining industry.

Buckhorn, Inc. - Buckhorn is one of the largest manufacturers of re-usable plastic shipping and storage containers of commercial, industrial and agricultural products.

Carhartt-Midwest - In addition to bib-overall production, the Madisonville operation warehouses and ships for the Midwest Division.

Ensign-Bickford Company - The Ensign-Bickford Company is a manufacturer of chemicals and explosive products used in mining, construction and quarry operation.

Filtration Sciences - The paper mill is capable of producing in excess of 15,000 tons of impregnated filter material per year for the automotive industry.

G. E. Aircraft Engines - The Madisonville operation manufactures turbine airfoils, both blades and vanes for commercial and military jet engine applications. Manufacturing incorporates some of the most sophisticated processes and technologies in the industry.

Goodyear Tire & Rubber Co. - Today the local plant is Goodyear's largest producer of pneumatic industrial tires for use on wheels under 12 inches.

Goldenrod Dairy Foods - Goldenrod processes, packages and distributes fluid and flavored milk, buttermilk, 100% orange juice, and fruit drinks, in addition to packaging more than 85,000 half pints of milk daily.

Kentucky Carbide - The plant manufactures comented carbide tips for American Mine Tool's coal mining and road construction tools.

Kris-Shan Plastics, Inc. - Kris-Shan Plastics is a producer of injection moldings products. Kris-Shan can mold a variety of large and small parts from a variety of materials.

Modern Welding Company - Modern Welding produces storage tanks in steel, glasteel, fiberglass and alloys metals. They also manufacture pressure vessels and processing tanks, structural steel, miscellaneous metals and coal hauler bodies.

Ottenheimer & Company, Inc. - Ottenheimer manufactures and distributes uniforms for the Medical, Grocery and Fast Foods Industry.

Polyweave Bag Company - As a producer of explosives packaging products, Polyweave ships finished products to all parts of the mining and quarrying regions of the United States.

Speed Queen Co. - A total of four different size dryers are manufactured at the Madisonville plant. These tumbler dryers are sold throughout the U. S. and some 75 foreign countries.

Versnick Manufacturing Co. - The company manufactures cylinder sleeves and engine block repair material. These specialized products are shipped to all parts of the nation and many foreign countries.

York International - The Madisonville Plant produces residential air conditioning equipment and heat pumps which are shipped to all parts of the nation and world.

Madisonville Building & Loan Association

"The Old Reliable"

The following business men met on February 16, 1923 to organize Madisonville Building & Loan Association. John L. Long, Harper Gatton, Edgar Arnold, Delmont Utley, E. G. McLeod, L. E. Ruby, S. R. Parker, J. Craig Riddle Sr., J. B. Ramsey and A. R. Cummings.

All papers had been filed and Madisonville Building and Loan Association was incorporated on March 3, 1923, with the following Officers: R. S. Dulin, President; Delmont Utley, Vice President; A. R. Cummings, Secretary & Treasurer. Directors were: L. E. Ruby, J. B. Ramsey, M. K. Gordon, E. P. Stum and E. G. McLeod.

The Association moved to the present location at 240 South Main Street in 1959.

The office of President has been held by R. S. Dulin, 1923-1926, Delmont Utley 1926-1961, A. R. Cummings 1961-1966, John F. Casner 1966-1971, Robert D. Fox 1971-1980 and William E. Howe 1980-present.

Other current officers are J. C. Arnold, Vice President; Leonard Villines, Secretary-Treasurer; Pearl Prince, Assistant Secretary; Rudy Stone, Consumer Loan Officer. Directors are J. C. Arnold, James Baker, Aubrey Cornette, Robert D. Fox, William E. Howe, J. C. Riddle Jr., Ralph Teague, Leonard Villines and Rash Wells.

Employees are: Terri Geiser, Debbie Howell, Marilyn Locke, Anita Mitchell and Barbara Rudd.

Madisonville Cablevision

Madisonville Cablevision started it's business in July, 1964. It was owned and operated by John McClendon, and employed 6 people. Later the system was sold to Meridith Avco, a Cable Business. In January 1969, the system was purchased by American Television and Communications Corporation. The growing business built cable to Earlington, Mortons Gap and the county area between the towns. In the spring of 1971, the company needing more space, moved to 55 Union Street. In November, 1978, the company merged with Time, Inc. In February, 1982, the business moved to its present location at 30 Oakdale Avenue. Since that time the company has added service to the Hanson and White Plains areas.

Madisonville Cablevision now serves approximately 9,500 subscribers and has 18 employes.

CABLE VISION

MADISONVILLE

IT'S TELEVISION WORTH WATCHING.™

(502) 821-6777

THE MESSENGER

THE MESSENGER
A NEW YORK TIMES COMPANY

221 S. Main
P.O. Box 529
Madisonville, Ky.

821-6833 advertising
821-0857 circulation

"The Messenger serving Hopkins County since 1917"

Published:
Mon-Fri evenings
Saturday morning

Circulation:
Everyday except Wed. 12,000
(Tmc) Wednesday 20,000

Publisher: H. Doug Miller
Ad Director: David A. Clevenger
Editor: Tom Clinton
Controller: Ken Duffield
Composing Manager: Henry Stoltz
Circulation Manager: Jeff Rutherford

"We're striving to serve you better!"

Parkway Ford Inc.

We opened our Dealership on June 11, 1982 in the depth of the worst recession since the 1930's. How could we succeed when other long established dealers were failing?
* THE BEST PRODUCT
* THE BEST SERVICE
* THE BEST FACILITY
BUT most of all * THE BEST PEOPLE

This combination attracts the best clientelle on a repeat basis. We are here to serve the people of Hopkins County.

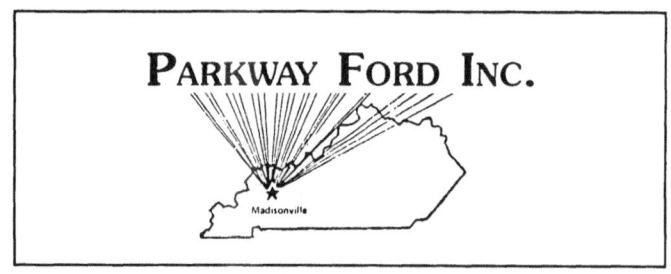

People's Bank

Peoples Bank was established on April 4, 1901. Its original location was at Earlington. The original capital stock of the bank consisted of 150 shares valued at $15,000.00. A report of examination conducted on July 9, 1902 showed deposits of $47,994.42, and loans of $41,772.50.

From this humble beginning the bank has grown throughout the years, providing essential banking services that have helped the community to grow, too.

In March of 1918 the Earlington Bank assumed the assets of Peoples Bank which was also located in Earlington. The bank continued as the "Earlington Bank" from that time until August 8, 1959. At that time, permission was granted by the supervisory authorities to move the main office to Madisonville, change the name to Peoples Bank and Trust Company, and to retain the old bank at Earlington as a branch office.

At the time of this change, total resources of the bank were approximately two milllion dollars. The bank in Madisonville was well received, and it enjoyed a good growth from the beginning.

In April 1959 the Bank Building and Equipment Company of St. Louis began construction of the new building, which was completed just in time for the opening on August 8th of that year.

In 1960 we purchased Farmers and Merchants Bank at Slaughters. Since this bank was located in Webster County, directors of Peoples Bank purchased the stock individually and operated it as a separate bank until such time as a new branch office could be built across the county line in Hopkins County for the establishment of a branch office. The building was completed and the old Farmers and Merchants Bank was liquidated, with the Slaughters Branch of Peoples Bank and Trust Company assuming all the assets and liabilities in early 1961.

The Farmers and Merchants Bank had assets of about one-half million dollars at the time they were assumed by Peoples Bank and has shown a steady growth since that time.

Prior to the time that the directors of the Earlington Bank decided to move the main office to Madisonville, plans were underway to construct a new building in Earlington. In fact, the building which was constructed in Madisonville was first designed to be built in Earlington.

In 1962 an architect was hired to design a new building at Earlington and a contract was awarded for the construction at a cost of approximately forty thousand dollars. The old building which stood on the corner of Main and Railroad Streets was razed upon completion of the new building, and the people of Earlington now have an attractive and modern banking facility.

By late 1963 the operation in Madisonville had outgrown its original facility and plans were made for the construction of a two-story addition. Work was begun on this structure on July 4, 1964, and it was completed and put to use in early January 1965.

In early 1971 application was made to the supervisory authorities for the construction and operation of a branch office in the north part of Madisonville. Permission was granted and in September 1971 construction was begun by Renshaw Construction Company of Madisonville. On December 20, 1971, the Northside Office Peoples Bank and Trust Company opened its doors for business.

On May 22, 1972, the directors of Peoples Bank and Trust Company purchased the Nortonville Bank. Application was made to the authorities to merge this bank with Peoples Bank, and this fact was accomplished in December, 1972.

In the spring of 1974, when the Main Office was once again bursting at the seams, construction was begun on an addition, which more than doubled the space available at that time.

Our Madison Square Office opened for business November 9, 1978 in the Douglas Oates building, located at the south side of the Madison Square Shopping Center. This location was chosen to serve our customers better on the east side of town.

With the growing need of service to our merchants, as well as other commercial and personal customers on the south end of town, we opened our South Side Office on December 29, 1980 for business.

In the Spring of 1984 an additional 8,300 square feet of floor space was started on the Main Office. Work on this addition was completed in April, 1985.

Peoples Bank and Trust Company has had a steady growth since 1959, and today we have four offices in Madisonville, and one each in Earlington, Slaughters, and Nortonville.

On June 30, 1986 Peoples Bank and Trust Company became part of a larger, much stronger financial organization. Our affiliation with Citizens Bank of Evansville and Posey County National Bank of Mt. Vernon, Indiana added impressive strength and new potential for economic growth in our region and better, more comprehensive service to our customers.

We look forward to a strong future of excellent service to our customers as, together with our new partners, we work each day to bring better banking to you.

Reid-Walters Funeral Home, Inc.

Reid-Walters Funeral Home, Inc. is a successor of Reid Funeral Home which was established in 1928 by Lewis H. Reid. The original location was on East Main Street in Earlington in the ground floor of the Victory Building. The business was later moved to another location on East Main Street and finally moved to another location at 302 East Farren Avenue, Earlington. In 1933, Hubert Reid (Lewis H. Reid's son) joined the firm as General Manager.

Lewis Elmo Reid (Lewis H. Reid's son) managed a branch operation at Mortons Gap for a number of years as well as assisting Lewis H. and Hubert in Earlington.

Lewis H. Reid died in 1958. Hubert and Elmo and Hubert's wife, Edith Price Reid, continued operation of the business until 1969. In 1969, John L. Walters purchased Elmo Reid's third of the partnership when Elmo went into semi-retirement, the business became Reid Funeral Home, Inc.

In 1972, John L. and his wife Patricia H. Walters, purchased the majority of the stock from Hubert and Edith and the business was renamed Reid-Walters Funeral Home, Inc. Patrick S. Walters, John's brother, came to work in the firm in 1974. In 1976, Hubert Reid suffered a debilitating stroke which forced his retirement. Prior to this, he had served as Coroner in Hopkins County from 1958 to 1966. He also served as Hopkins County Judge from 1966 thru 1970. Edith Price Reid continued to participate in the business until 1984. At her retirement, Lisa Walters Solise (John L. and Patricia H. Walters' daughter) joined the business. In 1985, John L. Walters was elected Coroner of Hopkins County. For 59 years, Reid-Walters Funeral Home, Inc. has been a family-owned and family-operated business.

The Salmon Memorial Clinic

The Salmon Memorial Clinic, located at 412 N. Kentucky Ave., Madisonville, was built in 1964. It sits on 1.689 acres, including a spacious parking lot and additional undeveloped real estate. It was designed by Architect Lawrence Casner, and is all masonry construction. Dr. James L. Salmon, 1905-84, had the clinic built and practiced general medicine and surgery there until shortly before his death. It is presently occupied by Dr. James L. Salmon's son, Dr. Thaddeus Robert Salmon, who began his practice of family medicine there in July, 1985.

The exterior of the 9,600 sq. ft. building is pale green glazed brick. The interior is unmistakably that of a medical facility, with gleaming asphalt tile floors and pale green ceramic tile extending to shoulder height, complimented by French ivory walls. The building was constructed to last indefinitely, with such unusual features as all lathe and plaster construction, all stainless steel fixtures, including door knobs, hinges, and cabinet hardware. Each of the 18 examination rooms has built-in cabinetry and a stainless steel sink. All door surfaces and cabinet tops are covered in formica. Even the roof has a concrete decking, which adds greatly to the overall strength and durability of the structure. The clinic is topped by a 600 sq. ft. penthouse, which contains a modern central heating and cooling system and auxiliary power generator. The Salmon Memorial Clinic is complete in itself with 18 exam rooms, minor surgical suite, recovery room, x-ray facilities, pharmacy, lab, and in-office laboratory testing.

SEXTET MINING CORPORATION

Coal for the Industries of the nation

Founded in 1962 by

Russell Badgett, Jr.
President - Russell Badget, III

Owners

Russell Badgett, Jr.
Mrs. Juanita Wadlington Badgett
Russell Badgett, III
Dr. C. B. Badgett
Claudia Badgett Riner
Bentley F. Badgett, II
Anne Badgett Smaldone
Joseph R. Badgett
Russell Moore
Paul S. Long

Trover Clinic

Loman C. Trover, M.D. began his medical practice in Earlington, Kentucky in 1948. After practicing there for two years, he was joined by his brother, Faull S. Trover, Sr., M.D., in 1957, and they moved their practice to Madisonville, Kentucky, choosing a little white frame house on Court Street for their offices. This house was directly north of the present location of Baker and Hickman's Tiny Town building. Office hours were from early in the morning until late at night. It was not unusual to see a line fo patients stretching down the sidewalk toward the old Capital Theater waiting to see one of the physicians. Their practice soon outgrew this location and in July, 1952, they occupied offices at 55 East North Street, which is the present location of the Clinic Convalescent Center.

Trover Clinic had its formal beginning July 1, 1953, at the North Street location when Drs. Loman Trover, Faull Trover, Sr. and three other physicians formed a five-man group with the goal of bringing quality medical care to this area of Western Kentucky. These three physicians were Merle M. Mahr, M.D., Frederick Scott, M.D., and John Haynes, M.D.

By 1962, the original clinic building had been expanded five times, and the staff had grown to twenty-one physicians with the following specialties represented: general surgery, ophthalmology, obstetrics/gynecology, thoracic surgery, orthopaedics, internal medicine, pathology, radiology and urology.

As the staff increased to twenty-six physicians, the Clinic outgrew both building and grounds. On October 26, 1962, the clinic was moved to new quarters at its present location. The new building consisted of four floors with 38,000 square feet. Later two below surface additions were added to the building, but by 1971, the 42,000 square feet was insufficient space for a staff of forty-five physicians.

In May, 1971 the clinic was expanded to 97,000 square feet, providing space for eighty-five doctors. In August, 1981, a nine story tower was added, providing an additional 80,000 square feet. Primary care practices are located in the Tower. Internal Medicine and Surgery specialties and subspecialties are located in the east wing.

The clinic has always been interested in extending its services through satellite clinics. The first satellite opened in 1954 in Earlington, the second in 1960 in Providence, the third in 1972 in Morganfield and the fourth in 1983 in Dawson Springs. An affiliate clinic was opened in August, 1984 in Hopkinsville. Also opening in the Fall of 1984 was Trover Clinic of Todd County, a satellite of the Hopkinsville affiliate clinic.

Trover Clinic, knowing that its goal of providing quality medical care is dependent in part upon well trained paramedical personnel, fostered training programs locally. The Medical Vocational School for technicians in may fields and the R. N. Training Program of the local community college have been developed with the encouragement of Trover Clinic.

Another development in the educational field was the designation of Trover Clinic as the first site to participate in the Area Health Education System (AHES) in conjunction with the University of Louisville and the University of Kentucky. Training based at Trover Clinic and Regional Medical Center is given to medical students and residents and includes a three-year Family Practice Residency Program.

The clinic presently has a staff of 100+ physicians covering approximately thirty-two specialties and subspecialties and employs approximately 400 employees.

by Daniel W. Dockrey

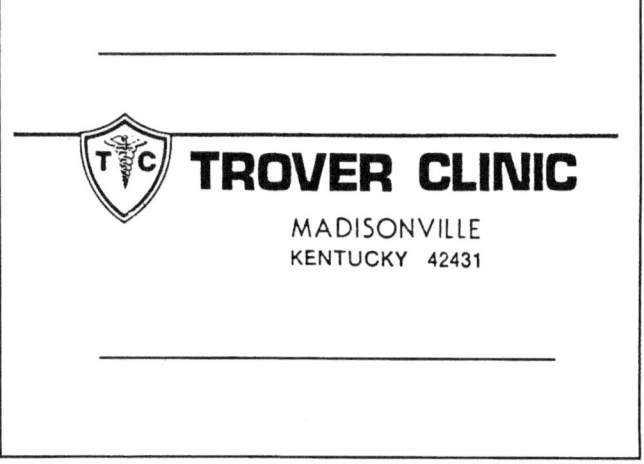

American Printing Co.

Where Ideas take shape...

COLOR LITHOGRAPHERS
249 NORTH MAIN STREET
MADISONVILLE, KENTUCKY 42431
(502) 821-5360

Brown & Holloway, Inc.

Our Agency dates back to 1902 when it was founded by T.M. Gooch, whose son-in-law, G. Frank Brown, Sr., and grandson, G. Frank Brown, Jr. continued the agency until each retired. I am proud to say I came on the scene in 1946 after returning from WWII and bought into the business in 1954.

People who have been around for awhile will remember that our present location here on Union Street was the site of a beautiful old theatre built in about 1885. There was also a residence on this same block where my grandmother and mother were born, so the location has special significance. When we razed the old theatre, we were careful to protect the sand mold brick, which was then used in the construction of our new building—similar in design to a magnificent colonial structure built near Williamsburg, Virginia in 1695.

This same pride and attention to detail is the basis of our business philosophy—we invite you to read a little about Brown & Holloway. Whatever you need, give us an opportunity to provide our very special style of protection.

Starling Holloway

...a Madisonville landmark of complete insurance protection!

Buckhorn's Dawson Springs Plant

The Dawson Springs facilities of Buckhorn started in one building in 1963 under the ownership of Mid-South Plastics, Inc., a wholly owned subsidiary of Metal Specialty Company of Cincinnati, Ohio. Production in the original building, which contained 30,000 sq. ft., started in October with four employees and one injection molding press. Building additions were completed in 1965, 1971, 1976 and 1978 to increase the facility's square footage to its present size of 75,000 sq. ft. Presently there are sixteen injection molding machines and two structural foam machines in operation at the facility.

In 1970, Vanguard Industries, located in Cincinnati, Ohio, purchased Mid-South Plastics. Vanguard's Sharonville, Ohio plant was merged into the Dawson Springs facility in 1971 and a second facility in Dawson Springs was purchased. This 65,000 sq. ft. building, located approximately one quarter of a mile away from the original plant, was established and continues to operate as a distribution center for small order quantities or stock items.

Cleveland, Ohio based Midland Ross purchased Vanguard Industries in 1973 and continued to operate the facilities until ownership was acquired by Buckhorn, Inc. in 1980. Buckhorn's original corporate office, located in Columbus, Ohio, was combined with the Material Handling Division's office in Milford, Ohio in late 1986.

During 1986, renovations of both Dawson Springs facilities started. New state-of-the-art, efficient equipment replaced some of the older equipment. Process related auxiliary equipment was replaced with new, increased capacity equipment to increase efficiencies in the production process also. The exteriors of both buildings were repainted and reroofed.

In June of 1987, controlling interest in Buckhorn, Inc. was obtained by Myers Industries by the purchase of common and preferred stock. Myers Industries, whose corporate headquarters are located in Akron, OH, manufactures storage bins and rubber tire processing equipment. Since Buckhorn has been involved in the plastic reusable container business for several years, everyone feels this venture will provide a profitable and enjoyable working relationship with Industries.

Cates Olds-Cadillac

Since 1947

New Car Showroom
Used Car Lot

744 S. Main
Madisonville
821-4791
825-1272

Founders
Brodie Cates
Maurice Cates

Cornette Engineering Services

CORNETTE ENGINEERING SERVICES

MINING CONSULTANTS

SINCE 1973

POST OFFICE BOX 271
2850 NORTH MAIN STREET
MADISONVILLE, KENTUCKY 42431
TELEPHONE 502 - 821 - 5149

Franklin, Gordon, Hobgood & Troop

Byron Lee Hobgood

W. Michael Troop

Charles G. Franklin II

Laurence T. Gordon

The history of this law firm is derived from two families of lawyers.

One law firm had its beginning in 1910 in Madisonville, Kentucky, when Charles G. Franklin began the practice of law. His firm became the law firm of Franklin & Franklin when his son, Carroll S. Franklin, joined as a partner in 1948. Charles G. Franklin died in 1959, and the firm was continued by Carroll S. Franklin.

B. N. Gordon began practicing law in Madisonville, Kentucky, in 1912, and later formed a partnership with L. R. Fox. Laurence T. Gordon, the son of B. N. Gordon, practiced law with the firm of Fox & Gordon from 1945 to 1950 when he became County Attorney of Hopkins County, Kentucky, a position that he served for twelve years; and after which time he became a law partner with Carroll S. Franklin, under the firm name of Franklin & Gordon. Bryon Lee Hobgood, City Attorney for Madisonville, Kentucky joined this firm as a partner in 1975.

In 1978 Laurence T. Gordon left the firm to become the first Hopkins County District Court Judge. Carroll S. Franklin died in 1980, and Byron L. Hobgood continued the law firm, and it was joined by W. Michael Troop, a former State Representative for Hopkins County, as a partner in 1981. Soon thereafter in the year 1982, Charles G. Franklin, II, a son of Carroll S. Franklin, joined the firm as a partner.

Laurence T. Gordon served as District Judge of Hopkins County until January, 1986, at which time he rejoined the law firm, and the firm now continues with the four partners: Byron Lee Hobgood; W. Michael Troop; Charles G. Franklin, II; and Laurence T. Gordon.

HAPPY'S

OFFICE SUPPLIES

OFFICE FURNITURE
Layout & Design

"YOUR SOURCE FOR EVERY OFFICE NEED"

Electronic Typewriters
Calculators
Word Processors
Personal Computers
Computer Printers

COPIERS

SALES & SERVICE

JORDANS FURNITURE

In the year 1937, the month of October, the Jordan Furniture Company came to Madisonville. It was owned and operated by W.D. Jordan. The Jordan Furniture Company succeeded what was then known as the J.D. Whitsell Furniture Company, which was located on West Center Street adjacent to the building once occupied by Jere's, which since then has burned down. The Furniture store opened with a staff of four people. After five years in that location, it became very evident that the Furniture Store had to move to larger quarters in order to properly display the merchandise.

In the year 1942, Mr. Jordan was fortunate to secure the building that was known as the Dulin Building, located at 31 South Main Street now housing the Madisonville-Hopkins County Public Library. W.D. Jordan's son, E.E. "Dave" Jordan was managing the company by then.

As the Furniture Company continued to grow, the staff increasing through the years to a total of ten people, it outgrew that location as well. Then in February of 1965 the company moved to the building it now occupies at 749 East Center Street. Here it has a 30 thousand square foot display and sales floor with an additional 10 thousand square feet of warehouse space, as well as a spacious parking lot.

Mr. E.D. "Dave" Jordan died in 1982 and the Company is now operated and managed by Vicky Gill (Mrs. James L. "Buddy" Gill) who has been with the company since August 15, 1955.

This year the Jordan Furniture Company will celebrate its 50th anniversary.

Madisonville-1940

E.D. "Dave" Jordan

PROW BROTHERS

Plumbing, Heating, Air Conditioning and Repair Work
18 Sugg Street Madisonville, Kentucky 42431

PROW BROTHERS is currently owned and managed by Russell Prow, who became active in the firm upon graduation from the University of Kentucky in 1966.

This firm had its origin in a business established in 1923 by Russell's grandfather, Samuel C. Ivey. Mr. Ivey had come to Madisonville from Nashville, Tennessee in 1921, as an employee of Bryant Plumbing Company.

Aubrey Prow, Russell's father, moved to Madisonville from Webster County with his family in 1910 when he was only four years old. Aubrey and his brothers E. L. "Doc", and Harold began working for Mr. Samuel Ivey in the early 1920's.

In 1925 the three Prow brothers formed their own company, at about the time that a natural gas pipeline came to town. The installation of home lines, gas furnaces and appliances required much plumbing work and this gave the Prow Brothers firm an opportunity to get well established.

Doc went into defense work early in World War II, leaving Aubrey and Harold to manage the firm until Harold's death in 1965. Aubrey continued the operation until he sold the firm to his son Russell in 1972. Russell has since operated a successful enterprise serving Hopkins County for the past fifteen years.

R. & D. ELECTRIC COMPANY

R. & D. Electric Co. was originated by Basil Richardson and Dorris Dixon mainly for the sale and repair of electric motors. They opened their shop at 105 Dempsey Street in July of 1962 and became dealers of Maytag appliances along with the motor service. Dixon sold out to Richardson in 1963.

In June of 1967 Richardson sold the building and business to Ben Tomblinson, who had been operating an independent business of electrical installations and maintenance and appliance repair service. Tomblinson combined his three employees with the two who had worked for Richardson, and eventually added the Kelvinator line of appliances.

In 1972, upon graduation from Western Kentucky University, with a degree in Industrial Technology, Mike Tomblinson became a partner in the business. After 13 years the business had grown to the point that larger quarters were necessary and it was moved to the present location at 276 W. Center St. in 1980. This building was previously owned by Ruby Jackson and had been used for a food and produce house, and later as a mine supply company on the east side, and housed the Salvation Army Store on the west side.

Mike Tomblinson now serves as General Manager; the business employs a total of 17 people at this time and uses 10 service trucks. It services all of Hopkins County with every type electrical installation or maintenance (industrial, commercial or residential), sells and services a full line of Maytag and General Electric major appliances, and sells and installs York heating and cooling equipment.

ROBARDS DRUG STORE, INC.

13 SOUTH MAIN STREET
MADISONVILLE, KENTUCKY 42431
TELEPHONE (502)-821-5511

Robards Drug Store opened in 1938 on West Center Street with W. A. Robards, owner. In July, 1940, J. W. Hatchel became a partner with Mr. Robards and in July, 1942, they moved the store to its present location of 13 South Main Street. In 1973, the store expanded north next to Kentucky Bank and in 1980 expanded south to include the card and gift shop. In 1975, Tim Gallagher bought into the store and upon the retirement of J. W. Hatchel in 1984 Tim and Judy Gallagher became the sole owners.

Free Advice, Free Charge Service, Free Insurance Claiming, Free Delivery. . . . . . . .WHERE CAN YOU BEAT IT?
OPEN 7 DAYS A WEEK TILL 10 PM. . . . . .365 Days A Year.

RUBY CONCRETE CO.

Rudd Insurance Inc.

A Part of the History of Hopkins County since 1925

Scott-McGaw Motor Company

SCOTT-McGAW MOTOR COMPANY

SALES AND SERVICE

Madisonville, Ky. 42431

Hopkins County's oldest automotive dealership was opened in 1924 by Ernest Scott and John Wesley McGaw. Their first location was on Sugg St. at the L & N Railroad. Within a short time they obtained the Pontiac franchise and later became the authorized Buick and GMC trucks dealers.

By merchandising high quality GM products and providing excellent maintenance service the firm prospered and in the late 1930's built a new facility at the present location on the Northeast corner of N. Main and Arch.

In 1933 Wesley's son N. S. "Scottie" McGaw returned from Purdue University and entered the motor car business. Scottie opened a dealership for the firm in Henderson, KY in the mid 1930s and there met his wife Anne. Anne and Scottie were married and moved to Madisonville in the late 30's.

Scottie remained active in the automobile business and exercised a positive influence in the community and civic affairs until his death in 1978.

Barry McGaw, the second son of Anne and Scottie, joined his father in the automobile business in 1965. He became the Buick Pontiac and GMC dealer in 1978 continuing the operations under the name of Scott-McGaw Motor Company.

Barry and his wife Mollie have two teenage children, Skip, a freshman at the University of Kentucky, and Anne Barret, a junior at Madisonville North Hopkins High School. Both showing interest in the automobile business, so the fourth generation is close at hand. With our many years of experience and great products, we thank you for your past and future business.

Speed Queen

Originally founded in 1908 as Huebsch Manufacturing Company of Milwaukee, the firm first manufactured hosiery forms, collar starchers, and other speciality items for the commercial laundry and drycleaning trade. In 1931, the firm invented what was called an open-ended clothes dryer, which was sold to commercial laundries.

A total of seven different size dryers, ranging in load sizes from 24 to 150 pounds are manufactured at the Madisonville plant. These tumbler dryers are sold throughout the U.S. and many foreign countries and are used in coin-operated laundries and laundry rooms of apartment houses, college dormitories, institutions and military facilities. All fabrication and assembly is done within the Madisonville plant.

The tumbler dryers that we enjoy today were introduced during the 1940's. The Madisonville plant was constructed in 1969 providing a total of 150,000 square feet of office and production space. In 1978, McGraw-Edison merged the operation of the Madisonville Huebsch plant and the McGraw-Edison Laundry Products Division. In 1979, the Laundry Products Division was purchased by Raytheon and the name was changed to the Speed Queen Company.

The Raytheon family consists of names such as Amana, Caloric, Speed Queen, Beechcraft Aviation. It is a diversified international company with more than 78,000 employees and is among the 100 largest industrial corporations in America.

Our reputation for quality, dependability and concern for our employees is the backbone of our growth and success.

U.C. Milk Co.

Since 1927

The original 333 shares issued-
U.C. Milk Co., Inc. 1928

Issued to:	No. Shares
Ruby Lumber Co. 5	U.W. Jenkins 5
R. Smith Dulin 5	Delmont Utley 10
A.R. Blanks 5	L.K. Bell 10
M.K. Gordon 10	James R. Rash 10
J. Craig Riddle 25	P.B. Ross 5
E.G. Tapp 50	J.W. Thomson, Sr. 10
Dr. E.B. Hardin 5	John R. Taylor-

Received Certificate #18 from
U.W. Jenkins

T.C. O'Bryan 10	Ashby Corum 31
John H. Utterback 31	Ashby Corum 50
John H. Utterback 50	D.W. Gatlin 6

Total Shares 333

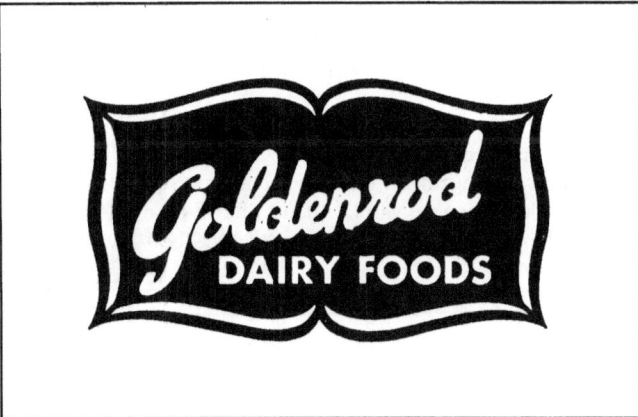

Vaughan Engineering

Vaughan Engineering was established in 1975 by William E. Vaughan as a Civil and Mining Engineering Consultant primarily to serve the coal industry in Western Kentucky. Since that date, the firm has expanded its field of expertise to include all phases of civil and mining engineering. From its original "one-man" company in rental property on North Main, the company has grown annually and now occupies a permanent office building at 173 West Lake Street, corner of Lake and South Seminary. The firm's structure and work ethic has constantly been modified to keep abreast of rapidly expanding technology, economics, governmental regulations, and many other aspects that influence today's engineering community; and consequently our society.

Vaughan Engineering was founded on a commitment to serve the best interest of its clients. Its ability to perform services within its field of expertise and experience coupled with honesty and a commitment to serve the best interest of its clients is evident in the growth of the firm over this short period of time.

A staff of three (3) Registered Professional Civil Engineers are supported by in-house office and field personnel, computer capabilities, and the latest electronic field equipment; enabling the firm to meet the challenges of today's complex engineering problems.

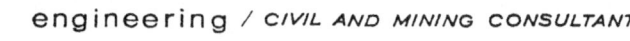

VAUGHAN engineering / CIVIL AND MINING CONSULTANTS
173 WEST LAKE STREET · MADISONVILLE KENTUCKY 42431 · TEL. (502) 821-2013

Weldon M. Brown Fuels Inc.

Weldon M. Brown Fuels Inc., one of the major coal brokerages in Kentucky, ships about 2 million tons annually.

"Brownies" reputation with the fuel buyers was built on his ability to put together required tonnages from multiple sources and to maintain product quality.

Weldon and his father, Carl, began operation at Coiltown in 1953 in partnership with others.

In 1962, he established W.M. Brown Fuels specializing in marketing and brokerage of fuel coal by both barge and rail. Electric utilities have always been our major customers.

Upon Mr. Brown's death in August of 1984, he was succeeded as President of W.M. Brown Fuels, Inc. by Ms. Vicky Foley.

Quality Coal by Rail or Barge

P.O. Box 369
Madisonville
(502) 821-6950

Baker and Hickman

"Madisonville's Leading Department Store"

For 86 years your hometown department store

Featuring nationally known brands at affordable prices

9 E. Center Street
Downtown
821-5686

Century 21

DOZIER-FAZENBAKER, INC.
100 West Broadway, PO Box 767
Madisonville, Kentucky 42431

Clark, Beshear and Clark

Clark, Beshear and Clark was founded in 1909 by the late Theodore Clark and the late Fred Beshear. Operating in those early years, the firm was an undertaking establishment as well as furniture business. Later the late Denny Clark, son of Theodore, entered the firm as a full partner. Hence the name Clark, Beshear and Clark.

In 1945, Russell Beshear and the late Ligon Beshear purchased both the undertaking and furniture and appliance firms from the retiring Fred Beshear and Denny Clark. These partners operated the firm until 1951 when Eddie Beshear purchased the interest of Ligon Beshear who moved away to Mississippi.

In 1953, the undertaking firm and the furniture and appliance businesses were separated. The undertaking firm became Beshear Funeral Home and the furniture and appliance store remained Clark, Beshear and Clark under it's new partners - Louis Franklin and Charles Simons.

Since 1909, Clark, Beshear and Clark has served Hopkins, Christian and Caldwell Counties and is Hopkins County's oldest furniture and appliance business.

Clements Jewelers Inc.

In 1935 Pat Clements moved to Madisonville, Kentucky from Marion, Kentucky where he had been in the jewelry business for a couple of years. He rented space from his brother and sister-in-law, Sam and Elizabeth Clements, who already were operating a beauty shop. The beauty shop was in the back of the building and the jewelry store was in the front. After about four years, Sam went into business with Pat. The original store was across the street and about four doors south of its present location. There was only one showcase to start with.

In just a few years the grocery store expanded and moved and Clements Jewelers moved to its present location.

In about 1945, Sam and Elizabeth left and moved with their two daughters, Gail and Martha, to Paducah, Kentucky where he opened up his own store and operated it until retirement about eighteen years ago.

In 1963, Carmel, Pat and Thelma's oldest daughter came to work at the store followed by Steve, their only son, in 1969. They trained under him until his death in 1973 at which time Thelma took over the store. She had worked there off and on since it's beginning. In 1981, she died and the store is now run by Steve and Carmel. On November 1, 1985 the store was Incorporated.

COLE & DURHAM INSURANCE INC.

SAM F. DURHAM
BERRY ADCOCK
STEPHEN P. DURHAM

This agency was established by T.C. O'Brien in the early 1920's and was later acquired by Charles Trathen. The agency had offices at several locations on South Main Street before moving to its present location at 446 East Center Street in the mid 1970's.

Dan and Wilma Mitchell owned and managed this agency from Apr. 1, 1957 until Jan. 1, 1970 when it was acquired by Frank Cole and Sam Durham. In December of 1986 Messrs. Durham and Adcock purchased Mr. Cole's interest and the three principals listed above currently operate the firm.

GREATER MADISONVILLE AREA CHAMBER OF COMMERCE

THE CHAMBER "WORKS" FOR YOU!
8:00 AM - 4:30 PM
MON-FRI

821-3435

140 S. Main   Madisonville

COMPLIMENTS OF HOPKINS COUNTY ASPHALT INC.

P. O. Box 1051
Madisonville, Kentucky 42431

Phone 502-825-8014

SERVING THE AREA'S PAVING NEEDS

Hopkins County Broadcasters

STEREO

24 HOURS A DAY

"THE WILDCAT'S DEN IS 1310"

821-1310

265 SOUTH MAIN
MADISONVILLE, KY. 42431

Compliments of Joe Leasure and Sons Inc.

Serving Mining and Industry Since 1935

READY MIX CONCRETE

Plus

- Stone
- Sand
- River Gravel
- Cement
- Kosmortar
- Plastic Wheel Stops
- Quikrete
- Quikwall

- Wire Mesh
- Rebar
- Expansion Joints
- Plastic Pipe
- Plastic Septic Tanks
- Concrete Sealers
- Bonding Agents
- Foundation Vents

RADIO DISPATCHED
DELIVERY TO THE GREATER HOPKINS AREA
MIXED TO YOUR SPECIFICATIONS
"NO JOB TOO BIG OR TOO SMALL"

Madisonville Concrete Co.
FULLY AUTOMATED PLANT
821-1478
2400 N. MAIN MADISONVILLE

McCOY & McCOY, INC.
Environmental Consultants
P. O. Box 907 • 85 East Noel Avenue • Madisonville, Kentucky 42431 • Phone 502-821-7375

The company was founded in 1952 to provide consultation in water and wastewater treatment plant maintenance supervision and analytical assistance to the Western Kentucky coal industry. It was founded by J. W. McCoy (father of the current President). Today the firm has expanded its capabilities far beyond the initial focus, to include additional municipal, industrial, commercial, and energy related clients in such ways as follows: supplying technical assistance to coal companies with mining feasibility studies; ensuring safety of drinking water for communities/public sources, as well as private sources; developing hazardous waste management plans for industrial and manufacturing clients; providing state-of-the-art assistance in asbestos abatement and detection; training of employees of clients in the right-to-know concerns; performing environmental audits; assisting clients with engineering and design services; and participating in the statutory/regulatory development, review, and compliance inspections processes. Because of the uniqueness of the firm's broad base of both analytical services and technical consulting the company serves many clients through a specialty of mitigation, handling specific aspects for the client with regard to communications between affected agencies. The firm services just shy of two thousand clients.

Principles in the firm are John A. McCoy - President, C. E. O.; Scott R. Smith - Vice President of Technical Services; Victor Scott Simms - Vice President of Analytical Services; and Barclay B. McCoy - Secretary/Treasurer.

The firm currently employs over one hundred and fifty individuals across the six offices located in Madisonville, Pikeville, Paducah, Lexington, Louisville, Kentucky and Evansville, Indiana.

McGary Bros. Furniture

Quality Furniture
Reasonable Prices

For Over 30 Years
Name Brands Such As
- Serta
- Broyhill
- Rowe
- Barcalounger
- Cochrane
- Sumter
- Dixie
- Catnapper
- Virginia House
- Waterbeds

We carry Our Own Accounts
• 90 Days Same As Cash
• Visa and Mastercard Welcome

19 North Main • Downtown

MELODY LANES

Melody Lanes opened Dec. 10, 1959 with 12 lanes and soon expanded to 20 lanes, and has for 28 years served the recreational needs of our many friends in Hopkins County.

We soon learned that when you entertain people, you are probably going to have to feed them. Meeting this need marked the beginning of Ballard Catering Service. We cater a delicious Bar-B-Q meal to any group, large or small. We also specialize in broasted chicken and all the trimmings.

This combination led to a wide range of friendships and opportunities for service that have been the hallmark of our success.

677 S. Main Street
Madisonville, Kentucky 42431

502/821-0016-Business

Dan McGary
OWNER/MANAGER

L.B. HOOVER, INC.

L.B. Hoover, Sr. came to Madisonville in 1916 and established the Chero Cola Bottling Co., a family owned business.

In 1932 Dr. Pepper was added and in the early 1930s Royal Crown Cola was introduced to the market. The first plant was located on West Center St. and the present plant is located at 308 West Center St., within two blocks of the original plant.

The business continues to be family owned. The son, L.B. Hoover, Jr., and the daughter, Laura D. Hoover Knight, are still involved in the business. Leslie B. Hoover III, the grandson of the founder, is manager of the business.

Ottenheimer and Company, Inc.

Dawson Springs, Kentucky

Manufacturers of
Professional Lab Wear
and
Corporate Image Identity Uniforms

META

State Farm Insurance

Frank A. Cheek, agent for State Farm Insurance opened his office on October 1, 1956 on S. Main Street over Kentucky Bank and Trust Company and remained in the downtown area until he built his office at the present location at 643 South Main Street and moved into it January 1, 1980.

Perry Cheek, son of Frank Cheek, became a State Farm agent September 1, 1983 and he shares the office building with his father. They employ three secretaries and all keep busy as State Farm is the largest insurer of automobile and fire insurance and is rapidly becoming the largest in life and health.

Perry A. Cheek
Frank A. Cheek

Steele, Hoodenpile & Roberts Agency, Inc.

AGENTS
Tommie Hoodenpile
383-2311

Bill Lansden
383-2311

Ed Steele
676-8434

Give Us A Try
Before You Buy

110 E. Main St.
Box 187
Earlington

Main St.-Box 315
Nortonville

Southern States

Southern States began operating in Madisonville and Hopkins County in 1948 on South Main Street and later moved to a new building on Seminary Street. In 1976 we moved to our present location at 1001 Pride Avenue and constructed a modern showroom and warehouse with ample room for any needed future expansion.

West Kentucky Plate Glass, Inc.

924 Main Street
P.O. Box 352
Madisonville

John "Doug" Inglis
O.M. Kington, Jr.
821-2646

Wilson & McPherson, Inc.

Wilson & McPherson, Inc. and its predecessor agencies have served the INSURANCE needs of Hopkins Countians for 118 years. It began with the founding of the R.M. King Agency on Oct. 13, 1869. Some of the other members of this firm were Rufus K. Arnold, James F. Dempsey, George W. Ramsey, W.E. Bourland, C.E. Morton, Ruby Laffoon, Sam D. Langley, Roy S. Wilson, Joel C. McPherson, Carl G. Vannoy and Everett Smith.

In 1897, the firm was known as Laffoon & Langley. In 1914, its name became Langley and Wilson and in 1916 Langley, Wilson and McPherson. In 1934, the present name of WILSON & McPHERSON was adopted and the firm has since been so known.

The C.B. Dillingham Store in White Plains in 1903

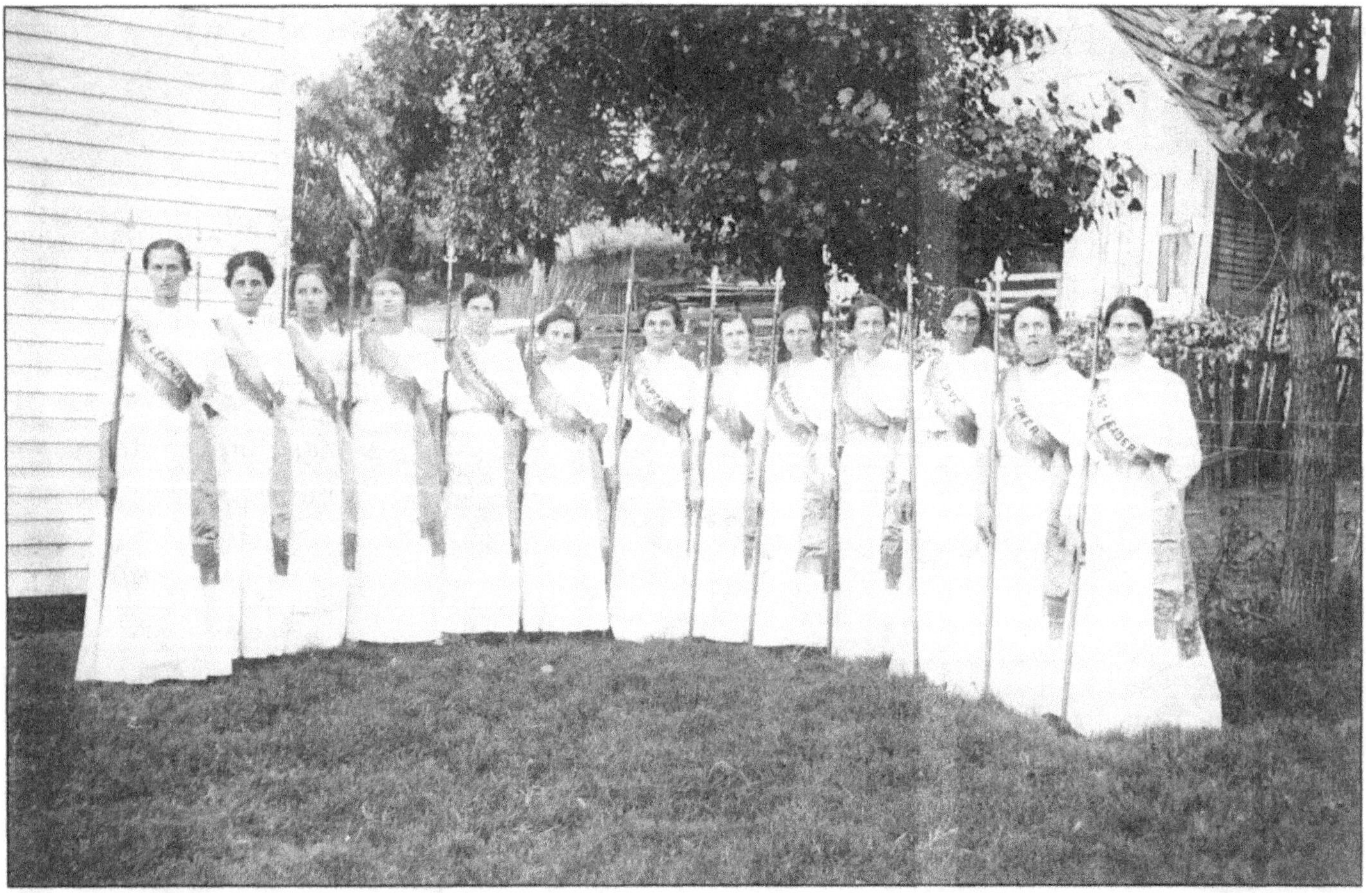

Woodmen of the World Ladies Auxiliary at Ashbyburg about 1910. From Left to Right: Emma Tomblinson Ashby, Unknown, Vaden Gentry (Mrs. Sam Corum), Emma Pritchett, Lesbia Corum (Mrs. M. Ashby Corum), Mallie Corum (wife of Dr. John R. Corum), Mrs. Jim Weldon, Beulah Cobb Allen, Dolly Tomblinson Carlisle, Miss Weldon, Mrs. Spicer, Clara Crabtree, and Nollie Anderson.

"I REMEMBER" STORIES

A Christmas Trip by Wagon

One of Hopkins County's outstanding citizens remembers a Christmas when he was a small boy.

Mr. J. W. (Will) Neisz traveled with his family from near Dawson Springs to Kuttawa by wagon to spend Christmas with Mrs. Julis Byard. Mrs. Byard was a sister of his grandmother, Mrs. Nancy Barnes. Mr. Neisz was about 5 or 6 years old at the time.

The family set out a few days before Christmas all bundled up in the family wagon for the trip which would take some time in those days. They spent the night in Princeton before traveling on.

There was Grandmother Nancy, Father John Barnes and his mother who was named James, and a brother Richard who was two years older than young Will and a sister Ruby who was 6 years older. So this was a trip with much preparation and anticipation.

An interesting thing is the mother's name "James" sometimes called "Jim". Shortly before she was born, her father who was named James died of typhoid fever at the age of 32. So her mother named her James.

Back to the wagon trip. After spending the night in Princeton, they traveled on to Kuttawa, where they enjoyed a happy Christmas with Aunt Julia and her family. There was plenty to eat, a Christmas tree and presents especially for the children.

When it came time to return home several days later, the weather had turned much colder and they considered the long trip home in the wagon. Father counted his money and left money for the family to take the train from Kuttawa to Princeton. Then early that morning he set out in the wagon to meet them upon their arrival later in Princeton.

You can imagine the excitement of three small children riding the train to go back home after having a happy Christmas. They were met by Father at the end of the train ride and then continued the trip home with Father in their trusty wagon.

In 1900 a train ride for a five year old boy was really an adventure worth remembering.

As told to Helen Wilcox

Circus Caused A Stir-1920's

There was one time of year that was always long awaited - the animal circus.

"The circus is coming!" someone would say. After hearing this call, Woodruff McGregor and his friends would hear their teacher dismiss school for the day. As they ran outside the Menser School, they would watch the fancy decorated wagons and trailers filled with all types of circus animals.

At this time the circus would travel dirt roads to go from place to place instead of traveling by train. When the caravan of fancy wagons and trailers would pass the school, the teacher would dismiss school because the students would all gather around to watch and she couldn't keep their attention with all this commotion.

The circus would then proceed into Dawson Springs where it set up in an old field that is now in the block between Kentucky 109, Hamby Avenue, Gilmore Street and Scott Street. People from all over Dawson Springs would come to see this annual event.

For someone who grew up on a farm, going to the annual circus was a long-waited-for event.

by David Paul Garrett

Watt Ridley's Recollections of Town Progress

Watt Ridley has lived almost all of his life in Dawson Springs.

Mr. Ridley remembers when Dawson Springs did not have electricity. A mill on Railroad Avenue had a generator and furnished electricity to four other buildings. The New Century Hotel furnished electricity to three other buildings and one store had carbide lights; otherwise, everyone else used kerosene lamps.

Mr. Ridley also remembers a steamboat that made regular runs carrying passengers on the Tradewater River and when one of four doctors could be consulted on a bench under a shade tree.

In Mr. Ridley's childhood, his father ran a livery stable on East Railroad Avenue. After Mr. Ridley's mother was widowed, she would rent two extra beds when the many hotels overflowed. She rented these beds for 25 cents a night per person.

Mr. Ridley also helped bring in extra money by going to work at Hamby's Well when he was 10 years old - selling papers, pumping water and working in the basement. He continued in this job until he went into military service.

by Lori Littlejohn

Early Dawson Springs

Many people from the southeast of the United States, especially from Tennessee, Mississippi and Alabama, have known of Dawson Springs as a health resort. Some of these people came to the Health Resort as children with their parents and then came back as adults with their families. This process continued over a half century and the number of people coming to Dawson Springs was substantiated by an advertisement of the I. C. Railroad which stated "We sold 50,000 tickets to Dawson Springs in a 3 month period." At that period in our history, it was the only way one could get to and from the city.

Now the health resort period was an outstanding time in the history of this early community, but I would like to address another phase of the city's history, which is, when Dawson Springs was used by professional baseball teams to hold their spring training.

In 1914 and 1915, the Pittsburgh Pirates came to train for the coming seasons. The New Century Hotel, one of the finest in the South at that time, was built in 1902 and consisted of the front part facing Main Street and the side wing running along Ramsey Street. Evidently the Pirate Organization wanted more rooms than the hotel could furnish, so they put up the funds for building another wing on the opposite side of the Hotel. During the spring of 1914 and 1915, they had free lodging and meals to repay the team for the money they had advance to the Hotel in the construction of this new wing.

Then the people of Dawson Springs built a barn-like structure, approximately 30 feet by 80 feet, wherein the team could work out in inclement weather. As you know, you can have some foul weather in March.

The best known player on that team was Hans Wagner who was considered the greatest shortstop at that time. He took a great deal of interest in the young boys of this community, helping them to become interested in baseball and teaching them the finer points of the game. This bunch of boys were known as "Wagner Recruits" and the majority of this group went on to become outstanding adults at home and in many places over the U. S. We are sure that the influence of Wagner on these boys gave them the desire to succeed in life.

There were, of course, other outstanding individuals on the team. The manager was Roger Brisnahan, a very successful former player as well as manager. Max Carey was the leading base stealer, not only on the Pirates team but in the National League. Babe Adams won 3 games in the 1915 World Series.

I was only a small boy at this time, but I can vividly remember the Pirates running through the Arcadia Hotel Park going to Pirate Park, which was named for them. I can remember they wore heavy Mackinaw Coats over their uniforms, running in basketball shoes with baseball shoes in their hands or hung around their necks. I would have given anything to have been in their place.

There were 3 Triple A teams from the American Association and a team known as an outlaw team, meaning they had been barred from other organized leagues which also trained here; namely the Toledo Mudhens, the Columbus Redbirds and the Louisville Colonels. These teams came here after World War I, with the Louisville team making about 5 trips to our town, one as late as 1935.

The Louisville team was my favorite, probably because I was older and able to go and watch them practice. The manager was a man named Meyers. One of the pitchers I will always remember, who was a full blooded American Indian that later played in the Major League, his name was Ben Tincup. Buy probably the individual I remember and liked best was the trainer, a black man that loved all kids. Our kid teams never lacked for bats and balls as he saw we were well supplied. Of course, the bats had been broken but we became experts in repairing the bats and we certainly didn't mind the balls being scuffed and dirty. I am sure Phil Bean is now a trainer for some Heavenly baseball team with a gang of kids following every play.

It is so great to look back and remember some of the things in the history of Dawson Springs, Kentucky.
by D. Fletcher Holeman

MADISONVILLE, AS I REMEMBER

I was born in Anton on November 25, 1908. As a child, I remember traveling to Madisonville every week by horse and carriage to shop during the week and go to church on Sunday.

The downtown area had the only street with sidewalks and were made of brick. The streets had no names at this time but were called by nicknames of something or someone in the area.

As we traveled along the road (known as Center Street now) the Madison Hotel sat on the corner of Center and Union. Across the street (now the Municipal Building) was Crowe's Livery Stable. We would do our shopping at the Grand Leader Department Store located in the area where Sharp's Bakery is now.

Across Main Street there ws the Grand Central Hotel, L & N Depot and the entrance to Tandy's Hall which was located where Jere's Department Store burned. Ben Elkstein Theater, Thompson's Restaurant, the Woolridge Restaurant, Charlie Woolridge Skating Rink, Dr. Lester's Drug Store, Carter's Livery Stable and Hipple's Saloon made up most of the lower level of Center Street.

Dempsey Street now as called the Jockey Ground. We took our corn for grinding to Thompson's Mill (where Foodtown Grocery is now).

On Main and Sugg Street was the Madisonville Hospital. A greek restaurant, the Post Office and Dulin's Store was the biggest part of Main Street.

Some of the most exciting times were spent at the Fair Grounds which were located where it is now. It had a board fence all around it. We hitched our horses across the street (in the area of Wiman Packing Co.) and we were off to a day at the fair. They sold lemonaid by the barrel, had horse races and the Merry-Go-Round now as called a Flying-Ginny which was run by steam. They had clowns and tent shows for entertainment.

I have seen Madisonville grow and prosper. I have seen good times and bad times, streets with no names and streets with names and I am proud to say I am glad to be a part of this community.
by Eldora Buckner

I REMEMBER ST. CHARLES IN THE EARLY 1900'S

On Aug. 7, 1900, I was born in Morton's Gap to Thomas M. and Dovie Emma (Jordan) Warren. We moved to St. Charles when I was 9 years old when I was placed in the 4th grade at the old St. Charles school. After a few months I was sent to the 5th grade in the "big room". My father went to work for Fox Run Mines of the St. Bernard Coal Company.

I lived in St. Charles from 1909 to 1967 when my husband, Charlie R. Jenkins, died in November.

St. Charles was a thriving coal town with lots of people living there in 1909. I remember how the town looked while I was growing up there. In the early years the roads were slack covered, there were no sidewalks, and the paths got very muddy in the winter. The main street through town was Greenville Street from Christian Privilege Church hill going east toward Crossroads and Nortonville. There were several mercantile stores, grocery stores, a drug store, restaurants, barber shop, dentist and doctor's offices along this street. There was a coal tipple just north of the Greenville Street operated by St. Charles Coal Co. which created a huge, smoldering slack pile right in the town, hauled there by mule and cart. It stayed there until after WW II and was an eye-catcher for strangers to the town for many years.

There were many "shot gun" type houses built and owned by the coal companies for the coal miners they employed; and there were some large, nice homes there also. They were called "shot gun" because the 3 rooms were lined up one room behind the other. We used kerosene (coal oil) lamps, and heated by coal grates and cooked with a coal stove. We had outside privies for many years.

A big Company store on Greenville St. owned first by St. Bernard Coal and later by West KY, had all kinds of groceries, clothing, shoes, furniture, hardware, appliances, coal oil—most anything a family needed. Metal tokens, called "flickers", of different money denominations, were issued by the coal company to miners who needed credit or some advance cash before payday. The flickers were as good as cash at the company store, and when turned in for an item, the amount was deducted from the miner's pay. A miner would do well to have any money coming to him at the end of the pay period.

A popular boarding house on Greenville St. was operated by Mrs. Annie Jenkins, who many years later was my mother-in-law. Wm. C. Jenkins was an early salesman for the St. Bernard Coal Co. The boarding house was for the drummers (salesmen) who came to St. Charles to sell their wares to the Company Store, and to other merchants. They had to come by the I. C. Train and stay overnight and catch the train out the next day, or they had to ride over from the livery stable at Earlington, which was more expensive.

The night train going east from Paducah, nicknamed "Whiskey Dick", would bring liquor orders to St. Charles residents. The application order and the money would have to be sent down the day before, and the next trip up it would bring the order. The person making the order had to take the order off from the baggage man. I remember my father lighting his lantern to go to the depot to meet the train to get his order of peach brandy.

One Saturday when I was a young girl, there was a tragic "shoot out" at the Company Store which was near our home. I was taking a bath when we saw people running to the store. Two men, the best of friends, had got into a big argument; one was the policeman and the other one had come to town drunk. When the policeman attempted to arrest the drunk, he shot the policeman. He fell, but raised up on his elbow and shot the drunk. He reeled out on the porch and fell off the porch dead. The policeman also died later. When the excitement started, I put my house coat on over my long handled underwear and rushed down to see what was going on. I walked up and looked at the dead man who had fallen off the porch. This was really sad as both men were well-liked around St. Charles.

We walked about 3 blocks to school every day, through all kinds of weather, and walked home for lunch—never heard of school being dismissed because of the snow, or bad weather. In winter we wore union suits (long underwear) down to our ankles, cotton ribbed stockings, and black sateen bloomers to the ankles covering the underwear. We wore either laced up or buttoned shoes, whichever our mother chose for us from the company store. Our dresses were home-made cotton print, made by mother and by Miss Alice Trover who was a seamstress for the community. Our coats were of coarse wool material.

Now and then, we had spelling bees with the whole four grades participating. All through the year we got "headmarks" for turning down everyone in spelling, where you went to the head of the line. I remember one time I won by being able to correctly spell "biscuit". I also got the most headmarks for the year one time, and we had been promised a prize from Dr. Curry, a community doctor. I remember my disappointment at receiving a little ball about the size of a golf ball for my prize from Dr. Curry.

A pump next to our school building supplied us good ole sulphur water for the school and to the entire town as well. We had a water bucket and dipper for the school, but some of us used little metal collapsible cups, and kept them in our desks. Some years later when another school building was planned for the same spot, Dr. Curry bought the lumber from the school building and built a nice house in St. Charles, up the hill from the pump, second house on the left which is still being used. The old sulphur-water pump was used for many decades, but is now capped over with only a concrete base to mark its place.

The toilets were boy's and girl's privies with a blind in front of each. The toilets were very unsanitary of course, with many flies and often you had to step over where the small girls "squatted" outside, because they were afraid to go in the toilet. We had "In-Out" paddles that hung by the doors of the boy's and girl's cloakrooms, and when you were "excused" you turned the paddle to "Out" and no one else could go out until you returned and turned the paddle to "In".

When I was a young teenager I was mostly interested in a certain boy, Charlie Jenkins, who was 4 years older than me. My mother thought he was too old for me, so I had to slip around to get to see him. He worked at a restaurant owned by Norris King, and he saved cigarette coupons and got a little silver spoon (called an orange spoon) which he gave to me. That was before we had even started "talking" (courtship), but we liked each other. One Christmas time he had a date with my older sister, May, and he gave her a box of candy, but I wouldn't eat a bite of it. He did things like that to mislead my mother about his feelings for me. He asked me what he could get for me, and I told him nothing because Mama would be sure to find it out.

When I was 17 and Charlie 21, we eloped to Clarksville, TN, taken by good friends, Harlan and Alma Kinnett, and were married. We observed our 50th Wedding Anniversary Sept. 23, 1967, before Charlie died in November, 1967. I left St. Charles after his death to be closer to my son, Charles W. Jenkins and family in Madisonville, but my heart and memories will always remember the days at St. Charles.

Many other memories of St. Charles may be read in the 1983 Yearbook of the Historical Society of Hopkins County which featured St. Charles.

by Opal F. (Warren) Jenkins

SARAH BARRON REMEMBERS

Some will doubt that a child of age 3-4 could recall happenings at such an early age, but my earliest memories are of the period between 1912-1914. I was born in Madisonville, May 15, 1909. By 1912, we were living in Nebo and by 1914, we had moved to our farm north of Nebo.

My brother Herbert, 22 months younger than I, took diphtheria while we live din Nebo. I have a vivid mental picture of my sick "buddy" in bed under a tent-like object and of standing in the doorway watching when the doctor saw me and shouted "GET HER OUT OF HERE".

The Will Porter family lived across the street. I remember Blanche Ray pulling her older brother, John Bradford, in a wagon. He had rheumatic fever and couldn't walk at the time.

I recall visiting my Granny Cox one day. Dressed in red from head to toe, high top buttoned shoes, red coat and hand-crocheted bonnet tied under the chin with a ribbon, I went by myself crossing the road on stepping stones. There was no danger of traffic as that was before the days of cars. I was about six when I saw and rode in a car, a Ford touring car owned by Mr. Joe Hobgood. He managed by grandfather's general store and farm in Richland. He and his wife visited my grandparents one Sunday. After dinner he took Grandad to one of his farms near Nebo and invited me to go along for the ride.

I have many memories of the four years we lived on the farm. The games I played were mostly "boy" games, as my brother Herb and I were constant companions. We wore out dozens of tobacco sticks using them as "stick horses". We rolled hoops, played marbles and he taught me how to "skin a cat" on low tree limbs. We rode Ole Rock, one of the horses, to the back of the farm to bring in the cows at milking time. We LOVED visiting the blacksmith shop about 1/10 mile down the road from our house to watch "Uncle" Charlie Pritchett shoe horses.

My brother Bill, four years my senior, rode saplings. One day he let me ride one after much begging from me. He said the second he let go he started to pray. He was afraid I would continue to "fly" but I held on for dear life. I don't remember begging to ride another one.

We had our own "private swimming hole" in Weirs Creek which flowed through our farm. Ruth, Bill, Herb and I spent many summer afternoons there. High above it on the bluff many beautiful wild flowers grew.

I remember our surrey (without the fringe on top). One Sunday afternoon, Mother loaded us into the two seated buggy and went for a visit to the Wash Hobgood family on Happy Lane. As we approached the railroad just out of Manitou, a train was coming. Mother didn't see it until we were almost on the track. By the use of the buggy whip, we made it across by the "hair of our chinney-chin-chin". Another day, she went to Madisonville grocery shopping and took me along. Among the items bought was a stalk of bananas. Coming home, the bananas and I rode in the back seat. When we arrived home I wasn't sick, neither was I hungry, but there were fewer bananas on the stalk. The last time I saw the surrey it was in the condition of the "Wonderful One Horse Shay". A little wren had taken possession and had built her nest in the slit lining of the back of the front seat.

Our feather beds were made from goose feathers. How cozy to hop into bed on a cold night and have the feathers fluff up around you. Water beds can't compare with them. I remember the medicine cabinet, every home had a well stocked one. Rural people had to rely on home remedies. The doctor seldom made house calls unless the sickness was serious, as pneumonia, diphtheria, typhoid fever, TB and to assist the stork. Before immunizations such childhood diseases as measles, chicken pox and whooping cough were dreaded, but endured. I remember the hot mustard foot baths and hot lemonade - minus the sugar - and a greased chest covered by a flannel cloth. Thank goodness our mother didn't hand as-a-fet-i-da around our neck, a gum encased in a small bag and tied to a string which was put around the neck and had a very offensive odor. People with germs wouldn't get near enough to you to share them.

I stayed with my grandparents a lot after I was six. My daily chore was to grind the coffee for the next morning's breakfast. The coffee mill was a large one that hung on the wall and the coffee beans were poured in the top. A small cup at the bottom held enough grounds for a pot of coffee. I remember a traveling sock company coming to town and the life of Frank and Jesse James was presented on the stage at the court house. Granny and Grandad slept in night caps, so did I.

I started school at age seven in 1916. I had had polio (called infantile paralysis then) before I was two years old and was small for my age. My first grade teacher was Miss Minnie Kington. I was the only girl in my class. That year our students went to the school fair at Madisonville in wagons. Each of us made something to exhibit - mine was a handkerchief.

It is good to remember the good times.

I Remember

Has it been so many years ago. We were staying with grandparents while my father and uncle built a tiny one room cabin. It was fall and getting cold. Watching in awe as the big sand rock chimney began to take place. Looking deep within those early years of childhood, unfolding like an inner TV screen, some memories are snowy, some sharp and in vivid color.

I remember that winter my father building a lean-to kitchen, so cold that first morning but nice as I was tired of fried foods from the fireplace. The cabin on a rolling knoll, the front door close to the ground, the back very high off the ground. "Perfect", I heard my father say, "to dig a root cellar". Memory fogs, the small hole under the house seemed so spacious to a small child not yet old enough to attend school. It had steps, board sides, sandrock from the caves at the lower end of the pasture where my young teenage aunt and I played the summer before. Left over rough wood and heavy orange crates were the shelves for onions, potatoes, turnips and pumpkins. The orange crated had been bought the year before. My father built a dressing table for my young aunt and my mother made a pretty skirt, she called it to cover it and one for the stool. The stool was given to me many, many years later and is in use in our bedroom now with my modern furniture.

Memory sharpens. The attending of revival meetings at Old Oakley Home Church morning and evening. My grandfather's little farm was nestled back off the main road, now Highway 630. The winding dusty land came out almost in front of the old church. We went barefoot carrying our shoes, my grandmother with two wet rags in her apron pocket. At an old, even then, unused log barn atop of the knoll just before the lane descended to the main road, we would stop, wash our feet, put on our stockings and shoes and leave the apron and wet cloth until services were over.

The screen snows over but images come through. I remember a visit to my great grandmothers. A house off the main road (Highway 630), near Cox's School, store and post office. My total memory was of the very large doll laying on the "company bed". The excitement brought a curious child running. The memory is sharp and in vivid color, RED. The whole world seems to be on fire. Shouts carried on the wind. I remember how the teenaged aunt and I clung to each other and cried. My grandmother's house burned, the wind picking up the sparks, the Cox's School burned also. Many homes were threatened. The students went back to school in Cox's Store. I remember my aunt taking me with her one day just to get me used to going for the next year.

This past summer I drove the old roads pointing out old memories to my teenaged grandson. Back on the winding dusty lane, now widened and graveled. Pointing out a special memory at this turn, a fallen log barn there. Then around the last turn and there was my grandparents old home (they sold it over 40 years ago). All sorts of I remembers tumbled out, the pond my parents giged frogs for breakfast in, the remains of the corn crib I played in and had a broken dish playhouse under. The white picket fence gone, the old well off the porch (broken rim but still had water). "Would it be alright to go in the house Mamaw?" Gingerly walking through the dusty mist that shrouded the rooms, "I remembers" flooded back. A young man's interest sharpened as I pointed out the mantel I hung Christmas stockings on and a naughty little girl received switches in the top of one. The merriment gave way to deep interest as we searched for the foundation rock and old chimney of the now gone log cabin. I pointed out the directions of the old caves. My now store house of old memories was flowing into a younger memory bank. "Mamaw, I wonder if the owners now would let my scout troop explore those woods and old caves?"

Turning a switch and my modern car came to life. It did not have to be handcranked as the one my father had. I barely remember hearing my young scout say "Gee, you must have had fun when you were a kid in the old days." I remember saying the same thing to my grandmother.

I Remember

It was during the fall and winter of the big snow and I was just a little girl. My brother and his wife (not much more than a girl herself) got snowed in during a visit. We were out playing in the snow when we decided to put snow in the old rock cistern. We put so much snow in the well, Daddy couldn't sink the bucket. Did he ever fuss! But the following summer, we had the coldest drinking water of all our neighbors and we had no frig.

By Betty Ruth Shoulders Osborn

HOPKINS COUNTY CENTENARIANS

This section was the idea of Dorothy Miller Shoulders of Nebo. It is through her efforts that this section is included in this book.

"Aunt" Mattie Alcock, a former slave, was born in Graves County, Ky., in 1818 and died in Nortonville in 1934. She was buried at Clements Cemetery. (Picture not available)

Myrtle Babb was born December 31, 1887 in Hopkins County. She is currently a resident of Kentucky Rest Haven. Mrs. Babb has four daughters, seven grandchildren, seventeen great grandchildren and two great great grandchildren.

Sallie Cain (1882-1985) Photo courtesy of Brown's Rest Home. See her family history.

Sarah (Sally) Temperance Cox born March 20, 1831 and died August 22, 1931 at the age of 100. See her story. (Picture not Available)

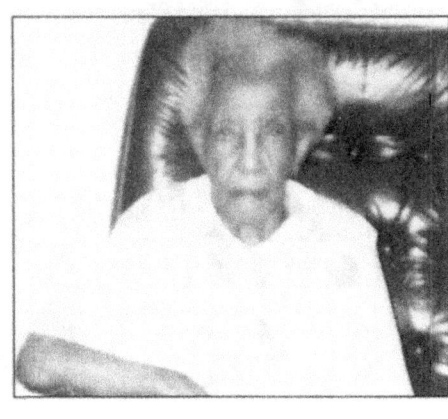

Blanche Lewis Goodridge, born Jan. 15, 1882. She still lives in her own home with her son Lester in Madisonville. See Blanche Goodridge family history.

Hilious E. Basham, 1884-1985, on his 100th birthday, see Hilious E. Basham family history.

Bernie V. Breedlove was born Aug. 5, 1878 in GLascow, Ky. She married William M. Breedlove in 1894 and they had nine children. The family moved to Hopkins Co. in 1919 and Bernie was widowed in 1920. She died Oct. 18, 1982 at the age of 104 and is buried at Bethlehem Church Cemetery.

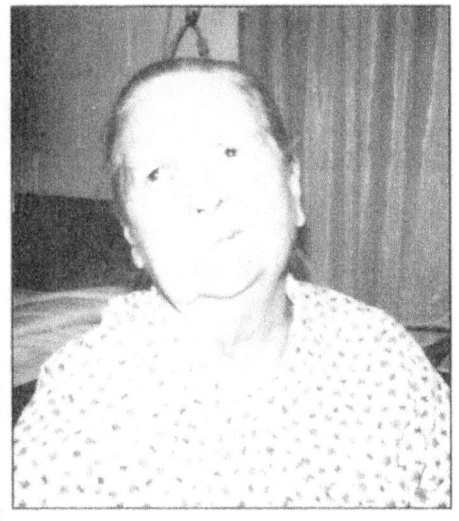

Miss Jessie Cooper was born Aug. 26, 1886 in Union Co., Ky. She was blind when she came to Brown's Rest Home in 1979. She remained very alert until illness sent her to Regional Medical Center in Sept. of 1987 where she is at this writing. She is 100 years old in this picture. Photo courtesy of Brown's Rest Home.

Frances Brown Harris Hart (1868-1968) on her 90th birthday, with Anne Dixon Hall Harris on the left and Reuben Cortez Harris on the right. For more info on "Aunt Fanny", see her family history.

John Richard "Uncle Dick": Bruce, 1869-1970. Photo taken at age 98-see his family history.

Iley Cates Cox, born July 13, 1883, pictured on her 100th birthday. Photo courtesy of her niece Opal Wilson. See Iley Cates Cox family history.

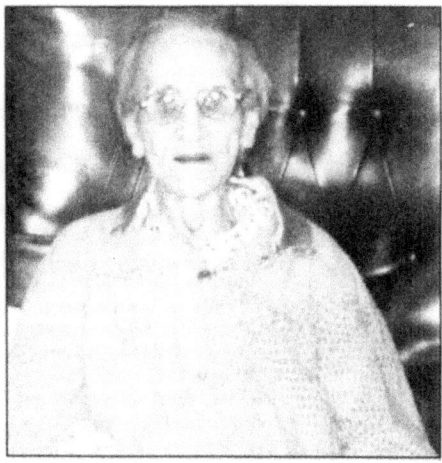

Pernicia Hart was born in Hopkins Co. June 11, 1881. She died at the age of 100, a resident of Brown's Rest Home. Photo courtesy of Brown's Rest Home. See Pernecia Hart story in family histories.

431

Mary May Tucker Hibbs born May 1, 1883. Photo courtesy of her grandson, Jim Rudd. See Mary Hibbs family history

James E. Huddleston (1886-1987) at the age of 94 in 1980. Photo Courtesy of Cloria Menser, a daughter. See James E. Huddleston's history

Mona McGregor, born in 1882, on her 105th birthday with her daughter Nana Lou Powell. See her family history

Ruben Hill 1875-1978, picture made on his 102nd birthday. Photo courtesy of his daughter, Gertie Hibbs. See Hill Hancock family history.

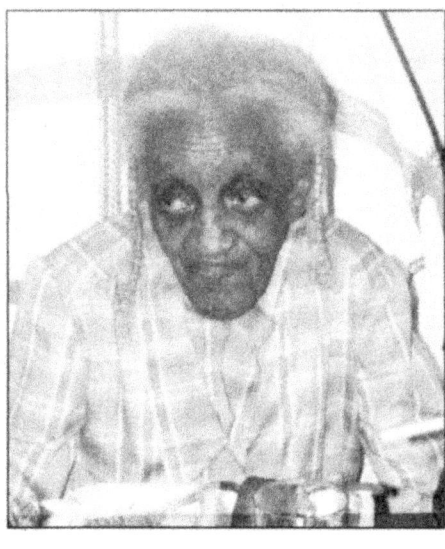
Bettie Ann Jones was born June 27, 1886 and died August 24, 1986. See her family history. Photo courtesy of Senior Citizens Nursing Home

Nancy Iona Martin, a resident of Senior Citizens Nursing Home, was born Feb. 14, 1887. Photo courtesy of her granddaughter, Mari Ola Madison See Martin-Baker story

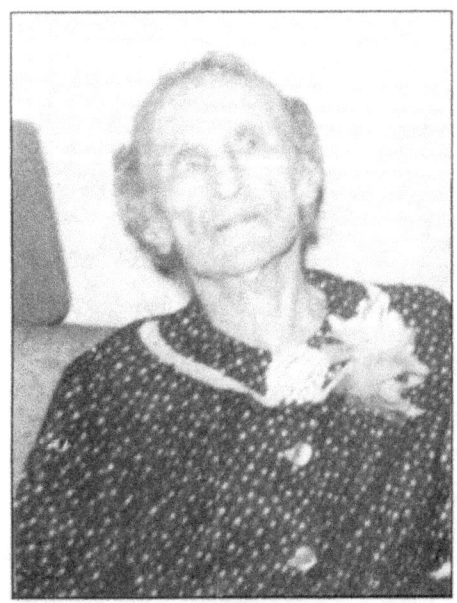
Eliza Cox Hoffman (1868-1970) on her 99th birthday. See her family history

Mary Elizabeth Yates Langzell, 93 at the time photo was taken, lived to be 101. She was born Oct. 22, 1883 and died June 4, 1984

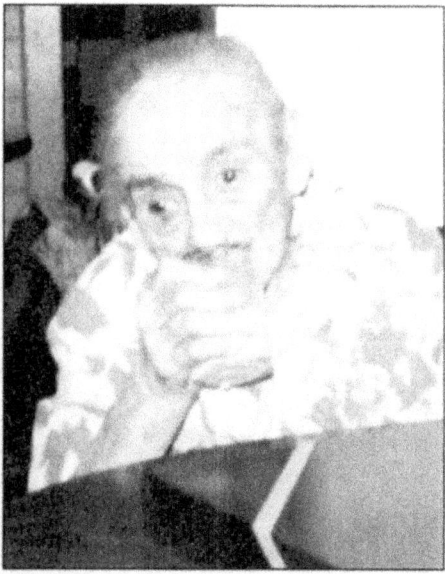
Sally (Sarah Elizabeth) Knight Maxwell born Nov. 16, 1880, died Sept. 27, 1981 on her 100th birthday. See Sally Maxwell family history

Essie L. Nichols was born May 26, 1883 in Hopkins Co., the daughter of James and Emma Nicholls. She worked as a seamstress for Dunlin's and McLeads of Madisonville. Essie died Jan. 21, 1985 at the age of 101 and is buried in Browder Cemetery east of Madisonville

Charles Frank Oakley was born Feb. 20, 1885 and died Sept. 12 1987. See his story

Lena Slaton Simons (1881-1982). See her story in the family history section

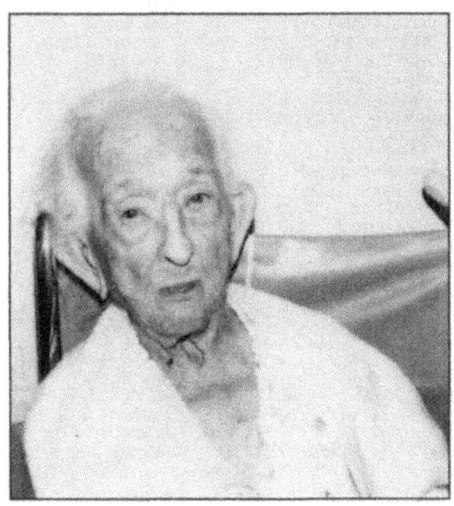
Mrs. Jessie Irene (Cavanaugh) White was born in Hopkins Co. on Dec. 14, 1884 the oldest of twelve children. She was the mother of nine children and was a life long member of the First Baptist Church of Mortans Gap where she served as a Sunday School teacher. She died on Dec. 17, 1985. Photo courtesy of David White, a son

The old Coke Ovens in Earlington-(1910-1920)-The man seated in upper row is Philmore Hoskins

Edith Morse, Birchie Cook and Lorene Pryor about 1942 at Daniel Boone

Gilliland School-teacher Ida Teague

INDEX

ABBAS, 42
ABBOTT, 70, 71, 79, 101, 262, 305, 342
ACHESON, 353
ACKLEY, 287
ACUFF, 173
ADAMS, 11, 12, 14, 19, 34, 35, 48, 54, 63, 67, 68, 75, 79, 84, 133, 157, 192, 205, 222, 229, 245, 262, 296, 301, 305, 309, 322, 323, 327, 333, 341, 346, 349, 353, 356, 369, 370, 398, 428
ADCOCK, 23, 34, 35, 54, 76, 94, 125, 180, 254, 278, 335, 377, 378, 422
ADDISON, 208, 215
ADKINS, 7, 71, 118, 119, 146, 174, 327, 335, 344
AGATE, 154
AGEE, 78, 127
AGNEW, 122
AINSWORTH, 42
AKINS, 75
ALANSON, 104
ALBRITTON, 172
ALCOCK, 431
ALCOTT, 35
ALDREDGE, 242
ALDRIDGE, 331
ALEXANDER, 19, 20, 24, 28, 35, 36, 37, 40, 70, 115, 126, 196, 201, 208, 214, 257, 262, 274, 286, 324, 326, 329, 335, 338, 349, 363, 365
ALFONSO, 157
ALFRED, 196
ALLAN, 259
ALLAWAY, 326
ALLDREDGE, 203
ALLEN, 13, 37, 38, 46, 47, 62, 68, 70, 104, 105, 122, 151, 155, 156, 174, 195, 197, 199, 213, 219, 248, 271, 275, 306, 320, 321, 322, 325, 326, 330, 334, 338, 339, 340, 347, 348, 363, 366, 385, 426
ALLERTON, 105
ALLEY, 210
ALLGEIER, 157
ALLIN, 64
ALLINDER, 38, 39, 110
ALLISON, 335, 345, 349
ALLSBROOK, 39, 173
ALMAN, 162
ALMON, 95, 209, 265, 267, 325, 357, 367
ALSBROOKS, 68
ALSOP, 101
ALSTON, 164
ALVEY, 93, 94, 364
ALVIS, 317
AMAR, 39, 40
AMOS, 170, 196
ANDERSON, 11, 12, 23, 34, 40, 63, 84, 161, 166, 173, 180, 187, 214, 229, 258, 276, 347, 355, 359, 365, 369, 426
ANDREW(S), 71, 92, 93, 143, 214, 312
ANGE, 133
ANGLIN, 317
ANNENSON, 42
ANTHONY, 251
ARBUCKLE, 73
ARCHEY, 354
ARDUESE, 113
ARIVETT, 345
ARLEDGE, 302
ARLIGE, 178
ARMSTRONG, 40, 41, 64, 131, 197, 198, 237, 370, 375, 390, 398
ARNETT, 17, 18, 72, 161, 245, 246, 252, 264, 289, 317, 319, 322, 348
ARNOLD, 34, 41, 42, 70, 71, 94, 102, 126, 143, 145, 146, 164, 178, 179, 183, 187, 190, 214, 227, 230, 243, 247, 272, 280, 291, 300, 321, 325, 336, 338, 342, 346, 347, 381, 403, 426
ARTE, 343
ARVIN, 317
ASBRIDGE, 132, 146, 147, 148, 240
ASBROOKS, 53
ASBY, 124
ASEBI, 43

ASH, 279
ASHBURNE, 116, 266
ASHBY, 8, 11, 12, 13, 14, 16, 17, 18, 23, 27, 34, 42, 43, 44, 45, 46, 54, 56, 59, 62, 67, 68, 82, 83, 85, 86, 89, 111, 112, 116, 132, 133, 136, 137, 140, 142, 153, 154, 158, 162, 166, 171, 172, 212, 221, 224, 228, 229, 232, 233, 235, 240, 261, 266, 278, 287, 288, 290, 294, 308, 311, 320, 323, 328, 334, 338, 340, 341, 344, 346, 369, 381, 398, 426
ASHE, 189
ASHLEY, 90, 253, 255, 321
ASHMORE, 101, 107, 111, 196, 204, 324, 331, 332, 345, 358
ATHEY, 112
ATKINSON, 21, 239, 253, 291, 316, 321, 375
ATNIP, 219
ATTERBURY, 64
ATWELL, 170
AUSENBAUGH, 44, 45, 100, 133, 156, 270, 334, 339, 341, 346
AUSTIN, 86, 132, 140, 256
AVERITT(S), 29, 85, 234, 280, 325
AYDELOTTE, 271
AVERY, 261
AYERS, 217, 271, 333, 346, 367, 398
AYOTTE, 214
AYRES, 206, 207, 236

BABB, 87, 96, 118, 431
BABINEAU, 398
BACHMAN, 358
BACK, 180, 223
BACON, 45, 54, 308, 350, 375
BADGER, 336, 366
BADGETT, 45, 46, 195, 377, 410
BADLEY, 286
BAGBY, 188
BAGGETT, 77, 129, 219
BAHLSTON, 350
BAILEY, 5, 8, 14, 22, 32, 37, 42, 43, 46, 62, 63, 84, 111, 132, 140, 159, 162, 163, 164, 174, 184, 188, 191, 207, 232, 264, 292, 303, 306, 308, 325, 334, 340, 342, 369, 382
BAIRD, 348
BAIZE, 90
BAKER, 14, 33, 37, 38, 42, 45, 46, 47, 48, 49, 51, 56, 71, 81, 87, 91, 105, 121, 127, 132, 137, 154, 155, 181, 192, 211, 223, 247, 260, 267, 272, 286, 291, 324, 336, 354, 363, 403, 432
BALCUM, 56
BALDWIN, 47, 94, 102, 166, 168, 212, 219, 320, 360, 365
BALE, 185
BALENTINE, 228
BALL, 41, 55, 77
BALLANCE, 258
BALLARD, 100, 160, 189, 234, 238
BALLINGER, 40
BALLOW, 95
BANAUGH, 336
BANDY, 47, 385, 398
BANGS, 36
BANKS, 47, 48, 116, 137, 138, 189, 190, 260, 319, 369, 390
BANNON, 18
BARBEE, 366
BARBER, 137, 160, 197, 293
BARD, 218, 363
BAREFIELD, 98
BARKER, 49, 71, 286, 343
BARLOW, 319
BARNARD, 119, 123, 342
BARNES, 38, 48, 55, 80, 94, 101, 106, 136, 167, 168, 212, 236, 245, 294, 335, 340, 343, 363, 427
BARNETS, 250
BARNETT, 8, 37, 60, 77, 89, 127, 175, 196, 257, 280, 281, 325, 341, 386
BARNHILL, 48, 49, 180, 203, 227, 316, 319, 325, 343, 345, 348, 350, 395

BARR, 154, 228, 229, 294
BARRETT, 204
BARRICK, 116
BARRINGER, 100
BARRON, 28, 49, 72, 73, 145, 158, 176, 222, 299, 323, 325, 340, 343, 349, 352, 361, 429, 430
BARTLETT, 153, 303
BARTON, 29, 49, 50, 236, 334, 344, 369, 398
BARWICK, 64
BASHAM, 50, 431
BASINGER, 183
BASS, 317, 318
BASSETT, 9, 22, 44, 50, 51, 55, 89, 122, 137, 144, 213, 223, 272, 350
BASTEIN, 198
BATES, 52, 78, 177
BATSEL, 17, 320
BATTAILE, 250
BATTALIA, 38
BATTERN, 92
BATTEY, 240
BATTS, 301
BAUGH, 153
BAULDWIN, 89
BAUMANN, 117
BAUNHOFER, 210
BAXTER, 231
BAYER, 52, 53, 202, 239
BAYLUS, 356
BEADLES, 64
BEAL, 60, 67, 89
BEALL, 216
BEALMEAR, 227
BEAN, 112, 149, 428
BEARD, 31, 51, 145, 146, 175, 313
BEARDEN, 53, 55, 67, 177, 178, 180, 207, 217, 218, 243, 251, 302
BEASLE, 332
BEASLEY, 54, 80, 159, 344
BEAUMONT, 100
BECK, 42, 307
BECKER, 239
BECKHAM, 118, 226
BECKTELL, 60
BEDWELL, 294, 339
BEELER, 173
BEENY, 50, 180, 302
BELAMY, 71
BELL, 14, 56, 57, 62, 72, 74, 75, 88, 112, 160, 207, 256, 289, 292, 301, 317, 327, 336, 339, 344, 345, 366, 419
BELLAMY, 98
BENIN, 47
BENNET, 286
BENNETT, 131, 137, 139, 164, 188, 192, 193, 229, 272, 327, 377
BENSON, 18, 57
BENTLEY, 54, 55, 91, 96, 208, 256, 263
BENTON, 54, 55, 72, 91, 167, 207, 276
BERESFORD, 199
BERKE, 313
BERNARD, 195, 358
BERNHARDT, 72
BERRELLEZ, 256
BERRY, 8, 11, 13, 16, 56, 57, 59, 116, 118, 134, 137, 182, 199, 218, 220, 239, 248, 282, 293, 308, 321, 332, 338, 342, 346, 349, 366, 367
BERRYMAN, 23
BERSHEARS, 197
BESHEAR(S), 29, 36, 37, 41, 57, 58, 60, 108, 114, 127, 165, 191, 195, 196, 214, 310, 324, 334, 335, 339, 346, 347, 348, 363, 385, 387, 390, 421
BEST, 347, 367
BETTS, 66, 353
BEVERS, 56, 60, 158, 222, 228
BIANCHI, 249
BIDWELL, 35, 49, 78, 292
BIGGS, 98
BILBRO, 55, 170, 325, 367, 385
BILLINGS, 115
BINGHAM, 291
BINKLEY, 233, 238
BIRD, 206
BISHOP, 14, 51, 89, 106, 119, 121, 125, 130, 224, 230, 309, 328, 352, 369, 398

BITTLER, 112
BIVIN(S), 141, 292
BLACK, 58, 74, 318, 363
BLACKBURN, 60, 196, 214, 304
BLACKERBY, 51
BLACKLEIGH, 291
BLACKWOOD, 288
BLADES, 59, 195, 208, 223, 280, 295, 343
BLAINE, 267
BLAIR, 183, 339, 366
BLAIS, 269, 313
BLAKE, 352
BLAKELY, 187
BLAKEY, 352
BLALOCK, 41
BLANCHARD, 142, 168, 284, 285, 299, 300
BLANE, 342
BLANKENSHIP, 59, 85, 160, 215, 217, 274, 323, 326
BLANKS, 154, 339, 342, 419
BLANTON, 68
BLAYLOCK, 197
BLICK, 90
BLIFFIN, 362
BLOODWORTH, 349, 363
BLOOMER, 294
BLOSSOM, 79
BLUE, 18, 42, 44, 56, 59, 89, 146, 171, 172, 228, 319, 326, 334, 336, 337, 342, 343, 345, 346, 374
BLYTHE, 367
BOARD, 369
BOATRIGHT, 72
BOBBITT, 97, 98
BODINE, 202
BOESE, 218
BOGGESS, 234, 258
BOGUS, 203
BOISSEAU, 209
BOITNETT, 113
BOITNOTT, 339, 347
BOJAK, 119
BOLD, 119
BOLES, 60, 349
BOLIN, 152
BOLLES, 354
BOND, 104, 175, 227
BONE, 36, 111, 122, 143, 174, 207, 238, 240, 293, 323, 325, 331, 334, 336, 344, 345, 350, 366, 369, 370
BONNER, 263
BOONE, 79, 182, 192, 196, 241
BOOTH(E), 2, 207, 231
BORAH, 227
BORDELY, 290
BORRUSCH, 161
BOSSUET, 188
BOSTIC, 214
BOSTICK, 60, 61
BOSWELL, 148, 214, 369
BOTELER, 398
BOUGHERS, 65
BOULDEN, 306, 308
BOUNDS, 44, 54, 56
BOURLAND, 11, 61, 62, 64, 77, 141, 163, 174, 191, 201, 203, 204, 256, 259, 321, 343, 369, 426
BOURNE, 116
BOWEN, 41
BOWERS, 65, 192, 336, 356, 357
BOWLES, 30, 66, 67, 100, 128, 134, 168, 179, 216, 227, 229, 261, 277, 278, 298, 379, 380
BOWLEY, 219
BOWLING, 134
BOWMAN, 62, 90, 118, 193, 261, 301, 313
BOX, 109
BOXLEY, 156
BOYCE, 90, 293
BOYD, 8, 42, 57, 67, 87, 121, 166, 176, 203, 251, 321, 337, 338, 340, 357, 370, 379
BOYLE, 2
BOYSMAN, 290
BRACKETT, 24, 62, 63, 102, 128, 223, 272, 347, 363
BRADDOCK, 44
BRADEN, 41, 65, 66, 210
BRADLEY, 2, 11, 12, 14, 118, 141, 145, 248, 317, 328, 336
BRADSHAW, 111, 220, 221, 349

BRADY, 334
BRANDON, 354
BRANDT, 128
BRANNON, 398
BRANSON, 8, 42, 51, 63, 89, 125, 142, 153, 160, 214, 228, 229, 232, 302, 324
BRANTLEY, 50
BRASHEAR, 160, 217
BRASHER, 45, 167, 184, 240, 274, 347
BRATCHER, 44, 275, 276, 279
BRATTON, 11, 70, 212, 213
BRAUN, 42
BRAWNER, 87
BREAKER, 362
BREEDLOVE, 100, 257, 258, 273, 431
BREIT, 307
BREWER, 179, 182, 184, 216, 261, 269, 356
BREWINGTON, 339
BREWSTER, 152, 335
BRIDGES, 202, 263
BRIEGEL, 72
BRIGGS, 161
BRIGHAM, 64
BRINEGAR, 354
BRINK, 201
BRINKLEY, 67, 98, 102, 106, 134, 166, 169, 171, 187, 217, 221, 227, 272, 325, 341, 371
BRISCO, 151
BRISNAHAN, 427
BRITT, 61, 118
BRIZENDINE, 216
BROADNAX, 14
BROCK, 103, 104, 105, 209, 216, 227
BROGDON, 153
BRONOUGH, 56
BROOKS, 44, 92, 128, 189, 195, 208, 213, 228, 232, 241, 257, 271, 313, 318, 323, 343, 347, 352, 367, 399
BROWDER, 11, 14, 34, 62, 63, 75, 119, 140, 142, 150, 259, 306, 307, 308, 323
BROWER, 60
BROWLEE, 213
BROWLEY, 317
BROWN, 2, 6, 8, 14, 34, 35, 36, 42, 43, 48, 47, 51, 56, 61, 64, 66, 67, 71, 75, 76, 77, 78, 81, 84, 85, 86, 92, 94, 99, 111, 115, 123, 124, 125, 128, 135, 136, 140, 150, 152, 154, 157, 163, 169, 171, 172, 188, 190, 191, 194, 205, 206, 216, 222, 228, 233, 234, 237, 238, 245, 247, 249, 251, 257, 267, 271, 272, 279, 280, 281, 286, 292, 296, 298, 302, 303, 306, 309, 310, 311, 312, 320, 321, 322, 323, 325, 326, 327, 329, 330, 331, 332, 333, 334, 335, 336, 337, 338, 339, 340, 342, 343, 344, 345, 346, 347, 349, 350, 360, 361, 362, 364, 369, 379, 398, 412, 420, 431
BROWNWELL, 44, 224
BROWNFIELD, 6, 100
BROWNING, 64, 96, 120, 130, 141, 145, 153, 208, 221, 274, 293, 313, 325, 338, 339, 356, 363, 370, 371, 398
BROXTON, 317
BRUCE, 6, 18, 64, 77, 98, 112, 126, 177, 280, 282, 338, 366, 370, 431
BRUMLEY, 271, 350
BRUNEAU, 67
BRUSWELL, 167
BRYAN, 98, 366
BRYANT, 48, 94, 95, 111, 121, 133, 166, 244, 327, 331
BUCHANAN, 34, 53, 64, 65, 76, 77, 96, 134, 136, 191, 200, 201, 217, 236, 256, 326, 331, 333, 342, 347, 379, 380
BUCHANAN, 77
BUCHETT, 65
BUCHHOLZ, 199
BUCKANAN, 180
BUCKNER, 2, 317, 319, 428
BUELL, 211, 260
BUFFINGTON, 65, 398
BUFORD, 52
BUHL, 213

BUIE, 68
BULL, 50, 52, 163
BULLETT, 79
BULLOCK, 36, 51, 274
BUMPASS, 63, 89, 116, 266
BUNBERRY, 57
BUNDY, 134
BUNTIN, 38, 63, 65, 76, 160, 321, 323, 334
BUNTON, 177
BURCHER, 94
BURCHFIELD, 274
BURCKEN, 17
BURDEN, 65, 66, 118, 127, 222, 366
BURDINE, 244
BURGESS, 106, 163, 276, 285
BURKE, 220, 293
BURNETT, 189
BURNS, 64, 207, 271, 292, 398
BURR, 242
BURRELL, 249
BURRIES, 101
BURRIS, 252, 339
BURSE, 339, 346
BURT, 129
BURTON, 53, 66, 67, 98, 104, 120, 210, 218, 244, 251, 291, 292, 321, 322, 331, 352
BUSH, 108
BUSHNELL, 97
BUTLER, 6, 69, 181, 188, 196, 257, 264, 274, 284, 301, 332, 343, 347, 353, 380, 398
BUTNER, 150
BUXTON, 371
BUZZARD, 180
BYARD, 427
BYERS, 90, 98
BYLES, 143
BYROM, 63
BYRUM, 67, 98, 157, 207, 323, 325, 352, 353
BYRUN, 279

CAHALL, 89
CAHUSAC, 116
CAIN, 67, 116, 136, 220, 431
CALDWELL, 263
CALFEE, 134
CALLAHAN, 95
CALLEN, 249
CALLIS, 195, 258
CALLISON, 307
CALLOWAY, 63
CALVERT, 100, 172, 173, 205, 251, 309, 310, 311, 324, 335, 336, 337, 344, 346, 347, 348, 367, 398
CAMBRON, 79
CAMERON, 271
CAMPBELL, 44, 68, 72, 74, 84, 98, 133, 137, 174, 232, 235, 286, 318, 321, 322, 329, 330, 332, 337, 338, 341, 342, 358, 362
CAMPLIN, 148, 264, 331, 336
CAMTON, 55
CANADAY, 257
CANEPA, 115
CANNADY, 295
CANNON, 366, 370
CANSLER, 40, 45, 68, 123, 149, 180, 214, 221, 244, 330, 341
CANTRELL, 7, 68
CAPLINGER, 170, 196
CAPPS, 18, 68, 77, 107, 194, 197, 224, 331
CARD, 69
CARDWELL, 7, 17, 42, 44, 69, 136, 138, 170, 195, 229, 232, 255, 276, 322, 326, 340, 363, 365, 370
CAREY, 80, 250, 428
CARGILE, 130, 317, 318, 365
CARITHERS, 196
CARLIN, 321
CARLISLE, 18, 44, 68, 95, 142, 221, 222, 357
CARLTON, 59, 69, 208, 301, 313
CARMAN, 366
CARMACK, 128, 156, 189
CARNAHAN, 136, 175
CARNAL, 158, 210, 221, 226, 287, 323
CARNEAL, 87, 160, 206, 320
CARNER, 68
CARPENTER, 36, 296

434

CARR, 166, 212
CARRAWAY, 137
CARRICK, 204
CARRICO, 331
CARRINGTON, 345
CARROLL, 36, 72, 74, 101, 175, 176, 177, 214, 234, 251, 263, 264, 325, 335, 365
CARSON, 69, 70, 208, 386, 398
CARTER, 48, 70, 119, 125, 167, 192, 201, 212, 245, 278, 292, 319, 326, 328, 390
CARTWRIGHT, 70, 71, 77, 95, 107, 209, 210, 340, 361
CARTY, 32
CARUTHERS, 280
CARVER, 116
CARY, 267
CASARES, 6, 36
CASEY, 156, 182, 317
CASH, 318
CASHER, 60
CASHMAN, 354
CASHON, 259
CASKEY, 366
CASNER, 7, 8, 80, 403, 409
CASSADY, 250
CASTEEL, 214
CASTLE, 71, 72
CASTLEBERRY, 110, 156, 163, 166, 172, 324
CASTRO, 256
CATES, 18, 41, 42, 44, 59, 65, 67, 72, 73, 85, 87, 94, 116, 133, 143, 153, 156, 158, 159, 160, 171, 176, 183, 188, 207, 209, 210, 220, 251, 304, 320, 321, 323, 331, 340, 341, 363, 413, 431
CATHEY, 122
CATO, 21, 73, 151, 241, 340
CAUDIL, 173
CAVANAH, 285, 321, 324, 335, 337, 382
CAVANAUGH, 294, 301, 325, 330, 335, 338, 367, 433
CAVANNAUGH, 192
CAYCE, 175
CAYWOOD, 350
CECIL, 100
CHADWICK, 127
CHAMBERLAIN, 244
CHAMBERS, 94, 124
CHAMLES, 201
CHAMNESS, 65
CHAMPION, 398
CHANDLER, 13, 28, 37, 73, 119, 132, 144, 207, 214, 228, 302, 331, 339, 344
CHANEY, 36, 234, 263, 298
CHANNELIER, 352
CHANNELL, 231
CHAPEL, (L), 150, 231, 309, 310
CHAPPELL, (E), 70, 80, 113, 128, 146, 181, 185, 324, 327, 334, 335, 337, 340, 346, 363
CHASTINE, 320
CHAUVIN, 269
CHEEK, 268, 269, 349, 425
CHERRY, 124, 236, 318, 354
CHESHER, 271
CHESLEY, 60
CHESNUT, 40
CHIGUDDER, 161
CHILDERS, 73, 74, 89, 262, 338, 349
CHILDRESS, 93, 262
CHILDS, 105, 367
CHILES, 105
CHOATES (S), 69, 249, 250, 301, 321
CHRIST, 68
CHRISTIAN, 46, 74, 122, 164, 188, 227, 229, 239, 255
CHRISTMAN, 65, 287
CHRISTOPHER, 74, 75, 330
CHURCH, 327
CLAPP, 65
CLARK, 5, 19, 36, 48, 60, 63, 69, 70, 75, 79, 90, 95, 99, 102, 115, 120, 128, 139, 140, 142, 145, 158, 159, 161, 169, 181, 185, 186, 190, 197, 207, 259, 262, 275, 281, 302, 305, 313, 316, 320, 322, 324, 326, 335, 337, 341, 344, 367, 369, 387, 398, 421
CLAXTON, 65, 124
CLAY, 55, 56, 72, 74, 122, 158, 199, 239, 307, 308, 356
CLAYTON, 33, 34, 35, 53, 64, 65, 68, 69, 73, 75, 76, 77, 78, 85, 87, 89, 116, 133, 134, 135, 157, 167, 177, 183, 188,
191, 214, 216, 224, 270, 273, 275, 279, 303, 321, 323, 326, 331, 333, 334, 336, 337, 338, 342, 343, 344, 349, 361, 363, 380
CLAYTOR, 213
CLEMENT (S), 10, 44, 70, 78, 79, 100, 213, 232, 325, 369, 421
CLEMONS, 317
CLENDENIN (G), 79
CLEVELAND, 259
CLEVENGER, 107, 157, 367, 369, 405
CLICK, 192
CLIFFORD, 252
CLIFT, 121, 128
CLINE, 158, 196, 197
CLINTON, 405
CLOPTON, 234, 238
CLOUD, 114
CLOUSE, 79, 80, 304
CLUM, 35
COAT(E)S, 5, 80, 109, 149, 225, 276, 334
COBB, 18, 44, 60, 81, 82, 85, 209, 226, 231, 253, 265, 320, 323, 347, 357, 426
COBLE, 42
COBURN, 185, 203, 204
COCK(E), 57, 77, 84, 145
COFFMAN, 18, 34, 71, 106, 116, 124, 149, 154, 210, 213, 214, 217, 228, 229, 240, 295, 298, 332, 357, 358
COGHILL, 98, 215
COIL, 18, 100, 174, 187, 189
COKE, 35, 36
COKER, 188
COLBERT, 318
COLBURN, 139
COLE, 255, 366
COLEMAN, 80, 98, 116, 172, 174, 188, 196, 286, 303, 317, 318, 339, 344, 352, 356, 369
COLLIER, 87
COLLINS, 40, 47, 60, 162, 168, 214, 245, 289, 324, 330, 356, 358
COLTHARP, 356
COMBS, 309
COMER, 161, 249
COMMER, 352
COMPTON, 14, 19, 42, 86, 356, 380
CONLEY, 71
CONN, 70
CONNALLY, 72
CONNELLY, 103, 104, 120
CONNERS(S), 39, 260, 286
CONNOR, 249, 286
CONOWAY,172
CONWAY, 54
CONYERS, 398
COOK(E), 47, 73, 90, 93, 196, 223, 224, 301, 306, 329, 330, 331, 334
COOKSEY, 46
COOMES, 93, 174, 255
COOPER, 80, 99, 100, 116, 296, 431, 433
COPELAND, 38, 80
COPELY, 325
COPPAGE, 65
CORBETT, 59, 60
CORBIN, 67, 325
CORBITT, 341
CORDIER, 371
CORNEAL, 263
CORNELIUS, 61, 129, 354
CORNELL, 224
CORNETT(E), 155, 358, 403
CORUM, 6, 80, 81, 82, 83, 89, 191, 238, 278, 320, 366, 399, 419, 426
COSTIN, 101
COTHRAN, 250
COTTON, 70, 83, 93, 114, 146, 147, 180, 234, 273, 342, 358, 363
COUCH, 73, 84, 158, 318, 320, 336, 398
COULTER, 84, 310, 311
COURTNEY, 44
COWAN(S), 253, 299, 325, 328, 339, 347
COX, 6, 28, 29, 49, 66, 73, 77, 84, 85, 102, 103, 104, 127, 128, 132, 144, 151, 152, 176, 205, 207, 222, 234, 238, 253, 261, 300, 301, 302, 303, 325, 328, 329, 333, 338, 341, 343, 345, 348, 350, 353, 354, 365, 370, 376, 429, 431, 432
COYLE, 313, 383

COZART, 158, 221, 222
CRABTREE, 23, 44, 54, 68, 69, 85, 86, 123, 253, 278, 207, 228, 229, 305, 320, 325, 335, 337, 343, 346, 377, 426
CRAFT, 146, 395
CRAFTON, 8, 230
CRAIG, 2, 34, 42, 133, 251, 328, 333, 336
CRAIN, 65, 249, 250
CRANE, 385
CRANOR, 169, 196, 326, 337, 344, 346
CRARY, 41
CRASK, 72, 133
CRAWFORD, 42, 104, 122, 127, 159, 204, 229, 304, 342, 343, 356
CRAWLEY, 320
CRAYTOR, 170, 196
CREAMER, 175
CREASEY, 157, 327, 336
CREEKMUR, 108, 235
CRENSHAW, 166
CRESS, 166
CREWS, 196, 228, 295
CRICK, 51, 69, 88, 127, 157, 274, 321, 325, 326, 331, 338, 340, 341, 342, 348
CRISCO, 117
CROCKER, 145
CROCKETT, 54, 234, 238
CROFT, 37, 86, 110, 115, 123, 150, 197, 273, 274, 305
CROKER, 298
CROOK(S), 148, 326, 335, 337, 346
CROSS, 75
CROSSON, 166, 336
CROWDER, 236
CROW(E), 27, 86, 87, 127, 133, 151, 160, 172, 181, 190, 224, 267, 279, 286, 319, 326, 327, 328, 332, 336, 339, 340, 341, 342, 345, 349, 366
CROWELL, 229, 369
CROWLEY, 232, 317, 323
CRUMBAKER, 57, 69, 321, 343, 367, 386
CRUMP, 261
CRUNK, 220, 267, 293
CRUTCHER, 42
CULLEN, 87, 148, 227, 247, 327
CULVER, 243
CUMBEE, 397
CUMMIN(G)S, 92, 297, 346, 403
CUNNINGHAM, 2, 6, 19, 37, 44, 51, 72, 75, 77, 87, 88, 109, 113, 114, 143, 155, 157, 160, 180, 201, 209, 222, 223, 227, 253, 254, 257, 259, 267, 273, 274, 275, 317, 325, 349, 363, 367
CURB, 88, 246, 288
CURLEW, 39
CURLEY, 328
CURNEAL, 78, 206, 290
CURREN, 89, 90
CURRIE, 354
CURRY, 354, 429
CURTIS, 184, 204, 216, 332
CURTRIGHT, 116, 267, 279
CURUAL, 65
CURTWRIGHT, 120
CUSHIONBERRY, 318

DADE, 248, 290
DAIL, 210
DAILEY, 220
DALLAS, 75
DALTON, 61, 280
DALY, 127
DAME, 39, 42, 43, 53, 59, 64, 76, 87, 94, 159, 176, 177, 180, 207, 215, , 243, 256, 267, 272, 278, 279, 363, 382, 398
DANIEL, 18, 34, 76, 77, 87, 89, 90, 168, 180, 243, 251, 272, 300, 341, 364
DANIELL, 38
DANIELS, 72, 86, 134, 140, 270, 306, 323, 326, 343
DANT, 93
DARDEN, 355
DARNELL, 147, 152, 153, 202, 305
DARR, 169
DAUGHTERTY, 62, 90
DAUGHTERY, 66, 70
DAVENPORT, 54, 55, 90, 91, 181, 207, 231, 263, 300
DAVES, 294, 304, 329, 331,
334, 345, 350, 398
DAVEY, 116, 266
DAVIDSON, 65, 303, 318
DAVIE, 266
DAVIS, 11, 12, 13, 14, 27, 36, 37, 38, 42, 45, 46, 50, 52, 54, 57, 59, 60, 61, 63, 65, 71, 80, 83, 87, 91, 92, 93, 94, 98, 101, 103, 105, 110, 112, 113, 114, 118, 129, 136, 140, 141, 146, 147, 153, 157, 160, 161, 162, 170, 174, 193, 199, 202, 205, 206, 207, 213, 220, 224, 229, 240, 243, 244, 245, 247, 255, 261, 262, 263, 268, 272, 274, 275, 280, 281, 290, 297, 301, 305, 312, 313, 321, 322, 324, 327, 331, 332, 336, 337, 338, 339, 340, 341, 345, 347, 350, 357, 358, 363, 369, 383, 389, 398
DAWNEY, 66
DAWSON, 20, 42, 94, 327, 328
DAY, 67, 76, 89, 160, 179, 188, 228, 290, 324, 342, 348, 357, 390
DEADE, 26
DEAN, 304
DEARING, 170, 197, 224, 225
DEARMOND, 83, 146, 147, 328, 329
DEAVERS, 342
DEAVOURS, 80
DEBANDY, 317
DE BORG,95
DE BOSTICK, 60
DEBOW, 94, 95, 133
DEERE, 321
DEES, 151
DELANY, 12
DELONG, 98
DEMENT, 34, 35, 243
DEMONBREUM, 249
DEMOSS, 167, 171, 230, 241, 349, 350, 354
DEMPSEY, 151, 302, 382, 426
DEMPSTER, 249
DENNEY, 217
DENNIS, 207, 262, 263
DENNISON, 268
DENNY, 200
DENSMORE, 310
DENSON, 44, 224
DENT, 248
DENTON, 91, 95, 96, 105, 186, 198, 229, 251, 258, 259, 273, 274, 275, 305, 332, 350, 353
DESHON, 373
DETWILER, 49
DEVAULT, 38, 64, 306
DEVENPORT, 85
DEVER, 189, 233, 236, 244, 327, 332, 345
DEVERAUX, 168, 290
DEVERS, 206, 327, 333
DEVOR, 238
DEW, 214
DEWITT, 42
DEXTER, 83, 96, 142, 146, 322
DICK, 357
DICKEN, 244
DICKERSON, 118, 196, 271, 325, 355
DICKEY, 161, 360
DICKINSON, 97
DICKMAN, 199
DICKSON, 240
DIGGS, 145, 255, 355
DILBECK, 167
DILL, 354
DILLINGHAM, 5, 44, 45, 59, 62, 77, 95, 97, 100, 105, 209, 229, 294, 322, 324, 325, 335, 347, 426
DILLMAN, 239, 240
DILLON, 354
DINSMORE, 305
DISMANG, 52
DITTO, 187
DIXON, 113, 140, 160, 177, 297, 324, 416
DOAN, 42
DOBBINS, 303
DOBSON, 64
DOBYNS, 57
DOCKERY, 5, 90, 97, 106, 113, 115, 125, 168, 169, 187, 246, 312, 313, 329, 335
DOCKREY, 7, 91, 97, 98, 112, 114, 115, 116, 129, 131, 135, 136, 140, 150, 167, 174, 175, 180, 210, 296, 313, 356, 411
DODGE, 363
DODSON, 80, 82, 83, 139, 320
DONALDSON, 6, 70, 98, 116,
173, 266, 267, 279, 303
DONAN, 22, 126, 363, 365
DONG, 88
DOOM, 38
DORR, 36
DORRIS, 67, 98, 99, 141, 161, 271, 352
DORRISS, 141
DOSS, 271
DOSSETT, 262
DOTY, 42
DOUGHTY, 56
DOUGLAS, 46, 50,
DOWDY, 151, 284, 350
DOWEL, 323
DOWLING, 42
DOWNEY, 71, 123, 347, 363
DOWNING, 106, 114, 120, 121
DOWNS, 258
DOYLE, 300
DOZIER, 99, 100, 142, 256
DRAKE, 109, 137, 138, 152, 191, 260, 346, 363, 365
DRANE, 271
DRENNAN, 92, 100, 236, 258
DREVECKY, 240
DRIVER, 36, 148, 216, 272, 365
DROPP, 214
DRYSDALE, 42
DUBOIS, 199
DUCKETT, 318
DUCKWORTH, 61
DUDLEY, 371
DUFF, 42
DUFFIELD, 405
DUFFY, 238
DUGAN, 116
DUKE(S), 32, 53, 56, 66, 69, 96, 217, 301, 365
DULIN, 100, 146, 156, 189, 199, 275, 318, 371, 403, 419
DUNBAR, 6, 100, 201, 147, 231, 247, 330, 334, 335, 342, 343
DUNCAN, 24, 32, 52, 53, 62, 63, 101, 102, 103, 128, 168, 169, 177, 178, 196, 217, 221, 223, 243, 244, 252, 272, 320, 321, 323, 338, 347, 348, 363
DUNHAM, 248
DUNKERSON,158, 308, 362
DUNLAP, 59, 98
DUNN, 49, 103, 120, 125, 172, 247, 291, 292, 341, 342, 344, 382
DUNNING, 17, 19, 95, 123, 124, 149, 150, 201
DUNVILLE, 34, 152, 222
DUPUE, 285
DUPUY, 192
DURANK, 257
DURBIN, 66, 164
DUREE, 66
DURHAM, 94, 103, 104, 105, 119, 120, 155, 163, 221, 227, 255, 265, 294, 326, 339, 422
DURRETT, 230
DUTTON, 52
DUVALL, 77, 95
DYE, 160, 161, 235, 245, 246, 252
DYER, 257
DYSON, 127

EADES, 36, 363, 365
EADS, 47, 181
EAGLE, 53, 177
EARHART, 51
EARL(E), 2, 11, 12, 21, 56, 59, 95, 96, 105, 166, 186, 199, 215, 229, 242, 275, 306, 307, 308, 324, 329, 332, 341, 342, 353, 378
EASTERLY, 189
EASTIN, 105, 106, 379
EASTMAN, 289
EASTWOOD, 23, 75, 270, 328, 343
EAVES, 225
EBA, 235
EBERLE, 199
EBERT, 147
EBINGER, 178
EBLEN, 348
EBRIGHT, 145
EDDINS, 175
EDENS, 80, 357
EDGE, 308
EDGER, 214
EDISON, 229
EDMISTON, 14, 76, 106, 114, 115, 313, 346
EDMONDS, 250
EDMUNDSON, 90

EDWARDS, 67, 78, 80, 93, 94, 98, 106, 139, 142, 207, 226, 292, 325, 339, 341, 346, 369
EGBERT, 40, 71, 74, 75, 101, 106, 124, 125, 182, 255, 257, 265, 276, 322, 327, 328, 331, 332, 344, 345, 361
EGEBERG, 253
EICKEL, 202
EIDEN, 398
EISENHAUER, 128
EISON, 58, 97, 150
ELAM, 42
ELDER, 336
ELDRIDGE, 125
ELGIN, 29, 341
ELI, 68, 107, 112, 147, 180, 245, 330
ELKINS, 43, 340
ELLIOTT, 93, 107, 108, 137, 158, 250, 282, 283, 284, 367
ELLIS, 42, 70, 90, 128, 152, 164, 203, 211, 245, 300, 350, 363, 365, 366
ELLISON, 212
EMANUEL, 282
EMPEROUR, 54
ENGLE, 325
ENGLISH, 58, 94, 234
ENNIS, 124
ENTZMINGER, 339
EPLEY,18, 196, 346
EPPS, 171
ERVIN, 324
ERWIN, 249
ESHELMAN, 188, 289
ESKRIDGE, 377
ESTIS, 89
ETHERIDGE, 80, 109, 225, 249, 266, 398
ETHRIDGE, 108
EUBANKS, 93
EUDAL(E)Y, 340, 341
EVANS, 109, 137, 138, 175, 275, 298, 313, 329, 383
EZELL, 57, 94, 114, 162, 174, 175, 195, 196, 240, 305, 367, 369

FAGAN, 90, 341, 344, 382
FAHNING, 228
FAITH, 240
FANCHER, 327
FARAR, 202
FARLESS, 151
FARLEY, 170
FARMER, 166, 194, 198, 214, 238, 269
FARRAN, 375
FARRIS, 96, 196
FAUCETT, 220
FAUGHENDER, 128, 274
FAULK, 47, 62, 193, 300, 301
FAULKNER, 42
FAULL, 109, 110, 141, 280
FAUQUAR, 66
FAUST, 96
FAVORS, 313, 345
FAWCETT, 161, 191
FAZENBAKER, 99
FEARS,183
FEATHERINGILLE, 56
FEATHERS, 271
FEILER, 269
FELKER, 55, 252, 327
FELLO, 42
FELTY, 66, 243
FERGUSON, 6, 49, 51, 81, 82, 86, 110, 168, 185, 331, 332, 339, 367
FERRELL, 71, 327, 361
FERRET, 332
FERRIS, 161, 246
FESNOT, 145
FIELDING, 54
FIELDS, 277, 339
FIGERT, 180, 379
FIKE, 41, 74, 107, 143, 178, 179, 214
FILIATREAU, 52
FINCH, 54, 258, 259, 317
FINDT, 119
FINLEY, 8, 110, 111, 114, 159, 165, 204, 213, 381, 346, 350, 367
FINN, 146
FIRES, 302
FISHER, 29, 64, 70, 104, 142, 313
FITCH, 215
FITTS, 149, 150, 151
FITZSIMMONS, 114, 142, 322, 325
FLEEHART, 286
FLEMING,111, 112, 212, 219,

435

220, 228
FLETCHER, 118, 124, 261, 327, 371
FLINT, 111, 240
FLOURNOY, 192
FLOYD, 154, 249, 259, 289
FOE, 92
FOLEY, 116, 174, 328, 420
FORBES, 66
FORCUM, 172
FORD, 37, 46, 49, 59, 73, 103, 104, 120, 189, 266
FORK, 36
FORKNER, 49, 279
FORREST, 51
FORSYTHE, 44, 66, 191, 224, 290
FORTNER, 71, 325
FOSTER, 44, 170, 196, 211, 224, 230, 260, 297, 373, 398
FOUNTAIN, 366
FOUST, 236
FOWLER, 13, 42, 69, 96, 128, 158, 172, 173, 207, 247, 259, 294, 328, 329, 340, 346, 365
FOX, 8, 44, 59, 60, 62, 90, 91, 98, 106, 112, 113, 114, 125, 126, 166, 180, 185, 206, 208, 209, 225, 229, 236, 253, 271, 281, 286, 301, 305, 313, 322, 324, 325, 326, 327, 328, 329, 331, 332, 335, 336, 337, 338,340, 342, 344, 346, 348, 355, 363, 365, 367, 369, 383, 385, 403, 414
FRAELICH, 8
FRANCIS, 320
FRANK, 309
FRANKLIN, 5, 8, 20, 24, 26, 41, 63, 65, 68, 75, 91, 98, 106, 110, 113, 114, 115, 125, 126, 128, 132, 133, 147, 150, 153, 170, 185, 217, 225, 227, 241, 264, 273, 274, 279, 280, 284, 298, 310, 311, 319, 322, 326, 327, 328, 330, 332, 335, 341, 342, 344, 347, 349, 353, 363, 390, 414, 421
FRANKLYN, 120
FRASER, 354
FRAZER, 243, 244, 325, 327, 344, 345
FRAZIER, 160, 162, 234
FREE, 290
FREEMAN, 36, 49, 95, 301, 366
FREER, 224
FRENCH, 39, 101, 214
FREY, 115
FRIDAY, 35, 217, 229, 320
FRIDY, 18, 134, 262, 331
FRIEDEL, 63
FRIEND, 95, 218
FRITZ, 70
FROST, 141
FRY, 65
FRYE, 132, 353
FRYER, 251
FUGATE, 12, 50, 52, 62, 94, 107, 115, 116, 130, 150, 174, 207, 221, 255, 259, 260, 279, 311, 333, 345, 363, 393, 398
FULCHER, 180
FULKERSON, 302, 303
FULLER, 5, 148, 262, 273
FULMER, 116, 172
FULTON, 276
FULTS, 61
FUQUA, 193
FUQUAY, 334
FURGERSON, 98, 116, 169, 187, 209, 213, 229, 310, 311, 331, 342
FURGUSON, 322, 345
FURLOW, 240, 241
FURMAN, 356
FUSON, 221
FUSTING, 203, 204
FYE, 47

GABBERT, 280
GABRIEL, 266
GADDIS, 200, 201
GAILOR, 324, 341
GAINS, 356
GALBRAITH, 112
GALBREATH, 207
GALES, 318
GALLAGHER, 417
GALLOWAY, 20, 44, 84, 89, 167, 177
GAMBLE, 38, 39, 149, 213, 223, 305, 306, 330
GAMBLIN, 19, 36, 88, 116, 120, 229, 240, 241, 324, 335, 337, 345, 346, 366
GAMER, 293
GAMMON, 159, 222
GANGLE, 42
GANNON, 19
GANTT, 117, 132, 146, 148, 240, 241, 242, 320
GARDINER, 117, 118, 248, 293
GARDNER, 47, 196, 233, 253, 293, 398
GARFIELD, 138
GARRARD, 62, 255
GARRETT, 112, 118, 286, 427
GARRIS, 286
GARST, 89
GARVIS, 60
GASS, 365, 369
GASTON, 217, 325
GATLIN, 59, 118, 130, 174, 188, 254, 321, 337, 339, 340, 345, 349, 356, 382, 385, 419
GATTON, 119, 348, 350, 403
GAUSE, 261
GAY, 98, 331
GEARY, 305
GENDRON, 116
GENTRY, 65, 320, 333, 340, 341, 352, 369, 426
GEOBEL, 191
GEORGE, 54, 273
GERENCER, 195, 246
GERRY, 178
GIANIMMA, 304
GIBBLE, 42
GIBBS, 155
GIBSON, 80, 96, 128, 157, 197, 219, 227, 228, 294
GILBERT, 229
GILES, 65, 77
GILFORD, 161
GILKEY, 150, 371
GILL, 6, 64, 70, 85, 104, 119, 120, 121, 127, 154, 161, 162, 346, 361, 366, 388, 415
GILLESPIE, 56, 57, 74, 121, 122, 123, 239
GILLILAND, 331
GILLON, 240
GILLON, 220
GILMORE, 18, 222
GIOVANNINI, 154
GIPSON, 7, 208, 305, 337, 338, 341
GIRTEN, 306
GISH, 102
GIST, 51
GIVEN(S), 2, 14, 51, 52, 56, 70, 74, 120, 122, 123, 130, 143, 159, 199, 209, 220, 239, 296, 306, 307, 308, 325, 336, 338
GIVINS, 133, 276, 330, 336, 345
GLADDISH, 5, 68, 123, 321, 341, 342, 367
GLADEN, 56
GLADWELL, 56
GLASS, 124, 167, 224
GLAZER, 348
GLEAVES, 73
GLENN, 2, 46, 100
GLOSS, 251
GLOVER, 73, 197, 332
GOAD, 37, 89, 328
GOCEY, 230
GOLD, 297
GOLDEN, 56
GOLDING, 57
GOLDSMITH, 54
GOLIDAY, 37
GOLLADAY, 46
GOOCH, 7, 8, 23, 45, 63, 78, 86, 124, 125, 135, 138, 153, 171, 178, 191, 212, 221, 222, 223, 226, 228, 290, 323, 333, 340, 344, 347
GOOD (E), 80, 98, 317, 324, 344, 348
GOODACRE, 332
GOODAKER, 19, 40, 125, 185, 298
GOODLOE, 85, 129, 216, 256
GOODMAN, 61, 63, 98
GOODRIDGE, 125, 126, 431
GOOLSBY, 197
GORDON, 8, 11, 12, 13, 56, 57, 115, 120, 126, 127, 130, 151, 153, 157, 162, 166, 188, 190, 203, 205, 230, 242, 243, 311, 354, 398, 403, 414, 419
GORE, 209, 233, 235, 236, 237, 253, 289, 369
GOSSETT, 96, 142
GOTHARD, 257
GOUGH, 304
GOULD, 213
GRABLE, 76, 270, 344

GRACE, 43, 120, 127, 181, 201, 220, 241, 293, 340, 342, 367
GRADDY, 98, 229, 255, 259, 325, 338, 346, 370
GRADY, 75, 317
GRAHAM, 33, 45, 48, 51, 58, 64, 65, 70, 106, 121, 127, 128, 143, 172, 185, 260, 265, 271, 306, 336, 339, 343, 346, 366, 390
GRAND, 253
GRANT, 62, 63, 94, 95, 125, 138, 157, 160, 259, 350, 354
GRASTY, 158
GRAVEN, 156
GRAVES, 65, 336
GRAY, 34, 97, 120, 132, 192, 209, 245, 263, 294, 353, 398
GRAYSON, 98, 127, 333
GREEN, 65, 66, 71, 72, 93, 113, 116, 198, 218, 291, 293, 309, 325, 343
GREENE, 297
GREENFIELD, 255, 328
GREENUP, 11, 12, 16, 172, 381
GREENWELL, 231
GREENWOOD, 303
GREER, 34, 131, 164, 184, 264, 271, 272, 291, 350, 382
GREGERY, 253
GREGORY, 177, 231, 268, 326
GREGSTON, 50
GRENIER, 96
GRESBY, 201
GRESHAM, 214
GRIBBLE, 60, 154
GRIFFEY, 280
GRIFFIN, 33, 230, 247, 328
GRIFFITH, 89, 124
GRIFFOR, 258
GRIMAND, 42
GRIMES, 221
GRISHAM, 68
GRISSELL, 212
GRIZZELL, 153
GROOM, 62, 259
GROPENGEISER, 74
GROSS, 191
GROVER, 65
GROVES, 65, 77, 132, 134, 158, 262, 274
GRUBBS, 224
GUESS, 251, 269
GUGE, 128, 227, 353
GUGGENHEIM, 205
GUILFOIL, 161
GUINN, 60
GULLY, 14
GUNN, 47, 196, 241, 257, 262, 263, 369, 385, 398
GUNNIS, 141
GUTHERIES, 65
GUY, 163

HACKLEY, 271
HADLEY, 53
HAGAN, 61
HAGEN, 124
HAGOOD, 138
HAHN, 41
HAIG, 293
HAIL, 87
HAILE, 68, 272
HAILEY, 271, 280
HALE, 55, 61, 63, 105, 128, 131, 164, 182, 184, 219, 225, 257, 263, 291, 324, 327, 335
HALEY, 25, 139, 218, 221, 247, 255
HALL, 2, 14, 21, 44, 55, 66, 103, 104, 115, 119, 120, 129, 130, 131, 135, 140, 174, 202, 203, 204, 205, 208, 212, 213, 224, 228, 229, 238, 263, 280, 288, 302, 318, 326, 330, 332, 344, 347, 354, 356, 358, 379, 386, 431
HALSALL, 269
HAMBY, 20, 42, 63, 128, 157, 167, 224, 244, 310, 325, 330, 333, 335, 336, 338, 342, 373, 390
HAMILTON, 49, 65, 191, 202
HAMMACK, 248, 339
HAMMERS, 6, 71
HAMMOND, 350
HAMMONDS, 4, 5, 6, 20, 68, 128, 129, 131, 132, 134, 137, 164, 182, 221, 228, 240, 242, 266, 293, 358, 375, 379
HAMPTON, 37, 60, 217, 256, 278, 322, 336, 346, 382, 383
HAMRICK, 295
HAMTON, 150
HANCOCK, 48, 107, 111, 143,

184, 220, 221, 273, 339, 340, 344, 432
HAND, 47
HANKINS, 112, 162, 185, 188, 241, 263, 265, 334
HANKS, 132, 262, 310, 328, 340, 341, 382
HANNER, 18, 69, 108, 292, 311, 323, 340
HANSON, 23, 27, 85, 86, 214, 375
HARBOR, 213, 214
HARDEGREE, 209
HARDESTY, 71
HARDIN, 56, 65, 139, 229, 292, 419
HARDING, 54, 60
HARDISON, 363
HARDWICK, 112, 322, 338, 356
HARDY, 72, 134, 229, 358
HARGROVE, 61
HARKINS, 41, 323, 337, 343
HARL, 244
HARLAN, 377
HARM, 251
HARMON, 132, 148, 240, 241, 337
HARNED, 106, 114, 136, 390
HARPE, 15
HARPENDING, 125
HARPER, 56, 95, 203
HARRALSON, 12, 133, 144, 179, 253, 323, 324, 333, 338, 341, 369
HARRELL, 6, 114
HARRELSON, 89, 140
HARRELSTON, 78
HARRIGAN, 280
HARRIMAN, 145
HARRINGTON, 296
HARRIS, 3, 34, 36, 39, 42, 57, 63, 70, 72, 77, 78, 84, 89, 94, 95, 96, 100, 101, 102, 103, 106, 120, 121, 130, 133, 134, 135, 136, 142, 144, 152, 177, 191, 210, 221, 230, 248, 254, 255, 256, 262, 309, 310, 316, 322, 327, 334, 335, 339, 341, 342, 343, 346, 352, 363, 366, 369, 370, 374, 395, 431
HARRISON, 34, 78, 110, 119, 163, 174, 189, 212, 297, 311, 316, 340
HARSHBARGER, 226
HART, 3, 67, 87, 111, 124, 134, 135, 136, 178, 191, 224, 271, 292, 324, 339, 376, 431
HARTFORD, 320
HARTIS, 71
HARTLINE, 279, 398
HARTWIG, 192, 233
HARVEY, 11, 40, 64, 136, 137, 293, 306, 308, 327
HARVIE, 61
HARWICK, 89
HASENMUELLER, 42, 235
HASKINS, 77
HASSLER, 109
HATCHEL, 417
HATCHER, 8, 60, 116, 131, 137, 164, 328, 348
HATFIELD, 86
HATLER, 366
HAUGH, 216
HAUMAN, 80
HAUN, 284
HAUPRICH, 120, 121, 162
HAVENHILL, 178
HAWES, 66
HAWKINS, 6, 33, 51, 54, 160, 209, 210, 218, 247, 253, 300, 317, 318, 340, 344, 357, 396
HAY, 203
HAYCRAFT, 203
HAYDEN, 260, 320
HAYES, 6, 8, 34, 47, 48, 74, 85, 137, 138, 157, 211, 260, 267, 286, 294, 350, 363, 390
HAYNES, 44, 153, 411
HAYS, 281, 332
HAYWOOD, 54, 138, 139, 159, 183, 187, 204, 280, 336, 357
HEAD, 67, 277, 309, 336, 357
HEADLEY, 136
HEARIN, 51
HEDGES, 139
HEDRICK, 120
HEFFLIN, 337
HEFLEY, 217
HEFLIN, 219
HEHL, 157
HEID, 196
HEIFFEY, 253
HEIL, 230

HEINA, 206
HELM, 111, 177
HELSTY, 350
HELTON, 150, 191, 306
HELTSLEY, 47, 398
HENDERSON, 10, 80, 96, 120, 147
HENDRICKS, 208, 229, 334, 345, 364
HENDRIX, 127, 301
HENERY, 168
HENIFY, 242, 243, 291, 296, 297
HENLEY, 290, 335
HENNEBUT, 144
HENNING, 353
HENRETTY, 340, 347
HENRY, 72, 74, 90, 127, 135, 139, 140, 178, 303, 319, 320, 339, 347, 348, 350, 370
HENSLEY, 72, 109, 158, 254
HENSON, 116, 129, 130, 140, 162, 166, 334
HENTY, 238
HERALD, 160
HERB, 173, 174
HERBER, 116
HERN, 191
HEROD, 80
HERREN, 207
HERRIN, 62, 140, 191, 223
HERRING, 215, 340, 342
HERRON, 5, 104, 327
HERZET, 199
HESSELBEIN, 61
HESSON, 354
HESTER, 124, 221, 222
HEULITT, 293
HEWETT, 57
HEWITT, 235
HEWLETT, 8, 42, 52, 132, 133, 136, 140, 141, 183, 216, 254, 255, 370
HEYSE, 402
HIBBETTS, 100
HIBBS, 8, 53, 62, 64, 66, 90, 91, 96, 103, 104, 110, 119, 120, 136, 140, 141, 143, 159, 163, 178, 179, 187, 191, 207, 214, 217, 232, 242, 251, 253, 259, 279, 280, 281, 302, 311, 321, 322, 325, 326, 328, 336, 339, 345, 361, 369, 398, 432
HICKERSON, 141, 170, 354
HICKEY, 363
HICKLIN, 17, 43, 95, 142, 151, 152, 188, 271, 338, 363, 398
HICKMAN, 42, 43, 63, 96, 99, 133, 142, 208, 256, 311, 348
HICKS, 5, 108, 142, 157, 208, 220, 278, 313, 322, 327, 331, 339, 341, 348
HIDGEN, 85
HIGBEE, 357
HIGDON, 218, 325, 336, 338
HIGGENS, 340
HIGGINS, 141, 300, 333, 342
HIGHT, 36, 127, 195, 215, 367
HIGHTOWER, 245, 321, 340, 347
HILBURN, 206
HILL, 49, 61, 67, 71, 133, 142, 143, 157, 158, 166, 178, 179, 219, 224, 230, 251, 255, 273, 300, 324, 325, 335, 341, 344, 345, 348, 352, 366, 369, 370, 432
HILLIARD, 397
HILLYARD, 72, 94, 133, 143, 150, 366
HILYARD, 203
HINES, 278
HINKLE, 333
HINTON, 349
HOAGLAND, 240
HOARD, 24, 72
HOBBY, 190
HOBGOOD, 49, 50, 52, 74, 86, 96, 125, 126, 140, 144, 157, 158, 159, 160, 278, 287, 300, 304, 328, 334, 382, 414, 429
HOBSON, 234
HOCKER, 317
HOCKERSMITH, 350, 374
HOCKING, 120
HODGE, 65, 203, 355
HODGES, 61, 63, 259, 320
HODIAC, 196
HOFFMAN, 8, 49, 54, 94, 143, 144, 145, 185, 214, 333, 341, 345, 349, 365, 382, 432
HOGAN, 125, 293, 398
HOGART, 304
HOGGARD, 264
HOGGART, 65

HOGUE, 120, 189
HOKET, 133
HOLBROOK, 105
HOLDER, 97
HOLEMAN, 96, 100, 358, 428
HOLLAND, 47, 134, 145, 261, 286, 363
HOLLEY, 150
HOLLIE, 75
HOLLIS, 75
HOLLOMAN, 145, 173, 183, 235, 290, 297, 298, 336, 363
HOLLOWAY, 283, 412
HOLSAPPLE, 263
HOLT, 80, 270, 278, 362
HOLZHAUSER, 338
HONEYCUTT, 209
HOOD, 34
HOODENPYLE, 425
HOOK, 83, 96, 145, 146
HOOKER, 187, 334, 339
HOOPER, 94
HOOVER, 205, 390, 424
HOPES, 96
HOPEWELL, 124, 333, 356
HOPGOOD, 29, 89, 200
HOPKINS, 6, 11, 16, 27, 50, 51, 272, 381
HOPPER, 55, 68, 196, 201, 217, 221, 224, 253, 274, 375
HOPSON, 214, 318, 322
HORTON, 292
HOSKINS, 187, 289, 433
HOUG, 380
HOUSE, 146
HOUSEHOLDER, 251
HOUSTON, 236, 363
HOWARD, 67, 72, 80, 84, 94, 98, 121, 177, 277, 278, 311, 350
HOWE, 375, 403
HOWELL, 37, 115, 116, 214, 222, 231, 232, 255, 256, 274, 281, 334, 339, 347, 363, 377, 403
HOWERTON, 263
HOWEY, 105
HOWSER, 41, 146
HOWTON, 5, 70, 71, 80, 84, 99, 108, 109, 116, 132, 146, 147, 148, 157, 168, 197, 240, 241, 246, 264, 322, 326, 327, 328, 329, 334, 335, 336, 337, 339, 344, 347
HOYLE, 57
HUBBARD, 327, 330, 333
HUBBERT, 142
HUDDLESTON, 38, 92, 94, 144, 147, 148, 149, 170, 196, 209, 305, 398, 432
HUDSON, 36, 57, 72, 222, 244, 324, 330, 332, 333, 335, 336, 346
HUECHTEMAN, 49
HUEY, 213
HUFF, 350
HUFFENSTUFER, 231
HUFFMAN, 61
HUGGINS, 70, 71, 325
HUGHES, 12, 61, 85, 93, 175, 178, 207, 260, 278, 310, 311, 324, 347, 357, 360
HULSEY, 147, 152, 362
HUMPHREY, 89, 116, 291, 365
HUMPHRIES, 65
HUNSAKER, 40, 125
HUNT, 41, 54, 128, 171, 209, 229, 273, 322, 332, 333, 334, 338, 365
HUNTER, 53, 69, 70, 187, 197, 357
HURLEY, 149
HURST, 105, 240, 398
HURT, 91
HUSTED, 214
HUSTON, 50, 272
HUTCHESON, 302, 303
HUTCHINSON, 87, 196, 234, 269
HUTCHISON, 86, 240
HYAMS, 97
HYATT(E), 94, 325
HYDE, 194

IBIS, 183
ILSLEY, 23, 24, 335, 377
IMUS, 195, 246
INGLIS, 58, 214, 231, 331, 342, 343, 425
IPOCK, 207
IRELAND, 358
IRVIN, 302, 363
IRWIN, 136, 292
ISBELL, 139, 222
IVEY, 230, 416

IVY, 223

JACKSON, 15, 44, 52, 64, 66, 67, 98, 112, 113, 114, 115, 120, 139, 141, 142, 143, 149, 150, 151, 152, 162, 179, 196, 197, 207, 213, 214, 221, 222, 223, 230, 277, 294, 301, 305, 309, 311, 313, 317, 330, 338, 340, 349, 357, 398, 416
JAGOE, 2, 152, 153, 160, 188, 203, 212, 213, 229, 326, 336, 342, 350, 379
JAHN, 129
JAMES, 18, 34, 48, 49, 73, 96, 127, 146, 153, 159, 212, 220, 226, 227, 326, 331, 430
JAMESON, 153, 154, 363
JARNAGIN, 82
JARRATT, 234
JARRELL, 222
JARVIS, 60, 240
JASPER, 154
JEFFERIES, 148
JEFFREY, 267, 268
JENKINS, 5, 6, 19, 43, 44, 71, 119, 136, 139, 145, 154, 155, 161, 168, 169, 170, 176, 195, 201, 202, 212, 213, 217, 221, 222, 224, 236, 240, 258, 263, 270, 271, 306, 309, 310, 324, 325, 335, 340, 341, 342, 345, 346, 347, 357, 382, 419, 428, 429
JENNINGS, 91, 125, 167, 173, 201, 206, 209, 224, 226, 235, 252, 269, 295, 323, 325, 383, 398
JENSEN, 112, 114, 172, 286, 287
JENT, 38, 139, 155, 156
JERNIGAN, 139
JESSUP, 97
JEWELL, 172, 173, 243
JOHNSON, 47, 48, 51, 52, 54, 58, 60, 75, 109, 112, 116, 128, 156, 167, 196, 199, 202, 205, 211, 213, 214, 224, 233, 235, 236, 252, 253, 260, 261, 262, 266, 274, 287, 293, 297, 306, 309, 318, 326, 333, 336, 340, 342, 369, 371, 379, 398
JOHNSTON, 5, 8, 24, 30, 60, 67, 71, 98, 112, 115, 156, 157, 181, 245, 327, 365, 366, 367, 369, 370, 378
JOINER, 57, 58, 65, 165, 342
JOLSON, 176
JONES, 7, 19, 43, 49, 51, 52, 54, 55, 65, 69, 72, 77, 80, 83, 92, 94, 96, 98, 100, 104, 113, 124, 126, 157, 158, 159, 161, 162, 168, 183, 185, 196, 207, 213, 217, 222, 223, 225, 228, 233, 234, 236, 240, 249, 251, 252, 272, 276, 282, 283, 292, 299, 300, 305, 308, 309, 310, 324, 326, 327, 333, 334, 337, 339, 340, 342, 352, 255, 263, 266, 267, 269, 380, 382, 383, 398, 399, 432
JORDAN, 44, 61, 106, 154, 161, 185, 224, 230, 356, 415, 428
JORDON, 77, 158
JOSEY, 19, 37
JOYCE, 150, 160, 216, 238
JOYNER, 57, 63, 112, 160, 168, 232, 276, 290
JUDGE, 161
JUGAS, 140
JULIAN, 112, 114
JUNTUNEN, 140
JUREY, 293

KAAKE, 154
KAISER, 324, 331, 337
KANE, 180
KARR, 234, 238
KAVANAUGH, 306
KAY, 127
KEEL, 150
KEELING, 109
KEEN(E), 39, 110, 160, 207, 301, 346
KEHR, 161
KEISLING, 60
KEISTER, 282
KEITH, 36, 69, 127, 301
KELLER, 120, 151, 214
KELLEY, 38, 61, 126, 140, 141, 142, 228, 306, 339
KELLO, 84
KELLY, 135, 177, 178, 179, 202, 358, 398
KEM, 170
KEMP, 2, 369
KENDALL, 57, 234
KENDRICK, 324
KENNEDY, 29, 48, 50, 111, 112, 160, 161, 174, 175, 220, 246, 252, 270, 336
KENNER, 44
KENNETT, 271, 358
KENYON, 228
KEOWN, 55, 269
KERBY, 244
KERR, 18, 112, 122, 162, 172, 286, 287, 334
KEY, 19, 94, 183, 340, 341, 352
KEYKENDALL, 190
KEYSER, 305
KIESEL, 90
KEITHLER, 280
KILGORE, 72
KILLEBREW, 57, 58, 61
KILLOUGH, 77, 116, 265, 267, 279, 282
KIMBERLAND, 34, 192
KIMBERLINE, 341
KIMBRELL, 172, 287
KIMMETT, 94
KINDER, 366
KING, 39, 44, 65, 87, 88, 137, 143, 146, 154, 160, 161, 176, 203, 205, 220, 230, 244, 263, 284, 288, 309, 318, 346, 350, 354, 371, 373, 429
KINGHAM, 213
KINGREY, 132, 146
KINGSMEN, 231
KINGTON, 6, 27, 158, 161, 162, 183, 280, 306, 323, 339, 340, 376, 425, 430
KINNETT, 429
KINNEY, 63, 304
KINSEY, 94
KINSOLVING, 80
KIRBY, 71
KIRCHOFF, 158
KIRKHAM, 98
KIRKPATRICK, 306
KIRKSEY, 338
KIRKWOOD, 19, 46, 51, 52, 116, 120, 121, 132, 140, 146, 157, 160, 162, 163, 164, 172, 173, 184, 187, 188, 207, 210, 251, 261, 262, 299, 317, 318, 320, 321, 325, 326, 331, 334, 336, 341, 344, 345, 356, 369
KIRTLEY, 356
KISER, 332
KISS, 190
KISTNER, 223, 271
KITTINGER, 128, 164, 269
KIZER, 332, 335
KLINGER, 58
KNAPP, 279
KNIGHT, 20, 68, 69, 74, 108, 114, 129, 131, 132, 134, 137, 153, 164, 182, 195, 221, 225, 228, 240, 242, 293, 311, 327, 357, 362, 375, 379, 401, 424, 432
KNOCHEL, 252
KNOWLES, 62, 294, 301
KNOX, 72, 133, 143, 166, 336, 341, 349
KOEHLER, 154
KOENIG, 244
KOH, 127
KOLTINSKY, 257
KONDZE, 42
KORB, 35, 36
KORNEGAY, 98
KOSURE, 8, 130, 296, 348
KOTCH, 307
KOWSKI, 42
KRAUTHEIM, 164, 165
KRIETZER, 72, 133
KRUSINSKI, 398
KUEHN, 258
KUMLIN, 36
KUYKENDALL, 224
KYLE, 6, 259, 325

LACEY, 195
LACKEY, 119
LACY, 2, 38, 91, 103, 165, 176, 199, 206, 225, 267, 268, 269, 311, 328, 356, 369
LADD, 34, 165, 166, 192, 335, 363
LAFFERTY, 240
LAFFOON, 2, 7, 8, 9, 26, 36, 42, 46, 57, 110, 11, 119, 121, 125, 128, 130, 137, 140, 142, 153, 166, 167, 181, 189, 207, 212, 216, 226, 256, 263, 270, 279, 281, 291, 292, 305, 324, 334, 346, 378, 398, 426
LAFON, 166
LAFOND, 166
LAFOUNTAINE, 94
LAKIN, 65, 362
LAM, 48, 80, 97, 98, 104, 201, 369
LAMAR, 142
LAMARR, 331
LAMB., 5, 49, 61, 121, 150, 167, 177, 224, 253, 265, 270, 282, 309, 317, 324, 335, 346, 398
LAMBERT, 45
LAMSON, 97,98, 156, 167
LANCASTER, 95
LANDER(S), 11, 158, 232
LANDIAI, 272
LANDINI, 50
LANDRUM, 160, 167, 176, 190
LANDSEN, 425
LANDSON, 323
LANG, 307
LANGFORD, 261
LANGLEY, 2, 63, 64, 234, 238, 290, 299, 326, 358, 365, 426
LANGZELL, 168, 259, 321, 325, 432
LANHAM, 52
LANIER, 29
LANSDEN, 143, 176, 345, 370
LANTAFF, 168, 169, 187, 322, 331, 334, 388
LANTRIP, 87, 165, 169, 197, 217, 258, 291, 321, 326, 330, 398
LARABEE, 42
LARIMIRE, 307
LARIMORE, 72, 144
LARKIN, 159, 160, 237, 238, 278
LARMOUTH, 8, 64, 212, 228, 329
LARUE, 163
LASH, 189
LASKOWSKI, 362
LATHAM, 102, 147, 188, 294
LATIMER, 86, 302
LATURE, 68
LAUDERDALE, 201
LAUGHLIN, 293
LAVILLION, 192
LAVIS, 36
LAW, 146, 212
LAWRENCE, 219
LAWSON, 104, 120, 265, 266, 280, 293, 363
LEACH, 110
LEAR, 259, 346, 347, 349
LEASURE, 335, 350, 398, 423
LEATH,146
LEAVELL, 355
LE CHERE, 159
LEDBETTER, 5, 7, 169, 170, 242, 258, 329, 334, 340, 345, 356, 375, 378
LEE, 71, 157, 219, 220, 261, 316, 318, 319, 324, 340, 398
LEECH, 34, 236
LEEPER,44
LEGRAND, 41
LEMON, 104, 230
LENNINGS, 335, 343
LESTER, 261, 317, 327, 328, 336, 341, 344
LETTON, 129
LEWIS, 64, 72, 81, 107, 113, 115, 122, 125, 132, 137, 139, 163, 170, 177, 195, 220, 250, 255, 274, 322, 325, 340, 367, 431
LIGHTSEY, 170, 193
LIGON,8, 41, 94, 129, 145, 207, 235, 257, 268, 323, 325, 341, 347, 348, 366, 382
LIKENS, 390
LILE, 196
LINCOLN, 38, 132, 159
LINDLE, 333
LINDLEY, 152, 305
LINDSAY, 296, 306
LINDSEY, 37, 86, 166, 231, 253
LINEAR, 24, 378
LINKENBERG, 119
LINN, 163
LINVILLE, 49, 196
LIPSCOMB, 219, 220
LISANBY, 170, 196
LISMAN, 343
LITTLE, 53, 173, 293, 398
LITTLEJOHN, 170, 427
LITTLEPAGE, 65, 95, 116, 170, 171, 175, 191, 255, 260, 262, 273, 279, 303, 318, 325
LIVELY, 385
LIVINGSTON, 125, 142, 151, 171, 333, 374
LLOYD(S), 116, 171, 172
LOCK(E), 38, 56, 303, 343, 403
LOCKBRIDGE, 248
LOCKER, 6, 185
LOCKRIDGE, 98, 172, 286
LOFTON, 377
LOGAN, 11, 33, 41, 59, 60, 85, 98, 163, 172, 173, 211, 222, 228, 233, 237, 243, 260, 262, 283, 322, 324, 332, 336, 337, 344
LOGSDON, 95
LONDON, 175
LONEY, 194
LONG, 41, 42, 59, 63, 64, 173, 174, 251, 313, 322, 344, 346, 403, 410
LONGFELLOW, 153
LONGSTAFF, 173
LOREAN, 287
LOVALL, 36
LOVAN, 8, 67, 116, 120, 130, 136, 161, 162, 174, 175, 193, 257, 259, 279, 318, 322, 325, 327, 328, 335, 337, 339, 341, 343, 345, 367
LOVE, 68, 207, 354, 382
LOVELACE, 32, 37, 38, 42, 174, 326, 342, 354
LOVELETTE, 104
LOVELL, 133, 234, 329, 334, 346
LOVIN, 347
LOVING, 37, 62, 91, 92, 93, 112, 143, 162, 174, 206, 324, 370
LOW, 49, 84, 98
LOWE, 152, 214, 235, 383
LOWERY,143, 189, 336, 342, 346
LOWREY, 167
LOWTHER, 6, 7, 175, 176
LOYD, 217
LUCAS, 176, 180, 205, 323
LUCK(S), 18, 42, 256
LUCKETT, 165, 176, 268, 269
LUCKY, 180
LUCZAJ, 271
LUNSFORD, 75, 223, 242
LUSK, 116
LUTZ, 41, 52, 53, 67, 85, 102, 131, 134, 136, 143, 176, 177, 178, 179, 180, 188, 190, 214, 217, 243, 252, 272, 292, 293, 302, 320, 321, 324, 329, 336, 347, 348, 398
LYALL(S), 199, 206, 269
LYELL, 36, 88, 109, 114, 127, 267, 274
LYLE, 40, 184, 296
LYNCH, 79, 91, 96, 114, 164, 172, 183, 324, 326, 336, 339, 343
LYNN, 19, 59, 67, 106, 141, 163, 172, 233, 236, 237, 243, 262, 293, 324, 330, 398
LYNNE, 89
LYON(S), 18, 33, 135, 180, 210, 245, 261, 270, 296, 343, 375, 397

MACARTHUR, 203
MCABEE, 236
MCALISTER, 180, 299, 328
MCALLISTER, 110
MCARTHUR, 140
MCATEE, 158
MCBEE, 42
MCBRIDE, 349
MCCAIN, 316, 317
MCCALISTER, 145
MCCALL, 119
MCCANDLESS, 119
MCCANN, 356
MCCARLEY, 258
MCCARTY, 77
MCCARVER, 112
MCCHESNEY, 180
MCCLAREN, 261
MCCLEAN, 37
MCCLEARN, 6, 80, 181, 349
MCCLENDON, 404
MCCLOWD, 56
MCCLURE, 56, 363
MCCORD, 40, 97, 338, 366
MCCORMACK, 177
MCCORMICK, 44, 52, 297, 334, 341
MCCOY, 39, 41, 63, 65, 66, 70, 71, 76, 86, 207, 323, 337, 423
MCCRACKEN, 69, 301, 399
MCCUE, 96
MCCULL(E)Y, 8, 18, 23, 181, 198, 216, 256, 281, 320, 327, 330, 335, 346, 382
MCCULLOCK, 214
MCCULLOUGH, 54, 293
MCDANIELS, 96
MCDONALD, 36, 44, 112, 181, 349, 357, 363, 365, 366
MCDOW, 213
MCDOWELL, 56, 199, 236, 237, 239, 380, 308
MCELROY, 108
MCELVAIN, 64
MCEUEN, 158, 171, 178, 179, 183, 357
MCFARLAND, 84, 231, 292
MCGAR, 128, 131, 182, 332
MCGARY, 11, 12, 13, 14, 16, 38, 129, 162, 163, 164, 182, 183, 184, 187, 216, 295, 299, 334, 358, 378, 424
MCGAW, 184, 185, 418
MCGEE, 332, 354
MCGEHEE, 370
MCGLINCH, 154
MCGOUGH, 90
MCGOWAN, 267
MCGRADY, 74
MCGREGOR, 35, 94, 96, 105, 109, 113, 132, 168, 185, 186, 196, 202, 213, 259, 264, 273, 275, 327, 328, 331, 332, 334, 336, 338, 342, 344, 349, 382, 398, 427, 432
MCGREW, 153
MCGRIFF, 116
MCGUIRE, 163, 187, 343
MCGUYER,163, 169, 183, 187, 227, 259, 260, 261
MCINTIRE, 219
MCINTOSH, 127, 214, 301, 324, 326, 332
MCINTYRE, 252
MCKAY, 56
MCKECHNIE, 120
MCKENNY, 36
MCKINNEY, 156, 286, 305
MCKINSEY, 77, 152, 187, 188, 289
MCKNIGHT, 24, 36, 37, 53, 63, 67, 112, 149, 167, 177, 224, 232, 330, 339, 342, 345, 347
MCLAIN, 42, 45
MCLANATHAN, 14
MCLAUGHLIN, 164
MCLEAN, 188, 356, 369
MCLEER, 63
MCLEMORE, 188, 201
MCLEOD, 38, 100, 188, 189, 317, 318, 358, 403
MCLESKEY, 207
MCMILLAN, 267
MCMILLIN, 246
MCMULLIN, 63
MCMURTIE, 356
MCNAMER, 97
MCNARY,59, 137, 189, 190, 366
MCNEAL, 61
MCNEEL(E)Y, 39,90, 101, 173, 190, 302, 347
MCNUTT, 277
MCPHERSON, 47, 203, 208, 426
MCREYNOLDS, 199, 317, 355
MCSWAIN, 87
MCVEY, 73
MCWHORTER, 213
MCWILLIAMS, 357, 398

MABREY, 190, 238
MABRY, 209, 275
MACE, 236
MACKY, 164
MADDEN, 258
MADDOX, 49, 136, 153, 161, 214, 306, 344
MADISON, 13, 16, 53, 66, 96, 125, 143, 158, 171, 191, 192, 217, 218, 222, 250, 251, 327, 387, 432
MAGAGNA, 47
MAGRUDER, 199, 307, 308, 348
MAHAM, 116
MAHAN, 344
MAHON, 65
MAHONEY, 50, 356, 358
MAHR, 411
MAHURIN, 398
MAIAMI, 42
MAJOR(S), 24, 37, 45, 46, 80, 191, 192, 335, 343, 355, 363
MALAIER, 291
MALIN, 110, 111, 138, 166
MALLORY, 225, 234
MALONEY, 57
MANGRUM, 124, 128, 217
MANGUM, 136, 191, 200
MANION, 65
MANIRE, 301
MANN, 175
MANSEL, 335
MARCUM, 231
MARETICH, 306
MARINE, 361
MARION, 215
MARKHAM, 124, 371
MARKS, 72, 96, 171, 262, 273, 295, 385
MARONEY, 52
MAROZZI, 202
MARROW, 150
MARSH, 120, 203
MARSHALL, 41, 136, 170, 301
MARTIN, 12, 13, 18, 19, 34, 41, 47, 49, 56, 57, 62, 88, 97, 105, 106, 108, 114, 123 148, 175, 178, 179, 184, 192, 214, 219, 222, 247, 251, 252, 256, 259, 263, 267, 270, 274, 276, 320, 323, 324, 331,335, 336, 338, 344, 345, 377, 432
MARZONIA, 119
MASHBURN, 157
MASON, 62, 92, 94, 114, 154, 170, 192, 193, 194, 196, 215, 277, 301
MASONCUP, 94, 159, 251, 278
MASSAMORE, 68, 194, 198, 205
MASSEY, 67, 250, 298
MASTIN, 296
MATHEIS, 224
MATHENEY, 340
MATHENY, 143, 194, 196, 222, 363
MATHER, 161, 195, 246, 252
MATHEWS, 365
MATHIS, 53, 169, 177, 178, 236, 292
MATHISEN, 120
MATNEY, 328
MATTHAI, 269
MATTHEWS, 106, 112, 114, 357
MATTINGLY, 89, 157
MAUK, 195, 258
MAUMEE, 287
MAUZY, 69
MAXWELL, 157, 175, 195, 334, 343, 344, 432
MAY, 93, 246, 340,
MAYERS, 42
MAYFIELD,34
MAYS, 146
MAZYAK, 116
MEADOWS, 390
MEAZLES, 210
MEDARIS, 40
MEDEIROS, 137
MEDLOCK, 339
MEELIN, 142
MEFFORD, 397
MEIGHAN, 49
MEJIA, 97
MELTON, 195, 196, 224, 240, 258, 270, 285, 300, 326, 343, 398
MENSER, 24, 36, 41, 58, 94, 125, 142, 149, 150, 170, 196, 214, 327, 349, 363, 432
MENTZER, 196
MERCER, 220, 294, 302, 320, 326
MEREDITH, 203
MERIDETH, 196
MERREL, 43
MERRELL, 134, 196, 197, 262, 328
MERRICK, 42
MERRILL, 349
MERRITT, 230
MERRYMAN, 134
MESSAMORE, 84, 197, 214, 337, 340, 398
MESSINGER, 66
MESTAN, 167, 224
METCALFE, 198, 224, 273, 358
METHENY, 225, 311
MEYER , 234
MEYERS, 428
MICHAELS, 35
MIDKIFF, 198
MILES, 271
MILLER, 13, 19, 34, 40, 50, 59, 67, 76, 84, 85, 88, 91, 94, 108, 116, 118, 126, 136, 141, 143, 145, 149, 153, 158, 159, 161, 165, 170, 172, 176, 181, 186, 192, 195, 197, 198, 199, 215,

217, 226, 231, 244, 252, 253, 255, 257, 268, 298, 299, 300, 307, 310, 312, 317, 321, 326, 327, 328, 335, 341, 350, 352, 353, 363, 365, 366, 367, 369, 370, 378, 380, 405, 431, 530
MILLIGAN, 36, 233, 397
MILLS, 42, 114, 120, 121, 132, 175, 249, 282, 309, 323, 371, 374
MILTON, 139
MILUM, 87
MIM(MS), 5, 63, 199, 200, 234, 277, 318
MINNICH, 45
MINOR, 216
MINTER, 192, 224, 325
MINTON, 35, 95
MISCHKE, 263
MISSICK, 357
MITCHELL, 8, 48, 49, 86, 89, 95, 107, 110, 116, 147, 160, 172, 173, 174, 175, 177, 191, 200, 201, 207, 217, 232, 236, 237, 253, 266, 297, 302, 311, 312, 313, 316, 317, 318, 319, 332, 340, 345, 347, 366, 373, 403, 422
MITCHEM, 72, 144
MIZE, 164
MOCK, 162, 200
MOFFET, 74
MOLTON, 346
MONGER, 192
MONHOLLON, 66
MONKS, 170
MONROE, 64, 114
MONTELLE, 159
MONTGOMERY, 77, 128, 193, 202, 327
MONTS, 34
MOODY, 56
MOONEY, 267
MOORE, 2, 14, 52, 70, 80, 87, 133, 134, 150, 153, 155, 158, 166, 170, 187, 188, 201, 202, 203, 204, 205, 210, 214, 221, 227,229, 232, 238, 251, 294, 300, 303, 312, 318, 319, 325, 328, 330, 332, 338, 340, 345, 347, 350, 355, 363, 365, 388, 398, 410
MOOREFIELD, 180
MOREMAN, 98
MOREMEN, 145
MORGAN, 6, 39, 42, 51, 52, 74, 75, 82, 87, 91, 110, 116, 120, 125, 160, 165, 166, 205, 206, 207, 212, 213, 219, 235, 245, 251, 255, 268, 269, 322, 323, 325, 334, 335, 349, 353, 338, 339, 344, 346, 347, 349, 353
MORPHEW, 220
MORRIS, 74, 153, 165, 228, 245, 256, 260, 319, 326, 327, 349, 380
MORRISON, 175
MORROW, 6, 8, 18, 46, 49, 54, 55, 73, 91, 96, 133, 159, 207, 208, 256, 263, 302, 325, 326, 333, 343, 348, 352, 354, 366, 398
MORSE, 157, 188, 281, 327, 328, 331, 342, 344
MORTON, 2, 11, 27, 61, 67, 91, 130, 135, 208, 215, 249, 255, 256, 261, 290, 316, 325, 326, 331, 332, 339, 340, 348, 350, 362, 371, 375, 379, 386, 426
MOSELEY, 112, 261, 287, 358
MOSELY, 154
MOSS, 242, 260, 271
MOTHERSHEAD, 321
MOTT, 304
MOULTAN, 257
MOUNT(S), 247, 361
MULLENIX, 191, 326, 343
MULLENNIX,222
MULLIGAN, 65
MULLINIX, 188
MULLINS, 71, 145, 171, 187, 235, 298, 327
MUNDAY, 397
MUNNS, 208, 382
MURPH(E)Y, 17, 69, 123, 142, 199, 228, 229, 253, 261, 274, 287, 295, 299, 300, 304, 325, 342, 345, 346, 349, 363, 382
MURRAH, 59, 69, 87, 208, 209, 301
MURRAY, 318
MURRELL, 354
MUSE, 124
MUSGROVE, 230
MUSIC, 209
MYERS, 41, 100, 135, 136, 145, 180, 198,209, 210, 237, 253, 278, 323, 326, 350, 354, 366, 367, 398
MYRE(S), 94, 323

NALEVANKO, 178
NALL(S), 17, 154, 337, 346
NANCE, 44, 69, 77, 94, 118, 159, 195, 207, 210, 226, 232, 298, 329
NAPIER, 210, 211, 328, 354
NASH, 272
NATIONS, 312, 313
NAUE, 65
NEAL(E), 34, 215, 221, 319, 369
NEATHERY, 215
NEBLETT, 291
NEEDHAM, 98
NEIBERT, 46
NEISBET, 211
NEISBETH, 336
NEISZ, 144, 230, 258, 333, 337, 342, 347, 398, 427
NEITZ, 348
NELSON, 18, 265, 290, 310, 317, 366
NESBIT(T), 50, 52, 325, 345, 358
NEWBOLD, 306
NEWBURY, 163
NEWCOM, 79
NEWCOMB, 171
NEWHOUSE, 362
NEWKIRK, 51
NEWMAN, 118, 367
NEWMANN, 183
NEWSAM, 249, 266
NEWSOM, 343
NEWTON, 159, 207, 225, 253, 269
NIBLICK, 52
NICHELSON, 212
NICHOLS, 8, 33, 37, 54, 57, 75, 91, 114, 121, 127, 134, 136, 207, 211, 221, 224, 245, 260, 325, 360, 379, 433
NICKELSON, 146
NISBET, 2, 11, 13, 38, 44, 100, 152, 153, 166, 189, 211, 212, 213, 234, 239, 240, 263, 306, 320, 324, 327, 333, 339, 344, 347, 357, 382
NISWONGER, 41, 146, 179, 213, 214, 333
NIX, 76, 165, 326, 343
NIXON, 37, 51, 79, 141, 149, 181, 214, 281, 304
NOE, 50, 51, 272
NOEL, 14, 19, 283, 305, 308, 321, 323, 325, 347, 365
NOF(F)SINGER, 71, 195, 288, 357
NOLAN, 196
NOLES, 94
NORMAN, 116
NORRIS, 77, 353
NORSE, 331
NORTHERN, 143, 251, 333
NORTON, 28, 29, 230, 341
NORVELL, 366
NORWOOD, 34, 35, 327
NOURSE, 29, 324, 344, 348, 349
NUCHOLS, 333
NUCKOLS, 349
NUTALL, 54

OAKLEY, 6, 74, 85, 102, 158, 160, 191, 215, 285, 299, 326, 433
OATES, 29, 46, 68, 161, 162, 164,183, 184, 215, 216, 229, 261, 295, 296, 303, 321, 326, 340, 342, 348, 385
O'BANNON, 373
O'BER, 36
O'BRIEN, 317, 422
O'BRYAN, 129, 140, 162, 163, 187, 217, 220, 251, 259, 337, 340, 356, 369, 370, 382, 419
O'BRYANT, 158, 339
O'DANIEL, 36
OFFUTT, 99, 216, 256, 257, 258, 262, 271, 287, 320, 333, 345, 398
OGDEN, 208
OGILVIE, 57
OGLESBY, 39, 61, 133, 193, 263, 325, 342, 349
OLDHAM, 64, 79, 80, 91, 112, 121, 129, 143, 171, 177, 212, 216, 217, 252, 254, 260, 263, 282, 313, 320, 325, 340, 343, 349, 353, 357
OLIVER, 26, 61, 139, 147, 149, 150, 217, 223, 257, 356
OLP, 164
OMER,240
O'NEAL, 398
OOST, 327
ORAN, 220
ORANGE,52, 97, 150, 224, 328
O'ROARK, 38, 107
O'ROURKE, 63
ORR, 198
ORSBURN, 299
ORTEN, 34, 111, 153, 196, 262, 321, 390
ORTON, 42, 44, 166, 221, 316, 334, 338, 347
OSBORN, 59, 177, 217, 220, 253, 323, 325, 326, 347, 358, 430
OSBORNE, 213, 267, 279
OSBURN, 46, 50, 53, 110, 127, 178, 179, 180, 181, 183, 217, 292, 296, 340, 369, 382
OSBURNE, 37
OSGOOD, 287
OTES, 215
OUTLAND, 180
OUTLAW, 44, 98, 295, 326
OVERALL, 202, 203, 204
OVERAND, 72
OVERBY, 65, 72, 77, 214
OVERSHINER, 281
OVERTON, 39, 219
OWEN(S), 28, 53, 56, 61, 67, 78, 95, 118, 177, 217, 218, 300, 304, 320
OXFORD, 49

QUALLS, 42, 151, 157, 158, 170, 232, 287, 321, 329, 349
QUARTRON, 203
QUEEN, 361
QUINLAN, 307
QUINN, 123, 324, 330, 336, 337
QUISENBERRY, 129, 209, 340

PACE, 53, 72
PADDOCK, 91
PADGETT, 128, 164, 218, 219
PAFFORD, 64
PAGE, 111, 139, 219, 220, 222, 229, 270, 271, 349
PAGUE, 238
PAIGE, 35
PAINE, 89
PAINTER, 78
PALMER, 38, 100, 116, 181, 193, 220, 293
PARCHER, 168, 290
PARHAM, 65, 291
PARIS, 152, 157
PARISH, 23, 67, 102, 159, 167, 177, 220, 221, 228, 244, 272, 308, 345, 350, 381
PARK, 47, 366
PARKER, 6, 42, 43, 54, 73, 87, 96, 107, 111, 121, 122, 123, 128, 135, 136, 144, 157, 166, 167, 196, 197, 201, 207, 221, 222, 276, 278, 287, 313, 317, 325, 330, 331, 334, 336, 342, 346, 354, 366, 403
PARKEST, 255
PARKS, 128, 174, 316
PARNELL, 373
PARRIS, 302, 358
PARRISH, 56, 60, 70, 106, 157, 158, 160, 191, 204, 222, 287, 325, 327
PARROTT, 243
PARSONS, 36, 196, 239, 332
PASCOE, 72
PATE, 8, 73, 151, 220, 238, 253, 280, 333
PATTERSON, 70, 161, 240, 293, 301, 307, 347, 398
PATTON, 319
PAUL, 80
PAYNE, 51, 89, 169, 170, 196, 222, 223, 251, 270, 292, 341, 343
PAYTON, 334
PEAK, 197
PEARCE, 213, 317, 350, 374, 382
PEARCY, 96, 179
PEARL, 51, 52
PEARSON, 19, 47, 227, 342
PEAY, 356
PECK, 336
PEMBERTON, 214, 326
PENDGRAPH, 50
PENDLEY, 37, 59, 62, 63, 71, 102, 223, 243, 271, 272, 321, 328, 346, 367, 369
PENDLY, 56, 58, 298
PENN, 175
PENNINGTON, 223, 224, 367
PEPPER, 6, 128, 131, 202
PERALTA, 284, 285, 299, 300
PEREZ, 42, 235
PERIMAN, 356
PERKINS, 60, 89, 144, 210, 212, 270, 322, 342, 344, 345, 352
PERRY, 56, 97, 135, 167, 224, 327, 338, 378
PERSHING, 153
PERSLEY, 336
PETERS, 157, 199, 354
PETERSON, 72, 73, 95, 325
PETSCH, 291
PETTUS, 77, 316
PETTY, 363
PETUS, 48
PETWAY, 93, 94
PEVELER, 152
PEYTON, 19, 44, 49, 72, 94, 120, 121, 128, 143, 144, 157, 191, 224, 225, 244, 317, 324, 325, 327, 330, 332, 334, 335, 336, 339, 344, 345, 348, 352, 358, 383
PHAUP, 128, 353, 364
PHELPS, 80, 96, 108, 109, 197, 225, 265, 349
PHILLIPS, 60, 62, 94, 128, 134, 136, 177, 180, 205, 237, 262, 296, 304, 320, 324, 332, 341, 357, 367
PHILPOT, 124
PICKENS, 213, 273, 303, 344
PICKERING, 158, 225
PIDCOCK, 13, 65, 153, 175, 228
PIEPER, 357
PIERCE, 104, 174, 307, 329, 367, 398
PIERCY, 324, 344, 369,
PIERSON, 282
PIGG, 62, 259
PIKE, 70
PILAND, 235
PILLOW, 135, 212
PINCKARD, 248
PINCKLEY, 61
PINDAR, 45
PINKSTON, 200
PINNEGAR, 170
PIPPIN, 65
PITCHFORD, 170
PITTMAN, 300, 323
PITZER, 359
PLAIN, 210, 335, 341, 344, 348
PLANK, 36, 332
PLETT, 173
PLUNKETT, 272
POE, 91, 114, 157, 324, 332, 334, 335, 347
POGUE, 39
POINDEXTER, 363
POLK, 75
POLLARD, 92, 225, 310, 311
POLLEY, 54, 69, 85, 159, 173, 225, 226, 232, 252, 260, 300, 325, 334, 340, 343, 349, 381, 382
POLLION, 213
POLLITTE, 57
POLLOCK, 96, 350
POLLY, 398
POOL, 58, 125, 130, 133, 226, 333, 342
POOLE, 78, 87, 134, 149, 170, 196, 203, 204, 227, 256, 331, 380
POPHAM, 161
PORTER, 14, 28, 37, 91, 179, 214, 227, 229, 322, 326, 333, 338, 339, 341, 342, 346, 363, 366, 369, 370, 377, 390, 429
PORTERFIELD, 104, 227
POTTER, 2, 287, 377
POTTS, 6, 128, 162, 188, 210, 227, 228
POWELL, 8, 37, 46, 73, 75, 84, 186, 230, 331, 332, 349, 432
POWERS, 56, 57, 200
POWLESS, 87
POYNTER, 106
P'POOL, 170
PRAIM, 131
PRATHER, 54, 60, 85, 86, 111, 112, 228, 229, 253, 321, 329, 333, 336
PRATT, 26, 322, 358
PRESLEY, 299
PRESNELL, 39
PRESSLEY, 181, 294, 337
PRESTON, 17, 60, 190, 229, 276, 295, 320
PREWITT, 88
PREZ, 226
PRICE, 122, 132, 136, 138, 205, 209, 242, 265, 271, 294, 295, 335, 336, 366, 408
PRIDE, 153, 166, 203, 204, 205, 229, 369
PRIEST, 7, 46, 157, 229, 230, 266, 354, 381
PRINCE, 90, 105, 132, 146, 165
PRITCHETT, 44, 47, 50, 52, 85, 130, 137, 138, 150, 159, 174, 211, 212, 213, 229, 230, 260, 272, 307, 317, 319, 350, 358, 362, 426, 429
PROCTOR, 96, 135, 338
PROW, 42, 144, 230, 231, 332, 416
PROWSE, 48, 195
PRUITT, 61, 231, 248, 288
PRUITTE, 187
PRUNTY, 212
PRYOR, 19, 20, 317, 318, 328
PUCKETT,133
PUGH, 6, 74, 323
PULLEN, 355, 360
PULLEY, 19
PULLMAN, 352
PURDY, 46, 70, 91, 139, 146, 231, 265, 315, 329, 330, 331, 334, 335, 336, 344, 347, 348, 356
PURVIS, 129
PURYEAR, 49, 72, 73, 158, 231, 232, 276, 290, 305
PUTMAN, 32, 38, 39, 56, 69, 157, 204, 259, 293, 294, 338, 342, 349, 367, 385
PUTTY, 243
PYLE, 71
PYLES, 69

RADEBAUGH, 190
RADZIEJEWSKI, 140
RADFORD, 149, 158
RAGLAND, 166
RAILEY, 300
RAINES, 116
RAINEY, 271
RAINWATER, 243, 263, 300, 340
RAKESTRAW, 358
RALEY, 296, 297
RAMAGE, 114
RAMBO, 262, 348
RAMM, 177, 178
RAMSEY, 2, 5, 6, 40, 41, 42, 43, 49, 52, 65, 67, 88, 116, 126, 145, 159, 160, 161, 209, 213, 214, 230, 232, 233, 234, 235, 236, 237, 238, 239, 246, 252, 253, 269, 270, 289, 290, 291, 298, 323, 324, 332, 335, 337, 338, 350, 356, 369, 382, 403, 426
RAND, 60
RANDALL, 371
RANDLE, 56, 57, 74, 122, 123, 239
RANDOLPH,126 141, 172
RANES, 42
RANKIN, 23, 56
RANSAW, 137
RAPPOLEE, 302
RASCO, 336, 363
RASH, 28, 70, 111, 213, 235, 239, 240, 350, 358, 371, 383, 419
RASMUSEN, 202
RATHMAN, 70
RATLIFF, 29, 33, 116, 117, 132, 146, 148, 240, 241, 242, 247, 270
RATZLAFF, 218, 219
RAU, 126
RAY, 43, 56 69, 90, 112, 164, 182, 278, 347, 348, 398
RAYNOR, 236
REA, 401
READ, 271
RECTOR, 223
REDD, 192
REDDICK, 37
REDENOUR, 203
REDMOND, 94
REEB, 271
REECE,244
REED, 253, 263, 288, 306, 324, 335
REEDER, 208
REES, 230
REESE, 44, 175, 337
REEVES, 113, 114, 249, 250
REHLING, 217
REICHMUTH, 80
REID, 53, 177, 242, 408
REIMER, 99, 178
REINECKE, 375
REIS, 90
RENFRO, 19, 246
RENICK, 162
RENSHAW, 95, 156, 196, 220
REYNOLDS, 96, 134, 150, 164, 165, 197, 226, 229, 231, 260, 261, 262, 278, 280, 307, 308, 343, 345, 349
RHEA, 172, 242, 243, 327, 367, 369
RHENN, 65
RHEW, 62, 101, 102, 103, 179, 221, 223, 243, 272, 279, 300
RHOADES, 37
RHOADS, 243
RHODES, 18, 19, 37, 157, 224, 243
RIBERS, 318
RICE, 14, 51, 71, 136, 172,202, 203, 222, 266, 286, 318, 339, 340
RICH, 49, 50, 190, 214, 279, 327
RICHARDS(S), 49, 62, 74, 172, 206, 243, 244, 276, 318, 324, 327, 330, 331, 336, 337, 343
RICHARDSON, 74, 91, 96, 96, 302, 398, 416
RICHETTS, 286
RICHEY, 282, 366
RICKARD, 44, 60, 128, 228
RIDDLE, 74, 192, 399, 403, 419
RIDENOUR, 244
RIDGE, 84, 108
RIDGWAY, 353
RIDLEY, 6, 57, 58, 114, 339, 427
RIES, 279
RIGGINS, 46, 196
RIGGLE, 353
RIGGS, 24, 30, 132, 146, 157, 244, 245, 335, 339, 346, 363, 365, 366, 369, 378, 380
RIGNEY, 241
RIGSBY, 61
RILEY, 44, 67, 86, 101, 258, 349, 388
RINCK, 293
RINGO, 88, 160, 161, 195, 235, 245, 246, 251, 252, 269, 270, 288, 289, 333, 365
RINGOLD, 317
RIODAN, 349
RIORDAN, 40
RIPLEY, 367
RISHER, 73
RISTON, 312
RITTENBERRY, 255
RITTENHOUSE, 133
RIVERS, 188
ROACH, 55, 78, 370
ROAKE, 129
ROAM, 45
RO'ARK, 107
ROARK, 37, 46, 121, 155, 367
ROBARDS, 5, 109, 148, 157, 246, 247, 322, 329, 417
ROBERSON, 228, 333, 349
ROBERTS, 41, 43, 66, 72, 87, 96, 100, 109, 142, 146, 175, 181, 211, 222, 229, 240, 247, 259, 276, 285, 294, 322, 326, 328, 329 , 358
ROBERTSON, 33, 39, 43, 44, 54, 74, 98, 141, 149, 212, 213, 229, 247, 255, 256, 269, 328, 332, 334, 340, 354, 358, 369, 370, 375
ROBINGTON, 339
ROBINSON, 27, 28, 33, 34, 41, 42, 65, 75, 105, 109, 127, 149, 151, 153, 161, 166, 167,190, 208, 247, 248, 262, 270, 275, 276, 278, 286, 305, 313, 321, 326, 335, 336, 339, 346, 353, 378
ROBISON, 369
ROBLING, 363
ROCK, 41
RODDY, 220
RODGERS, 2, 65, 66, 96, 128, 171, 183, 184, 214, 229, 253, 255, 276, 321, 345, 358, 380
ROE, 302
ROEHRENBECK,227
ROEHRIG, 199, 298
ROGERS, 28, 29, 45, 51, 57, 58, 95, 106, 167, 183, 187, 196, 223, 224, 274, 329, 341

ROGERSON, 51, 52
ROLAND, 248, 278
ROLLINS, 270
ROLLY, 178
ROMBEAU, 98
RONE, 366
ROOKER, 100
ROOT, 84
ROSE, 129, 274
ROSER, 2
ROSKOSKY, 205, 206
ROSS, 42, 43, 44, 67, 145, 158, 248, 261, 266, 269, 290, 293, 317, 319, 320, 419
ROSSNER, 259
ROTHROCK, 308
ROUSE, 47, 189
ROVER, 50, 52
ROWLEY, 55
ROY, 340
ROYSTER, 54
RUBENS, 348
RUBY, 99, 150, 161, 208, 246, 249, 288, 299, 350, 358, 382, 386, 403
RUCKER, 135
RUDD, 6, 78, 181, 191, 326, 328, 329, 333, 346, 363, 403, 432
RUDY, 336, 348
RUDOLPH, 380
RUFF, 155
RULE, 373
RUMPH, 183
RUMSEY, 55
RUNYON, 222
RUSH, 220
RUSS, 59
RUSSELL, 23, 74, 91, 112, 113, 114, 139, 142, 148, 159, 165, 183, 186, 236, 237, 272, 300, 335, 336, 347, 354, 364.
RUST, 124, 138
RUTHERFORD, 405
RUTLEDGE, 194
RYAN, 326

SAILOR, 199
SAINT, 341
SALLEE, 353
SALMON, 23, 24, 42, 67, 111, 131, 239, 249, 250, 270, 333, 335, 377, 409
SALSBURG, 132
SAMPLES, 79, 107, 398
SAMS, 318
SAMUELS, 107, 125, 126, 217, 250
SANCHEZ, 50
SANDEFUR, 90, 363
SANDERS, 170, 229, 253, 280, 281, 297, 303, 357, 369
SANDIDGE, 248
SANDIFER, 34
SANDFORD, 35
SARGENT, 234, 238
SARGOUS, 255
SATERFIELD, 297
SATTERFIELD, 66, 89, 191, 217, 250, 251, 331, 379
SAULS, 133
SAUNDERS, 165
SAVAGE, 52
SAVICH, 40
SAVINO, 91
SAWYER, 44
SBRAVATI, 304
SCALES, 60
SCEARCE, 63, 142
SCHAUT, 267
SCHEETZ, 202
SCHELLEBURG, 170
SCHERER, 176
SCHIMMEL, 218
SCHLOTMAN, 208
SCHLOTTMAN, 378
SCHMETZER, 251, 280, 323, 377, 386
SCHMITT, 267
SCHMITZ, 139
SCHNEIDER, 199
SCHOCH, 202
SCHOEFIELD, 114
SCHOLAR, 170
SCHRIENER, 36
SCHROLLER, 72
SCHULTZ, 49
SCHWAN, 42
SCHWANKERT, 206
SCHWARTZ, 287
SCISNEY, 43, 75, 264
SCOBEE, 279
SCOTT, 18, 41, 72, 87, 121, 138, 167, 170, 171, 175, 182, 209, 211, 220, 224, 229, 244, 248, 251, 258, 260, 261, 279, 285, 287, 306, 317, 322, 330, 341, 349, 350, 367, 399, 411, 418
SCROGINS, 332
SEABOUGH, 257
SEABURN, 167
SCUDDER, 172
SEARS, 69, 282
SEBREE, 375
SEELBACK, 238
SELBY, 94
SELF, 98
SELLARS, 43
SELLERS, 69
SELLS, 150
SETTLE, 272
SETZER, 29, 49
SEVERANCE, 179
SEWELL, 387
SEXTON, 204, 214
SEYMOUR, 161, 245, 246, 251, 252, 253, 348
SHACKELFORD, 284
SHACKLEFORD, 327
SHADOIN, 129
SHADRICK, 298
SHAFER, 95
SHAH, 117
SHAIN, 6, 76
SHANE, 192, 242
SHANKLIN, 18, 281
SHANKS, 96, 210, 298
SHARER, 90
SHARKEY, 197, 252
SHARKY, 177
SHARLITE, 350
SHARP, 112, 133, 244, 370
SHAVER, 269
SHAW, 38, 51, 306, 307, 308, 322, 345
SHECKLES, 309
SHEETS, 69
SHEFFER, 213
SHELBY, 13, 15
SHELTON, 137, 138, 156, 209, 210, 232, 233, 263, 264, 317, 321, 332, 337, 338, 341, 348
SHEPHERD, 54, 131
SHEPPARD, 225
SHERIDAN, 143
SHERROD, 260
SHIMMER, 71
SHIPMAN, 65
SHIPP, 192, 252
SHIRK, 361
SHOATE, 71
SHOEMAKER, 280
SHOLAR, 346
SHORE, 308
SHORT, 17, 152, 195, 354
SHOULDERS, 5, 19, 50, 59, 67, 76, 85, 88, 116, 126, 136, 141, 143, 145, 149, 158, 159, 172, 186, 192, 195, 215, 217, 226, 231, 244, 252, 253, 255, 299, 300, 322, 326, 327, 341, 352, 363, 365, 366, 369, 370, 430, 431
SHRAWDER, 222
SHRUM, 252
SHULL, 125
SHUMATE, 43, 44, 54, 139, 140, 228, 229
SHURTLEFF, 104, 105, 120
SIGHTS, 322
SIGLER, 71, 160, 161, 195, 209, 220, 237, 238, 246, 253, 310, 327
SILKWOOD, 11, 12, 13, 182
SILVOSO, 161
SIMKO, 214
SIMMON, 204
SIMMONS, 61, 98, 102, 103, 207, 254, 334, 342, 388
SIMMS, 77, 125, 217, 264, 272, 280, 326, 358, 423
SIMONS, 101, 157, 194, 197, 254, 255, 280, 326, 421
SIMPSON, 132, 161, 219, 291, 297, 301, 318, 398
SIMS, 36, 37, 253, 349
SINCLAIR, 167, 258
SINGLETON, 36
SINN, 36, 37, 166
SIRIA, 65, 76, 243, 337
SISK, 5, 11, 13, 14, 19, 35, 36, 43, 46, 51, 52, 54, 55, 63, 89, 91, 92, 93, 96, 99, 106, 112, 114, 115, 118, 120, 136, 140, 142, 156, 158, 161, 172, 174, 178, 181, 187, 196, 197, 198, 212, 213, 230, 251, 255, 256, 257, 262, 266, 269, 293, 312, 317, 320, 322, 3236.
SISSON, 298
SISTLER, 190
SITTLER, 52
SIVING, 350
SIVLEY, 61
SIX, 207
SIZEMORE, 128, 129, 164, 207, 257, 363
SKAGGS, 134, 135, 237, 257, 274, 299, 328, 336, 341, 342
SKEENS, 301
SKILES, 261
SKILLMAN, 328
SKIMERHORN, 127
SKINNER, 66, 211
SLACK, 128
SLADEN, 64
SLATEN, 162
SLATON, 7, 17, 18, 23, 46, 56, 61, 62, 63, 64, 100, 116, 128, 149, 152, 162, 163, 168, 170, 195, 200, 217, 221, 229, 232, 248, 251, 254, 257, 258, 259, 260, 261, 262, 309, 319, 323, 325, 333, 334, 338, 339, 341, 343, 344, 346, 347, 349, 369, 386
SLAUGHTER, 57, 75, 76
SLAYDEN, 163, 259
SLAYDON, 63
SLINKARD, 257
SLOAN, 150
SLYGH, 128
SMALDONE, 410
SMALLWOOD, 119
SMILEY, 173
SMILY, 16
SMITH, 12, 14, 17, 30, 33, 36, 39, 51, 54, 56, 63, 64, 69, 77, 89, 90, 91, 92, 95, 103, 104, 109, 113, 120, 128, 129, 134, 137, 154, 156, 164, 165, 166, 167, 182, 183, 184, 185, 191, 196, 201, 202, 203, 205, 208, 218, 221, 223, 224, 231, 240, 241, 243, 247, 249, 252, 253, 257, 261, 262, 263, 264, 265, 271, 274, 294, 295, 297, 301, 306, 311, 317, 318, 319, 321, 324, 325, 329, 330, 331, 332, 334, 336, 339, 341, 349, 353, 363, 366, 370, 423, 426
SMOHL, 65
SMOTH, 95
SNAP, 54
SNEED, 62, 95, 264, 265, 266
SNELL, 249
SNELLING, 62, 190
SNELLINGS, 187
SNODGRASS, 65, 162
SNORTON, 260
SNOW, 49, 160
SNYDER, 36, 125, 184, 398
SOFRANKO, 257
SDMON, 347
SOLOMAN, 63, 325, 342
SON, 325, 254
SORRELL, 105
SOUEBER, 244
SOUTH, 98, 137, 138, 142, 188
SOUTHARD, 115, 128, 169, 313
SOUTHERD, 50
SOUTHWORTH, 43, 64, 266, 383
SOWARDS, 360
SPAIN, 61, 157, 248, 249, 266, 398
SPANN, 64
SPEARS, 231
SPECK, 43, 320
SPEED, 322
SPENARD, 398
SPENCE, 398
SPENCER, 34, 46, 327
SPICER, 161, 426
SPICKARD, 58, 328
SPILLER, 56
SPILLMAN, 373
SPINKS, 194, 303
SPIVEY, 162, 213
SPRIGG, 54
SPRADLIN, 307
SPRINGER, 228
SPRINGFIELD, 41, 65, 111, 116, 141, 179, 208, 213, 217, 218, 220, 259, 266, 267, 279, 318, 326, 379
STADER, 216
STALEY, 352, 356, 369
STALIONS, 167
STALLARD, 242
STALLINS, 146, 147, 245, 337, 339
STANFIELD, 184
STANFORD, 36
STANLEY, 118, 198, 273, 287, 301, 325, 328, 329
STANNINGER, 390
STAPLES, 17, 103
STARKE, 74
STARKS, 92, 154, 170, 193, 194, 277, 280
STARR, 109, 228, 353, 362
STASER, 300
STATON, 157, 255, 350
STEADMAN, 112
STEARMAN, 181, 317, 322, 346
STEARSMAN, 71, 107, 256, 342
STEEL, 84, 317
STEELE, 201, 267, 425
STEELEY, 363
STEEN, 38, 116, 266, 267
STEFFY, 292
STENNETT, 227
STEPNEY, 54
STEPPE, 260
STEVENS, 31, 209, 215, 220, 235, 236, 267, 275, 289, 293, 324, 339
STEVENSON, 61, 371
STEWART, 42, 157, 165, 176, 194, 195, 199, 206, 267, 268, 269, 296, 310, 325, 327, 331, 338, 344, 357
STILES, 302
STILLS, 6
STILWELL, 302
STINNETT, 307, 322, 340, 362, 382
STIRSMAN, 234
STITES, 324
STODGHALL, 65
STODGHILL, 69, 118, 322, 325, 326, 338, 342, 343, 347, 358
STODGILL, 43, 160, 382
STOKELY, 134
STOKES, 12, 64, 160, 195, 202, 214, 247, 265, 269, 274, 330, 395
STOLTZ, 405
STONE, 60, 95, 135, 143, 168, 208, 221, 272, 297, 358, 388, 403
STONEY, 371
STORMS, 114
STORY, 42, 132, 152, 345, 365
STOUT, 52, 194
STRADER, 135
STRADLER, 80
STRAIGHT, 346
STRAUSS, 195
STRAWBRIDGE, 290
STREET, 151
STRIBLING, 56, 57
STRIDE, 116
STRINGER, 267
STRIPLIN, 127
STRODE, 158
STRONG, 363
STROTHER, 57, 69, 269, 303, 386
STROUD, 150, 330
STRUCK, 59
STRUM, 124, 200, 210
STUBB, 109
STUBBLEFIELD, 56, 230
STUDEBAKER, 46
STUM, 195, 258, 317, 337, 338, 346, 403
STURGEON, 333
SUGG, 8, 40, 77, 85, 115, 130, 162, 198
SUGGS, 347
SUGIMOTO, 252
SUINO, 140
SUIT, 210
SULLENS, 253
SULLIVAN, 41, 53, 88, 146, 160, 161, 177, 195, 197, 209, 233, 234, 235, 236, 237, 238, 246, 252, 253, 269, 270, 288, 289, 331
SUMMEROW, 234
SUMMERS, 33, 34, 65, 71, 170, 215, 219, 241, 242, 247, 270, 271, 301, 322, 356, 398
SUMMES, 366
SUMPTER, 174
SUTHARD, 153, 212, 213, 223, 240, 256, 271, 281, 328, 336, 341, 342, 349, 370, 388
SUTHERLAND, 271, 272
SUTTLE, 118, 272
SUTTLES, 34
SUTTON, 77, 255, 262, 284, 285, 320
SUWELL, 353
SWAIN, 217
SWAINIGAN, 158
SWAN, 340
SWANZY, 88, 288
SWEARINGEN, 207, 273
SWEENEY, 305
SWINNEY, 38
SWOPE, 177, 178, 250, 331, 339, 347, 365
SYMES, 36

TABOR, 41, 240
TAFT, 136
TALERICO, 233, 239
TALGLOE, 332
TALIAFERRO, 340, 356, 371
TALLANT, 356
TALLEY, 317
TANDY, 224
TANNER, 65, 94, 195
TAPP, 43, 50, 51, 53, 73, 75, 76, 79, 89, 116, 159, 165, 168, 193, 199, 221, 223, 234, 238, 272, 302, 303, 325, 365, 379, 419
TAPSCOTT, 187, 289
TARTER, 52, 63, 66, 102, 103, 177, 178, 221, 243, 252, 272, 273, 354
TATE, 328, 339, 342
TAYLOR, 66, 72, 75, 77, 80, 87, 99, 104, 120, 135, 137, 143, 154, 183, 184, 187, 196, 214, 217, 219, 320, 264, 271, 273, 287, 296, 303, 318, 343, 353, 367, 419
TEAGUE, 7, 29, 31, 35, 62, 65, 75, 87, 88, 90, 109, 114, 143, 150, 185, 186, 264, 267, 273, 274, 275, 324, 328, 333, 336, 337, 339, 341, 342, 344, 349, 382, 398, 403, 433
TEMPLETON, 249, 250
TERRY, 58, 132, 146, 150, 157, 201, 287, 324, 326, 327, 330, 332, 333, 336, 342, 346, 389
THAXTON, 65
THIESON, 72
THIESSEN, 73
THOMAS, 42, 45, 52, 64, 68, 83, 86, 88, 96, 135, 150, 160, 167, 170, 172, 180, 196, 221, 222, 224, 232, 275, 276, 284, 286, 288, 290, 291, 298, 321, 323, 332, 340, 350, 354, 360, 362, 367
THOMASON, 124, 338
THOMASSON, 111, 129
THOMISON, 271, 360
THOMPKINS, 67, 135
THOMPSON, 18, 25, 36, 63, 72, 74, 79, 93, 152, 167, 188, 224, 276, 277, 296, 326, 346, 350
THOMSON, 309, 363, 419
THORNBERRY, 123
THORNHILL, 125, 250
THORNLY, 56, 57
THORNSBERRY, 273
THORP, 239
THORPE, 169
THORTON, 100, 312
THRELKILE, 177, 178, 217, 292
THURMOND, 360
THURSBY, 34, 142
TIDWELL, 167
TICE, 120
TICHENOR, 292
TIERNEY, 145, 190
TIFFINS, 74
TILFORD, 318
TIMBERLAKE, 277, 319
TIMMONS, 18, 44, 56, 71, 80, 109, 228, 258, 298, 328
TINCUP, 428
TINDER, 374
TINES, 224
TINSLEY, 167, 193, 277, 371
TIPPETT, 34, 76, 160, 191, 342
TIPTON, 279
TIREY, 150, 194, 197, 198, 313, 325, 328
TODD, 17, 19, 55, 79, 87, 90, 96, 110, 112, 141, 148, 151, 152, 158, 159, 166, 171, 181, 190, 256, 277, 278, 281, 298, 309, 329, 337, 346, 357, 375, 382, 398
TOLAND, 81
TOLBERT, 305
TOMASSON, 80
TOMES, 78, 135
TOMBLINGSON, 168
TOMBLINSON, 18, 59, 68, 90, 298, 320, 416, 426
TOMLINSON, 44, 138, 278
TOMPKINS, 158, 278, 369
TOOMBS, 43, 152, 224, 266, 278, 279, 333, 347
TOOMES, 341
TOON, 128
TORAIN, 61
TORIAN, 318
TOWE, 87, 148, 246, 247
TOWL, 231
TOWLES, 11, 12
TOWNES, 14, 28
TOWNSEND, 42, 98, 116, 125, 267, 279, 323, 335, 341, 343
TOWNZEN, 41, 324
TRABUE, 10, 192
TRAHERN, 269, 357
TRAMMEL, 219
TRATHEN, 73, 128, 161, 162, 230, 279, 280, 422
TRAVIS, 91, 236
TRAYLOR, 108, 234, 235, 398
TREADWAY, 163
TREECE, 234
TRENT, 29, 49, 50, 54, 329, 336, 337, 344
TRICE, 191, 210, 248, 261, 301, 319, 326
TRIGG, 143
TRIMBLE, 74
TRIPLETT, 106, 114, 278
TROOP, 126, 280, 344, 345, 369, 414
TROTTER, 34, 147, 274, 330, 349
TROUT, 166, 363
TROUTMAN, 240
TROVER, 84, 110, 141, 146, 274, 280, 281, 346, 411, 429
TRUITT, 42
TRUNKFIELD, 36
TRUSTY, 73
TUCKER, 42, 44, 48, 51, 101, 141, 179, 180, 213, 232, 270, 342, 347, 432
TUBERVILLE, 56
TURLEY, 348
TURNBOW, 353
TURNER, 40, 54, 60, 61, 95, 103, 116, 161, 175, 210, 212, 228, 249, 277, 390
TURPIN, 64
TUTT, 321
TYLER, 68, 317
TYSON, 98, 195, 220, 293, 367

UIERCE, 324
UMFRESS, 293
UMPRIES, 172
UMSTEAD, 350, 373
UNDERDOWN, 207
UNDERWOOD, 154, 286, 371
UPLINGER, 134, 262
UTLEY, 5, 7, 8, 38, 49, 64, 71, 94, 120, 127, 139, 140, 156, 181, 186, 191, 198, 214, 216, 231, 246, 281, 282, 317, 326, 327, 330, 332, 334, 335, 337, 338, 340, 344, 350, 352, 361, 367, 369, 377, 382, 386, 403, 419
UTTERBACK, 136, 139, 180, 243, 251, 419
UZZEL, 220
UZZLE, 134, 139, 201, 262, 274

VAGNONI, 127
VANADA, 321
VANCE, 93, 120, 128, 131, 182, 205, 354
VANDIVER, 19, 94, 263, 272, 321, 344.
VAN HOECK, 282
VAN HOOK, 282
VAN LEER, 107, 108, 250, 282, 283, 284, 365
VAN METRE, 51
VAN NESS, 65
VANNOY, 55, 255, 284, 285, 300, 324, 326, 383, 426
VANOVER, 217, 219
VANVACTOR, 159, 218, 226, 252
VASSEUR, 94
VAUGHAN, 280, 420
VAUGHN, 49, 61, 158, 167, 231, 233, 238, 282, 331, 361
VAUGHT, 188, 197
VEAL, 19, 20

439

VEASEY, 218, 220, 267
VEATCH, 255
VEAZEY, 31, 46, 164, 183, 215, 285, 286, 321, 323, 324, 331, 341, 379, 380, 382
VELLER, 210
VENNERI, 164
VERCHER, 34
VERTRESS, 203
VICKERS, 204, 292, 343
VICKERY, 83, 196, 280, 281, 341, 367
VILLIANS, 102
VILLINES, 48, 71, 74, 77, 78, 133, 157, 223, 253, 326, 403
VINCENT, 18, 55, 62, 337, 346, 356, 369
VINSON, 61, 108, 238, 373
VIRE, 354
VOGT, 201
VON STEUBEN, 10, 20, 26

WADDILL, 2, 8, 238, 334, 358
WADE, 36, 69, 95, 113, 146, 172, 263, 278, 286, 287
WADLEY, 69
WADLINGTON, 410
WAETZEL, 217, 256
WAGGONER, 87
WAGNER, 144, 333, 358, 427
WAGONER, 42, 43, 287, 323
WAHL, 293
WAID, 185
WAIDE, 41, 72, 88, 143, 146, 160, 161, 195, 209, 233, 234, 235, 236, 238, 246, 252, 253, 270, 288, 289
WAINWRIGHT, 96
WAKE, 230, 371
WALDEN, 298
WALDROP, 97
WALKER, 24, 34, 37, 47, 50, 53, 61, 62, 65, 66, 67, 90, 96, 200, 102, 113, 160, 162, 167, 168, 170, 187, 188, 190, 195, 213, 221, 225, 232, 252, 258, 259, 271, 272, 274, 276, 289, 290, 317, 320, 323, 332, 336, 341, 344, 348, 349, 357, 363
WALL, 292, 320
WALLACE, 34, 39, 79, 94, 95, 100, 120, 158, 161, 170, 243, 304
WALLER, 42, 78, 125, 145, 234, 235, 238, 285, 290, 291,
296, 339, 379
WALLIS, 89
WALLS, 189
WALTERS, 72, 111, 220, 226, 398, 408
WALTON, 222, 223, 265, 291, 292, 322
WALTRIP, 4, 136, 292
WAMOS, 326
WARD, 128, 222
WARDER(S), 189, 192
WARENNER, 177
WARFIELD, 75
WARINNER, 292, 293
WARNER, 220, 230, 293
WARREN, 43, 44, 78, 111, 154, 201, 222, 224, 302, 428, 429
WARRINER, 178
WARWICK, 98
WASHINGTON, 15, 26, 43, 81, 93, 96, 122, 212, 213, 352
WATKINS, 75, 99, 133, 358
WATLINGTON, 39
WATSON, 49, 83, 97, 98, 126, 276, 290, 325, 337, 345
WATWOOD, 350
WATTS, 109, 219, 240, 350
WAY, 273
WEAKLEY, 291, 296
WEATHERLY, 118, 136, 137, 293, 371
WEBB, 42, 55, 75, 80, 115, 138, 172, 174, 187, 196, 287, 323, 324, 329, 353, 363
WEBER, 99
WEBSTER, 53, 112, 118, 177, 193, 217, 218, 243, 367
WEBSTERFIELD, 196
WEDDING, 135
WEEKS, 112
WEESTON, 117
WEGRICH, 90
WEINEBURGH, 94
WEIR, 11, 14, 23, 37, 46, 116, 143, 156, 212, 234, 238, 277, 280, 303, 327, 344, 350, 369
WELBURN, 204
WELBY, 42
WELCH, 104, 196, 255, 265, 293, 294, 297, 317, 335, 398, 402
WELDON, 18, 34, 201, 204, 205, 426,
WELLER, 53
WELLS, 19, 54, 55, 66, 77, 115,
123, 124, 156, 219, 249, 273, 285, 294, 303, 401, 402, 403
WELSH, 342
WERNER, 311
WEST, 45, 53, 64, 133, 166, 223, 249, 282, 294, 309, 398
WESTBROOK, 311
WESTBY, 278
WESTER, 57, 71
WESTMAN, 216
WETZEL, 51
WEVER, 197
WEVERSTAD, 42
WHALEN, 213
WHALEY, 228
WHALING, 89
WHEAT, 354
WHEATLEY, 240
WHEELER, 57, 123, 158, 300, 317, 341
WHELAN, 94
WHELCHELS, 86
WHETSTONE, 65
WHICKER, 294
WHITAKER, 177
WHITE, 42, 61, 62, 65, 71, 75, 150, 192, 193, 196, 227, 257, 313, 317, 324, 331, 344, 370, 433
WHITEHEAD, 145
WHITESIDE, 355
WHITFIELD, 19, 46, 85, 98, 127, 132, 136, 171, 187, 224, 229, 254, 259, 261, 274, 294, 295, 307, 320, 321, 328, 339, 340, 341, 345, 347, 348, 367
WHITFORD, 213
WHITLEDGE, 82, 143
WHITLEY, 42
WHITLOCK, 70
WHITMER, 298
WHITMORE, 85
WHITSELL, 46, 164, 184, 215, 216, 295, 296, 415
WHITSON, 309
WHITTAKER, 355
WHITTINGHILL, 124, 180, 210, 296, 356, 369
WHITTINGTON, 296
WHOBEY, 375
WHYTE, 13, 182
WIAR, 43, 287
WICE, 369
WICKLIFFE, 14, 303
WICKS, 49, 65, 110, 357
WILBERN, 236
WILBOURN, 234
WILCOX, 5, 6, 59, 135, 242, 243, 291, 296, 297, 369, 427
WILDMAN, 49
WILES, 74, 227
WILEY, 18, 56, 71, 139, 327, 353
WILGUESS, 209
WILHAM, 36
WILHITE, 307, 325
WILKERSON, 47, 51, 215, 217, 262, 302, 328, 332, 342, 363
WILKES, 59, 69, 297, 339
WILKEY, 5, 8, 41, 97, 114, 128, 142, 170, 198, 212, 247, 322, 325, 327, 329, 331, 333, 336, 341, 344, 382
WILKIE, 86, 324
WILKINS, 54, 279, 280, 330
WILLETT, 184
WILLIAMS, 16, 42, 50, 51, 52, 56, 59, 62, 79, 91, 98, 100, 103, 107, 120, 137, 138, 141, 144, 145, 154, 182, 199, 212, 219, 235, 257, 260, 261, 263, 275, 283, 287, 297, 298, 302, 303, 309, 318, 325, 342, 350, 357, 363, 399
WILLIAMSON, 102, 278, 298
WILLINGHAM, 54, 113
WILLIS, 14, 36, 116, 157, 165, 199, 269, 350
WILLOUGHBY, 43, 318
WILSON, 8, 14, 18, 36, 40, 42, 43, 45, 50, 63, 65, 69, 71, 72, 74, 77, 93, 97, 112, 113, 114, 116, 126, 128, 134, 135, 151, 157, 159, 163, 164, 166, 171, 172, 174, 183, 187, 190, 197, 198, 209, 210, 224, 226, 235, 243, 252, 255, 260, 263, 264, 266, 279, 282, 284, 285, 286, 292, 295, 299, 300, 301, 303, 305, 309, 316, 330, 332, 338, 343, 344, 345, 356, 361, 365, 366, 373, 395, 399, 426, 431
WINBADGER, 96
WINDES, 356
WINDERS, 62, 118, 300, 301
WINEBARGER, 229
WINFREE, 170, 196
WINFREY, 38
WINGO, 280
WINN, 335
WINSETT, 69, 301
WINSTEAD, 19, 25, 49, 50, 52, 53, 63, 65, 89, 106, 116, 144, 150, 167, 176, 178, 179, 189, 207, 212, 213, 214, 221, 231, 232, 234, 238, 243, 249, 270, 272, 273, 276, 290, 301, 302, 303, 317, 320, 325, 327, 332, 336, 341, 370, 398
WINSTON, 60
WINT, 68
WINTER, 230
WINTERS, 214, 262
WISE, 43, 116, 236, 266, 284, 290, 299
WISEHART, 139
WISEHEART, 217
WITHERS, 240, 333
WITHERSPOON, 143, 303, 304, 338
WITTEG, 42
WOFFENDALE, 57
WOLFE, 95, 357
WOLFENBERG, 150
WOLFORD, 5, 304
WOMACK, 80, 225
WOMOCK, 111
WOOD, 79, 80, 95, 96, 149, 166, 214, 232, 304, 305, 329
WOODALL, 80, 166
WOODARD, 326, 342
WOODBURN, 212, 234
WOODIS, 346
WOODRUFF, 30, 38, 44, 54, 60, 92, 123, 148, 149, 151, 154, 166, 212, 240, 263, 275, 305, 306, 326, 335, 349, 363, 382
WOODS, 7, 84, 90, 247, 322, 338
WOODSON, 11, 12, 13, 14, 16, 75, 121, 150, 178, 230, 304, 316, 375
WOODWARD, 190, 294
WOOLARD, 148
WOOLBRIDGE, 260
WOOLF, 167, 224
WOOLFOLK, 123, 199, 306, 307, 308, 316, 318, 320, 375
WOOLFORD, 2
WOOLFOLK, 239
WOOLRIDGE, 256
WOOSLEY, 95, 139, 274
WOOTEN, 134, 258, 260, 323, 325, 338
WOOTON, 77, 152, 176, 259, 308, 309, 333
WORD, 156, 369
WORKMAN, 5, 84, 112, 225, 309, 310, 311, 324, 334, 344, 382
WORTHAM, 6, 153, 188, 215
WORTHINGTON, 275
WRAY, 63
WRIGHT, 12, 36, 42, 112, 114, 117, 118, 119, 121, 126, 167, 210, 214, 216, 219, 229, 244, 257, 280, 282, 295, 305, 311, 312, 317, 328, 339, 341, 342, 349
WRISTEN, 92, 93, 312
WROTH, 116
WULF, 371
WYATT, 54, 64, 98, 106, 108, 109, 112, 113, 128, 150, 167, 173, 183, 234, 269, 270, 296, 297, 310, 312, 313, 315, 327, 332, 334, 336, 337, 339, 344, 357, 398
WYGAL, 251
WYMAN, 197
WYNN(S), 48, 127, 132, 151, 366

YANCEY, 297
YANDELL, 36, 150, 205, 344, 349
YARBROUGH, 41, 53, 64, 116, 143, 207, 250, 272, 273, 303, 336
YARLBROUGH, 89
YATES, 145, 168, 188, 263, 313, 363, 382, 432
YATSKO, 174
YEAGER, 77
YEANEY, 285
YELL, 77
YOCUM, 182
YOHO, 307
YOUNG, 2, 47, 60, 80, 98, 127, 129, 135, 183, 190, 208, 235, 262, 265, 271, 274, 306, 307, 310, 339, 340, 345, 356, 366, 374
YOUNGER, 163, 261

ZAPARANICK, 231
ZYNDA, 309

The rebuilding of Loch Mary Dam at Earlington

The Crabtree Company Store at Ilsley

The Masonic Temple in 1907 in Madisonville

Nortonville in 1911-The L & N and IC Railroad Station on left and Nortonville Hotel on right-25 Passenger Trains per day